How To Be
Well
Read

'A dazzling array of genres, periods, styles and tastes . . . chatty, insightful, unprejudiced (but not uncritical) and wise.' *Times Literary Supplement*

'Generous, enjoyable and well informed.' *Observer*

'Anyone hooked on fiction should be warned: this book will feed your addiction.' *Mail on Sunday*

'500 expertly potted plots and personal comments on a wide range of pop and proper prose fiction.' *The Times*

John Sutherland is Lord Northcliffe Professor Emeritus of Modern English Literature at University College London and previously taught at the California Institute of Technology. He writes regularly for the *Guardian*, *The Times* and *The New York Times*. He is the author of many books including *A Little History of Literature*, *Curiosities of Literature*, *Is Henry V a War Criminal?* (with Cedric Watts), biographies of Walter Scott, Stephen Spender and the Victorian elephant Jumbo, and *The Boy Who Loved Books*, a memoir.

How To Be Well Read

A guide to 500 great novels and
a handful of literary curiosities

JOHN SUTHERLAND

PENGUIN BOOKS

PENGUIN BOOKS

UK | USA | Canada | Ireland | Australia
India | New Zealand | South Africa

Penguin Books is part of the Penguin Random House group of companies
whose addresses can be found at global.penguinrandomhouse.com

First published in the UK by Random House Books in 2014
Published in Penguin Books 2022
002

Copyright © John Sutherland, 2013
Appendix © John Sutherland, 2022

Printed and bound in Great Britain by Clays Ltd, Elcograf S.p.A.

The authorised representative in the EEA is Penguin Random House Ireland,
Morrison Chambers, 32 Nassau Street, Dublin D02 YH68

A CIP catalogue record for this book is available from the British Library

ISBN: 978-1-529-15729-1

www.greenpenguin.co.uk

Penguin Random House is committed to a
sustainable future for our business, our readers
and our planet. This book is made from Forest
Stewardship Council® certified paper.

Contents

Preface

During the half-century I've worked in the university sector the study of my subject, English Literature, has changed radically. It has, nowadays, a more technical tool-kit than it used to – 'theory' has raised the professional game. It's cleverer. 'Bellelettrism', 'appreciation' and self-sufficient 'close reading' are no longer approved.

At the same time the focus of critical attention has narrowed to laser-like intensity. The 'monograph' (literally 'writing about one thing') is the principal medium of critical exchange. Generalism and 'big pictures' are no longer the norm.

I approve of what has happened in English studies: the new seriousness, one could call it. A couple of things I regret, however. The first is the relegation of the 'common reader' with whom, unlike Dr Johnson, the academic critic no longer always rejoices to concur. The second is the above mentioned narrowing of vision. To be 'well read' nowadays is not the unqualified term of praise it once was.

In my opinion, literature is a library, not a curriculum or a canon (I would not go quite as far as Umberto Eco, and claim that God, if he exists, is a library, but I'm half way there). In three large books, of which this is last, I have tried to sketch out larger than usual maps.

The Longman Companion to Victorian Fiction (1989, second edition 2008) contains some 650 lives and close on a thousand narrative summaries, together with ancillary entries on publishers, forms of publication, 'movements'. *The Lives of the Novelists: a History of Fiction in 294 Lives* (2011) is what the title (which annoyed some reviewers) states it to be. In brief these ventures are an attempt to think big, and companionably. In keeping with its predecessors this book is not a guide, a reference book, or a 'best of' compilation. It is a companion.

In the 500 or so entries which make up this book I have not, except in a handful of instances, recycled material from the Victorian companion. Nor have I, in a number of cases, included entries on novels on which I have written extensively elsewhere or for which, alas, I have no feeling worth putting on paper. I have, however, done my best to give a sense of the many different zones and genres of fiction, and the rewards.

Thomas Gray once jested that if heaven existed it would be a comfortable sofa and an endless supply of new novels. If so, my life has been a foretaste of heaven. Although I have been paid, one way or another, to read novels all my life (and am now pensioned to do so) I do not regard myself as well read in the genre. I do not think, given the number stored dustily in the British Library vaults (is it two million?) anyone can be. But one can be better read – more fish in one's net, on life's long reading trawl. The intention in what follows is to share a lifelong enthusiasm for that wonderful human invention, the prose novel. And, most importantly, to register the many different kinds of pleasure the prose novel can give.

I am very grateful to Nigel Wilcockson, Imogen Lowe, and Gemma Wain for their assistance, encouragement, and guidance. I exonerate them entirely from any errors that may be found in what follows.

John Sutherland
London, February 2014

Aaron's Rod, D. H. Lawrence, 1922

Aaron's Rod is a novel fated, like 'aardvark' in dictionaries, always to come first in any alphabetised collection. Rarely, however, is it the first novel reached for by Lawrentians. It was conceived in 1917, the bleakest year of the war. Lawrence had eloped with a married German woman (whom he persuaded to abandon her children) to set up a commune in Cornwall. The move culminated in his trying to throttle his fellow *communard*, John Middleton Murry – an event immortalised in the genital-dangling wrestling scene in the Ken Russell film of Lawrence's *Women in Love*. Ranamin (as the utopian community was called – don't ask why, it's complicated) led, by a series of misadventures involving semaphoric underwear on washing lines, drawn curtains, blackout violations, and submarines, to the Lawrences being persecuted as German spies. It was a bad time for a suspected 'conchie' to be married to a woman called Frieda von Richthofen – a distant relative of the fabled Red Baron flying ace.

Aaron's Rod was finally published in 1922 at the period in his life when Lawrence had resolved to shake the dust of England (coal dust, specifically) off his shoes for ever. The narrative opens crisply in the author's, and the hero's, mining country:

> There was a large, brilliant evening star in the early twilight, and underfoot the earth was half frozen. It was Christmas Eve. Also the War was over, and there was a sense of relief that was almost a new menace.

Aaron Sisson, a collier 'checkweightman', ups and leaves, with nothing but his flute and piccolo, to become a musician. He deserts his wife and daughters. His reasons are, literally, obscure. These harmless female impedimenta elicit a 'dark rage' in his soul. He craves light. In floodlit London, Aaron finds employment as a flautist in metropolitan opera. It is as likely an event, in the real world, as banjoist George Formby leading the London Philharmonic. Aaron's new career is interrupted by a bout of Spanish flu (an epidemic which killed more Englishmen than the Kaiser). His recovery marks his rebirth. Aaron moves, sardonically, among the chattering Bloomsbury intelligentsia, whom he finds unsatisfactory, before drifting on to Florence, the city of renaissances, where he finds living with a Marchesa similarly *ennuyant*. The narrative climaxes with a proto-Fascist bomb outrage in which his flute is smashed.

Aaron's Rod focuses on the dilemma which every major novelist of the time faced: home or away? 'Follow your soul', the hero's Virgilian guide advises. But what, precisely, does that mean? Is Aaron destined for exile, pilgrimage, or the kind of purification inflicted on the Israelites during their forty years in the desert? In that purgatorial episode, biblical Aaron features as the older brother of Moses, whose 'rod' outdoes the wands of the Egyptian soothsayers, brings down three of the plagues, and finally flowers. Where, and how, will the Lawrentian rod flower? Not, one gathers, in the pits – whether of the mine or the orchestra.

Abba Abba, Anthony Burgess, 1977

Abba Abba was written during a period of his career when Burgess had become the darling of the literary theorists – attention he relished rather more than most novelists do. In its first half, the story centres on the last months of the poet Keats spitting out his lifeblood in Rome, accompanied, as he historically was, by the artist Joseph Severn. One of the principal conclusions Burgess' novel comes to is that the writer, like wine, needs decades of lived existence to progress from precocious brilliance to seasoned maturity. It's not a young man's game. At one point in *Abba Abba* Keats, barely out of boyhood, is conducted round the Sistine Chapel to wonder at what Michelangelo achieved in his later years. His guide is a friend he has made in Rome, Giovanni Gulielmi. In the chapel, he encounters the local poet Giuseppe Gioachino Belli. Keats died in his mid-twenties. What would he have done given seventy more years of writing life? Or even the seventy-two in total that Belli enjoyed?

Keats' brief encounter with Rome (in Burgess' version) thrusts into prominence two other needful things: dirt and sex. The poet's own name, as mangled by local dialect, comes out as *cazzo* – slang for penis. It inspires a Keatsian *vers d'occasion*:

> Here are some names, my son, we
>   call the prick:
> The chair, the yard, the nail, the kit,
>   the cock,
> The holofernes, rod, the sugar rock,
> The dickory dickory dock, the liquo-
>   rice stick.

It goes on (Burgess always does go on) cataloguing penis synonymy for many lines more. More years of life, and more hanky-panky (something of which he had been sadly starved by the Brawne woman), and Keats would have been an author in the Burgess class, we apprehend. He himself was a ripe sixty years old at the time of writing *Abba Abba*. Why the odd title? A repetition of 'Abba', as in the above penile quatrain, is the rhyme scheme of the first octave of the sonnet – a form used by both English and Italian poets. It is also the Aramaic ejaculation ('Lord, Lord!') of the dying Christ on the Cross. Christ, like Keats, was taken early. The second half of *Abba Abba* comprises English translations of some seventy Belli sonnets by John Wilson, a descendant of Keats' friend Giovanni Gulielmi (i.e. John Wilson), whose C.V. is precisely that of Anthony Burgess, whose birth-name was John Anthony Burgess Wilson.

ABBA was also, of course, a Swedish pop group, formed in 1972, the name assumed as an acronym of the initials of their Christian names. After winning the 1974 Eurovision Song Contest Abba had a string of hits in the mid-1970s. 'Mamma Mia' was in 1975 particularly popular in Italy, where Burgess was resident. In 1977 one would have had to be immured in a dungeon in the Château d'If with an iron mask on one's head not to have known about the Swedish songsters. Constitutionally mischievous, Burgess certainly did. ABBA is also a palindrome for the initial letters of 'Anthony Burgess Burgess Anthony'. Clever, clever.

Absolute Beginners, Colin MacInnes, 1959

> A spectre has arisen in our cities – the spectre of lawless, carefree youth... In *Absolute Beginners* Colin MacInnes has gone right inside the 'teenage' world – of coffee bars, motor-scooters, casual and alarming elegance – and race riots... Though the language is jazz and the mood very hip, this is the truest, shrewdest and kindest eye that has looked over the new world made by the 'kids' themselves – right slap in the middle of the enemy.

So ran the blurb on MacGibbon & Kee's first edition. Which idiot wrote this balderdash is not recorded, but it is clear it was no 'teen-aged' idiot. Nor, as it happened, was the 'kind-eyed' MacInnes in the first flush of youth. He was forty-five years old in 1959. *Absolute Beginners* is the second in MacInnes' so-called 'London trilogy' – an overture to the soon-to-swing 1960s – along with *City of Spades* and *Mr Love and Justice*. The unnamed hero-narrator is a teenage photographer. There are echoes of Christopher Isherwood's 'Herr Issyvoo' – of *I Am a Camera* fame – but the character is based more directly on Soho's 'prince of the beatniks', Terry Taylor. He is on the verge of being twenty. 'I'll soon be out there among the oldies', he laments. The narrative opens with the narrator in discussion with 'the Wiz' in Simpson's restaurant. The Wiz is sixteen. No oldie he. Even younger is the chart-topping singer they are talking about as a sign of the times, Laurie London, whose April 1958 Number One, 'He's Got the Whole World in His Hand', came out when the singer was thirteen years old, if 'old' is the right word here.

MacInnes makes some depressing attempts at teenage argot, which grate on the ear like Klingon. The substance of the novel works better. The narrative climaxes, historically and topically, with the 1958 race riots in Notting Hill. At the height of the disorder two thousand white youths went on the rampage in West London, beating up any black people they could find. The main offenders were what were called Teds. These were working-class kids whose uniform was faux-Edwardian: a statement of some vague kind. Teds would later mutate – via a change of garb – into Rockers, sworn foe to the Mods (among which tribe are MacInnes' narrator and the Wiz). Mods rode Vespas not 'bikes', sipped coffee, listened to cool jazz, and affected parkas, winkle-picker shoes and drainpipe trousers. MacInnes depicts the Notting Hill riots graphically and with total sympathy for the victimised. The hero despairs and resolves to emigrate to somewhere he has been told has no race problem: Brazil. But at the airport he meets 'a score or so Spades from Africa'. They all look 'dam [sic] pleased to be in England', despite the pelting rain. The hero relents, and hope for his country is reborn in him. The sixties, we apprehend, will swing after all. Tinkerbell is saved. Right on.

Accordion Crimes, E. Annie Proulx, 1996

Proulx's tricky authorial name witnesses proudly to French-Canadian lineage, although most of her life has been spent in Vermont. She became internationally famous with her second novel, *The Shipping News* (1993), which, strange to say, is about exactly what the title says it's about. She became more famous still after the film *Brokeback Mountain*, adapted in 2005 from one of her short stories, a chronicle of gay sex in the American West – a lot wilder West, apparently, than one perhaps thought it was. But for me, Proulx's most impressive work is *Accordion Crimes*; not, sadly, one of her most-read works. It draws on a bestseller of 1760–5, *The Adventures of a Guinea* by Charles Johnstone, which follows the course of a gold coin as it passes randomly from hand to hand, telling the story of each of its successive owners. The connecting strands in Proulx's story are the adventures of a small green accordion made by a craftsman in Sicily at the close of the nineteenth century. The accordion-maker (unnamed) leaves his native country in 1890 for 'La Merica'. He takes with him his son Silvano and his instrument. In New Orleans, with ten of his Italian compatriots, he is promptly lynched in a riot orchestrated by local community leaders. Welcome to La Merica.

The little green accordion passes into the hands of a German immigrant farmer, Hans Beutle, who settles in Iowa. The instrument no longer plays plangent Sicilian melodies, but lusty Teutonic marches and ballads. Beutle is possessed of titanic physical energy and libidinal drive. Over the decades, the German farmer builds up a prosperous business, defying deep-rooted Iowan antagonism against 'sourkrauts'. It seems like a textbook American success story until Beutle dies, ignominiously and agonisingly, from postoperative infection following a goat-gland transplant into his sadly enfeebled testicles. In the same week – it is October 1929 – his fortune is wiped out by the Wall Street Crash. American quacks and hucksters have done him in. 'The old green accordion', as it now is, falls into the dexterous hands of a Hispanic virtuoso musician, Abelardo Salazar. We follow its tuneful career through the 1930s and 40s, as Tejano music builds its huge constituency among the migrant underclass. Abelardo is popular but never rich. He is bitten by a venomous spider and neglected to death by the American health system.

It is now the 1950s and the tempo accelerates. The accordion spends some time with Franco-Canadian owners before going south to Louisiana, where Zydeco is born from its now wheezy bellows. In the 1960s, it is briefly in the possession of African-Americans in the civil rights struggle. Polka-playing Poles and melancholy Minnesotan Norwegians have their turn before the old, exhausted accordion finally attains its quietus in the 1990s. The magic of the accordion is that, like America, it can absorb all styles, all cultural idioms, and harmonise them. And, like America, the accordion is profoundly delusive. Most of its various owners have been dirt poor, blissfully unaware that in its passage through America the instrument has acquired a hidden store of thousands of dollar bills in the recesses of its pleats. Proulx loves irony.

Across the River and into the Trees, Ernest Hemingway, 1950

By 1950, Hemingway – the most admired war novelist in America – had not published a novel for ten years, during which the greatest war in history was fought and won. The novel he came out with, after this authorially constipated decade, is generally regarded as his worst. Every great novelist, said Cyril Connolly, is allowed one bad work. The reason for the almost universally critical contemporary badmouthing of this book was, we can see with half a century's hindsight, chagrin that the work, awaited for so long, was faux Hemingway. In fact, read with that same hindsight's objectivity, it's a very interesting novel. It's almost as if Hemingway is playing games with the styles and idioms he has made peculiarly his own, a kind of 'how far can I go?' experiment.

Across the River and into the Trees chronicles the last day in the life of Colonel Richard Cantwell. Once a Brigadier General, he was 'broken' for losing three battalions (following bad orders too well) in the bloody Hürtgen Forest slaughter. Cantwell wants, literally, to get his ducks in a row before dying. The novel opens with a stunningly beautiful description of a morning shoot on the frozen Venetian Lagoon. He has, in his life as a soldier, some 122 'sure' kills. The last things he will kill are three birds and himself. It is 1948. The US Army is still occupying the Europe it conquered. 'Half a hundred years' old, Cantwell has a 'gladiator's broken nose', a thrice-wounded hand and a dicky heart. He cheats his way his way through a medical exam with the aid of (medicinal) nitroglycerin and then has himself chauffeured to spend his last days in Venice, the city he loves. And which loves him. 'You have to be a tough boy in this town to be loved,' he complacently muses. He is surely tough. En route to his death in Venice (the obviousness of the literary allusion vexed some critics) he stops at Fossalta, where, fighting for the Italians, he had been badly wounded in 1918. As a ritual act he pisses on the spot where his blood was spilled. As he says, 'tough'.

In Venice, Cantwell dines richly (omelettes garnished with truffles, crab enchilada). But there is nothing sissy about his gourmandising. Even at his simple breakfast:

The Colonel breakfasted with the leisure of a fighter who has been clipped badly, hears four, and knows how to relax truly for five seconds more.

If you're wondering – eggs over easy and Canadian bacon. More intensely than his chow, he chews over in his mind his comradely pre-war friendship with Rommel and Udet. They had skiied together and, as soldiers, had a martial code in common above any petty disagreements about politics. 'I can't hate Fascists,' Cantwell thinks, 'Nor Krauts, either, since unfortunately, I am a soldier.' Lucky he wasn't a German Jew. His real reason for coming to Venice is love (his heart is good for one more day of that). Renata, thirty years his junior, 'loves him true' and is 'good'. A tall striding beauty with 'unkempt hair', she has what is obscurely called 'a properly built body' and a face worthy of Tintoretto – 'if he were still around'. Her desire to have five sons by Cantwell is, alas, frustrated. She has to make do with a tumble in a gondola (a big bird flies from the craft at the moment of climax). Having lived his last day, his shotguns and the portrait of his young love he leaves 'to their rightful owners'. While writing the novel Hemingway was infatuated with a young woman: Adriana Ivancich, the original of Renata. *Across the River and into the Trees* was dedicated to his wife Mary – who, as she put it, kept her mouth shut.

Adam Bede, George Eliot, 1859

Adam Bede was Mary Anne Evans' first full-length (i.e. three-volume) novel. So keen was Miss Evans not to be grouped with the gaggle of 'silly lady novelists' she despised that she published her fiction under a hearty male pseudonym and built the story of *Adam Bede* round a hero named after the first man. To strengthen further the masculinism, he is a carpenter – the Son of Man's manly trade. She would have put chest hair on her pages, if the printers knew how to do it.

The date of the action is 1799. The Evangelical Revival – the movement which 'moralised' Victorian England – is spreading via itinerant field preachers throughout the English rural heartland, changing the social fabric of the country. Adam loves the beautiful but empty-headed milkmaid, Hetty

Sorrel. His brother Seth loves the charismatic 'Methodee' preacher, Dinah Morris. Both relationships are fraught. Hetty is seduced (all too willingly) by the dashing grandson of the local squire, Arthur Donnithorne. Dinah finds Seth, although a good man, an ineffably *dull* good man. Even Methodists like a bit of the Devil in their lovers. The novel features heavy debates on the nature of the universe (notably Chapter 17, in which the existence or non-existence of free will, when it comes to seducing attractive milkmaids, is debated). The third volume descends, as was conventional with the 'three-decker', into melodrama. The pregnant Hetty sets out to find insouciant Arthur, who has been posted with his militia to put down rebels in Ireland. She gives birth in a ditch, kills the baby, and is duly convicted of infanticide. Partly redeeming his sin, Arthur gallops – neck and crop – to the Home Secretary to procure a reprieve as she is trundling to the gallows. He succeeds in the nick of time. Adam marries Dinah. Seth embraces bachelorhood.

Adam Bede conflates a bundle of Eliot's favourite moral themes: principally the perception that old feudal organisation was doomed (contradicting Thomas Carlyle's romantic ideas). It was impossible to go back to some sentimentalised world of the past. As Eliot saw it, a new moral regime was necessary for modern times. This was one element in her thinking about the world and where it must go. In the ruthless depiction of airheaded Hetty the novel makes painfully clear another of the author's strongly held beliefs – namely that, as the proverb puts it, fine feathers do not make fine birds. Mary Anne Evans and her consort George Henry Lewes were proudly unbeautiful and proudly unmarried. Most trenchantly, Eliot makes the point in *Adam Bede* that Christian evangelicalism was a more potent instrument of real reform (which needed to originate in individuals, not political parties) than the 'vote' – a measure in which she never entirely believed, as her later, politically conservative, novel *Felix Holt, the Radical* testifies. The vote does not make people better. People make people better – and, possibly, novels.

It's ironic – an irony Eliot was surely aware of – that the most powerful woman in this woman's novel, Dinah Morris, is imminently to be rendered mute and impotent; a fact the novel strangely ignores. Methodism originated in the 1730s and, as part of its defiance of the established Church, encouraged female preachers. This changed after the death of John Wesley. From 1803 women of the faith were allowed only to address other women, under conditions almost as strict as the scold's bridle. The ban was not lifted until 1910. Mrs Dinah Bede would be transported not to Australia, like the luckless Hetty, but the kitchen.

Adrian Mole: The Prostrate Years, Sue Townsend, 2009

It was a dramatic monologue, broadcast in 1982 on BBC radio (featuring 'Nigel' Mole), which was the forerunner of the first instalment of *The Secret Diary of Adrian Mole, Aged 13¾*. The name was changed to Adrian to avoid too obvious a lifting from the 1950s 'skuleboy' hero, Nigel Molesworth, the immortal creation of Geoffrey Willans and Ronald Searle. The difference was, 'as any fule kno', that Nigel was minor public school-educated ('St Kustard's'). Adrian is very much a product of the bog-standard comprehensive system. His secret diary went on to become the bestselling fiction title of 1982, inspiring TV and film adaptations and a cult following.

Like Joe Orton (brought up in a neighbouring house in Leicester), Townsend had an unerring ear for the dialect of her uneasy class and place. She also had an acute insight into the trials of early adolescence. One of the early covers of her books portrayed a bathroom cup containing a Noddy toothbrush and a disposable razor. Adrian (Albert) Mole is trapped between the two. A child of the 1960s, life never swings for Adrian. The diary begins at the high point of the Thatcher years, an administration Townsend loathed (she has, however, a certain fondness for the Iron Lady's successor: 'I didn't see Adrian's face,' she once mused, 'well – not until I saw John Major on the telly').

The triumph of her first volume launched the 'Moleiad': a nobody's progress to nowhere in life. There followed another seven instalments of Adrian's career, ruefully chronicling his misfortunes, each volume becoming progressively darker in tone. The darkness spilled over from Townsend's own life. She was diagnosed with diabetes in her thirties, and registered blind in 2001. In 2005 her kidneys failed, and in 2009 she had a transplant. For the latter volumes she was wheelchair-bound and obliged to dictate the books to her son Sean – who also donated his kidney to her. The Mole diaries are increasingly bitter about New Labour, reaching a climax in *Adrian Mole and the Weapons of Mass Destruction*. Pandora – Adrian's Helen of Troy (she has launched a thousand masturbation fantasies) – is, in the later instalments, a Blair Babe and the focus of Townsend's unreconstructed Old Labour satirical venom. The author announced her intention to do away with Adrian in 2007. But in *Adrian Mole: The Prostrate Years* (2009), he was given a stay of execution.

It is c.2007. The diarist-hero is aged 39¼. He is living (if you can call it that) in a converted pigsty, semi-attached to his dysfunctional parents' house, on the outskirts of Leicester. He works in a second-hand bookshop which is going bust. His (illegitimate) son Glenn is serving in Afghanistan. Thank heavens his parents' savings are in Northern Rock and Adrian's own meagre hoard in an Icelandic bank. He is up all night with a worrisome bladder (more worrying, it transpires, than he suspects) and has not had sex with his wife Daisy for six months. He has, he discovers, galloping cancer of the sex organs. Sue Townsend did her research for *Adrian Mole: The Prostrate* [sic] *Years*. At thirty-nine Adrian is not, technically, in those red-zone years for prostate cancer: commonly assumed to be a man's late sixties onwards. But it can strike young – if you're unlucky. No one is unluckier than Mr Mole.

The Adventures of Augie March, Saul Bellow, 1953

Augie March is the novel which redrew the map of American fiction. By the 1960s the metropolitan Jewish novelists (Philip Roth, Bernard Malamud, Norman Mailer, pre-eminently Bellow) had seized leadership of

the form from the Southern novelists (William Faulkner, Robert Penn Warren, Katherine Anne Porter). The opening of *Augie March* reads like a declaration of literary independence – war even:

> I am an American, Chicago born – Chicago, that somber city – and go at things as I have taught myself, free-style, and will make the record in my own way. . .

The last word in the novel is 'America'. Martin Amis, never one to mince his words, goes so far as to proclaim: '*The Adventures of Augie March* is *the* Great American Novel. Search no further.' Even those who demur would concede that *Augie March* was instrumental in creating a new fictional 'voice' for its period.

The setting is Chicago in the 1920s. Bellow largely sidelines the city's legendary criminal gangsters, although there are occasional glimpses of Capone, Torrio, and sundry bootleggers (Bellow's own father, the novel's dedicatee, was once in that line of work). The eponymous hero is, to invoke the one epithet sidestepped in the novel's opening declaration, Jewish. At one point he and a companion, about to embark on some dubious job, are asked if they are 'Yehudim'. 'Yes, I guess,' says Augie. Of his Americanness he is surer. No guesswork required there. The novel more or less follows Bellow's own life history. Augie has a mother whom he loves, but who has little influence over him. One of his brothers, George, is mentally deficient (both George and their mother are eventually institutionalised). Another brother, Simon, is a go-getter, forever on the make. The father is long gone. Augie labels himself 'the by-blow of a traveling man'. The children are brought up by a 'grandmother' (adoptive), a first-generation, 'Eastern' Jew. Augie and Simon, unlike her, melt into America.

Bellow, among his other pre-eminent qualities, is a terrific storyteller. This, in impoverishing summary, is how it goes. The novel opens in the 1920s, in the run-up to the Wall Street Crash. Chicago is a city where 'illusions' (particularly illusions of a Scott Fitzgerald kind) are not possible and life is more *real* than elsewhere. The first sex that

Augie has, with a paid prostitute, makes sense to him because: 'that's what city life is. . . there wasn't any epithalamium'. His early life chronicles a bewildering series of menial jobs and fiddles, while he saturates himself in private reading. Augie's C.V. includes, as things go bad for him, that of dog-washer to the well off. At one point he takes up stealing books for fellow students, to pay for his own courses. The second half of the novel becomes increasingly surreal. Augie falls in love with a rich, beautiful woman who drags him off to Mexico to train eagles and hunt gila monsters. He subsequently joins the merchant marine on the outbreak of war (as did Bellow). His vessel is torpedoed (as Bellow's wasn't) and there is a long lifeboat episode in which Augie finds himself alone with a crazed fellow survivor determined to explain the meanings of life and death to him. The narrative wraps up in Europe, where Augie is still hustling and still asking of life the great question, 'What for, what for?'

According to James Atlas in his 2000 biography of Bellow it was the sight of water flowing down a street in Paris which inspired the author to develop the 'cascade of prose' in *The Adventures of Augie March*. His prose was taught how to flow by a French bucket.

The Adventures of Baron Munchausen, Anon. (gathered and written up by Rudolf Raspe), 1785

Few novels have loaned a name to medicine, which prefers terms with an authoritative Latin or Greek tang. The best known is 'the Pickwickian Syndrome', so named by the physician C. S. Burwell after the fat boy in Dickens' novel whose Bozian description, Burwell discovered, is astonishingly accurate symptomatically. No novel(ist), I think, can be credited with the name of two conditions listed in the medical textbooks other than the (unknown) author of *The Adventures of Baron Munchausen*. The conditions are: (1) Munchausen Syndrome, described by Dr Google as 'a psychiatric factitious disorder wherein those affected feign disease, illness,

or psychological trauma to draw attention or sympathy to themselves. It is also sometimes known as hospital addiction syndrome or hospital-hopper syndrome'; and: (2) Munchausen by Proxy Syndrome, in which fabricated symptoms are projected on to a second party (usually a child) for the gratification of the first party. The nomenclature is a tribute to the most wildly fictional work of fiction in literature.

Accounts of Baron Munchausen's 'marvellous travels' ('I am a traveller of veracity', he blandly informs us) and 'comical adventures' began in folklore before being assembled into book form, under the authorship of Rudolf Raspe, in 1785. Münchhausen was an actual German aristocrat, but he does not seem to have been the originator of the work put out under his name. The various tales are surreally preposterous (a feature lovingly developed in Terry Gilliam's 1988 film). One day while hunting, as the Baron tells us with the straightest of faces, he had run out of shot for his gun and used a handful of cherry stones instead. He managed to hit a fine stag in the middle of the forehead, but the beast ran off:

> A year or two after, being with a party in the same forest, I beheld a noble stag with a fine full grown cherry-tree above ten feet high between his antlers. At once I recollected my former adventure, looked on him as my property, and brought him to the ground by one shot. This gave me the haunch and cherry-sauce; for the tree was covered with the richest fruit, and I had never tasted anything like it before.

Munchausen makes two trips to the moon. The second begins:

> I went on a voyage of discovery at the request of a distant relation, who had a strange notion that there were people to be found equal in magnitude to those described by Gulliver in the empire of BROBDINGNAG. For my part I always treated that account as fabulous: however, to oblige him, for he had made me his heir, I undertook it. . . On the eighteenth day. . . a hurricane blew our ship at least one thousand leagues

above the surface of the water, and kept it at the height till a fresh gale arising filled the sails in every part, and onwards we travelled at a prodigious rate; thus we proceeded above the clouds for six weeks. At last we discovered a great land in the sky, like a shining island, round and bright, where, coming into a convenient harbour, we went on shore, and soon found it was inhabited. Below us we saw another earth, containing cities, trees, mountains, rivers, seas, &c., which we conjectured was this world which we had left.

'Hello, Houston,' we hear in our mind's ear. Munchausen's *voyages imaginaires* look backwards to Sinbad and Gulliver (as he acknowledges) and forward to Jules Verne, H. G. Wells and the rich twentieth-century genre of science fiction. A slightly different offshoot can be followed through to Harry Potter and Terry Pratchett.

The Adventures of Huckleberry Finn, Mark Twain, 1885

As D. H. Lawrence sardonically noted, great nineteenth-century American novels have tended, in the twentieth century, to be relegated to the status of children's books. Perversely, however, the greatest of them all, *Huckleberry Finn*, has been serially judged unsuitable for the juvenile American mind. In earlier years it was proscribed for encouraging young boys to imitate Huck's 'smart' tricksterism, his 'sass' (cheek), and his bad grammar. In recent years, *Huckleberry Finn* has been found objectionable – by libraries and school boards – for its promiscuous use (some 219 times) of the toxic 'N— word'. In January 2011 Professor Alan Gribben of Auburn University, Alabama, published an edition of *Huckleberry Finn* in which those 219 uses of the word 'nigger' were replaced with 'slave'. Professor Gribben's initiative brought down on his well-meaning head worldwide condemnation from infuriated defenders of the integrity of great fiction – to the joy of his publishers who, doubtless, ordered another few thousand copies from the printer.

As the title page proclaims, the story is set in 'The Mississippi Valley, Time Forty to Fifty Years Ago'. Huck had made an earlier appearance in *Tom Sawyer* (1876) as 'the juvenile pariah of the village. . . son of the town drunkard. . . cordially hated and dreaded by all the mothers of the town'. The Finns are Irish – at the time scarcely a notch, socially, above those we would call African-Americans (and whom Twain signally doesn't). The implied persecution of the Irish is often overlooked by modern readers, who see only black and white in the novel's demography. Also tricky for the modern reader to take on board is that, unlike its predecessor, *Huckleberry Finn* is narrated autobiographically in what Twain calls 'the ordinary "Pike County" dialect'. This is a novel which requires a keen ear.

Huck is semi-'sivilized' (much against his will) thanks to the iron discipline of the Widow Douglas and her sister Miss Watson, who have adopted him. The plot machine is got going when Huck's obnoxious father returns, hungry for his son's $6,000 (the fortune that came his way at the end of *Tom Sawyer*). Things get very Oedipal. Huck escapes by faking his death and as a runaway lives an idyllic life on the deserted Jackson's Island.

The novel gets interesting, thematically, when Huck's Man Friday appears in the form of Jim, Miss Watson's runaway slave. Jim has taken to his heels on overhearing that his penurious owner plans to send him to the New Orleans slave market. The new comrades, divided by race but united by misfortune, drift down the Mississippi past Cairo and Memphis, experiencing a series of adventures. They eventually fall in with a pair of criminal itinerant actors, the *soi-disant* 'Dauphin' and the 'Duke of Bridgewater'. In a complicated finale, Huck is mistaken for Tom by some distant Sawyer relatives. The luckless Jim is locked up as an escaped slave. Tom reappears on the scene and the two boys (under the influence of Tom's fevered enthusiasm for *The Count of Monte Cristo*) plot a daring escape for Jim. It goes badly wrong, but finally it emerges that Miss Watson had anyway freed her slave, something that the sly Tom knew all along. The narrative ends with a grudging Huck again facing the prospect of 'sivilization', and plotting to light out to the Indian territories with Tom (a sequel Twain did not, alas, get round to writing). Doubtless the promiscuous use of the word 'Redskin' would have got Huck into hot water again.

The Adventures of Sherlock Holmes, Arthur Conan Doyle, 1892

This was the first book-length collection of Holmes stories, reprinted from the *Strand Magazine*, in which the great sleuth's 'adventures' (i.e. brilliant crime-solvings) were first launched. Advance news that there was a new 'Holmes' coming would drive sales of Newnes' sixpenny magazine up to a phenomenal quarter of a million copies.

The hallmark physical appearance of Holmes (his aquiline profile, cape, Meerschaum and 'deerstalker') was supplied not by the author but by Sidney Paget, Conan Doyle's gifted illustrator in the *Strand Magazine*. The profile was further patented by the hatchet-faced Basil Rathbone and persists down to Robert Downey Jr's portrayal of the detective in the 2009 film *Sherlock Holmes* and its successor.

The *Adventures* volume contained a dozen of the amateur detective's earliest cases, including: 'The Five Orange Pips', 'The Adventure of the Speckled Band' and 'The Man with the Twisted Lip'. Conan Doyle had begun his series in the *Strand* very speculatively, with 'A Case of Identity'. Thereafter the stories followed a set formula: the Baker Street detective and his confidant Dr Watson would be presented with a fiendishly complex mystery which the inscrutable Holmes would solve by the application of pure intellect – usually keeping the doltishly gullible Watson (and the doltish reader) in the dark until the very last moment. Conan Doyle himself always underrated the Holmes stories, thinking them inferior to his historical romances. But the public adored, and still adore, 'the unofficial detective', and Holmes became a literary cult object and a franchise. Some twenty thousand copies of the *Adventures* were sold within the year. Conan Doyle was constrained

to write a sequel, *The Memoirs of Sherlock Holmes* (1894), which ends with the hero apparently plunging to his death in the Reichenbach Falls, while grappling with his mighty adversary Professor Moriarty, on 4 May 1891 – the blackest day in the Holmesian calendar.

American publishers induced Doyle to resuscitate the detective for yet another series, *The Return of Sherlock Holmes*, in 1905. He's still returning, in reprint after reprint and screen adventure after screen adventure – most recently in the above-mentioned film series starring Robert Downey Jr. Like Holmes, Downey Jr has had (well-reported) brushes with the 'seven per cent solution' – cocaine. It adds to his haunted charm.

The Aerodrome, Rex Warner, 1941

Kafka arrived late on the English literary scene, with Willa and Edwin Muir's translation of THE CASTLE in 1930. His leading English disciple ('The only modern novelist I like is Kafka') was Rex Warner. He was a young, brilliant, and highly impressionable Oxford student at the time when he first read *The Castle* in English. Warner wrote his masterpiece, *The Aerodrome*, in the run-up to the Second World War and published it during the conflict. Fictionally it echoes the dramatic opening sentence of Orwell's 1941 essay, 'The Lion and the Unicorn': 'As I write, highly civilised human beings are flying overhead, trying to kill me.' Like Virginia Woolf's BETWEEN THE ACTS, it dates from those awful months when it seemed as if the English Novel would for a near-certainty be crushed to extinction under the all-conquering Nazi jackboot. *The Aerodrome*'s narrative pivots on the binary opposition of an old English village (presided over by the 'Rector') and a new aerodrome (presided over by the 'Air Vice Marshal'). One represents totalitarian 'apparat', the other liberal English 'muddle'. Neither 'the Village' nor 'the Aerodrome' has a name. They are generic. The AVM's doctrine sounds suspiciously like English Fascism. He tells the novel's ingenuous hero:

'Remember that we expect from you conduct of a quite different order from that of the mass of mankind. . . Your purpose – to escape the bondage of time, to obtain mastery over yourselves, and thus over your environment – must never waver. . . . [T]his discipline has one aim, the acquisition of power, and by power – freedom.'

It all translates easily enough into German: *Freiheit durch Macht*. To win the war, Old England has to ape its enemy, destroying the principles for which it fought that damned war in the first place. Victory merely recreates the enemy in yourself.

Woven into the novel's design is a complicated love story centred on the orphan hero, Roy (an alternate version of Rex). Roy – who joins up as an airman – does not know where he belongs. He is a man in freefall. The novel opens on his twenty-first birthday when he discovers he is not, as he previously thought, the Rector's adopted child (the Rector has a terrible crime in his background). The narrative opens:

It would be difficult to overestimate the importance to me of the events which had taken place previous to the hour (it was shortly after ten o'clock in the evening) when I was lying in the marsh near the small pond at the bottom of Gurney's meadow, my face in the mud and the black mud beginning to ooze through the spaces between the fingers of my outstretched hands, drunk, but not blindly so, for I seemed only to have lost the use of my limbs.

In his perplexity, the Aerodrome offers 'structure'. It will, the Air Vice Marshal assures him, free him from 'shapelessness'. That freedom is, as every Kafka novel and story depicts, an illusion. The plot goes nowhere. But where could a narrative like Warner's go in 1941? *The Aerodrome* is an exquisitely uncertain novel, which belongs to a teetering moment in British history when (as in the Austro-Hungarian Empire when Kafka was writing) everything was falling apart.

The African Queen, C. S. Forester, 1935

Aside from the Hornblower series, this one-off novel remains the most popular of Forester's books, thanks to the 1951 film version, which won Humphrey Bogart his sole, late-in-life Oscar. The novel was begun in 1934 after a suggestion by the novelist's agent that he write a story for daily newspaper serialisation. The resulting novel is set in 'German Central Africa' (i.e. German East Africa) in late 1914. The book was conceived at an anxious time for non-Fascist Europe – Hitler had just come to power. Forester was rabidly anti-German, Nazi or otherwise. To him, they were all Huns. His previous book had been about Nurse Cavell – the British martyr in the First World War. In *The African Queen* (which made his name), Forester, long before most politicians, astutely foresaw another war coming. And, like former Lord of the Admiralty Churchill, he believed that sea power was the needful thing to preserve Great Britain's greatness (another of his hits, much later in his career, was the script to the jingoistic film *Sink the Bismarck*).

The novel, as serialised in the *Daily Express*, opens with Rose Sayer, the spinster sister of an English missionary, finding herself alone in the jungle after her brother dies in a brutal German raid. She is befriended by a cockney sailor, Charlie Allnutt, commander of the rundown river craft misnamed the *African Queen*. Rose nags the arrant coward Charlie into taking his boat down the Ulanga River, past German fortifications. The intention is to ram and sink a German warship in Lake Tanganyika. Vividly described, the hardships of the journey bring the couple together as lovers. They almost reach their target, but the *African Queen* sinks in a storm before they can make their suicidal strike. They are taken prisoner by the Germans. The enemy ship is eventually sunk by more orthodox Royal Navy warships.

John Huston's film drew successfully on the hitherto largely unexploited acting talents of forty-four-year-old Katherine Hepburn (playing Rose as considerably older than Forester's thirty-three-year-old heroine). Rather than having Bogart do his worst with cockney, the director made him Canadian so he could drawl his way through the part in his habitual lisping way. Huston, an infuriating man to work with, shot the film (while shooting everything else four-footed, furry, or flying) on location in Africa. It inspired two entertainingly irritable books. Katherine Hepburn published *The Making of the African Queen: Or How I Went to Africa with Bogart, Bacall and Huston and Almost Lost My Mind*. Peter Viertel, who wrote the script, published the roman-à-clef *White Hunter, Black Heart*, which sardonically portrays the megalomaniac Huston's lust for big game – something indelibly linked to his genius as a director. Viertel's novel was made into a well-regarded film in 1990, starring Clint Eastwood. Huston was three years dead by then and could neither sue nor enjoy the movie.

After Midnight, Irmgard Keun, 1937

Exile, James Joyce decreed, was a necessary state of literary affairs. To be fully creative, authors must sever the umbilical cord connecting writer to country – even when choosing to write about that country. This was certainly the case for Irmgard Keun (1905–82). She wrote *After Midnight* (*Nach Mitternacht*) after fleeing from Nazi Germany in 1936 with her lover Joseph Roth. An increasingly difficult relationship with the Reich Literary Chamber (i.e. the office of state censorship) had made writing as she wanted to write impossible. Quixotically she sued the Gestapo for lost earnings. Keun escaped the Nazis a second time by fleeing to America when war was imminent. In 1940 she fabricated a report of her suicide to be published in newspapers. This allowed her to return, under an assumed name, to wartime Germany. The last – post-war – years of her life were passed mainly in the mental wards of several hospitals. She was 'discovered' as a great German writer (and rebel) in the 1970s, when fame meant nothing to her.

After Midnight was published (in German) in Amsterdam in 1937, but not translated into English until 1985. Novella-length, and perfunctory in structure

(reflecting the pressures on the author as she wrote it), the plot revolves around a careless remark made in a Frankfurt *Bierkeller* on the day the Führer, newly installed in office, is visiting the city. A young woman, Gerti, tells an SA man who is trying to pick her up that 'the Reichswehr have nicer uniforms and are better looking'. She has a half-Jewish sweetheart, a fact which should make her watch her mouth more carefully.

Gerti's friend Sanna (Susanne Moder) has been in Frankfurt for only a year or so. She hails from the Moselwein country. In the city she has been farmed out by her family to an unpleasant aunt, a loyal Nazi, with whose strange and obstinately anti-Nazi son, Franz, Sanna falls in love. Franz is a clerk and generally regarded as an oddball. He has a strangely inexpressive face and 'ape-like' arms. Nobody but Sanna has any time for him. Things are not helped by Franz's decking himself out in red, a highly provocative colour in a world going Fascist black. Franz and Sanna resolve to marry but he, inevitably, is denounced to the Gestapo as someone to keep an eye on. Sanna's aunt denounces her niece to the same authorities. Denunciation is endemic. No one is safe; everyone lives in a state of nervousness. Sanna has a novelist step-brother, Algin, who has fallen foul of the Nazi censors. Rather than run for his life he pens a poem celebrating Hitler. Will it save him? Or will it simply draw attention to the fact that he was not, before the Nazis came to power, a pro-Putsch 'campaigner'?

Images of the 'new Germany' and 'reconstruction' pervade the novel. The whole population is 'only gradually getting the hang of the things you cannot do' – such as speak carelessly or write freely. The story makes its points by a series of striking, but in themselves historically insignificant, images. A little girl, Berta, is coached to read out a doggerel poem to the visiting Führer and drops dead with strain. Hitler himself sails through Frankfurt in his motorcade, 'just raising an empty hand'. Faint screams are heard from over a prison wall – it is communists being beheaded (a patriotically Teutonic mode of execution, reintroduced by the Nazis). Like spiders at the corner of their web, the Gestapo watch, wait, and strike ruthlessly. Sanna is a woman of the people – a 'little person'. She is neither political nor intellectual. Things are brought to a crisis when Franz kills the man who denounced him to the authorities. The narrative climaxes with the couple fleeing to the safety (dubious, as history will soon prove) of Holland, on stolen papers. The novel ends with the plea: 'Please God, let there be a little sunlight tomorrow.' Tomorrow would be a long time coming.

Against Nature, J.–K. Huysmans, 1884

Huysmans's original title, *À rebours*, is symptomatically untranslatable – this is a novel which resists being not French. *Against Nature* and *Against the Grain* are two preferred alternatives. Even Huysmans could not make up his mind about what to call it. His first choice was *Seul* (*Alone*). The book has proved similarly uncategorisable. Best call it a thought-game about literary and sensory excess – satirically chronicled, but with such a light touch that at most points it seems to be a celebration of what it satirises. Huysmans, on his modest civil-service salary, was not able to indulge in anything excessively – certainly not in the Rajah's lifestyle of his wealthy upper-class hero. Imagination, as in masturbation, supplied what the author's wallet could not. Jean des Esseintes, *fin de ligne*, finds himself rich, alone and '*ennuyé à mourir*'. Bored to death. Near-incestuous endogamy has reduced his family, once grand and potent, to short-lived 'effeminate males'. He has been left with ample 'means' but no purpose in life. The 'carnal repasts' of sex he finds 'stupid'. Opium and hashish are 'coarse stimulants'. They offend his refined palate. A student of Baudelaire's dandyism and Verlaine's symbolism, he resolves to undertake a voyage into his own sensibility. His five senses will be what Africa was to Rimbaud. A dark continent, awaiting exploration.

Embracing the decay of the des Esseintes heritage, he becomes a connoisseur of decadence. To this end he leaves Paris, where 'all is syphilis'. In his château in the country he embarks on his great aesthetic experiment.

It is a place of 'refined solitude, a comfortable desert, a motionless ark in which to seek refuge from the unending deluge of human stupidity'. He throws a banquet which is a symphony in black. The food is served 'to the sound of funeral marches played by a concealed orchestra, nude negresses, wearing slippers and stockings of silver cloth with patterns of tears'. As a companion he has a tortoise, its shell so encrusted with inlaid jewels that the luckless animal dies, 'unable to support the dazzling luxury imposed on it, the rutilant cope with which it had been covered, the jewels with which its back had been paved, like a pyx'. He becomes a virtuoso in décor – wallpapers, ornaments, fine books, chromatic synthesis (orange, he finds, has the most exquisite effect on the senses).

The sensory experiment is a failure. Des Esseintes is driven back to life by the most banal thing – indigestion and a rebellious stomach. The road of excess, *pace* William Blake, leads to diarrhoea. The novel ends with a hint that, Jesuit-educated, he may re-embrace Catholicism (the 'consoling beacons of ancient faith'). Discipline, fasting, ritual and incense may supply what 'nude negresses' did not.

Against Nature is the 'poisonous French novel' which depraves the hero in Oscar Wilde's THE PICTURE OF DORIAN GRAY.

Alfie, Bill Naughton, 1966

Alfie began as a BBC Third Programme radio drama, *Alfie Elkins and His Little Life*, broadcast on 7 January 1962. Naughton's play chronicled the doings of a low-life spiv – a 'wide boy' – born in 1916. Notable scenes featured young Elkins in the East End rag trade and such comic episodes as his trying to stuff purloined trousers (he wore several pairs when 'nicking gear') down the lavatory while, outside, the owner patiently explains the plumbing impossibility. Alfie's strongest interest in life is 'birds', how best to 'chat them up' and, if all goes well, 'pull them'. But is there not, the play intimates, something more to life than this – even a 'little' life like his? SATURDAY NIGHT AND SUNDAY MORNING, ROOM AT THE TOP, and *Look*

Back in Anger would ask the same question, more angrily. Naughton (1910–92) was not, however, an angry young man but an ironic middle-aged man, not far off retirement. The play was successful, although it provoked protest at its 'disgustingness' from those whose radios were normally tuned in for the channel's classical music, or Louis MacNeice's exquisite verse drama.

By this point the sixties were swinging ('like a pendulum do' as the popular song put it). Cockney low-lifes, like Alfie, were being recast as 'rebels' – heroic refuseniks, Dostoevskyan 'outsiders'. *Alfie* went on to be adapted for a big-budget movie in 1966. Michael Caine's smart, dry, wholly cynical voiceover to the movie set its tone. Alfie was now a chauffeur – a driver of smart cars. A (fast-fading) Hollywood star, Shelley Winters, was recruited as one of Alfie's 'birds' – ripe for the pulling. The film co-incided with the wide distribution of 'the pill' among the kind of bird who makes young Mr Elkins' life worth living. Sex without consequence, at last. The liberating contraceptive followed on the heels of another magic pill – the antibiotic – which, at a stroke, cured dreaded TB (and a whole range of pesky STDs, which meant even fewer consequences for the modern Don Juan). *Alfie*, however, remains stuck (true to its origins) in the pre-pill dark ages. The film retains the play's strongest scene, in which Alfie impregnates the wife of one of his fellow patients in the TB sanatorium and procures a horrifying illegal abortion for her. Abortion reform came later. *Alfie* is routinely cited as having made a strong collateral case for the 1967 Act.

The film inspired a novelisation which proved to be a bestseller. The novel is magnitudes more interesting than the film. Naughton took on the existential challenge of the famous theme song, 'What's It All About, Alfie?', to explore the pathos and cosmic pointlessness of the hero's existence. The 'What's it all about?' question is left hanging, pressingly, at the end of the novel. *Alfie* was recycled yet again as a Jude Law vehicle in 2004. This time the hero was a New York, high-end limousine driver. What next? Alfie on Mars?

Alice's Adventures in Wonderland, Lewis Carroll, 1865

Middle-aged clergymen and lifelong bachelors with an interest in photographing little girls in a state of undress would probably be looked at somewhat askance nowadays. A Reverend Charles Lutwidge Dodgson *de nos jours* might well find himself answering some pointed questions in Oxford police station. In Victorian times attitudes about such things were more relaxed. Perhaps it was as well in this case, since the evidence strongly suggests that Dodgson was impeccably correct in his behaviour. Nonetheless, the fact is that Dodgson (a maths don) did love the company of little girls and wrote *Alice in Wonderland* specifically for Alice Liddell and her sisters – a colleague's daughters. But should he publish it? A novelist who was staying with him, Henry Kingsley (brother of the better-known Charles, author of *The Water Babies*), was strongly of the opinion he should put it into print. A perplexed Dodgson sent it to George MacDonald – author of *At the Back of the North Wind* – who agreed. The unworldly Dodgson first thought of Oxford University Press, the text to be illustrated by himself. OUP would jump at it now: in 1862 this was not the case. Eventually it went to Macmillan (Kingsley's publisher), with illustrations by John Tenniel. A dedicated artist, Tenniel stringently insisted the first edition of 2,000 copies be pulped because his designs were imperfectly reproduced. For professional reasons (Oxford University was strict on such matters) Dodgson used a pen name, 'Lewis Carroll'. It was a pun, inevitably – and one which his colleagues at high table doubtless had a high time puzzling out (Lewis is etymologically linked, via Latin, to 'Lutwidge'; Carroll, likewise, to 'Charles'). The two Alice books (the successor to the bestselling adventures in Wonderland was *Through the Looking-Glass*) are unusual among children's literature in appealing equally to adult readers. Ideally, clever adults.

In the first volume, Alice is discovered reading under a tree in high summer. She sees a white rabbit rush by, feverishly consulting his watch. She rashly follows him down a hole in the ground, encounters various locked doors, eats and drinks substances which enlarge and shrink her, encounters mythical creatures like the Gryphon, extinct creatures like the Dodo, toothy but smiling creatures like the Cheshire Cat, breaks in on the Mad Hatter's tea party, and is finally sentenced to be beheaded by the irascible Queen of Hearts. As the playing card entourage falls on her with decapitation in mind, Alice wakes with dead leaves brushing her face. It was summer, and now it is autumn. The little girl is growing up. How sad, the story intimates, that – as the Frenchman put it – 'little girls get bigger every day'.

Alien, Alan Dean Foster, 1979

'Great movie', most will idly think, while calling up (the men, anyway) a vivid mental image of an underpanted and interestingly perspiring Sigourney Weaver saving the world from a fate worse than Godzilla. But *Alien* also merits attention as an interesting mutation of written fiction – a new high point of novelisation. There had, of course, been 'books of the film' before – one thinks of Graham Greene's *The Third Man* and Arthur C. Clarke's *2001: A Space Odyssey*. But these afterthought productions were shadows of shadows. It was Alan Dean Foster with *Alien* and his coeval David Seltzer, with *The Omen*, who pioneered the genre. Their 'novelisations' coincided with, or preceded, the film they were (artistically) 'following'. Liberties could be taken with the plot – often resuscitating ideas lost on the cutting room floor or that never even made it to the lens.

In *Alien*, set in 2087, space has been commercialised. The 'enemy' is as much big business as scaly green monsters (though they too will do their worst). A beat-up company freighter, mischievously called *Nostromo* (after one of Joseph Conrad's more inaccessible narratives), is making its lumbering return flight from Thedus, laden with twenty million tons of ore. The seven-man (actually five men, an android, and a woman) crew are roused from cryogenic sleep to answer a mysterious distress call from a nearby planet. On its surface (bril-

liantly conceived in the film by the Swiss artist H. R. Giger) they find evidence of a dead civilisation. What has killed it? They soon find out: an alien parasite, in its maturity a gigantic gila monster with acid for blood and an insatiable appetite for flesh. An egg explodes in the face of one of the crew and the alien is transported back to the ship in his unconscious and impregnated body. The company becomes very interested – but wholly uninterested in the risks it poses to their employees. Headquarters scents commercial possibilities. The alien meanwhile, having undergone a rapid gestation, tears limb from limb all the crew other than the resourceful female warrant officer, Ripley (another sly literary allusion). She is mankind's only hope. If, as programmed, *Nostromo* lands on earth, every breathing thing on its surface will be consumed.

Although some of the basic idea and novelisation was credited to Foster there was another finger in the *Alien* pie. Dan O'Bannon had made his name at film school with a brilliant student exercise, *Dark Star*, which went on to become a cult classic. O'Bannon came up with the *mise-en-scène* of *Alien* (cryogenic slumber, distress signal, etc.). He then left to work on *Dune*, leaving Foster in charge. O'Bannon is engagingly frank about his modus operandi: 'I didn't steal *Alien* from anybody. I stole it from *everybody*!'

All Quiet on the Western Front, Erich Maria Remarque, 1929

The bestselling novel of the period in America, Britain, and Germany (as *Im Westen nichts Neues*), Remarque's novel follows the doomed fortunes of six classmates from a small northern German town; privates all. It is narrated by Paul Bäumer, an eighteen-year-old 'veteran' who, before the war and what it did to him, had poetic aspirations. Early chapters focus obsessively on what soldiers at the front really care about: rations (the old sweat Katczinsky is forever scrounging extra fodder), tobacco, sleep, boots (a strand in the novel follows the fortunes of Kemmerich's superior footwear, which passes from comrade to comrade as a string of successive owners are killed), lice, sex, letters from home, the next attack – in which all the foregoing may become irrelevant.

The unit in which the six comrades serve sustains horrific casualties. The soldiers reserve their particular hatred not for the enemy but for their own officers and, directing them, the politicians. In their free time, they philosophise about the horrors of war: 'The war has ruined us for everything', they conclude. In one horrific episode, Paul bayonets a French *poilu* in a shell crater, and has to spend hours with the dying man. Paul goes home on leave, where he finds his mother dying of cancer. His jingoistic elders – men whom he once respected – now revolt him. He is glad to return to the front. One by one the six comrades die. Finally, on the day that the Armistice is being signed, Paul, realising that he can never readjust to civilian life, walks into no-man's-land and is shot. The news the day he dies 'confined itself to the single sentence: All quiet on the Western Front'. Remarque himself had served in the infantry in the First World War, and in 1916, as a sapper, was serving only a couple of miles from Adolf Hitler, a company runner, at the third battle of Ypres.

The novel was made into a film in 1930 by Universal Studios, directed by Lewis Milestone. The film elaborates the ending into a famous, non-suicidal moment. Paul leans out of his trench towards a butterfly, and is picked off by a French sniper. The emergent Nazi Party in Germany succeeded, by violent demonstrations outside cinemas, in having Milestone's film withdrawn. The novel was ceremonially burned in the great Berlin book-burnings of 1933. Four years later the author was stripped of his German citizenship. Remarque, sensing what was coming, had already departed to live as a refugee in Switzerland. His sister Elfriede did not. The Nazis arrested her on a trumped-up charge and beheaded her. For them, a cutting review meant just that.

All Souls, Javier Marías, 1989

In 1979 Javier Marías – a dyed-in-the-wool Anglophile – won the Spanish National Translation Award for his version of THE LIFE AND OPINIONS OF TRISTRAM SHANDY, GENTLEMAN – that 'Cervantick' *jeu d'esprit* which is a bow of Hercules for the translator. It was followed by two years as a 'temporary don' at Oxford, between 1983–5. This was the prelude to his first novel to be published in English, *All Souls* (*Todas las Almas*). To the Spanish ear, 'Don' calls up the following word, 'Quixote'. *All Souls*, too, is a chronicle of magnificent failure. There is the conventional protestation about 'no resemblance' in the novel's prelims. It is, we may assume, not the least fictional thing in this work of fiction. Marías (who clearly inherited a streak of mischief from his admired Sterne) compounded the joke by writing a subsequent 'false novel' (as he rather inscrutably called it), *Dark Back of Time*, complaining about the many Oxonians who had complained about being satirically depicted in *Todas las Almas*.

The unnamed hero of *All Souls* falls in love with a beautiful academic lady on windy, dark Didcot Parkway station – a facility which would qualify as Dante's tenth circle of hell. Clare Bayes is the leggy wife of a more permanent don, who interests the hero not at all. Her child, 'the boy' Eric, he finds even less interesting. As his prey is pursued, the novel ponders the oddity of Oxford, its out-of-worldness. The hero's college porter, for example, has escaped the bonds of time and in his dementia exists some days in 1941, others in 1961, some days today, some days tomorrow. Among the dreaming spires human beings do not matter; 'the only things that count here are the institutions'. People have no more permanence than sunbeams, or gusts of wind shuffling dead leaves. The hero gets his carnal way with Clare but, finally, she declines – scornfully – to elope with him. He is, she informs him, a lover who has stayed too long. A temporary don who would be a long-term Don Juan.

During his years in Oxford the hero makes two college friends. Cromer-Blake is a dandy homosexual who is dying, with exquisite good manners. The other friend is Toby Rylands, also dying (of old age). Rylands is a retired scholar of great distinction who is writing what is promised to be the finest study of Sterne's *A Sentimental Journey*. On his death, the study is discovered to be nonexistent – a Shandean joke. Haunting

Oxford's second-hand bookshops, the hero develops an obsessive interest in the minor writer Arthur Machen and, through him, the poet ('excessively minor', as Barry Humphries has called him) John Gawsworth. Gawsworth befriended Machen and became a fanatic disciple of the slightly less excessively minor novelist M. P. Shiel. Things, at this point, get slightly complex. Shiel was mixed-race, and West Indian by origin. When he was fifteen his father bestowed on him the monarchy of Redonda – a rocky islet in the Caribbean, used by seagulls as a handy latrine. Gawsworth inherited the title 'King of Redonda', but died a hopeless, homeless, pointless alcoholic. This, Marías infers, is the lot of the author. The king who lives in beggary, with a kingdom covered in shit.

In acknowledgement of his tender portrait of Gawsworth, Marías was himself anointed King of Redonda. He has ennobled his fellow authors *en masse*. Among them William Boyd (Duke of Brazzaville), W. G. Sebald (Duke of Vértigo), Umberto Eco (Duke of la Isla del Día de Antes), A. S. Byatt (Duchess of Morpho Eugenia). I have hopes (as the editor of the founder-king's THE PURPLE CLOUD) of at least a viscountcy myself.

The Ambassadors, Henry James, 1903

There are many dragons at the gate of 'late James'. *The Ambassadors* is second in fear-someness only to *The Sacred Fount*. The plot is, once detached from the Jamesian prose which encases it, simple enough. Lewis Lambert Strether, a Yankee businessman from Woollett, Massachusetts, made an early impulsive marriage. His wife died, to be followed by their ten-year-old son, from diphtheria. Strether is consumed by guilt – had he mourned his wife less, could he have intervened to save his son sooner? He edits a highbrow journal. It is, he is at pains to proclaim, a thing of no importance – but, in its way, 'distinguished'. His name is inscribed on the title page – as it might be on a tombstone for the living.

Now in the shadow years of his life he is again involved in an affair of the heart – old

though that organ is (Strether's teeth, James is at odd pains to let us know, are in good shape). He intends to marry a rich Woollett widow, Mrs Newsome. She dispatches Strether on an 'embassy' to Paris to bring back her errant son Chad, who has fallen into 'foreign ways'. On his journey to Paris the ambassador from Woollett teams up with a frighteningly busybody-ish fellow American, Maria Gostrey, who regards herself as a kind of Virgil, helping Yankees negotiate the infernal circles of Europe. A Sancho Panza simpleton, Waymarsh, who sucks a cigar and indulges in 'sacred rages', attaches himself to Strether. Chad finally makes an appearance – in the box of a theatre where the 'ambassadors' are watching an opera. The thirty-something man Strether finds is not the victim of European decadence he had anticipated. At a garden party, the two women who have captivated Chad are intro-duced to Strether – the countess Marie de Vionnet and her daughter Jeanne. But which of the women has captivated him most? Strether finds himself dangerously drawn to Marie. Mrs Newsome grows fretful. Chad's sister Sarah, another ambassador, is dispatched to sort things out.

Completely out of his depth, desperately in search of 'some idea that would simplify', Strether leaves Paris for a tour of the coun-tryside where, unexpectedly, he finds out the truth about Chad and the countess. It could be sex. The irrepressible Marie Gostrey offers Strether marriage – he refuses and turns his back on everything Paris has stirred in him with the rueful, and comically inadequate, summing up: 'Then there we are!' But where? Whether or not Chad will return home is left hanging. Has he been ruined or saved? Has Strether? Paris stirred something in him. It leads to his ejaculation which James, in his preface, directs the reader to as the key to *The Ambassadors*: 'Live all you can; it's a mistake not to.' What ejaculations is Strether capable of? E. M. Forster slyly points out that the man from Woollett could no more take off his trousers than he could take off his skin and dance about in his bones.

James says a lot, but often not what the reader desperately wants to know. Miss Gostrey presses Strether closely on the 'little nameless object' in whose manufacture

Woollett leads the world. 'It's a little thing they make – make better, it appears, than other people can, or than other people, at any rate, do,' Strether explains, adding vaguely that it is 'a small, trivial, rather ridiculous object of the commonest domestic use, it's just wanting in – what shall I say? Well, dignity, or the least approach to distinction.' Is it shoe polish? ventures Gostrey. Apparently not. Various plausible objects have been suggested: button hooks, toothpicks and – by the novelist David Lodge – chamber pots.

An American Dream, Norman Mailer, 1964

According to the novel's epigraph: 'There are too many American Dreams'. Few, however, are as nightmarish as Mailer's. Or, some thought, as downright awful. 'A dreadful novel', the Dean of New York critics, Stanley Edgar Hyman, called it. Mailer could plead that his dreadful novel was born in a dreadful time. An American Dream was published in 1964, the year after the assassination of JFK in Dallas, while the paranoia storm generated by that mysterious atrocity was still raging. It was also the year that saw the first meeting of the National Organization for Women, destined to be sworn foes to male-sexist-pig Norman Mailer. The novel can be seen as getting his retaliation in first. Or, more likely, an expression of the pugnacious relationship the younger Mailer had with America. Always had with America, one might say.

The narrative opens with a scene which has become famous as the quintessence of the Mailerist in-your-face offensiveness. Stephen Rojack (the Ukrainian name is never explained) – Harvard graduate (a buddy of JFK's on jolly student 'poon' hunts, as the future president called them), decorated war hero, and former congressman – is nowadays scraping by as a talk-show host and a professor of existential psychology. It's a living. High on booze, he breaks into the apartment of his former wife Deborah (an ultra-fashionable woman whom he met through 'Jack') and murders her. An existential act – just like Meursault's in THE

OUTSIDER. 'She was bad in death', we are told:

> A beast stared back at me. Her teeth showed, the point of light in her eye was violent, and her mouth was open.

Before calling the cops, Rojack takes time out to sodomise the German maid below stairs. Her name is 'Ruta' (Roto-Rooter, a sewage and drain-cleaning firm, is evoked). 'There was canny, hard-packed evil in that butt', he solemnly observes. It has been nominated as the most unconsciously funny line in the whole Mailerian oeuvre. There are other strong candidates. 'You are absolutely a genius, Mr Rojack,' Ruta says, after being violated. Rojack blandly explains to the police that his wife committed suicide by throwing herself off the balcony of the high-rise apartment. The cops are sceptical but give him a pass. He's a stand-up guy – and everyone knows what a pain in the ass wives can be. Over the following twenty-four hours Rojack plumbs the very depths of the Manhattan underworld, crossing the paths of assorted Mafiosi, a black jazz musician named Shago Martin (clearly based on Sammy Davis Jr) and Shago's blonde nightclub-singer girlfriend, Cherry McMahon. She, too, thinks Rojack a genius and offers no resistance to his manly demands

He is, meanwhile, receiving transmissions from the moon. Loony rather than lunar, one might think. He learns that Deborah had been involved in high-profile cases of espionage. Was she, though? His ex-wife's father, Barney Oswald Kelly (the middle name is significant) – a magnate with Mafia connections – is exposed as an incarnation of the Devil. In a Dostoevskyan episode Rojack is forced by the Evil One to traverse the inches-wide Waldorf Towers window ledge, confronting obscure cosmic truths all the while. He survives and walks out a truly free man at last. He has passed the supreme existential test. On arriving for some rest and recuperation at Cherry's apartment, he finds an ambulance and a police car waiting in front of the building. Cherry has been beaten to death by a friend of Shago's, and Shago himself has been beaten to death by an unknown assailant in

Harlem. Rojack drives to Las Vegas, and wins enough money to pay all his debts. As the novel ends, he makes plans to go to Guatemala.

It is a narrative that is beyond implausible – even borderline psychotic. The novel bears reading, though, for its extraordinary paranoid energy. And for those interested in the author it can be linked to events in Mailer's own life. A few years before writing it, at a party he reportedly threw to announce his intention to run for Mayor of New York on the 'Existentialist' ticket, Mailer got drunk and stabbed his second wife Adele, nearly killing her. Adele declined to press charges and Mailer escaped with a fortnight in Bellevue for psychiatric observation.

American Gods, Neil Gaiman, 2001

'I wanted to write a book that was big and odd and meandering', said Gaiman. One of *American Gods*' more daring meanders is across traditional genre lines. The novel scooped up a Hugo and a Nebula, the two premier SF awards (a double which puts Gaiman in a very elite club – up there with Asimov and Clarke). It also won the Bram Stoker Award for Horror and a Locus Award for Fantasy. Arguably it should also have won an Edgar as the best detective novel of the year. The first one hundred and fifty pages (a mere sliver, compared to the seven-hundred-page whole) shape up as a hard-boiled crime novel. Shadow is doing three years' hard time. He took the rap for something he didn't do, but he's a stand-up guy. Prison has made him existential in his outlook, scholarly in his reading (he knows his Herodotus backwards) and a skilled prestidigitator. The coin tricks he picked up from a cellmate, Low-Key (i.e. 'Loki' – there's a lot of that kind of wordplay). Prison evidently prepared Shadow for something. But what?

> He did not awake in prison with a feeling of dread: he was no longer scared of what tomorrow might bring, because yesterday had brought it.

In fact, tomorrow brings something very scary. His wife Laura has been looked after by his best friend Robbie while he's inside. A job in Robbie's body-building business is in prospect on Shadow's release. A day before the prison gate swings open, he learns his wife and best friend have been killed in a road accident. He will (somewhat later) learn that Robbie's genitals were in her mouth when the fatal accident happened.

On the flight to her funeral Shadow finds himself sitting alongside a corpulent gent who mysteriously knows all about him. Mr Wednesday ('Odin's Day', we later learn) invites Shadow to come and work for him as a kind of factotum. 'You could be the next King of America', he says. Shadow is, we gather, the Chosen One. Or, perhaps, just a gofer. Wednesday/Odin, a God with 'as many names as there are ways to die', has died many times and will die again. By the time we take all this on, the novel has changed genre gear. Gradually the central conceit reveals itself. All those immigrants to the New World – from the Vikings onwards – brought gods with them. But once arrived, they ceased to worship them. Without observance (but with a bit of blood sacrifice) the Gods live on as old codgers – mere shadows of their once-divine selves. America has become an old-gods home. It's a sad and rather comic comedown. One of the Egyptian deities, for example, custodian of the Book of the Dead, finds himself reduced to running a small-town funeral parlour. A leprechaun bums Guinness in bars. The gods are angry as hell (a region they know better than most) and intend to make war on the new pantheon – 'gods of of plastic, beeper, and neon'. Odin – Mr Wednesday – will lead them into Armageddon.

At this point, the plot gets very fuzzy. Shadow's wife returns in his dreams to warn him of something bad about to happen. It's lonely being dead. She wants him to bring her back to life. Oh, and why not some sexual intercourse to warm her up? Forget the blow job: she was just thanking Robbie for the lift – mere courtesy. Things get fuzzier still. There is a protracted pseudo-crucifixion of what may be a pseudo-Odin and a hint that Shadow is, indeed, 'The One'. Gaiman confirmed it in a live interview at UCLA when he disclosed that Shadow was (as astute Gaimanists had guessed) Odin's son, another Lord of Asgard. Watch that space.

An American Tragedy, Theodore Dreiser, 1925

Dreiser's novel coincides, chronologically, with THE GREAT GATSBY. The question *An American Tragedy* poses is: 'What did Fitzgerald's "Jazz Age" mean on $15 a week?' Dreiser was born, the twelfth child of poor German immigrants, in 1871. He dropped out of college to earn his living and – a clever young man with no advantages – drifted into journalism, thence into writing fiction. Before *An American Tragedy* his work had received respectful notices but no great sales. The idea for the novel was an actual murder. In 1906 Chester Gillette, a junior clerk at a skirt factory, having impregnated a factory girl, hoped to rise in life by marrying the boss's daughter. He solved the problem by taking the mother of his unborn child to an idyllic lake in the Adirondacks where he clubbed her with a tennis racket and allowed her to drown. It is possible that at the last moment Gillette lost his nerve and did not intend to do it. No matter: he went to the 'chair'. Dreiser moved the action of *An American Tragedy* to the 1920s. 'I call it an American tragedy', he explained, 'because it could not happen in any other country in the world.' America's 'tragic error', he believed, was the belief that you could rise in life to fulfil your dream and were justified in whatever means you chose to do so. Like clubbing an inconvenient girl to death with a tennis racket.

The novel opens and closes with parallel scenes of itinerant street preachers sermonising to indifferent passers-by as their offspring yearn for more out of life. Not for 'pagan' Clyde Griffiths the grim austerities of a street preacher's life. He lands a job as bellhop at the finest hotel in Kansas City, where he observes rich people's 'fun'. On an excursion in a purloined Packard, he is involved in an accident in which a little girl is run over. He flees to Lycurgus in upper New York state where an uncle owns a profitable factory making collars. Possessed of good manners and good looks, Clyde is taken on in a junior capacity. Like Gillette, he seduces a factory girl, falls in love with a wealthy girl, and solves his problems with a forehand smash on a deserted lake. But Dreiser leaves unclear, in his warty Germanic style of writing, what is actually going through Clyde's mind as he does the act – or does not do it:

> At this cataclysmic moment, and in the face of the utmost, the most urgent need of action, a sudden palsy of the will – of courage – of hate or rage sufficient; and with Roberta from her seat in the stern of the boat gazing at his troubled and then suddenly distorted and fulgurous, yet weak and even unbalanced face – a face of a sudden, instead of angry, ferocious, demoniac – confused and all but meaningless in its registration of a balanced combat between fear (a chemic revulsion against death or murderous brutality that would bring death) and a harried and restless and yet self-repressed desire to do – to do – to do – yet temporarily unbreakable here and now – a static between a powerful compulsion to do and yet not to do.

'I spent the better part of forty years trying to induce him to reform and electrify his manner of writing', wrote Dreiser's friend and patron, H. L. Mencken. He failed. Nonetheless, *An American Tragedy* was to America's taste in 1925. Reviews were ecstatic. It was, wrote one critic, the 'Mount Everest' of American fiction. At 400,000 words to *Gatsby*'s puny 50,000 it was certainly big.

Amok, Stefan Zweig, 1922

There are those who think Zweig is the greatest of interwar German-language fiction writers (not quite a novelist – the novella, or long short story, was always his preference). Much translated, his work is a prime example of the brilliance which flared up among the embers of the Austro-Hungarian Empire: his achievements, his supporters aver, rank with those of Schoenberg, Wittgenstein, and Koestler. But there are also those who maintain that Zweig is minor compared to his friend and protégé Joseph Roth, and a veritable pygmy compared to Kafka. Michael Hofmann is notably severe: 'He's the Pepsi of Austrian writing.'

'Amok' is, on the face of it, reminiscent of Joseph Conrad ('The Secret Sharer') and Somerset Maugham ('Rain'). But it has a metallic coldness that is distinctly Germanic and which rings hard, even in translation. The narrator – as blank as cellophane – is returning from a tour of India, where he was, we deduce, terminally bored. On the journey home he is appalled by the vulgarity of his fellow passengers and keeps to his cabin by day, venturing out on deck only in the cool of the night. A dry hard cough alerts him to another nocturnal escapee. Cigarettes are shared and – on the second night they meet – the other passenger tells his shipboard tale.

A doctor, originally from Leipzig, he was caught up in a scandal involving a woman and gunplay. Things got too hot for him and he took a contract job in the Dutch East Indies back country. It was not done out of humane motives; he regards the natives as 'scum'. Among the maladies peculiar to Indonesia is 'running amok' – a placid Malay suddenly takes a knife or axe and, for no reason at all, goes on a killing rampage. 'It's madness, a sort of human rabies,' the doctor explains.

In his station in the back country, the doctor was visited by a glamorous, limousine-borne European woman. After some coy interchange, it emerged she wanted a child (not her husband's) aborted. The doctor was instantly infatuated. He agreed to do the operation not for the large amount of money she offered, but for the enjoyment of her body (whether before or after is not clear). Rather than succumb she put herself in the hands of a filthy abortionist, who botched the operation fatally. The woman would not let the doctor save her, and insisted on dying with her secret (and her reputation) intact. Suicide – or, from another angle, manslaughter. The doctor duly lied to the woman's husband and threw in his job (and his pension – due in a couple

of years) in order to accompany the corpse back to civilisation in its lead-lined coffin. Her body, as he speaks, is rotting a few feet beneath them in the cargo hold. When they land at Naples, and it is in the process of being winched ashore, he throws himself on the coffin, taking it (and his luckless self) to the bottom. Irrecoverably.

Suicide figures centrally in much of Zweig's fiction, in his life, and in his death. Born the son of a Jewish millionaire, his adult life, after the Nazi takeover, was one of constant flight. In 1942, as German victory seemed certain, he and his wife took an overdose of Veronal together. In his suicide note he wrote:

> I thus prefer to end my life at the right time, upright, as a man for whom cultural work has always been his purest happiness and personal freedom – the most precious of possessions on this earth.

And Then There Were None, Agatha Christie, 1939

The retitling of this novel over the years is itself an interesting piece of social history and a register of what fiction is and is not permitted to say. It was first published as *Ten Little Niggers*, and subsequently as *Ten Little Indians*. That second title was, in its turn, deemed insensitive to Native Americans and it was laundered into *And Then There Were None*. The original title was drawn from a 'minstrel' song in the 1860s in America. Christie may, more plausibly, have known it not as a song but as one of the 'counting out' rhymes – like 'one potato, two potato, three potato four', or 'eeny, meeny, miny, mo' – still used by children in the playground

The novel opens with eight guests and two housekeepers being invited by a mysterious 'Mr Owen' to visit 'Indian [Nigger] Island', off the coast of Devon. They are: Mr Justice Lawrence Wargrave (a judge), Miss Emily Brent (an aged spinster), Captain Philip Lombard (a ladies' man), General John MacArthur, CMG, DSO (an old soldier), Dr Edward Armstrong, Tony Marston (a bland young man-about-town), Mr William Blore, and Vera Claythorne (a youngish school-teacher). All of them, it emerges, have committed a murder in their pasts for which they have never been punished. An 'indictment' is read out, by gramophone, and one by one (as in the nursery rhyme) they are killed – by shooting, poisoning, drowning, bludgeoning. The action ends with Vera, the sole survivor, hanging herself. In an epilogue, Judge Wargrave reveals that he is the executioner, and that he has carefully rigged his own suicide by shooting to look like murder to the investigating policeman, Inspector Maine. A dead man's trick. It is not merely the title which has been messed about with over the decades. *And Then There Were None* was very successfully dramatised by Christie in 1943. In the play Wargrave appears on stage and is foiled in his attempt to drive Vera to suicide by the last-minute heroics of Phil Lombard. The two young people survive to marry. The play was filmed as *Ten Little Niggers* by René Clair in 1945. This too has been serially retitled. 'What's in a name?' A lot of cultural history sometimes.

Angel Pavement, J. B. Priestley, 1930

Like its predecessor *The Good Companions* (1929), *Angel Pavement* was a runaway best-seller and what Priestley liked to call his 'golden gusher'. It continued to gush throughout his long writing career, subsidising many more ambitious ventures in authorship. Not everyone took pleasure in Priestley's triumph. Graham Greene, at an early struggling stage of his career, published his would-be bestseller *Stamboul Train* with the same publisher, Heinemann. Priestley, through the publisher, got a sight of Greene's proofs, in which he was portrayed as 'Quin Savory', a vulgar, fourth-rate Dickensian, 'Sold a hundred thousand copies. . . Two hundred characters.' And with a lustful eye for the ladies (which Priestley did indeed possess). Using his power in the firm, and the threat of libel action, Priestley enforced changes to Greene's text.

Resolutely middlebrow in tone (it flew off the shelf like hot cakes in the 'tuppenny' cornershop libraries of the time), the mood

of *Angel Pavement* is notably grimmer than that of *The Good Companions*, registering the traumatic impact of 1929's Great Depression. It retains a period charm.

The action centres on the firm of Twigg & Dersingham, London dealers in veneer and inlay. Their establishment is in 'Angel Pavement', a sleepy cul-de-sac in the City of London. The firm is an old-fashioned enterprise run with old-fashioned decency under the management of the middle-aged and 'gentlemanly' Howard Dersingham, assisted by his similarly antique head clerk, Hubert Smeeth. Enter James Golspie, a vulgar businessman who has come from the Baltic states with a consignment of suspiciously cheap timber. There is something 'faintly piratical' about Golspie, but he gains the confidence of the gullible Dersingham. Less effectively, he tries to seduce the firm's secretary, Miss Lilian Matfield, offering to take her on a dirty weekend to Brighton. Within six months Golspie has ruined the firm. He leaves Dersingham and Smeeth both unemployed and, at their age, unemployable. The last we see of the villain is on board a luxury liner, with his coquettish daughter (who has broken the heart of one of the firm's clerks), sailing off to South America. The novel's principal assertion – one of meagre comfort to the British people, facing ten years' grinding 'austerity' (i.e. deprivation and poverty) – is that bad things like this always come, like Dracula, from abroad. As I write, the same ('it's the Eurozone, stupid') line is being trotted out while Britain faces another 'austere' decade.

The Angels of Mons, Arthur Machen, 1915

War was declared between Britain and Germany in August 1914. A British Expeditionary Force was sent across the Channel. Jingoism on the home front was at hysteria level. The BEF was outnumbered and ordered to defend positions against the invading Germans which they had no time to fortify. Theirs not to reason why. Seasoned regulars – who had shot everything from 'fuzzy wuzzies' to 'Johnny Boer' (conscription had not yet cranked up) – were accepted into the force, and with wry humour christened themselves 'the Old Contemptibles'. At Mons, on the Belgium border, the BEF held their ground before effecting an orderly retreat. It was a defeat but, like Dunkirk in the Second World War, a glorious one.

Arthur Machen, a venerable writer with a strong line in finely drawn supernatural horror fiction, had been, along with the rest of the nation, gripped by newsreel and newspaper coverage. He wrote a short story for the London *Evening News* of 29 September 1914, called 'The Bowmen'. It features a 'Latin scholar' on the front line, facing the Teutonic foe, who invokes the spirit of Henry V. And:

as the Latin scholar uttered his invocation he felt something between a shudder and an electric shock pass through his body. The roar of the battle died down in his ears to a gentle murmur; instead of it, he says, he heard a great voice and a shout louder than a thunder-peal crying, 'Array, array, array!'

Enter Harry's archers. They help stem the Hun Horde – some of whom, to the mystification of the invader, have arrow wounds when their corpses are examined. Machen's text is laced with the 'buckets of eyeballs' propaganda about German beastliness which had been whipped up by the British authorities to induce the necessary blood lust among a population who, in summer 1914, could not quite work out why a world war was necessary or, if it was, why they should lead the fight. In 'The Bowmen', Machen has a vivid scene in which German soldiers crucify a baby on a church door. 'The baby was only three years old. He died calling piteously for "mummy" and "daddy".' Swine.

The newspaper did not clearly identify 'The Bowmen' as a work of fiction. It yielded Machen very little money but, in the weeks after it appeared, he was asked many times (mainly by clergymen) for the right to reprint or recite it. It merged with a confluent stream of war propaganda reporting that, during the Battle of Mons, British soldiers had seen not bowmen but 'angels' assisting their heroic efforts. It has been suggested that this nonsense was encouraged by 'black arts' propagandists in the war ministry.

Machen reissued his story ten months later, plumping it out to novel length with news reports, as *The Angels of Mons*. His original story had not mentioned angels. As an author (he penned some of the best ghost stories in the language) he was certainly susceptible to elements of the supernatural, but he loathed formal religion. As he wrote in his introduction to *The Angels of Mons*:

Well, I have long maintained that on the whole the average church, considered as a house of preaching, is a much more poisonous place than the average tavern. . .

Nonetheless, the Mons Angels lodged in the public mind as an enduring war legend, even if the troops serving in the British Army always had their doubts about receiving angelic reinforcements. When I was doing my national service in 1960, at a camp in Aldershot called 'Mons', one of the favourite complaints about something that had gone wrong was that it was 'the biggest fuck-up' ('cock up' if ladies were present) 'since Mons'.

Anna Karenina, Leo Tolstoy, 1877

The opening sentence about happy and unhappy families is famous and everywhere quoted. Also famous is the account of how the forty-four-year-old Tolstoy (with *War and Peace* behind him) happened on the idea for a novel so domestic, and 'unhistorical', in its plot. In 1872 a thirty-five-year-old woman, distantly related to him, had committed suicide-by-railway, near the author's estate. An interested Tolstoy attended her autopsy. The other, more literary, inspiration was his reading of one of Pushkin's short stories, which began – without any ado – 'The guests were arriving at the dacha of X.' The Pushkinian directness excited Tolstoy. Could he not do something similar? Discarding all circuitousness, exposition or scene-setting, he followed Pushkin's headlong example:

Happy families are all alike; every unhappy family is unhappy in its own way. Everything was in confusion in the Oblonskys' house. The wife had discovered that the husband was carrying on an intrigue with a French girl, who had been a governess in their family, and she had announced to her husband that she could not go on living in the same house with him.

Anna Karenina was serialised, and its first instalment landed like a bombshell in 1873. All Moscow was agog for the next section. Following the narrative to Anna's final act would, however, require unusual patience. It would be four years before Tolstoy released the last instalment, with the heroine's shocking solution to her problems.

The narrative architecture is more precise than in WAR AND PEACE. Tolstoy's narrative opens 'happily', with Anna married to the rising politician Karenin (aristocratic, like all the principal characters). They have a son, Seryozha. She travels from St Petersburg to Moscow to visit and aid her sister-in-law, Dolly, who has found herself suddenly unhappily married after the business with the French governess, which Tolstoy rushed out in the novel's second sentence. Anna resourcefully patches things up between 'Stiva' and his wife. Happiness is restored. But on her arrival at Moscow railway station she encounters a dashing young(ish) cavalry officer, Vronsky. This meeting will ruin her own marriage. The adultery that follows is complex. A practised philanderer, Vronsky has, in Anna, met a woman whom his predatory sexual code cannot manage. Anna, for her part, has met a man immune to her trite home cures for the Oblonskys' marital trials. After a prolonged siege, 'that which he asks for' is given Vronsky (Tolstoy tactfully evades description of the event itself) and Anna discovers herself pregnant. Karenin is twenty years older than Anna and, we apprehend, marital relations have ended. But not legal relations. In pre-Revolution Russia, only the innocent party could apply for a divorce. Vronsky resigns his commission. He is aristocratic, rich, cultivated, and for the first time genuinely in love. He fondly believes that society has progressed 'beyond its ancient prejudices'. It hasn't, he discovers. Russia winks at adultery – finds it an exciting spectacle, even. It tolerates mistresses. Peasant girls are fair game for any sexual marauder with a handle to his name. But Russia will not tolerate new forms of marriage.

Tolstoy never went in for simple narratives. He called his novel *Anna Karenina* but he could, as aptly, have entitled it *Anna Karenina and Konstantin Levin*. There is a second story that centres on 'Kostya' Levin, and is quite separate in its thematic concerns. Kostya's wife 'Kitty' (as adorably childlike as her nickname suggests) was once one of Vronsky's sexual targets before he was distracted by Anna. Levin believes that if there is hope for Russia it lies in the peasants. He experiences a Pisgah-like vision of an agrarian utopian future (he hates railways) in a haymaking scene when, *enfilade* with his peasants (a decade earlier they had been serfs), he finds himself at one with his swinging scythe and his fellow mowers. Levin's solution to the world's woes is that of Voltaire's CANDIDE. He will cultivate his garden. With the difference that Levin's garden is an estate of some 6,000 acres. Utopianism, like conventional marriage, is sceptically examined.

The final complications of the narrative consistently surprise the reader. Some years on Dolly visits Anna, now living with her paramour on his country estate. Dolly, the 'respectable' woman, is worn out, dowdy, and wretched. Anna, the 'fallen' woman, is blissful: 'I'm ashamed to confess it, but I . . . I am inexcusably happy. Something magical has happened to me.' But Tolstoy lifts the cover on her 'happiness'. Dolly, wholly innocent about such things, discovers Anna is using contraceptives. She has not told Vronsky, who is longing for a son. And she is a *morphiniste*. Her happiness, part of it at least, comes from a laudanum bottle. She finally finds peace under the wheels of a railway engine. The massive narrative ends, enigmatically, with a terrible thunderstorm. What comes next – the rainbow or the fire?

Anna of the Five Towns, Arnold Bennett, 1902

With the growth of the Suffrage Movement, powerful male novelists made efforts in print to protest that they understood the

'New Woman' phenomenon. Three superior novels which fall into this category are Lawrence's *Women in Love*, Wells' *Ann Veronica* and Bennett's *Anna of the Five Towns*. Not merely do these novels claim to understand women – they imply they understand women better than women understand themselves. Bennett's is a proudly provincial novel. 'Bursley' is one of five towns which, collectively, make up the Staffordshire 'Potteries', a region so called for their principal industrial product:

> The horse is less to the Arab than clay is to the Bursley man. He exists in it and by it; it fills his lungs and blanches his cheek; it keeps him alive and it kills him. His fingers close round it as round the hand of a friend. He knows all its tricks and aptitudes; when to coax and when to force it.

Bursley is home to a non-conformist belief system which adds energy to industry. There is a fine chapter, describing a religious revival campaign, which probes the happy marriage of Methodism and capitalism. The narrative opens with the heroine, Anna Tellwright, emerging from Sunday school, a creature of 'foal-like' beauty, with a good-conduct prize Bible in her hands. It is a sunny day, but she feels vaguely imprisoned by

> the various Connexional buildings which on three sides enclosed the yard – chapel, school, lecture-hall, and chapel-keeper's house. Most of the children had already squeezed through the narrow iron gate into the street beyond, where a steam-car was rumbling and clattering up Duck Bank attended by its immense shadow.

Anna's father, a coarse man and a lapsed Wesleyan, adopted 'brass' (i.e. money) as his great aim in life. By skinflintery, he has acquired a great deal of brass. At twenty-one, Anna inherits (from a relative) even more – £50,000, a huge sum. Her father has a lock on it – which she initially acquiesces to:

> Practically, Anna could not believe that she was rich; and in fact she was

not rich – she was merely a fixed point through which moneys that she was unable to arrest passed with the rapidity of a train.

As part of her inheritance she is a slum landlord. In this capacity she must exact rent from Titus Price and his son Willie, whose family business is on the rocks. 'But', she asks herself, 'would Christ have driven Titus Price into the bankruptcy court?' Matters are complicated by a growing romantic attachment to Willie. Anna's attractions, not least her fortune, attract the attention of Henry Mynors, a successful salesman who is 'rock-solid chapel'. Her father, Ephraim, approves. Mynors 'has his head screwed on'. A great crisis arises for Anna when Titus hangs himself, driven to the act by the shame of having forged a promissory note to save his business. Anna burns the incriminating document. Henry Mynors' offer of marriage is accepted. Bennett called the play he spun off from the novel *Cupid and Commonsense*. The second is now in ascendant. Willie goes off, it is believed, to Australia. The last words of the novel let the reader in on a sinister secret – he actually threw himself down a disused mine shaft. *Anna of the Five Towns* was a huge success and inspired a career in writing which made Bennett one of the wealthiest novelists in Britain and Virginia Woolf's *bête noire*. 'Brass' did not impress her.

The Apes of God, Wyndham Lewis, 1930

Lewis called his memoir of the Great War *Blasting and Bombardiering*. He liked hurling explosives around and would declare (literary) war in order to find targets for his irrepressible belligerence. Taking a wide-angle view, *The Apes of God* is the angry side of his cool – and amazingly perceptive – Vorticist portraits of leading figures of the modernist movement (Ezra Pound, T. S. Eliot, et al.) and the Bloomsbury coterie (the Sitwells, Strachey, et al.). It has been suggested that the 'moronic' Dan Boleyn spoofs the young Stephen Spender, a writer novelists just could not leave alone.

The two men had met when Spender invited Lewis to Oxford to address the Poetry Society. Lewis was evidently not much impressed with his host – although he later painted a very fine portrait of Spender.

Few artists (none ranks with him for ambidexterity) could blow so hot and so cold as Wyndham Lewis. *The Apes of God* blows very hot indeed. It is wilfully disorganised ('author in a rage') and – as angry people will – goes on at inordinate length. One episode, 'Lord Osmund's Lenten Party', is, at over 250 pages, of novel-length in itself. And tedious.

The narrative is set in the mid-1920s, climaxing in the General Strike of 1926, when it looked as if the whole country might go bang. Emergent Blackshirtism and Redflagism are described prophetically (Lewis was an acute political observer). The plot pivots on a version of Julien Benda's *trahison des clercs* thesis – the clever people have let the country go to pieces. Not villainy, but weak knees and degeneracy are to blame. Lewis satirises an anaemic artistic London, its reddest blood having been spilled by the riverful in France while aesthetes (of deviant sexual inclination, typically) thrived at home alongside the soft-faced businessmen who did very well out of the war, thank you very much. Everything enfeebled in British culture was, Lewis felt, incarnate in writers like the Sitwells, skewered in his novel as the 'Finnian Shaws'. They responded to his assault with what Lewis described as the 'sly Bloomsbury sniff'. The novel takes wild haymaking sideswipes at James Joyce (Lewis makes him Jewish – a poke at Leopold Bloom), Virginia Woolf, and – most vituperatively – Gertrude Stein. All these are 'apes' in the sense of 'aping', going through the motions, capable of nothing original.

The ingénu hero, Dan Boleyn, is a would-be *littérateur* (there is an obvious echo in the name, but the allusion to Henry's luckless queen goes nowhere obvious). Dan finds himself adrift in London, where he receives his education in literary apedom. He is instructed by such sages as the albino homosexual Horace Zagreus (who is as grotesque as his name); he regards Dan's 'moronism' as a tabula rasa on which he can inscribe his teachings. Somewhere in the background is Pierpoint (a name traditionally associated with hangmen), who seems to be a Lewisian mouthpiece. A papal figure, deistically above it all, the offstage Pierpoint communicates by written 'bulls'. One of the problems with the book was that, for all its ferocity, it was never entirely clear – three miles outside Soho anyway – who was being targeted. This is a problem which has become more acute with the passing of time. As Lewis' targets have faded into the obscurities he gleefully predicted, *The Apes of God* has found itself comprehensively and respectfully noted in literary historical chronicles purely because of its sheer percussive force. Its bang. It is, as one critic neatly puts it, 'no one's favourite novel'. But, read with some judicious skipping, the bangs are highly enjoyable.

Around the World in Eighty Days, Jules Verne, 1873

Verne's novel was first serialised in *Le Temps* between 6 November and 22 December 1872, the last instalment cunningly designed to coincide with the hero's return to the Reform Club at 8.45 p.m., on Saturday 21 December 1872. The most reprinted and enduringly successful of Verne's *voyages imaginaires*, the story enlarges on his first successful work, *Five Weeks in a Balloon* (1863). Verne's global theme was given contemporary currency by the travel agent Thomas Cook's advertising campaigns, by the opening of the Suez Canal, and by the completion of the American transcontinental railway link. The world was getting smaller.

The story opens in the Reform Club, where the inscrutable Phileas Fogg (the very incarnation of English sang-froid) is playing whist. In the course of conversation, he wagers £20,000 with his fellow club members that he can circumnavigate the world in eighty days: something which a newspaper has said is, theoretically, possible. The other members take him up on the bet. Fogg employs a French valet, Jean Passepartout ('goes everywhere'). Every Englishman needs one. The plan is to go by rail and ship from London to Suez (via the recently constructed Mont Cenis tunnel), through the great canal (dug by a Frenchman), by ship to Bombay, rail to Calcutta, ship to

Hong Kong, and on to Yokohama and San Francisco, rail to New York, and finally back by ship to London. Fogg's departure coincides with a robbery from the Bank of England, and his journey is tracked by a Scotland Yard detective, Inspector Fix. In their hectic travels Fogg and his servant encounter obstacles which they ingeniously surmount (travelling by elephant, or – in one climactic leg – purchasing the vessel they are travelling on so as to feed its wooden superstructure into the boilers until it arrives in port a metal skeleton). In India Fogg rescues a lady, Mrs Aouda, from suttee and eventually makes her Mrs Fogg.

On their arrival in London, with minutes to spare, Fogg is arrested by Fix. He is not, of course, the bank robber but it seems he will now be too late to win his bet. Then he realises, in the nick of time, that he has gained a day travelling west to east and thunders into the Reform Club on the stroke of 8.45 p.m. The narrative ends:

> What had he gained from all this commotion? What had he got out of his journey? Nothing . . . Were it not for a lovely wife. . . In truth, wouldn't anyone go round the world for less?

In 1889 the American reporter, Nellie Bly (pen name of Elizabeth Cochrane) was commissioned by the *New York World* to 'do a Phileas Fogg'. She left equipped, it is recorded, with 'two light satchels, a ghillie cap, flannel underwear, a bankbook, a 24-hour watch, and a goodluck ring'. She completed the circumnavigation in seventy-two days, six hours, and eleven minutes, taking time out to meet the sixty-one-year-old Verne in Amiens.

As I Lay Dying, William Faulkner, 1930

Faulkner wrote *As I Lay Dying* before he was earning enough from his writing to live by his pen. He wrote the novel while working on a building site with an upturned wheelbarrow as his *écritoire*. The first of the author's Yoknapatawpha County stories, it is routinely regarded as his finest achieve-ment and has been hugely influential. Faulkner's fellow Nobelist, Peter Carey, cites it as the book that made him a novelist. *As I Lay Dying* takes the form of fifty-nine chapters organised around the death and funeral of a back-country matriarch, Addie Bundren. She has a deformed toothless Quasimodo of a husband and five children. The narrative is assembled from the 'care-kin's' converging streams of consciousness, interspersed with sections from their preacher, their doctor, and their closest neighbours. It's a hard read.

And it's set in hard times. The Bundrens are cotton farmers in 1920s Mississippi, with eight square miles of 'sweated' land. They are dirt poor, close to the soil, and see little beyond it. Not a single 'public' event is alluded to in the novel – even the Great War is no big thing in Yoknapatawpha. Scott Fitzgerald's Jazz Age is worlds away. The only historical date supplied is that of the construction of a rotten bridge built in 1888. Like everything else it is in terminal decay. The first chapter describes two Bundren sons, Darl and Jewel. They are walking across a cotton field. A torrential summer storm threatens. They have a load to get to town – it means three dollars. That matters as much to them as does a dying mother.

As she lies dying, we go back in time to follow Addie's history. A former school-teacher, she was schooled by her father to believe that 'the reason for living was to get ready to stay dead a long time'. She (inexplicably) accepted the marriage offer of Anse Bundren: a suitor who wanted a wife merely as a human brood mare – to bear him sons to till his soil. One of the four sons is, however, not Anse's. During a brief spell of religious mania Addie was seduced by the local preacher. Jewel, the offspring of that episode, is the child she loves most. Jewel, on his part, reserves his love for his wayward horse. He has not inherited his father's faith in the Almighty: '. . . if there is a God', Jewel asks, 'what the Hell is *he* for?' Addie's only daughter, Dewey ('a wet seed wild in the hot blind earth'), has been casually impregnated by a field hand. Her blundering attempts to procure an abortion lead to a series of subsequent predatory seductions. All the Bundren children are, in their various ways, 'queer' (that is, touched in the head). Darl, the queerest of them all, has prophetic powers. He is given to such pronouncements on the human condition as: 'We go on, with a motion so soporific, so dreamlike as to be uninferant of progress'. Where precisely he has picked up his vocabulary the novel does not explain. Another son, Cash, lives for his woodworking tools. Addie watches him, through the window, making her coffin with elaborate care. Ten-year-old Vardaman, the youngest child, has caught a large fish whose struggling death is indivisible in his mind from his mother's expiration. He has the shortest chapter in the novel: 'My mother is a fish.' Soon she will become 'not fish'.

Addie's dying wish is to be buried with her 'own' folk, in Jefferson, the far-off (by mule wagon) county town. Getting her body to Jefferson involves biblical hardships for the family, all of whom trail along. There is trial by water, in the form of a hazardous river crossing, and trial by fire in which Addie comes near to cremation. The narrative ends with a finely conceived surprise. Having stolen the $10 Dewey was saving for her abortion Anse appears, carrying a new graphophone and a gleaming set of false teeth. He then blandly introduces 'the new Mrs Bundren'. She is the lady from whom he borrowed the spades to bury the old Mrs Bundren. It's a bleak novel. One puts it down with relief, but with a certain gratitude for having read it.

Ask the Dust, John Fante, 1939

Fante is a novelist best known, posthumously, through the homage paid him by Charles Bukowski ('Fante was my God'). Bukowski was instrumental in getting Ask the Dust back into print in 1980 after it, and its (then dead) author, had sunk into obscurity. Like Bukowski, Fante is a writer artistically rooted in Southern California, who framed a voice appropriate for that region – without, however, the factitious SoCal gloss ('Live the Dream') of the place that also gave the world Hollywood, Disneyland, and Governor Schwarzenegger. Fante's is, like Bukowski's, an artfully broken voice. This is how we first hear it:

One night I was sitting on the bed in my hotel room on Bunker Hill, down in the middle of Los Angeles. It was an important night in my life, because I had to make a decision about the hotel. Either I paid up or I got out: that was what the note said, the note the landlady had put under my door. A great problem, deserving acute attention. I solved it by turning out the lights and going to bed.

No tinsel in Arturo Bandini's Tinseltown. He lives off the 'zest' (i.e. unpalatable skin) of oranges, California's emblematic fruit. In his mouth it is as distasteful as the apples of Sodom, which look wonderful but turn to dust in the mouth. He is tortured with Catholic guilt.

What could be the matter with me? When I was a boy I had prayed to St Teresa for a new fountain pen. My prayer was answered. Anyway, I did get a new fountain pen. Now I prayed to St Teresa again. Please, sweet and lovely saint, gimme an idea.

Ask the Dust was published in 1939: the year that the Joads, Steinbeck's 'Okies', trundle along Route 66 from the Dust Bowl to the promised land – California. There they find another kind of dust. One recalls God's punishment of Adam and Eve:

By the sweat of your face you shall
    eat bread
Till you return to the ground,
For out of it you were taken;
For dust you are, – And to dust you
    shall return.

Fante's roots are not Oklahoman, or German (like Bukowski's), but Italo-American. His first hometown was Denver, Colorado. What he offers in Ask the Dust is autobiography with a fringe of fiction, constructed around his confessional alter ego, Arturo. The novel has as its epicentral moment the (historical) earthquake of 1933 – harbinger of the 'Big One'. That LA will go the way of Gomorrah is, of course, a favourite theme in literature – Ask the Dust belongs alongside Nathanael West's The Day of the Locust in the 'LApocalypse' section of modern literature. Arturo has published a story – 'The Little Dog Laughed' – and has gone on to write a novel. No one cares, least of all the 'literary world'. The plot, what there is of it, chronicles his utterly pointless love affair with Camilla Lopez, a crazy Mexican waitress. She loves her workmate, Sam the bartender. Things go wrong. Camilla, high on drugs, runs off into the desert. Only the Joshua trees and the coyotes, Fante records in a later novel, know what has happened to her. The novel concludes with Bandini throwing his novel into the same, unanswering, desert dust.

The Aspern Papers, Henry James, 1888

There are certain novels everyone in my profession should read and ponder. Nabokov's *Pale Fire* (that hilarious study of critical megalomania – 'I own the author'); Flaubert's *Bouvard et Pécuchet* (the chimera of encyclopaedic completeness – know-allism); David Lodge's *Changing Places* (The Don's Life: career, vocation, or total waste of time and intellect?). Topping the instructional list would be *The Aspern Papers*. James' long short story was inspired by the scholarly hunt for the literary remains of Shelley, which had, via one of the many women he ruined, Claire Clairmont, come into private hands – it was deduced – in Venice.

In the novel, the unnamed narrator directs himself to Julia Bordereau, the aged repository of poet Jeffrey Aspern's remains. Her path crossed that of Aspern when he arrived – seventy years before – to sit for her portrait-painter father. Acting on the advice of his agent, the narrator offers himself as a lodger in Miss Bordereau's decayed apartment. 'I don't think that unaided I should not have risen to that', he says:

I was beating about the bush, trying to be ingenious, wondering by what combination of arts I might become an acquaintance, when she offered this happy suggestion that the way to become an acquaintance was first to become an inmate.

Absurdly, he claims he is a horticulturist – attracted by the Bordereaus' ruined, but still fine, garden. He is wise to disguise his motives. Miss Bordereau ('such a subtle old witch') has little time for the lice on the locks of literature of his ilk:

'Oh, I like the past, but I don't like critics,' the old woman declared with her fine tranquillity.
'Neither do I, but I like their discoveries.'
'Aren't they mostly lies?'

A shrewd blow. Miss Bordereau has a niece, Tita. The least likely of gigolos (any gondolier on the Grand Canal has ten times the sexual attraction), the narrator woos the younger Bordereau. Things come to a head when, doors being left open, he raids the old lady's room for the treasured papers. She surprises him in the felonious act and realises it is not horticulture that is his interest.

I never shall forget her strange little bent white tottering figure, with its lifted head, her attitude, her expression; neither shall I forget the tone in which as I turned, looking at her, she hissed out passionately, furiously: 'Ah, you publishing scoundrel!'

Unmasked! He flees and she, overcome with the shock, dies a few days later, leaving everything to Tita, who contacts him with the delicate hint that he can have the papers – if he takes her along with the package. How strong is his scholarly lust? Not strong enough. He tactfully declines, the papers are burned, and he will live with remorse all his life. Publishing rascals, we deduce, will never make the ultimate sacrifice. 'When I look at it,' he concludes, 'my chagrin at the loss of the letters becomes almost intolerable.'

L'Assommoir, Émile Zola, 1877

There are few convincingly accurate novels about alcoholism. This is one of the few nineteenth-century novels which can lay claim to qualifying. The heroine, Gervaise, appeared earlier in Zola's vast, multi-volume Les Rougon-Macquart cycle. *L'Assommoir* chronicles her short, doomed and sodden life. Gervaise is first encountered living in Paris with the layabout Lantier, by whom she had the first of their two children when she was fourteen. Lantier takes off when the money dries up and Gervaise takes up with a worthier partner, the roofer Coupeau. They marry. Coupeau is, at this stage, abstinent and a model husband. Gervaise, a talented laundress, sets up her own business. Years pass and a daughter, Nana, is born to them. The family is ruined by something very small and poignant. Nana sees her father at work, high on a roof fitting a chimney cap. She cries out, excitedly, and claps her little hands:

> 'Papa! Papa!' she cried. 'Look!'
> The father turned; his foot slipped; he rolled down the roof slowly, unable to catch at anything.
> 'Good God!' he said in a choked voice, and he fell; his body turned over twice and crashed into the middle of the street with the dull thud of a bundle of wet linen.

In his convalescence Coupeau falls prey to L'Assommoir, the local bar with its infernal machine, for ever dripping poisonous absinthe. Lantier returns and panders to Coupeau's drunkenness the better to seduce Gervaise again. She submits, takes to drink herself, loses her business and her respectability. Nana will (as a subsequent novel in the cycle chronicles) grow up to be a whore. Coupeau dies of delirium tremens – graphically described. The most powerful section of the novel follows Gervaise's degradation, in which at her lowest point she eats dog droppings so as to be able to buy the liquor that is killing her.

None of the central characters acts out of free will. They are all creatures of circumstance with no more power over what happens to them than a jellyfish has to swim against the ocean current. This condescension is evident in the most acclaimed chapter in *L'Assommoir*, 'A Marriage of the People'. It rains on Gervaise's wedding day and the party take shelter – and, as they hope, find some amusement – in the Louvre.

It is another world, one which they can never aspire to understand:

> The party entered the museum of Assyrian antiquities. They shivered and walked about, examining the colossal statues, the gods in black marble, strange beasts and monstrosities, half cats and half women. This was not amusing, and an inscription in Phoenician characters appalled them. Who on earth had ever read such stuff as that? It was meaningless nonsense!. . . How many statues! How many pictures! They wished they had all the money they had cost.

The episode brings out Zola's serio-comic brilliance and, less admirably, the social aloofness (let's call it snobbery) at the heart of his 'naturalism'. It can be summed up in the proverb: 'Drink is the curse of the working classes'. The implication in *L'Assommoir* is that only the proletariat are at risk. They can no more handle their drink than they can read Assyrian inscriptions in the Louvre. You, members of the novel-reading class, can sozzle yourselves with impunity.

At Swim-Two-Birds, Flann O'Brien, 1939

O'Brien's is a novel which pulls off the difficult trick of being both 'modernist' and side-splittingly funny – when, that is, it is not being wilfully boring in order to ram home some artistic point. The novel was published on the enthusiastic recommendation of Graham Greene, then a lowly office employee reading unsolicited novels for Longman. It is not the least of his services to literature. *At Swim-Two-Birds* has never reached a wide readership partly because of its off-putting title, which looks as if a few words have mysteriously gone missing. Readers like a little hand-holding at the gateway to their novel. Or is there, perhaps, some code at work, of the THIRTY-NINE STEPS kind? Those caring to investigate the enigmatic title, by going on to read the book, may well end up as baffled as they ever were. O'Brien plunges headlong into hyperfictionality –

creating something equivalent, in its narrative entirety, to the 'Cretan Paradox' (i.e. 'everything I say is a lie, including this'). Everything is fiction – including fiction. Trust the tale, not the teller, decreed Lawrence. Don't trust either, decrees O'Brien.

This, I fancy, is how it goes. A student, Dermot Trellis, lodges grumpily with an uncle, an employee of Dublin's Guinness brewery. More precisely, the student lives in bed. He has bought himself a ream of foolscap paper (the name is significant: the paper serves a double purpose – it can record great thoughts and it can be cocked into a dunce's headgear). The book he has in mind to write is a grand cogitation 'on sin'. But the one sin available to him, wilfully bedridden as he chooses to exist, is Rousseau's 'solitary vice' – like writing a 'sin of the hand'. The novel (if that is what it is) is more like masturbation fantasy than theology. And like masturbation, its fantasies are wild, freewheeling and, from any practical point of view, utterly fruitless. At least three intertwining narrative strands can be followed, each leading nowhere in particular.

In one of the strands Dermot (if it is he) invents a character, Sheila Lamont, as the incarnation of virtue, and impregnates her. Like God and Mary (the deity's creation). A child with the Dickensian name Orlick ensues. He will go on to become a writer in his own right. And, as a writer, he will bring his father to justice. Characters from Celtic lore and the gun-toting American West flit across the narrative. It is, as John Updike calls it, 'a many-levelled travesty of a novel'. Like its ancestor THE LIFE AND OPINIONS OF TRISTRAM SHANDY, GENTLEMAN, it affirms (while denying the fact by the achievement of its own existence) that the novel is an impossible form. A glass slipper that life simply will not fit into. The novel ends with the student passing his exams. Oh – one should say again, At Swim-Two-Birds is a hugely funny read.

Atlas Shrugged, Ayn Rand, 1957

Rand's is the most reviled yet influential novel of the postwar period. With its book-length appendix on 'Objectivism' and its breeze-block bulk (1,168 pages in Random House's first edition), Atlas Shrugged was generally off-putting for the average consumer of novels. Early reviews did not help. Robert Kirsch declared in the Los Angeles Times that 'It would be hard to find such a display of grotesque eccentricity outside an asylum.' The charismatic Rand, however, had access to the new medium of TV talk shows and used the exposure to popularise her novel. American sales of five million were claimed by 1984, and three times as many by 2010. Rand's philosophical movement took her hero John Galt's oath ('I swear by my life and my love of it that I will never live for the sake of another man, nor ask another man to live for mine') and his iconic 'sign of the dollar' as articles of faith. 'Selfishness', to paraphrase Wall Street's Gordon Gekko, 'is good.' Rand propagandised the ferocious anti-collectivist doctrine that helped form Thatcherism in Britain in the 1970s and 80s, and strongly influenced American fiscal policy through the appointment of Alan Greenspan, a Rand disciple, as head of the Federal Banking system in the 1990s.

Atlas Shrugged has a simple plot: the leaders of American industry, art, medicine, and learning, tired of the 'looters' and 'socialisers' (i.e. the Democratic Party and unionised labour), resolve to go on strike. They, like the titan Atlas, have been holding up the world on their shoulders. Now they choose to 'shrug' off that burden. So there.

The human interest segment of the novel centres on James Taggart (slimy and villainous) and his younger sister Dagny Taggart (radiantly heroic), president and VP respectively of America's main railroad company. James sells out to the 'looters' in the form of Washington politicians and union leaders. Dagny resists. She lives for two things – railroads and the thrilling music of Richard Halley. Dagny is taken by a congenial friend to 'Galt's Gulch', a valley in Colorado protected by a ray-shield from the outside world. Here, the leaders of free America – artists, industrialists, thinkers, and businessmen – have congregated. Dagny at last meets Halley and the mastermind who, although not yet seen, has dominated the narrative, John Galt. He is, it transpires, a great philosopher and the Atlas strike is his idea. Overwhelmingly attracted though she is to Galt, intellectually and sexually, Dagny chooses to return to a civilisation which is rapidly falling apart.

Rand gives graphic descriptions of power failures and a magnificent train disaster. Finally, John Galt usurps the nation's airwaves to broadcast a long statement, extolling the virtues of the dollar, of capitalist selfishness, and of 'rationalism'. He is arrested and tortured with electric shocks. When the machine breaks down (as all the other machinery in the country is doing), Galt calmly informs his torturers (ignoramuses all) how to mend it, 'speaking in the brusque competent tone of an engineer'. They admit defeat in the face of a Christ figure who can repair his own cross. Dagny and Galt are united. The novel ends with the messianic hero announcing, 'The road is cleared . . . We are going back to the world', and making the holy sign of the dollar. 'Despair not, America!' Rand might have declared had she been clairvoyant, 'Reagan is coming.'

Atonement, Ian McEwan, 2001

The novel opens in 1935 with a thirteen-year-old girl, Briony Tallis, at her family's country house during a blistering summer heatwave. The setting is reminiscent of L. P. Hartley's THE GO-BETWEEN and (more distantly) E. M. Forster's HOWARDS END. Briony is an inveterate 'story-teller', and the ambiguity of that term – 'story' – will be the thematic core of the novel. 'In a story', Briony has discovered, 'you had only to wish, you only had to write it down and you could have the world'.

Precocious in every way, Briony has a 'pash' on Robbie Turner, one of the adults present. Turner, the son of the cleaning lady, has been sent by Briony's father to Cambridge, where he has repaid his patron's kindness by performing brilliantly. He plans to return to the university and postgraduate brilliance. He loves Cecilia Tallis, Briony's sister, but class and his own sexual clumsiness complicate things. Invited to supper at the big house, he pens a letter to Cecilia in which, for his own fun, he tells her he longs to kiss her 'cunt'. He then writes a proper letter. The two missives get confused. Briony, charged with delivering the letter, reads it. Furious, she decides Robbie is a 'maniac' – something confirmed when she spies on him and Cecilia making violent love that evening in the library. Her pash has taken a dangerous form.

One of the pubescent girls in the house is later the same night sexually molested in the woods. Briony – ever the Keyhole Kate – witnesses that event as well. She informs the police the assailant was Robbie. It is a 'story', but sufficient for him to be sent to prison for three years. Robbie, a ruined man, is taken off to the shout of 'Liars!' from his mother. There is only one liar behind it all – Briony, the 'story-teller'. It gives her a god-like sense of power. Cecilia, who believes Robbie to be innocent, breaks with her family.

The narrative jumps to the Second World War and the chaotic Dunkirk evacuation. Robbie, now a serving soldier, is wounded but makes it to the French coast. In England, a remorseful Briony has become a wartime nurse. The narrative takes another abrupt jump to later in the war. Robbie and Cecilia are reunited in a cheap London lodging house. Briony finds out where they are living and confesses the story she made up, offering to make amends with a confession to the authorities. Justice will, belatedly, be done. A final jump takes the novel to the late 1990s. A successful novelist, Briony is losing her mind – and her story-telling powers – to dementia. It emerges that the reconciliatory wartime meeting with Cecilia and Robbie was merely another of her 'stories' – a wish-fulfilling fantasy. Robbie actually died of his wounds at Dunkirk. Cecilia died in the Blitz. The novel ends with Briony asking herself the question: 'The problem of these fifty-nine years has been this: how can a novelist achieve atonement when, with her absolute power, of deciding outcomes, she is also God?'

In a *Paris Review* interview, McEwan revealed that he had given his father – who had served and been wounded during the Dunkirk evacuation – a 'cameo' in *Atonement*:

A dispatch rider from the Highland Light Infantry came by on a Norton.

His bloodied legs dangled uselessly, and his pillion passenger, who had heavily bandaged arms, was working the foot pedals.

It was, apparently, McEwan's father who had the leg injuries, and the strange tandem partnership actually happened.

August 1914, Alexander Solzhenitsyn, 1972

The action covers not a month but one fateful week in the first year of the Great War. The Russians opened the conflict by dispatching a whole army into the heartland of their traditional foe, Prussia. They did so in support of their 'Slav Brothers' in far-off Serbia. History records what followed as the Battle of Tannenberg. It was, more accurately, a series of conflicts over hundreds of square miles of lake and borderland wilderness. In a few days the Russian army was humiliatingly vanquished, losing a quarter of a million men. No Russian boot would touch German soil again for thirty years. The Revolution, three years later, can be traced from the disastrous campaign chronicled here.

The writing of *August 1914* coincided with a turning point in Alexander Solzhenitsyn's life. He was expelled from the Union of Writers in 1969 and awarded the Nobel Prize for Literature a year later. The country's most renowned – and, as the USSR saw it, loud-mouthed – dissident, he was arrested on 12 February 1974 and deported the next day. Solzhenitsyn took two models for his narrative: Zola's *Le Débâcle*, and, nearer home, WAR AND PEACE. *August 1914* opens with a young student, a fervent follower of Tolstoy, Russia's greatest man. He visits (uninvited) the author at his estate, before going off as a volunteer to fight the Prussians at Tannenberg. What, he asks, should he devote his life to? 'Love', answers Tolstoy, enigmatically. But love is not enough on the battlefield if you are fighting with an army ossified into incompetence by rank, privilege, and aristocratic command. 'The ruin of the Russian army', Sozhenitsyn writes, 'was the system of seniority'. There is a climactic

scene in *August 1914* when the Russian senior officers – whose incompetence has brought the disaster about – tear off their epaulettes. It is as if they are tearing off their limbs.

Novels typically condense the fog of war into some kind of clarity. Solzhenitsyn chooses a different technique. A repeated word in the novel is 'chaos'. Chapters flit, without warning, from one sector to another. The brain whirls trying to remember characters (the more confusing for the Russian patronymics and nicknames). At points the narrative dissolves into Eisenstein-like film montage. There is, amongst all this chaos, occasional focus. Instead of Tolstoy's Pierre, wandering gormlessly through Borodino, a clear-sighted colonel, Vorotyntsev, tries in vain to find out what is going on. Another recurrent focus is the field commander, General Samsonov (a historical figure). Samsonov is the incarnation of what was both good and hopelessly bad in the Russian army. Dull, decent and godly, he finally kills himself. There are some arrant villains. One General, who has never seen active service before Tannenberg, kills more Russians than the Germans he is supposed to be fighting by ordering a *sauve qui peut* retreat rather than hold his ground. Military history sees what its practitioners call the 'big picture'. Solzhenitsyn sees it differently: the feel of battle, its smells, its taste and the individuals involved – the 'drops', as he puts it, 'of the great lake which is the life of Russia'. Not the big picture, but handheld snapshots.

Aurora Leigh, Elizabeth Barrett Browning, 1856

The 'novel in verse' has never found much favour with modern readers. The Victorians loved at least a couple: *Aurora Leigh* and Tennyson's *Enoch Arden* were bestsellers to rival Dickens. Why did these novels in verse 'work' for Victorians and not for us? Because, one suspects, they routinely read them aloud to each other, at the speed of speech; they did not gobble them down, as the silent reader does, faster than the human mouth can handle. You want to enjoy *Aurora Leigh*? Find an armchair, a free evening, a friend with a good voice, and turn off the TV. Browning's narrative hybridises (miscegenates?) two usually incompatible forms: the social problem novel and the epic poem. It is an early literary effusion of feminism – something that would, over the following decades, harden into protest, female revolt and, at last, in 1928, the franchise. Essentially what this novel argues is that women can say important things too. It is, as the fifty-year-old Browning grandly stated in her preface, 'the most mature of my works, and the one into which my highest convictions upon Life and Art have entered'. The intention is reiterated, through the novel's heroine, in the no-nonsense opening lines:

> Of writing many books there is no end;
> And I who have written much in prose and verse
> For others' uses, will write now for mine,–
> Will write my story for my better self. . .

Aurora ('dawn') is born in Florence, to an English scholar and an Italian beauty. The mother dies early, leaving the daughter to the care and education of the father. A man of 'heavy mind', he had come to study Da Vinci's sewage systems, intending to stay only a month. Florence – and the Catholic Church – captivate him. He dies when Aurora ('a bleating lamb') is thirteen, and her upbringing continues with an uncongenial spinster aunt in England. She finds solace in the company of her father's library and a cousin, Romney Leigh. Already her remarkable mind is brewing sedition:

> The works of women are symbolical.
> We sew, sew, prick our fingers, dull our sight,
> Producing what? A pair of slippers, sir,
> To put on when you're weary. . .

No man, we deduce, should expect a pair of slippers from Aurora. Romney is heir to the family fortune and marriage with him would be 'good', as the world sees such things. But not for Aurora, who, aged twenty, wants more from life. Romney is scornful

when his proposal is rejected, her aunt is furious, and she is disinherited, with a paltry £330 per annum to her name. She goes off to London to 'write': prose for money by day, poetry for herself by night. The plot thereafter becomes intricate. Romney impregnates a lower-class girl, Marian; now a 'friend of the people', he intends to marry her. His project fails. Aurora returns to her native Italy. En route she discovers Marian working as a prostitute in Paris. Thinking herself decently in service (to one of Romney's lovers, the wicked Lady Waldemar), Marian was tricked into a brothel, raped ('man's violence / Not man's seduction' has made her what she is) and, her victimisers' lusts satisfied, loosed on to the streets to support herself and her child by vice. Aurora adopts the 'castaway'.

Like Brontë's Rochester (and Samson before them) Romney has, in the interim, been blinded. Thus 'neutralised' union with Aurora is possible. Whether slippers are in prospect is not disclosed. Aurora is the kindest of mistresses to the abused Marian. Elizabeth Barrett Browning, however, dismissed a maid-servant who had been with her for eight years when she married and got herself in the family way. The contradiction is explored in Margaret Forster's 1990 novel, Lady's Maid.

Auto-da-Fé, Elias Canetti, 1935

Canetti has always been a slightly iffy Nobelist – if not as unequivocally so as Pearl S. Buck or Winston Churchill (for literature?). Canetti published one novel, Auto-da-Fé. A long and bizarre work, its composition was completed in 1931, when Canetti was twenty-five. It was published in Vienna (where Canetti had spent most of his nomadic life hitherto), a few months after the Nazi takeover four years later, under the title Die Blendung – The Blinding. The novel's subsequent progress was disrupted by the Second World War – as was Canetti's. Jewish and left wing, he found refuge in England in 1938. An English translation of Auto-da-Fé, as it was renamed, was accepted for publication but held over until 1946 by the austerities of wartime book production. On publication it sank without trace, but resurfaced with the author's later fame – culminating in the award of the Nobel in 1981.

The central character ('hero' doesn't fit) of *Auto-da-Fé* is Dr Peter Kien, a Sinologist. He lives immured in his apartment by the 'most important private collection of books' in Vienna – twenty-five thousand of them. Kien is not a bibliophile but a student. He reads to fill his head. (The word 'head' appears in each of the novel's section titles.) Is the cranium capacious enough to live one's life in – the so-called 'life of the mind'? Or is that life, as the German title suggests, 'blindness'? Kien has no sensory contact with the 'real' world other than that he breathes its air and consumes its written word. He haunts bookshops every morning – waiting, like an alcoholic outside his bar, until they open at eight o'clock. From motives of sheer convenience and ineffable innocence he marries his housekeeper Therese Krummholz, the better to keep his library in tip-top, daily dusted condition. Women, he discovers, are not as easily shelved. Marital battles ensue when she discovers almost all his money has gone to the booksellers. The two of them end up occupying separate, sealed-off zones of the house. Separation from half his library pains Kien more than being deprived of the marriage bed. Codex means more to him than coitus.

Eventually Therese boots him out and his life becomes a phantasmagoric wander.

His path crosses that of the chess fanatic Fischerle, who is, as his second occupation, the least likely pimp in the history of prostitution. A dwarf, and hump-backed, he lies under the bed on which his whore (devoted to him) is servicing clients only to jump out and challenge any likely-looking punter to a game on the board. They tend to acquiesce and he always wins. He is probably the best player in the world – but he despises tournaments so no one will ever know. Kien offers him a job cataloguing the library, which no longer exists except in his head. Small as he is, Fischerle can't get in there. Kien has other random experiences, including a course of treatment by his psychoanalyst brother. He is not cured. He finally meets up again with Therese (whom he thought dead), who is negotiating the sale of his books with the local pawnbroker. The end of the novel spirals into total, homicidal confusion, climaxing with the image which – ever since he saw an example of it in Vienna in 1927 – haunted Canetti, namely a public book burning. The novel ends with a madly mirthful Kien committing suttee on the pyre of his flaming volumes.

Although he took British citizenship in 1970, Canetti spent his last years in Switzerland. He died in Zurich in 1994 and his body finally rests in a graveyard next to that other literary nomad, James Joyce – whose first question would be, 'Why not me?' (for the Nobel, of course).

Babel-17, Samuel R. Delany, 1966

This novel, for lovers of the genre, marks either a dead end or a new future for the 'tale of the future'. I tend towards the former opinion, with the addition 'interesting dead end'. Delany was in the forefront of the so-called science fiction 'New Wave' which transformed the hitherto resolutely subliterary genre in the 1960s. Whether with academic respectability and post-modernist trickery SF lost its 'juice' is a continuing dispute. The Nebula-winning *Babel-17* brought the author fame in his mid-twenties. Delany was not, as they say, 'one from the cookie cutter'. Precocious, openly gay (in later life, after a divorce), black (one of ten children to an undertaker father living in Harlem, himself the son of a father born in slavery), and scholarly (he became a professor of literature at top-flight institutions), he is as far from the SF identikit author as it's possible to be.

Babel-17 fantasises a distant future in which mankind has colonised the galaxy but is unexpectedly confronted by a deadly alien foe, whose language *Homo sapiens* is not sapient enough to understand. Unlike the Klingons, no subtitles or dubbing are on hand. Salvation depends on the poet-linguist Rydra Wong (Delany's partner at the time was the National Book Award-winning poet Marilyn Hacker) being able to decode 'Babel-17'. But she discovers that by mastering the language she, herself, becomes an alien. The narrative, though it contains all the familiar space-opera scenarios, is the vehicle for weighty cogitations on language, thought, and communication. Delany himself is acutely dyslexic – he has to rediscover language every time he writes: which is all the time (five novels before he was twenty-five, for example). As in Delany's other Nebula-winning work, *The Einstein Intersection*, the futuristic décor is surrealistic (clone assassins, 'cosmetisurgery', discorporate entities, etc.) but is used with a deftness that justifies the award of SF's most prestigious prize.

The core idea, or central gimmick, in the novel is the Sapir–Whorf thesis (not nowadays much subscribed to by linguists but of perennial interest to philosophers) that language does not describe the real world so much as create it – or, at least, our sense of it. We are what we talk. It is a sophisticated version of what Orwell postulates with Newspeak in NINETEEN EIGHTY-FOUR. Control language and you control everything. Even the universe.

Babi Yar, a Document in the Form of a Novel, Anatoly V. Kuznetsov, 1966

In the 1960s, after the death of Stalin and the elimination of his mini-me crew, the USSR's new paramount leader, Nikita Khrushchev, initiated what was called the 'the Thaw'. The Cold War was no longer quite so cold. Nor were the disciplines imposed on the Soviet people as disciplinary. Novels which, in Stalin's day, would have been a one-way ticket to Siberia (or worse) were – very nervously – allowed to see the light of print. Alexander Solzhenitsyn's ONE DAY IN THE LIFE OF IVAN DENISOVICH was the most famous beneficiary. *Babi Yar* was another 'now it can be told' product of this warm spell. Kuznetsov's docunovel chronicles the spectacular massacres carried out in Kiev, in the Ukraine, by the Nazis in September 1941. It was published, in 1966, heavily censored – but the fact that it was published at all was, for the time and the place, historically significant.

Three years later Kuznetsov defected, arriving in the UK with a copy of the uncensored *Babi Yar* wrapped around his body as a coil of photographic negative. The allegedly authentic text was published in 1970 in English, by 'A. Anatoli'. The narrative opens, defiantly, with a witness oath: 'This book contains nothing but the truth.' In official Soviet historical accounts – willing as they normally were to blacken the Nazis – the 'truth' of the Babi Yar atrocity had been suppressed. The reasons for this were complicated. As everywhere during the Second World War, the Jews had been the Nazis' principal targets. It is reckoned as many as 34,000 were taken to Babi Yar, a huge ravine, and methodically machine-gunned over the course of a few days. Also exterminated were, according to Kuznetsov, 50,000 gypsies, Ukrainians and Russians. Before they left in the face of the Russian reconquest of the Ukraine, the Germans exhumed and incinerated the corpses.

Many Ukrainians had initially welcomed the Germans in 1941 and had collaborated in the killing of Russians, who were hated. Jews were not generally loved. Uniformed Ukrainian auxiliaries assisted in the rounding up of victims for the Babi Yar massacre. Anatoly Kuznetsov, visiting in the early 1960s, had noted that there was no memorial of any kind, nor any memory: 'Babi Yar no longer exists. In the opinion of certain politicians it never did exist. The ravine has been filled in and a main road passes over it.' The poet Yevtushenko (another notable beneficiary of the Thaw) also visited and, as background to his poem 'Babi Yar', observed: 'what I saw was absolutely terrible – there were lots of trucks and they were unloading stinking garbage on the tens of thousands of people who were killed. I did not expect that.' Somewhere in hell Himmler must have laughed.

Kuznetsov had Russo-Ukrainian parentage and was living close to Babi Yar at the time of the massacre. His family had survived without collaborating with the Nazi invaders. Babi Yar is based on records he kept from his fourteenth year (1941). Young Kuznetsov saw 'what others were not allowed to see'. He did not, however, personally 'see' the Jewish massacre. He heard machine-gun fire – not popping as in a firefight, but methodical, like target practice on a range. His account of the massacre itself is taken from the only identified survivor, Dina Pronicheva, an actress from the Kiev Puppet Theatre, who survived by faking death in the mass of corpses in the ravine. Her story is narrated horrifically in Babi Yar, and more vividly still (with acknowledgement) in D. M. Thomas' bestselling novel The White Hotel (1981).

The Ballad of Peckham Rye, Muriel Spark, 1960

Two mid-century novels, published within a few years of each other, pondered the role of the Devil in contemporary life. The more famous is William Golding's pig-headed LORD OF THE FLIES. Spark's study in contemporary diabolism is subtler and draws more thoughtfully on her (adopted) Catholic faith. Superficially The Ballad of Peckham Rye is a comedy of suburban manners, set in the 'austere' 1950s in (then) unfashionable south-of-the-river London – home of the primitive 'Peckish' language and people. The novel has an opening which hooks the reader as a skilled angler hooks a salmon:

> Here they were, kneeling at the altar. The vicar was reading from the prayer book. . .
>
> The vicar said to Humphrey, 'Wilt thou have this woman to thy wedded wife?'
>
> 'No,' Humphrey said, 'to be quite frank I won't.'
>
> He got to his feet and walked straight up the aisle. . . got to the door, and into his Fiat, and drove off by himself to Folkestone. It was there they had planned to spend their honeymoon.

A sacrament defiled. Why did Humphrey do it? Read on.

The textile firm of Meadows, Meade & Grindley, based in Peckham (happy days when there was industry in this God-forsaken borough), have hired Dougal Douglas, 'the Scotch man', to uplift their wholly disaffected workers by introducing some 'art' into their lives. MM&G make 'nylons' – nether garb of the contemporary whores of Babylon. Douglas has suspiciously diabolic physical deformations – a humped shoulder and vestigial horns on his forehead which he blandly claims are the result of surgery (for what?). The cloven foot and tail we do not see. Douglas does not quite confess to being who he is but admits to being 'one of the wicked spirits that wanders through the world for the ruin of souls'. Exactly what is expected by the firm which employs him (not, apparently, soul-ruining) is never clear. 'Morality' is mentioned. He's meanwhile immorally in cahoots with MM&G's principal rival, conspiring to bring about his employer's downfall. He likes things that fall down: he did himself, of course.

Douglas throws himself into his new assignment with sly relish, insinuating himself into the lives of the luckless subjects of his 'research', seducing females, corrupting males and unleashing 'the dirty swine' within his subjects. A drunken Irish woman, Nelly Mahone, recognises Dougal for what he is and denounces him with raucous Catholic anathema. But who pays attention to Irish drunks? Peckham is full of them. It all ends with an outbreak of the disorder the Lord of Misrule specialises in. Humphrey's landlady is felled by a suspicious stroke. His boss Mr Druce's mistress gets it in the neck with a corkscrew from her maddened lover. And, flashing back to the opening scene, Humphrey jilts his true love Dixie at the altar. Having done his worst, Dougal moves on, leaving the usual 'ruined souls' in his wake – although Humphrey belatedly does the right thing. Quite a lot of people come to the second ceremony, in the hope that 'he'll do it again'.

Why, the reader may wonder, closing this enigmatic book, 'ballad'? Spark has gone back to the word's etymological roots – which are the same as 'ballet'. The novel could as well, but less artfully, have been called 'Devil's Dance'. Or, as a Peckham onlooker says, 'It wouldn't have happened if Dougal Douglas hadn't come here'.

Bambi, a Life in the Woods, Felix Salten, 1923

You've *seen* it, of course. Probably twice. It's one of the rites of childhood, and one of the ordeals of parenthood, having to sit through Disney's tsunami of treacle. But have you *read* it? Originally published by a Viennese novelist, for adults, this anthropomorphic story of the 'childhood' of a deer was inspired by a holiday visit to the Italian Alps (Bambi is short for *bambino*). Bambi is born to a doe who cares for him through his babyhood. Things get more complicated as his antlers sprout. They are a fine rack. Horned Bambi feels the urge to fight and possess the fawn Faline. Things are sprouting all over – he is now a 'buck'. At

this point enter the hunter and the dogs and exit Bambi's mother – venison for the hunter's table, alas. Enter, too, Bambi's father, the Old 'Prince of the Woods'. He takes over the higher education of his son – the 'Young Prince' – and instils in him the most important lesson of life: 'you must live alone, if you wanted to preserve yourself, if you understood existence, if you wanted to attain wisdom, you had to live alone'. By showing his son the corpse of a shot poacher, he demonstrates that, powerful as 'Man' is, he is not all powerful. There is 'Another', a supreme being, to whom all animals, even the two-legged variety, are subservient. Bambi survives being shot himself to succeed his royal father.

The Walt Disney Corporation acquired rights to the story in the late 1930s and the thoroughly Americanised *Bambi* hit the screens in 1942: the darkest year of the war. There was, however, little gloom in the film, from the opening storm's sweet refrain ('Drip, drip, drop / Little April shower') onwards. Children loved *Bambi*, parents approved the roles given Bambi's loving doe-mother and his stern stag-father, absent from home fighting the good fight, as was a good chunk of the male population of the US during the war. There were, however, dissenters. Uncle Walt himself, for example. The film – a masterpiece of animated art – proved hellishly expensive to make. The Nazis had long banned the book – much as Hermann Goering, notably, loved deer; or, at least, shooting them. Salten, of course, was Jewish. Goering liked shooting Jews as well. But the fiercest opponents of little Bambi have been over the years, strangely, in the American heartland itself. The National Rifle Association deplored what it took to be an attack on the American male's right to shoot anything furred and four-legged in the forest. Gun-toting Sarah Palin was pleased to find on the menu at one of her fund-raising dinners 'Bambi's Mother' as the main course. Bam!Bi! Where did those damned liberals think their sautéed venison came from, Palin sarcastically asked. Road kill?

Bartleby the Scrivener, Herman Melville, 1853

With Melville the rule has always been: the shorter it is, the more readable it will be. *Bartleby* was written *pari passu* with the author's longest prose work, MOBY DICK, which has generally been found to be something less than easily readable. *Bartleby* is subtitled *A Story of Wall Street*. Do not, however, look for a mid-nineteenth-century Gordon ('greed is good') Gekko. The Bartleby of the title is a lawyer's scrivener. The easy definition of 'scrivener' is 'human Xerox machine'. Before photocopying came along legal documents needed to be hand copied (carbon was not acceptable – it had to be 'manuscript'). Scriveners figure prominently in nineteenth-century literature. Bob Cratchit in *A Christmas Carol* is one. Another, who may have sown a seed in Melville's mind, is the morose and eventually suicidal Nemo ('Nobody') in BLEAK HOUSE, the novel which came out a few months before *Bartleby*. The Grossmith brothers would pursue the theme later in their DIARY OF A NOBODY – their Mr Pooter is a scrivener.

Melville's story is a study in what Henry David Thoreau, Melville's 'transcendentalist' colleague, called the 'quiet desperation' in which most modern men pass their lives. The narrator is a benign lawyer. 'I am a rather elderly man', he says, but in thirty years of professional life Bartleby the scrivener was 'the strangest I ever saw or heard of'. Only three facts are divulged about Bartleby: his gender (though no one calls him 'Mr'), his name (but not his forename), and his occupation – copyist. Perhaps there are no other facts to know. One day, in response to a request that he do some of his usual work, he replies: 'I would prefer not to.' The HXM has broken down. Permanently. Bartleby is dismissed but he refuses to leave the office, where he now lives day and night and where he refuses to do any copying – always with the polite statement of his preference. The office is sold over his head. The new occupants evict him, but cannot get rid of him. He sleeps outside their door, or in the corridor. When asked to move on, he offers his courteous refusal. It is all he ever says. 'I would prefer not to.' Arrested for vagrancy,

he ends up in the Tombs prison and finally dies of starvation – preferring, apparently, not even to eat or drink. The story ends, 'Ah, Bartleby! Ah, humanity!'

Bartleby is a much discussed text – often at greater length than the story itself. The hero's dysfunction can be read as a satire on bureaucracy. Melville's scrivener is not a human being, he is office equipment – Weberian *Gesellschaft* incarnate. Or he can also be seen as the exemplar of what another sociologist, Émile Durkheim, called *anomie* – rootlessness. He has no family, no 'social' life, no home, no background. He is urban man incarnate. Most plausible, in my view, is that *Bartleby* is an ironic reflection on Thoreau's essay on 'Civil Disobedience', published four years before, and Thoreau's refusal – on conscientious grounds – to pay his taxes. His peaceable resistance landed him, like Melville's scrivener, behind bars. Bartleby is the epitome of civility and disobedience, no refusenik in history more so.

Batman: The Dark Knight Rises, Greg Cox, 2012

Although Cox's name is on the title page he merely services (with commendable efficiency) the pre-existing narrative created by the film's director, Christopher Nolan, and his brother Jonathan. Christopher Nolan took on the exhausted Batman film franchise with strict conditions as to his complete artistic freedom. There should be no genuflection to what Neil Gaiman would call an 'American God'. A Wunderkind and an (English) English Literature graduate, fascinated by post-modernism, Nolan had, in his late twenties, written and directed *Memento* – a detective story told backwards through a hero with pathological memory loss, who has to tattoo clues on his arms.

The *Batman* series was, by the twenty-first century, ritually formulaic. A dastardly criminal – typically some circus-themed villain like The Joker – threatened Gotham City. Enter Batman and Robin to save the day with Bat-cave gadgetry. Batman, of course, was – *in propria persona* – millionaire philanthropist Bruce Wayne. Rockefeller in cape and mask. Nolan, in his 'Dark

Knight' trilogy, complicated and ultimately destroyed the formula – creative destruction, one could call it. Robin went. The design was darkened to pitch black. In the first film, infant Bruce is traumatised by witnessing the street murder of his parents. In the second film, the opponent is The Joker (played as a blood-chilling sadist by Heath Ledger). The third instalment finds Batman eight years retired and a pariah. He is believed to be the killer of Harvey Dent – the man who, before Batman threw him off a high building to his death, 'cleaned up' Gotham. In fact, Dent was evil incarnate. It was the maligned Batman who was the cleaner up. Bruce Wayne, now closing on forty, is no longer as rich. He is also a physical wreck. He still has Alfred Pennyworth, the British butler, to bring his drinks (too many of them). Alfred agonises over what he sees as a deathwish in his master. Wayne's ally, James Gordon, one of the few honest cops in Gotham and someone who knows his secret, is at death's door in hospital.

Things perk up when Catwoman breaks into the Wayne mansion to steal some family jewels (normal enough for a cat burglar) and Bruce's fingerprints (why?). Out of uniform she is Selina Kyle, born working-class, with a grudge against the rich. Not a criminal, but a revolutionary. It emerges that Catwoman is working for the dreaded Bane, an old foe, who plans to destroy Gotham's soul – and Batman's body with it. The dead but not gone (he never will be) Ra's al Ghul and his League of Shadows resurface, with a sinister tinge of Osama bin Laden. He has his eye on Wayne's cold-fusion apparatus, which could give Gotham clean energy for ever, but which has never been activated – lest some villain convert it into a Doomsday machine. Doomsday is precisely what Bane wants.

Batman dies saving Gotham – or does he? Perhaps, like Hannibal and Clarice, he retires, more happily than first time round, to live an incognito life in Italy with Selina – political differences forgotten. Mother of God, can this be the end of Batman? As far as Nolan is concerned, it may well be.

Beau Geste, P. C. Wren, 1924

Wren's archetypal Foreign Legion ('I joined to forget') novel has been filmed and televised over and again and has misled many young men to join the notoriously tough French army unit, which asks no questions of its recruits and for that reason feels free to treat them like the dregs of humanity they probably are. The novel opens with a teasing mystery. The Saharan fort of Zinderneuf has been discovered with dead legionnaires propped up like mummies on the battlements, eerily preserved by the dry desert air. The attackers, whoever they were, did not succeed in breaching the fort. Within its walls the commander, Sergeant Lejaune, lies with a French bayonet, not an Arab lance, through his heart. Clasped in the hand of a legionnaire's body nearby is a note referring to the 'Blue Water' sapphire. This gem, we learn, was stolen from one Lady Brandon in mysterious circumstances.

The story now flashes back to Brandon Abbas, in England's rolling counties, and the three Geste brothers: Michael ('Beau'), his younger twin Digby, and John. They are the orphaned nephews of Lady Brandon – the cream of their country's youth. While her magnificent Blue Water is being admired by the gathered family, the electric lights are suddenly doused. When they are relit, the sapphire has disappeared. Who took it? Michael and Digby disappear and it is assumed they are the thieves. But why? John joins the French Foreign Legion to track them down. The three brothers find themselves (improbably) reunited as comrade legionnaires. Their regiment is posted to the Sahara under the savage command of Lejaune ('March, you dogs! March!'), who has discovered that Michael has a fabulously valuable 'diamond'. There follows the grand climax at Fort Zinderneuf, under attack from Arab insurgents. Lejaune kills Michael and finds the diamond (in fact the Blue Water), only to be killed in turn by a vengeful John who, alone of the three, escapes to tell the tale. On his return to Brandon Abbas, he tells Lady Brandon that Michael and Digby had discovered that the Blue Water was paste and stole it to spare her embarrassment (and, presumably, so she could cash in on the insurance – Wren is a bit fuzzy about this). Theft was Beau Geste's 'beautiful gesture'.

I read the novel as a thirteen-year-old and, sixty years later, the horror of the surviving brother's protracted journey back through the country of the barbarous Tuareg rebels remains as a nightmarish memory – almost as traumatic as the death of Bambi's mother had been to me, five years earlier:

> . . .I could tell of a fair-bearded man who stared at us with blazing *grey* eyes, a man whose tongue had been cut out, whose ears and fingers had been cut off, and who was employed as a beast of burden.
>
> I could also tell of a Thing that sat always in the Sôk, mechanically swaying its body to and fro as it crooned. Its lips, eyelids, ears, hands, and feet had been cut off, it was blind, and it crooned in *German*.

In various accounts of Wren's life, all originating with him, the *Oxford Dictionary of National Biography* records, 'Wren is described as a sailor, an explorer, a trooper in a British cavalry regiment, and a recruit to the French Foreign Legion. There appears to be no credible evidence for any of these suggestions'. I wish I'd known that when I was thirteen.

The Beautiful Room is Empty, Edmund White, 1988

In this novel (so to call it) the unnamed 'boy' of White's 1982 novel, *A Boy's Own Story*, is growing up. He now knows 'real' sex and reads Kafka. *The Beautiful Room is Empty* conforms 'autrebiographically' to the known facts of its author Edmund White's young life. It is the mid- to late 1950s. The 'youth' (a boy no more) has yet to break free of his 'square' divorced parents in boring Cincinnati. He still attends a boarding school and has a visiting relationship with the city's beatnik, not very vibrant, counterculture. But it's the best Ohio can do.

> Everyone ate the same food, wore the same clothes, and people decided this

is 'freedom' whether they were Democrats or Republicans. The three most heinous crimes known to man were Communism, heroin addiction, and homosexuality.

The hero's father is rich in his 'remote but solid way' and runs a haberdasher's business. The hero's bosom buddy is Maria – eventually to be a 'dyke' but not there yet. She is, however, a communist. He himself is not yet gay nor red. They pore over existential literature which instructs them that 'communication between any two individuals is impossible'. Genital conjunction is very possible, it transpires.

The subsequent narrative is remorselessly carnal. In his last year at school the boy meets a Texan with 'bad eyes, bad skin and the smell of Luckies on his breath', who politely enquires whether he is a 'suck queen' or a 'brownie queen'. He's never done either (so far) but it will emerge that he's both. He moves on to the University of Michigan, where, in his fraternity, he passes as a 'cocksman' – straight. He has a big penis, which helps. His real thrills are found, furtively, in the university toilets, where he sits for hours, listening, sniffing and hoping. Cottaging and cruising will be his main interests. He hates his sexuality – but is imprisoned by it. 'Once is never enough' for him. The point of satisfaction is never reached. There is no post-coital state. 'Everyone else in the world', he concludes, 'was less interested in sex than I.'

His father declines to pay for postgraduate study at Harvard. He drifts to New York, where he falls in with Lou – an addict. Sex becomes a nightly voyage of discovery. By day he works as a journalist – he is good with words. The army turns him down when he ticks the 'homosexual tendencies' box. He will be spared Vietnam. He takes up weight-lifting (boosted by amphetamines) and black leather. Judy Garland dies. The New York gay world mourns. He and Lou now hang out at Stonewall. When, in 1969, the cops do their customary disciplinary raid, it is, for the first time in history, resisted. Gay has become political. 'It's our Bastille Day,' says Lou. The novel ends, the revolution begins (it will be chronicled in *The Farewell Symphony*, 1997). The significance of the odd title is spelled out in the epigraph, from one of Kafka's letters. The 'beautiful empty room' is the uncrossable space between human beings.

Bel-Ami: or, The History of a Scoundrel, Guy de Maupassant, 1885

Maupassant's second-published novel is a biting satire on Third Republican Parisian society, as the nineteenth century drew to a close – and, even more bitingly, a satire on journalism at every period of its history. The story opens as briskly, and jaggedly, as any of the author's short stories:

> After changing his five-franc piece Georges Duroy left the restaurant. He twisted his moustache in military style and cast a rapid, sweeping glance upon the diners, among whom were three saleswomen, an untidy music-teacher of uncertain age, and two women with their husbands.
>
> When he reached the sidewalk, he paused to consider what route he should take. It was the twenty-eighth of June and he had only three francs in his pocket to last him the remainder of the month. That meant two dinners and no lunches, or two lunches and no dinners, according to choice. As he pondered upon this unpleasant state of affairs, he sauntered down Rue Notre Dame de Lorette, preserving his military air and carriage, and rudely jostled the people upon the streets in order to clear a path for himself. He appeared to be hostile to the passers-by, and even to the houses, the entire city.
>
> Tall, well-built, fair, with blue eyes, a curled moustache, hair naturally wavy and parted in the middle, he recalled the hero of the popular romances.

Whatever else, Maupassant is not offering the reader a 'popular romance'. The subsequent narrative chronicles the unstoppable rise of Georges Duroy – called Bel-Ami ('handsome friend') by his female victims. Georges is initially encountered as a penurious railway clerk. He determines to get to the top by whatever means he can. A former army buddy, Forestier, now a journalist, gives him the useful key to success in the newspaper business: 'The secret is not to betray your ignorance. Just manoeuvre, avoid the quicksands and obstacles, and the rest can be found in a dictionary.' Georges follows this advice and makes his way into the corrupt world of 'higher' Parisian journalism. Forestier has also advised him to exploit his good looks ruthlessly – which he duly does. Not without ability, Georges wins success as a writer. In journalism, as in love, he finds dissimulation is the best policy, given the ineradicable gullibility of the reading public. You can fool them on the page, you can fool them in bed. Why? Because they are fools and you aren't. He marries for money (now under the grander name 'Du Roy de Cantel'), divorces, callously discards his mistresses, all the while consolidating his eminence in the world of journalism. The novel ends with his second advantageous marriage as he salaciously – during the wedding reception itself – sets up a sexual liaison with his next mistress, and foresees the political career that awaits him:

> When they reached the threshold he saw a crowd gathered outside, come to gaze at him, Georges du Roy. The people of Paris envied him. Raising his eyes, he saw beyond the Place de la Concorde, the chamber of deputies, and it seemed to him that it was only a stone's throw from the portico of the Madeleine to that of the Palais Bourbon.

From railway clerk to president.

The Bell Jar, Sylvia Plath, 1963

The novel has the opening you'd take with you to your Desert Island, if Kirsty Young allowed you only one:

> It was a queer, sultry summer, the summer they executed the Rosenbergs, and I didn't know what I was

doing in New York. I'm stupid about executions. The idea of being electrocuted makes me sick, and that's all there was to read about in the papers – goggle-eyed headlines staring up at me at every street corner and at the fusty, peanut-smelling mouth of every subway. It had nothing to do with me, but I couldn't help wondering what it would be like, being burned alive all along your nerves.

Esther Greenwood, recently graduated, has come down from New England to take up a month's internship on a New York women's magazine. 'The one thing I was good at was winning scholarships and prizes', says Esther – with the intention of enlarging her skills into some unscholarly areas. It is summer 1953. The opening of the narrative coincides with the execution by electrocution of Julius and Ethel Rosenberg (alleged communist spies, convicted of giving America's atomic secrets to the Russians). Esther makes friends among her fellow interns at the Amazon Hotel, where they are lodged – particularly with Doreen, who smokes, and is blonde and 'fast'. Esther isn't either of those things.

The narrative flashes back to Esther's childhood: the early death of her father, her complicated relationship with her mother, her relationship with the tubercular Yale student Buddy Willard. Esther cannot throw herself into the 1950s version of Sex in the City (Doreen can). Esther resolves to lose her virginity to Constantin, a translator at the UN. Her virginity resolutely declines to be lost. On her last night in New York she has another date, which also goes wrong. On her return to the Amazon Hotel, she symbolically casts her clothes out of the window – she will leave naked, as she came. Back home, Esther learns she has not been accepted into the writing course she wanted. Life with her mother, over the rest of summer, is depressing. Clinically so. She attempts suicide (described at length), is hospitalised and subjected to ECT (less convulsively than Ethel Rosenberg, but traumatically), and gradually recovers. With the help of friendly Dr Nolan, she acquires a diaphragm to prepare herself for life outside. She finally loses her virginity to

Irwin, a maths professor. After the act, however, she finds herself haemmorhaging and returns to the hospital. The novel ends with Esther, ambiguously in control of her life, on the brink of joining a creative writing course. She will have much to write about – including, presumably, a novel rather like The Bell Jar.

Plath's novel was held back from publication by the author until a few weeks before her suicide. It was done, it has been suggested, so as to save her mother's and early boyfriend's feelings as it is transparently, and painfully, autobiographical. While still an undergraduate at Smith College, Plath won the nationwide competition for an intern editorship with Mademoiselle magazine in New York. This is a kernel episode of the novel, as are Esther's fraught relationship with her boyfriend, her nervous breakdown, suicide attempt, and ECT. When it was published – under a pseudonym – The Bell Jar (felt to be out of date in 1963) flopped. It went on to become a posthumous bestseller.

Berlin Alexanderplatz, Alfred Döblin, 1929

After the war, as Germany reconstructed its literary canon from the cultural rubble left by Goebbels, Döblin's novel was reinstated as the German ULYSSES. This honorific status was certified by Rainer Werner Fassbinder's fifteen-hour 1980 TV adaptation – a narrative which was doggedly faithful both to the text and Döblin's Neue Sachlichkeit (New Objectivist) technique. Set in 1928, as Weimar rotted, the novel chronicles a year and a half in the life of Franz Biberkopf – a 'little man' and by no means a nice little man. The narrative opens with his fearfully leaving Tegel Prison ('the punishment begins', is the ironic comment), where he has served four years for stabbing his partner Ida to death with a cream-whip. Franz wants to go straight but, as he will discover, there are no straight paths for someone like him to follow in Berlin. He is given sustenance by some Jews (there are many of them, described without animus, in the narrative – in five years' time they,

Döblin among them, would be an endangered urban species). He finds sexual relief with whores and gets some practical help from Ida's sister Minna, who bears no grudge. Handouts keep him afloat, principally those from his friend Gottlieb Meck. Unskilled at anything (he was a furniture mover before going inside), Franz peddles tie-clips and shoelaces in the street. He finds more customers by vending the Nazi paper *Völkischer Beobachter*, although he himself is as apolitical as a tie-clip. He acquires a Polish mistress, Lina. But one of his little coups (a bulk sale of shoelaces) goes wrong when her uncle Otto does the dirty on him. He sinks in the world, drinks wildly, and throws in his lot with a criminal, Reinhold – a thief and white-slaver. The perks (in the shape of Reinhold's cast-off doxies) are good. Other aspects of Reinhold's criminality prove to be less happy.

On a bungled heist (Biberkopf doesn't even know that is what it is) he is thrown out of the getaway car by the rat Reinhold, is run over by a police car, and loses his right arm. Should he survive until 1933, the maimed Franz will never be able to give a Hitler salute. On his recovery he takes up pimping and goes steady with a new woman, Mieze. For the first time, he is in love. Like a moth to the flame he falls in again with Reinhold's gang. The incorrigible white-slaver attempts to rape Mieze and, when that fails, strangles and buries her. The crime is discovered and Reinhold faces justice (not that murder is that severely punished in Weimar Germany – if Franz's penal servitude is anything to go by, Reinhold will be out in time to join the SS in 1934). In his grief (the third great 'hammerblow', as the novel sardonically describes it) Franz descends into near-mortal despair only to emerge with the perception – the first such in his life – that he is a social animal. 'A ship', he says, 'cannot lie in safety without a big anchor and a man cannot exist without many others.' He takes a job as assistant doorkeeper at a factory – 'a humble workman'. He waits. What is coming his way was contained in the pages of the *Völkischer Beobachter*, had he troubled to read it. A hammerblow is coming which will make the previous three look like strokes from a feather.

Between the Acts, Virginia Woolf, 1941

The novel, as a form, can be many things. Occasionally (see THE BELL JAR or THE CASTLE) it can be read, by the morbidly inclined, as a suicide note. *Between the Acts*, Woolf's last complete novel, was published posthumously, and unrevised (something which the perfectionist in her would have hated), a few months after her death. One cannot read *Between the Acts* without wondering, poignantly, how many interesting lines of English fiction died with the author, whose art was at a transitional stage. Old England itself could well have died with Virginia Woolf. The flat in which she wrote most of the novel in Bloomsbury (her intellectual as well as her physical home) was destroyed by bombs in the Blitz. In the early chapters of *Between the Acts* the characters are constantly looking up to the skies – at birds they cannot always identify ('is it a nightingale?'). The whole population of Britain (I was one) spent a lot of time looking skywards – not for nightingales but Dorniers, Messerschmitts. Planes we could not identify ('ours? or theirs?'). She finished her novel in the Sussex countryside – near the river where she would drown herself and the Channel over which, it was feared, in spring 1941, the Germans would cross and do to England what they were doing in France. The action of the novel takes place over one day in high summer 1939. War broke out in the first week of September, as the harvest was being brought in. 'Between the acts' alludes, directly, to the annual village pageant at the centre of the action. But it also hints at the tense interval between the two great historical acts of war and peace, in Tolstoy's titular phrase. Woolf's first chapter begins:

> It was a summer's night and they were talking, in the big room with the windows open to the garden, about the cesspool. The county council had promised to bring water to the village, but they hadn't.

Life, as they say, goes on – as do complaints about the council.

The setting is a traditional one for

'condition of England' fiction: a country house. The action takes place in Pointz Hall ('a middle-sized house'), seat of the Oliver family. The Olivers are headed by the patriarch Bartholomew ('of the Indian Civil Service, retired') and his widowed sister Lucy Swithin; the younger generation comprises Isa and Giles Oliver (he is 'something in the city') and their son George. The Olivers' marriage is going badly, and they bicker. Isa is poetic and yearns, Madame Bovary-style, for a larger emotional life, with a partner more Byronic than Giles. She has her eye on a local man (himself married). The big day goes badly. Lunch guests, the florid Mrs Manresa (on whom Giles' roving eye has settled) and the effete William Dodge (a 'degenerate' – i.e. gay), prove to be awkward company. The afternoon chronicles the pageant, a mockery of English history through the ages, presented by the busybodying Miss La Trobe. It flops. 'Her gift', she sadly concludes, 'meant nothing. If they had understood her meaning; if they had known their parts; if the pearls had been real and the funds illimitable – it would have been a better gift. Now it had gone to join the others. "A failure," she groaned.' Woolf, to the end, was not afraid of portraying herself with self-mockery. The pageant opens with 'Merry England', then to Elizabethan glory, the Industrial Revolution, Empire and. . . what next? The novel sidesteps that all-important issue, ending at bedtime with Isa and Giles about to fight, copulate, and sleep. From their grudging embrace another life might be born. But first they must fight, as the dog fox fights with the vixen, in the heart of darkness, in the fields of night.

During the war, the Woolfs (Leonard was Jewish and left-wing) were on the Gestapo death list. He, like her, had plans for suicide (carbon monoxide poisoning in the garage) if the Germans invaded. Virginia preferred the 'cleaner' method of asphyxiation.

Billy Liar, Keith Waterhouse, 1959

Sexual intercourse, the poet Larkin lamented, began in 1963, 'Which was rather late for me'. And too late for Billy Fisher (alias 'Liar').

Billy's agonies predate the pill that would liberate every wannabe provincial Don Juan. Billy lives in Stradhoughton – a Yorkshire town locked up in a Yorkshireness which the narrative despises:

> The very name Stradhoughton conjures up sturdy buildings of honest native stone, gleaming cobbled streets, and that brackish air which gives this corner of Yorkshire its own special piquancy.

An 11+ failure (like his creator, Keith Waterhouse), Billy lives at home with parents and a 'poorly gran'. His father copped out of the war with a dubiously dicky knee (Mr William Liar Sr). He is a haulier who has spitefully kept Billy out of the family business (called 'Fisher & Son' nonetheless). He would dearly like to kick his son out of the house. But his 'mam' wants to keep Billy at home as someone to nag at. Which she does. Billy, we deduce, somehow (like father, like son) dodged his National Service. He is, at nineteen years old, a junior employee in the town's 'undertaking establishment', Shadrack & Duxbury. Billy lives principally in his mind, where he rules as the dictator of Ruritanian Ambrosia (named, those of Billy's generation will recall, after a brand of rice pudding). He loves radio comedy. This was the era when the great music-hall comedians had turned to radio 'variety' programmes as the theatres closed down. The greatest of them, Danny Boon, has expressed interest in some gags Billy sent him. But does Billy have the nerve to take the Whittington road to London?

His other principal escape from being himself is philandering. He has, however, yet to lose his virginity. There are three women in his life: Rita, Barbara and Liz. Rita, who works in a coffee bar, is common as muck but smart as paint. Barbara is dull and 'respectable'; despite his plying her with 'passion pills', she has her thighs so firmly clamped together they could crack coconuts. He has proposed marriage (madly shuttling the same ring between them) to both women. But his soul partner is the bohemian, suede-coated Liz. She is not, she informs a stunned Billy, *virgo intacta*. She 'swings' and makes only occasional visits to Stradhoughton (Liz is magnificently played by Julie Christie in the John Schlesinger film adaptation of Waterhouse's novel). Who will receive Billy's shrivelled apple of discord?

Billy's problem is that he'll do anything rather than do something. The narrative begins with him getting out of bed into the old raincoat which he fantasises is an elegant dressing gown, with the stern declaration 'this is a day for resolutions'. Then it's off for a state visit to Ambrosia, recently victorious. Things finally come to a head. He aims to leave for London, hopefully with Liz, but there is a showdown with his other two ladies, late at night, at the railway station. 'You miserable, lying, rotten, stinking get!' Rita tells him (Barbara nodding in agreement). 'You think you're summat, don't you? But you're nowt!' Liz also refuses to come with him – she has business in Doncaster: 'every so often I just want to go away'. So does he. She does, he doesn't. It's back to Clogiron Lane, the 'chipper', too much beer and and a groping last waltz at the Roxy on Saturday night. And, of course, Ambrosia. Life's lies, as Ibsen put it, are what make life liveable.

Black Beauty, Anna Sewell, 1877

If there is one word which sums up the nineteenth century – 'England's Century' – it is 'progress'. The Victorian great leap forward depended on many things. But one thing above all: servants. Say 'servant' and one thinks of maids, cooks, butlers, governesses, groundsmen, valets. The downstairs listening ear subserviently cocked, for the summoning bell from upstairs. There was another branch of servitude even more necessary to that world – the four-legged variety. The horse was, if anything, an even more potent source of energy. The nineteenth century was an age of steampower, and brainpower. And, above all, horsepower. Human servants were exploited and abused. Equine servants were even more exploited and abused. We still use the phrase 'flogging a dead horse' – it comes down to us from the nineteenth century,

when horses were flogged, and worked, to death. It's a major event in Victorian fiction when a man (some swine) gets horsewhipped. No big deal for the millions of horses that suffered the lash. Millions is no exaggeration. When, in the opening of BLEAK HOUSE, Dickens talks of 'mud everywhere' in the London street, he means principally horse-droppings. Thackeray was much struck by a phrase used by a coachman (a servant) when he noticed the shafts had scraped down the flesh to the bloody shoulder-bone of the horse taking them to where he was going (the novelist's St James club, perhaps). 'Does it not hurt?' he asked. 'Lord bless you, sir,' replied the coachman, 'he don't feel it when he *warms to the task*.' So it is with me, thought the philosophical novelist. We may, however, think Dobbin between the shafts had it harder than Dobbin's creator writing VANITY FAIR at the Garrick Club.

Anna Sewell, a daughter in a Quaker family (a sect which believed in the education of girls and kindness to all living things), suffered an accident walking back from school in which both her ankles were injured. She was lamed for life and dependent on a pony trap for everyday movement. She came to love her four-legged friends, to admire their 'beauty' and to hate the way they were generally used – particularly the cruel 'bearing rein' (designed to raise the animal's head 'proudly'). In her late fifties, and given a few months to live, she jotted down and dictated to her mother what became the novel *Black Beauty*. It would be her only published work. The publisher Jarrold snapped it up for the princely sum of £20 and promptly sold 100,000 copies. The tale informs us that it is 'translated from the original equine'.

The narrative follows Black Beauty's career from foal to colt to broken-down hack. The early sections deal with his training ('breaking', as it is candidly called in America) and thoughtful dialogues with his equine pal Ginger. Black Beauty is sold to the Birtwick household, where he returns kindness for kindness by saving his master's life. Later on, under another owner, he experiences the sadism of the bearing rein. Thereafter he becomes a jobbing and, finally, cart horse – the lowest of the equine low. Thankfully he finds sanctuary at Birtwick again. The novel ends with an instruction to his human masters: 'We horses do not mind hard work if we are treated reasonably'. It was Nabokov who noted sardonically that the English always feel sorrier for the blind man's dog. But, as George Eliot said, if the novel has one function it is to widen the circle of 'sympathy'. Make us feel for others. Even equine others.

The Black Girl in Search of God, George Bernard Shaw, 1932

Shaw began writing as a novelist at a time when, as he said, any manuscript which wasn't actually misspelled could get published. Which, of course, is why there are so many bad Victorian novels. Shaw himself wrote five such bad Victorian fictions at the start of his career. Shavians from time to time try to whip up interest in, say, *Cashel Byron's Profession*. But it's poor stuff, and even devotees must yawn a bit. Nonetheless Shaw wrote, later in his career, what qualifies as one very good novel: *The Black Girl in Search of God*. It's an extended parable on the necessity of iconoclasm (never believing what you're told) and a critique of empire (a dominion which, at the time, included a big chunk of Shaw's Ireland). 'Where is God?' asks the 'Black Girl' of the female missionary who has converted her. 'He has said "Seek and ye shall find me"', replies the missionary – a sexual neurotic who 'At eighteen began falling in love with earnest clergymen, and actually became engaged to six of them in succession. But when it came to the point always broke it off'. The Black Girl, by contrast, is 'a fine creature, whose satin skin and shining muscles made the white missionary folk seem like ashen ghosts by contrast. . .' Knobkerry in hand, with which to smash false idols, the Black Girl goes off to seek the true creator. Her first encounter is with the God of the Old Testament – an awful brute, the prototype of every drunk father who comes home on Friday night and beats the kids. The New Testament God (her second encounter) is a namby-pamby. So much for the traditional deities.

Her most interesting encounter is with the new god of science – in the person of Pavlov, who has worked out why dogs do things by cutting out their brains and 'observing their spittle by making holes in their cheeks for them to salivate through instead of through their tongues'. 'The whole scientific world is prostrate at my feet in admiration of this colossal achievement', he tells her. Do you know you're sitting on a crocodile? asks the Black Girl. Pavlov promptly climbs a tree with an agility he didn't know he possessed. There was no crocodile, she then tells him. Why did you do it? asks the great scientist, forlornly, from high up in the branches. 'An experiment', she blandly replies. At least she didn't bore a hole in his face. So it goes, until returning home she finds 'a red-haired Irishman labouring in the back garden where they grew the kitchen stuff'. Is it CANDIDE? No, it is GBS, as famous in youth for his flaming red locks as he was in age for his pepper-and-salt beard. This garden, the Black Girl explains, belongs to 'the Old Gentleman'. Does he know he's trespassing? 'I'm a Socialist,' replies the Irishman. She likes the reply and converts to Socialism and proposes marriage. At first he is coy. 'Is it me marry a black heathen niggerwoman? Lemme go, will yous. I dont want to marry annywan.' But he finally yields. They go on to have a brood of 'charmingly coffee-coloured' children.

There was much to offend (Shaw's stock in trade) readers of the time in his fable – blasphemy and miscegenation, notably. But his choice of illustrator, John Fairleigh, and Fairleigh's aphrodisiac woodcuts, which made much of the Black Girl's unclothed *bella figura*, proved most offensive to Shaw's contemporaries. In its noble tradition of persecuting its nation's own great books, the Irish government banned *The Black Girl in Search of God* in 1933.

The Black Tulip, Alexandre Dumas (père), 1850

The fact that *The Black Tulip* has never been as popular as Dumas's stories about musketeers and swordsmen, gardening being less exciting than gore, has rendered it one of the less known of his works. Nonetheless *The Black Tulip* is among the most readable of Dumas's books. The action takes place against the background of a historically significant event: the modern world's first 'economic bubble'. The Dutch Republic was enjoying in the seventeenth century what Simon Schama called 'the embarrassment of riches'. It had money to blow on what another historian, Thorstein Veblen, called 'conspicuous consumption'. Tulipomania (surely one of the strangest follies of mankind on record) was emblematic of these woes of capitalism – vast quantities of money chasing a ludicrously over-valued commodity: in this case a flower bulb indistinguishable to the eye from an onion.

The narrative opens on 20 August 1672. It is what came to be called the 'Disaster Year' (*rampjaar*) for the Dutch Republic. They were fighting on two fronts, against the French and English, and were under threat of invasion. Under the pressure of events they half returned to monarchy, appointing William (of Orange) their king in all but name. He wanted the whole name – and England's throne as well, it turned out. There ensued an internal power struggle between William and the Republican leader (or Grand Pensionary) Johan de Witt. De Witt and his brother Cornelis are hunted down and lynched by an Orangist mob on the day Dumas's narrative opens. The cold-hearted William may have engineered the atrocity (Dumas tends towards that belief). The killing itself is graphically described. The brothers are bludgeoned and disembowelled while still alive:

And after having mangled, and torn, and completely stripped the two brothers, the mob dragged their naked and bloody bodies to an extemporised gibbet, where amateur executioners hung them up by the feet.

Then came the most dastardly scoundrels of all, who not having dared to strike the living flesh, cut the dead in pieces, and then went about the town selling small slices of the bodies of John and Cornelius at ten sous a piece.

Within this historical frame Dumas sets a romantic tale of love and tulips. Johan de

Witt entrusts an exonerating packet of his correspondence to his brother's young godson – Dr Cornelius van Baerle. A floriculturalist, van Baerle, is close to creating the black tulip for which a prize of 100,000 guilders has been posted by Haarlem's Horticultural Society. He knows nothing of the contents of the packet but is denounced to the authorities by a neighbour, and less virtuosic tulipophile, who lusts after the bulb. Cornelius is sentenced to death, but his execution is commuted as the axe is about to fall on his neck. He is condemned instead to life imprisonment in the notorious Loevestein prison. The narrative follows the subsequent love affair between Cornelius and the jailer's delectable daughter, Rosa, and the villainous Boxtel's theft of the black tulip bulb. All turns out well, with William undergoing a wholly unhistorical change of heart. *The Black Tulip* showcases Dumas's favourite subject matters – notably fascination with the effects of imprisonment on the personality, distrust of monarchs, and hatred of mobs. The last was sharpened by the bloodshed of France's 'Second Revolution' in 1848. A staunch Republican, Dumas wholeheartedly supported the principles of the Revolution but feared, correctly, that the monarchist cause would opportunistically reassert itself, which it did in 1851 with the coup d'état by Napoleon III. The event forced Dumas into exile. His fears are laid out in *The Black Tulip*.

Though tulipomania was very real, the holy grail of tulipomanes found in Dumas's novel – the black version of the flower – has never (unlike Oscar Wilde's green carnation) been truly achieved. Flower fanatics have had to console themselves with very deep purples, passing as black.

Blade Runner, Philip K. Dick, 1968

The title will recall, for most readers, not a book but a film classic built on the brilliant, but flaky, foundations of one of Philip K. Dick's impetuously written stories. The first version of the story, published in 1968, was entitled, wittily, *Do Androids Dream of Electric Sheep?* It would go on to have only a remote connection with Ridley Scott's movie conception, which made the novel a perennial bestseller (under the new title, however). Scott's title originated in a 1974 novel by Alan E. Nourse called *The Blade Runner* – 'a person who sells illegal surgical instruments'. Ridley Scott was told about it by a friend and purchased trademarked rights to the phrase. Dick died a few weeks before the film was completed. At a screening of the 'rushes', he is reported as turning to one of the crew and saying, 'This is what I had in mind when I was writing it.' There are, nonetheless, major changes, the first of which is that the film is set in Los Angeles, 2019; the book in San Francisco, 1992. The novel opens with Rick Deckard waking from sleep and adjusting his mood with his 'Penfield' (Wilder Penfield was, historically, a pioneer mapper of the cerebral cortex – he discovered that, by small electrical impulses, he could generate feelings and emotions). Later, Deckard will don his lead codpiece.

It is 1992. There has been nuclear war. 'No one today remembered why the war had come about or who, if anyone, had won', but a lot of nasty radiation lingers on. That radiation has killed off most living species on earth. Deckard keeps a mechanical sheep in his roof-garden. He used to have an organic sheep, but it died of tetanus. He dearly wants to own another 'real' animal (his wife Iran doesn't count). An owl – the rarest surviving species) would be wonderful. Deckard has himself been exposed to a few roentgens too many. He will have to be quick if he wants to die an animal owner. With that in mind he returns to his freelance occupation, bounty hunting. What he specialises in is hunting 'andies' (androids). Mass emigration to Mars has been encouraged by the authorities – Earth now being very inhospitable. As an inducement, biologically constructed robotic slaves are given to emigrants. But those androids may not return to earth. Deckard tests suspect illegal immigrant androids with questionnaires, designed to discover the small 'empathetic' differences that identify the real and the mechanical. For example:

> You're reading a novel written in the old days before the war. The characters are visiting Fisherman's Wharf in San Francisco. They become hungry and enter a seafood restaurant. One of them orders lobster, and the chef drops the live lobster into the tub of boiling water while the characters watch. What do you feel?

'Ouch!' says the human. 'How long before you can eat it?' says the android. At which point it's shoot the andy time. Deckard is an ace hunter. 'I've never killed a human being in my life', he boasts – although he's retired a lot of androids. But the new Nexus-6 model has proved virtually undetectable. The plot, as is usual with Dick, becomes impenetrably foggy. There are evil magnates, strange gurus (preaching the religion of the 'empathy box'), and characters who may be human or synthetic or a blend of both. As always with Dick it's 'don't bother', just let the story wash over you. The story ends with some uncertainty as to whether a toad Deckard has found is organic or synthetic. The film, of course, introduced a far sexier term – 'replicant' for 'android' – and a magnificent acting opportunity for Rutger Hauer as the replicant-in-chief.

Bleak House, Charles Dickens, 1852–3

In one of his letters Wilkie Collins – the writer who came closest to imitating 'The Inimitable' – describes being among the select 'at home' audience who listened to Dickens reading out his forthcoming instalment of *Bleak House*. If one had had a ticket on H. G. Wells' Time Machine, those evenings at Tavistock Square would have been high on one's to-do list.

Collins learned a lot from *Bleak House* – not least its introduction of a new genus, the Scotland Yard detective. If THE MOONSTONE is, as is often claimed, the first 'true' detective novel in English fiction, Sergeant Cuff, the Scotland Yard Man, is a brother in uniform to *Bleak House*'s Inspector Bucket (based on Dickens' 'thief-taker' acquaintance Inspector Field – whom he admired rather more than his character's surname in the novel may imply). More importantly in this novel, for the first time, Dickens worked out how best to handle 'suspense' – that is, leaving artfully placed black holes and deliberately ruptured links in the plot, designed to keep the reader on edge for the many months of serialisation. It was Collins who coined the much-repeated slogan for the serialist: 'Make 'em cry, make 'em laugh, make 'em *wait*'. He learned that lesson at Dickens' knee.

Bleak House begins with enigma swirling as thick as fog. Half the narrative is carried by the sweetest (too sweet for many) of illegitimate young women. Who is Esther's mother? Who is her father? Readers had to wait months to find out. Meanwhile, in a dank but majestic pile in the country, a frigidly beautiful woman, Lady Dedlock (ominous name), idly glances at a legal document. An expression of shock crosses her normally mask-like face – the lawyer who has brought the document notices. But what has she seen? And in seedy London lodgings, a 'scrivener' – copyist – known as 'Nemo' (i.e. 'nobody') is, a little later, found dead. An opium addict, he probably killed himself. But how did he, clearly a fellow of some breeding, fall to this low station in life? His only friend is a little street-sweeper, Jo. How are all these scenarios going to link together – or are they?

This is a mid-career novel – arguably the greatest of them in the Dickens corpus – and there are the by-now-familiar ingredients. These are prominent in the famous first paragraph:

> LONDON. Michaelmas Term lately over, and the Lord Chancellor sitting in Lincoln's Inn Hall. Implacable November weather. As much mud in the streets as if the waters had but newly retired from the face of the earth, and it would not be wonderful to meet a Megalosaurus, forty feet long or so, waddling like an elephantine lizard up Holborn Hill.

It was Trollope (the Wykehamist) who sniffily decreed in *An Autobiography* that no one should recommend a young person to read Dickens (early school leaver) for his correct English. That one-word first sentence may well have lodged in Trollope's mind, or stuck in his craw. Gentlemen did not write

that way. Trollope thought the writer's style best which, like the cut of a gentleman's clothes, no one noticed. It is impossible not to notice Dickensian tricks of grammar.

Clearly Holborn is chosen for its legal connections. The Megalosaurus, we apprehend, has wandered in from the Great Exhibition (recently relocated to Crystal Palace, where 'life-size' model dinosaurs, reconstructed by the man who invented the word 'dinosaur', were a huge draw). London is, in November, a version of the slimy primordial soup in which the great lizards ruled. Dickens' rhetoric adds muscle to the imminent metropolitan reform – in terms of *Bleak House*, the removal of 'mud' (the word should be rolled round the tongue to produce something that sounds like the French *merde*). A few years after the publication of *Bleak House*, Joseph Bazalgette set in progress (and completed in a remarkably short time) the capital's subterranean sewer and water mains system. Londoners, mostly without realising, walk over it to this day, unaware of how much better it makes city life.

Balzalgette's system meant no more catastrophic cholera epidemics (faecally infected wells, as John Snow proved just after *Bleak House*'s run, were the disease vector), and the introduction of mains water, street drainage, water closets. According to a German historian of the time, 'the English think soap is civilisation'. No, *sewers* are civilisation, Dickens implies. And the more fragrant London *Bleak House* promises is just one of the things to relish in a novel which rewards a hundred readings. Read on.

Bleeding Edge, Thomas Pynchon, 2013

Entropy posits that things become disorganised more easily than organised. Take a pack of cards: put them in sequence. Drop the pack on the floor. Pick them up and put them back in order. Which process takes more energy? And how does that apply to fiction? Plot is another term for 'order' – shaping the booming, buzzing confusion that is life. In Pynchon's fiction, plot is a constant process of construction and deconstruction. Paranoia is its opposite. It's plot run wild. *Bleeding Edge* is entropic in its plotting and joyously paranoid in its world view. Pynchon even cracks a little joke at his own expense. 'Paranoia's the garlic in life's kitchen, right, you can never have too much', says a character. But, of course, you can. It's called madness. And awful grub.

Central to *Bleeding Edge* is the idea that 9/11 (the event around which the novel revolves) released the biggest explosion of paranoia – most of it cyberspatial – in history. It coincided with the entropic rot of the Big Apple: the period between the dot.com bubble, Wall Street meltdown and the destruction of the Twin Towers – world-capitalism's cathedral. But why, the novel ponders, did shares in the two airlines whose Jumbos were involved start jumping around in advance of the attack? Why did 'Ay-rab' taxi drivers seem to be jabbering about conspiracy the day before the towers were hit? Who was *really* behind it all... the Russian Mafia? The CIA? The Israelis? George Bush and his puppet master Cheney, desperate to get their Patriot Act on the books?

The novel's heroine is Maxine Tarnow, a very classy Jewish mother. She's divorced, amicably, from a guy who always looks like he spent the previous night in a sensory deprivation tank. She totes a gun, is a computer über-geek, and a good mother to her two kids, Ziggy and Otis. Maxine was a fraud investigator, trained to disbelieve everything she sees and to look for hidden patterns. Recently 'de-certified' and now a PI, she sets out on the trail of a mysterious site called hashslingrz.com. Behind it is the elusive, never quite seen, Gabriel Ice. He could be a Mossad agent; he could be funnelling money to the Jihadists; he could be a CIA black ops specialist. Or he could be a maniac who wants to own every damn program, piece of software and operating system in the universe (as in the movie *Tron* – or in real life, as paranoids believe, Bill Gates). The trail leads Maxine into the 'deep web' and 'dark archives' where 'phantom-ware' lurks. She is constantly 'duked in on forces outside [her] normal perimeter'. Back on the surface she works a night or two as a MILF pole dancer at Joie de Beavre strip bar; something else that is outside her normal perimeter.

What makes the novel a peculiar delight is Pynchon's conviction that New York is a city so sui generis and up itself, and so cyber-savvy, that it needs its own twenty-first-century language (*Borpers*: people with borderline personality condition – epidemic in Pynchon's world; *Bleeding Edge*: technology of no proven use, high-risk, something only early-adoption addicts feel comfortable with). But it's not all buzzwords. The novel is salted with good old-fashioned wisecracks too. Grandparents are said to bond strongly with their grandchildren because they both hate the same people, and – one of the laws of the Pynchon universe – everything eventually becomes a Broadway musical. My advice? Read it, but don't try to follow it. It'll make you giddy.

Blue Nights, Joan Didion, 2011

Most readers of novels, where there's any doubt as to what they are looking at, adopt the 'if it walks like a duck and quacks like a duck, it's a duck' test. But some narratives quack ambiguously – none more so than *Blue Nights*. In 2011 Joan Didion was the most famous living woman writer in America. But no one was quite sure what kind of literary entity *Blue Nights* was. Most reviewers called it, as Didion herself did, a 'book'. Some called it less vaguely a 'memoir', and a few braver spirits ventured the word 'novel'. At the centre of the book were known events in the author's own life. Didion had recently suffered two hammer blows – her husband of forty years had suffered a fatal heart attack over dinner. 'John was talking; then he wasn't', is how she put it; never one to waste words, even in the extremity of grief. Two months later, after suffering a series of apparently quite curable ailments, the couple's only daughter Quintana Roo, culpably maltreated by the most expensive medical system in the world, fell into a vegetative state. Her life was switched off. *Blue Nights*, dedicated to Quintana, is a chronicle of maternal grief, a memoir, but the 'book' is shaped with a novelist's hand. The haunting title is explained in its first sentence:

> In certain latitudes there comes a space of time approaching and

following the summer solstice, some weeks in all, when the twilights turn long and blue.

'Blue(s)' – for someone as versed in American song as Didion – carries a world of pain within its monosyllable.

The narrative organises itself around a succession of impressionistic images. Dominating the early sections is the departure from the sea-front home in Malibu where the family had been happy. The house (as is routine in Southern California when property changes hands) is 'bagged' – enveloped in a plastic envelope full of lethal gas to kill the ever-present termites. The process also kills the surrounding garden flowers – tended lovingly by Didion over the years. The three of them move to New York, where things are less happy. Didion records it all in a chiselled prose that makes the white space speak as eloquently as the ink. The tone is, by design, oddly affectless. If she hates anything, it is only the American medical profession. 'I always put the word "diagnosis" in quotes', she says, 'because I have not yet seen that case in which "diagnosis" leads to "cure".' The writer is the better diagnostician.

No writer is a more admirable stylist than Didion. But this is a mother's chronicle. How admirable is Didion in that unwriterly department? Not very, thought Mary-Kay Wilmers, in one of the few critical notices *Blue Nights* received. Should she have not noticed, Wilmers asked, 'when, aged no more than five, Quintana told her parents that she had rung the local psychiatric hospital while they were out "to find out what she needed to do if she was going crazy"?' This is a chronicle of unbearable loss. There is grief in this book, but alongside that a more poignant anxiety that, in addition to losing her loved ones, Didion is losing – with the decay of her brain and the exhaustions of grief – her talent – the talent which is her identity:

What if the absence of style that I welcomed at one point – the directness that I encouraged, even cultivated – what if this absence of style has now taken on a pernicious life of its own . . . What if I can never again locate the words that work?

Losing a child is one thing. Losing one's brainchildren is the ultimate horror. For a writer, that is.

Bluebeard, Angela Carter, 1997

I am, among other qualifications, a certified 'Junior Leader' instructor. It means I am licensed to hold discussion groups with (American) pre-schoolers on fairy tales and nursery rhymes. It's harder, I've discovered, than most post-grad seminars. And it requires a different pedagogy. Central to the Junior Leader programme is the 'enigma question'. That is to say, the question to which the instructor ('Prof Knowall' to his post-grads) does not know the answer – or, put another way, to which no definitive answer can ever be found, even by professors. Call it kindergarten post-modernism. For example:

Why does Jack go up the Beanstalk the *second* time?

Why does the wolf *wait* to eat Red Riding Hood, going through that 'what big eyes you have' catechism?

Why do Jack and Jill go *up* the hill to fetch a pail of water, when water flows down hills and there are no springs on hilltops?

Angela Carter's 'Bluebeard' is the lead title in her sly rewrite of Perrault's *Fairy Tales*, first published in France in 1697. She 'versions' the famous stories ('Puss in Boots', 'Cinderella', etc.) in limpid prose. Carter always understood the power of narrative simplicity. By the deftest touches, though, she introduces into Perrault's fables sly discolourations – like the drop of angostura in pink gin.

The Bluebeard story is among the best-known of the stories. Bluebeard is feared by women for his blue beard and the fact that he seems to have had many wives, since disappeared. He currently has his eye on two young sisters, and entices one of them into marriage. He has to go away for six weeks on business, being a man, and leaves his young wife to her own devices. Before going he gives her a bunch of keys to the locked attics in which he keeps his valuables. He adds:

'... this is the pass key that will let you into every one of the rooms in my mansion. Use the keys freely. All is yours. But this little key, here, is the key of the room at the end of the long gallery on the ground floor; open everything, go everywhere, but I absolutely forbid you to go into that little room and, if you so much as open the door, I warn you that nothing will spare you from my wrath.'

She promises, he goes, she promptly opens the forbidden door and finds 'the corpses of all the women whom Bluebeard had married and then murdered, one after the other'. When he comes back she lies, but he perceives tell-tale blood on the key. He is about to chop off her head – for prompt dispatch to the wife-storage room – when she is rescued by her brothers, who kill Bluebeard. Happy ever after. The enigma question is, why did Bluebeard give her the key? The best answer is that the key is a test – he is looking for a wife who keeps her promise (particularly the one at the altar). Such women, it would seem, are hard to come by.

Bomber, Len Deighton, 1970

On Thursday, 28 June 2012 the Queen unveiled the absurdly belated memorial to the 55,573 young airmen of Bomber Command (including, as it happens, my father) who lost their lives during the Second World War. That morning the one still-airworthy Lancaster dropped the corresponding number of red poppies on the rain-soaked capital, wholly mystifying litter to most Londoners. There were sentimental editorials in the papers about 'our bomber boys'. The Dambusters theme echoed in the mind. The event was not celebrated in Dresden, Hamburg, or Berlin. But why so long on the victors' part? The reason, of course, was that the Allies' bombing campaign over Germany, even after all these

years, was still politically radioactive. There were those who saw the aerial bombardment as fighting back the only way they could. Others saw it as 'the most uncivilised means of warfare that the world had known since the Mongol invasions'. Tellingly Winston Churchill – whose executive decision the British bombing campaign was – blanks it out in his history of the Second World War (for which he received the Nobel Prize for Literature – there being no Prize awarded for war). Len Deighton's novel casts a cold eye on the event, tending towards the 'Genghis Khan' view of things. The epigraph to Bomber starkly records the vast quantity of ordnance that was being dropped on North Vietnam at the time Deighton was writing.

Bomber's narrative is 'circadian' – one day and night in June 1943. It climaxes with a night-time bombing raid on the industrial Ruhr by a force of 750 aircraft, which goes disastrously wrong when flares are dropped by Mosquito pathfinders on a harmless German village rather than a 'legitimate' industrial target. The novel skips about, at bulletin speed, between various key locations. They include the village which will suffer extermination by phosphorus and high explosive, a German anti-aircraft battery, a British RAF officers' mess, and the Lancaster bombers themselves on their mission. The plotline follows Sergeant Pilot Sam Lambert. He is 'uncommissioned'; he is by far the most able airman in the squadron but didn't go to the right school, so no officers' mess for him. For Deighton the RAF is as class-ridden as the Bullingdon Society (Harry Palmer, the prole MI5 agent in The Ipcress File, makes the same Deightonish point). Lambert's commanding officer wants him to play cricket in the camp's team. Sam declines to oblige, like Alan Sillitoe's long-distance runner. Lambert is also connived against by an ambitious officer (who did go to the right school), who wants to poach the aircrew he has trained. Lambert makes the mistake of voicing his socialist opinions and his scepticism about 'strategic bombing'. What have German children done to deserve incineration? A dangerous question.

Deighton is formidably well informed about aereonautics and the technical 'specs of the Lanc'. 'I'd flown in Lancasters and Mosquitos during my time in the RAF', he recalled, 'and I knew many, many veterans of Bomber Command.' He is as well up on the machineries and tactics of the German night-fighters – with whom, at times, his sympathies seem to lie. 'I spent a long time talking to Germans', Deighton records. For the British bomber crews the five per cent casualty rate every raid, and the sixty sorties which made up a 'tour' and marked retirement from active service, meant that they were 'three times dead' before the first take-off. Lambert survives the raid and – to humiliate him – his commanding officer grounds him, putting the reluctant spin-bowler on latrine duties for the duration. He will not, one guesses, vote for Churchill in 1945.

The Bonfire of the Vanities, Tom Wolfe, 1987

This is the novel which enriched our everyday language with the terms 'the perp walk' and 'the pimp roll', and a host of other useful vocables. Wolfe's hero is a WASP Yale graduate, Wall Street investment banker named Sherman McCoy. Thirty-eight years old, and over-extended on a million a year, McCoy is a yuppie who secretly pictures himself as a 'Master of the Universe'. He lives with his designer wife and cute six-year-old daughter in a Park Avenue apartment that has been featured in *Architectural Digest*. It is 'the sort of apartment the thought of which ignites flames of greed and covetousness under people all over New York, and for that matter all over the World'. Though one may perhaps doubt whether the eskimo in his igloo, the bedouin in his tent or the Englishman in his semi really lust for deep green marble floors, Tiffany glassware, five-foot-wide walnut staircases, private lifts and faux-Sheraton cabinets that roll back to reveal television screens. While furtively picking up his mistress Maria Ruskin from Kennedy airport, McCoy loses his way in the labyrinth of the South Bronx. A barrier of garbage and auto-detritus at an on-ramp forces his $48,000 black Mercedes roadster with its bucket seats to a halt. Sherman panics, and they roar off, sideswiping one of the young black men who they believe

are attempting to carjack them. It's more run and hit than hit and run. The white couple nervously congratulate themselves on having gone into the 'jungle', fought the 'beast', and come out alive. They are disinclined to report the matter.

But Sherman is abnormally unlucky. At the nearest hospital, the injured black youth is neglected to death. He has a subdural haemorrhage; the doctors treat him for a sprained wrist. The victim, Henry Lamb (born, it would seem, for sacrifice), was in life a wimpish nonentity, too timid to drop out of high school like the more enterprising eighty per cent of his peer group. Comatose and dying, the not entirely illiterate Lamb is martyred as an 'honor student' cut off in his prime, an upstanding credit to his family, his city and his race. The cause is taken up by a black leader, the Reverend Bacon, a hypocrite of Dickensian proportions, who is principally concerned to distract attention from the $350,000 given him for a day centre but which he has secretly invested in McCoy's firm.

Sherman is subsequently hounded, ratted on by his girlfriend, deserted by his wife, suspended on a wholly inadequate $100,000 per annum by his employer, and eventually destroyed by the combined forces of corrupt journalism, corrupt ethnicity, corrupt law, and corrupt municipal politics. A civil suit awards $12 million (which McCoy doesn't have) to the comatose Lamb and his heirs. He loses the $3.2 million apartment, his Globemaster credit card, his country house in Long Island, his wardrobe of $1,800 suits (custom-tailored in England), his $650 New and Lingwood half-brogues with capped toes. He is picketed daylong by the All People's Solidarity Party and has his life threatened by the Gay Fist Task Force. His appearances in court are routinely interrupted by political demonstrations in the courtroom branding him as the 'Wall Street murderer' and 'capitalist killer'.

Wolfe's broadside against Manhattan and all its works ends with McCoy as a 'career defendant' and a ruined man, no longer able to afford a lawyer, facing his second trial and eight to twenty-five years in prison for manslaughter (i.e. about twice what he would have got for premeditated murder). New York? Call it hell.

Bonjour Tristesse, Françoise Sagan, 1954

It was, as Britons (especially young Britons) said, 'good to be alive in 1955'. No more hunting for under-the-counter rashers of bacon, or scotch in the local ('only got rum left, mate') or 'utility' clothing – as unsexy as work overalls. One had, at last, the means not merely to 'get by' – but to live with 'style'. But what, precisely, was style? *Bonjour Tristesse* provided some valuable pointers: elegant *ennui* and whisky sipped, not to get blotto, but as an *apéritif* (one wasn't too sure about that word). And, of course, sex that wasn't a 'knee trembler' in some windy alley, but that 'sophisticated' thing – an *affaire*. *Chic* was the word. Even less than style was one sure about 'existentialism' – but it seemed to mean forgetting everything your parents believed in. Sagan's heroine resolutely fails her philosophy exams at the Sorbonne because it would be *banale* to pass them. If I (grammar school boy that I was at the time) failed my A-levels, it meant a life of brick-laying. The first line of *Bonjour Tristesse* encapsulates the whole heady *mélange*: 'a strange melancholy pervades me to which I hesitate to give the grave and beautiful name of sadness.' Sadness isn't, as an English word, grave and beautiful. *Tristesse* most certainly is. It's taken from a poem by Paul Éluard, 'Adieu tristesse / Bonjour tristesse'.

Sagan's novel sold a million. But it's not 'grave and beautiful'. In the mind's eye one saw Sagan's heroine, seventeen-year-old Cécile, as another Bardot – recently canonised by (who else?) Simone de Beauvoir. Cécile was a sex kitten with a touch of Sartre in her '*certain sourire*'. I was seventeen when I made my first trip abroad – to Paris – in 1955. Françoise Sagan was eighteen when she published *Bonjour Tristesse* the year before.

Ten years' convent schooling has not made the novel's heroine-narrator Cécile good, but starving hungry for sophisticated sin. Pre-pill she must have had that mysterious thing, a 'diaphragm'. She drinks like a fish – *vin rosé*, lightly chilled, one conjectured. 'RU18?' said the sign in British pubs forbidding any precocious experiments with (warm) brown ale. Cécile's fashionably dissolute and widowed father Raymond has, openly, a 'mistress' (not a ' bit on the side') called Elsa Mackenbourg. He changes his mistresses every six months. The novel's main action takes place in a 'large white villa' (with its own *plage*) on the Côte d'Azur (a thousand miles from Clacton-on-Sea). By day, they work on cultivating 'a healthy golden tan'. By night they motor to St Tropez (at speed) and 'dance to the soft music of a clarinet', or to the casino at Cannes, after midnight, where they drink too much 'and perhaps gamble as well' (don't even think about football pools). Cécile takes her playboy father as her role model. He does not work, having what is vaguely described as a 'fortune'. Cécile amuses herself with Cyril, a dark 'Latin' fellow, twenty-five years old, and a 'student'. Enter Anne Larsen, a former friend of Cécile's mother. Raymond dumps Elsa and offers the impossibly bourgeois Anne marriage. Cécile schemes to break up this new relationship. Incestuous motive is broadly implied. 'I was always more important to him than his love affairs', Cécile tells herself. Elsa is tolerable; a stepmother is *autre chose*. She manipulates the unwitting Cyril to persuade her father that Anne has been unfaithful. Anne promptly drives her (*sportif*) car off a cliff. In an epilogue, written six months later, Cécile records that:

> Life began to take its old course, as it was bound to... Winter is drawing to an end; we shall not rent the same villa again, but another one, near Juan-les-Pins.

The Book of Disquiet, Fernando Pessoa, 1991

The arrival of this novel (*Livro do Desassossego: Composto por Bernardo Soares, ajudante de guarda-livros na cidade de Lisboa*) into readable form is, itself, a beautiful narrative. Pessoa, a minor figure in the Lisbon literary world (itself a minor thing by world standards), kept body and soul together during his lifetime by office servitude and 'commercial' translation. It was not a long lifetime. He died of cirrhosis in 1935, aged forty-seven. He was a 'discreet alcoholic' – a discreet everything, in fact. Found among his literary remains was a large trunk stuffed with 25,000 sheets of manuscript. It led to literary resurrection. The manuscript remains were brilliant, but fragmented. They had to be jigsawed together – rather like the Dead Sea scrolls – by a troupe of Pessoan disciples. They finally assembled the bits and pieces into something coherent – but it was not, of course, Pessoa's coherence. The novel is arranged around the explication and demonstration of a subtle literary thesis and an impressionistically rendered protagonist. Protagonists are, in fact, Pessoa's most subtle constructions. He assembled his work (as a poet and prose writer) round what he called 'heteronyms' – fragments of himself. Some eighty Pessoan heteronyms have been identified. Bernardo Soares, in *The Book of Disquiet*, is regarded as closest to the author. We call *The Book of Disquiet* a novel because we can't call it anything else (Pessoa unhelpfully called it a 'factless autobiography'). It's a novel which seems, somehow, to have lost its story. A mere two hundred and fifty words is devoted to the *mise-en-scène*. Pessoa first sees Soares in a Lisbon café:

> . . . a man in his thirties, thin, fairly tall, very hunched when sitting though less so when standing, and dressed with a not entirely unselfconscious negligence.

Pessoa might as well be looking in a mirror. When later Soares looks into a mirror he sees someone who looks 'like a rather dull Jesuit'.

Soares was born, we gather, in a country village. 'My mother died very young. I never knew her', he confides. Nothing else about her is divulged. He was brought up by an aunt and uncle he didn't get on with before drifting, like human flotsam, to Lisbon and a day job as an assistant book-keeper. It is 'about as demanding as an afternoon nap [and] offers a salary that gives me just enough to live on'. He has no interest in society, women, or books. 'I have only the remotest ties with life', he observes, complacently. He passes the night smoking and writing. What he writes are *pensées*, pregnant thoughts, conceived out of the cosmic tedium of his existence ('It's like having a

cold in the soul'). The essence is best communicated by some snatches of Soares' 'orchestra of myself', the plangent sounds of Soares's 'cold soul':

I am the interval between what I am and what I am not

Who will save me from existence? It isn't death I want, or life, it's the other thing

I have lived so much without ever having lived

I have never wanted to be understood by other people. To be understood is akin to prostituting oneself

Tedium. . . it is thinking without thinking

I experience time as a terrible ache

Little by little I find in myself the pain of finding nothing

We are death

All I ever asked of life was that it should pass me by without my even noticing it

Life would be unbearable if we were truly conscious of it. Fortunately we are not.

The Book of Ebenezer Le Page, Gerald Edwards, 1981

Guernsey's literary heritage is not large. Its high point is Victor Hugo's Napoleonic exile there. Edwards' novel qualifies as the finest native work the island has produced (*The Guernsey Literary and Potato Peel Pie Society* (2008) offers little competition – charming as the novel by Mary Ann Shaffer and Annie Barrows is). *Ebenezer Le Page* is the only book Edwards wrote, and it was everywhere rejected in the early 1970s, when friends prevailed on him to show it to London publishers. He died as he lived, an unsuccessful author and an expatriate Guernseyman. The book was published four years after his death and has become, in a small way, a cult classic.

The Book of Ebenezer Le Page is the chronicle of an undramatic life, narrated undramatically by an eighty-year-old Guernseyman. The son of a quarry worker, Ebenezer has modestly risen to the condition of self-employed 'grower and fisher'. He never leaves the island, and what wisdom he gains is circumscribed in provinciality. Much happens around Guernsey between 1870 and 1960, but the island remains on the fringes of history. The hero, too, has a quiet, marginal existence. His best friend Jim is killed in the First World War; his next best friend, Raymond, is blown up in the Second World War by a German mine while injudiciously walking out of bounds. Ebenezer is crossed in love by a coquette and comically persecuted in later life by a widow with a wooden leg. He never marries. During the German Occupation he engages in some minor and random resistance, and some equally random fraternising with the enemy. Generally, he keeps himself to himself, and becomes an object of local curiosity – 'the funny old man'. He makes a pot of money, which he buries in the garden of his stone-built house: he expects the house to last for ever since 'it cost a hundred pounds; and that's a lot of money'. The last, mildly fulfilling act of a featureless life is the discovery of an heir, representative of the true Guernsey spirit, to whom he can leave his little wealth.

Ebenezer's strongest feelings are insular and reflexive: hatred for Jersey, and for the English who have prostituted his island into a resort-cum-tax-haven-cum-tomato-factory. In one of his shrewder moments he observes that it was certainly the occupation which ruined Guernsey – 'the English occupation'. The main stress in the novel is on Ebenezer's monolithic psychic continuity in a fluxile, disintegrating society.

What renders this book at all interesting is the background to its posthumous publication. Gerald Edwards was born in 1899 on Guernsey. He was the son of a quarry owner, a well-educated scholarship boy who saw service in the First World War and then took a degree at Bristol University. In the 1920s

he worked in the WEA and was obscurely connected with D. H. and Frieda Lawrence. It seems that he wrote, going so far as to describe himself as 'author' by profession. What he wrote cannot be traced. From the time of the break-up of his marriage in 1933 to his reunion (unsatisfactory) with his surviving family thirty years later, Edwards' life is utterly mysterious. No more can be retrieved than that he was a minor civil servant, probably living around London. From his retirement in 1960 until his death in 1976, it is known that he lived as a recluse in Weymouth, Dorset. The spot was chosen for its being the closest he could get to Guernsey. The island's inflated property rates made retirement for him there impossible, even if he could have claimed the islander's privilege of lower house prices. Like Hugo, he was a literary exile. But quieter.

Brave New World, Aldous Huxley, 1932

Brave New World is less a novel than an exuberant playground for ideas, the bulk of them dropped in raw from the author's recent, voracious reading. The plot is simple. In the not-too-distant future, a global pacification has been imposed on the human race. Happiness rules worldwide. But there are a couple of flies in the hedonistic ointment. Some members of the elite ('alpha-plus') class chafe a little, on the *et in arcadia ego* principle (i.e. even in arcadia they are unhappy). And a Rousseauistic 'noble savage' irrupts into the story, causing havoc before – realising he can never change this brave new world – he hangs himself. Things go on as before, and as they always will. There is no real characterisation or complexity of plot. The novel is all exposition, satire, and a firework display of the author's alpha-double-plus mind.

Brave New World is set in 'AF' (i.e. 'After Ford') 632. Given Henry Ford's birth in 1863 this means a narrative time setting of AD 2495. The globe (we only see what used to be England) is run by ten 'World Controllers'. Their instruments of control are ectogenesis (babies bred in bottles – no more of that nuclear family nonsense, with all its Freudian complications), hypnopaedia (sleep teaching), Pavlovian conditioning, and tranquillising 'Soma' – opium of the people, AF632 style. Humanity is bottle bred according the grades at Eton (where Huxley was educated), and stratified from Alpha plus to Epsilon minus.

The principal instrument of social control in Huxley's dystopia is 'Fordism'. Henry Ford ('Good Ford!') has been elevated to the status of a deity. His *My Life and Work* (1922) is (hilariously) a biblical text. 'T' (as in the 'Model T' automobile) is as sacred a sign as was the cross two millennia ago. On the face of it Huxley's obsession with Ford and his conveyor-belt industrialism seems excessive. There were, in 1932, more pressing threats to civilisation, thought many – some quite as intelligent as Aldous Huxley – than the factory on the Rouge River, the model town of Dearborn, and its non-unionised, well-paid and wholly content workforce. Such things, for example, as the imminent Nazi *putsch* in Germany, the Great Depression, war in China, and Stalin's purges in Russia.

So why this Fordian bee in Huxley's bonnet? Because of the so-called '1928 plan'. This was designed to expand Ford's enterprise from US continental giant to the first truly multinational company in history, with three headquarters – in Ontario, Michigan, and England. The cornerstone of Ford's leap into England (and thus the vast territories of the British Empire), was to be Dagenham. In this tract of ugly marshland on the Thames, some twenty miles from London, Ford purchased a huge estate of 475 acres in 1928. On 17 May 1929, Henry's son Edsel Ford turned the first, ceremonial, sod. There rapidly sprang up in Dagenham 'Fordopolis'. It incorporated model housing, well laid-out schools, some of the most bizarre public houses that are still to be found in ex-urban London, and the ultra-modern plant itself. The works was ceremonially opened in March 1931, a month before Huxley began writing *Brave New World*. Huxley had seen the future – and it was an 'Anglia' motor car (Ford's English product). He did not like it.

Brave New World is a prime vindication of the veteran science-fiction writer Brian Aldiss's argument that his genre is rarely 'prophetic' – a forecast (accurate or inaccurate) of the future. It is, typically, Aldiss argues 'prodromic' – symptomatic of the present in which it is written. Or, to put it equationally, '1984 = 1948'. And Huxley's novel is similarly more concerned with AD 1932 than far-off AF 632, when the action of *Brave New World* is ostensibly set. It was, in its day, the novel of the day. Huxley himself regarded the book (which has, ironically, become his hallmark work) as a *jeu d'esprit*. As fiction it's thin as tissue paper, and now quaintly dated, but the acrobatic play of authorial mind still dazzles. That would have been enough for Aldous. He was always worried about that plus on his alpha.

Brideshead Revisited, Evelyn Waugh, 1945

No country house has been more revisited. Waugh's most popular novel was televised to huge – verging on 'manic' – acclaim in 1981. The series is regularly re-rerun; the theme music, by Geoffrey Burgon, still evokes chimes at midnight and gaudy nights among the dreaming spires. Waugh's novel is a mixture of double-distilled snobbery, toffocratic allegiance, Catholic exceptionalism, Oxbridge snootery, and five-star gourmandising (in a later preface Waugh had the good grace to apologise for the last, blaming it on the austerities of wartime rationing).

The grammar-school boy ('oick') Lieutenant Hooper's invasion (simply by being there, uninvited) of the billeted Brideshead during the war is seen as something worse even than what the Vandals did to Rome. It's class contamination. But do the Flyte-Marchmains deserve the comfortable place in life which English history has, for centuries, given them? The tortured Sebastian (significant name) is a youthfully epicene alcoholic, and later a middle-aged syphilitic alcoholic, who has never done a useful thing in his life. His mother is a monster. His father has decamped to live a selfishly sybaritic life with his mistress in Rome on money supplied by toiling tenant farmers on the estate he neglects. The heir to the title, 'Bridey', is a dolt and a prig. Why respect these excessively 'top' people? And what about the narrator hero himself, Charles Ryder? He is as much a servitor as Nanny Hawkins, the faithful old retainer lodged in the attic.

For the principals – Charles and Sebastian – Oxford is not a place of learning but of class affirmation. Even at pre-war Oxford, however, Hooperism – the lower-class, meritocratic infection – is fraying the edges in the shape of hard-working grammar-school lads. World war opens the flood-gates. The playing fields of Eton simply can't supply enough officer-class cannon fodder. Hooper, who would never stand a chance of being commissioned in peacetime, is, despite his marginality in the narrative framework, central to its inner anxieties. His 'flat Midlands accent' and vulgar Americanisms ('okey-dokey') do not grate, they are omens. Was it 'to make a world for Hooper', the novel enquires, that the upper classes sacrificed the flower of their youth in the earlier world war? On the face of it, those tens of millions – ninety per cent of them, one guesses, of the Hooper class – who devotedly turned on their TV sets to watch *Brideshead*, did so to get a well-aimed slap in the face. Waugh, as his first biographer Christopher Sykes noted, had an 'instinctive dislike of the working classes', as if such a thing were an irrational thing like a fear of heights. The author's admirers might argue that this dislike was entirely rational and stemmed from horror of what was happening to 'his' and 'their' England. The Attlee victory of 1945 (a disaster for Waugh's class that coincided with the publication of *Brideshead Revisited*) brought the Hooper masses a health service and a fair crack at higher education.

But what was it, in Waugh's view, that had been so fatally lost in the twentieth century – most catastrophically in the two world wars? Deference, principally: that quality which, Walter Bagehot argued, held England together and revolution at bay. Carlyle more bluntly called it 'servantship'. In one of his startlingly candid remarks about himself, Waugh proclaimed that, in the lower classes, he tolerated 'servility' but abominated 'familiarity'. The only likeable working-class character one recalls in his twenty-novel-strong dramatis personae is Nanny Hawkins. Like the undimmed lamp-light in the chapel (whose walls Charles has dutifully decorated, in his own act of higher servantship), she survives. Like the chapel, her utter servility is a beacon of hope. Critics have asked whether Lord Marchmain's soul is more important than Hooper's. Yes, Waugh would have answered, were he being honest (and he invariably was). And Nanny's soul? Yes, too, although unlike Hooper she would gain entrance to Heaven solely on the Marchmain ticket. Someone must iron those celestial robes.

The British Museum is Falling Down, David Lodge, 1965

The British Museum is Falling Down commemorates the dark age of the department in which I have spent the greater part of my professional life (English, University College London). Lodge sees the novel as commemorating something else, peculiar to the time he wrote it: namely that brief interval between 1962 (when Pope John XXIII set up a Second Vatican Council) and 1968, when devout Catholics believed that there might be some relaxation in the papal prohibitions against contraception. There wasn't. The novel narrates one day in the life of Adam Appleby, a twenty-five-year-old doctoral student completing (belatedly) what was originally an ambitious thesis on 'language and ideology in modern fiction', which has been boiled down, by academic bureaucracy, to a study of long sentences in three novels. Adam married early – like his apple-eating namesake. The rhythm method of contraception, all the Catholic Church currently permits, is simple. So simple he has three children under the age of five. The narrative opens with the hero waking up, glumly:

> It was Adam Appleby's misfortune that at the moment of awakening from sleep his consciousness was immediately flooded with everything he least wanted to think about.

Topping the list is the possibility that (rhythmically) his wife Barbara may be pregnant again. He trogs off to the British Museum Reading Room for a day's work. 'I thought people who worked there wore uniforms', his uncomfortably precocious daughter observes. Adam is drably dressed apart from a pair of his wife's knickers – the only clean underwear he could find. 'What's a transvestite?' the same daughter enquires as he leaves.

The novel (the first comic work Lodge wrote, at the suggestion of his friend Malcolm Bradbury) is an extended description of the woes of postgraduate existence. Central to it is a depiction of the old British Museum Reading Room, as remodelled by Panizzi in the mid-nineteenth century, where virtually every great writer plunked their buttocks to change the world (like Karl Marx) or entertain it (George Bernard Shaw and virtually every other great writer you can think of). It no longer exists in its old form, with the dull echoing thuds of the books, and – in winter – wisps of fog wreathing the upper reaches of the great dome. Lodge offers one of the finer memorials to the institution and its luckless inmates:

> He weaved his way to the row of desks where he usually worked, and noted the familiar figures at whose sides he had worked for two years without ever exchanging a word with any of them: earnest, efficient Americans, humming away like dynamos, powered by Guggenheim grants; turbaned Sikhs, all called Mr Singh, and all studying Indian influences on English Literature; pimply, bespectacled women, smiling cruelly to themselves, as they noted an error in somebody's footnote.

And, somewhere in that toiling mass, me, working on my PhD on Thackeray's compositional methods. Adam almost gets a job at UCL but his doltish heads of department have mixed him up with someone else. He's only been in the place for two years, for heaven's sake, how could they be expected to know who he was? An American fairy godfather, loaded with dollars to buy manuscripts, comes along and Adam, as we leave him, has been liberated from his British Museum captivity. The narrative is enhanced by a series of ten cunningly embedded

pastiches, ranging from Kafka to James Joyce via Graham Greene (on whom Lodge wrote his own PhD dissertation). They are funny in themselves and make the larger point that there is so much literature in Adam's mind that he cannot see the real world.

Lodge initially intended to call the novel *The British Museum Has Lost Its Charm*. Late in the day – after the novel was set up in print – he was warned that he would need permission from the Gershwin estate. They refused to give it and he had to make do with a title he has always regarded as inferior.

Brooklyn, Colm Tóibín, 2009

In the last half-century no European country has undergone a more disruptive evolution than Ireland. Once the slowest to change, since its absorption into the European Union in 1973 it has been the fastest to alter. The carthorse became the tiger. In the 1950s, 'John Bull's Other Island' (George Bernard Shaw's sardonic term) was tradition-bound with hangovers of an apparently indestructible theocratic past. There was no divorce, or abortion. There was censorship – even of classic Irish literature such as ULYSSES. Ninety per cent of the population, it is recorded, attended church. Colm Tóibín arrived into this Ireland in 1955. *Brooklyn* is centrally about that period – always fascinating to children – just before and just after he was born. His 'moment'. One knows it, because one's family talks about it constantly. But one wasn't oneself actually *there* (yet). Nabokov describes it with his customary wit in his memoir, *Speak, Memory*:

> I know, however, of a young chronophobiac who experienced something like panic when looking for the first time at homemade movies that had been taken a few weeks before his birth. He saw a world that was practically unchanged – the same house, the same people – and then realised that he did not exist there at all and that nobody mourned his absence.

Brooklyn opens in the early 1950s, in Enniscorthy, County Wexford, in the south-east of Ireland. Tóibín was born there too. Put simply it is the story of an adolescent, Eilis Lacey, coming into adulthood. She has a widowed mother and an elder sister, Rose, who plays golf and is glamorous. Eilis is not glamorous. There are two brothers, working in Birmingham, whose remittances home support the family. Eilis' destiny, as she sees it, is to get a job as a shop assistant, to meet some 'fellow' at the dancehall, marry, give up the job, and have children. And die, duty done. She vaguely rebels, wanting more out of life. To that end she is taking a course in book-keeping – hoping that she might be able to get some middle-management job in a shop.

A local priest, now with a parish in New York, comes home for a holiday. He encourages Eilis to emigrate, which, with assistance from her brothers, she does. An innocent in Brooklyn (not until she has lived in the borough a year does she cross the bridge to Manhattan), she makes her way. With the help of fellow immigrants and the admirable Father Flood she finds work in a women's haberdashers: but one which has a dynamism lacking in Miss Kelly's musty establishment back in Enniscorthy (where she got 7/6d a day and was treated with insufferable haughtiness). She goes to Brooklyn College night school and meets an Italian plumber, Tony, at a dance, with whom she is not sure she is in love. A bolt from the blue forces her to a series of critical life decisions. Her sister Rose dies unexpectedly. Eilis returns to Ireland, having had her first sexual intercourse and a hasty marriage to Tony. In Ireland, she is tempted to stay. But that world is now too small. She returns to Brooklyn. It is less *vita nuova* than a willed desertion from her old life.

Brooklyn won prizes. Readers and critics admired Tóibín's handling of that most uneasy thing for a contemporary male novelist – the woman's 'point of view'. For example:

> She realised when she touched him after a while, his penis erect again, how smooth and beautiful he was, and how much stronger he seemed naked than when he was with her in the street or in the dancehall.

The strongest feature of the novel is, however, the depiction of an Ireland 'known' but lost. The Irish 'point of view', one concludes, is very complicated. Only the Irish can understand it.

The Broom of the System, David Foster Wallace, 1987

Wallace recorded that the initial idea for this, his first published novel, sprang from a remark made by an old girlfriend who said 'she would rather be a character in a piece of fiction than a real person'. The action is set in near-future Cleveland. Wallace describes the place bleakly, focusing on 'Great Ohio Desert (or G.O.D.)', a man (not a god) -made wasteland filled, artificially, with black sand, which, politicians hope, will inspire something profound. At the centre of the jittery narrative is Lenore Stonecipher Beadsman (a tribute, presumably, to the above 'old girlfriend'). She is, like BARTLEBY, human office equipment – a telephone operator, soon, did she but know it, to be 'automated' out of existence by what jaundiced users call 'voice-jail'. The time will come (perhaps it has already) when, for the jazz fan, 'Hello Central, give me Doctor Jazz' will be as incomprehensible as Sanskrit. Lenore suffers from mysophobia – 'hygiene anxiety', particularly where clothes and footwear are concerned. She goes for spotless white. She has a claim to fame: 'her grandfather designed a Cleveland suburb in the precise outline of Jayne Mansfield's body' (a macabre jest: Mansfield's head was apparently severed from her magnificent torso when she died in a car accident). Another transitory centre of narrative interest is the 'Gilligan's Isle' bar – themed on one of the most inane series (a tough field, competitively) ever to be run on American network TV. On the sideline is Rick Vigorous, Lenore's boyfriend, impotent except when he is reciting skin-crawling stories (the publishing firm he part owns boasts the phallic name 'Frequent and Vigorous'). Rick narrates portions of the narrative, in high post-modernist style.

Lenore has things to worry about. She has a now-demented great-grandmother (once a student of Wittgenstein) after whom she has been named, a difficult brother, and a yet more difficult cockatiel, Vlad the Impaler, possessed of a strangely enlarged vocabulary. 'Women need space, too,' Vlad likes to squawk. (Drugs are involved in the avian garrulity.) Gramma Lenore goes on the run with the priceless Wittgenstein notebook she owns.

The manager of her nursing home, David Bloemker, is another passing centre of interest. As his surname hints, Mr Bloemker is a grandiloquent blowhard, who, as Wittgenstein might say, always speaks whereof he knows bugger-all. But then, what else does the novel, as a genre, do? Is it anything more than eloquent windbaggery? Martin Amis' perceptive early appreciation of the congenial Wallace's novel is worth quoting for its suggestion that if you want the very best things in *The Broom of the System*, you have to pick them out very carefully:

> Among the good stuff, I was especially impressed by the underutilised Norman Bombardini, a grotesquely obese Mr Creosote-figure (see *Monty Python's The Meaning of Life*; see it immediately) who personifies the all-consuming gaping maw of corporate capitalism, the force that has transformed the book's Cleveland, Ohio, into a commercialised, corporatised toxic waste dump. Bombardini is a wonderfully Swiftian invention, but although he haunts the entire novel, he only appears in one brief scene (probably the funniest scene in the book).

The Brothers Karamazov, Fyodor Dostoevsky, 1880

Edith Wharton speaks for many:

> There are moments – to me at least – when somehow I stumble, the path fades to a trail, the trail to a sand-heap, and hopelessly I perceive that the clue is gone. . . people are behaving as I never knew people to behave.

In one word, they are 'different'. Different, too, are the Russians in their reception of fiction. At the period he was writing *The Brothers Karamazov*, Dostoevsky (a former convicted felon) was asked by Emperor Alexander II to be the spiritual guide of his younger sons. Queen Victoria had troublesome male children, too. One can hardly imagine her asking George Eliot to be their 'spiritual guide'. Mr Gladstone, perhaps.

One of the small, but irksome, obstructions for foreign readers of Russian novels is names. As forewords point out, 'Russian names are composed of first name, patronymic (from the father's first name) and family name'. The patronymic signifies something quintessentially Russian – paternalism. How to be free of that bond? As Shakespeare puts it (and every resolved Oedipus complex testifies), you must 'strike the father dead'. Otherwise, as Dostoevsky puts it, 'they take your soul'. *The Brothers Karamazov* is a novel of necessary parricide. The national act of parricide, that of the Tsar ('little father'), would have to wait, of course, until 1917. Its necessity was here forecast by Dostoevsky.

To get at what Doestoevsky is trying to do in this novel it's helpful to untangle the various threads of the plot. Three brothers conspire to murder their father – named Fyodor. He is the subject of the first chapter. Fifty-five years old, he is a worthless human being, an awful father and a skinflint. 'A Nice Little Family', as the first of the novel's twelve books ironically announces. The youngest Karamazov son, Alyosha, is a monk. Celibate, he is the nicest member of the family. The two elder (half-)brothers, Dmitri and Ivan, are neither nice nor celibate. Dmitri competes with his father for possession of the peasant-girl-turned-courtesan, Grushenka. Ivan courts Dmitri's former fiancée, Katerina – a woman of their own class. She is not easily possessed. Grushenka and Katerina hate each other. There is a lot of hate flying around the Karamazov circle.

When he comes of age Dmitri asks for the inheritance left him by his mother. His father scoffs at the request. Without money Dmitri cannot win Grushenka or pay off Katerina. Wild drinking, wild spending and wild orgies do not solve his problems. An elder of the church, Zosima, is brought in to conciliate. It ends with a mad scene of foot-kissing. Holy fathers are as irrelevant as biological fathers – Dmitri becomes virulently parricidal. Ivan, meanwhile, is consumed by *contemptu mundi*. He is the thinker in the family. He dreams of destroying the world. A close confidant is his illegitimate half-brother, Pavel, the epileptic offspring of 'Stinking Lizaveta', a mentally deficient vagrant who died giving birth to him.

Fyodor is murdered and Dmitri is witnessed running away, with a blunt instrument in his hand. Whether he kills Fyodor is unclear. Jealousy over Grushenka is suspected. What is certain is that in his haste to escape he kills a servant, Grigory. Pavel is the murderous Karamazov brother. Nonetheless Dmitri is arrested for parricide. Ivan descends into madness – tormented by visions of the Devil. The narrative climaxes with Dmitri's trial (in which Katerina gives maliciously perjured evidence), a guilty verdict and a sentence of twenty years, with hard labour, in Siberia. Dmitri and Katerina are, perversely, brought together by the miscarriage of justice. At the centre of the novel are Ivan's interrogations about the human condition, contained in the 'Grand Inquisitor' chapters. They contain the much-quoted remark: 'It's not that I don't accept God, Alyosha, I just most respectfully return him the ticket.' 'That's rebellion,' mutters Alyosha. Sartre grandly claimed all of existentialism was contained in any one of such Dostoevskian utterances.

Buddenbrooks: The Fall of a House, Thomas Mann, 1901

Marxist critics call the novel 'the bourgeois epic' – usually with the implication of D. H. Lawrence's snortingly angry poem 'How Beastly the Bourgeois Is'.

If there is a novel about the bourgeois (or 'burgher') class which genuinely deserves the classification 'epic' it is this one. Mann wrote *Buddenbrooks* in his early twenties. He himself was born into a dynastic Lübeck grain merchant family. His senator father stood high in the town and young Thomas was scheduled to follow him. Instead of which he became a Nobel Prize-winning novelist and died, an American, in Switzerland. How did that happen? Was it the flowering of the Mann family, or the wilting of its top branch? Read on.

Buddenbrooks is richly descriptive of the food, furniture, and décor of an embarrassingly rich class – fattened on 'heavy meals, heavy drinks'. The reader is burdened with an inventory of the disposition of old furniture whenever any principal dies. One is given to know sideboards and oaken tables much more intimately than the shadowy lower-class workers who sweat, for pfennigs, in the Buddenbrook warehouse. The text, oddly enough, never once mentions the word 'Lübeck' – although the novel's location is described with a detail that makes it unmistakable.

The narrative opens with a family feast in the 1830s. The patriarch, Johann, is Max Weber's 'Protestant ethic' incarnate. The great Bible, with its inscribed family chronicle, is at the centre of his world view. Along with the magnificent sideboards. The concrete embodiment of the Buddenbrook achievement is the grand house on Meng Street. Lübeck has prospered because of the peculiar geography of the country. Germany possesses a tiny coastline and a vast inland bread-basket. Grain is funnelled, like the sand in an egg timer, through the entrepôt Baltic ports. The Buddenbrooks are middlemen, speculating in crops 'in the blade', or grain 'in the sack'. Johann has two sons. One, Tomas, is a chip off the block. The other, Christian, is strangely wayward. The main section of the narrative follows 'Tom'. Indefatigably energetic and morally admirable, he, like his father, runs the business and rises to senatorial rank – a giant in his Lilliput-Lübeck community. Misfortunes fall on the family – primarily in the form of bad marriages. Tom, who has chosen a woman, Gerda, from outside the community, has one son, Johann. Puny and nervous, and from earliest childhood a gifted musician, he is no more capable of running the family business than a racehorse can pull a cart. Does the Buddenbrook house fall because of external forces (the unification of Germany, the 1840s revolutions, the Prussianisation of the state)? Or does it fall because of the loss of its own internal dynamic? All houses are, inherently, divided. And, as the Jewish proverb puts it, the blood runs thin in the third generation. Or, from another angle, is the artist the apex – where the family was all the while tending?

As history reshapes his world Tomas realises that the mixture of 'practicality' and Lutheranism which sustained his father works no more. At the nub of the narrative, he picks up a cheap edition of Schopenhauer and discovers that there is only one thing that matters: 'the problem of existence'. Suddenly a window opens from his physical world – sacks of grain, profit and loss – into something 'metaphysical'. He dies, not yet fifty, falling of a stroke into the Lübeck gutter. What is left is his son Johann, the artist. Is this the summit of the Buddenbrooks enterprise, or what the preface calls it, its 'fall'?

By the Lake, John McGahern, 2002

McGahern's massive reputation rests on a small and intermittent corpus: half-a-dozen novels in the best part of fifty years. For Irish writers, novels meant conflict with Ireland – the old sow that eats her farrow, as Joyce's Stephen Dedalus put it. How can the Irish writer survive Ireland ? Through silence, exile and cunning, Joyce said. For McGahern, as for Seamus Heaney, there were two Irelands to escape, rawly scraping against each other. He was brought up in County Leitrim – the margin between Eire and the 'North'. His childhood was that of other farmers' children, destined for labour on the land: 'There were few books in our house, and reading for pleasure was not approved of. It was thought to be dangerous, like pure laughter.' He left the land to become a primary-school teacher. McGahern published his first novel, *The Barracks*, in 1963, as he turned thirty. A second novel, *The Dark*, followed promptly in 1965. It was well received in England but not in Ireland. Its depiction of the priesthood was deemed obscene by the country's censorship board, and the book was banned. Bowing to the wishes of the Archbishop of Dublin, McGahern's employers removed him from his teaching post.

The requisite Joycean exile in London followed where he worked with his brother-in-law on construction sites for contractors with Irish names. He continued to write and strenuously winnow what he wrote. For every published page, he would discard six. The *By the Lake* given to the world is the redaction of a novel of more than a thousand manuscript pages. McGahern returned to Ireland in 1970. The books which followed confirmed his reputation as 'that fella who writes the dirty books'. There was further conflict. McGahern took a public stand against the 1987 Enniskillen atrocity, in which eleven Protestants were killed by an IRA bomb. He was denounced as a British sympathiser.

By the Lake distils this complex life-history. It opens on an uneventful Sunday, the bells ringing, distantly, for mass. A man enters a house by a lake. The subsequent narrative follows a year in a village in Leitrim – the place where McGahern was born and where he returned to live and die. Joe and Kate Ruttledge have also returned. Joe too was born there. He has bought a house with twenty acres from the local IRA man. The Ruttledges have been assisted in the purchase by Joe's uncle, nicknamed the Shah, a big man in this small world who has enriched himself as a contractor. We haphazardly assemble a picture of the community. Jamesie, the local busybody, is the most likeable; John Quinn, a violent sexual predator, the least. All the principal characters in *By the Lake* are in their sixties. McGahern recorded that the starting point for the novel was his mixed feelings about his own generation, many of whom decamped either to England or America. Some – like the Ruttledges and their creator – came home. What, Joe is asked, 'was wrong with England'? The country gave him a good job (in advertising) and a good wife. 'Nothing,' he replies, 'but it's not my country and I never feel it's quite real'. The Ruttledges are childless, but there is a vividly described birth scene in which Joe helps a favourite shorthorn cow to deliver her calf. Hay is cut. Lambs are born, dipped, shorn, fattened and sold in the nearby market town. The biggest event of the year is the arrival of a telephone pole. The outside world has come closer. But the lake will not change. Like the earth in

Ecclesiastes, it abides. As the Shah, a man of few words, says: 'The rain comes down. Grass grows. Children get old . . . That's it.'

Byzantium Endures, Michael Moorcock, 1981

His publishers gave up very early in the game trying to count Michael Moorcock's novel output: 'more than seventy' is the bland estimate usually offered. His work has always communicated a sense of authorial inexhaustibility and unpredictability (he has resolutely refused, for example, to get locked into the SF 'ghetto' – despite being routinely hailed as Britain's most distinguished living practitioner in the field). *Byzantium Endures*, the first volume of what would extend to a tetralogy, was unlike anything Moorcock had hitherto done – or that anyone has hitherto done, to be honest. The narrator-hero is 'Colonel Pyat', alias Maxim Arturovitch Pyatnitski, alias Dimitri Mitrofanovitch Kryscheff, alias Whoknowswhat – a rogue and a liar. We encounter Pyat in his birthplace, pre-Revolution Kiev, where he has some adventures with a one-man flying machine he has invented. Pyat is, of course, well ahead of his dishonest rival Sikorsky – witness, as he proudly tells the reader, the records of his flight in the foreign journals *Reveille* (a now defunct British wank-mag) and the *National Enquirer* (still active celebrity-scandal mag). His aeronautic experiments end with a plunge into Babi Yar: 'a strange coincidence', in view of his unending protestations that he is not Jewish but pure Slav (see BABI YAR).

We follow Pyat to Odessa, where he loses his virginity, becomes hooked for life on cocaine and indulges in seaport crime. Then it's off to St Petersburg, where a brilliant career as an engineer (as he would have us believe) is cut short by war and revolution. Thereafter his adventures are increasingly picaresque, as he is swept around by the gigantic historical forces that shaped the twentieth century. At one moment he is with the Cossacks, at the next with the Soviets, and then with Ukrainian nationalists, designing a prototype laser gun (some of Moorcock's SF habits die hard). He survives to old age, a Portobello Road trader in junk, literally in the dustbin of history. A violent racist, he dies of shock in 1977 during the Notting Hill Carnival, 'when a group of black boys and girls entered his shop (one of the few open) and demanded a contribution'. His eleven shoeboxes of papers, written in six languages, come into the possession of 'Michael Moorcock', for whose magnificently bearded face Pyat had always had a nostalgic respect. Me too.

Byzantium Endures is a narrative tour-de-force. Pyat's account, untampered with by the Moorcock editor figure, is all vanity, bigotry, deceit and obsession. And comical English in his Portobello phase. As he recalls with some perplexity, 'My attempts to apply it so as to put others at ease were not always successful. . . My affectionate and admiring "How are you, you old bugger?" to Mr (later Lord) Winston Churchill, at a function for celebrated Polish émigrés, was not as well-received as I had expected and I was never able to thank him, thereafter, for the hearty support he had given to the cause of Russia's rightful rulers.'

Cain's Book, Alexander Trocchi, 1960

Once considered a 'very dirty book', contemporary readers who dig up *Cain's Book* will find it no more offensive than *The Tiger Who Came to Tea*. Certainly a lot less offensive than *Little Black Sambo*. Times change. Exile was the theme of Trocchi's writing and of his life. His first major *départ* was from postwar Glasgow, where he had taken a philosophy degree. In the early 1950s he drifted into the coterie of bohemians, avant-gardists, existentialists, layabouts and pornographers in Paris clustered around Maurice Girodias's Olympia Press, where Trocchi presided as 'the erratic pope of my pagan church'. Girodias specialised in what he called DBs (dirty books) for the porn-starved Anglophone tourist. Under the pseudonym 'Frances Lengel', Trocchi turned out such hot numbers as *The School for Sin* and *White Thighs*. In the late fifties he followed the action to New York and became involved with the Beats, pop art (he was a gifted sculptor) and, pre-eminently, the hard-drug culture. Out of this cosmopolitan mix came *Cain's Book* – the story, as in Genesis, of a criminal wanderer. It is a random performance (High again, Alex? one rather wonders) – 'my little voyage in the art of digression' the author archly, but all too accurately, called it. It is presented as the journal of 'Joe Necchi' (does one hear a rhyme?), someone like the author (ritually denied in the prelims), living a hand-to-arm existence on a scow, somewhere on the Hudson River. 'Half an hour ago I gave myself a fix', opens the first chapter. The narrator's mind, memory and prose style apparently permanently disjointed by the heroin coursing through his veins, he muses – sometimes reminiscently, sometimes philosophically.

The philosophy that protrudes through the rhetoric is egotistic. Two sets of laws in particular are defied in *Cain's Book*: those imposing censorship ('I say it is impertinent, insolent and presumptuous of any person or group of persons to impose their unexamined moral prohibitions on me') and those prohibiting psychotropic drugs ('To think that a man should be allowed a gun and not a drug'). 'I demand that these laws be changed', Necchi/Trocchi tells his readers, the American authorities, the world at large, and possibly God. None of them seem to be listening. The most coherent passages in the book return to blackout Edinburgh (as a very young man, Trocchi served in the wartime Royal Navy):

> I made love for the first time with a prostitute. Princes Street, Edinburgh. Ten shillings for a short time in an air-raid shelter. I had never seen such ugly thighs nor ever imagined it like that, exposed for me in matchlight, the flaccid buttocks like pale meat on the stone stairs, the baggy skirt raised as far as her navel and with spread knees making a cave of her crotch, the match flickering... She told me to hurry up.

Even from his 'pope', one suspects that M. Girodias would not have been happy with a DB called *Ugly Thighs* or *Flaccid Buttocks by Matchlight*.

Hounded out of the US for supplying drugs to a minor (then a capital crime) Trocchi returned to the UK in the 1960s, where, promoted by the avant-garde publisher John Calder, he became a cult figure – Britain's Bill Burroughs. He now got his drugs from the NHS and claimed his habit was 'controlled' and 'experimental'. He was, however, hopelessly hooked and wrote nothing readable between *Cain's Book* and his death in 1984.

Caleb Williams, William Godwin, 1794

A Jacobin (i.e. radical) novel of ideas, *Caleb Williams* is often claimed to be English literature's first detective story: a title contested by Wilkie Collins' THE MOONSTONE. The novel depends on its plotting, which alternates between the primitive (understandably, since this is, in terms of genre, a pioneer novel) and the ingenious. Squire Ferdinando Falkland – an ostensible philanthropist – has been accused and acquitted, some time before the narrative begins, of stabbing to death an odious neighbour, Barnabas Tyrrel. A 'gentleman' of high breeding such as Falkland, the court decides, could never commit such a heinous deed. One of Tyrrel's tenants is later convicted of the crime, together with his son. Both are hanged on the evidence of a knife found in their possession. Falkland becomes a lonely recluse given to violent outbursts of rage.

Caleb Williams, the hero-narrator, is a self-educated man of the lower classes who has a position on Falkland's estate. Caleb's life is destined to be 'a theatre of calamity'. He discovers the truth about the Tyrrel murder, is blackmailed into keeping his mouth shut by Falkland, and is himself later framed, by his employer, for a robbery he did not commit. He is imprisoned, escapes and falls in with a band of thieves under the leadership of the 'Captain'. The two men have long discussions about crime and its social causes. The narrative picks up when Caleb goes on the run again, now pursued by a criminal called Jones who intends to kill him. Falkland too is hot on his trail. Caleb foils his pursuers by means of various ingenious disguises and finally contrives to persuade a magistrate to let him divulge in court what he knows about the Tyrrel murder, including Falkland's guilt. As a result of Caleb's dogged sleuthing the villain is at last unmasked, confesses, and dies, cheating the rope which readers (but not Godwin, who opposed capital punishment) will think he deserves. There is an odd scene in which Falkland and Caleb forgive each other. The novel was designed as a vehicle for Godwin's 'necessitarian' philosophical doctrines – principally that 'Circumstances create crime'. Change the circumstances from things as they are to things as they should be, and the problem will disappear. If only.

In his ground-breaking work it's clear at almost every point that Godwin is feeling his way, trying to work out how best to create a novel of ideas which will also be a 'whodunnit?' A discarded, and tantalisingly better, ending had Caleb unable to prove his case against Falkland, languishing in jail with the remorseless Jones as his jailer. This version concludes:

Well then, – It is wisest to be quiet, it seems – Some people are ambitious – other people talk of sensibility – but it is all folly! – I am sure I am not one of those – was I ever? – True happiness lies in being like a stone – Nobody can complain of me – all day long I do nothing and am a stone – a *gravestone!* – an obelisk to tell you, *here lies what was once a man!*

Readers, given the choice, have always been undecided as to which ending works best. Myself I prefer the above.

The Call of the Wild, Jack London, 1903

There was a veritable chorus of wake-up calls to American youth as the twentieth century dawned. Two, opposite in kind, coincided on the West Coast, where the 'frontier' meets the sea and American manhood has always believed it is tested to the limit in its purest form (men have to do what they have to do, etc.). In 1903 the Chancellor of Stanford University, David Starr Jordan, issued to the young men under his charge an uplifting address entitled: 'The Call of the Twentieth Century'. Essentially what Jordan called for was the birth of a new world based on progress, eugenics (he was all in favour of forced sterilisation), democracy (for those that survived the well-intentioned gelding shears), and – above all – 'peace in our time'. Jack London had several annotated books by Jordan among 'the tools of my trade', as he called his library. Jordan's hobbyhorse was that war destroyed the flower of a nation's manhood, impoverishing the racial 'stock'. It was a point on which London profoundly disagreed with Jordan. For London, nature *was* war. He believed struggle did not thin or dilute the nation's stock: it strengthened it, as fire strengthens steel.

The Call of the Wild came out within a few months of Jordan's 'call' and was London's answer. It is a dog-narrative. But it is not at all cosy. London took a hard line on his four-legged friends. In answer to a newspaper report that he so loved dogs that he set a place for his favourites at the dinner table, he replied that the only dogs which appeared at his table were either roasted or boiled. The novella is the story of Buck, a cross between a St Bernard and a Scotch Collie. He weighs 'only' one hundred and forty pounds (i.e. ten stone). The story opens with an anthem to atavism:

Old longings nomadic leap,
Chafing at custom's chain;
Again from its brumal sleep
Wakens the ferine strain.

It is 1897. 'Men, groping in the Arctic darkness, had found a yellow metal ... These men wanted dogs, and the dogs they wanted were heavy dogs, with strong muscles by which to toil, and furry coats to protect them from the frost'. Buck is first encountered as a pampered pooch, owned by a judge. He is dognapped by a Spanish gardener with a gambling habit, and sold as a draft animal. It his first step into the 'law of the primitive'. He learns 'the law of the club'. He is 'de-civilised'.

A prize beast, Buck passes through a series of owners who represent the best and worst of humanity. He is obliged to assert his superiority in the pack against the fearsome Spitz – a fight to the death is graphically described. 'Buck was inexorable. Mercy was a thing reserved for gentler climes.' Finally in the Yukon, Buck falls into the hands of a good owner – John Thornton. He earns the man $1,600 in a wager, by pulling half a ton dead weight. He saves Thornton from drowning. But when his owner is killed by Yeehat Indians, Buck surrenders to the atavistic, primal urge and joins the wolf pack. He lives on in legend:

The Yeehats tell of a Ghost Dog that runs at the head of the pack. They are afraid of this Ghost Dog, for it has cunning greater than they, stealing from their camps in fierce winters, robbing their traps, slaying their dogs, and defying their bravest hunters.

Once a year Buck returns to grieve at Thornton's grave. The rest of the year he is 'ferine'. You want to understand the difference between American (violent) football and British (gentle) soccer? Read *The Call of the Wild*. Like BLACK BEAUTY or Kipling's *Jungle Book*, London's animal fable goes well beyond zoology. It articulates a position about humanity. History, on the whole, tends to come down in favour of David Starr Jordan. Jack London supplies the better read.

Candide, Voltaire, 1759

Voltaire dashed off *Candide* in three days in 1759. Dr Johnson wrote RASSELAS – the satire with which *Candide* is routinely compared – in a more leisurely week. The 'Great Cham of Literature' made his foray into fiction (not a genre he much respected) to raise money for his mother's funeral. Voltaire wrote his book to bring down France – or, at least, its *ancien régime*. Call it nuclear satire. The narrative opens with mock simplicity:

In a castle of Westphalia, belonging to the Baron of Thunder-ten-Tronckh, lived a youth, whom nature had endowed with the most gentle manners. His countenance was a true picture of his soul. He combined a true judgement with simplicity of spirit, which was the reason, I apprehend, of his being called Candide.

He is illegitimate and as virtuous as he is ingenuous – the knowing (the very, very knowing, Voltaire intimates) are rarely paragons of virtue. His education is taken in hand by Pangloss, a professor of 'metaphysico-theologo-cosmolonigology'. He instils in his pupil the belief that all is for the best in this, 'the best of all possible worlds'. This benign view of things will be sorely tested.

His suit to the baron's daughter, Cunégonde, leads to banishment and Candide is pressed into military service. Brutally flogged as his introduction to the soldier's life, he walks off – assuming that as a free-born man he is free to do so. He is recaptured and told, yes, he is indeed free to be shot or 'whipped six-and-thirty times through all the regiment'. He chooses the milder option, but after the second running of the gauntlet 'which laid bare all his muscles and nerves, from the nape of his neck quite down to his rump' changes his mind and opts for death. He is fortuitously pardoned by the passing King of the Bulgars – a demonstration that this is, indeed, the best of possible worlds – and is soon well enough to fight in the King's army. They win a great battle and Candide walks over the dead and past the dying to witness what 'victory' means:

> Old men covered with wounds, beheld their wives, hugging their children to their bloody breasts, massacred before their faces; there, their daughters, disembowelled and breathing their last after having satisfied the natural wants of Bulgarian heroes; while others, half burnt in the flames, begged to be despatched. The earth was strewed with brains, arms, and legs.

He learns, when Pangloss reappears on the scene, that he and Cunégonde have also had a bad time of it. 'She was ripped open by the Bulgarian soldiers', the great optimist reports, 'after having been violated by many; they broke the Baron's head for attempting to defend her; my lady, her mother, was cut in pieces.' In fact Cunégonde survives to be sold to a Jewish white-slaver – lucky her. Pangloss is now rotted to the bone with syphilis. The sado-comedy continues as Candide travels through the 'best of worlds' and is everywhere whipped, robbed, and mutilated. He, Pangloss and Cunégonde – what is left of them – end up in a cottage in the countryside. No more metaphysics for Candide. When Pangloss gets on his philosophical high horse he is cut off by the curt instruction: '*il faut cultiver notre jardin*' – 'let's dig our garden'. They end up peasants: soon, historically, to be France's revolutionary class.

As the moralists argue, pornography rots a country's moral fibre. Which, of course, is precisely what Voltaire had in mind with the outrageous sexual scenes in his novel. He wanted to undermine the old regime. *Candide* is a satire which has outlasted its historical moment by rendering, as it does, comically absurd all the spurious optimisms, faiths, and 'beliefs' which societies promote to keep themselves in business. Voltaire's, of course, is a totally destructive kind of satire. But sometimes the wrecking ball is just what is needed.

Candy, Terry Southern and Mason Hoffenberg, 1964

Candy was the first work of avowed 'pornography' (as defined in 1964) to figure in the *New York Times* bestseller list. It made number two. Porn as it may be, *Candy* remains readable as a prophetic satire on the idiocies of the sixties. As the title candidly indicates, it is a rewrite of Voltaire's CANDIDE – but with a female ingénue. The sexually innocent heroine, Candy Christian, undergoes a series of comic and erotically described adventures at the hands (and other bodily parts) of her college ethics teacher, Professor Mephesto; a semi-literate Spanish gardener; a psychotherapist called Dr Krankheit (who believes in masturbation as the sovereign remedy for all ills); her satyromaniac Uncle Jack, a mentally retarded cripple (on whose hump she finally ruptures her long-assailed hymen); and a mystical guru, the Great Grindle (rhymes with Great Swindle), whose frequently and ingeniously penetrated sex slave Candy becomes. When she becomes pregnant, Grindle gives her a one-way ticket to Tibet. In a temple there, Candy finds herself 'accidentally' being made love to by a 'holy man' from the front and the 'warm wet nose' of a collapsing statue of the Buddha from the rear. The holy man's identity is the novel's final outrage on propriety:

> With a sigh of indulgence she stopped her shy squirming . . . as [his] eyes glittered terrifically while the hopeless ecstasy of his huge pent-up spasm began, and sweet Candy's melodious voice rang out through the temple in truly mixed feelings:
> 'GOOD GRIEF – IT'S DADDY!'

Segments of *Candy* were published in uncensorious Paris from 1958 onwards. Mason Hoffenberg, in a *Playboy* interview of 1973, supplies the background, in a somewhat jaundiced way:

> Terry Southern and I wrote *Candy* for the money. Olympia Press, $500 flat. He was in Switzerland, I was in Paris. We did it in letters. But when it got to

be a big deal in the States, everybody was taking it seriously. Do you remember what kind of shit people were saying? One guy wrote a review about how *Candy* was a satire on *Candide*. So right away I went back and reread Voltaire to see if he was right. That's what happens to you. It's as if you vomit in the gutter and everybody starts saying it's the greatest new art form, so you go back to see it, and, by God, you have to agree.

Hoffenberg's bluff comments do not invite pointy-headed professorial contradiction. But *Candy* (which is still a delightful read) is not a satire 'on' *Candide*. It makes much the same broad point: don't believe the upbeat guff they try and sell you. The 'sexual revolution' was just another con.

Cape Fear, John D. MacDonald, 1957

First published as a factory-line pulp thriller in 1957 (as *The Executioners*), *Cape Fear* qualifies as one of the most successfully 'homaged' works in its 'man's gotta do, etc.' genre. MacDonald's original novel has a simple, wholly unoriginal, scenario. During the war Sam Bowden, a 'desk officer' with legal training, witnessed a brutal back-alley rape in progress. He rescued the fourteen-year-old victim and testified at the assailant's court martial. Max Cady – a psychopath with a hillbilly background – was sentenced to hard labour for life. The discharged Bowden went on to subside, happily, into life as a small-town lawyer in North Carolina, with a wife, three children (one, Nancy, on the cusp of 'womanhood' at fourteen), a mansion, two cars and a dog called – saucily – Marilyn. Cady gets early release and comes for revenge. What he has in mind is to rape the women and kill the dad. Bowden is powerless. The law will not help him until Cady has struck. Civilised lawyer that he is, he hires thugs to beat Cady up. Cady proves a tougher thug, even poisoning harmless Marilyn. A desperate Bowden, acting on off-the-record advice from the police, sets up a

trap in the woods, with his wife and himself as 'judas goats'. Cady easily evades the defences, and as near as dammit does the raping and killing he has in mind. But he is finally put to flight and, winged by a lucky shot from Sam, bleeds to death. Bowden, 'a sedentary, forty-year-old office worker, with a family and an insurance policy' has become a killer – to preserve his 'civilised' life.

The book's argument, as the original title proclaims, is that capital punishment is the only way to deal with the incorrigibly criminal. It advocates, as vigilante fiction routinely does, a return to the 'dusty and archaic code' which predated modern ideas of 'law'. The narrative ends with Sam and Carol, enjoying the beach on Labor Day: 'They walked down to the water hand in hand. Suburban husband and suburban wife. A handsome, mild and civilized couple'. Thanks to the gun and that blessed Second Amendment.

The book was filmed as *Cape Fear* in 1962. The driving force was Gregory Peck (star and producer). It was Peck who came up with the new title. Robert Mitchum played Cady and walked off with the film – although the sexual violence was toned down. The climax was relocated to the swampy, ominously named, Cape Fear River. Bowden does not kill Cady – having overcome him in man-to-man combat, he lets him live to 'rot in jail' – a fate worse than death. *Cape Fear* was remade in 1991, Martin Scorsese directing, starring Robert De Niro as Cady. It was De Niro's enthusiasm which persuaded Scorsese to take on the film, and he made further changes. Bowden is now a lawyer who was so disgusted with Cady's crime that he withheld evidence that would have cleared him (technically). He is a weak man – an adulterer, cowardly. Cady, a Pentecostalist maniac, has mastered law and has inscribed his body with tattoos from the Book of Revelation. He is straight out of the Apocalypse ('Do you know what it is to be *sodomised*, Counsellor?'). He cunningly charms the daughter (now an only child) with porn and pot, and in the climax of the film succeeds in raping the wife, who reacts ambivalently. He dies, trapped on the deck of Bowden's sinking pleasure boat in a tempest, shouting 'in tongues' to his cruel God.

Captain Corelli's Mandolin, Louis de Bernières, 1994

It is, all agree, a very strange title, by an English writer with a very strange name, virtually all of whose fiction has been set in very un-English places. De Bernières's career crested with this, his fourth effort, *Captain Corelli's Mandolin*. The novel, after a quiet start, took off as a word-of-mouth success – boosted, largely, by a BBC *Book at Bedtime* adaptation. The action is set on the Greek island of Cephalonia during the Second World War, and the story chronicles the invasion of the island by the Italian Axis forces, the resistance (or lack of it, in de Bernières's version) of the Greek Communist partisans, the massacre of five thousand Italian servicemen by the Germans after Italy switched sides in 1943, and the anti-Communist regime put in place by British force of arms after the war. At the heart of all this historical complexity is a love story. Pelagia, the daughter of a patriotic Cephalonian doctor, has two suitors: the Communist resistance fighter Mandras, and a musically minded Italian captain of artillery, Antonio Corelli. The invader of Cephalonia is a nobler man than his native rival. Debased by his experiences with the inept forces of ELAS, Mandras returns to ravish his former sweetheart:

> This violation of women was something that he could not help, it seemed. It was some irresistible reflex that welled up from deep inside his breast, a reflex acquired in three years of omnipotence and unaccountability that had begun with the armed appropriation of property and ended with the appropriation of everything.

While *Captain Corelli's Mandolin* was selling in its millions in the English-speaking world it was stirring up immense resentment among millions of Greeks – particularly those who had been there and remembered what actually happened in the war years. De Bernières's jaundiced depiction of Greek resistance fighters (which goes so far as to suggest that they assisted the Nazis in their massacre of the Italians) was opposed by the balance of expert historical opinion, as well as the mass of Hellenic patriotic sentiment.

When presented with the evidence against the 'history' in his novel, in a series of articles in the *Guardian* by Seumas Milne in July 2000, de Bernières emailed the journalist to say that he was 'no longer as sure of anything as I once was' and that he would be prepared to change his mind on the 'production of convincing evidence'. The makers of the film (in production while this dispute was hotting up) had already drastically amended their source text, from motives of prudence, presumably, and fear of affronting the powerful Italo-American and Greek-American lobbies. The film transforms the Communist villains into heroes, cuts out the homosexual relationship between Corelli and his comrade Carlo, and pastes on a happy ending. They might as well have called it *Captain Corelli's Banjo*, complained one critic.

Carmilla, J. S. Le Fanu, 1872

A pioneer vampire story, 'Carmilla' was first published with other Le Fanu stories under the collective title of *In a Glass Darkly*, supposedly all from the casebook of Dr Hesselius, a German practitioner of 'metaphysical medicine' – an occultist with a doctor's bag, ancestor of a string of literary exorcists of whom Stoker's shamelessly imitative Van Helsing is the most famous. Le Fanu's narrative is set in Styria, where motherless Laura (who tells most of the story) has been brought up in the stately, empty castle owned by her English father. Not an everyday upbringing. Laura is prey to dreams in which her neck is punctured by a beautiful (female) lover. Her loneliness is relieved by the arrival of the captivating Carmilla, who mysteriously resembles Laura's dream lover. The physical relationship which ensues is described in the most overtly lesbian terms to be found outside Victorian pornography:

> She used to place her pretty arms about my neck, draw me to her, and laying her cheek to mine, murmur with her lips near my ear, 'Dearest,

your little heart is wounded; think me not cruel because I obey the irresistible law of my strength and weakness; if your dear heart is wounded, my wild heart bleeds with yours. In the rapture of my enormous humiliation I live in your warm life, and you shall die – die, sweetly die – into mine. I cannot help it; as I draw near to you, you, in your turn, will draw near to others, and learn the rapture of that cruelty, which yet is love; so, for a while, seek to know no more of me and mine, but trust me with all your loving spirit.'

And when she had spoken such a rhapsody, she would press me more closely in her trembling embrace, and her lips in soft kisses gently glow upon my cheek.

Laura withers and an old family friend diagnoses vampirism and identifies Carmilla as the culprit. A series of clues reveals her to be 'Mircalla', Countess Karnstein, dead (or rather undead) for some century and a half. 'Depart from this accursed ground, my poor child, as quickly as you can,' Laura is advised. 'Drive to the clergyman's house.' The necessary exhumation and exorcism by a stake through the heart is duly performed by the Baron Vordenburg at the Karnstein tomb:

The grave of the Countess Mircalla was opened; and the General and my father recognised each his perfidious and beautiful guest, in the face now disclosed to view. The features, though a hundred and fifty years had passed since her funeral, were tinted with the warmth of life. Her eyes were open; no cadaverous smell exhaled from the coffin. The two medical men, one officially present, the other on the part of the promoter of the inquiry, attested the marvellous fact that there was a faint but appreciable respiration, and a corresponding action of the heart. The limbs were perfectly flexible, the flesh elastic; and the leaden coffin floated with blood, in which to a depth of seven inches, the body lay immersed.

'Carmilla' was plundered by Le Fanu's fellow Irishman, Bram Stoker, for DRACULA. In his manuscript Stoker first thought of Styria as the location for the Count's castle. To the eternal gratitude of the Romanian Tourist Agency, he changed it to Transylvania.

Carry On, Jeeves, P. G. Wodehouse, 1925

If the author (usually canny about his business affairs) had trademarked 'Jeeves', as the homonym search engine has done, his literary estate would be even richer than it is. Jeeves, as conceived by 'Plum' Woodhouse, is a 'man's man', – a valet, or personal factotum. The type goes far back in literature, via Phileas Fogg's Passepartout to the 'witty servant', a prominent character type in Terence's Latin comedy. A proud pedigree. Jeeves has, however, become the proverbial name for 'butler'. He does indeed 'buttle' when needs must, but Jeeves is a more intimate attender to his employer Bertie (Bertram) Wooster's person. Most people – particularly Hollywood people – think that butlers are very Olde Englishe. The term certainly is. The modern image of a flunkey bringing a hot-ironed copy of the morning paper on a silver tray with a 'Will there be anything else, sir?' in a strangulated accent as abnormal as Darth Vader's, isn't. The word 'butler' originates in the Old French bouteleur (cup bearer), from bouteille (bottle). These were upper servants trusted not to poison the master – something of a hazard in Old France. The image of 'ye olde Englishe butler' was popularised by J. M. Barrie's play The Admirable Crichton. It continues to be popularised, to the present day, in high literature such as Kazuo Ishiguro's THE REMAINS OF THE DAY, and low fiction such as BATMAN, where (Alfred) Pennyworth 'does' for his billionaire master, Bruce Wayne. Somewhere in between is Mr Carson in Downton Abbey.

The first of many collections of 'Jeeves and Wooster' stories came out in 1925. At the start of the opening story, 'Jeeves Takes Charge', Bertie has just fired his previous valet for 'sneaking my silk socks, a thing no bloke of spirit could stick at any price', and has asked the agency for a replacement less prone to insufferable larcenies. He wakes with a 'morning head' to find a 'kind of darkish sort of respectful Johnnie' at the door. He has a 'grave, sympathetic face' and an ability to glide, soundlessly, not 'clump'. Bertie's head is too sore to accept any clumping. Jeeves' first act is to mix an infallible hangover cure – raw egg, Worcester sauce and pepper. (The recipe would go on to become legendary as the Prairie Oyster – Wodehouse could have made another pretty penny trademarking that.) For a moment 'I felt as if someone had let off a bomb in the old bean' and then 'everything seemed suddenly to get all right'. Jeeves, destroyer of hangovers, is hired on the spot.

He goes on to be similarly invaluable at a country-house weekend, where the inept Bertie has been charged by his imperious fiancée to do a Raffles on the manuscript of a dangerously frank memoir that a senior member of the household intends to publish. Jeeves takes charge, and, in the process, breaks his master's engagement to the young lady of the house ('You would not have been happy, sir') while discreetly disposing of an 'unsuitable' checked suit to the under-gardener. The pattern is set. Bertie gets into some 'bloomin' scrape', the omnicompetent Jeeves comes to the rescue, and, brooking no contradiction, decrees what his master simply must wear. Who is the man and who is the master? The question often perplexes Bertie.

'Jeeves Takes Charge' was published in the *Saturday Evening Post*, in November 1916. This was the grimmest period of the war but Wodehouse passed it ungrimly in New York, where (in his early forties) he had taken up residence for the duration. As the *Oxford Dictionary of National Biography* dryly records: 'For Wodehouse the most important event of the First World War in professional terms was his work with Guy Bolton and Jerome Kern', on such Broadway hit musicals as *Sitting Pretty*. Bertie is twenty-four in 1916, but there is no record of any military service in his past. Why, one wonders, were no white feathers stuffed down the bally fool's plus fours?

Casting the Runes, M. R. James, 1911

Ghost stories work best when short, and few have been compressed to such diamantine perfection as 'Casting the Runes'. No other writer in the genre has been as effective, using fewer brushstrokes than a Chinese calligrapher in creating a world around his fantasies. In this story it is M. R. James' own world – old manuscripts and ivory towers. James, the epitome of literary donnishness, was a medievalist who served as Provost of King's College, Cambridge, and later of Eton College (still serving when he died in 1936). His stories achieve their effect by delicately manipulated 'turns of screw', as Henry James (himself a ghost-story writer, no relative) called it.

'Casting the Runes' is set in the present and touches on one of the woes in James' professional milieu. As any academic will testify, having an article rejected is one of the most humiliating experiences of that normally comfortable existence. It leads (as I will confess) to wild fantasies of revenge – seldom if ever (never in my case) carried through. The story opens with the frigid *politesse* of the rejection note:

Dear Sir, – I am requested by the Council of the — Association to return to you the draft of a paper on *The Truth of Alchemy*, which you have been good enough to offer to read at our forthcoming meeting, and to inform you that the Council do not see their way to including it in the programme.

Mr Karswell, the applicant, hoped to have his paper accepted for a forthcoming conference. His offering has been spurned on the advice of Edward Dunning – a don and 'almost the only man in England who knows about these things'. Karswell emerges as a very undonnish kind of fellow, a 'person of wealth', enriched by 'trade', whose new money has purchased Lufford Abbey. He is nicknamed 'the Abbot' by the locals, who hate him – and he them. Further investigation reveals that Karswell brought out a *History of Witchcraft* ten years previously.

John Harrington (a don), who gave it a well-deserved savage review, fell to his death in mysterious circumstances. Karswell, it is clear, has sinister 'powers'. He discovers Dunning's identity from an unwitting official in the British Museum's manuscript readers' room. Thereafter strange things happen. In a tram in which Dunning is riding home from his day's research in the BM, a flickering advertisement appears before him saying 'In memory of John Harrington, FSA, of The Laurels, Ashbrooke. Died Sept. 18th, 1889. Three months were allowed.' Dunning consults Harrington's brother, Henry, who confirms that the same eerie kind of event happened to John before he mysteriously killed himself. Most significantly, he found himself in possession of 'a strip of paper with some very odd writing on it in red and black – most carefully done – it looked. . . more like Runic letters than anything else'. In a bundle of papers, Dunning finds a similar strip of paper with runic inscription. He, like Harrington, has been 'allowed' three months.

Dunning and Henry conspire to pass it back. They ambush Karswell, who is leaving the country twenty-four hours before the three months is up, on the train to Dover from Victoria and secrete the rune in his ticket wallet. Later the French newspapers report that:

> an English traveller, examining the front of St Wulfram's Church at Abbeville, then under extensive repair, was struck on the head and instantly killed by a stone falling from the scaffold erected round the north-western tower, there being, as was clearly proved, no workman on the scaffold at that moment: and the traveller's papers identified him as Mr Karswell.

The downbeat, remote ending is of a piece with this most delicately assembled of stories. Those, like myself, who wore out their eyes on rare books in the 'North Room' of the old BM Reading Room could never enter that dusty place without thinking, with a shiver, of 'Casting the Runes'. The new manuscript and rare books room, as unatmospheric as an intensive care unit, doesn't have the same thrill.

The Castle, Franz Kafka, 1926

A young man – an estate agent – arrives at a village, somewhere in Middle Europe. His mission is to call on the count who lives in the castle which looms, ominously, over the village. But he has come at dusk and at the village inn he finds himself unwelcome. Peasants glare at him and fall silent. What novel comes to mind here? Two novels, in fact: Bram Stoker's DRACULA and Franz Kafka's *The Castle*. These narratives, which begin so similarly, illustrate how Franz Kafka took fiction like Stoker's apart and reassembled it to serve a new phase of the literary form's evolution – the phase loosely termed 'modernism'. The very un-modernist *Dracula*, after its suspenseful opening, rattles along to a wholly expected ending, with purification of the world from the vile infections of the evil Count. A happy-ever-after. *The Castle* goes nowhere. In the traditional sense it is plotless. The narrative finally breaks off mid-sentence. Kafka was not in the business of making novel-readers happy. They mattered little to a writer who held that the whole human race was the product of one of 'God's bad days'. His final instruction, to his friend and executor Max Brod, was that his literary remains (including presumably this unpublished last novel) should be 'burned, preferably unread'. We read Kafka in spite of Kafka.

He is the master of the disconcerting opening as, famously, in 'The Metamorphosis':

> As Gregor Samsa awoke one morning from uneasy dreams he found himself transformed in his bed into a gigantic insect.

The opening paragraph of *The Castle* is less of an assault, but equally pregnant:

> It was late evening when K. arrived. The village lay under deep snow. There was no sign of the Castle hill, fog and darkness surrounded it, not even the faintest gleam of light suggested the large Castle. K. stood a long time on the wooden bridge that leads from the main road to the

village, gazing upward into the seeming emptiness.

Everything quivers with enigma. 'K.' is a name, but no name. It is twilight – that nothing time between day and night. K. stands on a bridge – suspended in the space between the outside world and the village. Fog, darkness and snow shroud the castle. Is there anything in front of K. at all but 'emptiness'? Or behind him. Where has he come from? The narrative makes vague reference to his 'home' (the word in German can mean 'home-country'). He is in his thirties and has been on the road for a long time. What country are we now in? The village inhabitants have, most of them, German names, but with the fractured break-up of the Austro-Hungarian Empire into a mosaic of independent states, that means nothing. Kafka, dying as he wrote The Castle, had immersed himself in Schopenhauer. One of the philosopher's observations in The Will and the Idea evidently struck him:

We resemble a man going round a castle seeking vainly for an entrance, and sometimes sketching the façades.

'K.' is not to be confused with the 'Josef K.' of The Trial, whose character is markedly different. 'K' was, of course, the initial of Kafka's own surname and officials like him often initialled, rather than signing, office materials. 'K.' also carries an echo of the Italian Che – 'What?' What indeed.

The Castle of Otranto, Horace Walpole, 1765

The archetypal Gothic novel, Otranto has racked up some two hundred editions over the years. Walpole – not a novelist by profession – claimed to have written the work as a kind of stream-of-consciousness thing, 'without knowing in the least what I intended to say or relate'. The Castle of Otranto popularised the new cult of anti-quarianism and the fashion for decorating houses with armour and other antiques. Walpole (1717–97) was the son of the politician Sir Robert Walpole, later Earl of Orford.

Horace was educated at Eton and Cambridge. He undertook the Grand Tour as a young man and began the flow of personal correspondence on which his literary fame principally rests. His place as a writer of fiction is arguable (more pioneer than genius). His place as a writer of letters is assured.

The story is set in eleventh-century Italy. It opens on the wedding day of Conrad – only son of Manfred, the ruler of Otranto – to Isabella of Vicenza. The ceremony is interrupted when a huge helmet flies from the statue of Alonso, the former Prince of Otranto, killing Conrad. Personally I can never read the passage without thinking of the great crushing foot in Monty Python. Absurdity is piled joyously on absurdity.

Manfred, who is desperate for sons to carry on his royal line, promptly offers to divorce his wife Hippolita and marry Isabella himself, with the cryptic proposal: 'In short, Isabella, since I cannot give you my son, I offer you myself.' 'Heavens!' she retorts. Rather than take on her putative father-in-law, Isabella flees through the castle's subterranean vaults and is rescued by a mysterious young man, Theodore. The young couple are given succour by Father Jerome, who turns out to be Theodore's father, the Count of Falconara. In an increasingly convoluted and ever-accelerating series of denouements and crises in cloisters, caverns, and recesses of the Castle and adjoining monasteries, Isabella is revealed to be the daughter of Alonso (the helmeted one), who was, it later emerges, murdered by the tyrannical and libidinous Manfred. In a confused churchyard mêlée, Manfred stabs and kills his own daughter Matilda (who has meanwhile fallen in love with Theodore). At the end of the story a chastened Manfred and Hippolita take on themselves 'the habit of religion in neighbouring convents'. Theodore and Isabella marry and assume their rightful place as enlightened rulers of Otranto. So ends one of the most enjoyably absurd confections in the history of English Literature. Walpole, alas, elected to write no more fiction.

Catch-22, Joseph Heller, 1961

'Catch-22' has become shorthand for a world view which is particularly relevant to the period in which the novel caught on and took off – the mid 1960s to early 1970s – as is the other maxim put into general circulation by Heller's novel: 'Just because you're paranoid doesn't mean they aren't after you.'

The 'catch' itself is life's small-print clause. Airman John Yossarian has had enough of war, and wants out. He's come to the conclusion, after doing his 'bit' (and more) for victory, that: 'It doesn't make a damned bit of difference who wins the war to someone who's dead.' His military physician, Doc Daneeka, explains that Yossarian's only way out, other than a coffin, is to be certified insane. But if he claims to be insane, he must be sane. Underlying the universal Catch-22 is the fact that the people in charge can, when it comes down to it, always make you do what they want you to do.

What novelists who served in – and wrote about – World War Two seem to agree on is that they were fighting two enemies. Those in front of them, and those Heller calls 'the people in charge'. As Yossarian comes to realise, 'The enemy is anybody who's going to get you killed, no matter *which* side he's on.'

Catch-22 was Heller's first novel. It was published many years after the war in which he served gallantly. Aged nineteen, Heller enlisted in the US Army Air Corps. He was based in the Mediterranean theatre and flew sixty combat missions in B-25 light bombers, as a wing bombardier. He killed people. Many of them, doubtless, innocent Italians who got in the way of the bombs he dropped on them. Given the deadly flak thrown at his plane (particularly on sorties in southern France) he was very lucky not to be killed himself.

Heller survived, to be discharged from the Air Corps as a decorated first lieutenant. *Catch-22* recycles the author's personal history. Yossarian is a B-25 wing bombardier, based on the island of Pianosa, in the Mediterranean. The year is 1944. The war is effectively won. But the number of bombing runs before the aircrew can retire with a full 'tour' has been raised progressively from twenty-five to eighty (this ratcheting-up actually happened to Heller). As Yossarian tells a fellow airman:

> Christ, Danby ... I've flown seventy goddam combat missions. Don't talk to me about fighting to save my country. I've been fighting all along to save my country. Now I'm going to fight a little to save myself. The country's not in danger any more, but I am.

Yossarian 'lost his nerve' after the horrific death of a gunner in his crew, Snowden, in a mission over Avignon. The exact details are withheld until late in the narrative. Yossarian crawled back to help his wounded buddy, first-aid kit in hand. As he unzipped the gunner's flying suit, Snowden's intestines spilled on to the floor of the aircraft in a 'soggy pile'.

According to Clausewitz war is politics by other means. Heller's sour view is that war is capitalism by other means. Milo Minderbinder, a fellow airman, has made the rational decision that world war is just another branch of multinational big business. He runs his own firm – 'the Syndicate'. When Yossarian opens the first-aid kit mentioned above, in order to ease Snowden's dying, he finds all the syrettes of morphine missing, replaced with the note: 'What's good for M&M enterprises is good for the country.' On another occasion Minderbinder contracts with the German military to strafe his own base – for profit. Good business.

Heller had soaked up, as did other American writers, the Sartrean–Camusian doctrine of absurdity. There is, for example, a minor character whose father jestingly named him 'Major Major'. The USAF's IBM computer duly promotes him to major, with disastrous results for his men. *Catch-22* was not an immediate success with the American reading public but connected instantly with Europeans, in whose thinking absurdity had taken firmer root. The novel eventually caught on in the US, not because the population was now remembering World War Two without nostalgia, but because *Catch-22* articulated general discontent with the intrinsically absurd Vietnam adventure. In interviews, Heller conceded he was very happy about that.

The Catcher in the Rye, J. D. Salinger, 1951

Everyone has read it, of course. And, you could argue, everyone tends to misread it in their own way. Most blatantly among the misreaders must be Mark Chapman, who understood the book as an instruction to shoot John Lennon dead. However one (mis)-reads it 'Catcher', most would probably agree, is the best novel ever written about adolescence. Among teenage readers one suspects the praise might well be universal and acclamatory. It speaks to them. It might surprise some of them that the novel was published by a grizzled war veteran twice the age of his sixteen-year-old, 'mixed-up', hero-narrator.

Incredibly given its later success, *The Catcher in the Rye* had difficulty finding a publisher. One of them went so far as to call Holden Caulfield 'crazy'. Perhaps he is: by the best guess one can make the story is supposed to have been written in what Holden would call a nut-house and his parents a sanatorium.

The story covers three days in December (Saturday to Monday) in 1949. Holden is an unhappy rich kid, a senior running poor grades, and no 'jock', at an exclusive boarding school, Pencey Prep in Pennsylvania. He is punished for a minor misdemeanour, is bested in a scrap with the dorm bully, and bunks off for a three-day jaunt in New York, before the school breaks up for Christmas. It will mean expulsion. He and his little sister, Phoebe, love Central Park and its ponds. They also share a love of the Burns poem about bodies meeting bodies coming through the rye. Holden misremembers 'meeting' as 'catching' and weaves a fantasy about lifeguards saving children from falling over cliffs.

He is, it is clear, trying to work it all out. More important he is trying to sort out what is 'phony' and what is 'real' in the world around him. Only the children close to him are wholly unphony – Phoebe and his dead brother Allie. He has run away from school – but he will never arrive at where he is running towards, any more than Dorothy will get over the rainbow. Holden will never, in his own mistaken image, be the catcher, saving children from the 'fall'. What he needs – and will never get – is someone to 'catch' him.

On the lam in New York, staked by a handout from his grandmother, Holden drops out for three days, putting up at a swish hotel: he drinks, has an unsuccessful date with an old flame, calls up a prostitute, and is mugged by her pimp. Having returned home – his virginity still intact but his wallet empty – he is hit on by a gay teacher (a 'flit') whom he wrongly thought trustworthy. The world is not merely phony, but treacherous. His big city experiences have been unful-filling. The 'real' eludes him. He and Phoebe visit the Central Park Zoo and he is moment-arily happy.

By one's best guess he is writing all this up from a hospital in California. It's a longish stay – he talks of going to a new school, as a 17-year-old, in the coming September: nine months after the date of the story. Is the narrative what therapists nowadays call 'journaling' – an introspective exercise to facilitate cure? Or is it a memoir for his own children as they are growing up? Or is it, what vox populi would say, merely the best novel about adolescence ever put on paper? If the last, we are lucky to have it. The novel ends with a resolution not to tell anyone anything in future. It mixes you up even more than you were before. Salinger, who went on to be the most famous uncom-municative novelist in literary history, can be thought to have taken his own advice. This is the only full-length work of fiction, among the many millions of words which he is known to have written, that he chose to release to the world. On the strength of this one work he lived rich. 'There is a marvellous peace in not publishing', he said, twenty years after he went silent.

The Cave, José Saramago, 2000

The Cave (*La Caverna*) came out a couple of years after Saramago won his Nobel Prize in 1998, it being Portugal's turn that year, perhaps. For those coming at it from un-Portuguese traditions it's a bracingly unfamiliar kind of novel. Saramago was an unreconstructed Marxist who lived most of his life in Europe's longest-lasting Fascist dictatorship. Allegory – not saying exactly what he meant – was his preferred literary mode. It can be wearing. The opening paragraph (Saramago favours long paragraphs) describes a man driving a truck. He is called Cipriano Algor (Saramago, throughout the text, never shortens the name). He is a third-generation potter and is sixty-four years old, 'although he certainly does not look his age'. The truck contains a load of fragile crockery and is being driven carefully over the pot-holed road. Algor's passenger is his twenty-something son-in-law Marçal Gacho. The country – as is one of Saramago's hallmarks – is unnamed, though the characters' names rather give the show away. The truck lurches through the green belt, the industrial belt, and the slum belt, on its way to 'the Centre' – a vast urban complex. Marçal works there as a uniformed guard. He has hopes of promotion to 'residential' status, which would mean that he and Marta, his wife (Algor's daughter), can move there.

Algor's consignment of crockery is turned away – the buying public has discovered plastic. The Centre is a monopoly purchaser. Marta comes up with the idea of making dolls. She's making one herself – she has, she informs her father, what crude Anglo-Saxons call a 'bun in the oven'. There's another little stranger in the Algor household – Algor has found a stray dog called, somewhat unimaginatively, Found. Presumably he first toyed with the name Dog. Found is by far the most interesting character in the novel. As he learns how to make the dolls, Algor is described as feeling what God must have felt, forming man out of clay, getting it wrong and trying again: 'When our creator opened the door of the kiln and saw what was inside, he fell to his knees, amazed'. The Centre is mildly interested in the dolls, but will not buy. Marçal gets his promotion and the three of them leave their village, and Found, for the Centre and a soulless flat on the thirty-fourth floor. They ascend by glass elevator, passing

a succession of arcades, shops, fancy staircases, escalators, meeting points, cafés, restaurants, terraces with tables and chairs, cinemas and theatres, discotheques, enormous television screens, endless numbers of ornaments, electronic games, balloons, fountains and other water features, platforms, hanging gardens, posters, pennants, advertising billboards, mannequins, changing rooms, the façade of a church, the entrance to the beach, a bingo hall, a casino, a tennis court, a gymnasium, a roller coaster, a zoo, a racetrack for electric cars, a cyclorama, a cascade, all waiting, all in silence, and more shops and more arcades and more mannequins and more hanging gardens and things for which people probably didn't even know the names, as if they were ascending into paradise

Algor ventures into the foundation of the structure and discovers Plato's Cave, even down to the six chained spectators (now mummies), destined to see nothing but shadows of the real world projected on the wall. Allegory thickens to cement consistency. The Centre, we apprehend, is based on an illusion – capitalism. They return to their village, and a jubilant (re)Found hound. They are replanted in the Good Earth – the real world.

The Charterhouse of Parma, Stendhal, 1839

Stendhal is a novelist that novelists read. Balzac thought his work 'supreme'. Henry James thought The Charterhouse of Parma among the best dozen novels ever written (the other eleven being by Henry James, perhaps). The core elements of WAR AND PEACE owe much to The Charterhouse of Parma. One takes away from Stendhal's novel two unforgettable episodes. The first is the sprawling depiction of the Battle of Waterloo. The second is the compressed final chapter – reducing the last half of the hero's life to a tablet-sized chronicle of total pointlessness. Stendhal wrote the novel at a pointless period in his own life, during fifty-three days late in 1838. He was serving at the time as a minor French official in Italy – the Consul at Civitavecchia. A veteran of several Napoleonic campaigns (he was one of the survivors of the retreat from Russia in 1812), he was now a worn-out, diseased old man (something depicted in W. G. Sebald's novel VERTIGO).

The novel is a jaundiced investigation of a young man's romantic delusion. Fabrizio del Dongo is born a second son of a family ennobled since the fifteenth century. His early years are passed in the family's castle on Lake Como. Brought up by Jesuits, he hates his preposterously self-important father, and his avaricious elder brother Ascanio. Napoleon, a youth who 'passed for the oldest man in his army', becomes Fabrizio's god. He is taken under the wing of a patroness, the widowed Countess Pietranera, who finds him 'a 'very pretty boy'. Fired up by his hero worship, in 1815 the seventeen-year-old Fabrizio goes off (discarding the traditional allegiances of his family) to fight for Napoleon in his 'Hundred Days' campaign. The countess helps by giving him her last diamonds. Fabrizio travels via Switzerland inspired by the sight of an eagle flying in that direction. He disguises himself, surreally, as a dealer in barometers (passport complications recur as a feature throughout the narrative). There follow the Waterloo chapters. When he reaches the field of the battle which will change the course of European history, Fabrizio fully intends to speak to the Emperor: 'It had never crossed his mind that this might prove difficult'. It's deliciously comic, but soon to be eclipsed by horror. The young man's first experience of the reality of war is coming across a corpse, shot in the eye. War, he discovers, is a world of blood, mud and excrement. A *vivandière* (travelling caterer) who takes to him warns him about 'this filthy trade'. A *cocotte* (an army whore) befriends him. He is mistaken – as he will be many times – for a spy. 'Everyone's a traitor in this war', he is informed. He is arrested and escapes the firing squad in a dead hussar's uniform.

As a soldier Fabrizio is comically useless. He cannot even load his gun, let alone fire it. He finally takes the advice to 'get out of it' given him by a friendly corporal. 'Have I really been present at a battle?' he wonders. He will never know. He receives a wound in the thigh and 'the quantity of blood he had lost had rid him of the entire romantic side of his nature'.

On the way home he is once more arrested as a spy and is denounced by his brother. The Parma he returns to is now a totalitarian state. The rest of Fabrizio's life is a sequence of anticlimaxes and an upwardly rising career, helped by his patroness Pietranera – now a political player in alliance with the power behind the Parmesan throne, Mosca. Fabrizio goes into the Church on the grounds that 'a gentleman can't become a doctor or a lawyer'. Neither can he be celibate. He has love affairs, spawns bastards (disowned) and murders a rival in love. After his conviction for this last act, the ever-faithful Countess arranges his release from a lifetime of bread and water. He ends his life an archbishop. But nothing he has ever done *means* anything. Too late he sees himself for what he is: a bystander in epochal times.

Chéri, Colette, 1920

Chéri was published by Colette (a wonderful *nom de plume*) in 1920. In the novel, the First World War has not happened. War-weary readers could fantasise a world that went straight from 1913 to 1920, *sans détour*. Chéri ('loverman') is the nickname, hard-earned in many beds, of Fred Peloux. Twenty-five years old, Fred is about to marry a young woman, Edmée. This arrangement, of necessity, complicates his relationship with his mistress of six years standing, the forty-nine-year-old Léa de Lonval, a 'courtesan' of fastidious taste – or a Mrs Robinson figure, a later generation of readers might possibly think. The illicit lovers have enjoyed a relationship of sensual luxury, cosmopolitan culture and blasé indifference to bourgeois morality. Léa pleasures herself – when Chéri's youthfully hasty lovemaking palls – with a prize-fighter, Patron, who is always good for the whole fifteen rounds. He receives a generous purse for his efforts. The opening line of the novel hints that Fred – clad in 'silk pyjamas above doeskin mules' – is not going to break off from his mistress empty-handed: 'Give it me, Léa, give me your pearl necklace!' It sounds better (as, indeed, does the whole novel) in French:

'Léa! Donne-le-moi, ton collier de perles! Tu m'entends, Léa? Donne-moi ton collier!'

Aucune réponse ne vint du grand lit de fer forgé et de cuivre ciselé, qui brillait dans l'ombre comme une armure.

'Pourquoi ne me le donnerais-tu pas, ton collier? Il me va aussi bien qu'à toi, et même mieux!'

Au claquement du fermoir, les dentelles du lit s'agitèrent, deux bras nus, magnifiques, fins au poignet, élevèrent deux belles mains paresseuses.

'Laisse ça, Chéri, tu as assez joué avec ce collier.'

'Je m'amuse . . . Tu as peur que je te le vole?'

The *lit* (bed), with its lace coverings over an iron frame, and the woman's *bras nus* (naked arms – no lace) are caught as if they are the subject of a snapshot. And will Fred make off with the *collier de perles*? No, he's playing games. He's wealthy – a playboy, not a gigolo. Colette's novel continues in the same relaxed style, depicting very sophisticated but infinitely subtle romantic relationships. The narrative switches between different principals' viewpoints, evoking a world of conspicuous consumption in which one half expects larks' tongues to be on the menu. 'No *crème surprise*,' Léa instructs her maid, Marcel: 'Tell them to make an ice from the juice of strawberries. And now serve coffee in the *boudoir*.'

Having done the deed and ended things, Chéri discovers that he still loves his cast-off mistress – this despite the fact that his eye discerns 'that her throat had thickened and was not nearly so white, with the muscles under its skin growing slack'. On her side she discovers previously unsuspected deep feelings for him. After six months of marriage, which bore Chéri mightily, he and Léa enjoy an adulterous night together and tentatively project something permanent. But Léa, perceiving an essential lack of commitment in her lover, 'lets him go' – more precisely, she dismisses him. It is a moral act. French morality. Fred is last glimpsed from Léa's window. Who, she asks herself, glancing to the side, is that 'gasping

old woman' in the mirror? It is herself. For a moment she thinks he's coming back. But no.

> Chéri lifted his head towards the spring sky and the flowering chestnut trees and. . . in walking he filled his lungs with air like a man escaping from prison.

It is the end. For Léa.

A Child of the Jago, Arthur Morrison, 1896

I spent twenty-five years living and working in Los Angeles. Not once did I visit East LA, Compton, or Inglewood. I drove over them, many times a year, on the Century freeway to and from LAX airport. The nearest I got to 'being there' was listening to Tupac Shakur and Ice Cube on Power 105. Sometimes on that very freeway.

Victorians called the equivalently unvisitable areas of of their capital 'Darkest London' – as impenetrable to 'decent' people as the jungle, and inhabited by similarly dangerous fauna. Morrison offered his readers a chronicle of slum life in the Jago, in the East End of London. Historically it was the Old Nichol slum, behind the east side of what is now Shoreditch High Street. Very much a no-go area, the Jago was what Victorians called a 'rookery' – somewhere dark things hide out. Fagin is a rookery bird in *Oliver Twist* (his hangout is Jacob's Island, in Bermondsey). The Old Nichol rookery was razed in the same year as Morrison's novel came out, which is, in a sense, a grim elegy. Before the place came down, he spent eighteen months in Shoreditch, immersing himself in its degradation.

The 'child' of the title is Dicky, whose father, Josh Perrott, is a good man fallen into drink. Dicky, out of self-preservation rather than inherent villainy, apprentices himself to the 'Igh Mob – the street gang that runs the Jago. He is taken in hand by the villainous fence Aaron Weech, a hymn-singing hypocrite.

Dicky makes some feeble attempts to reform under the influence of the saintly clergyman Father Sturt. But after his father murders Weech, and swings for it, Dicky's downward path is unstoppable. He dies in a street knife-fight and 'honourably' declines to name his killer. Scenes such as the fight with broken bottles between Norah Walsh and Sally Green shocked reviewers, and still have the power to shock modern readers:

> Norah Walsh, vanquished champion, now somewhat recovered, looked from a window, saw her enemy vulnerable, and ran out armed with a bottle. She stopped at the kerb to knock the bottom off the bottle, and then, with an exultant shout, seized Sally Green by the hair and stabbed her about the face with the jagged points. Blinded with blood, Sally released her hold on Mrs Perrott and rolled on her back, struggling fiercely; but to no end, for Norah Walsh, kneeling on her breast, stabbed and stabbed again, till pieces of the bottle broke away. Sally's yells and plunges ceased, and a man pulled Norah off.

Morrison's novel was much reprinted and can be credited with many narrative conventions which later become clichés in romances of the 'Dead End Kids' kind, in literature and on the screen. The bloody clan fights in the Jago, between the Ranns and Learys, can be detected as far away as Scorsese's ultra-violent film *Gangs of New York*. And, of course, the South Central LA battles celebrated by rap artist Tupac Shakur.

The Children of Men, P. D. James, 1992

P. D. James' novel, a striking departure from the detective fiction for which she is famous, was adapted into a film in 2006 of which the author approved, despite its altering her analysis of what has gone wrong with England. The plotline recalls Margaret Atwood's THE HANDMAID'S TALE and James' theme recalls Günter Grass' HEADBIRTHS: OR THE GERMANS ARE DYING OUT. The dominant voice in the narrative is that of Theo Faron, an Oxford don, chroni-

cling the extinction of his species in his diary. What he records is a world which has lost its genetic potency – it no longer procreates. Male sperm is at fault. By 1995, the 'Year Omega', it is as unfit for purpose as curdled mayonnaise. Since that year no children have been born. Nor will they ever be, apparently. A bleak newspaper report announces:

> Early this morning, 1 January 2021, three minutes after midnight, the last human being to be born on earth was killed in a pub brawl in a suburb of Buenos Aires, aged twenty-five years, two months and twelve days.

The last generation to be born – the 'Omegans' – are wanton sybarites. 'Without hope of a future', the novel asserts, 'man becomes a beast'. The population at large is subjected to regular medical inspections which merely confirm the worst. Household pets – from kittens to budgerigars – have grotesquely displaced parental love lavished on them. What little vitality ageing England possesses has been sucked in, vampirically, by immigration. State-enforced euthanasia at sixty (by mass drowning) is enforced. Democracy, without a demographic foundation, collapses. The country is run by a 'Warden', Xan Lyppiatt (a relative of Theo's). The plot develops when Theo becomes involved with an underground group, the Five Fishes (named after the biblical miracle), who plan counter-revolution and the re-establishment of democracy. Their resistance becomes violent and the climax comes when one of their number, a woman called Julian, becomes pregnant. The narrative ends with a duel in the woods (where Julian's baby is being born) between Theo and Xan. The good guy wins, and there may be hope for the future. The novel makes no promise on the matter.

There is supporting science as well as fiction in James' scenario. In the 1960s, the World Health Organisation became concerned about the fall in male sperm counts. As the *Independent* reported in 2010:

> Professor Niels Skakkebaek of the University of Copenhagen presented data [to the WHO] indicating sperm

counts had fallen by about a half over the past 50 years. Sperm counts in the 1940s were typically well above 100m sperm cells per millilitre, but Professor Skakkebaek found they have dropped to an average of about 60m per ml. Other studies found that between 15 and 20 per cent of young men now find themselves with sperm counts of less than 20m per ml, which is technically defined as abnormal. In contrast, a dairy bull has a viable sperm count in the billions.

Mother of God. Will dairy bulls inherit the earth?

The City and the Pillar, Gore Vidal, 1948

Gore Vidal's death, at the great age of eighty-six, was commemorated in acres of newsprint and newscast. As they dusted off and updated their stock obituaries, however, the commemorators confronted a dilemma. Vidal was – among many other things – a novelist. Was his fiction any good? Well, not very. The best that could be said – and it was said everywhere – was that his third novel, The City and the Pillar, written when he was twenty-one, was 'brave'.

The allusion in the title is to Lot's wife, who, fleeing Sodom, defied her husband's instruction by looking back at the city – and was turned into a pillar of salt for her intransigence. What this novel says is: turn me to salt, if you like, but I'll damn well look at the sin of Sodom and not, like that prig Lot, turn my eyes away. It was brave but it was also foolish – as bravery often is. Publishers warned the young man. As he ruefully recalled, in later life:

I was told that so sordid a story about fags could never be considered tragic, unlike, let us say, a poignant tale of doomed love between a pair of mentally challenged teenage 'heteros' in old Verona.

He heard everywhere that most dispiriting of sounds for a young writer: doors slammed in the face of his genius. The New York Times would not advertise the book and 'no major American newspaper or magazine would review it or any other book of mine for the next six years'. The City and the Pillar went on to become, as a paperback, an 'underground' word-of-mouth bestseller.

The story opens and concludes in a bar 'where men meet men'. Jim Willard is very drunk. The action returns to the hero's college years, before the war, in the late 1930s. Jim was then a golden youth, of high southern breeding, brilliant of mind, superbly athletic of body, but unsure of what he wants from life. He visits his lush, luxurious home, with his closest friend, Bob Ford. In a post-mortem BBC programme, produced shortly after Gore Vidal's death, TV footage was recovered of him revisiting the riverside spot (on the family estate in Virginia) where the author's own first fulfilling sexual encounter took place, on a camping trip. It was immortalised in The City and the Pillar. Vidal read out the relevant passage from the novel, in his rich, high southern drawl:

The eyes opened again. Two bodies faced one another where only an instant before a universe had lived; the star burst and dwindled, spiraling them both down to the meager, to the separate, to the night and the trees and the firelight; all so much less than what had been.

It's tosh ('two dim-witted jocks getting it on – what's the big deal?' asks one sardonic blogger). But even to hint at such things in 1946 was explosive. Bob is ambivalent about man-on-man sex. Jim not at all ambivalent. After the starburst night they go their separate ways. Jim yearns for union with Bob, but drifts. He is, for a while, a tennis teacher in Los Angeles. He has various affairs and eventually moves on to New Orleans with Paul, a writer. War intervenes. Jim is enlisted and promptly discharged on medical grounds. Bob, meanwhile, has married. The two men meet again in New York, after the war. In the 1948 version of the novel Jim forces himself on his unwilling partner and, in a rage of frustrated passion, strangles him. In the novel as Vidal rewrote it in 1965,

Jim rapes Bob then leaves for the bar in which he was found at the beginning of the story, intending to 'drink his dream away'.

City of Glass, Paul Auster, 1985

The book world was not ready for Paul Auster. The manuscript received seventeen rejections before it was accepted by the small, extravagantly hippyish Sun and Moon Press in Los Angeles. *City of Glass* is a 'metaphysical detective story' set on the other side of the continent in the 'inexhaustible space' of New York, Auster's home town. The novel's famous narrative 'hook' is a midnight phone call: 'It was a wrong number that started it, the telephone ringing three times in the dead of night, and the voice on the other end asking for someone he was not.' The not-someone is 'Paul Auster, of the Paul Auster Detective Agency'. The recipient of the call is 'once ambitious' thirty-five-year-old author Daniel Quinn, who has sold out and now writes 'mystery' fiction under the pseudonym 'William Wilson'. Since the death of his wife and child, his life has been wholly vacuous. For reasons Quinn himself cannot explain, he pretends to be Paul Auster and takes on the case for his client 'Peter Stillman'. In following it up Quinn/Auster draws on the expertise of 'Max Work' (the private investigator hero of Quinn's moderately successful series of mystery novels). Genres bend. 'What interests' Quinn/Wilson 'about the stories he wrote was not their relation to the world but their relation to other stories'. Our old friend 'intertextuality'. In mystery stories, he notes, nothing is wasted – everything is a clue, however irrelevant it may seem. Life is something else. Peter Stillman Jr, Quinn/Auster discovers, was kept in solitary, lightless confinement for nine years of his childhood by his father, Peter Stillman Sr, a former Columbia University professor, so that the child might develop the primeval language of Adam – or, following another line of research, so that he might demonstrate whether the 'New World' of America can accommodate truly innocent human beings.

Young Peter emerges a jabbering idiot, but rich. It is his former nurse, Virginia, now his wife, who has hired Quinn/Auster because the father has been released from prison, and has threatened to kill his son. Quinn trails the released Peter Stillman, who dresses like a street person and is wholly self-engrossed. He goes for long walks every day. Eventually Quinn/Auster works out that the walks are tracing out letters of the alphabet. The transcribed words are mysterious: 'Ower of Bab'. 'Tower of Babel'. He accosts his man, and a long discussion of how to make the world 'coherent' ensues. Humpty Dumpty, Stillman believes, can be put back together again. Eden can be regained. Stillman manages to escape Quinn/Auster's trailing.

In the most perplexing chapter of the novel, the sleuth/author looks up the real Paul Auster and has another long discussion on the nature of fictionality. Two Austers talking about Austerism. Auster's (historically real) wife Siri Hustvedt and son Daniel make an appearance (see WHAT I LOVED). Quinn/Auster – quixotically (Daniel Quinn = Don Quixote) – sets out on a futile search for the now missing Stillman. At the end of the narrative, all the principal characters have mysteriously disappeared. The narrator (another Paul Auster) finishes by saying that 'Auster. . . has behaved badly throughout'.

City of Night, John Rechy, 1963

City of Night (with its echo of Céline's JOURNEY TO THE END OF THE NIGHT) was the first overground work of fiction to detail, close up and physically, the nature of the gay urban underground in America. It takes the form of a Jean Genet-like journal, with some chauvinistic nods to Rechy's compatriot beatniks – notably, in its urban restlessness, Kerouac's ON THE ROAD. William Burroughs is another detectable influence.

The reading world was ready for *City of Night* in 1963. It was the first overtly gay novel to make the *New York Times* bestseller list – at a time when gay sex was still criminal. It began, as Rechy recalled, 'as a letter to a friend. . . the day following my return to my hometown in Texas after an eternity in New Orleans':

It had been a dissolute eternity: In that Carnival city of old cemeteries and tolling church bells, I slept only when fatigue demanded, carried along by 'bennies' [Benzedrine tablets] and on dissonant waves of voices, music, sad and happy laughter.

The hero-narrator goes on to continue his exploratory travels into and across America – principally in Los Angeles (and its gay hub, Pershing Square) and Manhattan (and its gay hub, Times Square). Carnival – that brief season when morality and self-control slip – is a major theme, as is 'night-time'. As the popular song of the day put it, 'Night-time's the right time / for huggin' and kissin' / Day-time's the right time / for just reminiscin' – and, of course, writing up what happened the night before.

The narrative opens: 'Later I would think of America as one vast City of Night'. The young Latino narrator 'hustles' for a living and for kicks. Rechy uses the generic term 'youngman' for such hustlers. He experiences all kinds of sex, much of it violent BDSM. The work is punctuated with 'rules of life', given in imperative italic print; for example:

> After all there's this to consider: The world's no fucking good. You've got to pretend you don't give a damn and swing along with those that really don't – or you go under.

Or:

> You can rot here without feeling it.

After he has been through the long night of alternative sexuality the 'youngman' hero returns to El Paso, the desert where he grew up. What awaits him – the banality from which he was initially escaping? Is it defeat? The novel leaves the reader cunningly suspended between disappointment and hope, obliging them to supply their own ending:

> The clouds are storming angrily across the orange-grey sky . . . And the fierce wind is an echo of angry childhood and of a very scared boy looking out of the window – remembering my dead dog outside by the wounded house as the grey Texas dust gradually covered her up – and thinking: It isn't fair! Why can't dogs go to Heaven?

The Clockwork Testament: or, Enderby's End, Anthony Burgess, 1974

Famously, Burgess wrote spoof reviews of novels by his pseudonymised hack alter ego, 'Joseph Kell'. 'Be warned', he solicitously warned (unwitting) readers of the first volume of Kell's Enderby saga, this is 'in many ways a *dirty book*'. This, the last in the Enderby sequence, is, be warned, reader, dirtier by far. *A Clockwork Orange* is the best-known of Burgess' novels – for the perverse reason, as the author persisted in believing, that an American film-maker adapted his novel and got it all wrong. 'Clockwork Marmalade' was what Burgess called Stanley Kubrick's *A Clockwork Orange*. The 1962 novel is a quasi-theological meditation on the youth of the day – their 'teddy boy' dandyism, their 'cosh boy' violence, their inherent good and evil. The narrative is given in a sub-Joycean patois (Nadsat) not easily understood. Stanley Kubrick bought the rights to *A Clockwork Orange* (for a pittance, as Burgess complained) and made it entirely understandable. In both versions it is framed around the virtuoso juvenile delinquent Alex DeLarge (evoking that other juvenile hero, Alexander the Great). The film features orgiastic Technicolor violence. Burgess resented the gratuitous savagery, but even more the fact that Kubrick came from a different religious tradition. A cradle Catholic, Burgess believed, as did St Augustine, that goodness can only be achieved by a progress through sin. You cannot be programmed into virtue: it is as unnatural as the titular orange. Judaism takes a less stark moral line.

Theological dispute was one problematic element in the background of the *Clockwork Orange* adaptation. A second was the copycat crime committed, allegedly, by youthful British fans of the movie. Kubrick (resident at this stage of his life in the UK) withdrew his film from circulation in Britain. A third element was the year Burgess spent as a professor of creative writing at the City College of New York in 1972. While he was there he contrived to get up everyone's nose.

Burgess was, in 1972, aged fifty-five (Enderby's age), getting very cranky and feeling his years (the book could as well be called *The Clockwork Last Will and Testament*, though in fact he lasted until 1993). The narrative opens with the poet Enderby waking in his squalid New York apartment. He feels bad, and has lots to feel bad about. He is lying 'naked also on a fast-drying nocturnal ejaculation'. The wet dream was inspired by having seen some twelve-year-old Puerto Rican girls playing in the street, their dresses flying up. Enderby, in earlier life, wrote a narrative poem about Gerard Manley Hopkins' 'The Wreck of the Deutschland', a poem, by a Catholic priest, about five German nuns fleeing persecution, who were drowned in the English Channel in 1875. Why, the tormented Jesuit poet asks himself, did God do it?

Rights to Enderby's poem about Hopkins' poem have been picked up for a pittance ($750) by a 'famed' Jewish film director, Melvin Schaumwein ('Wine-scum'), who has shot it as a nun-slasher movie with 'over-explicit scenes of the nuns being violated by teenage storm-troopers'. Enderby is unconsentingly 'credited' and is now reviled in the tabloids and on TV. He can handle it. He rather likes being reviled. Worse, however, is that in a bar-room conversation he discovers that his fellow drinker is the grandson of the boy commemorated in Hopkins' tender poem 'The Bugler's First Communion'. He now learns that Hopkins ('he was a fag') took the opportunity to bugger the boy. Could even St Augustine (about whom Enderby is writing another long poem) handle that? He has three heart attacks during the course of the day and dies during an extremely unwise sexual bout with an admirer of his poems. His last words are: 'Oh, this is all too American'.

The Clown, Heinrich Böll, 1963

One of the first things the Nazis did when they came to power in 1933 was to stamp out Berlin's 'cabaret culture'. No more clowns – except behind barbed wire. Clownery revived after the war – but it was a peculiarly unfunny variety if we credit Heinrich Böll. The hero of *The Clown*, Hans Schnier, is the son of a millionaire whose income held up very well during the years that destroyed the rest of Europe. Now twenty-seven, Hans was ten years old at war's end in 1945 – too young to fight, but old enough to have been earlier recruited into the *Hitlerjugend*. His elder sister Henrietta had been sent off to 'man' a flak gun. She never came back.

Hans cohabits with Marie Derkum, whom (although he was born Protestant) he met at his Catholic school. Her father was a shopkeeper and a socialist who narrowly escaped the concentration camp. Hans had sex for the first time, aged twenty, with Marie. Scandal forced their departure from Cologne to Bonn, the excessively dull West German capital. As the novel opens Hans, now a clown by profession, has damaged his knee and can't perform. He recuperates in his apartment – a residence utterly without style. He has the odd knack of being able to pick up smells through the telephone. He is, in a rather more commonplace way, alcoholic. He is not much of a clown – especially when he goes on stage drunk, as he has been doing recently. Bookings are tailing off, his agent tells him. We never see Hans in action but are told he is better at 'Harlequin' than 'Pierrot'. His 'Charlie Chaplin' is well thought of. The novel takes the form of a written 'confession' as Hans 'rests', suffused all the while with 'animal melancholy'. He is alone, 'as monogamous as a donkey'. Marie, after a series of miscarriages and an 'abortive event', has returned to her Church and the arms of a more amenable lover, Zupfner, whom Hans cordially hates. Hans himself no longer has any religious belief, although he sings litanies in the bath.

Marie never appears in the novel except as a creature of his fevered imagination. Hans' only human contact is with his housekeeper Monika. 'I hate untidy rooms', he explains, 'but I am incapable of tidying them myself.' For seventy years and despite two (profoundly lost) world wars, the Schnier family has enriched itself with its brown (horrifically polluting) coal. 'If our era has a name', Hans thinks, it is 'the era of prostitution'. His commercially prostituted father, who wholeheartedly supported Hitler, is now a 'democrat'. His mother, a rabid anti-Semite during the war, now works to promote race relations through her Committee for the Reconciliation of Racial Differences. Their meetings are held in 'Anne Frank House'. Does he look like a Jew? Hans wonders. But he does not know what a Jew looks like – he's never met one. Hans refuses to take any money from his father. His brother Leo has broken with the family's Protestantism and is training for the priest-hood – another kind of clownery. 'Everyone in this world', Hans concludes, 'is an outsider in relation to everyone else'. At the end of the novel Hans takes his guitar to the train station and plays as people throw coins into his hat. The clown is now a busker.

Böll was also translating THE CATCHER IN THE RYE into German at the time he was writing *The Clown*. He had no great hopes for his book but, such is the perversity of public taste, it made the bestseller lists in the US and was instrumental in getting him his Nobel Prize in 1972.

Cockfighter, Charles Willeford, 1962

Cockfighter was first published as a 'paper-back original' (i.e. 'drugstore novel') in 1962. The publisher went bust and the whole print run was pulped ('pulp thou art, and shalt to pulp return'). The novel was republished in 1972, to coincide with the film rights being taken up. The ensuing film is regarded as an all-time turkey. Willeford went on to achieve fame with his Hoke Moseley novels – now regarded as classics of Miami noir. He himself regarded *Cockfighter* as his legacy book. Its hero, Frank Mansfield, has taken a vow of silence until he wins the Southern Conference cockfighting champion title. 'To a cocker', we are informed, 'this medal means as much as the Nobel Prize does to

a scientist.' Frank has left his long-suffering fiancée and will only return with the medal.

Willeford, who liked literary epigraphs, attached to *Cockfighter* Ezra Pound's 'What matters is not the idea a man holds, but the depth at which he holds it'. Frank Mans-field's idea is held very deep. The narrative opens with him down on his luck. His last rooster Sandspur ('a Whitehackle cross in peak condition') has been eviscerated in a contest with the mighty Little David. Frank, who wagered all he had, loses his Cadillac, his trailer, and the sixteen-year-old bedwarmer he's shacked up with. He feels no remorse about the last ('She was pretty, young and a good lay. She could get by anywhere'). When she dares to complain he confirms his adieu with a sharp punch to the belly. The Cadillac, by contrast, he misses sorely: 'All I had left was a folded ten dollar bill in my watch pocket and one dead chicken.' He hustles his way back into enough money to be a player again with his prize bird Icky (the true name, 'Icarus', he keeps to himself).

Cockfighting is presented as something archetypally manly (only male birds fight) and quintessentially American. 'As every cocker knows', Frank tells us, 'honest Abe Lincoln was once a cockpit referee'. George Washington was a fan. Cockfighting is illegal in the US, although it is still very popular, particularly in the south. Ten years into the twenty-first century, the state of Georgia was vainly attempting to 'block loopholes' in its anti-cockfighting legisla-tion, and failing. The cockpit incarnates the American frontier spirit as symbolically as did the *corrida* for Hemingway. Cock-fighting, Frank believes, is the only sport left that can't be fixed. The novel has plenty of flying claws and feathers, but lacks plot. There is casual sex, sharp-dealing, and lots of blood (not all of it chicken blood). Frank takes on a Polish partner, Omar Baradinsky. He finally wins his 'goddamned medal', finds his voice again, and loses his fiancée, who tells him that cockers are not, after all, her cup of tea. A pneumatic divorcée takes her place. They go off to celebrate his victory in Puerto Rico.

Cold Comfort Farm, Stella Gibbons, 1932

Cold Comfort Farm is an unusual novel in that it is a parody which has proved more popular than the popular vein of fiction (notably the gloomy regional melodramas spawned by Mary Webb's PRECIOUS BANE) which inspired it. What Gibbons offers the reader is not subtle parody. The novel is dedicated to 'Anthony Pookworthy [i.e. puke-worthy], Esq. ABS., LLR [absolute liar]'. The narrative continues in the same vein, poking fun at literary pretension. According to Gibbons (then an *Evening Standard* journalist), she was writing for:

> all those thousands of persons, not unlike myself, who work in the vulgar and meaningless bustle of offices, shops, and homes, and who are not always sure whether a sentence is 'Literature' or whether it is just sheer flapdoodle.

Flora Poste, twenty years old, finds herself orphaned and with 'one hundred pounds a year and no property'. Her mother, god bless her, has left her a 'slender ankle'. Flora takes herself off to her aunt Judith Starkadder's farm at Howling, in Sussex. Dominating the gloomy household is Seth, an insolent, priapic and beautiful male animal. Also present are Uncle Amos, a hell-fire preacher; Big Business, the massively endowed bull (always locked up in the barn, kicking in frenzies of taurine lust); Mrs Beetle the 'char'; Meriam, Mrs Beetle's daughter and mother of Seth's four children, with the likelihood of at least a dozen more; and Reuben the farmhand, given to utterances such as 'I ha' scranleted two hundred furrows come five o'clock down i' the bute', to which Flora finds she has no ready reply. Most delectable among the dramatis personae is Elfine, the fey young beauty. Aunt Ada Doom, meanwhile, is immured in her bedroom, whimpering incessantly about the 'something nasty in the woodshed' which she witnessed as a little girl.

Flora brings her 'higher common sense' to the farm. She has 'a tidy mind and untidy lives irritate me' – just like 'Miss Austen'. The author of *Pride and Prejudice*, she believes, 'liked everything to be tidy and pleasant and comfortable around her, and so do I.' As part of the tidy regime Big Business is put out to graze in a field. His priapism is munched away. Aunt Ada is introduced to the liberating pleasures of amateur aviation (and leather). Woodsheds no longer trouble her. Seth is recruited by a Hollywood movie studio to throb female hearts all over the world. Elfine is married off to the local squire. Having tidied everything up and made the farm thoroughly warm and comfortable, Flora flies off into the sunset with her own young lover, Charles Fairford. *Cold Comfort Farm*, Gibbons' first novel, won the Femina Vie Heureuse prize for 1933. Rarely has a novel brought more happiness into life – feminine and male. She wrote an unnecessary follow-up, *Conference at Cold Comfort Farm*, which no one reads.

Cold Comfort Farm was banned in Ireland on account of Flora's suggestion that Seth might limit the increasing number of illegitimate offspring populating the area with some easily acquired rubber appliances.

The Color Purple, Alice Walker, 1982

Boosted by Pulitzer and National Book Award prizes, and a quick-off-the-mark Steven Spielberg film, Walker's novel has sold vastly. One of its notable side-effects has been to help make Oprah Winfrey, who plays the sassy 'not gonna take it' Sofia in the film, the richest African American in history. Winfrey, ever since she ran out her house in her pajamas to buy an early copy of *The Color Purple*, has remained loyal to the author, some of whose later political interventions – such as her criticisms of Israel – have been controversial.

One can start with a mind game. Suppose Harriet Beecher Stowe's saintly Uncle Tom, in the privacy of his cabin, was portrayed as whipping his wife, the lovable 'Aunt Chloe', as savagely as Simon Legree whips Uncle Tom. Suppose, regarding his daughters as his chattels Uncle Tom, as do slave owners with female slaves who catch their eye, sexually and incestuously abused them. It's unthinkable in an evangelical protest novel of the 1850s and provocative even in the 1980s. Alice Walker's venture into this dangerous revisionism is one of the factors that has led to *The Color Purple*, for all its success, being banned on occasion from American schoolrooms.

The novel is set in 1930s Georgia – an unregenerate time and place. The first half consists of letters from a semi-literate girl called Celie to God. The second half consists of letters between the grown-up Celie and her more worldly sister Nettie. Celie's first address to her Maker is eloquent, despite her stumbling literacy. Her mother is dying. The letter opens, 'Dear God, I am fourteen years old. I have always been a good girl. Maybe you can give me a sign letting me know what is happening to me'. Her father has 'needs'. His daughter must supply them, 'ugly' as she is:

He never had a kine word to say to me. Just say You gonna do what your mammy wouldn't. First he put his thing up gainst my hip and sort of wiggle it around. Then he grab hold my tittles. Then he push his thing inside my pussy. When that hurt, I cry. He start to choke me, saying You better shut up and git used to it.

Celie has two children, incestuously engendered on her, before she is fifteen. She supposes her father has killed them. In fact he sells them. Nor is he, she will much later learn, her father but her stepfather.

The great endeavour of Celie's life is to save her pretty younger sister Nettie from suffering what is happening to her. To this end she marries a man, 'Mr –' (he has no surname, because he is, in a sense, every man) who has asked her father to sell him Nettie. He beats and rapes her. When asked why he blandly replies, 'Cause she my wife'. Nettie, who runs away, aided by Celie, is given a small chance for a better life.

As an abused woman Celie is inspired by two women. One is Sofia, who stands up to her husband. The other is her husband's mistress, the blues-singer Shug Avery, with whom she eventually forms her only sexually gratifying relationship. Nettie, now as free as any black woman can be, goes off to Africa with a missionary couple. British

colonialism is, for the colonised, as cruel as life in Georgia, she discovers. But Nettie finds that Celie's children, by her first abuser, are still alive.

Among the controversial things in this consistently controversial novel is the late turn of the story centred on Celie's lost son, Adam. In Africa he assimilates, marrying an African woman of the Olinka tribe. Adam's wife, Tashi, voluntarily undergoes the horrors of facial scarring and – at a late age (it usually happens to girls at eleven) – female circumcision, now renamed Female Genital Mutilation. It is done as a protest against imperialism: 'it is a way the Olinka can show they still have their own ways, even though the white man has taken everything else'.

The novel ends, vaguely, in the early 1940s with the expectation that things will get better, as they undeniably have. But the depiction of black-on-black sexual abuse and violence, and the 'cultural' vindication of FGM, remain contentious. Whatever else, Walker stirs things up. The film, despite outstanding performances (not least by Winfrey) received no Oscars. The judges have never much liked films which stir things up too much.

Compulsion, Meyer Levin, 1957

In 2000 a batch of letters was released, taking us, as the newspapers excitedly put it, 'Inside the mind of Britain's most reviled murderer'. Myra Hindley, of course, the partner of Ian Brady in the 1960s 'Moors murders'. The letters had been sent over the years to a journalist, Duncan Staff, and were transparently designed by Hindley as a fresh line of defence to coincide with her latest appeal. In earlier, fruitless pleas for mercy, Hindley presented herself as the hypnotised victim of Brady-Svengali: a rabbit to his stoat. Her letters to Staff offered a version of the more modish Menendez brothers' defence. In their first trial, the American siblings got off by claiming that childhood molestation and sexual abuse by their father and mother left them so powerless that there was no choice but to shoot both parents, pocket the insurance money and buy themselves watches and Ferraris to ease the pain of filial bereavement. In her letters Hindley recorded that Brady had repeatedly violated her. There was no mention of this sexual abuse in the 1960s trial testimony or in any previous appeal.

Another new piece of evidence was that Brady 'introduced her to the idea of killing' by giving her a book called *Compulsion*. In it a twelve-year-old child is abducted and murdered. 'I told him it was a very disturbing book,' Hindley recalled, 'but why exactly had he wanted me to read it?' At the time of the trial, in the late 1960s, much was made of the Moors murderers' reading matter. But interest focused on Brady's possession of a paperback of De Sade's JUSTINE (newly available since the *Lady Chatterley* obscenity trial) and a bootlegged copy of *Mein Kampf*. The mysteriously poisonous *Compulsion* was not alluded to. What kind of book, readers of newspapers in 2000 must have wondered, would incite a good Catholic girl like Myra to murder little children?

Compulsion was, in fact, the third-best-selling novel of 1957 in the US, read by millions. Written by Meyer Levin, it was a 'lightly fictionalised' account of the 1924 Leopold and Loeb murder case (Levin, then a young journalist in Chicago, covered the trial; he had been at the University of Chicago with the defendants). Nathan Leopold and Richard Loeb, two young men from wealthy and cultivated Jewish families, resolved to commit a kidnap for ransom and a 'perfect murder'. They bungled the deed (as perfect murderers invariably do) and were easily caught. Clarence Darrow, the greatest defence lawyer of his time, saved them from the death penalty with his dazzling oratory.

The case inspired Patrick Hamilton's play, *Rope*, and *Compulsion* itself was made into a memorable 1959 film. Levin novelised the crime to forestall libel action from the murderers' (still powerful) families. Nathan Leopold did in fact bring a suit against Levin (farcically) for invasion of privacy. Basically his objection was that Levin's book (which suggested sexual motives) hurt his feelings. A fellow prisoner cut Loeb's throat in 1936, which probably hurt more. Early in 1958, after thirty-three years in prison, Leopold was released on parole. In April of that year,

he set up the Leopold foundation 'to aid emotionally disturbed, retarded, or delinquent youths'. He lived on to become a respected ornithologist.

Levin was a writer of impeccable liberal credentials, the principal populariser in the US of *Anne Frank's Diary*. It beggars the imagination that the Jew-hating Brady would have admired Levin's book or that anyone could read it as an incitement to serial torture and murder. He would have seen *Compulsion* as a bleeding-heart, anti-capital-punishment tract.

Confessions of a Shopaholic, Sophie Kinsella, 2000

The 2009 paperback tie-in had a rosette splashed on its cover – 'Now a Major Motion Picture' – alongside a cut-out, in full high-fashion fig, of the lead actress, Isla Fisher. The picture bombed. It was sad because the film Hollywoodised a source text (first called *The Secret Dreamworld of a Shopaholic*) which came out in 2000 and was, for its time, witty, chick-litty, and hugely readable. But the times, as the songster says, were changing. In the UK in 2007 Northern Rock, and Lehman Brothers a year later in the US, collapsed – taking down much of Western civilisation (as chick lit would see it) with them. Kinsella's 2000 novel is a comedy about maxing out credit cards. There was nothing comic about debt in 2009.

The novel opens, in *Bridget Jones' Diary* fashion:

> OK. Don't panic. Don't panic. It's only a VISA bill. It's a piece of paper; a few numbers, I mean, just how scary can a few numbers be?

Rebecca (Becky/Bex) Bloomwood is employed in the open-plan office of (irony of ironies) the magazine *Successful Savings*. A heroically unsuccessful saver, she cannot resist the allure of new clothes, shoes, and knick-knacks. She shops till she drops – but has yet to drop. Her annual salary of £21k, even in 2000, doesn't stretch to A. P. C., Margaret Howell, or Liberty. She makes it stretch by stretching the plastic. But now she's maxed out. Her stack of credit cards has suddenly turned into a pack of hungry wolves, slavering for the money (£6k in total) she owes – at 21 per cent APR. Becky was brought up in a middle-class 'semi' and educated at a red-brick university. She lives in a flat with rich, hooray-Henrietta layabout (but lovable with it) Suze, whom she comes close to poisoning when – in a vain attempt to economise on takeaways and restaurants – she tries her hand at home-prepared curry. It's hopeless. Becky's attempts to parlay her desk-journalist job into something more important in the City come to nothing. Fund managers, a friend who has made the leap tells her, earn £40k a year. Becky converts this sum in her mind to wardrobes full of haute couture she could buy.

Kinsella's novel has no plot, as such. It is situational, episodic, and formulaic – something which enabled the first novel to extend into a bestselling series. Until 2008, that is. There is an on-off entanglement with a 'Mr Big' – Luke Brandon – who seems to be truanting from *Sex and the City*. Handsome Brandon, research discovers, is 'the thirty-first richest bachelor in the country'. With him in her sights Becky deftly fends off a creep called Tarquin (named after Shakespeare's ravisher), despite him being the fifteenth most wealthy bachelor in the country. It's not that Becky is frightened of sex – she lost her last boyfriend, she confides, because he wouldn't uncross his legs, 'saving it for marriage'. The narrative concludes when Becky's shopaholic smarts get her a slot on daytime TV. 'I was made to go on TV', she complacently announces. And, of course, 'spend, spend, spend'.

A Connecticut Yankee in King Arthur's Court, Mark Twain, 1889

'I am not an American. I am *the* American.' So Mark Twain is supposed to have boasted. But what, this most American of American writers wondered, did it mean to be American? The core question, as Twain saw it, was the new country's relationship with the old country. Twain loved England. He enjoyed

visits there and wrote them up as witty travel books. He appreciated that fundamental chunks of his country (its language, its democratic system, its founding ideology) derived from Britain. And yet America had formed itself by bloody war *against* Britain. It was this contradiction that Twain set his imagination to probe in *A Connecticut Yankee in King Arthur's Court*. The novel opens with Twain meeting a stranger who has an amazing story to tell. Henry (Hank) Morgan has returned from King Arthur's Camelot. Hank (the Yank) was, before he took off into the past, an engineer with a firearms manufacturer that we can identify as Colt – the gun that won the West. It was the armaments manufacturers of America (Gatling, Winchester and Colt) who had made possible the unprecedented slaughter during the American Civil War. But, you could argue, they had also made possible the unity of the United States. Is violence, then, the active ingredient in America's greatness?

In Hank's tale, he is bashed on the head with a crowbar and finds himself time-transported from Hartford, Connecticut, in 1879 to a field just outside Camelot, England, in AD 528. Our hero's first reaction, on being told by a passer-by where he has landed, is despair. This gives way to terror when a passing knight picks on him for a bit of lance-practice. Hank takes a tour of England, only to be disgusted by what he sees. Merlin turns out to be fake – no more skilful than a third-rate circus magician. England is riddled with a corrupt class system. It doesn't make sense to a freeborn Connecticut Yankee. Worse than that, it horrifies him: 'The most of King Arthur's British nation were slaves, pure and simple'. What the sixth century needs, Hank perceives, is some good old (that's to say 'new') American know-how. Technology, industry, factories, steam power, telephones, bicycles, guns. Hank's crash programme to drag the sixth century kicking and screaming into the nineteenth pays off. Not least for him. In no time at all he is the most important man in the country, more important indeed than the king. He assumes a title – Sir Boss. The plot thereafter becomes complicated. Hank marries and has a baby. He sets up (secretly) a military training institution, based on

West Point. His men are trained in modern warfare, with modern weaponry. They are few in number but formidable. Civil war breaks out and the Round Table breaks up (very differently from Sir Thomas Malory's version). Arthur is slain, the Church mounts a coup, and Hank mounts a counter-coup, appointing himself protector. The Church throws a huge army of medieval knights and soldiers against Hank's tiny force. They confront a series of electric fences and machine guns, which mow them down. The novel ends with mass slaughter:

> The thirteen gatlings began to vomit death into the fated ten thousand. Within ten short minutes after we had opened fire, armed resistance was totally annihilated, the campaign was ended, we fifty-four were masters of England. Twenty-five thousand men lay dead around us.

But at the moment of his triumph, Hank is wounded. Merlin, in disguise, poisons him. He returns to the present, a wiser man.

The book, one should note, was not written for America, Twain protested, it was written for England. It has never been popular in England, however, probably because the English have great difficulty spelling Conecticut, Connecticut, Connecticutt.

The Constant Gardener, John le Carré, 2001

When John le Carré finally brought George Smiley in from the cold in 1990, he announced that he intended to turn from espionage to 'modern problems'. *The Constant Gardener*, his eighteenth work of fiction, certainly represented a new departure as le Carré approached seventy. Set in what he describes as the 'dangerous, decaying, plundered, bankrupt, once-British Kenya', it is his first 'novel with a purpose' (as Victorians called the genre). Like his idol, Graham Greene, le Carré never forgets that the novel is, ultimately, an 'entertainment'. *The Constant Gardener* throws an opening punch worthy of Frederick Forsyth: 'The

news hit the British High Commission in Nairobi, at nine-thirty on a Monday morning.'

A young British woman has been raped and murdered in one of Kenya's national parks. A 'Force Twelve scandal' is inevitable. The young wife of a middle-aged career diplomat, Tessa Quayle was a saintly aid worker. Shortly before her death, she delivered a dossier exposing the multinational companies who have pillaged Africa. Whitehall has buried her report in the interests of 'British trade'. Tessa may have been the victim of bandits; she may have been killed by her black companion (another aid worker, and probably her lover); or – the suspicion gradually grows – she may have been the target of a 'corporate job'. The atrocity was committed at Lake Turkana, where a few years before the paleontologist Richard Leakey had dug up the oldest hominid bones ever found. The crime scene is the 'the birthplace of civilisation', the omphalos, or navel, of the human race. Symbolism is tactfully stressed.

The subsequent narrative moves smoothly on to the worms beneath the stone. The Quayles' marriage was unusual, even for the strange human specimens in the Foreign Office 'circus'. She was in her twenties, Justin Quayle is 'fortysomething. Menopausal, heading for injury time'. His single passion is gardening – creating a small, tidy plot in the wasteland of post-colonial Africa. After Tessa's death, Quayle's overwhelming feeling is that he has 'failed' her. He sets out not to avenge her (le Carré leaves that kind of 'entertainment' to Forsyth) but to understand who, or what, has killed her. 'Kenya', it emerges, did the deed.

Le Carré was in the intelligence service before he became a bestselling novelist with *The Spy Who Came in from the Cold*. As he sees it the principal purpose of British diplomacy and intelligence is what it has always been: espionage and the promotion of 'business interests'. Here the villains are Swiss (mainly) multinational pharmaceutical companies. 'Drugs are the scandal of Africa,' the novel asserts. The 'pharmas' have created an even darker place than Conrad pictured. Kenya, of course, can never be a worthwhile market for the big pharmaceutical companies. The 'scandal' is that Africa has been made to serve as the West's pharmaceutical laboratory. Concurrent with the publication of le Carré's novel, newspapers reported that ten Ugandan villages were allowed to fester (without medicine or treatment) to 'observe' whether syphilis predisposes sufferers to HIV. It would not be a le Carré novel if it did not go further into paranoid fantasy. Africa, he suggests, is not just where the pharmas carry out their obscene 'field trials'. It is (as with the AIDS and Ebola viruses) where they are concocting new diseases to make themselves even richer. It is out of Africa that the next rider of the Apocalypse, plague-2000, will gallop. We deserve it. Why? Because we didn't care. And still don't.

Cosmopolis, Don DeLillo, 2003

What book (other than Shakespeare and the Bible) would one prescribe for the bankers swelling the jails of the UK and US (in most cases those establishments, known sardonically as 'Club Penitentiary', for whiter-than-white-collar crooks)? Robert Harris, *The Fear Index*? Justin Cartwright, *Other People's Money*? Frank Norris, *The Octopus*? John Lanchester, *Capital*? Theodore Dreiser, *The Financier*? My vote would go to *Cosmopolis*. DeLillo's hero, Eric Packer, is a twenty-eight-year-old billionaire asset fund manager. 'We're all young and smart and raised by wolves' is his motto. He possesses an asymmetric prostate – something which seems obscurely central to the narrative, which covers one day in April 2000 (always an ominous month in literature, viz *The Waste Land*, *Nineteen Eighty-Four*, etc.). Eric inhabits a world where cyber-money has leached out all meaning from currency other than digits – electronic cash moving at currents faster than human thought can keep up with. Reality has become 'zero-oneness', in which transaction is measured in 'zeptoseconds' and 'yoctoseconds' (one septillionth of a second). The Wall Street office is not now merely paperless, it is the ante-room to the stillness of eternity. History has ended and so has economics. They have reached their destination. Capitalism, when it took form in the late Middle Ages, based itself on a

tick-tock or calendar relationship between time and money. For example: how much do you earn an hour, a week, a year, a lifetime? But digitalisation has accelerated time so that – if you're clever enough and have the right algorithm – you can earn a million dollars in a zeptosecond. Eric is clever enough. The whole system now depends on his intuitive, faster-than-thought skill. As the novel portentously declares (in one of its italicised apophthegms): '*When he died he would not end. The world would end.*'

Eric lives in a forty-eight-room triplex with a lap pool. He is borne aloft to it in a pair of 'mood' elevators, one that plays Sati and the other a Sufi rap artist, Brutha Fez. Among all this luxury he has a monastic cell in which he recites poetry to himself. The April day the book describes is passed in a journey – epic in its endeavour – across Manhattan in his 'proustified' (cork-lined), armour-plated, all-mod-cons (including a toilet) limo. Eric has just made a huge bet on the yen going down. It goes up – is his touch going, or is it self-destruction? En route his limousine crosses the path of a presidential motorcade. 'Do people still shoot at presidents?' he asks himself. 'I thought there were more stimulating targets.' He himself is being stalked by two men out to get him. One is a pastry assassin (who wants to give him the custard pie treatment); the other, Benno Levin, is overtly homicidal. He is a former employee who Eric 'let go' (i.e. fired). Eric stops by his wife of three weeks, Elise, a European heiress and minimalist poet, and then calls in on a prostitute. He also has 'bottle sex' with one of his employees, interrupting her Central Park jog to do so. He shoots his chief of security for no reason whatsoever. He drives, like a Blitzkrieg panzer, through an 'Occupation'-style demo. The yen turns against him big time. He transfers his wife's $750 million nest-egg into losing investments. He has been meaning all day to have a haircut. He ends his circadian journey in the slum area where he grew up, and asks the barber who first cut his hair to give him a final trim before he meets his end at the hands of Levin. He should, the novel enigmatically concludes, have listened to his asymmetric prostate.

Crampton Hodnet, Barbara Pym, 1985

'I'd sooner read a new Barbara Pym than a new Jane Austen', said Philip Larkin – who, more than anyone else, rescued his favourite novelist from oblivion. Larkin never read *Crampton Hodnet*. He died the year it was published. Pym had herself died in 1980, and it was published without her permission. The novel has an unusual title which makes a little more sense in the light of her whole name, Barbara Crampton Pym. The manuscript was finished in April 1940, just as Pym joined up to do her bit for the country's war effort. Her 'North Oxford novel', as she vaguely called it, was not published until almost half a century later. Although she privately thought it her funniest work, it had, she felt, rather dated over the decades and she kept it back from publication. The narrative opens, with prim exactitude, 'It was a wet Sunday afternoon in North Oxford at the beginning of October.' The academic term called (mysteriously, for outsiders) Michaelmas has begun. It will end in what is, equally mysteriously, called the Hilary term. There are no precise dating references except that it is after the Abdication (1936) and before the War (1939).

Miss Maude Doggett has Sunday tea parties for carefully selected students. All of them are a credit to their ancient institution. It is probably harder to get into the tea party than Balliol. Not for Miss Doggett 'young men from the poorer colleges, who came from Huddersfield and had state scholarships and wouldn't wear suede shoes even if they could afford them'. She has a paid 'companion' – Miss Morrow, 'a woman of definite personality'. Miss Doggett hovers over the subsequent action like a severe spinster goddess in some Greek tragedy. Another centre of interest is her nephew, Francis Cleveland. A don of a certain age, he has been giving the same lectures for twenty years while studiously not finishing his great work on the libertine poet John Cleveland, his ancestor. During a one-on-one tutorial (a practice Miss Doggett disapproves of – whatever the pedagogic merit) with Barbara Bird – the only student of her year likely to get a first – Francis notices how beautiful she is. '"Well, now you know," said

a chirpy voice inside him. "What are you going to do about it?"' What he does is very silly. But:

> it made him feel fine and important, a swelling ranting Don Juan with a dark double life, instead of a middle-aged Fellow of Randolph, ignored or treated with contempt by his wife and daughter.

The contemptuous daughter, Anthea, has set her cap at Simon, an undergraduate who aspires one day to be prime minister and is merely trifling with her affections. Francis' wife finds her husband 'rather a bore nowadays'. So, after a term listening to his lectures, do his students. Sharing the narrative foreground is a curate, the Reverend Stephen Latimer – thirty-five years old, handsome, and 'distrustful of all women under the age of fifty'. He is currently a 'PG' (paying guest) at Miss Doggett's and becomes entangled with Miss Morrow (a woman narrowly below the fifty threshold). He proposes and – to his amazement – is rejected. Even though she is, as one of her friends kindly informs her, a 'plain woman and no longer young' and he 'an attractive man with a natural charm of manner' (although there are some worrying touches of 'rheumatiz' coming on). It is the Reverend Latimer who invents the fictional parish of Crampton Hodnet to cover his tracks. Such devices are necessary. Oxford is Jeremy Bentham's panopticon – the Cotswold stone walls have prying eyes, eavesdropping ears, and gossiping tongues. Serious scandal is averted when the grand Cleveland passion fizzles out because Barbara doesn't like 'kissing and that sort of thing'. Put another way, Oxford doesn't like it. But, a few months away, and wholly unanticipated, is the war which will change the city, the university, and Pym's serene England for ever.

Crime and Punishment, Fyodor Dostoevsky, 1866

Few novelists have known crime and punishment as intimately as the author of *Crime and Punishment*. In 1849, Dostoevsky was arrested. As Constance Garnett records, in a foreword to her translation of the novel:

> Dostoevsky was one of a little group of young men who met together to read Fourier and Proudhon . . . Under Nicholas I this was enough, and he was condemned to death. After eight months' imprisonment he was with twenty-one others taken out to the Semyonovsky Square to be shot. Writing to his brother Mihail, Dostoevsky says: 'They snapped words over our heads, and they made us put on the white shirts worn by persons condemned to death. Thereupon we were bound in threes to stakes, to suffer execution. Being the third in the row, I concluded I had only a few minutes of life before me. I thought of you and your dear ones and I contrived to kiss Plestcheiev and Dourov, who were next to me, and to bid them farewell. Suddenly the troops beat a tattoo, we were unbound, brought back upon the scaffold, and informed that his Majesty had spared us our lives.'

The sentence was commuted to ten years' hard labour.

The novel opens with a briskness worthy of Elmore Leonard:

> On an exceptionally hot evening early in July a young man came out of the garret in which he lodged in S. Place and walked slowly, as though in hesitation, towards K. bridge.

The young man – 'exceptionally handsome' and clearly 'refined' – is a student, recently dropped out of the university, and dressed in rags. His landlady is close to calling the police to evict him. He muses, enigmatically: 'I want to attempt a thing like that'. Like what? He has, it will emerge, a 'plan' – in fact, it might more accurately be described as a moral experiment. It will all become clearer later.

On this July evening he is on his way to a money lender – an old woman who extorts what she can from those poorer even than herself. If anyone symbolises Proudhon's maxim, 'property is theft', it is she. Raskolnikov pretends to have a watch to pawn. In fact he is snooping, to see where her strong box is. She cheats him, as she cheats all her clients. It confirms to Raskolnikov the intrinsic worthlessness of most of the human race. He seems, however, to have little remorse for his family who have ruined themselves to furnish him an education.

The early section is dominated by a recurring nightmare Raskolnikov has of a horse which, as a child, he saw battered to death in the street with crowbars and axes. He tried to protect the beast, but could not. He returns to the moneylender, with an axe covered in a sack. As she turns away from him, to find a receipt:

> He pulled the axe quite out, swung it with both arms, scarcely conscious of himself . . . The old woman was as always bareheaded. Her thin, light hair, streaked with grey, thickly smeared with grease, was plaited in a rat's tail and fastened by a broken horn comb which stood out on the nape of her neck. As she was so short, the blow fell on the very top of her skull. She cried out, but very faintly, and suddenly sank all of a heap on the floor, raising her hands to her head. In one hand she still held 'the pledge'.

Why did he do it? Robbery, self-evidently. But, much later in the novel, another explanation emerges. The detective who solves the murder, Porfiry, turns up an essay Raskolnikov once wrote 'On Crime'. In it he divided mankind into two classes. One, the majority, was destined to be servile. There are, however, 'extraordinary' individuals – such as Napoleon – who are not bound by the laws, moral scruples which shackle ordinary people.

The murder of the money-lender, an *acte gratuit* will demonstrate that Raskolnikov, too, is 'extraordinary'. He is not, he discovers. He eventually confesses. As he tells Sonia, the humble women who stands by him during his eight long years in Siberia, 'I wanted to become a Napoleon, that is why I killed her . . . Do you understand now?' No, she does not. But she loves him.

Ironically Raskolnikov is spared the death penalty he deserves not because he is extraordinary but because he is, as a criminal, mentally defective. Less than ordinarily capable of making moral decisions.

The Crimson Petal and the White, Michel Faber, 2002

In the critical afterword to *The Quincunx*, his 1989 attempt at a Neo-Victorian novel, Charles Palliser advises that the main ingredient of the recipe is 'inversion'. Take *Jane Eyre*, turn it upside down, shake well, and you get what? WIDE SARGASSO SEA. What is prescribed for the 'Neo-Victorian novel' – a thriving genre after the 1960s – is Victorian fiction which is somehow 'beyond' the original Victorian fiction's reach. Dickens or Brontë couldn't do this, it asserts: they wouldn't *dare*.

Faber spent twenty years writing and researching his (appropriately massive) novel. Some think it time well spent. Faber's 'genteel' heroine, Sugar, has a second career (the first is prostitution), writing pornography for the woman reader, and her pseudonymous tales of male lechery and female revenge carry an epigraph worthy of Trollope's Baroness Banmann's objurgations against 'Ze Tyrant Sex' – 'Vile man, eternal Adam, I indict you!' Early on in *The Crimson Petal and the White*, Faber describes a whore looking out of her grimy garret window,

> Outside it is almost completely dark, as the nearest street-lamp is half a dozen houses away. The cobbled paving of Church Lane is no longer white with snow, the sleet has left great gobs and trails of slush, like monstrous spills of semen, glowing in the gas-light. All else is black.

This broad brushwork, drawing on the favourite colours on Faber's palette (dark phlegm and pale semen) doesn't quite come off. Nor do his finer touches of detail, carefully researched though they may be. Later in the novel, another whore (Sugar) – higher in the ranks of her trade – looks out of a nicer window: 'A warm reflux of semen trickles down her thighs and into her pantalettes as she stands sniffing; she winces, clutches herself, pushes the windows shut with her free hand. What to do next?' The nearest the author will have come to that interesting item of underwear is the display case in the V&A. And wouldn't a working girl like Sugar wear the 'free trade' crotchless variety? *The Crimson Petal and the White* boils down to the tale of an 1860s whore with a lot of what TV people call 'set dressing'. Late in the narrative the male protagonist wants to send a message home. 'If only,' he thinks,

> he could make contact with his household here and now, to confirm Agnes' safety. Only last week, he read an article in *Hogg's Review*, about a device very soon to be produced in America, a contrivance of magnets and diaphragms, which converts the human voice into electrical vibrations, thus making possible the transmission of speech across vast distances. If only this mechanism were in general use already! Imagine: he could speak a few words into a wire, receive the answer, 'Yes, she's here and sleeping,' and be spared this misery of uncertainty.

Clunk, clunk, bloody clunk, the jaundiced reader may think. But, somehow, the ponderousness of Faber's whore's tale piledrives its way into the reader's mind and one finds what one has is a page-turner, but an awful lot of pages (836 in the first hardback edition).

Cry, the Beloved Country, Alan Paton, 1948

The novel is subtitled 'A Story of Comfort in Desolation'. Paton's novel can be credited with putting global force behind the long process to South African democracy – something which the author, alas, who died in 1988, did not live to see. It's a technically primitive and avowedly sentimental novel, regarded with the cold eye of literary criticism. But it raises a familiar problem: if a work of literature manifestly does good, is it a good work of literature? One could call it 'the *Uncle Tom's Cabin* conundrum'.

Despite the lyrical rhapsody to the beloved country with which the narrative begins ('There is a lovely road that runs from Ixopo into the hills. These hills are grass-covered and rolling, and they are lovely beyond any singing of it. . .') the story was substantially written in exile in the US, where it was first published under the aegis of Maxwell Perkins (Hemingway's and F. Scott Fitzgerald's editor). The book's publication in 1948 coincided with the election of the National Party to power in South Africa and the installation of apartheid.

Paton, a teacher and liberal politician, wrote *Cry, the Beloved Country* with the intention of mobilising worldwide protest. The problem, as with Harriet Beecher Stowe, was that it is awkward to speak 'for' the oppressed. It encourages a kind of condescension – as if 'they' cannot speak for themselves. The problem is clear enough in the little scene that kicks off the novel's main action:

The small child ran importantly to the wood-and-iron church with the letter in her hand. Next to the church was a house and she knocked timidly on the door. The Reverend Stephen Kumalo looked up from the table where he was writing, and he called, Come in.

The small child opened the door, carefully like one who is afraid to open carelessly the door of so important a house, and stepped timidly in.

—I bring a letter, umfundisi.

—A letter, eh? Where did you get it, my child?

—From the store, umfundisi. The white man asked me to bring it to you.

—That was good of you. Go well, small one.

There is a kind of baby talk infecting the idiom here (e.g. 'Go well, small one'), but one cannot see how it could have been better done.

The letter which Kumalo has been sent is from a fellow minister, asking him to travel from back-country Natal to Johannesburg. His sister, Gertrude, needs him. And Kumalo's own son, Absalom, has gone missing in the city. After arriving in Johannesburg, the innocent pastor witnesses the cruel degradations and indignities imposed on the black majority. 'The white man has broken the tribe', he realises, bitterly. The Zulu were once a proud people.

Things go from bad to worse. Gertrude is found to be a whore, a vendor of illegal liquor and the mother of an illegitimate child. Kumalo persuades her to come home to Natal. Absalom remains elusive. Kumalo is helped by his brother John, who knows city ways. But Absalom, it emerges, has gone entirely to the bad. He is imprisoned for the murder of a white man who, ironically, was a campaigner for black rights. John's son is also involved in the crime. Both young men are tried and Absalom is sentenced to death. The white victim's father and the black murderer's father are reconciled and, over the following years, work together in Kumalo's village for a better world. The novel ends with dawn – but when the dawn of freedom will break remains 'secret'.

Like many of my generation I was made aware of the huge crime taking place in South Africa by the 1958, two-and-sixpence Penguin edition of *Cry, the Beloved Country*. It is, as I say, a not very good novel, which did an awful lot of good.

The Curious Incident of the Dog in the Night-Time, Mark Haddon, 2003

Freud claimed to have 'discovered' nothing. Creative writers had got there first. He merely gave their discoveries scientific names. 'Oedipus complex'? Read *Hamlet*. Hans Asperger gave his name to a mental condition he identified in the early 1940s. Up to this point, what is now recognised as a clear-cut syndrome had been regarded as a variety of schizophrenia. Much of Asperger's research was lost in the London Blitz (ironically, Asperger was a refugee from Nazi Germany). It was not until forty years later that his syndrome was accepted as a valid diagnosis of a highly specific kind of 'autism spectrum disorder' by the medical profession. Since then it has inspired a thriving genre of fiction. There are supportive 'aspie' websites which catalogue works and discuss new arrivals – recently, for example, Jodie Picoult's *House Rules* (2010). 'Aspergers'/'aspie' does not, interestingly, carry the same derogatory charge among the general population as, say, 'spastic' ('spazz'), 'moron' or even 'simpleton'. As one definition puts it:

> Compared with those affected by other forms of Autism Spectrum Disorder those with Asperger syndrome do not have significant delays or difficulties in language or cognitive development. Some even demonstrate precocious vocabulary – often in a highly specialised field of interest.

Asperger called his subjects 'little professors'. Like that woolly-headed profession, they could be brilliant but 'absent-minded'. Haddon's novel takes the form of the journal of fifteen-year-old Christopher John Francis Boone. A precociously brilliant mathematician, he is confident he will one day teach at a university. He will be an unusual teacher. Socially Christopher is drastically dysfunctional. He has what are called 'splinter skills' – numerical calculation, notably, causes him no problem whatsoever. 'Prime numbers', he says, 'are what is left when you have taken all the patterns away. I think prime numbers are like life. They are very logical but you could never work out the rules, even if you spent all your time thinking about them.' But he has huge difficulty telling the difference between truth and lies (for that reason he hates novels). He and his gas-fitter father live in Swindon. His

mother, Christopher has been told, died of a heart attack in hospital: even though, he says, she always ate muesli for breakfast. The novel opens with a vivid scene, described with aspergic exactitude:

> It was 7 minutes after midnight. The dog was lying on the grass in the middle of the lawn in front of Mrs Shears' house. Its eyes were closed. It looked as if it was running on its side, the way dogs run when they think they are chasing a cat in a dream. But the dog was dead. There was a garden fork sticking out of the dog.

Christopher loves dogs (they only have four emotions, unlike humans) and loves Sherlock Holmes (an aspie *avant la lettre*, some would argue). He sets out to solve the mystery. He solves an even more tangled 'incident' than the pitch-forked poodle. His mother, he discovers, did not die in hospital as his father told him. She ran off with the man next door (Mrs Shears' husband). His father did the vengeful business with the garden fork. A cache of letters reveals his mother is living in London. He takes off to find her, which, after many misdirections and errors, he does. He will live with her henceforth and visit his father – with whom he is partially reconciled (although the paternal 'lies' will always perplex him) – and, after A-levels, he expects, go to university and on to an academic career. The little professor will become a big professor. Christopher's narrative has no nuance, requiring the reader to read *through* it. Not much happens but it bears out the comedian's rule – it's not the joke, it's how you tell it.

The Dain Curse, Dashiell Hammett, 1929

Many dedicated readers of detective fiction, as I've observed (me among them), vary 'English Cosy' with 'American Hardboiled'. It's a kind of literary good cop/bad cop. *The Dain Curse* (wonderful title) should be in every literary medicine cabinet for a discreet swig after injudiciously swallowing too much Marple, Wimsey or Father Brown. An early work, *The Dain Curse* is one of the two major novels in which Hammett's 'Continental Operator', aka 'the Op', appears – a lawman to stand alongside Philip Marlowe, Perry Mason, or – dare one say it – Jack Reacher. 'Continental Operator' means that, like the newly created FBI, the 'Op' is a private agent licensed to operate across state lines – 'federally'; which he does.

Like its predecessor, *Red Harvest*, *The Dain Curse* began as a three-part serial in *Black Mask* magazine, the crucible in which 'hardboiled' crime fiction (Hammett, Cain, Chandler) was boiled very hard indeed. The narrative opens with the Op being hired to investigate a diamond burglary in the San Francisco home of a scientist, Edgar Leggett. A jewel merchant's, Halstead and Beauchamp, had loaned the gems to Leggett and they suspect the burglary is a scam. The case, however, proves to be something more than any 'two-penny insurance swindle'. Another private detective, Louis Upton, is murdered. The initial suspect in the theft, a housemaid, is a false lead. Attention turns to the daughter of the Leggett household, Gabrielle, a mysterious young woman (apart from anything else, she has no earlobes: no diamond ear-rings for Miss Gabrielle). She is also a *morphiniste* and – when not high – prone to psychotic episodes. A typical Jazz Age flapper. Gabrielle is engaged to a young millionaire, Eric Collinson. As he conducts his investigation, the Op confers with a friendly novelist ('my business is with souls and what goes on in them') called Owen Fitzstephan – manifestly a surrogate Hammett.

The plot thickens well beyond thick when Edgar Leggett commits suicide, leaving a long explanatory note. ('Spoiler Alert' from now on – skip if you wish.) His real name

was Maurice de Mayenne. In early life he married Alice Dain – the bearer of a 'curse'. Their daughter Gabrielle is the inheritrix of that curse. Upton was blackmailing Maurice. It emerges that the murderess (actually a serial killer) is Mrs Leggett. She employed Gabrielle as her accomplice, hence the girl's mental derangement. In the wrap-up section of the narrative (it's not easily wrapped up) Fitzstephan explains the 'psychological basis' of the crime to the stolidly unimpressed Op. In the final episode, Gabrielle's partner Eric is murdered. The Op unmasks the culprit, who turns out to be none other than the novelist Fitzstephan. It emerges he too is spawn of Dain. He escapes the chair on grounds of incurable insanity (the novelist's professional disease):

> He was sent to the state prison at Napa. A year later he was discharged. I don't suppose the asylum officials thought him cured: they thought he was too badly crippled ever to be dangerous again.

The novel ends with Gabrielle 'cured'. 'Stay away from the morphine', the 'Op' advises, by way of farewell. This is not a novel one reads for the plot or 'whodunnit?' suspense (hence I've broken a cardinal rule by giving the end away). One reads *The Dain Curse* for its brutally beautiful style, its nihilistic *Weltanschauung* – and the way forward for detective fiction that those then-revolutionary features made possible.

The Daughter of Time, Josephine Tey, 1951

One of the many services Allen Lane performed for the British people was 'domesticating' genre with lower-division Penguin Books lines – notably science fiction (Ray Bradbury first appeared in Penguin livery) and crime. My first encounter with Raymond Chandler, like my fellow school enthusiasts, was via Penguin's green-liveried crime and detection series – so coloured to indicate 'sub-literary, but still worth reading'. Thanks to the Penguin seal of approval, *The Daughter of Time* has done what all but a handful of its peers haven't. It has lasted. And – once one gets past the absurdly misleading title – it merits the longevity it still enjoys. The title is, as few will recognise, a quote from Francis Bacon, inventor of the 'scientific method': 'Truth is the daughter of time, not of authority.'

Tey's series hero, Inspector Alan Grant (first introduced in The Man in the Queue, 1929, and by this time rather long in the tooth), has been confined to a hospital bed after breaking his leg by falling through a trapdoor while in pursuit of a robber. The inspector is peevish in his unaccustomed inactivity. He wants to be 'doing', even if it's only 'armchair detection' he can manage. Grant is famed for his ability to 'read' criminal faces. To occupy his mind, a friend brings a set of postcard pictures of famous historical figures for him to apply his powers to. One of them is of Richard III – the famous picture, by an unknown artist, that resides in the National Portrait Gallery. It portrays a thoughtful, preoccupied man of attractive appearance. It is not, Grant's infallible instinct tells him, the face of a mass murderer. What he sees instead is 'a candidate for a gastric ulcer' – someone whose only failing is that he worries too much. Surely 'forty million school books can't be wrong?' he reasons. Surely Shakespeare can't be wrong?

He sends off a young American student friend, Brent Carradine, to rifle through the primary sources in the British Museum. Grant, by logical analysis of the documentary evidence, 'clears' Shakespeare's villainous king from the crime of killing the princes in the tower and all the rest of the blood spilled in the play. Richard, in the language of Grant's world, has been 'stitched up'. Finally Grant uncovers the real murderer – well, read it yourself and find out.

It confirms what Grant has always believed. If Henry Ford believed 'history is bunk', Grant believes that history – or, at least, the versions of the past historians put into circulation – is mainly lies, myths, and self-serving 'Tonypandies', as he calls them. The word is from one of his hobbyhorses. Ask the man in the street what happened when the miners went on strike in the Rhondda in 1910 and he'll tell you they were mown down by police, sent there by that bastard Churchill. In fact, Grant believes (not all historians do), the police were armed with nothing more lethal than 'rolled-up mackintoshes' (Tey, of course, was writing only a few years after Churchill 'won' the war for his grateful nation). Historians, Grant concludes, are lousy detectives (you can include Shakespeare's 'history plays' in that). He resolves to 'go back to the Yard, where murderers are murderers' as soon as those damned doctors will let him.

The Day He Himself Shall Wipe Away My Tears, Kenzaburō Ōe, 1972

Virtually all I know about science fact has been picked up from science fiction. Everything I know about the technicalities of murder and a shame-making quantity of my historical knowledge, ditto – from crime novels and historical romance. And Japan? I've never been there and probably never shall go there. Fiction and films (Kurosawa, principally) are my passport – yours too, perhaps. Ōe's novel is, for the literary tourist, as richly informative as any package tour. It is – reaching for one's own familiar literary touchstone – a Japanese MALONE DIES (Beckett's bleak ramblings and rumblings of a M[an]alone dying). As in other in articulo mortis works, the focus is on horizons closing inexorably in, until the mind can barely escape the body. Strange things – it is commonly thought – happen as one dies. If it is quickly, as in drowning, 'the whole of your life flashes before your eyes'. If it is a protracted process, the final act of mind is different. The phenomenon is allegorised in Kafka's 'In the Penal Colony', where convicts are tattooed to death with a machine which pricks and inks their body. As they die, they can 'read' through their pain, seeing what has been inscribed on them – the nature of their crime. They die 'knowing'.

The protagonist of The Day He Himself Shall Wipe Away My Tears is a thirty-five-year-old man. It is 1970, in a Tokyo hospital, and the man is not named. He is dying, or so he thinks, of liver cancer. His physicians do not agree. He is wearing goggles, with green lenses, that once belonged to his father. As the narrative opens it is night and he is

> trimming his nose that would never walk again into sunlight atop living legs, busily feeling each hair with a Rotex rotary nostril clipper as if to make the nostrils as bare as a monkey's.

His relationship with his disease is mystical. He sees his body as a garden flowering, like a 'bed of yellow hyacinths or possibly chrysanthemums bathed in a faint, purple light'. This is not a description to be found in the medical textbooks. Less mystically, the hero-narrator is given to outbursts of the song 'Happy Days Are Here Again'. His Japaneseness is disconcertingly infused with Westernness. There are references to Dostoevsky and Yeats (a particular favourite of Ōe's). The hero's relationship to his cancer is complicated when a man who looks like a monkey ('perhaps a lunatic') breaks into his room to tell him that 'I'm liver cancer'. He is driven away by the hurled nostril-clipper. There is someone else who may, or may not, be actually present in the hospital room, 'the acting executor of the will', who is taking down as dictation everything said. She may be his wife.

Like a puzzle in which most of the pieces are missing, elements of the past are assembled. The man in the bed revisits his childhood and the last thirty years of Japanese history. He had a close relative (his brother?) killed (or perhaps not) in the invasion of Manchuria, which began hostilities and the war that, ultimately, would change Japan for ever. He recalls the epochal moment in 1945 when, under the nuclear assault by America ('brighter than a thousand suns'), the Emperor admitted to his people that he was not a god. Just a little man. Over the years the narrator's father has been deeply implicated in various plots, culminating in a failed assassination attempt on the Emperor himself in August 1945, to prevent surrender and extinguish what was once Japan 'nobly'. His father dies and a gigantic chrysanthemum is glimpsed in the sky. Like much in the story this may be delusive. The narrative is as wispy as night-time mist. And for readers not Japanese, or steeped in Japanese culture, fascinatingly strange. Worth, as the travel guides say, the detour.

The Day of the Triffids, John Wyndham, 1951

Aka 'Giant Mangel Wurzels Run Wild', this is one of the most perennially popular science-fiction novels among those who have never learned to love science fiction itself, and a prime example of what Brian Aldiss calls 'the cosy catastrophe'. It's one of those books in which reading about the near-total extinction of the human race leaves the reader with a warm glow. It still does – although when the novel first came out over half the British population, surveys confirmed, stoically expected nuclear annihilation with only four minutes' warning. ('What would you do with it?' students like myself asked each other, with a knowing leer.) *The Day of the Triffids* coincided with the first detonation of the H-bomb, a planet-destroying weapon. Wyndham's novel, however, starts from a charmingly perverse and quite different catastrophe: the 'Groundnut Scheme'. Britain's post-war government planned to relieve the country's acute food shortages (the population was getting by on three ounces of butter per person per week) by turning Tanganyika, one of its colonial possessions, into a vast groundnut plantation. Prime Minister Attlee did not say 'I have seen the future, and it is a peanut' – but that is what he fondly had in mind. As Wikipedia bleakly records:

> The Labour government cancelled the project in January 1951. The total cost over the years had risen to £49 million and the land had been ruined in the process, leaving it an unusable dust bowl.

The novel is set a few years into the future. Its hero-narrator, William (Bill) Masen, is a plant biologist who has devoted his career to a bizarre vegetable life form called 'triffids'. They may have arrived by meteor from outer space, or have recently mutated into existence (spurred by all the nuclear weapons being detonated in the 1950s), but most probably they are the creations of some Soviet laboratory: Frankenveggies. If that is the case:

> these gardener's nightmares didn't stay behind the Iron Curtain long because they spread to the rest of the world when a smuggler's plane was shot down and triffid seeds were scattered to the four winds.

Triffids are ten feet high, ambulant on their three foot-pods, and armed with a lethal whip-like sting. They have what appears to be rudimentary intelligence, and no love for the human species. They secrete a valuable oil and have been cultivated in huge numbers as a cash crop. A night-time meteor shower – which may or may not be induced by man – blinds everyone on earth who looks up at it. Masen is saved from this fate by accident. His eyes are bandaged after he has been stung in the face by a triffid. When he removes the coverings in a deserted hospital he finds that he is now in H. G. Wells' country of the blind: 'When a day that you happen to know is Wednesday starts off by sounding like Sunday, there is something seriously wrong somewhere.'

The triffids are now free to prey on the helpless human population: it is their day. Masen moves out of London to set up a colony with a young sighted woman, Josella, who was lucky enough to have been sleeping off a bad hangover on the fateful night of the blinding meteor shower. Josella is upper-class and a good sort. Hockey sticks seem to be around somewhere. With a few other kindred spirits (mainly unsighted) they set up a commune in the country, barricaded against the ravening hordes of triffids and totalitarian-minded fascists who want to create a slave state in what is left of England. Their plans come to nothing when a plague sweeps across the world, killing what's left of the human race. Six years pass. The hero and heroine, their friends and children, finally escape to the triffid-free Isle of Wight, where sighted civilisation is in the process of being reborn. Cosily.

The word 'triffid' has – a high honour – made it into the Oxford English Dictionary, with the following, pricelessly stuffy, definition:

one of a race of menacing plants, possessed of locomotor ability and a poisonous sting, which threaten to overrun the world. Hence used allusively of vigorous plants, or *transf.* of anything invasive or rapid in development.

The Days of Anna Madrigal, Armistead Maupin, 2014

One of the most acclaimed fictional sagas of our time – an everyday story of 'transfolk' – reached its end with this volume. The nine-volume *Tales of the City*, one of the monumental constructions of contemporary fiction, began as a newspaper column in May 1976 about how San Francisco would strike an out-of-town-gal from Cleveland who needed a more liberated sexual identity than the American Midwest permitted.

The editor of the *San Francisco Chronicle* commissioned more of the same. At the time Maupin was crashing on film-star Rock Hudson's living room floor. The epitome of beefcake (more 'butch' than 'nelly', in SF argot) Hudson found refuge from being American womanhood's fantasy lover in the city's anonymous bath house and leather bar culture.

Hudson would later die, gallantly outing himself to bring the notice of the world that AIDS must be confronted. The 'plague' (with a cameo of Hudson), the concurrent Jim Jones massacre, and the abomination of paedophilia, feature in the darkest of the instalments, *Further Tales of the City*. Maupin was in his mid-20s when the *Tales* began. He chose to come out to his parents via his alter ego character, Michael ('Mouse') Tolliver. The old folks were understanding and Maupin dedicated the first volume to them.

When, hot foot from Cleveland, Mary Ann Singleton, arrives in the city she finds a home in the boarding house of Anna Madrigal ('as in "medieval"') at 28 Barbary Lane. It's a place where characters move out of sexual identity as easily as putting on today's clean underwear. The Bradie Bunch is a biological family. Anna's is what she calls 'logical'. They fit together like a jigsaw puzzle, no one piece like the other.

Or themselves. Anna Madrigal herself was born Andy Ramsay and brought up in a god-forsaken Nevada whorehouse. He escaped to San Francisco, served in the military, married, had a child, made the 'transition'. Anna Madrigal is an anagram of 'a girl and a man'.

In the last of the series Anna is now in her early nineties and wobbly. The novel opens with her, 'spiffed up' in her trademark Chinese silk pajamas, trying to ignite an electric candle with a fire-lighter. She's saved from in-life cremation by her carer, Jake. He works with Michael in his landscape garden business and is in a relationship with a transitioned partner, Amos, who used to be a butch sergeant in the marines. Michael is now happily married (twice – 'to make it stick') to a much younger guy. His HIV meds take their toll, but he's getting by. Mary Ann's 'inherited' daughter, Shawna, has written a best-selling novel, in txtese. Lesbian, she intends to get pregnant using the 'turkey baster' insemination technique. No guy required.

The story climaxes with two trips out of the city into the desert. A cohort of long-serving characters go to the Burning Man festival, in the Black Rock Desert. It's an actual festival. Hippydom rules for both 'Burners' and 'Burgins' (Burning Man virgins). It's a place where people can 'birth their inner voice'. Everything climaxes with a Wicker Man incineration. No Edward Woodward-style human sacrifice: just a celebration of life, in all its craziness.

Anna Madrigal makes a detour to the god-forsaken town in the desert where she was brought up and finally confronts the very bad thing she did there. She will now die 'unburdened' and the last we shall ever see of her is as the Queen of Burning Man. It's a noble exit, and a fine terminus for the series, one of whose signal achievements has been to help 'normalise' what used to be cruelly regarded as criminally abnormal. Novels can sometimes do a lot of good. Maupin's have done exactly that.

The Dead, James Joyce, 1914

'The Dead' is a long short story in which James Joyce pictures what James Joyce might have been had he not opted for his vaunted 'silence,

exile, and cunning'. The story's attractions are threefold. It is short. It retains the accessible realism of Joyce's early phase – it's 'readable', in a word. And it's the best gateway into the less easily readable masterworks of the novelist's maturity. 'The Dead' (the final piece in the volume *Dubliners*) was written in spring 1907, three years after Joyce, self-exiled, had left Dublin for Trieste. He would never be a Dubliner again – except in his writing.

The action takes place on Christmas Eve, 1904. That had been the pivotal year of Joyce's own life. He met Nora Barnacle, the woman who would be his lifelong love. Restless, jobless and homeless, he spent six days in the Martello tower which features in the opening of ULYSSES. He had begun his first novel, *A Portrait of the Artist as a Young Man*. Lest we miss the fact that 'The Dead' is another portrait of the artist (as a not quite so young man), Joyce offers a mirror image of himself in the early paragraphs:

> He was a stout, tallish young man. The high colour of his cheeks pushed upwards even to his forehead, where it scattered itself in a few formless patches of pale red; and on his hairless face there scintillated restlessly the polished lenses and the bright gilt rims of the glasses which screened his delicate and restless eyes. His glossy black hair was parted in the middle and brushed in a long curve behind his ears where it curled slightly beneath the groove left by his hat.

Rembrandt could not have done it more accurately. If one saw someone of that description wandering wild in Arabia one would shout 'Joyce!'

The central event in the story is the annual party given by Gabriel Conroy's aunts, the Misses Morkan, music teachers of immaculate respectability. As the hostesses' 'favourite nephew', Gabriel carves the bird, serves the pudding and gives the expected platitudinous speech – after which there is song and dance. His wife Gretta (who is not a Dubliner – she comes from Galway) arrives late. She has never been a favourite with his family, who think he should have 'done better for himself'. A pert young Irish nationalist, Molly Ivors, has discovered that Gabriel writes for arch-imperialist English newspaper the *Daily Express*, and upbraids him as a 'West Briton'. A slow crisis is triggered when, late in the evening, after drink has been taken, one of the guests sings a ballad from the west of the country, about a lover who dies after being drenched from standing all night outside his true love's window. When they get back to their hotel, an exhilarated Gabriel hopes to make love. But, to his surprise, Gretta is weeping. There was, she explains, 'a young boy I used to know . . . named Michael Furey. He used to sing that song. . . He was very delicate.' He died. Of what? ' "I think he died for me," she answered.'

A 'vague terror' seizes Gabriel. The story ends with him slipping off into sleep, his mind drowsily taking its own direction:

> The time had come for him to set out on his journey westward. Yes, the newspapers were right: snow was general all over Ireland. . . It was falling, too, upon every part of the lonely churchyard on the hill where Michael Furey lay buried. . . His soul swooned slowly as he heard the snow falling faintly through the universe and faintly falling, like the descent of their last end, upon all the living and the dead.

Will he make that trip to the west? No. Who is truly dead? Not Michael Furey but Gabriel Conroy – the James Joyce who might have been had he not, fortunately for literary posterity, refused to sell out and stay put.

Dead Cert, Dick Francis, 1962

Why read it? One reason is that you'll be in better-than-usual reading company. Francis was a favourite bedtime companion for (one is reliably informed) Queen Elizabeth, the Queen Mother – and, as he told us aggressively, Kingsley Amis. Philip Larkin went on record to declare that Dick Francis was 'always twenty times more readable than the average Booker entry' (and, he implied, as good as anyone who won that prize). Presumably they have an exclusive reading group up there in the sky, when the hymns pall, where they discuss whether *Whip Hand* or *Longshot* is the better read.

Francis was late in leaving the starting gate as a novelist. He first achieved national fame as a jump jockey. He was reckoned to be in the top ten of his gruelling sport, and between 1953 and 1957 he was jockey to the Queen Mother. But in 1956 Francis' life, as he liked to say, 'ended'. It was a dramatic final act – although whether comedy or tragedy is a moot point. Leading the field by many lengths in the Grand National that year, his mount Devon Loch mysteriously collapsed only yards short of the finishing line. Francis had never won the National, the peak of a steeplechase jockey's career, and his disappointment was bitter. Was Devon Loch nobbled? Perhaps – it's a recurrent theme in Francis' thrillers. But, experts suggest, the most likely explanation seems to have been a gigantic fart which was so explosive as to prostrate the unluckily flatulent beast. Francis retired at the age of forty-two, having ridden 2,305 races and 345 winners, and took to writing fiction.

Dead Cert draws on the unhappy race that so dramatically ended his career. It opens aromatically: 'The mingled smells of hot horse and cold river mist filled my nostrils.' It's the 2.30, three-mile 'chase' at Maidenhead. Young Alan York is ten lengths behind top jockey Bill Davidson, who is leading the field on the favourite, Admiral. At the last fence, for no apparent reason, Admiral falls, mortally injuring its rider. Why? Some sleuthing by a suspicious Alan reveals the last fence has been 'wired'. The trail thereafter leads, after much winding, to a sinister 'Mr Big' in Brighton. This mysterious kingpin runs a radio-taxi service, a razor gang, a protection racket and a bookie's shop. He bumps up his income by fixing races. Hence the wire, hence the fall. But who *is* the arch-criminal? York, who narrates (all Francis' novels had male narrators), is a white millionaire's son from Southern Rhodesia – an area which was destined a couple of years hence to become very uncomfortable for white millionaires and their sons. Francis' fiction is wholly uninterested in such things. Leave geopolitics to Freddy Forsyth. Romantic interest is generated by reader curiosity as to whether young York will marry Davidson's widow, Scilla, or the delectable horse owner

Kate Ellery-Penn, a beauty not yet fully bloomed. As the following indicates, Francis is stronger on four-legged fillies than the two-legged variety:

> And there it was. Kate the beautiful, the brave, the friendly, was also Kate the unawakened. She was not aware yet of the fire that I perceived in her at every turn. It had been battened down from childhood by her Edwardian aunt, and how to release it without shocking her was a puzzle.

Will Alan succeed in 'unbattening' her? Who cares. The fascination in Francis' first novel, and the many that followed, is the insider stuff about 'nobbling', the intricacies of handicapping, the mysterious mathematics of betting odds, the ambience of the weighing room. In short, the horsey smell evoked by that first sentence.

Francis was engagingly modest as to his narrative technique: 'I start at Chapter 1, page 1, and plod on to THE END.' His invariable practice was to begin a new book every 1 January, and deliver the manuscript to Michael Joseph on 8 May for publication in September. It has plausibly been suggested that his fiction was partially, perhaps entirely, ghosted by his wife Mary.

Dead Souls, Nikolai Gogol, 1842

Among the greatest literary achievements of the nineteenth century is the Russian novel. Its pioneer, as leading practitioners such as Dostoevsky candidly admitted, was Gogol. This, his last and best work, explains why his successors thought so highly of him. It is also, even across the notoriously deadening process of translation, as funny as anything any of the great Russian writers came up with. Funny – but also serious. Among the many revolutions in the nineteenth century was Western society's move from what the sociologist Max Weber called *Gemeinschaft* (community) to *Gesellschaft* (society) as its organising system. The one was essentially feudal, the other 'rational'. Bureaucratic rationality was efficient, but had, as its downside, a chilling, dehumanising, effect. As Weber put it in a famous passage from *The Theory of Social and Economic Organisation*:

> No machinery in the world functions so precisely as this apparatus... [It] reduces every worker to a cog in this bureaucratic machine and, seeing himself in this light, he will merely ask how to transform himself into a somewhat bigger cog... The passion for bureaucratisation drives us to despair.

Or, in fiction like Gogol's, it can be turned to wry comedy.

Gogol's novel pivots on a paradox. Can a soul die? Holy writ assures us it will live for ever, in heaven or hell. In the bureaucratised universe it will live for ever as 'data' – on lists, catalogues, and 'the census', that other revolutionary nineteenth-century innovation. Gogol wrote *Dead Souls* while feudal serfdom was still the great engine powering the Russian state machine. In it, he fantasises that serfs can serve that machine dead as well as alive. There is no emancipation, even in the grave. The narrative opens in sprightly fashion:

> To the door of an inn in the provincial town of N. there drew up a smart *britchka* – a light spring-carriage of the sort affected by bachelors, retired lieutenant-colonels, staff-captains, land-owners possessed of about a hundred souls, and, in short, all persons who rank as gentlemen of the intermediate category. In the *britchka* was seated such a gentleman – a man who, though not handsome, was not ill-favoured, not over-fat, and not over-thin. Also, though not over-elderly, he was not over-young.

Enter the Don Quixote of the Steppes. He has a Sancho Panza in attendance, a 'soul' (indentured servant) called Selifan. The visitor's official description, as he informs the town's authorities, is 'Paul Ivanovitch Chichikov, Collegiate Councillor – Landowner – Travelling on Private Affairs'. Where the Chichikov estate might be is not divulged. He takes up residence at the town's leading inn, where the cockroaches fight with the guests for territory and the mattresses are as thin as pancakes 'and possibly as greasy'. He rises serenely above such things. He has a mission. Serfs ('souls') were designated property before 1860, and taxed according to the most recent census – a notoriously inaccurate and out-of-date ledger. Typically serfs who had died were still registered as alive for decades after. Chichikov sets out to buy them up, at fifteen roubles a soul (in 'good paper money', he says – not that old-fashioned gold or silver) – and use that soul-property as equity to raise loans from banks. There ensues a series of negotiations with close-fisted locals. Chichikov ends up with four hundred non-existent souls. He is now a man of means. Gogol's judgement is indulgent:

> Again, although I have given a full description of our hero's exterior (such as it is), I may yet be asked for an inclusive definition also of his moral personality. That he is no hero compounded of virtues and perfections must be already clear. Then WHAT is he? A villain? Why should we call him a villain? Why should we be so hard upon a fellow man? In these days our villains have ceased to exist. Rather it would be fairer to call him an ACQUIRER.

Or, as our own commentators would say, a wealth-creator. *Dead Souls* was written at the end of Gogol's life. A second volume was destroyed, apparently in a frenzy, by the author himself, who seems to have gone rather mad at the end of his life. On his gravestone Gogol had inscribed, defiantly, 'I shall laugh my bitter laugh'.

Deadwood Dick on Deck: or, Calamity Jane, the Heroine of Whoop Up, Edward Lytton Wheeler, c. 1878

This is one of the most popular of the 'dime novels' that catered to a mass readership in late-nineteenth-century America. These ten-cent products were often westerns and sold in their hundreds of thousands – mainly to readers in the urban east. They were the subsoil in which Hollywood sank its roots when the entertainment industry cranked up at the turn of the century. Your dime could now get you into the Kinematograph, where you could see what previously you could only read about. Two things killed the cowboy dime novel: the continental spike, commemorating the completion of the transcontinental rail link that opened the way to mass movements of population ('Go West, young man!'), and the moving picture. To dip into dime novels (this is one of the best) is to savour the rich literary smell of the Hollywood subsoil. If you don't know the novel, how many movies come to mind reading the following summary? A lot, I predict.

Deadwood Dick on Deck is, chronologically, the eighth in the long-running *Deadwood* series, and the most famous for its depiction of the all-action, gun-toting, buckskin-wearing, man-hating heroine – Calamity Jane. Calamitous, that is, for any man (particularly any 'redskin') who crosses her. The action is set in the Black Hills of Dakota, in the gold-mining town of Whoop Up. The main line of the novel's action centres on two prospectors: Sandy and his rather mysterious 'pardner', Dusty Dick. In another part of the narrative Deadwood Dick, 'the handsome knight of the hills', is the leader of a gang who have appointed themselves as 'regulators' – unofficial agents of law and order who keep down the area's outlawry. Deadwood Dick disappears and is presumed dead. Call him Dead Dick. His disappearance from the scene leads to a predictable outbreak of lawlessness. In fact, Dick is not dead but has disguised himself as 'Old Bullwhacker', a superannuated bushy-whiskered 'regulator'. His reasons for doing this are not altogether clear. There ensue various 'diabolical plots' which climax in a bloody shoot-out in a goldmine.

In the denouement of the tale, Sandy the prospector is revealed to be Earl Beverly – a man falsely accused of forgery in the east who took the trail west to forget and be forgotten. Dusty Dick is revealed to be a girl, Edna Sutton. Sandy marries her. Pardners indeed. Calamity Jane remains resolutely single and misanthropic.

She was, historically, Martha Jane Canary (1852–1903). Reputedly she was a formidable Indian fighter, horse-lover and man-hater. Photographs confirm Ms Canary looked nothing like Doris Day, who played her on screen.

Death of a Hero, Richard Aldington, 1929

On 11 October 2012, David Cameron announced his government's plans for a 'truly national commemoration' of the start of the First World War, to climax, at the centennial moment, of the first day of conflict, 4 August 2014. There was, said the prime minister, 'something captivating' about 'stories of the First World War'. Harry Patch, the last surviving British soldier to have fought in the 'war called great', died in July 2009. His verdict was, to the end, bleak. It was, he said, 'organised murder'. The best writers of the time concurred, although it took some time for the bruises of the First World War to come to the literary surface. Aldington's novel, along with Graves' memoir *Goodbye to All That*, and Remarque's ALL QUIET ON THE WESTERN FRONT all appeared within a few months of each other in 1928–9. One reads these books not to revisit, in some Goyaesque sense, 'the horrors of war' (though there is plenty of that), but in search of an answer to the vexing question: why did men as sensible as Graves, Remarque and Aldington throw themselves so voluntarily into this global meat grinder? It is not a question they found easy to answer themselves.

Death of a Hero is less a novel than a symptom of what was not yet called post-traumatic stress disorder. The 1920s gave it the lovelier name 'neurasthenia'. Aldington, bohemian by nature, began his literary career as a poet. Unlike many of his peers (Rosenberg, Owen, Sorley) he survived the trenches, gas, and shell shock. Survived, that is, after a fashion. A patriot when he joined up to fight for king and country, he lost his belief in the trenches. 'Nationalism', he discovered, 'is a silly cock crowing on its own dunghill.' Kings, kaisers, tsars, and nations simply weren't worth sixteen million lives. The pointlessness of it all imbued him with a sense of cosmic despair – he claimed to have attempted suicide twice while serving (courageously). For the rest of his life he maintained, 'There are two kinds of men: those who have been to the front and those who haven't'. It was his personal heart of darkness.

'Kill the hero', instructed Zola. Field Marshal General Haig and Kaiser Wilhelm had done that for the writers of Europe. Aldington began writing *Death of a Hero*, his first novel, almost the day the war finished. It would not see print until 1929. Transparently autobiographical, it tells, via an unnamed narrator, the story of George Winterbourne. It opens bleakly: 'The casualty lists went on appearing for a long time after the Armistice – last spasms of Europe's severed arteries.' On this bloody list is the name of the novel's hero. The narrative spins back from this prelude. George was born middle-class into a family with the generic middle-class woes – a professionally unachieving father and a snobbish, dissatisfied mother. But he is a 'gentleman'. Defying his heritage, he hangs out in pre-war London with the leading lights of art and literature – he is himself artistic. He and his lover marry, with the understanding that the union will be 'open' – or adulterous, as their parents' stuffy generation would call it. George volunteers, in the spirit of Rupert Brooke-like patriotism, when General Kitchener points his finger. Fighting a war will be simpler, he expects, than his private life, which, in the way of 'open unions', has become rather tangled. In the trenches George discovers the real enemy is not 'the Hun' but England – 'a country where there are so many old fools and so few young ones'. Wholly disillusioned as armistice approaches, he hurls himself into a hail of machine-gun fire: 'The universe exploded darkly into oblivion'.

Chatto (who had just rejected LADY CHATTERLEY'S LOVER) agreed to publish Aldington only if he submitted his text to some savage blue pencilling. Aldington insisted on asterisks to mark the f****ing 'mutilation'. He gave as his reason: 'it is better for the book to appear mutilated than for me to say what I don't believe'.

The Death of Ivan Ilyich, Leo Tolstoy, 1886

This is for the older reader. One might go so far as to suggest that local authorities should give 'seniors' a free copy with their euphemistically named 'Freedom Pass', as a reminder of the biggest journey they will ever take. Perversely, because it is short and written by a writer whose name is better known than his work, *The Death of Ivan Ilyich* routinely appears on 'Great Books' courses for the young – to whom the story manifestly does not speak, since the young know they will never die. The narrative opens with the announcement of the death of a senior public prosecutor, Ivan Ilyich, to his assembled colleagues. Their faces are properly grave on receiving the sad news. Secretly, 'the first thought of each of the gentlemen in that private room was of the changes and promotions it might occasion among themselves or their acquaintances.' After a vivid description of the corpse, the narrative proceeds as a jaundiced obituary, beginning: 'Ivan Ilyich's life had been most simple and most ordinary and therefore most terrible'.

Ivan Ilyich is a child of the time – a careerist and wholly happy in the groove that history has carved out for him. He is professionally lucky because, with the abolition of serfdom, 'new and reformed judicial institutions were introduced, and new men were needed'. Ivan Ilyich is just such a new man, marked for fast-track promotion. Life is good. As an investigating magistrate in the provinces he meets Praskovya. She 'came of a good family, was not bad looking, and had some little property', and so he marries her. It starts well but continues less well: 'married life, with its conjugal caresses, the new furniture, new crockery, and new linen, were very pleasant until his wife became pregnant'. She loses her *gaieté de coeur* and her prettiness, and turns shrewish. Ilyich finds consolation in his official work, which, over the next two decades, goes swimmingly – climaxing, when he is forty-five, in the lusted-for senior post in St Petersburg. With it comes a luxurious new residence, 'a delightful house, just the thing both he and his wife

had dreamed of'. Ilyich 'himself superintended the arrangements, chose the wallpapers, supplemented the furniture (preferably with antiques which he considered particularly *comme il faut*), and supervised the upholstering'. Here Count Leo Tolstoy allows himself a flick of aristocratic scorn: 'In reality it was just what is usually seen in the houses of people of moderate means who want to appear rich'.

The house kills Ilyich. He falls from a ladder, seeing to the new curtains, and bruises his side. It turns cancerous. The first symptom is 'a queer taste in his mouth'. Doctors are vague and unhelpful. It gets worse as the months pass. The dying of Ilyich takes up over half the story. 'Anger choked him. . . "It is impossible that all men have been doomed to suffer this awful horror!"' It is alas, not impossible but inevitable. He is, he discovers, 'alone with *It*: face to face with *It*. And nothing could be done with *It* except to look at *It* and shudder'. And die. But before that release comes unbearable humiliation.

> For his excretions also special arrangements had to be made, and this was a torment to him every time – a torment from the uncleanliness, the unseemliness, and the smell, and from knowing that another person had to take part in it.

In his extremity he faces the question he has been able to avoid all his life: 'What does it mean?. . . Why must I die, and die in agony?' Agonising his dying most certainly is. He screams in torment for three days and nights. 'He had begun by screaming "I won't!" and continued screaming on the letter "O"', struggling all the while against 'that black sack into which he was being thrust by an invisible, resistless force'. Finally, 'He drew in a breath, stopped in the midst of a sigh, stretched out, and died'. Tolstoy was fifty-eight when he wrote *The Death of Ivan Ilyich*. He himself died aged eighty-two. His last words were, reportedly: 'But the peasants, how do they die?'

The Death of the Heart, Elizabeth Bowen, 1938

The Death of the Heart is the novel of Bowen's which routinely makes the 'One Hundred Best' lists. What, then, is 'best' about it? Two things, one might suggest. Few novels more scathingly catch the spiritual vacuity of between-the-wars, middle-to-upper-class English life. This is a 'condition of England' novel in which not the heart, but England itself, seems to have withered into a dry husk. A few months later, as history would have it, the war would change everything. It was an ill wind, wholly unanticipated in the novel. The Death of the Heart can also be recommended as the novel which is most suggestively informative about its author. 'I am fully intelligent only when I write', proclaimed Bowen (she was a boomingly self-important writer). One could add: 'or fully honest with myself'. Biographical detail enriches one's reading of this novel. Bowen's father suffered a catastrophic mental breakdown when she was six. Elizabeth and her mother moved to pokey lodgings in Hythe, on the south coast of England. Here her mother died of cancer, five years later. A remote committee of aunts took charge of the still-young girl.

This grossly disturbed childhood echoes plangently throughout The Death of the Heart in which Portia, the pubescent heroine (sixteen years old but 'looks ten', as one character puts it), finds herself an 'odd', orphaned child, neglected by indifferent or hostile guardians and prey to any sexual predator who looks at her twice. When her widowed mother dies, after a nomadic childhood with never a place to call home, Portia is packed off to London to live with her older half-brother Thomas and his wife. The family background is tangled. Her father, who was married, had fallen in love with Portia's mother, who was married to another man. Complicated divorces and remarriages ensued. Anna, Thomas' wife, is getting slightly too old for adultery (which her cuckolded husband has always found vaguely 'stimulating'). She has 'ash blond' hair, but 'the personality more of a dark woman'. Neither she nor her husband have the slightest desire for children, let alone a child

as strange as the one just landed on them – temporarily, as they hope.

Bowen can create stunningly good scenes. The novel opens in Regent's Park (alongside Bowen's own Crown Estate flat) in leafless winter. On a wooden bridge (it still stands) over one of the pools, Anna is in conversation with a novelist friend about the problem of Portia:

> That morning's ice, no more than a brittle film, had cracked and was now floating in segments. These tapped together or, parting, left channels of dark water, down which swans in slow indignation swam.

Anna has been secretly reading Portia's diary, which does not endear her to the cuckoo deposited in her nest. The unwanted girl is sent off to stay with Anna's former governess on the coast. In London Portia has fallen prey to a young wastrel, Eddie, an employee in Thomas' 'modern' advertising firm. Vulnerable to the slightest show of kindness or interest, she entrusts him with her diary. He uses his 'proletarian, animal, quick grace' to win her heart but his nerve fails at the last moment and he does not deliver the seduction she craves. He gives her five shillings (the going rate for a whore) and sends her out into the London streets. Rejected by Eddie and by an old buffer, Major Brutt, to whom in desperation she offers herself, Portia is alone, unwanted, not heart-broken but heart-dead. Innocence, the novel concludes, 'always finds itself in a wrong position'.

The book was published in the year I was born. People (those who survived the war, or were still around to talk about it) would sentimentally picture 1938 as Edenic – a paradise lost, a world I would never know. I find Bowen's depiction a useful antidote. Like much medicine, it tastes bitter.

The Decameron, Giovanni Boccaccio, c. 1350

The Decameron was, by best guess, written in the middle of the fourteenth century. Before print, that is, and some would say before 'the novel' itself as a discrete literary form. It bears reading 660 years later, if only as a highly enjoyable literary-archaeological dig – although I would suggest it has much more to offer. Is it what one could call 'the novel in embryo'? Does it reveal that necessary but elusive link between the flexibly 'told' oral tale and the inflexibly 'written' fictional text? 'Yes' to both questions, in my view.

However one chooses to classify it, *The Decameron* became hugely popular across Europe, particularly after it was printed in 1470. Popular and inspirational. Few works have disseminated themselves with more fecundity in distinguished literary places. Boccaccio's stories resurface in Chaucer, Shakespeare, Keats, and Tennyson. There was a major difference, however. Boccaccio was not, like them, a poet. The novel is, generically, 'prose fiction'. Prose lends itself to what we loosely call 'realism'. The novel, the French novelist Stendhal neatly observed, was like a 'mirror in the road', reflecting what it saw without pre-existing pattern or imposed structure. 'Realistically', that is. No prosody, no rhyme, no 'poetic diction'.

The frame story of *The Decameron* is simple and terrible. The Black Death is ravaging Florence – as it routinely did in the fourteenth century. Ten young people (seven of them female) of wealth and breeding hole up in a villa in the countryside for a fortnight till the plague burns itself out. To pass the time they tell each other *novellas*, one hundred in all. The word – pioneered by Boccaccio – means 'little new thing'. These tales are told in the warmth of the evening, under the olive trees, to the soft chirp of cicadas, with refreshment to hand. The subjects range from the fabulous and neo-classical to the bawdy, with a stress on the infinite variety of life as it is actually lived. Or so the novellas would have us believe. They are cunningly plotted and overwhelmingly subversive in tone. This 'new thing' is a literary genre which breaks literary rules and flouts convention. That is part of its newness.

The fourth tale, told by Dioneo (a character who is said to be closest to Boccaccio), illustrates the witty naughtiness of the Boccaccian novella. The hero is a young novice monk of such 'hot and lusty disposition (being in the vigour of his yeeres)' that

'neither fasts nor prayers had any great power over him' (a young person, that is, with whom the youthful company can readily 'identify'). While his fellow monks are having their afternoon siesta he walks around the monastery where 'hee espyed a prettie handsome Wench (some Husbandmans daughter in the Countrey, that had beene gathering rootes and hearbes in the field) upon her knees before the Altar'. To cut a short story shorter, he persuades her to come to his cell, where he has his unmonkish way with her. Her 'frailty' offers no opposition (the young women listening to Dioneo doubtless looked saucily demure at this point).

Afterwards, as the couple relax, naked, he hears a soft footfall outside. Looking through a crack in the door he sees, to his horror, the Lord Abbot on the prowl. The consequences could be dire for him. But, quick as a flash, he 'conceits an apt stratagem'. He goes out and gives the key to the abbot, saying he must go off and gather some wood. The abbot, who is suspicious, enters the cell and, despite his best intentions (as the young monk suspected he would), surrenders to his own lust. The young monk is not, meanwhile, in the woods, but up in the loft, spying. His 'stratagem' has worked superbly. He confronts his superior and assures him, ironically, that he will follow his pious example 'dayly'. The 'damosell' (a maid no more) will, we understand, be a frequent visitor. In John Florio's charming 1620 translation (from which the above quotations are taken), Boccaccio's novella reads as freshly as the latest novel on the bookstore shelf.

Delta of Venus, Anaïs Nin, 1940s

Pornography – particularly the 'softer' variety – does not normally have a long life. Nin's soft-and-literary offering has lasted better than most and – even in a less buttoned (zipped?) up period than that in which it was written – repays reading, if only as '*erotica curiosa*', the curiosity not least being that a woman, not a man, wrote it. Dogs walking on their hind legs and all that.

Delta of Venus is a bundle of loosely connected stories with a good story behind their composition. It was the 1940s, New York, and Nin was stony-broke. She was pals with stony-broke Henry Miller – virtually all of whose writings (notably TROPIC OF CANCER) were available only in Paris, as 'dirty books' for the dirty-minded Anglophone tourist. There was, however, a growing appetite in America for dirty books. As Nin records:

> A book collector offered Henry Miller a hundred dollars a month to write erotic stories. It seemed like a Dantesque punishment to condemn Henry to write erotica at a dollar a page. He rebelled because his mood of the moment was the opposite of Rabelaisian, because writing to order was a castrating occupation, because to be writing with a voyeur at the keyhole took all the spontaneity and pleasure out of his fanciful adventures.

The commission was passed on to Nin, who had no fear of the gelding shears or peeping toms and wanted the dollars. Screw artistic integrity. The book collector, whose identity has never been revealed, was – probably – not in the market for personal stimulation. Most likely he was making up private-press *editions de luxe*, for which there was a high-priced connoisseur's market. 'Rare item' booksellers were, at this time, main outlets for erotica – something that forms a central plot element in Raymond Chandler's *The Big Sleep*. Doubtless the 'rare items' circulate to this day for tens of thousands of dollars.

Nin set to and did her monthly stuff. The 'collector' was not dissatisfied although he complained she was, at times, too 'intelligent'. A learned, as well as intelligent, woman, she had taken as her model the great Renaissance pornographer Pietro Aretino and his *Ragionamenti*, in which two harlots discuss the many 'varieties' of sexual pleasure, having themselves tried them all. *Delta* comprises thirteen stories covering incest, paedophilia, bondage, necrophilia, rape, sado-masochism, sex-instrumentation, troilism, exhibitionism, what Freud called 'renifleurism' (sexual arousal by smell) and more. A smorgasbord of sex. Two characters called 'the Baron' and 'the Anarchist' recur, but variety (proverbially the 'spice of life') is the theme. The crudest of the stories is 'The Boarding School' (a Jesuit institution), in which an angelic, fair-haired, boy is lured into the woods by his schoolmates and gang-banged. Others are witty. In 'Manuel', a flasher – constantly at risk of arrest for his predilection of publicly displaying his 'not unformidable' member – finds a middle-aged woman with a precisely matching fetish. They marry, have a rich life, but never 'possess' each other. An aspect of the 'intelligence' which worried the collector is prominent in 'Linda', in which the heroine, to her surprise, is told by the man who clearly 'wants' her, 'I am not interested in possessing you as other men do'. He then asks her to pass a handkerchief between her legs (twice) and give it to him, which (with some relief, expecting something more onerous) she does. He trembles from head to foot, looking at the soiled handkerchief 'as if it were a woman, a precious jewel'. He carries it to the bed:

> laid the handkerchief on the bedspread and then threw himself on it, unbuttoning his trousers as he fell. He pushed and rubbed. . . finally reaching an orgasm which made him cry out with joy. He had completely forgotten Linda.

It is, of course, Nin's satiric portrait of the collector, slavering over her pages. One wonders if he realised.

The Devil Rides Out, Dennis Wheatley, 1934

This ranks high, by my reckoning, on the list of what George Orwell called 'good-bad' novels. As in love and automobiles, one doesn't always go for the ones one should. And, if no one censorious is looking, this is as good a good-bad read as you could hope to come by. I thought so when I first read it, aged fourteen, and I loyally still think so. An 'English Musketeers' romance, *The Devil*

Rides Out is centred on Wheatley's series heroes, first introduced to the reading world a couple of years before. These 'four just men' (as Edgar Wallace would have called them) are led by the aristocratic Duc de Richleau – the drawling embodiment of cosmopolitan cool. He has 'devil's eyebrows' and a connoisseur's taste for Imperial Tokay (the author was a West End wine merchant until, after bankruptcy, turning to fiction) and Hoyo de Monterrey cigars – the characteristic whiff of a 'Wheatley'. Richleau's comrades include the subtle Jewish intellectual Simon Aron, the English gent Richard Eaton (the homophone is meaningful), and the supercharged all-American Rex van Ryn. A little league of nations.

The story opens with one of the musketeers in a jam. Simon has disappeared. In alliance with the beautiful white witch Tanitha, he has been engaged in a life-and-death struggle with a defrocked priest turned Satanist, Mocata. The three other comrades muster at Richleau's country house, Cardinal's Folly. Under the direction of the Duke, who is as adept in the magic arts as in Cuban nicotine, they set out to combat Mocata and rescue their friend. The Duke (champion of the 'right hand way') and Mocata (champion of the 'left hand way') struggle and chase each other through various astral planes, without result. Mocata succeeds in abducting Eaton's virginal daughter, Fleur d'amour (never let it be thought Dennis Wheatley pulled his punches) for the purposes of a vile ritual. The musketeers, now reunited, come together within the points of a pentacle, for the final struggle with the powers of darkness. They fall into a collective trance in which they are transported to Greece where, bound naked on an altar, is Fleur – awaiting unthinkable penetrations. The Devil himself is to be called up to violate her. Mocata is finally foiled and the heroes, along with Fleur, wake up, safe, sound, and virginal in Cardinal's Folly. Mocata is reported to have died elsewhere of 'natural' causes. He will return.

The Devil Rides Out was to be the first of eight such occult romances. In them Wheatley drew on 'research' (as he called it) about necromantic rituals which were in fact picked up, second hand, from personal

acquaintance with Aleister Crowley (known as the 'Great Beast') and Montague Summers (known as the 'Evil Priest'). *The Devil Rides Out* was picked up by Hammer Films in 1968 with Christopher Lee as a superbly OTT Richleau. It was Lee – a personal friend of Wheatley – who persuaded the studio to take the book on. The script was written by the much superior writer Richard Matheson (author of I AM LEGEND). The Hammer adaptations kicked off a Wheatley cult. He died very rich.

Devil's Cub, Georgette Heyer, 1932

If you like Regency romance – none is better. If you don't know it, this is a good one to start with. If you know Regency romance and don't like it, pass on. Pass on, too, if you're a devotee who likes to read for suspense – although so predictable are the plot twists in this genre that spoiler alerts are rarely called for. The 'cub' of the title is a marquess in his mid-twenties, Lord Dominic Vidal, a dashingly handsome 'rake' (short for 'rake-hell', for those new to Regency romance). As the son of the Duke of Avon – known universally among the *haut monde* as 'Satan' – he has the nickname 'Devil's Cub'. Lordly Dominic is introduced to the reader on his way to Lady Montacute's 'drum' (a gilded ball, for readers new to Regency romance). He likes to break the hearts – and, we intuit, hymens – of 'chits' foolish enough to submit to him. Many do submit. The carriage he is driving, with typical devil-take-the-hindmost recklessness, is accosted by a highwayman, whom Vidal casually shoots dead before proceeding on to his evening's pleasures at breakneck speed. He holds the record for the London to Newmarket race and drives better when drunk. Lady Marling, schemer that she is, intends that he shall marry her daughter – a 'belle' – Juliana. The cub shall be tamed. However, Juliana, a resolute wench, has decided on Frederick Comyn. He is heir to a baronetcy, but this would still be, in her mother's eyes, a *mésalliance*. A marquess or nothing for the Marlings. Frederick and Juliana elope.

Vidal's wicked eye is, meanwhile, caught by the handsome daughter of a 'cit' (a burgher, for those new to Regency romance), Sophie Challoner. After a victorious duel in a gambling 'hell', Vidal is obliged to decamp to Paris – the authorities being unsympathetic to murder, even when it is an affair of honour between peers of the realm. Sophie, Vidal decides, shall come with him – as his mistress. 'In France these things are perfectly understood', he blandly explains. Life is not a Sunday school. Noblemen's beds must be warmed. Flighty Juliana's virtuous and less beautiful sister, Mary, intercepts Vidal's letter and, *masquée*, attempts to foil Vidal's scheme. But, rake that he is, he goes on to abduct Mary on his yacht and imprisons *her* in Paris (they perfectly understand that kind of thing as well over there). A strange attraction develops between captor and captive. Enter Comyn. Juliana's haughtiness has forced him to withdraw from the proposed marriage, for which they eloped. He offers to marry the unhappy Mary, and they run away to Dijon, pursued by a furious Vidal. There is the inevitable duel. Comyn is saved from being killed by Mary, who hurls her coat on Vidal's weapon as it is about to fire its deadly bullet (he never misses). She herself is wounded in the ensuing fray. Vidal now realises he loves her. He takes her in his arms

so fiercely that the breath was almost squeezed out of her. His dark face swam before her eyes for an instant, then his mouth was locked to hers, in a kiss so hard that her lips felt bruised.

A chastened Juliana makes it up with Comyn. No bruising kisses there.

The Devil's Cub has never been out of print since being first published in 1932. It is regularly cited as her faithful readers' favourite 'Heyer'. Mine too, although male readers are a bit skittish about confessing to liking this author.

The Devil's Elixirs, E.T.A. Hoffmann, 1815

A much-imitated Gothic tale, *The Devil's Elixirs* is itself an act of imitation (in litera-

ture, as elsewhere, the sincerest form of flattery) of M. G. Lewis' *The Monk*. Gothic writers are the worst jackdaws in literature. Hacked about, in *Blackwood's Magazine* as a 'Tale of Terror' where it was promptly imitated by Hogg's PRIVATE MEMOIRS AND CONFESSIONS OF A JUSTIFIED SINNER. Hoffmann's novel takes the form of a collection of manuscripts which the editor has mysteriously come by. Pages and sections are artfully left missing, creating anachronistic postmodern fractures in the narrative, which tells the story of a capuchin monk, Medardus.

He has been brought up in ignorance of his parents. A good monk (initially), he is entrusted with the care of his convent's reliquary chamber and its most precious contents, a small square box containing the 'elixir' (drink it and live for ever) with which the 'Arch-fiend' tempted St Anthony. So devout is Medardus that he is regarded as 'the pride of the institution'. A haughty aristocrat visits and demands to know whether these rumours about 'the devil's elixirs' are true. Medardus opens the box to display the bottle. The count promptly whips out a corkscrew and gulps down a swig. 'Delicious', he reports. After he has gone Medardus, too, is tempted.

That night the monk rises from his chilly cot, enters the reliquary, unlocks the cabinet, opens the box, uncorks the bottle, and swallows a 'deep and powerful draught'. 'It seemed immediately as if fire streamed through my veins', he discovers. He is 'alive' at last. Farewell those stuffy monastic vows. Farewell too to any shape to the subsequent story. After that deep and powerful draught the narrative disintegrates into a summary-defying 'phantasmagorie'. Mortal sin is piled on mortal sin. Medardus indulges in pleasures of the body – most of them criminal. Aurelien, his chosen 'paramour', may (if I read correctly) be his half-sister. Medardus hurls to his death in an abyss a prince who has foiled him. Or perhaps a lookalike does it. He is haunted by a doppelgänger – Count Viktorin (one of the numerous progeny of *The Devil's Elixirs* is Stevenson's *Doctor Jekyll and Mr Hyde*). Viktorin carries out what Medardus only fantasises.

After a string of murders the former monk is imprisoned but contrives to escape when the doppelgänger takes his place (and himself escapes). He adopts false, ludicrously pretentious identities and becomes a player in the Vatican's deep conspiratorial schemes. Who knows? He may himself one day occupy the papal chair. History has known evil popes. He carries with him a strange, magical, work of art – the precursor of Dorian Gray's picture. Finally, he discovers who he really is – the son of a father as evil as Medardus has now become. Chastened, he reassumes his early identity and returns to his old monastery where, coincidentally, Aurelien is about to take the veil. Medardus, breviary in hand, experiences a sudden resurgence of lust – the elixir still works in his veins. He yearns 'to rush up to the altar, to press her in my arms in one last delicious embrace, and then stab her to the heart'. He is about to rape her when Viktorin comes in and saves her from violation – by himself stabbing to death the would-be but now never-to-be nun:

> 'Ha, ha, ha!' screamed the madman [Viktorin] in a thrilling tone, 'would'st thou rob me of my Princess? – Ha, ha, ha! – The Princess is my bride, my bride!'

He then disappears for what will be a brideless honeymoon. Medardus dies, as an afterword records, raving diabolically.

The Diary of a Mad Old Man, Jun'ichirō Tanizaki, 1961

Most of us read novels most intensely at two stages of life. First in early adolescence – when one lives with one's nose in a book. Secondly late in life, when one has time to 'get round' to the books one has always promised oneself to read. With reference to 'sunset reading', much interesting fiction nowadays seems directed to the question 'how to live old'. I am struck in bookshops by racks, newly erected in the last decade, offering 'teen fiction'. If walk-in bookshops survive (not a certainty) I shall expect soon to see racks spring up labelled 'old guys' novels'. Prominent among such fiction's themes is how should the old male – 'old devils', as Kingsley Amis called them – deal

with their inconvenient sexual desire? Amis gives one (English) answer; Philip Roth another (American) answer (see THE DYING ANIMAL); Tanizaki offers a third, distinctively Japanese, answer. *The Diary of a Mad Old Man* is a fascinating mid-to-late-life read. It was published when the author was seventy-five – three years before his death, and already inexorably on the way there. The 'Mad Old Man' of the title, 'Mr Utsugi', a couple of years older than his author, keeps a diary in which he records his (very) private thoughts.

He lives prosperously in 1950s Tokyo, a rebuilt city he loathes, in a house which he shares with his wife, who is never named and does not much matter. His son Jokichi is a busy businessman – rarely at home. His daughter-in-law Satsuko is a former cabaret performer. The marriage was not initially pleasing to the Utsugi family. The young couple have an eight-year-old son whose occasional intrusions infuriate his grandfather. The diary records visits to the Kabuki theatre, afternoons in a tea-house, evening meals ('I have been hungry for eel recently' – he particularly relishes the viscera). The diary records in meticulous detail his ailments – due to a growing debility, neuralgia, he can now barely walk to his pavilion with his snakewood stick, and he requires a night nurse, whose very occasional nights off provoke intense irritation. He is a prescription drug addict (he knows more about pharmaceuticals, one of his doctors observes, than any intern). He is physically decayed and brutally honest with himself on the subject:

> I know very well that I am an ugly, wrinkled old man. When I look in the mirror at bedtime after taking out my false teeth, the face I see is really weird . . . not even monkeys have such hideous faces.

He is wholly impotent, but sexually alive – it is the only thing in him, in fact, which is not dying:

> I haven't the slightest desire to cling to life, yet as long as I live I cannot help feeling attracted to the opposite sex. . . I can enjoy sexual stimulation

in all kinds of distorted indirect ways.

At present I am living for that pleasure.

His desire – obsessional in its intensity – is directed at his flighty daughter-in-law, who lives for American movies and good times. But she has beautiful feet – Utsugi's fetish (necks he also rather likes). Seeing her advantage, Satsuko cunningly teases her 'father', allowing him to dry her feet after a shower. For a cat's eye ring – costing a cool three million yen (around $40,000 dollars in current value) – she intimates, he may have even more exciting privileges. He stumps up and she allows him some 'heavy petting'. His systolic blood pressure count soars to 240.

The second half of the diary recounts a visit to Kyoto (an unspoiled city Utsugi loves) to arrange his tombstone and final resting place. He intends to have casts of Satsuko's feet (anonymously) carved into the stone which will accompany him through eternity. The *Totentanz* comes to its inevitable climax and Mr Utsugi has a second stroke. The novel tails off with bleak medical reports on his near-vegetative condition. The story is wonderfully whittled down to an obsession – what Hardy (echoing Dido) called *veteris vestigia flammae* – 'the last flames'. There is not a single mention of the Second World War in the novel.

The Diary of a Nobody, George and Weedon Grossmith, 1892

The term 'a nobody' has proved a nightmare for translators. The French *inconnu(e)* doesn't do it. It comes across as 'unknown'. Nor does the German *niemand* work. It comes across as 'no one'. In English the term – as in *Diary of a Nobody* – has a whole socio-semantic framework around it. Without the English social system as context it is as meaningless as the Esperanto *neniu*. 'Nobody' doesn't, in this context, mean 'you don't exist' – it means 'you don't matter, you don't count'. To the people who do count, that is: the 'somebodies'. Reading the Grossmiths' comic epic can be recommended as either: (1) a guide to; or (2) a good reason to

laugh at, that grotesquely stratified thing, 'English class'. The laughs predominate.

The work was first published as serial 'papers' in *Punch* and retains that miscellaneous form. The 'nobody' is Charles Pooter, who works in a City office as a clerk under Mr Perkupp (another nobody, but one who thinks he is a somebody). Mr Pooter lives in a rented villa – The Laurels, Brickfield Terrace, Holloway – 'a nice six-roomed residence', with his wife Carrie. They have just moved in. To honour the great event, 'I resolve to keep a diary'. The diary goes on to recount his Lilliputian daily adventures at work and in his social life, in which the biggest event is an invitation to the Mansion House Ball. Mr Pooter is a little man for whom little life events loom large. For example:

> APRIL 8, Sunday. – After Church, the Curate came back with us. I sent Carrie in to open front door, which we do not use except on special occasions. She could not get it open, and after all my display, I had to take the Curate (whose name, by-the-by, I did not catch), round the side entrance. He caught his foot in the scraper, and tore the bottom of his trousers. Most annoying, as Carrie could not well offer to repair them on a Sunday. After dinner, went to sleep. Took a walk round the garden, and discovered a beautiful spot for sowing mustard-and-cress and radishes. Went to Church again in the evening: walked back with the Curate. Carrie noticed he had got on the same pair of trousers, only repaired. He wants me to take round the plate, which I think a great compliment.

Pooter's son, Willie Lupin Pooter, is a chronic source of worry. He arrives to live at home uninvited and proceeds to get himself engaged to a highly unsuitable young lady, Daisy Mutlar. She is older than he, and Pooter, who knows a thing or two about the world, suspects that the Mutlars are 'loafers'. Daisy eventually elects to marry Mr Murray Posh (meaningful name – untranslatable) and Lupin is saved. Somewhat unwillingly (he likes to lie in of a morning) he joins his father to work under Perkupp but is discharged, disgracing the name of Pooter throughout the length and breadth of the City of London. All ends well with Pooter, however. After a £100(!) raise, he is able to buy his own house at last, a consummation he regards as 'the happiest day of my life'. Lupin makes good in a new position where his 'dash' is appreciated and, to his parents' immense relief, marries sensibly.

The Grossmiths' charming work was hugely popular and inspired a whole genre of pseudo-diaristic successors (see, for example, *The Secret Diary of Adrian Mole, Aged 13¾*. THE DIARY OF A MAD OLD MAN, comes from a different place). The dominant creative force in the fraternal composition was Weedon, who perfected his 'voice' as a music-hall comedian. He specialised, as the *Oxford Dictionary of National Biography* notes, 'in acting "dudes" and small, under-bred, unhappy men': sad sacks (American term: untranslatable). Charlie Chaplin drew fruitfully on the same tradition.

The Diary of a Nobody has enriched the English language with the genus 'Pooter' (you can still see armies of them wending homeward from the City of an evening) and the epithet 'Pooterish'. Both are wholly untranslatable.

Dinner at the Homesick Restaurant, Anne Tyler, 1982

There are novels so good that you pass them on to others to read. There are other novels so good that you want to keep them to yourself, as a kind of secret, like Silas Marner's gold under the floorboards. *Dinner at the Homesick Restaurant* is such gold. The narrative opens:

> While Pearl Tull was dying, a funny thought occurred to her. It twitched her lips and rustled her breath, and she felt her son lean forward from where he kept watch on her bed. 'Get . . .' she told him. 'You should have got . . .'

What death cuts her off from saying is 'You should have got an *extra* mother'. It's a flashback. When her first and then only child,

Cody, fell dangerously ill, her motherly thought was she needed extra children – otherwise 'What would I have left?' So, like-wise, should children have a 'spare' mother or two. Already, at its outset, the novel is permeated with Tyler's unique narrative flavour – a kind of melancholy that never quite topples into bitterness. No writer has a better control of tone.

Pearl's deathbed reverie paints, for the reader, the picture of a very good mother indeed. Her salesman husband, Beck, walked out on her in 1944, leaving her with three young kids – Cody and the two 'extras' – to raise. She resourcefully got a job as a checkout assistant in a local Baltimore super-market and has lived to see all her offspring do well despite their deadbeat dad. Cody is a hotshot factory efficiency consultant (an asset stripper, more honestly). Ezra – 'dreamy', wholly 'inefficient' and home-loving – runs a local eatery, to which he gives the rueful name 'Homesick Restaurant'. Jennifer is a doctor. To have brought her brood up single-handed is, the dying Pearl thinks, 'the triumph of her life'. It should be a happy family. Except the Tulls all dislike each other and, even more, can't stand their mother. Cody resents the 'extras' – especially Ezra. He plays cruel practical jokes on him as a child. Requesting a home visit from a mortuary salesman, for a 'before need' ceme-tery plot, is one of the crueller. Leaving empty vodka bottles under Ezra's bed, for their mother to find and chastise him for, is another. In later life Cody steals Ezra's fiancée – not because he loves the homely Ruth (dashing and rich, he could have any woman he wanted) but because he's damned if Ezra is going to be happy. Jennifer goes through husbands at an extraordinary rate; unable ever to settle down. Every time she gets close to a man she wants to leave him. All the children think their mother is 'a dangerous person – hot-breathed and full of rage and unpredictable'. The narrative switches between the children's three different perspectives on their family history. Every now and then, over four decades, the Tulls try and have a 'family dinner' – at Thanks-giving, Christmas, or someone's birthday. It always ends disastrously.

Ezra – the most filial of the unfilial siblings – tends his mother as she dies.

Sorting out her things, he reads her old diaries. Their contents astonish him:

> Why, that perky young girl was this old woman! This blind old woman sitting next to him! She had once been a whole different person, had a whole different life separate from his.

After Pearl's death the Tulls finally have the family meal they were never able to have while their mother was alive. Cody delivers the non-eulogy, addressing it to his father, who, after forty-three years' absence, silence, and non-payment of child support, has chosen to turn up for his wife's funeral (they never divorced):

> You think we're a family. You think we're some jolly, situation-comedy family when we're particles, torn apart, torn all over the place, and our mother was a witch.

His siblings faintly demur, but secretly agree. Beck sneaks off. Ezra may have cancer, but is afraid to go to the doctor in case it's cancer. The novel tails off into an ending which is no ending. A half-dozen other novels are hinted at, never to be written.

Disgrace, J. M. Coetzee, 1999

Disgrace won the 1999 Booker Prize – whose grand award ceremony Coetzee declined to attend, dispatching a video instead. He'd won the prize sixteen years earlier for *Life & Times of Michael K*, whose award-giving ceremony he also chose to skip. He won the Nobel Prize for Literature in 2003, whose ceremony he did attend.

Disgrace precedes by seven years his changing his nationality and becoming an Australian (as his not-too-distant ancestors had changed their Dutch nationality to become South African). The novel is profoundly involved with the complexities of post-apartheid South Africa. It's a kind of 'goodbye to all that'. Two complexities in particular preoccupy *Disgrace*: the power relations involved in sexual harassment, and the facile delusion which lay behind

South Africa's everywhere-lauded 'Truth and Reconciliation Commission' and national 'rebirth', during whose proceedings the novel was written. As Robert McCrum put it, reviewing the novel in the *Los Angeles Times*, *Disgrace* 'asked awkward questions'.

Being awkward, or disgusted, has never deterred J. M. Coetzee. He is (among his many other parts) a former professor of literature, and the first half of the novel is set in a South African university. I recall a notice, shortly after the novel was published in America, posted for an on-campus women's discussion group at a university where I was at the time a visiting professor. 'Come and Talk About *Disgrace*', it said, without any mincing of words, 'The Story of a Professor who Sexually Harasses one of his Women Students and is Fired'. Crudely, if unflatteringly, that is indeed what the first half of *Disgrace* is about.

The hero, David Lurie, is fifty-two and a middlingly esteemed professor of 'communications' in a South African university. He is twice separated, maritally, and has recently found sexual relations with prostitutes unsatisfactory. He embarks on a predatory affair with one of his students, Melanie Isaacs. Scandal and a 'hearing' (i.e. commission of inquiry) ensue. Lurie declines the weasel's way out – public confession, apology, and a rigorous course of 'sensitivity training'. No truth and reconciliation for him. 'Was it serious?' he asks his tribunal. 'I don't know. It certainly had serious consequences.' Believing he has done nothing intrinsically wrong, he declines to kiss the rod and chooses disgrace instead. He is duly fired. Excommunicated. The reasons for Lurie's stiff-neckedness (why doesn't he just swim with the politically correct tide?) are never clearly articulated in the novel – other than as a brooding suspicion that sensitivity training courses, codes of conduct, and sexual-harassment tribunals are not the way to solve the deep-rooted, intractable (perhaps insoluble) problems at issue. Nor are 'commissions' with high-sounding names. 'I am sure', Lurie says, with scathing contempt,

> the members of this committee have better things to do with their time than rehash a story over which there will be no dispute. I plead guilty to

both charges. Pass sentence, and let us get on with our lives.

He denies his prosecutors the 'spectacle' they crave.

But what is it 'to live your life'? The second half of the novel is set on his daughter Lucy's farm in the country, where David, now jobless, washes up. Lucy is gang-raped by a band of black men – one of whom, Petrus, she continues to employ even though he seems to have been involved in the assault. She declines to lodge any complaint about the rape. Why will she not pursue criminal action? Because, one gathers, she sees it as reparation. Reconciliation, honestly defined, requires private suffering – not merely public bleating about how sorry one is. Perhaps 'they see me as owing something', Lucy muses. 'They see themselves as debt collectors, tax collectors. Why should I be allowed to live here without paying? Perhaps that is what they tell themselves.' The novel leaves this radioactive notion hanging. David gives up writing (he had an opera about Byron in mind) and finds his vocation 'putting to sleep' (kindly) unwanted dogs and disposing, respectfully, of their bodies.

The African National Congress issued an official denunciation of Coetzee's novel, accusing him of 'subliminal racism' and of trading in stereotypes about black male sexual violence. Coetzee did not respond – other than by self-imposed exile.

Doctor Zhivago, Boris Pasternak, 1957

I first came across the novel as a national serviceman during basic training. Newly published in the West, it was being extracted in the *Daily Express*, which hailed it (mistakenly) as an anti-Soviet tract. In the situation in which I then was, one scene struck me: that of a company of prisoners being detrained in the wastes of Siberia and, seeing nothing but snow and trees, wondering where they are going to live. Build it, they are instructed. It made perfect sense to someone involuntarily in khaki. I later read Pasternak's novel more

objectively. And its largest propositions continued to make perfect sense to me during the never-ending Cold War. *Doctor Zhivago* outlines the tenuous connection which any individual who is not a 'great man [woman]' will have with the great events of history. In its entirety the novel is an oblique history of the Russian Revolution – refracted through 'ordinary lives'. Sub-revolutionary lives, one might call them.

The hero, Yuri Zhivago, is a poet and a doctor: in reverse order. His story intertwines with that of Lara, whom he loves but will never possess. Both are eventually married to others: he, lovelessly, to a relative, she to the dynamic soldier Pasha, who will become a ruthless general in the Red Army, nicknamed 'the killer'. Yuri is, by contrast, a 'healer'. For much of the novel Lara is unsure whether she is a wife or a widow. Once rich, Yuri's father Andrei, in Karamazov style, squandered the family wealth. Much of it was embezzled by a corrupt lawyer, Viktor Komarovsky. Andrei committed suicide – jumping out of a train to his death. After the subsequent death of his mother, the orphaned Yuri is brought up by an uncle, an intellectual, formerly a priest. Having ruined the Zhivagos, Komarovsky – as lecherous as he is constitutionally dishonest – seduces the youthful Lara. Yuri is at this stage a student doctor and becomes embroiled in this complicated affair, which climaxes with Lara attempting to shoot her seducer dead at a Christmas party. She fails and escapes prosecution. Behind this low human drama, the defeat of Russia by Japan sets in motion the events leading to revolution, civil war, and the Stalinist tyrannies under which Pasternak wrote his novel.

The narrative resists easy summary because the lives of the principals bounce about like corks in stormy waters. They themselves are never sure whether things are falling apart, or actually taking new – probably terrifying – shapes. The novel ends inconclusively and exhaustedly. Yuri fades away in Moscow, having made a second passionless marriage. He dies of a heart attack in the city street. Lara is swept up in the 1930s purges. As the narrative bleakly records:

One day Lara went out and did not come back... She died or vanished somewhere, forgotten as a nameless number on a list which was afterwards mislaid.

Doctor Zhivago poses a searching question. What historical part did Yuri (and millions like him) play in the Revolution – if any? Irreverently one is reminded of Spike Milligan's *Adolf Hitler: My Part in His Downfall*. Zhivago and Lara survive. But is that all life is? Dodging the bullet? The question is articulated in one of Zhivago/Pasternak's poems, beautifully translated by Donald Davie, with its haunting end line: 'To live your life is not as simple as to cross a field.' Pasternak, unlike many other independently minded writers, survived the Stalinist purges – largely by keeping his head down. *Doctor Zhivago* was prohibited from publication in the USSR, although it evidently circulated in *samizdat*. The manuscript was smuggled out and published in Italy in 1957. Pasternak was awarded the Nobel Prize for Literature the following year but was not allowed to go to Sweden and collect it. He died in 1960.

Don Quixote, Miguel de Cervantes, 1605 (Part One), 1615 (Part Two)

Don Quixote is a work everyone *knows* but very few (I indict myself) will actually have read cover to cover. Or, if they have, they will have done so with, perhaps, less than studious attention. Nonetheless, if one had to locate the single foundation stone on which the novel (or at least the post-1800 novel) rests, this is it. The plot is simple – one could go so far as to say there is no plot. *Don Quixote* popularised a variety of fiction known as 'picaresque' – narratives which wander all over the place (the term does not fit exactly, *picaro* being Spanish for 'rogue', which Quixote most certainly is not). The protagonist is Alonso Quijano, to give him his Spanish name, a middle-aged gentleman living in quiet retirement in La Mancha. It is not, however, a serene retirement. His brain has been poisoned by

ancient romances, tales of chivalry and knight errantry. He hallucinates himself into the role of a knight – 'Don Quixote de la Mancha' – and sets out, in homemade armour, on a 'quest'. As his squire he recruits a fat peasant, Sancho Panza. An old nag, Rocinante, serves as his charger. The comedy arises from the disparity between what he sees, and what the uninfatuated world (not least Sancho) sees. There ensue a series of comic adventures, or 'sallies', the most famous of which is the battle with the windmills, which the don mistakes for giants. After a series of similar disasters he returns home, dejected but sane at last. Once again he is Alonso Quijano. On his deathbed he draws up his will and repudiates all the fiction which has ruined his life, declaring:

> My reason is now free and clear, rid of the dark shadows of ignorance that my unhappy constant study of those detestable books of chivalry cast over it. Now I see through their absurdities and deceptions, and it only grieves me that this destruction of my illusions has come so late that it leaves me no time to make some amends by reading other books that might be a light to my soul. Niece, I feel myself at the point of death, and I would fain meet it in such a way as to show that my life has not been so ill that I should leave behind me the name of a madman; for though I have been one, I would not that the fact should be made plainer at my death.

He dies plain Alonso Quijano. It's a noble end to a comic career. Nonetheless, there is something touching – admirable even – in the memory of that rickety old codger, his spavined nag, and his fat cowardly 'page', bravely taking on the windmills (and losing). Even at his deathbed, his mind now 'rational', his attendants testify to the fact that Don Quixote de la Mancha, for all his absurdity, was a good man. 'Quixotic' has never been a pejorative. And reading works of imagination may not be all bad.

Cervantes' novel articulates a dilemma at the heart of this book. Is the life spent reading fiction (as mine has largely been) a life wasted ('up, up and leave your novels', to misquote Wordsworth)? Or is a life so invested a voyage of life-long exploration? What does fiction do to us and for us? Putting that grand question aside, *Don Quixote* is a hugely entertaining experience even if, as most of us will, one dips into rather than wades through its thousand pages. Many novelists – from Henry Fielding and Laurence Sterne, through Scott, Dickens and Thackeray, to James Joyce – have paid homage to it. William Faulkner re-read it every year. Uncle Toby, Parson Adams, Jonathan Oldbuck, Samuel Pickwick, Colonel Newcome, Leopold Bloom, and Anse Bundren are all prize fruit of the great 'Cervantick' root. I would even make a case for Harry Potter and his Sancho Panza, Ronald Weasley. The broomstick and Rocinante might be a longer stretch.

Don't Look Now, Daphne du Maurier, 1971

Du Maurier's ghost story would be one's nomination for that which comes closest to the ideal that Henry James predicated in his preface to *The Turn of the Screw* – namely 'the subtler the telling, the more chilling the tale'. Du Maurier turns the screw very subtly indeed. John and Laura Baxter, recovering from the death by meningitis of their daughter Christine, take a therapeutic trip to Venice. It is a period (the 1950s) when such vacations were less common than now. The action opens in a restaurant on the outskirts of Venice with the remark:

> 'Don't look now,' John said to his wife, 'but there are a couple of old girls two tables away who are trying to hypnotise me.'

The 'old girls' are Scottish spinsters, twins apparently. One of them is staring unblinkingly their way. The Baxters make a joke of it. A few minutes later in the ladies' lavatory, Laura is informed by one of the Scottish ladies that her blind sister, Heather, is a 'seer' (the Scots specialise in them) and has 'seen' a little girl, cheerfully sitting alongside the couple. The little girl is not of this world, the seer perceives, describing Christine's appearance and dress with eerie accuracy. Laura is persuaded. Her husband, when told, is brutally sceptical. More so when he is informed that the women recognise him as having 'psychic' powers himself. Later that day, walking through the city, he sees a young girl skipping over some moored gondolas. The sisters warn the Baxters to leave Venice; something bad is coming their way. John pooh-poohs the advice.

An emergency interrupts the couple's holiday when their son, at boarding school, comes down with appendicitis. Laura flies back to England, but from a *vaporetto* John sees her – after she is supposed to have left – in a crimson coat, deep in conversation with the weird sisters. Have they somehow 'alienated' her? He reports them to the police as possible kidnappers and they are brought in for questioning. The *carabinieri* are, as it happens, preoccupied with other things. A serial killer is disembowelling Venetian prostitutes and tossing their corpses into the canals. It seems evident that what John 'saw' was a hallucination or, a sister tells him, prophetic. Of what? The climax of the story is shocking and, for most (even the most practised readers of 'mysteries'), as unanticipated as it is plausible. Enough to say John's final verdict on himself is that he has been 'bloody silly'.

Du Maurier's work adapts wonderfully well to film (e.g. REBECCA, 'The Birds', *Frenchman's Creek*). *Don't Look Now* was adapted by the director Nicolas Roeg in 1973, with Donald Sutherland and Julie Christie as John and Laura. The result is regarded as a classic film. Roeg made changes. His narrative begins, in medias res, with Christine, clad in a red plastic raincoat, drowning at the family home. The colour red overlays the Technicolor story which follows. John is an architect, charged with restoring a decayed Venetian church. Du Maurier hated Hitchcock's 1963 adaptation of 'The Birds' and was, apparently, cool towards his 1940 *Rebecca* (her stage version, performed in the same year, is very different, particularly as to whether Max de Winter was a murderer). The author wholly approved of Roeg's *Don't Look Now*.

Dorian: An Imitation, Will Self, 2002

Self is – to echo an entry above – a quixotic writer. He resolutely cleaves to what one of his (unfairly) jaundiced reviewers called 'antique modernism'. At the 2012 Booker Prize ceremony he proclaimed his allegiance to James Joyce. He lost. But then so did the Don. And, like Quixote, there is something both endearingly high minded and admirable in Self's fiction, of which *Dorian* is a fine example.

There is little need to point out what is being 'imitated' – THE PICTURE OF DORIAN GRAY. Wilde's fable of the rottenness at the heart of 1880s *jeunesse dorée* is translocated, with its cargo of outrageousness updated, to the 1980s. There is a lurid socio-historical backdrop: the Brixton riots, Babylonian excess, punk, and – centrally – the fanatic Princess Diana cult. Or, as the novel characterises her, '"Di" – because she must die' – die because such transcendent physical beauty cannot live for more than the briefest of periods, unless it makes some pact with the powers of darkness. The doomed 'Di' figures as a disconnected montage of glimpsed TV images – sometimes with AIDS victims, sometimes with celebrities (Armani, Elton, et al.), limbless mine casualties, sleazy paramours, and – of course – on the balcony after 'the royal fucking wedding' before the 'royal fucking'.

Dorian, a beautiful idealistic ingénu, just down from Oxford, is first encountered as a 'youth worker' in Soho – saving young lads from sin. He is casually debauched ('druggery and buggery') by the ultra-decadent Henry Wotton, a bisexual dandy-junkie-aristocrat-degenerate who describes himself as a 'fistula' on the 'anus of London'. As with much of Self's fiction it's wisest not to visualise the words too precisely. The other principal character is the sub-Warholian artist Basil (Baz) Hallward, who produces a multi-monitor video installation, *Cathode Narcissus*, showcasing images of Dorian. Dorian goes to the bad. His first victim is a teenage Soho rentboy called Herman. Other vile crimes follow. By the necromantic power embedded in Baz's video picture, Dorian remains young and beautiful – more to the point, he remains uninfected by the AIDS epidemic despite taking up to twenty 'rough and bareback' partners a night during the years of his unblemished juvenility.

Di duly dies. Dorian lives on – as long, that is, as his flickering, narcissistic image retains its life. Wotton dies in the Middlesex (nicely apt name – he never knew whether he preferred 'pricks or pudenda') AIDS ward. Baz dies at the hands of Dorian, who turns the artist's blood-spattered studio into something quaintly resembling a Jackson Pollock. Dorian himself expires when his 'image(s)' decay – as video tape invariably does, whether used or stored.

As with Wilde the novel is a vehicle for incessant modish witticism. 'I adore destructive spectacles', sighs Wotton, 'they are the last refuge of the creative.' Not all the epigrams are as quotably Oscarish. But they come at the reader like bunches of over-ripe, sharp-tasting radish. Which reminds me: 'Dorian's penis', we are told, 'was curved, red and gnarled with veins, like the dagger of an alien warlord' (why 'alien'?). Wilde's novel ends melodramatically. Self's ends in a welter of hyperfiction when it is revealed in an epilogue, if I read it right (the mind rather whirls at this point), that what we have been reading for four hundred pages is a slanderous masturbation fantasy by Henry Wotton, the actual Dorian being a perfectly decent gay man. I could be wrong, but don't tell me.

Dracula, Bram Stoker, 1897

'I am Dracula, and I bid you welcome'. The words still thrill. And behind the thrill are billions of dollars, pounds and, doubtless, Transylvanian 'leus' generated by the vampire franchise. The twentieth and twenty-first centuries' obsession with the toothy villain supports a commercial empire – books, films, cartoons, TV dramas and novelties. Like the great Transylvanian monster himself, it would seem that the vampire industry cannot die. Just when you think time has driven a stake into its heart, along comes a new wave of vampirophilia, such as *True Blood*, or the *Twilight* blockbuster series.

The trail of blood leads back to one name – Abraham Stoker. The son of an Irish civil servant, Stoker's life was transformed in 1878 by two events. Aged thirty, he married the wispily beautiful Florence Balcombe, winning her hand from a mortified Oscar Wilde. It may be that Bram had the more winning smile: his rival had what Florence saw as 'curly teeth'. The other event involved the theatre. From childhood, Bram had been stage-struck. Henry Irving's touring company played Dublin regularly in the mid-1870s. Stoker, a confirmed 'Irvingite', wrote an admiring review of the actor's Hamlet, in 1878. It was well received and he was summoned to Irving's suite at the Shelbourne, where the two men talked until daybreak. The next evening, Stoker was informed that the Great Man had a 'special gift' for him. It turned out to be a recitation of Thomas Hood's melodramatic poem 'The Dream of Eugene Aram'. At the end of his performance, Irving tore off his necktie and collapsed in a swoon. 'The recitation was different, both in kind and degree, from anything I ever heard,' Stoker recalled. His own response, he described as 'hysterical'. Irving impulsively invited Stoker to be his 'stage manager' (his Renfield, as commentators like to jest). It's plausible that Irving contributed something distinctive to the idea of Dracula – the *frisson* of the 'master'. It was an aspect of his hypnotic stage presence, most spectacularly displayed in his barnstorming performance as Mephistopheles in *Faust*.

Stoker claimed that inspiration for the novel came to him in a dream. For six years in the 1890s, while serving Irving, Stoker worked on and researched a work provisionally entitled 'The Un-Dead'. Eventually he came round to the Wallachian word for devil, 'dracul'. Stoker boned up on Transylvania in the British Museum; other sources of the novel were nearer to hand, notably fellow Irishman Joseph Sheridan Le Fanu's vampire fable, CARMILLA (1872). Du Maurier's sinister Svengali is also there somewhere. Stoker himself looked towards Jack the Ripper as a topical inspiration. But the fact is, so opaque are *Dracula*'s symbolisms and historical origins that one can read virtually anything into them – and critics have.

Stoker eventually settled on the historical figure of 'Vlad the Impaler' – a ruler who had tyrannised over Wallachia in the fifteenth century and whose patronymic was in fact 'Dracula' – as his villain-hero. He elected to tell the story in a high-impact, multi-narrative style (borrowed from Wilkie Collins). *Dracula* unfolds through various diaries (including, topically, a 'phonograph' journal), letters and press cuttings. The story is a simple crime and chase. A young solicitor, Jonathan Harker, is sent to Transylvania on the ostensible business of Count Dracula's house purchase. (Why the great bloodsucker should want to come to England is never quite clear.) Jonathan is thoroughly vampirised, but escapes. The Count, meanwhile, has had himself transported by coffin (first class) to Whitby, devouring the ship's crew on the way. Once arrived, the ghoul deposits fifty hideaway coffins round London and renders the Harkers' friend, Lucy Westenra, one of the 'undead'. The vampirologist Professor Van Helsing and his companion Dr Seward put the illegal immigrant to flight, track him back to his castle in Transylvania, trap him at sunset, and decapitate him.

The novel was in the event not an overwhelming sales success. It would not take off as an international bestseller until the 1922 screen version, *Nosferatu*, turned it into a goldmine – though not for Irving, nor for Stoker's widow, Florence, who survived him by twenty-five years, most of them tormented by *Dracula* copyright squabbles.

The Dream of the Red Chamber, Cao Xueqin, 1791

In the *Daily Telegraph*, 28 July 2012, John Minford, a professor of Chinese literature, published an article under the provocative headline 'the Best Book You've Never Heard Of'. In it he lamented the fact that 'China's greatest work of literature, the eighteenth-century novel *Dream of the Red Chamber*. . . is still virtually unknown in the English-speaking world'. He went on:

In its native land, *The Story of the Stone*, as the book is also known – *Stone* for short – enjoys a unique status, comparable to the plays of

Shakespeare. Apart from its literary merits, Chinese readers recommend it as the best starting point for any understanding of Chinese psychology, culture and society.

The need for that 'understanding' is urgent, some would argue, given the western world's worrying economic dependence on China. Napoleon is supposed to have said of the country, 'Let her sleep, for when she wakes she will shake the world.' The Napoleonic moment has surely come. It was significant that a few weeks after Minford's article, the Nobel Committee awarded the 2012 Prize for Literature to Mo Yan.

The Dream of the Red Chamber is not an easy read (it's twice as long as *War and Peace*) but it has a consistently fascinating strangeness for the literary tourist. It starts in heaven with a stone politely requesting passage to earth from a Taoist priest and a Buddhist monk. A child is duly born with a piece of jade in its mouth. This fusion of the mystical, allegorical and realistic continues throughout, with a vast overarching narrative and a seething mass of episodes centred on some 600 characters – the population of a small town.

The long story follows the rise and fall of a double-yoked clan, the Jias, in dynastic Beijing. One branch rises, the other falls. But both are ultimately blighted at the root. The 'throughline' is the career of the boy born with the jade in his mouth, Pao-yü. It is an open question as to whether his life – largely devoted to self-cultivation and pleasure – is the symptom of generational decay or aesthetic fulfilment. Consider, with that question in mind, Chapters 5 and 6 (the chapters, like the novel itself, are immensely long). The plum blossom is in full bloom. Having eaten well (the usual 'family banquet', nothing special) Pao-yü takes a post-prandial nap. He finds himself in heaven and is taken in charge by an astral guide whose abode she tells the sleeping but wakeful young man:

is above the Heavens of Divested Animosities, and in the ocean of Discharged Sorrows. I'm the Fairy of Monitory Vision, of the cave of Drooping Fragrance, in the mount of Emitted Spring, within the confines of the Great Void.

To cut a long chapter short, she gives the still virginal Pao-yü a sex lesson via the 'Supplementary Secondary Record of the Twelve Girls of Chin Ling'. In Chapter 6 the young man wakes – his trousers soaking. Unbidden I recall a playground joke I heard – it must be sixty years ago: 'Confucius he say: boy who go to sleep with sex problem on his mind wake up with solution on his pyjama trousers.' Pao-yü goes on to have his first 'licentious experience' with the servant girl who helps him change his clothes. It's hard to find a wet dream and first sex more delicately narrated. Redologists (scholars who devote their lives to the book) dispute among themselves whether their great work is a critique of feudalism, a comedy of manners, or a saga. For the western dilettante it is one of those novels which, like THE LIFE AND OPINIONS OF TRISTRAM SHANDY or DON QUIXOTE, can be read without having to do more than stick in your thumb and pull out a plum. Or a sprig of plum blossom.

A Dreary Story, Anton Chekhov, 1889

So are they all, a cynic might mutter, turning the last page of any collection of Chekhov's short stories. But few, perhaps, contain 'drearier' (as the author idiosyncratically defines the word) stories than this. And few tell their story with more effervescence. The opening sentence is brisk and sardonic:

There is in Russia an emeritus Professor Nikolay Stepanovitch, a chevalier and privy councillor; he has so many Russian and foreign decorations that when he has occasion to put them on the students nickname him 'The Ikonstand'.

The cartoon image of the 'ikonstand' hooks the reader. And, with a sharp tug of the hook, the second sentence reveals to our surprise (no one handles them better than Chekhov) that what we have here is the professor talking about himself:

The bearer of that name [i.e Nikolay Stepanovitch], that is I, see myself as a man of sixty-two, with a bald head, with false teeth, and with an incurable *tic douloureux*. I am myself as dingy and unsightly as my name is brilliant and splendid.

The name will look well on a tombstone – and that chiselled inscription is not, we apprehend, far off. Professor Nikolay is convinced that he will die in precisely six months. He is one of the country's leading medical scholars and knows what he is talking about – even if the albumen content in his urine is judged to be somewhat ambiguous. 'Was it worth it?' he asks himself in the long cogitation that follows.

He reviews his life with the long view of the hostile obituarist. He is still lecturing. Once the podium exhilarated him. 'Now lecturing is nothing but sheer torture for me'. And his lectures are, like him, rather whiskery nowadays. He no longer has the energy to keep up with his subject. He is racked with insomnia. 'Strange things are happening to me', he notes. His colleagues secretly look down on him. 'I am no longer a king'. His wife, never a queen, is now a nag – particularly on the subject of money, which, as his career wanes, is running short. His daughter Liza is thriftless and is pressuring him, through her mother, for permission to marry a man he career suspects is a sponger, Alexander Gnekker. His son, an officer in the army of occupation in Poland, is a neverending drain on his pocket. No member of his family acknowledges the sacrifices he makes for them or, apparently, loves him. He does not *matter* any more. His one consolation is a ward, Katya, left to his care – with a considerable fortune – by a colleague who died early. Katya, a girl of spirit, insisted on taking to the stage. She fell in love imprudently and too often. Neither drama nor romance worked out for her. She has had an illegitimate child – now got rid of. She lives wildly beyond her means, lying on her couch all day long, reading 'mostly novels and short stories' (a sheer waste of time, the world's greatest writer of short stories slyly intimates). She alone loves the professor and visits him daily, at tea time (the mysterious *samovar* features prominently). It is his last pleasure in life. His wife nags him into journeying to Kharkov to check up on Gnekker but before he can begin any investigation there is a telegram. The couple have married, secretly.

Then, finally, high drama. Katya appears, wholly unexpected and distraught, at his Kharkov hotel. Why has she come all this way? 'Nikolay Stepanovitch,' she bursts out, 'I cannot go on living like this! I cannot! For God's sake, tell me quickly, this minute, what I am to do! Tell me, what am I to do?' 'What can I tell you?' he replies. 'I can do nothing.' Hearing this Katya, suddenly frigid, holds out her hand and leaves – for where? he asks. She does not know, or care. 'I want to ask her, "Then, you won't be at my funeral?" but she does not look at me. . .I've seen her black dress for the last time: her steps have died away. Farewell, my treasure!' The story begins with dreariness and ends with pain. Which is the worse?

The Dressmaker, Beryl Bainbridge, 1973

Her career, Bainbridge said, took a leap forward when Karl Miller wrote a piece in the *New York Review of Books* in 1974, hailing her as 'possibly the least known of the contemporary English novelists who are worth knowing'. Miller dearly wanted *The Dressmaker* to win the Booker but was outvoted on the 1973 panel, which he chaired. He was still upset at the injustice a quarter of a century later.

The novel is set in a Liverpool home, occupied entirely by women, in 1944. 'Nellie had her hair net on and her teeth out', opens an early scene, and the novel recreates, with uncanny solidity, a house in which the three female inhabitants have their night-time 'cat's lick' in a tin bowl in the scullery before sharing a bed 'to shut out the cruel night air and the heart-beat of the alarm clock set for six'. The actual first word in the novel is: 'Afterwards'. The bulk of what follows builds up what has happened before that teasing introduction.

Bainbridge, before she found her vocation as a novelist, played a bit part in *Coronation Street*. Her novel belies the cosy view of life in Lancashire working-class terraces celebrated in that neverending soap. The three women in the story resemble nothing so much as the incompatible souls locked up for eternity in Sartre's *Huis Clos*. They are each other's hell.

Nellie, the dressmaker of the title, has been thrown out of work by the German bombs that destroyed her factory. She works 'on the side', wielding her 'sharp steel scissors' like some Fury. She has a fetish: her dead mother's furniture, which she preserves in the never-to-be-entered 'front room' and the attic, like 'things in the bloody British Museum', her brother-in-law, 'Uncle Jack', says. Nellie is unmarried. The bane of her life, Margo, a still flighty fifty-year-old, lost her husband to influenza after the previous war. The third member of this wretched conventual ménage, Rita, is the offspring of a dead sister and Uncle Jack, a homburg-hatted butcher of old-fashioned views good for an under-the-counter joint every Sunday. He wields a handy knife.

Pale, sensitive, anaemic Rita falls in with a GI called Ira. He is illiterate and stupid but trails behind him, as the 'Yanks' did (and no 'Tommy' could) an aura of Hollywood. Repulsed when he makes a none-too-expert assault on Rita's intimate elastic (working women kept their rayon stockings up with elastic bands in 1944), Ira makes a play for Margo, consummating things in the attic where Nellie stores items of the sacred maternal furniture. The fornicating couple are surprised by Nellie, come to kill the mice she thinks she has heard scuffling. Ignoring Margo's stockings round her 'pale knees' she observes a scratch, from Ira's belt, on 'Mother's rosewood table'. She stabs the luckless soldier through the throat. Uncle Jack is summoned to dispose of the body. Ira will end up as sausages or a body in the river. We shall never know, nor will Rita when she comes home that night. 'Afterwards' the ladies go to bed as usual. Only six months to VE Day.

Bainbridge, 'the Booker bridesmaid', was five times shortlisted for the prize. After her death Man Booker ran a 'Beryl's Booker'. It was won by *Master Georgie*.

The Dying Animal, Philip Roth, 2001

One can usefully read this novel – not usually thought one of Roth's more distinguished performances – for its update on the changing demographic of fiction. More specifically, its 'greying'. Anthony Trollope's last completed novel, a race-with-the-undertaker effort, is called *An Old Man's Love* (1884 – Anthony lost the race, it was published posthumously).

In it a superannuated gent, William Whittlestaff, falls for a slip of a girl, only to realise that, at the end of the day, there's no lead in his pencil. He lets her go to a younger rival, whose staff is less whittled by anno domini. The 'old man' of the title is fifty years old. In MIDDLEMARCH, 'ancient' – and, as we apprehend, wholly impotent – Casaubon (husband of the nineteen-year-old Dorothea) is in his early forties. All those patriarchal husbands in Dickens' fiction, manifestly incapable of impregnating their young wives (Dedlock, Dombey, Bounderby, et al.), are in their fifties but well over the sexual hill. Limp members and whittled staves are everywhere in Victorian fiction. Oats are in very short supply after a man's middle years. In *The Golden Bowl*, Charlotte tells the lusty young prince that she and the millionaire Verver will 'never' have children. Why not? Because they will never have sex. At his age? Fifty-something? It is the law of the literary universe.

But the literary universe has now changed utterly. Much of the change is down to a little blue pill. The first flagrant work of Viagra fiction was (seventy-year-old) Tom Wolfe's *A Man in Full* (1998). Charlie Croker ('just turned sixty') is full of vim. In the first paragraph he enters riding a stallion. Charlie, we are told, never lets his young wife forget 'what a sturdy, cord – no, what a veritable cable – connected him to the rude animal vitality of his youth'. It's not just broncos that buck in Mr Croker's world. And in 2000 the reading world received Saul Bellow's RAVELSTEIN – his last major novel. The two heroes, Abe and Chick, are (like their author) decades into their bus-pass years. Both of them (gay and straight respectively) are wheeled into the intensive care ward with proud hard-ons.

Abe's last request, as he succumbs to HIV, is for a hand job. Chick will, we assume, survive his near-death experience to sire a child on his new wife, Rosamund. That, of course, is what newly married Bellow did in the late 1990s and his late eighties.

Roth came out with *The Dying Animal* at the age of sixty-eight. Dying he may be, but the seventy-year-old hero, David Kepesh, goes out screwing, his animal energies undiminished. As his admiring young Cuban mistress tells the old Jewish goat, he is the only man who has ever given her 'real' pleasure. Those young Hispanic guys? Nowhere. If Hemingway were still around, he'd probably give us *The Old Man and the Semen*. Since Viagra was released to the American public at $10 a pop, 80 per cent of the millions of prescriptions have gone

to fifty-and-over males. The results, inside and outside wedlock, have been dramatic. There's a Niagara Falls of vintage sperm washing through American life, radically changing the sexual norms of literature. How different the classics would be if you could take your Wellsian time machine and slip some energising Viagra to Edward Casaubon, William Whittlestaff, Adam Verver and Sir Leicester Dedlock. And, while you're at it, to Ebenezer Scrooge, King Lear, Ivan Ilyich, and all those other sadly drooped patriarchs of the freshmen's literature course. As Roth puts it: 'Not too many years ago, there was a ready-made way to be old, just as there was a ready-made way to be young. Neither obtains any longer.' Add the blue pill and literature's a whole new ball game, my old cock.

East of Eden, John Steinbeck, 1952

Steinbeck's novel (his 'first novel', he grandly called it, although it was his nineteenth to see print) was the recipient of three lucky breaks: (1) ten years after it was published, Steinbeck won the Nobel Prize; (2) a popular film version was produced in 1955, starring James Dean – whose death-cult kept the title alive; (3) Oprah Winfrey chose it as a lead title for her book club in 2003, shooting it to the top of the *New York Times* bestseller list. The wider reading public has always preferred Ms Winfrey's sage critical opinion to that of the *New York Review of Books*, which sniffily dismissed *East of Eden* as 'bloated, pretentious, and uncertain... a wretched and meretricious book'. In fact it's a book well worth the effort of visiting or returning to. If nothing else it's the most ambitious work the author attempted – and nearly pulled off, in my judgement. One admires the literary pluck.

The time span covers the period from the American Civil War to the First World War and the book is set mainly in the Salinas Valley, lyrically evoked, where Steinbeck himself was brought up. A shadowy narrator – Mr John Steinbeck, we presume – steps forward to pontificate in a series of 'interchapters'. These innovatory (for Steinbeck) features allow him to preach. He enjoys the authority of the pulpit. At the heart of the novel are the sixteen morally ambiguous verses in Genesis that recount the fratricidal story of Cain and Abel. Steinbeck's opening 'genesis' section chronicles the story of two half-brothers, Adam and Charles Trask. 'A' and 'C' (Steinbeck never lays on the allegory with a light hand) grow up close, but different in character, on the family farm in the east of America. They are divided for ever by the irruption into their lives of Cathy Ames, an artful Jezebel possessed of a 'malformed soul'. 'I believe,' the narrator informs us, 'that there are monsters born to human parents.' Her monstrosities are closely recorded and survive in the reader's mind as the most interesting parts of the novel. Having nonchalantly locked her parents in the family house and set fire to it – first stuffing her bags with what valuables she can find – Cathy finds her vocation in a brothel. She traps goodly Adam into marriage, drugs him on the wedding night, and sleeps instead with less goodly Charles. Enriched by a mysterious (and certainly criminal) legacy from their father, Adam goes west with his bride to farm in Edenic Salinas. Charles stays in the east, seething with fraternal guilt. Cathy sleeps with Adam once only, for duping purposes, and nine months later bears twins – Charles offspring – Aron and Cal. She then shoots Adam ('you're a fool', she tells him, bluntly) and takes off to become a prostitute in Salinas. Things, thereafter, get very complex indeed.

The novel climaxes with Cal's futile attempt to win Adam's blessing by speculating on cash crops for the army during the war. His father objects, on the grounds that it is blood money. Cathy, having killed a few more people and comprehensively wrecked the Trask family, and already crippled with syphilitic arthritis, poisons herself. Aron goes off to war, to die (he succeeds), his belief in things wholly destroyed by a vengeful Cal. Adam, worn out by it all, gives up the ghost, tended to the end by his faithful 'Chink' friend and adviser Lee (there is a lot of racism in the novel, including promiscuous use of the N–word, which Oprah's advisers clearly did not tell her about). His last, feeble, utterance before he closes his eyes for ever is to forgive Caleb with the word '*Timshel*', Hebrew for 'thou mayest'. The novel is Steinbeck reaching out as far as he can as a novelist. It was clearly much admired in Sweden.

'East of Eden' is a biblical quotation: 'Cain went out from the presence of the LORD, and dwelt in the land of Nod, on the east of Eden.' Steinbeck wisely chose not to call his novel *The Land of Nod*.

L'Éducation sentimentale, Gustave Flaubert, 1869

Read it, and then turn to the simultaneously published MIDDLEMARCH. The channel dividing us may be only twenty-one miles wide and nowadays swimming it an unremarkable athletic feat. But it's a million miles and a different planet where Second

Empire French and Victorian English sexual attitudes are concerned. The common translation, *Sentimental Education*, hits a clangingly false note. There is nothing 'sentimental' – in the *Brief Encounter*, thundering Rachmaninov, English sense – about Flaubert's novel. The action opens in the years just before the Second Empire on a steamer leaving Paris. The youthful Frédéric Moreau sees a married woman standing on the first-class deck and – on the spot – falls in love with her as the city, bathed in autumnal morning light, drifts away:

> What he then saw was like an apparition. . . she wore a wide straw hat with red ribbons which fluttered in the wind behind her. Her black tresses, twining around the edges of her large brows, descended very low, and seemed amorously to press the oval of her face.

That one, transient image will deform the whole course of Frédéric's life. This is, he learns, Madame Arnoux – the wife of a fine-artwork publisher, and a mother. In his home town of Nogent, Frédéric's inseparable friend is Charles Deslauriers. The two young men resolve to go into law – Charles with far fewer social advantages to help him on his way.

On his return to his studies at the Sorbonne Frédéric sets out to win (i.e. seduce) Madame Arnoux. It's never clear whether lust or idolatry is driving him. The law is of not the slightest interest to him: he blithely fails his exams. Unexpectedly, he inherits a large fortune. With money in his pocket, he now 'counts' in Parisian society. The revolution of 1848 is brewing somewhere in the background but Frédéric pays as little attention to that as to his law lectures. His blood will not run in the gutters. He takes to art in a dilettante way and, in the bohemian way, takes a mistress, Rosanette, who shares her favours with Arnoux. A double cuckolding in prospect.

In Nogent, there is the prospect of Frédéric's marrying a rich young woman of lower social standing, Louise. Monsieur Arnoux, whose 'industrial art' business teeters on bankruptcy, is drawn to the young man with money like a fly to a honey jar. But his wife remains resistant to Frédéric's advances. Rosanette, by contrast, is wholly unresistant. Frédéric fights a duel (comically unbloody) to defend his true love's honour when it is impugned during a drunken evening out with other fashionable layabouts. A stab at political life comes to nothing. He takes yet another mistress, the wife of a banker, Dambreuse, who was haughty to him in his days of Parisian poverty. Revenge between the sheets is sweet. When she is widowed he toys with the idea of marrying her until he discovers she has been left nothing. Frédéric Moreau is an idealist about one woman only.

Rosanette becomes pregnant by him but, simultaneously, Madame Arnoux seems – at last – available: she and her husband are bankrupt. Frédéric's child dies (without any of the lachrymosity one would expect in English fiction of the period). Several years go by. Madame Arnoux visits him. Consummation at last? No. When she removes her hat, Frédéric sees that her hair is grey. He loses interest, she leaves. For ever. At the end of the novel Frédéric and Charles – who have lived life to the full – ask themselves when they were happiest. It was the summer of 1837 when, aged fifteen, they made themselves smart, picked some bouquets of flowers and presented themselves at the local brothel in Nogent. 'All the girls burst out laughing' and the two young bashfuls ran away. 'That was the best time we ever had', they agree. It's hard to imagine George Eliot's Will Ladislaw and Fred Vincy coming to the same conclusion about their first visit to a house of ill-repute, assuming such a thing could be allowed to exist in MIDDLE-MARCH.

Edwin Drood, Charles Dickens, 1870

You haven't read it? Don't fret. No one has – at least, not in its finished, Dickensian form. Boz's last novel is the 'Fermat's Last Theorem' of fiction – the equivalent to that fiendish problem the great seventeenth-century mathematician left for posterity to solve. If they could. The full title is *The Mystery of Edwin Drood*. 'Mystery' is the key word; *Drood* is a 'whodunnit?' But, in what follows here, there's no need to insert a spoiler alert. Since Dickens died halfway through writing it, and kept his cards very close to his waistcoat (he loved fancy waistcoats), we can only speculate what denouement he had in mind. The action opens in, of all places, a London opium den where a man, surrounded by sleeping addicts and lascars, is hazily coming round. He is, we immediately register, not one of the scum who are the regulars of Princess Puffer's evil garret, but a 'gentleman'. A clergyman, no less – and, as the world believes, an eminently respectable man of the cloth. John Jasper is the precentor (choirmaster) at Cloisterham Cathedral. It's recognisably Rochester Cathedral, just down the road from the fine house Dickens lived in, Gad's Hill Place. Dickens apologises, in the novel, for the pseudonym – but it's understandable. The authorities in the place where he himself worshipped on a Sunday might not have appreciated the world being told they were in the habit of appointing junkies to lead the choir.

Dickens liked teasingly complex plots in his late career and none is more complex than *Drood*. But at its centre is a familiar crime scenario involving sex, money, and homicide. Jasper, we learn, is uncle and guardian to an orphaned young man coming into his majority (twenty-one years). This young man is Edwin Drood, and he has what Dickens elsewhere calls 'great expectations' – a substantial cash inheritance. But there is a catch. He will (as their respective parents agreed before they died) only inherit if he marries another orphan, Rosa Bud. Jasper secretly lusts after Rosa, who is still at school in Cloisterham, under his tutorship. The name 'Rosa Bud' (her nicknames are 'Pussy' and 'Rosebud') is straight from the pages of Victorian pornography – as gentleman readers of the time would chortlingly have realised. The plot is thickened by the arrival of twins, Neville and Helena Landless, who have come from Ceylon to finish their education at Cloisterham. They may, or may not, be of mixed race. Ever since the Indian Mutiny of 1857 – in which he favoured the mass execution of the rebels by tying them to the mouths of cannons and blowing them to pieces – Dickens had had mixed feelings about the sub-continent.

Edwin goes missing after a violent storm.

The male twin, Neville, is suspected by the police of having killed him – he, too, has designs on Rosa. Jasper is suspected by the reader, who knows, as the police do not, about his opium habit. But since Dickens inconveniently died at this point in the narrative, we can't get beyond suspicion. *Drood* remains a mystery wreathed in mystery. How did Dickens intend it to end? He hinted to his future biographer, John Forster, that Jasper killed his nephew, and buried the body in the crypt of the cathedral, the easier to have his filthy way with Rosa. A mysterious character, Dick Datchery, makes an appearance in the last chapters we have. He is clearly someone in disguise – but who? Edwin? The truth is, we'll never know. But perhaps our great-great-grandchildren may. It took mathematicians 358 years to crack Fermat's Last Theorem. Which means we (they) can expect a solution to the *Drood* conundrum in 2228.

Elective Affinities, Johann Wolfgang von Goethe, 1809

This is not a novel which, on the face of it, has much going for it in the readability stakes. Written by a scholar more interested in chromatics than novels, it has a title whose meaning could be one of the tougher questions on *University Challenge*. The German is even more of a mouthful: *Wahlverwandtschaften*. There's a nice surprise, however, for anyone who clambers through the titular barbed wire. What follows is a lucid, crystalline novella which poses a teasing everyday question: why do we fall in love with some people and not others? What 'chemistry' is at work to create the sexual sympathies and antipathies which shape our lives?

Goethe's narrative is laid out with the simplicity of a fable and, at some points, a scientific formula. The Baron, Eduard, is a happy man. He has a fine castle and a beautiful wife, Charlotte. The Napoleonic Wars are raging somewhere but have not troubled the couple's quiet nook of Germany. Eduard was obliged, in his earlier life, to make a marriage of convenience to a superannuated rich woman who even more conveniently predeceased him. Charlotte, too, is now *en deuxièmes noces* and similarly happy. The story opens on a 'fine April morning' – Edenic perpetual spring is hinted at. Eduard has been occupied 'in his nursery-garden, budding the stems of some young trees with cuttings which had been recently sent to him'. His wife, meanwhile, has been planning a new summer house (the fourth) prettily set against an ornamental rock. Landscaping the estate will be of principal interest behind the drama to come. It expresses a feeling that the human species, in its present advanced condition, can make its own environment – no longer merely living as the inhabitant of its habitat. As the narrative puts it:

> Man is a true Narcissus; he delights
> to see his own image everywhere; and
> he spreads himself underneath the
> universe, like the amalgam behind the
> glass.

The couple's approaches to life are, however, different. She is intuitive and artistic, he is scientific and logical.

Eduard springs a surprise which serves to get the plot moving. He has invited a childhood friend, the Captain, currently down on his luck, for an indefinite visit. Happy as they are, he asks, must they be happy 'hermits'? Charlotte is wary but is overruled. There is another factor. It so happens than her niece Ottilie has been doing badly at boarding school. Although clever, she is strangely wayward. 'It is singular', her teacher reports, 'that Ottilie knows a great deal, and knows it well, too; and yet when she is asked a question, it seems as if she knew nothing.' Charlotte takes the ingénue under her wing.

The two newcomers are warmly received and the social arrangements are, initially, harmonious. The men happily continue the landscaping schemes together. But, inexorably, 'chemical' forces begin to complicate things. Life's test tube now has a new, ominously bubbling, mixture. Eduard is drawn to Ottilie, the Captain is drawn to Charlotte, Ottilie is drawn to the Baron. Is it adultery which is in prospect, or merely some new chemical 'compounding' of a purely innocent nature? The ending of the novel is powerful, teetering, as it does, just the right side of melodrama. The Baron and the Captain leave the estate – in an attempt to unmix the dangerous 'affinities' which are brewing. The women are left in residence at the castle. Divorce, it seems, is now the only solution, with the four parties making new partnerships.

In the background the park's symbolism becomes darker: a church and graveyard are despoiled in the name of 'art'. Charlotte has a child. Eduard looks at it and sees . . . what? The Captain's face. The novel which began so coolly ends in tragedy. Ottilie drowns Charlotte's baby in a boating accident. She is reconciled with the mother but herself dies of infection. Eduard pines and dies soon after. He decrees that his corpse shall be placed in contact with Ottilie's in the family vault and that no other human body should be interred there. A rather terrible chemical compound will happen, as their bodies decompose in unison. Together at last.

Emma, Jane Austen, 1816

Emma will, I suspect, be one of the most widely 'read it [or 'saw it'] already' found in this book. No need to summarise the mistakes, and the final salvation, of Miss Austen's match-making busybody – the heroine whom 'no-one but myself will much like' (but most of us do – even though Miss Woodhouse would, for a certainty, not like most of us). So well-worn are the standard 'readings' of *Emma* that the novel has an irresistible fascination for those who want to approach it from a perverse angle. To pick it up, so to speak, and shake it like a kaleidoscope. More so if, like me, you've marked a batch of A-level scripts all parroting the same weary staff-solution line. When I was doing my A-levels (at a period half a century closer to Jane Austen's world than now) one particular critical text was routinely hauled out for excoriation by my instructors. Namely Marvin Mudrick's ('These damned Americans!') monograph in which he proposed that there was manifestly inadmissible homo-erotic love between Emma and her protégée Harriet Smith. Lesbos at Hartfield. How we dutifully sneered. Such arguments became less sneerworthy as the decades rolled by, and with them a series of sexual revolutions. Nonetheless the Janeite hardcore constituency was slow to come round. A huge fuss was provoked by Terry Castle in 1995 when, under the *LRB* headline 'Was Jane Austen Gay?', she revisited the Mudrickian thesis that such things might, indeed, have been in the Highbury undergrowth. Or even the vicarages, dominated by women, in which Austen was brought up. Castle looked closely at the sleeping arrangements in Austen's family home – particularly the recorded fact that Jane and her sister Cassandra shared a bed. They 'slept with one another'. Not even the most loyal Janeite would query the fact that Cassandra (who, like her sister, remained unmarried) was the closest relation in Jane's life. The letters bear that out. Where, then, does Harriet Smith sleep at night, at Hartfield?

There are three large questions hovering over the narrative of *Emma*: one explicit, the others implied. Whom Emma will marry, is the first. The second is, why isn't she – an heiress and verging on twenty-one – married, like her sister Isabella, already? The third is, 'why on earth did she pick up with Harriet Smith – a young woman of no breeding (a tradesman's bastard), of no intelligence, no wit, no conversation?' All Miss Smith has is a doll like 'prettiness'. The point is forcefully made:

> She was a very pretty girl, and her beauty happened to be of a sort which Emma particularly admired. She was short, plump, and fair, with a fine bloom, blue eyes, light hair, regular features, and a look of great sweetness, and, before the end of the evening, Emma was as much pleased with her manners as her person, and quite determined to continue the acquaintance.

Harriet also recommends herself by her willingness to do anything (anything?) her patroness demands: even to the extent of giving up the man she loves, Robert Martin. Why? Because, as she says (it is the nearest she comes to eloquence in the novel), 'I would not give up the pleasure and honour of being intimate with you for any thing in the world.' Intimacy? Either we have to assume that, as one critic puts it, 'her characters have no sex at all', or we have to assume the sexuality is repressed and channelled in ways about which we can only speculate.

Mudrick and Castle were not the first to speculate. Charlotte Brontë noted in Austen's fiction a lack of interest in 'what throbs fast and full, though hidden, what the blood rushes through'. Edmund Wilson, in his 'A Long Talk about Jane Austen' (1944), instructed that Emma's putative lesbianism is 'something outside the picture which is never made explicit in the story but which has to be recognised by the reader before it is possible for him to appreciate the book'. That 'him' is slightly objectionable.

Empire of the Sun, J. G. Ballard, 1984

As everyone who has read the novel or seen the Spielberg film knows, *Empire of the Sun* relives its author's trauma as a young boy swept up by the Japanese capture of Shanghai at the outbreak of the Second World War, and his subsequent internment in the Lunghua airfield camp, outside the Chinese city. James Ballard's narrative, pitched ambiguously between autobiography and fiction, records the lost childhood of a lad variously nicknamed Jim and Jamie (the surname is never given – but is easy to supply). Jim is first discovered as one of the privileged foreign trading community living in Shanghai's 'concession' areas. The empires of Britain and Japan are at war, but Shanghai preserves an artificial cocoon of mercantile neutrality. Capitalism has its own rules.

After Pearl Harbor and all-out hostilities, Jamie is split up from his parents and camps out, living on cocktail snacks and soda water in the deserted mansions of the European quarter. He tries, without success, to give himself up to the Japanese, whom he admires intensely. (His abiding ambition, maintained throughout the hostilities which victimise him, is to become a Japanese combat pilot.) He passes under the wing of a series of more or less exploitative, deranged or uncaring adult guardians. 'In real war,' Jim realises, 'there were no enemies' – or friends. The camp, death and destruction become madhouse normality for him. Suffering bestows prophetic powers (the maimed seer is a recurring figure in Ballard's fiction): in visions of terrible incandescence, Jim foresees the American firebombing of Japan, the atomic destruction of Nagasaki, and – ultimately – World War Three.

In clinical terms, 'real' war fashions Jim into a psychopath. He has no normal 'human' responses to what is going on around him: patriotism, nationalism, even fellowship in misery with other prisoners are beyond his power to feel. In this null condition, he does not distinguish between Doctor Ransome, the noble Brownlow who self-sacrificingly protects him, and the Fagin-like American seaman, Basie, who loots his way through the course of the novel. (Jim first encounters Basie ripping gold teeth from Chinese corpses.) Jim somehow survives internment, death marches and a final bizarre episode with a bandit gang led by the indestructible Basie. Like the 500 million Chinese, he gets by because he has the advantage of knowing that he has always been half-dead. Jim's experience unrolls like montage in a strange newsreel: his parents, going to an eve-of-war fancy-dress party dressed as pierrot and pirate, their Packard crunching indifferently over a persistent beggar camped at their gate; three hundred hunchbacks, recruited by the management of the Cathay Theatre for the opening of Laughton's *Hunchback of Notre Dame*; children's coffins launched off Shanghai's funeral piers, always washed back to the mainland with the flowing tide, unable to leave China. This is the image with which Ballard chooses to end his novel. A routine tramride through peacetime Shanghai is a typically violent sideshow:

> Outside the tram station in the Avenue Haig the hundreds of passengers were briefly silent as they watched a public beheading. The bodies of a man and woman in quilted peasant clothes, perhaps pickpockets or Kuomintang spies, lay by the boarding platform. The Chinese NCOs wiped their boots as the blood ran

into the metal grooves of the steel rails.

In one of his many solitary spells, Jim comes across Lewis Carroll's *Through the Looking-Glass*. Its world seems enviably normal compared to his.

We are invited to accept *Empire of the Sun* as both cathartic and self-revealing. It tells us more about Ballard than the memoir, *Miracles of Life*, he wrote as he was dying from prostate cancer (stoically). This novel, which evidently rose like a slow bruise from Jim/Ballard's childhood, will always exercise a claim to be considered the best British novel of the Second World War. But admiration for the fineness of the novel merges into sympathetic pain at what it must have cost to be able to write it. Ballard later recorded: 'My mother never showed the slightest interest in my career until *Empire of the Sun*, which she thought was about her'.

The End of the Affair, Graham Greene, 1951

The word 'austerity' is much in vogue nowadays. Any Briton over the age of seventy (more of them graduate into that demographic bracket every year, I'm glad to say) will have already lived through what historians call 'The Age of Austerity' – roughly from Churchill's victorious two fingers in May 1945 to Macmillan's 'You've never had it so good' in 1957. Anyone under seventy interested in that first age of austerity should read the opening chapters of Greene's novel. It's a world of darned socks (not washed as often as they should be), turned collars on shirts worn for a week till 'wash day', everything one liked to eat 'on ration' or (for 'utility' clothing and furnishing) 'on coupons', fuel cuts, and long queues outside cinemas – the flicks being the only fun available. And often the only warm, if malodorous, place in town.

Greene's story opens with the declaration 'A story has no beginning or end'. But love affairs and marriages have endings. Lives too. The hero, Maurice Bendrix, an author living alongside Clapham Common (as did Greene, until his house was bombed in the

Blitz), goes out for a drink at the local – the Pontefract Arms (the pub is still there). Wars end, too, and the last one – the most cataclysmic in the history of mankind – had concluded seven months ago. Leaving the pub, walking down its 'war damaged' flight of outside steps (still there, now repaired), Bendrix encounters, standing in the rain under the 'black leafless trees', a man whom he had once cuckolded, Henry Miles. Miles is a stuffy civil servant. Probably his soul is pin-striped, bowler-hatted and brolly-carrying. Bendrix invites Miles back into the saloon bar for a drink. What's his poison? 'I wouldn't mind a whisky', says Miles. 'Nor would I', replies Bendrix wryly, 'but you'll have to make do with rum.' Making do was the norm in 1946 – as in 'make do and mend'.

The story unravels from this bleak encounter. Bendrix had originally taken up with Sarah Miles, Henry's wife, as 'research' for a character he had in mind for his novel in progress. They went on to have a passionate affair. The affair 'ends' (in a sense) in a doodle-bug raid in which the missile comes down on the house where they have been making love. Afterwards, for reasons Bendrix has never understood, Sarah broke off the relationship. Piqued by his encounter with Miles on the common, Bendrix employs a private detective to investigate. He is convinced that there must be a third man (that archetypal Greene character) somewhere.

The plot, revealed in Bendrix's stream of consciousness, fractured flashbacks and Sarah's diary, hinges on the peculiar character of the V1 pilotless 'buzz-bomb'. They were different from the manned bomber. The V1, a proto-cruise missile, had an unmistakable ram-jet 'buzz' and was programmed simply to cut out over London (and a few other major towns). It then fell – silently. For up to thirty seconds it was 'Do you feel lucky?' Bendrix and Sarah are unlucky. His body, in the rubble after the blast, seems to be lifeless under a fallen door. Sarah falls to her knees, and promises God that if He brings Maurice back to life she will break the seventh commandment no more. Bendrix 'miraculously' revives. An Act of God.

Sarah, a cradle Catholic, has – effectively – become a bride of Christ. She records in her diary: 'I've caught belief like a disease. I've fallen into belief a little like I fell in love'. She goes on in the novel, before catching another deadly disease (tuberculosis – like darned socks, a fact of pre-antibiotic 1946 life), to exhibit miraculous powers. She is, *in potentia*, a saint (fellow Catholics, like Evelyn Waugh, thought this last plotline 'mad', and Greene himself saw it in later life as a mistake). 'I am a jealous man', says Bendrix. But so too is God jealous. It was Frank Kermode who suggested that God is the 'fourth party' in this *ménage à quatre*. The lover who wins out.

Ender's Game, Orson Scott Card, 1985

In September 2012 there was a strange newcomer on the *New York Times* paperback bestseller list. In fact it wasn't a newcomer. *Ender's Game* was first published in short story form in 1977, then full-length in 1985. Twenty-seven-year-old novels rarely rise from the grave to become books of the day, and science fiction works almost never. The reason here was that a big-budget film was in production and, it was rumoured, would feature stars of Harrison Ford calibre. In point of fact, Card's novel has always sold strongly among two groups. Exceptionally gifted teenagers is one such group, and the US Marine Corps the other. *Ender's Game* has featured for years in the Corps's 'recommended reading' list given to all new recruits. I taught for a quarter of a century at the California Institute of Technology, one of the most elite schools of science in the world. It is the institution which (via its subsidiary the NASA Jet Propulsion Laboratory) successfully launched the Curiosity vehicle, which will be crawling round Mars for years to come. Caltech hosts a small body of undergraduates – around 1,000 in all (nearby UCLA has 26,000). You need to be in the top fifth percentile of the nationwide maths SATs even to qualify to apply to Caltech. It's an educational filter designed to trap what the outside world might see as precocious nerds. Teaching literature at Caltech was challenging – not least because one was dealing with classes whose average

IQ was double one's own. To work out what would appeal I ran regular questionnaires: (1) What authors are you reading?; (2) What is your favourite novel? Year-in, year-out the answers were: (1) Orson Scott Card; (2) *Ender's Game*. One doesn't need Freud to work out why. All that's required is to read the book.

Card's novel is set in the distant future. Earth is locked into a series of wars with an extra-galactic enemy – the 'buggers' (in the computer, not the sodomitic, sense), a 'Formic' culture which has the efficiency, and insectoid indifference to loss of individual life, of the ant colony. Earth has so far saved itself from destruction by the genius of its warrior leaders. Future war is analogous to the computer game. And who are the virtuosos of the game console? Kids. A military programme to raise 'genius' children has been put in place. The Wiggins family have three offspring. Peter is a genius, but sociopathic. He will go on in the novel, and its many sequels, to become a 'Hegemon' – a dictator. The sister, Valentine, is too soft and liberal (she will become a political force under the pseudonym 'Demosthenes'). Ender (the end child, birth name Andrew), by contrast, is just what the military-industrial complex needs to kick interplanetary butt. He is taken from the bosom of his family at six to be trained in 'Battle School'. He is conditioned to be absolutely lonely. That is what 'leadership' entails. At twelve, Ender commands the most powerful military force in history, with the expertise of Tommy the pinball wizard. At the end of the novel comes a big surprise – buggery is not what it seems.

Particularly in its opening chapters, *Ender's Game* allegorises the pathos of the gifted child. Society's practice of training such children like prize racehorses robs the little Enders of normal childhood and the adolescent Enders of the complex social and interpersonal lessons involved in 'growing up'. They are orchids and for them life is a constant hot-house. One can understand why Caltech students nod in assent. But why the USMC? For Enders 'winning' is not the best thing – it is the only thing. The first chapter describes the six-year-old hero being bullied at school by an older bigger boy. By skilled feints Ender fells his oppo-

nent. Then he walks over and 'kicks him in the crotch', killing him, as it turns out. He then goes on, calmly, to his next computer skills class (where, effortlessly, he is 'ace' pupil). That's how wars are won. Kick the buggers in the balls.

Enemies, a Love Story, Isaac Bashevis Singer, 1966

A Jewish novel, originally written in Yiddish and serialised in New York's *Jewish Daily Forward* newspaper (with an English translation published in 1972), this tale of love and genocide offers the gentile reader both enjoyment and a stimulating sense of literary gatecrashing. Singer's novel is set in 1949. The hero, Herman Broder, is a Holocaust survivor – or, more precisely, a Holocaust evader. He has lost his faith but it has not entirely lost him. He is by nature a Don Juan but no Apollo: 'Herman always woke up shabby and rumpled, looking as if he had spent the night wrestling.' Or copulating.

There are two women currently in Herman's life. One is Yadwiga, the woman (originally his maid) who hid him from the Nazis in a hayloft. She is Polish and a gentile. After the war he emigrated to America and passed her off as his wife which, it will later emerge, she was not. He works in New York as a speechwriter for a crooked rabbi, although to the world at large he pretends to be a travelling book salesman. This supplies ample opportunities for non-conjugal visits to his lover, Masha, who lives with her mother in the Bronx. She is a camp-survivor. Meanwhile Yadwiga, who cannot speak English, is housebound in their Coney Island apartment, under the huge, defunct Ferris wheel. Things are complicated beyond complexity when Herman's wife, Tamara, whom he thought dead in the camps, unexpectedly arrives in New York.

> This hysterical woman, who had tormented him and whom he had been about to divorce when the war broke out, had risen from the dead. He wanted to laugh. His metaphysical joker had played him a fatal trick.

He is, in effect, a trigamist. Herman's life is a tissue of deceit, evasion and escape from consequences. He is haunted by paranoid fantasies of jackbooted thugs coming for him. His women are his only friends: the rest of the world is his enemy.

The novel is an extended comedy of survivor's guilt. How do you live a good life in the presence of the historical fact of genocide? However far you flee, it is inescapable: 'The further removed they were from the holocaust, the closer it seemed to become.' Herman's life is finally simplified by a restored marriage with Tamara. But the ending is complicated by his disappearance from the narrative, leaving only his women present. Has he escaped again?

England, England, Julian Barnes, 1998

Contempt is not an ingredient much encountered in English fiction and, as the second millennium approached, contempt for England was an increasingly uneasy topic. What, precisely, was there to celebrate? Everyone with eyes in their head and a history book on their shelves knew there had been 'decline and fall' – lost an empire and not found a role, and so on. The Anglo-Saxons were no longer lords of creation. But there was a lingering sense of superiority – our unmatched 'heritage' was, surely, evidence of that. The 'heritage industry' (not to mention the 'Heritage Lottery Fund') would have been seen, in the years of Great Britain's true greatness, as stuff for Swiftian satire. Julian Barnes duly rose to the challenge.

A formidably knowing writer, his title has resonant echoes. D. H. Lawrence and George Orwell penned works called *England, My England* and 'England Your England', respectively. Lawrence's story centres on a market garden, a little Eden, which has supplied a family's needs for generations. The First World War breaks out. The owner of the garden despairingly throws away his life, fighting for an England he no longer believes in. The garden ('green and pleasant land') can be preserved no longer. It will be paved over. The story forecasts the theme of

Lawrence's last novel, LADY CHATTERLEY'S LOVER, and its *j'accuse* is that the great tree of life, 'Yggdrasil', is dead in England (Yggdrasil, incidentally, is an ash tree; enough said). Alluded to, ironically, in Lawrence's title is the full-throated Victorian anthem by W. E. Henley which opens:

WHAT have I done for you,
England, my England?
What is there I would not do,
England, my own?

Behind Henley is John of Gaunt's dying speech in *Richard II* ('This blessed plot, this earth, this realm, this England'). Football fans like Barnes would irreverently recall the war chant at international soccer matches: 'ENGERLAND! ENGERLAND!' Orwell, writing 'England Your England' as the German bombers flew overhead, felt there were indeed English things worth being blown to smithereens for, although his patriotism was more nuanced than Henley's.

Julian Barnes' *England, England* is, by contrast, a work of full-blooded, virtuoso Anglophobia by England's most distinguished literary Francophile. A financier-cum-newspaper tycoon (he owns *The Times*, the 'paper of record'), Sir Jack Pitman (transparently based on the seven-years-dead Sir Robert Maxwell), undertakes the creation of a theme-park England (half-size) on the Isle of Wight. Call it (although Barnes was careful not to annoy Disney's fearsome lawyers) 'Englandland'. Old England can't compete. A new royal couple, including the improbably named Queen Denise, move there to take up residence in a half-size Buckingham Palace. Samuel Johnson splutters ponderously, firing off his 'Sirs!' like musketballs. Battle of Britain pilots lounge in deckchairs waiting for the 'scramble' phone call. Pitman's England joins the EU, another synthetic construct. The tycoon's right-hand woman is fortyish Martha Cochrane – lower-middle-class, and ruthlessly careerist. Together they bring their project to fruition.

The novel is based on the conceit that England has nothing left but its 'heritage'. And Pitman's replica will be more real, more sanitary – above all more saleable – than the real thing. A French theorist is hired to give it philosophic sexiness:

It is important to understand that in the modern world we prefer the replica to the original because it gives us the greater *frisson*. I leave that word in French because I think you understand it well that way.

And, when push comes to shove, the English nation really can't be bothered with all the hassle of real things. Pitman's England is 'everything you imagined England to be, but more convenient, cleaner, friendlier, and more efficient'. He is finally brought down by turncoat Martha, who uses incriminating evidence of his strange doings in brothels. Having disposed of him, she retires to a hermit existence in 'Anglia' (mainland England), which has reverted to its antique 'Wessex' character. Thomas Hardy's *faux* England, that is.

Entropy, Thomas Pynchon, 1960

The academic George Levine once wrote an article describing how he had taken three months off from university teaching to read, in hermit-like isolation, Thomas Pynchon's magnum opus, *Gravity's Rainbow*. By which calculus five hundred novels – if reading as conscientious as Prof. Levine's lay behind them – would require a hundred or so years in the hermit's cave. Nonsense, of course. Most novels require hours, not months. Pynchon, though, is something else. Even his shortest novel, *The Crying of Lot 49*, is – to use the favoured euphemism – 'challenging' (i.e. like eating brazils without a nutcracker). What the notoriously incommunicative Pynchon is on about in his fiction is the stuff of 1,001 doctoral dissertations and pandemoniac conferences. But it's generally agreed that somewhere in the engine room of his novels are two energy sources: paranoia and entropy.

Paranoia is a wonderfully creative mental disorder. Everything, for the paranoiac, is narrative. A glance from a stranger indicates the CIA are hot on your trail. In Woolf's *Mrs Dalloway* the shell-shocked paranoiac Septimus Smith believes the pigeons in Regent's Park are talking to him (in Greek). In her paranoid state, Muriel Spark believed

that T. S. Eliot was sending her messages in his verse plays. He gravely wrote to reassure her that he wasn't.

Entropy, energy loss, is something else. When you start, say, a novel it winds down (losing energy) to its final page, like a pre-digital watch. Everything tends inexorably towards terminal equilibrium. Everything, put another way, breaks down. The entropic idea was popularised by Henry Adams and reformulated in a book influential on Thomas Pynchon, Norbert Wiener's book on cybernetics and society, *The Human Use of Human Beings*. What can rewind the clock? Paranoia. But paranoia is ultrafictional. Madness. At the beginning of *Gravity's Rainbow*, set in London in 1944, the hero is convinced that V2 rockets fall wherever and whenever he has an erection. Makes perfect sense. If you're paranoid. Pynchon laid out his cards in his early short story 'Entropy', first published in the *Kenyon Review* in 1960, and republished (after he became world famous) in 1984 in a collection called, self-disparagingly, *Slow Learner*. The story opens with an epigraph from Henry Miller, 'The Weather will not Change.' Paradoxically breaking weather – breaking everything ('disequilibrium') – will be the theme of the story.

In Manhattan, Meatball Mulligan is having a 'lease breaking party' fuelled by a plentiful intake of booze and dope. It is early February, and the weather is breaking. The party is in its fortieth hour and breaking up. Sandor Rojas – Hungarian freedom fighter and refugee virtuoso of Don Juanism, a serial heart-breaker – is one of the more prominent guests. A musical group, the Duke di Angelis Quartet, is also in attendance. The musical among the company discuss such topics as whether the Gerry Mulligan/Chet Baker quartet's dispensing with the piano is a breakthrough, or just a broken concept. A neighbour, Saul, who has just had an argument with his wife Miriam, breaks in through the window. Their argument, improbably, was about communication systems (another of Pynchon's hobbyhorses) and the 'disorganising' impacts of 'noise' (things coming in through windows) on circuits, breaking them down. It's 'sort of wet out', Saul reports.

The party breaks up into chaos. Five

sailors, on liberty leave, break in thinking the apartment is a 'hoorhouse'. A fight ensues. The refrigerator breaks down. Meatball contrives, temporarily, to cool things down. But the party will never return to what it was forty hours earlier – disequilibrium decrees that. Meanwhile, upstairs, a Princetonian graduate called Callisto has created what he fondly hopes is a 'closed system' – a hermetically sealed apartment, with his partner Aubade ('daybreak'). He clutches a dying bird to his chest, in the hope that 'heat transfer' will bring it back to life. It dies. Callisto breaks a window, and the inside and outside temperatures equalise at thirty-seven degrees (coincidentally the temperature of human blood in a living organism). The story ends. Or, put another way, having broken up, it winds down.

Esmé, Saki, 1911

Saki creates stories as compact and intricate as the movement of a jewelled Swiss watch, and as tart, in their brevity, as a drop of Angostura bitters. 'Esmé' (the title itself vibrates like a tuning fork) opens:

> 'All hunting stories are the same,' said Clovis; 'just as all Turf stories are the same, and all —'
> 'My hunting story isn't a bit like any you've ever heard,' said the Baroness. 'It happened quite a while ago, when I was about twenty-three. I wasn't living apart from my husband then; you see, neither of us could afford to make the other a separate allowance. In spite of everything that proverbs may say, poverty keeps together more homes than it breaks up. But we always hunted with different packs. All this has nothing to do with the story.'

At this particular meet her companion is Constance Broddle. Constance, the Baroness recalls, was 'one of those strapping florid girls that go so well with autumn scenery or Christmas decorations in church'. 'I feel a presentiment that something dreadful is going to happen,' she says to the Baroness before the hunt sets off, 'am I looking pale?'

She is, thinks her companion, 'looking about as pale as a beetroot that has suddenly heard bad news'.

There ensues a stiff run. The two women, now separated from the field, come across something which is certainly no mortal fox. 'It stood more than twice as high, had a short, ugly head, and an enormous thick neck'. A stray from the Baskerville estate, perhaps? '"It's a hyaena," I cried; "it must have escaped from Lord Pabham's Park."' The beast attaches itself, affectionately, to the two ladies. They christen it 'Esmé', because they don't know its sex and are disinclined to physically ascertain the fact. Now trailing the hunt by miles they pass some caravans. Esmé, keen to impress, picks up a 'half naked gipsy brat' and brings it back, wailing between its jaws, as a trophy for its new friends. When it is clear they do not want it, Esmé bounds 'into some thick bushes, where we could not follow; the wail rose to a shriek and then stopped altogether'. Constance goes the colour of an 'albino beetroot' and feebly asks, 'Do you think the poor little thing suffered much?' 'The indications were all that way,' replies the Baroness blandly.

They are now on the high road, Esmé padding behind. A car, driving at reckless speed, runs into the beast and kills it – sparing the ladies some tricky explanations to the Master of Hounds. The owner of the vehicle is frightfully apologetic. It was a prize animal, the Baroness sternly informs him. It won the puppy prize at Birmingham the year before. He helps bury Esmé and offers 'reparation'. The Baroness refuses but ensures he has taken her address.

> 'There was a sequel to the adventure, though. I got through the post a charming little diamond brooch, with the name Esmé set in a sprig of rosemary. Incidentally, too, I lost the friendship of Constance Broddle. You see, when I sold the brooch I quite properly refused to give her any share of the proceeds. I pointed out that the Esmé part of the affair was my own invention, and the hyaena part of it belonged to Lord Pabham, if it really was his hyaena, of which, of course, I've no proof.'

It is, as the Baroness says, an 'unusual' hunting story.

Saki, as his first readers would have realised, was poking fun at Lord Rothschild's (here 'Lord Pabham') estate at Tring – England's first wild animal park, where hyenas and other exotic animal life roamed free. It was first opened to the public in 1892. Lord Rothschild himself was often seen riding round his estate in a zebra-drawn carriage. Saki, one feels, could have made something of that.

Ethan Frome, Edith Wharton, 1911

Wharton's tale of love in a very cold climate is a New England *Wuthering Heights*. There is also, one must confess, a touch of COLD COMFORT FARM in this tale of 'Ethan Frome of Starkfield' (Seth Starkadder comes irresistibly to mind). Wharton was not, like Yorkshire through-and-through Emily Brontë, *of* the world she described. She was cosmopolitan, a Francophile, and a creator of magnificent country house gardens. This 'anecdote in 45,000 words', as she called it, is the work of a thoughtful and sensitive observer.

The West Massachusetts town of Starkfield has been left behind. Urbanisation, the great migrations, and above all the railway have pushed it to the side of America. 'Most of the smart ones get away', a local glumly observes. The narrator, unnamed, described as an 'engineer', has come to Starkfield as an agent of 'progress'. To do what is not clear – possibly to help bring in a trolley (i.e. tram) transport system for the town – which still runs on horsepower. The story opens:

> I had the story, bit by bit, from various people, and, as generally happens in such cases, each time it was a different story. If you know Starkfield, Massachusetts, you know the post-office. If you know the post-office you must have seen Ethan Frome drive up to it, drop the reins on his hollow-backed bay and drag himself across the brick pavement to the white colonnade: and you must have asked who he was.

In the house where he is lodging the narrator hears references to a mysterious 'smash up' in Frome's life, twenty-odd years ago. Frome now ekes a penurious living with his obsolete water-driven saw timber mill. The engineer hires Ethan to drive him around – it being deep winter and there being no work on the farm till spring. During a savage snow storm (this is very much a novel about weather) he is forced to stay overnight in the Fromes' run-down house. He hears two women angrily quarrelling upstairs.

At this point the story abruptly jumps back to the 'smash-up', in third-person narration. Ethan, we learn, almost 'got away'. He was enrolled as a student at a technology college. But his father's death pulled him back, after a year's study, to the family sawmill. He married a woman seven years older than he, Zenobia ('Zeena') Silver. There are no children. Zeena, after a year, turned into a chronic hypochondriac ('what Starkfield called "sickly"') whose one pleasure in life was to maltreat her husband. There was a third member of the Frome household, an orphaned relative of Zeena's. Mattie Silver was young, pretty, vivacious, and penniless. In return for bed and board she did the housework that Zeena claimed to be too ill to do. Ethan fell in love with their young lodger. Zeena, no fool, noticed. Why else would Ethan shave every day? She schemed to get rid of Mattie.

Ethan was paralysed between love and duty. He sadly acquiesced to his wife's scheme but insisted, at the very least, on driving Mattie to the station. On the way they kissed for the first time and stopped for a 'coast', a sleigh ride, which – as they hurtled down the steep hillside – allowed them at last to embrace. After the first run Mattie suggested that they do it once more, killing themselves by smashing into the elm tree at the bottom of the run. It was to be like Romeo and Juliet – *Liebestod*. But as with Shakespeare's star-crossed lovers, it went horribly wrong. She broke her spine, he pulverised a leg.

The story jumps forward to the present. The two women the narrator hears arguing are Zeena and Mattie, now grey-haired crones. Zeena it is who now, a hypochondriac no more, cares for the paraplegic Mattie. Ethan has two shrews under his roof – for as long as he can keep a roof over their heads. Who is to blame for this domestic tragedy? The flighty Mattie with her suicidal romanticism? The would-be adulterous Ethan? Or the vindictive wife Zeena? None of them. Starkfield is the villain. The smart ones get away.

Ever After, Graham Swift, 1992

Swift – a worthy Booker winner – has published nothing undistinguished. This could be judged his best work, I think, but perhaps because the hero is one of my profession and the novel delicately probes the perennial angst of the professor's career. Be warned, it is not, if you're new to it, a 'happy ever after' novel. The narrative opens with a fifty-two-year-old don convalescing in an Oxford college garden. 'These are, I should warn you, the words of a dead man', we are bleakly informed. It is summer: he is in a chair with a blanket over his knees. Corpse-cold. Bill Unwin hates his 'dodo' profession (when so many other species are extinct, why has dodo-academicus, aka 'the greater pointy-headed professor' survived, he wonders). What he is convalescing from we shall not learn until the last chapter, although the frequent references to *Hamlet* are a broad hint.

What emerges from the narrative he is scrawling on a pad is a history of his doomed family and, in the background to that, a chronicle of the collective death of religious belief in England. Three people close to him have died over the last year and a half: his mother, his wife Ruth and his American stepfather, Sam, a businessman who made an obscenely large fortune in plastics. Bill hates the commercial world, even though it has endowed the fellowship he unprofitably occupies. His wife Ruth – an internationally famous actress – fell a premature victim to lung cancer. They first met when he worked, as a holiday job, in a smoky Soho club in the 1950s. Bill's mother died of cancer of the larynx. It was a cruel affliction. She had been a 'gifted' singer.

The casualty list continues. Going decades back, his father, a serving army officer, committed suicide in Paris in 1946 – because, Bill has been given to believe, he had been cuckolded by the young American plastic merchant who later became his stepfather. With his mother's death, a packet of his great-grandfather's notebooks have come into Bill's possession. He intends to edit and publish them. His ancestor, Matthew Pearce, was a geologist and surveyor who worked alongside Isambard Kingdom Brunel building the great Saltash Bridge, in 1855. The bridge was majestic, but financially it was a disaster and precipitated Brunel's early death. The event coincided with Matthew's spiritual crisis. On the West Country cliffs, he came face to face with a prehistoric 'icthyosaurus' (i.e. its skull and skeleton – fleshed out by his imagination):

> The long, toothed jaw; the massive eye that stares through millions of years. He is the creature; the creature is him. He feels something open up inside him. . . and feels himself starting to fall, and fall, through himself. He lurches on to the path, as if outward movement will stop the inward falling. . . as if to stop himself falling he must get to sea level.

The vision converted him (a clergyman's son) to Darwinism some years before Darwin. He took off alone for the New World, only to be drowned en route.

Finally the truth emerges about Bill's own father. He did not kill himself for love, or out of mortification at his wife's betrayal, but because he was deep into murky dealings, between Britain and America, on the development of Weapons of Mass Destruction – i.e. the extermination of the human species. His suicide was an act of 'ideological anguish'. A series of yet more twists and discoveries lead Bill to an attempted suicide. It fails. But he is, nonetheless, 'a dead man'. It's a beautifully morbid novel.

The Exorcist, William Peter Blatty, 1971

Everyone read it once upon a time – shuddering as their predecessors Catherine Morland and Isabella Thorpe did over *The*

Mysteries of Udolpho. Fewer, I think, read it now. And those who do, don't much shudder. I've even seen the film, about which there was a huge moral panic when it hit the screen in 1973, shown on network TV before the watershed. *Autre temps, autre moeurs*. Blatty's *The Exorcist* was one of the pioneer 'frighteners' of the 1970s, with 'demoniac' children as their gimmick. Others were *The Omen*, *The Fury*, *Carrie* and *The Shining*. They dominated the bestseller lists and converted, profitably, into movies – often with distinguished directors (William Friedkin, Stanley Kubrick, John Carpenter, Brian de Palma). *The Exorcist* is the best of the bunch, and well worth a quick read. Smelling salts will not be required.

The kernel idea, the 'germ' as Henry James would have called it, can be traced back to James' own *The Turn of the Screw* and diabolic little Miles and Flora. Blatty's plot is simple, but the screw is turned very artfully. Eleven-year-old Regan MacNeil is the daughter of an actress single mother, Chris. They live in Washington DC. Regan, a model 'A-student', begins to behave strangely. The usual remedies and therapies (counselling, medications) do not work. Regan continues to decline into someone ugly, violent, and, ultimately, demonic. She is 'possessed'; unspeakable things are done with body parts and crucifixes. Finally a driven-to-distraction Chris is advised to turn – where else? – to Mother Church. She consults Jesuit priest and psychiatrist Damien Karras (a man haunted by apparitions of his dead mother, whom his vocation forced him to neglect), who summons 'the exorcist', Lankester Merrin. After a gruelling ceremony Damien sacrifices himself to lure the demon (Satan himself?) out of Regan's body, plummeting to his death through a window. The demon is defenestrated with him.

One of the reasons for the runaway success of *The Exorcist*, and a clutch of novels like it, was that it centred on situations familiar to families with young children – the desperate parent who, despite having followed Dr Benjamin Spock to the letter, just doesn't know what to do. Take, for example, the description of Chris in the psychiatrist's office, early in the narrative:

For a time, no one spoke. Chris was on the sofa. Klein and the psychiatrist sat near her in facing chairs. The psychiatrist was pensive, pinching at his lip as he stared at the coffee table; then he sighed and looked up at Chris. She turned her burned-out gaze to his. 'What the hell's going on?' she asked in a mournful, haggard whisper.

Out of context this could be an everyday 'parent worried about daughter's progress' scene. In fact, Regan has just been speaking in tongues, has psychokinetically lowered the temperature of the room to sub-freezing, and is exuding an overpowering smell of corpse. Doubtless worried parents in colonial Salem faced the same problems and came up with their own radical cures.

Eye in the Sky, Philip K. Dick, 1957

During his all-too-brief lifetime (1928–82) Dick shot out science-fiction novels at machine-gun speed. This is not uncommon with genre writers. What made Dick uncommon was the extraordinary inventiveness of his scenarios. A price was paid, however, and his plot work is typically chaotic. *Eye in the Sky* is early Dick and should be read for two reasons. The first is its sheer readability. It is, for this writer, singularly well plotted. Secondly, early as it is, *Eye in the Sky* distils what one could call the 'Attar of Dickism'. Dick's fictional universes are permeated with the paranoid sense that one is not in one's own reality. Or even one's own universe.

Eye in the Sky opens in the near-present for Dick – 1959. The paranoid theme is clued by the fact that Richard Nixon, the evil puppetmaster, is in the White House (Nixon did not in fact win the presidency until 1968 – well prophesied, Dick). A scientist, Jack Hamilton, has been working at the California missile maintenance labs for ten years, helping design the ICBMs that will, quite likely, destroy the planet. He is summoned into the top office, where he is informed that FBI monitoring has determined that his wife

Marsha is a security risk. She has signed a petition and reads 'liberal' newspapers. Lose the wife or the job, Jack is bluntly told. Nixon may be in the White House but witch-hunting Joe McCarthy is ruling the roost. Jack walks out and takes the day off to tour, along with Marsha and a party of six other sight-seers, the new particle accelerator – the Beva-tron at Belmont (i.e. the Cyclotron at Berkeley). They are conducted by a tour guide, Bill Laws, a brilliant Physics PhD who happens to be black and can't get a job worthy of his mind because, when employers discover his ethnicity, 'the job is always "filled"'. The platform they are all standing on collapses, and they are irradiated by six billion volts of proton energy.

Jack wakes to find himself in a familiar, but strange world. He and all the others are now inhabiting a universe constructed by the rabid thought waves of a right-wing racist religious bigot among their zapped company. In this world priests have a hotline to God – a gigantic eye in the sky. Divine punishment for dereliction is quick – either a wilderness of scorpions (if the sinner is lucky) or the lightning bolt. Old Testament rules apply. Tell a lie and a swarm of locusts gives you half an hour's hell. Curse and a bee stings your backside. Car mechanics repair cars by reciting their skilled prayers over the offending engine. The 'negro', Laws, is deformed into a shuf-fling 'Amos and Andy' caricature of his race. Hamilton himself nearly gets the light-ning-bolt treatment as a suspected 'nigger lover'.

The narrative then switches to another universe, created by the mind of a prim old maid (another unlucky visitor to the accel-erator) who has 'abolished' sex (no one has genitalia any more) and everything else that vexes her:

Garbage men who rattled cans. Door-to-door salesmen. Bills and tax forms of all kinds. Crying babies (perhaps *all* babies). Drunks. Filth. Poverty. Suffering in general.
It was a wonder anything was left.

There follows the Piranesi-like world of a full-blown paranoiac, and that of a Reds-under-the-bed Marxist. These alternative states of being are spun out of the minds of the half-dozen irradiated visitors to the Bevatron, as they lie, like cooked kippers, on the accel-erator floor. When they regain consciousness in the 'real world', a chastened Hamilton and Laws defect from the field of advanced weapons technology and devote their scien-tific skills to the making of more advanced hi-fi equipment. The hippy universe beckons.

What *Eye in the Sky* intimates is that each of us carries in our head our personal Utopia, which quite likely would be any other person's dystopia. Hell, declared Sartre, is other people. For Dick it's what goes on in other people's minds. Whose mind-constructed universe would you want to live in: Richard Nixon's? Mrs Thatcher's? Jimmy Savile's? Philip K. Dick's? None, for a certainty, but your own. Call it Planet Solipsis.

The Eyre Affair, Jasper Fforde, 2001

Jasper Fforde has gone where no fictioneer has gone before. Millions of readers now follow. After its legendary seventy-six rejec-tions, *The Eyre Affair* went on to become a cult bestseller inspiring a string of formu-laic sequels: *Lost in a Good Book*, *The Well of Lost Plots* and *First Among Sequels*. All feature the 'literary detective and registered dodo owner', the pride of Swindon town ('Jewel of the M4'), Thursday Next. Think *Dragnet*'s Joe Friday; think Chesterton's *The Man Who Was Thursday*. Think excruciating puns and heavy-handed allusion – funnier because both we and the author know it's heavy-handed ('geddit?'). Fforde is addicted to literary in-jokes ('up-themselves' jokes, one might call them) and lays them down on the reader like a First World War artillery barrage. In his literary fantasias Fforde employs two basic plot devices. One is the 'Alternative Universe' scenario, pioneered by Philip K. Dick in the 1950s. In Dick's *The Man in the High Castle* there are parallel worlds. In one world (our world) America won the Second World War; in the other world Germany and Japan won. The hero slips between these two universes. In Fforde's novels, Thursday Next's father is a

'ChronoGuard' – a time-cop – entrusted with keeping a multitude of parallel universes straight. He and his comrades have not been entirely successful. In fact they've been downright sloppy. Thursday inhabits a 1985 in which the Crimean War is still raging. She herself is a veteran of the doomed charge of the Light Brigade into the valley of Death.

Fforde's other gimmick is that the world of fiction and the real world ('outland') run into each other. Thursday's uncle Mycroft (occasional interloper into the adventures of Sherlock Holmes) has invented a 'Prose Portal' – a kind of literary TARDIS. Characters such as Edward Rochester or Miss Havisham come out; detectives like Thursday go in. The multi-volume story chronicles an extended duel between Thursday and her Moriarty (in fact her former English teacher – those damned A-levels again), Acheron Hades. Another sworn enemy is Jack Schitt, head honcho of the Goliath Corporation, which owns everything. Thursday resourcefully contrives to trap Schitt in Poe's 'The Raven', from whose textual depths he croaks out furious memoranda to his minions, all ending 'Nevermore!' In The Well of Lost Plots, Thursday (now pregnant by her husband, who has gone missing and has mysteriously slipped her memory) goes on the run from the real world into the magma of fiction, where all its vague primal inspirations reside: the id of literature. The well is under the jurisdiction of JurisFiction, an agency with responsibility for keeping the genre shipshape. The usual jokes are present in (over)abundance. Among the best is a JurisFiction Rage Counselling Session in which the characters in Wuthering Heights work, twelve-steps style, through their joint hatred of Heathcliff. A routine task for JurisFiction is to shift books around, so as to keep up with cultural climate change: 'The subgenre of Literary Smut has finally been disbanded,' Thursday learns in one Ffordian opus, 'with Fanny Hill and Moll Flanders being transferred to Racy Novel and Lady Chatterley's Lover to Human Drama.' More complicated are the dry-dock 'refits' which great novels constantly need if they are to be kept readworthy. One is particularly tricky. 'Even the biggest refit', one JurisFiction mechanic complains, 'never took more than a week but John Fowles' The Magus has been in for five.' The fitters 'removed all the plot elements for cleaning and no one can remember how they go back together again'. 'I'm not sure it will make a difference,' Thursday mutters.

One of the woes of being a literary critic is that novelists habitually ignore you. 'Lice on the locks of literature', and all that. Vain as it may be, I think that Fforde has noticed me. In my literary puzzle book, Is Heathcliff a Murderer? (one for the JurisFiction agency), I devoted a chapter to pondering how Jane Eyre managed to hear Rochester exclaim 'Jane! Jane! Jane!' at Thornfield Hall, when she was miles away. All is explained in The Eyre Affair. Thursday, wanting to revise Brontë's original ending in which Jane ends up with 'drippy' St John Rivers, crept up to Jane's window and imitated Rochester's bellowing voice. Result: the ending we all know and love. Elementary, dear professor.

Fair Stood the Wind for France, H. E. Bates, 1944

Bates was a serving officer in the RAF at the time this, his best and best-known novel, was published. It evokes the mood of the time so powerfully that one is tempted to start burrowing for one's gas mask. On the old side for active service (he was born in 1905) but with an established reputation as a popular writer (particularly of 'country tales'), he had been recruited and commissioned specifically to write morale-raising fiction – his way of doing his 'bit'. A series of short stories of service life under the pseudonym of 'Flying Officer X' was a great hit, leading the way to this full-length military romance. The title comes from the first line of 'Agincourt', a poem by Elizabethan poet Michael Drayton. The more familiar evocation is Henry V (in 1944 Lawrence Olivier, similarly smiled on by the War Department, was making his Technicolor film of Shakespeare's play).

A Wellington bomber under the command of Captain John Franklin is hit and forced to crash land in France. Bates was careful not to make the unlucky mission one of the '1,000 bomber' RAF raids that were still, in 1944, slaughtering hundreds of thousands of German civilians. This was not something the War Department wanted to publicise. Captain Franklin, having done the requisite number of combat flights, is nearing the end of his 'tour'. The bomber's crew, Franklin and four sergeants, survive the crash and, after walking for a day through fields, they are taken in by a mill-owner's family, who are sympathetic to the Resistance and conceal them in an upstairs bedroom. The plan is for them to make their way to neutral Spain. But Franklin's arm has been badly injured and a friendly doctor prescribes rest. His comrades fear betrayal – and as there are five of them, detection is probable: Germans constantly patrol the area. Fake documents are procured and the crew, less Franklin, leave.

He remains behind to be nursed by the mill-owner's daughter, the inevitably beautiful Françoise. And, inevitably, they fall in love during the long summer days and nights (Bates, the spinner of country tales, romanticises wildly at this point – but why not? There wasn't much to romanticise about in 1944). Franklin has a 'best girl', Diana, back in England – but the heart has its reasons. Françoise decides to accompany him, by bicycle and boat, to Marseilles (Vichy-controlled, and less dangerous) after her father commits suicide. In Marseilles they meet up with one of the flight crew, O'Connor, who sacrifices himself for his skipper and his new love. The couple make good their escape over the Pyrenees to safety.

Fair Stood the Wind for France is a cunning mixture of warm romance and hard-headed propaganda. It remains enjoyably readable for the rural description which was always Bates' strong suit. (After the war he would gain immense popularity following the television adaptation of The Darling Buds of May.) The propaganda element lay in the way the novel distracted attention from the brutal, and morally dubious, British 'terror bombing' of the civilian German population. An uneasy conscience on that topic delayed until 2012 the erection of any post-war monument to the 55,573 Franklins who lost their lives in Bomber Command (see BOMBER).

Following the success of Fair Stood the Wind for France Bates was commissioned by the Air Ministry to write a quick novel about the V1 and V2 rocket assault on Britain. After various disagreements, the author no longer being willing to toe the propaganda line, the manuscript was shelved and was not printed until 1994. There is other fiction by Bates, apparently, still kept in cold storage for 'security' reasons.

The Family Fang, Kevin Wilson, 2011

Wilson's novel ponders, fascinatingly, what one could call the 'Elizabeth Siddal conundrum'. Siddal – Dante Gabriel Rosetti's lover, Pre-Raphaelite Brotherhood muse and stunningly beautiful model – posed for Millais' acclaimed picture of the flower-bedecked Ophelia drowning. 'Posing' meant floating, day after day, in a tin bath heated, inadequately, by candles underneath. The ordeal precipitated chills and ill-health which conduced to her eventual death. And aesthetic immortality. Was it worth it? Put another way: 'What price art?' Life itself? Other peoples' lives? The great writer, said George Bernard Shaw, will write in his wife's mother's milk if necessary.

The Fangs are a family whose parents, Caleb and Camille, are avant-gardist performance artists – they use 'human' materials, 'not paint and canvas or even plastic'. The human material most readily available to them – on the domestic palette, so to speak – is their children. The couple put on outrageous performances in shopping malls in order to provoke 'reaction'. Their mission is to 'make something crazy happen' in a world dominated by the conventional, the banal and the script-written. The Fangs 'simply threw their own bodies into space as if they were hand grenades and waited for the disruption to occur. They had no expectations other than to cause unrest.' Their two children, Annie and Buster, are recruited to magnify that explosive 'unrest'. In one 'Fang event', entitled 'The Sound and the Fury', the children thump and blast on musical instruments they can't play, the parents passing round a collection box for an 'operarshun' (as the scrappy billboard says) to save their pet dog's life. 'Mr and Mrs Fang called it art. Their children called it mischief.' In a particularly mischievous 'event', the Fangs engineer a school production of *Romeo and Juliet* in which Buster and Annie play the lead parts. 'A play about forbidden love will now have the added layer of incest', says a complacent Caleb. Good art, as they see it. Not very wonderful parenting, as the children see it. 'They fucked us up, Buster,' says grown-up Annie. 'They didn't mean to,' he replies. 'But they *did*,' she insists.

When they are old enough the fucked-up children leave home to make their own more conventional careers in traditional forms of art. For Annie it's high-concept 'action' movies. As the novel opens she has recently starred in *Date Due*, in which she played a 'shy drug-addicted librarian who gets involved with skinheads with tragic results'. It wins an Oscar nomination. Her own 'dependencies', and some unhappy display of her private parts on the web, lead to her being written out of subsequent instalments in the blockbuster series – *Date Due II*, et al.

Buster is a minimally successful journalist and a wholly unsuccessful novelist. He writes for 'men'. As the novel opens he is in Nebraska writing a story for a gun magazine on 'the most high-tech potato cannon ever seen'. He gets a high-tech tuberous round smack in the face and is hospitalised. The children are, and they know it, 'second raters. . . human beings doing whatever they can to stop being bored to death'. On the side Buster teaches 'postmodern art' and has an unsatisfactory relationship with one of his students.

The grown-up children return home only to discover their parents have disappeared without trace. It is assumed they have been kidnapped and killed. They were last seen at a location with a history of such crimes. In fact they are engaged on their 'life work' – erasing their lives. They have cunningly created an alternate family, with different names and histories (and different children). The artistic imposture has taken them seven years to complete – longer than Michelangelo and the Sistine Chapel. The children track down their parents following clues embodied in a track by a punk group called the Vengeful Virgins. Revenge is the theme. The novel offers the gloomy – Oedipal – conclusion 'kill all parents'. If you don't, they'll kill you. Or, worse than that, they'll 'use' you.

Family Matters, Rohinton Mistry, 2002

Could you, off the top of your head, explain the difference between Parsi, Hindu and Muslim – three major groupings in the vast Indian subcontinent? If not, this novel would certainly help.

Mistry, one of the finest novelists of the Indian diaspora, was born in Bombay and now lives near Toronto. *Family Matters* is a title pregnant with significance. Ostensibly, the subject is domestic: family affairs. But the book also poses a larger question: *does* family matter in the modern age? Particularly in the increasingly strife-torn extended family that is India? Nariman Vakeel, a seventy-nine-year-old Parsi patriarch and former professor of English literature, is dying, lingeringly, of Parkinson's disease, in what used to be called Bombay and is now

Mumbai. As the novel opens, he has become bedridden after breaking his ankle in a fall.

Nariman has bequeathed separate apartments to the two branches of his family. His stepchildren, Jal and Coomy, occupy the larger, in a building called, absurdly, Chateau Felicity. His daughter and son-in-law and their two children live in a smaller apartment in a block named Pleasant Villa. Despite their cheery names, both establishments are decaying. So too are the bonds of kinship within them. One household is reluctant to care for 'Pappa' as he slowly expires; the other is not equipped for the filial task. Nariman ruefully observes that the setup is reminiscent of *King Lear* – Bombay-style.

As he wastes away, the secrets of Nariman's early life unfold. Forty years before, as an eligible, secularly inclined young intellectual in newly independent India, he had wanted to marry a Goan Christian. Reluctantly, and with tragic consequences, Nariman succumbed to family pressure and instead took a Parsi widow (with two children) as his wife. Meanwhile, the second generation of the family is gradually becoming corrupted. His clever young grandson starts taking bribes at school, helping classmates to cheat in order to earn money to care for Nariman, and his son-in-law Yezad embarks on an elaborate and criminal scheme to engineer promotion and a higher salary for himself. The two stepchildren meanwhile fabricate damage to their apartment to provide an excuse for not taking Nariman in.

All this unfolds against a mid-1990s Bombay that is itself stewing in corruption. What is the solution? Obedience to the Mahatma's supra-sectarian ideal of 'one India', or a return to the parochial loyalties of ethnic subgroup, caste, clan and family? Mistry's novel gives no easy answer. Good novels never do. Clearly, he is not wholly infatuated with what Rushdie has called 'the city of mixed-up, mongrel joy'. The pervasive image of Mumbai is of gangsterism, cronyism, impervious bureaucracy, destitution and decay – a landscape of 'crumbling plaster, perforated water tanks and broken drain pipes'. This is an India to escape from, not an India to reform.

As the narrative progresses, the focus of *Family Matters* shifts from Nariman to Yezad. Nariman's son-in-law is manager of the Bombay Sporting Goods Emporium, a store owned by a good-hearted, ecumenical Hindu, Mr Kapur. But Mr Kapur is destined to die – cricket bat in hand – while fending off a couple of Shiv Sena enforcers who have demanded that he call his establishment the 'Mumbai Sporting Goods Emporium', acknowledging the Hindu name of the city. Before they stab him to death, he threatens to 'knock their heads for a sixer'. The knife, alas, proves stronger than the cricket bat. *Family Matters* ends with an epilogue set five years on. Yezad, who once yearned to be 'a little Englishman of a type that even England did not have', has returned to Parsi ideals and principles with a vengeance. A family man who enforces his renewed faith with iron severity, he is now a Persian of a type that Persia may never have had.

To return to the original question, where does the Parsi religion originate and what is it? Followers of the prophet Zarathustra went into exile in India in the eighth century, after the Muslim conquest of Persia. Never numerous, the Parsis were esteemed by the British during the period of the Raj, particularly for what was seen as their extraordinary skill in the English language.

Fanny Hill: or, Memoirs of a Woman of Pleasure, John Cleland, 1748–9

A rake fallen on hard times, Cleland is supposed to have written *Fanny Hill* (an Anglicisation of *mons veneris*, 'mount of Venus') in debtors' prison as a kind of extended masturbation fantasy. An alternative legend has it that he wrote it as a result of a wager with James Boswell, to prove the point that a work of pornography could achieve its erectile effects without ever resorting to crude 'four letter words'. Skilful English could do it just as well. The narrative takes the form of a confessional letter, describing a 'harlot's progress' – but with less severity than Hogarth's morality-tale engravings. Cleland had a soft spot for harlots (of both sexes, it is suspected).

Fanny is born in a small village in Lancashire, 'of parents extremely poor, and, I piously believe, extremely honest'. When they die of smallpox (her cheeks, luckily, are spared) the fifteen-year-old Fanny travels down to London. Here she is taken under the wing of the benign procuress Mrs Brown. Her patroness tries to sell Fanny's maidenhead to an ill-favoured customer, but the girl cannot bring herself to cooperate. Eventually she surrenders her pearl beyond price to a 'young Adonis' called Charles (a gentleman of the same relaxed morality as the monarch after whom he is named). Her ecstasies of pain and pleasures in her devirgination are recalled with florid but 'modest' euphemism. Fanny goes on to become the mistress of a rich merchant, Mr H—. But, bored by the condition of kept woman, she seduces a massively endowed manservant called, bluntly, Master Dick, and is cast out with fifty guineas.

So ends the first volume. The second opens with Fanny the occupant of a brothel run by the good-natured Mrs Cole. Fanny, becoming more experimental, tries the joys of (very restrained) flagellation with Mr Barvile, and witnesses a male homosexual episode at Hampton Court (of which she is very censorious). Finally she is enriched by connection with an old and grateful benefactor. Prosperous, and just nineteen, she is united with Charles and becomes a respectable wife and mother. The narrative ends with an encomium on virtue.

John Cleland (1709–89) was variously a diplomat, servant of the East India Company and a versatile man of letters. In 1740 his fortunes took a bad turn and for a year, between 1748 and 1749, he was imprisoned in the Fleet prison for debt. In this extremity he wrote *Fanny Hill*. He was paid £20 for the copyright (legend has it that the publisher gained £10,000 by the bargain). Publication led to Cleland being summoned and told off before the Privy Council. The fact that the novel contains no 'four-letter words' and is elaborately 'polite' in its descriptions of sex gave it a kind of underground respectability and *Fanny Hill* sold steadily throughout the eighteenth and nineteenth centuries. It was successfully kept banned in London in 1963 (following the *Lady Chatterley* acquittal in 1960) but subsequently slipped back into print, where it now enjoys a place in the World's Classics and Penguin Classics lists. Call it a 'libertine classic', never 'porn'. Cleland was reputedly awarded a £100 a year pension by the government on condition that he publish no more pornography – which he did not. The pension may be apocryphal. A farthing for every copy of the novel sold and read over the centuries would have made the author and his estate as wealthy as J. K. Rowling.

Farewell, My Lovely, Raymond Chandler, 1940

Chandler is the master of the narrative opening. *Farewell, My Lovely* has one which is outstanding, even by his standards:

> It was one of the mixed blocks over on Central Avenue, the blocks that are not yet all Negro. I had just come out of a three-chair barber shop where an agency thought a relief barber named Dimitrios Aleidis might be working. It was a small matter. His wife said she was willing to spend a little money to have him come home.
>
> I never found him, but Mrs Aleidis never paid me any money either.
>
> It was a warm day, almost the end of March, and I stood outside the barber shop looking up at the neon sign on a second floor dine and dice emporium called Florian's. A man was looking up at the sign too. He was looking up at the dusty windows with a sort of ecstatic fixity of expression, like a hunky immigrant catching his first sight of the Statue of Liberty. He was a big man but not more than six feet five inches tall and not wider than a beer truck.

Marlowe is, as usual, a *flâneur*, drawn, not diving, into events. The big guy is 'Moose Malloy'. He is looking for the woman he loved, 'my little Velma', before he was put away behind bars for eight years. Dragging Marlowe behind him Moose enters the bar to be told, politely, by the bouncer, 'No white folks, brother. Jes' fo' the colored people. I'se sorry.' Moose beats the bouncer to pulp. After a refreshing draught of whisky he then goes upstairs and shoots the manager dead before leaving, still in search of 'Little Velma'.

While Moose has been behind bars, the world has changed. Los Angeles has 'mixed' into something very different from the sleepy West Coast city of the early 1930s. The reference to the Statue of Liberty is not accidental (nothing is in Chandler). The city had undergone immigrations and ethnic blending equivalent to those New York had experienced forty years earlier. Marlowe (as WASP as Cotton Mather) is, when Malloy grabs him, tracking down a Greek-American. He then falls in with this massive Irish-American who busts up an African-American bar which used to be American-American. All this on a 'mixed block' in Central Avenue, Los Angeles (now known as 'South Central', the home of West Coast rap music). The racial epithets ('shines', 'dinges', 'smokes', 'niggers') which speckle the opening chapter are distasteful. But they signal that – irrespective of any 'mystery' plot as to missing lovelies, jailbirds and stolen necklaces – that this is a novel about race and ethnic shift.

The narrative thereafter follows the tangled byways of every Chandler novel. In one episode Marlowe is incarcerated and drugged in a private hospital by a Scandinavian-American physician, Dr Sonderborg, and his sinister Native-American assistant who has 'the earthy smell of primitive man'. There is a Jewish-American, or possibly French-American (Jules Amthor), mixed up in things somewhere. Velma is eventually found. But like the bar on Central Avenue, she has changed utterly. We never quite know her ethnicity, any more than the real colour of her hair. At one point she is the kind of blonde 'who would make a bishop kick a hole in a stained glass window'. When Moose catches up with her she is as raven-haired as the stepmother in *Snow White*. And just as deadly. She puts a magazine of rounds into his belly. 'Velma' is short for 'Wilhelmina', so German-American (usefully sinister in 1940) is a good bet. But her surname, Valenta, suggests Italian-American. Who knows?

Farewell, My Lovely has always fascinated Chandlerologists for its tantalising hints as to the sexuality of Marlowe. As usual he fends off the women who throw themselves at him, but when he is helped by an ex-cop whom he has just met, Red Norgaard (Norwegian-American), he records a strange, instant, bond:

> He smiled a slow tired smile. His voice was soft, dreamy, so delicate for a big man that it was startling. It made me think of another soft-voiced big man I had strangely liked.

Who was that soft-voiced big man whom he 'strangely liked'? Certainly not the loud-mouthed Malloy. Does Marlowe have a gay past? Does he have a gay present, even, that he tells us nothing about? It would explain a lot, not least his habitual *noli me tangere* where 'lovelies' are concerned. With Mr Marlowe, it's always 'farewell', baby.

Farewell to the Sea, Reinaldo Arenas, 1982

Born in Cuba in 1943, Reinaldo Arenas was one of the expelled 'Marielitos' who came over to the US in 1980, living there until his suicide in 1990. Castro's main aim in enforcing the mass emigration was to punish his American persecutors by emptying the contents of his jails and lunatic asylums on them (this is the background to Brian de Palma's 1983 film *Scarface*). In his gift package there were also some dissidents and awkward writers – notably Arenas – who took literary advantage of their new country. For Arenas it meant a double freedom – he was gay, which was something persecuted in his own country. Suffering from Aids, Arenas committed suicide in New York in December 1990. He left a noble last note for publication. It stated:

> Due to my delicate state of health and to the terrible emotional depression it causes me not to be able to continue writing and struggling for the freedom of Cuba, I am ending my life. . . There is only one person I hold accountable: Fidel Castro. . . Cuba will be free. I already am.

A film, *Before Night Falls*, was made of Arenas' life, exile, and death in 2000. Directed by Julian Schnabel and starring Javier Bardem, it is regarded as a classic of modern gay cinema.

Farewell to the Sea is the middle volume of a five-part work of Himalayan scale, the *Pentagonia* – a literary Pentateuch conceived as a secret history of Castro's Cuba. It serves as a useful sampler for those intending to scale the whole; few, I suspect, will be tempted by that fictional Everest. But this portion, like the Russian *samizdat*, witnesses to how – despite all oppression – fiction will find a way to the light. Subtitled 'A Novel of Cuba', *Farewell to the Sea* might more accurately be called 'a novel in spite of Cuba'. A stark epilogue records the manuscript's trials. The first version of the book was stolen in Havana in 1969; the second version was confiscated by the Cuban authorities in 1971; a third version was smuggled out of the country (some six years before the author himself could escape) in 1974. It was published in Spanish in Barcelona in 1982 and finally this fourth version (translated by a professor of English at San Juan) became available to the English-speaking world in 1987. *Farewell to the Sea* has a tiny plot buried under an overgrowth of prose poetry. As far as I can make out, it goes like this. Hector and his wife take a cabin by the seaside for six days. They have their baby boy with them. Their aim is to recover the spirit of their early marriage. Hector is a poet, a disillusioned revolutionary and, it emerges, a covert pederast, a life-sentence crime in Cuba. His wife suspects that he has already visited the resort without her. In the course of the week Hector has an affair with a young boy in a neighbouring cabin, who commits suicide when he realises the bleak future for homosexuals in Castro's regime. The novel ends with the now entirely uncommunicative couple driving back to Havana.

A plot summary cannot convey the heroic effort that *Farewell to the Sea* demands from its reader. The narrative is divided into two separately introspective sections. The first is the wife's day-by-day stream of consciousness. Each of the six mornings starts with a factual observation of the world around her, and ends with an apocalyptic reverie as she drifts into sleep. She is, apparently, 'done with words for good' and consoles herself with glum stoicism: 'I must accept my existence, as others accept an incurable disease.' Her dull resentments against the revolution are inarticulate, but insistently talkative and nag away interminably. The second half of the novel is a 230-page-long Whitmanesque poem in six cantos which Hector has composed, presumably in his mind. It is obsessively homosexual and varies relatively lucid scabrous fantasy with wild flights like the following:

> swallows were gliding
> fornicating above the ocean

More poetic than ornithologically plausible, perhaps. Like the sea on a cold day, this is a book to dip into rather than hang around in.

Farnham's Freehold, Robert Heinlein, 1964

'Heinlein has gone mad', said one pungent review of *Farnham's Freehold*. In (re)visiting the novel and judging the author's sanity, some dates are helpful. In 1962, the world had teetered on the brink of nuclear self-destruction during the Cuban Missile Crisis. In 1964, Malcolm X was on a global tour, forging links between American Black Muslims and the new African leaders. The American Civil Rights Act was passed. 'Free at last', proclaimed Martin Luther King. While writing *Farnham's Freehold* Heinlein was living in rural Colorado Springs, a few miles from the headquarters of NORAD, the brain-centre of American's missile defence system, in the nuclear bunkers of Cheyenne Mountain. If war broke out with the USSR, Mr Heinlein would be a prime target. In preparation the author built himself a fallout shelter as impregnable (hopefully) as the innermost bunker of the Cheyenne complex.

The narrative of *Farnham's Freehold* opens during a bridge party *chez* Farnham. One of the players is distracted by a small button buzzing in his ear. '"It's not a hearing aid," Hugh Farnham explained. "It's a radio, tuned to the emergency frequency.'" He sleeps with it on. Why? Because the Russkis could attack any moment – with just four minutes' warning to get into the shelter. A 'coloured' servant, Joseph, brings cocktails to the card-players as required, with the equally required 'yessir/yes ma'am!' The Farnham family is in smouldering crisis, we learn. The hero's wife, Grace, is alcoholic and peevish. Hugh despises his lily-livered son Duke. His schoolgirl daughter Karen is, it will emerge, illicitly pregnant. Hugh himself is drawn sexually to a guest at the party, the divorced and busty Barbara. She is drawn to Hugh. Not every busty divorcee would be:

> Mr Farnham was fiftyish, she decided. And looked it. Hair thinning and already gray, himself thin, almost gaunt, but with a slight potbelly. [Yes, Heinlein was 'fiftyish', etc., in 1964.]

Nonetheless, Barbara suspects, there is a manliness under that potbelly a 'real woman' like her would be curious to explore: 'a panty girdle wouldn't be much protection against it'. The party ends prematurely when the Russians, 'those lying, cheating bastards', do, true to form, throw their 'murder weapons at the US'.

One nuke scores a direct hit on the Farnham fall-out shelter. It withstands the impact, but is knocked hundreds of years into the future. The bridge party, plus faithful retainer, emerge to find global warming has turned America into Africa. After a period living in the woods (no need for panty girdles any more; the adulterous Farnham impregnates Barbara while his wife hoovers up the shelter's booze cabinet) they discover the truth. The nuclear war of '64 wiped out most of the planet's white races, leaving the 'coloureds' – Muslims – 'free at last' to take over. 'The Chosen' keep the few surviving whites as a slaves for breeding ('studs'), as concubines, for manual labour, and as house servants whom they 'temper' (geld) and keep additionally docile by the generous supply of a narcotic drug, 'Happiness'. Discipline is kept, less happily, by electronic 'quirts' or whips.

In the house of a local leader called Ponse, Farnham's wife is recruited into the ruler's harem. His son Duke sacrifices his testicles and lives, contentedly sodden, on Happiness. Barbara survives, intact, now the mother of Farnham's twin children. Ponse has his seigneurial eye on her. The black elite live on a stew which Farnham finds too greasy for his taste. Later he discovers that it is, literally, 'white meat'. The 'Masters' have raised cannibalism to *haute cuisine*. By an improbable series of events Farnham, Barbara and their twins return to their own time to regenerate America and help prevent its being taken over by the 'dark people'. Page turner or stomach turner? Both.

Fathers and Sons, Ivan Turgenev, 1862

In December 1925 a young American went into Sylvia Beach's Shakespeare and Company bookshop at 12 rue de l'Odéon, Paris. Ernest Hemingway had been advised to read the Russian master Turgenev. Miss Beach duly loaned him a couple of volumes, *A Sportsman's Sketches* and *Fathers and Sons*. It was a Damascene moment – the young would-be writer saw his future (Hemingway would publish his homage, in the short story 'Fathers and Sons', in 1933). Ten days later, he wrote in a passion of enthusiasm to a friend: 'Turgenieff to me is the greatest writer that ever was. Didn't write the greatest books but was the greatest writer.' What Hemingway perceived in the Russian's fiction was how historical change – the movements of history, 'progress', the fate of nations – could all be boiled down and crystallised to the relationship of fathers and sons. No daughters need apply – it was strictly a matter of 'manhood'. But who possesses it truly – the young men in battle or the old men in the sea?

Turgenev's story was published at the pivotal moment when the emancipation of the serfs was setting in motion Russia's slow tumble to 1917. The action takes place over a few months in the late 1850s. Two students (in their mid-twenties – education is rarely a hurried thing in Russia) spend their summer vacation visiting their parents in the country. Central to the plot is Bazarov – a doctor in training, a passionate 'nihilist', and a 'new man' with a luciferian pride in himself. The nihilist philosophy advocates the negation, by an act of mind (no blood need be spilled), of all that 'old Russia' – the fathers' Russia – represents. What is needed is a generational purge. Alexander, the 'little father' of the nation, is never directly mentioned. The censors would have not allowed it. But tsarist arch-paternalism is evoked throughout. Bazarov's admiring, less clear-minded friend, Arkady, is pulled along in the nihilist's charismatic wake. He believes his friend 'knows everything'.

Their first visit is to Arkady's father, Nikolai, on his country estate. A widower of 'forty summers' he is already an 'old man'. He lives with his serf mistress, Fenichka (by whom he has a child), administers five thousand acres and rules over two hundred 'souls'. Many of the younger may be his offspring. He has a patriarchal beard. Bazarov and Arkady are 'shaven' – the badge of intellectual newness. Nikolai has done his best to be a 'reformer' – going broke and regarded as a dangerous 'red' by his neighbouring land-owners for his pains. The Romantic-by-temperament Pushkin is his god. Nikolai's brother Pavel lives with him. An Anglophile, Francophile, Germanophile dandy – now in middle age and somewhat frayed round the edges – Pavel falls out with Bazarov. He is particularly enraged by such brutally materialistic assertions as: 'A decent chemist is twenty times more useful than any poet'. Nikolai is similarly disturbed but ruefully thoughtful about the two young men: 'could their superiority be that they bear fewer characteristics of the ruling class than we do?'

Bored by rural hospitality and 'these funny old romantics', the young men cut short their stay. As they take their leave Nikolai foresees, sadly, 'the inevitable strangeness of his relationship with his son'. The sons' next visit is to Odintsova, the daughter of a beau, gambler, and philanderer, and widow of a rich old bourgeois who did her the favour of dying promptly. Both Bazarov and Arkady fall madly in love with the *femme fatale*, though Bazarov hates himself for succumbing to her charm. Such passions are wholly un-nihilistic. Their next port of call is Bazarov's father – an eccentric, former military doctor possessed of a mere twenty-two serfs. A poor rich man. The novel

climaxes with a comic duel between Bazarov and Pavel, and – thereafter – an anti-climax. Arkady marries and is destined to become his father's son. Bazarov, the man of the future, cuts his finger treating a peasant, contracts typhus and dies a banal death.

Turgenev's novel was hugely controversial on its publication in Russia. It engendered, as do the plays of Chekhov, an uncomfortable sense of something very big, but unclear, happening there. Turgenev never married. He had one child, a daughter, by one of his father's serfs.

Fear of Flying, Erica Jong, 1973

In 2012 *Fear of Flying* made *Time* magazine's list of 'top ten racy novels'. It's both hugely read (twenty million sales are claimed) and (still) hugely worth reading. At the time it was seen as a feminist counter-punch to the outrageously 'frank', chauvinist PORTNOY'S COMPLAINT – a kind of 'Two can play at that game, Mister!' But, over the years, it's become rather more than a simple kick in the tyrant sex's gonads. Jong's novel recounts the life story (like Portnoy's, framed as a confession to her analyst) of Isadora, a sexually repressed, twice-married, Jewish, childless New Yorker. Born Weiss, Isadora's maiden name was 'blanched' to 'White' by her upwardly mobile family. She now carries the compound nomination Isadora Zelda White Stollerman Wing – indicating a string of male ownerships and two melancholy allusions: to F. Scott Fitzgerald's 'mad' wife, Zelda, whom the psychoanalysts could not help, and Isadora Duncan, the dancer killed by her flowing feminine scarf and a perverse automobile wheel.

After some unfulfilling adolescent sexual experiences, Isadora studied English at Columbia, but never finished her doctorate (on Fielding – whose story of the sexual adventurer Tom Jones is frequently alluded to in Jong's narratives). At college Isadora met her first husband, Brian Stollerman, who later went schizophrenic on her. Now twenty-nine, the author of two volumes of (wholly unregarded) poetry, she has for five years been married to a psychoanalyst, Bennett Wing. Her 'mock memoir' begins, 'There were 117 psychoanalysts on the Pan Am flight to Vienna and I'd been treated by at least six of them.' The title alludes to her most intense phobia, a belief that if she relaxes for a moment the plane will fall out of the air. Isadora resolves to lose the sexual fears which have hitherto ruled her life. Following a casual copulation with a stranger on a train, she has a 'carefree' affair with an English psychoanalyst, Adrian Goodlove (the name is not one of the subtlest things in the novel). There is a *ménage à trois* with Adrian and Isadora's husband, Bennett. The novel ends with Isadora, liberated, lying in a warm bath, caressing her body, waiting – serenely postcoital and pre-coital – for her husband to whom she is, at last, happily married. It is 'A Nineteenth-Century Ending' as the title of the last chapter wryly declares.

Historically, *Fear of Flying* was taken up by the women's movement, launched a decade earlier, as a treatise for 'second-wave feminism'. A woman, the novel insists, can be wholly independent (a victim neither in the marriage bed nor on the analyst's couch) and, in Jong's chosen term, 'juicy' with it. The assertion crystallises around the novel's famous central concept – the 'zipless fuck'. This is the true index of women's liberation. It's defined rhapsodically in the novel although it's not till page 100 that Isadora gets there. What she experiences, having lost her fear of flying, is 'the true, the ultimate A-1 fuck. . . The zipless fuck was more than a fuck. It was a platonic ideal. Zipless because when you came together zippers fell away like rose petals, underwear blew off in one breath like dandelion fluff.' It is, she says, to sex what the Holy Grail was to the Knights of the Round Table. Her phrase is now proverbial; Jong, thirty years on, would concur: 'I used to worry that they would put "zipless fuck" on my tombstone', she sighed. In 2011, she publicly stated she no longer believed in her most famous invention. 'When I look back at the one night stands and zipless fucks, they were *terrible*. . . The best sex, generally, is with somebody where you really have a connection.' Long live zips.

Le Feu: journal d'une escouade, Henri Barbusse, 1916

Typically translated as *Under Fire: The Story of a Squad*, the title carries more punch in the original French. Henri Barbusse volunteered at the age of forty-one to fight in the First World War and was himself 'under fire' by the first winter of the conflict. His novel was published at a point when it had become obvious that the combatants were engaged in a war of attrition, not the quick conquest or defeat once expected. The side willing to sacrifice most blood would win. Barbusse lost enough of his own blood to write his manuscript in red. He would go on to be seriously wounded four times but – unlike a million of his compatriots – he survived the carnage. He wrote and published his novel, comprised of notes jotted down while under fire, he claimed, while he was later working (having been invalided) behind the lines in the War Office – a desk soldier. The English translation came out in 1917, at the very lowest point of the war for the Allies. It was accused of spreading 'alarm and despondency'. The British taste – until well after the war – was for works which were more bugle-blowingly inspirational. Jingoism is not a term which translates into French (Google gives me the dull '*chauvinisme*').

Le Feu has no plot as such – the only story is that of the war itself. It is narrated anonymously by one of the squad – a pseudo-Barbusse, we assume. The characters are the non-commissioned members of this single small unit. They are to a man brave volunteers but not thoughtless patriots. No officers figure centrally in the narrative and particular contempt is reserved for 'trench tourists'. *La tranchée* is a bog, in every sense of the word:

> It is carpeted at bottom with a layer of slime that liberates the foot at each step with a sticky sound; and by each dug-out it smells of the night's excretions. The holes themselves, as you stoop to peer in, are foul of breath.

Criss-crossing the landscape, the trenches are 'internal wounds' on the body of France, bleeding its life away.

Barbusse was staunchly communist. He found his creed made manifest in the camaraderie of the trench, where the human condition is reduced to elemental form. 'We are not soldiers,' declares one of the squad, 'we're men.' There is no hatred for the German 'men' across no man's land. 'Ah, *mon vieux*,' says another member of the squad, 'we talk about the dirty *Boche* race; but as for the common soldier, I don't know if it's true or whether we're codded about that as well, and if at bottom they're not men pretty much like us.' Hatred is reserved for the class enemies who started the war – a war started for what? No one in the squad has an answer. But they nonetheless fight, endure the fire, and die. French slang, *argot*, translates comically – as when characters in affectionate hostility call each other such things as 'shoe-sole face'. But the descriptions of the mutilations which bullets, shells and shrapnel inflict on the human body are vivid (e.g. 'And little Godefroy– did you know him? – middle of his body blown away. He was emptied of blood on the spot in an instant, like a bucket kicked over'). Most vivid are the descriptions of corpses (e.g. 'No doubt a bomb had exploded in his hands; and since all his face is alive, he seems to be gnawing maggots').

The novel ends enigmatically:

And while we get ready to rejoin the others and begin war again, the dark and storm-choked sky slowly opens above our heads. Between two masses of gloomy cloud a tranquil gleam emerges; and that line of light, so black edged and beset, brings even so its proof that the sun is there.

Reading between those terminal lines the end of the war is of little historical significance. The coming, post-war, revolution is what matters. Barbusse did not have long to wait. It came in 1917.

The Fifth Child, Doris Lessing, 1998

Theologians – and parents – have always been in two minds as to whether 'little strangers' (as Victorians called their newborn) are angelic, being more recently in God's company than we have been, or little demons infused with the 'Old Adam'. Novelists have always found richer inspiration in the demonic child. A notable example is Miles in Henry James' *The Turn of the Screw*. In 1988, Doris Lessing (a future Nobelist) followed the Master with *The Fifth Child*. It's not her usual line of fictional work, but it's an infant-horror story as good as any ever written.

The narrative opens at a London office party in the 1960s. Two middle-ranking employees of a firm in the business of 'putting up buildings' (Centre Point monstrosities) fall in love. David and Harriet are – despite the decade – resolutely unswinging. He is sexually 'honourable', she is a virgin (and resolutely 'anti-pill'). 'They were', they discover, 'made for each other'. They marry and buy a large house they cannot afford. His parents (classier than hers) help out. Harriet's widowed mother, Dorothy, is recruited as a future childminder. She will not have to wait long. On buying the house, the first thing the couple do is make impregnating love in the 'babymaker' bedroom. 'They meant to have a lot of children'. Four duly follow in quick sequence as the dreary 1970s, with the decade's 'winters of discontent', throw their pall over Britain. The Lovatts are a 'happy family'. David and Harriet are, they believe, 'blessed' and throw annual parties at the two festivals of the year associated with procreation – egg-hunting Easter, and Christmas. The children are named after apostles. TV is 'not much watched'. The world the newscasts display is becoming uglier by the year. The fifth child is born in what would be recorded as the worst year of post-war Britain – 1973. It saw social division, the three-day week, strikes so savage they verged on revolution, double-digit inflation brought on by the 'oil shock', and defeat for the west in Vietnam. A poisonous time.

Unusually for Harriet, whose previous births have been easy, this fifth pregnancy is 'horrific'. It feels as if the child is kicking to get out. Benjamin is born weighing a massive eleven pounds. He is not pretty: 'He did not look like a baby at all. He had a heavy-shouldered hunched look.' His hair is clumped in a 'wedge', his eyes are 'greeny-yellow, like lumps of soapstone' hooded by ridged eyebrows. He looks like a monster and gives clear signs of being one. While still in his playpen, endowed with more than infantile strength, he strangles the family dog. The parents fear for the necks of their other children and Ben is institutionalised. When she discovers that the 'home' is, in fact, a place where children are medicated to death, Harriet's maternal instincts, despite her loathing for the child, induce her to rescue him. He grows up a street yob and, at the end of the novel, takes off, leaving a permanently shattered family behind him. 'Whatever made the Lovatts think that just because they were baby boomers they had any right to be happy?' asks the novel. Harriet concludes, 'We are being punished... For thinking we could be happy'. As for Ben, 'he isn't really one of us' – he is a throwback, the incarnation of something unregenerate and savage in the human makeup. She foresees him, 'in Berlin, Madrid, Los Angeles, Buenos Aires... standing rather apart from the crowd... with his goblin eyes... searching the faces in the crowd for his own kind'.

In interviews Lessing recalled that she was embarrassed by readers of *The Fifth Child* writing to her to say that, as parents of 'special needs' children (unhappily afflicted with Down's syndrome, autism, or cerebral palsy), they had found her novel 'immensely helpful.' That was not what she had in mind at all, Lessing explained. She was thinking of 'imps of satan', 'trolls', 'goblins'.

Fifty Shades of Grey, E. L. James, 2011

In summer 2012, *Fifty Shades of Grey* was the most-read novel worldwide. Overwhelmingly, one was told, by women. No one could plausibly explain why – something I find immensely reassuring. Now that the Gadarene rush has abated, read it yourself and come up with a theory. Mine is below. First, however, a bit of the story. The heroine-narrator of *Fifty Shades*, Ana Steele, is a twenty-one-year-old final year student at Washington State University on the hippy upper West Coast of America – the current destination of Anglo-white flight from increasingly Hispanic southern California. Ana

catches the eye of a local billionaire entrepreneur – imagine Steve Jobs with flowing hair, eyes smouldering like the pits of Hades, whipcord muscles, and some strange 'preferences'. Why, Ana wistfully wonders (and so might we), would Christian Grey pick on the likes of little her: 'I'm too pale, too skinny, too scruffy'? And, she might add, in the words of the old song, 'never been kissed before'. One of the jokes in the spoof movie *Dragnet* (starring an exuberantly youthful Tom Hanks and Dan Aykroyd) was the problem the local Satanists were encountering nowadays in finding virgins for sacrifice in the greater Los Angeles area. Local Don Juans having got there first, Satan was feeling distinctly itchy. *Dragnet* was set in the 1980s. There may, in the first decade of the twenty-first century, be twenty-one-year-old virgins in the Portland area so attractive as to inflame the diabolic lusts of billionaire sex fiends, but my guess is that they are less thick on the ground than even twenty years ago. Ana – in one of the more sexually free-wheeling communities in the world (we are not talking Riyadh or Tehran) – has retained her pearl beyond price for longer than most Jane Austen heroines. And it takes the story 117 pages (as long as it takes Fanny Hill, in her harlot's progress chronicle, one recalls) to lose that jewel.

What Ana gets next would have been quite familiar to John Cleland's amiable woman of pleasure. Ana graduates to become not merely a bachelor of arts but, in the same week, sex chattel. From BA to SM in a night. The opening of Chapter 14 says it all:

> Christian is standing over me grasping a plaited leather riding crop. He's wearing old, faded, ripped Levis [these unmentionables are named and dropped so often in the text that one wonders about a product-placement deal] and that's all. He flicks the crop slowly into his palm as he gazes down at me... I cannot move. I am naked and shackled, spread-eagled on a large four-poster bed.

That vignette will be reassuring to the few men who furtively riffle through their partner's copy of *Fifty Shades*, with the guilt of a husband going through his wife's underwear drawer. It's Edward Rochester, teasing his poor little governess-girl; it's mustachio-twirling Alec d'Urberville forcing the strawberry between Tess's virginal lips (Hardy's novel is frequently cited by E. L. James); it's the second Mrs de Winter, cowering submissively before the masterful, pistol-wielding Max. In other words, it's get lost Steinem, Dworkin, Greer. Nothing has changed. The male chromosome is back where biological destiny meant it to be – in the saddle, with riding crop raised.

Fifty Shades poses a moral dilemma for the thoughtful woman reader. The book's egalitarian assertion – why should men have all the porno-thrills? – is something, perhaps, to applaud. Mommy-porn is democratic. An overdue slice of the cake. But Jong (see FEAR OF FLYING) surely did it better. And the atavistic sexual theme which James' novel celebrates – woman as (happy) sex slave – is troubling. Ana plays little coquettish games with her dominator. But, at the end of the day (and for the long, long night that invariably follows), she's exactly where poor Clarissa Harlowe was in Samuel Richardson's foundational novel (1748). In male bondage, that is. So what's my theory? I think I'd have to go along with Sylvia Plath: 'Every woman adores a Fascist / The boot in the face, the brute / Brute heart of a brute like you'. At least, now and again, they like to kick that idea around where it can't do any harm – in fiction.

Fingersmith, Sarah Waters, 2002

Fingersmith is one of the best of the Neo-Victorian works, which have evolved over the last thirty years into a vibrant genre. If not quite as good as POSSESSION (no NVF work, so far, is – and, short of a George Eliot reincarnation, is ever likely to be), Waters' homage to Dickens – and Dickens' acolytes (notably Wilkie Collins) – is highly accomplished. It helps that the author has a PhD in Victorian Fiction and, more importantly, that she hasn't let her doctorate put the leaden boots of scholarship on her imagination. *Fingersmith*'s historical veneer is thinly applied, although Waters has an admirable, and among her school of writers unique, sense of how radically nineteenth-century decades differed from each other – something

routinely fudged by less knowledgeable romancers. Her lesbian-bohemian romance *Tipping the Velvet* had been *fin-de-siècle*, and her gloomily Foucauldian second effort, *Affinity*, caught the more stolid mood of the Victorian heyday. In addition to identifying the precise and peculiar flavour of any decennial period, Waters contrives to choose exactly the right contemporary literary style. *Fingersmith* draws on 1860s 'sensationalism' – the popular literary flavour of those years.

The story opens, preludically, in Mrs Sucksby's thieves' kitchen and baby farm (the two were traditionally associated) in the Borough, where the heroine Sue Trainder (born in 1844 and now sweet sixteen) has been brought up. The inmates are described – among them John Vroom, 'a thin, dark, knifish boy of about fourteen' whose doxy is (implausibly) 'stitching dog-skins onto stolen dogs, to make them seem handsomer breeds than what they really were'. Vroom is meanwhile making

> a deal with a dog-thief. This man had a couple of bitches: when the bitches came on heat he would walk the streets with them, tempting dogs away from their owners, then charging a ten pounds' ransom before he'd give them back. That works best with sporting dogs, and dogs with sentimental mistresses.

There is a section on dognappers like Vroom and their tricks in Mayhew's *London Labour and the London Poor*, where we read that

> another method of decoying dogs is by having a bitch in heat. When any valuable dog follows it is picked up and taken home, when they wait for the reward offered by the owner to return it, generally from £1 to £5. The loss of the dog may be advertised in the *Times*, or other newspapers . . .

Waters does not cite Mayhew among her sources, but it is clear that, as her heroine would, she has dipped into his pockets and lifted what she needs. In her opening chapter, Waters makes knowing reference to *Oliver Twist* ('fingersmithing', pick-pocketing, is the trade taught in Fagin's crime-kitchen) and to

Charlie Wag (according to Mayhew, the penny dreadful most responsible for the corruption of London youth), but the Victorian novel that Waters principally sets out to invert, pervert and subvert in the thief's progress of her heroine, Sue Trinder, is *The Woman in White*.

The events of *Fingersmith* recognisably track Wilkie Collins' narrative, but they are overhung with seditious hypotheses. What if Wilkie's Walter Hartright, the drawing master sent to tutor Laura Fairlie at Limmeridge House, were a rogue and pervert? What if Laura were herself criminally inclined – and willing to join in a roguish plot with Walter? What if Mr Fairlie were not collecting fine pictures but pornography? What if Laura had a lesbian relationship with Marian Halcombe (something hinted at, but not developed, by Collins)? What is admirable in *Fingersmith* is the expert but relatively straightforward way that Waters, while pursuing these 'what ifs', masters Collins' sensationalist devices – playing, as it were, on the other novelist's instrument. 'Make 'em laugh, make 'em cry, make 'em wait', Wilkie instructed. Waters does all this and, most difficult of all, makes us 'ooh-ah' with occasional surprise as well.

First Among Equals, Jeffrey Archer, 1984

My favourite 'Archer'. Not everyone will have one. A British political melodrama, *First Among Equals* was the author's most successful novel to date, drawing teasingly on his insider experience as an MP between 1969 and 1974. The novel clearly gave no offence to his former colleagues. The year after publication Archer was appointed deputy chairman of the Tory Party – then riding high after Mrs Thatcher's leading the country to victory in the Falklands War. Archer was at the time the most popular public speaker in his party and a sure-fire vote-winner. He made no secret of the fact that since childhood he had aimed, one day, to become prime minister. And not too late in life. Pitt, not Gladstone, was the Archerian role model. There is a jaunty buoyancy to the novel that suggests he himself regarded

future residence in Number 10 as a dead cert. Top of the 1984 bestseller list would have to do in the meantime.

The novel opens seven years into the future. It is 27 April 1991. There has been a dead-heat general election and 'King Charles III' (not Archer's most successful prophecy) must decide which of three eligible members of the House he should invite to form the new government. The narrative flashes back to summarise the intertwining careers of these three rivals. All were part of the 'new boy' Westminster intake of 1964 (Archer himself had been the youngest MP in the house when he was elected in 1969). Simon Kerslake is Oxford-educated and middle-class: a 'new Conservative'. The Honourable Charles Gurney Seymour, the younger son of an earl, is patrician, selfish, and Eton- and Oxford-educated – a traditional Tory. Ray Gould is Yorkshire-born working-class, and Labour to his woollen socks. In the wings is Andrew Fraser – Scottish, a dark horse in tartan.

The three front-runners have been resolved, all their lives, to be prime minister of England, and have taken different routes to the top of the slippery pole. Gould became a union-backed apparatchik. He strategically distanced himself from Harold Wilson as the leader's reputation faded, and has survived a prostitute's attempt to blackmail him. (This was an eerie subplot. Archer was obliged to resign his deputy chairmanship in October 1986 when the *News of the World* ran the headline 'Tory boss Archer pays vice-girl'. Archer sued for libel and won.) Kerslake, the most honest if least likeable of the three candidates, had shrewdly backed Thatcher in the 1975 Conservative election contest, and thus edged ahead of Seymour. He is a junior minister, while Seymour is merely a junior whip (in which capacity he earlier assisted Edward Heath in winning his European Community vote). Seymour illicitly uses his power as a banker to attempt to bankrupt Kerslake. Kerslake's gynaecologist wife, Elizabeth, uses her clinical knowledge to blackmail Seymour with the information that his son, the apple of his eye, is not his child. All three have messy marital situations.

The narrative climaxes with the monarch summoning Gould to the Palace – only for the curtain line: 'I thought it would be courteous to explain to you in detail why I shall be inviting ****** to be my first Prime Minister' (the name is given, but it should really be taped over in the printed copy – it's far too easy for the reader to peek at the last page). Archer spices his narrative by introducing walk-on historical characters – Alec Douglas-Home, Harold Wilson, James Callaghan – and, most daringly, Mrs Thatcher herself, his 'number one fan'. All, however, in a prudently non-libellous fashion. Would he had been as prudent in other matters.

The Fixed Period, Anthony Trollope, 1882

The Fixed Period, the author's only science-fiction novel, has always been discordantly out of key with what we commonly regard as 'Trollopian'. In consequence, the book has enjoyed less popularity than the forty-six other works of fiction which gushed from the author's inexhaustible pen. The gushing had, sadly, almost dribbled to a conclusion by the time of The Fixed Period. He was anything but hale during the writing of this novel. Since 1873 he had been entirely deaf in in one ear. His eyesight was poor. He was grossly overweight (sixteen stone on a medium frame). He had suffered a hernia and was obliged to wear a truss, which rendered him virtually immobile. Cardiac asthma was suffocating him slowly. In late 1881, he went to his local Hampshire doctor with chest pains. He received the dreadful news that he had angina pectoris. 'I may drop dead at any moment,' he glumly told a friend. He did not have long to wait – Trollope died in 1882, aged sixty-seven and a half. It was during the months after his diagnosis that he wrote The Fixed Period. Anthony Trollope was not one to stop working hard simply because his heart was worn out.

The action of The Fixed Period is set in summer 1980, on the small former British colony off New Zealand, Britannula – specifically its capital Gladstonopolis (the Grand Old Man of British politics was a vigorous seventy-two, with two premierships ahead of him, as the novel was being written). The mother country has granted Britannula its independence. Under its president, John Neverbend (an obstinate man), it has introduced a law by which every citizen on reaching the age of sixty-seven and a half shall be 'deposited' in a college, grimly called 'Necropolis', and educated in oncoming death for a year, before being disposed of. The novel delicately hints at how the final act shall be carried out – exsanguination. Classicist that he was, Trollope thought the warm bath, the razor and the cut vein the best way to achieve what Keats called 'easeful death'. Cremation (becoming fashionable as rational corpse disposal in England) would follow. Neverbend is a lusty fifty-nine as the narrative opens. His best friend Gabriel Crasweller, however, is sixty-six and fast approaching the deadly age. He will be the first Britannulan to be deposited in the college. Crasweller is not at all looking forward to deposition. He attempts to wriggle out of it by lying about his age. This fails. He must go into the dark – it is the law. Things are complicated by a young suitor for his daughter who wants (via her) to inherit Gabriel's wealth, while another more likeable suitor (Neverbend's son, ironically) wants to scrap the fixed period.

There are three events in this fascinating but rather eventless novel. Crasweller finally submits to the law. But to forestall this judicial murder Britain sends out a gunboat with a massive '25olb swiveller gun'. Britannula is recolonised, Neverbend is arrested and the narrative ends with him on his way to England on the gunboat John Bright (named after the Liberal politician, who was seventy-one years old when the book was published), ruefully anticipating what awaits him when he reaches England. The core of The Fixed Period is not its SF gadgetry, which is unimpressive – steam-powered bicycles and rather alarming improvements on the piano and violin called the 'mousometor' and 'melpomeneon'. Nor is the novel interesting for the love triangle between the young people. Trollope was too old to work himself up about such juvenile nonsense. The power of the novel lies in its meditations on age, and what follows age.

The central event, oddly, is a cricket match between Britannula and England. The 'Tests' had begun in 1877 and the antipodeans had proved to be alarmingly good at the game. So much so that in 1882 (as *The Fixed Period* was published, by happy coincidence) they beat England so convincingly at the Oval that the *Sporting Times* declared cricket 'dead' and 'cremated'. Thus were the 'Ashes' born. Trollope died the same year. He was not cremated.

Flashman at the Charge, George MacDonald Fraser, 1973

As already discussed in the entry on THE CRIMSON PETAL AND THE WHITE, the main element in Neo-Victorian fiction is inversion. The simplest, and best-selling, example of this is George MacDonald Fraser's *Flashman* sequence, begun in 1969. Fraser turns *Tom Brown's Schooldays* arse-over-tip (as Flashy would say) by making a hero out of the bully who roasts Hughes' hero over the dormitory fire to 'persuade' him to hand over his lottery ticket. Flashman is subsequently expelled by Dr Arnold after being brought back on a shutter, dead drunk, from the local gin palace. Perversely (or inversely), in Fraser's extension of the subplot, Flashy goes on to great glory: he is ennobled, promoted and decorated – but, of course, remains the same unregenerate cad, bounder, lecher, knave, and coward who bullied and basted the lower forms at Rugby. In Fraser's version he is lovable with it. And, when he has to be, oddly heroic. After reading the twelve-volume saga one ends up thinking, 'Stap me – one wouldn't let one's wife alone with him, but, all in all, he's a damned fine Englishman. Rather be up the Khyber with him than that puling priggish bore Brown.'

In the first of the Flashman books Flashy is indeed up the Khyber, in the disastrous First Afghan War (he wins a Victoria Cross – although 'wins' is perhaps the wrong word and VD is more his style than VC). *Flashman at the Charge* is the fourth of the *Flashman Papers*, covering the period 1854–5. The hero, born in 1822, is now in his caddish prime. A captain in the cavalry, he is promoted to colonel during the course of the book. The VC has helped immensely. The novel opens briskly: 'The moment after Lew Nolan wheeled his horse away and disappeared over the edge of the escarpment with Raglan's message tucked in his gauntlet, I knew I was for it.' Into the valley of Death, and all that. From the imminent charge of the glorious six hundred, there follows a long flashback to London in the period leading up to the Crimean War. Flashy has been angling for a cushy berth in ordnance, where the bullets don't fly but are stored safely in their ammo boxes. He was earlier dismissed from Lord Cardigan's Hussars for having married (a paternal shotgun at the nape of his neck) a Scottish tradesman's daughter called Elspeth, who now has a son (whose? She's as much of a rogue as her husband). Much against his self-preserving instincts, Flashy finds himself ordered by Lord Raglan back to an active posting.

In a state of pure funk, and purely by accident, he finds himself galloping in the Charge of the Light Brigade by Cardigan's side. 'It was bloody lunacy from the start, and bloody carnage, too', is his old soldier's un-Tennysonian verdict, although he kills his share of Russians. Ever the survivor, he is taken prisoner and, as a high ranking enemy officer, billeted with a Tsarist nobleman, whose daughter he inevitably rogers. In a mad sled ride he later throws her overboard to stave off a pack of pursuing wolves – Flashman always dumps his ladies in style. He subsequently teams up with his old schoolmate (and dormitory victim) from his Rugby days, 'Scud' East, who is also a prisoner-of-war. They come across a Russian plot to invade India through the Khyber Pass and resolve to escape and warn the British authorities (or at least Scud resolves; Flashy would be happy to remain in his comfortable Russian berth until the war is over).

Many adventures ensue, culminating in our anti-hero – disguised as a tribesman – leading an Afghan rebellion against the Russians, transformed into a bloody warrior ('utterly against nature, instinct and judgement') by a potion of hasheesh, administered by his exotic Mongol lover. More glory awaits on his return back to a grateful queen and nation, proud to have such warriors as Colonel Harold Flashman, VC, protecting – nay, enlarging – an empire on which the sun never sets. *Flashman at the Charge* was serialised, in full, in *Playboy* magazine, April–June 1973. The 'centrefold' and 'Playmate of the Month' would have been of great interest to our hero.

Flush: A Biography, Virginia Woolf, 1933

What is literature's best dog novel? It's not a hotly contested field. Dr John Brown's *Rab and His Friends* would be a contender, so too would John Berger's *King* and Jack London's CALL OF THE WILD. *Flush* would be a front-runner among this select pack. Historically he was a Cocker spaniel owned by Elizabeth Barrett. Flush became his mistress' bosom companion in the invalid years at 50 Wimpole Street before her runaway marriage with Robert Browning – the great romance of mid-Victorian poetry. The book is, surprisingly perhaps, given Woolf's reputation, extraordinarily funny. And the dog's-eye view of a legendary story (immortalised in the play *The Barretts of Wimpole Street*, which Woolf saw in 1930) is oddly true (given the presumably sub-verbal nature of dog-thought) to Woolf's trademark stream-of-consciousness technique.

Flush, we are told, began life in 1842 in a 'working man's cottage'. Not for him a life of labour. He was given as a gift to Miss Barrett by fellow writer Miss Mary Mitford. The couple's first meeting is, as Woolf describes it, epic:

Each was surprised. Heavy curls hung down on either side of Miss Barrett's face; large bright eyes shone out; a large mouth smiled. Heavy ears hung down on either side of Flush's face; his eyes, too, were large and bright: his mouth was wide. There was a likeness between them. As they gazed at each other each felt: Here am I – and then each felt: But how different! Hers was the pale worn face of an invalid, cut off from air, light, freedom. His was the warm ruddy face of a young animal; instinct with health and energy... She spoke. He was dumb. She was woman; he was dog. Thus closely united, thus immensely divided, they gazed at each other.

Then with one bound Flush sprang on to the sofa and laid himself where he was to lie for ever after – on the rug at Miss Barrett's feet.

The rest is literary history. Miss Barrett begins to take the air in Regent's Park (in a bath chair, initially), and recovers her health and (importantly for what is to come) her beauty.

There are two things Flush loves in life, his mistress and smells:

To him religion itself was smell. To describe his simplest experience with the daily chop or biscuit is beyond our power. Not even Mr Swinburne could have said what the smell of Wimpole Street meant to Flush on a hot afternoon in June.

There is an exciting dognapping episode when Flush has to be rescued from some *canaille* in Whitechapel who threaten to dismember him and post the Flushy bits back to Wimpole Street (historically Flush was kidnapped, and bought back, three times). When Flush is an adult of some five years, he perceives a certain eagerness in his mistress. Her hands tap in expectation of a letter or, later, the knock on the door announcing a visit by a hooded man. Apprehending a rival, Flush bites the stranger's leg. Should he do it again, he is warned, his mistress will cease loving him. A worse thing could not happen. Finally the three of them escape to Italy, where Flush lives a long (in dog years) life. The novel ends with his end:

She was growing old now and so was Flush. She bent down over him for a moment. Her face with its wide mouth and its great eyes and its heavy curls was still oddly like his. Broken asunder, yet made in the same mould, each, perhaps, completed what was dormant in the other. But she was woman; he was dog. Mrs Browning went on reading. Then she looked at Flush again. But he did not look at her. An extraordinary change had come over him. 'Flush!' she cried. But he was silent. He had been alive; he was now dead.

Virginia Woolf herself owned, over the course of her writing life, a Cocker spaniel called Pinka (given to her by Vita Sackville-West, in 1926) and a dog of indeterminate breed called Hans, notorious for his incontinent droppings on household carpets.

Focus, Arthur Miller, 1945

What are the best novels about the subtle workings of American post-war anti-Semitism? A toss-up, one would think, between Philip Roth's THE HUMAN STAIN, Laura Z. Hobson's *Gentleman's Agreement* (1947), Bernard Malamud's *The Assistant* (1957), Edward Lewis Wallant's *The Pawnbroker* (1961) and Arthur Miller's *Focus*. The latter is the earliest and, as reviewers (even sympathetic reviewers) noted, somewhat clunky in its narrative technique. Miller's strengths would prove to be theatrical. But this, the one novel he wrote, carries an angry man's punch and is all the stronger for its straight-from-the-shoulder, rough-house technique. The main contention of the novel is that persecution is not merely located in far-away Nazi Germany. It can be found on the underground pillars of the New York subway, in the scrawled graffiti reading 'Kill Kikes!'

The story opens with a night scene of a young woman screaming pathetically in the street for help after she has been sexually assaulted and beaten up. No householder on the block helps, or even calls the cops. She has a Puerto Rican accent and this is not a 'Spic' neighbourhood. She'll be carted away by the garbage trucks, not an ambulance. The narrative which follows is bare-bones simple. A middle-aged New Yorker, Lawrence Newman, lives in Manhattan with his paralysed mother and works in a Manhattan firm as a 'personnel manager'. One of his principal responsibilities is keeping the personnel gentile, by tactful rejection of any applicant openly or secretly Jewish, or even 'Jewish-looking'. He carries out that duty with an applicant who angrily, and correctly, protests that she *isn't* – even though she may *look* it. One day Newman is reprimanded. His standard of work is falling off. He's letting them through. The fault is easily fixed – his eyes need to be corrected. He cannot tolerate

the contacts available in 1945 (few could, the lenses were as large and rigid as goldfish bowls). But when he puts on framed spectacles he 'looks Jewish'. And yet, without the visual aids, he will be dismissed for incompetence. It's Kafka's *Metamorphosis*:

> One morning, as Gregor Samsa was waking up from anxious dreams, he discovered that in his bed he had been changed into a monstrous verminous beetle.

Newman's boss kindly suggests he move into a back office, out of public view. He resigns angrily but getting a new job proves impossible. Everywhere it's 'the polite smile of refusal'. It doesn't help that 'Newman' is a common Anglicisation of Jewish names (as, for example, with the actor Paul Newman). It's hugely unfair, Newman thinks. His family came over in the nineteeth century from England: he even knows the village's name. He served his country in the First World War and killed a 'Fritz'. His best buddy, Fred, is an active member of the 'Christian Front', a neo-Fascist organisation devoted to cleaning the Jews out of America. (This actual organisation flourished in the late 1930s and early 1940s, fuelled by the 'radio sermons' of 'Father [Charles] Coughlin'. Among other racist nonsense Coughlin promoted the belief that President 'Rosenvelt' was part of a worldwide Jewish conspiracy.) Miller's novel is set in the early forties, with the Front going strong. A campaign is mounted in Newman's own street, directed against the corner shopkeeper Finkelstein. 'They'll be moving niggers in on us next,' says Fred.

Newman finally gets a job at a Jewish firm. One of his colleagues, he discovers, is Gertrude, the woman he turned down earlier for looking what she wasn't. They marry. On the honeymoon the couple discover hotels mysteriously don't have their booked rooms. It's 'how they look'. Gertrude becomes a self-hating Jew who is not even a Jew. Newman, after getting roughed up at a Christian Front rally, leaves her. There is a powerful last scene. Finkelstein and Newman are physically attacked on their street. Newman goes to lodge a complaint. The Irish cop asks where he lives and, as an afterthought, 'How many of *you people* live there?' Just the two of us, says Newman.

Focus was belatedly filmed in 2002. It was co-produced by Michael Bloomberg, who was elected Mayor of New York the same year. He evidently felt his city still had something to learn from Miller's novel.

For Esmé – with Love and Squalor, J. D. Salinger, 1950

On its publication in the *New Yorker* this short story was Salinger's first success as a writer. It has been called – by the author's partisan biographer, it should be said – 'the best piece of fiction to come out of World War Two'. Salinger personally had what would once have been called a 'good war'. He would not have called it that. This story contains a sensitive depiction of what would later be called post-traumatic stress disorder. Salinger was drafted in April 1942 and became an infantry counterintelligence NCO. He had intended to be a writer, but the war interrupted that plan. In 1944, Salinger was posted to England. His unit, the 12th Infantry Regiment, landed on Utah Beach as part of the Normandy invasion and suffered extensive casualties. Salinger went on to win five battle stars and a decoration for valour. He never spoke publicly or wrote about his experiences on the front line. It was, his daughter later recalled, 'the unspoken'.

'For Esmé – with Love and Squalor' opens in Devon two months before the Normandy invasion. 'Sergeant X', a counterintelligence officer, has been on a course for three weeks. This ends on a rainy day, and with nothing to do X walks through the nearby town and enters a church where a girls' choir is rehearsing. His eye is caught by one thirteen-year-old chorister in particular whose voice soars above all the others, containing within it not merely the purity of childhood, but English 'class'. Upper class, that is. X retreats to a tea room, where he sees the girl again at another table. She flashes him 'a small, qualified smile' and comes over to make conversation. Did not Yanks despise tea, she asks, by way of introduction. Would she like to join him, he asks. She would, it

transpires, for 'just a fraction of a moment'. He is, she goes on to inform him, the eleventh American she's met, and she's surprised to find him 'quite intelligent'. She thinks he has a sad face and looks lonely. She intends a *haut en bas* kindness – or perhaps it's just good manners. British manners, that is. Her name is Esmé, she half confides, preferring not to tell him her full name for the moment. Or her 'title'. Americans do not understand such things.

Esmé is an orphan. Her mother was killed in the Blitz; her father fighting against Rommel (she wears his man-sized wristwatch in remembrance). Her new American is, he confides, a writer – as yet unpublished. Esmé lodges a request for a story. She is an avid reader; he agrees that she shall be one of his first. She puts in a readerly request for 'squalor'. It's something she is partial to. A little 'love' would be welcome, as well. They exchange addresses. Her last words to him are 'I hope you return with all your faculties intact.' The story jumps to several weeks after VE Day. X's faculties are anything but intact. He is in Germany, in the throes of a nervous breakdown. Looking through a backlog of letters he comes across one from Esmé. It encloses a 'lucky talisman': her father's watch. Profoundly moved, he begins the long process of recovering his faculties. The story has, as its prelude, an invitation in 1950 to a wedding in England – Esmé's presumably. And this is the love and squalor story.

The Forsyte Saga, John Galsworthy, 1906–21

Soames Forsyte was first introduced in *The Man of Property* in 1906. It was only late in subsequent novels about Soames and his family that Galsworthy decided to refashion his narrative into a massive five-part dynastic 'saga' on the Trollopian–Barchester model. The sequence would conclude in 1921 with *To Let* traversing the First World War and chronicling the extinction of the Edwardian heyday and its high society. The war had knocked the stuffing out of old England. Galsworthy's reputation did not hold up after his death in 1933, but *The Forsyte Saga* rose from the grave to enjoy an unanticipated success in 1967 on BBC 2 (then a minority interest channel) as a twenty-six-part TV serialisation. A new literary-dramatic form was born: 'the miniseries'. Seven hundred thousand viewers tuned in (in those days it meant walking across the room to change the channel manually against competition from Hughie Green and *Opportunity Knocks*). The saga was rerun on BBC 1 the following year, attracting a record-breaking sixteen million viewers, and sparking off 'Forsyte Mania'. Clashing as it did with Sunday evensong, church services across the country were postponed. God must wait until the nation found out whether Irene succumbed to Soames. Baby Jolyons (the character was played, charismatically, by Kenneth More) were christened en masse in those same churches in the months that followed. The twelfth episode, 'Birth of a Forsyte', which – despite its title – centred on the death and funeral of Queen Victoria, was the most-watched episode drama ever broadcast on British TV. The funeral was daringly intercut with actual newsreel footage; the Dead March from *Saul* boomed, as ancient members of the clan – like Uncle Nicholas Forsyte, who had cheered at the Coronation in 1838 – struggled to their rickety pins to salute not just the death of a 'great lady', but the end of the era that made Britain great. Eye-moistening stuff.

Penguin Books sold over a million 'Forsyte' paperbacks on the coat-tails of the television series. The saga follows, with many digressions, the career of Soames, who finally dies in 1926. One needs a good genealogical head to follow the narrative (skip the next few sentences if you haven't). The patriarch of the Forsyte family, Jolyon the first, is eighty years old as the saga opens. He has been twelve years widowed. He has a namesake son – the scapegrace of the series, Jolyon ('Jo') Forsyte (1847–1920). Young Jolyon is professionally an underwriter but by temperament an artist. He has a reckless few years as an undergraduate at Cambridge. Later he deserts his first wife, Frances, to father an illegitimate child by the family's Austrian governess, Helene Hilmer, whom he later marries. Jolyon has

a son, yet another Jolyon (known as 'Jolly'), who is born in 1879 and killed in the Boer War.

Soames (1855–1926) – the central character in the saga – is the only son of old Jolyon's brother, James Forsyte (some ten years younger than the patriarch). Young Soames is a solicitor and co-director of the tea firm on which the Forsyte fortune is founded. Soames has long courted Irene, who declines to love him. He is not lovable. Irene eventually marries Soames, only to desert him to become Jo's third wife (following? It's much easier spread out over six months, with *Radio Times* recaps). Soames makes a second marriage, with Annette, in 1901. They have a daughter, Fleur, who then falls in love with Jon, the offspring of Irene and Jo. According to John Galsworthy: 'This idea, if I can ever bring it to fruition, will make *The Forsyte Saga* a volume of half a million words nearly; and the most sustained and considerable piece of fiction of our generation at least'. D. H. Lawrence's comment, on reviewing the whole enterprise, was the pungent two-word comment: 'Just money!' How right he was.

But Galsworthy, alas, did not survive to enjoy the big money his saga made. He did however win the Nobel Prize for Literature in 1932. It has never been regarded as the Foundation's most inspired choice. Presumably the Swedish translation of the saga had gone down very well.

The Four Horsemen of the Apocalypse, Vicente Blasco Ibáñez, 1918

This is the only novel translated from the Spanish ever to top the American bestseller list. It enjoyed a similar success in Britain. *The Four Horsemen*'s appeal was boosted by the First World War (which figures centrally in the narrative). Reviewing the first English translation in December 1918, the *New York Times* saw it as showing definitively 'that war was inevitable from causes deep in the German national character'. *Publishers Weekly* instructed that 'No red-blooded American should fail to read and ponder this thrilling, tremendous novel'. Millions of red-blooded Americans answered the call. Excitement was heightened to a stratospheric pitch by the sensational success (particularly among women) of the 1921 film based on the novel starring Rudolph Valentino (as Julio) in his most glamorous role. The book (with its Argentinian hero) was further boosted by the 'tango mania' which swept Europe in the immediate post-war period.

It is as a period piece that the novel remains highly readable. The melodrama has somewhat dated; the tangoism hasn't. The narrative opens with the cosmopolitan artist Julio Desnoyers waiting impatiently in a Paris park to meet his lover, Marguerite. She plans to leave her engineer husband Laurier for Julio, who has just returned from Argentina with a large portion of his family wealth. It is the darkening eve of war. A long flashback describes how Julio's father, Marcelo Desnoyers, left Paris at the time of the earlier Prussian invasion in 1870, in order to make his fortune in South America. He married his rancher patron's daughter and named his firstborn Julio. Another daughter of the old Argentinian rancher married a German, Karl von Hartrott, and named *their* firstborn Julius. The German and French lines of the family, both now immensely rich, have retired to France and Germany respectively. A Russian artist, Tchernoff, mystically foresees the imminent tragedy about to break on Europe in the allegorical imagery of Dürer's Four Horsemen of the Apocalypse (plague, war, famine, and death).

On the outbreak of fighting, the cuckolded Laurier is quick to join up. He performs valiantly for France and is shell-shocked. Marguerite, now a nurse, loyally resolves to stand by him out of patriotism. She gives up Julio, whom she still truly loves – country must come before heart. The most vivid section of the novel (Part Two) describes Don Marcelo's ordeal at the Desnoyers family château on the Marne. The unspeakable German hordes sweep through, plundering, looting, raping – all the atrocities described with propagandistic vividness. The château is ransacked (ironically, one of the von Hartrotts lends a hand). The ancient Marcelo Desnoyers is physically manhandled and

comes close to losing his life. The 'Huns' are eventually thrown back at the Battle of the Marne; the huge carnage is lovingly described. One of the liberators is Julio, who has at last joined up. A distraught Marcelo tells him:

'Men of your blood are on the other side. If you see any one of them. . . do not hesitate. Shoot!. . . Kill him!. . . Kill him!'

In the event it is Julio who dies in battle. The novel ends with Marcelo touring the endless military cemeteries, somewhere among whose acres of identical white wooden crosses his son lies buried. Julio's sister Chichí and her lover René embrace in this field of death, giving hope of life and regeneration to come.

The Spanish version of the novel was written in 1918. *The Four Horsemen of the Apocalypse* was filmed again in 1962, with the setting moved to the Second World War, directed by Vincente Minnelli. But it is the 1921 version – with its famous tango scene and Valentino's 'tragic eyes' – which is the true movie classic.

Ibáñez was a politically active Republican and pacifist. Radically anti-monarchist, he spent many years in exile, dying in France in 1928. His ashes were reburied in his native Valencia in 1933.

The Fox in the Attic, Richard Hughes, 1961

The Fox in the Attic has a forlorn foreword indicating that this is the first part of a work 'conceived as a long historical novel of my own times culminating in the Second World War'. The reader, Richard Hughes says, may wonder why 'a novel designed as a continuous whole rather than as trilogy or quartet should appear volume by volume'. The plain truth, he confesses, 'is I am such a slow writer that I have been urged not to wait'. The advice was sound. The trilogy, after a somewhat less good second part, never reached completion.

Whoever urged Hughes to publish *The Fox in the Attic* prematurely deserves the thanks of posterity. It ranks as arguably one of the very finest works of the post-war period – if one of the very least conventional. It can itself be considered as tripartite. The narrative opens with a passage of breathtaking beauty:

Only the steady creaking of a flight of swans disturbed the silence... It was a warm, wet, windless afternoon with a soft feathery feeling in the air: rain, yet so fine it could scarcely fall but rather floated. It clung to everything it touched; the rushes in the deep choked ditches of the sea-marsh were bowed down with it, the small black cattle looked cobwebbed with it, their horns were jewelled with it.

Two men appear in this damp Welsh landscape – back from shooting birds in the coastal marshes. One is carrying something over his shoulders. It is not the usual brace of duck but a dead child. The first section of Hughes' novel is, despite the little corpse, a country-house comedy – P. G. Wodehouse crossed with COLD COMFORT FARM. The hero, Augustine, has just escaped the First World War. He was about to be called to the Front when the Amnesty came. His cousin Henry was killed in the trenches and Augustine inherited the decaying mansion, Newton Llantony. It is now 1922. His world, what is left of it, is dying. Nothing new is being reborn to replace it. Augustine flagrantly neglects the traditions of his class. He is falsely suspected at the inquest of having killed the dead girl. In fact, he removed the body merely to protect it from water rats.

The middle section is a prose essay on the death of Liberal England and the scar of the war, which will never heal. It is a lump of historical discourse framed in fiction. The third section is set in Munich, in the days surrounding the failed 1923 Nazi *Putsch*. The young Adolf Hitler flares, darkly, across the narrative, 'an ego virtually without penumbra'. Augustine, now living in Germany, falls in love with a cousin, Mitzi, who is going blind and has symbolic visions of imminent catastrophe. If England's interwar plight is symbolised in the dead child, Germany's is the stinking

fox in the castle attic. Mitzi joins a convent and Augustine drifts on, aimlessly, as history prepares for something worse even than the First World War.

The Fox in the Attic is one of the very great novels of its time. That it is not universally acknowledged as such is attributable to its author's inveterate reticence and obstinate indifference to working his career as a writer. Every reader, in consequence, has to discover Richard Hughes. He is well worth the effort. The book was also the first novel – and still one of the best – with Hitler as a principal character. Equally good, I think, is Norman Spinrad's *The Iron Dream*. Other works in contention might be Beryl Bainbridge's *Young Adolf* and Ira Levin's *The Boys from Brazil*, in which the Führer is regenerated by the magic of DNA.

Foxfire: Confessions of a Girl Gang, Joyce Carol Oates, 1993

Oates, writing as a Princeton professor of great distinction, has a teasing dedication to *Foxfire*: five girls' names followed by a glum 'in memoriam'. They are dead, we assume. This is a trip down Memory Lane. And the professor, we are led to guess, was herself once a 'girl gangster' – not easy for those familiar with her work to picture. Professor Oates has herself confirmed the fact in interviews, calling the novel, set in her own early teenage period, 1953–6, 'emotional autobiography'. The five dedicatees were 'girls whom I knew – a composite of girls, not necessarily all in one group, some I went to school with'.

Whatever the label, *Foxfire* is, for my money, one of the best of the author's multitudinous works of fiction. The narrator is Madeleine Faith Wirtz, aka 'Maddy-Monkey', the 'gang chronicler'. Maddy is gifted with 'the power of words'. 'It was between the ages of thirteen and seventeen', her chronicle begins, 'that I belonged to FOXFIRE' (the gang name is capitalised, violently, throughout the narrative). The setting is 'Hammond' – transparently, for those who know the region, Oates' home-town of Lockport, New York state. The Foxfire crew are teenage vigilantes. Their target is the male sex *in toto*. Every male who figures in the novel – young, old, single, married – is a rapist or child molester. 'Men are our enemies' is the gang slogan. The one exception is a raddled, drunken, 'saintly', defrocked Catholic priest. 'Oh Jesus', exclaims Maddy, exulting in her sexual aggression, 'the very sound "girl gang" had the power to send the blood racing!'

The leader of Foxfire is 'Legs' Sadovsky (motto: 'I'm Legs Sadovsky I'm FOXFIRE I don't fuck around with guys'). All the girl gangsters come from broken families, or (in Maddy's case) 'dull' families. After making their vows in blood, Foxfire's first chronicled act of sex-vigilantism is directed at a lecherous maths teacher. They daub his car – which he then unconsciously drives through town – with the slogan:

> I'M A DIRTY OLD MAN MMMM GIRLS!!
> I TEACH MATH & TICKLE TITS.

He is promptly dismissed and goes on the run. A child-molester shopkeeper is himself molested by the teen Euripidean furies (Maddy gets a typewriter out of this exploit, on which she records the gang's doings). By virtuous vandalism they close down a pet store which mistreats animals. Foxfire becomes an 'urban legend'.

The gang breaks up when they steal a car and are arrested. Legs is put into a brutal correctional facility and on her dismissal the now near-adult girls move into a commune, which they call the 'FOXFIRE Homestead' and make available as a battered women's refuge. They pay their way by 'hooking' – duping would-be 'johns' who think the girls are prostitutes and pay richly for the mistake. Things begin to veer off the rails when Legs ventures into kidnap and extortion (penalty, the electric chair). What was once aggressive feminism is now feminist felony. Legs may, or may not, escape to Cuba. A girl gangster no more, Maddy becomes an astrophysicist and leaves Hammond for ever.

Frankenstein; or, The Modern Prometheus, Mary Shelley, 1818

A thousand 'know' Frankenstein for every one who has actually read Shelley's romance. Which is the more reason for giving it 999 new readers. The original readership was five people. But what a starry quintet. The poet Shelley and the sixteen-year-old Mary Wollstonecraft Godwin had eloped in July 1814, he leaving his wife Harriet (whom he had married in similar runaway circumstances). In February 1815, Mary gave birth to a daughter who died after a few days. A year later, still well shy of twenty years old, Mary gave birth to a son. She and Shelley were at this point not free to marry, his wife still being alive. The family left England for Switzerland, where they passed some months in the company of Byron. John Polidori, the poet's personal physician, was also present, and 'Monk' Lewis – so nicknamed after his notorious novel – was in the neighbourhood. As Mary recalled, 'it proved a wet, ungenial summer'. Rarely has rain had a happier literary result.

Byron proposed that each of the party should write a ghost story in the German *Schauerroman* ('shudder-novel') style. He himself apparently conceived a tale about a vampire which was later enlarged by Polidori in 1819 (thus were two of the most popular franchises of popular entertainment launched on their nineteenth-century career). As was de rigueur in Gothic romance (a tradition which goes back to Walpole, see THE CASTLE OF OTRANTO), Shelley claimed that the *donnée* for *Frankenstein* came to her in an enigmatic dream. The central story is encased in an elaborate narrative frame. On 'a voyage of discovery towards the northern pole', Captain Walton (a bluff, self-taught, upright Englishman) comes upon a lone and exhausted traveller in the Arctic wastes. In letters to his sister in England, Walton recounts the traveller's tale. It's worth summarising Shelley's narrative since it's been so mangled in its many stage, film, and 'knock-off' adaptations. Her version, as they say, still 'stands up'.

Victor Frankenstein is a brilliant Genevan chemist who has learned how to animate 'human clay'. The process involves galvanic shocks, and – apparently – an assemblage of criminally acquired dead body parts. Having succeeded in his experiments, Victor is overcome with horror at his 'Creature', and flees the country. Murders ensue, and the wrong people are arrested and executed. In a pathetic complaint to his 'Creator' (a word that caused consternation among contemporary readers for its blasphemous overtones), the creature (who has attained a commendable level of self-education from some improving books he has found left in a climber's rucksack) explains that his antisocial violence is the consequence of his being rejected by humanity. The novel's action (set indefinitely in the late eighteenth century, without reference to world events) moves to Britain. In the Orkneys, Victor fashions a mate for his monster, but then destroys his work, fearing to loose a race of such beings on mankind. In revenge (with the terrible promise 'I will be with you on your wedding night!') the aggrieved creature slays Victor's bride, Elizabeth.

When Walton picks him up, the scientist is on the trail of the monster, who has resolved to live in perfect isolation from mankind, at the most desolate tip of the planet. Having told his story, Victor dies. The monster returns to grieve over his Creator's corpse, then jumps overboard on to his ice-raft, with the intention of destroying himself on a funeral pyre. The creature's last word is that of Goethe's Werther: 'Farewell.' It was from that novel, stolen from the stranger's rucksack, that he learned the nature of human sympathy.

Despite Mary Shelley's impressive intellectual credentials, her novel was plundered by the unscrupulous makers of melodramas (there were over ninety stage versions in the nineteenth century), 'bloods', 'penny dreadfuls', and, in the twentieth century, mass-market films (notably the James Whale, Universal Pictures 1931 version, starring Boris Karloff). The writer and critic Brian Aldiss salutes *Frankenstein* as the foundation text of modern science fiction ('the first great myth of the industrial age'). All very impressive for an eighteen-year-old first-time author.

Freedom, Jonathan Franzen, 2010

The chauvinistic term 'Great American Novel' was coined by the anything-but-great novelist John William De Forest, in an essay in 1868. It has hung, like an Edgar Allan Poe curse, over the country's fiction ever since. Inevitably De Forest's grandiose label attached itself to Jonathan Franzen's hyper-hyped *Freedom*. The literary messiah had arrived. At last we had it. Or did we? The excitement lasted for all of Andy Warhol's fifteen minutes.

Freedom begins and ends in St Paul, Minnesota – one of those cities most visitors to the US rarely visit. It has, however, powerful literary resonance. St Paul is where F. Scott Fitzgerald was born, and *The Great Gatsby* regularly heads polls of twentieth-century GAN candidates. *Freedom* is strikingly Gatsbyesque. Fitzgerald's novel chronicles the 1920s Jazz Age (the term he coined) and a generation living on 'borrowed time' before the 'Crash'. Franzen in *Freedom* calls the coming cataclysm the 'Collapse'. It's very close, he calculates (AD2010). St Paul is also where Sinclair Lewis located the novels that won American fiction's first Nobel Prize in 1930. Why did Franzen choose St Paul? As homage to Fitzgerald, and for the same reason as Lewis chose St Paul – because that modest city is what, nowadays, is called the 'Heartland'; and, if the GAN is about anything, it is about America's heart.

In his novel *The Great American Novel*, Philip Roth nominates MOBY DICK as the GAN. It's a shrewd choice. What is *Moby Dick* about? Oil (whale oil was what America ran on, before they found black gold in the ground). How far, Melville asks, will America go to get what it needs to fuel its unstoppable growth? To the point, like Ahab, of the destruction of nature and the destruction of itself? It would seem so. Put another way, is America prepared to tear out the heart from its heartland?

Franzen poses that question in the image of rampant MTR (mountain top removal): corporate America comes into the virgin forests and hills of a region such as West Virginia and bulldozes the hills into flat, poisonous slurry to retrieve the coal beneath the surface. Whales, mountains, forests, wildlife – what's the difference? Birds gotta fly, fish gotta swim, GDP gotta grow. Say 'growth' to an economist and he'll smile. Say 'growth' to an oncologist and he'll frown. No country in the history of the world has grown itself so wonderfully as America. The machines that make our modern world so convenient (jumbo jets, the web, the iPad on which I'm writing) are all American, the fruits of its relentless techno-industrial growth. One's grateful. But is it the vitality of carcinoma gone wild? As the vast, 563-page narrative of *Freedom* moves to its conclusion, following the emblematic fortunes of the Berglund family, the authorial opinion is unequivocally stated. America is not the world's engine; America is the world's cancer. Probably around Stage 3 – not quite terminal, but don't hang around.

Franzen chose *Freedom* as his title. It's a heavily loaded term. America was born out of a defiant assertion of national liberty. Its overwhelmingly immigrant population has been drawn by two things, Franzen would have us believe: a desire to be free and the lust to be rich. Only where capitalism is unbridled ('free') can a person indulge that dream of wealth. In his novel, Franzen boils down the titular freedom conundrum into a neat Aesopian fable. There are, it is estimated, some 75 million domestic cats in America. They kill a million songbirds every day. House cats are not a native species. Everyone in America is free to own a cat. It's not (like the freedom to bear arms) in the constitution, but any politician mad enough to offend the cat-loving lobby can sell their Washington apartment: they won't be needing it. Tom Kitten exterminates more wildlife than all the shotguns, deer rifles, and crossbows in America combined. That's freedom for you. The big miaow.

The French Lieutenant's Woman, John Fowles, 1969

He wanted to write a Victorian novel, said Fowles, but how could he, living in the time of the *roman nouveau*? Out of that aesthetic conflict *The French Lieutenant's Woman* was born. The telescopic opening takes the reader by the scruff of the neck:

An easterly is the most disagreeable wind in Lyme Bay – Lyme Bay being that largest bite from the underside of England's outstretched south-western leg – and a person of curiosity could at once have deduced several strong probabilities about the pair

who began to walk down the quay at Lyme Regis, the small but ancient eponym of the inbite, one incisively sharp and blustery morning in the late March of 1867.

The mole, the Lyme Regis walled breakwater also known as the Cobb, has featured in fiction before: it is where Louisa Musgrave 'falls' (double-edged word) in Austen's PERSUASION. The 'woman' of Fowles' title is a fatal and fallen female. Sarah Woodruff fell in love with and was jilted by a French lieutenant, recovering from illness in the town. She has been abandoned by her (objectionably Catholic) lover and is now ostracised by her moralistic fellow citizens. There is another conventionally Victorian plot in the narrative's foreground. Charles Smithson (one of the telescopist's couple), who 'calls himself a Darwinist', is engaged to marry Ernestina (Tina) Freeman, a local beauty with a conventional mind and a vague horror of the carnal implications of the marriage bed:

Ernestina wanted a husband, wanted Charles to be that husband, wanted children; but the payment she vaguely divined she would have to make for them seemed excessive.

Tina's family is enriched by trade; Charles has aristocratic connections and fortune. A match made in Victorian heaven.

Everything is complicated by his falling in love with the mysterious Sarah. In his distraction he consoles himself with a whore in London. Fowles gives a vivid picture of the capital's underworld, drawing (with citation) on Steven Marcus' recently published *The Other Victorians: A Study of Sexuality and Pornography in Mid-Nineteenth-Century England* (1966). A breach of promise action is brought against Charles by the mortally affronted Freeman family. He is obliged to sign an affidavit admitting that he has forfeited for ever the name of 'gentleman'. He is a pariah, but a free pariah. Sarah goes off to live in sin with the ultra-Bohemian Pre-Raphaelite Brotherhood – Dante Gabriel Rosetti's amoral crew – steeped in free love, opium, untrimmed beards, and new ways of thinking about art. Two years pass. Charles travels the world, hoping to 'forget'. In vain.

Fowles offers an ambiguous double ending to the narrative in which the hero may, or may not, be united with Sarah.

The French Lieutenant's Woman is densely researched, rich in literary allusion, and self-consciously artful, notably in the proclamation thrown in the reader's face in Chapter 13:

> If I have pretended until now to know my characters' minds and innermost thoughts, it is because I am writing in (just as I have assumed some of the vocabulary and 'voice' of) a convention universally accepted at the time of my story: that the novelist stands next to God. He may not know it all, yet he tries to pretend that he does. But I live in the age of Alain Robbe-Grillet and Roland Barthes; if this is a novel, it cannot be a novel in the modern sense of the word.

This new/old novel, a bestseller on publication (particularly in America), enjoyed a second lease of bestsellerdom with the 1981 film, starring Meryl Streep and with a brilliant script by Harold Pinter. Not normally wordy, Pinter gave Streep such powerful dialogue as:

> It is my shame that has kept me alive, my knowing that I am truly not like other women. I shall never, like them, have children, a husband, the pleasures of a home. Sometimes I pity them. I have a freedom they cannot understand. No insult, no blame, can touch me. I have myself gone beyond the pale. I am nothing. I am hardly human any more. I am the French Lieutenant's whore.

Streep's hooded image, as portrayed on the film's poster, became emblematic. It was even, bizarrely, taken up by the Scottish Widows' Insurance Company.

From Here to Eternity, James Jones, 1951

The bestselling novel of the year in America, and the work with which Jones aimed to 'blow the lid off the war', it belongs alongside such similarly lid-blowing works as *The Caine Mutiny* by Herman Wouk and Norman Mailer's *The Naked and the Dead*. Jones' is the grittiest of the three. And, in my opinion, the best, although that may be attributable to my fondness for the film it inspired. Literary polish (in short supply here) is not a first requirement of war novels.

The action is set in Hawaii, at Schofield Barracks (where Jones himself had earlier served as a non-commissioned officer), on the eve of the sneak 1941 Pearl Harbor attack which drew an unwilling USA into the Second World War. The sprawling narrative centres on Sergeant Milton Warden, a cynical master sergeant, and Robert E. Lee Prewitt, a private (his forenames are ironic). Warden is having a steamy affair with his commanding officer's wife, Karen. She wants him to become an officer (and thus marriageable to a Captain's lady) but he refuses. He despises officers. Manliness is exclusively an 'other' ranks' thing. Prewitt was in civilian life a champion boxer who has vowed never to fight again – having killed a man in the ring. It's possible, sometimes, to be too manly. He is subjected to sadistic victimisation by his commanding officer (Karen's cuckolded husband) for his 'cowardice' in refusing to represent the regiment in interservice tournaments. Prewitt's reason is neither cowardice nor pacifism, but disgust at what boxing represents:

> Two men who have nothing against each other get in a ring and try to hurt each other, to provide vicarious fear for people with less guts than themselves. And to cover it up they called it sports and gambled on it.

Prewitt subsequently falls in love with a Hawaiian prostitute, Lorene, and is wounded in a bar-fight with knives, avenging his buddy Maggio who has been beaten to death by a sadistic NCO in the stockade. As he attempts to rejoin his unit during the Japanese attack, Prewitt is killed by an American sentry who mistakes him for the enemy.

From Here to Eternity ran into inevitable censorship problems in its use of barrack-room language. In his manuscript Jones disdained the 'fug' of compromise, adopted by Mailer in *The Naked and the Dead*, or the timid asterisk (see DEATH OF A HERO). America was ready (at a pinch) for three-letter words. Four-letter words were unprintable. Jones' fidelity to the language that soldiers really use was toned down – against, his wishes 'You can't have a tough master sergeant go around saying "gee whiz",' he complained. *From Here to Eternity* was filmed in 1953, starring Burt Lancaster as Warden, Deborah Kerr as a classy Karen and Frank Sinatra as Maggio. The 'gee whiz' factor was even stronger than in the novel, but the film broke new ground with a scantily clad kiss, lying on the beach, between Lancaster and Kerr. Hot stuff for 1953.

The title, as few readers of the book and fewer in the film audience would have picked up, is from Kipling's poem 'Gentleman Rankers' – familiar from its glee-club renditions:

> Gentlemen-rankers out on a spree,
> Damned from here to Eternity,
> God ha' mercy on such as we,
> Baa! Yah! Bah!

Gentleman rankers are soldiers like Warden (and James Jones), qualified to hold an officer's commission, who decline the promotion.

From the Earth to the Moon, Jules Verne, 1865

First published as *De la Terre à la Lune*, this is the first plausible lunar-voyage novel. It is also, arguably, the first novel to put a respectable quantity of science into science fiction. Nonetheless, as ever with Verne, there is a crazy comedy playing over the narrative – particularly its early sections.

The action is set precisely when the novel was published (no novelist was more topical than Jules Verne) in post-Civil War America. Hostilities concluded, the Baltimore Gun Club (a forerunner of the National Rifle Association) finds itself at a loose end. There's nothing to shoot. But as with the 'Revenge Weapons' of World War Two (the V1, V2), the recent war has come up with ballistic innovations that can be put to peaceful, post-war use. (Armstrong's 1969 small step for man, interestingly, could trace its origins to the same rockets that, in 1944, killed thousands of Londoners.) As a result of the Civil War, America now leads the world in the science of artillery. At a meeting of the gun club – the members sitting in seats made out of cannon, the hall lit by candelabra made out of musket-barrels – the president, Impey Barbicane, proposes that they construct a gigantic artillery-piece wherewith to send an expedition around the moon. It will relieve their itchy-finger boredom and equip the nation to win the next war. For ten or so chapters the novel then gets off-puttingly technical. There is more about perigees, apogees, propulsion, vectors of approach and escape velocity rates than anyone other than the most geekish of 1860s readers can have enjoyed. This mumbo jumbo skipped over, the moon-shot, the club calculates, must take place at 10.46.40 hours on 1 December 1866. The circuit of the moon (it will be a voyage around, not a voyage to) will take place four days later.

The necessary millions are raised from America and various interested nations. England contributes not a single farthing. They still haven't forgiven America for 1776. The craft will be manned by Barbicane himself, his great Philadelphian adversary Captain Nicholl (who has designed the aluminium plating) and – to placate Verne's home readers – a Frenchman, Michel Ardan, who has shrewdly proposed replacing the original spherical 'diving bell' design with a cylindro-conical projectile: a rocket. The launch will take place in Tampa, Florida (prophetically close to the present Kennedy Space Center).

In flight, the craft is knocked off course by a meteor. There being no radio communication, the world is in suspense until the rocket splashes down in the Pacific, to be rescued by diving bell. The club goes on to raise $100 million in order to set up the 'National Company of Interstellar Communication' – NASA, *avant la lettre*. Verne does not indulge in any nonsense about Selenite 'little green men', as H. G. Wells did in his follow-up, *The First Men in the Moon* (1901). Wells did, however, work out a way that a 'landing' as opposed to a circumnavigation might be achieved. He conceived a substance called 'cavorite', which blocked gravity, and could be used to calibrate acceleration and deceleration. Wells was sceptical about Verne's cannon-concept and use of explosive, believing that even with the 'water cushion' shock absorbers, the human cargo would be gelatine from the G-force impact of the explosive detonation.

Among the many 'firsts' in Verne's novel is, as provender for the astronauts, use of the Oxo Cube, or as the novel puts it:

> Tenderloin beefsteaks, which, though reduced to a small bulk by the hydraulic engines of the American Desiccating Company, were pronounced to be fully as tender, juicy, and savoury as if they had just left the gridiron of a London Club House.

Ardan serves as chef, of course.

Funeral Rites, Jean Genet, 1948

In French it's the more sonorously entitled *Pompes Funèbres*. In his early manuscripts, Genet also toyed with the title 'The Ghost of a Heart'. He had plenty of time to work on what to call it – *Funeral Rites* had a hard road to full publication. Genet began writing it in 1943, when any publication would have had to be licensed by the German Occupation authorities. Some hope. They would more likely have shuttled its author off to a concentration camp. The narrative in progress was sharpened emotionally by the pointless death of the author's lover, Jean Decarnin, on the eve of liberation, in August 1944. Decarnin was an active member of the Resistance and was shot by a collaborationist member of the *milice* (militia). Genet's own career during the war was not distinguished but fruitful. He joined the army in 1934 and deserted in 1936. He was tried as a deserter in 1938 and during the wartime years was in and out of prison for that and other offences, mainly theft. It was during this period, and in prison, that his first major works were conceived.

Much of the novel was written during autumn 1944. Early, curtailed versions of the text were published in 1948 and 1953 – the latter boosted by Sartre's absurd celebration of Genet as an existentialist 'saint'. A full text, and English translation, was finally issued in 1969. *Funeral Rites*, as we now have it, is a work of artful chaos, summed up by Genet's recommendation: 'this book is true and it is bollocks'.

The work begins and ends with descriptions of Decarnin's funeral. The ceremony 'has no style' because it is just like other funerals. Would a cannibalistic devouring of the corpse, the author muses, be a more appropriate memorial than burying all that meat? There are two other love objects in the narrative, both defined by their wartime roles. One is Erik, 'a handsome *boche* tank-driver'. The other is a young *milice* man, Riton, who is fantasised as the sniper who shot Jean Decarnin. Genet – gay, proletarian, and a criminal himself – sees Riton, the killer of his lover, as kin:

> Members of the Militia were recruited mainly from among hoodlums, since they had to brave the contempt of public opinion which a bourgeois would have feared. They had to run the risk of being murdered at night on a lonely street, but what attracted us most was the fact that they were armed. So for three years I had the delicate pleasure of seeing France terrorised by kids between sixteen and twenty.

The novel has many scenes of wilful offence and blasphemy. Hitler is introduced as a kind of benign pederast, with the compliment:

> Jewellers call a good-sized, well-cut diamond a solitaire. One speaks of its 'water', that is its limpidness, which is also its brilliance. Hitler's solitude made him sparkle.

The war was, for its prime instigator, a masturbation fantasy on a massive scale: 'The Führer sent his finest-looking men to death. It was his only way to possess them all'. Jeanne d'Arc is described menstruating on the day on which she is martyred, a dusty rose staining her white smock as the flames play about her. In one particularly nauseating scene Riton batters a cat to death, then eats it.

There are scraps of plot floating in all this sewage of the mind. Jean D, who is bisexual, has a child (the outcome of rape) who dies. Erik seduces Jean D's mother as well as Riton. There is a pivotal episode in which Erik shoots a young French boy. Why? Because the German had 'realised the moment had come to know murder'. Jean D – 'the ostensible reason for this book', as Genet calls him – dies simultaneously with orgasmic liberation and the accompanying orgy of patriotism from which Jean G is sublimely detached. The necessary chaos of his book, of all art, is pondered by Genet:

> To write is to choose among ten materials that are offered you. I wonder why I was willing to set down in words one fact rather than another of equal importance.

One can see what he means, but it does not make *Funeral Rites* easy to read with one's conventional reading approach. Reading it is a disturbing and unforgettable experience. Do so, with sick bag at the ready.

Funes the Memorious, J. L. Borges, 1944

The contents of *New Scientist* magazine are not for everyone. Occasionally, however, the mass media become interested in an article that first appears there. On 2 August 2012 newspapers picked up a piece in the magazine on what are called 'super memorisers'. These super memorisers are wholly ordinary people whose brains are so wired (or whose wiring is so kinked) that they can remember every single thing that has ever happened to them. Indelibly. Superficially, super-memory might seem to be a gift. But for those so endowed it is a curse. It is not that they have good memories. They are *afflicted* by memory. It blights their lives. It was Freud who said that psychoanalysis 'discovered' nothing. It merely imposed

scientific order and terminology on what the great writers had always known and written about. The technical term psychologists nowadays apply to super-memory is 'hyperthymesia', or 'Highly Superior Autobiographical Memory (HSAM)'. The condition was first clinically described by psychologists in 2006. Super memorisers were, however, anticipated years before in Borges' story, the wonderfully titled 'Funes the Memorious'.

Ireneo Funes, a ranch-hand, first crosses the path of the young Borges (a fictional Borges) in Fray Bentos, Uruguay. There is nothing special about Ireneo other than that he can tell the time, accurately to the second, without a watch. 'The chronometer Funes' Borges names him. He is the illegitimate son of an ironing woman and, it is rumoured, an Englishman, long gone. Borges – himself young – spends summers in the region on vacation with his family. Ireneo and his mother live nearby. In 1887 Borges sees Funes for the last time. He is a changed man. He is now wholly disabled, having been thrown from a horse. When he regained consciousness his brain had mysteriously altered. As he tells Borges:

> On falling from the horse, he lost consciousness; when he recovered it, the present was almost intolerable it was so rich and bright; the same was true of the most ancient and most trivial memories. A little later he realised that he was crippled. This fact scarcely interested him. He reasoned (or felt) that immobility was a minimum price to pay. And now, his perception and his memory were infallible.

He lives alone, in a dark room, wholly solitary, with his memory. It is an anything but empty life:

> We, in a glance, perceive three wine glasses on the table; Funes saw all the shoots, clusters, and grapes of the vine. He remembered the shapes of the clouds in the south at dawn on the 30th of April of 1882, and he could compare them in his recollection with the marbled grain in the design of a

leather-bound book which he had seen only once, and with the lines in the spray which an oar raised in the Rio Negro on the eve of the battle of the Quebracho. . . He told me: I have more memories in myself alone than all men have had since the world was a world.

Such memoriousness is too much for the human constitution. Funes dies, aged twenty-one.

Futility, William Gerhardie, 1922

Not a paperback of this novel exists that does not feature prominently on its front cover Evelyn Waugh's encomium: 'I have talent, but he [Gerhardie] has genius'. Posterity, unfortunately, has not concurred with Waugh. The author's name is known (the spelling uncertain – there are two official versions – and pronounciation even more uncertain) but his novels, alas, are unread. They deserve to be read, *Futility* particularly. Its presuppositions about the human condition anticipate DOCTOR ZHIVAGO, not entirely to Pasternak's advantage. The principal theme in both novels is identical: most human beings live their lives 'underneath', or 'alongside', history – not 'in' history. There are few good Russian novels by British writers. *Futility* is by far the best. There was a reason for this. Gerhardie had the unusual background of being born British but brought up as a child in Russia. He returned in a military and diplomatic role to that country as it was undergoing the cataclysm of the First World War and the Russian Revolution. *Futility* has the terse epigraph: 'The "I" of this book is not me'. And the moon is green cheese and cows jump over it. Hey-diddle-diddle.

The narrative opens: 'And then it struck me that the only thing to do was to fit all this into a book.' The aim is to make some sort of sense of what is otherwise overwhelmingly incoherent. The Bursanovs are the living incarnation of Russian 'futility' – a complex, lovable, admirable, infuriating

thing. Not least to the Russians themselves. In his novel *Wild Berries* (1984), Yevgeny Yevtushenko laments:

> Why do we still have lines [queues]? Because we're poor? Ludicrous. . . No country is richer than ours. But take a look into our railroad stations: they're mobbed, people sleeping there, piled up on one another. . . When will we get *organised* like normal people?

Futility asks the same question. The only answer is a forlorn 'we are a holy people' – and who expects 'organisation' from a nation of saints? The Russians are not what Yevtushenko calls 'normal people'.

Central to Gerhardie's narrative are the three Bursanov daughters: Nina, Sonia, and Vera. The first section of *Futility* is called, with rather too obvious a nod to Chekhov, 'Three Sisters'. Chekhov's depiction of the paralysis of the Russian soul is endorsed throughout. The Bursanov paterfamilias, Nikolai, has gold mines in Siberia which produce not an ounce of metal but warrant him taking charge of a horde of dependants. He has a wife who will not divorce him but who requires he support her and her Jewish dentist lover, who sees more gold in his patients' mouths than Bursanov will ever see from the steppes. Bursanov lives with his German common-law wife, Fanny Ivanovna, a former governess to his daughters, who, in her turn, declines to give him his freedom when his roving eye lands on the sixteen-year-old Zina. Among the hangers-on is a faux-baron and writer so intensely involved in his creation that he cannot stop to put a word on paper. The whole *ensemble* live on mortgage, overdraft, debt and hope. They are not a 'family' but a 'protectorate'.

The first section is set in St Petersburg on the eve of war. There is an interval in which the story's hero, Andrei, returns to Oxford. The second part, 'The Revolution', picks up events in 1917. Now a diplomat, Andrei returns on a 'special mission' to St Petersburg (not long, as he apprehends, before it's Leningrad). The third section ('Intervening in Siberia') jumps forward to 1921. Andrei has been posted again to the new post-Revolutionary Russia. The Burs-anov *caravanserai* has gone on a pilgrimage in search of its mine-wealth in the far steppes – wealth as illusory as the rainbow's pot of gold. On the endless and pointless train journey, Kostia, the writer who never writes, cries out: 'Where are we going? Why are we going?' No answer is forthcoming. But wherever the great engine of life is going it is not towards happiness for Andrei. Nina rejects him.

> 'Will you marry me?' I said.
> 'No.' She shook her head. 'I am tired of you.'

So it all ends as it began. In futility.

Gain, Richard Powers, 1998

Gain marks a departure for Richard Powers – for me the most powerful novelist of ideas currently writing. Powers' fiction is normally austerely intellectual. *Gain*, by contrast, is a tale of cancer and capitalism – what the Victorians would have called a 'social problem novel' – without any direct reference to the digitalisation of the human condition that is the normal Powers theme.

Gain nonetheless has his hallmark binary structure. One narrative traces the growth over a century and a half of the multinational company Clare Products, whose billions have been built on soap. Or, more precisely, on crime, like all great fortunes: the original chemical process was stolen by the Clare brothers from an ingenuous Irish immigrant. The setting is the firm's agricultural division in Lacewood, Illinois (to forestall libel suits, names have been changed). The other strand of the narrative follows, in harrowingly technical detail, the death of Laura Bodey, a divorced, forty-two-year-old realtor and mother of two. Clare owns or sponsors everything in Lacewood, including Laura, who 'hums the corporate theme song to herself sometimes, without realizing'. Everything in her little domestic world comes courtesy of the company:

> Two pots in her medicine cabinet bore the logo, one to apply and one to remove. Those jugs under the sink – Avoid Contact with Eyes – that never quite work as advertized. Shampoo, antacid, low-fat chips. The weather stripping, the grout between the quarry tiles, the nonstick in the nonstick pan, the light coat of deterrent she spreads on her garden.

The company may also have given her the malignancy that is destroying her. They supply the chemotherapy that doesn't cure her, but succeeds in bankrupting her. *Gain* ponders the great ambiguities of mature industrialism. Let's call it American capitalism. Is progress inevitably paid for by human loss? Does profit, like tobacco tar, cause cancer?

The dilemma runs through the novel, down to its smallest detail. This is Laura at the supermarket checkout:

> 'Paper or plastic?' the 55-year-old bagger asks her. What is she supposed to say? Liberty or death? Right or wrong? Good or evil? Paper or plastic? The one kills trees but is 100 per cent natural and recyclable. The other releases insidious fumes if burned but requires less energy to make, can be turned into picnic tables and vinyl siding, has handles, and won't disintegrate when the frozen yogurt melts.

She panics. 'Whatever is easiest,' she blurts out to the bagger, who grimaces. Powers accepts (and brilliantly demonstrates) Procter & Gamble's confident assertion that 'soap is probably the greatest medical discovery in history'. But at what cost? No answer is possible. 'We can't tell yet whether we've created an epidemic or not,' he has said in interviews. 'All we have is statistics, the vague math that only partially connects little to big.' And how, Powers wonders, turning to the biggest puzzle of all, did America, 'a country formed more or less by religious extremists', become 'this nation of insane consumerism'? Unlike Upton Sinclair and John Dos Passos (clear influences on *Gain*) he doesn't impose an answering thesis on the narrative, which ends with a twist which is, even for Powers, supremely ironic. Read this novel. You'll recall it every time you wash your hands or take a shower.

Galápagos, Kurt Vonnegut, 1985

My second-favourite Kurt Vonnegut novel. Not everyone will agree (see below, SLAUGHTERHOUSE-FIVE, for the first – with which most readers will, I think, agree). *Galápagos* finds Vonnegut authorially, if not geographically, on old ground. All the trademarks are here: the cute narrative manner belying an apocalyptic message (the end of the world is once again nigh); the little 'so it goes' tics of style (here an asterisk placed before the names of characters about to die); comic-scientific periphrasis (marriage is 'biologically significant copulation'). It's as if, having labelled himself a boring old fart, as he did in the prologue to *Breakfast of Champions*, Vonnegut decided to play the part for all it's worth. 'Here comes good old Kurt, again.' It still amuses.

The narrator of *Galápagos* is Leon Trotsky Trout, son of our old friend Kilgore Trout, the science-fiction writer (and frequent presence in Vonnegut's work) who has wonderful ideas for novels but can't write worth a damn. Leon has odd narrative qualifications. His mind, like Billy Pilgrim's in *Slaughterhouse-Five*, has been damaged beyond repair by war. Leon volunteered for the US Marines, fought in Vietnam, took part in a My Lai-type operation in which fifty-nine villagers were murdered (to make the world safe for democracy), deserted to Sweden, became a ship-worker, was decapitated by a falling sheet of metal (lost his 'big brain', as the novel would put it), became a ghost haunting the boat which is to be mankind's second ark, and now – a million years from next November – is writing the last story 'on air'. Hi ho.

Boiled down, Trout Jr's *Genesis II* goes like this. In 1986, mankind is extinguished by world-wide economic collapse, war, and epidemic sterility – the result of a new, Aids-type, ovary-eating virus. The only survivors are a random handful of passengers aboard a luxury liner off Ecuador. These comprise a megalomaniac German captain (the new Noah), six female Kanka-bono Indians, a con-man, an elderly widowed biology teacher, an industrial tycoon's blind daughter, a Japanese computer genius and his pregnant wife (whose mutant offspring – thanks to Hiroshima – is covered with fine fur). By a series of accidents, this motley-est of crews is marooned on the Galápagos, where Darwin made his conclusive observations about natural selection. After sexual intercourse with the captain, the biology teacher digitally transfers his semen from her uterus to the Indian girls' wombs. The resulting offspring mate with the Japanese couple's mutant son, and humankind is launched on an excitingly new genetic route. Like the flightless cormorant of the Galápagos which exchanged wings for fins, humanity surrenders its 'big brain', the

better to catch fish. So, over the million years covered by the novel, our species evolves into a furry, unintelligent, finned amphibian.

Galápagos has two premises. One is that, though we won't admit it, the Third World War will happen and, as Einstein predicted, if mankind is even around for the Fourth, it will be fought with rocks. Or flippers. The other premise (Einstein is again relevant) is that mankind's greatest enemy is its 'big brain'. According to Vonnegut, this organ – as absurdly overdeveloped as the elk's antlers – is 'simply no damn good'. At the heart of *Galápagos* is an exhausted misanthropy trying unsuccessfully to change its mind. But Vonnegut hasn't quite reached the Swiftian point of no return. There is an interesting exchange between Kilgore and Leon Trout, in which the author/father tells the author/son to give up on 'these animals' and join him in the great blue yonder. 'The more you learn about people, the more disgusted you'll become,' he tells Leon. But Leon stays on, sustained by his mother's favourite quotation (which stands as the novel's epigraph): Anne Frank's 'In spite of everything, I still believe people are really good at heart.' But, of course, Anne wrote that before the Germans got her.

The Gambler, Fyodor Dostoevsky, 1867

One hesitates to say it, since it's Dostoevsky, but *The Gambler* is a killingly funny novel. The story behind its writing witnesses to the sheer craziness of the novelist's life. He had made an agreement with a publisher that if he did not come up with a novel-length manuscript within a month, all his literary earnings, for the next nine years, would be forfeit. It was a reckless gamble. But Fyodor Dostoevsky knew all about gambling. He was an addict – maddened by the sight of green baize, *rouge et noir*, and the casino's wheel of fortune. *The Gambler* was duly dictated, rapid-fire, to a woman stenographer (one of the first of that profession in Russia), Anna Grigorevna Snitkina, whom he later married. That was a bad bet on her part. He would, when down on his luck, routinely pawn his wedding ring for gambling cash.

There is, Dostoevsky claims in this novel, a religious bond between roulette and the Russian soul. If Russians have money, they must waste it 'wantonly' as a test of whether or not God favours them. No answer has yet been received. *The Gambler* is set in the German town of 'Roulettenberg' (recognisably Wiesbaden). The story is told by Alexei Ivanovich, who is employed as a tutor in the household of 'the General'. We never see Alexei teach, any more than we see the General do anything military. Alexei loves the General's beautiful daughter, Polina. He would throw himself off a cliff for her, he says. She is cold, haughty – but teases whether him with remote possibilities. Is it because he is a penniless 'upper servant'? Or is there another man? She instructs him to go to the casino and lay a bet for her. Alexei is a casino virgin. But he takes the money, lays a wager, and – to his amazement – wins a large sum for her. Was it a test of his love? Or did she desperately need the money? The latter, we learn. The General has mortgaged all his property to play the tables. He is deeply in debt to a French patron, De Grieux, and the family is facing destitution. The General's hopes of salvation have been raised by telegrams from Moscow informing him that an ancient, wealthy aunt is dying. He calls her 'grandmother' and 'mother' – not because she is either of those things but because she can give him life, by dying. Streams of telegrams keep him informed as to whether this lucky event is about to happen. When it does he will be able marry the eligible French heiress he has his eye on.

Out of the blue, the aunt appears. She has dismissed her doctors, swallowed some folk-medicine and is now right as rain. 'Well, here I am – and instead of a telegram, too!' are her first 'catastrophic' words. Catastrophe multiplies. The old lady decides to look in at the casino she has heard so much about. Alexei is instructed to take her (in her bath-chair). She immediately catches the bug and – not quite understanding the rules – lays a mad series of bets on 'zero'. She wins consecutively and sees it as a sign from God. She is in her *seconde enfance*, mutters the Frenchman De Grieux. No – she is merely Russian, the novel affirms. Inevitably she proceeds to lose every penny she possesses. Only a loan from a good-natured Englishman,

Mr Astley (a magnate enriched by the sugar industry), enables her to make her way back to Moscow, a poorer and wiser old woman.

Alexei too is now infected. To win Polina he gambles 'unsystematically', and wins hugely. God loves him. But, even though he has banknotes spilling from his pockets, Polina spurns him. She has always (and prudently) loved Astley – the safest bet. In a downbeat last section Alexei departs for Paris with a French family, whose daughter the General once hoped to marry. They spend all Alexei's money in weeks. The novel ends with his meeting Astley in Bad Homburg (another German gambling town). The Englishman gives him a handout. It will, of course, end up on the tables. Alexei, now a professional gambler, meditates on the necessity of wagering even one's last coin and makes the bleak remark, 'No: tomorrow all shall be ended!' Suicide? Not before Astley's money is gone the way of all the rest.

The Garden of the Finzi-Continis, Giorgio Bassani, 1962

Ghetto, camp, garden: what do the three enclosures have in common? Lawn tennis and the Holocaust, what do they have in common? Answers are to be found in *The Garden of the Finzi-Continis*. The body of the novel covers just over two years – from the Indian summer of 1938 to the awful winter of 1940/1. In November 1938, Mussolini, hitherto lax about Italian Jewry, ingratiated himself with Hitler by bringing in 'race laws'. Bassani's novel chronicles what that meant for the Jewish community in the northern Italian city of Ferrara. For hundreds of years there had been no gross persecution. The ghetto had been abolished in 1859. A highly cultivated Jewish-Ferrarese elite had flourished – Bassani himself belonged to it. By 1945 it would be extinguished.

The narrative opens with a prelude in April 1957. A group of friends goes on a sight-seeing expedition to 'a famous Etruscan necropolis' near Rome. The Etruscans, of course, had been liquidated, as a people and a culture, by the Romans. A nine-year-old child in the party asks why the tombs are so gloomy-looking. 'They have been dead for such ages,' explains the narrator, 'it's as if they'd never lived, as if they'd *always* been dead'. For years, he then tells us, 'I wanted to write about the Finzi-Continis'. Now he does so, in a spirit of requiem, commemoration and resurrection – bringing them back to life as best a novel can.

The narrator (un-named, but called 'Giorgio', logically enough, in De Sica's film of the novel) first sees the Finzi-Contini siblings, Alberto and Micòl, at school in Ferrara. Not in the schoolroom. They only turn up for exams and are expensively home-tutored. Sephardic Jews, they are wealthy and socially superior. In summer 1929 Giorgio (let's call him that) finds himself at the wall of Barchetto del Duca, the grand Finzi-Contini house, with thirteen-year old Micòl whose 'large, light, magnetic eyes' entrance him. They always will. Giorgio almost climbs the garden wall and almost kisses her – but his nerve fails him. She is 'above' him, in every way. He has a horrifying image of what she sees: 'an extremely middle-class brat in short trousers'.

The narrative jumps to late summer 1938. They are all now students. Micòl is in Venice, working on a thesis on Emily Dickinson. As Jews, they have received formal letters of expulsion from the local tennis club. They form a club of their own in the garden of the Finzi-Continis – part *locus amoenus*, part ghetto. They are not over worried about world events. The crisis will blow over. It always does. Their foursome is made up by a gentile communist, Malnate, a burly, outgoing industrial chemist. The Indian summer is blissful, 'strung in a kind of magical suspense, a glassy, glowing stillness and sweetness'. The narrator now loves Micòl utterly but she toys with him, seeming to prefer the manlier Malnate. Life, he thinks, is coming between them. In truth she finds him dull. His 'dreary, absurd, everlasting courtship' is doomed. She is cosmopolitan, he is provincial. And, anyway, Malnate is the better player.

The games must end as the world outside the garden walls moves to the 'fatal last days of 1939'. In the last section Giorgio and Malnate visit a brothel together. Their conversation confirms Giorgio's suspicions

that he is not Micòl's preferred suitor. But he is never sure. The novel winds down as European horrors wind up. Alberto has the good luck (in the circumstances) to predecease the rest of his family in 1942, of lymphogranulomatosis. Malnate disappears without trace after being drafted to fight for Hitler on the Russian front. Most likely the Russian communists kill the Italian communist. In 1943 all the living Finzi-Continis (along with most of the other Ferrara community) are 'taken by stages to their deaths in German camps'. The novel ends with the narrator ruefully thinking that he never had a 'real kiss' from the woman he loved.

The novel does not record how the narrator avoids the Finzi-Continis' fate and that of virtually all the other Ferrarese Jews. Bassani and his wife (whom he met at a tennis club, before his being expelled) managed to make their way to Florence and Rome where he contrived to stay out of harm's way, under forged ID, until the liberation of the city. He was active in the Resistance.

The Garlic Ballads, Mo Yan, 1988

Mo Yan's novel was published a few months before the Tiananmen Square protests (and massacre) of June 1989, and afterwards promptly withdrawn from print. The author was constantly in hot water with the authorities – 'Mo Yan' is a pen-name meaning 'don't speak'. This early dissidence did nothing to dissuade the Nobel Committee from making him their 2012 laureate. The award of the Nobel to Mo Yan – by then a government-approved writer in China – was celebrated there. The more radical 2009 Nobel winner, Herta Müller, called it a 'catastrophe' and a 'slap in the face' for writers more resolutely opposed to their regimes than the author of *The Garlic Ballads*.

Although he is better known for his *Red Sorghum* series (and the 1987 film adapted from it), *The Garlic Ballads* warrants reading – particularly in Howard Goldblatt's racy 1995 translation. Mo Yan asks some very heavy questions. Like other states founded on Marxism-Leninism, China sees its 'soul' as located within the peasant class: the 'workers'. 'Re-education' in the brutal Cultural Revolution (during which Mo Yan himself was 're-educated') typically took the form of 'back to the land', to slave with the peasants in the fields. But what happens, historically, when an age-old peasant culture comes into contact with new-fangled Party bureaucracy? Can the two co-exist? The dedication in *The Garlic Ballads* is to the region in which Mo Yan (born into a farming family) grew up among peasants. The epigraph is a quotation by Stalin:

> Novelists are forever trying to distance themselves from politics, but the novel itself closes in on politics.

Stalin's solution was simple. Exterminate the peasants (in the Kulak reforms) and send any dissident novelists to Siberia. China's way forward has been less clear-cut.

The Garlic Ballads is set in 'Paradise Valley' – a fertile region based on Yan's own Gaomi County. Anything grows well – there are fields of fragrant coriander, jute, and millet. But the local council has decreed that only garlic shall be grown this year. Bureaucrats love monoculture. When the warehouses overflow they refuse to buy the bulk of the crop. Enraged, the peasants (facing a winter of starvation) attack and burn down the council headquarters. The narrative – drenched in aromas throughout (this is a novel one reads with twitching nose) – opens in the blackening, stinking garlic fields. It follows the misfortunes of two cousins, Gao Yang and Gao Ma. The first is a dutiful father, husband, and smallholder. A good man who minds his own business. He politely addresses the police thugs who are beating him up as 'Comrade Officer'. Gao Ma was discharged from the army for seducing his commanding officer's concubine. He is lusty, and loves a local girl, Jinju, in spite of the fact that her family have sold her in marriage to an aged, wealthy member of the community. They need the money so that their two sons can buy their own land. The sons beat up Gao Ma mercilessly. But in an idyllic interlude in a jute field (the dry leaves rustling tunefully and fragrantly) he impregnates Jinju.

Both cousins are arrested, brutalised, tried in a kangaroo court, and sentenced to the labour camp. This, the novel makes clear, is how 'revolution' will be brought to the unregenerate masses. In one scene Gao Yang, hung up by his thumbs, has a thorn branch thrust up his rectum by interrogating police officers. They want him to reveal where he buried his mother (a member of the 'landlord class'), in defiance of the edict that all corpses (to eliminate Confucian heresy) must be cremated. He will not betray her resting place – even in his agony. And he asks, 'Brothers, why are you doing this to me?' The police chief blandly replies: 'We're talking about class struggle here.'

While he is in prison Gao Ma's lover hangs herself. Coincidentally the old man she was destined to marry dies too. Her family arrange an 'underworld' marriage (for cash) in which the corpses will be mingled. When he hears of this, Gao Ma runs 'like a man possessed' out of the prison and into the surrounding snowy wastes. He is shot:

> He sensed something hot and sticky spurting out of his back. With a soft 'Jinju. . .' on his lips, he buried his face in the wet snow.

Gaslight, Gaiters, and Gonophs, Jack Northcliffe, 2012

The Neo-Victorian novel has flourished and is now a distinguished, specifically British, fictional genre. It is aptly represented in this compendium in works by Sarah Waters, A. S. Byatt, Michel Faber, and George MacDonald Fraser. None of them, however, has Northcliffe's slangy *brio* when it comes to period mise-en-scène. Take the opening to *Gaslight, Gaiters, and Gonophs* – a finely concerted sensory assault on the reader's 'inner' nose, ear, and eye:

> London, 1860. November. A peasouper billowing up from the flotsam bobbing in the Thames. The gas lamps already blearing. Good things of day begin to drowse. The rookeries are

emptying, and their birds of prey making wing to the West End.

Dollymops, cracksmen and gonophs are on the prowl.

Susan (up from Mrs Sucksby's kitchen in the Borough) and Caroline (one of Mrs Castaway's girls in St Giles) will hunt together tonight. Caroline is on the game, an alley-cat who'll lift her chimmy for two bob (and a tanner for Mrs C). Sue has been brought up 'by hand' by Mrs Sucksby to be a palmer, a pogue-hoister, a dipper, a flimp: what in Borough argot they call a *fingersmith*.

Tonight, though, she's a mutcher – a predator on drunks. Caroline will button for Susan – lure some tipsy greenhorn into a dark alley. One tap with the cosh then it's off with his unmentionables to the translators. Mrs Sucksby will fence the wipers, the repeater and the pins.

No great risk. The garrotting panic and legislation against footpads is still two years away. It's Liberty Hall on the London streets in 1860.

They walk down to St James'. Nothing. Normally Caroline's had her nancy jiggled two or three times by now. Reeling out of the Minor Club come a couple of swells. 'Why,' says Caroline, loud enough to be heard in Green Park, 'if it ain't Captain Flashie, VD – I mean VC – sorry, Soldier Boy.'

The swell, a military man with magnificent moustaches, turns to his pal and says, just as loudly: 'Hoist that dollymop's sail, Speedicut, and you'll be pissing fish-hooks for three months. Got the chats out of your bush yet, Caroline?'

'I'd rather be a martletop and steal snot rags from buses than do you, you toff bastard,' she shouts back, good-naturedly as he tosses a sov in the gutter. 'Bet it's snide,' she shouts at the men's backs as they saunter off to Kate Hamilton's place.

The girls amble on to the Arches – where, at last, they spy a four-square rig reeling out of a bar: kerchief, diamond stud and all. 'Shop!' whispers Caroline. 'Our first customer.'

Was ever backdrop better done? The plot follows a winding track, via the stolen wallet and what it reveals, culminating in a 'tremendous' climax in the Eagle Tavern on City Road, where more than an easel is popped that night.

Actually, there is no *Gaslight, Gaiters, and Gonophs*, nor any 'Jack Northcliffe'. The above is a pastiche by John Sutherland (aka Lord Northcliffe, Prof Emeritus), author of the *Longman Companion to Victorian Fiction*. And wannabe (all his life) novelist, rather than a louse on the locks of the particular variety of fiction he loves but cannot himself aspire to reproduce. Everyone who presumes to write authoritatively about novels should try to write one, if only as an act of humility and self-revelation. A very few critics are ambidextrous in this regard. I, as the above will make clear, am not. If any publisher thinks differently, please get in touch.

The Gates of Ivory, Margaret Drabble, 1991

The Gates of Ivory is the conclusion of Drabble's 'Headland Trilogy'. *The Radiant Way* (1987), the first in the series, begins with a chaotic end-of-decade party in Harley Street. It is 1979 – the 'Ice Age', as Drabble calls it. England is a frozen corpse of what it once was. There are some two hundred guests – many of whom flit past the bemused reader's gaze, never to be seen again. Specifically, the party introduces three 'highly selected' and self-made women – contemporaries at Cambridge in the early 1950s and now middle-aged. One, Alix Bowen, wants to 'change things'. An evangelical Leavisite, she teaches English to prisoners and has chosen to live in quintessentially provincial Northam (Sheffield). The second of the trio, Esther Breuer, wants to 'know things'. She is a Jewish émigrée art historian and connoisseur. Liz Headland is a psychotherapist who wants to 'make sense of things'. Liz is London-based (although Northam-born).

The long ensuing narrative follows these three lives, centrally Liz's. The process begins with her second divorce and the painful memory of being abused in childhood by her father. Life, we gather, is no 'radiant way' (Drabble's title refers to the simplistic imagery of a popular children's reading book in the 1930s). Running alongside the five years of *The Radiant Way*'s panorama is the career of the Horror of Harrow Road – a serial killer inspired by the Yorkshire Ripper. Alix comes within a hairsbreadth of being one of the Horror's victims. He is eventually discovered to be a rather mild fellow living in a flat above Esther. After he is put away, Alix visits him regularly to advise on such things as vegetarianism and his Open University degree.

A Natural Curiosity (1989), the second book in the trilogy, is a tighter effort, covering a few months in 1987. The focus is firmly on Alix, whose sleuthing uncovers the something nasty in the woodshed that made young Paul Whitmore the Horror of Harrow Road.

The allusion in the title *The Gates of Ivory* is to Penelope's declaration in the *Odyssey* about false dreams (or fictions) coming through gates of 'traitor ivory', while true dreams come through gates of horn. The narrative centres on Liz Headland's Marlovian quest into the heart of Cambodian darkness. Her Kurtz is Stephen Cox, a Booker-winning novelist with whom she had a pregnant conversation at Bertorelli's in January 1985, recorded long ago in *The Radiant Way*. Liz's obsession with Cox is triggered by an enigmatic parcel of his literary and possibly human remains (in the form of human finger bones). Why he went to Cambodia is a mystery: to research a play on Pol Pot is his unconvincing 'alibi'. And why Liz should choose to follow him to the most dangerous country on earth is another.

In her journey to the interior she encounters horrors almost beyond imagining. Descriptions of torture and mass killings abound. One account of eating live monkey brains will put the reader off variety meats for a day or two. Much other blood is spilled in protracted descriptions of menstruation. This is a novel which does for those unmentionables, the used tampon and sanitary pad, what PORTNOY'S COMPLAINT did for liver. It is all worlds away from the West End party where the story began.

Drabble's trilogy has never, I think, received proper recognition as one of the most monumental, and unblinkingly depressed, achievements in twentieth-century fiction. You'll need a fortnight – and a regular supply of cheering drink – to read it. Stock up and do so.

Gaudy Night, Dorothy L. Sayers, 1935

Sayers has not weathered the decades as well as Agatha Christie. But for those who can stand her donnishness and arch-snobbery this novel has always been of special interest. It is unusual in dealing less with murder and its solution than with sexual politics – more particularly gender discrimination. *Gaudy Night* was, as Sayers enigmatically informed her publisher, a novel which was 'important to me'. Why it was important to her, the reader is left to work out. The narrative chronicles the middle act of the [Lord Peter] Wimsey–[Harriet] Vane relationship, which began five years previously in *Strong Poison* with the trial in which Harriet was falsely accused of murdering her lover. The series was to end in *Busman's Honeymoon* (1937) with the couple's marriage.

'Gaudy Nights' are Oxford high-table college feasts. Harriet, now a successful mystery novelist, is invited back to her alma mater, Shrewsbury College, for such a dinner. She resides in Bloomsbury with a little car and a rising literary reputation, and 'lives with a man who was not married to her', as the censorious world notes. These writers! Although she took a brilliant first there she has never before been back to her college, and among the strongest parts of the novel are her impressions of 'Shrewsbury' (transparently Somerville College) as she walks again through its precincts. Crossing the quad by evening, Harriet comes across a sheet of paper with an obscene depiction of:

> a naked figure of exaggeratedly feminine outlines, inflicting savage and humiliating outrage upon some person of indeterminate gender clad in cap and gown.

It is the first of many such poison-pen missives. The culprit must be a member of the Senior Common Room, the English lecturer, Miss Lydgate, maintains.

Some months later Harriet is invited down again and asked to use her detective skills in investigating the outrage. She, in turn, calls on Lord Peter. Some idyllic, and for the time explicit, love-making in punts and meadow grass ensues. Finally, after sleuthing and shrewd deduction, Wimsey stages a denouement scene in the SCR. Who is 'X'? [Spoiler Alert: stop here if you do not wish to know.] Inexorably he demonstrates that it must be one of the college 'scouts' (servants), Annie Wilson. She is, it emerges, the widow of a scholar who was disgraced when one of the present fellows at Shrewsbury exposed him as an academic fraud. He subsequently drank himself to death. The high point of the novel is Annie Wilson's diatribe against the 'unnatural' life of a woman at Oxford:

> It is women like you who take the work away from the men and break their hearts and lives. No wonder you can't get men for yourselves and hate the women who can.

This outburst precipitates Harriet's decision that she and Peter must marry.

Generation X: Tales for an Accelerated Culture, Douglas Coupland, 1991

The title of Coupland's novel (the first he published) has broken loose to take on a life of its own as a demographic label, used promiscuously by commentators on the 1980s. Synchronically, the novel owes much to the North American twelve-step (famously AA) concept of 'sharing' life stories, without dialogue or 'cross-talk'. The stories, at a 'participation' meeting, are simply dumped into the heap of narrative in the middle of the room. Diachronically, the structure of *Generation X* goes way back to THE DECAMERON – a group of high-fashion kids escaping the current plague and amusing each other with their 'tales'. The key difference in *Generation X* is the modifier 'accelerated' –

things are breaking up faster here than in fourteenth-century Florence.

The frame-narrative, within which the little narratives nestle, is located in the Mojave Desert, near to Palm Springs. 'The Springs' is a futuristic city pasted on to primeval desert – a creation of urban whimsy. It has, someone has counted, 269 golf courses on a sandy wasteland in which not even scrub can grow. 'Palm Springs', sneers the novel, is 'a small town where old people are trying to buy back their youth'. And all they succeed in buying is very old age and looking like the lizards who originally owned the place.

Coupland, Canadian by origin, relocated to the Mojave to get its feel while writing the novel. He made the disarmingly modest (and probably sly) claim: 'I just want to show society what people born after 1960 think about things.' The narratives are spun out of a bunch of young layabouts who 'came of age', as the antique phrase puts it, in the 1980s. They are now in their late twenties. They have been condemned to live in a period of 'historical underdosing', when nothing seems to be happening. They are not rich and are disinclined even to do the work that might make them middle class. They simply hang out, housed by Helen, aged fifty-two, the most indulgent of landladies. 'They're my children,' she says. 'Adults or not, I just can't kick them out of the house . . . And besides – they're great cooks.'

The ruptured text allows each of the three principals – Andrew, Dag, and Claire – their own voice. Andy, who heads the trio, used to be an office worker. Now he picks up what few dollars he needs working bars. Claire is a refugee from a family split by divorce into human shrapnel – she bears the wounds. Dag used to work in advertising and is not likeable. He is diagnosed as a lesbian trapped in a man's body. None of the three is 'street' (or streetwise), all are college-educated. They are the living incarnation of Freud's *Civilisation and Its Discontents*. Everything, sighs one of them, seems 'to be from hell these days: dates, jobs, parties, weather'. They have tissue-thin relationships, between themselves and with 'significant others'. They call themselves the 'Poverty Jet Set' and their only mode of transport is a 'syphilitic Saab'. The layout of the narrative says it all. It is fractured into chapters and mottoes that say much more than the characters themselves.

I Am Not a Target Market
Dead at 30 Buried at 70
Shopping is Not Creating
Purchased Experiences Don't Count
Adventure Without Risk is Disneyland
God, You Get Old So Quickly!
Brazilification

Generation X introduced the term (which like the title has taken on a life of its own) McJob. The novel is as much a lexicon as a narrative. If Coupland had trademarked his more famous Couplandisms he would never have had to write another novel. With hindsight one views *Generation X* as a jaundiced anatomy of Reagan-revised America. Jaundiced and vaguely terrifying and, when you get down to it, too disengaged to protest – or even gripe interestingly. The novel has two endings. One is apocalyptic, a glimpsed end of the world, for which this has just been the waiting room:

It was a thermonuclear cloud – as high in the sky as the horizon is far away – angry and thick, with an anvil-shaped head the size of a medieval kingdom and as black as a bedroom at night.

The other ending is a hailstorm of tendentious statistics; e.g. 'Percent of US budget spent on the elderly: 30. On education: 2'. Gloomy stuff. All one can say is, it hasn't happened yet.

Gentlemen Prefer Blondes, Anita Loos, 1925

The teasing subtitle is 'The Intimate Diary of a Professional Lady'. The oldest profession, that is. Loos' novel underwent a successful transition from 1925 magazine serial to bestseller, with *New Yorker*-style illustrations by Ralph Barton. The brittle comedy installed into British and American folklore the indelible image of the 'dumb blonde', who is really not as dumb as she looks – nor, around the roots, as blonde as she looks. *Gentlemen Prefer Blondes* had to wait a quarter of a century before finding its perfect articulation in the person of Marilyn Monroe, who starred in the 1953 film adaptation (raven-tressed Jane Russell co-starred).

The novel takes the form of a series of archly semi-literate journal entries by Lorelei Lee, a New York 'gold-digger' (or 'professional lady'), mixing naivety and shrewdness: notably where diamonds and furs are concerned. The blonde diarist was born, we learn, in Little Rock, where she narrowly escaped imprisonment for shooting one of her faithless lovers by seducing the judge. Currently she is the protégée of Gus Eisman, the Chicago 'button king' (married, needless to say, to an unwitting Mrs Eisman). Gus has taken it on himself to 'educate' Lorelei. She also wins the heart of a penniless British novelist, Gerry Lamson, who is so taken with her that he promises to divorce his wife and make her an honest, not a professional, woman.

Lorelei is alarmed and is packed off by Gus on a European trip, first class, on an ocean liner, chaperoned by her hard-headed friend Dorothy. London, the girls decide 'is really nothing', though the heroine dances with the Prince of Wales and wins the heart of an aged British aristocrat, Sir Francis ('Piggie') Beekman – as well as some gratifying jewels. Alas, the Koh-i-noor escapes her grasp. Paris, they decide, is 'devine'. Not least the 'Eyeful Tower'. Lorelei's 'education' continues apace. One important lesson she learns from her experience of continental gallantry, which expects to get results free of charge, is:

I really think that American gentlemen are the best after all, because kissing your hand may make you feel very, very good but a diamond-and-safire bracelet lasts for ever.

In other words, leave '*l'amour*' to Colette.

The girls move on to Vienna where the heroine flummoxes 'Dr Froyd', whose psychoanalysis cannot handle Lorelei Lee. The eating habits of the Germans displease her mightily: 'You can say what you want about the Germans being full of "kunst", but what they are really full of is *delicatessen*.'

The ladies return to New York, the heroine now having won the heart of a Philadelphia millionaire, Mr Henry Spoffard, and a penniless Hollywood gigolo, Mr Montrose. Juggling all her suitors (including the long-suffering, long-paying button king) and making a final, respectable marriage (with promise of much infidelity) with Spoffard (whom she converts from Presbyterianism and abstinence to the more congenial doctrines of the jazz age) brings the diary to its jaunty conclusion. It is now July and Lorelei's 'education' has taken five months. Edith Wharton, perhaps not entirely seriously, called *Gentlemen Prefer Blondes* 'the Great American Novel'.

Miss Lorelei Lee's incontrovertible truth about the only thing a young lady can trust ('a diamond lasts forever') was taken over – unironically – by the retail diamond trade in the 1990s in its TV advertisements and popularised, pithily, in the 1949 stage and 1953 film adaptations as 'diamonds are a girl's best friend'.

Gilead, Marilynne Robinson, 2004

For the many readers who were impressed (who wasn't?) by Marilynne Robinson's first novel, *Housekeeping* (1980), it was a frustrating two decades' wait for the follow-up. *Gilead*, when it finally arrived, scooped up a basketful of prizes for its by then sixty-year-old author.

It is dedicated 'For John and Ellen Summers, my dear father and mother'. That touching semi-private detail cues us that this is a novel about inter-generational love. *Gilead* takes the form of a letter addressed by an unusually aged father to his seven-year-old son. They are only a few feet apart as he writes, dwelling under the same roof. But direct communication by speech, across the gulf of years that divides them, is impossible. The writer, John Ames, is in his seventies. He has been diagnosed with angina pectoris (it has a 'theological sound', he likes to fancy). The letter he composes opens:

I told you last night that I might be gone sometime, and you said, Where,

and I said, To be with the Good Lord, and you said, Why, and I said, Because I'm old, and you said, I don't think you're old.

As old, alas, as he's likely to get. And, he adds, by the time his son reads it:

I'll have been gone a long time. I'll know most of what there is to know about being dead, but I'll probably keep it to myself. That seems to be the way of things.

What began as a letter soon becomes a memoir.

John Ames is a third-generation Congregationalist minister. He likes quiet. He is ecumenical by nature. His closest friend is a 'staunch Presbyterian'. He has good relations with Methodists and the 'negro churches', as well as a particularly close affinity to the Quakers. Religion has been his life. Upstairs, neatly stacked, are 2,250 sermons. He is rather glad his doctor has advised against climbing stairs. Piece by piece the narrative of his life assembles.

His grandfather came from Maine to Kansas in the 1830s and took up arms for the Unionist cause in the Civil War. John's father, in reaction to *his* father, became resolutely pacifist. John himself is somewhat of this same mind. It is the mid-1950s and he thinks he may vote for Eisenhower. Not that he likes Ike. He just wants a quiet life in a quiet country. He was brought up in the small Iowa town of Gilead, where his father had a ministry. He was not the cleverest child in the family – that was his elder brother Edward who went to Germany, soaked himself in Higher Criticism and came back an atheist, provoking a family crisis and excommunication. John stayed on track and married young before being ordained. His wife and child died soon after, during childbirth. He held their baby while she was momentarily alive: 'It was a blessing'. Will he meet them again soon? he wonders.

He married again, very late in life, a member of his congregation thirty-five years his junior – a newcomer to Gilead, an adult convert whom he baptised. They have just the one child – a shy, serious little boy.

John dearly wishes his wife and son could have known him in his manly strength. 'Why d'you have to be so damn old?' she asks him amiably. 'I ask myself the same question', he thinks:

> The fact is I don't want to be old. And I certainly don't want to be dead. I don't want to be the tremulous old coot you barely remember. I bitterly wish you could know me as a young man, and not really so young, either, necessarily. I was trim and fit into my sixties.

Even now, 'For a dying man I feel pretty good. And that is a blessing.' Another blessing is that the son of his closest friend – who was thought to have gone to the bad – returns to Gilead to explain that the cruel race laws and prejudices of the time have enforced a separation from his common-law wife. He is, despite the gossip of Gilead, a good man after all.

Robinson's novel is – there is no other word – moving. An effect which is achieved with the quietest, least ostentatious, of literary materials. *Gilead* was disclosed by his press office to be one of President Obama's favourite books. Good for him.

Giovanni's Room, James Baldwin, 1956

Baldwin's novel opens with an elegant variation on the 'depiction by mirror image' expository device:

> I stand at the window of this great house in the south of France as night falls, the night which is leading me to the most terrible morning of my life. I have a drink in my hand, there is a bottle at my elbow. I watch my reflection in the darkening gleam of the window pane. My reflection is tall, perhaps rather like an arrow, my blond hair gleams. My face is like a face you have seen many times. My ancestors conquered a continent, pushing across death-laden plains, until they came to an ocean which faced away from Europe into a darker past.

For anyone who knows anything about Baldwin – and in 1956 anyone who picked up *Giovanni's Room* most certainly would – this self-portrait would perplex. It was the author's second novel. His first, *Go Tell It on the Mountain*, had been memoir-true to Baldwin's own life – growing up black, gifted, sickly-small, and two generations away from slavery – in Harlem, New York. Now we're faced with a blond beast in the *Côte d'Azur* – what is this book about? It is, the reader soon gathers (assuming the blurb hasn't filled them in already), about the other prejudice Baldwin faced: towards his sexuality. While writing *Giovanni's Room*, the author had come to France to 'find himself'. This, muses David, the American hero-narrator of the novel:

> is an interesting phrase, not current as far as I know in the language of any other people, which certainly does not mean what it says but betrays a nagging suspicion that something has been misplaced.

As for many American creatives of colour (jazz musicians like Sidney Bechet; novelists like Richard Wright and Chester Himes), France offers David a liberal atmosphere in which to develop his gifts and personality ('find' himself), unhampered by discrimination. There should, for many Americans, have been another statue of the Lady with the Torch at Orly Airport in Paris. Most important for Baldwin, the man and the author, was the French tolerance of homosexuality.

David, as it happens, is (or was, a few days before the novel begins) engaged to a woman. 'My girl, Hella, and I', he says, 'rented [a room] in Paris, from photographs, some months ago. Now she has been gone a week. She is on the high seas now, on her way back to America.' Something else is happening on this very day. A convicted murderer, Giovanni, is about to be guillotined. David first met Giovanni – a handsome Italian, with charming manners – as a bartender in Paris. A love affair ensued, conducted in the room of the title (a continuously darkened room, significantly).

As he stands at the window in the south

of France, David recalls the first gay experience he had as a child, which he has kept secret (even from Giovanni, whom he told he was a gay virgin). He dealt with that crisis by retreating into defensive homophobia. 'The idea that such a person could have been my best friend was proof of some horrifying taint in me.' In France, far from finding himself, David lost himself in a complicated series of denials – Giovanni for Hella, Hella for Giovanni. It led, eventually, to Giovanni losing his job and, in a frenzy of confusion, murdering the owner of the bar where he worked. Hella, meanwhile, discovered David in a gay bar, recklessly cruising for sex, and left him in disgust. Both, in a sense, are David's victims.

He has been supported, grudgingly, by his father back in America, who has shrewd doubts about whether David is a 'real man', but further support is unlikely. What, the novel leaves one wondering, will (can, should) David now do? Write *Giovanni's Room*, perhaps.

The Go-Between, L. P. Hartley, 1953

If anyone knows anything about this novel it's the opening line, a portentous maxim worn threadbare with repetition: 'The past is a foreign country; they do things differently there.' This leads into the opening enigma in the narrative. A hero who had a good start in life regards himself, with justice, as a failure:

> If my twelve-year-old self, of whom I had grown rather fond, thinking about him, were to reproach me: 'Why have you grown up such a dull dog, when I gave you such a good start? Why have you spent your time in dusty libraries, cataloguing other people's books instead of writing your own?'. . . – what should I say?

The answer he gives merely adds to the enigma:

> I should have an answer ready. 'Well, it was you who let me down, and I will

tell you how. You flew too near to the sun, and you were scorched. This cindery creature is what you made me.'

L. P. Hartley was born in 1895 into a family enriched by his solicitor father's canny investment in a local brickworks. It was a comfortable, middle-class domestic environment whose main discomfort for young Leslie was that it wasn't quite upper-class. That chafed. As his biographer records, 'Much of his life was spent in a seemingly ceaseless grand tour of the houses of the rich and famous.' A rather nice snob, in other words.

In 1909, when he was a nine-year-old lad, Leslie was invited by his school chum Moxey, a boy of higher status, to stay at Bradenham Hall in Norfolk. It was a heady but socially nerve-wracking experience. He wrote a sweet letter home to his mother recording that he had been met 'in a motor car' driven by a chauffeur(!). He added, 'there is going to be a cricket match today, the Hall against the village. I am going to [keep] score'. If, to this day, you want to understand the English class system, go and watch the village cricket match.

The Bradenham visit was a primal, life-formative event. *The Go-Between*, nearly fifty years later, germinated from those summer days in 1909. In the interim, Hartley – who had a private income thanks to bricks (he was one of the few novelists of his age to be bothered by supertax) – spent as much time as he could living well and writing well-received fiction and reviews. It was all prefatory to this, his masterpiece, which came out in one of the mundane years of the post-war period.

Leo Colston, a dried-up librarian bachelor in his sixties, finds a diary from 1900. In it he recorded how he had been invited, aged twelve, to a great country house, Brandham, in Norfolk. The invitation came about as the result of a series of misperceptions by his school chum, Marcus Maudsley. Marcus is unaware that Leo is a 'scholarship' boy and that his widowed mother makes do on a small income. He thinks that Leo's address – Court Place – indicates a residence as grand as his own, which it doesn't.

Leo arrives, in baking August, wearing

wholly inappropriate winter clothes (a Norfolk jacket, for example). Everyone is kind but condescending – they kit him out. They appreciate, now, that he is not (quite) one of them, but are good-natured about it. Leo finds himself appointed a kind of upper servant, carrying love letters (whose content he only dimly understands) between the beauty of the house, Marian, and her wholly unsuitable lusty farmer lover, Ted. It all climaxes in the great annual cricket match: the Hall versus the village. The gents turn out in flannels and display the repertoire of strokes they learned at public school. The village oicks look as if they'd just come in from mucking out the stables, and aim wild but shrewd haymakers at the spinners and quickies that their betters serve up to them. Leo is first scorer, then twelfth man, in which role, by 'catching out' Ted, he precipitates a terrible sequence of discoveries climaxing in blood and shame. Hanging over it all is the parching sun and the poisonous belladonna plant by the wood-shed – a place where evil lurks, like the serpent in Eden.

After the catastrophe Leo will live on as the emotional eunuch who introduced himself to us in those early pages. Why did things go so life-changingly wrong? Because he is inherently weak, or because, like Icarus, he flew too near the sun? The novel gives no direct answer, beyond the sense that it would have been wonderful if that last 'high' Victorian summer of 1900 had never ended.

Go Now, Richard Hell, 1996

Could the patriarch of punk, the lead anarcho-instrumentalist-vocalist of the Voidoids (their breakthrough track was 'Love Comes in Spurts') write a novel? More importantly would it be a novel anyone other than a loyal fan with spiked hair and safety pins through his conk would want to read? William Gibson (king of the punk-SF writers) had no doubt.

Go Now is vile, scabrous, unforgivable, and deserving of the widest possible audience.

That Richard Lester Meyers (b. 1949) intended to do the literary thing at some point is evident from his adopting his *nom de guerre culturelle* from Rimbaud's *Une Saison en Enfer*.

Go Now, like the Voidoid's hallmark track, 'comes in spurts'. The narrative is summarised by one disaffected blog-reviewer (cheerfully disregarding the finer points of capitalisation) as: 'i got high, i Had sex, I drove Around a bit. Heh!' Aptly put, bloggist. In form, Go Now is a 'drugalog', dramatising, and glorifying, the existential loneliness of 'junk'. Only junk can transport us to where the essential truths of the human condition are found, we, the uninitiated (unhooked?), are to understand.

It is 1980. The sun comes up. Billy Mud (born Michael Bernstein) is no early riser. His eyes open, his nostrils flare. Smell of the bed ('nasty, but like home'). Armpits (whiffy). The New York apartment ('sharp chemical-metallic smell that sweat glands make when deprived of heroin'). Autumn outside ('exhaust fumes mixed with the wet air. . . It smells like just-cooked junk'). All this olfactory assault and it's still page one. It's time to get up and cook some junk for breakfast. The only problem is our hero has run out. Nothing in his trusty teaspoon. He goes to his French girlfriend-turned-dealer to 'cop' some junk. He scores, injects, and luxuriates in the high:

I sit there. There's my dick inside my pants, really warm and heavy and potent. Maybe I should jerk off. I haven't come in days – it's like pissing or taking a shit, you can only do it on the outskirts of highs.

It is, we infer, a somewhat sluggish bodily member, but (male readers will enviously register) when unsluggish extendable past his navel. Or so he tells us.

Billy Mud is lead guitarist in a group whose vogue has passed. He still picks up the necessary money in 'dingy nightclubs' where 'the girls, as a rule, are there to be abused'. Which he does – out of *ennui*, not sexual interest. Something at last happens to relieve his boredom. A girlfriend, Chrissa, has been commissioned to deliver a classic automobile to LA – a fire-coloured '57 De

Soto Adventurer (the colour of New York methadone, Mud thinks; the analogy would not occur to everyone). 'The road!' – that sovereign remedy for all adventure-seeking Americans. On the drive across, his agent suggests he write a book about America – a 'Kerouaciad' for the 1980s.

Off they go, following the two-lane blacktop over prairies where once the covered wagons trundled. *En route* Mr Mud scores dope everywhere, and screws (to Chrissa's intense exasperation) anything screwable. It climaxes in Mud-Bernstein's (and Hell-Meyers') native Kentucky. He hasn't been in touch with his family for ten years. He celebrates by screwing his aunt Jane. She finds the reunion gratifyingly out of the ordinary. He steals all the Percodan from her medical cabinet, and then it's back on the road. Incest in Kentucky is one of the few things that happen in this novel, though Mud's anabasis takes in some sharp topographic observation. For example, you are *in* New York – but only *on* Los Angeles, like a fly on a window pane. To Mud, the West Coast city is, if anything, even less congenial than New York:

> The conspicuous electric signs and elaborate architecture are like smiles pasted onto fear. And then there's the frightening sweet smell of the place, like an orchid's ulterior motive, disgustingly attractive, like the smell of your own farts.

Mud survives, despite the world an unkind fate has dumped him in. 'The way things are now', he says, 'a few bags of dope make me feel lucky. And you know I think it's true. I've always been lucky'.

Gibson is right. It's a nauseating novel – but damnably readable.

The Godfather, Mario Puzo, 1969

The background to *The Godfather* was blatantly self-proclaimed by its author. He had written two well-received 'art novels' which, between them, made him $6,500. Mario was in food-stamp territory: 'I was

forty-five years old and tired of being an artist . . . It was time to grow up and sell out'. And, he complacently added, 'write the fastest and bestselling fiction paperback of all time'. A paperback that would – in addition to making its author rich – throw light on the most secret society in America: more secret than rabid anti-Semites believe the Elders of Zion to be; more secret than that strange club at Yale, the Skull and Bones; more secret than the Masons; more secret than the Grand Wizard conclave of the KKK; more secret than Opus Dei (whose superselling chronicle would come, thirty years later, courtesy of Dan Brown). Who are they? In a nice little joke, the M-word is never used in the novel. The author, *echt* Italian, knew all about *omertà* and what happened to those who infringed that savage law.

Puzo's only error, in an otherwise triumphant 'selling out', was to part with *The Godfather*'s film rights for a measly $12,500. Francis Ford Coppola went on to create an 'American classic' out of 'Puzo pulp'. The germ of *The Godfather* is an exuberantly paradoxical essay which Puzo wrote for *Cavalier* (a girly mag) in 1966, entitled, 'How Crime Keeps America Healthy, Wealthy, Cleaner and More Beautiful'. Critics of his novel (they were legion) wholly overlooked its 'casual irony', Puzo complained. He himself saw *The Godfather* as a work in the Swiftian 'Modest Proposal' class. In his essay Puzo puts forward an argument for an end to being law-abiding, which is as perversely 'logical' as Swift's argument that the Irish could solve the problem of starvation by eating their babies:

> How are we to adjust to a society that drafts human beings to fight a war, yet permits its businessmen to make a profit from the shedding of blood? . . . As society becomes more and more criminal, the well-adjusted citizen, by definition, must become more criminal. So let us now dare to take the final step.

Put another way: the more criminal America becomes, the more American it becomes. It's a variant on Black Panther ('gangster') H. Rap Brown's remark, made at roughly the same time: 'Violence is as American as cherry pie.'

The more violent America becomes, the more American it is. Is the Mafia a cancer, eating away at the vitals of the country (as the authorities like to present it) – or is it the country's soul, and its manifest destiny? The Puzo-esque answer is given in the description of Don Corleone's funeral:

> Michael... went out into the garden to join the host of mourners. Behind him came the *caporegimes*, followed by their soldiers and then all the humble people the Godfather had blessed during his lifetime... There were even some who had been his enemies, come to do him honour.
>
> Michael observed all this with a tight, polite smile... He would follow his father. He would care for his children, his family, his world. But his children would grow up in a different world. They would be doctors, artists, scientists. Governors. Presidents. Anything at all.

The 'family' will become the country. The epigraph which Puzo chose for *The Godfather* is Balzac's 'Behind every great fortune there is a crime'. And behind every great country there lies an awful lot of crime. *The Godfather*, dismissed by most commentators at the time as a heavy-handed gangster melodrama, invites serious critical attention as a Great American Novel about the dubious nature of American greatness.

The Gold-Bug, Edgar Allan Poe, 1843

This is a short story which can, plausibly, be credited with winning – or, at least, shortening – a world war fought one hundred years after its publication. It has always been the most popular and imitated of Poe's efforts – perhaps because it is one of his 'tales of ratiocination' or 'brain teasers'. It still teases. It has also benefited from becoming a cult classic among intellectuals in France. Baudelaire, no less, translated it under the beautiful title 'Le Scarabée d'or', while Jacques Derrida and Jacques Lacan, those gods of deconstruc-

tionist theory, also had a high regard for Poe's story. (Despite the title of Poe's story translating beautifully into French – *scarabée*, etc. – for British readers 'bug' means just one thing. Bedbugs. The story was retitled 'The Gold Beetle' by its first English publishers, which throws the narrative out of joint at any number of points.) These days, 'The Gold-Bug' has become wholly unfashionable as an object of study in American high schools and colleges for its grossly comic ('I'se here, Massa Will!') depiction of the hero's black servant, Jupiter, who is manumitted but so fond of slavery that he declines to be freed.

The story is narrated by a sceptical unnamed friend of the hero. After losing his considerable fortune William Legrand has taken refuge, Crusoe-style, on a god-forsaken island off the South Carolina coast, with only the clownish Jupiter as his Man Friday. It is not the kind of the place to raise a man's spirits.

> It consists of little else than the sea sand, and is about three miles long. Its breadth at no point exceeds a quarter of a mile. It is separated from the main land by a scarcely perceptible creek, oozing its way through a wilderness of reeds and slime...

The narrator is asked by his worried family to visit Legrand, who apparently is in the grip of some crisis. It turns out he has been bitten by a 'bug' – a handsome, gold-mottled thing (entomologically plausible; Poe had an actual beetle in mind). It happened near an offshore wreck. He no longer has the bug but made a sketch which he shows the narrator – who says, quite reasonably, it doesn't look like a bug at all but a human skull. Legrand is furious and the narrator leaves. A few months later he is called back.

To cut a short story shorter, it turns out the skull – and a cipher – were inscribed in invisible ink on the parchment. The heat of Legrand's fire (the narrator's first visit was during an unusual cold spell) brought out the inscription. Legrand has broken the code (this story includes the first use of the term 'cryptography'), which gives the location of Captain Kidd's buried treasure (hence the drawing of the skull and crossbones). They dig up the treasure – over a million dollars' worth.

The last third of the story is an account of how the code, reproduced graphically, was cracked. It was a simple substitution system ('f' for 'e', etc.). A child could work it out nowadays. But for the readers of 1843, it was heady stuff.

So where does the business about the Second World War come in? The most brilliant of American code-breakers during that conflict was William F. Friedman. It was he who managed to break Japan's 'Purple Code', which meant – among other things – that the US knew exactly what the enemy navy's next moves would be in the Battle of Midway, the naval engagement which swung the war America's way. Friedman was to America's victory in the Pacific theatre what Turing, Enigma, and Bletchley were to the Allies' victory in Europe. Friedman, it's good to record, was inspired, as a lad, to his career in cryptanalysis by reading Poe's story. If 'The Gold-Bug' hadn't come his way, who knows? History might have taken the course described in Philip K. Dick's *The Man in the High Castle* and the rising sun would have flown over the White House.

The Golden Apples, Eudora Welty, 1949

Welty is the *doyenne* of the Southern Fiction school, alongside William Faulkner. This work owes much, she recorded, to *The Sound and the Fury*. Like Faulkner, Welty does not yield herself easily to the reader. This is not a page-turner, except in the sense that one is for ever turning the pages back to work out just what is going on. In form *The Golden Apples* is a 'cycle' novel – a short-story cycle – which depicts a whole community by bundling together a set of individual stories. Other classic examples in American literature are Sherwood Anderson's *Winesburg, Ohio* and Hemingway's *In Our Time*. Turgenev is routinely credited with being the form's inventor; it has never really taken off in Britain.

The Golden Apples begins with a monologue, 'Shower of Gold', which may (like Benjy's monologue in *The Sound and the Fury*) be interior, or else ramblingly conversational. The speaker, Mrs Fate Rainey, runs a small convenience store in the small Mississippi town of Morgana. She is not a literate woman, but very talkative:

> That was Miss Snowdie MacLain. She comes after her butter, won't let me run over with it from just across the road. Her husband walked out of the house one day and left his hat on the banks of the Big Black River. – That could have started something too.

Snowdie's husband is King MacLain. He left his wife with twins – odd offspring, one of whom is albino. He has scattered other, illegitimate, offspring throughout Morgana. King is glimpsed from time to time, but never seems actually to be resident. The cycle ends, six stories later, with Mrs Fate Rainey's funeral.

King presides over the whole book. One story, 'Sir Rabbit', describes his coming upon a young married woman, Mattie Will Holifield, and her hunter husband in the woods. He stuns the husband and has his violent way with the delectable Mattie. Another illegitimate child will be coming. No one seems to hold it against him.

There is a profusion of hints, some so broad as to be heavy-handed, that overlaying this depiction of rural life in the south (as steamily realistic as Erskine Caldwell's *God's Little Acre*) is a framework of mythology. Critics of an exegetical cast have perplexed themselves trying to work out the significance of 'Morgana' (where does Morgana le Fey come in, exactly?) and what, precisely, the titular allusion to the golden apples of the Hesperides means. One thing critics agree on is that King MacLain is a 'Zeus figure' – the inexhaustibly lustful sovereign deity who takes his victims in 'a shower of gold'. Compare the description of the taking of Mattie with that of Leda, by Zeus metamorphosed into a swan, in the Yeats poem:

> When she laid eyes on Mr MacLain close, she staggered, he had such grandeur, and then she was caught by the hair and brought down as suddenly to earth as if whacked by an unseen

shillelagh. Presently she lifted her eyes in a lazy dread and saw those eyes above hers, as keenly bright and unwavering and apart from her life as the flowers on a tree.

A sudden blow: the great wings
    beating still
Above the staggering girl, her thighs
    caressed
By the dark webs, her nape caught
    in his bill,
He holds her helpless breast upon
    his breast.

The Yeats connection is significant and intentional. Ireland (after its civil war) and the American South (after the Civil War) were both depressed to a condition of near primitivism. Both Yeats (with his mythic celebration of pagan Ireland) and Welty assert that this offered, perversely, spiritual riches: a closer contact with the essentials of the human condition, as recorded in myth, than 'civilisation' could ever know. It's a dubious theory (rape in the woods is rape in the woods – not communion with the divine). But it makes for literature of which the *New Yorker* reviewer Hamilton Basso could enthuse, 'I doubt that a better book about "the South"... has ever been written'.

The Golden Ass, Lucius Apuleius, c. AD 160

This is the only novel to have survived the ruin of ancient Rome whole. But it has much more than literary-archaeological interest. *The Golden Ass* offers a vivid depiction of 'low life' in the Roman Empire and is – strangely – the first work of 'Black Fiction' we have (although it never appears on that shelf in the bookshop). Both Lucius the author and 'Lucius' the hero originated in what is now Algeria.

Flashing forward 1,800 years, 2 November 1960 is a day which lives in literary fame for the 'acquittal' of *Lady Chatterley* at the Old Bailey. The age of unfettered fiction had dawned. In fact Penguin, the publishers of Lawrence's novel, had been methodically

'liberating' fictional expression for a decade, using the impregnable shield of the Penguin Classic imprint. I recall how, with gleeful amazement, I took delivery of the newly published *Gargantua and Pantagruel* (translated by J. M. Cohen) in 1955. *The Golden Ass*, which came out even earlier in 1950, had an extra layer of literary impregnability in that it was translated by the eminent poet Robert Graves. It was, by the standards of the time, a 'filthy' book – but wrapped in exonerating livery. I came across a thumbed and battered copy when I was around fifteen. It fell open, suspiciously, at certain obviously much re-read sections.

In form *The Golden Ass* is a bundle of loosely linked tales. It opens with the hero-narrator, Lucius, travelling by horse in the mountains of Thessaly in Greece. A companion tells him the story of a vengeful witch who punishes lovers who betray her in terrible ways. One line sticks, to this day, in my mind: 'She then squatted and *staled* over my face' (I am sorry to see Graves' wonderfully antique word replaced by 'urinated' in the current 'revised' Penguin text). When he arrives at Hypata, Lucius stays with some friends. He has cruel jokes played on him (there is a vast amount of cruelty in this novel), but has a friendly slave, Fotis, to warm his bed at nights. He is fascinated by necromancy. His host Milo's wife, it emerges, is able to metamorphose by magical spells into a bird and (important detail) back again. This excites Lucius to near madness. He must find out how to do the trick. He fancies himself as an eagle. Fotis agrees to arrange it secretly, and his excitement takes a more carnal form.

Before we had quite finished discussing my plan, a sudden wave of longing swept over both our hearts and bodies. We pulled off our clothes and rushed naked together in amorous Bacchic fury; and when I was nearly worn out by the natural consummation of my desire she tempted me to make love to her as though she were a boy.

This, you will recall, was published in 1950 when buggery was a serious criminal offence. If 'hot' paperbacker of the time

Hank Janson (*Torment for Trixie* was his big seller in 1950) had gone anal, it would have meant the magistrates' court and righteous incineration. There was to be no corruption or depravity on Britain's bookshelves. Unless, of course, it was 'classic'.

In the story Lucius' metamorphosis goes sadly wrong – he finds himself not a bird but an ass – and Fotis fails to secure the antidote for him. A life of humiliation as a lowly beast of burden beckons. But:

> the only consoling part of this miserable transformation was the enormous increase in the size of my member, because I was by this time finding it increasingly difficult to meet all Fotis' demands on it.

In fact it is, indirectly, that vast member which will be Lucius' salvation. A respectable housewife, hungrier for more love than her husband can supply, uses Lucius as an asinine dildo. So impressive is his performance it is decided that he will be put on public display, doing the same with a condemned murderess, before both of them are torn to pieces and devoured by wild animals. More fun than gladiators, apparently, for the Roman mob. The goddess Isis finally takes mercy on the poor animal, restores him to human form, and Lucius lives his life thereafter as her faithful (celibate) acolyte.

Goldfinger, Ian Fleming, 1959

A strong contender for the 'everyone's favourite Bond' prize, *Goldfinger* was the work which converted to the most interesting film (1964). The novel opens with 007 missing a plane in Miami. While Bond is on a break from state-licensed homicide (most recently the Mexican kingpin Capunga), a friend asks him for a favour. A mysterious magnate – flamboyant in person, obnoxious in manner – has been winning too consistently at canasta. He is Auric Goldfinger. A little smear of anti-Semitism is streaked across the narrative, then erased – but not entirely. 'You won't believe it, but he's a Britisher. Domiciled in Nassau. You'd think he'd

be a Jew from the name, but he doesn't look it.' Can Bond help? He can.

In one of the 'gamble to the death' scenes which were Fleming's stock in trade, 007 takes on Goldfinger and discovers the villain's hearing aid is, in fact, a radio. Coincidentally, in London 'M' assigns Bond to investigate Goldfinger, who is, somehow, 'cornering' and illicitly exporting gold. He is, M suspects, a Russian SMERSH operative, financing that sinister agency's activities with his loot. It doesn't ring quite true. If Goldfinger is an agent, he's hardly secret. His clothes, hair, car and even his cat are golden-hued. His kink is to daub his hired escorts with gold paint before having sex with them. On the golf course another lengthy man-to-man battle ensues. Again Bond comes out on top – despite Goldfinger's trickery.

The scene moves to Switzerland, the entrepôt for Goldfinger's smuggling. Bond discovers that Goldfinger's car has pure gold panels. The metal is then smuggled, in the form of aircraft seats, to India, where it is sold at huge profit on the black market. Cunning devil. Bond is caught and tortured by Goldfinger's huge, silent valet, Oddjob – karate expert, cat eater, and sadist. The Koreans, Goldfinger cheerfully tells him, are 'the cruellest, most ruthless people in the world'. Escaping from being cut in half by a circular saw, Bond contrives to get himself recruited into Goldfinger's entourage. At this point the narrative soars into glorious surrealism. A titanic heist is being planned. Goldfinger – using the combined forces of America's two leading crime families (the improbably named 'Spangled Mob' and the Mafia) and Pussy Galore's crew of lesbian commandos – intends to rob Fort Knox. He will poison the water supply then simply walk in and help himself . A fleet of hired vans will carry away the thousands of tons of gold to some port where the customs authorities will conveniently not have heard about the biggest bullion robbery in history.

Bond goes to work. He seduces Pussy and saves her for heterosexuality. He also saves America's gold reserve by getting a message out to his old CIA buddy Felix Leiter. There is a final encounter on the plane on which Goldfinger and Oddjob are making their escape. Bond strangles the master criminal and shoots out a window through which the Korean is sucked into the outside air like so much golden toothpaste. Pussy, as she and Bond find themselves afloat in a rescue raft, will receive a gentler cruelty:

> His right hand came slowly up her firm, muscled thighs, over the flat plane of the stomach to the right breast. Its point was hard with desire. He said softly, 'Now.' His mouth came ruthlessly down on hers.

What Fleming (outrageously) calls the 'sweet tang of rape' is in prospect. The film improves on the Fort Knox caper by having Goldfinger irradiate the American gold with a Chinese nuclear device, thus driving up the value of his hoard.

Goldfinger has drawn objections to its perceived racism over the years. Few objected to the depiction of Koreans – the 1950s war had left a xenophobic score to settle. But 'Goldfinger' is a common German-Jewish name. The distinguished architect (and refugee) Erno Goldfinger threatened legal action and had to be mollified. Oddly, in the film Goldfinger was played by a former Nazi, the German Gert Fröbe, which led to the film being banned for a while in Israel.

Gone Girl, Gillian Flynn, 2012

Looking over the one hundred and twenty years since the first lists were published in the 1890s one thing is undeniable – *en masse* the bestseller is technically better than it once was. A whole lot better. Flynn's is a novel that proves the point. *Gone Girl* topped the US charts in summer 2012, vying for top place with FIFTY SHADES OF GREY.

The novel takes the form of alternating diaries – a narrative device which originated with Wilkie Collins' *The Woman in White*. Nick Dunne is born and brought up in North Carthage, Missouri (Mark Twain territory). He goes off to make his fortune in New York, as a journalist (more faint echoes of Twain). It is the 1990s, 'the last gasp of the glory days'. He lands a good job on a top-ranked magazine (transparently *Entertainment Weekly*). He falls in love and marries Amy Elliott – a beautiful 'girl' with butter-coloured blonde hair. She writes magazine quizzes. Things look very good. Then, three years into their marriage, the Internet takes off and the bottom drops out of the printed-word industry. 'I had a job for eleven years and then I didn't, it was that fast', Nick bleakly reports. They go back, tails between legs, to North Carthage. Amy still has a pot of gold from her parents' trust fund. Nick opens a bar. It fails. The remaining money is plundered by her parents, who are sucker-investors in the dot-com boom. A dreary future looms on the couple's fifth wedding anniversary: the 'wood' anniversary. Nick is – incompetently – having an affair with a student at the college where he teaches the odd class in journalism.

The plot – not to give away its many pretzel-like twists – centres on a malicious scheme by Amy. She disappears without trace, leaving a diary which is found by the police. It records (mendaciously) Nick's violence, drug-taking, addiction to sadistic pornography (there is, mysteriously, a revolting stash of it he has never seen in the house), his vast credit-card debt, a serious attempt to poison his wife, and – the clincher – the fact that she is inconveniently pregnant. It all points one way. He killed her and disposed of the body. Missouri still has the death penalty. Nick is loyally defended by his twin sister but public opinion passes an immediate guilty-as-charged, execute-the-bastard verdict. (Spoiler alert: stop here if you don't want to know more.) That the black widow Amy is still alive is developed in the 'true diary', which takes up most of the second part of the book.

Her motive in this elaborate, deadly charade? Revenge. Her first intention was to throw herself in the Mississippi and, when the corpse was found, it would be the lethal injection for Nick. Perversely, she then decided she wanted to live. Things get very complicated thereafter. She summons the help of a previous lover, who incarcerates her in his lake house. A second cunning, homicidal scenario is set up which, ingeniously, negates the first. In a riot of terminal irony, the novel ends 'happily' with Nick's acceptance that Amy will be his 'forever antagonist'. Few novels wrong-foot the reader as skilfully as *Gone Girl* – on every other page, almost. But what sticks in the mind, after the book is closed, is the chronically depressed, hopeless America which is the backdrop: Nick's violent, demented father with whom no one knows what to do, the closed-down printing factory on which the town depends (the computers stole their jobs), the locked-up mall. All families – not least Nick's and Amy's – are unhappy their own way. But the US is singularly unhappy too in this accomplished novel.

Gone with the Wind, Margaret Mitchell, 1936

Gone with the Wind (*GWTW* to its fans) has a story behind it as romantic as the novel itself. The author was born in Atlanta, Georgia, where her father was an attorney with a distinguished Southern bloodline. Her mother, Maybelle, was Irish by ancestry and fiery by temperament, and – one may plausibly suppose – the original of Southern belle Scarlett O'Hara. As a child, Margaret saturated herself in the history of the South, specifically of Atlanta during the Civil War and Reconstruction. There were still those living who could remember the burning of the town, which is the disaster at the centre of the novel and film.

Personal disasters, and the need to start over again and again in her life, just like Scarlett, afflicted the young Mitchell. Her fiancé was killed fighting in France in 1918. Her mother died in the 1919 influenza epidemic, and her father became an invalid. The academically gifted Margaret was obliged to give up her studies at college to come home and take charge – all of which can be tied in with the fictional sufferings of the indomitable Scarlett, and her return to Tara, after the sack of Atlanta and the ruin of her plantation, with the stoical observation 'tomorrow is another day'.

It was then still the custom for young Southern ladies to 'come out', and Margaret made her debut in 1920. She is reported as being lively – a 'flapper', even – and unafraid of risk. Whether like Scarlett she had a seventeen-inch waist and a 'well matured' figure, photographs demurely neither confirm nor disprove. Margaret contracted a disastrous marriage with 'Red' K. Upshaw in 1922 (clearly the original of Rhett K. Butler), an ex-football player, rogue and bootlegger. He is reported to have raped his wife on their honeymoon and the couple parted, bitterly, after a few months. Mitchell went on to make a wiser second marriage to the sedate newspaperman John Marsh in 1925. He had been the best man at her first wedding. The sequence is reversed in the novel. Scarlett secretly wants to marry the refined and intellectual Ashley Wilkes, but ends up with the swashbuckling blockade runner, and sexual predator, Rhett. Was there a lingering regret that she had lost 'Red', the brute she had loved?

Mitchell made herself a successful local journalist over the next ten years. Legend has it that she began writing her 'Civil War Novel' while recovering in bed with a broken ankle. Her husband brought her the necessary research materials, and she polished off the work in a few months – then, famously, left it to moulder in a cupboard for six years. There it might have remained for ever had it not been for the fact that, in 1935, Mitchell was assigned to show a Macmillan publishing executive around her town. He was scouting for new material and persuaded her to let him see the dilapidated manuscript of *Gone with the Wind*. It was accepted instantly and rushed out, with mammoth publicity, on 30 June 1936. The book was a runaway bestseller under the slogan: 'One million Americans *can't be wrong*. Read *GWTW*!' and won the Pulitzer. Macmillan's director, a gentleman publisher, awarded all the firm's employees an eighteen per cent bonus.

Mitchell sold the film rights to MGM for $50,000 and *GWTW* was adapted, using the new process of Technicolor, by David O. Selznick. Amid huge publicity, the studio recruited the unknown (in the US) British actress Vivien Leigh to play Scarlett. Clark Gable (very well known in the US) was chosen for Rhett. Selznick kept to the main outlines of Mitchell's plot, although the film softened Mitchell's favourable references to the Ku Klux Klan, and Rhett's killing a freed black slave who dared to affront the virtue of a white woman. The movie was launched in Atlanta in December 1939 (ten-year-old Martin Luther King was one of the cheerful 'picaninnies' hired to entertain during the interval). Book and film combined made the best history lesson America had ever, collectively, had and firmed up a useful sense of national unity prior to the country's entry into the Second World War.

Mitchell enhanced the *GWTW* mystique by never publishing another novel. But who would be so churlish as to want more? Read it. Ten million (and counting) Americans can't be wrong, can they?

The Good Earth, Pearl S. Buck, 1931

When Truman Capote was asked if he regretted not winning the Nobel Prize, he sighed and said, 'Pearl Buck, *alors*!' By which he meant, 'Who would want to be a member of that club?' *The Good Earth* is no classic. But it has a raw melodramatic power and an authenticity to its historical moment which make it worthily readable. It also served to lodge in the popular mind an image of the Chinese people rather more dignified than the examples of Charlie Chan, Fu Man Chu and Chu Chin Chow. It's interesting to compare *The Good Earth* with Mo Yan's even more authentic THE GARLIC BALLADS.

Buck's novel was published seven years before she was honoured by the Nobel Committee, but it was the main reason they leaned her way. On publication in 1931 it shot straight to the top of the bestseller list, won a Pulitzer, and sold strongly for the rest of the decade. It popped back to the top of the lists in 2004 when Oprah Winfrey selected it for her book club. The press release described this 'cultural masterpiece' in neon-glowing terms:

Told in the tradition of Chinese literature, Pearl S. Buck's *The Good Earth* runs the gamut of universal themes: women's rights, the importance of family, class conflict, spiritual and moral trials, and the hardships of the modern world. It also brings into focus a theme· that stretches far beyond the boundaries of Chinese society: the importance of simplicity.

'Simplicity, *alors*!' Buck's sympathetic depiction of peasant Chinese courage and moral virtue was highly topical and congenial to a 1930s American public reading in their newspapers about current Japanese atrocities in the Sino-Japanese war. *The Good Earth* was filmed in 1937 – the year of the Rape of Nanking. Of epic (137 minutes) length, it had Paul Muni (an Austrian famous for his depiction of Al Capone in *Scarface*) made up to look Chinese. Oscars were won. The film critic David Thomson offers faint praise:

The acting is heartfelt but empty epic, with strained accents and makeup struggling to be exotic and understandable at the same time. Far and away the best things are the landscape shots and especially the locust-attack montage which [Karl] Freund and Slavko Vorkapich contrived with coffee grounds in water.

It is, concludes Thomson, a 'big' picture.

Buck's big narrative opens with the arranged marriage of a small farmer, Wang Lung, to a former slave, O-Lan. The marriage works well. O-Lan keeps house, bears children, and labours like a man in the fields (even on the day after delivering their first son). Wang Lung prospers and buys some fertile land from the more prosperous farmer who previously owned O-Lan. Then the harvest fails. Wang Lung, O-Lan and their three children are forced to find refuge in the city, where he ekes out a living as a rickshaw man. During one of the many outbreaks of violence that are ravaging the country, Wang Lung and O-Lan contrive to enrich themselves with plunder: 'When you are hungry, theft is no crime'. With their booty they can return to the farm. O-Lan (a plain-faced woman) is permitted to keep some pearls for herself, but later Wang Lung takes them from her. She weeps.

Wang Lung prospers once more and brings a concubine, Lotus Flower, into his house. O-Lan dies of cancer. Wang Lung realises, too late, how much he loved his wife, and how much he owed her. His sons (the eldest of whom has been consorting with Lotus Flower) thrive. The latter part of the novel covers the ruses Wang Lung resorts to in order to keep his land from falling into the hands of bandits and thieves. In old age he finds love once more with a young slave, Pear Blossom. The novel ends, vividly, with him protesting to his sons that they must not, as they intend, sell the good earth. 'If you sell the land, it is the end,' he feebly protests. They smile knowingly at each other over his head.

The daughter and wife of Chinese missionaries, Buck was brought up in the country. A modest woman, when she heard on the radio that she had won the Nobel Prize she commented, 'It should have gone to Dreiser.' Her first astonished reaction – 'I don't believe it!' – was said in Chinese.

The Good Soldier, Ford Madox Ford, 1915

It's been called 'one of the most puzzling works in modern fiction' – a judgement with which few would disagree. Critics have driven themselves into the academic equivalent of melancholy madness trying to work out the chronology and whose testimony to trust in the narrative the novel releases to us – grudgingly and, in places, provably mendaciously. The puzzlement begins with the title. Ford, we are told, wanted to call the book *The Saddest Story*, echoing the first sentence, 'This is the saddest story I have ever heard.' His publisher John Lane did not like that title and the author wrote back, in a spirit of exasperated irony, '"Dear Lane, Why not *The Good Soldier*?". . . To my horror six months later the book appeared under that title.'

Whatever else, the hero Captain Edward Ashburnham is not a good soldier. As a military man in India (that part of his career is well behind him – he is no longer in uniform), he seduced his brother officers' wives remorselessly. Mrs Major Basil and 'little Maisie Maidan' are cited as notches on his bedpost. Where sex is concerned he's not a good role model. Ashburnham, for example (one of many such examples), is prepared to bankrupt his estate and publicly humiliate his wife, Leonora, by buying the favours of a courtesan (La Dolciquita) for an outrageous £20,000 (it translates into a half million in modern currency). He is a prime

candidate for the sex addiction clinic – had such places existed in the Edwardian period. (There was plenty of satyromania, as it was then called, not least around the royal satyr himself, Edward VII – the hero's forename is meaningful.) Failing a clinic, the gelding shears might serve.

When Ashburnham can't buy sex, he takes what he wants by force. He has compromised his position in English society by assaulting a servant ('the Kilsyte girl') in a third-class railway carriage – that being the drab's natural habitat. For nine years he callously cuckolds his best friend, the gullible American John Dowell. Dowell's wife Florence denies the luckless John his conjugal rights on the comical grounds that her 'heart' isn't up to it. An orgasm, she asserts, would do for her. She is, meanwhile, in other adulterous relationships with rougher trade than her husband or lover.

The narrative opens in 1913 (ominous year). The two men and their wives came nine years earlier – for health reasons – to Nauheim in Germany. The subsequent events, post-Nauheim, are chronicled by Dowell – a man possessed of an impercipience which verges on idiocy. 'Unreliable narrator' flashes over his narrative throughout, like a flickering light bulb, as the story works up to a multiple marital crash. When Ashburnham turns his attention to his wife Leonora's young ward, Nancy Rufford, Florence kills herself – unnecessarily painfully – with a dose of prussic acid. The widower Dowell is very perplexed. Leonora offers Edward a divorce, then withdraws the offer. He then commits suicide. He, too, does not choose an easy way out, slitting his throat with a pen-knife. Nancy collapses into catatonia, to be looked after by Dowell. Leonora marries the normal (but dull) Rodney Bayham. All very sad. In the last twenty years, critics have compounded their melancholy madness by speculating that Nancy is Edward's illegitimate daughter, adding incest to the adulterous, fornicatory brew.

Ford called *The Good Soldier* his 'auk's egg' – 'having reached my allotted, I had laid my one egg and might as well die'. That remark, like everything connected with this fascinating puzzle-piece of a novel, is not crystal clear. Read it and come up with your own interpretation.

The Good Soldier Schweik, Jaroslav Hašek, 1923

For the various authorities to whom he was answerable Jaroslav Hašek was a very bad Austro-Hungarian. He thought they were bad authorities. Worse than that, absurd authorities. Hašek, to draw up a longer charge sheet, was a bad son (of an even worse father, it must be admitted), a bad husband (to two wives, simultaneously), and (yes) a bad soldier in an army itself so bad it lost not just a war but bungled a whole empire away in the process. But there was a vein of redeeming mischief running through Hašek's malefactions, even the most reprehensible – an irresistible joy in anarchy (the only political movement he believed in).

That subversive sense of mischief – Kafka with laughs – is distilled in this sprawling chaotic, incomplete-but-vast chronicle. Hašek's great work (for himself and his readers, not the Emperor Franz Joseph) began when he was conscripted into the 91st Infantry Regiment of the Austro-Hungarian Army. There followed a wholly inglorious military career in which he would serve (never 'fight') under three flags (the Imperial Army, the Czech breakaway nationalists, and the Bolsheviks). It was nothing more than a series of uniforms to Hašek. *The Good Soldier Schweik*, which came out of this wartime experience, takes the form of a bundle of satirical-episodic papers. In many editions they are accompanied by the cartoons of Hašek's pre-war roommate, Josef Lada. The narrative opens with characteristically crude briskness:

> And so they've killed our Ferdinand [i.e. Archduke Franz Ferdinand] said the charwoman to Mr Schweik, who had left military service years before, after having been finally certified by an army medical board as an imbecile, and lived by selling dogs – ugly, mongrel monstrosities whose pedigrees he forged.

Schweik hies off to his local pub, the Chalice, where he predicts – quite correctly – that the assassination of the emperor's namesake nephew in Sarajevo will start something very big indeed. When the call comes he cunningly volunteers to do his bit, old soldier that he is, arranging to have himself pushed to the recruiting office in a bath-chair. The 'patriotic cripple' is hailed in the Prague papers. Alas, someone has informed the paranoid authorities of Schweik's pub-talk about the international conflict to come. How did he know? He must be party to a cunning plot to plunge the world into war – perhaps the mastermind behind it all.

After questioning, he is released into a lunatic asylum. These are the happiest days of his life, he later claims, because a madman can say exactly what he wants and no one punishes him: 'a freedom not even the socialists have dreamed about'. He is once again officially certified an 'idiot' and loosed on the world – no bath-chair is now required. The use of his legs has miraculously been recovered. After some disastrous setbacks in 1915, 'the Ministry of War suddenly remembered Schweik'. He is a soldier again. He pulls his routine sickness stunt but, in the hospital for malingerers, the regular and unsympathetic application of enemas produces a rapid return to fitness.

Survivor that he is, Schweik goes on to secure for himself a series of cushy berths, well away from the cannon's roar. He is a serial Sancho Panza, first as batman to a chronically drunken chaplain, who loses him in a game of cards to a lieutenant. All goes well until a misadventure with a general's dog leads to the officer and batman being posted to the front with the 91st, Hašek's old unit. 'Catastrophe' is the title of the chapter. Neither man relishes battle. Schweik never quite makes it to the front line. But its horrors loom ever closer and make clear why no sensible person (only real idiots) would want to go there. In a train, travelling through territory bombarded by the enemy, Schweik sees:

> entangled in the branches of an old burnt-out pine there was hanging the boot of an Austrian infantryman with a piece of shin bone.

His bones will never hang in a tree, if he can help it. In one of the story's comic high-points Schweik goes for a refreshing dip in a lake. A Russian deserter steals his uniform, leaving his own. Schweik faces the firing squad as an enemy spy. He survives. He always does. And his type always will. Long live Shweikism.

Schweik's creator, alas, did not survive as long as his admirers would have wanted. *The Good Soldier Schweik* is only half as long as Hašek planned. He led a life of dissipation until his premature death at the age of thirty-nine. It is thought Schweik would have continued his wartime career as a survivor in a Russian POW camp.

The Graduate, Charles Webb, 1963

Ask most people which names come to mind when you say *The Graduate* and the reply will be Dustin Hoffman, Anne Bancroft, Simon and Garfunkel, and – if they are into movies – director Mike Nichols. The name which is least likely to come up is Charles Webb, who sold the film rights to his novel for a one-off payment of $20,000. The contract earned him a spot in the *Daily Mirror's* list of 'World's Biggest Mugs'. But at the time the money looked good for a first novel by an author just a couple of years graduated from one of the 'potted ivy league' colleges on the East Coast. Twenty grand looked a lot less good when the film cleared more than $100 million. It must have irked Webb that the film, in plot and character, was so damnably faithful – word for word in many places – to its source. There were, however, distinctive differences. Nichols presented *The Graduate* as hip comedy – his stock in trade. The novel is full of angst and moral confusion, and is much heavier going. Nichols (turning down Robert Redford) cast the virtually unknown Dustin Hoffman as the lead. The actor protested that in the book Braddock is a large blond twenty-one-year-old WASP and he, Hoffman, was a small, saturnine, thirty-year-old Jew. Nichols replied, 'But don't you think the character is Jewish inside?' We all, it seems, have our 'inner Jew'.

The novel and film open with Benjamin's return, mortar board recently thrown in the air, to his hometown of Pasadena, where his father is a respected local lawyer. For those who know Pasadena (I taught there for twenty-five years) the novel is saturated with that quiet place's sleepy mood – seven miles from downtown LA but connected to it by the first freeway in America (the 'Arroyo Seco parkway' features centrally in the film). One of the things Hoffman had going for him was that he too was brought up (in less salubrious circumstances) in the same southern California as Webb, and cut his teeth at the Pasadena Playhouse. Webb's narrative is brisk and dialogue-heavy (something that doubtless recommended the novel to the film studio scouts). It opens:

> Benjamin Braddock graduated from a small Eastern college on a day in June. Then he flew home. The following evening a party was given for him by his parents. By eight o'clock most of the guests had arrived but Benjamin had not yet come down from his room. His father called up from the foot of the stairs but there was no answer. Finally he hurried up the stairs and to the end of the hall.
> 'Ben?' he said, opening his son's door.
> 'I'll be down later,' Benjamin said.
> 'Ben, the guests are all here,' his father said. 'They're all waiting.'
> 'I said I'll be down later.'

It is clear that he 'prefers not to' (see BARTLEBY THE SCRIVENER).

Larger refusals are in play. What does this 'graduate' want to do with his life? Like many in that turbulent decade, the one thing he knows is that he does not want to follow the script that has been written for him. Until he works it out he has a generous allowance and, as a reward for graduating, a new sports car – that necessity for leading a fully Californian existence.

Things begin to happen when he lets himself be seduced by the wife of his father's partner and best friend, Mrs Robinson, who uses him as indifferently as she might her bathroom loofah. ('Couldn't we talk, before?'

Benjamin plaintively enquires. The implied answer is a cold 'no'.) He turns his attention to Mrs Robinson's daughter, Elaine. She is not interested and, now a stalker rather than a sexual-satisfaction-for-the-older-woman gizmo, Benjamin pursues Elaine to Berkeley. Mrs Robinson goes to war. She's a fearsome adversary. In the climax Benjamin motors down the Arroyo Seco (it translates, unromantically, as 'dry gulch') to interrupt the church service in which Elaine is in the process of marrying another man. Like Lochinvar, he carries her off. His sports car has run out of gas and they leave on a bus. But where are they going, and what will they do?

Le Grand Meaulnes, Alain-Fournier, 1913

John Fowles, who did much to raise interest in Le Grand Meaulnes in the English-speaking world, called it 'the greatest novel of adolescence in European literature' (and, of course, the inspiration for that equally great novel in English literature, The Magus). Praise hovers ambiguously over Fowles' term 'adolescence'. It's a psychological category of relatively recent invention. The pioneer in the field was the American G. Stanley Hall, author of the magisterial Adolescence: Its Psychology and Its Relations to Physiology, Anthropology, Sociology, Sex, Crime and Religion (1904). Hall's doctrine of adolescence was a pragmatic response to the unnaturally long extent of American higher education – from kindergarten to college graduation – ending as late as twenty-two. Such an education necessitated the extension of childhood's mental pliability to well past what had traditionally been adulthood (adults, 'set in their ways', are notoriously harder to teach). Adolescence was the 'not quite yet' phase of life.

There is an alternative view, which celebrates adolescence as the most intensely honest phase of life. When, in Romeo and Juliet, the adolescent man (boy) falls in love with a thirteen-year-old woman (girl) he has never seen before, across a crowded room, is it 'true love' or 'childish infatuation'? Your answer to that question will determine your

response to Le Grand Meaulnes (and, of course, Shakespeare's play).

There is an initial hurdle for the Anglophone reader – that vexatious title. It translates as something like 'Meaulnes: Champion of the World' (apologies to Roald Dahl) or 'Big-Boy Meaulnes' (pronounced 'moan'). Unthinkable. Some translations plump for 'The Wanderer', 'The Lost Estate' or 'The Lost Domain', but most simply go with Le Grand Meaulnes and let the reader fend for themself. It has done the novel no good in the English-speaking world.

Alain-Fournier's story falls into three parts. It opens in St Agathe, a provincial boarding school, one of those peculiar French institutions which is part educational, part small hotel, or pensionnat. The narrator is the principal's fifteen-year-old son, François Seurel. A sweet, lonely, disabled boy (adolescent?), his life is brightened by the newcomer Augustin Meaulnes, a year older and soon to become what, in England, would be called the cock of the school. During the Christmas break, Meaulnes absconds with a pony and trap. He loses his way and – as he later recounts to François – blunders into a strange domaine (another tricky term), where a wedding fête is taking place. He mingles among the guests at the château in a bal masqué, and befriends the groom, Frantz de Galais. Momentously he catches sight of Frantz' young sister, Yvonne, and falls desperately, and for ever, in love with her. 'You are beautiful,' are his first words to her. 'I don't even know who you are,' she replies. . . 'and then she was gone'. The bride doesn't turn up, Frantz is suicidal. The fête winds down in disorder. Meaulnes blunders back to St Agathe, forgetting the route by which he got there. Yvonne, the love of his life, might as well be in fairyland.

At this point the novel, too, loses its way. Frantz turns up as a penniless vagabond – his debts have ruined the de Galais family. Meaulnes – soon to graduate – discovers where Yvonne lives. There intervenes a complicated episode in which he unknowingly seduces Frantz's skittish former fiancée, Valentine, and eventually marries Yvonne. It is not blissful. She tells him, chillingly, 'We are two children; we've been foolish.' While Meaulnes is off with Frantz, looking for Valentine, Yvonne dies in childbirth, never knowing why her husband has abandoned her. The novel ends with François picturing Meaulnes, 'in the night, wrapping his daughter in a cloak, to carry her off to some new adventure'.

So which was the more 'real' element in the novel? That ecstatic, love-at-first-sight moment in the *domaine*, or the wreckage of the later marriage? The answer will depend on whether the reader sees it as worthy of being, according to a recent poll, 'the most popular novel in France', or what a critic has called 'a creaking collection of old tricks', fuelled by infantile delusions about human relationships. Its author's first novel, *Le Grand Meaulnes* was published nine months before the outbreak of the First World War. Alain-Fournier was never able to publish a second novel. He died in action in the first few months of the conflict. He was twenty-eight.

The Grapes of Wrath, John Steinbeck, 1939

The Grapes of Wrath was the first American 'muck-raking' (i.e. social problem) novel to head bestseller lists both in the US and in the UK, boosted by the quick-off-the-mark film in 1940. Steinbeck's narrative sets out to expose the dreadful social consequences for the farming community in America's south-western states of the 'Great Depression'–exacerbated to catastrophic proportions by the mid-1930s – and wind-and-drought-whipped 'dust-bowl' erosion (to which the farmers themselves contributed). In the wake of these economic and environmental disasters, an army of so-called 'Okies' (displaced Oklahomans) migrated to California in search of a better life. In the Golden State, a false Eden, they were destined to encounter exploitation by Californian landowners, who used them as 'stoop labour', and prejudice from middle-class urban Californians, who regarded the Okies as sub-human peasants.

The Grapes of Wrath follows the (mis)fortunes of an Okie family – the Joads ('Job' is distantly echoed). Young Tom Joad, just out of prison, joins his family at their devastated farm as they are loading up a clapped-

out truck with all their belongings (including a paralysed grandma) to travel west. *En route* the old family cohesion disintegrates and Ma Joad gradually takes charge. 'Women can change better'n a man,' she says. 'Woman got all her life in her arms. Man got it all in his head.' At every stage, from the dishonest dealer who sells them their Hudson truck to the Californian farm-owners who use them, when needed, as seasonal fruit pickers, the Joads are cheated, abused and exploited. Tom is finally driven back to crime – or, as he sees it, revenge: 'wherever there's a fight so hungry people can eat, I'll be there'. Only in a communal camp, under a kind of consensual socialist regime, do the Joads find justice and any hope for the future.

Steinbeck's 'radical' political assertions (e.g. 'the quality of owning freezes you forever into "I", and cuts you off forever from the "we"'), and the novel's sexual explicitness – especially the last scene in which the Joad daughter, Rose of Sharon, having lost her baby, gives suck to a starving (adult) fellow Okie – provoked huge protest. Californians felt that Steinbeck was slandering the state to which he belonged. Woundingly, even Steinbeck's former high-school teacher, Miss Cupp, gave it as her opinion that *The Grapes of Wrath* was not an 'authentic' book. Steinbeck (who was not Jewish) was accused of peddling 'Jewish propaganda'. Ruth Comfort Mitchell wrote a novel of refutation, *Of Human Kindness*, vindicating California's treatment of its immigrant farm workers. It wasn't the ranchers who were to blame but the communists, she believed.

The 1936–41 La Follette Civil Liberties hearings in the US Senate supported Steinbeck's version – if anything, they suggested that he had understated the programmatic violation of migrant human rights in California. Steinbeck received support from Pearl S. Buck (who would for her part go on to highlight the abuse of Chinese-American workers) and Eleanor Roosevelt, who visited the migrant labour camps where Steinbeck had done much of the research for his novel. The abuse still goes on, of course, although now it's of 'undocumented' Latinos, not Okies.

In the 1940 film John Ford chose to finish not with Steinbeck's semi-cannibalistic ending (all the poor have to eat is the poor) but an upbeat exchange between Ma and Pa Joad, as they bounce along in their truck. The movie fades out with her hopeful words:

> 'Rich fellas come up an' they die, an' their kids ain't no good an' they die out. But we keep a'comin'. We're the people that live. They can't wipe us out; they can't lick us. We'll go on forever, Pa, 'cause we're the people.'

It was not weak-kneed. This was now the era of the Rooseveltian New Deal. The Depression was a thing of the past.

Great Expectations, Charles Dickens, 1861

If there was one story which everyone knew in 2012 it was the one about the blacksmith's boy who was told he had 'great expectations', made himself a gentleman (i.e. 'snob'), and discovered that his fortune was all thanks to a convict in Australia to whom he had once given a pork pie. In honour of the bicentennial of Dickens' birth there were two lavish adaptations of *Great Expectations* – one for the TV screen in January, the other for the cinema screen in December. The TV adaptation adopted a fashionable feminist line. Miss Havisham (played by a decades-too-young Gillian Anderson) was the 'de-centred' centre of interest – a version of the 'madwoman in the attic', man's perennial victim. The film version, scripted by *One Day* author David Nicholls, brazenly re-inserted the 'unhappy' ending the author had resolutely discarded.

Endings are not a mere matter of preferred phraseology in *Great Expectations*, as they are in the forty-seven *Farewell to Arms* variants. One ending renders Pip's life worthwhile. He gets the woman he has always loved. The other ending makes his life pointless. He loses the only woman he has ever loved.

In the routinely printed 'happy ending' Pip has, by eleven years' drudgery abroad, become a respectable businessman. He returns to Joe's forge, where he began life. Estella, he learns, is now a widow. He takes a stroll to Miss Havisham's Satis House – now wholly ruined. Night is falling. A figure emerges, ghost-like, through the 'cold silvery mist'. 'Estella!' The 'freshness of her beauty' is gone but 'its indescribable majesty and its indescribable charm remained'. They sit down on a bench and talk. He takes her hand in his,

> and we went out of the ruined place; and, as the morning mists had risen long ago when I first left the forge, so, the evening mists were rising now, and in all the broad expanse of tranquil light they showed to me, I saw no shadow of another parting from her.

This 'happy' ending is, one notes, not unequivocally 'happy' – it hints, broadly, at 'shadows' and gives no clear promise of marriage. An alternative was only divulged after Dickens' death. In it, fifteen years have passed. Estella is again widowed – but has remarried a kindly old doctor. She and Pip meet by accident in Piccadilly. He is accompanied by Joe's son, 'little Pip'. Estella assumes the child is his. They exchange meaningless pleasantries before going their separate ways into the London crowd, never to meet again.

On the advice of a friend – the novelist Edward Bulwer-Lytton – Dickens opted for the happy alternative. Was he right? And why take the advice of Lytton on the matter, a writer whose memory lives nowadays only as the literary buffoon who inspired the annual 'dark and stormy night' competition, for the worst opening line of the year? George Bernard Shaw, ever the realist, thought Dickens chose the rose tints from commercial motives. There is, arguably, a more interesting reason. Lytton was a famously awful husband. So vexing had his wife Rosina become to him that, a couple of years earlier, he had had her locked up in a lunatic asylum. In the period immediately preceding *Great Expectations*, Dickens had decided he could no longer live with Mrs Dickens. He was to console himself, for the remainder of his life, with Ellen Ternan, a woman twenty-seven years his junior, in what most presume to be unmarried bliss. Lytton was Dickens' close adviser over this period of marital rupture and total disgust with marriage. Dickens' grim scepticism about the institution rendered him unwilling to condemn Pip to it. But Lytton – who shared the scepticism – suggested that, to protect his own reputation, Dickens should nuance the negativity. Shadows and a distinct absence of wedding bells – astute readers would get the point. So which ending is 'right'? No question about it – the more delicately nuanced Dickensian–Lyttonian ending is the right one. Leave the text be, Nicholls.

There is yet another ending in the classic 1946 David Lean film. Satis House still stands as the shuttered, prison-like, place that it was during Miss Havisham's lifetime. Enter Pip, played by John Mills, who – while claiming Estella (still in her blooming youth) – tears down the curtains and throws open the shutters, letting in the blinding sunlight. No mist, no shadows, no uncertainties. It was, of course, the year the lights went on in London and blackout restrictions became a thing of the past. I loved it (aged eight).

The Great Fire of London, Peter Ackroyd, 1982

This is a novel to interest followers of Ackroyd in that it is about his favourite non-novelistic subject – London. It is not an easy read but well worth the effort. *The Great Fire of London*'s preface is a scenario based on *Little Dorrit*, but artfully falsified by an inauthentic sentimental climax. The reader is uneasily teleported to an alternative literary universe. Dickens' novel and his fiction generally echo disconcertingly through Ackroyd's. The main character, Spenser Spender (a poet manqué, what else?), is struggling to get a film version of *Little Dorrit* off the ground. At the time the novel was published, Spender was a culturally resonant name. While he was writing *The Great Fire of London*, Ackroyd had been actively helping the poet Stephen Spender (who had been in the National Fire Service when London burned during the Second World War) with his *Collected Poems*, published in the same year as this novel. 'He talks to me like a contemporary', wrote the sixty-year-old Spender, in his journal, approvingly, about his thirty-two-year-old adviser.

Spenser Spender's twentieth-century Circumlocution Office is found in the shape of the Film Finance Board. Various Dickensian look-alikes cross Spender's path. BLEAK HOUSE's Miss Flite appears for a moment in the King's Road, pushing a pram 'filled with scraps of old clothes and newspapers, empty tins of Horlicks and old bottles stuffed with rags'. *Our Mutual Friend*'s Bradley Headstone (here, Job Penstone) pops up as a grimly self-righteous polytechnic lecturer, pontificating on Dickens' male chauvinism to a troop of doltish students. Spender is destroyed by a schizoid female Barnaby Rudge, who sets fire to his Marshalsea set. 'London' burns. Spender, unlike his namesake, is no fireman and dies fighting the flames. Meanwhile a Quilpian dwarf throws open the prison where the film has been shooting.

It would be a mistake to think from the last episode in his book that Ackroyd is at all deferential to such readings as Lionel Trilling's: 'the informing symbol, or emblem, of the book . . . is the prison.' The novelist is known to be of John Carey's contemptuous persuasion on the subject of the Dickens industry's symbol-hunting. He makes his point with a heavily satirised gay Canadian Cambridge don who is researching 'his' author, surrounded by congenial works like *Dickens: The Baroque Lamp* and *Dickens and the Twisted Metastasis*. So much for the academics.

Ackroyd is a versatile writer. One of his earlier productions was the Eliot-homage treatise *Notes for a New Culture*. It recalls T. S. Eliot's maxim about the impossibility of gumming leaves back on trees: the culture of the past, that is to say, cannot easily be brought into line with that of the present. *The Great Fire of London* plays with this idea of cultural irrecoverability. The Cambridge expert (whom Spender hires as a script-writer) cannot bring back the world of Dickens. Nor can Audrey, a lunatic telephonist who claims to be in contact by séance with Amy Dorrit and thinks herself possessed by the Victorian heroine. Least successful of all is Spender's film reconstruction, for all its authenticity of set and location. In elaborating this pattern, Ackroyd may have had in mind that Dickens himself was describing the Marshalsea not as it stood, but consciously inventing it. As Dickens tells us in the preface to *Little Dorrit*, in this case he deliberately neglected his customary fieldwork:

Some of my readers may have an interest in being informed whether or not any portions of the Marshalsea Prison are yet standing. I myself did not know, until I was approaching the end of this story, when I went to look. I found the outer front courtyard, often mentioned here, metamorphosed into a butter shop.

Spender is thus engaged in reconstructing not Dickens' London, but Dickens' *imagination* of London.

The Great Fire of London, despite being the author's first foray into fiction, is cleverly resonant and sharply observed as to scene and character. Ackroyd is especially good on Cambridge high tables and low London gay bars. But – denying the reader any easily anticipated experience (he loves playing with us) – there is no Hollywood-style disaster climax. The narrative ends apocalyptically with another great fire of London, but the event is presented with all the drama of a *Keesing's Archive* entry: 'it inflicted disaster and destruction on the city', we are told. Nothing more.

The Great Gatsby, F. Scott Fitzgerald, 1925

Is *The Great Gatsby* the Great American Novel – a beast as elusive as the Himalayan yeti? The short answer is 'yes, it is' – or, at least, *The Great Gatsby* is one of that select group which can plausibly claim a ticket to the exclusive GAN club. But what makes this story of a 'big bootlegger' – a petty hoodlum, an utter phony (Holden Caulfield's most extreme term of contempt), stupidly in love with a woman unworthy of him (or anyone) – the classic literary expression of 'The American Dream'?

Or should that be 'The American Delusion'? There are those who read Fitzgerald's novel as a damning indictment of a civilisation which is in decay without ever having managed to flower. Respectable critics have put their name to that derogatory view. But it's wrong. The novel's final message (green lights and beating against the current, etc.) is overwhelmingly, if fuzzily, 'on the side of

life', as D. H. Lawrence would say. Dreams not delusions. But making the Lawrentian case is tricky. One thing is certain. Whatever critical disputes swirl around it, *The Great Gatsby* is here to stay.

The overwhelming majority of novels come, enjoy their brief moment, and fall into oblivion never to return. As George Orwell put it, 'Ultimately there is no test of literary merit except survival'. As every bookstore and educational syllabus testifies, the story of Jay Gatsby's doomed quest for Daisy Buchanan has survived. But why has a novel so intimately rooted in its own time 'lasted' into ours? What is it that posterity, nine decades later, finds fascinating in this chronicle of the long-gone Jazz Age (a term Fitzgerald invented), with its flappers, speakeasies, and anything-goes parties? What is it that the novel says to us in our anything-but-jazz age?

One very relevant thing the novel says is, 'don't get old'. No one, Fitzgerald proclaimed after the triumph of his first book, *This Side of Paradise*, should live beyond the age of thirty. That novel was published when he was a precocious twenty-three.

The Great Gatsby is a novel about the 'twenties', written by a novelist still in his twenties. It has a narrator in his twenties and a hero only a year past them, attempting to recover the woman he loved when he was twenty-seven. Our twenties is not only the best time in our lives, *The Great Gatsby* asserts, it is the *only* worthwhile time in our lives. That time alone is when it can be said we truly live. The novelist Jacqueline Susann once observed that 'for every woman, forty is Hiroshima'. Fitzgerald's view was even more apocalyptic. In his world thirty is, as he would have put it, the 'far side of paradise'. The point is stressed when, late in the novel, driving back with Tom Buchanan from New York, Nick Carraway, the narrator, suddenly realises that it's his birthday. He has passed, without realising it, what Joseph Conrad called the 'shadow line' in his life. Darkness awaits:

> I was thirty. Before me stretched the portentous, menacing road of a new decade ... Thirty – the promise of a decade of loneliness, a thinning list of single men to know, a thinning

brief-case of enthusiasm, thinning hair . . . So we drove on toward death through the cooling twilight.

The novel, like Susann, has no sympathy for the proverbially consoling truism that life 'begins at forty'. As the critic Matthew Bruccoli has observed, the primary emotion *The Great Gatsby* generates is regret: regret for the loss of youth and of youthful dreams and 'for depleted emotional capacity, a regret as intense as the emotions that inspired it were'. While writing *The Great Gatsby*, Fitzgerald acknowledged this was indeed his intention in a letter to a friend:

> That's the whole burden of the novel – the loss of those illusions that give such colour to the world that you don't care whether things are true or false as long as they partake of the magical glory.

Do you 'buy' it? 'Magical glory'? I'm not sure most of us do – but we *want* to. That, I suspect, is why the novel 'lasts'. Like Gatsby, we want something we can't have, but won't let go of.

The Groves of Academe, Mary McCarthy, 1952

My academic career (1959–2004) coincided almost exactly with the rise of the so-called 'campus novel' and, some would say, its decline and fall. The two facts are unrelated. I actually read what are credited as the pioneer American campus novels – Mary McCarthy's, and Randall Jarrell's *Pictures from an Institution* – before I entered the university world. I was flummoxed by both but, having paid good money for them (one from Boots' Library old-copy shelf, the other in Penguin livery), I soldiered on. What, I wondered, was 'tenure'? And why did academics (in America) all have PhDs? (And what were they?) Why were they so worked up about 'witch-hunts'?

Oddly, both these novels were inspired by sojourns as visiting professors in the late 1940s at the same institution – Sarah Lawrence College. It's located in Bronxville, a few stations from New York's Grand

Central rail terminus. SLC was, and still is, anything but typical of the famous institutions of American higher education. It was founded in 1926 as a Liberal Arts College on a handsome campus (literally woods and fields) by property magnate William Van Duzer Lawrence in memory of his dead wife, Sarah. Mrs Lawrence had believed passionately in education for women, and SLC was established as a sex-segregated institution. After the Second World War, as an act of gratitude to the armed services, a small forty-strong contingent of military veterans was admitted. They were regarded as the luckiest men in America, surrounded as they were by 350 of the most nubile and affluent young women in the land. Mary McCarthy – ex-Catholic, politically radical, un-nubile, unaffluent, and perpetually furious – taught at SLC as a visiting professor between 1947 and 1948. She needed the money. The college gave her a paltry $200 a month; a lot less than she needed or deserved. She hated the teaching 'because the students were so poor'. She meant, of course, that they were 'ignorant rich kids'. The college was being shaken up by Harold Taylor – known (behind his back) as the 'boy president'. McCarthy had no time for him. Neither did Randall Jarrell, who was there at the same period. Taylor is cruelly satirised in both writers' novels.

McCarthy's novel opens at 'Jocelyn College' (transparently SLC) with a letter informing the English Literature instructor, Henry Mulcahy, that his services are no longer required. He has an ailing wife, four children and no future job prospects. He prides himself on having introduced modern literature into Jocelyn's stuffy classrooms. He is a Joycean (he carries, ostentatiously, an ashplant walking stick, in honour of Stephen Dedalus). He resolves to fight – and, if necessary, to fight dirty. His opponent is the youthful president, Maynard Hoar, a liberal with – like all his kind – 'a wobble of uncertainty' at his core, which totally disables the new broom in his hands. This is the period of the (Joseph) McCarthyite witch-hunts. Mulcahy may have been a communist once. His liberal colleagues rally round him – without, however, imperilling their own positions. Good hearts and weak knees. They like to boil serious political issues down to such questions as 'What would Tolstoy do?' and then do nothing. It does not help that Mulcahy is cross-grained, tactless, a conscienceless liar where his self-preservation is concerned, and physically repulsive. He is described as: 'A tall soft-bellied, lisping man with a tense, mushroom-white face, rimless bifocals, and graying thin red hair'.

By underhand tactics, Mulcahy wins the contest. It is Hoar who is forced into resignation, having made the cardinal error of being good-hearted and wishy-washy. Liberals always finish last. McCarthy's trail-blazing novel left a useful instruction for the campus novelists who followed her (see, for example, THE HISTORY MAN). Contempt makes for far richer comedy than affection. Oh – and if you want to get ahead in American universities, fight dirty. The title is from one of Horace's epistles, *Atque inter silvas academi quaerere verum*. It translates as 'And seek for truth in the groves of academe'. Some hopes, McCarthy's novel suggests.

Guerrillas, V. S. Naipaul, 1975

He's a great novelist – we have the Nobel Prize Committee's assurance for it. But which is Naipaul's greatest novel? My vote would go to *Guerrillas*. Like much of his best fiction it has a hard kernel of historical fact, laced with the author's particular brand of acidic contempt and some plausible fictional extrapolation. Marxist analysis likes to see guerrillas as proto-revolutionaries. The dyspeptic Naipaul sees them as harbingers of chaos. The novel's epigraph (repeated in the body of the text) is:

When everybody wants to fight there's nothing to fight for. Everybody wants to fight his own little war, everybody is a guerrilla.

The central 'guerrilla' in *Guerrillas* is based on 'Michael X', self-named in imitation of the American Malcolm X. He was born Michael de Freitas, of mixed race, in Trinidad (Naipaul was born there a few months earlier). The son of a Portuguese father, he could had he wished have 'passed' for white. He chose, instead, to embrace a black

Muslim identity; another of his self-awarded names was 'Abdul Malik'. Before he became political, de Freitas worked in London as a thug enforcer for the crook/property tycoon, Peter Rachman – linked through Rachman's mistress, Mandy Rice-Davies, to the Profumo scandal. After being 'radicalised', he attracted publicity as an evangelist for Black Power and Black Pride. Having fleeced various rich *bien-pensant* dupes in the UK (John Lennon, famously), and falling foul of the law, Michael X fled back to Trinidad as a self-declared revolutionary leader. Among the 'commune' he set up there was an English convert, Gale Benson, the daughter of a Tory MP. She was killed – hacked to death like a side of beef. De Freitas was convicted of murder and hanged in 1975.

A fascinated Naipaul wrote a long essay on the subject, 'Michael X and the Black Power Killings in Trinidad' (1979), and a fictional version of de Freitas appears as the central character, Jimmy Ahmed, in *Guerrillas*. The novel complicates things well beyond the strict historical record. The action is set on an unnamed West Indian island, manifestly Trinidad, polluted – atmospherically and socially – by a multinational bauxite mining company. The three principals are: a white South African intellectual, Peter Roche, exiled for his Black Liberation sympathies; his mistress, Jane, an upper-class white woman; and Jimmy Ahmed, on the run from the UK, where he is wanted for rape. Ahmed has a 'catamite', one of the many boys he keeps, as a kind of posse, on his farm. He also, when he feels the need, borrows Jane from the complaisant Roche, who sees it as furthering the revolution. The multinational finances Ahmed with bribes – as insurance, in case he really does trigger a popular uprising and take things over.

The title – *Guerrillas* – is ironic: these are not freedom fighters, they are degenerates. The irony permeating the whole novel is implicit in the first sentence: 'After lunch Jane and Roche left their house on the Ridge to drive to Thrushcross Grange.' The allusions are mischievously obvious. Jane [Eyre] and Roche[ster] leave for the house which represents civilisation (as opposed to the savagery of Heathcliff's house) in *Wuthering Heights*. The first Mrs Rochester, we recall, originated in the West Indies. Unlike Charlotte Brontë's Jane, Naipaul's will end up raped by her super-potent black lover and murdered by his accomplice. Everything, every value – moral, spiritual, ideological – is decayed. Naipaul contrives a landscape which breathes irremediable corruption:

> The cleared land had been ridged and furrowed from end to end. The furrows were full of shiny green weeds; and the ridges, one or two of which showed haphazard, failed planting, were light brown and looked as dry as bone.

Looking at it through the car window, Jane says: 'I used to think that England was in a state of decay.' Roche replies, ironically, 'Decayed from what?'

The narrative is laced with ineffable contempt for the author's birthplace and what, after independence, it has more or less become. The plot follows the Michael X story, but with the difference that (having murdered his male lover) Jimmy goes on the run and escapes the rope. Roche leaves for a safer part of the world in which to play at guerrillas. The novel ends with Roche phoning Jimmy, warning him to keep his head down. God help the world if Naipaul's world-view is accurate.

Gulliver's Travels, Jonathan Swift, 1726

It's not a novel, you may say. But if it isn't, then what is it? Very broadly, fiction as a modern genre begins with a fork in the road, and two *voyages imaginaires* written within seven years of each other. One, ROBINSON CRUSOE, is by Daniel Defoe, who (intimately as he knew every region of England) never even crossed the Channel, let alone resided for twenty-seven years on an island off South America. And Swift, for a certainty, never went to countries where the population was as diminutive as tin soldiers, or as large as Titans, or where horses could discourse learnedly about the good life. Defoe's novel ('lies like truth', Leslie Stephen – Virginia Woolf's father – called it) is strenuously realistic. Inevitably, its *vraisemblance* was mistaken

for 'authenticity', the 'real thing', by its first readers, whereas *Gulliver's Travels* was, from the first, seen for what it is: a 'fable', fabulous in the true sense.

For scholars specialising in the eighteenth century, *Gulliver's Travels* is a rich trove of socio-political satire. Lilliput? The entourage of Queen Anne, populated as it was with small-minded little people. Laputa? Swift's conservative (why, incidentally, are all satirists conservative?) loathing of the Royal Society. For biographers, *Gulliver's Travels* is the most illuminating register of the Doctor's many phobias and hang-ups. For children, with their simplified and illustrated texts, it is a fairy story to go to sleep to, as comforting as a night light. For those who read it as a novel, *Gulliver's Travels* is a fascinating study of a man who begins life as merely 'gullible' – the standard ingénu hero-narrator – and goes stark staring mad. It belongs alongside that other 'slide into mania' masterpiece, Nabokov's *Pale Fire*. Swift anticipated his own personal decline into what we would see as Alzheimer's, and his physicians would have called 'softening of the brain', in his terrifying poem, 'Verses on the Death of Dr Swift':

> That old Vertigo in his Head,
> Will never leave him, till he's dead:
> Besides, his Memory decays,
> He recollects not what he says;
> He cannot call his Friends to Mind;
> Forgets the Place where last he din'd:
> Plyes you with Stories o'er and o'er,
> He told them fifty Times before.

So it happened. Swift, as Dr Johnson sadly puts it, expired 'a driveller and a show' (his servants would, for a fee of twopence, show off the drooling idiot).

Gulliver's Travels depicts another variety of madness. Not mental decay, but body-dysmorphic disorder. Orwell, in his essay 'Politics vs. Literature: An Examination of Gulliver's Travels', notes the eighteenth-century author's near-lunatic distaste for human excrement, expressed in such poems as 'The Lady's Dressing Room' with its disgusted line: 'Oh! *Celia, Celia, Celia* shits!' The inescapable fact of human excretion smeared, for Swift, the whole human condition. The first thing that happens to Gulliver, on his fourth, and most traumatic, voyage is that he finds himself in a terra incognita inhabited by Yahoos (i.e. 'noble savages', humans in a state of nature). They climb up trees and 'discharge their excrements' on the stranger's head by way of welcome to Yahooland. Gulliver then moves on to reside with the Houyhnhnms (horses) whom he finds rational, clean, and in every way preferable to Yahoo-humans: not least in their excremental functions and the nature of the waste. When he returns to ('shitty') civilisation he resolves to live in a stable, like the cleanly horse. Orwell speculates, plausibly, that Swift felt that 'horseshit', the animal being graminivorous, is the least offensive of animal droppings. One can't like it, but one can live with it.

'Body dysmorphia' is something that novelists have always been aware of. It's one of the 'nothing human is alien' rules of their game. Most ignore the excremental facts of life – too tricky. James Joyce, that other great Irish novelist, doesn't. Early in *Ulysses* we witness Bloom 'asquat on the cuckstool', reading the day's paper, 'seated calm above his own rising smell'. It's supremely sane. Joyce was able to solve fiction's waste-disposal problem. Swift was not. Both of them were novelists.

Gun, with Occasional Music, Jonathan Lethem, 1994

Jonathan Lethem's first novel made a hit on its appearance, signalling a new-wave moment in genre bending. *GWOM*, as admirers call it, is an acrobatic act of homage to two classic authors in the Californian canon. One is Raymond Chandler – something cued by *GWOM*'s epigraph, which is taken from *Playback* (in which PI Philip Marlowe is waiting for his suspect at the San Diego railway station):

> There was nothing to it. The Super Chief was on time, as it almost always is, and the subject was as easy to spot as a kangaroo in a dinner jacket.

It's a wild simile of the kind Chandler made his trademark. Lethem 'evolves' the image with a gun-toting hoodlum kangaroo named Joey Castle who is stalking *GWOM*'s PI hero, Conrad Metcalf, with homicidal intent.

Evolution is no longer something that happens over eons but a fast technology – patented by the pioneering Dr Theodore Twostrand (Dr Moreau, where are you?). You can now, as Lethem's opening chapter depicts, find yourself riding the lift alongside an evolved sow on the way up to your office, where an evolved rabbit in a miniature three-piece suit is waiting impatiently. The murder of a sweet-natured evolved ewe called Dulcie is going to cause Metcalf much grief, as will a rival PI called Walter Surface who happens to be an evolved chimpanzee and very persistent. This higher-zoological fantasy (Dr Dolittle, where are you?) is rationalised by Lethem's other idolised writer, Philip K. Dick ('pkd' to fans), in whose world (see BLADE RUNNER) 'animaldroids' would seem no stranger than androids or selling dreams wholesale. Metcalf is based in 'Bay City' – San Francisco.

His Marlovian (Philip Marlowe, that is) origins are proclaimed, stylistically, in such flamboyant Chandlerisms as:

> I got up next morning with a head that felt like the change you get from a five-spot when you spent it on a $4.98 bottle of wine.

This is a future world in which not just the animal kingdom, but California itself, has evolved into its ultimate selfhood. No coinage, no notes. The currency is 'karma'. Citizens have a spending limit. Max out your cards – 'zero your karma' – and it's cryogenic suspension for a year or two, or a slave camp for three-strike offenders. Metcalf is forever running short of karmic points. His 'PI' acronym does not denote 'Private Investigator' but 'Private Inquisitor'. He is licensed to ask questions. This is otherwise a prerogative of the 'Office' – the government. Cocaine, like everything else, has been 'evolved'. The state's principal industry ('Office' controlled) are 'makeries' in which designer drugs are made. They have specific functions, indicated by their trade names. 'Forgettol' blanks out unhappy memories. There is the heavier-duty 'Avoidol', 'Regrettol' for melancholics, and 'Believol' for sceptics.

Metcalf, fatalistic by nature, 'is skewed heavily towards Acceptol'. He's got some serious issues to be fatalistic about. He opted for a 'temporary orgasm exchange' with a floozy called Delia Limetree. She's gone who knows where with his neural penis and Conrad's sexual pleasure is now entirely vaginal.

The plot, as with Chandler and Dick, is a hook on which to hang things of greater interest than 'who did it?' Metcalf is hired by a mega-rich urologist. 'Everything was pretty about Maynard Stanhunt except the job he hired me to do for him', which is to beat up his unfaithful wife, Celeste (who, inevitably, when found, lavishes some infidelity in Conrad's direction). Stanhunt is murdered. Unravelling the crime involves a bewildering array of shady suspects, and a criminal kingpin with the unlikely name (they all are) of Phoneblum. The investigation is necessarily put on hold when Metcalf finally overdraws on his karma account and is put into cryogenic rest for six years. He returns (like H. G. Wells' Sleeper) to an even stranger soft-totalitarian world, now dominated by 'babyheads' (adults in juvenile physique), where it is illegal even to ask yourself what you do for a living. Frankly GWOM has given up all it has to give the reader by page 100 – but they are very readable and zestful pages. Chandler and Dick, had they lived to read it, would have welcomed the babyhead into their club.

The Guns of Navarone, Alistair MacLean, 1957

Most readers will have a soft spot for novels which are not good fiction but which are, nonetheless, 'good reads'. This is a strong candidate. MacLean's narrative is set in the dark days of the Second World War, in 1943, following the ignominious British retreat from Crete. Navarone, we are to believe, is a strongly fortified island off the Turkish coast with an impregnable battery of guns – or so, at least, the enemy fondly believes. This fearsome artillery, perched on sheer cliffs, imperils the British attempt to evacuate their troops from the nearby island of Kheros. A commando force is assembled by

SOE (Special Operations Executive) for the 'mission impossible' of disabling the Navarone guns.

The intrepid New Zealand mountaineer, Captain Mallory (of the Long Range Desert Group), is chosen to command. Mallory is backed up by Corporal Dusty Miller (an American and a 'genius with explosives'); by young Andy Stevens, who fears he may be a coward; by the massive Andrea (a Greek partisan who detests Germans, his family having been massacred by their Bulgarian allies); and by Casey Brown, the 'sparks' of the squad. They land, and with the help of patriotic islanders make their way to the fortress. But, as always in MacLean's adventure stories, there is a spy within – in this case a treacherous Greek, Panayis.

Mallory's group is captured by a German officer, Oberleutnant Turzig – like Mallory, a mountaineer and a 'good German' (unlike the vile Gestapo scum, who await them in Navarone's dungeons). The heroes contrive to escape, on the 'with one bound he was free' principle. The novel has a countdown structure and maps to help the reader see the events strategically. Mallory's men finally achieve the impossible feat, scale the unscalable cliffs, and blow up 'the two great guns of Navarone'. Stevens dies, bravely, proving he is no coward. Good chap.

The band of heroes – as in all MacLean's war fiction – is sexless as a company of worker bees. In one of his rare interviews the author harrumphed: 'Sex? No time for it. Gets in the way of the action.' For the MacLeanian action man, war itself can also be a perfunctory matter. Mere hostility pales beside the task of scaling Navarone's 'vast impregnable precipice' – the first, flash-forward, scene in the novel. The British and German mountaineers forge an instant manly bond. 'How easily one could respect, form a friendship with a man like Turzig if it weren't for this damned, crazy war', thinks Mallory. As they part (Mallory has meanwhile killed Turzig's superior officer, overpowered the German guards holding him, and guaranteed that his German chum will face a court-martial) he chivalrously invites his opponent to come climbing with him when this damned, crazy war is over. Nonsense, of course, but readable nonsense – so long as no one catches you.

Hadrian the Seventh, 'Fr Rolfe' (Baron Corvo), 1904

There is a very respectable category of literature called 'Nonsense Poetry' (Edward Lear and Lewis Carroll are luminaries). There could usefully be a respected niche for 'nonsense novels'. Corvo's best-known work would be a prime candidate. It was written by Fred Rolfe, who assumed a name almost as long as this entry (you can find it in guide books) and posed on his title pages as 'Fr Rolfe'. You get the point if you picture him writing away with a tonsure and biretta. *Hadrian the Seventh* (also known as *Hadrian VII*) opens with one of the most memorable depictions of the miseries of the writing life. A middle-aged hack – George Arthur Rose – is starving in his garret. Scant supplies of bread and sweet tea are brought to him by a maid. He is indifferent – cigarettes are all he needs. *Qui fume, dine*:

PROOIMION

In mind he was tired, worn out, by years of hope deferred, of loneliness, of unrewarded toil. In body he was almost prostrate by the pain of an arm on the tenth day of vaccination. Bodily pain stung him like a personal affront. 'Some one will have to be made miserable for this,' he once said during the throes of a toothache.

It is typical that Rolfe should start with a word most readers will have to look up in the dictionary (prooimion = opening). Payback, we apprehend, will be very much the theme of the novel. Rather more than a toothache is at issue. He tries to write, but cannot:

Dazed in a torrent of ideas, he painfully halted for words: stumbling in a maze of words, he frequently lost the thread of his argument: now and then, in sheer exhaustion, his pen remained immobile... His little yellow cat Flavio lay asleep on the tilted board, nestling in the bend of his left elbow. That was the only living creature to whom he ever spoke with affection as well as politeness.

He scans the papers. Disorder is everywhere. Socialism is rotting the world.

We pick up his background, piece by piece. A Roman Catholic convert in his twenties, he was discharged from the Scots College in Rome for obscure offences before he could take orders. He nonetheless regards himself as a priest in the wilderness. Enter two dignitaries of the Church, overflowing with apology. They shower him with thousands of pounds and take him off as a private chaplain to Rome where – there being a papal election, and, unable to choose between the corrupt Italian candidates – the conclave of cardinals elect him with the obligatory puff of white smoke. He will be the first English pope since Adrian – hence his choice of papal title. (Saint) George (King) Arthur (English) Rose is now Hadrian the Seventh. Justice has been done. He will, following the pragmatic way of his nation, save the world from itself.

He has long, instructive audiences with such dignitaries as the Kaiser and the King of England. He melts the useless gold ornamentation of the Vatican and plucks out its jewels to sell, using the funds in furtherance of his campaign against international socialism. He is, finally, assassinated near the tomb of the Emperor Hadrian, shot by one of the 'Kelts' (Scots) whose 'degenerate race' he has always despised. His work, however, is done:

The hand and the dark eyelashes drooped, and fell. The delicate fastidious lips closed, in the ineffable smile of the dead who have found out the Secret of Love, and are perfectly satisfied. So died Hadrian the Seventh, Bishop, Servant of the servants of God, and (some say) Martyr. So died Peter in the arms of Caesar. The world sobbed, sighed, wiped its mouth; and experienced extreme relief.

The body of this unique (in its bizarreness) novel is a wonderful clutter of ritual, liturgy, ceremonial ornamentation, Latin – Rolfe wallows in it. One can almost smell the incense rising from the pages. Rolfe, like Rose, was kicked out of the Scots College in Rome, in obscure disgrace. He was not, sadly, elected Pope Fred the First. But exploiting a slight relationship with an aristocratic patroness (infatuated with him, despite his being generally celibate, and homosexual when he lapsed), he ennobled himself as 'Baron Corvo'.

The Handmaid's Tale, Margaret Atwood, 1985

Where to put this feminist-futurist fable has, generically, always been a moot question. But the fact that it was nominated for a Nebula and won the Arthur C. Clarke Award (not easy for a woman who, as in other competitive fields, has to be twice as good as her male rivals to be recognised) indicates that the science-fiction community were prepared to admit it as one of theirs. Nonetheless it is as what the Victorians called 'a novel with a purpose' – fiction aiming to change an unfair world – that The Handmaid's Tale has secured a permanent place as a long-term bestseller, much-studied educational text and bone of critical contention. In schools and universities it has slotted into the place formerly occupied by the culturally and historically obsolescent NINETEEN EIGHTY-FOUR and BRAVE NEW WORLD, neither of which are enlightened on women – Orwell's Julia is as deceitful as Milton's Eve, and all the women in Huxley's fable are genetically 'pneumatic' and dumb.

Atwood's novel is set in a post-catastrophic, late twentieth century. Fundamentalist Christians have taken over the United States, which they have renamed the Republic of Gilead. African-Americans (Children of Ham) have been transported elsewhere. Women are again in their subordinate place. In the same period, male and female fertility has declined disastrously. As a result the few fecund women who remain are designated 'Handmaids' – breeders, at the disposal of men. A woman's role is indicated by the coloured uniform she must wear: green for the 'Marthas' (houseworkers); blue for (sterile) Wives; vivid red for the fertile, and much prized, 'Handmaids'. The biblical allusion is to Bilhah in Genesis who bears children for Jacob when his wife Rachel cannot conceive. A surrogate mother, in modern parlance.

As Mary McCarthy pointed out in her rather snippy New York Times review, Gilead is a matriarchy – but of a perverse kind. Feminism's worst nightmare. Gileadian Handmaids have no rights, no social life and are given the chattel-name 'Of[their owner]'. The heroine is Offred ('property of Fred'). She was captured with her husband and child trying to escape to liberal Canada (a small chauvinism; Atwood is Canadian). Offred is allocated to a powerful male called 'the Commander', with whom she suffers monthly, loveless couplings ('the Ceremony'). For those of the Commander's station, secret brothels are available with 'Jezebels' decked out in traditional whorehouse/Playboy style. Offred is persecuted by the Commander's infertile wife, Serena Joy, who is present at the monthly Ceremonies – vicariously orgasming.

It transpires that the Commander is sterile and, to preserve what little security she has, Offred has an affair with his chauffeur, Nick, to get herself pregnant. Nick eventually persuades her to join the underground, with the inducement of being reunited with her daughter. The novel ends ambiguously. The whole narrative is framed within a conference on 'Gileadian Studies' in the 'distant future'. Offred's 'tale' has survived on tape and is now, in a more liberated age, of historical interest only.

Atwood disclosed in interview that she was inspired to write The Handmaid's Tale by newspaper reports of a drastic decline in male fertility. It was caused, some scientists suggested, by the build-up of female contraceptive hormones (via urine) in the drinking water. A kind of Handmaids' revenge on the tyrant sex. The dedication of the novel is to Perry Miller, the Harvard historian who had been Attwood's mentor, and Mary Webster. As Atwood later revealed: 'Mary Webster was an ancestor of mine who was hanged for a witch in Connecticut.' The hangman bungled the job and she survived. Is this a hint that Offred does, as well?

Hangover Square, Patrick Hamilton, 1941

Hamilton, a sad case personally, enjoyed some success as a novelist of London in the 1930s. By 1945 he had drunk himself into terminal stupefaction. This is his best novel. His reputation was kept alive and his bar bills paid by his play *Rope* (with its body-on-the-stage-all-the-while gimmick), which Hitchcock adapted brilliantly into his most claustrophobic film. As the public forgot him, Hamilton retained a loyal corps of admirers and a reputation as an author's author. Doris Lessing, notably, led her praise nose-first with the commendation: 'Patrick Hamilton was a marvellous novelist ... Now people have forgotten the kind of smell that came out of England in the Thirties, the cheese-paring and the obsession with money.' 'You can almost smell the gin', agreed Keith Waterhouse, a Soho drinker almost in Hamilton's class.

Hangover Square carries the cheeky subtitle, *A Story of Darkest Earl's Court*. The action is set in the late summer of 1939 – the last days of pre-war England. The narrative is punctuated by radio bulletins, announcing the ever-closer approach of war. The novel was published during the Blitz which was methodically destroying London by night. It seemed at the time that Britain might lose the war. Hamilton's hero (not the kind of hero who wins wars) is George Harvey Bone, a lumbering ox of a fellow with 'great golfer's wrists' who, nonetheless, is possessed of a good nature. He is easily exploited and has fallen into a 'wrong set' whose life is drinking, sponging, and sleeping around. Their stamping ground is West End's Han(g)over Square, with its drinking dens (after-hours 'clubs' outside the licensing regulation). George has fallen in love with a second-rate actress and first-rate whore, Netta. She and her friends use George, who has an income, and spitefully sabotage his attempts to drink less.

There is one interesting feature of George's personality. When a certain 'click' happens in his brain, he enters what he calls a 'dead mood'. Split personality is commonplace in literature, going back through Jekyll and Hyde to Hoffmann. But by 1939 the condition had acquired a scientific name, which Hamilton's novel was instrumental in popularising. It is explained in the epigraph:

Schizophrenia: a cleavage of the mental functions, associated with assumption by the affected person of a second personality.

George's second personality fantasises about murdering Netta. She is, to use D. H. Lawrence's term, a prime 'murderee'. She torments George by giving others what she denies him.

The action climaxes on a banal dirty weekend in Brighton. Netta is spending it with her lover (a Mosleyite British Fascist, we learn). In one of his dead moods George, having heard the copulation next door, breaks in, kills the lover with one of his (George's) golf clubs, a carefully chosen number seven iron (one remembers those wrists), and drowns Netta in her bath by pulling up her legs and dunking her head under the foam. It will be the first time he has seen her naked. 'I'm sorry. I didn't hurt you, did I?' he politely enquires of her corpse. He then goes to Maidenhead, still in his other self, and takes up residence in a boarding house, where he kills himself, leaving a note asking that the cat in the London hotel he lived in be looked after. The newspapers pick up the detail with the screaming headline:

Slays Two. Found gassed. Thinks of Cat.

The novel ends with Chamberlain's address to the nation on the radio, telling them that the country is now at war with Germany.

Hollywood optioned *Hangover Square* to produce an all-time worst-ever film in 1945. The action is retro-set to Edwardian England. George is now a brilliant concert pianist. It gets more preposterous. Laird Cregar (who played the George character), an actor with a weight problem, ballooned up to three hundred pounds during the film's shooting. He crash dieted, with the aid of drugs, and lost one hundred pounds, killing himself two months before the film was released. Lucky, some said, not to have to sit through the damn thing.

Hannibal Rising, Thomas Harris, 2006

The Silence of the Lambs is one of the most-read novels of the late twentieth century. Interestingly Harris went on to do what

Conan Doyle had not attempted with Professor Moriarty, or Ian Fleming with Ernst Stavro Blofeld – that is, explain, in a prequel, what events had combined to make his arch-criminal so inhumanly and superhumanly arch-criminal. It resulted in a novel much less good than *The Silence of the Lambs*, or that other fine novel in which Hannibal Lecter appears, *Red Dragon*, but nonetheless fascinating.

Is it wise, or unwise, to 'explain' monsters? Harris takes up the challenge. His monster, we now learn, was born (unmonstrous) in far-off Lithuania, as heir to Count Lecter. The child was named after Hannibal the Grim, who built the family castle five centuries before, but Hannibal's early years reveal the young fellow as anything but grim. He was a completely normal child – apart, that is, from his maroon eyes, a Lithuanian title, six fingers on his left hand and genius-level intelligence. While barely a toddler, he masters Euclid and a clutch of Middle-European languages. As I say, completely normal. Little Hannibal is kind to animals – particularly horses and swans (remember that, it will be important) – servants and Jews. He loves his parents and, above all, his baby sister Mischa. However, Hannibal's familial destiny to become the nicest Count Lecter in five hundred years is rudely interrupted when he is eight, by Hitler's invasion of Russia. The family takes refuge in a forest lodge that affords them a couple of years' precarious safety. During the Nazi retreat from the country, the parents are blown to bits by a tank explosion but the children manage to survive.

A gang of brutal brigands, led by the villainous Vladis Grutas, ends all that. The priceless family treasures are looted, and, crowning horror, little Mischa is boiled in a pot when the brigands' rations run short. Hannibal is struck dumb by the Thyestean horror of it all and represses the memory of something awful he saw floating in the cooking pot – of whose cannibalistic stew he unwittingly partook. No chianti on the side.

After some time in a communist orphanage (Harris hates orphanages) Hannibal is adopted by his Uncle Robert, who lives in high-bohemian style in Paris, but unfortunately dies not long after.

Hannibal is taken in by his aunt, Lady Murasaki, a namesake of the author of *The Tale of Genji* – 'the first great novel in the world', as Harris informs us, slyly. From here on in, young Hannibal's progress towards full-blown monsterhood follows four tracks. One is the gradual recall (given in shuddering *italic* interludes) of what happened in the hunting lodge. Another is immersion in Japanese high culture by his aunt. Under Lady Murasaki's instruction, Hannibal can soon throw off haikus and watercolour sketches of herons in moonlight, and twirl the *tanto* knife as if to the manner born. A third track is a brilliant medical career. Lecter is the youngest student ever to be enrolled in the Parisian medical schools. He reads his textbooks once, and returns them (memorised) the same week for a full refund. But the most interesting track is his revenge on the swine who ate his sister. The deaths he comes up with out-gruesome even the final banquet of blood in *Hannibal* (the victim tricked into lipsmackingly eating his own fried brain – prepared, as haute cuisine, by Lecter: the chef from hell). At a critical moment in the action, a French detective observes, sententiously, 'What is he now? There's not a word for it yet. For lack of a better word, we'll call him a monster.' More fittingly, perhaps, a monster-chef. *Bon appétit*, readers.

To return to the question of whether monsters should be explained, *Hannibal Rising* highlighted an illuminating paradox in gothic fiction. The novel was greedily awaited and the initial American print run, promptly exhausted, was 1.5 million. Yet the book was a disappointment and, more significantly, diminished the effect of its predecessors. Where monsters from Grendel onwards are concerned, their monstrosity is, demonstrably, enhanced by our *not* knowing what made them. Conan Doyle made the right decision. Preserve the mystery.

Hanta Yo, Ruth Beebe Hill, 1979

In Olvera Street – the heart of (kitsch) Mexican Los Angeles and a favourite gringo-tourist resort – there is a monument. It is raised in memory of the Gabrielino Indians, many of whose bones, it was recently discovered, lie underneath the busy fajita and refried beans kitchens above. There are, alas, very few Gabrielinos left and there have been no speakers of their language for a hundred years. What was once their land, the stone piously records, is now 'held in stewardship by their successors'. Until the Martians arrive, presumably. The current owners (the 'paleskins'), one may confidently predict, will put up a sterner fight than the Gabrielinos, a peaceful, chestnut-munching people with a low level of craft and art. After the 1964 Civil Rights Act there was, in the American conscience, a distinct uneasiness about how they had treated what were increasingly called 'Native Americans' – not, nowadays, 'Indians' and never 'Hostiles'. Films and novels reflected the need to revise old prejudices: such works as Larry McMurtry's Lonesome Dove and Thomas Berger's hugely undervalued LITTLE BIG MAN come to mind. The revision became surreal with Marlon Brando dispatching Sacheen Littlefeather to collect his best actor Oscar in 1973, and the 1990 film Dances with Wolves. Hanta Yo is part of the nostra culpa process. Or would have been, had the novel not become entangled in doubts about its authenticity.

An ostensibly reverential and deeply researched 'documented novel' (in Hill's words), it chronicles a small band of Teton Sioux over the years 1759 to 1835. Hill (b. 1913) was a journalist by profession, principally active in southern California. Her preparation for what was to become Hanta Yo began in 1951 and took decades to complete. It would be the only novel she published; a lifetime's work. As research, she lived with Native Americans and learned the Lakotah tongue. She translated the eventual novel into that dialect, then back into English to get the timbre exactly right. Hill was assisted by a Sioux collaborator, Chunksa Yuha, who declared in his introduction that Hanta Yo (which, he explains, means 'clear the way' in Lakotah) 'will survive the generations for in its pages flows skan . . . spiritual vitality'. In her preface Hill asserts that the Native American 'attained perhaps the highest working concept of individualism ever practiced'. An obscure compliment.

The narrative follows the fortunes of the Mahto band over the last eighty years of their independence. It centres on a series of Sioux tribal heroes: Wnagi, Olepi, and other great unpronounceables. The novel chronicles the nomadic migrations into Missouri, seasonal practices, tribal wars, old and newly devised ceremonies, early contacts with the white man, consequent epidemics, and various strategies of self-preservation after the first immigrant wagons are encountered. And noble extinction.

Hanta Yo, and its author 'who made herself an Indian' (as one laudatory headline proclaimed), went down big on publication. The bestselling novel was optioned as a mini-series on the Roots model, which had glued almost 150 million Americans to their TVs in 1977. It was fondly hoped it would do for the Native American what Alex Haley's chronicle had done for the African-American. It was shot in the outskirts of Los Angeles (no reservation would host it), and sank without trace.

Harry Potter and the Deathly Hallows, J. K. Rowling, 2007

This is the seventh and last novel in the superselling series, in which Rowling frankly pitched her narrative to a mature, as well as to a juvenile, audience. The novel opens with something rarely, but always strategically, employed by the author: a scene in which Harry is not present. Voldemort, alias 'He Who Must Not Be Named' (his fiendish radar can tune into any reference to him), is plotting to terminate the hero as he comes up to his seventeenth birthday. From this point on, the defences which have preserved the lad throughout his childhood years will drop away. The game's afoot. How Voldemort plans to dispose of his adversary is not entirely clear, but a man-guzzling snake called Nagini (which seems to have slithered into the novel from the film-set of Anaconda) may be involved. Adult life, we apprehend, will bring problems not to be entirely solved by the 'enchanted razor' which Fleur gives Harry for his birthday ('eet will give you ze smoothest shave you will ever 'ave,' the worldly Mademoiselle Delacour tells him).

After the opening scene in Voldemort's lair, the story cuts to the chase. And a very bloody chase it is. There are no Marquess of Queensberry Quidditches in Harry's world. The battles are for real, with sizeable body counts. After a series of hairsbreadth escapes, the plot resolves itself into a duel between the two mighty opposites. On the one side, Harry and the three 'hallows' (holy thingies); on the other, Voldemort and the seven Horcruxes (particles of the evil one's soul). It's hammer and tongs. But why, one wonders, are these two so magnetically drawn to each other? How does Voldemort always know what Harry's next move will be? How is it that Harry, with a little throbbing of his clairvoyant scar, can visualise Voldemort's dastardly plans and even, at times, become Voldemort? This is something that Must-Not-Be-Told, but Which-Will-Be-Revealed when you reach page 593. Or sneak a look.

There are few historical dates in the Potter novels, but early on in HPDH we learn that in 1945 there was an epic, and decisive, struggle between a then-youthful Dumbledore and the Germanic 'Dark Wizard' Grindelwald. Dumbledore and the forces of light won. But the Grindelwaldian symbol, a runic 'sign' suggestive of the swastika, survives, as does its filthy baggage. In HPDH, Voldemort's Death Eaters take over the feeble 'Ministry' by putsch and introduce a ruthless programme of blood purity and racial hygiene. Their venom is particularly directed against 'Mudbloods'. Storm troopers ('Snatchers') roam the streets, seizing suspect Britons at will. Rowling must have known (although her younger readers might not have done) that 'mud people' is the vile appellation used by American Neo-Nazis for black people. The horrors of ethnic cleansing do not lie oppressively on the narrative and wouldn't ruin any young reader's fun, but there is a black cloud faintly looming over HPDH.

There is an artistic justification for Rowling closing the proceedings with HPDH. Seven ranks high in occult and popular numerology (seven orifices in the body, deadly sins, dwarfs, horcruxes, etc.). A septennial clock was factored in when, with the first sequel (Harry Potter and the Chamber of Secrets), Rowling decided to have her schoolboy age a year with every instalment. Unlike William Brown, Billy Bunter or Marty McFly, Harry moved forward until, inevitably, with this novel, he was on the furthest edge of the narrative frame his author initially created for him. The sixth-form of life.

The Haunting of Hill House, Shirley Jackson, 1959

Ask those who love the form what the best-ever horror story is and brows will wrinkle. Chances are it will be a toss-up between 'The Turn of the Screw', anything by M. R. James, and The Haunting of Hill House. Jackson's novel has the formal simplicity of a bridge game. Dr John Montague, an anthropologist, has been looking for 'an honestly haunted house' all his life. He intends to run an experiment. Is 'honestly haunted house' a contradiction in terms? He finds what he wants in New England and recruits three volunteers to reside there with him, over summer, as human litmus paper. Eleanor Vance is a chronically repressed spinster whose life has been 'wasted' looking after an invalid mother. She volunteers because nothing has ever happened to her in her thirty years. This will be an 'experience' – at last. Theodora is a life-loving artist with extraordinary, laboratory-tested powers of extra-sensory perception. The quartet is made up with a playboy of dubious honesty, and eventual heir to the house, Luke Sanderson.

Hill House is some eighty years old. It was built by a domestic tyrant, Hugh Crain. The women in his family who lived there all came to wretched premature ends. The narrative centres principally on Eleanor. That Hill House is sinister is signalled less by gothic horrors than by hints. There is a gibbering housekeeper who seems to have wandered out of the pages of Mrs Radcliffe's tales of terror. Grass in the grounds rustles – is it rabbits, a breeze? Temperatures plummet. The layout of the house is strange. The occupants are for ever losing their way. The house is not haunted – this is not Canterville Ghost territory – the house haunts. The other principal point is made by Montague:

'No physical danger exists,' the doctor said positively. 'No ghost in all the long histories of ghosts has ever hurt anyone physically. The only damage done is by the victim to himself. One cannot even say that the ghost attacks the mind, because the mind, the conscious, thinking mind, is invulnerable; in all our conscious minds, as we sit here talking, there is not one iota of belief in ghosts. . . No, the menace of the supernatural is that it attacks where modern minds are weakest, where we have abandoned our protective armour of superstition and have no substitute defence.'

We are vulnerable to the supernatural because we no longer believe in the supernatural. It's a subtle point. The four occupants establish one thing. Hill House is indeed evil.

This house, which seemed somehow to have formed itself, flying together into its own powerful pattern under the hands of its builders, fitting itself into its own construction of lines and angles, reared its great head back against the sky without concession to humanity. It was a house without kindness, never meant to be lived in, not a fit place for people or for love or for hope. Exorcism cannot alter the countenance of a house; Hill House would stay as it was until it was destroyed.

It is not destroyed. The party – all but one – leaves.

Jackson had been inspired by reading about the British Society for Psychical Research's investigations into Ballechin House in 1896. She modelled the physical appearance of Hill House on a property which belonged to her own great-great-grandfather. *The Haunting of Hill House* has never been out of print since publication. It was superbly filmed in 1963. The gifted Richard Matheson (see I AM LEGEND) wrote an homage, *Hell House*, and Stephen King's *The Shining* is another. King pays a disciple's tribute to Jackson in *Danse Macabre*.

Headbirths: or, The Germans are Dying Out, Günter Grass, 1982

Take a bleak statistic. China has a population of 1.3 billion (996 million in 1980, when Grass' novel was written), a figure that is rapidly increasing. Germany has a shrinking population of 81 million. Where can a novel go with that fact? Into head-dizzying complexities and a new kind of fiction if Günter Grass is the novelist. He always believed German fiction had to start again, after 1945, from a zero baseline. All the literary foundations had been rotted by Hitler. 'The past must be overcome', said Grass. But without the past, where does a writer start? In *Headbirths*, one's first reaction is that Grass isn't writing what one would regard as a novel at all. That privilege, we apprehend, no longer exists for novelists of his culturally shattered background. What he offers is a journal of 1979–80, with some fanciful digressions.

Floating in this narrative primal soup is an extraordinarily frank personal essay (although not quite frank enough to reveal that he served in the Waffen SS, a fact that only emerged in 2006). 'By a dubious stroke of luck', the novelist was born in 1927. But the current purge of an older, unluckier generation of German writers, condemned to silence by their Nazi pasts, leads him to speculate on his own career had little Günter been born ten years earlier, in 1917. In an eerie bio-bibliography of this tainted self, he provides an oeuvre which runs from the late Expressionist, rhapsodic poetry of his Hitler Youth period, through the post-Stalingrad 'poetry of lasting significance', to the 'fresh start' mode of de-Nazified 1947. All of which pertains to Grass's main literary-historical datum: that the ideology of National Socialism has laid waste the German language as extensively and less reparably than bombing laid waste the country's cities. If the German writer wants a tradition, he has to make it up out of his head. As regards what's bothering Grass's head most in this novel, it's the politics of carnal/cerebral fertility – 'Creativity'. During the war, the German people had been instructed to breed for the Reich. 'Fuck for the Führer' was not how they put it, but what was meant. So not to breed is, for the post-war German, an act of freedom. But what does that mean for Germany? The ultimate freedom is the freedom to think. But the Germans are thinking themselves to extinction. Falling birthrates confirm that Germany is now *Raum ohne Volk*, as dependent on fast-breeding immigrants to keep up the population figures as it is dependent on fast-breeding reactors for its 'power'.

The overarching – and non-fictional – event in the novel/non-novel is a tour by Grass and Volker Schlöndorff (director of the film of Grass' *The Tin Drum*) of various Third World locations. Seethingly populous India, Java or China are preferred settings for the new film they have vaguely in mind. The film never happens. But the scenario survives in another strand of the novel.

The main line of narrative centres on a model German teacher couple, Harm and Dörte Peters, from Itzehoe, Holstein. They worry their heads perpetually about whether or not they should have a baby. The poor thing might, for instance, have to grow up in a nuclear-powered Germany. The Peterses are children of the late 1960s: 'they met in Kiel, at a sit-in against the Vietnam War, or the Springer Press or both.' Now they are lost souls. Rudi Dutschke, their student rebel hero, is dead (drowned in a bath, after being shot in the head – a head death). Dörte has grown up to become a member of the FDP (Free Democratic Party) while Harm belongs to the SPD (Social Democratic Party). They now vote like headless chickens. A residue of student-protest romanticism takes them on an Asian trip (with 'Sisyphus Holidays') parallel to that of their creators. But Grass' couple exists only *in potentia* – 'unjelled'. The Peterses never happened – except, somewhere, in the heads of the two German 'creative' artists.

What, then, did Grass and Schlöndorff give birth to? Or abort? What – when all the cards are in play – is more important: to create a novel (or a film) out of your head, or a child out of your loins? To create literature, or population? The future will tell.

The Heart is a Lonely Hunter, Carson McCullers, 1940

McCullers' original title for the novel was *Mute*. She could as aptly have plucked one word out of the eventually published title: 'Lonely'. Conrad's sad truism 'we live as we dream – alone', with a vowel change to 'love', would serve as an apt epigraph. The lover and the beloved, McCullers believed, 'live in different countries'. The narrative opens with a vignette of separate togetherness:

> In the town there were two mutes, and they were always together. Early every morning they would come out from the house where they lived and walk arm in arm down the street to work.

John Singer is intelligent, a jeweller (as was McCullers' father), and an oracle to the lost souls of the town:

> One by one they would come to Singer's room to spend the evening with him. The mute was always thoughtful and composed. His many-tinted gentle eyes were grave as a sorcerer's . . . they felt that the mute would always understand whatever they wanted to say to him. And maybe even more than that.

Is the silent Singer a confessor or a scapegoat? He finally kills himself – does he take the woes and sins of his interlocutors with him? The other 'dummy' (cruel word) is fat, amiable and stupid. After an illness he becomes wholly anti-social and is institutionalised. The setting is the late 1930s. Hitler and Mussolini are mentioned – but so far away that they might be on Mars. 'The town' is in the 'deep south' where:

> The summers were long and the months of winter cold were very few. Nearly always the sky was a glassy, brilliant azure and the sun burned down riotously bright. . . The town was a fairly large one. . . the largest buildings in the town were the factories, which employed a large percentage of the population. These cotton mills

were big and flourishing and most of the workers in the town were very poor. Often in the faces along the streets there was the desperate look of hunger and of loneliness.

Which is worse, hunger or loneliness? McCullers wrote this novel about her native Georgia while an undergraduate at New York's Columbia University. In the storyline attached to fourteen-year-old Mick Kelly, the narrative hints at what she might have become had she not made her escape.

One of six children of a boarding-house proprietor, Mick is in love with music. She tries, pathetically, to make herself a violin as a black slave might fashion a banjo out of a cigar box. The classical music she hears on the radio – particularly that of 'Motsart' – speaks to her. But she is unable to respond – muted – and dreams forlornly of travelling to a 'foreign country where there's snow' – and music. She ends up working in Woolworths. McCullers, a lonely gifted child herself, aspired to be a concert pianist.

The town is barren ground for artistic aspiration or the big ideas transforming the world beyond. The one intellectual is an aged 'negro' (the politer term of the period) doctor, dying of consumption. Dr Benedict Mady Copeland has named his children Portia (after Shakespeare's heroine) and Karl Marx. Neither rises in life above the underclass. A third child is crippled for life in jail. The only white man who offers Copeland any kindness – or pays attention to him – is the deaf mute, John Singer. Copeland proselytises for the advancement of coloured people. It must happen, the novel insists. But not in this town.

McCullers' novel was published to huge acclaim. Deservedly. A few months later, aged only twenty-four, she suffered a severe stroke. As her friend, the dramatist Edward Albee, recalled: 'She was a very different person before she had her stroke, a very, very different person.' Nothing she wrote thereafter rivalled her first wonderful novel. She died aged fifty. At least she escaped Woolworths.

Heart of Darkness, Joseph Conrad, 1899

This is a very famous novel. As Dr Johnson once put it, to his ever-listening Boswell:

Fame is a shuttlecock. If it be struck only at one end of a room it will soon fall to the floor. To keep it up, it must be struck at both ends.

If the Great Cham was right, Heart of Darkness will surely last for as long as there are human eyes to read fiction. No work has been more batted about by critical reassessment over the last century.

The biographical seed for the story was Conrad's being commissioned around 1890 to skipper a decrepit steamer up the Congo River to an inland station, run by a dying manager called Klein (changed, though not very much, to Kurtz in Heart of Darkness). For a few months Conrad – a man of inherent decency, if not quite immune from the prejudices of his age and class – was an employee of the most iniquitous colonial agency, one that Europe should, for ever, be ashamed of, the Société Anonyme Belge pour le Commerce du Haut-Congo.

The so-called Congo Free State was founded in 1885 by Belgium. 'Free' in this case meant free to plunder. King Leopold parcelled out the million square miles to whatever firm would pay most. What they thereafter did with their colonial leasehold was up to them. The result was what has been called 'the first genocide of the modern era'. The river voyage had a profound influence on Conrad: 'Before the Congo I was a mere animal,' he later said. It took eight years for the 'horror' (a key word in the novel) to settle sufficiently in his mind for him to write Heart of Darkness: first as a three-part serial in Blackwood's Magazine, then, three years later, as a book which included two other novella-length works.

The story is simple. Marlow (Conrad's series hero-narrator) in his mature years entertains some friends on his yacht, the Nellie, bobbing in the mouth of the Thames as the sun sinks over the yardarm. In a momentary lull in conversation he says, musingly, 'And this also has been one of the dark places of the earth.' He is thinking of the Romans and ancient Britain. Behind every empire lies crime. He goes on to spin a yarn about a command he had in his early thirties. He was recruited in Brussels (a 'whited sepulchre' of a city) to go on a mission in Africa ('the heart-shaped continent'), up the Congo to the heart of the Belgian colony, where a station manager, Kurtz, had gone crazy in the process of harvesting elephant ivory. The voyage is one which takes Marlow into the dark truth of things – empire, human nature, and, ultimately, himself. Originally, Conrad intended Kurtz to be a journalist. A relic of that intention survives in the text as the pamphlet among his remains which opens with the lofty aim to bring civilisation to the savage world and ends, madly, 'Exterminate all the brutes!' Which Leopold's regime come criminally close to achieving.

Blackwood's first marketed *Heart of Darkness* as a nautical yarn and it sold well. Critics liked it – although some, like E. M. Forster, complained about 'opacity'. You can't see in the dark, Conrad would have replied. With the global wave of post-Second World War decolonisation, *Heart of Darkness* was universally prescribed, in the schools and universities of former imperial powers, as a kind of testament to present-day enlightenment. Sales soared, as did a sense of pedagogic self-righteousness. This was reversed by an explosive lecture at the University of Massachusetts-Amherst, on 18 February 1975, in which the eminent Nigerian novelist Chinua Achebe singled out *Heart of Darkness* to denounce Conrad as 'a bloody racist'. Why, Achebe asked, should the sufferings of his continent, and its millions of inhabitants, be utilised as so much background décor to the mental breakdown of one neurotic European? The novel now resides in that most uneasy of literary categories 'tainted classics', if not quite as untouchable by the syllabus-setters as Conrad's regrettably named *The Nigger of the Narcissus*. Read it and judge.

The Heart of Midlothian, Walter Scott, 1818

It requires an act of imagination to picture how successful Scott was in his day. 'The Author of *Waverley*' (he was still writing anonymously) demanded £5,000 for this work. His publisher happily stumped up a sum representing around half a million in current terms. Scott was worth it. A cargo ship carrying nothing but copies of the novel (printed at the James Ballantyne Press in Edinburgh, which Scott co-owned) was dispatched to London in July 1818. A week after publication Scott's aristocratic friend, Louisa Stuart, described being in a house 'where everybody is tearing it out of each other's hands, and talking of nothing else'.

That was then. Once the 'Great Unknown', Scott is nowadays the 'Great Unread'. But of all the Waverley novels, *The Heart of Midlothian* has retained the greatest residual interest for readers of the present day. A primary reason could be the fact that it has a Scottish working-class heroine – a genuinely heroic woman of the people – at its centre. But there are other features to recommend it. It is jested that the best way to start a Scott novel is to begin at page fifty. *The Heart of Midlothian* is an exception to this. It opens explosively with a recreation of the Porteous Riots. During the hanging of a smuggler, Andrew Wilson, in Edinburgh's Grassmarket on 14 April 1736, Captain John Porteous of the City Guard fired on the crowd (they had considerable sympathy with the smugglers, who brought them brandy at prices they could afford), killing and injuring many citizens who were only there to enjoy the show. Porteous was tried and himself sentenced to hang, but was reprieved by Queen Caroline. An enraged mob later stormed the Old Tolbooth gaol where Porteous was held, and lynched him.

Scott's plot complicates itself from this point beyond worthwhile summary. But a main strand centres on Jeanie Deans, who helps her father with his small herd of cattle on the common grazing land of Edinburgh's Arthur's Seat. Her sister, Effie, gets herself pregnant and – by the cruel law of the land – must hang when she refuses to name the father (the law was devised to inhibit abortion by discouraging secret pregnancies). The girls' father, 'Douce' (i.e. 'sober') David Deans, effectively disowns Effie. If either he or Jeanie told the court, on oath, that Effie had told them about her condition, she would be reprieved. Neither can bring themself to compromise their religious principles by committing perjury.

Instead Jeanie sets off on the long tramp to beg for mercy from the English Sovereign. On the way she falls in with highwaymen and a mysterious, witch-like woman, Madge Wildfire. In London, Jeanie finally meets Queen Caroline in the Great Park at Richmond. The Queen is impressed by her and grants a royal pardon. The third volume of the novel (which Scott struggled with) becomes very complicated and the plot runs off the rails. But all ends happily. Jeanie Deans has always been the most-loved of Scott's characters. But the deeper point the novel makes is that, ultimately, power (in this case the sovereign power to execute, reprieve, or commute) lies in London, not Edinburgh.

What, then, is the 'Heart of Midlothian'? I quote from the Best of Edinburgh tourist website:

> On the High Street [Royal Mile], just next to the west entrance to St Giles, you will notice this heart-shaped mosaic on the pavement. This represents the Heart of Midlothian and marks the entrance to the old Tollbooth (built around the beginning of the 1400s and demolished in 1817) which served as Edinburgh's prison, court and municipal offices. Over the years many public executions were held here, including that of William Brodie. It is also the site of the infamous Porteous Riot. Citizens of Edinburgh continue to this day to mark their contempt for the old prison and public authority by spitting into the Heart of Midlothian!

The Heart of Redness, Zakes Mda, 2000

HEART OF DARKNESS enjoys an achievement shared by very few other works in having provoked fellow novelists and artists to engage creatively with it. Francis Ford Coppola's film *Apocalypse Now* and Mda's novel, with its deliberately echoic title, top the list of Conrad challengers, with Graham Greene's THE HEART OF THE MATTER not far behind.

Mda's novel ponders South Africa's modern (i.e. colonial and post-colonial) history. Are there continuities, or just a for-ever-broken chain of misfortunes and a wholly disrupted future? The novel has two narrative centres and attempts, painfully, to forge a link between them. One centre is an 1850s Xhosa uprising against the hated British rulers. The other is the period immediately after South Africa's first democratic elections in 1994. Mda's hero, Camugu, was brought up in Johannesburg and has been thirty years (a short lifetime) in the US, where he has made a career in the communications industry. In these years abroad he has lost his inner self: his 'redness'. He comes 'home' to free South Africa in the 1990s only to be wholly disillusioned by the 'new Africa'. Nepotism bars him from obtaining any work he is qualified for. The 'Aristocrats of the Revolution' have no use for someone who is clever, highly trained and idealistic – but not one of them. Those who chose exile have no right to the spoils of victory bought by red blood, it seems.

Disillusioned, Camugu resolves to return to the US. But the night before his departure he hears a young woman singing on the roof of the building in the slum where he is staying. She is NomaRussia, who has named herself in tribute to the Russian soldiers who killed a former governor of the Cape Colony in the Crimean War. An infatuated Camugu follows NomaRussia to her birthplace, the small coastal village of Qolorha. This is the 'heart of redness' because it was also the birthplace of Nongqawuse, a teenage prophetess, who inspired the Xhosa nation to rise up in the mid-1850s. First she instructed her people to kill their cattle and burn their crops as a propitiatory sacrifice to the gods. The Xhosa dead would then rise from their graves and, in their hundreds of thousands, drive out the British robbers from their sacred land. And, she promised,

> the new people who will arise from the dead will come with new cattle, horses,

goats, sheep, dogs, fowl and other animals that the people may want. But the new animals of the new people cannot mix with your polluted ones. Destroy everything. Destroy the corn in your fields and in your granaries.

The village was divided between those who followed the 'cattle killing' instruction and those who did not. The 'Believers' won. The subsequent uprising proved disastrous for the Xhosa. Those who were not killed by the colonial forces, starved – 20,000 of them, it is estimated.

In the 1990s, Nongqawuse's village is still divided between Believers and Unbelievers. Those who want to wipe the slate clean – and then smash the slate – and others who want to build a casino and tourist resort and embrace the Westernised future. Camugu finds a middle way. He instructs the men in the village how to harvest and market the abalone (sea snails) from their shores, and teaches the women how to set up co-operatives for their indigenous textiles and Xhosa clothes. Their customers extend from local hotels to the great city itself. Traditional dress is much in fashion – and restaurants are voracious for sea-food. The casino would have prostituted Qolorha. Camugu has liberated it. He is, the novel implies, the true heir to Nongqawuse – and more sensible. The novel, which opened with a devastatingly downbeat verdict on the decadence of Johannesburg, ends in a surge of upbeat optimism.

The Heart of the Matter, Graham Greene, 1948

In his autobiography Ways of Escape (1980), Greene recalls that as he began The Heart of the Matter he was in two minds whether to write a serious 'novel' or one of his 'entertainments':

a crime story in which the criminal [Scobie] was known to the reader but the detective [Wilson] was carefully hidden, disguised by false clues which would lead the reader astray until the climax.

He finally chose the novel. A pity, perhaps, that he did not write both. It could have been something as powerful as The Third Man, whose screenplay he was working on at around the same time.

The action of The Heart of the Matter is set in a West African port (clearly Freetown, Sierra Leone, where Greene himself was posted as an intelligence agent) in 1942. It is a fetid backwater. Henry Scobie, a deputy commissioner of police, is middle-aged, unhappily married, and has just been passed over for promotion. An honest man in a singularly dishonest place, he is strenuously Catholic. He is known among his colleagues – sarcastically – as 'Aristides the Just'. This is not a place where justice thrives.

Scobie and his wife had a daughter who died. The wife, Louise, wishes to move from this wretched existence in the 'white man's grave' (and white woman's hellish boredom) to South Africa. Scobie dearly wants to oblige her. He is racked by guilt, pity and a hypertrophied sense of responsibility for the sufferings of others. He is, however, refused the necessary loan by his bank manager – a man harassed by the fear that he has cancer. When the manager discovers he is indeed doomed, he becomes much more generous with his bank's cash. But it is too late. Scobie, compromising a lifetime's probity, has raised the money criminally. In an environment where crime is universal, his is insignificant. But for him it is enormous – and it is a sin.

His life spins out of control. He falls in love with Helen, the young survivor of a torpedoed ship – she reminds him of his daughter. He is, meanwhile, being investigated by Wilson, an intelligence agent sent from England. The various betrayals overwhelm Scobie, who makes his own suicide look like a fatal heart attack so that Louise (who is having a wholly guilt-free affair with Wilson) will benefit and Helen, whom he can never make an 'honest woman' (divorce is impossible for a Catholic of his stringency), will be free. Wilson, by close examination of Scobie's diary, uncovers his ruse. Scobie confidently expects eternal damnation but after his death a Catholic priest, Father Rank, opines to Louise that God's mercy may be extended to her husband, despite his mortal sin: 'the church knows all the rules. But it doesn't know what goes on in a single human heart.' That generosity is confirmed by the paradoxical epigraph to the novel, from Péguy:

The sinner is at the very heart of Christianity ... No one is as competent as the sinner in Christian affairs. No one, except the saint.

George Orwell, among others, took huge exception to the exceptionalism of Greene's denominational prejudice, the notion 'that there was something rather special and distinguished in being damned; Hell is a sort of high-class country club, membership in which is reserved for Catholics only'.

The Heart of the Matter was the novel with which Greene broke through into international fame and bestsellerdom. It was, however, never a favourite with him because it was, as he believed, grossly and almost universally misread (by readers as distinguished as Orwell, for example). There was, Greene protested, nothing 'saintly' about Scobie. The man was a prig, who thought that he could play God. In the 1970s Greene made some crucial changes to the text and in a preface declared: 'The character of Scobie was intended to show that pity can be the expression of an almost monstrous pride.'

Heat and Dust, Ruth Prawer Jhabvala, 1975

Jhabvala is known for two things: her collaborations as screenwriter with the Merchant-Ivory film-making team and for having won the Booker Prize. Her Booker was controversial for not being controversial. *Heat and Dust* was judged 'slight', 'dull' and, that most deadly of things in the annual literary gladiatorial bloodbath, 'safe'. The judgement was unfair. The novel needs to be seen of a piece with the many delicately inflected screenplays Jhabvala wrote for James Ivory and Ismail Merchant. The 'three-headed monster' (as Merchant called them) are acknowledged as the most gifted translators of E. M. Forster on to the large screen. Merchant-Ivory did not, alas, 'do' *Passage to India*, which was

adapted, clumpingly, by David Lean. It was like Chopin played by a brass band.

Heat and Dust makes one ache a little for that might-have-been Merchant Ivory film. The novel runs on two tracks, the narrative as perforated as lace, leaving unfilled gaps at every stage of its unfolding. A young woman of the present day is curious about a relative no one in the family talks about: her dead grandfather's first wife, Olivia Rivers. There is, she guesses, some scandal dating back to 1923, when her grandfather was a civil servant in Satipur. The young woman (un-named, and we learn virtually nothing of her background) goes to India and goes native. The opening sections describe her exciting experiments with Indian dress (not entirely successful: she is mistaken in the streets for a *hijra* – a eunuch whore). She lodges in an Indian house. One of the few things we do pick up is that she is sexually uninhibited.

Her chronicle is intertwined with Olivia's – told in the form of diaries and third-person narrative. Olivia's husband Douglas is an impeccable civil servant: a just and generous Assistant Collector. British to the core. His office works uneasily with that of the local ruler: the Nawab of Khatm. A playboy charmer – the owner of Rolls-Royces and every gilded luxury wealth can import – the Nawab subsidises his extravagance by protecting criminal gangs. He is devoted to his mother, a distantly omnipresent Begum, and anything but devoted to his wife. Predatory and bi-sexual, he keeps a homosexual British man as a kind of house catamite. 'When he wants something', one of the British residents says, 'nothing must stand in his way.' And he wants Olivia. So overpoweringly that she becomes pregnant. Her lovemaking with Douglas has been barren. She has been metaphorically impregnated by India.

Unable to face the likelihood of a wrongly pigmented baby, Olivia turns to an Indian abortionist. But her secret leaks out and scandal ensues. In a world where respectable Memsahibs will not let male servants iron their underwear, she has not merely disgraced herself but let down the Empire. Her marriage shatters and she is confined by the Nawab as a kept woman – in a hill-station, 'Town X' – away from the 'heat and dust' of low-lying Satipur, which has been reaching its pre-Monsoon scorching pitch during the course of this drama. Olivia's step-granddaughter takes a parallel course, with the deviations allowed in an independent India for an emancipated woman. 'India always changes people, and I have been no exception', is her bleak verdict. She seduces her Indian landlord and – having toyed with the thought (for convenience, not any fear of 'scandal') – rejects abortion. She, too, moves to 'Town X'. The novel ends with a landscape-shot of stunning richness.

> I rarely look down. Sometimes, when the rains stop, the mist in the valley swirls about and afterwards the air is so drenched with moisture that the birds seem to swim about in it and the trees wave like seaweed. I think it will be a long time before I go down again. First, of course, I'm going to have my baby.

The effect of this scene is cinematic and climactic. The pent-up energy of the novel's terseness is released, explosively. *Heat and Dust* may be minor. But its touch is so deft, and so artistically cunning, that one cannot resent its winning any prize going.

A Hero of Our Time, Mikhail Lermontov, 1840

Lermontov's novel is often titled in translation as 'The Heart of a Russian'. It depicts, in the character of its 'hero', the 'spirit of the age'. That spirit is imbued with spiritual malaise and Byronic ennui (the English poet was Lermontov's god). The novel falls into five separate stories, or parts, anachronistically assembled. A traveller to the Caucasus, un-named, intending to write a travel book, falls in with a bluff old soldier, Maksim Maksimych, who tells him about a remarkable officer under whom he once served. What emerges is not a 'novel', the narrator insists, 'but a collection of travelling notes'.

Grigori Aleksandrovich Pechorin 'was a splendid fellow' recalls Maksim, 'but a little peculiar'. He gives the narrator a bundle of Pechorin's writings, which Maksim had intended to use for cartridge paper, thinking they might be of interest to his new friend.

The reader, given the fractured nature of the narrative, which is jig-sawed together, finds it hard to form any physical image of Pechorin. A few, tantalising physical hints emerge: his fanatical insistence on dazzling white linen for his person. His small aristocratic hands (gloved and spotless), with thin fingers. He was, muses Maksim:

> a very eccentric man; and he must have been wealthy too. What a lot of expensive trinkets he had!... but I noticed that he did not swing his arms – a sure sign of a certain secretiveness of character.

Among the notes passed on are some tantalising autobiographical recollections of early life in St Petersburg:

> I fell in love with fashionable beauties and was loved by them, but my imagination and egoism alone were aroused; my heart remained empty ... I began to read, to study – but sciences also became utterly wearisome to me ... Then I grew bored ... Soon afterwards I was transferred to the Caucasus; and that was the happiest time of my life. I hoped that under the bullets of the Chechenes boredom could not exist – a vain hope! In a month I grew so accustomed to the buzzing of the bullets and to the proximity of death that, to tell the truth, I paid more attention to the gnats – and I became more bored than ever, because I had lost what was almost my last hope.

The five stories are set against a sordid war with the unruly Chechens (Putin's Russia is still fighting it) among beautiful Caucasus landscapes, glowingly described by the travel-writer narrator. In the first of the stories, 'Bela', a Circassian girl of high birth, catches Pechorin's eye. The 'fragrance' of young girls is stressed (Lermontov was of the class which used serfs for sexual relief but he himself did not 'because they stink'). He bribes the girl's brother with a prize horse in order to take possession of her. 'I am your captive,' she says after the abduction, 'you can compel me.' He doesn't and she falls in love with her refined captor. He develops feelings of tenderness for her but as the months pass, she, like everything in life, bores him. Until, that is, in an act of revenge, she is stabbed by one of her own people who had hoped to marry her. She dies, lingeringly. Pechorin withers, spiritually, and dies. But of what?

'Bela' casts its mood over the four stories that follow. In one of them a fellow officer proves that he is predestined to die at some later date by holding a loaded pistol to his head and pulling the trigger. It misfires. His eventual death is more horrible. The last and longest of the stories, 'The Princess Mary', finds Pechorin taking some R&R at a spa-town. He becomes inextricably entangled with two women and fights a duel on a cliff-edge (so that the death of one of the duellists is ensured) with a rival in love, in which he behaves disgracefully. He rides back to war – loveless, bored and, obscurely, doomed. What will happen to him eventually we already know from the first story.

A Hero of Our Time has a twenty-five-year-old army officer hero. It was written by the twenty-five-year-old army officer Lermontov, largely in the Caucasus. He died, the next year, in a duel (like his literary idol, Pushkin) to the accompaniment, it is recorded, of resounding thunder claps.

High Rise, J. G. Ballard, 1975

By the time he got round to writing High Rise Ballard had been very hard on the world. He had visited Planet Earth with storms (The Wind from Nowhere), with deluge (The Drowned World) and with global scorching (The Burning World). There's nothing cosy about Ballardian catastrophe. Leave that to Wyndham. In High Rise he identified yet another disaster: the council house. Or, more specifically, the council high-rise block.

The action of High Rise is set in a thousand-unit residential structure populated by a planned mix of two thousand residents. Upper-class, upper-middle-class and middle-class owner-occupiers are all inserted into

their hierarchical slots. At the apex, in the penthouse, is the architect 'A. Royal'. The building itself is a tribute to the utopian Corbusian ideal of a 'machine made for living'. Alas, human beings are sadly unmechanical. Treat them like cogs and you end up with savages. Gradually the closed environment folds in on itself. Social and architectural engineering break down and fragment. Stress precipitates tribalism and the inhabitants of High Rise group into warring clans of child-keepers or dog-keepers, upper- and lower-class residents. It's Hobbesian war of all against all, or the Roman amphitheatre, or a sackful of hungry rats – however you want to picture it. The super-hygienic building is befouled with garbage, excrement and, ultimately, corpses. It is the familiar Ballardian regression to primal states. 'Back to basics', as John Major would have put it, meaning something rather different.

Among the horrors, weird fulfilments are found. The central character, Dr Robert Laing (the name is mischievous – R. D. Laing was the evangelist of 'love your madness, don't cure it'), ends up butchering an Alsatian to feed his children. Doc eats dog. A film critic (Eleanor Powell – not, of course, to be confused with the most famous film critic of the day, Dilys Powell) suckles her cats from her opened veins. Wilder, a TV producer and sexual athlete, paints his body and is finally devoured by a Bacchic band of High Rise wives. 'Everything was returning to normal', the narrator wryly observes as Laing ignites a pyre of telephone directories in order to roast Alsatian steaks for the kids. Ballard normal, that is. Apparently the outside world takes no notice as detritus flutters from the top floors, urine dribbles down outside walls, windows smash, lights go out and bodies fall like bombs on to the car parks below. Ballardian normality sometimes strains plausibility. In a perversely cosy last paragraph the hero observes the lights going out in the neighbouring high rise: 'Laing watched them contentedly, ready to welcome them to their new world.'

Britain went crazy for high-rise housing after the war – the English nation, our leaders felt, should be treated like battery hens. Ballard had a number of specific targets in mind. One was Ronan Point, the jerry-built twenty-two-storey tower block in the East End, designed for proles relocated from the slums. It collapsed, killing four people, in 1968. Another target was the upmarket Barbican Estate, by the City of London, with its three sky-high residential towers. But Ballard's prime target was Trellick Tower in west London, designed by Ernö Goldfinger (see GOLDFINGER). Labelling it 'The Tower of Terror', the tabloids saw it less as homes in the sky than a factory for crime, drug addiction, and social disintegration. It was, Ballard himself said, 'an environment built not for man, but for man's absence'. Oddly, Mrs Thatcher's radical privatising of council housing led to Trellick Tower becoming a 'des res', as estate agents call them. The larger flats, when they come on the market, are now snapped up for nearly half a million pounds. And it's listed, Grade II. It can console itself on missing the top category by having inspired a first-rate novel.

A High Wind in Jamaica, Richard Hughes, 1929

Hughes' novel is founded on his jaundiced belief that if adults admitted to themselves the truth about children, the human race would die out. Like LORD OF THE FLIES, with which it is routinely compared, High Wind dismantles many fond myths about the young – particularly the British young. But unlike Golding, Hughes introduces sex into the mix.

The framework of Hughes' novel is a hand-me-down pirate yarn: the Jolly Roger has always flown merrily over children's fiction. Despite the title, only a sixth of the novel is set in Jamaica, a ruined Eden for the adult world. The narrative opens around 1870 with the glum observation:

> One of the fruits of Emancipation in the West Indian islands is the number of the ruins, either attached to the houses that remain or within a stone's throw of them: ruined slaves' quarters, ruined sugar-grinding houses, ruined boiling houses; often ruined mansions that were too expensive to maintain.

All around is the seethingly verminous ever-encroaching jungle: nits in the hair, jiggers under the toe-nails, cockroaches that nibble the skin off your feet by night, feral cats, red ants, ringworm, snakes. It is, the narrator wryly concludes, 'a kind of paradise for English children'. Five of them are at the centre of the story – the Bas-Thorntons. Their paradise of ruin and jungle is lost after a violent hurricane. Only the eldest child, ten-year-old Emily, discerns that it has been accompanied by a tsunami. The knowledge of the imminent flood is, mystically, her private possession and eventually leads her to believe she is God.

The alarmed family dispatch their five children back to England. En route their vessel is taken by pirates – half of whom are dressed as women (so that the pirate vessel looks like a passenger ship). The captain who has been entrusted with their care saves himself, reporting to the children's parents that their offspring were shot by the fearsome buccaneers – but, the Thorntons may console themselves, not raped first.

Piracy, like the sugar trade, is a declining business. The pirate captain intends to retire to his native Lübeck after the next capture. Meanwhile he takes over the care of the five children. Strange relationships develop. The children are now free to become themselves. Eventually the pirates are captured by the Royal Navy. Despite the quite decent treatment they have received, the children blithely testify that their captors were as brutal as Barbarossa himself. They hang. The children feel no remorse, nor much interest. High Wind remains in the reader's mind, indelibly, as an album of vivid scenes, vignettes and episodes. The pirate vessel has a mascot – an aged ship's monkey. The beast's tail becomes cancerous. The crew resolve to amputate it and to this end get the monkey drunk. Seeing what's coming, in the form of a kitchen knife, the monkey shoots up the rigging and drunkenly falls to the deck, breaking its neck. The description is given a couple of pages. A little later one of the children, John, falls from a high window in Santa Lucia and breaks his neck. It's given a paragraph and the boy is promptly forgotten by everyone – including his siblings.

Hughes' novel rests on a set of disturbingly unsentimental propositions. Primary among them is that children are an alien species, and the younger they are, the more alien: 'they are animals, and have a very ancient and ramified culture, as cats have'. Children, the novel proposes, do not care a fig for their parents or siblings. They are indifferent to the sufferings of animals and habitually torture them. And not just animals. Emily stabs an innocent man to death and promptly forgets about it. Adults, the novel proposes, have sexual feelings towards very young children. The uneasiest episode in the book is when the drunken pirate captain begins to caress Emily – who bites his thumb, savagely. Fellatio is hinted at. An even younger girl, Margaret, ends up in the first mate's cabin. One should mention that the novel, whatever its nastiness, is beautifully written.

High Wind was filmed (intelligently but unfaithfully) in 1965, directed by Alexander Mackendrick. Young Martin Amis played the doomed John Bas-Thornton and – when he got round to reading the novel – became a staunch advocate of Hughes' genius.

The History Man, Malcolm Bradbury, 1975

It pleased Auberon Waugh to say he would have given the Nobel Prize to Bradbury on the strength of *The History Man* and then lit a celebration bonfire of universally unread (Waugh alleged) copies of the simultaneously published *Humboldt's Gift* (1975) – written by the actual recipient of the 1976 Nobel, Saul Bellow. This is too harsh on the American, but it makes a point. Judged solely as a campus novel, Bradbury's is indeed *non pareil*.

There are two dates it is essential to know when reading any of Malcolm Bradbury's fiction. One is 1956, the other 1963. It's also useful to know something of the author's background. A grammar-school boy of provincial upper-working-class background, Bradbury (b. 1932) was one of the very first to benefit from the 1944 Butler Education Act, which provided free secondary education for all. He went on to attend an excessively provincial university, Leicester, where he spent three years writing a satirical novel

about a provincial university, identifiably his alma mater ('academic dear old mum' would fit the place better). This novel was published in 1959 as *Eating People is Wrong*. For all its provinciality Leicester was, as it happened, a leader in the new discipline of sociology. The refuseniks who cultivated the subject there had not been wanted at Oxbridge, any more than the new-fangled discipline. The embryo of anti-heroic Howard Kirk, Bradbury's most famous creation, was formed over the author's three years' observation of the new men on the Leicester campus.

To return to dates – in Bradbury's view of things 1956, the year of Suez and the Hungarian Uprising, was the year that 'barbarism' won. The old 'gentle' (as Orwell called it) English liberalism went under for ever. Forster's wych-elm was felled. The title of Bradbury's first novel picks up a line from a Flanders and Swann song. After 1956, 'eating people' is OK. It's what Howard Kirk does – with the relish of a cannibalistic gourmand.

The second momentous year, 1963, was when the Robbins Report was put into operation, setting up a whole tier of 'new universities' with 'new maps of learning' – in which sociology had a place of curricular honour. In 1965 Bradbury went on to the gleamingly 'new' University of East Anglia, Norwich, one of the campuses created by the Robbins expansion. *The History Man* is set in the composite-mythic campus of 'Watermouth' – which feels more like Sussex than UEA (albeit Bradbury loved Norwich, and served UEA loyally despite its Robbinsonian newness). Watermouth has been designed as a 'total environment' by a Finnish architect in the modish new-brutal (call it 'barbarous') style. Bradbury devised a congenially brutal narrative style – present tense, brusque, and rough-edged. The novel begins and ends with a Fellini-esque New Year ('out with the old') party thrown by the Kirks. Wives are swapped, students are laid, pot is smoked, suicide is attempted.

The book chronicles the rise and rise of Howard Kirk. His ruthlessness (justified by the most strenuous social analysis) means the overthrow of what the fuddy-duddy English department represents. Bradbury offers a sly vignette of himself in the novel:

The door of a room adjoining opens a little; a dark, tousled-haired head, with a sad visage, peers through, looks at Howard for a little, and then retreats... this depressed-looking figure is a lecturer in the English department, a man who, ten years earlier, had produced two tolerably well-known and acceptably reviewed novels, filled, as novels then were, with moral scruple and concern. Since then there has been silence...

When it looks as if an English student (who wears a tie, a sports jacket and a college scarf, egad) is causing trouble, Kirk extinguishes it by seducing one of the female teaching staff from that department and setting in process the necessary expulsions. Liberalism cannot stand in the way of the History Man. Kirk wins. For Kirk, sociology means getting what you want. The future belongs to Kirk. *The History Man* received a huge boost with its 1981 televisation, adapted for the screen by Christopher Hampton and scripted by Bradbury. It was a showcase for Anthony Sher's Howard Kirk, sporting Cuban heels, Zapata moustache, leather jacket, and flares – predatory, dangerous, unprincipled on principle. He was, said one critic approvingly (me, as it happens), the 'Thinking Man's JR'.

The Hitchhiker's Guide to the Galaxy, Douglas Adams, 1979

Probably the UK's most popular work of science fiction in the 1980s, Adams' fable is marked by a distinctive offbeat humour. Its origins can be traced by the curious reader back to THE DIARY OF A NOBODY. The narrative began as a radio serial on BBC Radio 4 (what used, charmingly, to be called the Home Service) in March 1978, to an insomniac audience not habituated, for the most part, to SF. The paperback publisher Pan (another charming name) commissioned a book version. It came out in October 1979 and duly 'appeared on the *Sunday Times* bestseller list and stayed there', as the author recalled.

In January 1980, six new radio episodes were broadcast. The book which resulted

from the second series was called *The Restaurant at the End of the Universe*. It was published in 1980, incorporating later material, and enjoyed similar cult popularity to the first. Following a TV series a third Hitchhiker book, *Life, the Universe and Everything*, was published in 1982. Adams completed the tetralogy in 1984 with *So Long, and Thanks for All the Fish*. Deep readers were doubtless drawn to it by recent mindboggling discoveries about the nature of the universe. That it was not merely unimaginably vast, but expanding ever faster. That there were things called black holes. That the more astronomers discovered, the more ignorant they discovered their astronomy to be. There was a yearning for the old, comforting simplicities – whether creationist, Copernican, or cows jumping over moons.

Shallow readers merely enjoyed Adams' inexhaustible whimsy. It's caught in the opening lines of the first instalment:

> Far out in the uncharted backwaters of the unfashionable end of the western spiral arm of the Galaxy lies a small unregarded yellow sun. Orbiting this at a distance of roughly ninety-two million miles is an utterly insignificant little blue green planet whose ape-descended life forms are so amazingly primitive that they still think digital watches are a pretty neat idea.

This planet is scheduled for demolition to make way for a new hyperspace express route – a motorway of the ether. Adams' amiable hero, Arthur Dent, is rescued from the cosmic bulldozers by an alien from a small planet 'somewhere in the vicinity of Betelgeuse', pretending to be an earthling, 'Ford Prefect', from Guildford. Ford is researching a new *Hitchhiker's Guide*, portions of which are generously quoted. There follow a series of surreal adventures.

In *The Restaurant at the End of the Universe*, the heroes (joined by Ford's cousin Zaphod Beeblebrox, President of the Universe, and his earthling friend Trillian) have further adventures. *Life, the Universe and Everything* finds Arthur living as a caveman on prehistoric earth. *So Long and*

Thanks for All the Fish (the dolphin species' last message as they leave earth before the cataclysm – it emerges that they have been all the while more intelligent than humans) is the most loosely knit. It ends with God's valedictory message to His creation: 'We apologise for the inconvenience.' Adams' own final remark at the conclusion of this 'trilogy in four parts' is: 'There was a point to this story, but it has temporarily escaped the chronicler's mind.'

The Hobbit, J. R. R. Tolkien, 1937

It is estimated that as many as one hundred million people have read *The Hobbit*. But for every thousand of that fan-horde, I would guess that less than one has read Tolkien's most authoritative work of scholarship – the article (based on the lectures in his Anglo-Saxon classes) 'Beowulf: The Monsters and the Critics'. Tolkien's argument is simple. During his career as a don at Oxford, archaeology (notably the wonderful discoveries at Sutton Hoo) had passed Anglo-Saxon studies into the hands of the historians. More and more was known about their physical 'world'. Well and good. But when it came to the wonderful literature which has descended to us from that heroic age, Tolkien believed attention should be directed not to what the poetry reflects of the Anglo-Saxon 'real world', but its 'imagined world'. Grendel (whom Beowulf defeats) and the dragon (which kills Beowulf) are the central elements in the great epic. We should not read 'through' the ancient stories, poems, and riddles for supposed 'realities' which lie behind their fictions. We should honour them for what they are.

Tolkien disdained 'allegory' – the idea that literature could be 'decoded' into something other than itself. In his preface to the second edition of *The Lord of the Rings*, he wrote:

> I cordially dislike allegory in all its manifestations, and have always done so since I grew old and wary enough to detect its presence... I think that many confuse applicability

with allegory, but one resides in the freedom of the reader, and the other in the purposed domination of the author.

A warning sign stands at the entrance to all Tolkien's writing (as it does to Twain's *Huckleberry Finn*), 'Allegorists will be Prosecuted'. Dragons are dragons, not metaphors for Danish invaders or whatever. If you want to know about the Anglo-Saxon unliterary world get a shovel and join an archaeological dig.

On, then, to *The Hobbit*. Bilbo Baggins is a home-loving, supremely bourgeois hobbit (a diminutive species) who lives in his underground home, Bag End, in the Shire. He is selected by the wizard Gandalf to assist a band of thirteen warrior dwarves in recovering their gold and their kingdom under the Lonely Mountain, which has been usurped by a dragon, Smaug. They need someone who will break and enter – a criminal activity, beneath their knight's dignity. Reluctantly Bilbo joins in their quest, although their leader, Thorin Oakenshield, despises the un-martial civilian. There follow struggles with goblins, monster spiders, trolls, wargs, orcs and an uneasy alliance with the mystical elfish people. Bilbo is interrogated by Gollum, a riddler who lives in the heart of a mountain. A wrong answer means death for the hobbit and supper for Gollum. Bilbo comes by a magic ring, and with it powers of invisibility, which raises his stock. Smaug is eventually overcome, the Lonely Mountain is lonely no more and Bilbo survives (Thorin doesn't) to return home a very rich hobbit.

It will prove irresistible to some readers, despite Tolkien's stern prohibition, to allegorise this charming tale. The entirely male world of *The Hobbit* surely recalls the single-sex community of Oxford University. The oafish, proletarian 'Orcs' surely recall that supremely snobbish term of collegians for townies, 'Oiks'. Gollum gives Bilbo what in Oxford would be called a 'viva voce' exam (a life-or-death matter if your doctorate is at stake). The continual conflict of all against all in Hobbitworld reflects 1937 – still bleeding from one world war, knowing a second is coming. One could go on. But these decodings take the juice out of the story.

Avoid them. Read in the intelligently super-ficial terms that Tolkien insists on – letting the story be itself – it is an intensely enjoyable experience. So enjoy.

Hollywood Wives, Jackie Collins, 1983

Collins' starting point was, clearly enough, THE VALLEY OF THE DOLLS. Jacqueline Susann's novel was the progenitrix of the 'pills and shopping' genre. Collins' novel has been similarly inspirational. It's less a product of its time than a highly profitable franchise. Topping the list was a TV minise-ries and Collins-authored spin-offs with their hallmark titles: *Hollywood Husbands*, *Hollywood Divorces*, et al. The hugely successful *Desperate Housewives* is another offshoot, as is the docu-fantasy *Real Housewives* franchise. In Britain the sublimely absurd *Footballers' Wives* enjoyed a couple of top-ranked seasons on TV. I suspect Gareth Malone's splendid Military Wives Choir (who serenaded the Queen in her 2012 Christmas Broadcast) is a stretch too far.

Susann's setting was New York, where her own induction into the shark-infested world of celebrity and modelling had happened. For Collins, it was Hollywood. Aged seventy-two, she recalled her induction into the life (the quote is from *Entertainment Weekly*):

> The author was out partying in Holly-wood with big sister Joan Collins when she caught the eye of the actor, Marlon Brando. She recalls, ' . . . He sent someone over to me to say, "Marlon thinks you're great-looking and have a great body and would like to meet you."' Collins admits she didn't hesitate and jumped into bed with Brando days later . . . 'We had a very brief but fabulous affair . . . He was at the height of his fame, and gorgeous.'

He was twenty-nine, and 'white hot' from his stage performance as Stanley Kowalski in Tennessee Williams' *A Streetcar Named Desire*. Jackie was what, in another play of the time, Williams called a 'baby doll'. Desired. That experience, and others like it, evidently opened her eyes to the way of the Hollywood world. Less beloved by the lens than her sister Joan, she decanted her sexual allure into fiction. In my view she writes atrociously – reading her fiction is like being pelted with a hailstorm of used cotton buds. But the experience fascinates. Book One of *Hollywood Wives* opens with the wifely heroine waking on a day which will change her life. Elaine Conti is married to a Hollywood actor, Ross, whose star is declining.

> Elaine Conti awoke in her luxurious bed in her luxurious Beverly Hills mansion, pressed a button to open the electrically controlled drapes, and was confronted by the sight of a young man clad in a white T-shirt and dirty jeans pissing a perfect arc into her mosaic-tiled swimming pool.
>
> She struggled to sit up, buzzing for Lina, her Mexican maid, and at the same time flinging on a marabou-trimmed silk robe and pressing her feet into dusty pink mules.
>
> The young man completed his task, zipped up his jeans, and strolled casually out of view.

Elaine drags herself up for the first ordeal of the day – her shower:

> She gritted her teeth. Cold water was best for the skin, tightened everything up. And, God knew, even with the gym and the yoga and the modern-dance class it still all needed tightening.
>
> Not that she was fat. No way. Not a surplus ounce of flesh on her entire body. Pretty good for thirty-nine years of age.

Time is clearly running out. Before it does Elaine resolves to get Ross back to the top and establish herself as a ruling Hollywood hostess. And why just Hollywood? 'The day Ronald Reagan was elected President was the only day she gave a passing thought to politics. If Ronald Reagan could do it, how about Ross?' The novel, as it unwinds from this reflective moment, is plotless and hugely readable – if, that is, you are not too hyper-critical in your judgement of its literary value.

Hombre, Elmore Leonard, 1961

Choosing one's favourite Leonard is tricky, because of the uniformly high standard in the many fields of fiction in which he has excelled. He began, however, by writing Westerns. Two, above all, have been recognised as classics – the short story 'Three-ten to Yuma' (1953) and Hombre. Both led to films as good as the originals. Hombre was written at an interesting moment. Its success – not least the reassuring film-option money – led to Leonard, then in his mid-thirties, giving up his day job in advertising to devote himself full-time to fiction. And 1961 was, in terms of literary and film history, the end of the line for Westerns. It was an exhausted genre and the 'frontier thesis' underlying it had worn thin. Hollywood moved on, as did Leonard. Some were disappointed. 'Why don't you write those Westerns any more?' his mother asked. 'They were so nice.' The next phase of his career would exploit crime in the urban east. Less nicely.

Hombre has a number of historical backgrounds. One is the closing down of the stage-coach networks as the railroads open up Arizona (in 'Three-ten to Yuma', the newly opened railway is changing the whole nature of crime and punishment in the 'wild' West). Generically Hombre is put together with two large, well-tried components. One, borrowed from Jack Schaefer's Shane, is heroism viewed through the innocent eye of a young person – here Carl Everett Allen, the employee of a stagecoach firm. The other is the firm's last journey – a little epic with its 'all life is there' cargo of passengers: homage to John Ford's classic film. Leonard's plot is bare-bones simple. Among the coach's six passengers are: a white woman, recently rescued from the Apaches; an Indian Reservation agent on the run with stolen government funds; a bandit who has set up an ambush to steal the money; and John Russell – part white American, part Mexican – who has lived with the Apaches, by preference, all his life. A 'half-breed', in the cruel parlance of the time.

After an ambush in the desert the passengers find themselves dependent on Russell who, despite his hostility to whites, saves them at the cost of his own life. What gives Hombre its extraordinary power – particularly for those who first read it, and saw the film in the 1960s – is its political topicality. An opening scene has Russell, accompanied by two full-blooded Apaches, enter a bar to be refused service. Not for him a 'sit in' (one of the Gandhi techniques for breaking the Color Bar in the American South), but a rifle butt to the face of the racist scum. On the stagecoach itself, when Russell's Apache affiliation is discovered, he is made to sit outside. The allusion to Rosa Parks, refusing to sit in the 'Colored' section of the bus, is unmistakable.

More significant is the historical background. The principal events are, unusually for a Western, given a specific date: 12 August 1884. There are frequent references to the San Carlos reservation, from which Professor Favor (like many of the administrators of the place, a Lutheran pastor) has stolen federal funds meant for feeding the inmates, and where Russell was, for a period, impounded. San Carlos (Hell's Forty Acres) was America's first concentration camp. The Indians, forcibly encamped there after the long-running Apache Wars, died in their thousands. The character Professor Favor is based on a convicted criminal who defrauded federal funds designated for feeding the starving inmates. The San Carlos institutional crime led to Geronimo's last resistance on behalf of his people. All this is touched on lightly by Leonard. It is a heavy load for a mere Western to carry. But it gives Hombre a ballast that is unusual in the genre. The book is a powerful, if oblique, plea for civil rights – which were finally delivered in the epochal 1964 legislation.

Homesickness, Murray Bail, 1980

Bail is one of a select company of indisputably world-class Australian novelists currently practising. One can justifiably rank him alongside Carey, Keneally, and Coetzee in the Oz pantheon. But although his peers are famous the wider reading world has not taken much notice of Murray Bail. *Homesickness* was first published in the author's home country in 1980, where, among the discriminating, it enjoys classic, or Patrick White, status. ('Great Australian Novel' is not, as satirists might think, a contradiction in terms.) *Homesickness* was not published by a British or American publisher until 1999. Bail's career as an international writer has not been helped by his snail-slow rate of production. By his late fifties he had a scant three novels to his name. At the time of writing (2013) the count is five, and he's seventy-two. Neither does it help that Bail rarely gives interviews, and the fabric of his fiction is notably lacking in self-revelation. Bail-watching is not an easy sport. But it's well worth rising to the challenge.

Homesickness is a fictional cogitation on the dubious pleasures of mass tourism, that debased descendant of the heroic emigration that, a century ago, made modern Australasia. The form of the novel is simple (Bail reveres the native tradition of the 'yarn' – embodied in the fiction of Henry Lawson). We follow a 'package' (meaningful word) of thirteen Australians (meaningful number – the disciples plus Judas, or Christ, take your pick) on a 'trip-of-a-lifetime' world tour. Their peregrinations take them to Africa, Britain, South America, the United States and the Soviet Union. The itinerary would make more sense to the Flying Dutchman than a travel agent. The tourists are uninteresting and some downright repulsive. They include a foul-mouthed drunk; a zoologist who has fallen out of love with his profession and whose wife ('she was in zoology too') has just died of cancer; a couple who photograph everything obsessively (the husband may be blind, or just pretending – one of the few notes of suspense); a sexual predator; a sex-starved spinster; and a married couple who indulge in unsavoury sex games faintly audible through the hotel walls. None of the tourists are presented to us in depth. We do not get to know them, nor – frankly – do we regret the omission. It's rather as if Chaucer had made his entire band of pilgrims as unappealing as the Pardoner.

Tourism means, literally, going round in circles. Bail's narrative coils around itself repetitively. The tourists land at a featureless international airport and check in at their featureless international hotel. They gawk at the strange landscapes and townscapes. Their principal activity is to visit museums – all of which are surreal and baffling collages. Among the clutter in an African museum of handicrafts there is a colour television that, because 'there is no television in Africa, the dark continent', is filled with 'lime green water and three brightly colored fish. . . chased by a baby crocodile'. It gets stranger. In the lost property office of a London train station, the *objets trouvés* include 820 umbrellas and a stuffed galah from western New South Wales. (Don't ask.) At the Science Museum, Bail's travellers inspect the 'Great Brains' on pickled display, then go on to a Corrugated Iron Museum. In Ecuador, they visit a Museum of Legs. No odder, one well-travelled member of the party thinks, than Reykjavik's Museum of the Potato – and legwork is, after all, the essence of tourism. In New York, they solemnly visit an Institution of Marriage. The establishment features a slice of Queen Victoria's wedding cake and live (married) sex shows. Bail, one deduces, does not much like New York. Or anywhere else.

The novel ends in a brightly lit museum in the Soviet Union where – to the tourists' consternation – there is nothing on display. They look at themselves and realise, in a moment of brilliant enlightenment, that they are the museum's bric-à-brac.

If there is a theme to *Homesickness*, it is that thanks to late-twentieth-century tourism, nothing is real any more. Nowhere is home; everywhere is abroad.

Hotel du Lac, Anita Brookner, 1984

Brookner is an acquired taste and one well worth acquiring. This, her fourth and Booker-winning novel, is a good place to start. The narrative opens with the confident high-stylistic touch of a writer as accomplished in art-history connoisseurship as she is in fiction:

> From the window all that could be seen was a receding area of grey. It was to be supposed that behind the

grey garden, which seemed to sprout nothing but the stiffish leaves of some unfamiliar plant, lay the vast grey lake, spreading like an anaesthetic towards the invisible further shore, and beyond that, in imagination only, yet verified by the brochure, the peak of the Dent d'Oche, on which snow might already be slightly and silently falling.

We are not, it is clear, in Arthur Hailey's Conrad Hilton-inspired establishment, nor Vicki Baum's vulgarly grander hotel. It takes a page or two to tune one's receiver to Brookner's sweeping syntactic line, with its regular insurance clauses taken out in mid-sentence to guard against anything as crass as a straight statement of descriptive fact. Her paintbrush dabs, pointillist-style, barely touch the fictional canvas. But once cultivated, the taste for her prose is addictive.

The situation which is artfully unfolded in *Hotel du Lac* is one of minor intensities – 001 on the fictional Richter scale. Edith Hope, thirty-nine and unmarried, is staying at an end-of-season hotel on Lake Geneva. She looks like Virginia Woolf but, as 'Vanessa Wilde', writes moderately bestselling romances of the traditional, Georgette Heyer kind. She has resisted the urging of her agent to produce the more fashionable 'bodice rippers' which are currently all the rage. As well ask Henry James to write spine-chillers (hold on though, he did) or Edith Wharton to write incest-porn (well, as it happens, she did). It gradually emerges that Edith has been sent to Switzerland by well-meaning friends to atone for 'an apparently dreadful thing'. She jilted her fiancé at the register office door. She is also embroiled in a long, unhappy affair with a married auctioneer.

In the course of her supposed recuperation at the hotel, Edith – an incorrigible sexual recidivist – has a sudden romance with a masterful electronics engineer. He is a divorcé who resembles, she notes, the Goya portrait of Wellington, and has a rather well-known collection of *famille rose* dishes (such things count for a lot in Brookner's novels). A lover of fine objects, he proposes marriage to Edith – a fine object herself. She accepts. But in a surprising climax, things go wrong

again for her. This time, however, Edith takes charge of her own destiny, acting – at last – like a 'grown-up'. The heroine's misadventures keep the reader wriggling on the narrative hook. But the active ingredient is the heroine's sharp, novelistic detective work on her fellow guests as they gradually coalesce into a rather nasty little community. In one sense, there is very little in the story: some social comedy, a daub or two of Swiss scene-painting, a few conversations, a little seduction and betrayal. But Brookner contrives to spin out her matter, creating effects of silken, cobwebby fineness. She could, one feels, get six novels out of Jane Austen's two inches of ivory and have room left over for a landscape or two.

The Hound of the Baskervilles, Arthur Conan Doyle, 1902

This is the acid-test Holmes. Buy it and you will buy anything with a deerstalker on the dust jacket. The case against (let's call it the *argumentum ad codswallop*) was mounted by Edmund Wilson in an essay entitled 'Mr Holmes, They Were the Footprints of a Gigantic Hound!', published in the *New Yorker* in 1945. Wilson did not have to go much farther than his title to make his point. On the other side the vox pop judgement is clear, loyal and indomitable. This is the most filmed of all the full-length novels, and the most cherished.

Sir Charles Baskerville, a Devonshire nobleman, dies of a heart attack, supposedly precipitated by the apparition of a demon hound. The centuries-old Baskerville estate borders the Dartmoor region of bogs – the most sinister of which is the Grimpen Mire. Sir Charles, it is suspected, is the victim of an ancient family curse. One of his wicked forebears, Sir Hugo, abducted a peasant girl with the aim of exercising his seigneurial rights. She escaped and the pitiless aristocrat pursued her across the moor with his pack of hounds and had her torn to pieces (Grimpen Mire is not, one would have thought, ideal hunting country).

The heir to the estate, Sir Henry, returns from Canada to assume his title, house, huge wealth and lands. And, perhaps, the family curse. He recruits the Baker Street duo, suspecting there is mischief afoot. There is a prelude in London in which Holmes and Watson are mysteriously trailed and items of the new baronet's clothing are stolen. Watson is dispatched to Baskerville Hall unaccompanied. Meanwhile, unbeknownst to the doctor (as ever, slow off the mark), Holmes goes down as well, in deepest disguise, to reconnoitre. After a number of twists, close shaves and adventures, it emerges that the apparitional hound is actually a flesh-and-blood dog ('large as a small lioness') – a cross between a mastiff and wolfhound – loosed on the Baskerville heirs by a frustrated relative called Stapleton, who hopes to inherit if he can scare the legitimate heirs to death. Stapleton expires horribly in Grimpen Mire. Sir Hugo's crime, we apprehend, is now exorcised. The mythic hound can go back to its kennel in the sky. And now, the acid test. Do you buy it? The spectral canine, that is. This is how Watson describes it:

> I sprang to my feet, my inert hand grasping my pistol, my mind paralysed by the dreadful shape which had sprung out upon us from the shadows of the fog. A hound it was, an enormous coal-black hound, but not such a hound as mortal eyes have ever seen. Fire burst from its open mouth, its eyes glowed with a smouldering glare, its muzzle and hackles and dewlap were outlined in flickering flame. Never in the delirious dream of a disordered brain could anything more savage, more appalling, more hellish be conceived than that dark form and savage face which broke upon us out of the wall of fog.

They shoot the hell-hound dead. And,

> I placed my hand upon the glowing muzzle, and as I held them up my own fingers smouldered and gleamed in the darkness.
> 'Phosphorus,' I said.
> 'A cunning preparation of it,' said Holmes, sniffing at the dead animal. 'There is no smell which might have interfered with his power of scent.'

Cunning indeed. Phosphorus is an irritant and highly toxic. Getting the beast to terrify specific humans on command (having sniffed those stolen articles of Baskerville's clothing) rather than leap in the nearest bog to rinse the horrible stuff off its jowls and eyes would require the skills of Dr Dolittle and the cruelty of Dr Moreau. And the most vividly luminous phosphorus paint of the day, as Swiss watchmakers had recently been exploiting, would have the candle power of a safety match. Codswallop wins – but we still love it.

In the same year as the *Strand Magazine* concluded its serialisation of the novel, 1902, the American jewellery firm Tiffany patented a decorative radio-luminescent, phosphorus paint product, devised by the eminent scientist Charles Baskerville with George Kunz (amazing, but true). 'The girls doing the painting were said to be easily recognisable at night – flecks of paint in their hair and on their faces made them sparkle in the darkness'. No Manhattan heart attacks are recorded.

The Hours, Michael Cunningham, 1998

I spent twenty-five years, on and off, teaching in southern California. I was very happy there and had more opportunity to read novels than anywhere else in my life. Happy hours were spent walking in the mountainous Los Angeles Forest, often with a novel in my rucksack to read in the hills whose range divides the West Coast from the Mojave Desert. To get there, you drive east through La Cañada Flintridge along the 210 Freeway, on one of two great canyon systems ('the Valleys') that branch out from Los Angeles. La Cañada ('canyon') is low-lying, hot, parched, dusty and, as the smog barrels through the valleys driven by the afternoon onshore winds, not a good place to be if you have pulmonary problems. But it has good schools, having (unlike neighbouring Pasadena) chartered itself as a city in order to opt out from the bussing reforms of the 1960s, which – optimistically – dispersed kids from deprived inner-city areas (race came into it) for a better education in the suburban outskirts. Aspiring parents pay over the odds for house in La Cañada, whatever it might do to their little ones' lungs.

But La Cañada is a long way from Woolf-land, and the damp leafy squares of Blooms-bury and Fitzrovia where, when it rained (it always rained), Virginia Stephen (later Woolf) said the tree trunks looked as black and glistening as the humps of seals. How, then, did a boy from this southern California (waterless) backwater become the most widely read Woolfian of the 1990s with his Pulitzer Prize-winning novel? This is how Cunningham himself explains it:

> I was drifting along at fifteen in La Cañada High School, smoking a ciga-rette one day, trying to look dangerous, when I found myself standing next to the pirate queen of the entire school. (These were the sixties, when the poor teachers, desperate to look cool, had us analysing rock lyrics.) She was beautiful and smart, dressed in the skins of the animals she'd slain, and I was desperate to impress her. I mentioned Leonard Cohen. 'Have you ever thought of being less stupid?' she said and gave me a copy of Mrs Dalloway.

Did he find it difficult – somehow 'alien'? – Cunningham was asked:

> It was opaque to me. I wasn't so young and stupid that I couldn't see the balance of those sentences. I was like an aborigine hearing Beethoven. She was doing with language what Jimi Hendrix was doing with music, reck-lessly flirting with chaos.

Cunningham paid off his debt to Woolf with The Hours (Woolf's working title for MRS DALLOWAY). It is a complicated fantasia on Woolf's novel, moving between 1920s London, 1940s Los Angeles, and 1990s New York – each time-setting with its version of the Woolfian archetypal heroine and Bloomsbury resonances.

To respond fully to The Hours requires a daunting range of intertextual reference (not merely to Woolf's novel, but also to the 1997 film adaptation starring Vanessa Redgrave). Cunningham's novel would be a very thin experience as a freestanding literary object. On the horses-for-courses principle an ideal sequence would be to read Mrs Dalloway, watch the Redgrave film, read The Hours, then watch the Meryl Streep film of Cunningham's book. Assuming, that is, you have a couple of weeks to spare.

Howards End, E. M. Forster, 1910

Howards End is a permanent fixture in canonical English fiction. It figures routinely as an A-level text; no student in any self-respecting English department will graduate without being able to prate knowledgeably about 'only connect', 'prose and passion', etc. It is, in short, a classic – and among the more readable for the author's waspish take on the absurdities of the English class system, as viewed, quizzically, from a Bloomsbury window, with a bone-china teacup in hand. What is routinely overlooked is just how wrong Forster's novel is in its social analysis and forecasts. Jack and the Beanstalk scores higher.

Howards End has a simple plotline, dependent to an almost Hardy-esque degree on coincidence. A young woman of careful breeding and high cultivation makes what she immediately recognises to be a mistaken choice of fiancé, and peremptorily breaks off the engagement. Her erstwhile fiancé is the youngest son in a family – the Wilcoxes – enriched by colonial trade. They inhabit a world of 'telegrams and anger'. They do things. Helen Schlegel, the unwilling fiancée, is half German and wholly cultured. An umbrella is picked up, by accident, during a Beethoven recital (whimsically described), by Helen and her elder sister Margaret. It is reclaimed by a young clerk, Leonard Bast, who – via a strenuous course of reading, theatre and concert attendance – is doggedly 'improving' himself. But he is, despite his aspiration, just another one of H. G. Wells' comical 'little men', and always will be. What Leonard wants requires three generations and more money than he will earn in three lifetimes as a thirty-bob-a-week pen pusher.

The Schlegels take a philanthropic interest in Leonard. Over the following months Margaret Schlegel enters into a mystical relationship with the mother of the Wilcox family. A daughter of the landed gentry, Mrs Wilcox owns a fine country house, Howards End, dominated by an ancient wych-elm. The tree symbolises long organic continuities in English life. Mrs Wilcox is dying and, in a pencilled, unwitnessed, codicil to her will, leaves the great house to Margaret. The family, sensibly enough, suppress the document. But Margaret marries the widowed Wilcox, Henry, and comes into possession of the house anyway. It is not a union of love, but – as she explains to Helen – cultural necessity:

'You and I and the Wilcoxes stand upon money as upon islands. It is so firm beneath our feet that we forget its very existence. It's only when we see someone near us tottering that we realise all that an independent income means... the very soul of the world is economic, and that the lowest abyss is not the absence of love, but the absence of coin.'

In an attempt to help Leonard, she passes on Henry's (inaccurate) information that the firm he works for is facing bankruptcy. Leonard falls into that 'lowest abyss'. No money island for him. He has married a woman who is, by unconvincing happenstance, a cast-off mistress of Henry's from his wild-oat-sowing days in Cyprus. It ends with disaster and reassurance. Leonard is killed by Henry's obnoxiously snobbish son Charles. But Helen (adulterously) bears Leonard's child. The Germanic culture, incarnate in the Schlegels, is 'connected' with Wilcox money. Helen's working-class Bast bastard will inherit that conjoined world. The novel ends with hay being gathered under the great wych-elm. England endures (at least until the 1970s and Dutch Elm disease).

The novel was published in 1910. Any remaining connection between Prussianised Germany and old England would be broken, bloodily, four years later. If they were sensible the Schlegels (like the royal Saxe-Coburgs, soon to be the Windsors) would change their family name to 'Shepherd'. Equally wrong-headed was the idea that class conflict between the Bast morlocks and the Bloomsbury elite could be solved by a simple act of sexual conjunction. Russia, seven years on, would shatter that illusion. The analysis underpinning *Howards End* is profoundly rose-tinted. Nonetheless, all those millions of admiring readings, and viewings of the 1992 Oscar-winning film, would seem to demonstrate Eliot's grim truth: 'humankind cannot bear very much reality'. Thank God, then, we have fiction to keep it at bay.

The Human Beast, Émile Zola, 1890

One of the more popular Zola works outside France, thanks largely to the superb 1938 film by Jean Renoir starring Jean Gabin, and the less good, Hollywoodised *Human Desire*, directed, clumpingly, by (German expressionist) Fritz Lang. A late work by the avatar of 'naturalism', *The Human Beast* is a sardonic meditation on modern machinery – particularly the terrifying velocities, and passionate energies, inherent in the express train service which was transforming France. Ironically, in Zola's bleak vision of the human condition, it is the ultra-modern machine which releases the atavistic 'bestiality' in men and women. The more technological the world, the less human mankind becomes. One can trace a direct line from *The Human Beast* to *Terminator IV*.

Zola's narrative is set in the dying days of the Second Empire, and forms a part of the massive Rougon-Macquart metanovel (a cycle of twenty works). Jacques Lantier is a railway engineer, working on the line between Paris and Le Havre. He is subject to homicidal urges, which he represses with great difficulty. Jacques's urges are specifically aroused by any woman he loves. He only feels safe from his demons when riding trains at speed. Lantier was brought up by his aunt who, with her husband, operates a crossing in the open country. Trains whizz past them, a metaphor of the transience of contemporary life. Elsewhere in the plot the station master at Le Havre, Roubaud, discovers that his wife, Séverine, has been seduced by one of the railway directors, Grandmorin, who is also her godfather (a patriarch sadly defective in his sacred duties). The enraged cuckold and (less than willingly) his errant wife join forces to kill Grandmorin in his private compartment on board a train. The murder is witnessed by Jacques. He says nothing – for he too has carnal feelings for Séverine. Human beastliness is everywhere above the thundering wheels.

Encouraged by Roubaud (who sees it as a means of securing Jacques's silence) the couple engage on an affair and, at Séverine's instigation this time, they plot to kill her husband. It is she, however, who is killed – having aroused her lover's always-latent homicidal urges. Meanwhile, Jacques's aunt has been poisoned by her husband for her life's savings. Flore, Lantier's cousin, loves Jacques. In a fury of unrequited passion she attempts to engineer a crash that will kill him. Failing, she hurls herself under another train's wheels. The novel ends with an orgasm of techno-carnage. Lantier, driving a train packed full of troops for the front in the war with Prussia, fights with his fireman over a woman. Both fall to their deaths, leaving the train – driverless – hurtling ever faster through the night. The last sentence reads:

> It travelled on, it travelled on, loaded with this cannon-fodder, these soldiers, already exhausted, and drunk, who sang on their way.

What a way to run a railway.

Zola's most distinguished American disciple is Tom Wolfe (see THE BONFIRE OF THE VANITIES), and The Human Beast is the novel that Wolfe most admires. He began a lecture to the National Endowment for the Humanities entitled 'The Human Beast':

> I take that term, the human beast, from my idol, Émile Zola, who published a novel entitled The Human Beast in 1888, just twenty-nine years after Darwin's The Origin of Species broke the stunning news that Homo sapiens – or Homo loquax, as I call him – was not created by God in his own image but was precisely that, a beast, not different in any essential way from snakes with fangs or orang-utangs. . . or kangaroos. . . or the fang-proof mongoose.

The Hunchback of Notre-Dame, Victor Hugo, 1831

The English title (which Hugo hated) is at variance with the French, Notre-Dame de Paris. But 'Our Lady of Paris' would be confusing and 'Notre-Dame of Paris' sounds wrong. There is the perverse justification that the English title reflects the casual verbal cruelties which – even after 2012's glorious Paralympics – the physically disabled routinely experience. But then, I suppose, 'The Kyphotic Campanologist of Notre-Dame' wouldn't work.

Never a writer to linger in composition, Notre-Dame's 200,000 words were dashed off by Hugo in six months. He aimed to move the topographic genre beyond Scott's 'prosaic' treatment of a heroic building (in Kenilworth), imbuing it with his own brand of exalted Romanticism. The narrative opens on 6 January 1482. The year was chosen because of its connection with the invention of printing – something that the novel portrays as destroying the ancient and more venerable script of architecture ('the book was to kill the building'). The day is the festival of Twelfth Night. Quasimodo (so called because he was found on the cathedral steps on the morning of 'Quasimodo Sunday', or 'Low Sunday'), the hideously deformed and deaf cathedral bell-ringer, a living gargoyle, is elected Pope of Fools and carried in carnival procession through the streets.

It is the first time in his life the 'monster' has received anything but horrified scorn from his fellow man. But his happiness is cut short by his severe guardian, the cathedral archdeacon, Claude Frollo. For all his public rectitude and ostentatious celibacy, Frollo has a guilty secret. He loves the gipsy girl, La Esmeralda, who has been dancing in the festival. With the help of Quasimodo, Frollo attempts to abduct Esmeralda but is foiled by the captain of the King's Archers,

Phoebus de Châteaupers. Frollo escapes undetected. Quasimodo (who has acted unwittingly in the failed abduction) is caught, publicly flogged, and set in the stocks. Esmeralda gives him water and thereby wins his everlasting love. Frollo stabs Phoebus, furious that he has won Esmeralda's love. She is accused of the act, found to be a witch, and condemned to be burned alive, only to be rescued at the last minute by Quasimodo, who carries her off from the execution scaffold to the Cathedral – allowing her the ancient right of sanctuary.

The novel has a terrific climax. The cathedral is stormed by a mob of street riff-raff. Frollo hangs Esmeralda when she refuses to give herself to him. Watching her death-throes, he laughs 'demonically':

Quasimodo did not hear that laugh, but he saw it.

The bellringer retreated several paces behind the archdeacon, and suddenly hurling himself upon him with fury, with his huge hands he pushed him by the back over into the abyss over which Dom Claude was leaning.

The priest shrieked: 'Damnation!' and fell.

The spout, above which he had stood, arrested him in his fall. He clung to it with desperate hands, and, at the moment when he opened his mouth to utter a second cry, he beheld the formidable and avenging face of Quasimodo thrust over the edge of the balustrade above his head.

Then he was silent.

The abyss was there below him. A fall of more than two hundred feet and the pavement.

Thus die the only two people Quasimodo has ever loved. Some time later the hunch-back's skeleton, recognisable by its deformity, is found embracing Esmeralda's in an old vault where the corpses of the executed were thrown. When they try to detach the skeletons, the bones crumble into dust.

Hunger, Knut Hamsun, 1890

Hamsun is one of a group of writers of whom he, Ibsen and Strindberg are best known internationally. Labelled 'New Romantics' by their contemporaries, they are seen by literary history nowadays as pioneer modernists. For a brief moment, Scandinavia was doing the cutting at the cutting edge of world literature.

Hamsun's impact was concentrated in three end-of-century works: *Hunger* (1890), *Mysteries* (1892) and *Pan* (1894). *Hunger* is a challenging title – in both Norwegian and English. Hamsun could as aptly have called it 'Alienation', or 'Perversity', or – if feeling censorious that day – 'Idiocy'. It is well into the novel before we learn the name of the protagonist: Andreas Tangen. Identity doesn't matter. He's a man without roots except that he seems to feel, oddly, that Christiania (i.e. Oslo) is where he belongs. Tangen has no family, profession or direction in life. He has no religion, no philosophy no sexual drives or need for love. Wilfully he strips himself of the one thing which binds a person to corporeal existence – food. All that is left, in Tangen's self-imposed inanition, is 'mind' – fed by perceptions, thoughts, ideas liberated by the need to serve nothing but themselves. Unsurprisingly the only philosopher who interests him is Kant.

The novel opens:

It was during the time I wandered about and starved in Christiania: Christiania, singular city, from which no man departs without carrying away the traces of his sojourn there.

Sojourning? He *lives* there, surely. 'Starving' means keeping his intake down to the very minimum needed to keep on starving indefinitely. It requires a precarious equilibrium between just living and nearly dying. Tangen has parted with everything that could be thought of as a possession:

How regularly and steadily things had gone downhill with me for a long time, till, in the end, I was so curiously bared of every conceivable thing, I had not even a comb left, not even a book to read.

In summer he sits in churchyards (where the dead lie) or parks (where the children play) and writes. His mind buzzes with ideas. Sometimes, although payment means nothing to him, he places a piece with a newspaper and picks up a penny or two. Most of his pieces are rejected. He never writes on commission.

The narrative, bleak as it is, has strangely comic episodes. Tangen breaks his fast by recklessly (for him) buying a cheese sandwich. He can hardly control the energies it looses. His mind riots with the prospect of 'crushing Kant's sophistries'. The energy subsides with digestion and, presumably, is all gone with excretion. He does not repeat the experiment. He later sees a poor old man down on his luck and rushes to the pawnbroker, tears off his waistcoat, and pawns it for a few coins. He gives the old man the money and receives, in a return, an old-fashioned look. Tangen is furious:

> The man took the money and scrutinised me closely. At what was he standing there staring? I had a feeling that he particularly examined the knees of my trousers, and his shameless effrontery bored me. Did the scoundrel imagine that I really was as poor as I looked?

Well, yes; he is.

In his wanderings and cogitations he thinks of writing a play, and doesn't. He thinks of work, but does none. Women? No interest. Is he falling apart, or distilling himself down to his essence? The novel does not answer the question. Finally he signs on as a seaman (he has no nautical qualifications) on a merchant vessel leaving for Spain via England. He may disembark at the first port of call, who knows? As the ship leaves harbour, he looks back, nostalgically, 'to Christiania, where the windows gleamed so brightly in all the homes'. But no home for Andreas Tangen.

Hamsun won the Nobel Prize for Literature in 1920. He lived through the Second World War and, perversely, backed the German invaders of his country, and their stooge, Quisling. In 1943, he sent Germany's minister of propaganda, Joseph Goebbels, his Nobel Prize medal as a gift. He was rewarded with an audience with Hitler. Hamsun spoke so volubly (Hitler was not a good listener) that, reportedly, 'it took the Führer three days to get over his anger'.

A Hunger Artist, Franz Kafka, 1922

In early autumn 2003 an American performance artist (self-styled 'illusionist'), David Blaine, had himself suspended for forty-four days (forty days would have had a more Lenten significance), scantily dressed, in a Perspex box thirty feet over the River Thames, alongside Potters Fields Park – now a pleasing green space, but historically where the indigent (and often starved) poor were interred. He ate nothing over his incarceration, and sipped only enough water (four and a half litres daily) to keep himself alive. He emerged fifty pounds lighter. Was it 'endurance art' or a 'stunt'? For Blaine, starvation had a truly Christlike, soul-purifying significance. As the (wholly unimpressed) American news channel CBS reported:

> 'This has been one of the most inspirational experiences of my life,' Blaine said feebly, pausing and looking as if he might pass out. 'I have learned more in that box than I have learned in years. I have learned how strong we are as human beings.'

Underlying Blaine's ordeal was the perennial belief that hunger is a requirement for the highest (or, at least, the most genuine) artistic achievement, and a means of spiritual purification; that it is the ultra-ascetic Trappists – as trapped in cellular self-deprivation as Blaine – who are nearest to God. It may be so. But what was interesting over the weeks was the effect of Blaine's art-event on the normally good-natured pedestrians on London's South Bank where once Shakespeare's Globe stood a few yards away from a bear-baiting pitt).

The public were, perversely, stimulated

to cruelty as much as to admiration. Barbecues were lit under Blaine's box, the aromatic smell of sausage and bacon wafted up. A remote-controlled helicopter lifted a Big Mac to just outside his cage. There was an atavistic urge, it seemed, to torment Blaine more than he was tormenting himself. Few, if any, reports (that I saw) drew attention to the eerie congruity of the Blaine performance with Kafka's 'A Hunger Artist'.

Kafka's short story begins with the observation that:

> During these last decades the interest in professional fasting has markedly diminished. . . At one time the whole town took a lively interest in the hunger artist; from day to day of his fast the excitement mounted; everybody wanted to see him at least once a day; there were people who bought season tickets for the last few days and sat from morning till night in front of his small barred cage.

The 'hunger artist' goes from town to town, routinely fasting for forty days. No Christian symbolism is intended. It is merely that the artist and his manager have observed that people lose interest after this period. He could always have gone on for longer. Alas, over the years, his art loses its appeal. The hunger artist cannot stoop to showing himself 'inartistically' in a street booth at village fairs. He elects, instead, to join a circus, where he is demoted to the status of a sideshow. He is ignored by passers-by. There are more interesting things to gawp at. His feeders neglect to put even the minimum amounts he needs for survival in his cage. At the point of death he informs an overseer why he has followed this career:

> 'because I couldn't find the food I liked. If I had found it, believe me, I should have made no fuss and stuffed myself like you or anyone else.'

But what 'art' would a full belly have inspired? They bury the withered cadaver of the hunger artist, 'straw and all', in an unnamed grave and install a young panther in his cage. It proves a huge draw; particularly at feeding time.

There is a long history of hunger artists. The most famous and relevant for Kafka was Giovanni Succi, who fasted publicly in New York in 1890. Because of its biblical resonance, forty days was the traditional length of hunger performances. Blaine's choice of forty-four days was presumably so as to create a world record. *The Guinness Book of Records* announced, during his performance, that it would never condone starvation records, any more than goldfish swallowing.

The Hunt for Red October, Tom Clancy, 1984

Red October (as fans call it) is the best Cold War novel to come out of that happily heatless conflict, and arguably (an argument supported by President Ronald Reagan, no less) a work which helped bring down the evil empire and end four decades of MAD (mutually assured destruction – with the press of one button). It was Clancy's debut novel. He had even more difficulty than most new authors in finding a publisher. Eventually it was taken on by the US Naval Institute Press (as their first novel), who made enough money from it to buy their own submarine, had they cared to. Clancy did not, initially, want to be a novelist. But his poor eyesight denied him a life in uniform. In his enforced civilianship he remained geekily fascinated by things military – particularly new technology. The annual *Jane's Fighting Ships* was his Bible. In his fiction, hardware replaces the hard men of traditional male-action war fiction.

The plot of *Red October* is simple. It is set against historical fact. Under the brilliant Admiral Sergey Gorshkov the Soviet Navy was, by the early 1980s, technologically, and in terms of materiel, worryingly ahead of its US rival. Clancy moves on from that fact to the fiction that the Russians have developed a 'Typhoon' class of submarine with a virtually undetectable underwater sound signature. Armed with twenty-four MIRV rockets, these sinister craft have 'first strike capacity'. They can sneak through to the American coast and flatten everything on the mainland before any response can be mounted. Captain First Rank Marko Alexandrovich

Ramius, half Lithuanian, has lost faith in the USSR – a disillusionment sharpened by the death of his wife as the result of medical malpractice and political cover-up. He resolves to defect with the first of the Typhoon vessels, Red October, on its maiden voyage. Under his command, and that of his protégé, the skipper commanding *Red October*, he deludes the crew into thinking the nuclear reactor has malfunctioned. He kills the on-board 'political officer', giving himself time to get ahead of the Soviet submarines sent in pursuit. He has also to elude American submarines who have, resourcefully, tracked him. A supremely skilled mariner, Ramius eludes both pursuers.

The CIA analysis is that a first strike is coming (a couple of years earlier, the Soviet invasion of Afghanistan had ratcheted up Cold War tensions). A coded dialogue develops between Ramius and the junior agency analyst Jack Ryan (a future President of the US – something not foreseen in these early days). Ryan persuades his superiors that Ramius intends to defect, bringing with him the dowry of the enemy's state-of-the-art weaponry. It's a close-run thing, with the fate of the planet in the balance, but Ryan succeeds. 'I'm damned glad you're here', is Ramius' greeting when they finally meet. A scuttling of *Red October* is staged and the Kremlin is fooled. America has the new technology and can find ways to foil it. The war goes on, but the balance on which MAD depends is restored.

Red October, which was filmed – with huge success – in 1990, popularised the military 'technothriller' genre in which the heroes are metallic rather than flesh and blood. The submarine is much 'sexier' than even Sean Connery, who played Ramius in the film. There have always been complaints that Clancy 'fetishised' instruments of death. But, like much popular fiction, *Red October* educated. Millions of Americans, after reading or seeing it, had a better sense of what the underwater shield around their country was and why it was costing so painfully many of their tax dollars. *Red October*'s success was assured when President Reagan (his Irish name, incidentally, is an Anglicisation of 'Ryan') hailed it as a 'perfect yarn'. His wife Nancy also praised it publicly, and

the Reagan administration's leading Anglophile (he was later knighted by the Queen), Caspar Weinberger, reviewed Clancy's novel glowingly in the *Times Literary Supplement*. America's huge investment in the 'six-hundred-ship navy' during the 1980s is plausibly cited as one of the factors which brought down the Soviet Union, which could not match the expense, in 1989.

Huntingtower, John Buchan, 1922

It's a pity Buchan is only remembered, by many, for THE THIRTY-NINE STEPS – and for that thanks are due mainly to Alfred Hitchcock. But the fact was, he didn't care if he was remembered at all as a novelist. 'Writing is a delightful hobby', he once told a friend, 'but it becomes stale and tarnished if adopted as a profession.' His profession was politics. He died the Governor General of Canada and it was his hand which signed the country's declaration of war against Germany, in 1939. That same hand also wrote an impressive range of fiction.

Huntingtower is one of his once popular 'Die-Hard' comic thrillers. It's also one of Buchan's most generously Scottish works and a frank expression of his political beliefs (arch-Tory – but amiable with it). The novel opens with a prelude, set in wartime, just before the Russian upheavals of 1917, describing the tribulations of the Russian Princess Saskia. The main action then switches abruptly to post-war Glasgow, where Dickson McCunn has just retired from a long and prosperous career as a grocer, aged fifty-five. His wife, Tibby, is away at the Neuk 'Hydropathic', getting a water cure. The McCunns had one child, a daughter, Janet, who died tragically 'long ago in the Spring'. Dickson has displaced his paternal feelings to a gang of street urchins, the Gorbals Die-Hards, based in Glasgow's Mearns Street (a name with echoes of 'Mean Streets').

Dickson goes off for a fortnight's jaunt, tramping the high roads of Scotland. He puts up at the Black Bull Inn, Kirkmichael, where he falls in with a morose young poet, John Heritage, who coins lines such as 'the moon's pale leprosy sloughs the fields'. Not, as Dickson thinks, 'much cop'.

After some sparring (Heritage insists on calling Dickson 'Dogson') they join forces to investigate a mysterious house standing on a peninsula: Huntingtower. The building is eccentric: a 'mad' replica of a Tudor house, 'in a countryside where the thing was unheard of'. They hear a woman singing, which recalls an experience Heritage had in Italy during the war. In fact, in both cases the woman was Princess Saskia. McCunn and Heritage are reinforced by the Die-Hards, who are spending their annual summer vacation under canvas. Dougal, their leader, explains that two women, Saskia and Eugénie, are being held captive in Huntingtower. It emerges that Saskia's jewels – secreted during the Revolution – are the reason she is incarcerated. These gems are lusted after both by the Resistance and by the Bolsheviks. The Poet (Heritage), the Grocer (McCunn), the street arabs (the Die-Hards), and an incognito Russian prince mount an assault on Huntingtower to rescue the Russian ladies and their jewels. Dickson is relieved of his chronic boredom.

The poet Heritage (although he is denied union with the princess whom he loves) finds a new meaning in life. The Die-Hards prove they are something more than street garbage. The Bolsheviks are foiled.

Huntingtower has many charming touches, not least the Die-Hards' war chants, which they have adapted from a Socialist Sunday School song-book without the slightest idea what they mean or what the 'Boorjaysies' or 'Proley-Tarians' are. McCunn is rewarded with a necklet, which he passes on to his unwitting wife Tibby. 'Real stylish. It might be worn by a queen', she observes. The novel ends with a eulogy by the Russian Prince for the British values that McCunn embodies:

'He is the stuff which above all others makes a great people. He will endure when aristocracies crack and prole-tariats crumble. In our own land [Russia] we have never known him, but till we create him our land will not be a nation.'

Some would say we are still waiting.

I, Claudius, **Robert Graves**, **1934**

The best preparation for Graves' Roman novel is not Suetonius' *The Twelve Caesars* but the author's own soldiering memoir, *Goodbye to All That*. It is estimated that more than 700,000 British men died in the First World War for 'King and Emperor'. Graves survived. But what did the surviving 'heroes' like him come home to? Unemployment, strikes, mass discontent. A world not worth living in, let alone dying for. What, *I, Claudius* asks – focusing on the most ambiguous of Roman figureheads – are 'emperors' for?

There is much mystery surrounding Claudius. One thing, however, is certain: that he was the most literate of his imperial kind. Graves' novel presents the reader with a Claudian 'goodbye to all that', in the form of this novel and its successor, *Claudius the God*. Claudius survived a period of imperial intrigue, incest, unfathomably ingenious cruelty, war, internecine slaughter, a treacherous nymphomaniac wife, and epidemic madness. He 'floated' on its surface like 'King Log'. His survival was helped, as Suetonius and Graves argue, by cynically playing up his disabilities (possibly the result of polio), to make him seem even more handicapped than he actually was, and no threat whatsoever to whomever was in power. It worked. Even his own mother, Antonia, found him too repellent to take notice of.

The narrative opens with a self-mocking curriculum vitae:

I, Tiberius Claudius Drusus Nero Germanicus This-that-and-the-other (for I shall not trouble you yet with all my titles), who was once, and not so long ago either, known to my friends and relatives and associates as 'Claudius the Idiot', or 'That Claudius', or 'Claudius the Stammerer', or 'Clau-Clau-Claudius' or at best as 'Poor Uncle Claudius', am now about to write this strange history of my life; starting from my earliest childhood and continuing year by year until I reach the fateful point of change where, some eight years ago, at the age of fifty-one, I suddenly found myself caught in what I may call the 'golden predicament' from which I have never since become disentangled.

The 'golden predicament' was the imperial crown, which he, uniquely among his clan, never coveted. By nature, Graves' Claudius cultivates the privilege of the indifferent outsider – he can see more clearly than those involved what is going on. Nothing worth getting involved in, he concludes. Using an artfully 'modern' prose (Graves argues it is the 'true Roman' style), Claudius disentangles the skein of his life, and the series of accidents that made him – feeble specimen of humanity that he was – the most powerful man in the world and a god. Or else the gods' joke on humanity.

He is writing this life story to fulfil the prophecy of the Sibyl at Cumae, consulted in his childhood, that he will leave his testament to posterity, to be read two millennia after his death. His early life is dominated by his ruthlessly ambitious grandmother, Livia. 'The name', Claudius notes, 'is connected with the Latin word which means Malignity'. Livia lives up to her name and beyond. One husband (Claudius' father) fails her. The second, Augustus, succeeds. As emperor, he is her tool. She poisons any too-obvious rival – even her own children. Her schemes prepare the ground for her chosen successor to Augustus (whom, inevitably, she eventually poisons), Tiberius. Always crazed, supreme power renders him totally mad. Imperial madness reaches an unprecedented pitch with his successor, Caligula. When he is assassinated, the imperial guard – fed up with potentates – appoint the spectacularly impotent (and wholly unwilling) Claudius as emperor (with, of course, the divinity which is one of the perks of the post). 'Put me down!' he shrieks as they carry him out on their shoulders. 'I don't want to be Emperor. I refuse to be Emperor. Long live the Republic!' They laugh, and prophecy is inexorably fulfilled.

One wonders, with the success of the film *The King's Speech* (2010), whether a small part of Graves' inspiration was stammering HRH Prince Albert's epically embarrassing speech at the British Empire Exhibition on 31 October 1925. The prince was, as reluctantly as

Claudius, anointed King and Emperor two years after Graves' novel was published. Prophetic.

I Am Legend, Richard Matheson, 1954

I Am Legend has 'lasted' better than most genre novels. It routinely comes high in 'best ever' science-fiction polls. But it is, in essence, a work locked in the local paranoia of its own time and place – and the more interesting to read for that reason.

One of the tormenting ethical conundrums in the 1950s was the 'fallout shelter' dilemma. A majority of the American population expected 'hot' war to follow after the Cold War, as inevitably as night follows day. Municipalities built public shelters (you can still sometimes see the fading yellow insignia in American cities), as did businesses and schools. And the government's Office of Civil and Defense Mobilization issued the population with a booklet, *The Family Fallout Shelter*. Unlike those built in Britain in the Second World War, these were not mere burrows in the ground to cower in until the morning 'All Clear'. 'Fallout' indicated the poisonous radiation and contaminated dust which would, for a few lingering weeks, make the 'open air' uninhabitable. The fallout shelter had food, water and fuel supplies, air filtration, and was designed to house the family until the outside was safe. But what about those who weren't 'family'? The prudent shelter owner added guns to his supplies. And if a next-door neighbour, your former friend, came knocking, asking for shelter with his family in tow, what should you do? Let them in, dooming both families to death by overcrowding, or let them have it, with both barrels? Potentially every home was an Alamo.

I Am Legend is set in Los Angeles in the middle and late 1970s. Atomic war has left the planet devastated. Who won is not clear. Swirling clouds of toxic dust have swept across the planet carrying bacteria, which have infected survivors with a 'vampire' plague. The legendary monster, created by Bram Stoker (see DRACULA), is legendary no longer. The infected have formed bands of shambling, zombie-like nocturnal raiders – unintelligent, but terrifying in their sheer inhuman mass and hostility. The hero, Robert Neville, is 'the last man'. Why he alone has survived is a mystery. The narrative opens with a long description of him repairing his house, which he has converted into a fortress against the vampire hordes which attack by night. He shoots vampires in the head and, when he can, drives stakes through their hearts. He was obliged to carry out the requisite heart surgery on his own wife, Virginia.

Neville's main opponent is his former next-door neighbour (and former best friend), Ben Cortman, who comes to batter at his shelter every night with his family of fellow zombie-vampires. The situation – which looked to be one of perpetual war – changes when Neville meets Ruth, who may be a vampire or his Eve. She is neither, it emerges. The monsters are transitional – 'speciation' is happening fast. Ruth is one of the new vampires arising, phoenix-like, out of the ashes of nuclear war. Last man meets new woman. She betrays Neville, who is put on trial and sentenced to death. He will, he foresees, be for the generations to come the legend that Stoker's Transylvanian count once was – something to frighten the children with:

> Robert Neville looked out over the new people of the earth. He knew he did not belong to them; he knew that, like the vampires, he was anathema and black terror to be destroyed. And, abruptly, the concept came, amusing to him even in his pain.
>
> A coughing chuckle filled his throat. . . Full circle, he thought while the final lethargy crept into his limbs. Full circle. A new terror born in death, a new superstition entering the unassailable fortress of forever.
>
> I am legend.

I Capture the Castle, Dodie Smith, 1948

I have a friend who reads Smith's novel every time she feels she's coming down with a cold. Better than Lemsip, apparently. *I Capture the Castle* was Smith's first work of fiction – although her plays had made her one of the best-known, and better-off, writers in the country. Smith left for America shortly before the outbreak of the Second World War; her husband was a conscientious objector. Hollywood welcomed her with open arms and chequebook, but she was haunted by escapee guilt, described by her biographer, Valerie Grove:

> She lived in a perpetual state of wretched regret about having left London, where she longed to be, her ear pressed to the wireless reports, avid for letters from friends with their accounts of air raids.

The novel she wrote in this torn condition can be seen as a psychic retreat into a fantasy England – a kind of cheerful *Gormenghast* (see TITUS ALONE) where war never happens. The story is set in a rotting Suffolk pile, Belmotte Tower. The country house (Shandy Hall, Mansfield, Brideshead, Howards End, etc.) is an emblematic presence in English fiction. Here it is more Bleak House. The Mortmains have the property on long lease. ('Mortmain' was a concept popularised by Leonard Woolf for the 'dead hand' of the past, which throttles the present.)

The father of the Mortmain family is a 'blocked' writer who, long ago, wrote a modernist novel, which temporarily put him up with James Joyce. But fisticuffs with a neighbour got him three months in the nick. Since then, he has turned his back on life. He has a young second wife, Topaz, who has reached the end of her own working life as an artist's 'life' model. She is given to walking around the castle clad only in boots. Rose is the narrator's elder sister. She would marry Quasimodo if he had money to rescue her from this 'crumbling ruin surrounded by a sea of mud'. But no prince ever comes to Belmotte. The family's only source of income is the son of their former cook, Stephen, a loyal retainer, who gives the Mortmains his wages. The narrator-heroine is Cassandra. In Homer she is the girl who shouts out the truth to the Trojans and of whom no one takes the slightest notice. In Smith's novel, Cassandra is 'seventeen,

look[s] younger, feel[s] older'. She writes in exercise books. 'Partly', as she says, 'to practise my newly acquired speed-writing and partly to teach myself how to write a novel.' But, she ruefully confesses, 'I am not quite Jane Austen yet.' She is beloved by Stephen, which she finds 'awkward'. The novel opens:

> I write this sitting in the kitchen sink. That is, my feet are in it; the rest of me is on the draining-board, which I have padded with our dog's blanket and the tea-cosy... And I have found that sitting in a place where you have never sat before can be inspiring – I wrote my very best poem while sitting on the hen-house.

The strange world of Belmotte is the core of the novel; the plot and sub-plots are secondary. In one episode, the Mortmains inherit a vast trove of mothballed clothing from a distant aunt. Wearing one of the furs, Rose is mistaken for a bear escaped from a passing circus and narrowly escapes being shot.

Salvation comes in the form of a wealthy American family, the Cottons, who inherit neighbouring Scoatney Hall. There are two, highly marriageable, brothers. Rose gets her release. Cassandra ends the novel (exercise books having run short) longing for the wealthy (but absent) Simon Cotton:

> A mist is rolling over the fields. Why is summer mist romantic and autumn mist just sad? ... He said he would come back.
>
> Only the margin left to write on now. I love you, I love you, I love you.

Cassandra began on the margin of life at Belmotte, she finishes on the margin of life itself. What will follow?

I promessi sposi, Alessandro Manzoni, 1827

Italians one meets are invariably surprised that one hasn't read this novel. They are right to be – it is a very great work. Inspired by Scott's *Ivanhoe*, it knocks the Wizard of the North into a cocked hat. Or so, at least, the Italians would have us think. The work was actually written before there *was* an Italy. But rebellion, the seed of the *Risorgimento*, is at the novel's core: as is love (never Scott's strong suit – although Donizetti injected an intoxicating dose into his adaptation of *The Bride of Lammermoor*). *I Promessi Sposi* went through a series of revisions between 1821 and 1827, before being revised again in 1842, improving itself at every stage and cultivating, to a perfect pitch, its jaunty, ironic tone – narrated, as it is, by Manzoni himself. He has supposedly found the original materials in manuscript form and is now relaying them, as one might tell a close friend some interesting tale over a bottle or two of wine.

The setting is Lombardy in the early decades of the seventeenth century. Northern Italy was historically a cockpit for occupying powers (Spain in the narrative, Austria at the period Manzoni was writing). The story pinpoints two, historically unimportant, lovers: Lucia Mondella and Renzo Tramaglino. A poor but honest couple, they are peasant workers in the regional silk business. Their prospective marriage is sabotaged by a wicked (hispanically named) nobleman, Don Rodrigo, of feudal inclinations, who has laid a bet with his cousin ('his partner in rascality and debauch') that he can filch Lucia's maidenhead, as he has filched many others. The craven parish priest Don Abbondio, 'a man not possessed of the heart of a lion', goes along with the monstrous scheme. The lovers flee, separately. Lucia takes refuge in a convent at Monza. To be on the safe side, she takes a vow of perpetual virginity. Irresistibly desirable, she is abducted by a character known by the sinister incognito 'Innominato', the 'nameless one', in the employ of Don Rodrigo. She escapes again, only to be struck down by the plague that is ravaging Milan. She recovers to be reunited with Renzo. The virginity vow poses a few terminal problems but all is resolved. Don Rodrigo comes to his deservedly unhappy end, his face unrecognisable under the 'black spots' of the pestilence. The lovers return, as man and wife at last, to their silk mill and a happy ever after. We last see Renzo with a bouncing babe (Maria) on his knee. In the background, the

Thirty Years War has eighteen years yet to run. The author takes a friendly farewell:

> If this has not entirely displeased you, do feel a little warmth for the man who wrote it, and a little, too, for the man who patched it together. But if we've succeeded in boring you instead, believe me, we didn't do it on purpose.

Like Scott's, once one gets into the swing, Manzoni's story rattles along. But the reader should linger on Chapters 31 to 33, and their chronicle of the Milan plague of 1629–31. The city authorities initially attempt to control the outbreak by banning the word 'plague'. This is followed by endless argument as to who should pick up the bill. The body of San Carlos is paraded through the streets as urban medicine. Rich citizens put all their finery in gigantic piles and burn it – as acts of propitiation and purification. Spectres and comets are seen. With the failure of the Church's intercessions the populace reverts to paganism, and still the contagion spreads like wildfire. Paranoia takes hold. There must, it is thought, be malefactors 'anointing' the city walls with diseased lotions – *untori*, administering the extremest of unctions. Suspects are lynched; lazarets – houses of death – are established. Not everyone liked these 'nakedly historical' interludes, as Goethe complainingly called them. And Manzoni made little attempt to weave the history into the stories of the main characters – they are so many corks in the ocean. Nonetheless the pestilence chapters are scorchingly vivid. Poe read and reviewed *I promessi sposi*. It inspired his *Masque of the Red Death*. In literature as in life, imitation is the sincerest form of flattery.

The Ice House, Nina Bawden, 1983

The Ice House should carry a health warning for male readers: 'Read at your discomfort.' Bawden's own three-word summary was 'adultery in Islington' – a joke directed at the much-scorned 'orgasm in Hampstead' school of novels. The novel is acidically bitter on the subject of happy marriage – as mythical a beast as the unicorn, Bawden contends. The story opens in 1951, the year of the 'Festival of Britain' – a dreary jubilation, as any who were there may recall. Two pubescent schoolgirls, both of whose lives have been disrupted by war, become best friends. What seals their lifelong bond is when Daisy (a bouncy, outgoing lass) witnesses Ruth (a sly minx, as unfriendly classmates see her) undergoing a sexually sadistic whipping by her father – a martinet who has picked up his disciplinary techniques from his wartime Japanese captors. Ruth's offence was omitting to pick some strawberries in precisely the manner he instructed. Ruth is routinely punished for such infractions of domestic discipline by being incarcerated in a former ice house underneath the decayed grounds. The cold enters her soul. Bawden's art lies in withholding outcomes. Enough to say the ice house figures in the father's eventual comeuppance.

The plot jumps forward to the late 1970s. Ruth and Daisy are now 'happily married' to their respective partners, as the world sees it, living close together in adulterous Islington, in the sexually perilous premenopausal years of their lives. They are safely ensconced in the comfortable professional classes, with complex, interesting children. Ruth has made a career for herself as a boutique dressmaker. Daisy is more the woman about town. Something dramatic happens, followed by something highly unusual. Daisy's husband Luke commits suicide on the motorway. He had recently been edged into 'early retirement' – but not so painfully as to warrant self-destruction. Even less explicable is Daisy's choosing to proclaim to the friends who have come to console her that she doesn't give a damn. 'He was born second-rate', she says, contemptuously. Her widowed mother – a raddled old battle axe who is shacked up with a geriatric working-class gigolo – agrees that she felt the same about her own exemplary spouse. 'I wanted excitement and violence, pillage and rape, and what he offered was peace and kindness'. The spectacle of these un-merry widows frightens Ruth. Her own husband, Joe, has been acting strangely. She wheedles out of him that he has been having an affair with a younger colleague, Eunice

Pilbeam by (improbable) name. Ruth fantasises murderous revenge (the 'ice house solution'). 'I am more like my father than I thought', she discovers. She and Joe patch it up. But her contempt for the man in her life is ineradicable.

The bombshell moment (stop reading here if you don't want to know) happens in the last, cleverly withheld, section. Eunice Pilbeam is a fiction. Joe's secret lover is Ruth's best friend, Daisy. Luke discovered the affair – hence his suicide. The three survivors take a luxury holiday up the Nile, visiting the chambers of the pyramids (ice houses of a kind). The climax coincides with the assassination of Anwar Sadat on 6 October 1981. Bawden was herself vacationing on the Nile when Sadat was killed. She later recalled:

> how I had come to dread the cold Egyptian tombs. And how, when I was planning the novel, I connected them with an old ice house I had seen in Norfolk. And a story someone once told me about a brutal father, and some strawberries.

Ruth and Daisy have it out – but they are, after all, each other's 'oldest friends'. Husbands, they resolve, are irrelevant – the hell with them.

The main line of the plot is embroidered with subplots, all tending to the same jaundiced view about marriage and the visceral distaste which (all) women feel for men. There is painfully lingering attention in the novel, for male readers, on the unaesthetic properties of the naked (but hirsute) male buttocks, unsightly paunches and general smelliness. Flesh of their flesh? Not for the missus. Women, the novel implies, are closer to reality, because the world is unkinder to them. But they have themselves.

If on a Winter's Night a Traveller, Italo Calvino, 1979

The natural stablemate for Calvino's novel (hereafter *IWNT*) is Julio Cortázar's *Hopscotch* (in this compendium I've gone for another

Cortázar teaser, see LAS BABAS DEL DIABLO). Like *Hopscotch*, *IWNT* is best approached as a game of fiction, testing the reader's nimble-footedness. It was devised by Calvino at a period when 'theory' was revolutionising reading practices. Umberto Eco was flexing his neurons in the post-structuralists' house journal, *Tel Quel*, in preparation for THE NAME OF THE ROSE. *IWNT* opens with flagrant 'extradiegesis' (a sacred concept in the theory toolkit). That's when a novel reaches out from the ('intradiegetic') narrative goldfish bowl to pull the reader in – as, famously, with JANE EYRE's: 'Reader, I married him.'

IWNT opens: 'You are about to begin reading Italo Calvino's new novel, *If on a Winter's Night a Traveller*. Relax.' The joke is you *can't* relax – he's done a 'defamiliarisation' job on you, the reader. The chapter then goes on to ponder ideal sitting positions for 'your' assault on the book. 'In the old days they used to read standing up, at a lectern.' But 'you'? Try a sofa and cushions with a nearby pack of cigarettes and coffee pot. The prelude then segues into the browser's dilemma – the peculiar fact that in a bookshop, unlike an off-licence, you enter often without the faintest idea what you want to buy; you are a lost soul:

you are attacked by the infantry of Books That If You Had More Than One Life You Would Certainly Also Read But Unfortunately Your Days Are Numbered. With a rapid manoeuvre you bypass them and move into the phalanxes of the Books You Mean To Read But There Are Others You Must Read First, the Books Too Expensive Now And You'll Wait Till They're Remaindered, the Books ditto When They Come Out in Paperback, Books You Can Borrow From Somebody, Books That Everybody's Read So It's As If You Had Read Them, Too.

Gradually it dawns on you that 'you' (i.e. 'I, reader') are an actor in this theatre of reading. The dozen chapters which follow hopscotch alternately between two lines of narrative. One involves the reader in a more or less continuous flow, which becomes a perilous quest when they discover that a binding error has conjoined two separate books. The other line hops between ten stories – written in different generic styles, heavily pastiched, none of which gets beyond its opening. There are cunning echoes and overlaps – what Roland Barthes calls *lures* or traps. 'I'm producing too many stories at once', Calvino confides,

because what I want is for you to feel, around the story, a saturation of other stories that I could tell and maybe will tell or who knows may already have told on some other occasion . . .

Although *IWNT* is routinely labelled sub-Nabokovian, it has deeper, and more chauvinistic, roots – namely Pirandello, the playful Italian, in such plays (literally) as *Six Characters in Search of an Author* (1921). Who, then, are Calvino's six (plus two) characters in search of a novel to house themselves? Leading the pack is Ludmilla – the 'co-you' – sex-object, and consistently sceptical companion in 'travel'. She has a sister, Lotaria. As the name indicates, Lotaria is deep into romance. Ermes Marana is named after the gods' messenger Hermes in Greek mythology, also patron of liars. This Ermes lives up to his name. His role is to confuse. Cavedagna is a publisher who labours to edit Marana's messages into some kind of sense. Silas Flannery is an Irish novelist. Writing fiction has robbed him of all pleasure in reading it (an occupational hazard). Irnerio is an artist who uses books as physical matter for sculptures. Professors Uzzi-Tuzzi and Galligani offer (unsolicited) academic interpretations more baffling than the text itself. Much of the narrative is set in Cimmeria, a fictional world borrowed from Robert E. Howard, creator of *Conan the Barbarian*. There are lots of jokes of that kind.

The novel ends with Ludmilla asking 'you' to turn off the bedside lamp. 'Just a moment', 'you' replies, 'I've almost finished *If on a Winter's Night a Traveller* by Italo Calvino.' But has *he* finished it?

If This Is a Man, Primo Levi, 1947

Which particular shelf to put Levi's work on has always presented problems to the tidy-minded. The standard categorisation is that *The Periodic Table* is his one and only novel, there are two collections of short stories, and the rest of his work (including this) is classed as 'autobiography'. Those, however, are not Levi's categories. He consistently refers to *If This Is a Man* merely as a 'book'. A book about Auschwitz. There is a reason, one can deduce, for the refusal to specify more precisely than that it is paper, cardboard, and ink. After Auschwitz, pronounced Theodor Adorno, poetry is 'impossible'. Equally impossible is 'fiction'. Interestingly, Kurt Vonnegut refused to call SLAUGHTERHOUSE-FIVE (his revisiting of the apocalyptic bombing of Dresden) a 'novel'. Like Levi, he called it 'a book'. I'm prepared to give Levi's 'book' brevet-novel status. If you're not so prepared, skip this entry.

The narrative begins with a poem which, effectively, enquires whether you are more fully a 'man' in a warm house 'returning in the evening [to] hot food and friendly faces' or working in the mud, fighting for scraps of bread, dying or living because of 'a yes or a no' at the next SS 'Selection'. Is Lear a man in the royal palace with a crown on his head or 'a poor bare forked animal' on the heath with a coronet of weeds? The narrative is conducted in a prose which is reduced to crystalline simplicity by spiritual exhaustion:

> I was captured by the Fascist Militia on 13 December 1943. I was twenty-four, with little wisdom, no experience and a decided tendency – encouraged by the life of segregation forced on me for the previous four years by the racial laws – to live in an unrealistic world of my own. . .

The real world supervenes. Levi is writing only three years later – but it is a different person he describes in his book. He was a brilliant Jewish chemist, a prize graduate of the University of Turin (in his home city). He joined the partisans, was captured, and was sent to Auschwitz: not for his resistance but for his race – his bio-chemical composition. Of the six hundred-odd Italian Jews dispatched with him, he was destined to be one of only twenty survivors.

At Auschwitz he was designated a useful commodity – 'a superior kind of slave' – and worked with the chemical work *Kommando* in the construction of a factory to make synthetic rubber. It was as futile as the Tower of Babel, producing not an ounce of the stuff, though at the expense of thousands of lives. The commandant of Auschwitz would, one day – not far off in time – suffer execution for the murder of millions of innocent human beings.

At some kinds of factory the Nazis excelled. They were world-beaters. Many accounts of the camps, filmic and documentary, stress their horror. Levi records the banality, and the mad micro-organisation down to every level. The camp is a parody of the bureaucratised state – as those unfortunates who wheel round supermarket shopping carts, full of treasured garbage, parody consumerist society. A notice in the latrine over a tub of 'turbid filthy water' reminds the inmates 'to wash your hands after using the lavatory'. Regulations impose weekly haircuts and shaves for those 'about to die'. The inmates wear uniforms and there are three monthly-distributions of clean underwear. Prisoners are marked, by insignia, into a wide array of affiliation groups. Are they, at the penultimate end of this process (the ultimate end is crematorium smoke) still 'men'?

When the Russians arrive in January 1945 the crazed system breaks down. The death rate becomes virtually total and immediate in the chaos of liberation. They would have died anyway, but in a more orderly fashion, in the little SS state, a simulacrum of the larger. 'It seems to me unnecessary to add that none of the facts are invented', writes Levi. But they are 'shaped', as by the creative writer's – the novelist's – hand.

In the Second Year, Storm Jameson, 1936

Oblivion lies heavier on some novelists than on others – unfairly so in the case of Storm Jameson. Not even her teasing pen-name (she was born humble 'Margaret Jameson'), the Virago Press exhumation editions or an informative biography have managed to bring her back. Jameson was born – unstormily, solidly middle-class – in Whitby, Yorkshire, and went on to take a first-class degree in English at Leeds University. She was politicised into left-wing pacifism by losing a brother in the First World War. Her personal life was tangled and she supported herself writing well-received fiction for the huge inter-war library market. The germ of this novel – one of her best – was her attending, on 7 June 1934, the Nuremberg-style rally of the British Union of Fascists at Olympia, in the company of Aldous Huxley, Vera Brittain and some five hundred other protesters. When they heckled Oswald Mosley, posturing Hitler-style on the platform, the protestors were set upon by a thousand Blackshirt thugs. Several were badly beaten, others had castor oil forcibly thrust down their throats (inducing instant uncontrollable diarrhoea). As Jameson reported in the *Daily Telegraph*:

> A young woman [was] carried past me by five Blackshirts, her clothes half torn off and her mouth and nose closed by the large hand of one; her head was forced back by the pressure and she must have been in considerable pain. I mention her especially since I have seen a reference to the delicacy with which women interrupters were left to women Black-shirts. This is merely untrue ... Why train decent young men to indulge in such peculiarly nasty brutality?

Pondering the question, she came to the conclusion that British Fascism was peculiarly 'British'. It originated not in the streets, but in the public schools (of the kind Mosley attended – Winchester in his case).

Jameson's novel describes a British Fascist Putsch led by – who else? – Etonians. One of its leaders describes to the narrator-hero

> the England he would create when he and his friends were in charge. It made me wince. It was like nothing more than a frightful public school,

with willing fags, a glorious hierarchy of heroes in the persons of himself and his Volunteers, and floggings for the unwilling or rebellious.

In the Second Year is set over three months (April to June) at an unspecified point in the near future. Andrew Hillier is a cousin of the prime minister, leader of 'the National State Party'. Frank Hillier (a kind of echo of Hitler and Führer) is a man of fanatic temperament, elected on a wave of popular discontent with rampant strikes and mass unemployment. He is assisted in bringing 'discipline' to the country by his second-in-command, General Richard Sacker (Andrew's brother-in-law), who has recruited a 'Volunteer' force of five million men. The ruling pair are regarded (particularly in the newspapers they now control) as 'the saviours of the country'. Sacker's 'discipline' involves such measures as chopping up the poet Stephen Spender and throwing the bits into the Thames, forcing E. M. Forster into exile, and setting Virginia Woolf to work in a labour camp. And lots of flogging.

Andrew was a fag at Eton to both his relatives. But disabled, and incorrigibly liberal, he has taken refuge in Norway, where he is a university teacher. It is now the second year of the great reform and Andrew revisits a changed England. A Hitler/Röhm-style power struggle develops, based on Germany's Night of the Long Knives. Sacker is liquidated and his 'Volunteers' disbanded, as was Röhm's SA, to be replaced by the more military, SS-style 'Special Guards'. Andrew returns to Norway. As they viewed newscasts of the August 1936 Berlin Olympic Games, readers of Jameson's novel must have shivered. Was the lady right?

In the Skin of a Lion, Michael Ondaatje, 1987

It was Israel Zangwill who invented the 'melting pot' thesis. Politicians have always loved the idea that you can cook nationality into a homogeneous stew in the interest of the nation. Zangwill himself was sceptical about it. Most novelists, who look at things in a closer way than politicians, are also sceptical. Does a new 'skin' come with a new passport, the old one sloughed off like a snake's? That is the question posed here by Ondaatje. His career was jet-propelled by the success of the Booker-winning *The English Patient* (1992) and the Oscar-winning film which followed. This novel, from earlier in his career, is more self-reflective. Flirting as it does with post-modernist techniques, it is harder to read, but rewarding.

A 'new Canadian', as the country calls them, Ondaatje was born in 1943 in Sri Lanka (Ceylon), of mixed Dutch, Sinhalese and Tamil ancestry. Many skins. For *In the Skin of a Lion* he takes as his hero Patrick Lewis, a second-generation Canadian of rooted British origins. But which is Patrick's real skin? The opening sections relate his early life on an Ontario farm in the second decade of the twentieth century. Among all the vivid impressions of childhood, he makes his first attempts to grasp, mentally and manually, what Canada is:

> The house is in darkness except for the bright light in the kitchen. He sits down at the long table and looks into his school geography book with the maps of the world, the white sweeps of currents, testing the names to himself, mouthing out the exotic. *Caspian, Nepal, Durango.* He closes the book and brushes it with his palms, feeling the texture of the pebbled cover and its coloured dyes which create a map of Canada.

Patrick's father is later killed in an explosion in a feldspar mine and in 1923 the young hero goes to Toronto, where he first works as a 'searcher', a $4-a-week finder of missing persons. His quarry is Ambrose Small, a decamped robber baron (and a historical figure). Patrick becomes sexually involved with Small's mistress, Clara Dickens, and through her meets the love of his life, Alice Gull.

With the onset of the Depression, Patrick takes up work as a labourer on the great tunnel under Lake Ontario (it now houses the city's water-filtration system). This construction is the dream of Rowland Harris, a man who is gigantically selfish and driven. (Harris was a heroic real-life figure

in Toronto history. If anyone 'built' the town, it was he.) Grandiloquent in his schemes, Harris is fanatical about even the smallest detail. In his perfectionism, he imports herringbone tiles from Siena for his tunnel's toilets. Irrationally, these small ornamental touches radicalise Patrick and, although the narrative becomes misty at this point, what seems to happen is that Alice is blown up carrying dynamite for an anarchist demonstration. Patrick goes to prison.

On his release, he plants bombs in the hated tunnel and confronts Harris, blasting-box in hand. But Harris persuades Patrick that he really belongs to the newly made Canada of bridges, tunnels and conurbations: 'You must realise you are like these places, Patrick. You're as much of the fabric as the aldermen and the millionaires.' He is, in one of the book's dominant images, part of the mosaic of emergent Canada. But it will be his fate, unlike Harris, to be written out of history.

Ondaatje prepared himself to write this work with months of research in the Toronto historical archives. But he gave himself the novelist's licence to embroider. The Wikipedia entry on Harris sniffily notes: 'Harris is featured (and misnamed as "Rowland") in the Michael Ondaatje novel *In the Skin of a Lion.* The portrayal of him is fictitious.'

In the Year of Jubilee, George Gissing, 1894

Orwell, a staunch admirer, recommends Gissing thus:

> Everything of Gissing's – except perhaps one or two books written towards the end of his life – contains memorable passages, and anyone who is making his acquaintance for the first time might do worse than start with *In the Year of Jubilee.*

It is Gissing's wholly disillusioned, but curiously insatiable, relish for metropolitan 'sordidness', Orwell observes, that distinguishes this work. Gissing fingers filth like a jeweller fingering gems. The year in the title is 1887 and the jubilee in question is that commemorating Queen and Empress Victoria's 'golden' half-century on the throne. Victoria's was effectively the first such celebration. There has been one since which has not yet, as far as I know, been commemorated in fiction. Gissing casts a typically jaundiced eye on the junket. This was also the year of the 'Bloody Sunday' riot – by angry socialists and 'radicals' – on 13 November in Trafalgar Square (an event which 'fabianised' George Bernard Shaw), during which 2,000 police and 400 troops laid into the 10,000 protestors with truncheons, fists and boots. The 1880s were a period of depression – particularly in the countryside (something which cast a pall of gloom over Thomas Hardy's early fiction). Victoria's big day was nevertheless celebrated with a national holiday on 21 June – a blazing hot day. The crowds in London were unprecedentedly huge. Gissing's description reminds one of that of Eliot, surveying the morning crowd on London Bridge in *The Waste Land*, with the Dantean comment, 'I had not thought death had undone so many':

> Along the main thoroughfares of mid-London, wheel-traffic was now suspended; between the houses moved a double current of humanity, this way and that, filling the whole space, so that no vehicle could possibly have made its way on the wonted track. At junctions, pickets of police directed progress; the slowly advancing masses wheeled to left or right at word of command, carelessly obedient. But for an occasional bellow of hilarious blackguardism, or for a song uplifted by strident voices, or a cheer at some flaring symbol that pleased the passers, there was little noise; only a thud, thud of footfalls numberless, and the low, unvarying sound that suggested some huge beast purring to itself in stupid contentment.

The jubilee, as the title promises, is central to the novel. Multiple plotlines are constructed around two neighbouring families, the Lords and the Frenches, in Camberwell. Gissing had recently taken up residence in South London and was fascinated by its petit bourgeois horrors. The head of the Lord family deals in upright pianos. There are two children: Horace, a wastrel and Nancy, a vulgar flirt who has, nonetheless, 'something worthwhile' in her. There is some mystery about the absent Mrs Lord. The members of the French family in whom the novel interests itself are three correspondingly vulgar young women, possessed of a small inheritance from their builder father. The multiple wooings, marriages and ensuing complications (involving losses of virginity, secret marriages, and infinite manoeuvring for small inheritances) constitute the plot. Nancy Lord emerges as the principal character; Gissing's first thought was to call the novel 'Miss Lord of Camberwell'. She is eventually 'saved' and transported to a happier life in genteel Harrow.

The novel is principally a vehicle for Gissing's inveterate satire against the semi-educated (but inexorably 'rising') lower-middle classes; their awful reading matter and even more awful 'popular' music (much of it described and cited, scornfully, in the novel); and, above all, advertising. 'How', the novel sarcastically enquires,

> could we have become what we are without the modern science and art of advertising? Till advertising sprang up, the world was barbarous. Do you suppose people kept themselves clean before they were reminded at every corner of the benefits of soap? Do you suppose they were healthy before every wall and hoarding told them what medicine to take for their ailments? Not they indeed!

Gissing did not rejoice at a future dominated by 'Camberwell Man', carbolically clean as his armpits might be.

Independence Day, Richard Ford, 1995

This novel is the middle part of the 'Frank Bascombe trilogy' which made Ford's reputation. The hero, first introduced in *The Sportswriter*, is now in a slow tumbling breakdown. It is what he himself calls his 'existence period' – he is barely 'getting along'. It's 1988. Thirty-eight in the earlier novel, Bascombe is now in his bleak mid-forties. He is divorced from his second wife, Ann, who has remarried and has custody of their two children. Even Frank's relationship with his mistress, 'blond, tall and leggy Sally Caldwell', is on the rocks. He has given up sports writing, which was never that rewarding for him. Now he is that most hated species in American life – a realtor (estate agent) – a parasite on capitalism. 'You don't sell a house to someone, you sell a life', Frank intones to his (sucker) clients. He is currently having difficulty closing a deal with a couple called the Markhams, who are picky suckers. This is a period when mortgage rates are running at a ruinous and 'fixed' eleven per cent and the property bubble is about to burst (you're not selling a house, but a lifelong millstone round the neck).

The setting of *Independence Day* is (fictional) Haddam, NJ; easily recognisable, apparently, to readers living around Princeton, NJ. Frank, an incurably thoughtful fellow, is at that point of life when the future is clearly foreseen as a destiny you can no longer avoid:

> A sad fact, of course, about adult life is that you see the very things you'll never adapt to coming toward you on the horizon. You see them as the problems they are, you worry like hell about them, you make provisions, take precautions, fashion adjustments; you tell yourself you'll have to change your way of doing things. Only you don't.

He is a fatalist. Or, as he puts it, in a state of 'psychic detachment'; he is watching himself crash.

Nonetheless, there is some struggle left in him and the novel chronicles a futile attempt to put bits of his fragmented life back together again. On the 4 July weekend (all three of the Bascombe novels have narratives covering less than a week in time) he drives by in his 'air conditioned Crown Vic' to pick up his fifteen-year-old son Paul and take him to the Baseball Hall of Fame and

Museum in Cooperstown. They will 'bond', Frank hopes. They don't. Paul is a troubled youth. He was recently arrested for shoplifting 'three boxes of 4x "magnum" condoms'. He is fat, has shaved off his hair, and barks, constantly, in fond memory of his dog, who was run over by a car ten years before. He is also 'off the charts' on the Stanford–Binet Intelligence Scales. Paul's are not problems to which the solutions will be found in the self-help shelf of the local bookstore.

At the Hall of Fame he gets banged in the eyeball at a 'try it yourself' baseball machine, sustaining serious retinal damage. Frank, ever the negligent parent, wasn't there to make sure he was wearing the protective helmet and goggles. He is consumed by guilt. Much good guilt does. Underlying a rambling, excessively ruminative novel, is a nagging question. Where does 'independence' end, and 'loneliness' begin? Frank's *vade mecum* (he takes it with him on the road-trip) is Emerson's essay on self-reliance, with its lofty assertion that:

> the great man is he who in the midst of the crowd keeps with perfect sweetness the independence of solitude.

Sounds good. But how would an estate agent, failed husband, and lousy father put that Emersonian precept into practice? The novel ends, 'and that is simply that'. Simply?

Although some critics found the novel excessively prosy, it won a Pulitzer. Ford does not like critics and confesses to taking his handgun and using the books of those who criticise him for target practice. I am warned.

Independent People, Halldór Laxness, 1934 (Volume 1), 1935 (Volume 2)

The Icelandic title, *Sjálfstætt fólk*, means 'Self-Standing People'. It could as well be called 'Insularity'. Islands, like certain solvents, remove everything except the indissoluble truths of the human condition. No island more so, the novel implies, than Iceland, on the hostile rim of the habitable world. The Norsemen, who invaded in the ninth century (before invading that more clement island, Great Britain), left a culture and the seeds of a great literature which flowered, as Laxness reminded the world in his Nobel Prize acceptance speech, in 'mud huts'. The Norse sagas are, he said, 'as much a part of Iceland as her landscape', and 'An Epic' is the subtitle to this novel.

The hero is Bjartur ('bright'). His family have been subsistence farmers for thirty generations. Bjartur is introduced striding across a barren moor, spitting on the ground and addressing a cairn, 'Damn the stone you'll ever get from me, you old bitch.' He is, we learn, refusing to deposit a pebble on it in order to propitiate a witch who has long cursed the valley. A stone is not the offering with which to cajole the most ill-intentioned spirits, who would surely want at least a chicken and preferably a virgin. This is a harsh world.

Bjartur believes in nothing – not Christianity (all this misery for eating an apple?), nor the Socialist co-operatives which are, belatedly, rendering Iceland's land and seas marginally more profitable to those unlucky enough to live by working them. What he believes in is Iceland. He is a receptacle of the oral sagas, tales, and lyrics. He is most himself reciting them alone in the hills. Bjartur worked for a local 'bailiff' for eighteen years, but now has left to work on his own croft. He is 'Bjartur of Summerhouses' and the owner of a dozen animals, a starving dog, and a wife. Rósa is the least-valued animal – but he needs offspring. She is only marginally less valued when she discovers on her wedding night that she is pregnant by the bailiff's pampered son. Rósa later dies, horribly. Left alone in their hovel, in the last days of pregnancy, she kills a young lamb, cooks and guzzles its meat. It momentarily soothes the craving in her belly. She hides the carcass. Bjartur goes off into the hills for five days, looking for the missing beast. Left alone, Rósa dies in bloody childbirth. The babe survives, is named Ásta Sóllilja ('beloved sun lily') and, although not Bjartur's own, is loved (despite her cross eyes). At the age of fifteen he takes her to Reykjavik. In the city lodgings, to save money they sleep in the same bed. Something momentous happens:

> Little by little, almost without her being conscious of it, his hand had come nearer, involuntarily of course … one of the two buttons of her knickers had by some chance become unfastened, and the next moment she felt his hand, warm and strong, on her flesh. She had never felt anything like it.

Bjartur afterwards throws her out with blows and curses. The story then jumps thirteen years. Bjartur has remarried and lost a second wife, who has borne him three sons. He has prospered thanks to the 'beautiful' world war which has created an international demand even for his wormy mutton and straggly wool. He hopes they'll go 'blasting their brains out for ever'. Disastrously he over-extends himself and is ruined when, with peace, bust follows boom. He retreats into the moors and mountains, and another mud hut. He is again a subsistence crofter, wrenching a bare living out of the ungrateful soil. Bjartur remains there, obstinate to the end. He is ultimately reconciled with Ásta. The novel ends with them embracing and her promising, true to her name, to be 'the flower of your life'. This is a novel worth a Nobel, wherever it came from.

The Innocents, Francesca Segal, 2012

Segal's novel caught the spotlight by winning the 2012 Costa Prize for a debut novel. It is literary homage to Edith Wharton's The Age of Innocence. The connection is blatantly signposted in the title, the name of the principal character (Adam Newman – Newland Archer in the earlier novel), and its epigraph, which comes from The Age of Innocence:

> In the rotation of crops there was a recognised season for wild oats; but they were not to be sown more than once.

The scorpion sting in the second clause warns any tyro novelist that Wharton is not easily emulated. The 'innocent place' for Wharton was 1870s New York – before the mass immigrations at the end of the century. Segal's innocent place is Temple Fortune and the London Jewish community surrounding it, which is so glued together as to be almost monolithic. There is a hilarious excursion to Israel, where the principals find 'familiar faces plucked from around the upper branches of the Northern Line and deposited on the banks of the Red Sea'. Moses would have smiled, approvingly.

Like Wharton, Segal ponders whether life's marital decisions are made by the individual or the society around them. Twenty-eight-year-old Adam is a smart lawyer, about to marry the boss's daughter, the 'nice Jewish girl' Rachel Gilbert (May Welland, in Wharton's novel) – perhaps a little dumpy, but pretty enough to be regarded as a trophy. They have been in a relationship, sexual but decently so, since their schooldays. Having put it off, he now wants the thing over with quickly – because, as Rachel shrewdly perceives, he fears his own second thoughts.

Wharton's narrative opens at the opera when the arrival of Countess Ellen Olenska draws every eye from the stage:

> . . . a slim young woman, a little less tall than May Welland, with brown hair growing in close curls about her temples and held in place by a narrow band of diamonds. The suggestion of this headdress, which gave her what was then called a 'Josephine look', was carried out in the cut of the dark blue velvet gown rather theatrically caught up under her bosom by a girdle with a large old-fashioned clasp. The wearer of this unusual dress, who seemed quite unconscious of the attention it was attracting, stood a moment in the centre of the box . . .

Segal mischievously resets this pivotal moment to a Yom Kippur ceremony in which Rachel's cousin Ellie Schneider, a dazzling blonde, blows in from New York:

> exposing skin from clavicle to navel, wearing a tuxedo jacket with nothing beneath it and black trousers – trousers! – that clung and shimmered as if she'd been dipped in crude oil.

She has been kicked out of Columbia University for starring in a porn film. Not a nice Jewish girl. Adam has only once been unfaithful to Rachel, during a temporary break-up. His little crop of wild oats is sown. He and Ellie fall madly in love, but the marriage juggernaut is not to be halted. There is a wild, single, moment of adultery (Adam has tired of the big question being salmon or lamb for supper) but the extra-marital flame is doused by the arrival of a boy-child.

What Segal offers is deft play with parallel shapes. But there are darker things glimpsed beneath the surface. At a party, a Pinter-esque snatch of conversation floats by asking whether Anthony Julius' diagnosis of incorrigible anti-Semitism in the *politesse* of English life is correct. It's like a sudden bad smell, gone before one can take a second sniff. And why choose Wharton for a literary model – the most flagrantly anti-Semitic of gilded-age authors? On her deathbed she declared how much she 'hated the Jews'. Like Henry James, she bitterly resented the 'Hebrew conquest of New York'. The last third of the novel hinges on a Ponzi scheme, clearly modelled on Bernie Madoff's, which ruins Adam's father-in-law. Anti-Semites, round the world, had a fine time with that episode. Segal sees it as a trial – finally lived through.

'Homage' was perhaps the wrong word to use about *The Innocents*. To the superficial eye this novel looks like fluff. It contains a hard kernel.

Invisible Man, Ralph Ellison, 1952

As there are 'Great White Hopes' in the world of boxing so, in fiction, there have been great black hopes. It was unfair – and, as his life-story confirms, ultimately crippling – for Ralph Ellison to have that role imposed on him. *Invisible Man* is a minor classic of genuine social significance crushed by over-promotion and America's mistaken sense that misplaced literary praise is reparation for centuries of oppression. The author himself, in his speech accepting the 1953 National Book Award for the best novel of the last year, recorded his dismay that his 'attempt at a major novel' had been so honoured. It looked like tokenism in the year of Hemingway's *The Old Man and the Sea* and Steinbeck's EAST OF EDEN.

Like other African-Americans – Paul Robeson and Richard Wright, notably – Ellison had had premature hopes that Marxism would liberate his people. *Invisible Man*, which he began in 1945, was written in a spirit of total disillusion with Moscow. He initially planned a short novel and in 1947 published a core element – the 'Battle Royal', in which, for the delectation of jeering white men, black men are stripped naked, blindfolded, and made to fight each other in a boxing ring for delusory prizes. The full-length novel hinges on another conceit:

'I am an invisible man. No, I am not a spook like those who haunted Edgar Allan Poe; nor am I one of your Hollywood-movie ectoplasms. I am a man of substance, of flesh and bone, fibre and liquids – and I might even be said to possess a mind. I am invisible, understand, simply because people refuse to see me.'

In an interview with the *Paris Review*, Ellison elaborated the point:

There is the joke Negroes tell on themselves about their being so black they can't be seen in the dark. In my book this sort of thing was merged with the meanings which blackness and light have long had in Western mythology: evil and goodness, ignorance and knowledge, and so on.

Invisible Man is permeated by jazz – strictly the music that came from New Orleans. Although he revered T. S. Eliot's *The Waste Land*, and cited it as an inspiration, Ellison reportedly loathed modern jazz ('too white'). He loved the improvisational freedom of the great African-American art form: one of the few freedoms his people could claim.

Louis Armstrong's '(What Did I Do to Be So) Black and Blue' haunts the novel like a theme song.

The mainframe of *Invisible Man* is Dostoevsky's *Notes from Underground*. The nameless narrator-hero lives in a large cellar, siphoning off electricity from 'the Monopolated Light & Power Company' in a huge, subterranean light show (1,369 light bulbs). Southern-born, he is two generations from slavery. On his deathbed his grandfather instructed:

I want you to overcome 'em [the whites] with yeses, undermine 'em with grins, agree 'em to death and destruction, let 'em swoller you till they vomit or bust wide open.

Negro college-educated (his prize for excelling in the Battle Royal), the Invisible Man came north to Harlem. What follows is racial picaresque. There is a *Driving Miss Daisy* episode, an interracial sex subplot (explosive stuff in the 1950s) in which he is used by a white woman, and a period of minimum-wage employment in a factory making whitewash. He is subjected to electroconvulsive therapy – cerebral castration. Eventually he is radicalised into a Marxist 'brotherhood'. Fraternity ends, he discovers, with pigmentation. A (black) youth leader of the Brotherhood is shot dead for selling Sambo dolls in the Harlem street without a licence. It climaxes with bloody pointless riot and lynching. The Invisible Man takes refuge underground. What hope is there for him? None – or, at least, this novel can't see any. That grim conclusion is attested by the fact that, over the next forty years, Ellison could never produce another novel.

IQ84, Haruki Murakami, 2009–10

Murakami's novel is so called, apparently, because that is what 'nineteen eighty-four' sounds like in Japanese. It sets up the little meta-literary oddness that is this novelist's stock in trade and signals that the novel is taking place in that Orwellian year.

The narrative is hugely long, close on a

thousand pages. Fearful publishers, in Japan and the West, split its initial publication into three volumes across 2009 and 2010. Their reception was a major national event in Murakami's home country. Amazon Japan was obliged to delete five-star reviews posted before *IQ84* had even appeared. Its contents were kept wholly secret (*Harry Potter*-style) until the morning of publication. The novel was rather more grudgingly received in the West, which felt that it did rather go on. Three-volume novels, it was implied, went out with the Victorian crinoline. Life was too short for them nowadays.

For those unwilling to invest the many hours required, the separately published third volume will serve, given Murakami's incorrigible habit of summarising previous events at every stage. But first (and second) things first. The narrative opens with a young woman in a taxi in a Tokyo traffic jam. Her nerves are soothed by listening to Janáček's Sinfonietta – something she does at least once a day. Her name is Aomame (surely a near homophone for 'anonyma'?). It means 'green pea' in Japanese, apparently. She is a fitness instructor who doubles as an assassin. Her modus operandi is a fine needle inserted into the base of the skull; accidental death is invariably reported. Her victims are men who are guilty of unpunished domestic violence. Her current target is the child-rapist leader of a mysterious cult with offshoots everywhere. The taxi driver advises Aomame to take an iron staircase down from the expressway. He adds the warning, 'things might look different to you down there'. They do. There are, for instance, two moons in the sky. One of them is green.

And it might be paper. But generally things are more or less the same, just, somehow, arrhythmic and out of kilter.

The subsequent narrative alternates and intertwines (in single-focus chapters) with that centred on another character, Tengo. He teaches maths and writes fiction. He has to his name a novel called *Air Chrysalis*. But it is not his. It was written by a seventeen-year-old girl, Fuka-Eri, who is on the run from a cult. She has written (or dictated) the novel inspired by the 'little people', four-inch-tall mannikins who actually exist (in this novel). Aomame was herself an abused child. Tengo was the only person who – with just one touch of the hand – showed her kindness at that unhappy time of her life. The third book has as its main plotline a private investigator of egregious ugliness (it helps in his line of work) on the trail of Aomame. He has been recruited by the cult. Eventually she and Tengo are united, unharmed. A good thing, since she has become pregnant by him before their actual meeting. The novel ends:

> The two of them stood there, side by side, as one, wordlessly watching the moon over the buildings. Until the newly risen sun shone upon it, robbing it of its nighttime brilliance. Until it was nothing more than a grey paper moon, hanging in the sky.

Distantly the novel's epigraph, 'It's only a paper moon', echoes back.

Murakami says he was inspired to write *IQ84* by THE BROTHERS KARAMAZOV). It's an explanation as inscrutable as everything else about the novel.

Jack Maggs, Peter Carey, 1997

I've always had difficulty with Peter Carey's fiction – which seems to ask too much of its reader – but have the least difficulty with this novel. Probably because I've written a book of academic explication on GREAT EXPECTATIONS and this is a novel which springboards light-footedly from Dickens' version into a fantasia which, if the numerous awards which Carey has received mean anything (he must have a mantelpiece as long as the Great Barrier Reef to accommodate them all), certifies him as being in the same literary league as the Great Inimitable. *Jack Maggs* is at every point resonant, but at no point exactly congruent, with *Great Expectations*. It is an unsettling effect.

Carey writes with crystalline simplicity, as in the vivid opening sentences which hook the reader from the first:

> It was a Saturday night when the man with the red waistcoat arrived in London. It was, to be precise, six of the clock on the fifteenth of April in the year of 1837 that those hooded eyes looked out the window of the Dover coach and beheld, in the bright aura of gas light, a golden bull and an overgrown mouth opening to devour him – the sign of his inn, The Golden Ox.

It has the familiar Dickensian 'bounce'. The year, 1837, is chosen carefully. It's the year Victoria came to the throne. It's the year the twenty-five-year-old Dickens shot, meteorically, into celebrity. It's the year Dickens was most preoccupied with mesmerism ('animal magnetism') – something that features centrally in *Jack Maggs*. It's the year in which Dickens' love for his live-in sister-in-law, Mary Hogarth, reached its climax with her death. This quasi-incestuous relationship has always fascinated biographers. Carey (whose foreword admits to having 'stretched fiction to suit my fictional ends') creates a full-blown affair, something that no bona-fide biographer has done. The plot, like the characters' names, plays with the Dickensian source.

Jack Maggs, like Magwitch a convict transported 'for the term of his natural life', comes back to England without a 'ticket of leave'. He has taken the risk of being hanged to find his son, Henry Phipps (a version of Pip – aka Philip Pirrip). But he is not to be found. Maggs gets a position as a footman to a rich grocer who lives next door to Phipps' house, Percy Buckle (distantly recalling Pip's best friend, Herbert Pocket). While serving at Buckle's convivial table (comically clumsily), Maggs comes across Tobias Oates – Boz under another name, and the son of a murderer (Dickens was only the son of a debtor). Maggs and Oates are united in the search for Phipps. It ends with more murder, hypnotic revelation, and trauma for Oates, who begins to write it all up but cannot end it:

> The Death of Maggs, having been abandoned by its grief-stricken author in 1837, was not begun again until 1859 [around the time Dickens began *Great Expectations*]. The first chapters did not appear until 1860, that is, three years after the real Jack Maggs had died, not in the blaze of the fire Tobias had always planned for him, but in a musty high-ceilinged bedroom, above the flood-brown Manning River [in New South Wales]. Here, with his weeping sons and daughters crowded around his bed, the old convict met death without ever having read That Book.

Jack Maggs earned Carey his third Miles Franklin and his first Commonwealth Writers' Award. Mischievously he found it 'inconvenient' to come to Buckingham Palace to receive the CWA from the English monarch – the implied reason being he had no 'ticket' and feared, like Maggs and Magwitch, for his neck.

Jacques the Fatalist, Denis Diderot, 1796

Diderot, like Voltaire (see CANDIDE), is one of the novelists who could be said to have thrown a match to light the great conflagration of the French Revolution – a kind of witty

Gallic equivalent to the rifle shot that rang round the world. Both novelists were irrepressibly naughty. Some see the seed of *Jacques the Fatalist* as being sown upon his meeting with England's similarly naughty (but wholly unrevolutionary) Laurence Sterne in 1762. The two men hit it off – the author of THE LIFE AND OPINIONS OF TRISTRAM SHANDY said he would send Diderot his book in progress. 'Trim's knee' – a story which finds itself impossible to be told (and one of Sterne's most hilarious episodes) – duly became the core element in Diderot's plot.

Diderot was a writer of many parts. Literally. His most inflammatory work was his part-published *Encyclopédie* (1751–72), which he worked on for twenty years. The volumes were banned by the French censors. Knowledge was not the kind of thing which kept *anciens régimes* safe: ignorance and superstition were their foundation blocks. The science entries in Diderot's *Encyclopédie* promoted atheism; the political entries promoted republicanism; the historical entries promoted *lèse-majesté*. Irreverent fiction was held to be likewise seditious. The state-controlled 'privilege' was withheld from mockers and jesters. An injudiciously comic publication could land an author in the Bastille. The *Encyclopédie* was, necessarily, published outside France, in Switzerland. *Jacques the Fatalist* was held back for decades. Diderot probably started writing it in the early 1760s but it did not see the light of print until after the Revolution (and its author's death) in 1796.

The offence lies, among other things, in the novel's incorrigible refusal to obey rules. It rebels. It reverses, for example, the master–servant relationship found in, say, DON QUIXOTE. Jacques, the lower-born man-servant and factotum, is no Sancho Panza. He sagely instructs his master, throughout, on the inescapability of what is 'written above'. The sedition lies in the assumption that there is a power superior to that of sovereigns (Canute and the waves come to mind). God does not come into it. One can see Jacques's fatalism as a version of Marx's historical materialism. Diderot's main narrative gimmick, similarly unruly, is what theorists call extradiagesis – the narrator's hand, coming out of the text (like the hand in David Cronenberg's film *Vide-*

odrome, reaching out from the TV set) to grab the reader by the ear. The opening of *Jacques the Fatalist* demonstrates Diderot's extradiegetic manoeuvre:

How had they met? By chance, like everybody else. What were their names? What's it to you? Where were they coming from? From the nearest place. Where were they going? Does anyone know where they're going?

Does the writer know? Does the reader? Does it matter? *Jacques the Fatalist* has always been a novelist's novel. Milan Kundera dramatised it in 1971 and elsewhere proclaimed the novel a masterwork – a postmodern novel before even modernism happened. The novel can also be credited with inspiring Baudelaire's most famous line, in his poem 'To the Reader': '*Hypocrite lecteur, – mon semblable, – mon frère!*' The supreme moment of self-definition in the novel comes late on with the in-your-face-declaration by the narrator to his *hypocrite lecteur*:

Look, Reader, whichever view you take you get it wrong. If my book is any good, you'll like it; if it's bad, it won't do you any harm. There is no book more innocent than a bad book. I rather enjoy – pausing only to change the names – writing down the stupid things you do. . .

Diderot then turns savagely on any would-be censor:

Just leave me alone, you miserable hypocrites. Carry on fucking like rabbits, but you've got to let me say fuck. . . words like 'kill' and 'rob' and 'betray' come boldly to your lips but you don't dare say *that* word out loud.

Within all Jacques's tumbling anecdotage there are some perfunctory plot episodes. At one point there is a duel; the master (having killed his opponent) takes flight and Jacques is arrested in his place. How it works out is not entirely clear. There are three different endings offered. Take your pick, Reader.

Jane Eyre, Charlotte Brontë, 1847

Few novels, however great, can be credited with inspiring a whole genre of fiction. Charlotte Brontë's has done just that. *Jane Eyre* is credited as the pioneer of the 'Gothic governess tale' – of which all I've come across are inferior to hers (Du Maurier's REBECCA is a possible exception). The formula is simple. Humble girl, in some form of servitude, wins the heart of dashing man in authority over her. Brontë's tale is told autobiographically by a 'heroine as plain and as small as myself'. Jane is introduced as a young orphan, unhappily lodged with her sadistic relatives. She suffers further maltreatment at Lowood School, fifty miles away, which is run by evangelical tyrants, the Brocklehursts. After the school is ravaged by an epidemic of typhus – biblical in its severity – the Brocklehursts are dismissed. Jane remains for a while at Lowood as a teacher, but her restless nature craves more adventure than any mere classroom supplies.

She applies for a position as a governess at Thornfield Hall. So far, so realistic. Enter, at this point, the 'Gothic' strain. Jane discovers that her pupil is Adèle Varens, a spoiled girl of French origins. There is no mistress in the house. The 'master' is Edward Rochester, a man possessed of Byronic allure. Adèle, of course, is the offspring of one of his former mistresses – a French dancer. Enough said (or not quite said; this is, after all, a Victorian novel). Jane is by now aware that Thornfield Hall has a strange occupant, whose maniacal laughter she occasionally hears. Things become more complicated most improbably – and most readably. Following a series of events, Rochester, mysteriously converted to Victorian decency, offers marriage. At the service, in answer to the minister's routine 'any let or hindrance' query, things are enlivened when, by God, there is. Rochester already has a wife, incarcerated in the upper storey of his house. The (un)wedding party returns, and the would-be bigamist leads it, with Jane still in her wedding dress, to a cell in the hall's upper storey and shows them its hideous occupant, Bertha: a bloated, purple-faced, homicidal lunatic.

'That is my wife,' said he. 'Such is the sole conjugal embrace I am ever to know – such are the endearments which are to solace my leisure hours!'

But there are embraces other than conjugal for the 'leisure hours' of a man of the world. If not a wife, Rochester coolly suggests, why does not Jane live as his concubine? Orientals do it. Jane flees into the wilderness – not for her a life of adultery on silk cushions with her 'pasha'.

All is finally made good. Rochester solves his marital problems when, in a catastrophic fire started by his wife at Thornfield, she throws herself off the roof – he, meanwhile, is standing by. One's suspicion is he did the throwing or, at the very least, made no effort to stop the jumping. Divorce – Victorian-style. Blinded and physically mutilated in his escape from the burning building, he contrives, in his Samsonic state, to dispatch a kind of extra-sensory telegram across the ether: "'Jane! Jane! Jane!'" Her response is immediate: "'I am coming!' I cried. "Wait for me! Oh, I will come!'" Apparently she has overcome her scruples about adultery. On arrival she discovers they can, at last, marry without let or hindrance.

In addition to the governess tale (Mills and Boon cultivated a powerful line in them) Brontë's novel inspired a school of feminist criticism, which in turn has inspired a thousand doctoral dissertations. In their polemic *The Madwoman in the Attic* (1979), Sandra Gilbert and Susan Gubar argued that, at a sub-textual level (more accessible to women readers of the time than to any man), it was Bertha, locked in the attic like Dorian Gray's 'true' picture, who was intended as the 'true' image of incarcerated Victorian womanhood. Jean Rhys scooped them in 1966 with her novel WIDE SARGASSO SEA.

Jaws, Peter Benchley, 1974

Jaws – in its cunningly concerted barrage of hardback, Spielberg film, and film tie-in versions – inspired a mania of unprecedented pitch. Those who lived through that nonsense will remember it vividly. There have been manias since (see FIFTY SHADES

OF GREY) but Jawsmania was a landmark (seamark?) in modern popular culture. A spin-off industry extended its massive reach from the chic (and franchised) use of the *Jaws* motif and logo on pricey I. Magnin swimwear, to T-shirt transfers, right down to such novelties as strap-on shark fins. Shark's-tooth necklaces and pendants became de rigueur decoration at European resorts, although – at $400 a fang – few were genuine.

This whole industry began with the scrappy plot outline Benchley (a hitherto unknown novelist) sent to his publisher:

> The purpose of the novel would be to explore the reactions of a community that is suddenly struck by a peculiar natural disaster – not an earthquake or a flood. . . but a continuing, mysterious devastation that, as time goes on, loses its natural neutrality and begins to smack of evil. . . Suppose a Long Island resort community was suddenly visited by a great white shark? A young woman is killed . . . How does the community cope with this inexplicable menace?

The received opinion is that Spielberg's film is the silk purse and Benchley's book is the sow's ear. This is questionable. In order to get his necessary PG rating, Spielberg stripped away the motel adulteries of the sheriff's wife, Ellen Brody, and the ichthyologist Hooper (who is devoured by the shark he worships in the book, but survives in the film). And he brought in his trademark 'endangered children'. Spielberg also cut out the novel's subplot about Mafia land sharks devouring Amity, the beach-resort community, and Benchley's high-tone allusions to Ibsen's *Enemy of the People*. What the film foregrounded, cutting to the chase, was the mismatched trio who go out in the good ship *Orca* to destroy the whale.

Thalassophobic Sheriff Brody represents the feeble power of 'law and order'. At the helm is Quint the shark-hater, who, like Ahab, pursues a 'quenchless feud' with the great white (in the book Quint's bonding with the shark in a snarled rope directly evokes the end of MOBY DICK). The third is Hooper the ichthyologist, who believes the giant white to be 'perfect':

> Sharks have everything a scientist dreams of. They're beautiful – God how beautiful they are! They're like an impossibly perfect piece of machinery. They're as graceful as any bird. They're as mysterious as any animal on earth.

'Horseshit', responds an unimpressed Quint, for whom sharks are 'dumb garbage buckets' and 'cock-suckers'. One might as well lyricise cockroaches.

One of the oddities in *Jaws* was the way in which both book and film move from an initial Hooperesque, eco-friendly position to frank, Quintian delight in the struggle to the death between species. In the showing of *Jaws* that I saw in 1975, the audience was moved to cheer when Brody shoots the gas cylinder which detonates in the shark's jaws, blowing it to fish paste. Yet few, I imagine, would have consciously approved the use of the explosive harpoon to kill whales.

Jazz, Toni Morrison, 1992

In an interview Morrison explained 'the jazz-like structure wasn't a secondary thing for me – it was the *raison d'être* of the book . . . I thought of myself as like the jazz musician'. What kind of jazz? one wonders. 'Free form', one might guess, from her post-modernist way of writing – the kind of chaotic thing Archie Shepp and Ornette Coleman pioneered in the 1960s: no beat, no melody, no harmony. Morrison's novel has no numbered chapters, a 'group' of unidentified narrators, and no straight narrative line.

Or perhaps she had another kind of jazz in mind. The opening scenes are set in Harlem ('the City') in 1926, the middle of the Jazz Age in which THE GREAT GATSBY is also set. It was F. Scott Fitzgerald who actually invented the term to describe the 'Roaring Twenties'. In *The Great Gatsby*, African-Americans are as invisible as Ralph Ellison's hero. I would like to think Morrison intended to fill that blank. What comes to mind in her Harlem novel is Duke Ellington's exquisite

'Harlem Air Shaft'. As the musician himself eloquently put it:

> You get the full essence of Harlem in an air shaft. You hear fights, you smell dinner, you hear people making love. You hear intimate gossip floating down. You hear the radio. An air shaft is one great loudspeaker, you hear people praying, fighting and snoring.

Morrison herself could scarcely say it truer. Compare, for example, the following audio-visual shot of Harlem:

> Daylight slants like a razor cutting the buildings in half. In the top half I see looking faces and it's not easy to tell which are people, which the work of stonemasons. Below is shadow where any blasé thing takes place: clarinets and lovemaking, fists and the voices of sorrowful women. A city like this one makes me dream tall and feel in on things. Hep. It's the bright steel rocking above the shade below that does it. When I look over strips of green grass lining the river, at church steeples and into the cream-and-copper halls of apartment buildings, I'm strong.

'In *Jazz*', says Morrison, 'I put the whole plot on the first page.' The narrative opens with a woman in Harlem, on a bitter winter morning in 1926, opening a window to release all her caged birds (should one recall Maya Angelou? Or Miss Flite?), including a parrot whose refrain is 'I love you'. She is, we learn, a hairdresser called Violet Trace (nicknamed, for reasons which soon become apparent, 'Violent'). Her husband, Joe, is a travelling salesman in ladies' cosmetics (complexion has always fascinated Morrison). Joe, in his mid-fifties, abandoned his wife for the light-skinned, seventeen-year-old Dorcas – a banal sexual event, made highly eventful by post-menopausal, childless Violet becoming increasingly 'strange'.

The past gradually obtrudes. Joe (a generation on from slavery) fell in love with Violet in Virginia. They came to Harlem for a better life, and an escape from fieldwork. It was also an escape from the 'savagery' which

American history ('artificially' Morrison insists) imposed on them. Harlem was civilisation. Joe repudiated his mother – a woman called 'Wild', who lives naked in the Virginia woods. What the name implies is all we know of her. But by repudiation he created a 'nothing' inside himself. Time settings melt into each other. The narrative skips back to 1926, when Dorcas tires of her older lover and eventually dumps him in favour of a younger suitor. Jazz, its excitements and formal liberation, has infected her. Joe shoots her at a dance. Dorcas, instructing that no ambulance be called, bleeds to death. Joe is not prosecuted. At Dorcas' funeral, in a fit of wildness (not to be suppressed, even by this most solemn of ceremonies), Violet slashes Dorcas' face as her body lies in its casket. Thereafter things mend between Joe, Violet, and Dorcas' family. A small community forms. The marriage becomes loving again. The novel ends, enigmatically, with the unnamed narrator (closest of the bunch, one feels, to the author) lamenting that by narrating she has failed to live.

The Jewel in the Crown, Paul Scott, 1966

This is the novel which paved the way for Scott's so-called *Raj Quartet*. It was first necessary to clear the way with an act of literary demolition. 'Forster', Scott said, 'loomed over literary India like a train terminus beyond which no other novelist could be permitted to travel'. Scott ignored the ban. He was singularly immune to the 'glamour' of India, which had so gripped Forster. Scott wilfully put at the centre of his novel the central plot element in *A PASSAGE TO INDIA* – the rape of a white woman by an Indian. Whereas in Forster the rape is a fantasy – a symbolic product of the 'muddle and mystery' of racial relationships – in *The Jewel in the Crown* it is an actual gang rape. The period, as Scott sets the scene, is the endgame of empire:

> In 1942, which was the year the Japanese defeated the British army in Burma and Mr Gandhi began

preaching sedition in India, the English then living in the civil and military cantonment of Myapore had to admit that the future did not look propitious.

British control of the largest component in her empire (symbolised by the stolen Koh-i-Noor Diamond in the monarch's crown) is slipping away. Scott draws the reader's particular attention to an 'image' in the opening paragraph, which contains the essence of the novel:

> Imagine, then, a flat landscape, dark for the moment, but even so conveying to a girl running in the still deeper shadow cast by the wall of the Bibighar gardens an idea of immensity, of distance...

The captive is escaping. Or is she being pursued, prior to violation?

At the centre of the novel are three principal characters. Orphaned Daphne Manners has come to India to live with her relative Lady Manners so that she may escape the war against Germany, which Britain looks likely to lose. She falls in love with a young Hindu, Hari Kumar, educated in a British public school and more English than the English. Daphne begins to doubt the 'rightness' of empire. The third central character, and the most complex, is Ronald Merrick – a corrupt and brutal police superintendent as we first encounter him; a be-medalled Lieutenant-Colonel, and ostensibly happily married, as we (and India) take our leave of him at the end of the quartet. It is fiendishly difficult to establish any moral line on Merrick. Of lower-class origins (his father was a corner tobacconist), young Ronald was yanked out of school at the age of fourteen. An intelligent lad, he had 'just enough education to scrape into the Indian Police Service'. But not, of course, to hold the King's Commission – until, that is, the Japanese victories of 1941. Britain's officer class had run short of the right stuff. Merrick was later commissioned in the Indian Army Service Corps (an unsmart branch of the military). He could never have aspired to the promotion in peacetime.

Merrick is said, behind his back in the 'mess' and the 'club', not to be 'one of us' – white, that is, but not 'pukka'. An officer – but not *quite* a gentleman. His uneasy social pedigree means Merrick can never give the 'right' answer to that officer-class shibboleth: 'And where were you at school, Ronnie?' But the same *déclassé* status in the mess gives him a clarity of vision denied his class-blinkered colleagues. 'Amateurs', as he contemptuously calls them. He sees colonial India for what it really is: a racket, in which he intends to be a successful racketeer.

Merrick lusts after both Daphne and (as a repressed homosexual) Hari, who – although Indian – represents the 'Englishness' Merrick can never attain, because of his education and westward-looking upbringing. Vengeance for what the class system has done to him is within Merrick's grasp and he takes it. When Hari and Daphne make love in the Bibighar gardens they are seen by a mob. Daphne is blindfolded and multiply violated. She refuses to testify, so as to protect Hari – though she divulges that Muslims may be involved (identified by their circumcised penises), and possibly even Englishmen. Merrick arrests and rapes Hari during interrogation. Daphne, pregnant (by whom?), dies giving birth. And this, bear in mind, is only the beginning.

Jezebel, Irène Némirovsky, 1936

It's not a crowded category of fiction, but *Jezebel* can be put forward as arguably the best novel we have about the pathos of ageing. Women's ageing, that is. The heroine's biblical namesake had it easy, Némirovsky implies, in dying young. So what that the dogs fed on her (still beautiful) body? It's preferable to having that body eroded into ugliness by age while you still occupy it. Rich men who lose their wealth, the novel tells us, lose the most important thing in their lives. Poor them. But what of women, who do not merely *lose* their 'looks' but, agonisingly, *feel* them slip away, year by year?

On one level, then, *Jezebel* is a poignant meditation on ageing. But on another level it's an ingenious crime novel, with surprises for the reader. The narrative opens in a Paris courtroom in the mid-1930s:

A woman stepped into the dock.

She was still beautiful, despite her paleness and her drained, distraught appearance. Her sensual eyelashes were pale from crying and her mouth drooped, yet she still looked young. Her hair was hidden beneath a black hat.

Out of habit she placed her hand on her neck, no doubt feeling for the long strand of pearls she had worn in the past, but her neck was bare ...

It is not until late in the novel that we can calculate that the beautiful woman is sixty years old. Gladys Eysenach is rich and cosmopolitan, and has had many lovers and husbands. And one child. The crime for which she is arraigned is mysterious – a mystery she resolutely does nothing to clarify. The basic fact considered by the court is that a twenty-year-old man, the penniless student Bernard Martin, was shot dead by Gladys, in her bedroom. The prosecution's conjecture is that Martin was a young lover who was about to betray Gladys to her older, long-standing lover – an Italian count, whom she has for years refused to marry. Gladys offers no defence, asks for no leniency, and requests death. That would mean the guillotine – a mode of execution which, mercifully, does not disfigure the victim's face, as does hanging. The French justice system, ever more worldly than its Anglo-Saxon counterpart, assumes a *crime passionnel* and gives her a token five years.

The court proceedings occupy a quarter of the novel. 'She had played her part', the narrative concludes, 'it had been a rather banal part, in the end. A crime of passion ... A somewhat modest sentence... What would become of her? No one cared about the future; no one cared about her past.' The remainder of the novel unravels what really happened in 'her past'. It is anything but 'banal'. She was born Gladys Burnera, a Brazilian. From girlhood onwards her beauty gave her a power over powerful men, in which she exulted. She defies time, helped by her sylph-like figure and her blonde hair, which has paled to an even more fashionable 'ash'. Her swan-like neck is unwrinkled. The reason she has not married the Italian count, whom she genuinely loves, is that he

would see the incriminating date on her birth certificate. Her beauty remains as 'intact' as Dorian Gray's – although it requires more maintenance.

Her one child, Marie-Thérèse, obstinately insists on growing up. Aged eighteen (her mother insists she is fifteen), and now herself a beauty, Marie-Thérèse falls in love. Her lover dies in the Great War but she is pregnant and bears a son. Grandmotherhood is something that Gladys cannot, will not, endure. She allows her daughter to die in childbirth and has the baby disposed of, but he comes back, vengefully, into her life as Bernard Martin. And departs this life on her bedroom floor, her secret for ever secure. What is five years in prison compared to that?

Johnny Got His Gun, Dalton Trumbo, 1939

I first came across this book on a research trip to the US. Wearing my eyes bloody with Thackeray manuscripts during the day, I would afterwards read myself to sleep with a paperback. It was 1973 and the Vietnam War – under the contemptible Nixon slogan, 'Peace with Honor' – was winding to its end. I picked up Trumbo's book, expecting crime, and read the following from the author's 1970 preface:

> Numbers have dehumanized us. Over breakfast coffee we read of 40,000 Americans dead in Vietnam. Instead of vomiting, we reach for the toast. Our morning rush through crowded streets is not to cry murder but to hit that trough before somebody else gobbles our share.
>
> An equation: 40,000 dead young men = 3,000 tons of bone and flesh, 124,000 pounds of brain matter, 50,000 gallons of blood, 1,840,000 years of life that will never be lived, 100,000 children who will never be born.

Johnny Got His Gun was first published in 1939, the year after my birth, two years before my father added his bone and flesh to all that destroyed in the Second World War. The novel is set in the period after the previous world war (in which my grandfather lost an eye, weight negligible). *Johnny Got His Gun* won a National Book Award for the 'most original book of 1939', which it incontrovertibly is.

It opens with Joe Bonham, a 'doughboy', coming to consciousness in a hospital bed. He senses, strangely, that he is drowning:

> He shot up through cool waters wondering whether he'd ever make the surface or not. That was a lot of guff about people sinking three times and then drowning. He'd been rising and sinking for days weeks months who could tell? But he hadn't drowned. As he came to the surface each time he fainted into reality and as he went down again he fainted into nothingness.

He does a mental inventory of his body. He has no arms, no legs. 'He threw back his head and started to yell from fright. But he only started because he had no mouth to yell with.' He cannot hear, see, talk, taste, smell or feel. As consciousness returns he remembers the full frontal impact of a German shell. He is now living an Edgar Allan Poe nightmare – buried alive in what is left of his body. The narrative follows two tracks. One is a spate of memories: a strained relationship with his father, making love to his 'girl' before embarking for Europe, the war which rendered him the piece of insensate human steak he now is. In the other, he gradually attempts to *do* something. There is a small piece of skin on his neck which still has feeling. He uses it, and the shaft of sunlight which hits it, to create a clock and a calendar. Four years pass. Eventually Joe contrives to tap out, by bumping his head, Morse-code messages to the most responsive of his nurses. A medal is pinned on him, and, using this laborious mode of communication, he makes a request of the military authorities. Will they put him on display, as a living example of the horrors of war? No, he is told, it is 'against regulations'.

Johnny Got His Gun had a bizarre publication history. After winning awards, and becoming a favourite text with the Isolationist party in the US, it was suppressed in 1941 as a text promoting 'alarm and despondency'. After the war Trumbo's whole-hearted communism got him in trouble. A scriptwriter for Hollywood, he was blacklisted. Gradually he got back into the world of credits (Kirk Douglas bravely listed him as the writer for the 1960 film *Spartacus* – based on fellow-communist Howard Fast's novel). As the Vietnam War stoked up, *Johnny Got His Gun* became a resistance text, a bestseller, and a novel which I picked up in a drugstore in New Haven.

Journey to the End of the Night, Louis-Ferdinand Céline, 1932

Céline's hero is Ferdinand Bardamu and this novel takes the form of a globe-trotting picaresque, infused with bitter pessimism. Munchausen is a stay-at-home and Schopenhauer a comedian by comparison with Louis-Ferdinand Céline. The epigraph issues a tongue-in-cheek warning. What is it the reader has in their hand?

> It's a novel, only a made-up story. The dictionary says so and it's never wrong.

This 'made-up story' opens in Paris with the hero, a medical student, furiously denouncing the Great War, which is about to start: 'Whereupon, damn me, if a regiment of soldiers didn't come marching past the café where we were sitting'. Bardamu, in a mad moment of chauvinism, decides to join up. A mistake. War is, he discovers, cosmically absurd:

> This war, in fact, made no sense at all. It couldn't go on. Had something weird got into these people? Something I didn't feel at all? I suppose I hadn't noticed it. . . Anyway, my feelings toward them hadn't changed. In spite of everything, I'd have liked to understand their brutality, but what I wanted still more, enormously, with all my heart, was to get out of there,

because suddenly the whole business looked to me like a great big mistake.

Additionally, war is very dangerous. 'Could I be the only coward on earth?' he muses. So many others seemed strangely willing to die. Not Bardamu. Dispatched on a reconnaissance mission he meets up with the army's other coward – Léon Robinson (a name which evokes the first great voyager in fiction, Mr Crusoe). Robinson will be Bardamu's alter ego, his 'night self' (they always meet in the dark). The two of them hatch a crazy escape scheme – taking off their clothes and surrendering, as men of no nation, to the Germans. It goes wrong. Bardamu ends up an invalid in Paris with a medal pinned to his chest, and a pretty American nurse Lola (doing her bit) warming his bed. 'To tell the truth I was an appalling lecher', he confides. The authorities decide he is mad (he is) and consign him to a lunatic asylum which, after the Front, seems a very sane place. And safe.

He decides nonetheless to leave warring Europe and follow the Rimbaud trail to Africa. A 'maggot-ridden' continent, he discovers, and the mosquitoes 'fill your body with diseases that can't be got rid of'. Nor does the local population exactly charm him:

> The black race stinks in its poverty, its endless little vanities, the obscenity of its resignation: just like our own poor, in fact, except that they have more brats about the place and less dirty washing hanging up, and less red wine.

Burning with fever (syphilis, it is hinted), he takes off for the New World, where he ends up, Charlie Chaplin-style, working on the assembly line of Henry Ford's plant in Dearborn. It is a new kind of madness: 'One was forced to become a machine oneself'. At every point, the obscure Robinson crosses Bardamu's path. He returns to Paris, gets his qualification as a doctor, and sets up his practice in the capital's darkest quarter, where he becomes a connoisseur of 'mankind's stink'. In his morning surgery he rediscovers all the platitudes of the trenches:

I'd have liked to examine her, but she was losing so much blood, there was such a gooey mess I couldn't see anything in her vagina. Blood clots. A glug-glug between her legs like in the decapitated colonel's neck in the war.

He and Robinson become involved in shabby murder schemes for profit. As with everything, they mess up comically. Robinson gets shot in the belly and dies slowly. Bardamu watches, making no attempt to apply his medical expertise. 'One lacks almost everything that might be of use in helping someone to die', he observes, philosophically. Robinson expires unphilosophically. Summary, even with plentiful quotation, gives no clear impression of the elliptical (Céline loves the three-dot fracture), wholly delightful *perversity* of the narrative. It narrowly missed winning the Prix Goncourt. Perversely.

Juan in America, Eric Linklater, 1931

Every so often, during a bookshop browse, you come across a title which rings a bell but which for some reason you've never got round to reading. You pick it up and give it a go. And find a new delight. *Juan in America* falls into that category (for me, I hasten to add).

Linklater recorded the key element in the novel (his third) in his later memoir:

> I went to the Grammar School of Aberdeen, whose most famous pupil was Lord Byron. Before the school there was a statue of him in robes of flowing bronze: I read *Don Juan* and *The Vision of Judgement*, and my affection for romance was cut in two, and the other half of my mind fell far in love with wit. Dirty-fingered, we sat at our desks, – rough with deep-cut initials – and gave glum attention to *Samson Agonistes* and *The Cause of the Present Discontents*; but Byron, through the window, undid the schoolroom teaching that literature must be a solemn thing.

His life after school was suitably Byronic. By lying about his age Linklater got himself into uniform, and to the front line. He was a sniper in the Black Watch for years before he could legally vote. Unlike the martyr of Missolonghi the war did not succeed in killing him; he was invalided out with a severe head wound. He went on to university and, after some post-war knocking about the literary world, found himself a novel-writing academic at the University of Aberdeen, with a Commonwealth Fellowship to spend a year in the US. His latent Byronism was unleashed.

Juan in America was hugely successful – in Britain. It is one of the best of a small category of novels which could be called *contemptu americani*: in the same top bracket as Waugh's THE LOVED ONE and Huxley's *After Many a Summer* – if less bilious than either. Juan Motley is a bar-sinister descendant of the mad, bad, dangerous-to-know lord. He has spent the year or two after university in barren Australia (some bastard offspring of his own seem to be involved in the exile). Of a wandering disposition, he has been invited to an American college founded by one of his distant Motley kinsmen. He departs with zest, casting a coolly appraising look at the herd of passengers embarking with him for their home shore:

> Spectacled, fat, benign, alert, young, gay, hard-faced handsome, tidy, slov-enly, smart, stalwart, slim – three hundred holiday-makers going home stepping aboard the ship with casual Yankee unconcern as though it were a foot-plank crossing a creek. The heirs of Time and applied Science, they used a forty-thousand-ton liner like a row-boat or a penny ferry. Children of immensity, they were unabashed by immensity.

The snooty tone is sustained throughout. What follows is a ramshackle ingénu progress. In New York it is speakeasies, bodies falling from Wall Street skyscrapers, and Broadway chorus girls. On to Chicago, where he gets involved in a Capone-style shoot-out. The bootleggers like his style and he moves some booze across the border.

More bullets fly. Then on to Motley College where, after some lively stuff with 'co-eds' (nothing like it at Oxford), he dooms himself by fluffing a match-winning move on the football field. On he travels. He loses his cash in a stick-up, gets by 'slinging hash', is almost killed by an African-American (the now unprintable n-word is cheerfully sprayed about) hog-slaughterer. He meets up with the now happily married mother of one of his bastards (slightly sticky) and goes on the road with a vaudeville 'operacrobat' who sings Verdi hanging upside down from a trapeze. She's just as unusual between the sheets. Having arrived on the Atlantic coast, he leaves from the Pacific coast, with a charming Chinese girl, Kuo Kuo, his wander-lust, and every other lust, still running strong. All great fun.

Jules and Jim, Henri-Pierre Roché, 1953

A work of huge charm, *Jules and Jim* was published at a period when France – and Paris – was at its least gay. A bloody colonial war in Vietnam was coming to its climax at Dien Bien Phu, after which the European country would teeter for years on the brink of counter-revolution. 'La belle France' was the hollowest of epithets.

Jules and Jim was Henri-Pierre Roché's first novel. He was seventy-four. He had known everyone of artistic significance during the *belle époque* when Paris was the most cultivated city in the world. *Jules and Jim* escapes to that past, when things were indeed 'beautiful'. The narrative opens in 'about the year 1907'. The vagueness casts an aura of fairy-tale charm. Jim (pronounced English-style – 'Djim' not 'Zheem') meets the man who will be his bosom friend, Jules. Despite the name, and its French pronun-ciation, Jules is German. A stranger to Paris, he asks Jim – tall, thin and elegant – whom he 'hardly knew',

> to get him into the *Bal des Quat'z'Arts* [annual 'Ball of the Four Arts' – fancy dress] and Jim had found him a ticket and taken him to the costumier's. It was while Jules was gently turning

over one material after another and choosing a simple costume, that of a slave, that Jim's friendship for Jules was born. The friendship grew during the ball, which Jules took in serenely, his eyes round with wonder.

Neither partner in this Parisian Damon and Pythias relationship works, but they live at the highest pitch of cultivation. Jules is not just German, but Germanic: a little solemn and inexperienced with women. He demands too much from them, he confesses, which is 'why I get nothing from them'. He is not handsome (there are problems with his repulsively thick body hair). The two men box, cycle, eat well, and absorb – as by osmosis – the great art and good life happening around them. The first third of the novel is taken up with the women they pursue and drop, as gently as thistledown.

On a trip to the Greek islands Jules and Jim are enchanted by the statue of a woman with 'an archaic smile'. After returning to Paris (the novel is already half over) they meet, as by Kismet, a woman possessed of just that smile – Kate (or rather Kathe – she is German but, like Jim, her name is anglicised). As in the Pygmalion fable, the statue has become the woman. But Kate also resembles the female resident of another island, Cisthene. There is a touch of man-destroying Medusa about her. After her wedding to Jules Kate breaks up the ceremonial solemnity by jumping in the Seine. She will walk in naked, or dress publicly in men's clothes (with a 'bold cheeky stare'), for no reason other than that she damn' well wants to. She shoplifts. She believes in 'taking risks'. Meanwhile the war comes and goes. It is wholly irrelevant to the indestructible friendship of the men and their joint partner. The conflict is disposed of in two sentences. It comes. It goes. Jules and Kate now live in Germany.

Following the birth of a second daughter their relationship is no longer sexual (whether that between Jules and Jim ever was is left vague). 'That chapter's finished', Kate declares. A final chapter is about to begin. She gives herself, with Jules' blessing, to Jim. They resolve to marry and have children. Accidental death solves what looks like becoming a very sticky situation. The three

of them have experienced enough in life already.

Roché's novel made little impact on first publication: it was regarded as unserious. Then François Truffaut picked up a second-hand copy from a Paris bookstall. He found it 'a perfect hymn to love' and adapted it for his 1961 film, a classic of French New Wave cinema. On its coat-tails, Roché's novel was reappraised as the minor masterpiece it is. Jules and Kate are based on the author's best friends in the period covered by the narrative, Franz Hessel (the German translator of Marcel Proust) and his wife Helen. She survived to read the novel, which she rather disliked, and see the film, which – with herself played by Jeanne Moreau – she loved.

The Jungle, Upton Sinclair, 1906

In 2013 a new word claimed entry in the annually revised *Oxford English Dictionary* – 'horseburger' – and the British people were shocked to discover what the word 'process' in the term 'processed meat' actually meant: excrement. One might have recalled a high-point scene in Sinclair's novel. The sad-sack hero, Jurgis, a labour-slave in the gigantic Chicago meat-processing factories, has sunk to the lowest pits of Durham's huge processing plant:

> Worst of any, however, were the ferti-lizer men, and those who served in the cooking rooms. These people could not be shown to the visitor, – for the odour of a fertilizer man would scare any ordinary visitor at a hundred yards, and as for the other men, who worked in tank rooms full of steam, and in some of which there were open vats near the level of the floor, their peculiar trouble was that they fell into the vats; and when they were fished out, there was never enough of them left to be worth exhibiting, – sometimes they would be overlooked for days, till all but the bones of them had gone out to the world as Durham's Pure Leaf Lard!

'Manburger'. Have you never wondered? Sinclair pulled no punches in his descriptions of what went into processed meat – diseased animal parts, rat-droppings, syphilitic contamination (from brothel-using strike-breakers). But it was the Thyestean detail which hit home.

Sinclair had huge problems getting his novel published. Five publishers turned it down. Macmillan's reason was typical: nausea. They would take it, Sinclair was told, if he dropped 'the blood and guts'. He wouldn't and they didn't. *The Jungle* first appeared in the congenial pages of a socialist journal before Sinclair took the risk of paying for publication himself. Once published, word of the novel spread like wildfire. The president, Theodore Roosevelt, received a proof copy and was initially dismissive, regarding the book as 'Red' propaganda. He nonetheless dispatched government officials to Chicago – just in case. It was, they told him, even worse than Sinclair described. One can picture the fork stopping halfway between the breakfast table and Teddy's mouth. The result was, within months of the novel's publication, the Pure Food and Drug Act, and the Federal Meat Inspection Act of 1906.

Sinclair – who'd wanted to start a revolution, not improve the quality of salami – was displeased. 'I aimed at the public's heart,' he grumbled, 'and by accident I hit it in the stomach.' In truth he was aiming at the nation's voting slips. The novel ends with a rousing call to arms ('Organize! Organize! Organize') at a Chicago election, urging the city to lead the way to 'Socialism in America'.

The plot of *The Jungle* is simple and its prose basic – this is a novel whose primary readership, Sinclair hoped, would be the 'workingmen' to whom he dedicated the book. The open immigration of the turn of the century had sucked in huge, docile labour forces. Whole families, in some cases whole villages, would be transplanted from the Old World to slavery in the New. The narrative opens with the marriage of Jurgis Rudkus, a handsome, strong Lithuanian peasant, to his childhood sweetheart. The social culture of the old country is visibly eroding. The ceremony is a shambles. Jurgis' response to every crisis thereafter is: 'I will earn more money – I will work harder.' But it is the system which is working him. He is of no more significance than the carcasses

swinging their way to the cannery. Once his strength is used up by the meat-packing industry, and his family destroyed, Jurgis becomes a tramp and finally a broken-down janitor – all he has left is his vote. The great American melting pot is as effective a 'process' as the Durham Meat Packing Factory's fertiliser room.

In addition to clean-food legislation *The Jungle* did give literature the term 'muck-raker', invented by Roosevelt as a term of abuse. The reference was to *The Pilgrim's Progress* and the 'the man with the muck rake', whose 'carnal mind' makes him 'look no way but downward'. Novelists from Sinclair onwards adopted the term as a badge of pride. Downward was where the truth lay.

Jurassic Park, Michael Crichton, 1990

Michael Crichton was a unicorn among best-selling writers of fiction. He had a science degree from Harvard University, and a *summa cum laude* to go with it. *Jurassic Park* represents the fusion of a number of elements, of which that educational attainment is one. Another was the huge leap forward in life sciences during the period of Crichton's writing – particularly in the field of genetics. Another great leap forward – important in the afterlife of Crichton's novel(s) – was cinematic CGI. 'Special effects' (F/X) had reached a new level of technical sophistication. No more of the jerky stop-frame animation of *King Kong*.

A more personal ingredient in the novel's mix was Crichton's fascination with Disneyland. All that Southern California has given the world, Woody Allen once jested, is 'right on red'. For a generation of thoughtful popular novelists and film-makers, it has in fact given the world something else of great importance – the theme park. It was the family's annual trip to Disneyland that inspired the young George Lucas – *Star Wars* was born from that excited little boy's ride on 'Autopolis'. Ira Levin's *The Stepford Wives* is a riff on the 'animatronics' of the 'Pirates of the Caribbean' ride at Anaheim. As, of course, is *Pirates of the Caribbean* the movie franchise. Michael Crichton's vision was broader and more thoughtful. He saw the archetypal Californian theme park as the material embodiment of the Great American Dream – cross-hatched with nightmare. His miniature masterpiece *Westworld* (1973), a film over which he had total artistic control, is centred around a theme park which takes over the world that made the theme park. Westworld, in the brooding inhumanity of a robotic, unstoppably lethal cowboy (played by Yul Brynner and the inspiration for James Cameron's *Terminator*), unleashes not merely the joy, but the ineradicable violence in the American soul. *Jurassic Park* explores this idea further.

The novel's plot is simple and owes much to Conan Doyle's *The Lost World* (Crichton graciously acknowledged the debt by using Doyle's title for his follow-up dinosaur novel). It all hinges on a gimmick. There are insects trapped in amber washed up every day on the shores of the world. These fragments of semi-precious material are little time machines. The gem-substance is petrified gum, some of it from the prehistoric era. What if the entombed insect were a mosquito which had been sucking the blood of – say – a Tyrannosaurus rex or a Velociraptor? Enter the entrepreneur John Hammond, who has a dream. He will build a theme park on an island off the coast of Costa Rica, populated with the lab-regenerated dinosaurs which, thanks to children's books, we all love. Shortly before opening it to the public (who will, he is confident, pay many thousands a head for the trip) he brings in an eminent paleontologist (and his delectable research student), a mathematician and a marketing expert, to get a final pre-launch opinion. Bad things happen.

The novel takes as its fly in the ointment (flea in the amber?) the truths of chaos theory, enunciated throughout by the mathematician. Bluntly, it's a kind of sod's law which argues that consequences are never deductible from prior causes because 'boundary conditions' can never be precisely identified or controlled. Allusion is made to Ray Bradbury's 'butterfly effect'. Go back in a time machine to a prehistoric forest, tread on a butterfly, and when you return the modern world will be unrecognisable. The safety precautions set up by Hammond fail,

as theory predicts they must. The novel ends with the island being napalmed (the American solution) – but have some of the dinosaurs survived? Neither Crichton, nor Spielberg, was stupid enough to close the door to any sequel – more fiction, and film, duly appeared. The *Jurassic Park* franchise packed, as does much of Crichton's popular fiction, a hefty ideological punch. In the US many among the population hold the belief that God created the earth within the last ten thousand years and cast doubt upon evolution. A novel and a film in which the destruction of dinosaurs sixty-five million years in the past is reiterated as scientific 'fact' could only be incendiary or – as optimists might think – instructive.

The fly/amber/DNA gimmick is, scientists concur, only plausible to gullible readers of fiction. Ah, well. We can dream, can't we?

Justine, Lawrence Durrell, 1957

The prelims of *Justine* bear close examination. It is the first of *The Alexandria Quartet* (published entire in 1962). But this, a foreword sternly instructs us, is not a Proustian *roman fleuve*. 'A suitable descriptive subtitle', we are to understand, 'might be a "word continuum"'. Think Einstein and relativity. The epigraphs make the point. One is from Freud:

> I am accustoming myself to the idea of regarding every sexual act as a process in which four persons are involved. We shall have a lot to discuss about that.

The other is from de Sade's namesake novel (banned in 1957 Britain):

> There are two positions available to us – either crime, which renders us happy, or the noose, which prevents us from being unhappy.

This will be a play of quadrilaterality. But it is a novel, the foreword reminds us. 'Only the city is real' – Alexandria.

Nobody who did not personally suffer

post-war austerity, and whose chances of seeing Alexandria were as remote as a round trip to Mars, will appreciate the intoxication with which my generation devoured Lawrence Durrell's *Justine, Balthazar, Mountolive* and *Clea*. Even now, my saliva glands moisten and my pulse quickens at the opening words:

> The sea is high again today, with a thrilling flush of wind. In the midst of winter you can feel the inventions of spring. A sky of hot nude pearl until midday, crickets in sheltered places, and the wind unpacking the great planes, ransacking the great planes...

Or, at least, they moistened and quickened when I first read *Justine*, in its beautiful 'nude-ochre' Faber paperback covers. 'Do you know what they're saying about me?' Durrell indignantly asked one of his friends. 'That my prose is as sticky as *nougat*.' For those Britons (Durrell, working for the Foreign Office in Egypt at the time, was not one of them) who had endured a dozen years of sweet-rationing, prose-*nougat* was the next best thing. And for the bulk of the British population, cooped up with the measly £50 travel allowance, *The Alexandria Quartet* was the only tourism on offer – and if it was sex tourism (before *Lady Chatterley*, Durrell was considered very 'adult') so much the better. Alexandria, in Britain's sexually strangulated fifties, seemed like the fabled Pornotopia:

> Five races, five languages, a dozen creeds: five fleets turning through their greasy reflections behind the harbour bar. But there are more than five sexes and only demotic Greek seems to distinguish among them. The sexual provender which lies to hand is staggering in its variety and profusion.

Staggering indeed. Suddenly Friday night at the Corn Exchange dance hall (Ted Heath's dance, 'The Creep' was in) seemed very dull. And what on earth were the other two sexes? Eustace Chesser's *Love Without Fear* (one's manual in such things) offered no answers.

The plot of *Justine* is easily summarised once one unsticks the *nougat* from one's eyeballs. It is the eve of the Second World War. The narrator, Darley, a failed writer, depressed teacher and disciple of the poet Cavafy, permeates the novel without offering any clear image of himself. He is writing, nostalgically, on a Greek island, accompanied by a young girl – the child of a prostitute lover, Melissa, whose life he saved after an unfortunate overdose of aphrodisiacs. She is no longer around. The core event in the plot is his love affair with Justine, the beautiful Jewish wife of a Copt banker, Nessim – who may or may not be complaisant, may or may not be sharing Melissa, and may or may not be conspiring against British rule. There are other characters, all degenerate: Pombal, Darley's French diplomat flatmate, who occasionally throws a whore his way (sometimes venereally infected); the sarcastic English novelist Pursewarden; the cross-dressing policeman Scobie; the sleek, sharkskin-coated paedophile Capodistria. It ends bloodily with a duck hunt on Nessim's estate. Then it goes on, and on, and on, for another three volumes. Like *nougat*, one bite is delicious. A hundred less so. Enjoy *Justine*, though.

Justine: or, The Misfortunes of Virtue, Marquis de Sade, 1791

De Sade was an aristocrat born into a family of debauchees. He would, in the course of his life, raise their debauchery to the level of an art form. The first crime for which he was arrested set the pattern for what was to come. Five months after marrying (a woman to whom, perversely, *Justine* is dedicated) de Sade was arrested. He had disgusted a twenty-year-old prostitute whom he had hired for the night 'by talk of masturbating into a chalice and proposing to thrust communion hosts into her vagina'. He got off lightly. But over the following decades the punishments would be more severe. His life was spent, largely, in confinement – first in prisons, then in the Bastille, then in a lunatic asylum. He read widely and wrote profusely in these years. Jail, he could have said (echoing Gorky), 'is my university'.

While members of his *aristo* class were having their heads chopped off by the tumbril load, he actually worked, in intervals of freedom, for the Revolution. Pornography had been tacitly encouraged by the more thoughtful insurgent leaders as corrosive of a state sustained by a belief in divine monarchy. Rape, as de Sade presented it, could be conceived of as a revolutionary act. The outrageous doctrine is expressed frequently in *Justine*; for example, in the following pedantic explanation of his act by a child-rapist to his soon-to-suffer victim:

> This virtue that you make such a fuss about is of no use in the world. There's no point in kneeling before its altars, because its vain incense will not feed you ... In this world, my child, men value only those things that earn money or bring pleasure.

'Oh, Monsieur,' replies the little girl, 'do men no longer have any honesty or benevolence?' 'Very little,' replies her rapist, and proceeds.

The other 'Romantic' theorem underlying de Sade's work is (as in Wordsworth and Coleridge) the primacy of imagination. Anything that can be imagined can be written, his fiction asserts. The Marquis was possessed of an unusually powerful, if somewhat obsessive, imagination. He wrote *Justine*, an early work, in 1787, while imprisoned in the Bastille. One can fancy Dickens' Dr Manette ('Prisoner 105') decently cobbling shoes a few feet away in North Tower. *Justine* was published in 1791 and banned when the Bonapartist regime took over. Napoleon conceived a violent personal antipathy for 'the most abominable book ever engendered by the most depraved imagination', and had the author back behind bars for another thirteen years. Thereafter, like everything with the name de Sade on it, *Justine* was forbidden reading.

The story is simple – a peg on which to hang sexual fantasies. De Sade's revolve around ingenious violation of the female body, the BDSM (as it is now categorised) couched in coy circumlocution. It is set shortly before the Revolution. Justine, the respectable daughter of a banker, is kicked out of her convent school when her father speculates and falls into ruin. She is twelve – a picture of blonde, blue-eyed maidenhood. She goes straight to her confessor who, on hearing her plight, responds by diving into her bosom. An unhappy career ensues.

Any narrative which opens so climactically will face problems. One was how to 'turn the screw' (to borrow Henry James' phrase, from an entirely different context). De Sade comes up with more and more multiplications, variations, and surreally implausible sexual acts, in which the problem, increasingly, is to forestall boredom. The other problem is how to end the story. In one version (de Sade wrote three) a lightning bolt comes to perform a cosmic and terminal violation on the body of the 'unfortunate' heroine. Should we burn de Sade? asked Simone de Beauvoir – setting his fiction up as a problem for existentialist philosophy. Why bother? is the current response. But, out of curiosity as to what terrified our ancestors, read a page or two.

Keep the Aspidistra Flying, George Orwell, 1936

Orwell's novel kicks off with an epigraph of sheer bloody-minded blasphemy:

> Though I speak with the tongues of men and of angels, and have not money, I am become as a sounding brass, or a tinkling cymbal . . . *etc, etc.*

This biblical travesty goes on, unamusingly, for half a page. The reader, before even getting into the story is muttering 'enough already, George'. But on it goes, relentlessly. There are diatribes against the 'money god' on virtually every page.

Keep the Aspidistra Flying is an early novel and Orwell had not yet mastered narrative weights and measures. Nor had he mastered the art of the title, which in this case has dated catastrophically. Aspidistras, and what they represent, are rarer in households today than Venus flytraps. Orwell himself had little time for his first three novels. 'Bollocks' was his pungent verdict in later life. But *Aspidistra* has its loyal admirers. Norman Mailer, of all people, pronounced it 'perfect' ('fugging perfect'?). I recommend the novel for its rawness. It is Orwell ore, unrefined.

Composition was started in 1934, when the action is set. It was conceived in the shadow of certain calamity. As Orwell later wrote, 'I don't quite know in what year I first knew for certain that the present war was coming. After 1936, of course, the thing was obvious to anyone except an idiot.' *Aspidistra* uses life material gathered from what are 'lost years' to Orwell's biographers. He was, in the mid-1930s, down and pretty well out. The 'rather moth-eaten' hero, Gordon Comstock, is a victim of the damnable British class system. For ever below the toffs, for ever struggling (ever more feebly) to keep from falling into the 'abyss'.

Gordon has published a volume of poetry, which, because he didn't go to the right school or university, has sunk without trace. It's absolutely pointless submitting his poems to the 'good' magazines: 'he might as well have dropped his card at Buckingham Palace'.

The sods! The bloody sods! 'The Editor regrets!' Why be so bloody mealy-mouthed about it? Why not say outright, 'We don't want your bloody poems. We only take poems from chaps we were at Cambridge with.'

One knows the feeling.

Comstock scrapes a living as a counter jumper in a Hampstead bookshop (as, for a couple of years, did Orwell, selling the awful middle-brow fiction of the period to awful middle-class people). He has a loving woman, Rosemary. They meet, glumly and sexlessly, in Lyons Corner Houses. Neither of their landladies will allow 'visits' and creaking bed springs. Gordon is clear-eyed enough to see through the sham of the British class system but lacks the will to break through it.

Finally, in the spirit of Winston Smith loving Big Brother, he sells his writing talent to that most corrupt sideshow of capitalism, the advertising industry. *Vicisti, Aspidistra*. As a copywriter, he comes up with a winner: 'PP' ('pedic perspiration', or foot odour), a variant on the never-fail 'BO' ('body odour' – the acronym that sold carbolic soap for lower-class armpits). Smells were always a big thing, as well as a class thing, for Orwell.

Partisans claim Gordon to be the first Angry Young Man. But he's not. His 'rebellion' is that of the perpetually unclenched fist, suffused with hopelessness. Although Orwell didn't realise it at the time, it was to be that most feared thing, the coming war, which would consign the aspidistra, and the England it represented, to the dustbin of history.

Two reasons, then, for recommending you read this highly imperfect novel: it's Orwell unvarnished, and rich in its depiction of mid-thirties England.

A Kestrel for a Knave, Barry Hines, 1968

The beautiful title is explained by the novel's epigraph:

> An Eagle for an Emperor, a Gyrfalcon for a King; a Peregrine for a Prince, a

Saker for a Knight, a Merlin for a lady;
a Goshawk for a Yeoman, a Sparrow-
hawk for a Priest, a Musket for a Holy
water Clerk, a Kestrel for a Knave.

Hines' message comes through strong,
clear and extremely angry. This is a novel
about class. And class at a particularly
seething period of British social history.
Kes (to use its shorter title) was one of the
'angry', 'kitchen sink' works, which flowered – like ragwort in the English rose
garden – in the late 1950s and 1960s. It was
a period when, as Kenneth Tynan said, the
world was changed for ever by the first
performance of *Look Back in Anger*. Hines'
novel is another of the 'tracts for the times',
a manifesto of the provincial-proletarian
cultural revolt in the 1960s, which
produced, among other things, the Beatles
and David Bailey.

The narrative opens in a pit town (clearly
Barnsley), on a housing estate – 'a sink estate'
for the 'underclass'. Billy Casper's mother is
a drunken slag. Her husband walked out on
her. Wise decision. Her 'oldest', Jud, has gone
down the pit. He shares a bed (anyone can
share hers) with Billy, who is in his last weeks
at school before, at sixteen, he is loosed into
a world that doesn't want him. The narrative
opens with Jud going off to work at six in
the morning (stealing Billy's bike) and Billy
having to walk his paper round. The Casper
boys hate each other. At school Billy sleeps
through lessons, is cuffed and humiliated.
Just another day.

The school is a 'secondary mod'. The door
to that one escape route for kids like him
has been slammed in his face. He failed the
'eleven plus'. Deservedly. Billy is barely
literate and no good at sport – he does his
best to lose the game when 'picked' for football – echoes of Sillitoe's long-distance
runner.

His 'release' from being Billy Casper is
like that of the Birdman of Alacatraz. He
finds a kestrel hawk chick and with the aid
of a (stolen) book teaches himself the
complex craft of falconry. There are two
remotely kind strangers in his life: one is
the farmer in one of whose ruined buildings
was the nest from which 'Kes' came. The
other is a teacher, Mr Farthing, to whom
Billy explains what the bird means:

I know, Sir. That's why it makes me
mad when I take her out and I'll hear
somebody say, 'Look, there's Billy
Casper there wi' his pet hawk.' I could
shout at 'em; it's not a pet, Sir, hawks
are not pets. Or when folks stop me
and say, 'Is it tame?' Is it heck tame,
it's trained that's all. It's fierce, an' it's
wild, an' it's not bothered about
anybody, not even about me, right.
And that's why it's great.

It's Hopkins' 'The Windhover' – in a thick
Barnsley accent.

The novel, which is as social-situational
as a Bruegel 'genre' painting, has just one
central event. Billy keeps the money Jud
gives him to put on a horse, in order to buy
Kes food. The horse wins and the bird loses.
Vengeful Jud beats Kes to death with a poker,
and dumps him in the dustbin. 'You fuckin'
bastard,' screams Billy and runs off to a
derelict cinema ('the Palace'), where he was
once happy with his father and dreams of
revenge. Then he goes home, buries the bird,
and goes to bed. With Jud. What awaits?
Probably the pit or prison. There's no call
for falconers down at the 'exchange'.

Hines' Billy Casper is kindred with Billy
Liar and Billy Elliot – but without the first's
ruefully comic resistance or the second's
ugly-duckling prospects (from outside lavatory to Sadler's Wells and *Swan Lake*). Ken
Loach's film, *Kes*, retains the anger, the
impenetrable accent, the blunt-instrument
narrative, and the furious energy, which, in
that decade, welled up from the England that
was not London. It changed nothing, of
course. But at least, after the outburst, the
awfulness was clearer.

The Killer Inside Me, Jim Thompson, 1952

Thompson's novel first saw print as a 'paperback original'. It's pure pulp and impurely
noir – a masterpiece of its low literary kind.
Lou Ford, the hero-narrator, is deputy sheriff
in Central City, a roadside-stop town in West
Texas, which got lucky with the oil boom.
It's historically a region glorified in film and
romance by the 'frontier thesis' – the idea

that it is in these edgy places, in the 'Wild West', that true American manhood is tested. And, among the heroes of the Western myth, the 'man with the star' stands tallest.

Lou Ford looks the part – with Stetson, cigar and six-gun – but doesn't quite fit the bill. Beneath his reassuringly amiable, but strong as rawhide, exterior he's a homicidal psychopath. More Krafft-Ebing than John Wayne. The narrative opens in a coffee shop. Everyone there loves Lou and the sense of civic order he brings with him just by being around. He's a good old hometown boy. On his way out a panhandler extends his hand for any loose change. Lou ignores him.

Inside himself Lou is consumed by what he calls 'the sickness', a need to murder. His doctor father discovered early on that his son was a psychopath and sterilised him, after he was caught raping a three-year old girl to death. His adoptive brother took the rap for him and was later murdered. Frontier justice.

For almost fifteen years Lou's 'sickness' has been quiescent – apart from inconsequential acts of sadism. The novel's action – narrated autobiographically, with a chilling charm – gets going when Lou becomes involved with a new whore in town, Joyce Lakeland. He's been told to run her out of Central City but one thing leads to another, and he ends up whipping her with his sheriff's belt. She's a masochist, it transpires, and falls in love with him. Later in their relationship the foreplay gets out of hand and Lou batters her to death (as he wrongly thinks – she in fact survives), and sets up the son of a local businessman to pay for the crime.

The sickness has now, as it always threatened to do, taken him over. A string of other murders ensues. Lou strangles a Greek boy, who thinks Lou is his only friend, making it look like suicide, and beats his own fiancée Amy to a pulp after some particularly satisfying love-making. The novel ends in a bloody, fiery shoot-out, and Lou's conclusion that everyone like him (and you, perhaps) 'started the game with a crooked cue':

Plenty of pretty smart psychiatrists have been fooled by guys like me, and you can't really fault 'em for it. There's just not much they can put their hands on, know what I mean?. . . We might have the disease, the condition; or we might just be cold-blooded and smart as hell; or we might be innocent of what we're supposed to have done. We might be any one of those three things, because the symptoms we show would fit any one of the three.

The Killer Inside Me is, like Jack Finney's *The Body Snatchers*, a prime example of Cold War paranoia. You can trust no one – not even the lovable small-town sheriff. And the novel displays the greater freedoms of pulp fiction at this period in matters sexual. Although Middle America recoiled from the 'frankness', so called, of novels like *Peyton Place*, Thompson could create scenes such as that in which Amy, who has guessed during oral sex (by his 'smell') that Lou has earlier made love to Joyce, turns on him with: 'You screwed her. You've been doing it all along. You've been putting her dirty insides inside of me, smearing me with her.'

The novel was strikingly innovative at a period when the term 'psychopath' was becoming widely used and the reading public was wrestling with the idea. Among Lou Ford's more distinguished progeny is the TV mini-series character Dexter – 'America's favourite serial killer' as Showtime's advertisements describe him. Lou is less lovable, but more credible.

Kim, Rudyard Kipling, 1901

The novel has a terrific opening – a scene that shrinks the multi-volume *Jewel in the Crown* into crystalline brevity. The boy Kim – indistinguishable from the dusky native children – is described playing a version of King of the Castle near the Moti bazaar. He is currently 'king' astride the 'great gun Zam-Zammah', a paramount symbol of British power. Those of a morbid cast of mind will recall that in the then-recent 'Mutiny' – nowadays more properly called the Indian Rebellion – captives were strapped over the mouths of artillery pieces (perhaps even Zam-Zammah itself) and blasted to bloody death. This scene is less violent, but evocative of where colonial power lies:

He sat, in defiance of municipal orders, astride the gun Zam-Zammah on her brick platform opposite the old Ajaib-Gher – the Wonder House, as the natives call the Lahore Museum. Who hold Zam-Zammah, that 'fire-breathing dragon', hold the Punjab; for the great green-bronze piece is always first of the conqueror's loot.

There was some justification for Kim – he had kicked Lala Dinanath's boy off the trunnions – since the English held the Punjab and Kim was English. Though he was burned black as any native; though he spoke the vernacular by preference, and his mother-tongue in a clipped uncertain sing-song; though he consorted on terms of perfect equality with the small boys of the bazaar; Kim was white – a poor white of the very poorest.

At this point, Kim suddenly catches sight of a *lama*, whose *chela*, or disciple, he is destined to become. The narrative is set up.

Kim was born Kimball O'Hara, the son of a sergeant in the Mavericks, an Irish regiment. His mother died of cholera, his father took to opium and – an unwanted orphan – Kim has been brought up by a lady of easy virtue in the bazaar. He is sunburned to a pigment which means that, with his bilingualism, he can 'pass'. To use Kipling's terms, East and West meet, inextricably, in Kim. He is later reabsorbed by his own people and, after a public-school education, Anglican indoctrination and cricket, emerges a 'sahib'. Using his ethnic skills he enters the 'great game' of espionage. The blast of the cannon is no longer sufficient to keep India in English possession – something more cunning, but equally ruthless, is required. The novel ends with exciting intrigue in the Himalayas, and – with Kim's guidance – his *lama*, or guru, finally discovers his sought-after sacred river.

Kim allegorises Kipling's own first five years as a child in Bombay. The novel was illustrated by his father – the only time, I believe, this has ever happened in fiction. *Kim* can claim to be the finest novel about race and colonialism until *Midnight's Children* came along. Rushdie, of course,

has a Kipling problem. It's hard to make friends with the author of the 'White Man's Burden':

> Take up the White Man's burden—
> Send forth the best ye breed—
> Go send your sons to exile
> To serve your captives' need;
> To wait in heavy harness
> On fluttered folk and wild—
> Your new-caught, sullen peoples,
> Half devil and half child.

Nonetheless Rushdie concedes, 'every true Indian reader knows that no non-Indian writer understood India as well as Kipling'.

The author recorded that, as he put pen to paper, *Kim* 'grew like the Djinn [genie] released from the brass bottle'. It's an interesting comment and alludes to a Victorian bestseller, *The Brass Bottle* by F. Anstey, published a few months earlier, and an interesting work in its own right. In it, Horace Ventimore, a young architect, buys a brass vessel. It contains a singularly bad-tempered genie (djinn) called Fakrash-el-Aamash, whose attempts to help his 'master' go comically awry. A murderous feud develops. Horace finally tricks the djinn back into his bottle, which he throws into the Thames. The djinn will spend eternity in river sludge, while Horace returns to his bourgeois destiny. Like *Kim*, *The Brass Bottle* intimates that in the twentieth century the White Man's Burden might become very burdensome indeed. The old brass bottles, and great cannon, had had their day.

King Rat, James Clavell, 1962

King Rat is the second-best novel about being a prisoner-of-war of the Japanese in the Second World War. The best, for my money, is EMPIRE OF THE SUN. Third, by a long way, is *The Bridge on the River Kwai* – although, of the three film adaptations, David Lean's got the best out of the actors.

King Rat was Clavell's first novel, his shortest, and his best. He later went on to be given the (then) world's largest advance for a work of fiction in 1986: a cool $5 million. The resulting *Whirlwind* was as obese as the advance. Novelists can have too much royal jelly stuffed down their gullets. As a tyro, Clavell submitted his overlong manuscript of *King Rat* to his editor's knife. It's the better for it.

Clavell himself, as a young artillery officer, had been imprisoned by the Japanese after the shameful fall of Singapore in 1942 – the blackest day of the war for the British, and the first domino to fall in what would be the end of empire. *King Rat* is set in Changi, where Clavell was imprisoned. It opens:

> Changi was set like a pearl on the eastern tip of Singapore Island. . . Closer, Changi lost its beauty and became what it was – an obscene forbidding prison.

Clavell's fiction and films (he went on to co-write the script for *The Great Escape*) revolve around certain obsessive themes – notably the pressures of wartime defeat and, in the Pacific theatre, a fascination with the Japanese victor's chivalrous yet uncompromisingly brutal martial codes. Implicit throughout *King Rat* is the belief 'we won the war but they were the better soldiers'.

King Rat opens in early 1945 and chronicles the odd-couple friendship between an eccentric young RAF lieutenant, Peter Marlowe (a nod to Conrad, not Chandler), and an opportunist American enlisted man, known only as 'King'. King does not merely survive in what is for others a death camp. He prospers and grows fat by the ruthless 'entrepreneurial' exploitation of the prison black market. 'The King was the only man in Changi who wore underpants. He had six pairs.'

The novel's title alludes to King and Marlowe's enterprisingly imaginative scheme to market battery-raised rats as 'mouse deer'. The 'king rat' is the stud beast who survives by eating his weaker fellows. Changi is a 'rat eat rat' world. The narrative rattles along but Clavell does not simplify matters. The captors are beastly to their prisoners because the Japanese are the worthier military caste. The equivalent British officers are wholly despicable. They steal their men's food, while retaining, for internal camp 'discipline', all the perquisites of office (even

though none of them has underpants). It is only these Hooray Henries who are sold and unwittingly eat the 'mouse deer'. Marlowe represents a kind of decency but he throws in his lot with the wholly unscrupulous King, on the grounds that at least he's honest. The counterpoint figure is a British Provost Marshal officer, Robin Gray. Promoted from the ranks, despised by officers and other ranks alike, he is clearly modelled on Javert in *Les Misérables* (another great prison novel).

King Rat ends with the end of the war. The old ways reassert themselves. King is now just another corporal and is last seen being bundled off in a truck – a nobody on the way to nowhere. A 'tormented' question haunts Marlowe's mind. Has he somehow 'betrayed' king and country in his alliance with the King of Changi? A larger question plays over the book. Is not the way of the Samurai – 'honour or death', no compromise – a nobler code than that of the British? It's a question Clavell went on to explore in his longer, better-known novel (and hugely successful TV series) *Shōgun*, in which the Elizabethan Age hero, John Blackthorne, does not merely survive Japanese imprisonment but himself goes on to become a barbarian Samurai warrior.

King Rat, China Miéville, 1998

This is the first published novel by a writer who has since gone on to win every award worth winning in his genre, with his hallmark brand of 'new weird' science fiction. (More ominously, PhD dissertations are being written on him.) *King Rat* is a weirded-up children's story. Its nucleus is Browning's poem 'The Pied Piper of Hamelin', with Miéville probing its central mystery: he kills the rats, but what does the tootling old pervert do with all those children?

The novel opens with Saul Garamond rolling into North London by underground (theme alert!) train at night. Once home Saul takes to his bed, without saying goodnight to his father, with whom his relationship has recently been tricky. He is roughly shaken awake in the morning by the police. Someone has tossed his dad out of a high window and Saul is suspect number one. At this point, the narrative begins to fragment – interestingly, if you like that kind of thing. Saul is rescued from his prison cell by a stranger of dark and filthy appearance, who can squeeze through cracks and walk on rooftops. He talks, non-stop, in cockney rhyming slang (Miéville's first name, incidentally, derives, less exotically than it may sound, from china plate = mate).

The visitor is, it emerges, the Rat King, the last survivor (like that little cripple boy) of the Hamelin rodent holocaust. He introduces Saul to the rare pleasures of lunch from the garbage can and informs him that his dead mother was a rat princess (we later learn, when the narrative is well into its own entrails, that the Rat King is Saul's real father). The Rat King is engaged in a generations-old feud with – who else? – the Pied Piper, nowadays a virtuoso flautist called Pete, who has teamed up with a drum 'n' bass composer of particularly killing riffs.

Essentially *King Rat* is less a treatise on pest control than a meditation on a world where MTV is, for the young, more persuasive than any political ideology, and in which a superpower can be brought down by rock and roll. It connects with the unanswered question in Browning's poem. Exactly what kind of music is it that could lead children, en masse, away from their homes and loved parents into dark caverns where bad things happen? What sorcery is at work?

Miéville's 'Acknowledgements' go out of their way to thank 'Two Fingers and James T. Kirk for their novel *Junglist*'. This was an underground work of fiction, for cultists devoted to the extremely underground (rathole) music of the same name. To quote one authority:

> To identify yourself as a 'junglist' in 1993 meant you belonged to an outcast tribe, a scene feared by most London clubbers as a sinister underworld populated by speed-freaks and baby-gangstas. Born out of rave's Ecstasy-fuelled fervour, the music had mutated, under the influence of bad drugs and the desperation of the recession-wracked early Nineties,

until it was too hard, too dark, and too black for most people to handle.

Miéville calls it music you 'follow with your feet' – like Hamelin's rats and children did. Probably to destruction. But when the music plays, you have no choice.

The narrative explodes towards the end. The Rat King forms an alliance with other animal sovereigns (shades of Gaiman's AMERICAN GODS) but the Piper, and his new music, win this last (or is it?) battle. They are the future. At the end of the novel the King is deposed by Saul, who proclaims revolution for the furry long-tailed masses, promising to put the 'rat' back into 'fraternity'. The age of kings is over. All hail rodent democracy (don't even try to work out where it's going. The author himself wasn't sure). Miéville summarises what he's doing very simply. He's 'pissing in a cosy bedroom'. Your bedroom. You're never more than ten yards away from a rat.

King Solomon's Mines, H. Rider Haggard, 1885

I loved Rider Haggard as an eleven-year-old in the 1950s. I found him erotic. At that godforsaken time in England the most sexually explicit material a lad could find was in the African articles in the *National Geographic* where, for purely 'geographic' instruction, topless native maidens were photographed. And, for me, the African novels of Haggard (I didn't dare go into the 'novelty shops' and buy a Hank Janson).

Sex, from the first, was Haggard's main selling point. All those young (predominantly male) readers, elevated into literacy by the 1870 Elementary Education Act, gobbled up his tales insatiably. It wasn't just the adventure, although that certainly helped. The really enticing aspect of a book like *King Solomon's Mines* was pinpointed by one of the publishers who turned down the work in disgust:

> Never has it been our fate to wade through such a farrago of obscene witlessness. . . Nothing is likely in the hands of the young to do so much

injury as this recklessly immoral book.

The mammarian Sheba Mountains, and the omnipresent topless Zulu maidens decorating the action, strike the modern reader as quaint rather than erotic, but in the 1880s to the 1950s they were sexual dynamite. Lurking in the background was that book of the Bible, always skipped over in RE lessons, the *Song of Solomon*, and its erectile line:

Thy two breasts *are* like two young roes that are twins, which feed among the lilies.

All this eroticism is mixed into the directions contained on the treasure map, which lies at the heart of the plot:

I, José da Silvestra, who am now dying of hunger in the little cave where no snow is on the north side of the nipple of the southernmost of the two mountains I have named Sheba's Breasts, write this in the year 1590 with a cleft bone upon a remnant of my raiment, my blood being the ink. . .

Let him who comes follow the map, and climb the snow of Sheba's left breast till he comes to the nipple, on the north side of which is the great road Solomon made, from whence three days' journey to the King's Palace. Let him kill Gagool. Pray for my soul. Farewell.

Haggard's Africa is no heart of darkness. It's a naked female body waiting for the intrepid explorer. Or, at least, that's how it leaped off the page at me in 1950 (awful year).

Illicit excitements were one thing the novel offered. Travel was another. At a period when your chances of getting out of England were about the same as Papillon's of escaping Devil's Island, *King Solomon's Mines* was a safari in print. I still remember the primal thrill of Chapter 4, 'An Elephant Hunt', and its casual gunnery and white supremacy:

We were too tired to follow them, and perhaps also a little sick of slaughter, eight elephants being a pretty good

bag for one day. So after we were rested a little, and the Kafirs had cut out the hearts of two of the dead elephants for supper, we started homewards, very well pleased with our day's work.

The meat ration in 1950 was, I recall, eight-pence (2.5p) worth of scrag-end a week.

Haggard's plot is rattlingly simple. Allan Quatermain (a name universally and insultingly misspelled by those who do not love this novel), a big game hunter and old Africa hand, is recruited to make up a party with Sir Henry Curtis and Captain John Good, in order to search for Curtis' younger brother, who is lost in the interior of the dark continent. There's also the map, promising untold riches to make the trip *vaux le détour*, as the Michelin guides put it.

Accompanied by the necessary army of native bearers, they duly find and follow King Solomon's road, surviving tribal spears and witchcraft (notably practised by the sinister Gagool whose name Silvestra wrote in blood). The missing white man and the buried wealth are found. And, if you read cunningly between the lines, there's also a lot of buried sex along the way.

The Kreutzer Sonata, Leo Tolstoy, 1889

At the time of its publication *The Kreutzer Sonata* was seen as expressing what was called 'the higher thought'. High or not, the tsar's censors did not like it, and the novella was promptly pulled from publication. Tolstoy's motto could be D. H. Lawrence's line (in his poem about the carnal activities of tortoises): 'why were we crucified into sex?' The novella's epigraph is Matthew 5:28.

But I say unto you, That whosoever looketh on a woman to lust after her hath committed adultery with her already in his heart.

Be warned, sinner.

The action opens in a first-class compartment of a Russian train. Some readers may recall Mr Dombey's symbolic ride:

The power that forced itself upon its iron way – its own – defiant of all paths and roads, piercing through the heart of every obstacle, and dragging living creatures of all classes, ages, and degrees behind it, was a type of the triumphant monster, Death.

But Tolstoy had already done that, with THE DEATH OF IVAN ILYICH. And this is no two-hour trip from Euston to Leamington Spa, but 'two fatiguing nights' on the Trans-Siberian.

There are two men of interest in the carriage: the narrator, and a strangely quiet, but sardonically observant, passenger, who is swathed in an astrakhan-trimmed coat and a fur hat. More vulgar, and less interesting, is a merchant in an American skunk coat. Conversation passes the time and the subject turns to marriage, everyone sustained by pots of tea drunk 'fearfully strong'. The consensus is that 'we are still a long way from the European ideas on marriage'. 'Do not trust yourself to your horse upon the highway. Do not trust yourself to your wife at home', says the oldest passenger.

As the journey continues the narrator discovers the identity of the quiet passenger. His name is Pozdnyshev. It is a notorious name – he is a wife-killer. Pozdnyshev goes on to confide his life story and his philosophy of human relationships. It's a bleak philosophy. 'It is only in stupid novels,' he says,

> that it is written that 'they loved each other all their lives'. And none but children can believe it. To talk of loving a man or woman for life is like saying that a candle can burn for ever.

As a boy Pozdnyshev was plunged into an 'abyss of delusions'. He masturbated insatiably . He was taken early to a brothel – he felt the experience contained 'merit and valour'. 'I had become what is called a voluptuary', he says (in some translations the word is 'fornicator').

So it went until he was thirty when, as convention required, he took a wife. He was attracted by her curls and her 'well-fitted garments'. Like all marriages, it was a union based on mutual deceptions, soon stripped away. Things reached a crisis when Pozdnyshev discovered his wife was using contraception (after bearing six children). He was 'profoundly disgusted'. In her last mellow 'beauty of the end of the summer' she had an affair with a musician, their mutual lusts inflamed to madness by Beethoven's disgustingly erotic sonata. He plays the violin, she the piano. It is not clear whether the relationship was actually adulterous.

Pozdnyshev stabbed the wanton to death, taking down a crooked Damascus blade (the oriental weapon) from the wall to do so. Her neck, he discovered, is surprisingly tough. He would have gone on to stab his putative cuckolder, except the rogue prudently ran out of the house and Pozdnyshev was wearing only socks. He did not want to look absurd – just 'terrible'. He was given a light sentence. Male justice sees it as a *crime passionnel*. Now he rides trains, like a latterday Flying Dutchman, confiding his history, his apologia and his creed – seeking absolution and converts.

Tolstoy added an epilogue making it clear his views were identical with those of Pozdnyshev: no sex in heaven, and the gate yawns widest for those who have avoided it in life. Better the human race die out in purity than wallow in carnal turpitude. He himself had thirteen legitimate children, and probably many more illegitimate ones since none of his serfs, or female servants, was ever safe from his voluptuary's appetites.

Lace, Shirley Conran, 1982

I'd just published some dusty book on popular fiction in 1982, and found myself on a promotional event with Shirley 'Superwoman' (motto: 'life is too short to stuff a mushroom') Conran. We politely exchanged books after the event, in which I played a wholly Prufrockian role. She inscribed in mine, 'For John, who taught me everything I know about goldfish'. Odd, I thought, before tossing the massive 650-page tome (life was too short, etc.) on the way home: me by train, she by limo.

I didn't actually read the book until 2012, when Canongate – on the coat-tails of *Fifty Shades* mania – republished it, under the punchy slogan 'Rediscover the ultimate bonkbuster of the 80s!' I duly 'rediscovered' and found out, after a thirty-year hiatus, why Arab potentates keep goldfish bowls by their satin-sheeted beds. Still dusty to the core, I concluded that, as regards *Lace*, not much had changed since the fashionable 'silver fork' novel of the Regency period, which had once been of scholarly interest to me. The major difference was that no one called Mrs Gore's prurient romances 'shopping and fucking' novels. Or 'mummyporn'. But under whichever label, it was the same thing: envy and Keyhole Kate fantasy about what those enjoying the high life got up to behind closed doors.

Conran's narrative hinges on the opening question (the other thing everyone who read the novel in the 1980s remembers, apparently, along with the sexualised aquarium): 'Which one of you bitches is my mother?' It's directed at four women in their forties, each of whom has 'made it', who have been summoned to a meeting in a Manhattan hotel. The questioner is Lili, who has used a private investigator to track them down. Abandoned as a child, Lili has worked her way up from porn babe to Hollywood superstar. The 'bitches', it transpires, are four bosom friends who pledged to be loyal to each other through 'sick and sin'. Their high-flying careers have taken them to the four corners of the metropolitan world – five-star luxury all the way in Paris, London, New York, Cairo.

Judy, American by birth, is a fashion-magazine magnate. Kate, resourceful and English, is an intrepid war reporter. Maxine is French and an interior designer. Pagan (not a name one can imagine the vicar uttering with much relish at the christening ceremony) is the trophy wife of an Eastern potentate, Prince Abdullah, the literary offspring of E. M. Hull's 'Sheik' (immortalised by the Rudolph Valentino film), but whose oriental erotic skills are symbolised by goldfish rather than Hull's foaming stallions.

Twenty-odd years earlier, at their exclusive Swiss finishing school in Gstaad, one of the four fell pregnant. A pact was made that the mother should never be identified and the baby discreetly disposed of. Not quite left out on the mountainside for wolves, but as good as.

Under Conran's lace frills there are cunningly placed 'feminist' themes: the right to abortion, glass ceilings, pill-permissive sex, *Kama Sutra* female-dominant variations (never a missionary to be seen in the Conran bedroom). But throughout the novel's entire length the question is left hanging – which one of the bitches is it? Conran plays a teasingly sly game, and a parodic wink constantly hovers over the lacy pages. For the 2012 re-launch, with the very straightest of faces, she protested that:

> *Lace* started life as something very different. As an editor on the *Observer* and the *Daily Mail*, I had received many letters from confused and timid women, which made it clear that sex from a woman's point of view needed to be explicitly addressed at a time when, as I've said before, the average Englishman thought the clitoris was a Greek hotel and his sex education consisted of what his misinformed mates had told him. Originally intended as a textbook to teach teenage girls about sex, I finally wrote it as a novel, subsequently described as the book which taught men about women and women about themselves.

Pull the other one, Shirley.

Lady Audley's Secret, Mary Elizabeth Braddon, 1862

This is the most sensationally successful of all the so-called 'sensation novels' of the 1860s. The heroine is a beautiful governess when she catches the eye of rich, old and randy Sir Michael Audley of Audley Court. But there is a terrible secret in Lucy Graham's past – bigamy! Earlier in life, she married George Talboys, a devil-may-care dragoon. Talboys absconded to the Australian gold fields, leaving his wife and baby behind (divorce dragoon-style).

Three years later, and by now a reformed character, George returns with £20,000 to reclaim his wife (known by him as 'Helen') and child. Apparently he has never heard of the General Post Office, so efficiently reformed by Anthony Trollope. He is told his loved ones are dead, but in visiting the new residence of 'Lady Audley' he immediately recognises his wife. A woman of spirit and resource, she lures him to a deserted spot in 'her' grounds and pushes him down a well. Ding Dong Dell, hubby's in the well. She thinks she has murdered him but he survives, with a somewhat lower opinion of his wife. As he later recalls:

> God knows that from the moment in which I sunk into the black pit, knowing the treacherous hand that had sent me to what might have been my death, my chief thought was of the safety of the woman who had betrayed me. I fell upon my feet upon a mass of slush and mire.

His first thought being for his would-be murderess's 'safety' is a nice touch. And to ensure it he takes himself off, under one of the many false names in this novel, to America.

His bosom friend, Sir Michael's barrister nephew Robert, turns sleuth to uncover the truth about his suspicious aunt. Hand-writing connects her to 'Helen', the woman who married the now-disappeared Talboys. Increasingly desperate, the false Lady Audley tries to burn down the inn where Robert is lodging. He survives the flames to denounce her. Talboys returns, yet again.

Lucy-Helen-Lady Audley finally pretends to go mad and is incarcerated in a Belgian madhouse like the Man in the Iron Mask. The novel ends:

> Audley Court is shut up, and a grim old housekeeper reigns paramount in the mansion which my lady's ringing laughter once made musical. A curtain hangs before the pre-Raphaelite portrait; and the blue mould which artists dread gathers upon the Wouvermanns and Poussins, the Cuyps and Tintorettis. The house is often shown to inquisitive visitors, though the baronet is not informed of that fact, and people admire my lady's rooms, and ask many questions about the pretty, fair-haired woman, who died abroad.

There are many interesting aspects to *Lady Audley's Secret*, not least the fate of the villainess/heroine, incarcerated in a lunatic asylum. It was often done with inconvenient wives of that period. The novelist Bulwer-Lytton, for example, when his estranged spouse began yelling at his public election meetings, had her certified and locked up. She was absolutely sane, just hopping mad at her swine of a husband. The less swinish Thackeray had his insane wife locked up in Camberwell. Dickens threatened his wife Catherine with a similar fate if scandalous gossip about his relationship with her sister continued. His close friend John Forster was a commissioner in lunacy, and it could easily have been managed.

Braddon's own domestic circumstances also resonate interestingly. *Lady Audley's Secret* was published by John Maxwell. He and Braddon became lovers and their first child was born in 1862, the year the novel appeared. Maxwell had five children – and a wife residing in an Irish lunatic asylum. In 1874, when the first Mrs Maxwell died, Braddon was at last free to marry her publisher, and went on to bear the philoprogenitive Maxwell another five children, while continuing to be his principal commercial asset. Revenue from Braddon's fiction installed their growing family in a fine country house. The couple rode out the inevitable scandal when it became known to the world that they had been living, and breeding, in sin for years – although their servants resigned en masse.

Lady Chatterley's Lover, D. H. Lawrence, 1928

No novel has changed its literary landscape as radically as *Lady Chatterley's Lover*. Changing things was precisely what Lawrence had in mind with this – his last will and testament of a novel – which he threw over his shoulder, like a hand grenade, as he departed the world to instruct God how to run heaven.

And what was Lawrence's desired 'change'? He wanted to take the dirt out of sex. 'Hygienise' it. The process should start with the lexicon of four-letter words. Fuck. Shit. Piss. I can only print those words, un-muzzled and un-asterisked, because of Lawrence and this novel. I don't, however, have much cause to use them *en clair* in the stuff I write. Novelists manifestly do.

Epic court battles were fought in UK and US courts from 1959 to 1960 to 'acquit Lady Chat'. The acquittal effectively liberated *Hustler, American Psycho* and FIFTY SHADES OF GREY – which was precisely what D. H. Lawrence didn't have in mind with his hygienising campaign. Not that he lived to see the damage his quixotically well-intentioned novel had done.

Lawrence's story is, in essence, double-distilled Mills & Boon romance – love leaping across English class boundaries. Lady Constance ('Connie' – Lawrence liked the naughty French pun) Chatterley is a 'war wife' married to Sir Clifford Chatterley of Wragby Hall, a coal magnate in what Lawrence call the 'uneasy midlands' of England – his own country. Clifford was severely wounded in the war and is paralysed below the waist, wheelchair-bound, and wholly impotent.

Connie – denied sexual relations with her husband – has various unsatisfactory affairs. Clifford informs his wife that if she gets herself pregnant he will welcome the child as the heir Wragby needs. Connie meets Oliver Mellors, who works, menially, as a gamekeeper on her husband's estate. (He was promoted from the ranks to become a commissioned lieutenant during the war, but is now back where he belongs, raising birds for his employer's friends to shoot).

They fall in love, and they make love a symbolic seven times. For Connie it is an education in 'real' life. She is, at last, liberated sexually – not least by Mellors' Anglo-Saxon wooing lingo.

While the inconstant Constance is in Venice having, as her husband fondly imagines, an affair with someone from her own class, Mellors' estranged wife Bertha returns. She finds evidence of the lovers' affair and denounces them to Sir Clifford, who is appalled that his wife should cuckold him with a *servant*. Connie is now indeed pregnant and the novel ends, vaguely, with the expectation that she and Mellors will be reunited

Lady Chatterley's Lover is interesting on many scores. Most interesting is the fact that it is the first undeniably great novel to proclaim that England is not merely in a bad way, but utterly, finally, irremediably dead. The great tree of life Yggdrasil, Lawrence proclaimed, had withered beyond rebirth in England's barren soil. It was gone at the root. The novel opens with a diatribe against the present era that is worthy of Savonarola:

> Ours is essentially a tragic age, so we refuse to take it tragically. The cataclysm has happened, we are among the ruins.

More considered, and less sermon-like, is Connie's thoughtful car ride through the pit village, Tevershall, as she contemplates leaving Wragby and Clifford for ever:

> The car ploughed uphill through the long squalid straggle of Tevershall, the blackened brick dwellings, the black slate roofs glistening their sharp edges, the mud black with coal-dust, the pavements wet and black. It was as if dismalness had soaked through and through every-thing. The utter negation of natural beauty, the utter negation of the gladness of life, the utter absence of the instinct for shapely beauty which every bird and beast has, the utter

death of the human intuitive faculty was appalling.

The Victorians called novels like *Lady Chatterley's Lover* 'condition of England' fiction. For Lawrence the condition of the country which bred him is 'dead and rotting'. One comes away from the novel with a haunted feeling. What if he's right? Am I a novel-reading maggot munching on a corpse?

Lady Pokingham, or, They All Do It, Anon., 1879–80

This is one of the most popular works of Other Victorian Fiction, and is wildly inventive. It was serialised by an anonymous hand (perhaps a team) in the most-thumbed erotic magazine of the period, *The Pearl*. Oddly enough, *Lady Pokingham* was still circulating in the 1950s. I picked up a copy (or, more properly, it was grubbily and clandestinely passed on to me) as a schoolboy; the book was printed in Tangier. Vilely.

The novel carries a preface arguing, mischievously, that the heroine is a true Christian:

The natural instinct of the ancients instilled in their minds the idea that copulation was the direct and most acceptable form of worship they could offer to their deities, and I know that those of my readers who are not bigoted Christians will agree with me, that there cannot be any great sin in giving way to natural desires, and enjoying, to the utmost, all those delicious sensations for which a beneficent Creator has so amply fitted us.

Amen to that.

Lady Pokingham has a stronger narrative frame than most of its kind (it's congruent, in some interesting respects, with the foregoing novel about an even naughtier lady). The tale is narrated by her ladyship herself, at the end of an exhausting life, from her wheelchair. It takes the form of a letter addressed to 'Walter' – author of the Victorian porn-epic, *My Secret Life*. Lady Pokingham tells him in her prefatory epistle:

You will also find a fine lock of dark brown hair, which I have cut from the abundant chevelure of my Mons Veneris; other friends and relatives may have the admired curls from my head, your memento is cut from the sacred spot of love.

She, presumably, is one of Walter's 1,200 exhaustively notated partners in Victorian sexual experiment.

Beatrice Pokingham is the true-born daughter of a marquis. She undergoes the routine sexual initiations (birchings, lesbian delights, bedroom frisking) at her boarding school, and forms a bosom friendship with bosomy Alice Marchmont, 'a beautiful, fair girl, with a plump figure, large sensuous eyes, and flesh as firm and smooth as ivory', who is destined to be Beatrice's tutor in the ways of the world. The two of them go to live in a Roman Catholic household in London. Its main devotions are to 'liaisons' and 'orgies' and a 'Paphian Circle', specialising in climax by flagellation.

Beatrice marries the aged rake, Lord Crim-Con (a pederast by preference). He is thirty, but looks fifty and acts seventy:

His youthful vigour had been expended long ago, by constant and enervating debauchery, and now instead of being able to enter the lists of love in a genuine manner, he had a perfect plethora of disgusting leches, which he required to be enacted before he could experience sensual excitement.

Orgies are not for weaklings. He dies during a disgusting lech which is, even for him, too much, involving as it does concurrent carnality from two young male pages and his ever-willing spouse.

As a very rich widow Beatrice embarks on a strenuous career of debauchery. Sick with galloping consumption she is finally ordered to Madeira for her health and seduces the doctor treating her and every servant in her retinue (en masse) before returning to England, exhausted, to pen her chronicle for Walter. The novel is replete with evasive euphemisms borrowed from predecessors such as Cleland, among them 'engines of love' (see FANNY HILL), and 'the sacred spot of love'. Even for an adolescent schoolboy in the puritanical 1950s it was an unexciting text but it tells one everything that one needs to know about the 'Other Victorians'.

Lanark: A Life in Four Books, Alasdair Gray, 1981

Gray's novel is a lifetime's work. Begun in 1954, it finally saw print, in its complete and decorative form, twenty-seven years later with the small Edinburgh firm of Canongate. It has been, since then, showered with prizes and its author hailed as the greatest Scottish novelist since the Wizard of the North, Walter Scott. Unlike the *Waverley* novels, however, *Lanark* was, and remains, a tough nut to crack for most readers. Particularly Americans, for whom Gray's novel might as well have been written by the Klingons' General Chang.

Following the *in medias res* rule of the epic, *Lanark* begins at Book Three, with the Prologue and Epilogue similarly perversely displaced. The narrative adopts three distinctly different stylistic modes. Most striking to the eye are the exuberant and erotic cover illustrations Gray designed (a feature which made production of the book unusually expensive). In the primary storyline, a character who cannot remember his name, and so adopts that of a small town ('Lanark'), finds himself in a mysterious world which has the characteristics of Glasgow. It is identified as 'Unthank' (ungrateful place). The hero, searching for a few gleams of sunlight and his own identity, develops a scaly skin condition, 'dragonhide' (a transparent allegory of Gray's own eczema), which will eventually metamorphose him into the thing traditionally slain in literature. W. S. Burroughs' 'mugwumps' in NAKED LUNCH may also come to mind. Gray's prose is characterised by its air of surreal mannerism:

He looked at them and saw their faces did not fit. The skin on the skulls crawled and twitched like half-solid paste. All the heads in his angle of vision seemed irregular lumps, like potatoes but without a potato's repose: potatoes with crawling surfaces punctured by holes which opened and shut, holes blocked with coloured jelly or fringed with bone stumps, elastic holes through which air was sucked or squirted, holes secreting salt, wax, spittle and snot. He grasped a pencil in his trouser pocket, wishing it were a knife he could thrust through his cheek and use to carve his face down to the clean bone. But that was foolish. Nothing clean lay under the face. He thought of sectioned brains, palettes, eyeballs and ears seen in medical diagrams and butcher's shops. He thought of elastic muscle, pulsing tubes, gland sacks full of lukewarm fluid, the layers of cellular and fibrous and granular tissues inside a head. What was felt as tastes, caresses, dreams and thoughts could be seen as a cleverly articulated mass of garbage.

The second stream in *Lanark* – the story of 'Duncan Thaw' – is realistic, a recognisable transcript of Gray's own life in conventional narrative style. It is a grimly unvarnished tale, more reminiscent of the austere late 1940s and early 1950s than the swinging seventies. 'Let Glasgow flourish by telling the truth' is the motto on Gray's frontispiece. It's a grim truth. Duncan, believing himself to be a sex murderer, commits suicide.

Lanark is embellished with a number of flamboyantly eccentric features. For example, a genre-bending meeting between Thaw and his creator, Gray; an owlishly elaborate 'Index of Plagiarisms', covering everyone, from Kafka to Walt Disney, who may be thought to have been an influence on the author. Ralph Waldo Emerson, it is sagely recorded, is *not* plagiarised. Looming over the whole is a sense of vast, historical, social and personal deprivation. 'Why are you content with so little?' Lanark is asked. He replies with the question: 'What else can I have?'

Culturally the impact of *Lanark* has been momentous. James Campbell's verdict, 'probably the greatest Scottish novel of the century', attracted little contradiction (I might timidly venture the work of Lewis Grassic Gibbon). It was, as Joyce said of *Finnegans Wake*, a book to keep the professors busy, and a Gray industry subsequently cranked up in the Scottish universities. Gray himself was appointed writer-in-residence at Glasgow University. Wry as ever, he claimed *Lanark* was 'overrated'.

Las babas del diablo, Julio Cortázar, 1956

The Spanish translates as 'Drool of the Devil' but the story is universally known as *Blow-Up*, even among Hispanic commentators. *Blow-Up* is a title which lacks the unusual sheen of diabolic spittle but one which inextricably links Cortázar to the cult-classic Antonioni film. The latter punningly records explosive 'blow-ups' as well as the process of photographic enlargement (the ostensible subject of Cortázar's story). Antonioni gratefully acknowledged Cortázar's influence on his film.

Cortázar's calling-card novel *Hopscotch* also has a nudgingly meaningful title. I find that work challenging to the point of cruel and unnatural punishment for the reader. In *Blow-Up* (I'll call it that) Cortázar grasps the golden rule of fiction: if you can't keep it simple, keep it short. This, even more briefly, is how it goes.

It's Paris, 7 November, year unknown. A Sunday. A month ago to the day, an event occurred which is now recalled by a Franco-Chilean translator of political documents, Roberto Michel – possibly an exile. We don't know that for certain, nor any other fact about his life. He sits in front of his Remington typewriter, fingers twitching with a life of their own.

On that Sunday, last month, the sun shone – it was the last warm day of autumn – and, to enjoy it, he took a walk next to the Seine. Michel is a keen amateur photographer and had his 1.2.2 Contax round his neck. He stopped on the leafy Île Saint-Louis where, some distance away, he saw a beautiful woman of a certain age and a handsome, clearly nervous adolescent sitting on a park bench.

It might be the lad's first pick-up, he thinks, with an attractive lady of easy virtue – or perhaps a respectable older lady who felt a passing whim for young love. He takes their picture and is seen doing it. The boy runs away; the woman confronts Michel, angrily. Later, in his darkroom, he enlarges the photograph, vastly, to squeeze the narrative out of it. Everything changes. Now visible in the background is a 'horrible black car', and in it sits a male predator (?). Was the woman pimping the boy – or worse?

The characters and situation swim out of the photograph, in what may be Michel's trance or some Poe-like invasion of the Gothic. The story plays with the unreliability of the instruments and sense organs on which, frustratingly but necessarily, we have to rely. But what else do we have? Divine revelation?

The book opens:

> It'll never be known how this has to be told, in the first person or in the second, using the third person plural, or continually inventing modes that will serve for nothing.

Thereafter Roberto's typewriter keeps running wildly out of control. At one point it scolds the author's fingers with a peremptory 'cut it short'. At another Mr Remington tells Monsieur Michel he's fantasising – writing 'fabricated unrealities', for God's sake. Stick to the facts. But what *are* the facts?

A camera (who says it never lies?) says one thing in long shot, then something quite different in close-up. *Blow-Up* is a fable which boils down to acid-drop dimensions the problems which face all storytellers, from the child telling a bored parent what happened that day at school to Marcel Proust and his madeleine. It proffers an invitation to pontificate that critics have found impossible to resist. This is a taste of what more advanced minds make of *Blow-Up*:

> The sentence in 'Apocalipsis' [another self-referential Cortázar story] about *Blow-Up* and *Las babas del diablo* refers to a polysemiosis, to an exemplary complication of the relationship

between different sign systems. It announces or forewarns the apparition of the semiotic ghost. The semiotic ghost is an out-of-control, heterological appearance within the text. [*Julio Cortázar: New Readings*, Carlos J. Alonso]

Ah, now we understand.

The Last Evenings on Earth, Roberto Bolaño, 1997

Bolaño had fewer evenings on earth than most of us. This collection of snapshot stories is the best introduction to his remarkable, short-lived talent. The background to his life is visible everywhere, either as grim scenario or as black mood. He was a chronically uneasy man. The son of a truck driver, he dropped out of high school. He was dyslexic but intensely poetic, and fed his mind with stolen books. Theft added savour to them. As a young man of anarcho-socialist beliefs, he was briefly imprisoned after the 1973 Pinochet coup and afterwards fled the country where opposition could now mean death.

He lived mainly in Mexico, where he wrote for a tiny fraction of the Hispanophonic world. Even after democracy returned to Chile, Bolaño could never make peace with his home country. His constituency, for most of his writing life, before fame kicked in, was various coteries. It was a world in which editors of 'little magazines' (as dictatorial as Pinochet) would decree that 'one Chilean poet per issue' was more than enough. He was always conscious, Bolaño said, 'of our useless pointy heads and the abominable death of Isaak Babel'. He opposed everything – as anarchic in literature as politics – and offended every Hispanic literary establishment by declaring that 'magic realism stinks'. He achieved worldwide readership in his very last years (and ton-loads of it posthumously) but died aged fifty in Barcelona, of, it is assumed, drink, drugs, depression and unquenchable rage. It was one of the many ironies of his life that he died third-in-line for the next liver transplant that would have given him more years in which to rage.

The Last Evenings on Earth assembles shards of the broken life of the exile writer. No 'grounded' relationships are possible. The narrator-hero-observer in some of the strung-together chapters is 'B' – not quite Bolaño. A main character is Augusto Pinochet. His name is never mentioned but the old bastard is 'there'. He would outlive Bolaño by decades. His liver worked just fine.

In the opening story, 'Sensini', 'B' is a young Chilean writer working as a night-watchman in Spain. He opens a correspondence with an Argentinian exile, Sensini, whom he knows by name from the poetry competitions they both enter. They never meet, but the relationship – conducted by stamped envelope – is intimate and permeated with an 'odd sensation of fragility'. Sensini has lost contact with his son, Gregorio (named in honour of Kafka's Gregor Samsa), who may or may not be in a mass grave: one of the 'disappeared' in Argentina's 'dirty war'. Sensini dies after some years, without ever learning Gregorio's fate. Years later Sensini's daughter arrives to tell 'B' that the relationship her father had with him was the most important of the older man's life – more, evidently, than any relationship he'd had with her. They smoke on the terrace, as night falls, and silently ponder this fact. 'The little world of letters is terrible as well as ridiculous', the story concludes.

'Henri Simon Leprince', another story in the collection, centres on an excessively minor resistance hero, the merest of footnotes in French literature, who gains entry to his desired literary set only by running small errands for more talented writers as part of their resistance effort. His is a 'modest and repellent' marginality permeated with the terror of being insufficiently talented. Which he is. Is 'B'?

The best piece (best written, and best constructed, that is) in the collection, arguably the best thing Bolaño ever published, gives the book its title. 'B' and his philistine father, once a champion boxer and still in his lusty forties, go on vacation to Acapulco. It is 1975. B's father insists on hiring a Ford Mustang – a macho vehicle for a macho guy. 'B' has brought with him a volume of French surrealist poetry: a volume for a wimp. 'B''s only pleasure during the ghastly vacation is rising early to swim in the ocean. He is contemplating suicide. But the good times must roll. Father and son have iguana for lunch and drink too much. 'B''s father demands nocturnal 'action'. That climaxes in a whorehouse where, over a dispute at the card table, it looks as if the troublesome parent is going to be killed. 'B', throughout, has felt 'disaster is approaching'. He will never travel with his father again.

The Last of the Mohicans: A Narrative of 1757, James Fenimore Cooper, 1826

I saw the 1936 film version when I was eight years old (in 1946, in an Edinburgh flea-pit) and the 1992 version soon after it came out (more comfortably, but less excitedly). The first starred Randolph Scott, veteran of many Westerns. That's where (in my unregenerate childhood) I placed this version. Hopalong Cassidy, Hawkeye. . . what was the difference?

The 1992 film has a much more sensitive, and thought-provoking, portrayal of Hawkeye, as played by Daniel Day-Lewis, who blends civilisation and 'savagery' to create a complex kind of hero-type. Looking back, I now see the 1936 version as imbued with a sense of 'manifest destiny' – the assumption that God had brought the White Man into America to take whatever he needed from the country. If that meant extermination, whether of the passenger pigeon or the 'Red Man', so be it. No criminal actions involved, only the working out of God's will. The 1992 film, on the other hand, reflected the uneasy sense that modern America owes its emergence if not to genocide, then certainly to serious mistreatment of the indigenous population, which comes close. Perhaps America simply misconstrued God's will. What then of the raw material (Fenimore Cooper's novel) which produced these diverse ideological underpinnings?

The Last of the Mohicans is the second volume of the Leatherstocking Tales (Leatherstocking aka Natty Bumppo appears here as the scout Hawkeye). In conceiving the novel, Fenimore Cooper wanted to write something

celebratory for the fiftieth anniversary of the 1776 Revolution. Things had moved on. The novel was published just a few years before the decisive phase of the Indian Removal policy (ethnic cleansing, avant la lettre).

The action is centred around Fort William Henry in upper New York State. There is an improbable romantic plot centred on Alice and Cora, the two delectable daughters of the fort's commander. The latter attracts the villainous desires of a treacherous Indian guide, Magua (aka 'Le Renard Subtil' or cunning fox), who lusts to make her his squaw – a fate infinitely worse than death. Magua is a very bad Indian. The 'good Indians' are represented by the ancient Chief Chingachgook and his son Uncas – the fin de ligne of the Mohicans.

The novel and both film versions have as their big set-piece scene the (historical) massacre of the disarmed white men by massed Indians, incited by (unhistorical) Magua:

> [He] placed his hands to his mouth, and raised the fatal and appalling whoop. The scattered Indians started at the well-known cry, as coursers bound at the signal to quit the goal; and directly there arose such a yell along the plain, and through the arches of the wood, as seldom burst from human lips before. They who heard it listened with a curdling horror at the heart, little inferior to that dread which may be expected to attend the blasts of the final summons.
>
> More than two thousand raving savages broke from the forest at the signal, and threw themselves across the fatal plain with instinctive alacrity . . . The flow of blood might be likened to the outbreaking of a torrent; and as the natives became heated and maddened by the sight, many among them even kneeled to the earth, and drank freely, exultingly, hellishly, of the crimson tide.

Legend has it that thousands of white men died. The recent estimate, from archival study, is around a hundred. History records no blood-drinking.

Uncas attempts to rescue the abducted

Cora from Magua in a dramatic cliff-side struggle in which the good Indian dies and the bad Indian lives – only to be shot by the ever-present Hawkeye with his trusty 'Long Rifle'. The noble Mohican people are, with Uncas now bound for the happy hunting ground, well on their way to extinction. It gives a fresh twist to the old frontier proverb: the only good Indian is a dead Indian. The Delaware Indian sage, Tamenund, wraps things up with the declaration:

> The pale-faces are masters of the earth, and the time of the red-men has not yet come again.

What do the bloodthirsty (literally) savages expect? Civil rights?

Left Behind, Tim LaHaye and Jerry Jenkins, 1995–2007

Religious fiction fills endless footage in modern American bookstores. For people like me, these are the walk-by shelves: like the similarly uninviting massed ranks of 'teen fiction'. (Why don't they have old guys' fiction – *Me and My Prostate, I Can't Find My Glasses Without My Glasses*, etc.) I'm strictly science fiction, crime and classics.

Religious fiction isn't a new genre – PILGRIM'S PROGRESS still sells – but a new development in the recent decades is religious fiction's 'book of the day' bestselling popularity and, most strikingly, its doctrinal aggressiveness. The plot which has proved most successful recently is based around 'end times'. The end times themselves will begin with the Rapture, which, unlike other apocalyptic events, will be 'signless' – i.e. unannounced. Guiltless children (even those in the process of being aborted) and the Christian-minded will be instantaneously teleported into Heaven. For the Remnant, some of whom (although not the abortionists) can still be saved, there will follow seven years of Tribulation. During this period of pestilence, conflict and global catastrophe, the Antichrist will come to power. He will use diplomacy to create a New World Order, which will last three and a half years. In this time he will rebuild

Babylon and offer Israel a spurious covenant. Israel itself will be transformed by the 'ingathering', when many Jews repent their great error and accept Christ as Messiah, leaving the intractable 'Satanic Jews' to suffer damnation. The converted Jews will ally themselves with the army of the righteous for Armageddon. Inevitable victory in the battle will herald the return of Christ, who will establish his thousand-year kingdom on earth in a purged Middle East.

You don't buy it? According to a Time/CNN poll conducted in July 2002, fifty-nine per cent of Americans believe that 'the prophecies of the Book of Revelation will come true'. Chew on that, unbeliever. The site www.raptureready.com closely monitors current events to compile a 'Rapture Index' using forty-five measures, from 'False Christs', through 'Beast Government', to 'Floods'. It's currently, as I write, at an all-time high.

If you really seriously want to be rapture-ready, start with LaHaye and Jenkins' *Left Behind* and keep reading the sixteen-volume series (the last, *Kingdom Come*, was published in 2007) until people around you start, mysteriously, to disappear. The debut novel opens on a 747 flight to London. All the good Christians are suddenly teleported to Heaven, leaving little piles of clothes and uneaten lasagne behind them. (Stephen King had used this idea five years earlier in *The Langoliers*. But why should the Antichrist have all the good stories?)

Rayford Steele, the sin-stained pilot of the enraptured jumbo, lands at Chicago to discover that his wife Irene ('attractive and vivacious, even at 40') and most of the congregation of the church of which she is a born-again member have been beamed up. The novels go on to chronicle the seven-year Tribulation for those like Rayford (who's been casting lustful eyes at a neighbour – hence unraptured) and his daughter Chloe (a formerly free-thinking Stanford student) who were left behind. Unceasing battle rages between the Remnant (gun-loving American Christians) and the evildoers, easily recognised by the mark of the beast on their foreheads. In command is the Antichrist himself, Nicolae Jetty Carpathia, the thirty-three-year-old president of Romania, who uses his promotion to secretary-general of the UN to create a common European currency and then a Global Community of which he (after his death and resurrection) becomes Supreme Potentate – with his capital in New Babylon (Baghdad). From here he fights the bad fight with all his might. The good fight is led by the Trib Force: a motley guerrilla group with, at their head, ex-747 pilots and Jesus-accepting Jews.

This is not a novel I'd put on my 'must read before you die' list. But, on second thoughts, it might be wise to take a peek, though I wouldn't recommend it as airport-lounge reading. Can fifty-nine per cent of Americans be wrong? Pray that they are.

The Leopard, Giuseppe Tomasi di Lampedusa, 1958

In my experience, talk to any cultivated Italian about the world in general and they will come out with the statement 'things must change, in order to stay the same'. It's said with that automatic assent we give to proverbial truth: the accumulated wisdom of mankind in the homeliest of verbal packaging. The saying originates in Tomasi di Lampedusa's novel, where it is wreathed in ironies which slice its confident-sounding truth into so much salami.

The Leopard is a thinly veiled chronicle of the author's own family, centred on his grandfather. Up to that point in history, the Tomasi had been princes in Sicily. In the following three generations they became – the author himself among them – ordinary citizens. One of the highpoints of the novel – sumptuously staged in the Visconti film adaptation – is a huge ball to 'present to the world' the bride-to-be of the heir to the aristocratic Salina family. This occupies all of Chapter 6. It is 1862 and Italy is enjoying a momentary lull in the turmoil surrounding the Risorgimento. Fracturing the extended description of the ballroom (the author excels in interior description) is the following anachronism:

From the ceiling the gods, reclining on gilded couches, gazed down smiling and inexorable as a summer sky. They thought themselves eternal;

but a bomb manufactured in Pittsburgh, Penn., was to prove the contrary in 1943.

The palazzo of the author's family was similarly destroyed in the Allied bombing of Sicily, during the Second World War. The gods did not intervene. Nor did things thereafter remain the same. They went, for the Tomasi di Lampedusa family, to hell.

The narrative of The Leopard opens in 1860. The country that is soon to become modern Italy is in ferment. Palermo, in the Kingdom of the Two Sicilies, is under siege. In these momentous times Fabrizio Corbera, Prince Salina, elects to visit a brothel in the dark quarter of the city, returning to offer the same gift of himself to his wife later in the night. The big question for him is how to 'keep things the same'. Drawing on the kinds of survival techniques suggested to princes by Macchiavelli, Don Fabrizio encourages his heir and nephew, Tancredi, to marry the daughter of a rich, vulgar local politician rather than forging an obvious link (as would have happened in previous generations) with Don Fabrizio's daughter. It staves off the downfall of his house. But only for a generation. Tancredi (it is he who makes the pompous statement about change) proves to be a self-seeking opportunist.

Hanging over the narrative is the sense that the fin de ligne of the Corbera family is symptomatic of the weariness of Sicily – a land exhausted by its own contentious history. Don Fabrizio is offered a seat – and power – in the new senate. He declines. He and his region are too tired. As he explains to the diplomat from the insurgent north who offers the 'honour':

Twenty-five centuries of excellent, wholly diverse cultures: all of them came from outside, none of them originated within us and we have in no way dictated the tone . . . I do not say this to complain: it is our fault. But all the same – we are tired and empty.

Tomasi di Lampedusa made the odd comment that the most important character in the novel is the Don's Great Dane, Bendico. The novel's last image is of the disposal of the dog's stuffed body as it is thrown from the window of the small house where the last of the Corberas live:

> A few minutes later what remained of Bendico was flung into a corner of the courtyard visited every day by the dustman. During the flight down from the window his form recomposed itself for an instant; in the air one could have seen dancing a quadruped with long whiskers, and its right foreleg seemed to be raised in imprecation. Then all found peace in a heap of livid dust.

The Leopard is Tomasi di Lampedusa's only significant work of literature. He was dying as he wrote it and went to his grave with the work unpublished and everywhere rejected. It went on to become a worldwide bestseller and is routinely cited as the best Italian novel ever written. Some would even drop 'Italian'.

Life and Fate, Vasily Grossman, 1959

This is a big book, nine hundred pages or more in any readable version, on the very biggest of topics. And, for the author, a dangerous topic. The KGB not only confiscated the manuscript but the ribbons on which the text had been typed. Can a novel receive higher honour? Grossman's position within, and on the margin of, the Soviet Union was perpetually conflicted. Sometimes he presented the aspect of the despised 'running dog' (there are long analyses in the novel of the Russian 'slave soul'); sometimes he veered life-threateningly close to dissidence. During the cultural 'thaw' Khrushchev himself intimated approval of *Life and Fate* alongside his censors' wonderfully absurd caveat that it probably could not be published for three hundred years.

Life and Fate aligns itself knowingly with *War and Peace*, a book which Grossman read while covering – from the front line – the Battle of Stalingrad as a reporter for the party newspaper, *Red Star*. There was a

difference, as one of the characters in the novel explains to an unbelieving general – Tolstoy was not present at the war he chronicled.

The novel begins in autumn 1942, in a German concentration camp for Russian captives. 'These camps... were the expanding cities of a new Europe' and the USSR has its own 'labour camps' (a bureaucratic euphemism equivalent to 'concentration camp'), where millions of lives vanish 'beneath the ice of Siberia' in a quixotic bid to erase 'the birthmarks of capitalism'. Grossman's narrative switches intermittently and abruptly to Moscow, the provinces, and – looming over all – Stalingrad. A reporter by training, he captures domestic life at the front – the business of eating, shaving, defecating, letterwriting. The things that make soldiers human. As well as, of course, what robs them of their humanity: dying.

Among the huge cast of characters is Viktor Shtrum, a scientist and a self-portrait (Grossman was also a scientist by education). Viktor, a theoretical physicist by specialism, is the archetypal absent-minded professor. His research is constantly meddled with by the Party, which intends to bend even particle physics to its ideological template. The idea of Einsteinian 'relativity' plays over the narrative:

> Physics was determining the course of the twentieth century ... Just as Stalingrad was now determining the course of events on every front of the World War.

Stalin and Hitler have cameos in the novel. They are rabid anti-Semites, which in both dictators is depicted as a symptom of 'lack of talent'. But Stalin is the shrewder monster. In an extraordinary scene, after Viktor has been denounced (usually a one-way ticket to Siberia via the Lubyanka), the paramount leader phones him: does he have all the equipment and foreign research papers he needs? Why this extraordinary solicitude? Stalin foresees the bomb that the state needs. That need overrides ideology. Viktor remains unpurged.

For Grossman, Fascism and 'the concept of "a man"' cannot co-exist. But what has communism done to humanity? In Moscow a blind ex-soldier asks a woman for help to get on a tram: 'the woman swore at him and pushed him away. He lost his balance and sat down on the pavement'. The episode is in no way material to the plot. But it poses the question: where did this inhuman behaviour stem from? A German SS interrogator tells a Russian prisoner, 'You may think you hate us but what you hate is yourselves – yourselves in us.' These hints at totalitarian parallels were highly dangerous and are handled lightly.

In the largest sense (and the dimensions of this novel are cosmically large) war revives 'old Russia' for the salvation of 'New Russia'. The beauty of Stalingrad is that the ferocity of the battle makes ideology irrelevant. Questions can be left hanging.

Life and Fate was written in the culturally more relaxed period after Stalin's death, which did not stop the KGB scooping it up in 1960, lock, stock and ribbon. It was smuggled out as microfilm in 1974, published in the West in 1980 and, in the dying days of the evil empire, translated into English. Vasily Grossman had died, wretchedly, in 1964. He would never know the answers history would give to the questions his book posed. And that he was right.

The Life and Opinions of Tristram Shandy, Gentleman, Laurence Sterne, 1759–1767

Why, in his late forties, Sterne should have embarked on writing a novel has never been entirely clear. The first two books of *Tristram Shandy* were composed 'under the greatest heaviness of heart'. Sterne was pressed for money and his wife, maddened by her husband's flagrant sexual delinquencies, had been temporarily committed to an asylum. His lungs were giving out. Not the ideal circumstances in which to produce a comic masterpiece.

Tristram Shandy opens with one of the funniest, and cleverest, scenes in British fiction. Where, if you want to tell the story of your 'life', do you start? At the beginning, of course. Conception. That event for the homunculus who would become Tristram

happened in the master bedroom at Shandy Hall – which the embryo forming in his mother's womb is one day destined to inherit. Mr Shandy is a man who runs his household according to strict rules. Like clockwork, you might say. And, once a month, he does indeed wind the grandfather clock to whose chimes Shandy Hall runs:

> he had made it a rule for many years of his life, – on the first Sunday-night of every month throughout the whole year, – as certain as ever the Sunday-night came, – to wind up a large house-clock, which we had standing on the back-stairs head, with his own hands:— And being somewhere between fifty and sixty years of age at the time I have been speaking of, – he had likewise gradually brought some other little family concernments to the same period, in order, as he would often say to my uncle Toby, to get them all out of the way at one time, and be no more plagued and pestered with them the rest of the month.

As he is in the middle of the second 'little family concernment', assuring himself of an heir, his wife asks him if he's wound the clock.

> Good G. . . ! cried my father, making an exclamation, but taking care to moderate his voice at the same time, – Did ever woman, since the creation of the world, interrupt a man with such a silly question?

So at this, the moment of his conception, the homunculus who will become Tristram Shandy, gentleman, is for ever skewed.

Sterne's novel (so to call it, not everyone does) is replete with jokes which could have found a happy home in the movie *Airplane!* Tristram's Uncle Toby suffers from a carefully unspecified wound – though every indication is that it is somewhere in the vicinity of the groin. The Widow Wadman (who has marital designs) asks him where precisely he was wounded. 'The Battle of Namur,' he answers, hauling out maps to show exactly where the mysterious abdominal wound was incurred.

Other episodes in the novel could have come out of the more broadly comic *American Pie*. Little Tristram, for example, is circumcised by a falling sash window, which Mr Shandy (nothing really works by clockwork in the hall) has for years omitted to mend. Why was Tristram's little member in that spot? Because the servant had forgotten to put a chamber pot under the bed, and the most sanitary recourse was peeing out of the window. Help is called for. Mr Shandy rushes off, not for bandages (while Tristram is still, so to speak, undergoing the 'procedure' at the windowsill) but to find an encyclopaedia and relevant information as to what the ancients' opinions were on the merits of foreskin-snipping.

Technically, what *Tristram Shandy* bequeathed to English fiction was immediacy – 'writing to the moment.' Sterne's sign manual is the 'dash' – typically a 5-em thing which slices through the narrative (speeding up one's reading in the process). *Tristram Shandy*, with its expressive typography (super large capitals, different fonts, the creative use of white space and blocked pages) is, among other things, a tribute to the growing skill of the mid-eighteenth-century London printing trade. The fluidity Sterne aimed at was that of speech. 'Writing,' he wrote, 'when properly managed (as you may be sure I think mine is) is but a different name for conversation.' As Sterne 'managed' it, fictional narrative ceased to be a 'history', a past-tense thing. It ceased to lumber. Sterne, it might be said, put wings on the English novel. Tristram, incidentally, never gets his life down on paper because he's living 365 times faster than even he can write. Quarts and pint pots don't come into it.

Little Big Man, Thomas Berger, 1964

A turn-of-the-tide novel: the tide in question being American attitudes to Native Americans. Historically, Berger's novel and the spin-off film take their place alongside such things as Marlon Brando's sending a Native American, diatribe in hand, to collect his Oscar (for *The Godfather*). The collective mind was being corrected on the question of the previously misnamed Red Indians (they were neither). Too late for them, of course, but that's history.

Little Big Man is narrated by the 111-year-old Jack Crabb, who has survived into the mid-1950s. His reminiscences are taken down by Ralph Fielding Snell, a stuffily self-important 'man of letters'. The story opens:

> I am a white man and never forget it, but I was brought up by the Cheyenne Indians from the age of ten.

The novel begins and ends with bloody massacre, narrated in a kind of 'so-what?' comic tone, as by a man who is now so far beyond the normal perimeter of life that nothing matters much to him. It is the first massacre which makes him what the Cheyenne 'arrogantly' call a 'human being' (no other tribe – even the paleface – is seen as human). Young Jack's father, a certifiably mad preacher, has taken the family west, on a wagon train. They are met – in a fairly friendly way – by a bunch of 'redskins', led by a chief called Old Lodge Skins.

Before they move on, Jack's father gives the natives a few swigs of hard liquor. A big mistake. High on firewater, the Indians stake Jim's father (still preaching madly) to the ground with arrows to die, rape the more eligible women in the train, and kill the men. They refrain from scalping them, observing the nicety that this is not a war party. Jack they take with them, along with his sister Caroline. She thinks, wrongly, they intend to make her a squaw princess. Actually, she is so big and ugly they think she's a man. The next day the Indians return with some ponies, by way of reparation. The surviving women – safe from these savages when sober – give them the rough side of their tongues.

'Crazy Horse', the novel suggests, is an entirely appropriate name for all of them, redskin or paleface. Though it's sad about Crabb Sr, who didn't come west to end up like Saint Sebastian. The Indians hold on to the boy Jack as a kind of mascot, and rename him Little Big Man after he makes his first kill. He is reabsorbed into white society after one of the routine reciprocal massacres by the US cavalry. He saves himself by shouting out 'God Save George Washington', which the sabre-wielding cavalryman recognises as rather unusual for a Cheyenne war whoop.

Thereafter young Jack rattles around the frontier. He is adopted by a childless couple in Missouri, moves on, marries a Swede, falls into bad ways in saloons, tries gunfighting, mule-skinning and gambling. He takes a Mexican wife who puts so much chili in his tortillas that it's divorce for the sake of his liver. He returns to the Cheyenne and Old Lodge Skins and has another family, all of whom are wiped out in the Washita Creek massacre by the genocidal Custer. Most of the victims were women and children.

Revenge comes when, as a cavalry scout, he plays a dubious part in the Battle of the Little Bighorn in 1876: 'Custer's last stand'. Reunited with Old Lodge Skins, Jack/Little Big Man notes (the white man in him speaking chauvinistically):

'He [Custer] was not scalped, Grandfather. The Indians respected him as a great chief.'

Old Lodge Skins smiled at me as at a foolish child.

'No my son,' says he. 'I felt his head. They did not scalp him because he was getting bald.'

Custer's vanquisher, Sitting Bull, ended up in Buffalo Bill's 'Wild West' circus, for $50 a week, signing photographs. How was the West won? Pure craziness, answers Berger's wonderful novel. Don't believe everything you see on the screen.

The Lodger, Marie Belloc Lowndes, 1913

Lowndes' is the best of the many works of fiction inspired by the Jack the Ripper panic of 1888, in which some five (possibly more) East End prostitutes were savagely mutilated and killed by a still tantalisingly unknown killer. Over the years *The Lodger* has inspired a play, an opera, and at least four films, notably Hitchcock's classic silent version in 1927, subtitled 'A Story of the London Fog'.

The action opens in the boarding house of Mr and Mrs Bunting, retired servants who have fallen on hard times. Clothes are being pawned, rooms rented. A mysterious lodger, 'Mr Sleuth', takes up residence. Lowndes transplants the scene of the murders from the Ripper's actual East End killing ground to Regent's Park, which figures centrally together with Madame Tussaud's 'chamber of horrors'. The action is brought forward twenty years to the early twentieth century with forensic fingerprinting, tube travel, and – most atmospherically – gaslight, the street illumination whose velvety lustre turned foggy, night-time London into a theatre set.

Their Mr Sleuth is a very odd lodger, the Buntings discover. He appears to be suffering from religious mania. He has an endless supply of gold sovereigns. (Why, then, is he pigging it with them at ten bob a week?) He may be a medical man. He will not eat meat. He carries a bag, always locked, whose contents are wholly mysterious. He undertakes 'experiments', often using Mrs B's gas-stove for the purpose. There are dark suspicions of cannibalism. The increasingly distraught Buntings note that he is given to going out at night, heavily cloaked, and the next day the newspapers report the 'Avenger' has done it again. A letter is published in the press:

The culprit, according to my point of view, is a quiet, pleasant-looking gentleman who lives somewhere in the West End of London. He has, however, a tragedy in his past life. He is the husband of a dipsomaniac wife. She is, of course, under care, and is never mentioned in the house where he lives, maybe with his widowed mother and perhaps a maiden sister. They notice that he has become gloomy and brooding of late, but he lives his usual life, occupying himself each day with some harmless hobby. On foggy nights, once the quiet household is plunged in sleep, he creeps out of the house, maybe between one and two o'clock, and swiftly makes his way straight to what has become The Avenger's murder area . . . I give this theory, Sir, for what it is worth, but I confess that I am amazed the police have so wholly confined their inquiries to the part of London where these murders have been actually committed.

Signed 'Émile Gaboriau' (who was the father of the detective novel with his FILE NO. 113), it's manifestly from the hand of Mr Sleuth. There is a dramatic climax in Madame Tussaud's chamber of horrors, but the lodger eludes capture and disappears, never to be seen again. And 'as suddenly and as mysteriously as they had begun the "Avenger" murders stopped'.

Of its spine-chilling kind, Lowndes' novel is up there with The Silence of the Lambs. And the Ripper enigma continues to tickle the public fancy. Who was he? It was a challenge picked up by the most successful woman crime writer of the twenty-first century, Patricia Cornwell, who in 2002 came out with what was intended to be the definitive monograph: Portrait of a Killer: Jack the Ripper – Case Closed. The man in the dock (or rather a speculative dock, previously occupied by princes of the blood royal, innumerable medical students, and even Gladstone) was the artist Walter Sickert, famous for his 'Camden Town' pictures of blowsy ladies of the night. Did he from time to time lay down his brush and pick up a razor? Cornwell is widely alleged to have done some ripperwork of her own on her substantial collection of Sickert canvases, to get at his DNA. Neither Ripperologists, nor admirers of the artist, were much impressed by Ms Cornwell's sleuthing efforts, and felt she should have stuck to ripping yarns.

Lolita, Vladimir Nabokov, 1955

The name Lolita was virtually unknown in the English-speaking world before the 1950s. Google it now and you will dredge up some of the rankest filth the internet has to offer. It has been channelled to the slavering pornhound via a work of the finest prose in the English language – by a Russian author for whom English was a third language. The novel's twisted route to publication is a story of interest in itself. The typescript was universally rejected by American publishers in the early 1950s ('Do you think I'm crazy?' asked one). An émigré, of aristocratic descent, Nabokov was an American university professor at the time. Lolita was first published by Maurice Girodias, as one of his 'dirty books', under the Olympia imprint in Paris in 1955. Girodias did not have many university professors on his list. Lolita given mainstream American and British publication in the last few years before Lady Chatterley blazed a trail for the new 'permissiveness' in fiction at the end of the decade. It helped Lolita to slip through that Nabokov's novel, unlike Lawrence's, had no 'four-letter words'.

Lolita, or the Confessions of a White Widowed Male, is a prison journal: part confession, part plea-bargain with the reader. Humbert Humbert (preposterous name) is, we gather, facing a charge of murder, not child abuse. (If it were the 2010s, rather than the 1950s, his confessed paedophilia might well attract a heavier penalty than the homicide of the even worse paedophile, Clare Quilty). Humbert's defence is crime passionnel: he did what he did for love. Love, that is, of a twelve-year-old girl. A secondary, and riskier, line of defence is that the cunning little 'nymphet' made him do it (Your Honour). If one follows the contours of Humbert's criminal career it runs thus: he comes to the New World of America to take possession of an inheritance from his oncle d'Amérique. He has been fixated on nymphets (little girls verging on puberty) ever since an episode in his own childhood with one called Annabel. Now a rentier, and a dilettante man of letters, Humbert lodges with a widow, Charlotte Haze, in the nowhere town of Ramsdale. He is infatuated with her pubescent daughter Dolores, affectionately nicknamed 'Lo' and 'Lolita'. He marries the widow – although he secretly despises her and her crass American ways – planning to murder her. Humbert is spared the trouble when, after reading his private journal, Charlotte runs madly into the street and is run over.

The widow picks up the orphaned Lolita from her summer stay at Camp Q. On their first night at the Enchanted Hunters Hotel, where they are obliged to share a room, he discovers that she is not, as he'd fondly expected, an American maiden but has been 'debauched' at the camp by the proprietor's oafish, thirteen-year-old son, Charlie. Humbert's indignation at the non-existence of the hymeneal innocence he was planning incestuously to violate is comic:

> Suffice it to say not a trace of modesty did I perceive in this beautiful hardly formed young girl whom modern co-education, juvenile *mores*, the campfire racket and so forth had utterly and hopelessly depraved.

Other sordid details emerge, notably Charlie's habit of frugally recycling 'a fascinating collection of contraceptives which he used to fish out of a . . . nearby lake . . . called Lake Climax'.

According to Humbert, Lolita seduces him. He is insistent on the point:

> Frigid women of the jury! I had thought that months, perhaps years would elapse before I dared to reveal myself to Dolores Haze; but by 6 she was wide awake, and by 6.15 we were technically lovers. I am going to tell you something very strange: it was she who seduced me.

Things get complicated thereafter, culminating in the slaughter of Quilty, who abducts Lolita, and her later death, obscurely, 'in childbed'. Humbert's death, of a broken heart (or rather, a coronary thrombosis), takes place in jail before his trial. The novel, hugely entertaining and more disturbing by the year, poses a teasing question: can fine writing exonerate a crime the tabloids (with their anything but fine prose) routinely label 'vile'?

London Fields, Martin Amis, 1989

London Fields is a novel much concerned with dying. Our planet, by the novel's calendar, will have expired with the millennium fireworks: a dried-up cinder. It's not clear what the rider of the AD 2000 apoca-lypse will be: whether a colliding asteroid, a new configuration of the sun, a voracious black hole, an HIV-like plague, or 'mutually assured destruction'. The bomb. But the end is nigh.

In a teasing foreword Amis divulges that he spent sleepless nights before coming up with the title. Forget any topographical association with London Fields, E8 (Hackney). The novel's action is centred on the other side of the city, around Portobello Road and environs. The allusion, one suspects, is to Falstaff's babbling about 'green fields' on his deathbed.

Amis, finally unburdened of his tedious *enfant terrible* epithet, was 40 years old when *London Fields* saw print. Life begins at that age, says the dubious proverb. In interviews given around the period *London Fields* was published Amis confided that 'the message has got through'. He was mortal. The novel is narrated by a dying man delivering a final testament in a dying city in a dying world. Amis himself has glimpsed the fact that, as the singer Jim Morrison put it, 'Nobody gets out of here alive'.

The narrative opens, disarmingly with a set of pseudo-candid utterances which, like the title, set the reader running in entirely wrong directions:

> This is a true story but I can't believe it's really happening. It's a murder story, too. I can't believe my luck. And a love story (I think), of all strange things, so late in the century, so late in the goddamned day.

Docufiction, crime fiction, romance, and science fiction. It's none and all of these. The speaker is Samson Young. He is the novel's author but also a player in its action – and finally its villain. 'Man, am I a reliable narrator', he exclaims at one self-satisfied point. He isn't: the novel he is writing finally turns round and bites him on the backside. There's a lot of this kind of postmodernist jesting. The heroine, for example, asks Sam to 'edit out' another character who is getting on her nerves. He declines.

Sam, a novelist who hasn't made it, has done a flat swap with fellow writer Mark Asprey (nom de plume Marius Appleby) who has, having sold out, made it big in New

York. *Success* was the title of an earlier novel by Amis. It was, indeed, very successful. Sam has been a London expatriate in New York for ten years. He has returned to die in 'the iodized shithouse that used to be England'. What is killing him we are not told – but that his dead father was a scientist working with plutonium is a broad hint. His 'true' novel' (i.e. *London Fields*) is not, we learn, going down well with his agent, Missy Harter.

On arrival Sam is picked up from Heathrow by a dicey limousine driver, Keith Talent, a failed armed robber, deadbeat husband, and paedophile. He is suspected of stubbing his ciggies out on his baby Kim's bottom. He occasionally rapes ('something of which a man might not easily speak'). His single talent is darts. There was a huge revival of interest in the 'last working class sport' in the 1980s, boosted by TV 'world' championships. Keith is unworking working class: his income is cheating at which he earns 'three times as much as the Prime Minister' while still drawing unemployment benefit.

On the journey from Heathrow Keith stops his vehicle (meter running) at his 'local', the Black Cross. It is here that Sam will be introduced to the novel's other two leading characters. Guy Clinch is 'good guy' to Keith's 'bad guy'. He's a banker – 'pointlessly good looking' – married to a 'brightly American' wife with a child called Marmaduke, who could take on *The Exorcist*'s Regan in the projectile vomiting stakes.

Calling the shots in what follows is Nicola Six – nicknamed '666': the fatal woman. She has cast herself as a 'murderee', but is as yet unsure whether Keith or Guy will do the necessary. She is sure, however, that the deed will take place on the fifth of November, to coincide with her 35th birthday and the total eclipse which will herald the end of the world. A grand exit.

What epigraph would one suggest for this novel (Amis does not supply one)? For me it would be Sam's 'Death is killing me' or Keith's more demotic, 'Life goes on innit.' *London Fields* was blackballed out of Booker Prize contention in 1989 because of a perception of misogyny.

Lord Jim, Joseph Conrad, 1900

Lord Jim revolves obsessively around an act only very cloudily described in the novel. Jim is a lad who becomes infatuated with the sea. He is romantic: a lover of Marryat. Fifty years later he would have been a lover of Hornblower. Eighty years on, a lover of Patrick O'Brian. Following his youthful dream, Jim gets his mate's certificate and takes up a post on the *Patna*. Conrad, an old sea dog, describes it with a contemptuous eye:

> a local steamer as old as the hills, lean like a greyhound, and eaten up with rust worse than a condemned water-tank. She was owned by a Chinaman, chartered by an Arab, and commanded by a sort of renegade New South Wales German.

The cargo is eight hundred pilgrims. 'Cattle', the German captain calls them.

The *Patna* hits some unidentified object underwater. It slips over it 'as easy as a snake crawling over a stick', but the vessel has sustained damage below the waterline. Jim goes down to investigate. A bulkhead plate is palpitating, like a boil about to burst. As he later recalls:

> 'I tell you it bulged. I was holding up my lamp along the angle-iron in the lower deck when a flake of rust as big as the palm of my hand fell off the plate, all of itself.' He passed his hand over his forehead. 'The thing stirred and jumped off like something alive while I was looking at it . . . What could I do – what?'

There are seven lifeboats – enough for one-third of the souls on board. Once the bulkhead goes, the ship will sink to the bottom like a stone. What Jim 'should' (not 'could') do, of course, is stay at his post and offload in an orderly fashion those who can be saved. But his imagination is too strong. He jumps into a lifeboat, joining the rat-officers (all but him) who have already left what they *know* to be a sinking ship. But Jim is not a born rat, he is an Englishman, and from then on for him: 'There was no going back. It was as if I had jumped into a well – into an ever-lasting deep hole'. Exactly why he can never quite explain to himself. The *Patna* does not sink. It is towed safely to port. On board, taking command during that perilous passage, is a French lieutenant, a scarred veteran with no imagination whatsoever, who risks his life because that is what officers do. 'Man is born a coward', he says. But man does not have to behave like one.

The court of inquiry strips Jim of his certificate. He drifts around the harbours of the world, doing any menial job until people discover who he is, as they always do. The chance for redemption comes when he is befriended by Conrad's series hero, alter ego and all-purpose narrator (as here), Marlow, and Marlow's friend – the German trader Stein. Stein's philosophy is that a man must 'in the destructive element immerse'. Face up to it. He gives Jim a chance to redeem himself by appointing him the post-manager of an Indonesian island, Patusan. Jim becomes a 'White Rajah' there, and brings order and decency. After an invasion by brigands, led by Gentleman Brown (less gentlemanly by far than Jim is now lordly), Jim gives up his life for 'his' people.

Lord Jim has long been the favourite among Conrad's longer works. One critic explains the novel's popularity with the observation that most of us have a *Patna* in our lives, which we labour either to forget or to atone for. You will find mine, if you care to look, in the last chapter of my memoir, *The Boy Who Loved Books*.

Lord of the Flies, William Golding, 1954

I read the book two years after it came out. I was seventeen. What survives from that primal reading (it's still vivid in my mind) is the question: what schools do they all come from? I was myself at a grammar school which had deluded itself it was a minor public school, despite all the kids being day boys, from all classes, given entrance and ruthlessly 'streamed' by eleven-plus results. The atmosphere was one of utter institutional neurosis.

The three principals in the opening chapters of *Lord of the Flies* are Ralph, Jack and Piggy. Ralph is introduced, vividly, in the first paragraph:

The boy with fair hair lowered himself down the last few feet of rock and began to pick his way toward the lagoon. Though he had taken off his school sweater and trailed it now from one hand, his grey shirt stuck to him and his hair was plastered to his fore-head.

The school sweater and grey shirt are the giveaway. A grammar-school boy. His slightly off-the-target slang – 'Whizzo!' – but perfectly grammatical speech and chronic self-doubt are also clear markers.

The character soon to be identified as Piggy emerges from the undergrowth. He has what he would call 'the runs', and Ralph an 'upset tummy'. 'I can't hardly move with all these creeper things', he groans. The grammatical solecism is all we need to know about his social background. Piggy talks a lot and every time he opens his mouth a speech error pops out: double negatives ('I didn't expect nothing'), wrong verbal concords ('we was attacked!'), bad definite articles ('them fruit'), lower-class slang ('You can't half swim' – doubtless with an unaspir-ated 'h'). He wears a greasy zipped wind-breaker and no uniform. But, oddly, he knows about 'megaphones'. He is the only boy who has worked out the complicated destruction of the plane, and the safety capsule which has landed them, by para-chute, on the island.

Finally, enter Jack Merridew marching his little troops like *Hitlerjugend*. Each boy (despite the tropical heat) is wearing a long black cloak with a ham-bone frill, and a square black cap with a silver badge on it. Their leader has a golden cap badge. Clearly enough these are public-school pupils – a school connected with a cathedral. Winchester or Westminster, I'd guess. Jack is the choir leader, a boy with power. Now unchecked by any superior power.

Ralph I picked out as one of my kind, liberal and decent but socially insecure. Jack is the product of the public-school system, confident: a natural leader. Most interesting is Piggy. What's his school background? To answer the question it's necessary to know something about the system of state secondary education set up in the early 1950s.

There were 'grammars' (like mine and Ralph's), secondary moderns (for the hopeless), and 'techs' – short for technical schools. Techs were peopled (for the few years they lasted) by kids who were good with their hands: practical, technologically minded. 'Superior' working class. They were interesting. Many of my closest friends in adolescence were products of the 'tech' on Colchester's North Hill (it later became a distinguished art college). That, as I spotted, was Piggy's background.

Novels mean different things to you at different periods of your life. That's what *Lord of the Flies* meant to me in 1956. Golding himself was what in Colchester was called a 'grammar bug'. He once said he would happily blow up every public school in England – and every Jack Merridew with them. He felt he lived *under*, not *in* the British class system – and, he despairingly concluded (and *Lord of the Flies* confirms), that system was indestructible. Blast Britain to smithereens with nuclear bombs, dump a bunch of innocent kids on an Edenic desert island, and class reasserts itself like Funny Putty – Jack Merridew the toff, Piggy the oik – thus it was, and thus it ever will be. All we can do is hope our Jack Merridews are nicer than Golding's.

Lost Illusions, Honoré de Balzac, 1837–43

Lost Illusions is a long novel in its own right, and forms part of Balzac's immensely long *Comédie humaine*. Despite that grand allusion to Dante, Balzac's horizons are strictly metropolitan. Although he occasionally ventures into the provinces with his narrative, Paris is the centre of the Balzacian universe. It's never been as important a place as Parisians think: an 'illusion' they have never lost. The novel is subtitled *The Two Poets* and cues the reader to expect a narrative about literature. But Balzac is a materialist. Literature, in his view, is not the gift of the muse but the product of the machine. *Lost Illusions* opens with an apostrophe to an obsolete printing press:

> At the time when this story opens, the Stanhope press and the ink-distributing roller were not as yet in general use in small provincial printing establishments.

The novel goes on in this 'Bibliography 101' vein for several pages. The press was the instrument which had for four centuries created 'illusions', dreams, ideologies, utopian visions of a better world. Historians have argued that it was the printing press which made possible the French Revolution. But where, Balzac asks, is the now modernised press (the London *Times*' steam-driven monster, for example) driving mankind? To a world, *Lost Illusions* predicts, where there is no 'poetry'.

The narrative begins in provincial Angoulême. Genius may be born there, but it will never flower. As the young hero is instructed by his patron: 'Paris, my dear, is the only life for *superior* people'. The two 'poets' of the subtitle are Lucien Chardon, who does indeed versify, and David Sechard, a brilliant technologist, whose genius is directed towards the poetry of the machine. David is cheated by his father into buying the family printing shop and its wholly obsolete equipment. He marries Lucien's sister, Eve, the one good woman in the novel. But he is hobbled by lack of working capital from the start. Things look more hopeful for Lucien when he is taken up by an Angoulême bluestocking, Naïs. She persuades him, after the *de rigueur* seduction business, to elope with her to Paris, where, she assures him, his genius will be immediately recognised. It isn't and Naïs drops Lucien after a few days in the capital, to take up with a dandy-baron. Undaunted, Lucien renames himself de Rubempré (without heraldic licence) and embarks on the rocky road to literary success. This section is entitled: *Un grand homme de province à Paris*. Provincial big men, it transpires, are in Paris very little men indeed. His great work – a novel in the style of Scott – flops.

But, fortunately Lucien has a good angel, the writer Daniel d'Arthez, who sagely instructs him:

There is no cheap route to greatness . . . Any man who means to rise above the rest must make ready for a struggle and be undaunted by difficulties. A great writer is a martyr who does not die; that is all.

He also has a bad angel, the literary critic and hack Étienne Lousteau, who gives him the harder-headed advice:

In short, my dear fellow, in literature you will not make money by hard work, that is not the secret of success; the point is to exploit the work of somebody else. A newspaper proprietor is a contractor, we are the bricklayers.

Lucien is persuaded by his bad angel. A wise choice.

Things meanwhile are going badly for David back in Angoulême. He has invented a new process for making paper out of vegetable rather than textile materials (more Bibliography 101). But he is cheated out of the fruits of his genius and retires from life to cultivate his garden with his Eve.

The novel ends enigmatically. His illusions wholly lost, Lucien has resolved to commit suicide but is talked out of it by the escaped convict and predatory homosexual Vautrin who, in a public carriage, offers him a cigar and persuades him to renew his quest for fame in the Paris literary world. Disillusioned and with a mentor like Vautrin, his chances are now brilliant. No one does cynicism better than a French novelist on top form.

The Lost Weekend, Charles Jackson, 1944

Jackson's is the best novel ever written about alcoholism. I make that judgement about The Lost Weekend as an alcoholic myself. I read the novel before getting sober and after, and it terrified me on either side of that momentous threshold. Before, because of the uncanny accuracy of Jackson's depictions of the lies that the alcoholic's drink-raddled mind tells itself. After I cleaned up,

it was four curse-like words in the text which terrified me: there isn't any cure. It's said in the novel by the head nurse in the Bellevue closed ward, where the hero ends up:

There isn't any cure, besides just stopping. And how many of them can do that?. . . If they do stop, out of fear or whatever, they go at once into such a state of euphoria and well-being that they become over-confident. They're rid of drink, and feel sure enough of themselves to be able to start again, promising they'll take one, or at the most two, and – well, then it becomes the same old story all over again.

One celebrity alcoholic, Herman Mankiewicz (who wrote the script for Citizen Kane), is supposed to have attempted suicide after reading The Lost Weekend.

The story chronicles a five-day binge in 1936 Manhattan. Don Birnam is a talented, but not very talented, writer. He was kicked out of his Ivy League college some years ago, for indiscreet sexual advances towards a fraternity brother. He may, or may not, be gay. The uncertainty is one of the things 'driving him to drink'. Don is currently jobless. He has a girlfriend, Helen, who believes in him, and he shares an apartment with a salt-of-the-earth brother, Wick, who is coming round to the 'there is no cure' point of view. Don manipulates them both with the skill of the practised alcoholic.

Don manages to avoid leaving town for a short vacation with Helen and Wick and, now off the leash, goes on a glorious weekend bender. He's a 'periodic' (intermittent alcoholic) and the 'barometer of his emotional nature was set for a spell of riot'. He drinks himself into delirium tremens, graphically described. A tiny mouse emerges from a crack in the wall. A bat swoops, there is a crunch, and a stream of blood streaks down the wall. Birnam screams. Then he blacks out. Why, 'normies' (as 'alkies' call them) wonder, after experiencing that kind of torment, would alcoholics go back to drinking? But they do.

Jackson, himself bisexual, emotionally fragile and dipsomaniac, knew exactly what he was writing about. He had, as they say, done the research. He resolved to write the first novel to describe alcoholism as it really is, rather than as it is demonised in temperance-tract fiction such as *Ten Nights in a Barroom*, or romanticised as a ladder to the stars in novels such as *Tender is the Night*. Fitzgerald was, nonetheless, the writer Jackson idolised – there's a comic moment in the novel when Don, smashed, phones up the wearily sober great author (but not sober for long – Fitzgerald drank himself to death, aided by several heart attacks, in 1940, aged forty-four).

The Lost Weekend was snapped up for film adaptation by one of the best directors in Hollywood, Billy Wilder, who sniffed Oscar-material. And so it was. Ray Milland played Birnam to perfection: his rolling eyes alone were Oscar winners. Wilder kept close to the novel's realism (including the DTs scene). But the film, which is viewed nowadays on TV reruns more often than Jackson's novel is read, makes two damaging alterations to its source text. In the film Don is 'cured' and sets to work on a great novel, called *The Bottle*. That doesn't happen and isn't predicted in the book. Jackson's Don Birnam will have other lost weekends and bouts, until either the closed ward or the morgue brings him to the Last Weekend of all. Jackson denounced the film's ending as a 'betrayal'. The other change is to Birnam's latent homosexuality, which is glossed over entirely in the film. Too hot for 1945.

Jackson made a small fortune from the novel and its film rights. But his life went to pieces and, drinking again, he killed himself in a Manhattan hotel. There is no cure. If you're curious, I've been clean and sober thirty years and sixty-nine days at the time of writing.

Love in a Cold Climate, Nancy Mitford, 1949

A charmingly mischievous novel, and one that seemed outrageously mischievous when delivered to the 'socialist' England Evelyn Waugh (Mitford's co-conspirator in the writing) called 'Welfaria'. It is narrated by Fanny, who performed the same narrative service in *The Pursuit of Love* (1945). The action centres on that critical moment in a deb's life – after 'coming out' but before marrying, and the let-downs of 'domesticity, maternity, and the usual lot of womankind'. Heels are, for a few short years, joyously kicked. Fanny, however, rather disgraces herself by marrying a 'don'– not of the Spanish breed (where 'dons are somebody') but the Oxford sort. 'A fella [that] reads books', an uncle exclaims in palpable disbelief.

The novel is dominated by Sonia Montdore, wife of the Earl of Montdore though she was born a rank or two below. A formidable woman, her pragmatic approach to life is summed up in the following 'coming out' advice given to her daughter Polly:

> 'The important thing, dear, is to have a really good fur coat, I mean a proper, dark one.' To Lady Montdore, fur meant mink; she could imagine no other kind except sable, but that would be specified. 'Not only will it make all the rest of your clothes look better than they are but you really needn't bother much about anything else as you never take it off. Above all, don't go wasting money on underclothes, there is nothing stupider – I always borrow Montdore's myself . . .'

Lady Montdore urinates once a day, in the morning – declining those dinnertime niceties in the aristocratic routine which allow ladies to 'retire' while men break wind, pass port and 'unbutton'.

Having for twenty years failed to produce the required heir, she finds herself 'less well than usual', and out pops Polly, destined to be the most beautiful woman on the marriage market. After spending her growing-up years in India, where her father was viceroy, Polly returns to find love in England's cold climate. She has her pick of the crop but chooses, very queerly, an uncle – just within the degrees of incest, and well the other side of paedophilia. Called 'Boy Dugdale', he prefers little girls. A scholar specialising in the delinquencies of the aristocracy, he is nicknamed 'the lecherous lecturer'. Fanny is told by her friend Jassy:

He took Linda up on to the roof and did all sorts of blissful things to her; at least, she could easily see how they would be blissful with anybody except the Lecturer. And I got some great sexy pinches as he passed the nursery landing . . .

Linda was thirteen, and among the other juvenile recipients of his lecherous 'passes' was Polly. They went beyond sexy pinches, we deduce. After such a mismatch, disinheritance ensues as naturally as night follows day and the Montdore 'seat', Hampton Court, and title descend to a distant (in every sense) relative, Cedric. His arrival at Hampton is a foretaste of more than Wildean problems ahead:

> . . . the butler opened the door and announced 'Mr Cedric Hampton'.
>
> A glitter of blue and gold crossed the parquet, and a human dragonfly was kneeling on the fur rug in front of the Montdores, one long white hand extended towards each. He was a tall, thin, young man, supple as a girl, dressed in a rather bright blue suit; his hair was the colour of a brass bed-knob, and his insect appearance came from the fact that the upper part of the face was concealed by blue goggles set in gold rims quite an inch thick.

What plot there is serves merely as a vehicle for calculated affronts to the stuffy decencies of middle-class England. It's not easy to work out, from the high-life bubble the novel chronicles, what the historical setting is, but a couple of hints make clear it is the loathed (by Mitford and Waugh) Labour and coalition governments of Ramsay Macdonald, 1929–35. 'Yah boo sucks, you Socialists!' would be an appropriate subtitle. Great fun.

Love Story, Erich Segal, 1970

Segal's novel originated as a screenplay for Paramount Studios. He was, at the time, a young classics professor with an unusually enterprising literary agent. For the story, Segal drew on his own undergraduate experiences, where his Harvard contemporaries included the two future luminaries (and erstwhile roomies) Al Gore and Tommy Lee Jones. Gore has made great play of the fact that he was the inspiration for the novel's preppy hero. Segal suggested the athletic (and, frankly, sexier) Jones was more in his mind's eye. It was Paramount who suggested that a tie-in novelisation might put some lift under the movie. It proved to be an inspired decision. The novel made the number one spot on the *New York Times* bestseller list, while the film was the highest-grossing release of 1970. Both 'versionings' (as modern literary critics like to call them) immortalised a proverbial prefix: 'Love is. . .' (Fill in your own blank. In the novel/film it's '. . . never having to say you're sorry'.)

The story is told by Oliver (a man not terribly gifted in the word department) and opens:

> What can you say about a twenty-five-year-old girl who died? That she was beautiful and brilliant? That she loved Mozart and Bach? The Beatles? And me?

The 'girl', Jennifer Cavilleri, is a Radcliffe music student. The narrator, Oliver Barrett IV, is a Harvard senior. The institutions are neighbours, but there is a gulf separating them. Harvard is the tops; Radcliffe is merely 'respectable'. No ivy, no ivory. Oliver likes the quiet of Radcliffe's library and has reading privileges there. He has to bone up for a history exam which is looming:

> I ambled over to the reserve desk to get one of the tomes that would bail me out on the morrow. There were two girls working there. One a tall tennis-anyone type, the other a bespectacled mouse type. I opted for Minnie Four-Eyes.

Oliver asks for his book imperiously. There is a tiff between Minnie and the 'preppie', as she calls him to his face (actually he's more of a 'jock' – a star of the ice-hockey rink). He decides she's a 'Radcliffe smart-ass'. Actually she's working her way through college, defraying her Radcliffe fees with library counter service. Not the kind of thing Oliver has to do.

They make up in a local ice-cream parlour and, inevitably, it's love over the scoops. Oliver's background is old money. Lots of it. She is Italian, the daughter of a baker, clawing her way up from the bottom of the great American pile. Looked at more closely he observes, without the nerdy eyewear, she's beautiful. Oliver defies his family, who plan great things for him, by marrying Jennifer. He is cut out of wills and ordered never to darken doors again. Jennifer sacrifices her dream of studying in Paris on the music fellowship she's won. Ollie turns to and makes himself an honest New York lawyer (this is, remember, a romance). Love has conquered all – all, that is, except the one thing it never can. After failing to conceive the child they both long for, Jennifer is diagnosed with a fatal illness. What it is we never know but it renders her, like *la dame aux camélias*, even lovelier. The deathbed scene jerks tears with the ruthlessness of a street mugging:

> 'Would you please hold me very tight?' she asked.
> I put my hand on her forearm, Christ, so thin and gave it a little squeeze.
> 'No, Oliver,' she said, 'really hold me. Next to me.' I was very, very careful of the tubes and things as I got on to the bed with her and put my arms around her.
> 'Thanks, Ollie.'
> Those were her last words.

Love Story was submitted by its publisher for a National Book Award. The fiction jury threatened to resign as a body unless the novel was withdrawn. It was. And sold on.

The Loved One, Evelyn Waugh, 1948

Waugh spent all of six weeks in Southern California, the subject of this novella, drawn there by the prospect of selling BRIDESHEAD REVISITED for a big-screen adaptation. This 'time in the sun' was enough to convince Waugh that he was the incarnation of civilisation and Los Angeles the heart of darkness. The keynote is struck in the first paragraph:

> All day the heat had been barely supportable but at evening a breeze arose in the west, blowing from the heat of the setting sun and from the ocean, which lay unseen, unheard behind the scrubby foothills. It shook the rusty fringes of palm-leaf and swelled the dry sounds of summer, the frog-voices, the grating cicadas, and the ever present pulse of music from the neighbouring native huts.

Oddly, American readers, the residents of those 'native huts' (for which read Hollywood bungalows, duplexes and Bel Air mansions), were not outraged – something that rather irked Waugh.

The story, mockingly subtitled 'An Anglo-American Tragedy', is simple and relentlessly satirical. Dennis Barlow, an Englishman of the amoral Basil Seal kind, is an ex-serviceman (Squadron Leader) and the author of a well-received volume of verse. He is invited to Hollywood by Megalopolitan Pictures to work on a screen adaptation of the life of Shelley (somewhere, historically, in a neighbouring studio Aldous Huxley is working on an abortive pitch for the Disneyfied *Alice in Wonderland*). It goes nowhere but, liking the climate, Dennis resolves to lotus-eat for a while (England means living from ration books). Once 'let go' by the studio, he takes up work at the Happier Hunting Grounds, an animal mortuary. It's an establishment which has modelled itself on 'Whispering Glades', which, of course, is as near a depiction of Forest Lawn, the most famous cemetery in the world, as the lawyers would permit Waugh to go.

Dennis lodges with an elderly distant relative, a literary 'knight' whose long run at Megalopolitan is rapidly ending. His swimming pool is empty and overgrown with weeds. When the chop comes, Sir Francis hangs himself and Dennis is charged by the Anglo-Hollywood cricket club to arrange the funeral, which plunges him into what Waugh's friend Jessica Mitford would call 'The American Way of Death'. The way, that is, which was pioneered by Forest Lawn founder Dr Hubert Eaton, the seer who believed that death should be something to celebrate as much as birth and marriage. Eaton also saw a lot of dollars to be made from cheering up funerals. Waugh, a Catholic of the oldest school, found a 'deep mine of literary gold' in new-fangled American mortuary practice, something as elaborate in its denial of the plain facts of death as the embalmed mummies and pyramids of the ancient Egyptians.

Meanwhile, on the other side of Burbank's boulevards, the film studios are in the business of creating living mummies such as the movie star Baby Aaronson. Baby, as her handler Sir Francis recalls, was transmuted by the studio's cosmetics labs into Juanita del Pablo. She was 'surly, lustrous, and sadistic', he recalls over a whisky and soda with Sir Ambrose Abercrombie, character actor and leader of the English set in Hollywood. They 'had most of her nose cut off', he tells Sir Ambrose,

and sent her to Mexico for six weeks to learn Flamenco singing. Then [they] handed her over to me. *I* named her. *I* made her an anti-fascist refugee. *I* said she hated men because of her treatment by Franco's moors . . . And she was really quite good in her way, you know, with a truly horrifying natural scowl. . . And now there's been a change of policy at the top. We are only making healthy films this year . . . So poor Juanita has to start at the beginning again as an Irish Catholic colleen . . . they've pulled all her teeth out. She never had to smile before and her own set was good enough for a snarl. Now she'll have to laugh roguishly all the time. That means dentures.

It's the embalming of the still alive.

Waugh declined to sell Hollywood *Brideshead Revisited* ($140,000 was offered – enough to tempt a Pharaoh). Nor did he ever return to Southern California. Six weeks there sufficed. He is buried, unembalmed and decently decomposing, in the Somerset village where he lived.

Loving, Henry Green, 1945

'An acquired taste', one says knowingly. But, alas, too few people have acquired that taste. Green is, Sebastian Faulks neatly observes, a writer 'who always seems to need "introducing"'. The fault is his, and technical. It's less 'acquiring the taste' than 'learning' how to read him. Or, more properly, from which direction to approach him. Green believed in the truths of 'irrelevancy' (his master in this craft was Chekhov) and 'obliquity' (in which he, Henry Green, is the undisputed master).

In a wonderfully perverse interview with the *Paris Review* in 1958, Green observed that:

Most of us walk crabwise to meals and everything else. The oblique approach in middle age is the safest thing. The unusual at this period is to get anywhere at all – God damn!

Loving (that topic, incidentally, is wholly elusive in the narrative) is set during the most important battle in English history since 1066. It is the only battle dignified with the name of the nation: 'the Battle of Britain'. Obliquely, the narrative opens in Ireland, in an Anglo-Irish country house. The residents and servants are all as British as toad in the hole. The first paragraph is one designed to put the reader at sixes and sevens:

Once upon a day an old butler called Eldon lay dying in his room attended by the head housemaid, Miss Agatha Burch. From time to time the other servants separately or in chorus gave expression to proper sentiments and then went on with what they had been doing.

One name he uttered over and over, 'Ellen.'

The pointed windows of Mr Eldon's room were naked glass with no blinds or curtains. For this was in Eire where there is no blackout.

Why the fairy-tale opening?

The main business of what follows centres (not the right word, perhaps, but *faute de mieux*) on that great issue in country houses – succession. Not who will succeed to the bloodline, but who is going to get Eldon's butlership. Leading the pack is thirty-nine-year-old Charley Raunce, a Machiavelli in plush breeches. It will be an important step up for him. At Kinalty footmen like he is have no identity and no name of their own. The mistress of the house calls all lower servants 'Arthur'. If Charley (professional name above stairs: 'Arthur') gets the post, he will henceforth be 'Raunce'. A person at last. The other great thing in Charley's sights is his below-stairs love for the under-housemaid Edith.

The novel deals with events of ineffable inconsequence. A clutch of unbroken eggs in a gardening glove (misuse of property), clumsy handling of the peacock flock (a source of constant vexation), and exchanges like the following:

'You write to London for the blotting paper of course?'

'Yes Madam but this is all Mr Eldon could get. I believe he was going to speak about it.'

'No, he never did,' she said, 'and naturally it would be hopeless trying to buy anything in this wretched country. But tell me why if there are several pastel blues can they do only one shade of pink?'

'I believe it's the war Madam.'

Obliquely the novel is about 'old England'. The widowed mistress of Kinalty is surnamed, significantly, 'Tennant' – the family's tenure is precarious. There is no master in the house. Jack Tennant has gone off to war, leaving his mother and adulterously inclined wife behind. He figures not at all in the story. Perhaps he is killed.

All the important action is below stairs. The servants are homesick but fear any return to England. It will mean rationing, conscription and, who knows, German masters speaking an incomprehensible lingo in no need of butlers and housemaids. They fear Ireland: a 'neutral' country more sympathetic to Germany than England, and swarming with IRA gunmen. As a bomb shelter, Eire is not ideal.

The novel which began 'once upon a day' finishes with similar fairy-tale brevity:

The next day Raunce and Edith left without a word of warning. Over in England they were married and lived happily ever after.

Charley won't go to war. His stomach is playing up. Of course, it may kill him.

Once acquired, the taste for Green's 'crab-wise' narrative is addictive. Those who do acquire it don't stop until they've read everything with his name on it.

The Luck of Roaring Camp, Bret Harte, 1868

In 1868, Harte launched as editor and proprietor a new magazine, the *Overland Monthly*, in which he aimed to publish his Western stories, the first of which was 'The Luck of Roaring Camp'. The story duly made his name and kicked off a lifelong, bitter rivalry with Mark Twain. The story takes only half an hour to read.

The enduring interest in Harte's tale lies in its being an antidote to the 'frontier thesis' – the sustaining myth of the West that the struggle which life there imposes brings out the true American spirit. For Harte, the 'West' (he lived and worked there in its frontier days) is a barbarous, primitive place that humankind must rise above. And, given what humankind is, probably never will rise above. We're not that lucky.

Roaring Camp comprises a 'wild bunch' who have come west to California in 1849 in the hope of striking it rich in the gold fields. They have not struck it rich. The story opens in winter, when prospecting is slack. The tone is laconic:

There was commotion in Roaring Camp. It could not have been a fight, for in 1850 that was not novel enough to have called together the entire settlement. The ditches and claims were not only deserted, but 'Tuttle's grocery' had contributed its gamblers, who, it will be remembered, calmly continued their game the day that French Pete and Kanaka Joe shot each other to death over the bar in the front room. The whole camp was collected before a rude cabin on the outer edge of the clearing. Conversation was carried on in a low tone, but the name of a woman was frequently repeated. It was a name familiar enough in the camp, – 'Cherokee Sal.'

About five rattling Westerns are contained in that bleak *mise en scène*. What is it, then, that brings this god-forsaken crew into something temporarily resembling a community? The death of Cherokee Sal, the common-law wife (or, to be more blunt, whore), who services the otherwise all-male camp. Sal is not a doxy any Hollywood agent would let his client play onscreen: 'She was a coarse and, it is to be feared, a very sinful woman'. She is in the last stage of pregnancy, and dying in the act of giving Roaring Camp a child. (Whose? It could be any one of them.) The surviving infant 'ain't bigger nor a derringer'. He is named (no christening is possible in this god-forsaken place) Thomas Luck. It's a joke. Luck has been in very short supply in Roaring Camp.

Strangely, a child in their midst 'regenerates' the camp morally:

> Almost imperceptibly a change came over the settlement. The cabin assigned to 'Tommy Luck' – or 'The Luck,' as he was more frequently called – first showed signs of improvement. It was kept scrupulously clean and whitewashed.

Civilisation has been born with the child. 'Profanity' is given up. Gun play too. Sanitation is introduced. A 'golden summer' breathes, temporarily, over Roaring Camp. But Harte does not let the reader off with any easy sentimentality. The winter of 1851 is one of the harshest in memory. With the camp nestling under the Sierra Nevada, the springtime melt causes flooding. The gulch becomes a tumultuous, unpredictable flood plain. It is now the water that roars. It is, for the miners, good luck. The streams, eroding the hills and mountains, bring down gold dust in their currents. But a particularly savage flash flood drowns little Thomas Luck. He is too good for the world – at least the world of Roaring Camp.

Lucky Jim, Kingsley Amis, 1954

Kingsley Amis' chronicle of a junior history lecturer, struggling for tenure at a dull Midland 'redbrick' university, who rises above the mediocrity around him ('plucky Jim'), pioneered a thriving literary genre – the British 'campus novel'. The word which leaped from the reviews in 1954 was 'funny'. John Betjeman went so far as to hail this novel, by a hitherto unknown novelist, as 'the funniest book I have read since *Decline and Fall*'. It's a plausible claim. But with the difference that Waugh's novel begins with the thinly disguised Bullingdon Club on a glass-smashing rampage (the happiest sound ever heard by night at Oxford, one gathers). Lucky Jim begins with the glum vista of a university building converted from a lunatic asylum. 'Campus' is not perhaps quite the word as yet.

Fun, like other good things in life, was in chronically short supply during the 'Age of Austerity'. The reading public of 1954 wanted the relief of a belly laugh, which Amis offered. *Lucky Jim* flew off the shelves of bookshops and libraries. Humour is a fragile commodity. Like milk, it goes off very quickly. What inspires tears of laughter in one generation induces tears of boredom in the next. But *Lucky Jim* has retained its primal freshness. New, and even young, readers still split their sides at the famous set-piece of Jim's hangover, as he comes to painful consciousness in his professor's house, swaddled in the blankets his last unextinguished cigarette of the night before has violated.

Read it and keep a straight face, I challenge you:

> Dixon was alive again. Consciousness was upon him before he could get out of the way; not for him the slow, gracious wandering from the halls of sleep, but a summary, forcible ejection. He lay sprawled, too wicked to move, spewed up like a broken spider-crab on the tarry shingle of morning. The light did him harm, but not as much as looking at things did; he resolved, having done it once, never to move his eyeballs again. A dusty thudding in his head made the scene

before him beat like a pulse. His mouth had been used as a latrine by some small creature of the night, and then as its mausoleum. During the night, too, he'd somehow been on a cross-country run and then been expertly beaten up by secret police. He felt bad.

The other, very different, word bandied about in early reactions to *Lucky Jim* is 'angry'. Amis' anti-hero, Jim Dixon, is what was called in the 1950s an 'Angry Young Man'. There was, of course, anger on both sides of the age divide – 'scum', Somerset Maugham (born 1874) called the AYMs. But who cared what that angry (eighty-year-) old man thought?

Jim, much as we love him, is an out-and-out philistine. Mozart is 'filth' in his ears. He never reads a book unless he has to and sometimes not even then. He drinks hugely and, boozed up beyond his normal inhibition level, attempts sexual assault on his girlfriend Margaret, whom, when sober, he is aiming to dump. And climactically – inflamed by nips of hooch from a visiting donor's hip flask – Jim tells his audience of university shags (one of Amis' favourite words for those who incurred his displeasure) exactly what he thinks of them. In doing so he ruins a perfectly respectable public event and brings his institution into disrepute before diving, nose first, off the podium – a place of honour he will never, as a lecturer, grace again.

But this disaster is Jim's 'luck'. He gets the girl, and the rich man who got him so disastrously drunk rewards him with a top London job in the city. Jim is free. *Dixon agonistes* no longer. Rebellion has become life-change. It's double-distilled tosh, of course. Given a directorial salary and metropolitan freedoms (not to say the night-time lures of Soho), James Dixon would drink, laze and womanise himself out of his job long before (as Amis' pal Philip Larkin put it) sexual intercourse began in 1963. So what? Those five hundred hangover-describing words are the funniest thing ever written in British fiction.

I, incidentally, attended the model for Jim's redbrick, seven years later. It wasn't *that* bad.

Madame Bovary, Gustave Flaubert, 1856

A generation of modern readers will have arrived at Flaubert via his parrot courtesy of Julian Barnes, one of whose strands of satire is that *Madame Bovary* is far too good to be left to the teaching of academics. Barnes mounts a scathing attack on the Oxonian blue-stocking who presumed to pontificate to him on this novel – regardless of the facts that the narrative was so far removed from her own spinsterish experience of life, and her linguistic competence so defective, she might as well have been lecturing to the undergraduate Mr Barnes from the University of Mars.

As one of the despised academic profession, for many years I taught a course comparing Flaubert's novel – subtitled *Provincial Lives* – with MIDDLEMARCH, subtitled *A Study of Provincial Life*. A nifty correspondence, I thought. My French, like that of Barnes' teacher Enid Starkie, is inadequate to catch what Paul de Man calls 'the cadence of Flaubert'. In one of his letters, for example, the novelist records spending a day on 'shadings and refinements'. These, alas, are lost to me in even the best translation. Bigger things also. What the comparison between Eliot and Flaubert threw up was, essentially, an intractable fact of literary geography. Where novels are concerned, the English Channel is more than twenty-one miles wide. Both of the novels in my course have main narrative strands chronicling provincial doctors whose lives are ruined by flighty wives. . . and there the similarity ends. For Eliot the provinces, which had endowed her with her own intellectual character, are the foundations of the English nation. For Flaubert, the provincial world outside Paris is a dull, muddy nowhere.

There are three Madame Bovarys in the novel, and two deadly poisons. The first poison is romantic fiction, which pollutes Emma's mind. The second is the arsenic with which she commits suicide. Charles Bovary ('Monsieur Bovary') is introduced as a schoolboy mocked by his fellows because 'he came from the country'. Scraping a mediocre medical qualification, he practises medicine in a provincial town. He makes,

thanks to his mother's intervention, a sensible marriage to a rich, but otherwise excessively undesirable, widow who conveniently dies, allowing him to marry the pretty Emma Rouault – a woman with the inbred instincts of the peasant but a soul yearning for higher things. Emma is a victim of literacy: intoxicated by the terms 'bliss, passion, ecstasy', which she knows only from the romantic novels in which she loses herself. In the marital bed she discovers only a husband who snores. As for passion: '[Charles] embraced her at certain fixed times. It was one habit among other habits, like a familiar dessert after the monotony of dinner.'

Emma's discontent is inflamed during a ball given to the townsfolk by a marquis. Her attractiveness wins her a turn on the dance floor with a nobleman. She tastes a better life. 'Paris, more vague than the ocean, glimmered before Emma's eyes with a silvery glow . . . She wanted to die but she also wanted to live in Paris.'

Chasing her vision of things Parisian, and passionate by nature, she allows herself to become the mistress of a rich voluptuary, Rodolphe, who is 'something of a connoisseur' where women are concerned. To him, she is a new dish to try. To her, he represents the elusive other life she craves. 'I have a lover!' she exclaims, after consenting to adultery. Rodolphe, sensible man, declines to elope with her. She takes another, humbler lover – a law student, Léon – and borrows recklessly in order to shower him with gifts. Having ruined her cuckolded husband, she kills herself.

Flaubert, who observed himself closely in the act of writing, said that:

> The entire value of my book, if it has any, will consist of my having known how to walk straight ahead on a hair, balanced above the two abysses of lyricism and vulgarity.

This balance required the unflinching insensitivity of the surgeon's scalpel. On a trip to Egypt, Flaubert saw a lice-ridden beggar and said he was unsure whether to pity the man or the parasite, obliged to live on such a specimen of humanity. A key word for George Eliot is 'sympathy'. For Flaubert sympathy, as the old joke puts it, is in the dictionary between shit and syphilis.

The Makioka Sisters, Jun'ichirō Tanizaki, 1943–8

Translations of the fiction of Jun'ichirō Tanizaki (1886–1965) began to appear prominently in Western bookshops and on world literature courses in the 1970s and 1980s – contemporaneous with his country's post-war rise to economic superpower. His work is peculiarly relevant to Japan's changing status, displaying, as it does, an ambivalent attraction both to the Westernised modernism embodied by Tokyo and to the older Japan represented by his more beloved Kansai, where he moved after the 1923 earthquake that devastated the capital. There would be more than one such devastation of a city in Japan during his lifetime.

Tanizaki's narratives are fictional gossamer. As his translator Edward Seidensticker puts it, he 'always made a narrative virtue of vagueness, observing that "we Japanese scorn the bald fact"'. *The Makioka Sisters* is characteristically oblique. The Japanese title, *Sasameyuki*, means 'lightly falling snow'. Seidensticker (whose translation came out in 1957) struggled to find an equivalent and finally settled on a 'bald' description of the narrative content – which is the story of four sisters.

The novel has the quality of making the occidental reader feel clumsy. The Makioka sisters, we are told, make a ceremonial trip every year to see the cherry blossom. This visit is very important in the novel – but why?

> The ancients waited for cherry blossoms, grieved when they were gone, and lamented their passing in countless poems. How very ordinary the poems had seemed to Sachiko when she read them as a girl, but now she knew, as well as one could know, that grieving over fallen cherry blossoms was more than a fad or convention.

What exactly is the significance? Doubtless the Japanese reader has the same problem with Wordsworth's rhapsodies over daffodils.

One experiences the same awkward sense of incomprehension with the description of the twilight 'firefly hunt':

> In the last moment of light, with the darkness creeping up from the water and the moving plumes of grass still faintly outlined, there, far as the river stretched – an infinite number of little lines in two long rows on either side, quiet, unearthly. Sachiko could see it all even now, here inside with her eyes closed. Surely that was the impressive moment of the evening, the moment that made the firefly hunt worthwhile.

Bugs?

The novel is set in the thirties, and extends to the eve of the Second World War. It was actually written during the war and in the first years of the Occupation: something which injects an elegiac tone into the pre-war narrative. As the epigraph puts it, 'At the touch of sunlight, the snowflakes melt away'. Old Japan had well and truly melted away, and the new, post-war Japan was swiftly engrossed in the formation of a new national identity. But the political and world-historical never intrudes on the narrative. The invasion of China, one of the bloodiest events of the twentieth century, is mentioned, only parenthetically, as an 'incident'. The militarisation of the country, preparatory to world war, goes unremarked.

The four sisters belong to a class whose social supremacy is ebbing. They are unaware of the fact. For the many-branched Makioka family, life is preoccupied chiefly with observing rituals and, above all, arranging marriages. The main preoccupation throughout the book is contriving to find a suitable match for the 'difficult' third sister, Yukiko. Until a match is arranged for her, nothing can be done for the fourth sister, Taeko, who is something of a wild-cat, infected with Western ideas. Yukiko's various suitors have been judged ineligible by the family or undesirable by her, and now, at the age of thirty, she is on the awful verge of being unmarriageable. The final contender is someone older, and a widower. He, it is decided, will do. The senior, decision-making sister is Tsuruko. Her husband has deferentially taken the Makioka name, as have their six children. The second sister, Sachiko, runs the clan-connected Ashiya household. Her husband, too, has become a Makioka.

Yukiko's wedding in Tokyo finally happens in April 1941. The family has been saved. The last paragraphs of the work seem sublimely complacent and trivial, in the light of the national horror to come: 'Thus the future was settled . . . Yukiko's diarrhoea persisted throughout the twenty-sixth, and was a problem on the train to Tokyo.' The future, alas, was not settled.

Malone Dies, Samuel Beckett, 1951

My generation of readers was introduced, belatedly, to Samuel Beckett in two ways. One was repertory theatre performances, after the English premiere in London's Arts Theatre of *Waiting for Godot* in 1955; the other the late 1950s Calder and Boyars paperbacks of his work. *Malone Dies*, after that small publisher had done the ground-breaking, was picked up as a Penguin in 1962. My sad-looking copy sits in front of me now. Not quite dying, but stained from its long life and much use.

Malone Dies is a uniquely Beckettian 'Robinsoniad' – the title echoes 'man alone'. The novel's implication is that one is as alone at the moment of dying as previously in the womb. Death is merely less comfortable. Hell, to paraphrase Sartre, is not other people – hell is your lonely self. Every man is, whatever John Donne says, an island. And he'll never get off it.

When George Orwell was dying in a private ward in University College Hospital (with those less well-off than he, as he observed in his essay 'How the Poor Die', meeting their end in large wards, commu-nally), he retained his sanity in the face of terror by putting down on paper, in literal detail, exactly what was around him in the room. He was dying in 1950, the year before *Malone Meurt* was published in Paris.

Malone finds himself alone in a room in a 'plain ordinary house'. It is neither hospital nor prison. He calls himself an octogenarian but he cannot prove it. From time to time the door of his room half opens, and 'a hand

puts a dish on the little table left there for that purpose, takes away the dish of the previous day, and the door closes again'. The dish contains soup ('They must know I am toothless'). When his chamber-pot is full he puts it alongside the soup-dish on the little table. He does not sleep. 'Coma is for the living', not the dying. But he lies in bed. One is born in a bed, copulates in a bed, and dies in a bed. It is the item of furniture which most closely supports the cycle of life.

Malone never washes. All that matters to him is eating and excretion. And writing. He has been left, by whom he knows not, a thick exercise book and the stub of a pencil. While he is dying his mind and writing hand weave stories, which may be autobiographical. The narratives are punctuated with the ejacula-tion 'what tedium' – but it would be more tedious, we apprehend, not to tell stories.

The first focuses on a dull boy called 'Sapo'. The name is absurd, Malone decides, and replaces it with 'Macman' (the Scottish prefix means 'son' – hence 'son of man'). He ends up in a religious asylum for alcoholics tended by a nurse called Moll (nickname for Mary), revolting of face, with 'by way of ear-rings two long ivory crucifixes which swayed wildly at the least movement of her head'. Another story half-narrates itself around a family called the Lamberts. Mr Lambert, a 'pig-bleeder' by profession, treats his family as brutally as he treats swine. He beats his wife with the washing beetle before raping her. He has daughters, and 'incest [is] in the air'. They bury a dead mule.

The subject of the final story is Lemuel, evoking Swift's Gulliver. There is a voyage to an island and, at last, Malone dies.

> never anything
> there
> any more

It requires a strenuous effort of memory to recall the effect of this on a self-improving schoolboy. I seem to remember laughing, but – after a diet of more normal fiction – it was so hard to make sense of that it left one's senses disordered. On re-reading, not all that far from Malonian octogenarianism, it now makes a lot of sense.

The Man Who Died, D. H. Lawrence, 1929

One of Lawrence's finest poems, 'Piano', opens:

> Softly, in the dusk, a woman is singing to me;
> Taking me back down the vista of years, till I see
> A child sitting under the piano, in the boom of the tingling strings
> And pressing the small, poised feet of a mother who smiles as she sings.

The woman is his mother, the child under the tingling strings is young Bertie Lawrence, and the songs which the child would have thrilled to were Methodist hymns. Lawrence was, from childhood, marinated in non-conformist theology – particularly on the topics of blood and resurrection. His novels, as their rhetoric constantly insists, are religious. But it is religion according to the Gospel of San Lorenzo (as D. H. liked to be called), not Saints Matthew, Mark, Luke and John.

Awaiting death in Italy, Lawrence produced *The Escaped Cock*, later retitled *The Man Who Died*, a fable of resurrection. The first part of the story imagines Christ (never named, but distinctly Lawrentian) coming back to life in the tomb where his corpse has been laid. There is no miracle; he has been taken down too early. An Aesopian prelude, which gives the piece its original title, describes a 'dandy' cockerel whose vital energies are tethered by the peasant (clearly Italian) who owns him. It escapes as Christ rolls away the rock from before his tomb. Throughout life, the Eastwood lad in Lawrence had loved playground jokes about 'cocks' (see AARON'S ROD). And he had also always been fascinated by one of the central paradoxes of the New Testament. Does Christ have a cock – and, if so, what part does it play in his life? When Christ is resurrected not as a spirit but in the *flesh* (as all his followers will be, it is promised), what are the carnal implications?

In the full version of the tale Lawrence wrote, the man who died goes on, after resurrection, to lose his virginity to a prophetess of Osiris. Both partners in the congress are religio-sexually fulfilled by the act. The tale teeters on the brink of absurdity (never all that far away in Lawrence) when, looking down at his erect, throbbing cock, the man 'felt the blaze of his manhood and his power rise up in his loins, magnificent' and declares, 'I am risen.' Not something most early-rising churchgoers think about when reciting the creed on Sunday at matins. The story concludes with the man rowing away from the Temple :

> The man who had died rowed slowly on, with the current, and laughed to himself: I have sowed the seed of my life and my resurrection, and put my touch for ever upon the choice woman of this day, and I carry her perfume in my flesh like essence of roses. She is dear to me in the middle of my being. But the gold and flowing serpent is coiling up again, to sleep at the root of my tree.
> So let the boat carry me. Tomorrow is another day.

As Anthony Burgess perceptively notes, GONE WITH THE WIND ends with the same truism: 'Tomorrow is another day'. There were, alas, very few days remaining for D. H. Lawrence. He died a few months after the tale was published (not in the UK, where it would have been instantly banned). His ashes were buried under his favourite image of the phoenix, the bird which rises reborn from its death and incineration. In the flesh.

The Man with the Golden Arm, Nelson Algren, 1949

I first read the novel, as did most of its British readers, in the wake of the 1955 movie. I paid my one-and-ninepence (stalls) at the Colchester Hippodrome principally to listen to the Shorty Rogers cool West Coast jazz soundtrack. The film, one later learned, had been a grim experience for Nelson Algren. His novel had won a National Book Award and glowing reviews. Hollywood, and its slimy lawyers, secured the rights with a measly $15,000 payment and a broken promise about collaboration. It then turned his narrative into sentimental mush and advertised the movie (which won Oscar nominations) as 'Otto Preminger's *The Man with the Golden Arm*, Starring Frank Sinatra'. Hollywood, said Algren, had reduced him to 'the penny piper of American Literature'. It confirmed his perennially jaundiced view of life.

Preminger's version chronicles the ordeal of 'Frankie Machine' (Francis Majcinek). He's a hard-bitten, but decent-hearted, Chicago heroin-dealer and addict, just out of prison and 'clean'. The 'monkey' is off his back. He aspires to be a jazz drummer. He is married (chained) to a shrewish wife, Zosh, who pretends to be paraplegic but isn't. Frankie is in love with Molly – played by the delectable Kim Novak, the only authentically Chicagoan element in the film. Finding himself in debt to his old boss, Frankie begins to deal heroin again, and soon relapses into addiction. He screws up an audition with the Stan Kenton band (another plus for seventeen-year-old me), goes cold turkey, and when Zosh conveniently self-destructs, lives on happily ever after with Molly. The film was everywhere hailed as 'brave' because it touched on the taboo subject of drug addiction in marginally less gothic fashion than had *Reefer Madness*.

Algren's novel is something else. The epigraph signals that what is to come will be blackness beyond black.

> Do you understand, gentlemen, that all the horror is in just this – that there is no horror!

The quotation is from the Russian writer's Aleksandr Kuprin's story 'The Pit', a favourite Algren text. The world-view of the story is expanded on by Kuprin's narrator, Platonov:

> they write about detectives, about lawyers, about inspectors of the revenue, about pedagogues, about attorneys, about the police, about officers, about sensual ladies, about engineers, about baritones – and really, by God, altogether well – cleverly, with finesse

and talent. But, after all, all these people are rubbish, and their life is not life, but some sort of conjured up, spectral, unnecessary delirium of world culture. But there are two singular realities – ancient as humanity itself: the prostitute and the moujik. And about them we know nothing, save some tinsel, gingerbread, debauched depictions in literature.

Or, Algren would have said, the movies. No gingerbread for him.

Nelson Algren had a Jewish upbringing in Chicago and, after an unspectacular university career, bummed around the US as a hobo in the 1930s. He got himself a hard-time prison sentence for stealing a typewriter – an allegorical theft if ever there was one. 'America', he said, is 'a long dust road leading to nowhere'. It was nothing like the *idea* of America.

Algren's dealer (of cards, not dope) never gets the monkey off his back. He finally hangs himself in a 'Men Only' hostel. Molly-O is not fragrant Kim Novak, but a bar-room hustler and whore. Even the family dog, Rumdum, is a hopeless alcoholic. There is nothing in the novel's world but Kuprinian 'rubbish', seething with violent, pointless energy like a pile of maggots on a corpse. The most powerful scene in the novel has Frankie in a holding cell – it is just after Christmas, and he has been shoplifting his presents. Inscribed on the wall round him are graffiti of the kind one would find in a circle of hell:

> *Don't go by Dago Mary she give bad drink*
> *In for a bum rap too I never rolled a sober one*
> *All women are deseased*
> *We're all victims of circumstance*

Algren wrote *The Man with the Golden Arm* while in love (adulterously) with Simone de Beauvoir, Sartre's partner. She depicts him as Lewis Brogan in her Goncourt-winning novel *The Mandarins*. On reading it, Algren concluded he was the better writer. He is. You could even argue he's a better existentialist.

Manon Lescaut, Abbé Prévost, 1731

A 280-year-old French novel, with the authorial prefix 'Abbé', is not, for most lovers of fiction, an irresistible prospect. But *Manon Lescaut* is a welcome surprise, a lively study of what in French is called *amour fou* – the self-destructive and self-deceiving qualities of 'crazy love'. Prévost published the novel while in exile in Amsterdam. Then, as now, it was the most tolerant of European cities. Paris, at the time, was not tolerant and *Manon Lescaut* was banned in France for its perceived amorality, and less perceivable, but clearly implied, satire on the self-delusions and vanities of the aristocracy. The full title is *L'Histoire du chevalier des Grieux et de Manon Lescaut*. She (Manon) is a commoner; he (des Grieux – Knight of the Order of Malta) nobly born.

The story opens with a narrator who promptly disappears. On the way to Le Havre he sees a consignment of a dozen of the 'frail sisterhood' – prostitutes – in chains, bound for transport to the American colonies. There they will be disposed of at the whim of the governor. Meanwhile their captors sell them, for a few francs, to anyone who is interested. The narrator is struck by the extraordinary beauty of one of the captives, and by the sight of a pale, weeping young man, clearly of high birth. He intends to accompany the cargo of whores to the new world, says the young man, for love of the loveliest among them. The story then flashes back, and will pick up the scene at the dock many chapters later.

The young man is a second son in one of the 'first families in Picardy'. He was studying for the church in Amiens, alongside his *fidus achates*, Tiberge. Both lads were 'model students'. At an inn, des Grieux saw a beautiful young girl, Manon Lescaut, destined for a convent. He had never, to this point, even thought of the 'difference between the sexes'. The difference struck him hard and he fell in love on the spot. He and Manon ran off together. He was promptly disowned, and she – now a 'mistress', not a nun – became 'ruined' in the eyes of the world. But ruin, and its comforts ('affluence'), are what Manon wants. The desperate des Grieux

scrounged money from Tiberge – but could not stand the homilies that accompanied it.

What follows is structured around a series of captivity narratives. Des Grieux's family kidnap him, but he escapes. For a while, he supports a lavish lifestyle by card-sharping. Manon, meanwhile, is pimped out by her brother as a high-priced courtesan. All this is accompanied by lofty rhetoric about the 'purity' of the couple's passion. Manon's duplicity with an elderly lover lands her in the 'Magdalen' – a place of confinement for fallen women – and des Grieux in the prison of Saint-Lazare. He escapes, killing a guard as he does so, and contrives to rescue her. The pattern repeats itself until we arrive back at Manon being deported from Le Havre.

The story ends in the New World. New Orleans, they discover, is beyond provincial – a mass of huts, hovels and human dregs. The lovers decide, rather belatedly, to marry – they have little new to discover about each other's bodies. But the governor of New Orleans forbids the match. He has promised Manon to his nephew. Des Grieux provokes a duel and runs the nephew through. The lovers flee, hoping to make it through the wilderness to an English encampment (Prévost, whose American geography was not his strength, pictures Louisiana as a desert). Manon expires. Des Grieux keeps his lips clamped to her dead face for twenty-four hours, then buries her and prepares himself for death on her grave. Pursuers from New Orleans find him and take him back. The governor's nephew is not dead it transpires. Tiberge turns up, with the necessary francs to win his protégé's freedom. The two of them return to France where, we gather, des Grieux will make a successful career in the Church. As an experienced fornicator, pimp, gambler and murderer, he should do well.

Mansfield Park, Jane Austen, 1814

For most of its existence *Mansfield Park* was taken as the story of little ('nobody') Fanny Price, and the final success in life which vindicates her invincible moral rectitude and inherent goodness... Cinderella in a high-bosomed Regency dress. But for many of the millions who had read the novel there was a lurking sense of unease as to whether or not they really 'liked' Miss Price ('Miss Prig'). She weeps more than any other of Austen's heroines, says little, and what she does say lacks any of Elizabeth Bennet's sprightliness or Emma Woodhouse's spite. Knowing reference might be made, in more recent years, to that arch-Fanny-disliker Kingsley Amis, and his tart comment that a dinner party with Mr and Mrs Edmund Bertram would not be an event to look forward to. That category of response changed in the 1970s when critics like Marilyn Butler informed the reading world that:

> Mansfield Park is the most visibly ideological of Jane Austen's novels, and as such has a central position in any examination of Jane Austen's philosophy as expressed in her art.

There were, it seemed, 'ideas' in the undergrowth. And this from a writer who never so much as mentioned the French Revolution or the ongoing war with the Corsican tyrant. Thank God for critics.

Most revisionary of the post-1970s critiques was that by Edward Said in Culture and Imperialism (1993). 'Follow the money', Said instructed. Where does the wealth which keeps up the costly magnificence of Mansfield Park originate? Most of it, he informed us, from black slaves, working 4,000 miles away in the sugar plantations of the Caribbean, in conditions of inhuman exploitation. Those places which the head of the family, Sir Thomas, takes a year off to visit in the course of the novel, while the young people disgrace themselves with amateur theatricals and à la mode flirtations. According to Said, 'The Bertrams could not have been possible without the slave trade, sugar, and the colonial planter class'. In a just world, Said implies, Sir Thomas Bertram ought to be in the dock of the International Court in The Hague, for crimes against humanity. And not just Sir Thomas. Said's chapter on Mansfield Park finishes with the emphatic declaration, 'Yes, Austen belonged to a slave-owning society'. Since

she claimed to write on two inches of ivory one could also assert that, like Kurtz in HEART OF DARKNESS, she was also responsible for the extermination of the African elephant.

Not every reader will accept Said's J'accuse. But it demands proper consideration. There is, for example, a much-commented on episode early in the novel in which – her head splitting with a migraine (the standard circumlocution for period pains, as every female reader would have picked up) – Fanny, a constitutionally frail young woman, is ordered by Mrs Norris to go and cut some roses for the drawing room (guests are expected) in the blazing sunshine. One's heart goes out to her. Edmund notices, in company later, how deathly pale his cousin looks. But, if we go along with Edward Said, the clothes on Fanny's back, the (barely touched) dishes on the table in front of her at supper, even the secateurs with which she clips the roses, are all paid for by black slaves sweating in a much hotter sun, hacking away with machetes at the cane from dawn to dusk, whose overseers, whips in hand, would undoubtedly be even less sympathetic than Mrs Norris is. This view of the novel permeates the 1999 film version, which adds another element: the sexual exploitation of his slaves by Sir Thomas (played in the film, incredibly, by Harold Pinter), who not only forces them to sweat in his plantation fields by day, but makes the more delectable ones service him sexually by night.

I worry about this revision of Mansfield Park. Did I get the novel I first delighted in, before the Great Revision, wrong? Am I reading it 'right' now? Why don't I like it much any more?

The Master and Margarita, Mikhail Bulgakov, 1967

Bulgakov began writing The Master and Margarita in 1928. It was a brief interval of Muscovite thaw before the bloody purges which cranked up in 1934. Over the years that followed he was in the strange situation of being in Stalin's favour (he received a number of amiable phone calls from the 'great' man) and was employed by a state-approved theatre. Yet he was forbidden from either publishing or having his plays performed. He was, as he said, 'buried alive' – but then, just *being* alive was a stroke of luck for an experimental Soviet writer in the 1930s.

Bulgakov died, aged forty-eight, in 1940, having dictated the last revisions of *The Master and Margarita* to his wife. Portions of the text seeped out over the following years, but the full work did not see the light of day in print in the USSR (or elsewhere) until twenty-seven years later, when the authorities judged it could do no harm. Fiction, like plutonium, has a half-life.

The iron rule for Russian novelists between the wars was 'socialist realism' – fiction which depicted the world as it was, with some urgent forecasting of the world as it should be (and would be, with the fruition of the Revolution). Instead of following this convention, Bulgakov came up with one of the most flamboyantly metaphysical novels of the century. *The Master and Margarita* is a wonderfully crazed production. It shimmers with enigma at every point. An earlier discarded title, 'The Devil in Moscow', was evidently felt to be too obvious. The chosen title is deliberately un-obvious.

The first chapter, entitled 'Never Talk with Strangers' (a wise precaution in Stalin's Moscow), opens:

At the hour of the hot spring sunset two citizens appeared at the Patriarch's Ponds. One of them, approximately forty years old, dressed in a grey summer suit, was short, dark-haired, plump, bald, and carried his respectable fedora hat in his hand. His neatly shaven face was adorned with black horn-rimmed glasses of a supernatural size. The other, a broad-shouldered young man with tousled reddish hair, his chequered cap cocked back on his head, was wearing a cowboy shirt, wrinkled white trousers and black sneakers.

The elder of the two men is called (confusingly given the name's musical associations) Berlioz. He runs 'a fat literary journal' and is the chairman of the board of MASSOLIT (a clear swipe at the Union of Soviet Writers, set up while Bulgakov was writing the first draft of *The Master and Margarita*). The younger man, Ivan, writes poetry under the pen name 'Homeless'. A poem by him, about Jesus, is under consideration. It's a touchy subject.

Berlioz asks for a drink at a kiosk – nothing is available except some filthy-yellow apricot soda. He drinks the potion and in so doing summons up the Devil – in the guise of a 'Professor Woland'. He is not wearing gown and mortarboard but a 'peaked jockey's cap . . . [and] a short chequered jacket'. Both are made of air. Woland is seven feet tall and possessed of a 'jeering physiognomy'. He is accompanied by a large, talkative, pistol-packing, chess-playing cat called Behemoth. Socialist realism this is not.

Conversation becomes an argument about the authenticity of the New Testament. The Professor, in passing, prophesies that Berlioz will have his head cut off by a party member in an hour or two. (It duly happens. The executioner is an incompetent young communist cadet driving a tram.) The Professor, who was *there*, relates what *really* happened in Jerusalem between Pilate and the subversive Jew called Yeshua. Gospel truth is a contradiction in terms.

After they go their separate ways, Ivan pursues Woland with the intention of saving Moscow. It lands him in a lunatic asylum, where he comes across 'the Master' – a frustrated novelist who was writing a novel about Pontius Pilate and Jesus. Forbidden topics, as the authorities decreed. In frustration, the Master burned his manuscript and dumped his lover, Margarita.

Thereafter the story spirals into narrative swirls that may, or may not, be the products of the paranoid minds now released to frisk at will on the page. Margarita, still faithful to the Master, accepts the Devil's offer of witch-hood and takes to her aerial broomstick. Naked. She is reunited with her lover and recovers his novel ('manuscripts don't burn', the novel declares enigmatically), having taken terrible revenge on his critics. They drink a draft of Pontius Pilate's poisoned wine and die, but are resurrected into a kind of eternal half-life. The Homeless poet lives on.

Generation after generation has read *The Master and Margarita* in a spirit of entertained wonder. Just don't ask what it all means.

Memories of My Melancholy Whores, Gabriel García Márquez, 2004

Critics had to wait ten years for Márquez' novel. Suspense was sharpened by the fact that the author was seventy-six years old when he wrote it – would the obituarists beat the printers to the finishing post? The book was novella-length – wholly lacking in the trademark Márquez magic but containing some extremely uncomfortable realism. Viz the opening, which is as economical with words as a Scotsman's telegram:

> The year I turned ninety, I wanted to give myself the gift of a night of wild love with an adolescent virgin. I thought of Rosa Cabarcas, the owner of an illicit house who would inform her good clients when she had a new girl available . . . after the first ring I recognised the voice on the phone, and with no preambles I fired at her: 'Today's the day.'

It is the day he is ready formally to enrol himself as a very dirty old man indeed. The reader has to fill in the lightly sketched narrative frame around the unnamed narrator-hero. We can work out that the story is set in Márquez' home-town, Aracataca. It's the 1960s. Pre-computer, pre-mobile and pre-narco-state Colombia. He is the sole surviving relic of a once-grand family, and is now subsisting as a newspaper columnist – subject to bone-headed censorship from the state-appointed 'Abominable No-Man', with his 'blood-red pencil'. He has never had 'intimate friends, and the few who came close are in New York. By which I mean they're dead.'

There is still life in this old Colombian dog, though. He was twice elected 'client of the year' by the town's bordellos. (Who says there are no democratic elections in Colombia?) He is possessed of a 'burro's [donkey's] cock'. In his whole life he has never had sexual relations other than with whores and his servant – whom he takes in a humiliating servile posture, usually while she is bending down getting on with the housework.

The brothel-keeper, Rosa, duly supplies a fourteen-year-old from the country who has hitherto supported her family and crippled mother by sewing on buttons twelve hours a day in a clothing factory. Now a better source of income offers itself. Her virginity will cost the narrator five pesos. And afterwards? John Updike, who wrote a very uneasy review in the *New Yorker*, reminds us of a corresponding scene in Márquez' world-famous *One Hundred Years of Solitude* (1967), in which Aureliano Buendía visits a very young whore, an 'adolescent mulatto girl' with 'small bitch's teats'. He is her sixty-fourth customer of the night.

> Her back was raw. Her skin was stuck to her ribs and her breathing was forced because of an immeasurable exhaustion. Two years before, far away from there, she had fallen asleep without putting out the candle and had awakened surrounded by flames. The house where she lived with the grandmother who had raised her was reduced to ashes. Since then her grandmother carried her from town to town, putting her to bed for twenty cents in order to make up the value of the burned house. According to the girl's calculations, she still had ten years of seventy men per night, because she also had to pay the expenses of the trip and food for both of them.

This time, the madam takes the precaution of drugging the fourteen-year-old virgin. But he finds he can't deflower her – mysteriously, he falls in love. On successive visits he reads her fairy stories. He gives her the name 'Delgadina' (her birth name he does not trouble to discover). She too is mixed-race, with 'molasses-coloured skin. . . dark and warm'. Her 'newborn breasts still seemed like a boy's, but they appeared full to bursting with a secret energy that was ready to explode'.

It's a familiar problem in literature. Shakespeare's Juliet is thirteen. *Autres temps, autres moeurs*, one mutters. With this novel one might vary it to *autres pays, autres moeurs*. But in the second decade of the twenty-first century, it makes one uneasy. And that, one suspects, is exactly what Márquez set out to do.

The Message to the Planet, Iris Murdoch, 1989

This is a terrible novel. Terrible, that is, in the sense that it will terrify any thinking person who reads it. Put another way, it will terrify any person still (thank God) capable of thinking.

Murdoch published her first novel *Under the Net* in 1954. Her last, *Jackson's Dilemma*, was published in 1995. She was seventy-five and shortly afterward was diagnosed with Alzheimer's disease. It progressed thereafter blessedly fast and she died in 1999. Dr Peter Garrard, of UCL's Institute of Cognitive Neuroscience, analysed syntactic complexity and vocabulary ranges in the last novel and saw clear indicators of the disease at work. 'Alzheimer's', Garrard noted, 'is known to disrupt the brain's semantic system, but this can happen subtly before anyone has the remotest suspicion of intellectual decline.' Given this cue one looked, with gloomy suspicion, at other late-life works by Murdoch. Were any even subtler precursor signs discernible?

The Message to the Planet, published six years before the disease had progressed to a catastrophic state, is (to my un-clinical eye) the work of a writer in full possession of her abilities, although the novel has a palpably more confusing narrative line than one finds in the precise narrative geometries of *A Severed Head* (1961) or *The Bell* (1958). But, with the poignant knowledge of what was imminently to come for the author, *The Message to the Planet* is intensely interesting in terms of what it's about. It poses the question commonly confronted by thinking people as they come to the end of their life, when it's a toss-up whether brain-death comes before the grim reaper: what did it all mean?

Losing one's mind, one's hold over knowledge, was traditionally called 'madness'. It is now called dementia, which is Latin for the same thing but softer on the ear. Being 'medical' it also hints at possible cure, which, for Alzheimer's, there isn't. Dementia is most commonly a disease of the old. It would be more honest to call it an epidemic of the old. Statistically it affects one in fourteen people over the age of sixty-five, one in six over the age of eighty. 'Oh, let me not be mad, not mad, sweet heaven. Keep me in temper: I would not be mad!' pleads eighty-something King Lear. The sweet heavens take no notice of his prayer, any more than of those one-in-six afflicted.

The Message to the Planet opens:

> 'Of course we have to do with two madmen now, not with one.'
> 'You mean Marcus is mad too?'
> 'No, he means Patrick is mad too.'
> 'What do you mean?'

It takes a moment to work out that three people are talking about two other people. They are, it emerges, the novel's five principals; all men, and each representative of some mode of knowledge or creative discourse. They are 'minds' of a different kind. The central character – through whose viewpoint the narrative unfolds – is Alfred Ludens, a reader in history on sabbatical from London University. Gildas Herne (the first speaker) is a musician and ex-priest. He represents the weak magnetic force which holds the group together; the novel begins and ends with the main characters joining to sing as an amateur choir under his direction. Patrick Fenman is an Irish poet; Jack Sheerwater an artist. This quartet revolves around the pivotal figure of Marcus Vallar, a philosopher and mathematician who has travelled beyond knowledge as it is partitioned in academic departments and books. Marcus may be mad, or he may be a new Leonardo on the brink of devising a universal language, a kind of grand unified theory which will deliver a message to the planet. As the novel opens, he is a recluse living no one knows where.

From four of its five points of 'mentation' (Gildas serves mainly as a choric figure in both senses) the novel branches out. The main track is Ludens' hunt for Marcus in order to discover his messianic 'message'. He 'knows' something. When Marcus is finally located and persuaded to return and raise Patrick from the dead (as it is given out by the tabloids), the reclusive philosopher becomes the object of a hysterical cult. What he 'knows' remains a message in a cloud, depicted in a suspiciously cloudy novel.

Middlemarch, George Eliot, 1872

Middlemarch first came my way at university. The critical orthodoxy under which I was instructed was antagonistic to the novel. The favoured dismissal was Lord David Cecil's 'the dust lies thicker on George Eliot than on Thackeray and Dickens'. Eliot was, my tutor (the influential Monica Jones, mistress of Philip Larkin) informed me, the kind of novelist evangelicals permitted their children to read on Sunday. Cecil was a belle-lettrist who politely pressed his points home by means of a refined prose style and a sensibility more delicate than one's own. He was sternly opposed (I'm talking about the early 1960s) by the strenuously moralistic Leavisite regime, for whom George Eliot was one of the five pillars of the 'Great Tradition' of English fiction (Thackeray and Dickens weren't). The Leavisites had the bigger, noisier guns. And despite a few rear-guard pockets of resistance (one of which was mine and Monica's at Leicester), they won the day. That day, mercifully, has long passed. My tutor shifted me towards Thackeray – on whom I went on to write a PhD. Gold in your pocket for life, Monica said, as she recommended not just the big novels but everything – even *The Virginians* ('I heard,' observed Thackeray to Douglas Jerrold, 'that you said *The Virginians* is the worst novel I ever wrote.' 'No,' quipped Jerrold; 'I said, "It's the worst novel anybody ever wrote"').

The relative valuations shifted, as they always do with time. The emergent women's movement elevated Eliot's status. They saw things in the novel that Lord David hadn't. It became a tectonic shift, when, thanks to Andrew Davies' television adaptation in spring 1994, *Middlemarch* shot to the top of the British paperback bestseller list. Dust was meanwhile landing by the sackful on Thackeray. He's still buried under it. When I finally got round to reading *Middlemarch* carefully and objectively I found it oddly congruent with the novel I had taken as its anti-type, Thackeray's VANITY FAIR – subtitled *A Novel without a Hero*. Both large novels are 'antedated' – that characteristic Victorian habit of setting the action of their novels in the distant, controllable past. In Thackeray's case, it was the Waterloo era, and the great battle that made the century England's. In Eliot's case the setting was a decade later, in the months before the first Reform Bill, which rendered Britain the world's first 'mature' parliamentary democracy. Thackeray's main narrative throughline is the seesawing careers of a good woman (Amelia) and a bad one (Becky). He slyly inclines us to root for the bad woman. Both heroines end up, either side of a counter at a charity bazaar, as respectable high-Victorian ladies. The fact that one is brainless and the other an adulteress and possibly also a murderess is irrelevant. The novel ends with a long sigh about the human condition:

> Ah! *Vanitas Vanitatum!* which of us is happy in this world? Which of us has his desire? Or, having it, is satisfied?– come, children, let us shut up the box and the puppets, for our play is played out.

The corresponding throughline in *Middlemarch* centres on Dorothea Brooke. Her defining epithet is 'ardent' – she burns with desire to become the St Theresa of her day. After the woes of a self-sacrificing union and an undescribed second marriage, the novel's epitaph tells us:

> Her finely touched spirit had still its fine issues, though they were not widely visible. Her full nature, like that river of which Cyrus broke the strength, spent itself in channels which had no great name on the earth. But the effect of her being on those around her was incalculably diffusive, for the growing good of the world is partly dependent on unhistoric acts, and that things are not so ill with you

and me as they might have been is half owing to the number who lived faithfully a hidden life and rest in unvisited tombs.

St Theresa's tomb, of course, was, and is, much visited.

Both novels are in frank disagreement with Thomas Carlyle, and his notion that society depended on 'hero-worship' and hierarchy. It is ordinariness, unheroic behaviour and 'hidden lives' that characterise – and shore up – British society, the great Victorian novels assert. It took me a long time, and a lot of prejudicial decontamination, to work out what Victorian fiction was saying to me. But, renegade that I am, I still take more readerly joy in Thackeray.

Middlesex, Jeffery Eugenides, 2002

The great thing for lovers of fiction is that once you graduate from the dictatorship of education (see the foregoing entry) you can choose books at will, as whimsically as you fancy, and – unlike those you fall in love with – they never say no. I read *Middlesex* not because it won a Pulitzer. Nor because it was an Oprah pick. Nor because it sold three million copies and received, as far as one could see, not a single uncomplimentary review. The reason I bought a copy was because I saw someone reading it on the London underground (geographically thundering through subterranean Middlesex) with a perplexed expression on her face.

When I skimmed through the contents of my newly purchased copy and saw the chapter-heading 'The Oracular Vulva', I understood my fellow-passenger's perplexity. The first chapter ('The Silver Spoon' – i.e. what the hero was born with) opens:

I was born twice: first, as a baby girl, on a remarkably smogless Detroit day in January of 1960; and then again, as a teenage boy, in an emergency room near Petoskey, Michigan, in August of 1974. Specialized readers may have come across me in Dr Peter Luce's study, 'Gender Identity in 5-Alpha-Reductase Pseudohermaphrodites,' published in the *Journal of Pediatric Endocrinology* in 1975... My birth certificate lists my name as Calliope Helen Stephanides. My most recent driver's license (from the Federal Republic of Germany) records my first name simply as Cal... now, at the age of forty-one, I feel another birth coming on.

One might well be reminded of that surprise line in Virginia Woolf's novel, 'Orlando had become a woman'. Or the Kinks song, penned by Ray Davies, about the ambiguous Lola: 'Girls will be boys and boys will be girls'. Or Ovid's *Metamorphoses*. Or *Myra Breckenridge*. One might go on to wonder whether the author's name – which means 'well born' in Greek – is a pen-name (it isn't).

Eugenides' novel, in its largest sense, is about another odd mixture – what it is to be a Greek-American. They are, compared to, say, the Jews, Japanese, or African-Americans, a very 'unachieving' ethnic group. They could have had a Greek-American president, the narrator sadly muses, if Dukakis hadn't got himself photographed in that damned tank. And Spiro T. Agnew (born Anagnostopoulos) didn't exactly cover his compatriots of Greek descent with glory. The Stephanides family, of which Cal/Calliope is the chronicler, began three generations back as silk farmers in a village in Turkey. They emigrated to the US in 1922, in order to find some peace from the never-ending Greco-Turkish war and the death throes of the Ottoman Empire. The patriarch grandfather, nicknamed Lefty in the US, leads the family into the new world, where they first settle with a clandestinely lesbian relative in Detroit. Lefty marries his sister, the captain officiating, on the voyage across. The good-natured skipper loans him a gravy-stained tie for the illegal occasion. Incest increases the likelihood of gene problems.

After a spell working on Henry Ford's assembly lines and some bootlegging, the enterprising Lefty opens a saloon called the Zebra Room (the zebra being that classically miscegenated beast). The Stephanides family rises in the world. Perversely, thanks to some canny insurance scams, the 1960s Detroit riots allow them to move to swish Grosse Pointe. The narrator-hero is born, third-generation (when the immigrant blood, traditionally, 'runs thin'), in the 1940s. He is unaware of his genetic doom. Love affairs fizzle out mysteriously. Finally, after an accident with a tractor, a clever doctor discovers his ARD-5 status. Rather than accepting surgical-pharmaceutical 'cure', Cal/Callie goes on the run – a refugee less from his family than from his biology. Thereafter the narrative goes everywhere, finishing in San Francisco and Germany.

Middlesex is consciously 'epic' (he/she has, says Cal/Calliope, a genetic tendency to 'Homeric' expression), and chauvinistically follows that Aristotelian prescription that epic is a literary form which begins *in medias res*. Arguably *Middlesex* never quite emerges from the middle of anything. But neither, we apprehend, does life. It's an odd novel. I daresay my face, too, looked perplexed as I read it.

A Million Little Pieces, James Frey, 2003

In 2003 James Frey published a graphic chronicle of his alcoholic debaucheries and recovery. *A Million Little Pieces* shot to the top of the American non-fiction charts. But, while it was still up there in the bestseller stratosphere, making its (now clean and sober) author rich, the website The Smoking Gun disclosed, after strenuous research into court and police documents, that Frey's book was, as they challengingly put it, 'a million little lies'. Frey did not rise to the challenge and sue.

It should have meant disgrace. It didn't. *A Million Little Pieces* promptly shot to the top of the charts as a 'novel'. Was it a different book in its two super-selling categories? Or was it a book where the fact/fiction criterion was irrelevant? And how blurry are our minds to such things when we read?

The fictional / factual storyline runs thus. James Frey (or his novelistic avatar) comes to, after a three-week bender:

> I wake to the drone of an airplane engine and feeling of something warm dripping down my chin. I lift my hand to feel my face. My front four teeth are gone, I have a hole in my cheek, my nose is broken and my eyes are swollen nearly shut. I open them and I look around and I'm in the back of a plane and there's no one near me. I look at my clothes and my clothes are covered with a colourful mixture of spit, snot, urine, vomit and blood.

James is being transported, he discovers, like 180 pounds of probably unrecyclable human garbage, to a rehab centre. He is wanted in three states on felony charges. He is a twenty-three-year-old multi-drug abuser. A jailbird. A tough guy. Physicians regard him as a most interesting case. 'You have done', a doctor informs him – amazement in his voice,

> significant damage to your nose, your throat, your lungs, your stomach, your bladder, your kidneys, your liver, and your heart. I have never seen so much and such extensive damage in someone so young... If you start drinking or using drugs regularly, you will be dead within a few days.

The narrative of *A Million Little Pieces* covers his stay in the centre. It is not named but identifiably the Hazelden institute in Minnesota. It boasts the highest addiction-therapy success rate in the country: seventeen per cent, apparently. The roulette wheel at Las Vegas offers better odds.

Those who make it to the sunny uplands of 'clean and sober' get with the Hazelden programme. James does not. He has 'attitude'. The 'Fury' he calls it. (Frey/Fury – get it?) He picks fights with fellow patients, he breaks the institute rule against dating female inmates, he hangs out with a recovering Mafia don. He 'disses' his long-suffering doctors. He won't take his medication. He doesn't buy the twelve-step programme ('bullshit') which the institute regards as essential for recovery. He despises the 'disease concept of alcoholism'. Cancer is a disease, he sneers. Addiction isn't. A disease 'cannot be dealt with by... reading books with blue covers or saying prayers about serenity'. Nonetheless he ends up among the saved seventeen per cent. How? By willpower. He stays sober because he damn well decides to. Well done, you horrible person, one is tempted to say. Now bugger off.

Horrible sells. In October 2005, while Frey's drunkalog was still accepted as God's honest truth, Oprah selected *A Million Little Pieces* as one of her picks. She lauded it on her show, tears streaming. In interview with her, Frey vaunted his book's opening statement: 'I am an Alcoholic and I am a drug Addict and I am a Criminal.' Sales soared to near four million. Brad Pitt was interested in the film rights. Then six weeks of digging by The Smoking Gun website revealed that not all was quite as it seemed. Originally Frey had submitted the work as fiction. It was turned down by a series of publishers. Ironically, once denounced (after an embarrassing mea culpa on Oprah) James Frey was revealed not as an alcoholic/addict/criminal but – what else? – a novelist. Not a great novelist, some would possibly argue.

Misery, Stephen King, 1987

King has frequently raised a rueful protest against being typed as a horror writer. 'I could', he protests, 'be an "important" writer like Joseph Heller and publish a novel every seven years or so, or a "brilliant" writer like John Gardner and write obscure books for bright academics who eat macrobiotic foods and drive old Saabs.'

Instead of which he is the 'King of Horror', who has had his face on *Time* and probably earns as much in a year as the Saab motor company. He cries, in other words, all the way to the bank. Or, as he puts it, 'I don't give a shit what they call me, so long as I can sleep at night.' Nevertheless, for all his zest in being his triumphant self, it's clear he has mixed feelings about the loyal public who have made him 'Number One', with their vampiric demand for ever more of the same from him. The mixed feelings are worked through in *Misery*. The best of his novels, I would hazard.

A bestselling author, Paul Sheldon, crashes in a desolate area of the Rockies. It is winter, his car is buried in the snow, and his broken body is rescued by a homicidal and crazy nurse, Annie Wilkes, who before retiring under something of a professional cloud killed more than a few of her patients. But she is a devoted – not to say fanatical – fan of Sheldon's bodice-ripper heroine, Misery Chastain. Unluckily, Sheldon has just killed off Misery, so as to free himself from historical romance and write 'serious' novels of the Heller/Gardner kind.

Annie installs Sheldon in a wheelchair, hooks him on codeine, and keeps him locked up in a bedroom in her lonely farmhouse. Discovering that he has with him the manuscript of a new novel, she forces him to barbecue the only copy when she discovers it to be a 'literary' effort, a realistic study of adolescent slum life. Before the snows melt and his car is discovered, at which point she will kill him, she obliges Sheldon to write for her personal delectation *Misery's Return*, bringing the dead heroine back to pulp life. The deal is simple: no story = no drugs and a lot of pain. When Sheldon tries to escape, Nurse Wilkes chops off his left foot with an axe and cauterises the wound with a propane torch. A lesser offence results in his thumb being sliced off with an electric meat knife. Kings handles such scenes with infectious glee:

> Paul screamed as fire splashed over the raw and bleeding stump. Smoke drifted up. It smelled sweet. He and his first wife had honeymooned on Maui. There had been a luau. This smell reminded him of the smell of the pig when they brought it out of the pit where it had cooked all day. The pig had been on a stick, sagging black, falling apart.

Under Annie's sharp-edged regime, Sheldon actually contrives to produce *Misery's Return*, which he recognises as the best instalment of the saga. Nurse, it would seem, knows best.

In the inevitably gory climax Sheldon turns the tables. By a ruse, he manages simultaneously to incinerate his number one fan and the romance she has forced him to write. He finishes her off by choking her with the ashes of the novel. Rescued and patched together (what's left of him), Sheldon, a wiser and sadder author, writes up the experience as *Misery*.

Misery's writing-treadmill-with-torture expresses King's jaundiced view of the genre author–reader relationship, and its mutual imprisonments. The fan is a monster who first makes you famous and then traps you in the fame like a wasp in a jam jar, and does nasty things – like not buying your books – if you act out of character. There are many real-life confirmations of King's thesis that in popular fiction you create a success at your peril. Conan Doyle thought himself free from Sherlock Holmes ('he takes my mind from better things') when he killed the sleuth at the Reichenbach Falls on 4 May 1891. But reader demand obliged him to resurrect Holmes. Fans wouldn't let James Bond decently retire the service with the death of his creator Ian Fleming, but kept him going for an increasingly dreary series of adventures by John Gardner. For the true fan, once is never enough.

Moby-Dick; or, The Whale, Herman Melville, 1851

The world to which *Moby-Dick* was delivered was not ready for Herman Melville's masterpiece – nor would it be for seventy years. Some ultra-Melvilleans claim it still isn't. The critical exhumation of *Moby-Dick* was led by D. H. Lawrence in his 1923 book on classic American fiction. Lawrence had probably never caught anything larger than tiddlers in the Trent, but he apprehended that Melville's epic isn't to be read in the same way as one reads the yarns of old salts like Marryat – or even Joseph Conrad. It should be read metaphysically. 'What then is Moby Dick?' asked Lawrence. 'He is the deepest blood-being of the white race; he is our deepest blood-nature.' Forget blubber. The 'Melville revival' led, over the following decades, to the coronation of *Moby-Dick* as that most elusive of beasts, rarer even than pallid whales – the Great American Novel. Thar she blew.

After spending an unhappy spell as a wage-slave behind a desk – misery that gave, to grateful posterity, bartleby the scrivener – Melville's 'life began', he liked to say, when (like Ishmael) he answered the call of the sea. Bearded and wild-haired, he enrolled as a common sailor on the whaler *Acushnet* in January 1841. He was crammed for months into the forecastle – one of the only places in America where different races mixed on equal terms. The 'foc'sle' was a microcosm of America's multi-ethnicity; a melting pot on the waves. And it was a pot heated by more than race. As Melville's biographer Hershel Parker notes, 'mutual masturbation was commonplace'. Communal onanism was called 'claw for claw'– sailors going at each other's privates like fighting cocks. The description of life aboard the *Acushnet* (less the fighting cocks) was tempered by Melville's connection with the New England transcendentalists – notably Nathaniel Hawthorne, *Moby-Dick*'s dedicatee. The transcendentalists, under their presiding sage Ralph Waldo Emerson, were dedicated to finding the meaning of things. For them literature was a quasi-philosophical enterprise.

The story of *Moby-Dick* is simple. A young man of class and breeding, whose name and background are withheld, embarks as a common seaman on a whaler. Ishmael's motive is spiritual redemption. His life, he feels, is purposeless. The vessel on which he enlists, the *Pequod*, is under the command of Captain Ahab, who has lost a leg to a white whale that has determined to fight back against man. Killing Moby Dick is Ahab's quest – his reason for being. But it is, finally, the whale which wrecks the *Pequod*. Ishmael, the only sailor to escape, is saved by floating on the coffin made for the Native American Queequeg, with whom he has forged a close bond.

It's clear enough why Ahab dedicates his life to destroying a whale – he has a bone to pick with Moby Dick (a leg bone, specifically). But why was the species being hunted on such a vast scale? Whaling was, by the mid-1840s, one of the biggest industries in America. The mammals were not being slaughtered for their meat (as the Japanese now kill them) or for their bones (so useful for corsets), but for oil. A mature beast yielded as much as three tons of the stuff. Sperm whale oil created the most brilliant, and clean, source of illumination – as candlelight, and domestic and streetlight fuel – that mankind had yet come up with. What saved the sperm whale, on the brink of extinction, was the discovery in 1846 of 'kerosene' technology – this distilled a more conveniently available oil, along with petroleum (in an alternative Philip K. Dick universe mankind is driving blubber-fuelled cars). Extinction for Moby Dick's kind was postponed.

The 'Melville Revival' received a second boost in the 1970s with the arrival of queer theory as a force in literary criticism. This new explanation of Melville depended on a supposed 'encrypted sexuality' in the texts. Rich pickings for such cryptanalysts were located in Chapter 11 of *Moby-Dick*, in which Ishmael and Queequeg share a double bed, and such passages as that in the later section describing the removal of sperm oil from the whale:

> Squeeze! squeeze! squeeze! all the morning long; I squeezed that sperm till I myself almost melted into it; I squeezed that sperm till a strange sort of insanity came over me; and I found myself unwittingly squeezing my co-laborers' hands in it, mistaking their hands for the gentle globules.

'Surely the oldest piece of phallicism in all the world's literature,' D. H. Lawrence commented, thoughtfully.

The Moonstone, Wilkie Collins, 1868

In the outrageously prejudicial 2010 press hounding of the innocent schoolteacher Chris Jefferies over the murder of his young female tenant (for which the guilty parties later shelled out punitive sums in compensation), the *Sun* newspaper produced, as clinching supporting evidence, the fact that Jefferies was 'obsessed by death', and 'scared kids' in his classroom. He had, for example, taught pupils the 'Victorian murder novel' *The Moonstone*. Case closed.

Such power, I thought, is dangerous. As an English teacher at a high-ranked school, Mr Jeffries would surely have been using my edition of Wilkie Collins' novel – the only one, if I may toot my own trumpet, to make use of the manuscript and investigate the novelist's working materials. Pulp the edition, I thought, with a shudder, before it kills again. It is not, in fact, usually categorised as a 'Victorian murder novel' but, as T. S. Eliot (no less) put it, *The Moonstone* is 'the first . . . and the best of modern English detective novels'. For good measure Eliot added that it was also 'the longest', which I've always thought a bit hard on the author of BLEAK HOUSE.

Collins' story, blossom-fresh in its day, is now the oldest of genre hats. It begins with a prelude describing the storming of Seringapatam in 1799. A priceless gem is looted from a Hindu idol. It comes, by complex inheritance, into the possession of a beautiful young English woman and is stolen, by night, from the bedroom of the country house in which she lives. Incredibly, it turns out to have been stolen by the young lady's 'intended' – an ostensibly upright young fellow who even offers to investigate the mystery when it comes to light (there are shady characters, and three Hindu jugglers in the background). The drowsy, night-gowned heroine actually witnessed her intended, night-gowned, doing it (all this bedroom stuff was 'sensational' by the fictional conventions of the time).

What motivated him? The answer, we eventually discover, is somnambulism and opium. It's not clear when Collins – one of the great improvisers in fiction – hit on his 'Macguffin', as Alfred Hitchcock called the narrative device, during the year-long writing of the novel. But it is significant that during its serialisation he overdid the opium to which he was addicted (his eyes, one amanuensis reported, were like bags of blood) and composed a whole section of the novel in a trance. When his head cleared he could not recall what he had written. So, too, is Franklin Blake innocent of the crime he committed. A neat parallel.

The novel is enriched by any number of surrealistic touches – notably a piebald, mixed-race, persecuted scientist who uncovers the drugging ruse on which the novel's plot-work depends. It is one of any number of reasons for admiring *The Moonstone*. But principal among those reasons is the novel's educative value. Collins refines the 'evidence from the witness box' technique he introduced in *The Woman in White*. Different characters give 'their version' of the central events. It places the reader in the position of juror. Put bluntly, it makes the reader work harder. Not everyone was grateful for this: Anthony Trollope, for example, complained, in his bluff way, that 'When I sit down to write a novel I do not at all know, and I do not very much care, how it is to end'. Collins, on the other hand, seemed always,

> . . . to be warning me to remember that something happened at exactly half-past two o'clock on Tuesday morning; or that a woman disappeared from the road just fifteen yards beyond the fourth mile-stone.

'Such work', said the amiable chronicler of Barsetshire, 'gives me no pleasure', conceding that he was quite prepared 'to acknowledge that the want of pleasure comes from fault of my intellect'.

Trollope was right. What Collins demanded was a more attentive, cleverer kind of reader. Over the century and a half since *The Moonstone* had readers panting for the next instalment, readers have become, generation by generation, cannier participants in the detective-story reading game. So much so that *The Moonstone*, written when the genre was in its infancy, now seems clunky. But, like T. S. Eliot, we should salute it for its ground-breaking achievement and enduring charm.

Mr Lonely, Eric Morecambe, 1981

Literary history records some unusual novelists – Winston Churchill, Josef Goebbels, Saddam Hussein. Britain's greatest stage comedian (as many would rank him) belongs in that strange literary compartment with the 'Who would have thought. . .?' label.

He's nicer than Goebbels and, though untutored in the craft, a better novelist than any of the above. Tolstoy once complained that no one, asked if they could play the violin, would think to seriously reply: 'I don't know, I've never tried.' Yet everyone assumes that they could write a novel if they only had the leisure to do it. Eric Morecambe had the leisure to try his hand at fiction during convalescence from one of the many heart attacks which afflicted him from the age of forty-five onwards, and which would kill him three years after *Mr Lonely*, following what is recorded to have been a cracking performance at the Roses Theatre in Tewkesbury. 'Bring Me Sunshine' should have been playing.

To judge by *Mr Lonely*, had Eric ever picked up a violin he would have been able to play it straight off at least as well as Jack Benny. Which is to say that Morecambe is no Tolstoy, but nevertheless was capable of writing an extremely readable novel. It opens with a description of the lower-class Northern background in which most of Britain's great comedians originated, before the toff *Beyond the Fringe* crew arrived to up the social tone and convert 'Variety' into 'Satire':

> Sid Lewis came into this world exactly the same way as any other child. He weighed eight and a half pounds and had a shock of black hair. The trouble was, as he used to say, 'It wasn't on my head, it was all under my left arm.' His childhood was normal, lumps, bumps and mumps. His schooling was average – sums, bums, and chums. He left school when he was fourteen and went to work behind the counter of a tobacconist's shop earning fifteen shillings a week and all he could inhale.

Morecambe inhaled sixty a day. It didn't help with the heart attacks.

Sid Lewis moves on, in young manhood, to tread the music-hall boards. From early on he is happily married but never able to resist a bit on the side. Anything on the side that comes his way, in fact. But, as show business people say, 'it doesn't matter on tour'. One night, in front of a particularly difficult audience, he creates a new character – Mr Lonely. A man nobody loves. A BBC scout sees the perfomance, and is impressed, and Sid finds himself on his way up from the Pier End at Yarmouth to Las Vegas and best-ever thirty-five-million ratings for his BBC Christmas Show (a record in fact held by Morecambe and Wise in the mid-1970s). Sid dies at the height of his career, when a taxi bumps into him and drives two of the points of showbiz's supreme 'Star' award through his heart. As Sid's signature tune puts it: 'Hey Mr Lone-ly, Why can't you see, Suc-cess is no guar-an-tee.'

There's plenty of scope in *Mr Lonely* for Eric's psycho-biographers. Morecambe was not, like Sid Lewis, a solo artist, but half of a celebrated double act. Yet, as Conrad observes in *Heart of Darkness*, we live as we dream, alone. The thought may have occurred to the comedian-novelist that at death's door he wasn't, for once, dancing off into the blue with his little hairy-legged friend.

That there are other links between Eric and Sid is strongly suggested by various tricks in the novel. The author makes personal, rather John Fowles-like, interventions at various points in the narrative. For the rest, *Mr Lonely* has, as one would expect, some good one-liners, some hilarious sex-on-the-side scenes (there's a particularly funny episode in a massage parlour), and some corny mother-in-law and agent jokes: 'My agent's very unhappy. I'm getting 90 per cent of his salary.' There was, one might say, a novelist inside Morecambe, struggling to get out.

Mrs Dalloway, Virginia Woolf, 1925

It is not an easy novel to read, but *Mrs Dalloway* is the easiest of novels to summarise. 'A day in the life of a middle-aged upper-class London woman planning her party' is how the *Oxford Companion to Twentieth-Century Literature* encapsulates it. The 'day' is 13 June 1923 by the best guess an astute reader can make. The 'upper-class woman'

is Clarissa Dalloway, the wife of a 'sporty', middle-ranking Conservative politician who has never quite made it into cabinet. Mrs Dalloway (the narrative avoids any cosy 'Clarissas') is recovering from a serious illness and concomitant depression, for which she has been treated by eminent Harley Street physicians. But she is not yet entirely 'well' – in body or mind.

The long prelude to the party is Mrs Dalloway's morning walk through the West End of London to collect the flowers for the party she and her husband are throwing that evening. When she returns from buying the blooms (exclusive florist in Bond Street, of course) she finds she has a visitor, Peter Walsh. Thirty years earlier they had been on the brink of marriage, in an affair which reached its emotional climax at a country house, Bourton.

Young Clarissa declined Peter's proposal; the reasons are not clear. A temporary surge of lesbian rebellion is hinted at. Since then their lives have gone their separate ways. Peter migrated to India, and missed the war. There is a woman in India, Daisy, whom he may, or may not, have a relationship with. His conversation with Clarissa is unsatisfactory and he goes off, disconsolately, to ruminate in Regent's Park, fiddling all the while with the pen-knife in his pocket. He has, he may well feel, fiddled his life away.

The park is also where a World War One veteran, Septimus Smith, is walking distractedly with his Italian wife, Lucrezia (a hat maker). Septimus is still suffering from shell-shock, and is seriously deranged. The birds, he fantasises, are talking to him – in ancient Greek (this actually happened to Woolf in one of her recurrent breakdowns). His mind has been shattered. Before the war he was a sensitive, promising poet. During the conflict he had an intense relationship with his officer in the trenches, Evans, who was killed. It haunts him.

Septimus is about to go for a consultation with Clarissa's eminent Harley Street psychiatrist, Sir William Bradshaw. No help is forthcoming. Sir William's advice is platitudinous and useless. Septimus must be moved to an asylum.

The narrative focus shifts to Richard Dalloway, Clarissa's husband, at lunch with two friends, Hugh Whitbread and Lady

Bruton. They talk of grand affairs of state – pointlessly. They are not serious political players. Richard returns home with a bunch of roses for Clarissa. He senses their relationship has, obscurely, gone wrong. He is right.

The focus moves again to Septimus and Lucrezia at home, waiting for his removal to the asylum. In terror, he throws himself out of a window, impaling himself, fatally, on the spiked iron railings below. As the ambulance bell rings, Peter (who hears it) goes to Clarissa's party.

Also present is Sally Seton, with whom Clarissa was on the brink of being in love many years ago. Once a tomboy, Sally is now dull Lady Rosseter. News of Septimus' death arrives and is gossiped about, aimlessly. Clarissa feels a bond with the dead man – stronger, we apprehend, than that for her husband or her near-adult daughter, Elizabeth (on the brink of conversion to rigidly evangelical Christianity). The novel ends, inconclusively but pregnantly.

It is always wrong to read an author's life too directly into their creative writing. But the immediate circumstances in which Woolf wrote *Mrs Dalloway* are relevant. She was forty years old when she began writing the novel in 1922 and was in bad health, mentally and physically. 'Illness' is, at one point in the narrative, a euphemism for 'menopause', which she, and her heroine, may be supposed to be going through. Virginia and her husband Leonard visited a series of Harley Street physicians and therapists. As Claire Tomalin records:

> One specialist diagnosed diseased lungs, another inflammation of the heart, incurable and likely to prove fatal very shortly; a third discovered yet another incurable disease.

There is a mystery at the heart of Woolf's novel. Why make her heroine a conservative politician's wife when she, and more actively Leonard, were card-carrying Fabians and active socialists? The best answer one can come up with is a version of Kipling's 'sisters under the skin'. Whatever their 'party' women have more in common with each other than with any man.

My Ántonia, Willa Cather, 1918

As with George Eliot's *Romola* you can tell if the person talking to you has actually read the novel if they pronounce its title properly. As the hero of this one is instructed: 'the name is pronounced An-ton-ee-ah'. In *My Ántonia* Cather, as elsewhere, chronicles the pioneers – those who pushed American civilisation ever westwards. Steamrollered in the process were the indigenous 'redskin' population, who survive only in place names, as poignantly resonant as the inscriptions on tombstones – here Black Hawk (based on the original town, Red Cloud) and Nebraska (based on an ancient Otoe Indian word).

The novel opens elegantly. The narrator, an author by profession, meets a childhood friend on a train. As they speed westward across the great plains, 'flashing through never ending miles of ripe wheat' in the observation car, they reminisce about Nebraska, in its more primitive era, and particularly a girl they knew ('their' Ántonia) and both loved. The friend, Jim Burden, is a successful New York lawyer who feels he has lost something vital from his life. He married 'brilliantly' but is unhappy in his marriage and childless. The narrator invites Jim to tell his life story with a portrait of Ántonia – 'Tony'. He, with his professional skills, will lick it into shape. A few months later, in New York, Jim delivers the manuscript. So powerful is it that the narrator passes it to the reader 'unimproved'.

Jim, a child of genteel background, arrives in Nebraska from Virginia. He is a ten-year-old orphan who will be brought up by his grandparents on their farm. He is a migrant, of a kind – but white, prosperous, Protestant. On the train to his new home, reading a dime novel about the Wild West, he sees – in a lower class of carriage – a family of farther-flung immigrants from Bohemia (Czechoslavakia). The Shimerdas are bound for the same destination as he is. Clearly the brightest spark in the family ('bright as a new dollar') is a twelve-year-old girl who already knows a dozen words of English. 'We go Black Hawk, Nebraska', Ántonia (Tony) tells Jim.

He goes back to his comfortable farm house and the Shimerdas take up residence in a 'sod house' (a squalid mud cabin) as tenant farmers. The Burdens, as is common among pioneers, are kind and friendly to newer Americans than they. Tony's father implores Jim to teach 'my Ántonia', which, over the next year, he does. The ethnic patchwork of Swedes, Norwegians, Bohemians and older-rooted Americans is closely and respectfully described. Human beings, said the philosopher Schopenhauer, are like porcupines. They only huddle together when the weather is cold. Nebraska's cold is legendary. Spit is an icicle before it hits the ground.

Over two deliciously golden months in autumn, after the harvest has been brought in, the young Jim and Tony fall in love. The setting is Edenic and Jim's descriptions are lyrical. There is even a snake, which he kills to protect the terrified Tony. But her father, a weaver by trade (and a gifted fiddler), is not made for pioneer life and commits suicide in the depths of the following winter. Ántonia and her brothers keep the farm going. But there is no more 'teaching'

for her. Jim shines at school, and wins a place to study law at Lincoln. Eden is for ever lost. Back in Black Hawk, Tony is left pregnant, then abandoned, by a ne'er-do-well railway engineer. She buckles to and marries a new man, bearing another nine children.

Twenty years on an unrecognisable Jim, now a well-off if unhappy lawyer, makes a return visit. Tony is toothless, but

> The eyes that peered anxiously at me were – simply Ántonia's eyes. I had seen no others like them since I looked into them last, though I had looked at so many thousands of human faces. As I confronted her, the changes grew less apparent to me, her identity stronger. She was there, in the full vigour of her personality, battered but not diminished, looking at me, speaking to me in the husky, breathy voice I remembered so well.

The novel leaves poignantly open what Jim has gained and what he has lost. 'His' Ántonia.

Naked Lunch, **William S. Burroughs, 1959**

This is a novel which deals with pederasty, cannibalism, exotic ravishments and drug addiction – most of them calculated to put you off your lunch. Unsurprisingly, published when it was, *Naked Lunch* provoked a censorship crisis in the English-speaking world. The narrative of its bumpy road to publication is an interesting story in itself (the novel is not particularly strong as regards story).

Naked Lunch was written in the US but wholly unpublishable there as a book, although some excerpts surfaced covertly in small-circulation magazines. France, at the time, was indulgent to libertine works in languages in which the chauvinist authorities were not interested (i.e. everything but French). Burroughs offered his (reportedly) rat-gnawed manuscript to the Paris publisher of underground books, Maurice Girodias. It was sent back for tidying up and rodent decontamination before being published in Paris in 1959. Emboldened by the liberating 1959–60 *Lady Chatterley* trials, Grove Press, a boundary-pushing specialist in 'raunchy' literature (de Sade was their bestselling author), brought out *Naked Lunch* in America in 1962 (inevitably it was 'Banned in Boston' – a badge of pride for a Grove Press book).

In Britain, the book was published in 1964 by the consistently risk-taking John Calder, who adopted various canny tactics to avoid prosecution. This was a novel which took things well beyond wholesome 'Lady Chat' had done. Calder's hardback was duly priced at a whopping 42s. More provocatively, he took out large advertisements in the literary papers describing *Naked Lunch* as 'one of the most significant literary events of our era. . . a book that is lectured on in British university courses. . . British publication is a matter of historical necessity'. Some might have thought matters arising from the Cuban Missile Crisis were of greater historical necessity. Burroughs' own attempts at explaining the work to the British public were little help. He visited in early 1963 (under sufferance from the immigration authorities) and had a broadcast conversation, on the Third Programme. On further consideration the BBC chose to edit out Burroughs' comment:

> Did I ever tell you about the man who taught his asshole to talk? His whole abdomen would move up and down and, you dig, farting out the words. It was quite unlike anything I ever heard.

And quite unlike what the prim listeners to the Third were used to hearing via their wireless sets.

Naked Lunch has three main elements. It is: (1) an essay on drug withdrawal; (2) a 'scholarly' study of addiction; and (3) a paranoid-sexual fantasia. In themselves these themes could be handled in the early 1960s without raising any hackles except for Mrs Whitehouse's. But Burroughs' novel (if, indeed, it is a novel) jolted its readership with vividly described scenes of necrophilia and cannibalism particularly in the 'hanging' scenes, such as that of the underage boy, Johnny, by his tormentors Mary and Mark (Burroughs' trademark ellipses are as below, mine in square brackets):

> She [Mary] locks her hands behind Johnny's buttocks, puts her forehead against him, smiling into his eyes she moves back, pulling him off the platform into space . . . His face swells with blood . . . Mark reaches up with one lithe movement and snaps Johnny's neck . . . sound like a stick broken in wet towels. A shudder runs down Johnny's body . . . one foot flutters like a trapped bird . . . Mark has draped himself over a swing and mimics Johnny's twitches, closes his eyes and sticks his tongue out . . . Johnny's cock springs up and Mary guides it up her cunt, writhing against him in a fluid belly dance, groaning and shrieking with delight [. . .] She bites away Johnny's lips and nose and sucks out his eyes with a pop . . . She tears off great hunks of cheek . . . Now she lunches on his prick.

There were well-attested accounts of readers at the time vomiting. Sensibilities have hardened since. Who knows? We shall perhaps live to hear *Naked Lunch* as a Radio 4 'Book at Bedtime' and set for GCSE examination.

The Name of the Rose, Umberto Eco, 1980

I was lucky enough to have attended Frank Kermode's (literally seminal) 'theory' seminars in the early 1970s. Kermode, the greatest critic of his age, had long been fascinated by what he called (lovely phrase) the 'patience' of literature – its ability to return any number of variant, sometimes contradictory, 'readings'.

Theory – particularly that of the post-structuralists – put an interesting twist on literature's 'plurivalence', its many-meaningfulness. Roland Barthes – in *S/Z*, his exemplary reading of a Balzac story – and the cluster of writers around the journal *Tel Quel* ('As is') were particularly influential in propagating the new ideas. Eco, one of the sages of Bologna University (a city famous for its baloney, as wags pointed out), was a leading *Tel Quel* contributor. (He was fascinated, oddly, by James Bond, and wrote about 007 – post-structurally, semiotically, and hermeneutically – in the journal's pages.) In America, the theory revolution began with a momentous conference in October 1966 at Johns Hopkins University, when a clutch of French theorists turned up, and turned upside-down the way the Anglo-American academy read its literature.

The Name of the Rose, which made theory comprehensible to anyone who could read a Sherlock Holmes novel, was – to everyone's surprise – a runaway bestseller on its publication in the UK. The action takes place in 1327. Brother William of Baskerville (the Holmesian allusion is deliberate) is assigned an investigation of a possible heresy in a wealthy Italian Abbey. There are clues everywhere. Can one get beyond the empire of signs – the semiological barrier – to where that philosopher's pot of gold, the Kantian *Ding an sich*, is located? 'True learning', believes William, 'must not be content with ideas, which are, in fact, signs, but must discover things in their individual truth.' Easier said than done, Brother William.

Young Adso is assistant to William and the narrator-observer. William is a detective before the word existed, a man who can read the many meanings of the written word. 'Books', he says, 'are not made to be believed, but to be subjected to inquiry. When we consider a book, we mustn't ask ourselves what it *says* but what it *means*'. A deep proposition.

A monk, Venantius, has committed suicide. The circumstances (he is weltering in pig's blood) are mysterious. He has left a coded message. It is important to read the signs. It is believed the apocalypse is nigh. Gross sexual deviance in the abbey is hinted at. Signs everywhere, pointing everywhere.

A vast library of manuscript codices, the greatest in the Christian world, is secreted in a maze. Somewhere, on its inaccessible shelves, lies the truth. Perhaps. At the library's core, it is said, is a hitherto lost sequel to Aristotle's *Poetics* – the primal text of literary criticism. It may explain all.

There are seven (mystical number) more murders. These are not random. A homicide-code is inscribed in the gore. Feuds within the various bodies of the Church and disagreements about papal wealth and monastic poverty are aired, amongst all the blood in the cloisters and enigmatic writings in the library. It gets very intricate.

The Name of the Rose is a good, teasing, read. But what gives the book bristles is the theory interlaced with the whodunit narrative. The title, *The Name of the Rose*, picks up on two well-known quotes: Gertrude Stein's 'a rose is a rose is a rose' and Shakespeare's 'A rose by any other name would smell as sweet'. 'Semiology,' mutters the theorist. Adso discovers, in the mazy library, the facts of 'intertextuality' – that literature is principally interested in intercourse with literature: 'Until then', he says, 'I had thought each book spoke of the things, human or divine, that lie outside books. Now I realised that not infrequently books speak of books: it is as if they spoke among themselves.' The novel, we are told, is 'a machine for generating interpretations' (one recalls Sartre's definition in *Nausea*, that novels are 'machines that secrete spurious meaning into the world'). *The Name of the Rose* is not theory made easy, it's theory made fun.

Native Son, Richard Wright, 1940

Wright's title has a bitter taint. The word 'native' carries the meaning, as Bruce Springsteen grandly proclaims, 'Born in the USA', but also alludes to some kind of 'savage'. The hero, Bigger Thomas, is one of the mass of African-Americans sucked up from the agricultural South by the industrialisation of the North; from plantation shack to ghetto slum. In Chicago, black people and white people are socially wholly segregated but, in the city that pioneered the skyscraper, the two live as tightly packed together as sardines and riot is never more than minutes away.

The narrative opens one morning in the Thomases' squalid apartment on Chicago's South Side. Twenty-year-old Bigger is the man of the house. A huge rat (at least a foot long) joins the family for breakfast. Bigger batters it to death with a skillet:

> 'I got 'im,' he muttered, his clenched teeth bared in a smile. 'By God, I got 'im.'
>
> He kicked the splintered box out of the way and the flat black body of the rat lay exposed, its two long yellow tusks showing distinctly.
>
> Bigger took a shoe and pounded the rat's head, crushing it, cursing hysterically:
>
> 'You sonofa *bitch*!'

Bigger is a low-level hoodlum planning the burgling of a Jewish merchant's store. Normally he preys on his fellow African-Americans – the police don't care about solving that kind of crime. Before he puts his plan into action, Bigger has a stroke of luck. A rich white man, Dalton – a supporter, as he proudly proclaims, of the NAACP (National Association for the Advancement of Colored People) – offers Bigger a job as a chauffeur. Ironically Henry Dalton's wealth comes from property, and he owns the slum in which Bigger's family lives.

Bigger takes the menial ('Yes, suh! No, suh!') job. It's a *Driving Miss Daisy* situation, but with an angry member of the new urban slave class at the wheel. Bigger drives Miss Mary, the daughter of the house, and her communist lover, Jan, out for a night on the town. They make him take them to a 'colored' bar on the South Side. He brings Mary back, dead drunk, and carries her to her room. Overcome by sudden lust, he begins to caress her unconscious body:

> He lifted her and laid her on the bed. Something urged him to leave at once, but he leaned over her, excited, looking at her face in the dim light, not wanting to take his hands from her breasts. She tossed and mumbled sleepily. He tightened his fingers on her breasts, kissing her again, feeling her move toward him. He was aware only of her body now; his lips trembled. Then he stiffened. The door behind him had creaked.

It is the girl's blind mother entering the room. While she rebukes her daughter for stinking of whisky, Bigger covers Mary's face with a pillow (Othello's killing of Desdemona is evoked), and suffocates her. Panicstricken, he takes her body down to the furnace – it is his responsibility to keep burning during the winter. He cuts off her head (the body's too long to go in whole) and incinerates the body parts.

The plot, thereafter, goes awry. Bigger sends a ransom note to the Daltons, having cunningly suggested to the investigating authorities that it was Jan who did it. White Chicago despises the 'Blacks' but fears the 'Reds'. Bigger goes on the run, is caught, and – his crime having provoked the inevitable race riots – condemned to die. Wright cannot quite bring himself to exonerate Bigger's crimes by reference to the larger crime of American racism. But he comes close and suggests an element of redemption before Bigger's long walk to the chair.

Native Son was a novel peculiarly vulnerable to 1940s censorship. Most frequently cut from the various reprints was a scene in which Bigger and a friend go to a movie theatre and – excitedly watching a newsreel of white girls disporting themselves on a Florida beach – masturbate.

The Neon Bible, John Kennedy Toole, 1989

The circumstances surrounding John Kennedy Toole's works of fiction are as American Gothic as anything his idol, Flannery O'Connor, could have devised. Without any of his friends suspecting he had authorial ambitions, Toole wrote *A Confederacy of Dunces* in the early sixties, while doing his national service in Puerto Rico. Eerily apt in the light of later events, the title is taken from Jonathan Swift's jaundiced rule of literary life: 'When a true genius appears in the world, you may know him by this sign, that the dunces are all in confederacy against him.' The dunces in the New York publishing world rejected his manuscript and suddenly, while teaching at Dominican College, Toole disappeared. It later emerged that he had taken off on an odyssey to California. On his way back he called by Flannery O'Connor's house in Georgia. Then, outside Biloxi in Mississippi on 26 March 1969, he connected some garden hosepipe to the exhaust of his car and gassed himself. He was just thirty-one years old.

By sheer tenacity, his mother, Thelma Toole, got *The Confederacy of Dunces* published. It went on to win a posthumous Pulitzer Prize in 1981, became a bestseller and is now regarded as a cult classic. Toole's literary remains comprised the manuscript of another work of fiction called *The Neon Bible*. He had allegedly written it for a literary competition when he was sixteen, just after going up to Tulane University as a precociously clever student. It's arguably the best work of juvenile fiction ever to reach print.

The story covers a period from around 1937 to 1953 and is set in rural Mississippi, a landscape of baked clay and shacks with cinder yards. David, the hero-narrator, grows up an only child in redneck poverty. His father drifts from job to job, beats his wife and lets David get beaten up by young thugs his own age. The family are ostracised by respectable townspeople, because they cannot afford to pay church dues. Eventually the father dies as a GI in Italy. David's mother promptly goes insane. He receives love only from his eccentric Aunt Mae, a sixty-year-old

floozy. But she resurrects her show-business career and goes off to Nashville, leaving the boy wholly friendless. David's world thereafter is one of mysterious violence, utter solitude and a rock-hard Southern Baptist Church, whose neon sign on Main Street (a garishly coloured page of the Bible) threatens his eventual damnation. The personality that permeates the story is repulsive. While still a boy, David proposes marriage to the only girl he has ever dated. By way of reply she screams, claws his face and runs away, her hair flying. The novel ends with much blood and some spectacular violence against mothers, all of it filtered through David's anaesthetised gaze and eerily precocious schoolboy prose.

The power of *The Neon Bible* resides in its descriptions of the small town where David endures his childhood. But, even as the reader admires Toole's writing, questions form. Was he really only sixteen when he wrote it? Did he perhaps revise or wholly rewrite the text at a later date? There are tantalising gaps in the record of his life – about, for example, the mysterious writing competition in 1953. Thelma Toole was fanatical on the subject of her son's genius. As the work of a young man, *The Neon Bible* is interesting. As the work of a boy, it is prodigious. One would, however, like conclusive proof that it is, indeed, a boy's novel – a thing that is rarely done well. No one now is going to forget John Kennedy Toole; his mother can rest in peace on that score. He is a legendary figure – a Louisiana Rimbaud. But *The Neon Bible* perplexes.

Netherland, Joseph O'Neill, 2009

The paperback edition has, among all the other puff and guff on its cover, an endorsement to die for: '*A brilliant book: Barack Obama*'. For a novel published in 2009, this is praise equivalent to the pointing finger of God. One should, however, bear in mind that presidential tastes in fiction are not always awe-inspiring. Eisenhower was fond of Zane Grey; Kennedy, famously, had a soft spot for Ian Fleming; Clinton, reportedly, likes the inter-ethnic detective stories of

Walter Mosley. And since this is a novel that is centred on the English sport of cricket, one does wonder whether POTUS knows his leg cutters from his seamers, where silly mid off is, or what it is to vary your maiden over with chinamen or googlies. There are good American novels about baseball (Bernard Malamud's *The Natural*, for example) but the mind strains to think of a good novel about cricket. The best I can dredge up is Simon Raven's *Close of Play*, in which the hero kills a close-fielding rival in love by hitting a ball into his groin. Murder by on-drive.

Netherland has been hailed as the first great post-9/11 novel. It is set in bombed Manhattan, but the 'attacks' are only mentioned parenthetically. Nonetheless, it is patently an 'aftermath' novel. Pedagogically, the hero-narrator gives a little lecture on the word 'aftermath':

> This last-mentioned word, somebody once told me, refers literally to a second mowing of grass in the same season. You might say, if you're the type prone to general observations, that New York City insists on memory's repetitive mower.

Netherland is a novel very given to 'general observations'. The hero is a Dutchman in New York (once called New Amsterdam), Hans van den Broek (co-etymological with 'Brooklyn'), a Wall Street analyst. (It is estimated that 373 non-Americans died in the Twin Towers.) His speciality is oil futures. Arguably the future of oil was at the heart of the atrocity – the terrorists being mainly of Saudi origin. Hans has relocated from London with his wife Rachel and son Jake. In the aftermath of 9/11, they move into the Chelsea Hotel, where Dylan Thomas died and Bob Dylan wrote 'Sad-Eyed Lady of the Lowlands'. Less excitingly, Hans meets Arthur Miller in the elevator. He pays six grand a month for a two-bedroomed suite, reminding us that the Twin Tower atrocity slaughtered a cohort of the highest-paid office workers in the history of the planet. Hans' wife Rachel earns a quarter of a million a year as a lawyer; he pulls in twice as much 'gross'. Everyday Manhattan folk.

The plot is hand-me-down everyday marital breakdown. 'All lives', observes the hero, 'eventually funnel into the advice columns of women's magazines'. There is no infidelity. Rachel simply cannot live with Hans' distractedness, and returns to London. He is alone in post-apocalyptic New York. He achieves a kind of peace of mind by playing cricket every other weekend on the Staten Island Cricket Club pitch, where Sobers and Bradman once smote the ball and which offers the best view of the ruined skyscrapers. Hans' cricket buddy is a Trinidadian – a country with a more glorious cricketing record than the Netherlands – called Chuck Ramkissoon. He is not a player, but an umpire. Cricket for Chuck is the whole point of life. 'We have an expression in the English language,' he says:

> The expression is 'not cricket'. When we disapprove of something, we say 'it's not cricket'. We do not say 'it's not baseball'. Or 'it's not football'. We say 'it's not cricket'.

Off the pitch Chuck is a dabbler in street crime, which eventually leads to his hand-cuffed body sleeping with the fishes in the Gowanus Canal, Brooklyn. The Russian Mafia (not from a cricketing nation) are most likely responsible.

The marriage mends and the novel ends, alluding to the 'beating against the current' ending of THE GREAT GATSBY with a recollection of crossing on the ferry from Staten Island, at 'watery sunset', and little Jake excitedly pointing at 'two amazingly high towers going up above all others'. As the man says, a brilliant novel.

The New Confessions, William Boyd, 1987

It is mysterious that *The New Confessions* is not more widely recognised as the very great novel it manifestly is. This is how the story goes. On an island in the Mediterranean in 1972, an old man remembers his life during a series of walks and solitary meditations. He is John James Todd, born in Edinburgh in 1899. His mother dies giving birth to him. He cannot love his surgeon father;

he is idle and bored at school. Showing some aptitude for mathematics, John James is sent to a private academy where his only achievement is to ask a more gifted friend whether prime numbers are discovered or invented. The query inspires a brilliant career in mathematics – but for the friend, not John James.

He runs away to join the army in 1916 on the newly entrenched Western Front and survives the horrors of war – first in the odd company of a public schools regiment, and later on in the even odder company of murderously degenerate Scottish 'bantams' (under-regulation-height cannon fodder, but 'plucky' with it). After the war John James makes films in London and Berlin. The first instalment of his great Abel Gance-like epic, costing millions of pounds, is finished in 1929 – just in time to be totally eclipsed by the new-fangled 'talkies'. His favourite child dies, his marriage breaks up, his sexual infidelities lead nowhere. He moves on to Hollywood, where he subsists throughout the 1940s, making inferior 'B' Westerns. During the Second World War he is slandered by the British press as a traitor. After the war he is hounded out of America by the House Un-American Activities Committee. By the 1960s, film histories list John James Todd as dead. But he survives, quietly, in the sun, living in a villa loaned by a friend. Here, by the dried-out swimming pool, he voyeuristically spies on his maidservant through peepholes, indulges his raging persecution mania, and is 'discovered' by a resourceful band of German film students to whom he entrusts the print of his great film, thought to be long-since lost.

As story-telling The New Confessions is wholly engrossing. And Boyd's power of historical mise-en-scène is uncanny. Turn-of-the-century Edinburgh, the First World War trenches, 1920s Berlin, interwar and post-war LA, are all reconstructed with a density of detail that is as richly pleasurable as running your fingers over velvet. There is, however, a secret structure nestling within John James' apparently disordered reminiscences. His great doomed film venture is a five-hour version of Jean-Jacques Rousseau's Confessions. The double-barrelled Christian name (Jacques being the French for James) set up the allusion. And throughout, if one cares to check, John James' confessions artfully parallel those of Jean-Jacques. Thus the opening lines of The New Confessions:

> My first act on entering this world was to kill my mother . . . The date of my birth was the date of her death, and thus began all my misfortunes.

echo the first chapter of the Confessions:

> I was born as a poor and sickly child, and cost my mother her life. So my birth was the first of my misfortunes.

Boyd grafts on to the frame of the Confessions the mellower retrospection of Rousseau's Reveries of a Solitary Walker, which was left unfinished at the philosopher's death. Why Rousseau? Perhaps Boyd was piqued by the challenge laid down in the first sentence of the Confessions:

> I have resolved on an enterprise which has no precedent and which, once complete, will have no imitator.

Boyd, we are led to presume, sees in Rousseau's cast of mind a classic presentiment of modern angst. As Rousseau puts it in Reveries of a Solitary Walker:

> Wrenched, somehow, out of the natural order, I have been plunged into an incomprehensible chaos, where I can make nothing out, and the more I think about my present situation, the less I can understand what has become of me.

Todd puts it slightly differently, but with the same conviction that the highest understanding man can achieve is despair that he will ever understand anything:

> It has been deeply paradoxical and fundamentally uncertain. That's how I would sum the whole business up, my time on this small planet.

As I say, a great novel.

New Grub Street, George Gissing, 1891

It is a critical refrain that Gissing has never quite been awarded the status in literary history he deserves. This is his savage novel about how literary status is achieved. Or, in Gissing's own case, not achieved. He was too good for his literary world.

At the novel's centre is a novelist, Edwin Reardon. The author of two finely wrought 'literary' works, Reardon is destroyed by the drudgery and banality imposed by Mudie's lending library system – a leviathan purveying fiction to the masses. The 'system' has done for high literature what factory chimneys have done to London air. Edwin is insufficiently cynical to pander to the reading public. His sensibility crumples. His unsympathetic wife, Amy, brings him no dowry and their marriage withers under the strain of trying to keep up a genteel habitation in the Regent's Park area. When the failure of his books forces Edwin to return to menial clerking, Amy, snobbish to the illiterate core, protests at the loss of status, and the marriage is doomed. Even after she inherits a fortune – the traditional 'get out of disaster' card in Victorian fiction – the memory of Edwin's inherent shabbiness persists. The Reardons' child dies, and he follows soon after. A martyr to fine writing; one of the for ever to be forgotten of literature.

Edwin's career is contrasted with that of the cynical, but irresistibly genial, opportunist, Jasper Milvain – a child of his time. It is Jasper, the rascal, who eventually marries Amy, reaping the benefit of her £10,000. To win the prize, he is obliged to jilt a fellow writer, Marian Yule, who supports her father, a 'battered man of letters', and a small-circulation highbrow magazine. Mr Yule is going blind – which means lifelong servitude as a literary galley slave for Marian. The prudent Jasper decides she is not, when all things are considered, the proper partner for a rising young fellow in the literary racket such as himself, and leaves her to drudge pointlessly in libraries, checking quotations and citations and marking proofs.

What Gissing offers is a *Dunciad* for the nineteenth century. At its heart is not eighteenth-century Grub Street (home of the seething mass of literary maggots) but the majestic, post-Panizzi British Museum Reading Room: the home of books. For Thackeray that great dome, raised in the mid-Victorian period, was the nation's brainpan:

> Many Londoners – not all – have been to the British Museum Library... I have seen all sorts of domes of Peters and Pauls, Sophia, Pantheon – what not? – and have been struck by none of them so much as by that catholic dome in Bloomsbury, under which our million volumes are housed. What peace, what love, what truth, what beauty, what happiness for all, what generous kindness for you and me, are here spread out! It seems to me one cannot sit down in that place without a heart full of grateful reverence.

For Marx, the 'BM' was Marxism's quarry – where his ore was dug. For George Bernard Shaw, it was his university (he left a substantial portion of his wealth to the place). For Virginia Woolf, it was one of the few environments where intellect was gender-neutral. For Gissing's Marian Yule, it is a circle of hell.

> The days darkened. Through November rains and fogs Marian went her usual way to the Museum, and toiled there among the other toilers ... The fog grew thicker; she looked up at the windows beneath the dome and saw that they were a dusky yellow. Then her eye discerned an official walking along the upper gallery, and in pursuance of her grotesque humour, her mocking misery, she likened him to a black, lost soul, doomed to wander in an eternity of vain research along endless shelves. Or again, the readers who sat here at these radiating lines of desks, what were they but hapless flies caught in a huge web, its nucleus the great circle of the Catalogue? Darker, darker.

Read *New Grub Street* and understand, well below the super-structural literary achievements recorded in this book, there is a deep foundation of skulls, bones, and more forgotten literary misery than Thackeray's numerous volumes could ever chronicle. The forgotten, the unread, the never published. The Edwin Reardons.

Nightmare Abbey, Thomas Love Peacock, 1818

The nineteenth century is seen by posterity as glorified by 'the march of ideas' – the engines of 'progress'. Thomas Love Peacock was unimpressed by intellect on the move. He was particularly unimpressed by the expansion of the 'reading public' (a term he used with an invariable snort of contempt), courtesy of such institutions as the Society for the Diffusion of Useful Knowledge, which he satirised in his novel *Crotchet Castle* as the 'Steam Intellect Society'. In his fiction Peacock took on politics, philosophy, and in *Nightmare Abbey* – hilariously – his own craft. The novel would be, he forecast, a comic romance in which he intended to amuse himself 'with the darkness and misanthropy of modern literature'. It would be all the more effective for being handled with deadly affection. Peacock was a close friend of Shelley, who is lampooned in the person of the hero of the novel. There were tragedy and grandeur in the poet's short, brilliant life, but also, as Peacock perceived, absurdity. Shelley, for example, could not help falling in love with whichever young woman (some of them very young indeed) crossed his path.

Nightmare Abbey is constructed from very basic materials. It is largely backdrop and conversation, threaded through with a thin line of burlesque narrative. The owner of the titular abbey is Christopher Glowry, Esq., a widower whose view of the world is darkened by an 'atrabilarious temperament' and not much consoled by his lone offspring, Scythrop:

> This only son and heir Mr Glowry had christened Scythrop, from the name of a maternal ancestor, who had hanged himself one rainy day in a fit of *taedium vitae*, and had been eulogised by a coroner's jury in the comprehensive phrase of *felo de se*; on which account, Mr Glowry held his memory in high honour, and made a punchbowl of his skull.

The Glowrys are attended by a body of servants called Raven, Crow, Skelett and the singularly ominous Diggory Deathshead.

Scythrop's temperament is quite contrary to his parent's. He is a romantic utopian, what Coleridge called a 'pantisocrat'. A believer in 'mankind', Scythrop has less luck with women and, in his serial disappointments in love, is forever ordering Raven to bring him a 'pint of port and a pistol'. He drinks the one but never quite gets round to using the other. Scythrop has dropped out of Oxford, leaving a pamphlet behind him which he fondly expects will point mankind's way to the millennium: 'Philosophical Gas: or, a Project for a General Illumination of the Human Mind'. (Among all else, Peacock was profoundly unimpressed by the new-fangled gas lighting Walter Scott had introduced into his gothic pile, Abbotsford.) A mere seven copies of 'Philosophical Gas' have left the shelves, but Scythrop does not despair. After all, seven is a 'mystical number'. Shelley himself had dropped out of Oxford, leaving behind a pamphlet 'The Necessity of Atheism'. It did not change the world.

Nightmare Abbey has dramatis personae of ideas incarnate – characters such as the pessimist Mr Toobad and terminally *ennuyé* Mr Listless. There are also satirical vignettes of Byron, as Mr Cypress, and Coleridge, as Mr Flosky. No one, I hazard, having read the following, will be able to read 'Kubla Khan' or 'Christabel' (or perhaps even shake a saltcellar), with a straight face again (one of Scythrop's band of ladies, Marionetta, drops by Mr Flosky in his cell):

> It was noon, and the sun was shining in full splendour, much to the annoyance of Mr Flosky, who had obviated the inconvenience by closing the shutters, and drawing the window-curtains. He was sitting at his table by the light of a solitary candle, with a

pen in one hand, and a muffineer in the other, with which he occasionally sprinkled salt on the wick, to make it burn blue. He sate with 'his eye in a fine frenzy rolling,' and turned his inspired gaze on Marionetta as if she had been the ghastly ladie of a magical vision.

Literature needs its regular antidotes. *Nightmare Abbey* is one of the sweetest-tasting.

Nightmare Alley, William Lindsay Gresham, 1946

Nightmare Alley is a sick novel by a patho-logically sick author whose life was a pinball-bouncing progress through alco-holism, breakdown, and demented searches for cures in AA, psychoanalysis, Marxism, and, finally, mysticism. Nothing worked. Gresham killed himself in 1962, alone, in a hotel room taken for the night, his pocket full of business cards with the bleak inscription:

No Address. No Phone. No Business. No Money. Retired.

The last publication of a very sad man, but a man not lacking a wryly humorous approach to the inherent sadness of things.

Nightmare Alley is a novel about the most depraved, but in its way most symbolic, of things in the American enter-tainment industry: the 'geek'. The term was a word not originally applied to the big-brained ('nerds', 'swots') of the academic world, as it now customarily is, but to the carnival 'wild man' – the incarnation of the lowest depth to which *Homo sapiens* could sink. Gresham began writing the novel, as he records, while serving in the Spanish Civil War. He loved lost causes (he was himself one of the most lost). While at the front, a comrade who had worked in a trav-elling carnival, or 'carnie', told him about one of the failsafe attractions: the caged man who bit the heads off living chickens – known, among the trade, as the 'geek'. Invariably the part was played by some

down-and-out drunk, recruited for the price of his next slug of booze. Given their low cost for hours of entertainment, carni-vals thrived in the Depression Era. (Another popular entertainment was the 'dance till you drop' competition, chronicled in the novel and film *They Shoot Horses, Don't They?*) Central attractions were the monster show featuring 'freaks' and, central to this narrative, the 'mentalist' or mind reader. For Gresham, the carnival is a microcosm of America, populated by geeks, freaks, con-men, losers and grifters.

Gresham's novel opens with one such travelling carnival, in the 1930s. The hero, Stan Carlisle, twenty-one, is haunted by childhood memories of the brutal killing of his dog, and the unexpected revelation of his mother's adultery. Now in the carnival racket, he steals the 'code book' of the amiable mentalist, Zeena, having killed her drunk of a husband by giving him a bottle of booze containing a fatal dose of wood-alcohol (it is Prohibition – drinkers do not look carefully at labels). Having seduced and widowed her, he does not team up with Zeena but moves on to the more pneumatic bump-and-grinder, Molly. They go on to make it big as con-artists. It all culminates in Stan's offer to bring back from 'the other side' the childhood sweetheart of an aged multi-millionaire, for some posthumous hanky-panky (Molly, it is planned, will play the part of the randy revenant). It goes wrong and Stan goes to pieces. The narra-tive ends with him drifting back, broken down, into a carnie where the manager tells him:

I got one job you might take a crack at. It ain't much, and I ain't begging you to take it; but it's a job. Keep you in coffee and cakes and a shot now and then. What do you say? Of course, it's only temporary – just until we get a real geek.

The novel's ending was too strong for an otherwise faithful 1947 film adaptation (now regarded as classic film noir). On screen Stan is 'saved' by the ever-faithful Zeena. But both novel and film are permeated with ineffable scorn for the suckers who make up the carni-val's patrons: as Phineas T. Barnum might have said, there is one born every minute. 'How helpless they all looked in the ugliness of sleep', the narrative observes:

> A third of life spent unconscious and corpselike. And some, the great majority, stumbled through their waking hours scarcely more awake, helpless in the face of destiny. They stumbled down a dark alley toward their deaths. They sent exploring feelers into the light and met fire and writhed back again into the darkness of their blind groping.

Nights at the Circus, Angela Carter, 1984

Carter is a writer who is fun to read – none of her works more so than this, the penultimate of her unhappily short life. As the pages whisk by, it's hard to discern shapes or structures, but so lively is Carter's prose that one ignores that shortcoming. The opening of *Nights at the Circus* fizzes on the page like sherbet:

> 'Lor' love you, sir!' Fevvers sang out in a voice that clanged like dustbin lids. 'As to my place of birth, why, I first saw light of day right here in smoky old London, didn't I! Not billed the "Cockney Venus", for nothing, sir, though they could just as well have called me "Helen of the High Wire", due to the unusual circumstances in which I come ashore for I never docked via what you might call the *normal channels*, sir, oh, dear me, no; but, just like Helen of Troy, was *hatched*.'

It's magical realism with a cockney accent and music-hall brassiness. Fevvers 'Feathers' is a bird-woman, who has put her hybridity to work as a circus performer. Specifically she is an *aérialiste*, a trapeze artist who needs no trapeze to perform the 'impossible' triple somersault. Clad for her performances in the skimpiest *cache-sexe*, her beauty is, if anything, enhanced by her 'monstrous' wings. But are they real?

It is the turn of the century, a moment poised, ambiguously, between Victorian prudery and Edwardian relaxation. Fevvers is starring in the West End's Alhambra Music Hall (famous for its animal shows). As the novel opens she is being interviewed by a serious young American journalist, Jack Walser, who is engaged on a series of articles called 'Great Humbugs of the World'. Fevvers claims to have been hatched from an egg like Helen of Troy or, possibly, like Venus, to have emerged fully formed from the sea (despite the dropped aitches and glottal stops, it is clear, see above, that Fevvers knows her mythology). Firmer facts gradually emerge. She was left a foundling on the doorstep of a London brothel. As a little girl, she did *tableaux vivants* for clients. These became more lubricious when her wings sprouted after puberty, and she had a narrow escape from the clutches of a rich degenerate, Christian Rosencreutz, who wanted a bird-woman 'intacta' for some unspeakable pagan rite.

Having set out to unmask Fevvers' humbuggery, Walser is entranced and becomes her follower after the bird-woman joins Colonel Kearney's travelling circus. Sybil, the Colonel's porcine oracle (i.e. talking pig), recommends that Jack become a clown, which he does, sending dispatches all the while on circus life to his loyal, and presumably very perplexed, American readers. The circus travels through Russia, where things go badly wrong. The artists and the tigers fall out and jealous acrobats try to murder Fevvers. The attempt fails, but she is abducted by a Russian nobleman of wicked intent. She escapes (a Fabergé egg proves helpful). Fevvers and her loyal journalist clown find themselves on the Trans-Siberian express, reunited with the circus. They are kidnapped by bandits. Finally, still in the wastes of Siberia on New Year's Eve, Fevvers and Jack realise their love for each other. But there is one final twist in this most tortuous of plots. As she sits 'crouched above him' in sexual union at last, Fevvers ejaculates, 'Gawd, I fooled you! . . . To think I really fooled you!'

Meanings have been pasted, unconvincingly, on to Carter's extended frolic. It is 1899 – a new age dawns. Will women now fly higher? Is a feminist point being made about those wings? Is Fevvers an emblem for what was called in the 1890s 'the New Woman' – something implied by the final image of her domination of Jack? Commenting on her novel, Carter pointed in another direction: 'It's actually a statement about the nature of fiction, about the nature of her narrative.' The novel, that is, poses the question: is Fevvers fact or fiction, or something for which either word is inadequate? But, Carter seems to say with a wink, why be serious? Just read, chortle and wish she'd lived to write more fiction as enjoyable as *Nights at the Circus*.

Nineteen Eighty-Four, George Orwell, 1949

Orwell's dystopia is so well known that it needs no summary even for those who have not actually read it. The story is bare-bones simple. After an inconclusive, but atomic, Third World War, Winston (named after the great Second World War leader) Smith (viz, a 'nobody') is a junior *Times* journalist who resolves, quixotically, to mount a one-man rebellion against the dictatorship of 'the Party' and its dictator, the possibly non-existent 'Big Brother'. The world in 1984 is beyond ideology and nationhood. The former 'paper of record' exists only to falsify history ('who controls the past controls the present'). Britain is now 'Airstrip One' in the American conglomerate 'Oceania', a super-state in constant fluid rivalry with Eurasia and Eastasia. It is not a real war – merely a condition of mutually assured emergency, in which anything can be justified by the plea of wartime necessity. All that matters is power. 'If you want a picture of the future', an interrogator – part torturer, part father figure – tells Winston, 'imagine a boot stamping on a human face for ever.' Winston's one-man revolution is given a boost by his alliance with a sexual rebel, Julia, who principally wants to sabotage the Party's state-enforced chastity. They are caught in bed, and brainwashed by the ultimate horror of Room 101. Winston is last seen admiring 'BB', awaiting the inevitable bullet in the back of the neck (as he confidently anticipates). Orwell's working title

was 'The Last Man in Europe'. When the trigger which liquidates Winston is fired, mankind in any humane sense of the word will no longer exist.

Nineteen Eighty-Four has given its name to a social syndrome: 'Orwellian'. Like 'Kafkaesque', it originates in one of those rare novels which have framed public discourse. But when the novel first came out, in June 1949, it made no great impact. Secker and Warburg, its publisher, printed barely enough to satisfy the public library market. One of the things reviewers complained about was that, as a work of science fiction, is how it was interpreted at the time, *Nineteen Eighty-Four* was lamentably unimaginative. There were no time travellers, no ray guns, no Triffids. History has proved the novel was hugely prophetic in one sense – the power of TV, still latent in 1949. This was something contemporary reviewers and readers largely missed. Orwell foresaw a television which watches you, creating a 'soft' surveillance tyranny. 'Orwellian' was a term ubiquitously drawn on in the furore about the WikiLeaks and Snowden revelations in 2010 and 2013.

Interestingly, TV played a central part in boosting *Nineteen Eighty-Four* to long-term bestsellerdom, making it something more than just 'another novel'. Nigel Kneale's adaptation was broadcast in December 1954. You needed to be a sixteen-year-old schoolboy, as I was at that time, to feel the life-changing impact of that dramatisation. My family home didn't have a 'goggle box' (or a telephone, or a fridge, or running hot water) and I missed out on the first BBC broadcast, but inflamed by playground gossip ('Rats! Eyeballs!') I was careful to book a place to see the repeat a week later. At the time there was only one TV channel: the BBC. They took their monopolistic responsibility piously. On both evenings they issued the solemn warning that the upcoming *Nineteen Eighty-Four* was 'unsuitable for children or those with weak nerves'. I took the risk.

There was at least one fatal outcome. As the *Daily Express* reported on 14 December under the headline '1984: WIFE DIES AS SHE WATCHES', Mrs Beryl Mirfin, 'a local beauty queen of 1936', had expired on her sofa. 'A doctor who was called asked at once, "Was she watching the TV play?". Indeed the poor woman was. Whether the doctor wrote '1984' on the certificate as 'cause of death' is not recorded. 'Big Brother is watching you', 'doublethink', and the 'two-minute hate' became ubiquitous catchphrases. A waggish BBC weatherman began his bulletin on 13 December with the barked announcement, 'Stand by your sets, citizens, bad news coming up!' Sales of the novel boomed after the programme's airing, and have boomed ever since. But the shock-horror excitement of the innocent TV age that fuelled it has died away. The TV production can still be muzzily found on the internet. View it and wonder. No need to look for the book, of course. Copies are as ubiquitous as Gideon Bibles.

North and South, Elizabeth Gaskell, 1855

Gaskell's first 'social problem' novel, *Mary Barton* (1848), was thought to be unfair to Lancashire mill owners. An indomitably fair-minded woman, Gaskell wrote *North and South* in an attempt to do justice to the captain-of-industry class, which Dickens satirised in the person of Mr Bounderby in *Hard Times* (1854). That novel first came out in Dickens' own journal, *Household Words*, shortly before Mrs Gaskell's novel was also published in the same journal. One senses the odd phenomenon of a contributor kindly but firmly correcting her own editor. Dickens was not all that pleased with Mrs Gaskell's narrative, and hacked it about. He confided to a friend: 'If I were Mr Gaskell, O heaven how I should beat her!' For Disraeli, England was two nations: the rich and poor. For Scott, Scotland was two nations: the highlanders and lowlanders. For Gaskell ('Mrs Gaskell' to her contemporaries), England's division was between industrial North and agricultural South. She herself had been brought up in one and, on marrying a Unitarian minister in Manchester, transplanted to the other. The division she demarcated is still a fact of British life.

In a conscious parallel, Margaret Hale is transplanted from a comfortable life in the home counties to alien 'Milton-Northern' (i.e. Manchester) in 'Darkshire', when her clergyman father's religious 'doubts' (that perennial Victorian affliction) force him to surrender his church living in Hampshire. In Milton, 'Workshop of the World', Margaret is plunged into the hottest part of the furnace of the Industrial Revolution. She befriends a free-thinking mill-worker, Nicholas Higgins, and his invalid, mill-girl daughter, Bessy. Sexually, Margaret is attracted to John Thornton, a stiff-necked 'master'. The relationship, however, receives no encouragement from Thornton's equally stiff-necked mother. Things take a turn for the worse when Margaret, good-heartedly, becomes involved in a labour dispute, which ends up in a 'lock-out'. She courageously proves her love by protecting Thornton from a rioting mob of stone-throwing workers, who are infuriated by his bringing in Irish 'black-legs' to break the strike. The scene embodies the essential moral 'goodness' of Gaskell's writing, and her taste (shared with most of her readers) for high drama:

> Her eye was on the group of lads who had armed themselves with their clogs some time before. She saw their gesture – she knew its meaning – she read their aim. Another moment, and Mr Thornton might be smitten down – he whom she had urged and goaded to come to this perilous place. She only thought how she could save him. She threw her arms around him; she made her body into a shield from the fierce people beyond. Still, with his arms folded, he shook her off.
>
> 'Go away,' said he, in his deep voice. 'This is no place for you.'. . . she turned and spoke again:
>
> 'For God's sake! do not damage your cause by this violence. You do not know what you are doing.' She strove to make her words distinct. A sharp pebble flew by her, grazing forehead and cheek, and drawing a blinding sheet of light before her eyes. She lay like one dead on Mr Thornton's shoulder.

At the end of the novel Margaret, recovered in body but with her love life still unsettled, returns to London and the rural area of Helstone where she was brought up. But having experienced the more vital life of the North, she now finds the South unsatisfying. She inherits a fortune, that ubiquitous stroke of good luck in Victorian fiction, and is able to return and rescue a now-bankrupted Thornton. The couple return to Milton, where he becomes a model employer, striving incessantly for a relationship with his workers beyond that of 'cash nexus'. Endings were never a strong point in Mrs Gaskell's narratives, but her keen analysis of social geography renders *North and South* still resonates today.

Oblomov, Ivan Goncharov, 1859

In the 1940s – a peculiarly frantic era in British national life – the critic V. S. Pritchett wrote a witty piece in the *New Statesman* revolving around the paradox of what he called 'the Russian day'. He speculated on what he called the 'yawning hours' of Russian everyday life, whose number must have comprised many more than our quotidian twenty-four. The Russian upper classes seemed, if Tolstoy, Dostoevsky, Chekhov and Turgenev were to be believed, to have so much burdensome *time* on their hands. Clocks moved more slowly; weeks dragged; months crawled by under the vast Russian skies and across the endless steppes. Life, for the Sashas, Pierres and Mishas, seemed to be permanently on hold. Goncharov's novel is set in the period shortly before the emancipation of the serfs – a period in which, as in the antebellum American South ('Peel me a grape, Beulah'), serfdom has rotted all willpower in the serf-owning class. Goncharov eponymously calls the Russian disease 'Oblomovitis'. As the French wit put it, 'Living? Our servants will do that for us.'

Oblomov is 'a gentleman by birth and a collegiate secretary by rank' who could more accurately be called an upper-class layabout. Lying about is, in fact, his main occupation in life. He can barely be bothered to get out of bed (where's he's discovered as the story opens), unless it's to lumber across to his sofa and pass the day there, dressing-gowned, doing nothing other than wait for bedtime to roll round. He lives off the revenue from an estate, many miles away from St Petersburg. The estate is worm-holed by other parasites more energetic than he can be bothered to be. Oblomov does not care. No landlord is more absentee.

The novel describes, at extraordinary length, the Oblomovian day. He eats voraciously, and unmercifully nags his luckless serf Zakhar – who has 'boundless loyalty' to the master he nonetheless (like everyone else) cheats whenever he can. Friends call. Oblomov never calls back. This 'sublime sluggard', as Pritchett calls him, is contemptible but lovable, and even – in a perverse way – admirable. He embodies 'the poetry of procrastination'. Like Baudelaire's *flâneur*, idleness is his profession and his criticism of life. In the climax (so to miscall it) of Goncharov's narrative – after nothing happening apart from gorging, loafing, bickering, not working and not marrying (his friend gets the girl, Olga) – Oblomov is found, years on, now living in reduced circumstances in the country, still loafing, still scoffing, still serenely at peace with his world. He is stuffed, nowadays, on homelier fare than in St Petersburg, by his housekeeper Agafya, who treats him rather as French peasants might do a particularly valued Strasbourg goose.

Oblomov has a stroke and is paralysed (had he ever been anything else?) and a year later dies, well short of the statutory three-score-and-ten; although doubtless his lifespan felt positively Methuselean to him (psychological time, as it's called, passes more slowly in bed; in Joseph Heller's CATCH-22 there is a character, Dunbar, who is extending his life by never getting out of his bunk). Boredom makes life longer. Oblomov's departure happens off-stage. One cannot call it an 'event'. In a sense it can barely be said to happen. So torpid is his life in his final years that it is indistinguishable from rigor mortis. He drifts out of life as he drifted into it, and through it, leaving nothing behind him but a word, 'Oblomovitis'. His monument.

The novel can be read as a parable of Russia in terminal pre-Revolutionary decay. Or it can be read as high comedy (which is how Spike Milligan travestied it in his long-running 1960s stage version). Or one can read Oblomov as a one-off literary curiosity. Goncharov was deranged while writing the novel, and in later years was wholly paranoid. But V. S. Pritchett catches the beguiling charm of the novel, and of the long-day Russian novel in general, most eloquently:

> In nineteenth-century Russia, under the simpler feudal division of society, there is more room to breathe, to let the will drift, and the disparate impulses have their ancient solitary reign. In all those Russian novels we seem to hear a voice saying: 'The

meaning of life? One day that will be revealed to us – probably on a Thursday.'

Of Human Bondage, Somerset Maugham, 1915

I first came across Maugham's novel when I was a sixth-former and was soon so engrossed I took the risk of reading it under the desk. The teacher, hawk-eyed like all his kind, swooped, took one look, and snarled, 'He came to a bad end, and so will you.' I was never sure whether he was talking about Maugham or Maugham's hero, Philip Carey. Not that it matters. They are, essentially, one and the same. And he was right. I got terrible A-level results.

Of Human Bondage can be classed a *Bildungsroman*. We don't have a workable English word for it. Another relevant if off-putting German term for it is *Erziehungsroman* – 'development novel'. It's fiction concerned with the formation of human personality from childhood through youth to adult maturity. Deformation also comes into it. Philip Carey is given a club foot. Maugham was afflicted with two less Byronic disabilities: he had a stammer, and he was gay (with florid bisexual interludes – a Russian princess while writing *Of Human Bondage*). He wrote the novel in his thirties, while riding high from an unprecedented run of stage successes. He was the author of the day. How had he got there? The novel probes this question with a mixture of narcissistic self-love and self-disgust.

Maugham was, manifestly, taking his lead from the one of the novels he admired most, *David Copperfield*. Like Dickens' David, Philip loses his mother and father and is billeted on a clergyman uncle and his wife. They are childless. Philip's surgeon father has left only a tiny (for his class in life) patrimony of £2,000. Great things are not in prospect. It is the interestingly decadent 1890s – or *fin de siècle*. But Philip is trapped, like Ernest Pontifex in THE WAY OF ALL FLESH, in a Victorian-vicarage time warp. Philip loses his faith when the Almighty declines to make his foot whole after being fervently begged for this small favour. At

boarding school he is an outsider, but excels in classwork and examinations. His adolescent career takes the form of a series of breakings out of bondage, only to find himself ever more enmeshed.

He spends a *Lehrjahr* in Heidelberg, studying languages. University will mean going into the Church afterwards, which he does not want; Oxford is duly rejected. Accountancy proves too dry an activity – Philip has artistic yearnings. He tries his hand with brush and palette in Paris, but on discovering that he is gifted but not a genius that exalted future is closed to him. Philip is on the brink of his twenties when he loses his virginity to an older woman who, after the act, disgusts him. The wrinkles around her neck are a particular affront. He finally follows his father into medicine. The formative/destructive influence in his life is now sex. He falls hopelessly in love with a waitress. Mildred is 'common', vulgar, pasty-faced and flat-chested ('boy-like'). She despises her posh lover as a feeble cripple. She routinely betrays him, steals what little money he has, treats his love-making with contempt, and goes off for some 'fun' whenever the fancy takes her. On one occasion she returns pregnant by another man. But, mysteriously, she is the woman Philip must have. When she leaves for a dirty weekend with his best friend, he consoles himself with a descent into degradation:

> He walked up Piccadilly, dragging his club-foot, sombrely drunk, with rage and misery clawing at his heart. He was stopped by a painted harlot, who put her hand on his arm; he pushed her violently away with brutal words. He walked on a few steps and then stopped. She would do as well as another.

On Mildred's last return to him he realises he is no longer in love with her. When he refuses her poisonous embrace, she trashes his flat and cuts his clothes to ribbons. He last sees her on the game, feathered, rouged and rotting, in Shaftesbury Avenue.

The narrative has a happy ending which is best left unread and is a concession to the prissy age in which *Of Human Bondage* was published (the year, for example, in which the authorities banned and burned Lawrence's *The Rainbow*). For me, everything preceding it is still worth the reader's while.

The Old Gringo, Carlos Fuentes, 1985

Fuentes, who died in 2012, would have made the international *Who's Who* even if he had never written a novel. As a public man, Fuentes' career was directed to Mexico's chronically uneasy relationship with the outside world – he was the Mexican ambassador to France in the 1970s and held various other distinguished posts. It was revealed in 2013 that he also enjoyed the ultimate accolade of being 'a person of interest' to the FBI. As a writer, Fuentes tirelessly explored the internal character of his country. His novels feel their way among the paradoxes and social contradictions of Mexico: the complicated assimilations of its Indian, Spanish, French and North American legacies, its two natures as a state founded in socialist revolution yet effectively governed by feudal gangsters, or *jefes*. Mexico is a country where, as the sardonic proverb has it, 'the law is obeyed, then it is disregarded'.

Fuentes sees Mexico as the site of two great and conflicting myths: the myth of epic conquest, and the myth of a pre-existent utopia. And for Fuentes, Mexico is a country whose strangeness defies, and yet can only be understood by, the imaginings of fiction. Hence every worthwhile Mexican novel must, directly or indirectly, be a historical novel, a novel about 'our land', *nuestra tierra*. His lofty motto as an author was, 'write everything that history has not said, otherwise it will be forgotten'. As Fuentes puts it in the prelude to *The Old Gringo*, the very dust of Mexico is 'memorious' (viz Borges' FUNES THE MEMORIOUS). By contrast, the United States is 'the land without memory'. In the novel Fuentes suggests, extravagantly, that North Americans have lost their past by virtue of ancestral sexual timidity – the conquerors (unlike the *conquistadores*) killed, but they did not 'sufficiently' rape. The result was genocide, not miscegenation. As the North American hero of *The Old Gringo* puts it: 'we killed our Redskins and never had the courage to fornicate with the squaws and at least create a half-breed nation. We are caught in the business of forever killing people whose skin is of a different colour. Mexico is the proof of what we could have been.'

The action of *The Old Gringo* is set during the revolution of 1910–20, the most tormented passage of Mexican history since the conquest itself. Enter into the fiction 'the old gringo', aka the historical figure Ambrose Bierce (1842–1914). Very little is known of Bierce's origins. He served in the Civil War in the Indiana infantry with reckless gallantry, twice rescuing comrades under fire, apparently wanting to die but fated to survive. He did not seem to care one way or the other about the issues over which North and South fought. After the war he was a journalist. He hated American capitalism and imperialism, and yet perversely worked for William Randolph Hearst (Orson Welles' model for Citizen Kane), who owned over a million acres of ranchland in Chihuahua and supported any Mexican tyrant who did not threaten his landholding there. Bierce's sons died in circumstances of squalid debauchery; his wife divorced him after a long unhappy marriage. In 1913 Bierce apologised to his friends for still being alive and slipped incognito over the Mexican border, apparently to join the revolutionary army of Pancho Villa. To a friend, he wrote:

> Goodbye. If you hear of my being stood up against a Mexican stone wall and shot to rags please know that I think that a pretty good way to depart this life. It beats old age, disease, or falling down the cellar stairs. To be a Gringo in Mexico – ah, that is euthanasia!

In fact, nothing reliable was ever heard about Bierce's death. Perhaps, like the Flying Dutchman, he still wanders the northern Mexican deserts, unable to find the 'good, good darkness' he sought. Fuentes' magic realism fills the tantalising vacancy left by literary history. Read *The Old Gringo*, but first read 'Funes the Memorious' and Bierce's equally wonderful short story, 'An Occurrence at Owl Creek Bridge'.

The Old Men at the Zoo, Angus Wilson, 1961

Wilson's fiction deserves to be better remembered than it is. This is his masterpiece, one of the finest 'Condition of England' novels of the early sixties – a period when England's condition was in flux: one world dead, the other struggling to be born. Wilson had come to fiction late, in his forties. He was, by earlier profession, a talented civil servant. His major work was putting the British Museum Library holdings back together after the war, which had destroyed a quarter of a million of them. Wilson understood that Britain was most essentially embodied in its great institutions: Whitehall being the greatest and most labyrinthine.

The narrative is projected into the early 1970s (the novel is often classified, misleadingly, as science fiction). Simon Carter, the central character, had been a rising star in the Treasury, where the cleverest of the clever end up. He's a wizard with tables and statistics. Coming into money on his marriage to a rich American wife, as a lover of animals (particularly badgers) he chooses a more relaxed career by getting himself appointed Secretary of the Zoological Gardens (the 'Zoo') in Regent's Park – a government-run institution. Life there proves to be anything but relaxed. The two 'old men' at the top of the institution are locked in a struggle about how the zoo should go forward. One wants to keep the beautiful mid-Victorian 'gardens' as a museum of living things, with its wrought-iron cages, compounds, penguins, animal houses and 'rides'. His opponent wants a 'wild animal park', where animals can range freely. It's a version of the quarrel conducted in the 1930s between the institution and naturalists like Julian Huxley, which ended with the awkward dualism between Regent's Park and Whipsnade.

The first hundred pages of Wilson's narrative revolve around a symbolic event which crystallises moral issues. A young keeper is killed by a giraffe – killed horribly (it stamps on his testicles while he is impaled on a spiked fence). Giraffes are regarded as gentle. But this one, 'Smokey', was terminally ill and should have been shot. The advocate for Victorianism had declined to do so. And, of course, the accident would never have happened in a wild animal park. Meanwhile Britain – in self-imposed exile from the European Union – is increasingly in conflict with its continental neighbours and there is a nuclear exchange. The animals have to be evacuated and chaos ensues, in which the country reverts to 'savagery' – nature, red in tooth and claw. The nation now understands what the 'wild' in 'wild animal park' actually means.

Wilson's jaundiced narrative tone is infected at times with outright bitchiness; he does not love humans in general. It adds a sour readability to the novel. The following observation, as Simon strolls through the zoo, indicates his feelings about the British people:

> The high hysterical barking of the sea lions took me to their pool to watch the crowd watch the keeper throwing fish to feed the beasts. Automatically I registered faces – fat men, thin women, rhomboid children, figures all from a strip cartoon.

The animals, by contrast, are lovely; natural. Until, that is, they kill. There's a particularly nasty subplot involving an Alsatian dog which kills his mistress and sex-partner. Bestiality plays a central part in the second half of the novel, culminating in a scene in which Simon is obliged to eat one of his beloved badgers.

The Old Men at the Zoo focuses on a perennial crisis in British life, which was particularly acute in the sixties. Britain is the only major country in the world with a governing party which proclaims itself 'Conservative' – dedicated to holding on to the past. When the book was published in 1961, the PM was Harold Macmillan – the most fuddy-duddy of Tory leaders, lover of Trollope's fiction and wearer of wing-collars. Meanwhile, sex, drugs and rock and roll were brewing up. Old men or young rebels? Half a century on it would be good to think history has answered the big questions Wilson's novel asks. It hasn't.

On the Road, Jack Kerouac, 1957

I first heard about the movement of which Kerouac's novel is the vanguard text on the Third Programme (now Radio Three). It was late 1957, when those ahead of the game were beginning to talk knowingly about the 'Beats' and 'beatniks' (the Russian satellite, Sputnik, went into space in the same period that Viking published *On the Road* in America). Why, wondered the BBC sage (I seem to recall it was David Daiches), did these young men choose to call themselves 'Beats'. Was it the influence of jazz? They certainly improvised, and Kerouac liked to recite his poetry against a cool jazz accompaniment. Or was it 'beat' in the physical sense of being beaten up, or beaten down? The term 'beat' is used sixty-one times in the text of the novel (Professor Daiches, in 1957, did not have my invaluable word-count feature). The meaning varies between usages such as 'the sordid hipsters of America, a new **beat** generation', and 'the **beat** and evil days that come to young guys in their middle twenties', and 'California has 'the **beatest** guys in the country'. For Kerouac and his crew, the word 'beat', to echo Humpty Dumpty, means just what they choose it to mean. But it has a kind of dark, fluid glamour that still radiates powerfully.

On the Road is a novel much easier to taste than to describe (although it will never again taste as fresh as it did to me in the late 1950s). Kerouac is supposed to have composed it while high on Benzedrine inhaler pellets (the Beats' drug of choice), on an unbroken scroll of typing paper, rattling the keyboard like a crazed woodpecker. The opening tumbles on to the page – impatient with syntax, form and the drudgeries of exposition. It's winter 1947 in New York, around Columbia University, haunt of the poet Allen Ginsberg ('Carlo Marx' in the novel). The speaker-chronicler is 'Sal(vatore) Paradise' (imagine Erroll Garner tinkling on the piano in the background):

> I first met Dean not long after my wife and I split up. I had just gotten over a serious illness that I won't bother to talk about, except that it had something to do with the miserably weary split-up and my feeling that everything was dead. With the coming of Dean Moriarty began the part of my life you could call my life on the road. Before that I'd often dreamed of going West to see the country, always vaguely planning and never taking off.

The great journey west is now, at last, on, under the manic captaincy of Dean (a thinly disguised Neal Cassady, non-writing high priest of the Beats), who is just out of jail, footloose and ready to roll. The companions on the pilgrimage to anywhere are not hobos, nor vagrants, but peripatetic 'thinkers' – as high on Nietzsche as on amphetamines. Dean is all energy and 'will'. Sal is contemplative, reflective, rational and – in the final analysis – too weak for a continuous life on the road.

Over the next few years the companionable beatniks – sometimes apart, often together – take cross-country buses, hitch rides and, in one glorious phase of the journey, take charge of a Cadillac for delivery to Chicago. It's 'a beautiful big car, the last of the old-style limousines, black, with a big elongated body and whitewall tires and probably bulletproof windows'. The liveliest passages in the book describe Dean's cool madness at the wheel (imagine for this the accompaniment of a Shelly Manne drum solo):

> Dean was driving and driving and had not slackened his speed; he took the curvy corndales of Iowa at a minimum of eighty and the straightaway 110 as usual, unless both-ways traffic forced him to fall in line at a crawling and miserable sixty. When there was a chance he shot ahead and passed cars by the half-dozen and left them behind in a cloud of dust.

It is the journey, not the destination, which is the essence of *On the Road*. The novel still excites with its romantic fascination with 'movement'. At a deeper level, it articulates a blind urge to escape the bourgeois serenity of Eisenhower's America. Where to? It doesn't matter. Just move. Get out.

One Day in the Life of Ivan Denisovich, Alexander Solzhenitsyn, 1962

Few novels merit the epithet 'brave'. This one does. After the accession of Nikita Khrushchev in the 1950s there ensued a period of international thaw towards Russia. The Cold War wasn't quite as cold. Internally, it meant that Soviet writers could publish things that were previously unpublishable. For the world outside, a window on what Stalin's regime had really been like was opened.

Alexander Solzhenitsyn, like other well-meaning intellectuals, had fallen foul of the authorities. He fought gallantly for his country in the Great Patriotic War (as the commander of a sound-ranging battery) but had injudiciously criticised Stalin in a letter sent back from the front. It got him eight post-war years in labour camp and a period of 'internal exile' – that exquisite Soviet paradox by which, as the puritans said, you were not of the world but in it. Solzhenitsyn was released from provincial exile in 1956 and was able to take up work as a teacher. He wrote furiously – but only for himself. He did not even make use of the closed-coterie samizdat system. As he later said:

Not only was I convinced I should never see a single line of mine in print in my lifetime, but, also, I scarcely dared allow any of my close acquaintances to read anything I had written because I feared this would become known.

The 'thaw' temporarily relaxed censorship and, after Khrushchev himself gave it a *nihil obstat*, One Day in the Life of Ivan Denisovich (with some 'necessary' changes) was published in the country's leading literary journal, *Novy Mir*. All 95,000 copies were snapped up on the first day.

The story is set in 1951, in a 'labour camp' during deepest Siberian winter ('Twenty-seven and a half below, the bastard', complains one inmate, angrily berating the camp thermometer). Ivan Denisovich Shukhov's 'crime' is that he was captured by the Germans, and escaped. Any Russian captive was automatically branded a traitor. Others (like the saintly Alyoshka) are serving time for being Christians; or for their parents having had too much money; or for having the wrong books on their shelves. There are, of course, also dregs-of-Russia criminals.

The novel opens at daybreak:

The hammer banged reveille on the rail outside camp HQ at five o'clock as always. Time to get up. The ragged noise was muffled by ice two fingers thick on the windows and soon died away. Too cold for the warder to go on hammering.

The jangling stopped. Outside, it was still as dark as when Shukhov had gotten up in the night to use the latrine bucket – pitch-black, except for three yellow lights visible from the window, two in the perimeter, one inside the camp.

Ivan is feverish and oversleeps, which means punishment and a nearly missed breakfast – slops and gruel. He stores the meagre ration of bread to eat later during his working hours with Gang 104. The day is punctuated by rituals of humiliation in the name of 'security' – including strip searches. Anything 'irregular' (non-issue warm clothing, personal belongings) is punished. The camp is an 'orderly' institution. It is, in fact, a microcosm of the 'regime' – a theme Solzhenitsyn would enlarge on in The Gulag Archipelago. The penal 'labour' is constructive. Literally. Gang 104 is helping to build a power station – what was it Lenin said? 'Electrify, electrify!' – but, while building the Leninist Utopia, the minds and spirits of the camp's inhabitants are kept narrowly confined. These men are what Gogol called 'dead souls'; the new serfs. Nevertheless there is comradeship to be found in shared hardship. Paradoxically this is where true communism resides – or glimpses of it. Ivan is particularly close to the gang foreman, the intrinsically noble Tyurin (he's inside for having had a well-off father). The camp strips men down to what they really are.

The story chronicles tiny events – the lucky catch of a comrade's 'dog-end', a small piece of metal which might come in useful as an improvised knife for self-protection, four hundred grams of bread for work well done, and, most blissfully, a chunk of sausage from a friend's food parcel. Ivan falls into his bunk at

the end of an unclouded day. Almost a happy one. Just one of the 3,653 days of his sentence, from bell to bell.
The extra three were for leap years.

One Flew Over the Cuckoo's Nest, Ken Kesey, 1962

Egas Moniz pioneered human lobotomy in 1935. American surgeons had earlier noted that if you hacked the frontal lobes off chimpanzees' brains, the primates stopped jumping round the monkey house. The 1930s was a time when the medical profession was unimpeded by petty ethical restrictions, and Moniz – despite the lack of any notable surgical expertise – went to work on the (unconsenting) inmates of Lisbon's asylums. As with chimps, the results were dramatic. Moniz trumpeted to the world the beneficial effects of lobotomy. He duly received his Nobel Prize in 1949. He was, the committee said, a 'wonderful man'. Not all of his patients agreed; in the same year as he received the Nobel one of them shot him, shattering his spine.

The operation was popularised in the US by Walter Freeman, who trundled round the states in his 'lobotomobile', demonstrating his 'ice pick' technique to any hospital that would let him into their operating theatre. Failing that, he would operate in hotel rooms, lobotomising children for 'delinquent behaviour' and housewives who had lost the will to do the washing-up. The asylums loved lobotomy: it cost a mere $25 and kept the noise down in the wards. Protest came from some unlikely places: notably L. Ron Hubbard's Scientologists. But, mostly, it was writers and film-makers who got across to the public the full horror of carving up the human brain like a Thanksgiving turkey. Lobotomy inspired Tennessee Williams' 1958 play Suddenly Last Summer. Williams had a sister who had undergone the operation. He knew, too, that it was

sometimes inflicted on gays to render them 'morally sane'.

In One Flew Over the Cuckoo's Nest, the hero is lobotomised because the person in charge can't stand his unruly behaviour. By 1975, when the Oscar-winning film starring Jack Nicholson (at his manic best) came out, lobotomy was history. Freeman had lost his surgeon's licence in 1967, after killing a patient with his ice-pick treatment. But Moniz (who died in 1955) still has his Nobel Prize. The similarly brutal Electro-Convulsive Therapy – a high-voltage sledge-hammer to the brain – was still being used. Kesey's novel weaves together, as novels can, a number of strands of thought about the lunatic asylum. (Ironically, the word 'asylum' etymologically means 'safe refuge'.) It was a 'chamber of horrors', a 'snake pit' (the title of a melodramatic, asylum-based 1940s novel and film), where inmates were brutalised into sanity. It was a circus, where comically insane humans might be laughed at (in Hogarth's rendering of Bedlam, a couple of fan-holding ladies are taking the 'tuppenny tour'). In the post-war period, it was a place where dissidents and 'refuseniks' could be incarcerated and 're-educated'. Or warehoused. And, in the 1960s, there came along contrarian psychiatrists like R. D. Laing who argued the paradox that it was only in the insane asylum that sanity could be found – an idea dramatised in Peter Weiss' 1963 play Marat/Sade.

One Flew Over the Cuckoo's Nest is narrated from inside the 'cuckoo's nest' ('nut-house', 'loony-bin') by a half-Native American inmate, 'Chief Bromden'. The institution is 'radicalised' by the arrival of a life-loving Irish-American buckaroo, Randle McMurphy, who has faked insanity to get out of a prison sentence for battery and gambling so as to win himself what he fondly thinks will be a cushier berth. He embarks on a long feud with the wicked stepmother of the institution, (Big) Nurse Ratched. Randle demands 'rights' (watching baseball on TV) and sows mischief, and finally instigates outright rebellion, after he has managed to smuggle in liquor and prostitutes to the all-male ward. His diagnosis is that the inmates need a damn good party, not 'therapy'. He is routinely punished by ECT. It ends with Randle being lobotomised.

Bromden suffocates him, as an act of mercy, before himself escaping. As the novel opens, the Chief has been on the run a long time.

This bestselling novel, and the Oscar-winning adaptation, gave added impetus to the dissolution of state-funded mental institutions in the US and UK, in favour of 'care in the community'. The reform has proved about as efficacious as the snake pit – but cheaper.

Oranges Are Not the Only Fruit, Jeanette Winterson, 1985

Jeanette Winterson's novel (her first) is about a girl called Jeanette whose life – from the age of seven to her coming of age at twenty-one – conforms, more or less, with what has been revealed to the world about the author's own upbringing. The action is set in the north-west of England, where most of the country's great music-hall and radio comedians originate. There is a comic, Lancastrian effervescence running through what other writers (see Maugham's OF HUMAN BONDAGE) take all too solemnly. Winterson, in a sense, plays it if not for outright laughs, then for comedy with razor-sharp edges. Eric Sykes meets Proust.

The title picks up the heroine's mother's strict injunction that 'oranges are the *only* fruit'. That is, the only fruit worth eating. It is contradicted by the novel's saucy epigraph: – the sales pitch of a famous seller of oranges (and herself) to merry monarchs:

'Oranges are *not* the only fruit' – Nell Gwynn

Edenic proscriptions against forbidden fruit are distantly evoked. The dedication of the novel is to 'Fang the Cat' (Winterson is fascinated by witchcraft). Chapters in the novel are framed by allusive reference to books of the Bible. The opening, 'Genesis', is done in the ventriloquised voice of the seven-year-old Jeanette, who has been educated at home, mainly in Bible studies. The house is a kind of Accrington *madrasa*:

Like most people I lived for a long time with my mother and father. My father liked to watch the wrestling, my mother liked to wrestle; it didn't matter what. She was in the white corner and that was that.

She hung out the largest sheets on the windiest days. She *wanted* the Mormons to knock on the door. At election time in a Labour mill town she put a picture of the Conservative candidate in the window.

She had never heard of mixed feelings. There were friends and there were enemies.

Enemies were:

- The Devil (in his many forms)
- Next Door
- Sex (in its many forms)
- Slugs

Friends were:

- God
- Our dog
- Auntie Madge
- The Novels of Charlotte Brontë
- Slug pellets
  and me, at first.

Jeanette is an only child, and adopted. Her mother, like Mary, wanted a child without the messiness of sex. She dominates the novel like the Old Testament Jehovah:

She was a flamboyant depressive; a woman who kept a revolver in the duster drawer, and the bullets in a tin of Pledge. A woman who stayed up all night baking cakes to avoid sleeping in the same bed as my father. A woman with a prolapse, a thyroid condition, an enlarged heart, an ulcerated leg that never healed, and two sets of false teeth – matte for everyday, and a pearlised set for 'best'.

Revisiting the material for *Oranges* in a later, non-fiction book, Winterson delivered a mixed verdict on her mother: 'She was a monster. But she was my monster.'

The family's Pentecostal sect prizes eloquence, 'speaking in tongues' (Jeanette's mother's favourite glossolalia is via two-way radio), together with moral rigidity of an ultra-puritanical severity. The novel tracks Jeanette's growing up against a background which is so deeply ingrained in her that freedom means denying herself. At school she does not fit in – her apocalyptic vision of the universe contradicts the wishy-washy cheerfulness of the place. A kind teacher takes an interest in her, and, clever little girl that she is, she sops up culture like a sponge. She finds herself, after puberty, lesbian by nature. She prefers another fruit.

> As far as I was concerned men were something you had around the place, not particularly interesting, but quite harmless. I had never shown the slightest feeling for them, and apart from my never wearing a skirt, saw nothing else in common between us.

Exorcism and eventually exile from her church follow. By native intelligence, she wins a place at Oxford, and the novel ends with what might be reconciliation with her mother: 'I miss God,' the heroine concludes, wistfully.

The Ordeal of Richard Feverel: A History of Father and Son, George Meredith, 1859

The Victorians took little pleasure in reading difficult novels. 'There ought to be no need of sitting down before the thing with tools and dynamite like burglars at a safe', proclaimed George Saintsbury (a critic who loved wine even more than he loved fiction). 'It is the first duty of the novelist *to let himself be read*.' If asked in 1859 who was the novelist least willing to 'let himself be read', many Victorian readers would have nominated George Meredith. But as sometimes happens, they chose, on the whole, to give him the benefit of the doubt. He may have served up some tough literary viands, but that was because he was a cleverer writer than they were readers. Meredith led a long life and, as the era drew to an end, was much honoured by discriminating Victorians. They persisted in thinking there

was something important inside that Meredithean safe – if only they could crack the damn thing open. Some evidently did. James Joyce, it is recorded, was a fervent admirer of *Feverel*. Buried in some university vault, doubtless, is a doctoral dissertation on what it contributed to ULYSSES. I don't want to read it.

Feverel is far and away the most accessible for those tempted to make any assault on the Meredith strongbox. Its subject is how best to educate a child. Richard Feverel's mother deserts her husband, leaving her young son behind. Meredith's wife had done the same in the months before he began work on the novel (later deserted by her lover, she went on to kill herself). Young Richard is brought up by his father, Sir Austin, on scientific educational principles. At the centre of the novel is a meditation on Herbert Spencer's then recently aired views that non-institutional education was infinitely preferable to school education. The 'reform' which would soon deliver the 1870 Universal Education Act was in the air. Sir Austin's sub-Spencerian 'system' – which keeps Richard secluded at home – is tested to breaking point when the boy falls in love with Lucy Desborough, the niece of a neighbouring farmer. Sir Austin opposes the match, naturally enough (there is no provision in the system for such vagaries) but the young couple marry secretly and run away. In London, Richard and Lucy – both dangerously inexperienced in the ways of the metropolitan world (they have had no 'social education') – are exposed to various trials and temptations. She attracts the dangerous attention of Lord Mountfalcon, who sends a courtesan to seduce Richard. The couple separate. Lucy, unknown to her husband, bears a child. Sir Austin is finally brought round to approval of his daughter-in-law. But Richard is badly wounded in a duel with Mountfalcon in France. Lucy goes mad and dies while her husband lies paralysed, a casualty of his father's system. He is last seen on his sick-bed, 'striving to image her on his brain'.

The Ordeal of Richard Feverel was banned by the circulating library 'leviathan', Charles Mudie. The great librarian's Calvinist susceptibilities were particularly affronted by the seduction scene in which the married hero succumbs to the wiles of the seductive Bella Mount:

> as he looked down on her haggard loveliness, not divine sorrow but a devouring jealousy sprang like fire in his breast, and set him rocking with horrid pain. He bent closer to her pale beseeching face. Her eyes still drew him down.
>
> 'Bella! No! no! promise me! swear it!'
>
> 'Lost, Richard! lost for ever! give me up!'
>
> He cried: 'I never will!' and strained her in his arms, and kissed her passionately on the lips.

Torrid stuff for 1859, and too much so for Mr Mudie, whose boycott effectively killed sales of the novel – while stimulating considerable curiosity about its contents.

Getting through this book is like clambering, bare-kneed, over barbed wire, but at the heart of the novel, for those who make it there, is a still-relevant, and still-raging, debate over the best form of education for a young child. Should it be based on 'system' or should the child be allowed to range freely, as nature intended? At the time of writing, system is winning.

Oroonoko, Aphra Behn, 1688

Aphra Behn currently holds the title of Britain's first 'true' novelist – although there remain chauvinists who would back Defoe. She was born Eaffrey Johnson in 1640 near Canterbury. What scant evidence there is records that her father was a 'surgeon barber' (they specialised in treating venereal disease, as well as trimming beards) and her mother a wet nurse. In return for services rendered, the Johnsons received favours from powerful local families. It was thus, one assumes, that Eaffrey's father, the barber, was appointed in 1663/4 Lieutenant General of Surinam, a British colonial possession. It has a touch of Caligula's horse about it. But the Civil War had (temporarily) disturbed the usual power, patronage and privilege circuits. Surinam was put to the

cultivation of sugar. Slaves from Africa worked the plantations and were harshly treated. It was a black man's hell, and a white man's grave. Thus it proved for Aphra's (as she had renamed herself) father, who evidently died there. Did his daughter accompany him to Surinam? The question, with accompanying anxieties about 'authenticity', has always vexed commentators on Oroonoko. It seems, from the ostentatious accuracy of her local description and the introduction of actual historical figures, that Behn indeed knew the place first hand. Sceptics persist in wondering.

Aphra's adult life is shrouded in dimly recorded glamour, adventure and mystery. She may, or may not, have married a Hans Behn (who may, or may not, have been a slave trader). She was probably a state spy, putting her skills to work for her country in enemy-territory Flanders after the Restoration. Like Moll Flanders, she spent some time in debtors' prison. She was certainly the first woman to write for the Restoration stage, leaving a distinguished body of comedy. And, when the licentious London theatres were less open to her talent, she turned her ready pen to writing the primal novel, Oroonoko. It was published a few months before she died.

The 'True History', as the title proclaims itself (the term 'novel' was yet to be invented), is the manifestly untrue story of a 'Royal Slave'. The oxymoron is piquant in the context of the 1680s, with the recent incidences of deposed and restored monarchs. An African prince, Oroonoko, along with his wife Imoinda, has been transported to Surinam from West Africa, to live in slavery in the plantations. His history is 'set down' by an anonymous young Englishwoman, daughter of the newly appointed deputy governor. The narrator befriends the luckless African pair. Oroonoko, being a prince in exile (as was Behn's beloved Charles II in France), can speak both French and English – elegantly. Even in remote West Africa, he heard of the execution of Charles I and found it – as did all right-thinking people, we apprehend – 'deplorable'. The narrator is struck by the couple's native dignity. Their beauty is anything but native. Oroonoko (flatteringly renamed 'Caesar' by his captors) has straight hair and 'Roman' features. He is less a noble savage, a hundred years *avant la lettre*, than a noble, *tout court*. A black-skinned blueblood. We recall that the nickname for the notoriously swarthy Charles II was 'the black boy' (it survives as a common pub name in England).

Oroonoko is no common slave. He kills two tigers and has a closely described battle with an electric ('benumbing') eel. When Imoinda becomes pregnant, Oroonoko is determined that his son shall not be born into slavery. He organises an uprising, and is cheated into surrendering on the point of victory. Realising it is the end, Oroonoko cuts Imoinda's throat to save her from the misery of slavery, and then cuts off her face to ensure no one will ever see her beauty again. He disembowels himself, but is sewn up by surgeons in order to be executed, sadistically, for the delectation of a white rabble. Behn's Royal Slave is even more stoic, at the moment of regicide, than the Royal Captive, Charles I, calmly puffing away at his pipe as his genitals are cut off.

Behn died only months after the publication of *Oroonoko* and is buried in Westminster Abbey, the first woman author to be so honoured. On her tomb, instructed Virginia Woolf, 'all women together ought to let flowers fall. . . for it was she who earned them the right to speak their minds'.

Other People, Martin Amis, 1981

When his memoir, *Experience*, was published in 2000, Amis' publisher predicted at the launch party that it was a book which would still be read 'in 200 years' time'. An ebullition of millenarian fizz, one might think. But what, if readers look back in 2200, will they make of Martin Amis, canonical novelist of a time gone by? My guess is they will perceive a writer much more experimental than we conventionally take him to be. Two of his more interesting works, following this proposition, are among his slipperiest and least accessible: *Other People* and *Time's Arrow*.

The title of *Other People* alludes to Sartre's *'l'enfer c'est les autres'*, conventionally translated as 'hell is other people'. The narrative follows a heroine who has just

woken in hospital ('a white room') lacking all long- and short-term memory. She is both conscious (of where she is) and unconscious (of where she has come from). The amnesiac gimmick is common enough in the science-fiction and thriller genres (*Other People* is subtitled *A Mystery Story*). But Amis is less concerned with reconstituting the mysterious past of Mary Lamb (as she arbitrarily calls herself) than with exploiting her as a centre of disoriented consciousness. For Mary the familiar world is 'defamiliarised'. Thus, for instance, she tackles the problem of the telephone:

> Mary had watched people use the telephone several times and was pretty confident she could handle it. The bandy, glistening dumb-bell was heavier than she expected. But she had expected the call: she knew who this must be.
> 'Yes?' said Mary.
> A thin voice started calling. Telephones were clearly less efficient instruments of communication than people let on. For instance, you could hardly hear the other person and they could hardly hear you.
> 'I can't hear. What?' said Mary.
> Then she heard, in an angry whine, *'I said* turn it the other way up.'

Mary, as anyone who was au fait with what was 'hot' in the literary world in the 1980s would have apprehended, is a version of the poet Craig Raine's 'Martian', for whom the quotidian and domestic props of life are rendered bafflingly alien and wonderful. As Raine describes the telephone, in one of the anthems of what is called the Martian School of poetry: 'In homes, a haunted apparatus sleeps, / That snores when you pick it up.'

Raine and Amis were of the same generation, and of the same university, and their careers in literary journalism were intertwined at this period. They were held to belong to a coterie which has been termed – embarrassingly for them, doubtless – the 'New Oxford Wits' (wags intruded a 't').

Other People has a plot of kinds. Mary picks up with and is picked up by various wrong sets, from the criminal to the swinging. She has Candy-like adventures (see CANDY) as she discovers, with some surprise, what the different sockets in her body are for, and is a 'little girl' no longer. In the last brief section the heroine recovers consciousness of her original identity and history. In some very enigmatic fashion, the facts about her would-be saviour, Detective Prince, and her would-be murderer, Mr Wrong, are sorted out. There's an 'Occurrence at Owl Creek'-like ending in which Mary may be executed, or reborn, or returned by time-loop to the novel's opening situation. *Other People*, this is to say, does not easily give up its secret – at least not to me.

Amis' cleverness has always been of the kind which makes his clodhopping readers feel they are having rings run round them or, even worse, being sneered at. As a sustained exercise in *ostranenie*, the Russian Formalist term which translates uneasily as 'making strange', *Other People* is virtuosic. Very strange. As a mystery story, it's very mysterious. Perhaps in two hundred years it will all be much clearer.

Outerbridge Reach, Robert Stone, 1992

Stone started writing late in life and accumulated his now substantial reputation carefully and gradually. His first novel, *Hall of Mirrors* (1967), a study of moral decay in New Orleans, established him as a Graham Greenian novelist of the 'why this is hell, nor am I out of it' kind. Planet Stone is not a jolly place. His second novel, *Dog Soldiers* (1974) – often cited as the best novel to come out of his country's Vietnam trauma – projected an infernal vision of modern America, and mounted a powerful refutation of the Nixonian 'peace with honour' nonsense. A torture scene, enhanced by LSD, sticks in the mind as horrible in ways not even de Sade could imagine. *Outerbridge Reach*, Stone's fifth novel, is a profound meditation on spiritual loneliness, infused with cosmic pessimism. The plot is almost entirely situational. A Donald Trump-like magnate, of playboy temperament, resolves to compete in a round-the-world solo sailing race to publicise a new design of yacht his firm has developed. There is a financial scandal and the playboy mariner goes to ground, not to sea. His place at the helm is taken by one of his firm's salesmen. Owen Browne is a veteran of Annapolis and Vietnam, happily married, the world assumes, and clean-cut. But inwardly as his closest friend perceives he is a seething mass of spiritual discontent.

Browne's firm has recruited a film-maker to record his voyage from a shore-base (this dual-hero scheme – one who acts and one who watches – is standard in Stone's fiction). A decadent hipster, Ronald Strickland made his reputation with a documentary satirising America's involvement in Vietnam. He is totally cynical.

Browne's all-plastic-and-fibreglass vessel fails its great test. It's a flop. As he founders in the southern Atlantic he decides to fake his voyage, on the grounds that the only truth at sea is the truth you make. He sabotages his transponder, compiles false logs and marks time, intending to pick up his competitors on their way back and beat them to the finishing line. But as he drifts in the empty ocean, religious mania overtakes him and he walks off his boat having discovered, as he thinks, the secret of the universe. Meanwhile, back on shore, Strickland seduces Mrs Browne.

Stone served in the US Navy as a young man, is a lifelong yachtsman, and knows his nautical ropes. He was resident in the UK in the late 1960s during a period of national excitement about round-the-world sailing exploits, with heroes such as Sir Francis Chichester regarded as 'New Elizabethans' – modern-day successors to England's great sixteenth-century buccaneers. What seems particularly to have caught Stone's imagination was the strange voyage of Donald Crowhurst in the 1968, *Sunday Times*-sponsored 'Golden Globe' circumnavigation competition. Crowhurst set out in his 'revolutionary' trimaran. It proved inadequate. He hid himself in the southern Atlantic, faked his logs, and intended to pick up the race on the return leg and win by fraud. But, in his loneliness, Crowhurst succumbed to religious mania – as his increasingly odd logbook entries record – and his boat was later found enigmatically empty.

Stone's book sailed high for nine weeks on the *New York Times* bestseller list and still drifts, gloomily, in its oceanic pessimism a prose *Rime of the Ancyent Marinere*.

The Outsider, Albert Camus, 1942

Most of my generation learned everything they wanted to know about existentialism from this novel and everything they wanted to know about existentialists from Simone de Beauvoir's *The Mandarins*. *L'Être et le néant*, Sartre's treatise, was rather too knotty by comparison. But he instructed that to label Camus an existentialist was 'a grave mistake'. His colleague was a 'classic pessimist', of the Schopenhauerian kind, and a connoisseur of the 'absurd'.

However one classifies it, Camus's novel remains addictively readable and indefinably 'strange'. *L'Étranger* (literally 'the stranger') was published in occupied France in 1942. The first English translation was offered to the victorious (but knackered) UK reading public in 1946. It was the publisher, Hamish Hamilton, who came up with the title *The Outsider* for the novel. It was an inspired choice. 'The Stranger' would have missed the mark, as would 'The Alien' or 'The Foreigner'.

The action is set in Algiers – nominally part of 'metropolitan France' – soon to be the site of a post-war bloody colonial conflict. Camus's novel was written in a France angrily but impotently occupied by Nazi Germany. It had, humiliatingly, to pass through German censorship before a French man or woman could read it 'under licence'. Consequently the text is 'neutralised'– bleached of any political or nationalist content. The hero Meursault has a French name, but we do not know how ethnically French he is; he sees himself as different from 'the Arabs'. As Cyril Connolly, an early advocate of the novel put it (rather too snootily for contemporary taste), Meursault is:

the flower of a pagan and barrenly philistine culture. This *milieu* has a certain affinity with . . . those torrid American cities where 'poor whites' exist uneasily beside poor blacks.

The narrative is autobiographical. It opens bleakly, 'Mother died today. Or maybe yesterday: I can't be sure.' Nor does Meursault much care. He has not visited her in her old folks' home and has not paid her residential bills. He alludes to no other family. His filial indifference will, indirectly, lead him to the guillotine. It's not clear what Meursault *does* care about. He has an office job. He evidently does it efficiently. His employers may, it seems, send him to Paris – a big step up. 'I didn't care much, one way or the other', he says. He has 'lost the habit of noting his feelings'. Does he have any? His closest friend is Raymond, a pimp and gangster. The two of them are men who 'understand each other'. But he has no inclination to join in Raymond's criminal activities. He takes up with Marie, with whom he makes love listlessly. His one pleasure is swimming in the ocean, hence he frequents the beach. When Raymond provokes a fracas there with some Arabs, involving knives, it is Meursault who, for no particular reason, returns by himself and shoots one of the recumbent, unthreatening Arabs six times. His only explanation, not that he tries very hard to come up with one, even to save his life, is that it was very hot that day. All he misses in prison are cigarettes and the swimming. It's hard, he finds, to 'kill time'. Easier to kill Arabs and let himself be killed.

At the trial, his reported 'callousness' after his mother's death weighs heavily against him. He himself has nothing to say. He is condemned. He feels nothing but rage at the chaplain who, before his execution, attempts to put him in a properly religious state of mind. For the only time in the novel he is articulate, garrulous, and angry. The chaplain bursts into tears and leaves. Meursault feels, at last, that quality Camus most valued: defiance in the face of the accepted death:

All that remained to hope was that on the day of my execution there should be a huge crowd of spectators and that they should greet me with howls of execration.

The Painter of Signs, R. K. Narayan, 1976

The Painter of Signs is a novel about writing – or, to use the critical term that was trendy in the 1970s, 'semiotics'. It was published forty years into Narayan's career as one of India's great 'English' novelists, by which time he had whittled his use of the language down to bone-like simplicity.

The hero Raman paints signs for shops, offices and small businesses in the southern town of Malgudi – Narayan's favourite setting. It's fictional, in South India, and the nearest large city is Madras. Raman is college-educated and prides himself on being rational. He is a man of the modern world – the world of the 1970s. He scrapes a modest living by his craft. His reads English classics (Dickens, etc.) and they are his greatest pleasure in life. Orphaned, he lives in their 'ancestral house' with an aunt – a woman of profound superstition whose main household activities are making sure they are not cheated by the milkman (whose product comes via an ambling cow not a van) and the rice vendor, who sprinkles small stones in his wares. She is now elderly and yearns to spend her last days in a religious retreat. Raman, in his twenties, is unmarried and a virgin. Sex, he believes, is what has brought mankind to its present sorry pass: 'If Adam had possessed a firm mind, the entire course of creation would have taken a different turn.' If one wants to 'view women normally' one should look at them when they are 'past sixty and look shrunken-skinned', he instructs himself. But his desires for a younger variety of the sex worry him: 'An edifice of self-discipline laboriously raised in a lifetime seemed to be crumbling down'.

Other things are crumbling. In the background is the Prime Minister Indira Gandhi's controversial 'sterilisation' campaign. Nowadays, as his aunt observes, India is 'afraid of children'. Teams are being sent into the rural areas to bribe women (notoriously with the offer of a transistor radio) to submit their bodies to sterilising surgery. Raman falls in love with one of Gandhi's birth-control missionaries: a woman of fiery dedication to the cause of reducing population growth 'by at least five per cent'. Sex

education, Daisy believes, 'must be given from the kindergarten stage'. She needs signs and Raman accompanies her into the back country. The bullock pulling their cart becomes lame, and they are obliged to spend a night together – he under the cart, she on top of it. He does not sleep but:

> lay tossing on his bed of straw, looking up longingly at the bottom of the cart. He debated within himself whether to dash up, seize her, and behave like Rudolph Valentino in *The Sheik*, which he had seen as a student. Women liked an aggressive lover – so said the novelists.

Raman finds himself in love and wholly irrational. The object of his passion may, or may not, reciprocate. She is unreadable. Her 'signs' are ambiguous. He coerces her into marriage, she accepts – but then declines to live with him. His aunt, meanwhile, has decided to go off to die as she wishes in a religious commune, taking the bare minimum from her life outside:

> She packed into her jute bag her possessions: a couple of white saris, a little brass casket containing sacred ash for smearing on her forehead, a coral rosary for prayers, a book of sacred verse, and two tiny silver images of Krishna and Ganesha. 'These were given to me by my father,' she explained.

Daisy finally declines to join Raman in the ancestral house, with the implication that, although he does not admit or even know it, what he offers is old India: children, sifting rice, housework. This poignant story, and the big things it delicately implies about the author's 'developing' country, is beautifully done.

Pamela, Samuel Richardson, 1740

The full title is *Pamela; Or, Virtue Rewarded. In A Series Of Familiar Letters From A Beautiful Young Damsel, To Her Parents*. There were no blurbs, one is reminded, to whet the prospective reader's appetite in the eighteenth century. This novel's prospective reader was – in all likelihood – a woman. Young women were in fact so drawn to the novel that *Pamela* is credited with having inspired the first reading 'mania' – or 'stampede' to the bookshops and circulating libraries of the day. The author was neither young nor a woman. One of the oddities surrounding *Pamela* is how an ailing printer in late middle age came to write it at all – and what his motives for doing so were. First among them was a desire to preach to the largest congregation that would listen to him. From his earliest days (his schoolmates nicknamed him 'Serious'), Samuel Richardson had an urge to instruct the young. And he was the first popular British novelist to realise that fiction was the ideal pulpit from which to do so.

Samuel was a precocious penman. As a youth he acted as a scribe to girls of his acquaintance, wanting to write the right kind of love letter. He enjoyed 'secretaryship' and it led to his being apprenticed for seven years as a printer. Following the moral script laid down by Hogarth (in his 'Industry and Idleness' plates), he married his former master's daughter, Martha. The couple had six children (three of which were named 'Samuel'), none of whom survived beyond the 'prattler' stage of life. On the death of Martha in 1731, and that of the last of their surviving children, Richardson remarried in 1733. His second wife, Elizabeth, bore him five daughters and a son who died in infancy. As the 1730s progressed, Richardson became an increasingly respected figure in the London book trade. His personal health, however, deteriorated as his fortunes rose. There was a dangerous tendency to 'Rotundity and Liquor'. He decided, at the age of fifty, in his enforced more sedentary way of life, to compose a moral tale told in the first person for young women. A novel – since they seemed to like fiction.

He remembered being told some years before about a virtuous serving maid who had married her master. As Defoe's *Moll Flanders* records, it was more usual for servant girls to be sexually abused by their employers. In this case, the girl had, unlike Moll, evaded 'the snares laid for her virtue' – and gone so far as to threaten to drown herself rather than part with her virginity. While he was writing, Richardson recalled:

> my worthy-hearted wife, and the young lady who [was] with us, when I had read them some part of the story, which I had begun without their knowing it, used to come in to my little closet every night, with – 'Have you any more of Pamela, Mr R.? We are come to hear a little more of Pamela,' etc. This encouraged me to prosecute it.

The plot of *Pamela* is somewhat sarcastically summarised by Richardson's biographers in one, reductive, sentence:

> A virtuous servant girl rejects her master's lewd advances and is kidnapped by him and confined in a lonely country house where she continues to fight him off until he is overcome by her virtue to the extent of proposing matrimony, which is instantly accepted.

The novel, one of the longest and slowest in the language, was responsible for two literary innovations, signalled in the title. Together they set English fiction on a new course. Epistolary narration was one of these innovations. The technique created immediacy – albeit sometimes with a measure of improbability. Just as Byron said that no man shaves himself during an earthquake, so no young girl carries on writing a letter (or, nowadays, an email) even as some ravishing Tarquin lunges at her breasts – though Pamela manages to. The other innovation is the novel's grand assertion that 'little people' matter. 'Beautiful Damsels in Distress' in romance are not, before 1740, fifteen-year-old skivvies who empty the chamber pots and do the ironing for their betters. *Pamela* is not merely a love story, but an act of democracy. Respect it, even if you can't spare the hundred hours it requires (at least) to read it.

Parade's End, Ford Madox Ford, 1924–8

It's odd that a trio of the best English literary works about the First World War are by authors with German birth names: Robert von Ranke Graves, who wrote the memoir *Goodbye to All That*; Siegfried Sassoon, who wrote *Counter-Attack and Other Poems*; and Ford Hermann Hueffer (i.e. 'Ford Madox Ford'), who wrote a tetralogy – *Some Do Not . . .* (1924), *No More Parades* (1925), *A Man Could Stand Up* (1926), and *Last Post* (1928) – with the collective title *Parade's End*.

It opens in 1912. Christopher Tietjens and Vincent Macmaster are civil servants and statisticians: organised, scientific types. They keep the biggest show in the world, the British Empire, going. They are currently tooling down to Rye to get in a spot of golf:

> The two young men – they were of the English public official class – sat in the perfectly appointed railway carriage. The leather straps to the windows were of virgin newness; the mirrors beneath the new luggage racks immaculate as if they had reflected very little; the bulging upholstery in its luxuriant, regulated curves was scarlet and yellow in an intricate, minute dragon pattern, the design of a geometrician in Cologne. The compartment smelt faintly, hygienically of admirable varnish; the train ran as smoothly – Tietjens remembered thinking – as British gilt-edged securities.

All is well with the world, but not with Christopher Tietjens. His marriage has gone wrong. His wife Sylvia is a 'whore'. 'Their' child is probably not his child. Foul rumours have been circulated to which he has adopted a policy of 'complete taciturnity'. He would 'rather be dead than an open book'. His father would rather be dead than live with the shame his son has brought on the Tietjens name, and commits suicide. Christopher has been disowned by his family, while the family's large country house in Yorkshire, Groby, has been inherited by his elder brother Mark and Christopher is no

longer welcome there. Divorce? 'No one but a blackguard would ever submit a woman to the ordeal of divorce', he tells Vincent. Sylvia, Tietjens' wife, rather prefers blackguards and finds him a bore with his 'dull display of the English gentleman'. But, like a cat playing with a mouse, she will never let him go.

Tietjens is admirable but unlikeable. He is a member of an office class which resents the fact that 'Jews' and 'niggers' (i.e. cultivated Indians) have been allowed into their department. He is no Adonis. He has a 'nose like a pallid triangle on a bladder of lard'. By chance – on the golf-course at Rye – his life becomes entangled with that of a girl who shows up there, waving a placard and interrupting the men's game. The encounter leads to an unlikely love affair. Valentine Wannop is a short-skirted, ankle-flaunting, pacifist suffragette ten years Tietjens' junior. One of the new 'wild women', Valentine 'demonstrates' in public, blows up the king's letter boxes, and is serenely prepared to undergo the torture of force-feeding for the 'cause'. A cause Tietjens viscerally despises. Nonetheless, they find themselves irresistibly attracted.

War is approaching. Tietjens knows that it will be 'the end of the world. The last of England'. But, despite being in a reserved occupation, and over-age (as was Ford), he volunteers (as did Ford). Part two of the quartet jumps to 1917 – the lowest point of the conflict for the British and their Allies. Tietjens is a captain (he is too morally upright and cross-grained for the more senior post his abilities warrant). He has sustained acute shell-shock and chronic disillusion. He sees the war as systematised massacre; men die 'by the quarter million'. Tietjens is a logistics officer, entrusted with keeping the conveyor belt to front-line massacre running as smoothly as a high-street butcher's sausage grinder. He could get himself invalided out, but he will not. Going back to the trenches for a 'big push', which he suspects will be his death, he asks Valentine (now a rebelliously uncorseted PE instructress at a girls' school), 'Will you be my mistress tonight?' She consents. Despite the odds, Christopher Tietjens survives the war. England, as expected, doesn't. He ends up, uneasily united with

Valentine, making his living as an antiques dealer. He has always loved the past more than the present.

The years 2014–18 will see national 'celebration' of the Great War in Britain. It is to be hoped it will help to recruit the new readers Ford's majestic, and troubling, novelistic sequence richly deserves.

A Passage to India, E. M. Forster, 1924

Anyone who has had reading contact with it for fifty-six years (viz me) will have had two very different experiences of the novel. A Passage to India was conceived in 1913, completed in 1921, and published, after much wrestling with the last section, 'Temple', three years later.

Forster lived on until 1970, though he produced no further full-length works of fiction – long enough to witness the passing of the Sexual Offences Act, which decriminalised homosexuality. He himself was, before this date, 'an unspeakable of the Oscar Wilde sort' (as he put it in the post-humously published Maurice). By a wonderfully English absurdity, he had spent many of his later years in a happy (criminal) relationship with a tolerant (married) police constable, twenty-three years his junior, who took the Nelson's-eye view on what people did in their private lives. PC Bob Buckingham's laissez-faire attitude was not, alas, widespread in the force. In 1952, for instance, Alan Turing – whose brilliant work on cryptology had saved Britain in the Second World War – was charged with 'gross indecency' and chemically castrated. I read A Passage to India at school five years later, and studied it at university in the early 1960s. No direct reference was made in either place to Forster's sexuality, beyond the vague comment that he was never good with female characters.

A main narrative strand in the novel follows a young English schoolteacher, Adela Quested, who has been brought to India to marry a British official. Things go very wrong after she may, or may not, have been sexually assaulted in some local caves, which are imbued with ancient, but entirely

inscrutable, religious significance. Adela's innocent intention was to make friends with a 'native'. Near riots and a trial ensue in which the accused assailant is acquitted. Adela's 'passage to India' – and her marriage – ends in humiliating ruin. No one ever finds out precisely what happened in the Marabar Caves – it is part of the 'mystery and muddle' that is colonial India.

The novel's title echoes a poem of Walt Whitman's. His 'Passage to India' poses a question which goes to the heart of the imperial situation Forster's novel set out to probe. Namely: is it possible to have a fully human relationship if that relationship is complicated by colonial possession and racial difference? This is how Whitman puts it, rather spoutingly:

> Passage to India!
> Lo, soul seest thou not God's
>   purpose from the first?
> The earth to be spann'd, connected
>   by net-work,
> The people to become brothers and
>   sisters,
> The races, neighbors, to marry and
>   be given in marriage,
> The oceans to be cross'd, the distant
>   brought near,
> The lands to be welded together.

Whitman was as floridly gay as Forster was reclusively so.

At the core of the novel is the relationship between another British schoolteacher, Cyril Fielding, and a Muslim doctor, Aziz (Adela's alleged assailant). Their friendship is intense – verging, the novel hints, on passionate. But, by Kipling's law of imperial life: 'East is East and West is West, and never the twain shall meet'.

Forster found the novel almost impossible to finish. No ending was 'right'. It was not because of any writing block. What he was up against was the fact that fiction, by its nature, could not 'solve' the problems inherent in empire. A Passage to India ends inconclusively, but to fine artistic effect, with the two men who can never, because of the contradictions within the system in which they both live, be 'welded', as Whitman puts it. They are last seen riding horses through the monsoon-soaked Indian jungle, which forces them apart:

> But the horses didn't want it – they swerved apart; the earth didn't want it, sending up rocks through which riders must pass single file; the temples, the tank, the jail, the palace, the birds, the carrion, the Guest House, that came into view as they issued from the gap and saw Mau beneath; they didn't want it, they said in their hundred voices, 'No, not yet,' and the sky said, 'No, not there.'

It is a conclusion in which nothing is concluded because, in 1924, it could not be. Forster's 'not yet' would be nearly a quarter of a century coming, with Indian Independence in 1947. *Midnight's Children* were as yet twenty-three years unborn. And it would be twenty years after that as regards any possible union between Fielding and Aziz.

Perchance to Dream, Ray Bradbury, 1948

By their nature writers are a constitutionally sleepless profession. Much of our literature 'smells of the lamp' – as they used to say, before gas and electricity abolished the daily darkness which earlier, unluckier generations were obliged to live with. How much of Jane Austen, Dickens, Hardy, was written, sleeplessly, by candlelight? If only the manuscripts could talk. Or if, like our computer files, they were calendar- and time-dated. How interesting it would be to compare those passages of the books we love which were written in the dark watches of the sleepless night with those dashed off in bright sunlight.

Unsurprisingly, the most imaginative depictions of sleeplessness – the weary nocturnal wrestle with an obstinate Morpheus – have been accomplished by great writers: chronic insomniacs, by and large, and, many of them, indefatigable explorers of the condition. My favourite in the literature of insomnia is the science-fiction writer Ray Bradbury's short story 'Perchance to Dream' (incidentally Hamlet,

from whose 'to be or not to be' soliloquy Bradbury's title is taken, is a Class-A insomniac – viz his discovery, during a midnight ramble, of Claudius' instruction that he be executed on landing in England). In Bradbury's short story – subtitled 'Asleep in Armageddon' – an astronaut's spaceship crashes on an apparently uninhabited planet. It's a mishap, not a disaster. After his SOS, Leonard Sale can expect rescue within a week; and, until his rescuers arrive, obtain some welcome rest:

> The sun rose and was warm. He felt no sense of mortality. Six days would be no time at all. He would eat, he would read, he would sleep. He glanced at his surroundings. No dangerous animals; a tolerable oxygen supply. What more could one ask? Beans and bacon, was the answer. He touched the machinery in his helmet that popped food into his mouth.
>
> After breakfast he smoked a cigarette slowly, deeply, blowing out through the special helmet tube. He nodded contentedly. What a life! Not a scratch on him. Luck, sheer luck!
>
> His head nodded. Sleep, he thought.
>
> Good idea. Forty winks. Plenty of time to sleep, take it easy. Six whole long, luxurious days of idling and philosophising. Sleep.
>
> He stretches himself out, tucks his arm under his head, and shuts his eyes.

Sleep comes. . . and is just as instantly wrenched away. His brain, Leonard discovers, has been invaded. It is now the battle ground between two warring armies: those of 'Tylle of the Blood Mound and the Death Drum' and 'Iorr of Wendillo, Destroyer of Infidels'. Having destroyed their planet, eons ago, these brutal warriors have been waiting to pursue their never-ending combat – the astronaut's sleeping brain is where they will now carry on their fight. Leonard cannot sleep – the pain of the warfare in his head when he does is too great. Nor can he survive six days without sleep.

The two-man rescue party, when they

arrive, find him raving incoherently and helpfully inject him with a sedative – so he can rest. Having been thus abandoned to his night terrors, Leonard doesn't last long. 'Perchance to Dream' ends with the expected sting in the tail.

> They made a grave and said a word over it. They drank their evening coffee silently. They looked at the lovely sky and the bright and beautiful stars.
>
> 'What a night,' they said, lying down.
>
> 'Pleasant dreams,' said one, rolling over.
>
> And the other replied, 'Pleasant dreams.'
>
> They slept.

Or did they?

Peregrine Pickle, Tobias Smollett, 1751

It was George Orwell who diagnosed 'gentleness' as the essence of 'England' in his 1941 essay 'The Lion and Unicorn', with its Blitzkrieg opening: 'As I write, highly civilised human beings are flying overhead, trying to kill me.' Orwell, scribbling in his bomb shelter, rhapsodises on the theme:

> The gentleness of the English civilisation is perhaps its most marked characteristic. You notice it the instant you set foot on English soil. It is a land where the bus conductors are good-tempered and the policemen carry no revolvers. In no country inhabited by white men is it easier to shove people off the pavement. And with this goes something that is always written off by European observers as 'decadence' or hypocrisy, the English hatred of war and militarism.

It was also George Orwell who wrote a laudatory appreciation of the author of *Peregrine Pickle* in another wartime essay, 'Tobias Smollett: Scotland's Best Novelist' (1944). A rash claim, lovers of Scott and Stevenson

will think. Others might point out that in subject matter and location Smollett is as English as roast beef (or, in 1944, Woolton Pie – that meatless meat pie).

Orwell concedes that Smollett's 'picaresques' are 'long, formless' and 'frankly pornographic'. His two principal heroes, Peregrine and Roderick Random,

> go through great vicissitudes of fortune, travel widely, seduce numerous women, suffer imprisonment for debt, and end up prosperous and happily married. Of the two, Peregrine is somewhat the greater blackguard, because he has no profession – Roderick is a naval surgeon, as Smollett himself had been for a while – and can consequently devote more time to seductions and practical jokes. But neither is ever shown acting from an unselfish motive, nor is it admitted that such things as religious belief, political conviction or even ordinary honesty are serious factors in human affairs.

Wherein, then, lies the 'best'-ness? The novels, Orwell argues, contain 'some of the best passages of sheer farce in the English language'. And, he goes on to argue, they are 'realistic'. Or, put another way, brutally 'ungentle'. A novel like *Peregrine Pickle*, Orwell implies, takes the reader back to that unregenerate age before the great 'softening up' of British society.

> Peregrine devotes himself for months at a time to the elaborate and horribly cruel practical jokes in which the eighteenth century delighted. When, for instance, an unfortunate English painter is thrown into the Bastille for some trifling offence and is about to be released, Peregrine and his friends, playing on his ignorance of the language, let him think that he has been sentenced to be broken on a wheel. A little later they tell him that this punishment has been commuted to castration, and then extract a last bit of fun out of his terrors by letting him think that he is escaping in disguise when he is merely being

released from the prison in the normal way.

'Picaresque' is from the Spanish *pícaro*, meaning rogue, rascal, swine, cad, rotter. Peregrine fits the profile. He lazes and bullies his way through school, idles dissolutely at university, whores his way through the grand tour, loses his money at gambling hells, duels, murderously at the slightest provocation, only – at the end – to win the heart of the pure (rich) woman he has always, in his winner-takes-all fashion, had rather a soft spot for. He will not be a faithful spouse.

If one compares *Peregrine Pickle* to, say, a Surtees–Jorrocks adventure, or the election and Fleet Prison scenes in *Pickwick Papers* (a homage to Smollett's work, as the alliteration testifies), the 'gentling' that had come over England in a mere hundred years is palpable. Samuel Pickwick, for example, would no more cudgel a tradesman who displeased him (as Peregrine does) than he would 'sharp' at cards (as Peregrine does). The national character had changed. Historians would probably put it down to the Evangelical Revival, which 'reformed' Victorian society morally. For all that, there is something as irresistible in unregenerate Smollettian comedy as in the serial plates of Hogarth's 'Four Stages of Cruelty'. Sugar-coat it as you will, *Peregrine Pickle* insists, the world is not soft-centred, but, at its heart, hard as stone. But fun as well.

Perfume: The Story of a Murderer, Patrick Süskind, 1985

Norman Mailer once claimed that Hemingway 'didn't have three smells in all his work'. The Anglo-Saxon olfactory nervousness has had a patently impoverishing effect on creative literature, while the French interest in private odours, and their extinction, led not just to the best perfume industry in the world but to an 1884 masterpiece of olfactory fantasy: Huysmans's AGAINST NATURE, with its 'perfume-artist' hero, Jean des Esseintes. (Less well known is Huysmans's eulogy on the female armpit in *Le Gousset* – or 'Gusset'; not a title to sound

sweet to the British ear.) I suspect that one reason why ULYSSES remained banned for so unforgivably long in the English-speaking world (and was finally cleared in the US on the bizarre grounds that it was 'emetic' – vomit-inducing – rather than 'erotic' – arousal-inducing) was not the occasional 'four-letter word' but its passing references to Bloom's breakfast of grilled mutton kidney, 'which gave to his palate a fine tang of faintly scented urine', and his sitting asquat the cuckstool a few minutes later. In Anglo-Saxon literature, these are uneasy territories.

Patrick Süskind's *Perfume* was translated from the original German and published in 1986 in Britain and America, where it became a runaway bestseller. Set in pre-Revolution France, it tells the story of Jean-Baptiste Grenouille. Born in 'the most putrid spot in the whole kingdom' in sweltering July, under a fishmonger's stall, Grenouille inherits misfortune and the single talent of a preternaturally keen sense of smell, which he puts to good use.

The first phase of the novel chronicles the hero's apprenticeship to a Paris perfumer; the second his period in the wilderness. Living as a hermit for seven years, he makes the extraordinary discovery that every human has an individual smell, as unique as their fingerprints. He travels to Grasse, the scent-laden centre of the perfume industry. There follows a spell of olfactory vampirism in which Grenouille kills maidens so as to distil and relish their pure, and infinitely distinct, fragrances. Caught and condemned to death by breaking on the wheel, he escapes by releasing a pheromone (*his* smell, made up of the mingled scent of all the dead virgins) on the scaffold. The odour subliminally convinces the townspeople that he cannot be guilty, and they surrender themselves to a mass orgy of scent-induced sexual lust. Released, and now possessed of this latent political power over the masses, Grenouille returns to Paris just before the Revolution, which, we apprehend, his strange skill will trigger.

Süskind tries valiantly to get the reading nose as interested as the reading eye. Hence passages like the following (do your nostrils twitch?), describing malodorous eighteenth-century Paris:

There reigned in the cities a stench barely conceivable to us modern men and women. The streets stank of manure, the courtyards of urine, the stairwells stank of mouldering wood and rat droppings, the kitchens of spoiled cabbage and mutton fat; the unaired parlours stank of stale dust, the bedrooms of greasy sheets, damp featherbeds, and the pungently sweet aroma of chamber-pots. The stench of sulphur rose from the chimneys, the stench of caustic lyes from the tanneries, and from the slaughterhouses came the stench of congealed blood. People stank of sweat and unwashed clothes; from their mouths came the stench of rotting teeth, from their bellies that of onions, and from their bodies, if they were no longer very young, came the stench of rancid cheese and sour milk and tumorous disease. The rivers stank, the marketplaces stank, the churches stank, it stank beneath the bridges and in the palaces.

Every nose must sniff, approvingly or disapprovingly, for itself. I offer the ambiguous comment, 'it stinks'. But interestingly.

Persuasion, Jane Austen, 1818

I had intended to include in the P section of this book Borges' first non-pseudonymous work of fiction, 'Pierre Menard, Author of the Quixote'. But at six pages it wouldn't qualify as even the shortest of short stories. It would nonetheless have been good to have got it in as a powerful allegory of the problem of reading 'classic' literature. Menard sets out to 'understand' the historical world, and biographical circumstances, of DON QUIXOTE so intimately that he can, without ever having read the work, reproduce Cervantes' text, word for word. Borges' story poses a teasing problem, particularly for the modern reader of Jane Austen's work. How can we, without the aid of Wells' time machine, really *know* her fiction?

Before engaging with that problem, a summary of *Persuasion*. It was not Austen's

title. She was very ill – dying, in fact – while writing the novel, and neither named nor fully revised the text. The heroine, Anne Elliot, is twenty-seven years old, and has lost her 'bloom'. Her mother, who was fond of her, died early. Her father is not over-fond of her. Sir Walter cares more for his handsome elder daughter, his baronetcy and his own complexion – whose masculine bloom he preserves with cosmetics. He has no direct heir, which supplies the novel with its later plot complications.

Anne was persuaded by a friend of the family, some years earlier, not to marry a young naval officer. It was a 'prudent' act of persuasion. There was a war on and Frederick Wentworth possessed no fortune, while Anne could expect no great dowry. What that could mean Austen had previously portrayed in the Portsmouth chapters of MANSFIELD PARK. Now the war is over and Wentworth has returned, a bronzed hero (Sir Walter shudders at the spectacle of what sea air does to a man's face), promoted and enriched with prize money from the French ships he has captured. Captain Wentworth is in need of a wife: but is bloomless Anne now too old for him?

The episode in *Persuasion* that most piques my interest with regard to Menard's quixotic enterprise is that on the Cobb (breakwater) at Lyme Regis. Wentworth seems to be setting his cap at other, 'blooming', young ladies. One of them, Louisa, falls off the Cobb – attempting a reckless leap – and is rendered unconscious. 'The horror of that moment to all who stood around!' the text breathlessly ejaculates. Captain Wentworth, who has seen men killed around him in battle, should surely take charge. He does not. His reaction is histrionic. He kneels alongside the fallen lady, 'with a face as pallid as her own... "Is there no one to help me?" were the first words which burst from [him] in a tone of despair, and as if all his own strength were gone.' Anne takes charge and sends for a surgeon. Why is Wentworth (to use an un-Austenish word) such a wuss? The easy explanation – Jane Austen, spinster to the end, knows nothing of 'real' men – is wrong. She had brothers in the Navy who fought for their country. But why is Wentworth so feeble here?

To understand one needs, like Menard, to immerse oneself in the period of the book. Sailors, spending as they did years at sea in all-male societies, were notoriously shy around 'petticoats'. Clearly Wentworth should loosen Louisa's 'stays', put his ear to her exposed breast, tenderly feel her injured ankle. But nautical modesty prevails. In PEREGRINE PICKLE wooden-legged Captain Trunnion – who, like Wentworth, has valiantly faced death at sea – crumples like a girl when the formidable Mrs Grizzle commands him to dance with her. As Smollett gleefully explains:

> Trunnion, who had scarce ever been on shore till he was paid off, and never once in his whole life in the company of any females above the rank of those who herd on the Point at Portsmouth, was more embarrassed about his behaviour than if he had been surrounded at sea by the whole French navy.

The 'herd on the Point at Portsmouth' are, of course, prostitutes, offering Jack Tar quick relief before he sets off to sea again. One assumes that middle-aged Wentworth may well have also used them on his brief spells on shore. No problem with loosing *their* stays. A 'lady' is something else.

The point is, Austen's descriptions here, if we transport ourselves to Austen's world, ring true. For the whole novel to ring true requires, alas, for the modern reader an effort as immense as Menard's. But, like him, we keep trying.

The Picture of Dorian Gray, Oscar Wilde, 1890

It could be called 'A Portrait of the Artist as a (for ever) Young Man'. Wilde's only published novel is one of the vanguard works of British 'decadence', with an explosive (for Victorian readers) sexual subtext: the love that dare not speak its name, and was certainly not in the habit of writing novels about itself for public consumption. The story rings *fin-de-siècle* changes on the 'Faustian pact'. Every man has his price. How

much, then, is eternal youth worth? Your soul? Faust himself wanted knowledge and magical power, not physical beauty. Would he have parted with eternal salvation for the gift of a pretty face?

This is how the story goes. An artist, Basil Hayward, creates a magnificent portrait of a 'young Adonis', Dorian Gray – the embodiment, at this early stage, of 'youth's passionate purity'. But not, alas, for long. Dorian is corrupted by Hayward's worldly friend, Lord Henry Wotton. Following Wotton's lessons he breaks the heart of an actress, Sibyl Vane, who commits suicide. While dissipating himself utterly, Dorian remains for ever young and beautiful. Meanwhile, the Hayward portrait of him (hidden in an attic) secretly ages and turns ugly as sin. Hayward, becoming curious, is shown the picture and Dorian murders him. Finally Dorian attacks his portrait with a knife, thereby killing himself.

The novel serves as the vehicle for Wilde's witticisms, but it also works up a poignant theme. Dorian's name can be glossed as the French d'or – made of gold. And, mismatching that, the colour of old hair, 'gray'. The novel pirouettes nimbly around the pathos of those (lucky enough, as Mark Twain reminds us, given the grim alternative) to live beyond youth into the grey years: 'Golden lads and girls all must / As chimney-sweepers, come to dust'. So Shakespeare put it. But for many years before the dusty terminus come the grey years – alive, but no longer golden. At the age of thirty-six, when he published the novel, Oscar was probably himself sadly plucking out the odd silver strand from his flowing tresses.

Thomas Mann's *Death in Venice* (clearly influenced by Wilde's fable) plays with the same idea of paint and age. On his way by boat to the plague-ridden city, another passenger catches fifty-something Gustav von Aschenbach's eye:

> One in a bright yellow, excessively fashionable summer suit, red tie, and a boldly bent up panama hat, exceeded all the others with his shrill voice and gayness. No sooner had Aschenbach set eyes on him than he realised with a kind of terror

that this ephebe was false. He was ancient, there could be no doubt about it. Wrinkles surrounded his mouth and eyes. The meek crimson of his cheeks was make-up, that brown hair below the colourfully-banded straw hat was a wig, his neck was dilapidated and sinewy, his moustache was dyed, his yellowish and complete set of teeth which he laughingly presented was a cheap counterfeit, and his hands with signet rings on both index fingers were that of a very old man.

In Venice, after he has fallen in love with the Narcissus-like Tadzio – a golden youth he sees, but never speaks to – Aschenbach too 'paints' himself in the vain hope of regaining youth:

He felt compelled to rejuvenate himself; he frequently visited the barber of the hotel. In the hairdressing cape, under the grooming hands of the talkative barber, he looked at his mirror image with torment.

'Gray,' he said with a distorted mouth.

Would that Oscar – or Mann – had survived until the age of nip, tuck, cosmetic 'work' and 'new tints' shampoo.

The Pilgrim's Progress, John Bunyan, 1678

The Pilgrim's Progress was written by a working-class Englishman, probably self-educated, of dissident Puritan belief. If his contemporary John Milton set out in Paradise Lost to justify the ways of God to Man, Bunyan set out to perform the same service for Everyman. In 1660, with the return of the latest Merry Monarch and the downfall of the austere Commonweal – England's little experiment with republicanism – Bunyan, who had drawn his sword for Cromwell, was imprisoned for obstinately preaching without a licence. He would spend, with brief intervals of freedom, some twelve years in Bedfordshire county prison

as what we would call a prisoner of conscience – and he would have called a martyr for Christ. It was in prison that he conceived and began to write The Pilgrim's Progress.

The jail was situated in Silver Street, in the bustling centre of Bedford. It was in the prison day-room that Bunyan wrote. Inmates, even in this relatively humane penitentiary, could not expect candles. The clink in Silver Street was, for Bunyan, more like house arrest than incarceration, if not actually a 'club penitentiary', as Americans call their open prisons. Solzhenitsyn, who compiled The Gulag Archipelago in Stalin's vile camps, was obliged to consign his great narrative to memory; the incarcerated Bunyan evidently had access to writing materials. It wasn't quite Proust's cork-lined bedroom, but it was adequate. Victorian artists liked to picture Bunyan in durance vile, but the truth was less melodramatic. Something more like Virginia Woolf's room of one's own – but with the lock on the outside.

The full title of Bunyan's great work is:

The Pilgrim's Progress FROM THIS WORLD TO That which is to come. Delivered under the Similitude of a DREAM. Wherein is Discovered, 1. The manner of his setting out. — 2. His Dangerous Journey; and — 3. And safe Arrival at the Desired Countrey.

Bunyan's father had been an itinerant pedlar, tramping wearily round the country, a pack on his back, a staff in his hand. That, for the son, was an enduring metaphor for man's life. The story opens dramatically. Christian is reading a book (the Geneva Bible, we deduce). It raises a terrible question in his mind: what shall he do to be saved? He runs off shouting 'Life, life, eternal life'. His wife and four children try to stop him, but he puts his fingers in his ears and runs on, leaving them to fend for themselves. There are more important things than families. For Bunyan, life is a quest towards the gleaming city on the hill; Salvation; 'The Desired Countrey'. And what Christian has to conquer on the way are the obstacles which afflict the religious mind: depression ('the Slough of Despond'), doubt ('Doubting

Castle'), and, most dangerous of all, the seductive temptations of the city – 'Vanity Fair':

> at this fair are all such merchandise sold, as houses, lands, trades, places, honours, preferments, titles, countries, kingdoms, lusts, pleasures; and delights of all sorts, as whores, bawds, wives, husbands, children, masters, servants, lives, blood, bodies, souls, silver, gold, pearls, precious stones, and what not. And, moreover, at this fair there is at all times, to be seen juggling, cheats, games, plays, fools, apes, knaves, and rogues, and that of every kind. Here are to be seen too, and that for nothing, thefts, murders, adulteries, false swearers, and that of a blood-red colour.

Despite himself, Bunyan makes it sound rather fun.

The Pilgrim's Progress' influence on the subsequent history of fiction is massive. The pulpit was, thereafter, always vacant, for the novelist who chose to use it (many have). As VANITY FAIR went on sale (the title, of course, flagrantly lifted from Bunyan) Thackeray informed the editor of Punch – the wonderfully named Mark Lemon – that he regarded his mission as a novelist as 'serious as the Parson's own'. D. H. Lawrence went a step further along the 'serious' route: the novel was, he declared, 'the one bright book of life' – the Bible for modern man. At least, as written by Lawrence and, before him, John Bunyan, it was.

The Place of Dead Roads, William S. Burroughs, 1984

Burroughs published this novel aged seventy. He was, by this stage of his surprisingly long life (surprising because of his loudly proclaimed excesses), Literature's Grand Old Junky. Almost respectable. It was his habit (loaded word) to kick off his fiction in deadpan documentary style, thereafter spiralling away into increasingly wild fantasy. The Place of Dead Roads begins, lucidly enough, with an 1899 newspaper account of a doubly fatal shoot-out in Boulder, Colorado, between two men of mystery: William Seward Hall, a real-estate speculator and writer, and Mike Chase. Neither man fired his weapon (later we learn that Hall carried a .44 Special Action, Chase a .455 Webley; Burroughs had a great love of guns). Both Hall and Chase died by rifle-fire from an unknown third party. Hall, it is reported, wrote under the pen-name and in the person of Kim Carsons, the famous Western shootist (fictional, but evocative of historical gun-man Kit Carson). He is the central character of The Place of Dead Roads.

From this initial point, the narrative spills out like some nasty liquid, in any number of non-linear directions, following the oblique spurts of Burroughs' sado-sexual fantasies, paranoid obsessions, and surreal machineries. In the largest sense, Burroughs' career was dedicated to the discovery, or invention, of a territory for his outlawry; an 'interzone', or no man's (certainly no woman's) land where his immoralities could have free play. In his personal practices as a homosexual and an opiate user, Tangier served him best. In this novel, Burroughs presents an imagined community of 'Johnsons' living undercover (complete with female impersonators to fool the straights) in Johnsonville. The Johnsons plan an eventual escape from Planet Earth by spaceship. They meanwhile give their attention to evolution-enhancing experiments 'designed to produce asexual offspring, to cloning, use of artificial wombs, and transfer operations'. As an outlaw gang, the 'Wild Fruits', they dedicate themselves to merciless terrorism against 'normals', or the 'shits', as they are uncompromisingly labelled.

The conceit at the core of The Place of Dead Roads is that the 'shits of the world' are epidemically infected by a virus, a rabid alien parasite descended from outer space, apparently Venusian in origin. This 'RIGHT' virus (so called because its hosts are possessed with a frenzied sense of their own rectitude) leads them to fanatical persecution of such victimless crimes (normal behaviour for the virally uninfected) as homosexuality, obscenity, drink and drug use. Civilisation, religion, conventional morality and heterosexuality are (in the Burroughs universe) viral and pathogenic. In its wilder, more vindictive flights, *The Place of Dead Roads* fantasises about a mass clean-up (or 'shiticide') programme, in which Christians – the main vectors of the moralistic Venusian planetary virus – will be pinpointed and assassinated by Johnsons. Kim Carsons, in one comic sub-plot, destroys the inhabitants of the nearby town of Jehovah by distributing free illustrated Bibles impregnated with smallpox virus. Nazi genocide is evoked by the Johnsons' SS ('Shit Slaughter') commandos, who are formed to undertake a hygienic final solution and rid the universe of Christian, temperate heterosexuals.

Burroughs' burlesques of science fiction, Western dime novels and – in one hilarious excursion – *The Godfather* are brilliantly done. He ranks with Joyce as a parodist. But no author of the twentieth century was more calculatedly, and inventively, offensive. At one point in *The Place of Dead Roads* he lets rip with an emetic salvo of Anglophobia (he never forgave the country for its Crown prosecution of NAKED LUNCH). 'What hope', the narrative sarcastically enquires, 'for a country where people will camp out for three days to glimpse the Royal Couple?. . . Never go too far in any direction, is the basic law on which Limey-land is built. The Queen stabilises the whole stinking shithouse.' Never himself afraid to go too far in any direction, Burroughs goes on to devise a little fantasia in which Her Majesty, commiserating with the parents of Aberfan on the tragic deaths of 116 of their children under the 1966 tip slide, is stunk out by a virtuoso farting guerrilla attached to the Johnsonian underground army. She 'never made another public appearance', the narrative gleefully records.

Portnoy's Complaint, Philip Roth, 1969

Roth's novel takes the form of a long ejaculation – most of it about ejaculation. Only when he gets to the last page is the structure made clear:

PUNCH LINE
So [*said the doctor*]. Now vee may perhaps to begin. Yes?

Alexander Portnoy's complaint ('wail', 'lament', 'vent', 'kvetch', 'protracted belly-ache') is an attempt at the 'ranting cure'. Mere talking won't do it – things are too serious. He is lying on the couch, while Dr Spielvogel, sitting behind him in the classic Freudian position, listens. Portnoy's 'complaint'? The thing in his pants. He has been, since birth, a satyromaniac – 'schlong driven'. What a fellow sufferer, Roth's fellow Jewish novelist Norman Mailer, called 'a prisoner of sex'.

Alex masturbated wrist-sprainingly as a boy and womanises recklessly as a man. In his younger onanistic days his 'aids' ranged far beyond the traditional Kleenex: milk bottles, smelly socks (feet have more glands than any other part of the human body), his sister's underpants, a baseball mitt and, on one epic occasion, the liver for the family's meal. In his 'life as a man' (a later Roth title), Alex is the incarnation of Freud's 'most prevalent form of degradation': namely that once a man achieves sexual intercourse with the woman he loves, it can only be continued by mentally degrading her into a wanton slut. You can't, as Alex would say, get it up unless in your head you put her down. Aged thirty-three, he cohabits with a shiksa partner, whom he nicknames 'The Monkey'. As gymnastic as any simian, she performs whatever act his lusts can ingeniously demand. He despises her for it.

To the outside world, Alex is a son any Jewish mother should be proud of. His father was a hardworking, door-to-door insurance salesman, whose bowels are as locked by constipation as Alex's gonads are seething with lust. Alex's mother, Sophie, was once tricked by a 'goy' rogue into eating lobster and was thereafter wary of the traps the world lays for the unwary. Alex's primal memory (genuine, or 'screen' memory, hiding something even worse) is of her holding what he took to be the castrator's knife (doubtless to slice the family liver, not the little Messiah's foreskin). Alex grew up an 'honor student', possessed of an IQ of 158, and currently serves society as a civil rights attorney in New York. Sophie would have preferred him to become a doctor (there is much play in the novel with the joke about the Jewish mother running along the beach screaming: 'Help, help, my son the doctor is drowning!') and – even more importantly – to marry a nice Jewish girl and give his mother grandchildren. Legend has it that *Portnoy's Complaint* inspired a collective protest by Jewish mothers. Roth's own mother took it in her stride. 'All mothers are Jewish mothers', she told a reporter who enquired about her reaction to the novel. Leonard Bernstein's mother was similarly witty when asked. Yes, she confessed, indeed she nagged little Lenny: 'I nagged him to get him away from the piano so he could eat.'

Portnoy's Complaint inspired a hailstorm of wisecracks. It did for the Jewish mother, said one critic, 'what *Jaws* did for the shark'. While, in 1960s New York, Americans were – at last, thanks to the pills (contraceptive and antibiotic) – indulging in sex without guilt, Alex Portnoy, cracked another critic, had made an eloquent case for Guilt Without Sex. He had, said another, quoting from the novel, 'put the id into yid'. Forget Alex Comfort, said another, Portnoy was living, ejaculating proof of the 'Joylessness of Sex'.

Like radioactive substances, fiction has its half-life. After four decades *Portnoy's Complaint* no longer shocks. It endures as a funny book about being human, being Jewish, being alive and, above all, being honest about it.

The Portrait of a Lady, Henry James, 1881

Although he was sarcastic about the inartistic architecture of mid-Victorian British fiction (his sneer about 'large loose baggy monsters' is routinely cited), Henry James ('the Master') picked up useful serialist's tricks from writers like Dickens and Wilkie Collins. *The Portrait of a Lady* was first serialised in the *Atlantic Monthly* magazine and was indeed masterly in keeping the *Atlantic*'s readers 'waiting' – suspended on monthly tenterhooks.

It opens on what was for James the most Edenic experience in this fallen world: tea on an English lawn in high summer.

Presiding over the cups is Mr Touchett – New England-born, an Old England resident by choice (the anglicised French surname, 'Touchette', adds a whiff of the cosmopolitan). A fabulously rich banker, and a gentleman to the core, Touchett's is a minor portrait in the gallery but, in one of James' favourite terms, wonderfully 'achieved'. Touchett has a shrewd, estranged wife and a darling only child, Ralph, who is brilliant, fine-spirited, and consumptive. Enter into the teatime ensemble, fresh as a newly blooming flower, Touchett's niece, Isabel Archer. She has just arrived from America, where she was brought up an 'independent' girl. Now she is an orphan. There was money during her growing up, but no longer. How can one be independent without 'means'? the novel asks.

The first half of the book keeps the reader (the first reader of the serial parts, that is) 'waiting'. Who will 'win' Isabel? Ralph is too frail – although he would have been a good choice. There is a husky American suitor, Caspar Goodwood, the son of a wealthy millowner, who crosses the Atlantic to woo her. Isabel rejects him gently. It must be someone from the Old World, not the new. She wants refinement, not energy. The word 'class' resonates in her mind. It is only to be found in Europe. Lord Warburton – a moderately dashing nobleman who has generations of class behind him – duly proposes. She can like him, Isabel decides, but not love him. All three suitors, however, remain in play and a second round of wooing may win her.

There ensues at this point one of the two most important chapters in the novel. Ralph, who will inherit a fortune, persuades his mortally ill father to bequeath half his immense wealth to Isabel. As an heiress she will be free to make unencumbered choices. She will be a 'lady'. She will have 'power'. With it, her fine sensibility will have a chance to develop into something great. The gentleman overcoming the banker in him, Touchett Sr assents.

The setting then switches to Florence. Isabel, now rich, has befriended a woman of the world, Madame Merle. Hugely sophisticated, she represents in Isabel's eyes the 'aristocratic situation' – the higher breed, 'class'. Madame Merle deftly directs Isabel towards Gilbert Osmond – an American 'collector' of small means and renowned sensibility. Osmond has a wonderful eye for portraits. He is (he relishes the word as applied to himself) 'fastidious'. The unimpressed Ralph describes him as a 'sterile dilettante' and a 'humbug'. Osmond has a daughter whose origins are mysterious (she is, it will later emerge, the offspring of his affair with Madame Merle – of whom he is nowadays 'tired'). Isabel, despite her cousin's warning, succumbs to Madame Merle's manipulation. Another chronological jump takes us a couple of years into the marriage, when Isabel at last realises she has made a fatal mistake. Osmond is a monster of ego. The realisation is articulated in the other key chapter (42): '. . . she had not read him right'. Those six monosyllables resound like a funeral bell.

The Osmonds have a child who dies six months after its birth. The couple are not thereafter, we guess, intimate. The crisis comes with Ralph's death in England. Isabel defies Osmond's opposition and goes to his side as he slips away. The serial began by keeping the reader on the hook (who will she marry?). And so, in similar fashion, it ends – will Isabel stay married? She returns to Florence – is it to rescue Osmond's daughter, Pansy, whom she has come to love, and to leave her husband? Or is it to accept the fate of being 'Mrs Osmond'? James keeps us waiting for the answer. For ever.

Possession: A Romance, A. S. Byatt, 1990

The American term 'campus novel' has never been appropriate to its English literary counterpart. Possession is more properly described as 'a novel of university life' – and a candidate for the best such ever written. It also contends for the title of the best Neo-Victorian novel ever written.

One of the outstanding women of letters of her time, A. S. Byatt chose to spend a few years as a teacher at University College, London; English fiction is the richer for it. One of her motives, as one now appreciates, was to prosecute her fascination with Victorian poetry. Possession would be dedicated to the leading authority on the field, Isobel

Armstrong, and the narrative itself is interlaced with long passages of Browning-esque verse. They frightened her publishers but Byatt refused to drop them. Her defiance was justified: Possession won the 1990 Booker Prize and sold massively. Byatt's success arose in part from a canny blending of genres. She set out, she once said, to 'parody' both high and low literary forms. Subtitled A Romance, the novel draws on the work of Georgette Heyer (a 'low' novelist Byatt admires) and on John Fowles' THE FRENCH LIEUTENANT'S WOMAN. (Particularly influential on Byatt must have been the 1981 film version of Fowles' book and Harold Pinter's twin-track screenplay, which switched, as does Possession, between modern and nineteenth-century settings.)

A post-doctoral research student, Roland Michell, is working for a senior scholar, Professor Blackadder, on a prospective collected edition of the works of the great Victorian poet, Randolph Henry Ash. Nicknamed 'the Ash Factory', it is a sterile research mill. But things look up when Roland discovers in the London Library a letter hinting at a clandestine relationship between Ash and the woman poet, Christabel LaMotte. He steals the letter. All's fair in love and literary research. Roland sets out to find out the truth. He is helped by a young, new-feminist LaMotte scholar, Maud Bailey. Maud, it later transpires, is a distant descendant of LaMotte. Other scholars join the hunt – all eager, in their different ways, to 'possess' Ash. Heading the pack is the predatory American, Professor Mortimer Cropper, who wields a fat wallet in order to collect Ash manuscripts as trophies. A short way behind is the wild, New York-Jewish, feminist-Marxist Leonora Stern.

Byatt is not altogether kind to her erstwhile colleagues (I was one and, like the others at UCL, read the novel tremblingly). The secrets of the Ash–LaMotte relationship are buried in a box alongside Ash's coffin. The box is disinterred during the night of the great 1987 hurricane and the contents astound.

Possession is an extraordinarily knowing novel, and Byatt's narrative picks up innumerable echoes of actual literary history. Randolph Ash, man and poet, is patently based on Robert Browning. The affair with

LaMotte recalls Browning's intense friendship (only discovered in the late twentieth century) with Julia Wedgwood. As a poet, Christabel is as clearly based on Christina Rossetti. And the business of the buried manuscripts recalls G. H. Lewes' love letters, which George Eliot had buried with her (unless some latter-day Cropper has secretly disinterred them). More morbidly it recalls Dante Gabriel Rossetti's first burying the manuscripts of his unpublished 'House of Life' sonnets with Elizabeth Siddal, then having them dug up again when he decided, after all, that the world, rather than the corpse of his lover, should have the fruits of his genius. Victorianists can get a lot from the novel. But *Possession* is more than a work for insiders to chortle over. It transcends all categories (university novel, romance, 1980s satire) to emerge as a great work of fiction. And, one might add, not a bad work of poetry either, if you like Browning.

Post Office, Charles Bukowski, 1971

It was while he was a dropout from society (a 'bum') and in the Los Angeles Public Library that Bukowski came across the author who would be most influential on his writing, John Fante – specifically Fante's novel ASK THE DUST. Fante cultivated a style of fragmented immediacy, with low-life LA settings and a high autobiographical element (Bukowski later archly calculated there was ninety-three per cent autobiography in his own fiction). Bukowski's early attempts at writing were everywhere rejected. Over the ten years of his 'barfly' existence, as he called it, he created his fictional alter ego (and hero of five of his six novels), Henry Chinaski.

Over these years he kept body and soul together with short-term 'shit jobs'. He roomed in crummy lodging houses, bummed around America, and was regularly in and out of the drunk tank. When he had money, he drank it – or lost it at the race track, his other addiction. It was during this period that he fell in with his first long-term partner, Jane Cooney Baker. Like Bukowski,

she was alcoholic, morally dissolute – and considerably less of a catch than Faye Dunaway, who plays her in the 1987 film *Barfly*. He regarded her as his muse and they lived together on and off for eight years. But Baker lacked Bukowski's canny survival instincts. Their dissipation *à deux* broke up and she drank herself to death – an event commemorated in *Post Office*, his first published novel. Bukowski went on to marry the poet Barbara Frye in 1957. Physically disabled and acutely shy, Frye had never even had a boyfriend before Bukowski. The marriage lasted two years, giving neither party much satisfaction. It, too, is commemorated in the novel.

Some sort of stability entered Bukowski's life in the early 1950s when he entered the employment of the US Mail, in the Los Angeles division. He was happiest working on the anti-social shift, tossing parcels around by night and writing furiously by day. He took no more pride in his job, badge or uniform than the galley slave did in his vessel. 'It began as a mistake', the novel opens. But it was a mistake which worked out well for him. He began as a Christmas temp. What he saw around him, in the sorting office, was much to his liking: 'all these mailmen do is drop in their letters and get laid. This is the job for me, oh yes yes yes.' The novel narrates, with some embellishments, his long-term relationships with his partners and the woes of the postal life (Alsatians loom large, as sworn foes). There are vivid vignettes of fellow workers – a motley crew of layabouts, child molesters and oddballs.

Nothing really matters to Henry Chinaski. The novel's epigraph, 'This is presented as a work of fiction and dedicated to nobody', says it all. His is a world bleached of moral significance. He perpetrates a casual rape, for example, while on the delivery round. It is described as affectlessly as jamming a largish package through a creaky mailbox:

> I reached down with my mouth, got one of her tits, then switched to the other.
> 'Rape! Rape! I'm being raped!'
> She was right. I got her pants down, unzipped my fly, got it in, then walked

her backwards to the couch. We fell down on top of it.

She lifted her legs high.

'RAPE!' she screamed.

I finished her off, zipped my fly, picked up my mail pouch and walked out leaving her staring quietly at the ceiling . . .

And for him it's on with the next delivery. The mail has to get through. In short, Henry is utterly despicable. But what makes Bukowski's writing special is a quality of felt immediacy – one admires through the revulsion. That distinctive tang is summed up by the book's ending, as Henry, after eleven years (a life sentence), leaves the service with not a dime more than he had when he started there.

I got into the door, said goodbye, turned on the radio, found a half-pint of scotch, drank that, laughing, feeling good, finally relaxed, free, burning my fingers with short cigar butts, then made it to the bed, made it to the edge, tripped, fell down, fell down across the mattress, slept, slept, slept.

In the morning it was morning and I was still alive. Maybe I'll write a novel, I thought. And then I did.

Jean-Paul Sartre called Bukowski 'America's greatest poet'. What Bukowski called Sartre is not recorded.

The Postman Always Rings Twice, James M. Cain, 1934

Raymond Chandler loathed this author:

James Cain – faugh! Everything he touches smells like a billygoat. He is every kind of writer I detest, a faux naif, a Proust in greasy overalls, a dirty little boy with a piece of chalk and a board fence and nobody looking. Such people are the offal of literature.

Why did Chandler hate Cain? As the 'goat' reference indicates, because his heroes have animalistic sex. They 'rut'. Chandler's

Marlowe is as chaste as a Knight of the Round Table; Chandler called him a 'shop-soiled Galahad'.

My strength is as the strength of ten
Because my heart is pure

as Tennyson's chaste knight puts it. There is no such purity in Cain's heroes.

He left an economically depressed New York to work as a Hollywood scriptwriter in 1931. Two years later, at forty-two years old, having been fired by Paramount Studios for drunkenness and with a young family to support and a heap of alimony to pay, he produced his first novel, The Postman Always Rings Twice, with one eye on screen adaptation.

Frank Chambers is a drifter and a jailbird – a no-good. The narrative opens: 'They threw me off the haytruck about noon.' It's Depression-era Southern California. It would be unsurprising to see the Joad family's wheezing Hudson truck roll by (see THE GRAPES OF WRATH). Frank finds himself at a small roadside sandwich joint and gas station, the Twin Oaks Tavern, about twenty miles outside LA. He bums a meal, intending to leave without paying the trusting Greek owner, Nick Papadakis. Then something happens:

I saw her. She had been out back, in the kitchen, but she came in to gather up my dishes. Except for the shape, she really wasn't any raving beauty, but she had a sulky look to her, and her lips stuck out in a way that made me want to mash them in for her.

'Meet my wife.'

She didn't look at me. I nodded at the Greek, gave my cigar a kind of wave, and that was all. She went out with the dishes, and so far as he and I were concerned, she hadn't even been there. I left, then, but in five minutes I was back.

He decides to stay and wash dishes with the wife, Cora. And other things. 'Stealing a man's wife, that's nothing, but stealing his car, that's larceny.' Nick's car is safe enough.

Steamy sex, murder and intricate double-crossing follow. The novel is remarkable for the violence of the lovemaking ('I bit her. I sunk my teeth into her lips so deep I could feel the blood spurt into my mouth'). As noted above, it was this lubriciousness which appalled Chandler – whose hero always has his pants virtuously zipped. Frank's narrative takes the form of a death-row confession and ends, bleakly, 'Here they come.' The gas chamber awaits. Not, ironically, for the death of Nick (of which he is guilty) but the accidental death of Cora (of which he is totally innocent). That, obscurely, is the postman's second ring. You won't get off *that* easily, it warns.

The Postman Always Rings Twice was hailed as a masterpiece of the newly fashionable 'hardboiled' genre and established Cain as the leading rival of his fellow Baltimorean, Dashiell Hammett. 'I tried to write as people talk,' he said in explanation of his distinctively spare style. The Cain sparseness was much admired, particularly in his so-called 'California novels', and is cited as an influence on writers as far afield as Camus (specifically THE OUTSIDER) and David Mamet. *The Postman Always Rings Twice* was twice adapted for the screen. The first movie, made in 1946, starring John Garfield as Frank and Lana Turner as Cora, is judged film noir almost of the same class as *Double Indemnity*. You'll find it a useful accompaniment to the novel. Think of it as ketchup on the fries.

Postmortem, Patricia D. Cornwell, 1990

Patricia Cornwell is headline-famous for being super-rich and flaunting it – she is, I would guess, the only novelist currently writing who does her author tours by private jet. It was not always so. Scribner acquired the first Kay Scarpetta novel, *Postmortem* (written in the mid-eighties, turned down by seven publishers, revised in the late eighties, finally published in 1990), for $6,000. Scribner's measly payment was par for the course. Cornwell had no track record as a mystery writer (only a string of rejections). After a divorce which left her with nothing but the name Cornwell, she worked for six years as a computer analyst in the

chief medical examiner's office in Richmond, Virginia, where she was fortunate enough to make the acqaintance of Dr Marcella Fierro, the inspiration for Kay Scarpetta (a later novel is dedicated to Fierro with the coy epigraph: 'You taught Scarpetta well'). Scarpetta – a tough-talking, gun-toting, chain-smoking (in the early works), whisky-drinking chief medical examiner – is clearly cut from the same genre cloth as Sara Paretsky's V. I. Warshawski (introduced in *Indemnity Only*, 1982) and Sue Grafton's Kinsey Millhone (introduced in *A is for Alibi*, 1982). It was a woman editor who, while rejecting the manuscript, advised Cornwell to dump the male hero-narrator ('Joe Constable') of the early draft, and bring Scarpetta's character to the fore. But Cornwell's novel had a couple of genuinely new wrinkles. It popularised a type of detection which sought, forensically, for its key clues in the tissue of dead bodies ('corpse reading'), and it familiarised the novel-reading world with the way computers were revolutionising crime detection.

Postmortem went on to win an unprecedented five major prizes in its first year and rode to the top of the *New York Times* bestseller list. From a standing start, Patricia Cornwell made herself a one-woman fiction factory, and her Scarpetta novels became a cult. Cornwell's stormy personal life kept her in the public eye. The books have, over the years, coalesced into a genre soap opera: characters, situations, messy relationships and serial killers have been carried over from one novel to the next. Scarpetta's beloved niece, Lucy, grew from a pudgy ten-year-old schoolgirl to a twenty-three-year-old FBI field agent, the first woman ever to serve in the agency's elite Hostage Rescue Team, and is now closing on menopause.

The opening paragraph of *Postmortem* demonstrates the pluses and negatives of the Scarpetta novels. Put bluntly, she can tell a story, but she's no Raymond Chandler:

> It was raining in Richmond on Friday, June 6. The relentless downpour, which began at dawn, beat the lilies to naked stalks, and blacktop and side-walks were littered with leaves. There were small rivers in the streets, and

newborn ponds on playing fields and lawns. I went to sleep to the sound of water drumming the slate roof, and was dreaming a terrible dream as night dissolved into the foggy first hours of Saturday morning. I saw a white face beyond the rain-streaked glass, a face formless and inhuman like the faces of misshapen dolls made of nylon hose. My bedroom window was dark when suddenly the face was there, an evil intelligence looking in. I woke up and stared blindly into the dark. I did not know what had awakened me until the telephone rang again. I found the receiver without fumbling. 'Dr Scarpetta?' 'Yes.' I reached for the lamp and switched it on. It was 2.33 a.m.

A serial rapist-killer is on the loose. He only strikes on Friday nights, entering through open windows (thank God Scarpetta's is closed), leaves a sprinkling of glitter, and appears to have a strange hang-up about maple syrup. Inevitably, as happens in all the novels, he comes for Scarpetta: divorced, petite and blonde, but with a private arsenal to rival that of the Virginia National Guard and less compunction about using it. Having to deal every few months with a fiendishly ingenious serial killer is not good for the nerves. Over the course of the Scarpetta chronicles the heroine (motto: 'paranoia is a healthy condition') deteriorates from being a jumpy woman to a full-blown nut. Readers love it. So do I.

Precious Bane, Mary Webb, 1924

Precious Bane is an unusual novel in that its fame these days mostly results from another novelist having been very rude about it. Ironically, the rude novel in question, Stella Gibbons' COLD COMFORT FARM, won the same prestigious Prix Femina award (for the depiction of English life) as did Webb's book. Webb did not live to read Gibbons' merciless satire on her moody rustics and 'howling Sussex'; she died only three years after writing Precious Bane – a small mercy, some might think, as she was a hypersensitive

woman and hated mockery. Adding to its interest is that Precious Bane was hugely admired on its publication by the Conservative prime minister, Stanley Baldwin. He voiced his admiration for her 'neglected genius' in April 1928, in a speech at the annual Royal Literary Fund Dinner. It was written up in the newspapers the following day and, six months after her death, Webb became the novelist of the day.

Precious Bane is set during the period of the Napoleonic wars and in the author's beloved Shropshire – the county of whose soil she is the acknowledged laureate. The narrator is Prue Sarn, an uneducated farmer's daughter of fine sensibility. At the time of writing she is old and nearing death (as was Webb). As Prue explains, she was lucky in her childhood, being billeted on a literate family dominated by a patriarch, Beguildy, who claimed wizardly powers:

> It was at Plash that the Beguildys lived, and it was at their dwelling, that was part stone house and part cave, that I got my book learning. It may seem a strange thing to you that a woman of my humble station should be able to write and spell, and put all these things into a book.

Strange indeed.

Under her thin veneer of book learning Prue is a child of nature – beautiful were it not for a harelip (the link with Webb's own disfigurement – a neck goitre, which made her terribly self-conscious – is painfully obvious). The deformity breeds suspicion that she is a witch. Villagers believe that at midnight on the family farm, Sarn Mere, Prue becomes a hare and races over fields and woods. Woe betide anyone her path crosses.

The novel traces feuds and the domestic tyranny of a brother, Gideon, determined to make money, at whatever cost. He sells his soul by becoming a 'sin eater', ritually eating bread over the coffin of his dead father. He blackmails Prue into a life of servitude (the wages to be taken by him) with the promise that, one day, he will pay for an operation to mend her lip. He does not. Despite her disfigurement, Prue is chosen by a manly and comely weaver, Kester Woodseaves, to be his true love. The novel ends, unusually for Webb, happily, when Kester – like Lochinvar – scoops up Prue to gallop away with her on his horse. A barrage of erotic dialogue ensues:

> 'Tabor on, owd nag!' says Kester, and we were going at a canter towards the blue and purple mountains.
>
> 'But no!' I said. 'It mun be frommet, Kester. You mun marry a girl like a lily. See, I be hare-shotten!'
>
> But he wouldna listen. He wouldna argufy. Only after I'd pleaded agen myself a long while, he pulled up sharp, and looking down into my eyes, he said—
>
> 'No more sad talk! I've chosen my bit of Paradise. 'Tis on your breast, my dear acquaintance!'
>
> And when he'd said those words, he bent his comely head and kissed me full upon the mouth.

Webb's novels have all been lovingly immortalised on the web, free of charge, by her devoted band of admirers (most of them located in Shropshire) who do not find her funny in the least.

Pride and Prejudice, Jane Austen, 1813

Austen's most famous novel has been wrung, like a wet face-flannel, for every possible drop of elaborate exegesis that can be extracted. Topping the list of zany homage is *Pride and Prejudice and Zombies* (2009) and a soft-porn retread by 'Clandestine Classics' which, in 2012, gave the love story of Elizabeth and Darcy the FIFTY SHADES OF GREY treatment. In Winchester Cathedral the body of a long-buried lady must be spinning fast enough to smash atoms.

The narrative framework, inscribed with exquisite precision from the initial faux 'truth' ('universally acknowledged', etc) on the author's traditional 'two inches of ivory', is a simple tale of crossed love eventually uncrossed. Mr Bennet, comfortably set up in life, is a bibliophile and, one deduces, an extremely negligent farmer. The only calves

Mr Bennet now likes are those whose hides cover his books. When he was younger there were other calves that attracted him. The philoprogenitive Mr Bennet has a brood of five unmarried daughters and a wife whom he evidently married when she was a comely thing. She is now uncomely, irritably talkative and her unceasing, prattling ignorance keeps him, by preference, in his library.

His favourite is not the beauty among his daughters (Jane), nor the bluestocking (Mary), nor the 'coltish' wild daughter (Lydia), nor last-born Catherine, but 'witty' Lizzy. The size of his family witnesses to Mr Bennet's doomed and, doubtless, towards the end with gritted teeth, attempt to breed a male heir. The complex rights by which he owns his property means, without a male heir, Mr Bennet's house, land, and income will go to a distant relative – the stuffy clergyman, Mr Collins. The young Bennet women are, if not completely 'undowered', poor prizes in the marriage market.

Enter two eminently eligible bachelors: the newly enriched Mr Bingham and Mr Darcy, possessed of old money, aristocratic connections, a fine country house and a pedigree, judging by the latter's family name, going back to the Norman conquest (Jane Austen lived and wrote through the long war with France, and French names bring with them a whiff of moral danger). Eventually Jane and Elizabeth will be united with these two rich young men. But the path of love runs rough.

Pride and Prejudice was first drafted as 'First Impressions' in the mid 1790s, when the possibility of French invasion was running high. It's a wartime novel. If a new spin is required, the fizziest is supplied, I think, not by zombiephiles, or soft-porn merchants, but by the military historian Rupert Willoughby. Willoughby notes that Austen, with two brothers in the Navy (both would rise to be admirals), was well up with what was going on in her country's great struggle. She admired Britain's 'hearts of oak' nautical heroes. But her attitude to the army was 'more ambivalent'. She was not alone. The British have always disliked 'standing', home-garrisoned armies. If men with guns were required, let them rule the waves in Britannia's name, or spill their blood in the far-off Iberian peninsula. Or like Colonel Brandon, in even further-off India. Civilians were particularly ambivalent about the 'militias', raised in the 1790s in the face of expected invasion by the Corsican tyrant. These inexperienced troops were routinely used to put down civil insurgencies. Jane had a favourite brother, Henry, commissioned in the Oxfordshire militia a couple of years before she started to write 'First Impressions'.

A regiment of militia arrives in Merriton in the autumn of the novel's action. The little town would have been swarming with redcoated visitors – the other ranks billeted in public houses and inns or in makeshift camps. Bingley, when he calls on Longbourn, wears a blue coat (a style made fashionable by Goethe's Werther). It is noted as significant by the girls. Lydia, ominously, is more taken by the red coat of the caddish Wickham and fantasizes about 'the glories of the camp, its tents stretched forth in beauteous uniformity of lines, crowded with the young and the gay and dazzling with scarlet'. One can imagine the heartless, selfish young militia officer Wickham – resplendent in scarlet – rather enjoying the disciplinary floggings about which the younger Bennet girls heartlessly gossip.

I recollect seeing four major adaptations of *Pride and Prejudice* on screen. None of them, I recall, catches the overwhelming wartime mood, and military disruptions of civilian life, which fizzle, effervescently, below the surface of the narrative. Forget zombies. Concentrate on the red coats in the next wring of the flannel.

The Prime of Miss Jean Brodie, Muriel Spark, 1961

Spark called it her 'milch cow'. This was the novel which, after it was published in its entirety in the *New Yorker*, 'made' her. Conversing at dinner parties in the 1970s (I was teaching in Edinburgh at the time – in my 'prime') one would recall delicious moments in the text with companions who had read Spark's novel, or who had seen the Vanessa Redgrave stage adaptation or the Maggie Smith film. We knew the whole rollcall of the Marcia Blaine School's teaching

staff as well as if we attended daily assembly there ourselves: Miss Lockhart, the chemistry mistress, who has enough explosive 'to blow up this school'; Miss Gaunt, of the bony head and horse-blanket skirt; even the comic *tricoteuses*, the sewing misses Ellen and Alison Kerr. And, of course, the ruthless head teacher, Miss Mackay, dedicated to ridding her school of the trouble-making Miss Jean Brodie. All are lovingly depicted with the malice of the child's eye.

The novel's central theme is set up by a tea-time conversation in an Edinburgh hotel. The war is recently over and life is bleak. Miss Brodie – now well past her prime – wonders who it was 'betrayed' her, who got her booted out, six years previously, from Marcia Blaine Girls' School. Her interlocutor, formerly a pupil, now a nun, cannot help.

The action flashes back to the mid-1930s. Marcia Blaine is an all-girls' school like the James Gillespie High School on which it is based (as close as libel law would permit) and which the young Spark attended in the mid-thirties. Miss Brodie has her 'set' – the 'crème de la crème' as she grandly calls them. They comprise six ten-year-old girls: Sandy, Rose, Mary, Jenny, Monica and Eunice. We follow them through their school careers to the age of seventeen. For them, Miss Brodie *is* the school. Her boast is: 'Give me a girl at an impressionable age and she is mine for life.' Miss Brodie defies curricular orthodoxy. It is life she is educating her girls for. 'The word 'education' she says:

> comes from the root 'e' from 'ex', out, and 'duco', I lead. It means a leading out. To me education is a leading out of what is already there in the pupil's soul.

The stress is on 'leadership'. Mussolini is one of her idols.

Jean Brodie, legend records, once had a true love, Hugh Carruthers, one of the fallen in the Great War. In her prime, her sights have been lowered. Her first choice would be the art teacher, Teddy Lloyd. He lost an arm in the war and would be acceptable were he not married, a Catholic, and the father of six children. Divorce is impossible, and a prolonged affair too risky. Brodie instead targets the school's doltish music teacher,

Gordon Lowther, whom she seduces with womanly wiles and some rich cookery. All this is closely noted by her 'girls', for whom she is the most important subject of study in the school and for whom sex is a topic of growing interest (little Rose is their 'expert'). Sandy Stranger (the surname is a sly nod to Albert Camus) is a particular favourite and confidante. Since it is now unsafe for her physically to prosecute her affair with Teddy, Miss Brodie pimps out favourites like Sandy to 'sit' (i.e. pose) for him. Reciprocating, he invariably puts Brodie's head on the pubescent body.

Teddy finds Sandy, as he crassly tells her, 'just about the ugliest little thing I have ever seen in my life'. She does not forgive. As the novel progresses Sandy, having in her last years become Teddy's lover, sees through her one-time idol. 'She must be stopped'. The opportunity arises when – in line with her sympathy for fascist dictators – the teacher persuades a girl, Joyce Emily, to abscond and join Franco's forces. The girl dies en route and Sandy 'betrays' Miss Brodie, who can now (to Miss Mackay's huge relief) be dismissed to live on as a bitter, lonely spinster. Sandy, now 'Sister Helena', can find no forgiveness or explanation. But, in a sense, Miss Brodie does, indeed, have her 'for life'.

The Private Memoirs and Confessions of a Justified Sinner, James Hogg, 1824

Nicknamed the 'The Ettrick Shepherd' by the Edinburgh literati, Hogg spent his life battling with the debt collector. Things became serious when his wife Margaret's dowry did not materialise. They became critical when her father fell on hard times and came, with *his* wife, to live with (and on) the Hoggs in their cottage in rural Altrive, in the Scottish Borders. In a desperate attempt to raise money for family dependants – now as numerous as a small clan – Hogg dashed off *The Private Memoirs and Confessions of a Justified Sinner*. It was published in 1824, anonymously, by Longman in London.

The first half of the *Confessions* comprises an 'editor's narrative'. The editor is complacent, slightly dull, and very unlike the rough diamond Hogg. The historical setting is the 1680s, an unsettled moment in Scottish history (but when isn't?). The Laird of Dalcastle, an old-school rascal who loves life, takes a much younger, religiously hidebound wife. Her true mate, whom she brings in her entourage, is her spiritual adviser Robert Wringhim, an 'ultra-Calvinist', one of the antinomian sect whose creed presumes that the elect have been pre-ordained for salvation – whatever sins they commit. 'Works' are irrelevant.

Rabina, the newlywed bride, is violated in the marriage bed and, before making her escape to live by herself, bears two sons. The elder, George, the laird acknowledges as his. The younger, Robert, he believes (very plausibly) to be the offspring of Wringhim. The boys are brought up in their parents' now separate establishments. George grows up a lusty young heir, the apple of his father's eye. The hated Robert, who takes on the surname 'Wringhim', grows up a neurotic bigot, suffused with religious malignity. As he enters manhood Robert is egged on to ever more malicious acts by a mysterious companion, Gil Martin ('Gil' means 'fox' in Gaelic). Gil has the strange capacity to morph into anyone. He manipulates Robert into assassinating his brother in a midnight brawl which he, Gil, has orchestrated. The laird dies of grief and Robert inherits the estate. His crime is suspected, and finally detected, by two resourceful ladies of easy virtue: the laird's mistress, Miss Logan, and a branded prostitute (narrowly escaped from the gallows), Bell Calvert.

The second half of the novel takes the form of Robert's own 'private memoir and confessions'. He is mad, but not deluded as to the fact that Gil (who is witnessed in both accounts by third parties) actually exists. However, he takes his mentor to be Czar Peter of Russia, in disguise. This leads to such deliciously malapropos exchanges as:

> I asked, with great simplicity: 'Are all your subjects Christians, prince?' 'All my European subjects are, or deem themselves so,' returned he; 'and they are the most faithful and true subjects

I have.' Who could doubt, after this, that he was the Czar of Russia?

By now the reader apprehends, although Robert has not, that Gil is Satan incarnate. Strangely, and ambiguously, Robert confesses to more murders than we know him to have committed (including matricide). Indeed at one point it seems that Gil has persuaded him that they should unite to slaughter the whole human race. Even Robert is rather daunted by that prospect. As the new laird, he suffers blackouts after drinking that last for months, coming round to discover he has done ever more terrible things. His conviction that God will never punish him eventually dissolves into terror. He runs away but is pursued wherever he goes by his erstwhile 'friend' – now his 'tormentor'. Finally he descends to being a rural shepherd and hangs himself with a hay rope. This, too, is mysterious to those investigating his death:

> Now the fact is, that, if you try all the ropes that are thrown over all the out-field hay-ricks in Scotland, there is not one among a thousand of them will hang a colley dog; so that the manner of this wretch's death was rather a singular circumstance.

Poor Hogg wrote his novel to make money. But the *Confessions* failed spectacularly to appeal to the public taste of the time. It earned the author £2 in 'profits' (miscalled) in the two years Longman kept the book in print. Poor Hogg remained poor Hogg.

The Purple Cloud, M. P. Shiel, 1901

Matthew Phipps Shiel was born in Montserrat in the West Indies to mixed-race parents whose own parents had been slaves – something Shiel kept from public knowledge during his lifetime. His inflated image of himself, which verged on megalomania, was confirmed when, aged fifteen, he was reputedly 'crowned' by his father 'King Felipe of Redonda' (see ALL SOULS). Redonda is an uninhabitable four-hundred-acre rocky islet some fourteen miles off Montserrat. It is frequented by gulls, principally, as a convenient place to drop guano.

In 1885 Shiel went to England, where he briefly worked as a translator and tried his hand at teaching. In 1896 he published his first novel, and from then on earned a living by his pen. As a novelist he specialised in wildly imaginative science fiction, with a sideline in detective novels. It was *The Purple Cloud* (1901) which earned Shiel the status among his admirers (few but fanatical) of an apocalyptic prophet, and it is the work for which he is most remembered today. Less happily remembered is his private life. His preference for twelve-year-old girls led to sixteen months in Wormwood Scrubs in 1914.

The Purple Cloud began serialisation in the *Royal Magazine* at the turn of the century, in January 1901. The human race habitually predicts disasters at such epochal dates, Y2K being the most recent example. Shiel claimed to have received the novel word for word from a 'hypnotist' (he didn't). The narrator-hero of the tale, Adam Jefferson, is recruited as physician and botanist for an expedition to the North Pole. At the time Shiel was writing, the icy surface of ninety degrees North had not yet felt the footstep of man. But the first fall of that frost-bitten limb was not far off. The necessity of achieving the polar conquest had been stoked to the pitch of mania by the popular press worldwide. There were wild rumours of cannibalism, hot oceans, strange alien races and monsters. What would be found there? Nothing, as it turned out. The myths Shiel draws on so artfully would burst like bubbles when, eight years after the publication of *The Purple Cloud*, the American Robert Peary claimed to have planted the Stars and Stripes on the bleak, grinding, shifting ice of the North Pole.

But in 1901 the Americans' unexciting discovery lay in the future. Shiel could still fantasise, and did. Having made it to the Pole, Adam Jefferson discovers himself on the edge of a round lake, surrounded by a carpet of meteoric diamonds. He dimly perceives a pillar at the lake's steamy centre, with illegible writing around its base. He swoons. At this precise moment humanity suffers its second and most drastic fall. Has Adam

Jeffson, like his primal namesake, precipitated a universal disaster by his God-defying rashness?

Jeffson will discover, many months later, that a super-volcano in the South Sea erupted, releasing from the bowels of the earth vast quantities of gaseous cyanide which has drifted, in a lethal purple cloud, across the face of the earth. Fortuitously, he alone has escaped the fate of all other air-breathing things. He is now the last man on earth. He goes mad under the pressure of his cosmic solitude, surrendering to the 'dark voice' within him. In his desperate search for sexual gratification, he makes love, when his urges become overwhelming, to youthful-looking female corpses.

The reason why God has spared him gradually takes form in his crazed mind: he has been appointed to carry out the Almighty's threat to mankind – delivered after the biblical deluge – 'the fire next time'. That time has come. Jeffson ('Jehovah's-son') has been appointed Jehovah's arsonist, and it is his destiny to purge the world of sin with purifying flame. The dark voice in his soul keeps him resolutely at the task over the decades which the worldwide conflagration requires. 'City-burning', he blandly records,

> has now become a habit with me more enchaining – and infinitely more debased – than ever was opium to the smoker, or alcohol to the drunkard. I count it among the prime necessaries of my life: it is my brandy, my bacchanal, my secret sin. I have burned Calcutta, Pekin, and San Francisco.

Finally, Adam Jeffson finds his Eve, cowering in a wooded glen outside Constantinople. But another purple cloud is blowing down on them – will humanity survive? The hypnotist did not tell Shiel, and he does not tell us.

Quarantine, Jim Crace, 1997

Novelists, egotists all of them, yearn to novelise the gospels. Among those who have done it are D. H. Lawrence, J. H. Ingraham, Lloyd C. Douglas, Nikos Kazantzakis, Norman Mailer, Colm Tóibín – many more than the Four Apostles in the good book (the best novel ever written, say some infidel wags). Jim Crace is very good – in the St Matthew class, I'd say (up with Pasolini, who made the best stab in film, with *Il vangelo secondo Matteo*). In *Quarantine*, Crace concentrates his narrative on one of the more enigmatic episodes in the gospel narrative: Christ's forty days in the wilderness and the purification ritual that follows after the Annunciation ('this is the Son of God') by John the Baptist. It is, literally, a 'quarantine' – from the Italian *quarantina* ('forty') – a lovely word, now exclusively used in a medical context, its connection with its biblical source consistently forgotten.

As a literary form with a general tendency to agnosticism, the novel has chronic problems with 'fictions' about the Son of God. Crace, it would seem, pays oblique homage to his predecessor D. H. Lawrence's THE MAN WHO DIED, also known as *The Escaped Cock*. That novella begins with Christ returning to consciousness after his (botched) crucifixion. It is no miracle. They just took him down too early and buried him too soon. *Quarantine* pivots on a similar set of non-believer rationalisations. In interviews around the time of the novel, Crace declared, 'I'm not even a relaxed atheist, I'm a post-Dawkins scientific atheist.' His epigraph takes the form of a 1993 medical opinion:

An ordinary man of average weight and fitness embarking on a total fast – that is a fast during which he refuses both his food and drink – could not expect to live for more than thirty days, nor to be conscious for more than twenty-five.

Christ is possessed of a human body, which must mean the usual consequences of extreme hunger and thirst, Crace reasons. Death, in other words, and well before the fortieth day. How then did Christ ever get started on the gospel-chronicled saviour-of-the-world career?

Crace's Jesus is a 'boy', a weak-bladdered, under-sized, back-country dreamer nicknamed 'Gally' (for the northern region of Galilee he comes from). He undertakes his forty-day retreat, or quarantine, with four companions – his first apostles, in a sense: three Jewish zealots (a dying man, a barren woman and a mystic) and their guide. For them fasting means refraining only during the hours of daylight – as in Islam's Ramadan. For Gally, the fast is total. Their paths cross with that of the mercenary Musa, who has been left for dead by his caravan. Jesus comes on the apparently dying trader and mutters 'be well again' – a common greeting to the sick. Miraculously, Musa does get well again. It's not a helpful miracle. After flinging his donkey over a cliff, battering his pregnant wife Miri, raping the barren Jewess, and robbing her two gullible companions, Musa sets out to find out everything he can about Gally, the man who saved him. He is incorporated into Gally's hallucinations (visions?) as the devil, offering food, drink and wealth. All receive the biblical rejection 'get thee behind me, Satan'.

By glossing the biblical fast into total abstention from food and drink, Crace pricks the reader's curiosity and reveals – finally – an elegant and intellectually satisfying explanation for how the Christ-cult originated. To his chagrin, Crace recalled, he wound up the narrative with sufficient enigma not to demolish any believer's belief. Trust the (enigmatic) tale, not the (atheist) teller – as D. H. Lawrence would have said. *Quarantine* was short-listed for the Booker, which, that year, went to Arundhati Roy's *The God of Small Things*. I think I might have voted Crace's way.

The Queen and I, Sue Townsend, 1992

Until the 1960s it was near-treason to depict the reigning monarch on stage, on film, or in literature. After that liberating decade, the world of entertainment became more daring: no longer fearful of the Tower, nose-slitting, or being whipped through London at the tail of a cart. Prince Charles was made to play a part in a Tom Clancy novel and, horror of horrors, the monarch herself was spoofed by a professional look-alike in the film *The Naked Gun* (luckily, by 1988, cinema performances were no longer required to end the evening with 'The Queen' and the whole audience standing to attention).

No jester was jollier about the 'Royals' than Sue Townsend. And no popular novelist of the time started life lower down the class ladder headed by the House of Windsor. Sue Townsend, creator of Adrian Mole, is that rarity among novelists: *echt* working-class. She was born one of the post-war 'bulge' – the population explosion which brought the country's resources to rupture point (as the baby boomers enter retirement, they may well yet destroy the country's tottering finances). Townsend was the daughter of a postman, brought up in a 'prefab' – rabbit hutches for the heroes who won the war. The eldest of five sisters ('Very Chekhovian,' she says), her life expectations were minimal. Young Susan failed the eleven-plus and attended a 'secondary modern' (i.e. school for the second rate) a stone's throw away from the grammar school she did not attend. She left school at fifteen, at the earliest possible moment, married too soon and unwisely, and had three children (nothing Chekhovian about that), all the while reading Penguin Books ('my university') and cultivating her god-given talent as a 'secret writer' (she kept her manuscripts in a cupboard with the brooms). Then came Adrian and bestselling success.

In 1992, at a period when things looked peculiarly dark for England, Townsend produced *The Queen and I*. The story takes place after a bloodless revolution, in which the Socialists have taken over. The House of Windsor finds itself rehoused in a Midlands council house in Hellebore Close (nick-named 'Hell Close'). It's a 'learning experience':

> 'Mr Barker, there is no mention of dogs here,' said the Queen.
>
> 'One per family,' said Jack.
>
> 'Horses?' asked Charles.
>
> 'Would you keep a horse in a council house garden?'
>
> 'No. Quite. One wasn't thinking.'

> 'Clothes aren't on the list,' said Diana, shyly.
>
> 'You won't be needing much. Just the bare essentials. You won't be making personal appearances, will you?'
>
> Princess Anne rose and stood next to her father. 'Thank God for that! At least something good has come out of this bloody shambles. Are you all right, Pa?'

The monarch, along with her loyal 'dorgi' (corgi dog) Harris, ingeniously makes do on her state pension – 'Mrs Windsor' is now a welfare queen. Charles chats all day to his garden plants, and Diana misconducts herself with some racy fellows up the street. When the Queen Mum dies (she was going strong at the time the novel was published), Hellebore comes together to give her a mini-state funeral. At the end of the narrative what's left of England is bought by Japan – cut-price.

Townsend carried on her good-natured lèse-majesté (which had dated painfully with the death of Diana) in *Queen Camilla* (2006). Years have passed. Jack Barker is now running the Republic as head of the Cromwell Party. The country is owned by America. Hellebore is under the local dictatorship of Arthur Grice, a scaffolding contractor. The thoroughly proletarianised Windsors rub along contentedly enough, despite the electronic tagging and universal CCTV Grice has imposed on his compound. Camilla – fag in hand – handles it best of all, although things get a bit dicey when her and Charles's illegitimate son from way back appears on the scene. Princess Anne has married a man called 'Spiggy' – whose name says it all. Counter-revolution, under the old-school 'Boy' English, looks imminent. If it comes, says Mrs Windsor, she will abdicate on the spot. She is with her people, and will stay one of their number. Long may she not reign. *Vivat!*

A Question of Upbringing, Anthony Powell, 1951

A Question of Upbringing (1951) is the first volume of Powell's twelve-volume *Dance to the Music of Time* sequence and, as the title makes clear, is wholly concerned with school days and university years – the upbringing years. The first paragraph opens with a scene of road-mending in winter in some unnamed town (we can later work out it's Windsor, habitat of royalty and Etonians). Nothing is happening:

> The men at work at the corner of the street had made a kind of camp for themselves, where, marked out by tripods hung with red hurricane-lamps, an abyss in the road led down to a network of subterranean drain-pipes.

The description meanders on for another two hundred words, ending:

> The grey, undecided flakes continued to come down, though not heavily, while a harsh odour, bitter and gaseous, penetrated the air. The day was drawing in.

Where, the reader might well wonder, is all this going? Nowhere very quickly, it's safe to assume, like the hole in the road. But the effect is oddly hypnotic. A tempo has been set: adagio.

A young Etonian, Jenkins, regards the men at work. 'For some reason', he ruminates, 'the sight of snow descending on fire always makes me think of the ancient world – legionaries in sheepskin warming themselves at a brazier'. A more sympathetic onlooker might think what a bloody awful job for those poor sods to be doing in November. But manual labourers are human specimens for whom questions of upbringing are irrelevant. The music of time does not play for them.

The action moves, in leisurely fashion, to three young Etonians roasting bangers in their shared room. Templer, the most adventurous, comes back from London, having had a tart (his first) for a quid. Jenkins is the narrator (who even at this early stage thinks he might be a writer). It's 1921. Jenkins' father was something important in the military and involved with proceedings leading up to the Treaty of Versailles. The disastrous terms of the treaty will lead to another world war, half a dozen novels away.

Charles Stringham, another sausage feaster, comes from a rich aristocratic family who, as Alan Clark might have put it, did not buy their own furniture, or make their own position in life. It all 'came'. Peter Templer is the son of a very successful businessman, a 'tycoon'. The trio are boon companions. Jenkins confides, 'I liked and admired Stringham: Templer I was not yet sure about.' They are extremely unsure about another boy, Widmerpool, who is awkward, relatively underbred (the son of a solicitor, and bound for that lowly trade himself), chronically badly dressed (his overcoat has become an Eton legend), but driven by a Nietzschean will to succeed. Widmerpool is dangerous, because they cannot quite 'place' him. Such men are not to be trusted. They do not have upbringing.

The first third of the narrative covers the trio's final year at school. They play malicious pranks on their housemaster, Le Bas. Jenkins visits Stringham's appropriately magnificent country house and falls in love, not very disastrously. His shiftless uncle Giles drifts in and out of the narrative, leaving an aroma of tobacco and uselessness behind him. Then, as if arriving by escalator, the three find themselves at the gates of Oxford.

In what would now be called a gap year, Jenkins spends time in France, where he crosses paths again with Widmerpool – now even more worrying a presence than he was at school. Templer, drawing on his circle of influence, gets a good job in the city, deciding university offers nothing worthwhile to a fellow like him. Stringham follows suit, getting a job with a big firm, at board level. He no longer counts as a bosom friend of Jenkins and even stands him up in a restaurant. Jenkins is alone at Oxford. The last major event in the novel, the only event of any significance, is a crash in Templer's car. No one is killed. Like the hole in the road at the beginning of the narrative, it is described in an affectless prose. It's summed up as 'an exceedingly inconvenient occurrence from everyone's point of view'. But, if one's got this far, one's hooked for the whole dozen.

Rabbit, Run, John Updike, 1960

Written over three decades, the four-part Rabbit tetralogy (grand word) can claim to be the finest *roman fleuve* (grander words) in American literature. Updike began it when he was not yet thirty, having established a reputation for himself as a writer of short stories in the *New Yorker*. The first instalment, *Rabbit, Run* (1960), commemorated the end of the fifties in post-war America. Each of its three follow-ups would arrive at the end of successive decades, creating a summary of where the country had just been and where it was heading.

Harry 'Rabbit' Angstrom, blue-eyed and of Swedish stock, is 'a high-school athletic hero in the wake of his glory days'. Rabbit's basketball stardom lasted a mere two seasons. He now has some fifty unheroic years left to live in the shadow of his brief glory. 'After you're first-rate at something,' he discovers, 'no matter what, it kind of takes the kick out of being second-rate.' As we first encounter him, Harry is a minimum-wage salesman selling a new-fangled (and useless) vegetable peeler on commission. Not even second-rate. Unhappily married with one child, and another on the way, Harry decides he can't take it any more and goes on the run. He takes up with another woman, a part-time prostitute, whom he impregnates. His alcoholic wife Janice accidentally drowns their daughter while hopelessly drunk. It is 'the worst thing'. And it is he – not she – who feels guiltier about it. Harry remorsefully returns – abandoning his mistress and their child. More guilt. According to Updike, the Angstrom tetralogy is deeply immersed in the Lutheran creed of his childhood. He sometimes plotted his novels while sitting in church. Hovering over the whole sequence is the question: can a man be good (as Harry is) and yet do bad things (as Harry does)?

Updike picked up the story in *Rabbit Redux* (1971). Rabbit is now thirty-six years old and a linotype operator alongside his similarly employed father, both of them imminently to be made redundant by the offset printing process on which *Rabbit Redux* was itself printed. The US is in ferment. The Apollo moon shot is the novel's central metaphor, and the race riots rocking the country's cities are the big sub-lunar issue. The narrative gives a central role to a black dissident, Skeeter, from whom Harry learns the hollowness of 'civil rights' legislation. This time round his wife Janice has run away from him, and he is living with his pubescent son Nelson, Skeeter, and a hippy drop-out, Jill, whose death by arson (Rabbit having driven his neighbours to criminal revenge by lowering their property values) he provokes. Yet again, 'he knows he is criminal, yet is never caught'.

In *Rabbit is Rich* (1981), the hero is back with Janice and is now a well-off Toyota salesman, thanks to his in-laws' money. He makes a nice packet on the side, speculating in silver coins, and tries out some varieties of sex, outside marriage, which are new to him. His relationship with his son Nelson is fraught. Life may be comfortable for Rabbit, but it never ceases to perplex him: 'In middle age', he discovers, 'you are carrying the world in a sense and yet it seems more out of control than ever.' And where exactly is he going?

The final instalment, *Rabbit at Rest* (1990), commemorates the Reagan decade. Rabbit likes the Great Communicator's 'foggy voice' and 'magic touch'. Rabbit himself had the magic touch once, on the basketball court. America is now in a condition of happy 'anaesthesia'. Harry and Janice spend the cold months in their Florida condo. 'Most of American life is driving somewhere and then driving back wondering why the hell you went,' he concludes. But there is no happy ending. Nelson, addicted to cocaine, ruins the car sales business. Harry, addicted to sex, makes love to Nelson's wife Pru, and goes on the run again. In a Florida ghetto he has one last pick-up ball game with some mystified black kids, suffers a heart attack and dies in hospital – lasting long enough to confide in Nelson, 'All I can tell you is, it isn't so bad.'

The Ragged Trousered Philanthropists, Robert Tressell, 1914

Poor people, 'underlings', 'workers of the world' (as Marx hailed them), do not write novels. While researching, for a companion guide to Victorian fiction, some 3,000 nineteenth-century novels, I turned up just one which was written by a bona-fide servant. It was not very good. Servants proliferate in the world of Victorian fiction, and there are some very good novels *about* them (*Esther Waters* is the best, I would hazard). But, like the similarly omnipresent horse, and the well-behaved child of the period, they are seen but not heard. Occasionally novelists like Mrs Gaskell speak on behalf of the 'dumb people', as she called the workers of Manchester (or speak for the equine masses, as does Anna Sewell in BLACK BEAUTY), but that too is fairly rare. The voices of men with hods on their backs, or women with needles in their hands, go largely unrepresented.

Tressell's book is the exception to this. It's a novel whose conception, gestation and struggle into the birth of print are as interesting and instructive as the narrative content itself. The title, however, may have hindered the book's fortunes. 'Ragged trousered philanthropists' is a clumsy jest – the term indicates the working classes, who 'give' the fruits of their labour to their capitalist exploiters.

The author was born Robert Croker, illegitimate (then a shameful thing), in Ireland (where illegitimacy was particularly shameful) in 1870. He took on his mother's surname, Noonan, and emigrated to South Africa around 1888, where he worked as a house decorator and sign-writer. He prospered moderately, married and divorced, returning to England with a daughter at the turn of the century – driven out by the imminent Boer War (he was no imperialist). He had, while in South Africa, made some attempts to unionise exploited black workers. Around 1906, he began to write a story, giving himself the name 'Robert Tressell' – a homophone for 'trestle', one of the tools of his trade. He was, by now, a committed socialist. The manuscript was everywhere rejected. He tried to burn it, but the 1,600-page work was pulled from the flames by his daughter. Tressell was preparing to emigrate to Canada, but died of TB and was buried in a mass grave for paupers in 1911. He was just forty. A truncated version of the novel finally saw print in 1914, but the full text was not published until the 1950s.

The hero-narrator is Frank Owen, a house decorator He is first found working in a large house nicknamed 'The Cave' in Mugsborough (or Hastings, where the author lived – an unlovely place). The house is jerry-built and the workmen are a pick-up gang of journeymen cowboys, brutally driven by a foreman. They take no more pride in their work than if they were captive Israelites building pyramids in Ancient Egypt. The book abounds with graphic descriptions of the grinding hardships and daily humiliations of 'honest work'. What plot it has is simply so many fictional soapboxes on which Frank and, later, his better-off friend of the poor, Barrington, can stand and preach the moral force of socialism.

What is fascinating about the novel is the fatalism at its core. Although the narrative might be expected to finish with the ritual 'workers of the world unite' peroration, Tressell, in his heart of hearts, doesn't believe it. His pessimism about the invincible stupidity of the underclass is expressed in asides such as:

> He hated and despised them because they calmly saw their children condemned to hard labour and poverty for life, and deliberately refused to make any effort to secure for them better conditions than those they had themselves . . . *They* were the people who were really responsible for the continuance of the present system.

George Orwell was profoundly influenced by *The Ragged Trousered Philanthropists*, which, he said, 'has always seemed to me a wonderful book, although it is very clumsily written'. It's plausible that Orwell's own thinking drew from it. 'If there is hope', thinks Winston in NINETEEN EIGHTY-FOUR, 'it lies in the proles.' But there is no such hope. The only thing the proles will riot for is new saucepans. The only thing that ever excites them is football pools. In *Animal Farm*, the Joneses and the Pigs will always be in charge. Revolution, even where it happens, changes nothing.

Ragtime, E. L. Doctorow, 1975

Doctorow customised his novel about America for an upcoming big event – the 1976 bicentenary. The book was helped on its way by a revival of interest in the music of Scott Joplin, whose ragtime compositions were so influential in the creation of America's unique art-form – jazz. The novel has as its epigraph Joplin's instruction: 'It is never right to play Ragtime fast. . .' and the prose rhythm which Doctorow crafts for his narrative is sonorously 'plink, plink', reminiscent of the piano rolls which are Joplin's memorial.

Ragtime opens in 1902 with a (white) family in New Rochelle, New York. They have no names, only roles: 'Father', 'Mother', 'Mother's Younger Brother', etc. In other words: 'Every American'. They are prosperous from the manufacture of flags and fireworks (boom industries in 1976). Enter a black waif, Coalhouse Walker Jr., and Harry Houdini (the first of the narrative's historical characters), whose car breaks down in front of the family's home. Henry Ford, Emma Goldman, J. P. Morgan, Evelyn Nesbit, Sigmund Freud and Emiliano Zapata will all play walk-on parts in the narrative, weaving historical threads through the fictional fabric. But Houdini, escapologist of genius, plays a central role:

> His life was absurd. He went all over the world accepting all kinds of bondage and escaping. He was roped to a chair. He escaped. He was chained to a ladder. He escaped. He was handcuffed, his legs were put in irons, he was tied up in a strait jacket and put in a locked cabinet.

The catalogue tumbles on, plinkingly, for two more pages.

The other centre of narrative activity is a destitute immigrant Jewish family living on New York's Lower East Side. Here WASPs, black people and Jewish people are all thrown together in a melting pot in which nothing is evenly dispersed, certainly none of the riches of the country. *Ragtime* portrays an America dominated by robber barons. In one hilarious episode Henry Ford and the banker J. P.

Morgan secrete themselves in Morgan's 36th Street palace to discuss reincarnation (surely people like themselves deserve more than one life?) and set up 'the most secret and exclusive club in America, The Pyramid, of which they were the only members'.

The gulf between America's rich and poor is coolly satirised in Doctorow's sour depiction of the 'poverty balls' which were popular at the period (the historical research for the novel was meticulous):

> One hundred Negroes a year were lynched. One hundred miners were burned alive. One hundred children were mutilated. There seemed to be quotas for these things. There seemed to be quotas for death by starvation . . . It became fashionable to honor the poor. At palaces in New York and Chicago people gave poverty balls . . . One hostess invited everyone to a stockyard ball. Guests were wrapped in long aprons and their heads covered in white caps. They dined and danced while hanging carcasses of bloody beef trailed around the walls on moving pulleys. Entrails spilled on the floor. The proceeds were for charity.

Not ragtime, but a time of rags.

The novel climaxes when, in fury at the vandalising of his Model T automobile, Coalhouse and a band of fellow black rebels take over Morgan's private library, which is now a public institution, the Morgan Library and Museum. I was a visiting fellow there when I first read *Ragtime*: the venue added real zest to the experience – although I was careful not to flash the book around in the reading room. It all ends bloodily with Coalhouse killed by the cops:

> In the bright floodlit street the black man was said by the police to have made a dash for freedom. More probably he knew that all he must do in order to end his life was to turn his head abruptly or lower his hands or smile. Inside the Library, Father heard the coordinated volley of a firing squad. He screamed. He ran to the window. The body jerked about the

street in a sequence of attitudes as if it were trying to mop up its own blood. The policemen were firing at will. The horses snorted and shied.

The Black Panthers, and the assassination of Panther George Jackson in particular, are evoked as the narrative approaches the eve of the First World War, when the music turned off-key.

Rasselas, Samuel Johnson, 1759

One of Johnson's more objectionable (but much recycled) remarks is that which he made when Boswell says he has heard a woman preach at a Quaker meeting:

'Sir, a woman's preaching is like a dog's walking on his hind legs. It is not done well; but you are surprised to find it done at all.'

It is as surprising that the Great Cham (the word means 'khan' or 'king') should ever have ventured into fiction. He had scant respect for the masterworks of the new genre being created around him. When Boswell ventured to mention the greatest novelist of the age, it triggered the inevitable explosion:

Fielding being mentioned, Johnson exclaimed, 'he was a blockhead... What I mean by his being a blockhead is that he was a barren rascal.' BOSWELL. 'Will you not allow, Sir, that he draws very natural pictures of human life?' JOHNSON. 'Why, Sir, it is of very low life.'

Sterne received similarly short shrift:

'Nothing odd will do long. *Tristram Shandy* did not last.'

Richardson's moral decency Dr Johnson respected. But not the literary form he chose to express it in.

Nonetheless, Johnson himself wrote a novel and a very interesting one, if only for the circumstances of its composition, and

its cross-grained perversity as regards the art of fiction. In 1759, Johnson's aged mother was dying; his father had gone to his reward in 1731. Johnson was early on in his penurious career as a pen-driver. To cover the expense of his parent's last days and interment, he wrote, over the evenings of one week, *The History of Rasselas, Prince of Abissinia*. It is a mixture of thinly applied 'oriental' setting (drawn from travel books), and heavy moral dogmatising – as English as suet pudding (drawn from the fifty-year-old author's life experiences).

The ingénu prince leaves the comfort of his palace in 'The Happy Valley' in Ethiopia to range the world, seeking the secret of a happier, or more worthwhile, life than his home affords. He is accompanied by his sister and a philosopher, Imlac (alias Samuel Johnson). There is, Rasselas discovers, no happiness to be found anywhere in this world. Life is, as Johnson said elsewhere, a condition in which much is to be endured and little enjoyed. Patience is all. Few novelists, one imagines, could produce the statutory happy-ever-after with the 'Dead March' from *Saul* droning, incessantly, in their ears. *Rasselas* is no page-turner – sermons on the human condition seldom are. But it brought Johnson £75 – and another £25 for a speedy second edition.

The novel does have some fine conceits. Particularly memorable is the astronomer who, in a condition of advanced professional mania, believes he has been entrusted by God with the running of the universe. The sun itself 'has listened to my dictates', he tells his visitors. This watcher of the celestial bodies is the first of his kind to be found in fiction – 'the mad scientist'.

The marrow of the novel is in the tenth chapter, which Johnson uses as a conveyance for his literary credo:

'This business of a poet,' said Imlac, 'is to examine, not the individual, but the species; to remark general properties and large appearances. He does not number the streaks of the tulip, or describe the different shades of the verdure of the forest.'

Abstraction, not concreteness, is what literature should aspire to. But the novel, as a genre, aspires to the opposite of this John-sonian recipe. It relishes what Henry James called 'solidity of specification': detail. Individual tulip streaks everywhere. Ask a reader what they recall most vividly from ROBINSON CRUSOE and many will say 'that footprint in the sand'. We never know whose it was. It's one of the many threads left hanging in the narrative, but the unexplained detail contributes powerfully to the effect of realism.

One's glad Johnson got his mother decently buried and also glad he wrote *Rasselas*, because it's so illuminatingly wrong-headed. It's like one of those failed experiments which, scientists claim, are as useful to the progress of science as the eureka moments.

Ratking, Michael Dibdin, 1988

It's strange what you learn from novels. I reviewed Dibdin's *Ratking* when it came out and made the passing comment (in an otherwise appreciative notice): 'The title, incidentally, alludes to an unwilling syndicate of rodents, whose permanently tangled tails oblige them to act as a unit: I suspect the image is not zoologically sound.'

Dibdin wrote in a very civil correction:

SIR: Your reviewer's suspicions that the central image of my novel *Ratking* is 'not zoologically sound' are unfounded. At least forty authenticated examples of ratkings have in fact been discovered, mostly in Germany; six are still preserved. The history and probable causes of the phenomenon are discussed by Martin Hart in *Rats* (London, 1982), which also contains photographs of a king found in Holland in 1963, including the X-ray image reproduced on the cover of my book.

One lives and learns – even bone-headed reviewers. Dibdin's letter reminded me that all I knew about rats came from 'The Pied Piper of Hamelin', *The Wind in the Willows*, and (although I would never have confessed the fact in the columns of the *LRB*) James Herbert (see THE RATS).

Ratking is the inaugural novel in Dibdin's long-running, and highly superior, 'Zen' crime-novel sequence. The Police Commissioner (i.e. detective) hero, Aurelio Zen, is a Venetian seconded from Rome to solve the kidnapping of a rich industrialist in Perugia. Italy was historically late to unify, and there is a lot of quite complex play with ineradicable Italian provincial prejudices. A Venetian, the reader is led to understand, is as different from a citizen of Perugia as a Bedouin from an Eskimo. In the light of this, the 'Ratking' (rodents forced, against their natural instinct, into a collective) has an ironic aspect to it – if not an entirely flattering one. Dibdin was British, but taught for some years at the University of Perugia, and knew his Italy.

Zen is under a cloud for having botched the (real-life) Aldo Moro kidnapping investigation and his career is going nowhere. His personal relationships with his mother and his girlfriend are vexed. Before coming to Perugia, he was given a punishment posting in Rome, shuffling paper. The Perugia assignment represents his second chance. At the time *Ratking* was published, the Aldo Moro case still very much alive in public memory. The senior politician had been abducted by the Communist 'Red Brigades' in 1978, held for nearly two months, and then shot dead – after writing a number of letters to other politicians, his family, and Pope Paul VI – when the kidnappers' demands were not met. Europe felt its political foundations assailed by domestic terrorism. Zen is assigned to what looks like a copycat case. Ruggiero Miletti – a hugely powerful industrialist privy to much of what is going on, murkily and corruptly, behind the scenes in politics – is kidnapped. With the political stakes high, the captive's death might be the safest outcome. Miletti's own family are not desperately keen that he be rescued. As would be the formula in later novels in the series, Zen – a complicatedly honest man in a complicatedly corrupt world – has to penetrate walls of silence and entrenched regional distrust of the snooping outsider as he conducts his investigation. All the rats, he eventually discovers, are tied together by the tail.

Ratking deservedly won a Golden Dagger Award for the best crime novel of the year and Dibdin went on to write ten more 'Zens'; among their other pleasures as subtle, ironic thrillers, they offer a sensitive depiction of the author's adoptive country. Canny tourists would pack the latest volume in their bags before leaving for Italy. Dibdin died in 2007, leaving the appropriately named *End Games* to be published later that year. One wishes the Zen game could have lasted longer.

The Rats, James Herbert, 1974

For those of a perverse cast of mind, 20 March 2013 saw an interesting coincidence. The Queen and other members of the Royal Family visited Baker Street underground station, to commemorate the one hundred and fiftieth anniversary of the world's first, and still pre-eminent, subterranean transport system. On the same day, James Herbert's death was announced. Say his name and the person you're talking to will quite likely fire back: 'Rats in the underground!' Herbert, as the obituaries reminded us, broke into bestsellerdom in 1974 with a novel which featured the creatures breeding out of control in the warm, foetid entrails of the 'tube'. Having reached critical mass, the super-rats tumble out from their lairs to devour any Londoner in their way. My mind, as I read the two news-stories, pictured that Herbertian horde spilling out of the dark Baker Street tunnels, equerries gallantly hurling themselves in the rodents' path to protect the monarch and her heir-carrying granddaughter-in-law, with Prince Philip drawing the swordstick he always carries with him, holding the vile things at bay. (The rats, that is, not the reporters.)

James Herbert was an East Ender, the son of a stall-holder, and an early school leaver. His modern 'gothics' – of which *The Rats* is far and away the best – were in a direct line of descent from the 'penny dreadfuls' and 'penny bloods' which alarmed Victorian authorities to the point of moral panic and fired the juvenile imagination of the young Boz. Low as it may be on the literary scale of things, *The Rats* has a powerful kick to it. Stephen King (he was always generous about the writer called 'England's Stephen King')

said: 'Herbert does not just write. . . he puts on his combat boots and goes out to assault the reader with horror!' (Should have been Doc Martens, of course.)

The Rats has no story – merely a row of narrative hooks on which to hang blood-curdling scenes. Mutant rodents, a scientific experiment gone wrong, infest a metropolis where, it is said, even at the best of times you're never more than ten yards from a rat. The *scène à faire*, as the French (never James Herbert) would put it, centres on 'dingy' Shadwell underground station in the heart of the East End. It's the early 1970s, and late at night. 'Dave', an amiable yob, is on the way home, chugging a carton of milk. He's pissed off; his girl's 'a PT: prick teaser', he's discovered. She'll have to go. A lad has to have his oats.

The only other person around is a 'coloured station worker' (pubs closed at eleven in the early seventies; and many in that unregenerate era carried the sign 'no coloureds'). As Dave stands alone on the platform, something catches his eye:

> A dark shape was moving along between the tracks. He walked to the edge of the platform and peered down the track into the gloom. Nothing. Then he noticed the shape had stopped. Realising it must be a rat, he threw the empty milk carton to see if he could make it scamper back into the darkness of the tunnel, but it merely shrank beneath the electric rail. The boy looked up sharply as he heard noises coming from the dense black cave of the tunnel. It sounded like the rush of air, but not the sound caused by an approaching train. He glanced nervously back at the form lurking in beneath the track and up again as the noise grew louder. As he did hundreds, it seemed, of small black bodies came pouring from the tunnel, some between the tracks, others up the ramp and along the platform.

Farewell Dave, under a 'river of vermin'. Science eventually defeats the rat horde – or does it? A nasty white patriarch survives. First Hamelin, now London.

In the numerous tweeted and internet-posted tributes to Herbert, many recorded how, in their impressionable childhood, they were happily traumatised by the rats in the underground scene. I myself think of them every time I drop by (no longer dingy) Shadwell station.

Ravelstein, Saul Bellow, 2000

Bellow's last fictional bellow – published at the age of eighty-four. Could the creator of Augie March, one wondered, keep it up twenty years after the mandatory retirement age for most of his readers?

The novel is a frank (and acknowledged) tribute to Bellow's long-time friend and sometime colleague at Chicago University, Allan Bloom – 'Abe Ravelstein' as he's called here. In 1987 Bloom published *The Closing of the American Mind*, a book which savagely denounced the 'new enlightenment' ('theory', 'feminism', 'Neo-Marxism', etc.), and demanded a return from all this mumbo-jumbo to the 'liberal imagination'. Bloom was both an intimate of Bellow's and his intellectual *confrère*. Either of them could have come out with Bellow's grotesquely un-PC jibe against Black Studies: 'Who is the Tolstoy of the Zulus?' Some wags, when *The Closing of the American Mind* appeared, suggested that Bloom was actually a Bellovian invention.

Surprisingly, Bloom's jeremiad became a bestseller. It did for culture what Reagan did for the economy – took it backwards into the future. It didn't hurt Bloom's wallet, either. 'His intellect had made a millionaire of him', as Bellow dryly puts it in the novel. *The Closing of the American Mind* made Bloom a hero among the neocons on both sides of the Atlantic. Mrs Thatcher had him to tea at Chequers. Doubtless they discussed the necessity of returning English 101 and Virgil to the curriculum. Alas, Allan Bloom did not live long enough to enjoy his millions and his international fame. He died in 1992 of an illness vaguely described in the glowing obituaries as 'liver failure'.

The novel opens in the 1990s with Abe revelling in his well-gotten gains, enjoying the life of a Parisian bon vivant in the five-star Hôtel de Crillon with his lissom Malaysian lover, Nikki. Life is good for Ravelstein, and would be perfect were it not for a vexing physical ailment – Aids, as it turns out. Abe appoints his writer friend Chick to be his Boswell. *Ravelstein* covers the last year of the hero's life. Nothing very much happens except hospitals and talk. A lot of the novel is like hearing two old codgers rabbit on about what it's like being two old codgers. They reminisce, bad-mouth people (particularly Chick's ex-wife, the Romanian bitch Vela), and tell, over and over again, their favourite Jewish jokes. For those in the know, *Ravelstein* was breathtakingly indiscreet. The descriptions of Vela (clearly based on Bellow's second wife) and living colleagues at Chicago University went as far as lax American libel law permitted, and well beyond decorum.

'You don't easily give up a creature like Ravelstein to death', the novel concludes, portentously. When death did its worst, Chick/Bellow created a monumental likeness of his friend for posterity to admire. But *Ravelstein* offers a lot more than funerary portraiture. The novel explores, in its engagingly rambling way, two dauntingly large and touching themes: death and American Jewishness. 'As a Jew', says Chick 'you also are also an American but somehow you are not.' Is that a good or a bad thing?

The first half of the narrative chronicles Abe's struggle with full-blown Aids (this was before the arrival of modern medicines). What is it to die? the two old men ask themselves. 'No more pictures' is the best they can come up with. Or, as T. S. Eliot put it, 'Dark dark dark'. The second half of the novel chronicles Chick's own struggle with the Grim Reaper after eating some toxic fish in the tropics. As he lies in his hospital bed he has to decide 'whether I should or should not make efforts to recover'. He does make the effort. (The toxic fish episode actually happened, Bellow made the effort, and lived on for eleven years.) The novel caused great anger among some of Bloom's other friends. Bellow always took pleasure in getting people's backs up.

The Reader, Bernhard Schlink
1995

It's always fascinating to see a novelist gingerly approaching a topic of which they are profoundly nervous. For instance, how can a non-Jewish German – born in 1944 – dare to write anything about the Holocaust? Let alone anything that could be construed as special pleading? Schlink – a lawyer and part-time crime writer – finally took up the challenge of an Auschwitz novel fifty years on. *The Reader* proved hugely successful in Germany and was extravagantly praised in Britain and America.

Michael Berg, a fifteen-year-old schoolboy in an unnamed German city, collapses, vomiting, in the street. He has undiagnosed hepatitis. A uniformed woman (a comely tram conductress) cleans him up and helps him home. It is 1958. The *Wirtschaftswunder* (economic miracle) is going full steam. Michael's father is an emotionally distant professor of philosophy who kept his head down during the war. The conductress is Hanna Schmitz. Once he has recovered Michael tracks her down to give her some flowers. Her apartment is bleak. She has no family. Helping to fill her coal scuttle, he gets himself horribly dirty. She bundles him into a bath and, towelling his naked body down,

> She came so close to me that I could feel her breasts against my back and her stomach against my behind. She was naked too. She put her arms around me, one hand on my chest and the other on my erection.

They become lovers. It's criminal: he is, by law, a child. She is thirty-six. The relationship is almost entirely physical. She dominates him – sometimes cruelly. But it has another aspect to it. She loves him to read to her for hours at a time:

> We kept up our ritual of reading aloud, showering, making love, and then lying together. I read her *War and Peace*.

She also has a soft spot for Goethe.

The affair ends abruptly when Hanna disappears into thin air. Michael goes on to college to study law. Seven years after his affair with Hanna, a case crops up which interests him. A group of female Auschwitz SS guards are being tried for an atrocity perpetrated in the last months of the war. Hundreds of Jewish women prisoners were locked in a church and burned to death. To his surprise, Michael recognises Hanna as principal among the accused. Among other things, it is stated, she was responsible for 'selections' (to the gas chambers), and made favoured prisoners read books to her and submit to her sexual demands. Hanna accepts that she wrote the mendacious SS report which subsequently covered up the massacre.

Michael realises that she is illiterate, and so could not have written the report, but rather than admit the fact will accept life imprisonment in preference to the shorter sentences her equally guilty comrades receive. Her life has been one long flight from her inability to read and write – that was why she deserted Michael. At the time she had been offered promotion to an office job. The truth would have come out. Over the eighteen years of Hanna's imprisonment, Michael sends her audio tapes of great German literature. She painstakingly teaches herself to read and, one apprehends, becomes a civilised German. She hangs herself on the morning of her release on parole.

Not everyone had good words to say for *The Reader*. Frederic Raphael, in a biting critique, declared that to burn *The Reader* would put it in better company than it deserved. The notion that the SS recruited illiterates was nonsense, and the idea that a confessed mass-murderess would be converted to civilised decency by reading Goethe and Tolstoy obscene. One can appreciate the force of Raphael's denunciation, but *The Reader* remains hugely readable and thought-provoking.

Rebecca, Daphne du Maurier, 1938

Ask where *Rebecca* belongs on the bookshop shelves and the answer you'll most likely receive is 'Romance' (with the implied epithet 'women's romance'). Viewed more judiciously *Rebecca* classifies both as one of the best crime novels of a period (the 1930s) when the genre rode high, and as a pioneer tribute to Franz Kafka (see THE CASTLE) at a time when that writer's work was first percolating through into English – more of which below.

Du Maurier's novel is narrated by a woman looking back to a time when she was young, innocent and vulnerable. It opens with what is often cited as the most famous first line in fiction:

Last night I dreamt I went to Manderley again.

Like many people, I suspect, I tend to misquote this as 'I was at Manderley again'. Learned articles have been written on the difference. The narrator once lived in Manderley – a grand Cornish house. As an older woman, telling the story, she no longer lives there. Where she now lives, and what her current condition in life now is, remain mysterious until the end of the book.

The story opens with a whirlwind romance. The narrator was a paid 'companion' to a rich woman in Monte Carlo – playground then, as it still is, of the filthy rich. Enter a man of a certain age, Maxim de Winter, with an aura of mystery, who sweeps Mrs Van Hopper's companion off her feet, and proposes marriage in what will prove to be his habitually curt way:

'Either you go to America with Mrs Van Hopper or you come home to Manderley with me.'
'Do you mean you want a secretary or something?'
'No, I'm asking you to marry me, you little fool.'

The heroine goes to Manderley, as Mrs de Winter. She is not, she discovers, the first mistress of the house, which is still infused with the presence of the previous Mrs de Winter: Rebecca. The keeper of her flame (a woman over-fond of flames, it transpires) is the housekeeper, Mrs Danvers ('Danny'), who was also, we are led to suspect, Rebecca's lover. Her 'welcome' to the second Mrs de Winter oozes menace:

'Now you are here, let me show you everything,' she said, her voice ingratiating and sweet as honey, horrible, false. . . 'That was her bed. It's a beautiful bed, isn't it? I keep the golden coverlet on it always, it was her favourite. Here is her nightdress inside the case. You've been touching it, haven't you?'

Rebecca died mysteriously, a year before, in a solo yachting venture, at night. Improbable. . . but good enough for the coroner (a close friend of Max's). The true facts eventually emerge. Max killed Rebecca. He will never answer for it but, in a kind of suttee homage to her lover, 'Danny' burns down Manderley. The arson happens as the de Winters are motoring back from London, where Max has been warned to leave the country to escape the scandal.

The Kafkaism, so to call it, is found in the fact that the narrator has no more of a fore- or surname (at least before she becomes the second Mrs de Winter) than Josef K in *The Trial*. The un-dead Rebecca has vampirically sucked all identity out of her. Kafkaesque, too, is the crime at the heart of the novel. It happened in a cottage by the sea. Max went down there with a gun (why?), suspecting that Rebecca had betrayed him with her lounge-lizard cousin Jack Favell. He shot her, we are led to suspect, through the belly, when she taunted him with the fact that she was pregnant with Favell's baby – the future heir to Manderley. Mysteriously, another woman's body (which Max criminally identifies as Rebecca's) is washed up. Was she discovered *in flagrante delicto*? Did Max kill them both? Du Maurier artfully hints at all these possibilities, but leaves them unconfirmed. The plot has as many holes in it as a colander. This is a mystery novel which does not commit the cardinal fault of most 'mysteries' – denouement. The knot is left tangled, teasingly.

Culpably, Alfred Hitchcock in his 1940 film adaptation had Rebecca dying accidentally in the cottage, so as to exonerate Max. He should have left well alone.

The Red Badge of Courage: An Episode of the American Civil War, Stephen Crane, 1895

Crane's first working title was: 'Private Fleming: His various battles'. The original motive, it is reputed, was a boast that he could write a better battle story than Zola's La Débâcle (1892). At the time Crane was a twenty-three-year-old – born six years after the Civil War. He claimed to have learned everything he needed to know about human conflict from playing football. He was, at the time of writing The Red Badge of Courage, a newspaperman, and brought to the narrative a journalistic briskness.

The story records the character-forming war experience of Private Henry Fleming. As an eighteen-year-old farm boy, Henry volunteers to fight for the North. He has no political conviction, sense of history or quarrel with slavery. His is less a war story than a fictional study in the 'psychology of fear': his 'battle' with himself.

Crane claimed the opening paragraph came to his imagination fully formed, as a gift from his muse:

> The cold passed reluctantly from the earth, and the retiring fogs revealed an army stretched out on the hills, resting. As the landscape changed from brown to green, the army awakened, and began to tremble with eagerness at the noise of rumors. It cast its eyes upon the roads, which were growing from long troughs of liquid mud to proper thoroughfares. A river, amber-tinted in the shadow of its banks, purled at the army's feet; and at night, when the stream had become of a sorrowful blackness, one could see across it the red, eyelike gleam of hostile camp-fires set in the low brows of distant hills.

Henry runs away from his first fight. In the woods he comes upon:

> a dead man who was seated with his back against a columnlike tree. The corpse was dressed in a uniform that once had been blue, but was now faded to a melancholy shade of green. The eyes, staring at the youth, had changed to the dull hue to be seen on the side of a dead fish. The mouth was open. Its red had changed to an appalling yellow. Over the gray skin of the face ran little ants. One was trundling some sort of bundle along the upper lip.

A fleeing comrade hits Henry savagely, if accidentally, on the head. This is mistaken, as he continues to run through the rear lines, for an honourable war wound – his 'red badge of courage'. He finally composes himself and returns to the fray, where he carries his unit's standard and fights gallantly. 'He was a man.' The statement hangs, ironically, over the novel's final paragraph.

> It rained. The procession of weary soldiers became a bedraggled train, despondent and muttering, marching with churning effort in a trough of liquid brown mud under a low, wretched sky. Yet the youth smiled, for he saw that the world was a world for him, though many discovered it to be made of oaths and walking sticks. He had rid himself of the red sickness of battle. The sultry nightmare was in the past. He had been an animal blistered and sweating in the heat and pain of war. He turned now with a lover's thirst to images of tranquil skies, fresh meadows, cool brooks – an existence of soft and eternal peace.
>
> Over the river a golden ray of sun came through the hosts of leaden rain clouds.

The American army, I believe, is the only one to give its soldiers a medal for merely being wounded while serving in battle – the Purple Heart. The award, which originated in the American War of Independence but fell out of use for a while after the First World War, was reintroduced in 1932. Other armies see war-wounds as occupational hazards and not inherently valorous. Most armies, of course, agree on what cowardice is.

The Red Badge of Courage was serialised

in over five hundred newspapers. It was universally believed, from the vividness of the battlefield descriptions, that Crane himself had served as a soldier. One genuine veteran, a colonel no less, distinctly remembered serving with 'Stephen Crane' at Antietam – some nine years before the novelist was born.

Red Star, Alexander Bogdanov, 1908

Alexander Bogdanov is remembered – by those who keep up with such things – as the heretic flayed in Lenin's great polemic, *Materialism and Empirio-Criticism*. Bogdanov's error, in Lenin's infuriated opinion, was to deny the materiality of the world, so falling into 'Machian confusion and idealist aberrations'. Big stuff. But along with the infamy, Bogdanov should enjoy posthumous fame as a writer of science fiction. Lenin, one suspects, would have had little time for such frippery (the great leader's favourite story, one is told, was Jack London's TO BUILD A FIRE). Bogdanov trained as a doctor. Contact with poor patients led him to embrace Bolshevism; at the time of writing *Red Star* he and Lenin were comrades-in-arms. As a physician, Bogdanov undertook useful research into blood transfusion – an act which had Socialist symbolism for him. He died, in 1928, experimenting on himself with blood donations from an infected patient.

Red Star takes as its starting-point Schiaparelli's observation of so-called *canali* on Mars in the late 1870s. The word was meant to indicate 'channels' but was misapprehended as 'canals' – artefacts, not natural features. The myth that Mars presented the distant spectacle of a dead or dying mighty civilisation took firm root. It was bad astronomy, but excellent inspiration for romancers. Among the fantasies inspired by the Martian 'canals', the most famous is Wells' *War of the Worlds* (1898). Projecting the ways of his own people, Wells conceives the Martians as imperialists, ruthlessly employing superior military technology to invade, and then plunder, London (the inevitable target, as the heart of terrestrial colonialism). The origin of *War of the Worlds* is

Wells' conviction that a superior race would treat the English as the English had recently treated the luckless aborigines of Tasmania. 'Are we such apostles of mercy', his narrator asks, 'as to complain if the Martians warred in the same spirit?'

Bogdanov's Martians, by contrast, are interplanetary comrades, not colonisers. His logic is that Mars, being the older planet, must inevitably have preceded Earth, through war, to Socialist fulfilment; Mars is the red planet in all senses. The Martians elect to land in Russia, the cradle of revolution, where 'the pulse of life beats strongest'. The alien society is found to embody the future that the early Bolsheviks imagined themselves fighting for. 'In order to wage the struggle,' Bogdanov notes, 'one must know the future.' To supply this inspiriting knowledge is the aim of *Red Star*. There is an interesting scene, evidently answering Wells, in which Bogdanov's Martians, facing the exhaustion of their planet's natural resources, have the option of either colonising Earth (and exterminating its inhabitants) or sending out mining expeditions to the hazardous and unpopulated surface of Venus. Although the Venusian choice is infinitely more costly and risky, it is the one chosen. Bogdanov's Martians are ethical aliens.

Red Star was written immediately after 1905's abortive revolution, and scenes of contemporary battle form the opening backdrop. From this furnace of insurrection, the hero is carried off for a recuperative sightseeing tour of Mars in one of the visitors' 'etheronephs'. On the red planet, he discovers what the Communist future being fought for on Earth holds for earthlings. Individualism had been abolished (and with it, all vestiges of leadership). Martian society is organised as a benign industrial factory-cum-garden state. Eden.

Bogdanov hits a few prophetic bull's eyes, with his projections of mainframe computers, talking three-dimensional movies and dictaphones. But in general *Red Star* is as wildly inaccurate a predictor of the future as is the rest of its genre. There is a perfunctory wrapping-up of the action, in which the hero returns to Earth, throws himself even more vigorously into revolutionary struggle, and is wounded. He finally returns to Mars, and reunion with his Martian mate. On balance, one suspects – if it ever happens – the invading aliens probably won't be comradely. Wells, alas, is the more convincing prophet on that score.

Red Wind, Raymond Chandler, 1938

Not enough is known about Chandler's life; not a single letter survives from the first thirty years of it. He has always been barren territory for biographers. But Chandler's route into hardboiled fiction – of which he is the Shakespeare – is reasonably well chronicled, and fascinating.

For reasons known only to himself, Chandler – who had been a high-earning oil-company executive before losing his job in the Depression – decided, at close on forty-five years of age, to give up drink (he was acutely alcoholic) and become a professional writer. He cocooned himself in cheap lodgings with his wife Cissy – a woman old enough to be his mother – he married her not long after his mother's death, who seems, nobly, to have gone along with their sudden change in circumstances. For several years Chandler imposed a gruelling writer's apprenticeship on himself. He chose crime writing, he said, because it was 'honest'. Poverty, too, was 'purifying'. Chandler had set his sights on *Black Mask* – the magazine which had launched Dashiell Hammett. It pioneered in its pages 'hardboiled' detective fiction: a classier product than was purveyed in the pulps, and a tougher one than was produced by British 'tea-cosy' crime writers. Chandler realised there was space in this new crime-fiction genre to establish a whole other style. Over the latter years of the 1930s he created a niche for himself as a regular contributor to *Black Mask*, cultivating a specialism in the Los Angeles-based 'private eye' story. What Chandler perfected was 'voice'. His favoured narrative mode is autobiographical – the tone is laconic, wise-cracking, seen-it-all, world-weary. Above all, he aimed at what he called 'cadence' – a quality which American crime writing sadly lacked.

The great novels are all well known. Less

visited are his early trial runs perfecting the 'voice' – tuning it as a musician tunes his instrument before an important performance. Notable among these exercises is the long short story 'Red Wind', which centres on private investigator John Dalmas (who would eventually mutate into Philip Marlowe). It's the first Chandler I ever read (as a schoolboy), in its Penguin green livery. On the strength of it I went out and splurged 16/- on the Hamish Hamilton Marlowe quartet. It's looking down on me, battered by time and re-readings, at this moment.

'Red Wind' opens with a paragraph of pure Chandlerian 'cadence':

> There was a desert wind blowing that night. It was one of those hot dry Santa Anas that come down through the mountain passes and curl your hair and make your nerves jump and your skin itch. On nights like that every booze party ends in a fight. Meek little wives feel the edge of the carving knife and study their husbands' necks. Anything can happen. You can even get a full glass of beer at a cocktail lounge.

This overture leads into a *Nighthawks*-esque scene in an LA bar (a favourite opening in Chandler narratives). Dalmas, who has an apartment nearby, has drifted in for a nightcap. The bar is empty, apart from a drunk who is sitting sodden in the corner, a pile of dimes in front of him (a 'shot' only cost a quarter, twenty-five cents, in those days). It emerges that the drunk is no drunk but a contract killer, waiting patiently for his prey. That prey is the customer who has just walked through the door. He gets two expertly directed .22 rounds to the chest and falls to the floor. 'He might have been poured concrete for all the fuss he made,' Dalmas comments, laconically. As is usual with Chandler, the plot thereafter goes haywire. Famously, he himself never understood what was happening in his narratives. 'Who knows?' was his customary riddling response when asked about some peculiarly baffling twist. Dalmas, as the formula requires, cracks the case (and a few heads in the process). But no one reads Chandler for the story – it's the voice, stupid.

Redback, Howard Jacobson, 1986

Howard Jacobson began writing novels late in life. Born in Manchester in 1942, the young Howard went to grammar school and read English at Cambridge, where he was taught by the martinet F. R. Leavis. He did well enough to be invited on board. His subsequent academic career started in Cambridge, diverted to Sydney University and ended at Wolverhampton Polytechnic: a downward trajectory which Jacobson seems to gloomily find fit for such as him. Aged forty-one, he published his first novel, *Coming from Behind* (saucy title). Since then, he has come a long way. He won the Man Booker prize in 2010, for *The Finkler Question*, and commemorated his triumph with the funniest winner's speech ever heard at the Guildhall.

Redback chronicles Jacobson's time Down Under. It will be some way into the narrative before most English readers feel the full Antipodean force of the enigmatic title. But, to begin with, it's enough to register the suggestions of painful sunburn, humiliation and pommy gaucherie. The peculiarly nasty nature of Anglo–Australian relations (as lampooned by Jacobson) is outlined in a symbolic prelude to the action. An unnamed Oxford undergraduate meets a wholesome young Australian girl with powerful mandibles and an MA in fine art – 'let's give her an ordinary Australian name, say . . . Desley'. She and the undergraduate initially hit it off. But in his rooms later that evening, after a heavy supper of pasta and fish, the chemistry goes wrong and the sexual act misfires. He wakes in the morning,

> relieved to discover that the girl has gone; but an odd feeling, an unaccustomed tingling of the skin, a sensation of discomfort and unease around the heart, causes him, still on his back, to cast an eye over his person, whereupon he finds that she has left a little memento of herself – a Freudian gift, hard, compact, warm, in its own way perfectly formed, a faecal offering smelling of fish and pasta (of tagliatelle marinara) – nestling amongst the soft hairs of his chest, only inches from his gaping mouth.

The unfortunate undergraduate unburdens this tale to his friends. One amongst them – Leon Forelock – finds himself particularly intrigued, having never imagined that Australia contained girls 'capable of such erudition, athleticism and aplomb'.

Redback is not a novel for those with an easily tickled gag reflex. Like swimming, it should for safety's sake be undertaken at least two hours after eating. The nauseating tone of the work established, it continues in the form of an envenomed monologue, following the random progress of the hapless Leon. The Forelocks hail from 'Partington', the wettest spot in Europe. Leon goes to Malapert College, Cambridge, and wins a double-starred first in moral decencies. As the only non-homosexual attending the university, he is recruited by the CIA for covert service in Australia. There, it is his mission to dam the creeping tide of 'Tristanism', cultural sophistication that is sapping the country's robust philistinism. It's also an opportunity to crap on Aussies, which Leon enthusiastically does by setting up front organisations such as CACA – 'Campaign for a Cleaner Australia'.

The climax of Leon's Australian ordeal comes in a second encounter with his fatal woman, Desley, on the Bogong High Plains, where she is building a feminist community. But again the chemistry goes wrong. Having fortified himself with three bottles of Shiraz, Leon bursts, Mellors-like, into the lodge and announces: 'I have come back to fuck you, Desley.' She is nothing loath, but tells him first to use the non-sexist locution 'fuck with you'. Leon finds he has an inbuilt cultural incapacity to make the necessary verbal adjustment, so she tells him to 'fuck off'. Leon obediently stumbles out of the lodge into a storm. He takes refuge in a wooden dunny where, patiently, the redback's mandibles await him. The redback, we at last learn, is a poisonous spider, sister species to the better-known black widow. She (the sex is significant – only the females are venomous) bites Leon's exposed, dangling and unrequited member. Not funny ha, ha – but funny ouch, ouch.

Regeneration, Pat Barker, 1991

Barker (born in 1943) recalls that her interest in the First World War was inspired by a scar on her grandfather's body, visible when he stripped off for a wash at the family sink (we are not talking *Brideshead* here). She was told it was a bayonet wound, but he would not talk about it. My own grandfather lost an eye in the 'Great War'. He didn't talk about it either, and I, as a child, was too frightened to ask. He brought back from the war half-a-dozen brass-cased shells, which stood on shelves over the hob fire and which my grandmother polished every Friday afternoon along with the silver.

The non-combatant author writing about war faces the stern prohibition laid down by Richard Aldington (see DEATH OF A HERO): 'There are two kinds of men: those who have been to the front and those who haven't.' Those who haven't, it is implied, should choose some other topic for their fiction. And that, as regards the First World War, would seem to preclude all female authors.

Pat Barker's Booker Prize-winning novel is set well in the rear echelon, at the pioneering psychiatric hospital in Edinburgh which employed real-life psychiatrist William Rivers – a consultant familiar with the new-fangled ideas of Freud where broken minds were concerned. The specific mental ailment of the First World War was 'shell shock'. In the Second World War it would be 'battle fatigue', and after Vietnam 'PTSD'. In his thinking that mental war wounds could be as traumatic as physical injuries, Rivers was a trailblazer. In summer 1917, when *Regeneration* is set, he had two major figures in the history of English poetry, Siegfried Sassoon and Wilfred Owen, as patients at the Craiglockhart mental hospital. Sassoon was wangled into Craiglockhart ('Dottyville', as he called it) by another poet, Robert Graves, to avoid court-martial after he became increasingly pacifist, and – under the influence of Bertrand Russell – had declared, in a letter to *The Times*, 'in an act of wilful defiance', that the war was being deliberately prolonged. All three poets, who fought gallantly in the trenches, were of the same opinion in 1917. Each suffered from what Graves called 'the inward scream: the duty to run mad'. All three ran the risk of being despised, and punished, as cowards.

I wish I could read *Regeneration* with the innocence of those (many, I suspect, in the centenary years, 2014–18) who know little about the historical strands Barker artfully weaves into her narrative, because what one knows gets in the way of what she is doing. Take the opening of Chapter 11:

Sassoon was trying to decipher a letter from H. G. Wells when Owen knocked on his door.

'As far as I can make out, he says he's coming to see Rivers.'

Owen looked suitably impressed. 'He must be really worried about you.'

I can't help thinking at this point that Sassoon and Owen will be getting down to work in a day or two on 'Anthem for Doomed Youth' – I've seen reproductions of the scrawled-over manuscript. Fine poem. And, yes, Wells' handwriting really is indecipherable. I remember that from editing THE HISTORY OF MR POLLY. And what's Wells' 'new book' that Sassoon refers to a few lines later ? Must be, surely, *Mr Britling Sees It Through*. I simply can't read Barker's novel without all these distracting shadows passing over the text.

Regeneration is largely situational and is almost entirely set in Dottyville – the front is described only through the nightmare dreams of traumatised patients. There is little plot as such. Rivers' agonies of conscience supply a semblance of one: is he merely repairing shattered men to go back to war and be killed? One of the fictional characters has a love affair. Sublimated homosexual relations between the three poets are subtly implied. There's a horrific electro-convulsive therapy session. The war grinds on even more horrifically. Sassoon returns to the front and lives. Owen returns and dies – his family will receive the news on the day the bells are ringing for Armistice.

The Remains of the Day, Kazuo Ishiguro, 1989

It's not an English name, and the author was born in Nagasaki, but Kazuo Ishiguro understands the English better than any novelist living. And the English (he took British citizenship in 1982) revere him for it. The Remains of the Day won the Booker Prize in 1989 and, as a Merchant Ivory film, went on to be nominated for a clutch of Oscars four years later, only to lose out heavily to Schindler's List.

In outline it sounds like an unlikely prizewinner. The narrative takes the form of reminiscences by an ancient butler: a trusty but somewhat tongue-tied retainer at Darlington Hall. Stevens (butlers have no first names) is given a holiday, and permission to use the Hall's venerable Ford by Darlington's new American owner, Mr Farraday. Car keys in hand, Stevens resolves to make an 'expedition' to the West Country. There he will meet another former employee of the Hall – Miss Kenton, a housekeeper who left twenty years earlier. There was once a possibility the two of them might have been in love, but they fell out over an obscure below-stairs dispute. Their respective professional susceptibilities were mortally affronted. They have not communicated since she left in a huff. Stevens has recently begun to detect in himself 'small errors' in the performance of his duties. His edge has gone. He hopes that Miss Kenton (now Mrs Benn) can be persuaded to return to the Hall. With her help, he may be able to hold on a few years more. A letter from her, hinting at marital unhappiness, gives him grounds for hope that reconciliation is possible.

The novel takes the form of a six-day journal de voyage through mid-1950s England. The meeting with the former Miss Kenton in Weymouth is a disappointment. Her marriage is indeed unhappy; she has frequently walked out on her husband. But she has no intention of returning to the Hall:

My rightful place is with my husband. After all, there's no turning back the clock now. One can't be for ever dwelling on what might have been. One should realise one has as good as most, perhaps better, and be grateful.

Sound advice.

'At that moment, my heart was breaking', Stevens says. But he gives no sign of it. Butlers do not show their feelings. Imperturbability is the badge of all their tribe. His 'rightful place', he resolves, is at the Hall, where he will serve out his time as best he can. He takes strength from a chance encounter with a stranger whom he meets, walking along the sea front at evening. Stevens blurts out his misery. 'I gave my best to Lord Darlington. I gave him the very best I had to give, and now – well – I find I do not have a great deal more left to give.' His newfound friend advises: 'You've got to enjoy yourself. The evening's the best part of the day. You've done your day's work. Now you can put your feet up and enjoy it.' Duly bucked up, Stevens resolves to return to Mr Farraday's service in what he thinks of as a 'bantering' spirit. It is gallant but, as we apprehend, doomed. Stevens can no more banter than he can fly in the air.

Over the six days' confessions we gradually put together a portrait of the dignified, decaying, noble 'upper servant' – his little snobberies, intense professional pride, essential goodness, and ineradicable, but lovable, stupidity. It has, for example, entirely escaped his notice that his former master, Lord Darlington, was a Mosley-sympathising Fascist. Stevens, we deduce, is the best of 'his' England. An England that will, like him, soon be no more.

Revolutionary Road, Richard Yates, 1961

Those swept up in the early 1960s chic of the hit TV series Mad Men will find an antidote in Yates' story about Frank and April Wheeler. Yates' own life was a chronicle of self-willed failure and self-destructive waste – out of which came this first, and autobiographical, work.

After being discharged from the army after the war, with the most undistinguished of military records, Yates was, variously, a copywriter and a malcontent journalist. All the while he laboured at his own writing, which was all he really cared about. His best-paid day job was in the PR department of

Remington Rand, merchandisers of the first commercially viable computer (something that interested Yates not at all). He was trapped, like other Madison Avenue men in grey flannel suits, in a 'good job'. He married, entrapping himself further. His wife Sheila, a gifted woman who could possibly have done well on the stage, had settled for the life of a no-nonsense New York secretary. Their marriage produced two daughters before failing. It also generated the raw experience for the magnificent novel of suburban nightmare which is *Revolutionary Road*.

The Wheelers are young suburbanites in the 'house of their dreams' (in realtor-speak) on Revolutionary Road, Connecticut. April, passionate about the stage, joins a local drama society. A performance of *The Petrified Forest*, in which she has a leading role, flops. During a flaming row, Frank tells her: 'It's sure as hell not my fault you didn't turn out to be an actress', and, for good measure, that her 'imitation of Madame Bovary doesn't wash' with him. According to the 1950s rulebook they should be happy, but they are not. Frank 'commutes' (at the time a word totally mysterious to the British ear) to the Knox Business Machines headquarters in New York. The routine of salary slaves like him is sardonically described:

He did sleep on the train, riding with his head fallen back on the dusty plush and his *Times* sliding from his lap; and he stood for a long time over scalding cups of coffee in the echoing tan vault of Grand Central, allowing himself to be late for work. How small and neat and comically serious the other men looked, with their grey-flecked crew cuts and their button down collars and their brisk little hurrying feet! There were endless desperate swarms of them, hurrying through the station and the streets, and an hour from now they would all be still. The waiting midtown office buildings would swallow them up and contain them, so that to stand in one tower looking across the canyon to another would be to inspect a great silent insectarium displaying hundreds of tiny pink men in white shirts, forever shifting papers and frowning into telephones, acting out their passionate little dumb show under the supreme indifference of the rolling spring clouds.

One recalls T. S. Eliot describing the black-suited hordes flowing over London Bridge to their city offices and invoking Dante's 'I had not thought death had undone so many'. There is, for Frank, a grubby office romance with a secretary named Maureen Grube. For April, nothing but the imprisoning pinafore, childcare and meaningless *Kaffeeklatsch* mornings.

Revolutionary Road catches, almost before it had passed, the deep materialistic pointlessness of the Eisenhower 1950s (the 'you've never had it so good' era in Macmillan's UK). It was – there is no other word – ineffably boring. 'Soul-destroying' was the word used at the time:

Then it was Sunday, with the living room deep in the rustling torpor of Sunday newspapers, and no words had passed between Frank Wheeler and his wife for what seemed a year. She had gone alone to the second and final performance of *The Petrified Forest*, and afterwards had slept on the sofa again.

He was trying now to take his ease in an armchair, looking through the magazine section of the *Times*, while the children played quietly in the corner and April washed the dishes in the kitchen.

This is the 'American Dream'? In an interview Yates confided that the novel was intended to express the view that the road taken in 1776 had come, in the 1950s, to a 'dead end'. The narrative ends, horribly, with an abortion gone wrong. But so, to be honest, has everything else.

The Riddle of the Sands, Erskine Childers, 1903

A passionate yachtsman and a true British patriot, Childers had volunteered to fight in the Boer War and wrote a memoir (published in 1900) of his frustrating experiences, which mainly involved looking after horses. He returned to Britain opposed to the colonial war he had earlier thought worthwhile. But he retained a belief in the necessity of fighting 'just wars' and he apprehended, very early on, that a war of that kind was on its way.

As a novelist, Childers' principal, and abiding, achievement was his spy yarn, *The Riddle of the Sands*, published, to great sales success, a few years after his Boer memoir. It is subtitled *A Record of Secret Service* and written in pseudo-documentary style with accompanying maps. The chronicle which forms the narrative is dated '1903'. The hero-narrator is 'Carruthers of the Foreign Office'. He describes himself, with saving facetiousness, as 'a young man of condition and fashion, who knows the right people, belongs to the right clubs, has a safe, possibly a brilliant, future in the Foreign Office'.

Just at the moment the young man of condition and fashion is finding London tedious. It is late summer. The West End bores him and he longs for the four bracing winds of heaven and a little light relief from 'the dismal but dignified routine of office, club and chambers'. The 'big picture' is sketched in the background. Germany is secretly arming itself ('she grows, and strengthens, and waits').

Carruthers and his old college acquaintance, Arthur H. Davies, go off sailing the yacht *Dulcibella* in the sand-bar-bedevilled Baltic waters. There the young men stumble across, to their patriotic alarm, Germany's plans for the invasion of England. There is much accompanying descriptive detail of ropes, tackle and canvas. On their return, the Admiralty is informed. The necessary precautions must and will be taken against the wily Hun.

Childers' novel – simplistic as it is – can plausibly be credited with a number of achievements. The first is that it pioneered a genre – the spy/secret agent docu-novel. Secondly, it usefully (from the authorities' point of view) whipped up anti-German sentiment in the long run-up to the First World War. Thirdly, it inspired the creation of a number of naval bases on the North Sea coast, to increase British readiness for any

invasion from that direction. Winston Churchill, as first Lord of the Admiralty, was a staunch admirer of *The Riddle of the Sands*. A breathless postscript to the novel, dated March 1903 (a busy year, evidently), records:

> It so happens that while this book was in the press a number of measures have been taken by the Government to counteract some of the very weaknesses and dangers which are alluded to above.

And:

> Is it not becoming patent that the time has come for training all Englishmen systematically either for the sea or for the rifle?

Not even Winston was prepared to go that far. The notion of the burgeoning Labour Party with rifles at the ready was not to be contemplated.

After the war Childers settled in Southern Ireland in order to engage directly in the emergent state's confused and bloody politics. He opposed partition (as was agreed in the 1921 treaty with England) and joined the rebel Republican Army. He was captured, at his mother's house, by soldiers of the Irish Free State government. After a court martial in Dublin, on trumped-up charges of possessing an illegal weapon, he was shot by a firing party, with each member of whom, it is recorded, he cheerfully shook hands before his execution. He remains, as his biographer puts it, a 'riddle' – only his personal bravery is indisputable. And few novelists, with only one novel to their credit, can be said to have trademarked a whole genre.

Riders of the Purple Sage, Zane Grey, 1912

Zane Grey was, for a season, the most popular writer in the English-speaking world. At his zenith his American sales were reckoned to be second only to those of the Bible. He was one of only a few novelists, in the years 1915–30, to get 'Westerns' regularly into the

American bestseller lists. No one knows the exact figure, but his total lifetime and posthumous sales are calculated at around 250 million copies, which puts him in the stratosphere with Agatha Christie and Erle Stanley Gardner. Grey hit the jackpot with *Riders of the Purple Sage* (1912), the second of his chart-topping titles. As often happens with a genuinely innovative work, he had difficulty finding a publisher willing to take it. The book was eventually signed by the New York firm Harper, after the commissioning editor consulted his wife on the matter.

Riders of the Purple Sage has one of the best, and most imitated, openings in the history of Westerns. The narrative is set in 1871 (the year before the author's birth) and, as would become usual in Grey's stories, features a maiden in bondage. Jane Withersteen is heiress to a vast ranch among the purple sage of the Utah–Arizona border. She is a Mormon (somewhat lukewarm in her faith, it turns out) and is under siege from the lecherous and covetous 'Elder' Tull, who wants to make her one of his harem of wives (in film adaptations the Mormons tend to become Native Americans – pagan 'hostiles' both of them).

The action opens with a young 'rider' (a cow-puncher) about to be whipped by Tull, for the offence of being liked by Jane. It is, for the time and the place, a relatively mild punishment: Mormons, it is hinted, routinely castrate 'Gentiles' who hang around their women. But then:

The restless movements of Tull's men suddenly quieted down. Then followed a low whisper, a rustle, a sharp exclamation.

'Look!' said one, pointing to the west.

'A rider!'

Jane Withersteen wheeled and saw a horseman, silhouetted against the western sky, coming riding out of the sage. He had ridden down from the left, in the golden glare of the sun, and had been unobserved till close at hand. An answer to her prayer!

'Do you know him? Does anyone know him?' questioned Tull, hurriedly.

His men looked and looked, and one by one shook their heads.

'He's come from far,' said one.

'Thet's a fine hoss,' said another.

'A strange rider.'

'Huh! he wears black leather,' added a fourth.

With a wave of his hand, enjoining silence, Tull stepped forward in such a way that he concealed Venters.

The rider reined in his mount, and with a lithe forward-slipping action appeared to reach the ground in one long step. It was a peculiar movement in its quickness and inasmuch that while performing it the rider did not swerve in the slightest from a square front to the group before him.

'Look!' hoarsely whispered one of Tull's companions. 'He packs two black-butted guns – low down – they're hard to see – black akin them black chaps.'

'A gun-man!' whispered another.

This is Lassiter. One hears in the mind's ear a Sergio Leone jingle of notes. The stranger faces down Tull and his men and rescues Bern Venters from the Mormon lash.

Nothing in the subsequent plot matches the wonderful opening – but that alone was enough to create a genre formula. There is cattle rustling, gunplay, a masked rider who turns out to be a woman, and an exciting final chase in which the bad guys are cut off at the pass. The novel patented a veritable mine of what would become Hollywood clichés and, in the hands of directors of genius, like John Ford, the stuff of high art. Published a couple of years before the First World War – an event in which six-shooters were as irrelevant as pea-shooters – Gray's novel nostalgically looks back forty years to frontier days when 'men were... etc., etc.'. With Lassiter an archetype was born: the lone-wolf cowboy and gunman searching for something that he may never find (in Lassiter's case, an abducted sister); middle-aged and world-weary, but alert, hard and lean as whipcord; a man of few words, invincible in gunplay, and a dispenser of Solomonic justice. As portrayed first by Tom Mix, then by Randolph Scott, the Lassiter type descends directly to Clint Eastwood.

The Road, Cormac McCarthy, 2006

'This way the world ends'. If there were a catalogue of the gloomiest novels in this volume's round-up, McCarthy's novel would, for a certainty, head the list. Gloom sells (sometimes, if done well enough). *The Road* was a bestseller, won a shelf-full of prestigious literary prizes, and was adapted into an applauded film. Why McCarthy's novel should have hit the right note for the reading public in 2006 must remain a matter for speculation. But the fact that it carried what looked like visual flashbacks to lower Manhattan after 9/11, and that it distilled popular apprehension about climate change and its consequences, seem to point to plausible inspirations. The novel was hailed as a work of huge ecological significance by the leading eco-critic in the UK, George Monbiot, who saw it as a work of biblical significance. 'A few weeks ago', Monbiot wrote in October 2007,

> I read what I believe is the most important environmental book ever written. It is not *Silent Spring, Small is Beautiful* or even *Walden*. It contains no graphs, no tables, no facts, figures, warnings, predictions or even arguments. Nor does it carry a single dreary sentence, which, sadly, distinguishes it from most environmental literature. It is a novel, first published a year ago, and it will change the way you see the world.

McCarthy, Monbiot declared, was one of the fifty people who could save the planet. A heavy burden, one would have thought, for any novel to bear.

The story is as simple as a fable by Aesop, but considerably less cheerful. At 1.17 a.m., some years ago, something happened. The earth ceased to function as a biosphere – a planet with life. It died. It is said that lice on a human body survive for a day on a human corpse. That is a fitting metaphor for the condition of the two principal characters in *The Road*. A nameless man (he does not need his name – such things are no longer useful) is accompanied by his son as they make their way south to escape the cold. The man's wife committed suicide some time ago. What possessions the two travellers have are trundled along in a supermarket trolley (I suspect readers will remember *The Road*, as I do, every time they see a person homeless on the street doing the same – with the unspoken thought, 'the future of the human race').

Nothing grows any more. There is no vegetation or animal life; no seasons. Some fungoids seem to survive, along with *Homo sapiens*, who – the novel implies but does not explicitly state – is responsible for the planetary mess. The man and the boy make do on canned food they scavenge. They are the 'good guys'. The 'bad guys' have degenerated into cannibalism. There are horrific scenes, including one of a baby being turned on a spit like a barbecue chicken.

The man is spitting blood. He may be poisoned by the polluted air. But it is clear he is dying. His one purpose in what life remains to him is to protect his son. For what? They come to the end of the road at the sea. The man dies. Keeping watch over the corpse, the boy meets up with a family of 'good guys' who take him under their wing. The novel ends with a prose anthem to a world that is no more, and never will be again:

> Once there were brook trout in the streams in the mountains. You could see them standing in the amber current where the white edges of their fins wimpled softly in the flow. They smelled of moss in your hand. Polished and muscular and torsional. On their backs were vermiculate patterns that were maps of the world in its becoming. Maps and mazes. Of a thing which could not be put back. Not be made right again. In the deep glens where they lived all things were older than man and they hummed of mystery.

McCarthy dedicated the novel to his son. Let's hope young John Francis McCarthy lives to be a trout-fishing grandfather.

The Road to Wellville,
T. Coraghessan Boyle, 1993

The Road to Wellville is founded on a strange historical coincidence. At the turn of the century in Battle Creek, Michigan, the American breakfast food industry and the American health food industry sprang up side by side, destined to mingle for ever after.

The pioneers were the Kellogg brothers, who became deadly enemies after 1906, and their great rival Charles W. Post, who supposedly stole the ideas for Postum decaffeinated coffee and Grape Nuts from the Kelloggs. Post was the author of a booklet whose name tickled T. C. Boyle's fancy, 'The Road to Wellville'.

Boyle's central character is the dynamic but unlovable Dr John Harvey Kellogg, inventor of the cornflake, peanut butter and some 'seventy-five other gastrically correct foods'. He was swindled out of the cornflake franchise by his brother, Will. Not a man to surrender easily, John Kellogg went on to pour his energies into the Battle Creek Sanatorium (founded on the principles of the Seventh Day Adventists). With its programme of 'biologic living', the John Kellogg Sanatorium proclaimed itself the 'single healthiest spot on the planet', attracting such rich and famous patrons as Henry Ford (inventor of the cheap assembly-line-manufactured automobile), Harvey Firestone (inventor of the cheap rubberised automobile tyre), Thomas Edison (inventor of every damn thing you can think of), Upton Sinclair (see THE JUNGLE) and Johnny Weissmuller (Olympic Champion swimmer and the screen's most famous Tarzan). It was an all-American kind of place, devoted to the wellbeing of the intestine. John Kellogg, it is said, did for the alimentary canal what de Lesseps did for the Suez Canal. The author of 'The Itinerary of a Breakfast', he believed, fanatically, in complete bowel cleanliness and speedy throughput. One scene in The Road to Wellville has the ingenuous hero discovering that Kellogg's Bulgarian yoghurt diet involves not just eating the goo but having it shoved up him as an enema five times a day. He subsequently, and against his will, has his intestines shortened surgically for faster more efficient excretion. A shorter itinerary for the breakfast.

Kellogg retained from his Adventist upbringing a fundamentalist horror of alcohol, tobacco, caffeine and sex (in the novel he has forty-two children, thirty-two of whom were fostered and eight adopted).

His great sales gimmick was scientific apparatus. The Road to Wellville lingers over the description of such things as sinusoidal baths, Universal Dynamometers, and radium therapies (whose beneficiaries mysteriously turn green and die). Boyle himself admits to a past 'haunted by drug and alcohol demons', and does not like sanatoria (traditionally thought of as detox centres). One suspects he is not a great one for healthy breakfasts, either.

As cultural archaeology, The Road to Wellville fascinates. It throws satiric light on the odd link between the American breakfast and moral purity – the sense that by crunching matutinal cornflakes (soggies, shredded wheat, rice crispies, whatever) and swilling it down with 'decaf', you are a step nearer to saving your soul or, at least, making yourself a better person. Little matter that lab rats fare better on a diet of the cardboard box, that the milk furs your arteries, sugar drives up your blood pressure (stopping only in its 'itinerary' to decay your teeth), and decaf is suspected of being carcinogenic (as are the aflatoxins in peanut butter).

Boyle's novel works brilliantly as social history. The actual plot elements are correspondingly perfunctory: pegs on which to hang amusing things. The plot is diffused. At times the centre of things seems to be John Kellogg and his Oedipal struggle with his bad-seed adoptive son, George. At other points interest focuses on an amiable con-man, Charlie Ossining, who is touting a hopeless celery-flavoured breakfast food ('Perks up Tired Blood and Exonerates the Bowels!') that even hogs won't look at. In another part of the narrative, space is given to Eleanor and Will Lightbody, patients at the sanatorium. She falls into the hands (literally) of the unscrupulous Dr Spitzvogel, a specialist in therapeutic manipulation of the womb. The couple finally escape into a happy-ever-after of eggs-and-bacon breakfasts. Read this novel and you'll never thoughtlessly crunch another cornflake.

Robinson Crusoe, Daniel Defoe, 1719

If Daniel Defoe had died in 1718 he would be remembered as a prolific pamphleteer and pioneering English journalist. Living as he did until 1731, he ranks as a founding father of English fiction. Why, in his fifties (a great age in the eighteenth century), did he turn to writing novels? The biographical answer is that he was short of cash. The sociological answer that the rise of the novel is contemporaneous with the rise of capitalism. Defoe had, in one of his many different undertakings, been a 'speculator' – a player on the newly established London Stock Market. He was not successful. A scheme to harvest musk (from the anuses of civet cats) was unproductive, and he was arrested in 1692 for debts that may have been as high as £17,000 (around £680,000 in today's money). As the rise of the novel/rise of capitalism argument has it, Robinson Crusoe – marooned on his island, making his fortune by his own efforts – is a new (novel) kind of man for a new (novel) kind of economic system. He is '*Homo economicus*'. Defoe's novel is inextricably connected with what was going on financially in the City of London at the time of writing – in the counting houses, banks, shops, warehouses, offices and the docks on the Thames. It was an age of mercantilism and entrepreneurship.

The story of *Robinson Crusoe* is familiar, in outline, even to those who have not read the novel. A young man falls out with his merchant father and runs away to sea without a penny to his name. He becomes, after various adventures, a trader. Among the goods he trades in are slaves, coffee, and other things worth transporting between the old and new worlds. On one of his trading voyages from Brazil, Robinson's merchant ship is wrecked by a terrible storm. All the crew perish and he finds himself marooned on a desert island off the mouth of the Orinoco River in South America for twenty-seven years. Having made it to shore with nothing but the clothes he stands up in, he colonises the island. How does Robinson do this? By entrepreneurship – by (literally) making a fortune

from exploiting the island's natural resources. This ordeal encourages him to renew his faith in God. In fact, he believes that his Maker has placed him here, and approves of what he – Robinson – has done on the island. It is God's work as well as his own. We are now in the territory of Max Weber's Protestant ethic. God loves money-makers.

This economic-sociological interpretation does not explain the magic of Defoe's novel – its attraction, for example, for juvenile readers. It's an adventure story, after all. More interesting is the technique Defoe employs. The book was published as an 'authentic' tale – as the story of Alexander Selkirk's sojourn on a desert island (published seven years before *Robinson Crusoe*) was authentic. There are many delights for the modern reader in the book. For the younger reader: cannibals, shipwrecks, escape from slavery (and no sex whatsoever). For post-colonial critics, Robinson's illuminating relationship with his chattel (but not slave) Friday. And for lovers of sly fiction, such scenes as when Robinson is taking what he can from the wreck of his ship, for use on his new island home. He gives us a pedantically exact inventory of what he salvages. Revealingly, in the captain's cabin he finds £36. While noting that it will not be useful on the island, and that taking it will be theft, he spends a paragraph sermonising on the moral worthlessness of lucre. Then he takes the money. *Homo economicus* through and through.

Room at the Top, John Braine, 1957

I can date the precise moment I stopped using hair cream, which, up to that point, I had slathered on by the pot-full in homage to the Brylcreem Boy, dashing cricketer Denis Compton. What rendered my post-March 1957 cranium for ever unpomaded was the scene in *Room at the Top* where the upper-class Alice Aisgill runs her fingers through the working-class Joe Lampton's locks with the instruction to lose the hair-oil. 'Too too Palais de Danse, darling', she drawls. Remember that, Sutherland, I thought. You'll never get a sophisticated lady with gunk dripping like axle-grease from your bonce. And better give up the Palais, as well. For those wanting to be 'an angry young man', yet also 'cool', *Room at the Top* wasn't a novel – it was a how-to manual.

Braine had terrific trouble getting his novel published. It took him years. Eventually it was taken on by Eyre & Spottiswoode, who expected little attention to be paid. The author had no track record, and had laboriously hacked out the text over years in a TB sanatorium and at the Bradford Writers' Circle – not renowned in London publishing circles as a nursery of literary genius. To their surprise, the publishers discovered they had a runaway bestseller on their hands. The reading world had been, it was clear, waiting for *Room at the Top*. Eyre & Spottiswoode prefaced this most explosive of novels with a statement of comical pusillanimity: 'This book', they informed the prospective purchaser, 'is about the violence which a young man does to himself and to others in his struggle to rise above the world of his childhood.' Was it hell! The power of *Room of the Top* – what propelled it into bestsellerdom (readers of my age leading the way) – was its furious assault on the 'establishment'. And its chronicle of how a northern oick – with nothing but energy, good looks, native intelligence and vengeful ruthlessness – could, at this finally liberated point in English history, do a lot of violence to his class' traditional masters. Payback for a thousand years of oppression was what the novel angrily celebrated. The underdog's angry bark and bite.

The story is simple. Joe Lampton was born working-class in Depression-blighted Dufton – a place so polluted, he bitterly recalls, that the snow was black before it settled on the spittle-and-fag-end-coated pavements. His parents were killed in an air raid. Joe had a 'good war' in a POW camp. Not for him any 'officer-class' Colditz nonsense. He took an external qualification in accountancy behind the wire. On his return he got a promising job in the Municipal Treasury at Warley (clearly Braine's Bradford).

The novel opens with him arriving there by train – with a new trench coat and trilby, and a fierce resolve to rise in the world. He has got a room in an upper-class area of town, 'the Top', with an upper-class family, the Thompsons. Mr Lampton is not a 'lodger' but a 'PG' – paying guest. He joins the local amateur 'dram-soc' and thereafter becomes embroiled with two women: Alice Aisgill, married to a local potentate, and Susan Brown, the ingenuous daughter of the local magnate. The cuckolded husband and the protective father represent risks to a mere clerk. Joe loves both women. When Susan gets pregnant he (reluctantly) jilts Alice, who kills herself in a car accident – horribly. After a remorseful binge, Joe is driven off to the wedding and what he came to Warley to get: a future life at the top. It's like ashes in his mouth:

> Eva drew my head on to her breast. 'Poor darling, you mustn't take on so. You don't see it now, but it was all for the best. She'd have ruined your whole life. Nobody blames you, love. Nobody blames you.'
>
> I pulled myself away from her abruptly. 'Oh my God,' I said, 'that's the trouble.'

The 'gained the world but lost his soul' plot is merely a vehicle for the novel's 'sod you all' attitudinising. It doesn't work now, but it worked a treat in March 1957.

Rose Madder, Stephen King, 1995

When he was in one of what he called his 'fire-storms' King was capable of turning out as many as three big books in two years, making himself in the process a millionaire twenty times over. But more interesting than his hard-charging earning power is the fact that he has never been a formulaic crowd-pleaser. In fact, he hates the constrictions of genre fiction. In MISERY he wrote a novel about the tyranny of the 'number one fan' and the necessity imposed on the popular author of endlessly 'playing it again'. King earnestly wanted, throughout his career, to develop and play something different with every new novel. *Rose Madder* was very different. The fans didn't much like it, although as the web certifies, it was well regarded by some women readers. By the time he wrote the novel, King had come a long way from the horror-factory stereotypes of *Carrie* (1974). His technique had improved and the under-lying vision of his work matured. When, decades hence, the tell-all biography of the late Stephen King is published, it will be interesting to see why he became a feminist in the 1990s. That is what is at the heart of the book

On the face of it, *Rose Madder* recycles the plot of *The Shining* – immortalised not merely by the 1977 novel but by Stanley Kubrick's film (which King, reportedly, disliked). In that novel a demented, axe-wielding husband stalks his terrified wife and child through the corridors of a deserted Colorado hotel. In *Rose Madder*, a homicidal husband stalks his runaway wife, 'rambling Rose', who has left fourteen years of marital hell and gone to ground in a women's refuge in an unnamed big city (recognisably Chicago – unusual terrain for New Englander King).

In *The Shining*, the wife-killer is a novelist with writer's block who is, despite his demons, no bad guy (this paradox of likeable axe-murderer was hammed up magnifi-cently by Jack Nicholson in Kubrick's film). In *Rose Madder*, the stalker-husband, Norman Daniels, is a cross between Norman Bates and Hannibal Lecter: a cannibalistic, sexual-psychopathic, 'nigger-hating' (his obnoxious phrase) bad cop whose greatest pleasure in life is delivering kidney punches to his wife, beating up suspects, and tearing the breasts off prostitutes for supper. Not even the thespian art of Jack Nicholson could generate a shred of sympathy for the unspeakable Officer Daniels.

One of the implications in the punning title is that only when she gets murderously mad can Rose free herself from her brute of a mate. Rage and violence liberate her. The reader inwardly cheers as Norman gets his testicles righteously scrunched, his nose broken (twice), his jaw dislocated, is urinated on by a three-hundred-pound black lesbian (with a heart of gold and a bladder the size of the Goodyear blimp), and is finally devoured by the biggest, baddest black-widow spider that King's imagination can devise, as the novel – which began ultra-realistically – goes through the looking-glass into terminal surreality.

What is disturbing (at least to male readers) about this work is the implication that Norman is not a monster, he is everyman. More specifically he is every husband taken to his logical extreme. The women with leading roles in *Rose Madder* have all been abused by their partners, and are all good, gentle people whose mission in life is to help each other. With the excep-tion of the Woody Allen-ish pawnbroker with whom Rose finally ends up, all the men in the novel are lesser versions of Norman – but brothers under the skin. As Rose's alter ego tells her: 'Men are beasts. Some can be gentled and then trained. Some cannot.' For 'trained' read 'gelded'. For 'some cannot' read 'must be put down like mad dogs'. King never came up with a madder dog than Norman.

Salman the Solitary, Yashar Kemal, 1997

Say 'First World War' and what, precisely, does 'world' mean? French trenches if we have read REGENERATION; the Russian front if we have read AUGUST 1914; the Italo-Austrian campaign if we have read *A Farewell to Arms*; desert sands if we have seen David Lean's film, *Lawrence of Arabia*, or read *The Seven Pillars of Wisdom*. Few Anglophones, however well read, have any mental image of the domestic repercussions of the 'war called great' in Turkey. Yet it is on the Turkish–Iraqi border that one of the most corrosive residues of the conflict remains today, in the form of the 'Kurdish problem' – those luckless people dispossessed from 1914–18 and tossed about in every regional conflict since. As I write, they are streaming, 10,000 a day, out of Syria to another country (Iraq) which is not their own.

Salman the Solitary is a story of village life set against two cataclysms. One is the defeat at Sarikamish in 1915, which cost the Turks an estimated 23,000 dead and sealed the downfall of the Ottoman Empire eight years later. The other is the 'Great Crime' – the Armenian genocide (as Turkey prefers us not to call it). Yashar Kemal's novel never, as far as I can tell, directly mentions the First World War, but that conflict affects, disastrously, the little lives of all the principal characters he chronicles.

Kemal's narrative loops and twists in imitation of oral tale-telling. The central strand is the story of a good man, the Kurd Ismail Agha. He is a bey's (potentate's) nephew, and his clan lived in pre-war harmony with their ethnic neighbours under the mountains by Lake Van. This delicate harmony is shattered, for ever, by rampaging deserters from the front – Turkish soldiers turned dogs of war. Ismail, with the women of his family, takes flight. Eventually they find asylum in a village on the fertile plains of Chukurova. Ismail nobly refuses to take over any of the numerous houses vacated by the massacred Armenians. As his mother says, 'No bird will find rest in another's blighted nest.' Once settled, Ismail impoverishes himself to help other needy Kurdish immigrants. 'God rewards a good deed in the end' (this novel is rich in proverbs), and over the years he prospers and again becomes a great man in his little world. On his flight from Lake Van, Ismail picked up an apparently dying child. The women in the family clean the waif, pick the maggots from his wounds (there is a lot of strong stuff in this novel), and bring him back to life. Salman attaches himself fanatically to his 'father' and grows up to become Ismail's feared bodyguard. The only rival for Salman's loyalty is his bay filly, with whom – after puberty – he has daily sexual intercourse (strong stuff, as I say). The plot thickens with the arrival of a child of Ismail's loins, Mustafa. Salman is displaced as Ismail's favourite. Sibling rivalry in Turkistan is more readily solved by the dagger than the psychoanalyst's couch.

Kemal's narrative is occasionally baffling, dipping as it does into choric depictions of the susurrus of malicious village gossip and subplots dealing with the vendettas that interrupt the tranquil rhythms of rural life. And the chronology – lacking our familiar historical markers – is disorientating. One seems to be in a medieval world, and then a Ford car chugs across the scene reminding us that, 6,000 miles away, it is the Jazz Age and Scott Fitzgerald is drinking too much.

The real challenge is getting hold of the dynamics of tribalism – the relative placings of Turcoman, Kurd, Yoruk, Armenian, Yedizi, Alevi, and the occasional Arab. It's worth the effort. Reckoned to be Turkey's greatest living novelist, Kemal is also a human-rights warrior of heroic stature. He was born in 1923 in a village on the plains of Chukurova, and presumably much of *Salman the Solitary* is, if not autobiographical, derived from personal recollection. First published in 1980, the novel was translated in the late 1990s into English, its tragic relevance underlined by the resurgence of the Kurdish problem. For that part of the world, the First World War goes on. Few notice.

Sardines, Nuruddin Farah, 1981

Female genital mutilation became a headline issue in Britain in the second decade of the twenty-first century. There were frequent stories (many extremely harrowing) and much fist-banging comment in newspapers; help websites were set up; campaigns were organised to suppress the hideous practice. The previously current neutral terms 'clitoridectomy' and 'female circumcision' were universally dropped, in favour of the wholly condemnatory 'FGM'. But oddly, although since 1985 an estimated 3,000–4,000 procedures of wholly criminal 'cutting' have taken place every year among immigrant communities in the UK on girls as young as four (typically carried out with razor blades or scissors, without anaesthetic, by medically unqualified practitioners, mainly female), not a single court case has been brought. It is tolerance by legal paralysis – or self-inflicted blindness.

Somalian novels are rare birds in the English-speaking world. Farah is one of the few novelists from that country with an international profile. The 'sardines' of the title are a group of contemporary Mogadishu 'priviligentsia'. What cramps their Westernised cosmopolitan style, like the tiny fish in the tiny tin, is the police state in which they live (tyrannised over by an unnamed 'General') and the tribal traditions of a recent feudal past. They are, however, sardines – not martyrs. The novel takes as its epigraph Ho Chi Minh's ironic:

Being chained is a luxury.
The chained have somewhere to
    sleep
The unchained have not.

They get by, like the chorus in T. S. Eliot's *Murder in the Cathedral*, 'living and half-living'.

The novel's heroine, Medina, has thrown off the chains of marriage and deserted her husband, taking her eight-year-old daughter with her. Her abandoned spouse is a well-meaning, time-serving politician, feebly hoping to 'humanise' from within the regime he serves. She is a tough, westernised journalist. There are two reasons for her leaving the marriage – and all that goes with it. One reason is that she intends to write a book critical of the General (for the same reason, she has withdrawn her daughter from school, where she will only learn ninety-nine ways of praising the father of

the revolution). The second reason is that she has resolved that she will not allow her daughter to be circumcised by another dictator, her mother-in-law:

If they mutilate you at eight or nine, they open you up with a rusty knife the night they marry you off; then you are cut open and re-stitched. Life for a circumcised woman is a series of deflowering pains, delivery pains and re-stitching pains. I want to spare my daughter these and many other pains. She will not be circumcised.

Nothing much happens in the novel beyond the tracing of various tensions and frustrations. It ends with a minor purge. The husband is disgraced, beaten up and reconciled with his wife. There are deportations and possibly executions to come. The General remains, remote and patriarchally irremovable. Circumcision, matriarchally irremovable, goes on, but perhaps Medina's daughter will be spared. Perhaps. The novel leaves the outcome in the air.

Much has happened in Somalia since 1981, none of it good: it is one of the unhappier places in the world. But the practice of FGM remains a sanctioned and honoured institution. It is estimated that ninety-nine per cent of young girls in Somalia undergo it. Farah's novel artfully defines the critical issues that the practice raises. It is practised almost exclusively by women on women. Historically FGM was put down by colonial powers – prohibition led by Christian missionaries who found it an abomination. In the struggles of colonially oppressed countries, notably Kenya, it was aggressively revived during the period of insurgency as an assertion of cultural independence. Kenya's best-known – and defiantly post-colonial – novelist, Ngugi wa Thiong'o, has taken up what many see as an ambiguous position on the practice. In short, it's a fiendishly difficult issue. Farah's novel diagnoses the difficulty with a great novelist's sensitivity. Fiction is one of the few places where the complexities can be fully articulated.

The Satanic Verses, Salman Rushdie, 1988

On 14 January 1989 something unusual happened. A significant section of the population of Bradford became interested in a recently published novel (one which had received distinctly tepid reviews in the London press) and took to the streets to express their excitement. So excited were the Bradfordians that they burned the novel publicly, having first paraded it through the streets of the city, tied to a stake. The media were forewarned. Petrol does more for book promotion than a lead review in The Times or a big advertising budget, and the novel caught fire (literally). CNN picked up the event. Riots ensued in the Indian subcontinent. On St Valentine's Day, 1989, the author received – from the paramount leader of Iran, Ayatollah Khomeini – a 'love letter' in the form of a fatwa. Salman Rushdie relished the irony, and later inscribed it into the opening chapter of The Ground Beneath Her Feet (1999). He was echoing the ironic comment of Jean Cocteau that harsh criticisms of literature are the love letters of disappointed suitors. The word 'fatwa' was not one hitherto familiar in Western discourse; thanks to Rushdie, it will now for ever feature in everyday speech.

The unprecedentedly offensive novel was, of course, The Satanic Verses. The narrative opens with a symbolic episode. An Air India jumbo jet (named after one of the gardens of Paradise) explodes. Two Indians fall 29,002 feet on to Hastings – that historic beach where William the Conqueror ate his symbolic mouthful of sand before gobbling up the whole country. Gibreel Farishta and Saladin Chamcha are, like William, illegal immigrants. Or angel and devil. Or Hindu and Muslim antitypes. Christian resurrection is also invoked: "'To be born again," sang Gibreel Farishta tumbling from the heavens, "first you have to die."'

Mid-air explosions which slaughter hundreds of infidels were not, per se, enough to distress the Ayatollah Khomeini, the paramount religious ruler of Iran – now a rigid theocracy. What drew down his wrath was: (1) an impudent depiction of his fundamentalist self in The Satanic Verses; (2) an even more satirical depiction of the Prophet, under the insulting Western name 'Mahound'; (3) the implication that an earlier version of the sacred text, containing a concession to polytheism (these are the 'satanic verses' – inserted maliciously by Satan), had been added strategically, before absolute monotheism could be confidently insisted on; (4) the fictional allegation that the text of the Qur'an had been rephrased, after it emerged from the mouth of the Prophet, by a Persian scribe called 'Salman' (in fact the historical Salman Farsi, but Rushdie hints at another of that name):

> Little things at first. If Mahound recited a verse in which God was described as all-hearing, all-knowing, I would write, all-knowing, all-wise. Here's the point: Mahound did not notice the alterations. So there I was, actually writing the Book, or rewriting, anyway, polluting the word of God with my own profane language.

Rushdie's aim, as one interprets it, was not heresy but to suggest the same kind of imagination at work in the Muslim holy text that German 'New Criticism' had found, over a hundred years earlier, in the Bible. Put another way, the holy book was not unalloyed Revelation but the Almighty's novel. This, as Rushdie explained, was not to defame, or devalue: merely to argue that the Qu'ran could be believed in, and made sense of, by non-fundamentalist disciplines. It could even be played with.

Sacrilege is a risky profession. The fatwa against Rushdie laid on every devout Muslim the obligation to kill the apostate. The author was bundled into protective custody by Britain's Special Branch, under instruction from Mrs Thatcher – 'Mrs Torture' in the novel. No deep symbolism there. It was wormwood for the ruling Tory Party. Geoffrey Howe, foreign secretary in 1989, observed that 'The British government, the British people, do not have any affection for the book . . . It compares Britain with Hitler's Germany.' Diplomatic relations with Iran broke down. Rushdie would spend years in the ground beneath the world's feet. As his friend Martin Amis wittily put it: 'He vanished into the front page.' Salman Rushdie's own view was that it was like 'a bad Salman Rushdie novel'. In my opinion there aren't any.

Saturday Night and Sunday Morning, Alan Sillitoe, 1958

Sillitoe's first novel, *Saturday Night and Sunday Morning* has never (unlike every one of his other novels) been out of print. It takes the form of a long interior monologue by a new and interesting social animal: a worker of the world who thinks for himself, in a kind of eloquent primitivism.

The conclusion Arthur Seaton has reached, from twenty-one years' experience of the world around him, is that the only thing that matters in life is a good time. Sex, drink, and smart togs that catch a lady's eye. The rest – including the beneficence of the post-war welfare state – is just propaganda. In the favoured word of the period, Arthur is a 'rebel'. But (contrary to the fifties proverb) he does indeed have a cause. He embodies the intelligent, explosive, clear-eyed anarchism always latent in the working classes:

> Once a rebel, always a rebel. You can't help being one. You can't deny that. And it's best to be a rebel so as to show 'em it don't pay to try to do you down. Factories and labour exchanges and insurance offices keep us alive and kicking – so they say – but they're booby-traps and will suck you under like sinking-sands if you aren't careful. Factories sweat you to death, labour exchanges talk you to death, insurance and income tax offices milk money from your wage packets and rob you to death. And if you're still left with a tiny bit of life in your guts after all this boggering about, the army calls you up and you get shot to death. And if you're clever enough to stay out of the army you get bombed to death. Ay, by God, it's a hard life if you don't weaken, if you don't stop that bastard government from grinding your face in the muck,

though there ain't much you can do about it unless you start making dynamite to blow their four-eyed clocks to bits.

Fifties censorship blanked out the four-letter words one can nonetheless hear unsaid.

The action is set in Nottingham, which was then (the early 1950s) throbbing with industrial life – there were the historically famed lace workshops, the Player's cigarette factory and the Raleigh bicycle works, where Arthur, with National Service well behind him, operates a capstan lathe, pulling in a cool thousand a year with overtime (Britain still largely travelled on two wheels then). He has the wardrobe of the young working swell of the day: Slim Jim ties, Hardy Amies shirts, houndstooth jackets, chukka boots. All the gear. The novel opens with a Saturday drinking competition in a working men's club. Heroic quantities are downed – a dozen pints and more. Arthur wins and celebrates with a bedroom romp with his mistress – his mate Jack's wife, Brenda. When Brenda's not available he makes do with her married sister, Winnie. Life is good.

Life is less good after he gets Brenda pregnant. There's a messy abortion (gin, a hot bath, and blood), and Winnie's husband gives Arthur a beating. He complicates things by falling in love with (and marrying) a 'good girl', Doreen. Saturnalian Saturday nights are one thing. It's now the Sunday hangover. No more good times. 'Revolution' is, at best, five years from adolescence to 'maturity'. *Dolce vita* Nottingham-style. No wonder the unfairness of it makes young men angry. The system has won. It always does.

Saturday Night and Sunday Morning has dated more than the majority of AYM (Angry Young Men) tracts. Nottingham is now as different as Mars. If he were alive now, Arthur would probably have been on the dole for the last twenty years of his (un) working life. Adolescence is nowadays a much richer, more complicated business. But the raw energy of Sillitoe's novel still leaps off every page.

Saville, David Storey, 1976

The primal scene in David Storey's fiction (and, as it happens, my own erratic life) is to be found in this Booker-winning novel. Colin Saville, a miner's son, brought up during the war in the South Yorkshire village of Saxton, is taking his eleven-plus for selection to the local grammar school. The exam carries with it the sense of destiny implied by that concentration camp euphemism: 'selection'. Storey vividly evokes the huge, echoing, dusty examination rooms, the ink-stained desks, the shepherding, numbering and mysterious instructions, the nervy atmosphere of remembered threats and bribes, the sense of an inscrutable authority, the pointless questions designed to measure IQ ('How many other words can you make from the word "Conversation"?'). For those who underwent it, the eleven-plus was an experience recalling Beckett's 'Do not despair; one of the thieves was saved. Do not presume; one of the thieves was damned.' A right or wrong answer to an enigmatic question would determine the rest of your life.

Born in 1933, Storey himself took the exam in 1944, the year in which the Butler Education Act came into force. He was one of Beckett's saved and made it to Queen Elizabeth's Grammar School in Wakefield. The problems of a boy like Storey were anatomised by Richard Hoggart in the last chapters of his survey of modern British culture, The Uses of Literacy (1957). As it fed through to the creative writing of the sixties, the grammar-school boy's educated self-alienation gave rise to a lexicon of fashionable literary terms – 'roots' (invariably cut off), 'outsiders', 'rebel' (as in 'without a cause') and 'anger' (as in 'Angry Young Man').

Colin loses his accent (richly laid on in the early chapters). He begins to 'talk proper'. With that loss, a link to the historical past is severed. He is now adrift. 'Grammar school broke him in two,' Storey says of another of his heroes, Leonard Radcliffe. The abstract term 'deracination' doesn't catch the complexity of that break. Grammar-school education was a gateway to good things (as defined in terms of folk memories of the bad things of the 1930s): security, a steady, well-paid job, house ownership, a car, a body undestroyed by physical labour – all the amenities of 'cushy' middle-class life. But upward mobility meant class exile.

The grammar school recurs in Storey's fiction. Typically, having been crammed for the 'scholarship' and pushed into the school by his miner father, the Storey hero loses his way. He is bolshie, good at the wrong sports (he despises Rugby Union i.e. gent's football), plays truant and makes unsuitable friendships. He doesn't go to university (though he could) but to art college, the bohemian alternative, with its greater freedoms and less certain social destiny – 'the flight into Camden', as Storey called it. All this is chronicled in Saville; the archetypal Storey novel. Would the hero have been happier working in the pits than as a teacher in a classroom (a 'master', so-called)? Which is the 'manlier'?

The Storey hero such as Colin invariably finds himself at bay within society. His intelligence has promoted him, but has not given him the tools for survival. Physically, he is a wounded animal and the more dangerous for it. He has a craggy face, with some prominently broken feature (a bent nose, missing teeth). He often bears an ostentatiously Brontëan name in which 'cliffs' and 'heaths' are directly or remotely recalled (here 'savage'). He never 'belongs'. The problem is that mobility can take you in any number of directions. Which is the right direction for a grammar-school boy – up, down or sideways? Storey's novels explore various possibilities and destinations. Angrily and inconclusively.

Saville ends with the memorable Storeyism, 'The shell had cracked.' Colin makes his break, turning, like Paul Morel in Sons and Lovers, towards the light of the city on the hill. He's done with school-mastering. 'You haven't any lodgings or anything,' his lachrymose mother tells him, as he prepares to catch the train to London with nothing but a suitcase and fifty pounds. 'I don't need lodgings,' Saville replies, 'I can always sleep on the street.'

The 'Tripartite' education system associated with the eleven-plus was abolished in the same year as Saville was published. Nine years later Mrs Thatcher's victory over the miners in 1985 destroyed the mining village culture the first twelve chapters of Saville chronicle.

The Sea, John Banville, 2005

It's an unusual moment for literary historians when they feel they are making, rather than recording, literary history. It has happened to me just once: which is more, I suspect, than happens to many in my profession. In the final voting round of the Man Booker Prize in 2005, the five-person panel were split 2/2 between Banville's novel and Kazuo Ishiguro's *Never Let Me Go*. I had the deciding vote and, after a thoughtful moment, cast it for *The Sea*. Banville's standing, with the world's most prestigious fiction prize on his mantelpiece, shot up. I felt, for a moment, like a thumbs up/thumbs down Roman emperor. Ishiguro, in conversation with me later, observed smilingly, 'the goalkeeper jumped the wrong way'.

The Sea is short, grounded on the novelist's usual belief that although it is lived forward, life is only understood backwards – in hindsight. And the best time to understand what one's life amounts to is the moment when any forward progress has stalled and one is on the threshold of terminal darkness. As in detective novels, denouement comes on the last page, before the ominous word 'finis'. In this novel, that final moment is symbolised by a solitary, crocked old man, standing on a beach, looking at the indifferent sea. Behind him is the place where the most important event of his life happened. He does not, yet, quite understand that event. But he will.

Two Irish influences meet in Banville: Beckett and Joyce. His prose is florid but the situation of *The Sea* is quite as minimal as *Krapp's Last Tape* or MALONE DIES. A passage describing what is, titularly, the subject of the novel demonstrates the 'Joycett', so to call it, quality of Banville's prose (his main concern as a writer, he confesses, is to write well):

All morning under a milky sky the waters in the bay had swelled and swelled, rising to unheard-of heights, the small waves creeping over parched sand that for years had known no wetting save for rain and lapping the very bases of the dunes. The rusted hulk of the freighter that had run aground at the far end of the bay longer ago than any of us could remember must have thought it was being granted a relaunch.

It's simultaneously rich and bleak, leaving a strange taste on the tongue.

The narrator-hero Max Morden is a widowed art historian – his life is decoding pictures. His wife, Anna, has just died of cancer. He handled it badly. He is alienated from his daughter, Claire; nothing major, they just don't get on. He has returned (why?) to a seedy boarding house by the sea, The Cedars at Ballyless (a pseudonym for Rosslare, where Banville spent childhood summers). It was here something happened to change his life, half a century ago.

In those days The Cedars was a 'big house'. Rich tenants from England rented it through the summer. The occupants who coincided with Max's late adolescence, and entry into adulthood, were the 'Graces'. They brought with them, as Max calls it, 'the time of the gods'. Adolescent Max is excited by the mother, Connie, and even more so by her wayward daughter, Chloe. There is also Chloe's brother, Myles – who has a 'problem' – and a nursemaid, Rose, who looks after them. It gets complicated. Max, doing a Peeping Tom, observes the Graces. But, at a critical moment, he misinterprets what he sees, and assumes complicated sexual goings-on. The rest of his life will be determined by what Max thought he understood about the Grace family. But the novel finishes with a surprise revelation worthy of Agatha Christie. Max is finally consigned to the no-nonsense care of his daughter, Claire. He will not live long. His whole life has been grounded in mistake and incomprehension. But he will go into the darkness knowing, at last, what really happened.

The Secret History, Donna Tartt, 1992

The Secret History is a fable of corruption among a group of classics students in Hampden College, an elite (that is, for rich kids), private (that is, expensive) institution in Vermont. It was Donna Tartt's first published work of fiction and was promoted with monumental hype. Something wonderful had happened. Here was a Great American Novel by a prodigy who, as Zadie Smith said of herself by way of recommendation to her first agent, 'did not look like the back of a bus', Tartt was in her twenties and had read classics at Bennington College, an elite, private institution in Vermont. *The Secret History*, the reader was informed, had been rewritten many times, having been seen only by college friends including Brett Easton Ellis, of *American Psycho* fame, to whom the book is dedicated. An endorsement, as they say, to die for: although preferably not via Mr Bateman's staple gun.

An ingénu Californian, Richard Papen, comes to Hampden on a student loan ('poor kid') scholarship. Richard tells his new, and enviably wealthy, classmates that his family is 'in oil' – without specifying that Dad runs a gas station. It is the first filament in what is to become a web of lies. Imprudently, Richard elects to enrol on a classics course whose eccentric professor insists that his students take no other classes than his and restricts class size to half a dozen. In return, Professor Julian Morrow poisons his acolytes' minds with propositions such as:

> We don't like to admit it, but the idea of losing control is one that fascinates controlled people such as ourselves more than almost anything. All truly civilized people – the ancients no less than us – have civilized themselves through the willful repression of the old, animal self . . . And what could be more terrifying and beautiful, to souls like the Greeks' or our own, than to lose control completely?

Richard's classmates are patrician, bored and degenerate. Not for them the banal pleasures of 'drinking contests, wet-T-shirt competitions, and female mud-wrestling tournaments' or frat orgies. Corrupted to more creative degeneracies by their philosopher king, they indulge in a full-blown Bacchanalian frenzy in the Vermont woods. Incest happens – and worse. Dionysus himself appears and a luckless farmer is torn limb from limb. His murderers are rewarded with a 'state of *euphemia*, cultic purity'.

United by the mystic bond of human sacrifice the cultists, in their condition of euphemic exuberance, proceed to bump off the weakest of their number, who looks as if he may snitch. It all ends with cathartic spillage of blood, but nothing resembling poetic justice. Just secrecy.

While reading *The Secret History*, Leopold and Loeb (see COMPULSION) come to mind, as does Hitchcock's masterly retelling of their crime in *Rope*. Like Hitchcock, Donna Tartt builds her plot effects well; there are no great surprises nor much suspense (other than the nagging suspicion that Richard may be telling the story from Death Row). The surrounding structure of classical allusion and myth is deftly handled – even the glories of the New England spring, it is suggested, have been brought about by the mid-winter murders. The Nick Carraway-like narrator, who admits to having a mediocre mind and displays it by his every turn of phrase, never quite understands what he chronicles. The rich remain – as the creator of Gatsby said they were – incomprehensibly 'different'.

In passing, *The Secret History* throws some illuminating sidelights on the business side of American higher education. Fees at institutions like Hampden run, nowadays, at around $60,000 a year, and the 'package', for a four-year degree, will cost much more. Monastic austerity is not required. Tartt's undergraduates run BMWs, flash major credit cards, buy airline tickets (first-class) to faraway places on a whim. And, if that way inclined, write strange and wonderful novels.

For others from the Bennington stable see Ellis himself and Jonathan Lethem (see GUN, WITH OCCASIONAL MUSIC).

Senilità, Italo Svevo, 1898

Senilità (or *As a Man Grows Older*, as the title is usually translated) had more than one literary birth. In 1907, the forty-five-year-old Svevo (pen name of Aron Ettore Schmitz) was taking English lessons in Trieste from a young Irishman, twenty years his junior. Discovering this tutor 'wrote' (he was James Joyce – although not yet *the* James Joyce), Svevo shyly showed him his novel – called *Senilità* – which had been published nine years before; it was written in high Italian, rather than Svevo's native Triestine dialect. The novel had fallen still-born from the printing press. Joyce presciently smelled genius in his pupil's homework, and would over the coming years promote Svevo as the greatest living Italian author. Italy – snootily – did not concur. Joyce helped get Svevo's novels into print, to be greeted with as universal a lack of interest (or readers) as the first time round. There is, Svevo wryly observed, nothing quite so unanimous as silence.

The book is the chronicle of an enormous upheaval in the quiet life of Emilio Brentani. He is thirty-five years old, the Dantean *'mezzo del cammin'*, and has an office job, the description of which occupies a single line of the novel. He lives in Trieste, and many years ago published a novel. It flopped. His closest friend, among a collection of minor government officials and small entrepreneurs, is a talentless but indomitable sculptor, Stefano Balli. Emilio has a sister, Amalia, who represents his entire family. Their lives are uneventful.

Suddenly there is an event. Emilio falls for a lower-class woman, many years younger, who 'glistens like gold'. Impulsively he tells her, on the basis of no acquaintance whatsoever:

'I am very much in love with you, but it is impossible that I should ever consider you as more than a plaything. I have other duties in life, my career and my family.'

An affair – physical, furtive, but not quite consummated – ensues. Over the months it emerges that Angiolina has had affairs more carnal than the one she has with Emilio – affairs with (this hurts) virtually all his friends. Most hurtfully, he is betrayed by Balli. Events now crowd in, thick and fast. Amalia is revealed as a secret drinker. She has as secretly nursed a passion for her brother's best friend, and dies of delirium tremens, believing it is her wedding day. Balli never noticed either her addiction or her passion for him. After Amalia's death, Angiolina having made off with an embezzling bank clerk, Emilio returns to his old

routine. He feels, however, that 'an important part of his life had been amputated'.

The appropriateness of Svevo's translated title is revealed in the last paragraphs. As he grows older Emilio 'narrativises' his adventure:

Years afterwards he looked back with a kind of enchanted wonder on that period, which had been the most important and the most luminous in his life.

It evokes Falstaff, in the 'chimes at midnight' scene with Shallow – 'Lord, Lord, how subject we old men are to this vice of lying!' It's pathetic. But pathos, like passion, has its place in life; as, that is, a man gets older.

It was Joyce who suggested the English title *As a Man Grows Older*. *Senilità* had a third birth, under this Joycean title, translated by Beryl de Zoete, with an introduction by James's brother, Stanislaus, in 1932. Thus 'Englished' it finally received the admiration it deserves. Italy still disowns Svevo, however.

Separate Development, Christopher Hope, 1981

History, as they say, is written by victors. The ANC and Nelson Mandela will be commemorated by history as the heroic forces that ended what was euphemistically called by its (unvictorious) inventors 'apartheid' – 'separate development' – but which was, in practice, 'keep the black man down – for ever'. Gnawing away, like *bien-pensant* rats, at the foundations of the apartheid state, novelists played their part in bringing the obnoxious system down, either by protest fiction (as with Alan Paton's CRY, THE BELOVED COUNTRY), chronicles of Kafkaesque alienation (as in Coetzee's *Life & Times of Michael K*) or satire. Christopher Hope (better known in South Africa for his poetry than his fiction) was firmly in the satirist camp. On publication, *A Separate Development* was banned by the authorities ('temporarily suppressed' – they loved euphemism), a badge of distinction at that time, in that place. The main contention of the novel – its offence against the regime – was that it rendered apartheid a laughing matter. Absurd. It aligns Hope with that other satirist of South Africa, Tom Sharpe, but Hope, I think, is the subtler comedian of the two.

The novel takes the form of a comic monologue, delivered by Henry Moto. Moto, as we first meet him, is a 'coloured' who 'passes' for white. Later on he is a white who masquerades as a 'coloured' (a word with a unique resonance in the South African lexicon). For Henry, there is no separate development, only a pigmental confusion. He is 'an identity in search of a group' or – a supreme term of abuse – a 'white kaffir', a hybrid condition which in South Africa has none of Norman Mailer's 'White Negro' chic miscegeny. Verwoerd, the architect of apartheid, created a world more absurd than Ionesco's or Beckett's.

The main part of the narrative (a forced prison confession, we gradually realise) covers a chaotic period between Henry's running away from school, his going to ground in Koelietown, and his eventual capture by the police. His offence, apart from an indeterminate pigmentation, is the supposed rape of a white woman who was in fact so eager for his embrace that Henry could be considered the more qualified defendant.

The novel's structure is the simplest known to literary history: that of the picaresque string of adventures in which the rascally hero pinballs through society – now up, now down, always in motion. At the same time, A Separate Development has its sharp topicalities. It is set in the late fifties to the early sixties, and the first third of the book, dealing with Henry's white schooldays, has the feel of a transposed American Graffiti. Apart from the macabre final scene in prison, when reality kicks in, Hope sticks to broad, knockabout comedy. Some episodes work better than others. Funniest is when Harry is recruited as driver-cum-model for 'Epstein the Traveller', peddling his range of Gloria Sunshine Skin Care Products. As one enthusiastic apothecary tells the ambiguously tinted hero:

It's your sort of epidermis the Africans want. The trick is to make them believe it comes out of a can. I don't suppose you spare a little piece? As a

sort of sample, you know, the way they do with curtains. I'd have something to show my customers what to aim for. Just a small flap, Harry, from the wrist, say, or a couple of inches from behind the thigh. You'd never miss it. I'd have it mounted on cardboard like those colour-matching charts in paint shops.

To his parents, teachers, employers, and even to the sinisterly paternal police interrogators, Harry is a 'naughty boy'. And the novel itself is pervaded with a sense of mischief. Naughtiness can play its part in bringing about a better world.

Sideswipe, Charles Willeford, 1987

Readers addicted to Elmore Leonard will find in Willeford's *Sideswipe* a candidate for the best novel Leonard never wrote. Leonard thought so too, and graciously permitted the publisher to use his self-deprecating praise in their advertisements: 'No one writes a better crime novel than Charles Willeford.' A close-run thing, fans would say.

Like Leonard's *Swag*, *Sideswipe* is a story of that most banal of modern American crimes, the supermarket stick-up. It flirts with another threadbare cliché ('the gang that couldn't shoot straight') in the form of the inept band of villains who make up the dramatis personae. At the forefront is Stanley Sinkiewicz, a seventy-one-year-old retiree from Ford's Detroit assembly plant who is living (call it that) his last years in Riviera Beach, Florida. Stanley is the last of a breed – the men who used to hand-paint the decorative stripes on the sides of Ford cars. Under pressure from Japanese competition, he was automated out of a job just in time for retirement. And the cars have lost their last humanising touch, 'because a ruled line is a "dead" line, and a perfect, ruled line lacked the insouciant raciness a hand-drawn line gives to a finished automobile'. As with automobiles, so with modern America, we understand. As Updike's Rabbit Angstrom observes, modern cars don't express anything about America. They're tin cans on wheels. The same glum point was made on screen by Clint Eastwood in his valediction to old America, *Gran Torino* (2008). You want to know where the country went wrong – look at the freeways.

A bizarre series of accidents deposits the dumb but upright Stanley in jail for child molesting. In the cells, he meets a disarmingly friendly sociopath, Troy Loudon, who instructs him on how to manipulate the psychiatrists who will soon be examining him. Stanley is duly released, and in return dispatches a note which will discourage Troy's accuser ('If you don't drop the charges, I'll kill your baby and your wife and then you'). It works, Troy stays some time with Stanley (now deserted by his unsympathetically prudish wife) and continues to mesmerise the old man with romantic claptrap about the old, 'live' America that used to be before automated straight lines took over. Stanley follows Troy to Miami Beach, where the misfit gang musters. There is geriatric Stanley, sociopathic Troy, a Bajan nonobjective painter (whom Stanley helpfully instructs in the art of painting an unruled straight line), and Dale, a go-go dancer with a delicious body whose face was beaten into pulp by an enraged protector: 'Her nose was crushed almost flat and the left nostril was partly missing, as if cut away with a razor blade. Both of her sunken cheeks contained rough and jagged scars, and some of those holes looked large enough to contain marbles.' The delusion fostered by Troy is that the takings of the hold-up will allow the artist to study in New York and enable Dale to get plastic surgery in Haiti. Stanley goes along out of misplaced paternal motives, to look after Troy.

The trick in *Sideswipe* is keeping the preliminary comedy bubbling until a genuinely horrific and blood-curdling last chapter which fairly clubs the still chuckling reader. It's very well done. At the same time, and with the same consummate sleight of hand, Willeford contrives to connect the hold-up fiasco with the apparently irrelevant story of a burned-out detective-turned-hotel-manager he's kept going on the sidelines of the main business. That detective is Willeford's series hero, Hoke Moseley, who features in a string of novels, beginning with *Miami Blues* (1984), which may be aptly summed up by the words of a congenially sardonic Karl Kraus: 'Life is an effort that deserves a better cause'.

The Siege of Krishnapur, J. G. Farrell, 1973

Late in his career, in conversation with George Brock, J. G. Farrell confided that 'the really interesting thing that's happened during my lifetime has been the decline of the British Empire'. He did not lament or rejoice in that decline. Why not? Because when things break down you see more clearly how they work. That 'interested' Farrell. Very much.

While writing *The Siege of Krishnapur*, Farrell was chronically hard-up and pigging it in London bedsits. On the strength of his previous novel, TROUBLES, he had applied to the Arts Council for a grant-in-aid to help fund a new novel he had in mind on colonial India – a country he had never visited. With this and his prize-winnings from *Troubles*, he travelled (third-class all the way) across the sub-continent for two months, braving dysentery, heat exhaustion and dirt. It was a phantasmagoria of 'curiosities and horrors', but it gave him what he needed. Not that the trip made writing easier. 'I had a firmer idea of what India was about *before* I went', he said on his return. It is reflected in the original title for the novel, *Difficulties*.

Farrell had done his groundwork in the British Museum Reading Room. As he told his ex-India parents, in a letter from New Delhi, 'I . . . enjoyed visiting the Red Fort (did you go there?) particularly because I had read in the B.M. a gripping book by a certain Mark Thornhill called *Personal Adventures of a Magistrate during the Indian Mutiny*; the Europeans all piled into the Fort and lived there for some time.'

Thornhill gave Farrell his under-siege *donnée*. But the affair at the Red Fort (so called for its sandstone construction) was too minor an episode in the Sepoy Mutiny (now termed the Indian Rebellion) for what he had in mind. For his historical framework, Farrell drew on historical accounts of the Siege of Lucknow. Like Gordon at Khartoum, Rorke's Drift and the Relief of

Mafeking, it is an epochal event in British imperial history. Lucknow was in a region, Oudh, which had been annexed by the East India Company the year before the mutiny erupted. The East India Company was in India for one reason only – profit. The intertwining of Thornhill's personal account with the commercial rapacities of the British Empire combined critique and strong narrative line – the mix J. G. Farrell particularly wanted.

The novel chronicles a group of representative figures – principally the Collector, the Magistrate, the Soldier, the Poet, the Doctor and the Padre – going patriotically lunatic as they fight off the Sepoy hordes, retreating building by building to their final stronghold, the Residency. After months of holding out, the relieving force discover survivors who are indistinguishable, as one of the officers observes, from 'untouchables'. Fraternity at last.

As in most of Farrell's fiction there is no overwhelmingly sympathetic character. What presides is a bitter comedy, designed to evoke an odd uneasiness in the reader. In the last desperate stages of the siege, for example, the British defenders run out of cannon balls and use the heads from busts of literary figures which ornament the Residency library. They were installed to symbolise the values of the high civilisation the British are spreading across the globe, while the 'Company' grabs all it can:

> And of the heads, perhaps not surprisingly, the most effective of all had been Shakespeare's; it had scythed its way through a whole astonished platoon of sepoys advancing in single file through the jungle. The Collector suspected that the Bard's success in this respect might have a great deal to do with the ballistic advantages stemming from his baldness.

The Siege of Krishnapur went on to win the Booker Prize in 1973. Like John Berger the year before, Farrell used his prize-winner's speech to attack the 'unacceptable face of capitalism', incarnated in the prize's sponsors, who had allegedly made their millions out of sweated labour in sugar plantations. Every year, he jested (to a stonily un-applauding audience),

Booker should expect a yet more horrible monster to be washed up on its prize shores. This ('oh, and thanks a bundle for the cheque') was his monster.

A Single Man, Christopher Isherwood, 1964

Isherwood's novel covers the single man's single day. The season is irrelevant. The action is set in southern California where, as in Eden, it's always (boring) summer. The year is 1962, around the time the whole planet came close to extinction in the (not boring) Cuban Missile Crisis. Isherwood was always at his most creative as an Englishman in foreign cities. Weimar Berlin was one such – as in his early masterpieces, *Mr Norris Changes Trains* or his short story 'Sally Bowles' which, as adapted into the musical *Cabaret* (not by Isherwood), kept him in comparative luxury for the last twenty years of his long life. In *A Single Man*, the foreign city is greater Los Angeles – specifically its beach enclave, Santa Monica. On the whole, one suspects, Weimar Germany was more to Herr Issyvoo's taste.

The novel is virtually plotless. George Falconer is single because his lover, Jim, recently died in a car crash in Ohio. We get the briefest of snapshots of how they met in a singles' bar:

> years ago, when George walked into *The Starboard Side* and set eyes for the first time on Jim, not yet demobilised and looking stunning beyond words in his Navy uniform.

George, by contrast, is unstunningly English, fifty-eight years old (too much) and five foot eight inches tall (too little). His normal facial expression is 'a dull harassed stare'. He is an English Literature instructor at San Tomas State College (Isherwood taught at Los Angeles State College). He lives alone in a house he could not nowadays afford to buy (he and Jim got in the property market before the immigrant rush) – secluded, and not too far from the ocean. The air is smogless. His life is airless.

George is anything but 'mellow' – that

distinctive Californian response to the world. He is infused with loathing, encased in his starchy Englishness. Through George, in his 'I am a camera' style, Isherwood captures SoCal masterfully. He is uncannily sensitive, for example, to what it feels like to drive the freeways, those arteries of future urban life, as Reyner Banham evangelised them in *Los Angeles: The Architecture of Four Ecologies* (1971). For example, as Isherwood observes:

> There's always a slightly unpleasant moment when you drive up the ramp which leads onto the freeway and become what's called 'merging traffic.'

It's a little allegory of the immigrant becoming 'naturalised'. For 'merging' read 'melting pot'. But few 'alien residents' (as the American Immigration Service calls them) are as unmerged – in the final analysis – as George Falconer.

George hates his next-door neighbours, the Strunks, because they have seven children (no singleness there). And he hates their happiness. He 'knows' it's not the real thing:

> Oh yes, indeed. Mr Strunk and Mr Garfein are proud of their kingdom. But why, then, are their voices like the voices of boys calling to each other as they explore a dark unknown cave, growing ever louder and louder, bolder and bolder? Do they know that they are afraid? No. But they are very afraid.

Theirs is a world of 'annihilation by blandness'. The little smear of anti-Semitism, implied by 'Garfein', jars. George's students are dumb. And what he teaches them is useless because it cannot be converted to the top salary. His classes are meaningless palaver about what literature is 'about', to young barbarians who can no more understand it than he can explain it. In his blackest moments (there are many of them), George fantasises about spreading lethal diseases which will kill three-quarters of the American population. The bigots, that is: 'These people are not amusing. They should never be dealt with amusingly. They understand only one language: brute force.' But the 'force', of course, is on the bigots' side. It always will be.

George is in hell – why? Simply because he's alive. Jim, he thinks, 'was lucky at the end, the only time when luck really counts'. Jim was wiped out by a truck before he knew what had hit him. That night there is a moment of relief for George, when a flirtatious student comes over. But he goes to bed, alone, and dies of a heart attack, while sleeping. He, too, has been lucky at the end.

Slaughterhouse-Five, Kurt Vonnegut, 1969

On the night of 13 February 1945, three months before the end of the Second World War, Kurt Vonnegut was a POW cowering in an underground animal slaughterhouse during the devastating fire-bombing of Dresden. 'We got through it', Vonnegut wryly recalled,

> because we were quartered in the stockyards where it was wide and open and there was a meat locker three stories beneath the surface, the only decent shelter in the city. So we went down into the meat locker, and when we came up again the city was gone and everybody was dead . . . We walked for miles before we saw anybody else: all organic things were consumed.

Vonnegut and his fellow American POWs, exhumed at dawn from their underground coffin, were set to work 'corpse mining' – excavating blackened bodies for a second cremation on open piles. The live meat took care of the dead meat. What can a novelist do with that?

In *Slaughterhouse-Five*, Billy Pilgrim, the unheroic hero, is a POW in the same shelter as Vonnegut. Billy too survives the devastating fire-bombing – but he goes crazy. Lovably crazy. Vonnegut himself had almost insuperable personal difficulties writing his 'Dresden novel'. He had to forge an entirely new 'schizophrenic' technique, weaving realism, science-fiction schlock (little one-eyed green men from Tralfama-dore, resembling toilet plungers) and slap-stick social comedy into a startlingly innovative pattern. Chronically suicidal by nature (his mother killed herself on Moth-er's Day), the novelist uses all the resources of fiction to make sense of senselessness.

Billy Pilgrim, a time and intergalactic traveller (or, more likely, merely nuts), ends his post-Dresden pilgrimage incarcerated no longer by Nazi Germany but by aliens from the planet Tralfamadore, some 446,120,000,000,000,000 miles from earth, whither he has been transported by flying saucer (widely believed in during the 1960s). Billy's imprisonment on planet Tralfamadore is in a geodesic dome – a style of architecture much favoured by hippy communes in the 1960s (they too wanted to escape) – made tolerable by furniture from Sears, Roebuck (less favoured by hippies), and by the presence of the even more luxuriously upholstered, but wholly brainless, starlet Montana Wildhack. She was flying-saucered across the vast tracts of space to be Billy's 'mate' (on Earth she is one of Hugh Hefner's playmates). They will be earthling specimens in the Tralfamadorian national zoo, kindly treated and grateful for the dome, the furniture, and each other.

'I was there,' is a constant interruption in the text. In two places in the novel, Vonnegut actually gives himself a Prufrockian speaking part. Walter Scott was not present at Culloden. Tolstoy wasn't at Borodino, Thack-eray wasn't at Waterloo, nor was Stendhal. Norman Mailer – though the myth persists – didn't see a lot of action in the Pacific campaign. Interestingly, Vonnegut himself did not call Slaughterhouse-Five a 'novel' but, more awkwardly, 'my Dresden book'. However, Billy Pilgrim is not Vonnegut but is based on a fellow POW called Joe Crone who did not survive the war. Crone was, like Billy, comically mal-coordinated, a soldier doomed always to be the platoon klutz. He let himself starve to death before the fire-storm and was buried, wearing a white paper suit. Vonnegut resurrected him.

Vonnegut did not, in the conventional sense, write Slaughterhouse-Five – it rose out of his subconscious like a slow bruise. Immediately after the war he found he could not remember the event: 'There was a complete blank where the bombing of Dresden took place ... And I looked up several of my war buddies and they didn't remember either.' In his first, fuzzy, concep-tion of the book, he imagined something like the popular war movies of the period: 'I saw it as starring John Wayne and Frank Sinatra.' Ironically, these two 'dirty old men', as a friend's wife calls them in the first chap-ter's account of the novel's gestation, did not serve their country in the Second World War, but made millions out of playing war heroes onscreen where the bombs don't hurt.

Snow, Orhan Pamuk, 2002

Pamuk's novel was translated from the Turkish in 2004; he went on to win the Nobel Prize for Literature in 2006. There is always a political subtext to Sweden's laurel leaves. The judges recognised in Snow a novel which miniaturised, and aestheti-cised, the clash of civilisations in a country which had, historically, tried to be two contrary things: Islamic and Westernised. Snow was a novel for the time.

Pamuk's epigraph is from Stendhal's CHARTERHOUSE OF PARMA:

> Politics in a literary work are a pistol-shot in the middle of a concert, a crude affair though one impossible to ignore. We are about to speak of ugly matters.

The novel opens in a bitter February in the mid-1990s. The hero, 'Ka' (Kerim Alakuşoğlu), returns to Kars, the town in eastern Anatolia where he was brought up in a comfortably Europeanised household. Now he has no family. He has been a political exile in Germany for twelve years but has never learned the language, believing it would steal something of himself to do so. A poet, his creativity has run dry.

Kars (an actual town) is sealed off from the outside world for three days by snow. The downfall erases familiar outlines and releases conflicting ideological energies. Situated where it is, at the conflux of borders, Kars was once a cauldron of regional history: Russian, Ottoman, Armenian,

Kurdish and Turkish elements mingled to create its unique character. Now 'political Islam' is dominant. Under moral absolutism, the city is withering. And, as Ka perceives:

> it was not just the world of his childhood that was dying: it was his dream of returning to Turkey one day to live.

Ka has returned, on this occasion, ostensibly to research and write about the 'suicide epidemic' in nearby Batman (an actual historical event). Young girls are killing themselves. The reason, Ka discovers, is deeply rooted in what Turkey has become:

> the suicide stories he heard that day would haunt him for the rest of his life. It wasn't the poverty, or the helplessness, or the insensitivity that Ka found shocking in these stories. Nor was it the constant beatings to which the girls had been subjected; or the conservatism of their fathers, who wouldn't even let them go outside; or the constant surveillance of jealous husbands; or the lack of money. What shocked and frightened Ka was the manner in which these girls had killed themselves: abruptly, without ritual or warning, in the midst of their everyday routines.

They kill themselves as routinely as leaves fall off trees in winter – before the first snows arrive.

Ka's real reason for returning is to see the woman he once loved, and lost. İpek is now divorced from her fundamentalist husband. Through her and a young man, Necip, Ka meets the charismatic Islamic rebel leader – Blue (İpek's lover, we later learn). Ka's muse is woken. He is again a 'dervish'– a poet fizzing with verse: notably what will be a major work, 'Snow'. Little of Ka's verse is offered in the novel, although one line sticks in the memory:

> If you're unlucky enough to live in Kars, you might as well flush yourself down the toilet.

The first half of *Snow* (a long novel) is realistic. The second half veers into fantasy, including a theatre episode in which the police open fire on the audience during the televised performance of what the authorities deem a seditious play. Headscarves are the inflammatory issue. Necip is among the casualties.

The novel dissolves into complicated intrigues, only partly explained. Ka falls foul of the secret police and returns to Germany, where he is assassinated by some of Blue's followers, who blame him for their leader's capture. A narrator-protagonist called Orhan appears on the scene. He searches in vain for the notebook in which Ka's poetry was written. Orhan, we gather, has been the narrator throughout – but one cognisant of the limitations of ever knowing the reality of things:

> when Orhan the novelist peers into the dark corners of his poet friend's difficult and painful life: how much can he really see?

Not everything, one might respond, but Pamuk can describe dark corners beautifully. Turkey, it would seem, is one of the darker.

Solo, Rana Dasgupta, 2009

Rana Dasgupta is described by his publisher as a 'British-Indian novelist'. It does him an injustice. He was born in Canterbury, studied at Oxford, and in France and America; he lived in many places, and currently resides in Delhi. *Solo* was first published in Australia, then India and, belatedly, in the UK and US. The world, one apprehends, is Rana Dasgupta's oyster. *Solo* won the prestigious Commonwealth Writers' Prize. The award hangs inadequately round his neck, although it puts him in the company of Coetzee, Rushdie, and Carey (other wanderers). Something like the 'Here, There, Everywhere and Nowhere Prize' would be more appropriate.

Dasgupta's debut novel *Tokyo Cancelled* (2005) was an updated *Canterbury Tales* in which stranded airline travellers swapped stories about different cities of the world. *Solo*, on the face of it, is more rooted in the local – at least, for its first half. The novel is set in Bulgaria, a country which, to paraphrase Neville Chamberlain, is far away and of which we know little, and care even less. The hero is Ulrich – whom we first meet aged nearly a hundred. Bulgaria itself is scarcely older. It was invented, as a European constitutional monarchy, out of the Balkan cauldron in 1878. Ulrich is blind. Like Sophocles' Tiresias, this means he can see his country's history, and destiny, more clearly than those of his compatriots who have eyes to distract them.

The novel returns to Ulrich's childhood. His father was a visionary railway engineer, who dreamed of shining steel rails that would connect Baghdad, Sofia and Paris, and drag Bulgaria 'out of Asia'. When young Ulrich shows early stirrings of musical talent, it is savagely suppressed by his father, who smashes his son's violin and throws it in the fire, with the words: 'You won't do this, my son! I won't have you waste your life. Musicians, artists, criminals, opium addicts . . . You'll end up poor and disgraced. I won't have it!'

Ulrich is sent, instead, to Berlin, where his study of chemistry is cut short by hyperinflation of the currency. He returns to his native country to work as a book-keeper, then as a lowly lab-rat in a chemical products factory. He marries. The marriage fails. His father is mutilated in the First World War. Bulgaria fights on the German side, as it does in the Second World War. Thereafter, the country comes under the Kremlin's heel and Moscow's dullest stooge, Todor Zhivkov.

Uncorking a vial of sulphuric acid at the lab, Ulrich accidentally blinds himself. Like everything in the novel, it is described unexcitedly. These things happen.

Ulrich's mother is hauled off, for no reason, to a Bulgarian gulag and returns a madwoman. Rich in natural resources, Bulgaria is plundered and polluted by its communist masters, so much so that women's nylons dissolve at the first touch of Sofia's polluted air. Ulrich spends his last days, alone, in a shabby room by the bus station.

In interviews Dasgupta explains that *Solo*'s theme is music – the ways in which, out of group harmony, single voices can emerge. If there is hope in the world, it lies

not in European union but in that shattered violin, and the dream it represented for Ulrich. Or, cynics might suggest, the Eurovision Song Contest ('*Bulgarie: nul points*'). We recognise the theme: it is that of Salman Rushdie's *The Ground Beneath Her Feet*, in which an Orphic lyre alone can bring the world together But what Dasgupta studiously avoids, for his own effects, is Rushdie's exuberance of language – his verbal music. *Solo* is written in a stripped-down style: easy to read, but hard to be swept away by. It's a powerful novel, but an odd one. But then, how many good novels about Bulgaria has one read?

Something Happened, Joseph Heller, 1974

There was, for readers like me, a tediously long wait between the paperback of *Catch-22* (Heller's first novel), which swept the campuses in the early 1960s, and this, Heller's second novel. Buoyed by its predecessor, it was a *New York Times* '#1' bestseller for almost a year – but the reader response, as articulated at huge length in the *New York Times* by Kurt Vonnegut, was universally perplexed. *Something Happened* was, said Vonnegut in a back-handed compliment, 'black humor indeed – with the humor removed'. Very simply – nothing happens. Nothing worth writing a novel about, that is.

Something Happens takes the form of a long internal monologue. It opens with the hero-narrator in a strangely cowering posture:

> I get the willies when I see closed doors. Even at work, where I am doing so well now, the sight of a closed door is sometimes enough to make me dread that something horrible is happening behind it, something that is going to affect me adversely . . . Something must have happened to me sometime.

And so on, and on, and on – for five hundred pages. Did Heller, one fancifully speculates, toy with the idea of calling his novel 'The Willies'?

Slocum is, as Vonnegut sums him up, perplexedly:

> a nattily-dressed, sourly witty middle-management executive . . . who lives in a nice house in Connecticut with a wife, a daughter and two sons. Slocum works in Manhattan in the communications racket. He is restless. He mourns the missed opportunities of his youth. He is itchy for raises and promotions, even though he despises his company and the jobs he does. He commits unsatisfying adulteries now and then at sales conferences in resort areas, during long lunch hours, or while pretending to work late at the office. He is exhausted. He dreads old age.

And that's about it. Slocum served – like John Yossarian (see CATCH-22) and Joseph Heller himself – in the United States Air Corps in Italy in World War Two. All Slocum says about that episode is that he found the Neapolitan whores rather more to his taste than the Manhattan ones who beguile his post-war afternoons.

In one particularly distasteful episode Slocum records sexually molesting his young cousin: 'I gave her a dime and was sorry afterward when I realised she might mention that. Nobody said anything. I still keep thinking they will. I didn't get my dime's worth. She was a dull, plain child.' He despises his wife, whom he wanted to divorce, he says, before he even met her. But he is faithful to her, in his fashion.

> Sometimes when I'm in bed with another girl in the city or out of town and find I'm already sorry I started, I close my eyes and pretend I'm fucking my wife. Such fidelity.

He doesn't think he'll tell her.

Slocum may be responsible for the death of his nine-year-old son, by hugging him to death in a spasm of parental anxiety. His daughter, now a slobby teenager, disgusts him. As for his mentally deficient son Derek: 'I no longer think of Derek as one of my children' he says. 'Or even as mine. I try not to think of him at all.' He succeeds. We are never told what firm Slocum works for. Off the record, Heller confided it was the conglomerate Time Inc., Insurance division.

What, one has to wonder, was the 'something' that happened? Possibly his mother's deathbed curse ('You're no good'). Possibly the trauma of a gang rape in the stockroom during his first job, when he lost his nerve and couldn't perform (the victim later killed herself). Most likely, what has reduced Slocum to this unlovely shell of a human being is the war. As Vonnegut suggests, he is the spokesman (via his interminable unhappy burble) for the generation of 'victors' for whom 'everything has been downhill since World War II'. 'Absurd and bloody' as that event was, at least 'something happened' between 1941 and 1945. The post-war world? 'It's an idea whose time is gone.'

My favourite review of *Something Happened*, alongside Vonnegut's, is that by Jonathon Walter:

> 'This is a great novel. Please don't read it.'

A Son of War, Melvyn Bragg, 2001

When it came out in 2001, *The Soldier's Return* was judged by knowing critics to be one of the best novels of the year. At the age of sixty-one, Bragg the novelist had, it seemed, found his subject: Melvyn Bragg. The story of Joe Richardson, born working class in Wigton, Cumbria, during the war, was manifestly drawn from the author's own life. Trained as a historian, working as an arts journalist, with a Lakeland poet's sensibility, Bragg (b. 1939, in Carlisle) clearly faced a dilemma as to which literary instrument he should choose for this song of himself. Bragg chose fiction. *The Soldier's Return* (2000) would be the first in a quartet of novels, followed by *A Son of War*, *Crossing the Lines* (2003) and *Remember Me* (2008) bringing the Richards chronicle up to middle age.

The Soldier's Return covers the first seven years of Joe's life – the 'war years', in which the only child is in sole possession of his mother, before his father Sam comes back from Burma to reclaim his conjugal property and take charge of the infantile baggage that goes with it. This second instalment deals with Joe's next seven years, through the eleven-plus exam which, when he passed it, opened the door to a new life. For me, and other contemporaries of Bragg, it is the densely reconstructed feel of the late 1940s in the novel that entrances. Bragg has an eerily perfect recall of the little world of his (decently) working-class childhood. Reading this novel, I hear again the omnipresent Light Programme wafting out 'Give Me Five Minutes More' and 'Don't Fence Me In' on *Two-Way Family Favourites*, and programmes like *Take It From Here* and *Much-Binding-in-the-Marsh* (were they really as funny as I then thought?). Once more, the inner ear hears the lugubrious strains of Reginald Dixon at the theatre organ, Blackpool Tower, and the nose recalls the thrilling smell of Friday's new delivery of the *Wizard* and *Hotspur*. I had, until Bragg opened the lower vaults of my memory bank, almost forgotten the country's obsession, in 1946–7, with boxing (the glory when Freddie Mills beat Gus Lesnevich a year later!) and cricket (Compton and Edrich, the Middlesex twins, racking up unbelievable averages that baking summer). Smells and tastes of that distant time are evoked with the vividness of Proust's madeleine: the odours of the outside lavatory numbed by the fumes of Capstan Full Strength (a brand that probably killed more English servicemen than the Wehrmacht); the slimy feel and pallid look of powdered egg; the cold smear of Brylcreem on the brow.

Like its predecessor, *A Son of War* moves between three centres of consciousness. Still dominant is Sam, the father who made his leap at the end of the first volume, jumping (like Lord Jim) from the train taking him to Australian 'freedom'. Now he is truly returned, locked for the rest of his working life into a shift job at the local paper factory (unless the pools release him). Sam's wife, Ellen, is sensitive and intuitive, in a Mrs Morel kind of way. But, increasingly, the centre of the narrative is Joe – the boy moving towards adolescence and his own dilemmas of freedom.

A Son of War ends with a Conradian moment of choice for Joe, symmetrical with that of his father seven years before. Shall he leave school at fifteen for a 'good job' in

an office? Or should he stay on? Will he be true to his class? Or will he 'aspire', and join the upwardly mobile but deracinated ranks of scholarship boys whose only organic connection with their roots will be to write books about their childhoods, fifty years on? It's a poignant, deeply felt novel. But only those of a certain age will feel it most deeply. Everyone will have a novel they are grateful that the author wrote. This is one of mine.

Sophie's Choice, William Styron, 1979

Styron's last major novel, *Sophie's Choice* intertwines a portrait of the author (Stingo) as a young man in early post-war New York with the story of a mysterious Polish immigrant, Sophie Zawistowska. Styron's own life at this period is relevant. He narrowly missed war service (something he regretted) and after graduating from Duke University, North Carolina, he gravitated – by literary magnetism – to New York, a city that was in creative ferment and culturally inhospitable to Southerners. Styron had, as he put it, 'the literary syrup inside him but it would not pour'. He had a day job at the publisher McGraw-Hill. He wanted to be the next William Faulkner; they wanted someone to Roto-root through the slush pile of educational manuscripts. He walked out to become a full-time writer, barely surviving. The suicide of a girl he had been smitten by as a young man was the 'germ' of his first novel *Lie Down in Darkness*, which he struggled with for three years.

Stingo's city is congruent with his creator's. In the novel, he gets to know Sophie through an acquaintance, Nathan Landau, who is her lover. Both are fellow lodgers. Nathan is Jewish, Sophie Catholic. Both are, in a sense, 'phoney' – not what they seem. Stingo notices, for example, a tattooed number on Sophie's arm, and her scarred wrists. She has no teeth:

> She turned from the mirror with a startled gasp and in so doing revealed a face I shall never in my life forget. Dumbfounded, I beheld – for a mercifully fleeting instant – an old hag

whose entire lower face had crumpled in upon itself, leaving a mouth like a wrinkled gash and an expression of doddering senescence. It was a mask, withered and pitiable.

Nathan poses as a brilliant scientist. He's neither a scientist nor brilliant. Worse than that, he's crazy and into drugs. Nathan eventually turns homicidal To escape him, Sophie and Stingo go on the run to the South. On the way she confides her life-secret:

'Stingo, I must tell you something now that I've never told anyone before. Never before ... Without knowing this, you wouldn't understand anything about me at all. And I realise I must tell someone at last.'

'Tell me, Sophie.'

She is, it emerges, a non-Jewish survivor of Auschwitz. She lived in nearby Krakow and was arrested for smuggling food to her dying mother. Her two blue-eyed, Aryan-looking, 'racially pure' children were interned with her. She desperately attempted, and failed, to get one of them into the adoption programme, by which eligible Poles were farmed out to German families. In the camp, she was allowed to keep only one child with her. The other would face a Dr Mengele figure and the SS executioners. Her 'choice' was which child to sacrifice – her son or daughter.

'So you believe in Christ the Redeemer?' the doctor said in a thick-tongued but oddly abstract voice, like that of a lecturer examining the delicately shaded facet of a proposition in logic. Then he said something which for an instant was totally mystifying: 'Did he not say, "Suffer the little children to come unto me"?' He turned back to her, moving with the twitchy method-icalness of a drunk.

Sophie, with an inanity poised on her tongue and choked with fear, was about to attempt a reply when the doctor said, 'You may keep one of your children.'

'Bitte?' said Sophie.

'You may keep one of your children,' he repeated. 'The other one will have to go. Which one will you keep?'

'You mean, I have to choose?'

'You're a Polack, not a Yid. That gives you a privilege – a choice.'

Sophie sacrificed her daughter, Eva. What happened to her 'saved' son she never knows. One thing she does know is 'that my Redeemer don't live'. The virginal Stingo's consummating act of love with her, and Sophie's final, Styronian act (the self-chosen death, inevitably, and a final solution to the Nathan problem), are the novel's climax.

Styron received the record-breaking sum of $750,000 for the novel's film rights and the adaptation appeared in 1982. Meryl Streep won an Oscar for her portrayal of Sophie. She did not sacrifice her teeth for the role. The phrase 'Sophie's choice' went on to become proverbial.

The Sorrows of Young Werther, Johann Wolfgang von Goethe, 1774

Goethe wrote Werther when he was in his early twenties. In later life he came to hate this youthful effusion and the indisciplined fever of Sturm und Drang romanticism that inspired it. None the less, it has become the most read of his many and varied productions.

The story, distantly autobiographical, and epistolary in format, is thin but manifestly powerful. Werther, a young man of fashion, loves Charlotte ('Lotte'). But she is promised in marriage to Albert, a rather ordinary fellow. After the wedding, a chagrined Werther borrows Albert's pistols on a pretext. The husband charges his new wife to do the actual handing over. The fact that Lotte has handled the weapons triggers a detonation of fetishised love in Werther: 'They have passed through your hands – you have wiped the dust from them. I kiss them a thousand times – you have touched them. Heavenly Spirits favour my design – and you, Charlotte, offer me the weapon.'

He puts a pistol to his head, intending a

theatrically terminal gesture. In fact, his self-destruction is worthier of the Three Stooges than of a latter-day Hamlet. The clock strikes twelve, and with the forlorn cry 'Lotte! Lotte! Farewell! Farewell!' the lover looses a ball into his skull. Six hours later a servant comes in to find his master in a pool of blood, but still breathing. It is not until noon that Werther dies. His mistake was to shoot himself with a low-velocity pistol 'above the right eye'. The ball's impact was absorbed by the boniest part of the skull, an area which human evolution has specifically fortified against missile attack. Had Werther devoted his last hours to reading anatomy rather than Lessing's *Emilia Galotti*, he would have known to shoot himself through the right eye, or up through his open mouth. Goethe, a scientist as well as a novelist, had evidently thought this through, and meant the reader to see it as grimly comic.

W. H. Auden, who was fascinated by the novel, argues for the moral selfishness of the hero. Goethe had given us, claimed Auden, 'a masterly and devastating portrait of a complete egoist, a spoiled brat, incapable of love because he cares for nobody and nothing but himself and having his way at whatever cost to others'. It's moral satire and should be read as such. But that is not how *The Sorrows of Young Werther*, buoyed by the full tide of the German Romantic movement, was received. Werther became, for his generation, a hero.

On a superficial level the novel inspired a sartorial revolution. Yellow trousers, open shirt-collars and blue jackets – the alarming garb in which Werther chooses to meet his Maker – became all the rage among the fashionable young in Germany and Vienna. One recalls that one of the things that excites the Bennet girls in PRIDE AND PREJUDICE is Mr Bingley turning up at Longbourn in a blue coat. *Werther* would have been one of the books, for a certainty, in Mr Bennet's library. Goethe's novel was also much read by young women. Frankenstein's last word is, allusively, Werther's 'Farewell'. And Goethe's novel was one of the books that Victor's creature studied in order to become more acceptably human. Not, alas, with complete success.

More seriously, *Werther* inspired an epidemic of copycat suicides – as many as 2,000, it is claimed. The book was banned in Leipzig, Copenhagen, and Milan. Goethe thought the phenomenon 'confused'. There was no reason 'to turn poetry into reality'. Suicide, following Emile Durkheim's pioneering study of the topic, has always been of interest, as a tool of analysis, among sociologists. (Why do Protestants commit suicide more than Catholics, town dwellers more than country dwellers, etc.?) Durkheim himself pointed out suicide is 'contagious' (an idea played with at the end of ZULEIKA DOBSON). The American sociologist David Phillips immortalised the phenomenon in 1974 with the now-universal label for epidemic suicide: 'The Werther Effect'.

The Sot-Weed Factor, John Barth, 1960

At university, while working on Boccaccio for his comp-lit class, the young John Barth happened on a peculiar volume in the library. It could have qualified, one guesses, for the least-read item in the well-stocked stacks of Johns Hopkins University in Maryland (a significant regional detail). Ebenezer Cooke's 1708 doggerel poem 'The Sot-Weed Factor' is a verse 'satyr', set in seventeenth-century colonial Maryland. As the title-page of the poem announces, the work describes:

> The Laws, Government, Courts and Constitutions of the Country, and also the Buildings, Feasts, Frolicks, Entertainments and Drunken Humours of the Inhabitants of that Part of *America*.

It opens:

> Condemn'd by Fate to way-ward Curse,
> Of Friends unkind, and empty Purse;
> Plagues worse than fill'd Pandora's Box,
> I took my leave of Albion's Rocks:
> With heavy Heart, concerned that I
> Was forc'd my Native Soil to fly,
> And the Old World must bid good-buy.

Virtually nothing is known about Ebenezer Cooke. It may be a nom de plume or more likely the name of a totally forgettable nobody, as far as literary history or the annals of Maryland are concerned. But this epically obscure, and comically inept, poem – with its clodhoppingly Hudibrastic sarcasms against New World barbarism – remained on Barth's mind for another decade.

In 1960 he published *The Sot-Weed Factor*, with Ebenezer Cooke as its hero, to immense success. A picaresque tale in high-pastiche mode, it mixes elements of Voltaire's CANDIDE, Hervey Allen's *Anthony Adverse*, and what the 1960s revered as 'absurdism', all sauced up with post-*Lady Chatterley* trial 'explicitness' as to matters sexual. More importantly, *The Sot-Weed Factor* laid the ground for 'Literature of Exhaustion'. The phrase is Barth's and the concept is his singular, and fruitful, bequest to modern fiction. Its basic tenet is that once all the stories are told, or no longer tellable, all the writer has left is 'narrative' – the empty, but still functioning, fictional machine. Barth's 'exhaustion' thesis helped the experimental novel on to its next stage of literary evolution, 'post-modernism'.

The plot (so to flatter it) follows the fortunes of Ebenezer, 'poet and virgin' – an ingénu hero in a very worldly new world. His life's main aim is to advance his poetic career and preserve his virginity. He starts his epic string of misadventures in Restoration London. The narrative opens:

> In the last years of the Seventeenth Century there was to be found among the fops and fools of the London coffee-houses one rangy, gangling flitch called Ebenezer Cooke, more ambitious than talented, and yet more talented than prudent.

Ebenezer fails to make his way in London and his father ships him off to America, where he takes up work as a sotweed factor (i.e. tobacco merchant). Such is the literary impoverishment of the place, he is also appointed 'the poet laureate of Maryland'– roughly equivalent to being the best synchronised swimmer in Bismarck, North Dakota.

Among early episodes is Ebenezer's capture by pirates on the voyage across (he shares the vessel with a cargo of whores, destined for the brothels of the New World, who supply the crew with some lusty on-voyage entertainment). Pocahontas supplies a sub-plot of amazing improbability. In essence, the plot goes in all directions. At once. It's also a very bawdy novel. One commentator observes (disapprovingly):

> *The Sot-Weed Factor* surpasses any ribald work I've ever read. The book is larded with dick jokes, fart jokes, jokes about diarrhoea, jokes about sex and venereal diseases and so on.

At its centre, it's a meditation on what constitutes literary fame. Ebenezer's personal tutor, Henry Burlingame, argues that literary success, however great, is, illusory. Don't waste your small portion of life writing – live. That's all life is for:

> 'My dear fellow,' Burlingame said caustically, 'we sit here on a blind rock careering through space; we are all of us rushing headlong to the grave. Think you the worms will care, when anon they make a meal of you, whether you spent your moment sighing wigless in your chamber, or sacked the golden towns of Montezuma?... We are dying men, Ebenezer: i'faith, there's time for naught but bold resolves!'

Nonetheless Ebenezer Cooke writes on. Badly. Read the poem. It's good for a laugh. So, too, is Barth's novel – good for laughter of a much higher kind.

A Sound of Thunder, Ray Bradbury, 1952

As the nineteenth century drew to a close, a number of writers became fascinated by the idea of time travel as a fictional device. But those who exploited the gimmick such as, notably, H. G. Wells, were happier with travel into the future rather than travel into the past. The reason is obvious enough – what Ray Bradbury, in his brilliant short story, establishes as the 'butterfly effect'. *A Sound of Thunder* opens with the advertisement:

TIME SAFARI, INC. SAFARIS TO ANY YEAR IN THE PAST. YOU NAME THE ANIMAL. WE TAKE YOU THERE. YOU SHOOT IT.

The story's hero, Eckels, decides to take the plunge and travel back sixty million years to bag the biggest game of all, a Tyrannosaurus Rex. The AD 2055 America he's taking a break from has just narrowly escaped being taken over by a neo-Fascist dictator. Democracy hangs by a thread. Eckels (not, himself, much of a human specimen) discusses the close-run election as he makes his booking with Time Safari Inc.:

'Unbelievable.' Eckels breathed, the light of the Machine on his thin face. 'A real Time Machine.' He shook his head. 'Makes you think. If the election had gone badly yesterday, I might be here now running away from the results. Thank God Keith won. He'll make a fine President of the United States.'

'Yes,' said the man behind the desk. 'We're lucky. If Deutscher had gotten in, we'd have the worst kind of dictatorship. There's an anti everything man for you, a militarist, anti-Christ, anti-human, anti-intellectual.'

For 'Deutscher' read 'Joseph McCarthy', the blackest of beasts for liberals like Ray Bradbury in the early 1950s. There was serious fear that the demagogue Senator from Wisconsin might (a horrible thought) make it to the White House.

Together with a bunch of other time-travellers, Eckels is whizzed back to the prehistoric past and more primitive kinds of monsters. Once they arrive, the hunters are warned to stay on an 'anti-gravity' path which floats six inches above the earth. They must not touch so much as a grass blade, flower, or tree. 'Step on a mouse', they are told,

and you leave your print, like a Grand Canyon, across Eternity. Queen Elizabeth might never be born, Washington might not cross the Delaware, there might never be a United States at all. So be careful. Stay on the Path. Never step off!'

The prey have been carefully selected to be shot not more than two minutes before they would have died anyway. Queen Elizabeth will be born.

Enter, crashingly, Eckels' designated monster:

The Tyrant Lizard raised itself. Its armored flesh glittered like a thousand green coins. The coins, crusted with slime, steamed. In the slime, tiny insects wriggled, so that the entire body seemed to twitch and undulate, even while the monster itself did not move. It exhaled. The stink of raw flesh blew down the wilderness.

Eckels proves to be a coward – his companions are obliged to kill the Tyrant Lizard with a fusillade when he fails to pull the trigger. Worse still, in his terror he falls off the path and his boot touches the ground. He crushes, although he does not realise it, a butterfly. He returns to the present to discover the dictator, not the democrat, has won the presidential election. He has changed world history by treading on a butterfly. A 'Tyrant' has been killed, a 'Tyrant' has been born.

The paradox Bradbury plays with has proved infinitely rich in fantasy fiction and film – most delightfully in the *Back to the Future* movie series. One way out of the paradox was suggested by another brilliant science-fiction writer, Philip K. Dick. In *The Man in the High Castle* (1962), Dick popularised the idea of 'alternative universes'. If you went back in time and changed things you would not be changing the present from which you started but creating a parallel world, with different data. There were, the thesis suggests, an infinite number of such worlds. Dick's solution to the paradox is played with in the film *The Butterfly Effect*. Bradbury's witty story, like the crushed butterfly, has had momentous after-effects.

Sour Sweet, Timothy Mo, 1982

Sour Sweet tells an everyday story of the Chinese takeaway food-retail trade from what is an unusual angle in the Western world. The novel is set in the 1960s, and chronicles a period of miniature cultural revolution in London's Gerrard Street ('Chinatown') and its outlying dependencies. The plot has two centres, both concerned with clan groupings. Foremost is that of the immigrant Chen family, the head of which graduates from being a Soho waiter to opening a takeaway in outer London. The other main element concerns a triad, or secret society, fighting a rival for control of the heroin and protection rackets in 'the Street'. (The 'official bandits' – that is, the police – are fended off with no trouble at all.)

The way in which the honest little shopkeeper gets caught up in the Hung triad's web and is eventually killed (by having his 'face washed') is not the most original feature of Mo's novel. What is fresh and consistently comic is the quaint way in which familiar life is reflected back to the British reader off an alien ethnic surface. We see ourselves as these very different others see us. The trick is easier shown than described – such as in the following passage about the Chens' perplexity about 'Chinese Food', British-style:

The food was, if nothing else, thought Lily, provenly successful: English tastebuds must be as degraded as their care of their parents; it could, of course, be part of a scheme of cosmic repercussion. 'Sweet and sour pork' was their staple, naturally: batter musket balls encasing a tiny core of meat, laced with a scarlet sauce that had an interesting effect on the urine of the consumer the next day. Chen knew, because he tried some and almost fainted with shock the morning after, fearing some frightful internal haemorrhaging (had Lily been making him overdo it lately?) and going round with a slight limp until in the mid-afternoon the stream issued as clear as ever. 'Spare ribs' (whatever they were) also seemed popular.

If we credit Mo, the presiding thought in the Chinese catering mind is mild curiosity as to why foreign devils should eat the muck. And, more mystifyingly, pay to eat it.

Mo's novel shouldn't be read for its contribution to good race-relations in multicultural Britain. It is extremely funny. A particularly successful creation is Mui, Chen's sister-in-law. She has been housebound for years, despite being sound in body. But steeping in her favourite soap opera, *Crossroads*, gives her the happy knack of being able to tell one occidental face from another, and some sympathy with the host country's irrational ways. Gradually she emerges from her low status of unmarried hanger-on. By the end of the novel she is the Chen clan's matriarch, all set to open a fish-and-chip parlour.

The arc of the narrative traces a larger cultural adaptation. The Chens finally come to terms with car-owning, schools and taxreturns. It means 'the end of the old life, the life of the loving, closely knit family'. The triad gives up its heroic street-fighting ways, in which gang armies pulverise, cleave and shatter each other in epic, set-piece battles. The new line of crime is bureaucratic, discreet, and, like Mui's fish-and-chipper, highly profitable.

Stoner, John Williams, 1965

On 5 July 2013, addressing the nation at 8.35 a.m. on the *Today* programme, Ian McEwan instructed listeners to pack, along with their swim-wear, the novel *Stoner* – the beach book for 2013. '*Stoner* – a novel about drugs?' the 6-million or so listeners to the programme may idly have thought, before McEwan began his meticulous eulogy ('extraordinary', 'hits at human truths', 'prose as limpid as glass').

Even though the core of the story is set in the 1920s there's no booze, no flappers, no gangsters. It's a story about a second-rate English teacher, in a second-rate American university, whose career is a failure, whose marriage is a failure and whose one adultery is a failure. What makes William Stoner significant is that he loves literature. It is the most important relationship in his life:

The love of literature, of language, of the mystery of the mind and heart showing themselves in the minute, strange, and unexpected combinations of letters and words, in the blackest and coldest print – the love which he had hidden as if it were illicit and dangerous, he began to display, tentatively at first, and then boldly, and then proudly.

Stoner's undergraduate years coincide with the war years (for America, 1917–18). His fellow students rush to volunteer *en masse*. He does not. Not because he is a coward, but because he now loves literature more.

Stoner received respectful reviews when it was published in 1965. 'Well written', was the general verdict. It was eight years before it made it to Britain. The *TLS* dismissed it in under three hundred words as less interesting than Norman Mailer's current offering. It came, it was read, it was forgotten – like most novels, even the very well-written ones. But a few connoisseurs kept the word of mouth going.

Who was John Williams? He was a professor at a respectably middle-ranking American university. He was, as his brief obituaries testified, well thought of but not 'stellar'. His contributions to scholarship were minor. But, significantly, he was one of the first teachers of 'creative writing'. McEwan, coincidentally, is one of the earliest products of the UK's pioneer creative writing programme, introduced at the University of East Anglia.

The background to *Stoner* will probably elude – and possibly not interest – most of those who rushed their orders into Amazon on 5 July (the bestseller list went momentarily crazy). The orthodoxy in the teaching of literature at university level shifts every forty years or so, as the dinosaurs give way to the young Turks. Williams' hero comes from a dirt-poor farming background. He escapes the hard life which has been his family's destiny and, thanks to luck and scholarships, gets himself a higher education in English Literature. It's a forever-changing discipline, one that is always quarrelling with itself.

During William Stoner's career (1920–50) the struggle was between 'Philology' (English Literature studied alongside Latin) and 'New Criticism' (close reading, paying attention exclusively to the 'words on the page'). Stoner is a philologist – increasingly isolated but dedicated, body and soul, to the books he loves. His PhD topic (and one published book) is on the influence of the classical tradition on medieval lyric poetry. His courses on medieval literature are dry – but, in their way, passionate. He is at permanent war with the head of his department, who is a new man and a New Critic and who malevolently keeps Stoner down, teaching, year after year that un-sexiest of courses, 'freshman composition' – something normally assigned to 'adjunct' teachers. Stoner defies attempts to force him into early retirement, only to be diagnosed with cancer and retire almost immediately to his death bed. There, he caresses not his wife or daughter (both estranged), nor the mistress with whom he had a brief, unhappy, fling, but an old, much-loved book. McEwan went out on a limb, calling it the finest death scene in literature.

Academic institutional life is the smallest of beers. There are no corridors of power in the ivory tower. But it has its pathos and its martyrs. Williams (of a later generation than his hero, and by affiliation a New Critic) handles this world with tenderness.

Strait is the Gate, André Gide, 1909

The French title, equally resonant, is *La Porte Étroite*. The biblical reference (in both titles) resonates through the narrative:

> Because strait is the gate, and narrow is the way which leadeth unto life, and few there be that finde it. (Matthew 7:14)

Change 'life' to 'love' and the subject of Gide's novel emerges, crystallised. The plot is deceptively simple, as is the faux-straightforward opening:

> Some people might have made a book out of it; but the story I am going to tell is one which it took all my strength

to live and over which I spent all my virtue. So I shall set down my recollections quite simply.

Is this, then, a book – or not a book?

The narrator-hero is Jerome Pallissier. Every year, in his early life, he and his mother leave their meagre Paris apartment (his father is dead) for a summer vacation at their rich relatives' country estate in Fongueusemare, Normandy. Aged ten, he falls madly in love with his cousin, Alissa Bucolin – at two years older she is pubescent, he is infantile. The exact moment of 'falling' is when he sees her kneeling in prayer, sobbing. 'My whole life', records Jerome:

> was decided by that moment; even to this day I cannot recall it without a pang of anguish. Doubtless I understood very imperfectly the cause of Alissa's wretchedness, but I felt intensely that that wretchedness was far too strong for her little quivering soul, for her fragile body, shaken with sobs.

The following Sunday, the two of them, both religiously devout, hear a sermon in church on the 'strait is the gate' text. Their love is, literally, ecstatic – something outside things carnal.

Already teasing issues are raised. Can you, however precocious, 'fall in love' in any significant way aged twelve? In Jerome's case, it's complicated by the fact that Alissa has been put off romantic and erotic love by her mother's flagrant adultery and elopement and, we deduce, changes in her own body. That is why he saw her sobbing. She diverts her passion to God and rejects her cousin's overtures. Jerome is not deterred. About to leave for university, he proposes. They are too young to get engaged, Alissa argues. Her real motive, we much later learn, is to enable her sister to marry first. Juliette does so. Her union spawns numerous children. Jerome and Alissa exchange long letters in which a passion is expressed that they can never enact face to face. They enjoy the summer grounds of her family estate, and read poetry to each other, but both remain inhibited by their religious beliefs. For Jerome, the idea of 'forcing' (i.e. seducing)

her is unthinkable; the idea of not having her torment.

The years pass. She continues to resist him – searching instead, apparently, for religious fulfilment. There is a final meeting in the country, alongside a narrow garden gate which has figured throughout their relationship. She confesses:

> 'I feel happier with you than I thought it was possible to feel . . . but, believe me, we were not born for happiness.'
> 'What can the soul prefer to happiness?' I cried impetuously. She whispered:
> 'Holiness . . .' so low that I divined rather than heard the word.

Alissa pines. She is, apparently, mortifying herself, in a vain attempt to purge that which she feels for Jerome. She rids her shelves of the volumes of poetry that they both loved. She stops eating, and dies in a Paris nursing home. Her journal reveals she loved Jerome even more than he loved her. God, she concludes, as she is about to meet Him, was not the lover she should have chosen.

Strait is the Gate drew on early events in Gide's own life and on his fraught marriage in 1895 to his cousin Madeleine. Out of it he created a love story as short (one hundred and twenty pages) and simple as a fable by Aesop, and as complicated, in its inner workings, as ANNA KARENINA.

The Stranger's Child, Alan Hollinghurst, 2011

The Stranger's Child perplexed reviewers when it was first published in June 2011. James Wood summed up the perplexity neatly by noting that it was 'a frustrating book, both a large and a curiously small novel', and the story artfully obscured in the telling by a 'nice English blur'. It is a story which declines to tell the reader what it is about.

The Stranger's Child is not a story about strangers' children. The title is from Tennyson's memorial poem for his Cambridge friend (and probably more than friend) Arthur Hallam. The full quote is:

And year by year the landscape
  [will] grow
Familiar to the stranger's child

The idea, as pondered in the novel, is that the most important things in your life will matter less to you and yours than to someone who comes long after you, and whom you will never know.

The narrative opens in the year before the Great War. Cecil Valance, heir to a title and a landed estate (Corley Court), visits his Cambridge chum George Sawle at his family's nice little place in Stanmore. Called 'Two Acres', it's a window box compared to Corley – but nonetheless a handsome country house (soon to be engulfed by London suburbia). Cecil and George are members of an intellectual club called 'the Society'. Its membership is deeply secret. It is based, transparently, on a Cambridge society called 'the Apostles'. Tennyson and Hallam both belonged to it. The club was, at the period the novel is set, the cradle of British high-minded liberalism – and predominantly gay: Maynard Keynes, Lytton Strachey, and E. M. Forster were members. They were later moving spirits in the Bloomsbury Group. Cecil is a poet of what would be called the Georgian School – anti-modern and genteel. He is clearly based, in both person and poetry, on Rupert Brooke (an Apostle, and bisexual), but teasingly the novel poses the question whether Cecil is Brooke's equal, superior or a lesser talent?

At Sawle's house George and Cecil make love for the first time in the woods. Cecil has a massive cock and one which is wholly indifferent as to gender. He throws off a poem, 'Two Acres', commemorating the fruition of his relationship with George. To preserve the necessary secrecy (George's mother, Freda, is already suspicious) he inscribes the poem in the mauve autograph book of George's sixteen-year-old sister Daphne. She is duped, as are others. Although Hollinghurst's narrative traverses, chronologically, two world wars, the narrative never visits them. Cecil dashes off a 'Will you be my widow?' letter to Daphne and is killed in 1916. He becomes, in death, an icon of British patriotism. Churchill himself (as he did for Rupert Brooke) eulogises him as the flower of British youth. A marble monument is raised in the chapel of Corley and a whitewash biography is authorised. Daphne, who now knows the truth about 'Two Acres', marries Cecil's brother Dudley – a shell-shocked relic of the war. She has her own corrosive secret. It will ruin her marriage and her life.

The narrative jumps to a relationship between a schoolteacher, Peter (Corley is now a boarding school – with no expectation of a long future), and Paul, a bank-clerk in an establishment connected with the Sawles. They both have a literary interest in Cecil and each other. One of them will go on to write the biography which will 'out' Cecil.

The novel ends with the 'clearance' of Two Acres (which has gone through many changes, including a spell as an old folks' home) in 2008. One of the scavengers picks up an ancient copy of a newspaper and uncrumples it:

> puzzling vaguely over it as he came back into the relative brightness of the sitting room, he realised from the stiffened folds that the page of the *Telegraph* had been used to wrap some square object, it was a wholly random survival, of no interest in itself. He took it out to throw on to the fire.

It contains the autograph book that contained the poem. Forget the 'large' and 'small' paradox. It's a great novel by a novelist who, like his idol Henry James, determinedly keeps his distance from the reader.

Strangers on a Train, Patricia Highsmith, 1950

Highsmith's novel-writing career began on a top note with this novel about ingenious murder. Homicide is the rational response to the human condition in Highsmith's moral universe. 'Murder', she believed, 'is a kind of making love, a kind of possessing.' On the face of it, such apophthegms look like the bourgeois-offending small talk of the existentialists, whose left-bank doctrines Highsmith was infatuated with during the late 1940s. There is, however, a difference.

Unlike Meursault (she read THE OUTSIDER in 1947), Highsmith's killers positively relish their killing. For them, it's orgasmic.

The big difference between the classic 'noir' 1951 Hitchcock movie and its source is that in Highsmith's version Guy (literally a nice guy) does actually commit murder, honouring an agreement forged, over too many highballs, in the private compartment of an express thundering across the Texas plains. Everything one does in life, said Jean Cocteau, even love, occurs in an express train racing towards death. We are all of us strangers on the same death-bound train. Hitchcock's targeted cinema audience was not up for the savagery of Highsmith's world view. Or the wilful affronts to poetic justice. *Crime and Punishment* was one of Highsmith's favourite novels (she actually re-read it a couple of months before beginning *Strangers on a Train*), but her Raskolnikovs routinely escape the afflictions of law and conscience – and sometimes even punishment.

The skeletal plot of *Strangers on a Train* is as follows. Guy Haines, an architect (bizarrely transmuted into a star tennis player in the movie), dearly wants to be rid of his tramp of a wife, Miriam. He's in love with another woman – a socialite who can be very useful to his career. On the journey back to his hometown to talk Miriam into a divorce (it's complicated by her being pregnant by another man), he strikes up a conversation, over drinks, with Charles Anthony Bruno. Bruno is a rich ne'er-do-well who wants to kill his father (who is being very mean about his 'allowance'). Both men have people in their lives whom they want out of the way. Why not swap murders? Bruno ingeniously proposes. Both crimes will be apparently motiveless, random acts, and both the beneficiaries of this convenient double homicide can construct waterproof alibis.

Guy assumes it's just drunken fantasy and writes Bruno off as a nut. But Bruno goes ahead and kills Miriam while Guy is out of the country. Highsmith, knowingly, makes the act sado-sexual (murder as love-making):

> His hands captured her throat on the last word, stifling its abortive uplift of surprise. He shook her. His body

seemed to harden like rock, and he heard his teeth crack. She made a grating sound in her throat, but he had her too tight for a scream. With a leg behind her, he wrenched her backward, and they fell to the ground together with no sound but of a brush of leaves. He sunk his fingers deeper, enduring the distasteful pressure of her body under his so her writhing would not get them both up. Her throat felt hotter and fatter.

Guy, once he learns what has happened, is reluctant to shop Bruno. They did, after all, 'agree' to the murder. Over the following months, Bruno becomes insistent that Guy fulfil his end of the bargain. Blackmail is threatened: Bruno will tell the police Guy paid him to kill Miriam. Guy gives in and duly murders Bruno's father. He then marries the woman who can be useful to his career. He remains, though, ridden with guilt and fear. He is right to be fearful. Detectives are beginning to piece the plot together when Bruno, drunk, drowns while yachting. Guy is now clear. But he confesses to a friend. It leaks out.

The most interesting subtext in the novel is the sexual attraction between the two murderers. Highsmith drops heavy hints as to its nature:

> Each was what the other had not chosen to be, the cast off self, what he thought he hated, but perhaps in reality loved.

Raymond Chandler, who wrote the original script for Hitchcock, thought the swapping murders McGuffin was 'ludicrous'. Hitchcock thought differently; millions of moviegoers have agreed with him. They love the speeding carousel at the end. So do I. But I love the book more.

The Street Lawyer, John Grisham, 1998

Grisham's stock in trade is the 'legal procedural' – novels about the intricacies of American law – and he indisputably knows the subject from the inside. Born in 1955, he graduated from law school in 1981, and for nine years ran his own firm. He hails from Arkansas and is distantly related to that state's other successful lawyer, Bill Clinton (a relationship which did neither man any harm in their respective rises to the top). Grisham served as a state legislator in the Mississippi House of Representatives from 1984–90. Then came the success of his second novel, *The Firm*, and Grisham was up with the fiction-writing multi-millionaires.

His fiction after *The Firm* followed an invariable formula, and *The Street Lawyer* is no exception to the rule. All his novels pit an honest lawman – usually a Southerner about Grisham's age – against a corrupt system. In *The Firm*, the hero takes on the Mafia and the FBI. In *The Pelican Brief*, the heroine takes on environment-wrecking big business. In *The Client*, the evil system was the Mafia again, and in *The Chamber*, the Klan. So it goes. There are plenty of bad guys in America. Interestingly, in *The Street Lawyer* the evil system the lawyer takes on is the law itself. The slight introverted twist in formula ('read one you've read them all') makes it, I think, among the more interesting of Grisham's efforts.

The hero, Michael Brock, is a fast-track young professional with a top Washington firm, Drake & Sweeney. A Yale graduate, Michael earns $120,000 a year (princely in the late 1990s, chump-change nowadays). He is smart and confidently expects to make partner by thirty-five. That means at least a million bucks a year. Yuppie heaven. Michael has a Lexus and a beautiful wife called Claire (on her own fast track as a neurosurgeon). Sex hasn't been too good. How can it be when they are both working ninety hours a week? But divorce is less of a hazard for rising young lawyers such as Michael than clinching evidence that they seriously want to succeed – the job comes first. With his million bucks he can buy another wife and a bigger Lexus.

The Street Lawyer opens with the best scene Grisham has ever put on paper. It is winter in Washington and bitterly cold. As he does every day, Michael drives to work, averting his eyes from the capital's street people. One of them, a grizzled African-American, follows him into Drake & Sweeney's gleaming building. He is armed and takes a whole floor full of lawyers hostage. He doesn't want money or revenge. All he wants is to see the lawyers' tax returns, and to ask 'How much did you give to poor people?' last year. Not much, it turns out. It's a brilliant episode – taut, funny and disturbing.

The SWAT team intervenes and it ends bloodily, although no white lawyer's blood is spilled. Michael's first thought is that he may have contracted Aids from the African-American bodily fluids that have been splattered over him. His enquiries lead him into the world of Washington's homeless. His conscience is pricked and he gives up his job at Drake & Sweeney to become a 'street lawyer' at a measly $30,000 a year (Grisham clearly expects us to see this as barely one up from food-stamps). He throws away his designer suits and grows a beard. 'You look like a radical,' his worldly brother tells him. Michael now spends ninety hours a week advising crackheads and prostitutes about their 'rights'. He is the Mother Teresa of Washington lawyers. Claire divorces him, on the grounds that he has lost his mind.

But he has, of course, found his soul. All Grisham's novels cut very early to the chase (one reason that they adapt so well to the screen). Michael finds himself on the run from Drake & Sweeney, which turns out to be in cahoots with corrupt property developers. The suspense is handled competently and there are a couple of nice surprises. The novel ends with the familiar lawyerly pieties – values are endorsed. The law is good – whatever the lawyer jokes say.

Summertime, J. M. Coetzee, 2009

In 1999 I was a judge when J. M. Coetzee won his second Man Booker prize, for DISGRACE. He didn't turn up to collect his award, so the photographers were obliged to take a picture of the novel propped up on an empty chair. The unheld volume spoke volumes. Keep your distance, it said. You may read my novels but don't think you have any right to judge them. Or, perish the thought, 'know' me.

It's odd, then, that this pathologically private man should be so forthcoming in his 'fictionalised memoir' sequence, of which *Summertime* is the third part. The trilogy began with *Boyhood* (1997), which covered the (then unnamed) protagonist's upbringing in South Africa. It continued with *Youth* (2002), which followed the (still unnamed) character in his years of exile in London. Both books conformed exactly to the known facts of Coetzee's own career. With this last volume, the work is overtly autobiographical. The protagonist is finally given a name 'John Coetzee'– alias Yours Truly.

Summertime's narrative leapfrogs over the most dramatic period of Coetzee's life – his years as a postgraduate student and university teacher in the US, researching Beckett, and his deportation for taking part in anti-Vietnam War protests. As the book opens John Coetzee has recently returned from the US to live, grumpily, with his father in a South Africa that is falling apart. It is not a happy domestic arrangement. 'Fathers and sons', John says, 'were never meant to share a house.' He does manual work – something whites, in the early 1970s, would never usually deign to do. He also picks up a pittance tutoring – wasting his scholarly abilities. But in this trough of his life 'John', as did 'J. M.', produces his first novel, *Duskland*.

So far, so parallel. But at this point autobiography melts – perplexingly – into fiction. 'John Coetzee', we later gather, emigrated to Australia as did 'J. M.' in 2002. But 'John' died there in 2006, the year when 'J. M.' became an Australian citizen. His posthumous biography is now being written by a shadowy Boswell called Vincent. This extremely dull fellow is interested solely in John Coetzee's life during the early 1970s. He has some uninformative notebooks and the testimony of former lovers, colleagues and a cousin. They give very little away.

So is the dead 'John Coetzee' to be taken as the live 'J. M. Coetzee'? Experienced readers will be wary of this game. Young James Ballard, for example, in EMPIRE OF THE SUN, has experiences strikingly similar to those of the young J. G. Ballard when he was interned in the war by the Japanese. But the hero 'James Ballard' in J. G. Ballard's *Crash* is nothing like J. G. Ballard. You shouldn't do this kind of thing, said Kingsley Amis, when young Martin went ahead and did it by introducing 'Martin Amis' to Self, the narrator of *Money*. 'It's breaking the rules,' Kingsley protested, 'buggering about with the reader.' But who says novels have rules?

Assuming that *Summertime* is a bona fide self-portrait, it's the least flattering since Dorian Gray's. 'John Coetzee', his near and dear ones grimly recall, was 'scrawny', 'seedy' and exuded 'an air of failure'. He 'had no sexual presence whatsoever . . . as though he had been sprayed from head to toe with a neutralising spray'. His 'teeth are in bad shape'. He is 'sexless'; intercourse with him, reports one disgusted lover, 'lacked all thrill'. His cousin, with whom he has an arid fling in a broken-down pick-up truck, calls him '*slapgat*' – Afrikaans for a loose anus. Another lover comes as near as dammit to accusing him of an unhealthily pederastic interest in young girls. Above all, John Coetzee has no faith in his art. 'Why then', he asks himself, 'does he persist in inscribing marks on paper, in the faint hope that people not yet born will take the trouble to decipher them?' No answer is given.

Discussing Philip Roth's novel *Operation Shylock: A Confession* (1993)– in which the principal character is 'Philip Roth' – Coetzee observed: 'We are in the sphere of the Cretan Liar' (i. e. 'everything I say is a lie, including this'). The same, one suspects, is true of *Summertime*. Work that out.

Sunset Song, Lewis Grassic Gibbon, 1932

This is the first volume of Grassic Gibbon's 'A Scots Quair' trilogy ('quair' means 'quire' or 'gathering of sheets'). There were no silver spoons in Gibbon's mouth. Not the least of his disabilities was being Scottish in an English-dominated literary culture. Literature did not originally seem a likely option for James Leslie Mitchell (as he was born). 'Of peasant rearing and peasant stock', he was brought up on a farm near Stonehaven. He left school at sixteen and made a false start as a journalist. It ended with disgrace and attempted suicide when he was discovered fiddling his expense accounts. He then embarked on a ten-year stint in the armed forces, which was largely unprofitable but which took him to the Middle East, an experience that profoundly affected the development of his idiosyncratic view of world history. As an RAF clerk, Corporal Mitchell learned methodical writing habits that stood him in good stead when, on discharge in 1929, he became an author. He died of peritonitis brought on by a perforated gastric ulcer in 1935 at the age of thirty-three, in the middle of a creative burst that had produced seventeen books in seven years. Success eluded him during his lifetime, although some prescient fellow writers, notably Hugh MacDiarmid and H. G. Wells, had marked him as a major talent.

'A Scots Quair' is also called 'The Mearns Trilogy'. Say 'Scotland' and few people (and no travel agents) will think of the bleak, windswept, comparatively featureless north-eastern coastal region that separates St Andrews from Aberdeen. The Mearns is not a beauty spot and has no glamorous associations. But for Gibbon it is elemental Scotland. His descriptions of it constitute his most powerful writing. *Sunset Song* is divided into four seasonal sections: 'Ploughing', 'Drilling', 'Seed-Time', and 'Harvest'. 'Ploughing' opens on a parched, vividly described landscape:

> Below and around where Chris Guthrie lay the June moors whispered and rustled and shook their cloaks, yellow with broom and powdered faintly with purple, that was the heather but not the full passion of its colour yet. And in the east against the cobalt blue of the sky lay the shimmer of the North Sea, that was by Bervie, and maybe the wind would veer there in an hour or so and you'd feel the change in the life and strum of the thing, bringing a streaming coolness out of the sea.

The novel is set in the period from just before the First World War until just after it. Much of the power of the novel resides in the crofter (tenant farmer) John Guthrie, the heroine Chris' appalling father. Guthrie rapes his wife, who finally kills herself and her two youngest children rather than face the nightly ordeal of the marital bed. The clever Chris, a scholarship girl, is forced to give up education to skivvy for the widowed Guthrie and to labour in his infertile fields. She also has to resist her father's violently incestuous overtures. The surviving younger children are boarded out. After Chris' brother, Will, takes off for Argentina – the farthest point on the planet he can get from the batterings he suffers at John Guthrie's hands – Chris is left alone with her hated, dangerous parent.

Gibbon wrote nothing more affecting than the description of Guthrie, mortally wounded by falling against a stone, thrashing in his own farmyard, cursing and calling his daughter 'a white-faced bitch'. Yet, at his funeral, Chris grieves, reverencing 'the fight unwearying he'd fought with the land and its masters'. Only God defeated him.

Chris' first husband, Ewan, dies in the war (shot as a deserter). The novel ends with a dedication by a minister, who will figure in Chris' later life, of a war memorial: the elemental 'Standing Stone', a 'grey granite' symbol of the Mearns' enduringly hard character. It's a bitter Scottish novel that deserves to be better known in England.

Super-Cannes, J. G. Ballard, 2000

Super-Cannes continues the dystopian line Ballard began in the 1970s (see HIGH RISE). The Ballardian law of the universe runs thus: every idealistic attempt by human society to organise itself into progressive or 'higher' forms will, inevitably, precipitate catastrophe. Interesting catastrophe, of course. And so the high-rise block degenerates into a jungle; the motorway system (as in *Crash*) becomes a seventy-mile-per-hour, high-tech killing ground; the leisure city of the future (as in *Cocaine Nights*) decays into Sodom by the Med. Psycho-biography could doubtless connect Ballard's fiction with that grandest delusion of the author's youth – the Welfare State, the great British experiment in universal 'caring' that failed (test it out in an Accident and Emergency room on a Saturday night). No one cares.

An engaging feature in Ballard's fiction is his cavalier indifference to the laws that hobble lesser writers (who else would introduce Elizabeth Taylor into a novel in which the hero is called James Ballard?). As the preface to *Super-Cannes* informs us, the inspiration for Eden-Olympia, where the action is set, 'is the landscaped business park of Sophia-Antipolis, a few miles to the north of Antibes'. The website for 'Europe's leading science park' records that it is home to '1,414 companies, 30,000 employees, and 5,000 researchers and students' (did they also, one wondered apprehensively, have a couple of libel lawyers?). Sophia-Antipolis is '2,300 hectares, or one-fourth the size of Paris', and the plan is for it to double in size every five years. Fiction could not invent such a monster. It will, it is fondly hoped, make Silicon Valley crawl back up its canyon. It is the future, the grandest of grand projects. As one of Ballard's characters observes, the Riviera has always been a melting pot, but 'The solvent now is talent, not wealth or glamour.'

The novel opens with a newly married couple arriving at Super-Cannes. The forty-something hero, Paul Sinclair, is an amateur aviator, a child of the 1950s who wears sports coats and drives a Jag (preferably along the old, serpentine *routes nationales*). His twenty-something hippyish wife is taking up a position as a physician at the park. They met in hospital, where she treated Paul (with rather more imaginative therapy than our NHS normally provides) after he pranged his vintage Harvard plane. Jane Sinclair is replacing another English physician, David Greenwood (who may or may not have been her lover when they were interns). He went on a shooting spree and killed seven high-ranking officers at the park. Why? Nobody knows.

Sinclair sets out to solve the mystery. He discovers flaws in the official account. Greenwood, a saintly paediatrician, worked with orphaned children. His only recorded vice was an addiction to Lewis Carroll's Alice books (wasn't there something about Charles Dodgson and little girls?). Various hypotheses unfold. As with J. F. Kennedy, there could have been more than one

assassin. Greenwood may have been a fall guy. He could perhaps have been a random symptom of the park's totalitarian pathology. 'Meaningless violence', as one of the park's gurus puts it, 'may be the true poetry of the new millennium.' It may be that at Super-Cannes, where everyone works sixteen hours a day, seven days a week, 'going mad is their only way of staying sane'. It's vintage Ballard.

Swann's Way, Marcel Proust, 1913

There's a famous Monty Python sketch, 'The All-England Summarise Proust Competition', in which contestants have exactly fifteen seconds to sum up all of Proust, dressed first in a swimming costume and then in evening dress. *Swann's Way*, the first part of the seven-part novel *Remembrance of Things Past*, represents a similar challenge. It's a heptathlon event for any reader. Proust invested a huge amount of his life in the novel – published over fourteen years from 1913–27. He requires a similarly large investment from any reader. His brother Robert wryly suggested breaking a leg, and taking some extended convalescence, before embarking on it.

Swann's Way opens with an 'Overture', a long meditation on memory. Why do certain things 'stick in the mind' and other things 'slip the mind'? The adult narrator, Marcel (he is, and he isn't, Marcel Proust), recalls, involuntarily, a childhood bedtime. He is transported back to rural Combray, where his parents took him (an only child) for summers with his grandparents. Little Marcel hated going to bed – it wasn't from fear of ghosts, or the dark, but of being left alone with only his own mind for company. On the occasion he remembers, the family downstairs is entertaining a neighbour, Charles Swann. They do not realise how important a man he is and condescend to him. He is too modest and well-mannered to enlighten them. Marcel eavesdrops. Eavesdropping will be the pattern of his life.

Denied his mother's usual goodnight kiss, Marcel commits a 'sin': he sends, through a maid-servant, a pathetic note downstairs asking her to rescue him from the terrors of his bedroom. She comes up to read to him and his father permits her to stay all night. The boy's nerves are bad; it will keep him quiet. Marcel, for the only time in his life, sleeps with his mother. The Freudian-Oedipal implications (with which Proust was wholly familiar) are obvious.

The keynote struck by the Overture is that the person who remembers the most, lives the most. Proust, reportedly, was in two minds whether to make the first half of *Swann's Way* an essay rather than fiction. He chose fiction, as it offers more opportunity for imagery. And the most resonant image in the novel – one of the most famous in literature – is of a cake. Marcel has, he says, considerable sympathy with the 'Celtic' myth that certain past events are locked in objects, and can be released – often accidentally. It connects with that French noun, which Anglophones borrow (not having the right word themselves), '*souvenir*'.

The Anglo-Saxon 'association of ideas' (originating with John Locke) doesn't match the French one. Late in life, Marcel sips a cup of tea, and nibbles a cake – a 'madeleine' – which releases a 'gust of memory'. It all comes back to Marcel – the whole Combray story, that is.

The second half of *Swann's Way* breaks off and changes mode. The narrative goes back, fifteen years from the bedtime scene, to chronicle Swann's disastrous infatuation with a whore. It is not Odette herself but the idea of her, which has entrapped him. He marries her, only to discover that she has poisoned his existence with her incorrigible adulteries. It ends, forlornly:

> he cried out in his heart: 'To think that I have wasted years of my life, that I have longed for death, that the greatest love that I have ever known has been for a woman who did not please me, who was not in my style!'

The word 'style' – the same in English as in French – reverberates with the reader, colouring one's impression of the whole novel.

The title is awkward both in English and in French (*Du côté de chez Swann*). It refers to family walks in the countryside round Combray. A choice of routes is available: the 'Guermantes way' or the 'Swann way', so called because the paths border two estates. The Guermantes, a baron and duchess, represent aristocratic France. Swann – Jewish, cultivated, a Parisian art dealer moving in the highest intellectual and social circles – is *belle époque* in embryo: the new France. His 'way' (i.e. the Combray path) is rich with the flowering hawthorn which, for Marcel, is what draws him towards a life of the senses.

No more words. Break a leg. Read it.

Sweet Tooth, Ian McEwan, 2012

Sweet Tooth is something new, in fact several new things, in the long evolving career of its author. The novel's primary novelty is that it is a spy story. A secondary novelty is that it has a female narrator. For those in a long-term relationship with McEwan, *Sweet Tooth* contains a revealing chunk of autobiography, chronicling, with mixed nostalgia and self-mockery, the author's formative years, in the late 1960s, as one of the first students on the first creative writing course in the country (at UEA, where he was the prize pupil of Malcolm Bradbury and Angus Wilson) and, at the take-off point of his meteoric rise to fame in the early 1970s, in the London literary world, under the aegis of Ian Hamilton and his cultural HQ in Soho's Pillars of Hercules pub. It was in Hamilton's *New Review* that McEwan first attracted admiring attention with New Gothic short fiction of a quite startling violence.

The novel is dedicated to Christopher Hitchens, 1949–2011 – one of the most golden young literary men of the time. The theme is one which would have been congenial to 'Hitch' (as friends such as Martin Amis, McEwan, and Julian Barnes were privileged to call him). It's the British *trahison des clercs* of the 1960s – specifically the *Encounter* scandal, in which it was discovered that the country's premier opinion-forming magazine, *Encounter*, was funded by the CIA, through a cunning network of proxies.

The narrative has the crispest of openings:

My name is Serena Frome (rhymes with plume) and almost forty years ago I was sent on a secret mission for the British security service. I didn't return safely. Within eighteen months of joining I was sacked, having disgraced myself and ruined my lover, though he certainly had a hand in his own undoing . . . Nothing strange or terrible happened to me during my first eighteen years and that is why I'll skip them.

At nineteen Serena went up to Cambridge to read maths. It was a 'male' subject. Her mother, chauvinistically, insisted it was her duty 'as a woman' to break down the fences. Her father, a vicar on the way to being a bishop, concurred. It turned out rather badly: a third-class degree.

But the love of literature blooms in Serena over the three years at Cambridge – she realises English is the subject she should have chosen. It has now chosen her. Serena loves Trollope and spends a blissful four afternoons reading his masterpiece THE WAY WE LIVE NOW (my edition, I trust). She dislikes novelists (Thomas Pynchon, Borges, et al.) whom she regards as tricksters and double dealers. Her taste tends towards Byatt and Lessing.

Cambridge is the nursery of English espionage and she allows herself to be recruited for MI5. The agent in place who recruits her, and becomes her lover, is a middle-aged history professor, Tony Canning. Tony, at the highpoint of his double-agent career, passed nuclear secrets on to the Russians. MI5, Serena will later discover, has been pimping her out to probe Canning's reliability. It's all a dirty game. Her love of literature means she can be inserted into the booming literary world and facilitate the clandestine funnelling of funds to chosen places. It is also her assignment to manipulate usefully influential writers. One such is Tom Haley, who is making a name for himself as a critic of the persecution of writers in the Eastern bloc. Ian Hamilton and Martin Amis have walk-on parts. So, to be honest, does Ian McEwan, under the thin disguise of Tom Haley. Serena goes to Sussex University, where Tom is based, and offers him a stipend from the Freedom International Foundation – recognisably the Congress for Cultural Freedom, through which the CIA channelled its funding. Serena falls in love with Tom's writing (McEwan mischievously reproduces extracts from his own 1970s work), then falls in love with him. It's a career mistake.

McEwan likes to tie up his narratives with an intricate knot. Enough to say Sweet Tooth is, finally, revealed to be not the Sweet Tooth we thought we were reading. It is, to use Serena's word, 'tricky'. It is also McEwan's most playful novel and among his most uncomplicatedly enjoyable.

Tarka the Otter, Henry Williamson, 1927

Ted Hughes spent the last thirty years of his life living close to Tarka's watery Devon habitat. It was no accident. Hughes had first read the novel aged eleven 'and for the next year read little else'. Williamson is not an author the British public has much cared for: in the 1930s, his misguided compliments to Hitler made him, ever after, a 'non-person'. Hughes, the Poet Laureate from 1984–98, and very much a 'person', described *Tarka*, defiantly, in his memorial address for Williamson in St Martin-in-the-Fields, as 'a holy book, a soul-book, written with the life blood of an unusual poet'. Rachel Carson, the author of *Silent Spring*, saluted Williamson's novel as one of the sacred texts of the environmental movement she spearheaded.

Unlike other anthropomorphic fables discussed here (THE CALL OF THE WILD, BAMBI and FLUSH), *Tarka* is resolutely unsentimental. While revering nature, the events it chronicles are as unremittingly savage as Hughes' legendary pike, lurking in the weeds, a 'killer from the egg'. Williamson's own attitude to the animal world was far from cosy. He had nothing against otter-, fox- and stag-hunting, and his behaviour to animals could be brutal. 'He is alleged', according to his biographer, 'to have seized a kitten and smashed its brains out on the kitchen floor when he caught it destroying the fish dinner laid out in honour of a titled guest.'

Williamson's principal thesis is that to enter otter consciousness a new idiom must be fashioned. Only (as Hughes approvingly observed) a kind of prose–poetry would serve. *Tarka*'s opening sentence makes the point.

> Twilight over meadow and water, the
> eve-star shining above the hill, and
> Old Nog the heron crying *kra-a-ark!*
> as his slow dark wings carried him
> down to the estuary.

Old Nog the heron, it has to be said, becomes a bit of a bore over the course of the novel.

The plot is encapsulated in its full title: *Tarka the Otter: His Joyful Water-Life and Death in the Country of the Two Rivers*. The narrative opens with an otter cub's birth and the simultaneous death of his father between the clamped jaws of an otter-hunting dog. The cub is born 'in the hollow of the water-lapped trunk' and is called Tarka, 'which was the name given to otters many years ago by men dwelling in hut circles on the moor. It means Little Water Wanderer, or, Wandering as Water.' Tarka wanders the waters as soon as he is born, and grows into a lithe, furred, amphibious, beautiful killing machine. Frogs, fish and eels – when their migratory passage teems through the waters of his two rivers – are devoured. In the estuary, where the two rivers join the sea, he feasts on crabs. But from the first another killer (he who slew Tarka's father) is on his trail – Deadlock, 'the great pied hound with the belving tongue, leader of the pack whose kills were notched on many hunting poles' (the staves otter hunters, in their distinctive green garb, carry to test the depth of water). Deadlock kills not for food, but at the behest of the otters' only real enemy, man.

Lutrine wisdom is passed down to Tarka by the ancient matriarch Greymuzzle. While adolescent he courts the coy doe White-tip and is sent on his way by the formidable otter cry 'Ic-yang!' Badly wounded, he is tended by Greymuzzle who 'became dear to Tarka, and gave him fish as though he were her cub, and in the course of time she took him for her mate'. She dies in the harsh winter, when the arctic wind pours 'like liquid glass' across the rivers. In his second year, Tarka, now a warrior, fathers a brood on White-tip. The novel ends in a fight to the death with the remorseless Deadlock in which Tarka shrewdly goes for the hound's jugular. The cast-down otter hunters:

> pulled the body out of the river and
> carried it to the bank, laying it on the
> grass, and looking down at the dead
> hound in sad wonder. And while they
> stood there silently, a great bubble
> rose out of the depths, and broke, and
> as they watched, another bubble
> shook the surface, and broke; there
> was a third bubble in the sea-going
> waters, and nothing more.

Nog krarks.

Tarzan of the Apes, Edgar Rice Burroughs, 1912

Burroughs made many false starts in life. He was a cowboy, a gold panner, a railroad policeman and – at his lowest point – a door-to-door pencil-sharpener salesman. As a last resort (what else was there left?), he turned to fiction with *Tarzan of the Apes*. By the time the first film rolled off the reel in 1918, the Apeman was already a franchise. Burroughs disliked what Hollywood did with his creation but gratefully pocketed the dollars and used them to buy up large chunks of California real estate (most profitably the chunk now called 'Tarzana').

The novel opens in 1888 with 'a certain young English nobleman, whom we shall call John Clayton, Lord Greystoke', being dispatched by the British colonial authorities to investigate the dirty doings of the Belgian colonial authorities in the Congo (Burroughs had obviously read HEART OF DARKNESS – it's a nice question whether Joseph Conrad returned the compliment). Clayton is 'the type of Englishman that one likes best to associate with the noblest monuments of historic achievement upon a thousand victorious battlefields – a strong, virile man – mentally, morally, and physically'. Hip, hip . . . He and his wife are caught up in a shipboard mutiny, and left to fend for themselves in the African coastal jungle. Being English, they manage wonderfully. But Alice, after giving birth to a baby son – the future Lord Greystoke – sickens and dies; Clayton is later killed by marauding great apes. One of the more motherly simians, Kala, scoops up the orphaned baby, protects him, and gives him suck.

The nurseling is named 'Tarzan', which means 'whiteskin' (racial themes bubble close beneath the narrative surface of Tarzan fables). He grows up wholly ape, but is strangely fascinated by things which he finds in his parents' now-derelict cabin. A knife proves particularly handy in an encounter with an unfriendly gorilla called Bolgani, and the apes reward their white-skinned brother with an invitation to 'the fierce, mad, intoxicating revel of the Dum-Dum' – a cannibalistic rite in which they feast ('yum-yum') on their vanquished enemy.

Tarzan finds usefully lethal work for his knife. In the cabin he also finds his father's little library useful. 'The light of knowledge' dawns in his ape-dimmed brain. His reading instructs him that garb might be useful for a hairless simian like himself. A lioness, Sabor, supplies a jungle overcoat (and, as in the movies, a decently unflappable loin cloth). There follows the unhappiest sentence in this not always finely written novel:

> Deftly he removed the great pelt . . . When the task was finished he carried his trophy to the fork of a high tree, and there, curling himself securely in a crotch, he fell into deep and dreamless slumber.

Tarzan seems set for a happy life in the wilds. Enter, however, man – at first in the form of black people fleeing white colonialists. One of them kills Tarzan's 'mother', Kala. The vengeful knife plunges yet again. Tarzan, now in the strength of his years, defeats, in ape-to-ape combat, the chief of his tribe: 'And thus came the young Lord Greystoke into the kingship of the Apes.'

Ape kingship is not to be the limit of Tarzan's destiny. A newly marooned group of white colonialists, led by Professor Archimedes Q. Porter, has found the cabin. Porter's delectable daughter Jane is one of the party, who find a note ('trespassers will be prosecuted, etc.') pinned to the door by Tarzan. It ends in romance. To his credit Burroughs avoids 'Me Tarzan, you Jane' inanities. Through a series of adventures and misadventures the lovers are parted and Tarzan follows her, aided now by a French guide and tutor, D'Arnot, across the world to civilisation. Somewhat improbably (but what does probability matter?) he saves her from a forest fire in the woods of Wisconsin, swinging through the branches, probably yodelling tunefully as well. She is grateful, of course. But can a white maiden like herself marry an ape-man? Yes, it transpires, when fingerprints prove he is – who else? – Lord Greystoke. A blue-blooded, very wealthy ape.

But *will* she marry him? Readers were obliged to buy *The Return of Tarzan* (1913) to find out the answer. They did so, eagerly, and kept buying anything with 'Tarzan' on the cover for the next hundred years. To honour him in his centenary in 2012, the US Mail issued a Tarzan stamp. More Americans, one suspects, recognised his face, as they licked the back of the stamp, than that of George Washington.

The Tenant of Wildfell Hall, Anne Brontë, 1848

Published in the annus mirabilis for English fiction, 1847–8, it's no one's nomination as the 'greatest' novel of those twelve months, which also saw the publication of VANITY FAIR, JANE EYRE, Dombey and Son and WUTHERING HEIGHTS. Nevertheless, The Tenant of Wildfell Hall merits a high place on the list – not because it is as good as Dickens (or take your pick from the above), but because it contains the first chillingly authentic depiction of alcoholism in British fiction.

Asthmatic, the youngest, and always the most biddable of the surviving three Brontë sisters, Anne saw the most of Branwell – the son and great hope of the family. That great hope, of course, was dashed. Branwell, having failed to win the hoped-for place at university, went on to fail as a portrait painter. Even more catastrophic was his being dismissed from a clerical job with the local railway on suspicion of embezzlement. Despite his dissipations, Anne, who was at the time a governess, secured her brother a tutor's position with her own employers, the Robinsons. But Branwell was dismissed from that post for 'proceedings ... bad beyond expression' – thought to be misconduct of a vague sort with Mrs Robinson. Members of the Robinson clan threatened to shoot him; whatever Branwell did, it was beyond horse-whipping. On his dismissal in 1845 he fell into a spiral of despair, which he self-medicated with opium and alcohol. He died – of drink, drugs and galloping consumption – in 1848, aged just thirty-one. The great expectations of the family (and some incomplete works of fiction, alas) went to the family vault at Haworth with him.

The Tenant of Wildfell Hall reveals its plot twists gradually. Helen Huntingdon wishes to escape her brutally alcoholic husband, Arthur. Given the date, Mr Huntingdon would be quite entitled (an entitlement which lasted until 1857, well after the novel's publication) – should he find his errant wife in England – to repossess his conjugal rights (i.e. rape her at will), to repossess whatever personal things she has taken with her, which were legally viewed as his stolen property, and to reassume sole parental responsibility for their son, little Arthur. Since he has adamantly refused her permission to leave his (entirely his) house and denied her access to money, it is clear that Mr Huntingdon is in no mind to give up any of the chattels the marriage laws of England have made over to him. In order to escape, Helen changes her name to 'Mrs Graham' and takes refuge in a broken-down mansion, Wildfell Hall. In a melodramatic climax to the narrative, Huntingdon falls from his horse and Helen – her wifely instinct proving inextinguishable – elects to nurse him as he dies. When he does, she marries a decently sober second husband.

Descriptions of drunkenness are common enough in literature. Novels like TOM JONES are marinated in hard liquor. What is uniquely powerful in The Tenant of Wildfell Hall is the close description of the alcoholic's death. On his deathbed, quite aware it will kill him, Arthur demands strong drink. The consequence is delirious terror:

> 'Death is so terrible,' he cried, 'I cannot bear it! You don't know, Helen – you can't imagine what it is, because you haven't it before you! and when I'm buried, you'll return to your old ways and be as happy as ever, and all the world will go on just as busy and merry as if I had never been; while I—' He burst into tears.

The novel was published three months before Branwell's death – and it is his petulant voice one hears in the above outburst. Anne may have hoped that plain speaking, even through a fictional character, would effect a cure. It rarely does – as legions of spouses of alcoholics testify. Anne outlived her brother by only a few months, dying decently (but tragically early) of the family complaint, consumption.

The Tenant of Wildfell Hall had a

wretched publication history. It was first put out by the same rogue, Thomas Cautley Newby, who had scuppered *Wuthering Heights* on its initial appearance. He did the same for Anne's novel. Charlotte, who survived her sister, disliked the book for its graphic depiction of Branwell's dipsomania, and suppressed its publication. Meek and self-effacing, had she lived Anne would probably have acquiesced in Charlotte's verdict.

Tess of the D'Urbervilles, Thomas Hardy, 1891

How can one read Victorian literature like a Victorian? *Tess* is a useful test case. The basic story is straight off the romance shelf. A young Wessex milkmaid, of intelligence and possibly even noble blood (despite her family's peasant circumstances), finds herself ruined when, driving the family cart by night, she is responsible for the death of the horse on which her father's business as a 'tranter' depends. She goes to work for a family who have bought 'her' Norman name – 'Durberville' – and is raped by the young master, Alec. She bears an illegitimate child who dies in infancy. A young idealist, Angel Clare (as high-minded as his name), later marries her but Tess' confession of her sexual past is badly received by him. He leaves her when he discovers that she is a 'maid no more'.

To support her now fatherless family, Tess descends to agricultural work, labouring in fields which are increasingly mechanised by steam-driven machinery. She is, along with everything else she endures, a victim of the Industrial Revolution. Alec returns, a 'reformed man', and reclaims her. Having again become his mistress (preferring that, apparently, to fieldwork), she stabs him to death when he says something rude about her husband, Angel. Hardy spares us the bloody scene.

On the run she is briefly reunited with Angel before, lying on the sacrificial block at Stonehenge (never let it be said Hardy was afeared of melodrama), she is arrested. Since her union with her husband has been belatedly consummated, she may be pregnant.

British justice doesn't wait to find out. Angel, now a free man, maritally, consoles himself with her younger sister after they witness the divorcing black flag raised outside the jail where Tess is hanged. The novel ends with Hardy's hallmark irony:

> 'Justice' was done, and the President of the Immortals (in Aeschylean phrase) had ended his sport with Tess.

I have discussed Hardy's novel with highly intelligent people over many years. Invariably they cast Tess (a 'pure woman' as Hardy calls her) as the most innocent of victims – a casualty of the cosmic unfairness of things. Hardy, following this line of response, puts quotation marks round 'justice'. And, in addition to Aeschylus (and those captious Greek gods), the word 'sport' recalls Gloucester's bitter 'As flies to wanton boys are we to the gods; / They kill us for their sport'. The view is eloquently expressed by the critic Tony Tanner:

> Hardy's vision is tragic and penetrates far deeper than specific social anomalies. One is more inclined to think of Sophocles than, say, Zola when reading Hardy ... Tess is the living demonstration of these tragic ironies. That is why she who is raped lives to be hanged.

Life sucks, as a later generation would say.

However, the Victorians, by and large, saw Tess as a willing and active partner in her 'seduction', and as a murderess who (despite beauty and good nature) deserves condemnation – if not, perhaps, the rope. Compare Tanner's 'tragic victim' with Mrs Oliphant's robustly Victorian denunciation of a morally careless wench:

> A Pure Woman is not betrayed into fine living and fine clothes as the mistress of her seducer by any stress of poverty or misery; and Tess was a skilled labourer, for whom it is very rare that nothing can be found to do.

Hardy, writing at a period (the 1890s) when Victorian attitudes were mutating into modernism, blurs the reader's response by not closely describing the rape/seduction and by not giving any account of the trial nor the evidence against Tess. (Was it really necessary to murder Alec; could she not merely have left him? Why was she with him, voluntarily committing adultery?)

I was born a mere thirty-seven years after Queen Victoria died. After spending much time in my childhood with grandparents, I have a kind of Victorian grain to my thinking. (I can recall my grandmother describing seeing Gladstone – 'a bent little man'. She would have thought Tess a 'shameless hussy'; Aeschylus would have baffled her.) On the other hand, twentieth-century liberalism – that which would wholly exonerate Tess from being the architect of her own downfall – comes just as easily to my mind when I read the novel, as I regularly do. Hardy has left for posterity a little puzzle which will tease, I suspect, for as long as fiction is read.

Things Fall Apart, Chinua Achebe, 1958

Chinua Achebe, who died in March 2013, was never awarded the Nobel Prize he richly deserved. By way of consolation, he can claim authorship of the work routinely described as the most-read novel to have come out of Africa. *Things Fall Apart* changed the image of that continent in the Western mind – an achievement that Achebe saw as his primary mission in fiction.

He was born an Igbo, in an 'impressive zinc house', and raised middle class in a small town, Ogidi, in southern Nigeria. He described his father, Isaiah Okafo, as a Protestant 'missionary', 'catechist' and 'evangelist', who named his son Albert after Queen Victoria's consort – a colonial label the son later scornfully shed. Achebe's detachment from 'Victorian' (i.e. British nineteenth-century) hegemony was lifelong, fraught, and as painful as removing a slaver's brand. 'Chinua', his chosen first name, is the abbreviation of an Igbo prayer.

The opening paragraph of *Things Fall Apart* sets the narrative in the period when the colonising missionaries had just arrived in the Igbo hinterland, but had not yet 'taken it over'. The prose strikes a defiantly un-British note, bleaching English of all its Englishness to do so:

> Okonkwo was well known throughout the nine villages and even beyond. His fame rested on solid personal achievements. As a young man of eighteen he had brought honour to his village by throwing Amalinze the Cat. Amalinze was the great wrestler who for seven years was unbeaten, from Umuofia to Mbaino. He was called the Cat because his back would never touch the earth. It was this man that Okonkwo threw in a fight which the old men agreed was one of the fiercest since the founder of their town engaged a spirit of the wild for seven days and seven nights.

The syntax has the percussiveness of an African drum. Okonkwo is proudly heathen: his gods are Idemili, Ogwugwu and Agbala. But, one notes, the title of the novel comes from Yeats' chiliastic poem about 'The Second Coming'. In childhood reading of writers such as Rider Haggard, Achebe 'took sides with the whitemen against the savages'. He was brought up jointly steeped in Anglican theology (THE PILGRIM'S PROGRESS was the first novel he read) and the still-vital folklore and oral narratives of his people, outside the zinc walls of the church and household. His stance, as he developed his literary personality in later life, was that of resolute opposition to the mind-forged shackles of colonialism – specifically the Uncle Tom-ist, paternalistic ('benign') racism of novels like Joyce Cary's *Mister Johnson* (a particular object of detestation), Conrad's HEART OF DARKNESS (even more detested), and such lordly observations as Hugh Trevor-Roper's that 'Africa has no history'.

Things Fall Apart is the story of a yam farmer, Okonkwo, who – like Michael Henchard in Hardy's *Mayor of Casterbridge* (an occidental novel Achebe respected for its 'reality') – is a 'man of character' doomed by history. The harbingers of his downfall are the newly arrived missionaries to his village Umuofia. The date of the action is, by Western reckoning, the early 1890s.

Okonkwo is driven to justified murder and altruistic suicide, to spare his village punitive measures. The colonists are not mentally equipped to appreciate either act for what it is. The District Commissioner (later to reappear in Achebe's third novel, *Arrow of God*) muses, apropos of a book he is thinking of writing on the colony:

> The story of this man who had killed a messenger and hanged himself would make interesting reading. One could almost write a whole chapter on him. Perhaps not a whole chapter but a reasonable paragraph, at any rate. There was so much else to include, and one must be firm in cutting out details. He had already chosen the title of the book, after much thought: *The Pacification of the Primitive Tribes of the Lower Niger*.

A paragraph in the white man's history of his people? Okonkwo should count himself lucky. Oh, and what's 'this man's' name? It doesn't matter, and it's hard to pronounce anyway. Call him, say, 'Albert'.

The Thinking Reed, Rebecca West, 1936

There is a blaze of anger in everything she wrote, which is why Cicely Isabel Fairfield renamed herself 'Rebecca West' (the adopted name was from Henrik Ibsen's savagely anti-bourgeois play *Rosmersholm*. Reviewers of the time politely called her 'Miss West' – as inappropriate a politeness as 'Miss Medusa', or 'Miss Lucrezia Borgia'. West was a very fiery woman. And a man-eater.

The Thinking Reed was a success in terms of both sales and critical acclaim for West, a woman who contrived to live very well by her pen. The novel is a reaction against two sources of annoyance: one is Henry James, the other the male domination of women in general. The striking title and epigraph are taken from Pascal:

> Man is but a reed, the most feeble thing in nature, but he is a thinking reed.

And women, Monsieur Pascal? The question is left hanging. West's own gloss of her book was that it chronicled 'the effect of riches on people and the effect of men on women, both forms of slavery'.

The narrative is set in and around the favoured resort of the young American rich, the south of France. Somewhere around the place, we may fantasise, are Scott and Zelda Fitzgerald – he writing THE GREAT GATSBY, she cuckolding him with a dashing French aviator. When the novel opens, Isabelle, a hugely rich, twenty-six-year-old American widow (her husband, Roy, a dashing aviator, recently died in a plane accident), is resident in Paris. Her life, she has resolved, is a 'room which must be completely refurnished'. She has attracted the attention of André de Verviers. Isabelle is beautiful. More to the point, she is possessed of a 'competent, steely mind'. Verviers – handsome, vain, aristocratic, hedonistic – disgusts her. He wants her as a sexual trophy. But he is not the male furniture she had in mind.

As part of his charm offensive André sends her sprays of red and white roses every day. Her response is violent: she carries the offering to his front door and grinds the blooms 'into the mud' with her heel. He will see the debris when he comes out and understand what she means – '*Fou moi le camp!*' ('Buzz off!'). The act frightens off another suitor, a rich Southerner of refined manners and timid disposition, who prudently decides this wildcat is not for him and also buzzes off.

Making all her own life choices, Isabelle selects as her mate a gauche, physically unprepossessing Jewish industrialist by the name of Marc Sallafranque. The marriage is, as the world thinks, ill-assorted. Isabelle, however, has cast herself as an equal partner, not a helpmeet to the mate she has picked for herself. Marc, it transpires, is in danger from his gambling addiction. Isabelle, having gone into the casino where he is playing for ruinously high stakes and realised that desperate measures are required, creates 'a scene':

> She opened her mouth and listened to the high scream that came out of it. It passed like a wind through the room.

She further screams, to the embarrassment of all present, that he has taken as his mistress an expatriate Russian princess, Luba, whom (privately) Isabelle knows to be innocent of the charge. As the climax of the scene she strikes her supposed rival on the cheek. This controlled, wholly theatrical, act of madness works:

> Her heart leaped up in her for she saw Marc's face darken and change from the loose-fitting mask of a stupid, sodden man to the twitching muzzle of an anxious, faithful dog.

She has mastered her mate and brought him to his senses. He takes her off, a reformed man, though a heavy price is paid – she miscarries under the stress of it all. 'I am destroyed', she mutters. But the marriage is saved.

The charge levelled against Henry James is clear. The novel wilfully replays the theme of THE PORTRAIT OF A LADY. James' Isabel (the concurrence of names is wholly deliberate) is no thinking reed, but a wilting pansy. She should have decided more aggressively whom to marry. If it had to be Osmond, she should have mastered the man – not shrivelled under his feeble frigidities. 'James' women do not think,' said West, 'they are presented as sexual objects who behave by the most conventional standards and exhibit no sense of their own.' It's a shrewd criticism, and one James, dead for a decade, could not refute. Alive, he would have been wise, like all men in West's presence, to keep his mouth shut.

The Thirty-Nine Steps, John Buchan, 1915

From his earliest years a 'high flyer', Buchan did many things in his life. Had he done fewer of them, he might have made himself the greatest Scottish novelist since Sir Walter Scott (whose biography he wrote, with sympathetic flair).

As the First World War broke, Buchan, in his late thirties, was recovering from a duodenal ulcer, the occupational hazard of high achievers. To entertain himself, he wrote a 'shilling shocker' – and one which would also 'do its bit' for the war effort (he was too old and too crocked to fight). The story opens in May 1914: the last summer of Old England:

> I returned from the City about three o'clock on that May afternoon pretty well disgusted with life. I had been three months in the Old Country, and was fed up with it.

Richard Hannay, a thirty-seven-year-old Scottish bachelor and African 'old hand' (as was the then forty-year-old Buchan), is terminally bored. He has made his 'pile' cleanly in Southern Rhodesia. He's now dabbling in the City. It's tame work for a man who did his bit against Johnny Boer and has every big game trophy going. Returning to his Portland Place flat one evening, after dining alone at the Café Royal, Hannay is accosted at his front door by a stranger – a small man with 'gimlety blue eyes'. He is, we will learn, an American, Franklin P. Scudder. Why has he approached Hannay? Because, living in the same exclusive block, he has observed that his neighbour is 'not afraid of playing a bold hand'. For reasons which are left wholly mysterious he spills out to Hannay, whom he has known for all of twenty minutes, the fact that he is a secret agent working with British intelligence, and that he has uncovered a dastardly plot by the 'Black Stone' gang to precipitate worldwide conflict, in which Germany will have a strategic advantage – not least knowledge of Britain's 'naval dispositions'.

Scudder is promptly killed by the gang. Hannay, who is the prime suspect, goes on the run to Scotland, pursued by the police and the Black Stone crew, whose German-speaking leader can 'hood his eyes like a hawk' and has tracking skills to match. They hunt him up and down the glens, but Hannay's brilliant veldtcraft frustrates them. Meanwhile, he deciphers Scudder's little black book (which the agent ingeniously hid in Hannay's baccy jar) and, most importantly, the meaning of the cryptic sentence:

> Thirty-nine steps, I counted them – high tide 10.17 p.m.

The government is eventually informed, and the Hun is foiled. Berlin will gain no unfair advantage in the war, which will break out in a few weeks. Buchan was writing at a time when it was fondly anticipated that it would all be over if not this Christmas, then the next – a very unmerry *Weihnachten* for Johnny Bismarck. British amateurism has it over Prussian *Effizienz* any day of the week.

There have been innumerable adaptations of Buchan's shocker (best of all Alfred Hitchcock's gross-liberty-taking 1935 film). There's a comedic West End adaptation running as I write, and it will do so until the centenary month, May 2014. I have not seen it (nor will I), but one thing I am sure of is that the moustachioed derring-do is not underpinned by Scudder's hysterical explanation of what is going wrong with the modern world:

> The Jew is everywhere, but you have to go far down the backstairs to find him . . . a little white-faced Jew in a bath-chair with an eye like a rattlesnake. Yes, Sir, he is the man who is ruling the world just now, and he has his knife in the Empire of the Tzar, because his aunt was outraged and his father flogged in some one-horse location on the Volga.

Scudder's disgusting anti-Semitic rant has been a perennial source of embarrassment to lovers of Buchan. There are routine defences (Scudder's a deranged character, everyone was anti-Semitic in 1914, etc.). Best do what most readers do. Blank it out and enjoy the rest. It's highly enjoyable.

This is How You Lose Her, Junot Díaz, 2012

Díaz' charming-rogue hero, Yunior, also appeared in the Pulitzer Prize-winning novel *The Brief Wondrous Life of Oscar Wao*, and was first introduced in an earlier collection of linked short stories, *Drown*. Yunior (a corruption of 'Junot') is a first-generation Dominican immigrant, brought to New Jersey as a six-year-old to join a father who did not, as it happened, much want to be

joined and soon went his own way. One of the stories in *This is How You Lose Her*, 'Invierno' ('Winter'), recalls Yunior's bleak first months living in the so-called land of the free – in a freezing walk-up apartment alongside a gigantic garbage dump, his elder brother ailing with cancer, and his mother unable to cope. He is cooped up and learns English from the TV that is left burbling away all day. (All this corresponds with Díaz' own primal experience.) 'Back then, in those first days,' recalls Yunior, 'I was so alone that every day was like eating my own heart.'

The young Yunior has nothing going for him. He is a 'nigger' – dark-skinned. The first barber he goes to in America tells him his hair has too much of 'the African' in it, and recommends a shaved scalp. 'None of us wanted to be niggers,' Yunior says, 'not for nothing.' Yunior seems destined for the streets. Or worse. But (the progress is not described in any detail) he ends up a tenured professor of English, in his early thirties, at a prestigious Boston university (Harvard, it is hinted – Díaz himself is a tenured professor of literature at MIT).

The successful careers of Yunior/Junot are vindications that, in the US, anyone can make it. And do – viva America! Nonetheless Yunior's life, as confided in *This is How You Lose Her*, is unhappy. Why? Because he's a sex addict, a love rat; he can't keep his pants zipped. He gets into relationships, then wilfully 'fucks them up'. It's in his blood, he tells himself. 'You had hoped the gene missed you, skipped a generation, but clearly you were kidding yourself. His 'papi' was the same.

The first story, 'The Sun, the Moon, the Stars', opens with a half-apology:

> I'm not a bad guy. I know how that sounds – defensive, unscrupulous – but it's true. I'm like everybody else: weak, full of mistakes, but basically good. Magdalena disagrees though. She considers me a typical Dominican man: a sucio, an asshole . . . See, many months ago, when Magda was still my girl, when I didn't have to be careful about almost anything, I cheated on her with this chick who had tons of eighties freestyle hair.

Why did he do it? Why is Yunior – why are men generally – such suckers for 'culos and titties'?

Díaz' narrative dialect (when he's talking to himself, not his students) is salted with Spanish. Sucio is glossed above. Yunior calls his less-important women sucias – female filth. Not that his eye for detail isn't sharp even when describing his most disposable homegirls. One of his 'slips', we gather, is with 'an ecuatoriana with the biology degree and the *chinita* eyes' (i.e. a girl from Ecuador, with Chinese-looking eyes).

The stories, arranged unchronologically, chronicle Yunior's sexual career: schoolboy initiation, encounters with predatory MILFs, one-night stands. The last story in the collection, 'The Cheater's Guide to Love', spans five years. He is an adult and a successful academic, but yet again Yunior has blown it, 'fucked-up' Casanova that he is. His girl-friend has discovered his fifty love-cheats and resists all his attempts at reconciliation.

> You try every trick in the book to keep her. You write her letters. You drive her to work. You quote Neruda. You compose a mass e-mail disowning all your sucias. You block their e-mails. You change your phone number. You stop drinking. You stop smoking. You claim you're a sex addict and start attending meetings.

Nothing works. You cheated on her fifty (!) times in your six-year relationship. No way back from that. As Díaz has explained in author interviews it's the fact that Yunior is aware of his 'fucked-up-ness' that makes him interesting: 'He longs to do better and yet he can't'. End of story.

This Sporting Life, David Storey, 1963

Say 'David Storey' and readers of my generation will recall the final shot in the film of *This Sporting Life* (scripted by the author): Frank Machin (Richard Harris), mired, spav-ined, hauling himself to his feet on the rugby field so as to lurch back into hopeless battle. His life as a professional is over. Ten

years is a long career in this game. 'Football' (not to be confused with namby-pamby soccer) chews up its workforce faster even than the pits and the factories do. But Frank doesn't take it lying down: no longer a sportsman, he is still a man. He will finish on his feet.

Storey adapted his original novel for Lindsay Anderson, who directed the film, but he curtailed the ending. He also changed the hero's name from Arthur to Frank, to avoid confusion with Sillitoe's Arthur Seaton (see SATURDAY NIGHT AND SUNDAY MORNING). On the printed page, after Machin's legs have 'betrayed' him on the pitch, there is a final scene in the changing-room. The players have had their communal bath. Someone, inevitably, has pissed in it. Machin looks around him, 'had my ankles strapped, got dressed and put my teeth in'. As in the film, the scene expresses a refusal to be ground down, but in a grittier, less self-glorifying way. Getting your teeth knocked out can be glamorous: wearing dentures for the next forty years less so. Both novel and film open with the collision in which the hero, then a young hero, lost his teeth:

> I had my head to Mellor's backside, waiting for the ball to come between his legs.
> He was too slow. I was moving away when the leather shot back into my hands and before I could pass a shoulder came up to my jaw. It rammed my teeth together with a force that stunned me to blackness.

Unconsciousness is followed by toothless-ness. The shoulder charge, of course, was deliberate.

The titular 'sporting life' is ironic – 'sport' is what toffs call their poncey games. Rugby Union (the amateur game) and Rugby League (the professional game) are, histori-cally, class-separated. 'Union' was played on Saturday – a working day for the labouring classes in the pits and steel mills of the north of England. 'League' was played on Sunday, the working man's one day off. The philoso-phies of the respective games (which have now merged with the professionalisation of Union) were different. RU was 'Varsity Matches'; 'good sports' and 'good losers' were honoured. RL was ruthless; to lose was to be worthless.

The novel is set in Wakefield, the home of Rugby League – called here Primstone. Arthur, though never more than dimly aware of what is going on, tells his own story. He works as a lathe operator (a miner in the film) in a factory (like Sillitoe's Arthur). He gets a trial for the local League team and is 'picked' after breaking the nose of one of his own team who is hogging the ball. The owners like savagery: it wins matches. As it happens the team is owned by the same Mr Weaver for whom Arthur slaves in the factory. Selection means £600 a year plus winning bonuses – a fortune to Arthur. He buys a Humber car 'for just over three hundred' and a TV.

Lucky on the pitch, Arthur is singularly unlucky in love. He lodges with a landlady, Mrs Hammond, whom he loves but cannot communicate with. Her husband Eric, suicidal by nature, died in Weaver's factory. It's not clear whether or not he killed himself She was bought off with a 'couple of hundred'. It's all a member of his and her class is worth. She is traumatically embittered, and wholly unimpressed by the dolce vita Arthur hopes will win her heart. When rumours about his 'knocking off' other women circulate he is kicked out. Any reconciliation is impossible after she dies, unexpectedly, of a stroke. He sits in vigil outside her hospital room as, comatose, she slips away. All Arthur has left is the gladiator's death in the ring. For whom? The Weavers of the world. Damn them.

Three Men in a Boat, Jerome K. Jerome, 1889

The British reading public retain an inextinguishable fondness for Jerome K. Jerome. Other worthy humourists who had the 1890s in fits of laughter – Barry Pain, W. W. Jacobs, Eden Phillpotts, William Pett Ridge – have fallen by the wayside. Their names evoke not the mildest of chortles in the twenty-first century. Not so the writer with the odd, self-chosen middle name – Klapka – whose origin remains a perennial topic of dispute among his admirers.

One work is responsible for Jerome's afterlife: the merry story of three pals, and their faithful hound Montmorency (a fox terrier of distinction), messing about in a row-boat on the Thames. One sees them in the mind's eye, blazers blazing with garish stripes, peaked boating caps, 'big pipes' and big moustaches, pints of good bitter and a love of high jinks. This is how the jolly boating venture opens:

> There were four of us – George, and William Samuel Harris, and myself, and Montmorency. We were sitting in my room, smoking, and talking about how bad we were – bad from a medical point of view I mean, of course.
>
> We were all feeling seedy, and we were getting quite nervous about it. Harris said he felt such extraordinary fits of giddiness come over him at times, that he hardly knew what he was doing; and then George said that *he* had fits of giddiness too, and hardly knew what *he* was doing. With me, it was my liver that was out of order. I knew it was my liver that was out of order, because I had just been reading a patent liver-pill circular, in which were detailed the various symptoms by which a man could tell when his liver was out of order. I had them all.

High jinks ahoy. They will, to recover their normal good health and high spirits, row the seventy miles from Kingston-on-Thames to Oxford, spending the nights under canvas and the stars. Things go comically wrong from the start. Jerome first thought of it as a guidebook, and there is much about river landmarks (Hampton Court, Runnymede and Magna Carta Island, etc.). But mainly it's jollity.

Three Men in a Boat has always tickled the English people's funny bone; but nothing else by Jerome does. The Thames will freeze over before the National Theatre considers reviving any of his excessively trivial plays or his eminently forgettable other works of fiction. But what you can confidently expect is that at some not-too-distant point, TV, radio and perhaps even the big screen (it will be the fourth such film) will give us another version of the doomed voyage of the three chums and their pooch. Once more we shall laugh out loud at the trio lost in Hampton Court Maze, attacking tinned pineapple without an opener and the hilarious business of George's shirt.

A streak of black does thread its way even through this jolly chronicle of George, Harris and 'J' (the narrator). During one of the arguments between the chums about whose turn it is to row, George notices something drifting in the water and cries out with a 'blanched face':

> It was the dead body of a woman. It lay very lightly on the water, and the face was sweet and calm. It was not a beautiful face; it was too prematurely aged-looking, too thin and drawn, to be that; but it was a gentle, lovable face, in spite of its stamp of pinch and poverty, and upon it was that look of restful peace that comes to the faces of the sick sometimes when at last the pain has left them.

Jerome's most recent biographer, Carolyn W. de la L. Oulton, supplies the back story. It actually happened, as indeed the jaunt itself was based on a real boat trip (though Montmorency was fictional). Seduced, pregnant and abandoned, the woman drowned herself. It is quite possible that Jerome took the trouble to attend the inquest in July 1887 and read the local newspaper accounts. Death was prone to take a seat at even the jolliest of Victorian feasts.

The Tiger in the Smoke, Margery Allingham, 1952

The last of the great London smogs shrouded the capital in lethal murk in December 1952, three months after Allingham's novel was published. The air was filthy, yellow, and impenetrable to anything but radar. It had to be breathed to be believed (believe me, who wheezed through it) and is reckoned to have killed over 10,000 people.

London had been notorious for its smogs ('pea-soupers', 'old peculiars') for centuries. Climatic inversion, household fires, and factory chimneys were the culprits.

Allingham offers a prefatory note for her American readers, of whom there were many: 'In the shady ways of Britain today it is customary to refer to the Metropolis of London as the Smoke.' The opening paragraph of The Tiger in the Smoke is as evocative as Pissarro and Monet's London fog studies – although a closer influence on Allingham was Alfred Hitchcock's 1927 masterpiece, The Lodger: A Story of the London Fog (see THE LODGER, from which it was adapted). Allingham's novel describes it as follows:

> The fog was like a saffron blanket soaked in ice water. It had hung over London all day and at last was beginning to descend. The sky was yellow as a duster and the rest was a granular black, overprinted in grey and lightened by occasional slivers of bright fish colour as a policeman turned in his wet cape.

The Clean Air Act of 1956 would be a direct response to the Great Smog of December 1952. Smokeless fuel and the exurbation of heavy industry did the trick. Smoke, smog, and dingy fog became things of the past. Some even felt nostalgic for the mephitic atmosphere ('A foggy day, in London town' etc.).

'[T]he thriller proper', Allingham believed, 'is a work of art as delicate and precise as a sonnet.' The Tiger in the Smoke adds to her usual intricacy of plot an unusual sense of doom. It is generally regarded as the best of her 'Campions' although her series hero, Albert Campion, does not play a central role. Haunting the novel (literally; he is not seen in the flesh until halfway through) is Jack Havoc – the tiger, moving unseen through the murk. Havoc is a sadist who slits throats and eludes capture with the cunning of a cat burglar. When he finally appears, it is 'like seeing Death for the first time'. Contesting the moral ground with him is Campion's saintly uncle, Canon Avril, who knew Havoc as a boy and recognised him even then as 'of Evil'. 'Psychopath' is too exculpatory a word. The novel climaxes on a Dostoevskyan debate between Havoc and Avril. Has he been reading 'Frenchmen', asks Avril, those godless existentialists? No. He's just bad to the bone.

There is a personal reason for the novel's dark visions. Allingham had just discovered her husband's flagrant adulteries, which led to a three-year separation and emotional breakdown for her. Her later life was punctuated by periods in asylums.

The narrative grips from its first sentence – 'It may be only blackmail . . .' – to its last: 'The body was never found.' The opening chapter does not merely grip, but goes on to tantalise. A taxi is crawling through a traffic jam. Fog has oozed into the cab, 'ungenially, to smear sooty fingers over the two elegant young people who sat inside'. The couple are engaged to be married. Geoffrey Levett is something in the city: with a 'good war' behind him. Meg Elginbrodde is a twenty-five-year-old widow, and is beautiful. Her husband was a war hero, presumed dead. But is she indeed a widow? Someone has been sending her photos which, blurrily, seem to be of the dead (is he?) Martin. If it's blackmail, for what purpose?

Campion, and his no-nonsense assistant, Inspector Charles Luke, are called in. Ominously, Jack Havoc has recently escaped from prison, leaving a trail of blood behind him. But like Macavity the Mystery Cat, when they get to the scene of the crime, he's never there. The working out of the initial business of the mysterious photographs is replete with the usual Allingham surprises and pleasurable reversals of reader expectation. But brooding over the whole is Havoc. The fact that he disappears without trace – leaving a cloud of sulphur (that 'fog') – is of a piece with his life. He is (who else?) the devil, who is – however many wars we win – always with us.

Titus Alone, Mervyn Peake, 1959

Reading this novel, the last in the *Gormenghast* series, is like watching a slow authorial breakdown. The novel was never quite put together by Peake, who by then was in no state to do so. Perversely that failure, felt on every page, adds to the novel's painful fascination.

Titus – young prince of Gormenghast, the 77th Earl of Groan – has been cast out into the modern world. The frontispiece which Peake drew for the novel shows a boy clinging, panic-stricken, to the outside walls of an ancient castle as a futuristic aircraft shrieks past – carrying, one apprehends, a nuclear bomb. The modern world, Peake implies, finds its epitome not in the medieval castle, but the concentration camp (he was a commissioned war artist and depicted Belsen for posterity), the modern post-industrial city, and – that most horrific of institutions – the 'lunatic asylum'. Peake would die (shattered by 'therapy') in such an institution in 1968.

Titus Alone's opening picks up on the last words of *Gormenghast*, 'Titus rode out of his world':

> To north, south, east or west, turning at will, it was not long before his landmarks fled him. Gone was the outline of his mountainous home. Gone was that torn world of towers. Gone the grey lichen; gone the black ivy. Gone was the labyrinth that fed his dreams. Gone ritual, his marrow and his bane. Gone boyhood. Gone.

Gormenghast was decayed but – in its vestigial way – coherent. This new world flickers around Titus in fractured images. He finds himself pursued by a pair of ruthless policemen – for what? No one recognises him as the aristocrat he is. He is viewed as a vagrant from somewhere else. And, obscurely, a criminal:

> The hunger burned in his stomach but there was another burn, the heartburn of the displaced; the unrecognised; the unrecognisable.

No one in this new world has ever heard of Gormenghast – a castle as large as a small country, a few miles away on a vast mountain. It is, they assume, a fantasy. Perhaps it is. 'I have nothing to hold in my hand,' says Titus. 'Nothing to convince myself that it is not a dream.'

Things take some shape for him when he encounters Muzzlehatch, an authority figure who is first seen 'naked, except for a fireman's helmet'. He is hosing into obedience a couple of amorphous beasts who have 'reverted'. Muzzlehatch is a zoo-keeper.

He is the incarnation of dark anarchy – there is no point in building a structure, he believes:

> There is no value in a rule until it is broken. There is nothing in life unless there is death at the back of it. Death, dear boy, leaning over the edge of the world and grinning like a boneyard.

He has no reason for taking Titus under his wing other than whim and an instinctive nasal aversion to the police pursuing the young man:

> I dislike the police. I dislike their feet. I dislike that whiff of leather, oil and fur, camphor and blood. I dislike officials who are nothing, my dear boy, but the pip-headed, trash-bellied putrid scrannel of earth.

Gormenghast embodied organic decay. The modern world is one of hellish machinery – there are death rays, bombs with lethal flechettes; Muzzlehatch has a car in the form of a shark; rockets sear, threateningly, through the stratosphere. 'Money' (something irrelevant in Gormenghast) rules. Titus has an instructive encounter with a beggar who eats money (one of the more discomfiting images in the novel). Coming to any terms with this new world is complicated by the twenty-year-old Titus' dawning sexuality. The main episode takes place in a factory dedicated to the production of bad smells. Titus becomes involved with the owner's daughter, a modern young woman who gallivants around in a helicopter and is called, in tribute to Tarzan's companion apparently, Cheeta. Muzzlehatch blows up the factory before the relationship can go anywhere.

The novel ends with the hero still wandering, in no direction other than away from where he wants to be: 'With every pace he drew away from Gormenghast Mountain, and from everything that belonged to his home.' Alone for ever. As David Louis Edelman says: 'the first question to ask is this: how much of *Titus Alone* is Mervyn Peake switching gears, and how much is Mervyn Peake losing his marbles?' Good question.

To Build a Fire, Jack London, 1908

London is one of the select band of American authors – along with John Reed, Upton Sinclair, and Howard Fast – who were literary heroes in the early days of the Soviet Union. The man who made the USSR, V. I. Lenin, died on 21 January 1924, aged fifty-three. He had literally worked himself to death. Lenin's mind had become clouded by three strokes and he was confined, in a kind of house arrest, by his young, more ruthless, successor, Stalin. The law of life, as London would have put it. On his deathbed, Lenin asked his wife, Nadya, to read 'To Build a Fire' to him. The novel draws on the year young Jack had spent in the Yukon, mining for gold. He came back from the snowy wastes with less than $5 worth of gold dust, but having had a life-changing encounter with what he called the 'White Logic' – 'the argent messenger of truth beyond truth, the antithesis of life, cruel and bleak as interstellar space, pulseless and frozen as absolute zero, dazzling with the frost of irrefragable logic and unforgettable fact'. Dialectical Materialism reduced to the clarity of an icicle.

The story opens with a man walking along a trail in the snow. He is a newcomer here and this is his first winter. It is seventy-five degrees below zero: spit, and the spittle will turn to ice in the air before reaching the ground. The man has been warned by old hands never to walk the trails without a trail-mate when the temperature is below minus fifty. But he has no fear. He is on his way to a camp a few miles off, to register a new claim and have dinner in a warm cabin. He is making a brisk four miles an hour, and will be at his destination very soon. At his heels 'trotted a dog, a big native husky, the proper wolfdog, grey-coated and without any visible or temperamental difference from its brother, the wild wolf'.

The man takes a short cut along a creek. Here the bubbling water underneath the ice does not freeze, however cold the air above.

> And then it happened. At a place where there were no signs, where the soft, unbroken snow seemed to advertise solidity beneath, the man broke

through. It was not deep. He wet himself halfway to the knees before he floundered out to the firm crust.

Wet feet are nothing to worry about: except when the temperature is seventy-five below. If he wants to live the man must light a fire to dry out his footgear. He gathers twigs and branches to do so. By the time they are piled up he has lost all sensation in his feet. More ominously, 'to build the fire he had been forced to remove his mittens, and the fingers had quickly gone numb'.

He succeeds in lighting the fire, using as kindling some birch bark with his matches in his pocket. But, newcomer to this wilderness that he is, he foolishly builds the fire under a spruce tree. The wind blows lightly, snow falls heavily, extinguishing the flames. Even if he lights a second fire, he will lose some toes, at least – and possibly fingers. But is he able? His fingers are now paralysed. He has to extract a match with his teeth. He again contrives to light the fire, but a lump of moss falls from the tree, scattering the layer of twigs. To live he must light a third fire – but he will freeze to death before he can do so; his hands are already useless. Suddenly he remembers a tale he was told. If he kills his dog, its hot entrails will warm his hands sufficiently to render them usable again. But he cannot kill the dog: his arms are immobile, and the animal perceives his intent. The man drifts into unconsciousness, hallucinating that he is running effortlessly to the camp and safety. Soon it is all over: 'the man drowsed off into what seemed to him the most comfortable and satisfying sleep he had ever known'. The dog watches from a safe distance before making its own canine decision. 'It turned and trotted up the trail in the direction of the camp it knew, where were the other food-providers and fire-providers.'

A few hours after hearing the story, Lenin fell into his own last sleep.

To Kill a Mockingbird, Harper Lee, 1960

Lee's novel (her only published work) takes place in the depressed 1930s, and is set in the backwoods town of Maycomb, Alabama, in the Deep South. It arrived at the start of the fraught run-up to the 1964 Civil Rights Act, and made a potent contribution to the debate. The hero Atticus Finch's proclamation that 'You never really understand a person until you consider things from his point of view . . . Until you climb inside of his skin and walk around in it' ('skin' being the operative word here) has become as well known as the opening lines of 'The Star-Spangled Banner'. To Kill a Mockingbird won a Pulitzer Prize, inspired an Oscar-winning film, and to date is reckoned to have sold 30 million copies. In 1991, a Library of Congress survey of reading habits found that it was one of three books most often cited as 'making a difference', second only to the Bible.

The novel starts, obliquely, by describing a mysterious wound:

> When he was nearly thirteen, my brother Jem got his arm badly broken at the elbow. When it healed, and Jem's fears of never being able to play football were assuaged, he was seldom self-conscious about his injury.

The narrator is Jean Louise 'Scout' Finch – at the time of the story a six-year-old 'tomboy'. Jem is her elder brother. They live with their widowed father Atticus, a small-town lawyer, and a black housekeeper, Calpurnia. The story runs on two tracks. One is the children's relationship with the recluse – nicknamed 'Boo' – who lives in the sinister Radley Mansion. He communicates, in a clumsily friendly way, with the Finches by leaving gifts for them in a tree they pass on their way home. They try to entice him out, but 'Boo' (short for 'boogy man', or demon) remains resolutely unenticed.

The other plot strand opens mid-narrative when Atticus is appointed to defend a Negro (as the more polite term then was) accused of raping a white woman. The case strongly parallels the series of trials of the nine 'Scottsboro boys', accused falsely (by Alabama justice) and sentenced to death for raping two white women. They were wholly innocent and the trials dragged on from 1931–7, attracting worldwide outrage as time and again white juries found them guilty of what they did not do. Atticus, as were the defenders of the Scottsboro boys, is reviled as a 'nigger-lover' (hateful compound) and faces down a lynch mob who want quicker justice than all-white juries and judges supply.

The Finch children are banned from attending the trial and clandestinely watch proceedings from the 'Colored Balcony' – 'in another skin', so to speak. Atticus proves his client Tom Robinson's accusers, a white girl and her father, are lying. A clumsy overture on Mayella Ewell's part is to blame for the accusation: she 'tempted' Robinson, 'a strong young Negro man', and – taking the initiative – kissed him. He 'felt sorry' for her, and did not push her away. Her 'shamed' father caught sight of the event, beat his daughter 'savagely' and concocted a false charge of rape to uphold the honour of white womanhood. Despite Atticus' stirring speech for the defence Tom is convicted by a jury of anything but his peers, condemned to death, and shot dead while attempting to escape over the jail fence.

Bob Ewell, enraged by Atticus' humiliation of him in court, attacks the Finch children with murderous intent as they walk back through the woods from a Hallowe'en party. Enter, belatedly, Boo Radley, who saves them, killing Ewell. The fiction is concocted that it was an accidental death – but Jem sustains the arm wound mentioned in the book's first paragraph as a reminder of the truth.

Atticus, the embodiment of what is most redeemable in Maycomb, is prepared to take his gun off the wall to shoot a rabid dog (he's a dead-eye shot) but warns his children never to shoot mockingbirds: 'Mockingbirds don't do one thing but make music for us to enjoy . . . but sing their hearts out for us. That's why it's a sin to kill a mockingbird.' The National Rifle Association has never been able to make up its mind as to whether it likes Harper Lee's novel or not.

Tom Jones, Henry Fielding, 1749

Fielding's novel has, for most of its existence, been in and out of literature's doghouse. From Dr Johnson to Dr Leavis, 'doubts' have been expressed about the author of *Tom Jones*. The climate of disapproval has not been dispelled by the allegation of the novelist's most eminent biographers, Martin and Ruthe Battestin, that at the kernel of the definitive Fielding comedy is incest (a theme richly enlarged on in *Tom Jones* by the hero's romp in a bed with Jenny Waters, née Jones – his putative mother).

The story of *Tom Jones* is loose (in both senses). A foundling is discovered in the bed of a virtuous spinster, Bridget Allworthy. Her brother, an estimable magistrate who is well deserving of his epithetic name, takes in the unwanted little boy and he is named Tom Jones – the surname because he is assumed to be the offspring of Jenny Jones, a local woman of bright intelligence and relaxed morals, and a schoolteacher, Mr Partridge. As a magistrate, it is Allworthy's duty to put down bastardy. Nor is Mrs Partridge all that sympathetic. Jenny is banished and Partridge goes his own way, a ruined man.

Tom is brought up in rural Somerset, as a son of the Allworthy household. But not, of course, with the 'prospects' that legitimate offspring would have. He is a wild lad – fond of drinking, women, hunting – but good-hearted. Straitlaced observers confidently predict that he is born to be hanged. Meanwhile, Bridget Allworthy marries a soldier on the make, Captain Blifil, and produces a son. On his father's death from apoplexy, young Blifil, a sly hypocritical youth, devotes himself, cuckoo-style, to the eviction of Tom from the Allworthy nest. As the boys grow up his scheme is aided by the house tutors, Square and Thwackum, moralists of the old school.

Tom, a lad of spirit, falls in with the poacher Black George and his family. Molly, George's daughter, offers no resistance to Tom's sexual advances. He also sets his cap at a local squire's daughter, Sophia Western. Blifil, a much less enticing suitor to her, but entirely enticing to her guardians, is now Tom's rival in love as well as inheritance. Tom's chances are sadly damaged by Molly's falling pregnant – responsibility for which he confesses to Allworthy. He is, it emerges, not the father, but self-proclaimed fornication does not raise his moral standing.

On what looks like his deathbed, Allworthy reads out his will – leaving the bulk of his estate to Blifil. Tom celebrates

Allworthy's unexpected recovery by getting drunk, fighting Blifil (unlike Tom sadly disappointed by his uncle's reprieve), and having his lusty way, yet again, with the ever-willing Molly. The novel thereafter turns picaresque when Tom is banished and Sophia, to escape the awful fate of becoming Mrs Blifil, runs away. Tom finds his Sancho Panza in Partridge (his father?), and in a hilariously farcical episode in the inn at Ware makes casual love to a lady, 'Jenny Waters', who turns out (or does she?) to be his mother, the former Miss Jones. The reader is left to believe, uncomfortably, in the incest until virtually the last page, when Tom's actual (wholly unlikely) parentage is revealed.

Sophia is also, by chance, at the inn and is unimpressed by Tom's philandering. She angrily goes off on her own again. Thereafter in London things become climactically complicated and, after a duel, it seems Tom will indeed hang, while Sophia narrowly escapes rape by a licentious aristocrat. But all turns out well (un-incestuously, with maidenhead intact). Tom and Sophia become respectable, god-fearing, well-off country folk. All-worthy.

It was, of course, the sex which offended – particularly in the nineteenth century. As Thackeray complained:

> Since the author of Tom Jones was buried, no writer of fiction among us has been permitted to depict to his utmost power a MAN. We must drape him, and give him a certain conventional simper. Society will not tolerate the Natural in our Art.

Arguably it was not until the 1960s – that most uncensorious and un-Victorian of decades – that Tom Jones finally came into its own with the joyous Tony Richardson-directed, John Osborne-scripted, Albert Finney-starring film. Sales of the novel, in its classic reprint livery, boomed. It sold more copies than ever before in the year of the film, 1963 (also the year in which, according to Philip Larkin, sexual intercourse began to the thumping soundtrack of the Beatles' first LP). The film won four Oscars and is, unlike incorrigible Tom, very faithful.

Touch, Elmore Leonard, 1987

The unusually fraught background to Touch is outlined in its preface. Leonard wrote the work in 1977 and had it promptly rejected by a dozen hardback publishers. They were universally polite about the prose, in one case calling it 'the best writing you have done to date'. But they wanted nothing to do with the subject matter. Finally, the work was reluctantly accepted, as an act of goodwill, by Leonard's regular publisher, for issue as a humble paperback original. They went on to set Touch up in galleys, but made no apparent effort to publish the book. Meanwhile, on the strength of works like Glitz (1986), Leonard's reputation as a hard-boiled crime writer grew. After three years, he bought back the rights to his unwanted novel. And, in 1987, his star was high enough for anything with his name on it to sell, even the literary orphan Touch. So published it finally was.

Touch is set in Detroit's downtown (a favourite Leonard locale). At its simplest, it's a novel about healing – more particularly, miracle-working. In interviews, Leonard occasionally alluded to the drinking problems and breakdowns which plagued his life and career in the seventies. Touch would seem to have grown out of those episodes, and the well-trodden AA recovery route via the 'higher power', which the fellowship requires you to trust in. Leonard was, in short, a drunk who took his last drink at 9.30am on 24 January 1977. He apparently never touched the stuff thereafter, remaining clean and sober until his death in August 2013.

Touch's story is simple enough. A young priest, Juvenal, leaves the Franciscan order and takes up work in the Sacred Heart Rehabilitation Centre, a half-way house for recovering drunks. In the course of his Samaritan work, he finds himself able to perform miracles of healing. He makes the blind see and the lame walk. Furthermore, he bleeds from the marks of the stigmata. It seems he is the 322nd in the line of known stigmatics, the last of whom, Padre Pio of southern Italy, died in September 1968. As a saint in the making, Juvenal is stalked by the Gray Army of the Holy Ghost, who want to use him in their campaign to restore, by armed force if necessary, the traditional Catholic mass. He is also stalked by the entertainment industry, who see remunerative possibilities in the television world for the miracle-worker.

A resourceful woman publicity agent (with whom Juvenal eventually falls in love) fakes her way into the Centre and tracks the hero to his bedroom with the aim of securing an exclusive contract to represent him. She gets more than she bargains for.

> He stood in white undershorts by a dresser, his chest and legs bare. He stood on a white towel, his feet bare.
>
> Lynn said, 'Oh, my God—'
>
> She saw his mild expression, his eyes. She saw his hands raised at his sides, palms up, as if holding small pools of blood.
>
> She saw the crucifix on the wall.
>
> She saw the blood on his hands. She saw the blood oozing out of his left side, staining the waistband of his shorts. She saw the blood on his bare feet, red gouge marks on his insteps, the blood trickling to the towel.
>
> She saw the crucifix again, the agonised figure of Christ on the Cross.
>
> She saw Juvenal standing in his bedroom, bleeding from the same five wounds.

One can understand why those publishers turned tail and ran. There is no dissolve into irony, fantasy, science fiction or rational explanation. The novel quite straightforwardly dumps a medieval saint on to the streets of Detroit. Oh, my God, the reader echoes: Elmore Leonard believes in miracles and he wants to tell us about them. It's Conan Doyle and the fairies all over again.

Touch climaxes with Juvenal's appearance on a talk show. Before an audience of millions, he heals the crippled body of a man who earlier tried to assassinate him. The miracle is real enough, but the sensation-jaded American public disbelieve the plain evidence of their eyes, assuming that the whole thing is a hoax. The saint is without honour in his country.

Trainspotting, Irvine Welsh, 1993

One of the heartening events for the British book trade in the 1990s was the recruitment of a new cohort of young readers to fiction – readers who might, it was feared, have been lost for ever to TV, CDs, clubs, and, as the decade drew to a close, social networking and computer gaming. Irvine Welsh was at the forefront of bringing those lost readers back to the pleasures of the novel with *Trainspotting*, boosted as it was by the prize-winning film, directed by Danny Boyle and starring, among other future superstars, Ewan McGregor.

The narrative is set in Edinburgh, specifically the traditionally working-class Leith area of the city, in the late 1980s, before 'urban regeneration' robbed it of its character. The novel takes the form of a number of disconnected brief episodes featuring a quintet of young, nihilistic, work-shy Scots who live for drugs, rock and roll (Iggy Pop, principally), Kung Fu movies (Jean-Claude van Damme, usually), brawling and selfish sex (unprotected, of course: Aids will wipe most of them out in a year or two, if heroin and violence don't). The five principals in *Trainspotting* are: (1) Sick Boy, half Italian, half educated, a ruthless predator of underage girls whom he later pimps; (2) Second Prize, who never made it as a junior footballer and is now a hopeless addict; (3) Spud, the nicest of the gang, an incorrigible petty thief; (4) Begbie, a psychopathic sadist and drug dealer, who punches his pregnant girlfriend in the belly by way of domestic discipline; and (5) Rents, or, as he is more formally known, Mark Renton (the Ewan McGregor character).

Renton is the central character and the narrator. *Trainspotting* opens with him scoring heroin and ends with him absconding to Amsterdam with the group's drug stash. His pals will kick him to death if he ever again shows his face in Leith. Begbie might come up with something worse. Renton is the only one of the group whom we can conceive writing a novel like *Trainspotting*. From incidental comments we can assemble an identikit portrait. He is twenty-five. His parents are Catholic working class, originally from Glasgow. Sometime ago his disabled brother, Davie, died. This disturbed him. He has an elder brother, Billy, in the army – soon to be killed in Ulster – whom he does not like or mourn. This does not disturb him. At the funeral Rents seduces, for want of a better word, Billy's very pregnant girlfriend in a conveniently unengaged lavatory. At sixteen Rents was apprenticed as a joiner. But later he went to sixth-form college and from there to Aberdeen University. He was kicked out, after a year, for drugs, stealing books and sexual turpitude.

On the face of it, Rents is as grossly philistine as his comrades. But there are glimpses of something tantalisingly higher. Literary touches keep breaking in on his brutal street talk. At one point, for example, he describes the shivers that accompany heroin withdrawal as being like 'a thin layer ay autumn frost oun a car roof'. He routinely uses words like 'psychic vandalism'. In order to pick up some birds on a train down to London (he's hoping for more of that sex in lavatories) he discourses learnedly about Bertolt Brecht and *Verfremdung* – talk that makes Begbie dangerously suspicious.

Most impressively, when he and Spud are arrested for stealing from a bookshop, Rents explains to the magistrate, in very technical English, the essence of Kierkegaard's philosophy. 'I'm interested', he tells the court,

in his concepts of subjectivity and truth, and particularly his ideas concerning change; the notion that genuine choice is made out of doubt and uncertainty, without recourse to the experience or advice of others.

He gets off. The inarticulate Spud goes to jail for ten months.

For all its crudity of language, *Trainspotting* is a subtle novel. Subliminally it sends the message, 'Tough guys do read; books are a turn-on'. Good for Irvine Welsh, say I.

Treasure Island, Robert Louis Stevenson, 1883

The novel was initially published in the boys' weekly *Young Folks* and was Stevenson's first work of fiction. He was in his early thirties when he invented the one-legged rogue who has become folkloric. 'Sooner or later', Stevenson recalled, '. . . I was bound to write a novel. It seems vain to ask why. Men are born with various manias: from my earliest childhood, it was mine to make a plaything of imaginary series of events.' The genesis of *Treasure Island* was an even more rotten Scottish summer than usual, in which 'Louis', his new wife Fanny, and his stepson Lloyd were confined to their holiday cottage by weather which was 'absolutely and consistently vile'. As with FRANKENSTEIN, we owe a masterpiece to unseasonal downpours. To entertain himself Lloyd (a lad skilled with the paintbrush) devised an imaginary map, fed by the nautical tales of writers like R. M. Ballantyne, author of *The Coral Island*. It inspired his writer stepfather to join in for the amusement of himself, the family, and visitors (one of whom was a scout for *Young Folks*). He would, he later recalled, read aloud the day's instalment 'after lunch' to the family. Desert island as dessert. Later chapters were read in the evening, after the candles were brought in. His voice, recalled Fanny, was 'extraordinarily thrilling'. He enjoyed doing it, and that boyish joy comes through on every page. Defiantly, like Mark Twain at the beginning of THE ADVENTURES OF HUCKLEBERRY FINN, he warned critics away. 'Let them write their damn masterpieces for themselves', he expostulated, 'and let me alone.'

The young narrator-hero, Jim Hawkins, helps run a Devon coastal inn, the Admiral Benbow, with his mother and sick father, who soon departs the story. A mysterious sailor, Billy Bones, lodges with them. After a visit from Blind Pew (who delivers the dreaded 'black spot', the pirates' death sentence), Bones dies of shock. Resourcefully, Jim discovers Bones' map, locating where the notorious pirate Captain Flint buried his ill-gotten treasure on an island in the Spanish Main. Together with Squire Trelawney and Dr Livesey, Jim sets off on the good ship *Hispaniola* to find the trove. They recruit a one-legged sea cook, Long John Silver (in fact one of Flint's former crew), who cunningly foments mutiny. There ensues a series of treacheries and fights to the death on board the ship, and then on the desert island.

The island is not, however, entirely deserted. Jim discovers Ben Gunn (another of Flint's old crewmates), who has been marooned for years (his greatest longing is for a bite of cheese, poor fellow). Jim contrives to take the *Hispaniola* from the mutineers single-handed (shooting the villainous coxswain, Israel Hands, in the process). When a truce is called, and Flint's chests dug up (they are located by codes, drawing, confessedly, on Poe's THE GOLD BUG), they are found to be empty. Gunn has removed the treasure. This final trick defeats the mutineers. Silver escapes with a sackful of gold coins. Stevenson thereby left the door open for a sequel, which, alas, he never got round to writing. Others (most recently Andrew Motion) have.

The Tribe That Lost Its Head, Nicholas Monsarrat, 1956

It is one of the privileges of fiction – its licence so to call it – to advance very unfashionable causes. Monsarrat's novel is one such. In this regard it's of a piece with his other (more famous) novel, *The Cruel Sea*, whose subtext was that, however beastly the Germans were, Britain was a country which may not have been worth making the ultimate sacrifice for.

Monsarrat was, in the early 1950s, a Foreign Office official – moderately highly ranked. The five years he was stationed in Johannesburg, as Africa seethed in turmoil, had been formative. It was the period of what Harold Macmillan later called 'the wind of change' (the actual speech was delivered, bravely, to the South African parliament, in 1960). What Macmillan – arguably the last great orator to hold the prime ministerial post – told his largely unsympathetic, and that time wholly windproof, audience was:

The wind of change is blowing through this [African] continent, and whether we like it or not, this growth of national consciousness is a political fact. We must all accept it as a fact, and our national policies must take account of it.

Monsarrat had resigned from the Colonial Service in 1956. It was, with the inexorable process of decolonisation ('the end of empire', as it was grandly called – others called it a 'scuttle'), a rational decision. He was earning enough from his fiction not merely to get by, but to be interested in locations such as the Channel Islands and Malta, where he could evade the punitive exactions of Britain's Inland Revenue.

He could not anyway have stayed on in the service, what with the novel he published that year. *The Tribe That Lost Its Head* is far and away Monsarrat's best, and his most contentious. It is set in an imaginary island, Pharamaul, off the west coast of Africa, and allegorises the tensions resulting from old, complacent British colonial rule (more benign than that in the nearby Republic of South Africa) in the aftermath of Kenya's Mau Mau insurgency – on which Monsarrat had views which would have made Sanders of the River look namby-pamby.

The story's black hero, Dinamaula, is the Oxford-educated chief-in-waiting of the Maula tribe who returns to take up his position. He is clearly based on the occidentalised, Oxford-educated Sir Seretse Khama, who returned after the independence struggle to take up the leadership of Botswana. Monsarrat had personal dealings with Seretse Khama and despised him. Like Khama, Dinamaula has chosen to marry a white woman, which complicates things. His prospective subjects, the Maula – a childlike people who have lived quite happily under a regime which has not changed since the rule of their 'Mother across the Sea' (Victoria) – are inflamed by ideas of self-determination fed to them by mischievous British newspapermen and doltishly doctrinaire Socialist politicians. Rebellion ensues and the tribesmen, whose pagan Christianity demands blood sacrifice, ritually crucify and rape some luckless missionaries and white women. Summary executions follow and a press conference is given by a wholly disillusioned young administrator, David Bracken:

'You mean that they actually crucified him [Father Schwemmer]?'
'Yes,' said David.
'A deed of madness!' exclaimed

Father Hawthorne. 'Those poor, misguided children.'

David looked at him. 'Yes, indeed. Misguided, *greedy* children.'

'What do you mean by "greedy", Mr Bracken?'

'I should have told you that they ate him as well.'

That had been the end of the Press conference.

It echoes the blackly comic ending of Evelyn Waugh's *Black Mischief* (1932), when Basil asks the chief what was in the delicious stew they had last night and is told, 'Your girl friend.' But Monsarrat's view was not – like Waugh's – that of the satirical tourist. The novel expresses radical uncertainty about whether Empire was worthwhile, and whether letting go of it so precipitately was morally right or wrong. Monsarrat was no Blimp. Nor did he believe, like the novel's senior colonial official Macmillan (mischievously named after the PM), that in a couple of centuries or so the Africans might conceivably be about ready for emancipation. It was, he believed, all a mess – but the Englishman's mess. This novel was, in the context of 1956 (and with the Belgian Congo independence riots imminent), explosive. It offended, and was intended to. Novels are free to do that.

Tropic of Cancer, Henry Miller, 1934

I first read the 1934 Obelisk edition, picked up (with a furtive glance over the shoulder) from a *bouquiniste* on the Seine's *rive gauche*, aged seventeen. It had a powerfully aphrodisiac effect from the fourth paragraph on, when the book's great sexual fantasia begins. I had never before read fiction which was so headily out of moral control:

> Tania, where now is that warm cunt of yours, those fat, heavy garters, those soft, bulging thighs? There is a bone in my prick six inches long. I will ream out every wrinkle in your cunt, Tania, big with seed ... After me you

can take on stallions, bulls, rams, drakes, St Bernards. You can stuff toads, bats, lizards up your rectum.

I was not fool enough to try and get the novel past the Customs officer. ('Anything to declare, young sir?') No need. It was all etched on my mind. I could have recited it from memory. In the following years I came across Orwell's thoughtful essay, 'Outside the Whale', in which he ponders Miller's total freedom from social constraint. Is 'outside', ranting without fear of reprisal, where the writer should be? Or should he/she be a well-mannered citizen inside society? Outlaw or hack?

At a later period in life I picked up the 1963 Calder hardback of *Tropic of Cancer*, published in the great 'tidal wave of filth' (as a large part of England saw it) precipitated by the *Lady Chatterley* acquittal. The *TLS*, speaking for many, found it 'nauseating', a 'verbal cancer'. It was reviewed, more perceptively, by an undisgusted Richard Hoggart in the *Guardian*, as a spasm of raw, but essentially healthy, literary energy. Hoggart was a god to me at the time for his trial-turning evidence, which had won the case for the liberation of Lawrence's book.

Then, a year or two later, came the opinion-reversing feminists. For critics like Kate Millett, in her polemic *Sexual Politics*, Henry Miller – along with Lawrence and Mailer – was the quintessence of male chauvinist piggery. (Why, for instance, can't Tania shove toads up Miller's rectum?) Jeanette Winterson, speaking for her sex in the *New York Times*, on the fiftieth anniversary of the book's first publication, concurred with Millett:

> There is beauty as well as hatred in 'Cancer', and it deserves its place on the shelf. Yet the central question it poses was stupidly buried under censorship in the 1930s, and gleefully swept aside in the permissiveness of the 1960s ... The question is not art versus pornography or sexuality versus censorship or any question about achievement. The question is: Why do men revel in the degradation of women?

And, here I am, reading *Tropic of Cancer* again. It strikes me now as a thoughtful game with the rules of fiction. A self-reflexive novel, asking interesting questions about its genre. It's no more aphrodisiac, in the second decade of the twenty-first century, than the contents label on a ketchup bottle. The key to the work (I'm avoiding the word 'novel') is found in the epigraph:

'These novels will give way, by and by, to diaries or autobiographies – captivating books, if only a man knew how to choose among what he calls his experiences that which is really his experience and how to record truth truly' – Ralph Waldo Emerson

The novel, as Miller creates it, is in a condition of evolutionary mutation into something beyond and beneath realism (that 'mirror carried along a high road', as Stendhal called it), a closer contact with reality: more specifically the reality of self. There is a significant moment in the narrative when Miller says, in passing:

I have moved the typewriter into the next room where I can see myself in the mirror as I write.

Narcissus is the true creative spirit here. Miller is what he writes. Masturbation – Miller making love to Miller – is the appropriate analogue.

Nothing happens in Miller's novel worth writing a novel about. He spends two years comfortably in Paris cadging off people as aimless, rootless, amoral and worthless as the narrator is. But nonetheless Miller is doing something important and new in fiction, despite the willed crudity and the raving megalomaniac *non serviam* ('This is not a book. This is libel, slander, defamation of character' etc.). It's a work of (almost) fiction which contrives to be offensive, crass, and important. And worth reading and thinking about – at least to the fourth paragraph.

Trouble at Willow Gables, Philip Larkin, 2002

It's not unusual for writers of impeccable canonical respectability secretively to dabble in forbidden literary territory. Edith

Wharton left, among her unpublished papers, the sketch 'Beatrice Palmato', with its breathtakingly graphic – and outrageously erotic – description of a father's rape of his half-daughter (much enjoyed on her part). Mark Twain wrote, for his and friends' amusement, the fantasia '1601', which pictures Queen Elizabeth presiding over a farting contest between Shakespeare, Jonson and Sir Walter Raleigh. Swinburne and others' *Whippingham Papers* enjoyed an underground circulation among similarly disposed flagellophiles, and it is probable W. H. Auden's 'Platonic Blow [Job]' also found a willing audience. T. S. Eliot's *Inventions of the March Hare* surfaced into publication long after his death, featuring such bawdy and racist doggerel as: 'A wild and hardy set of blacks' possessed of 'great big hairy balls' and 'big black knotty penises'.

There's enough of the stuff to furnish an *Oxford Anthology of Literary Naughtiness*. And somewhere among its pages would be Larkin's *Trouble at Willow Gables*. He wrote the one hundred-and-twenty-page spoof in the idle, mentally knackered period after his finals at Oxford, confiding to a friend in 1943, 'I am spending my time doing an obscene Lesbian novel, in the form of a school story. Great fun.' As part of the fun he assumed the pen name 'Brunette Coleman'. He was spoofing, as those familiar with the girls'-boarding-school story genre would recognise, Angela Brazil and – more closely – Dorita Fairlie Bruce's 'Dimsie' series with their hallmark Wal Paget covers invariably featuring flashing young legs. (Both Bruce and Brazil are reputed to have been discreet lesbians.) Larkin's pen name was also, his biographer Andrew Motion suggests, a nod towards Blanche Coleman, the leader of an all-girl band, whose jazz-inflected swing was to Larkin's taste at this period of his life.

Accompanying the story is an owlish essay (in the Coleman persona), 'What are We Writing For?' The phrase echoes a question ('What are we fighting for?) much bandied about in the war years. Winston Churchill is supposed to have asked it when it was proposed to him that the West End theatres be closed. What was England fighting for? *Getting Gertie's Garter* and *Chu Chin Chow*. Larkin's is an extended joke along the same lines. Already possessed of the librarian's archival instincts, he kept the manuscript. It was resurrected, edited and published long after his death, doing his reputation little good.

Trouble at Willow Gables revels in a little world of gymslips, liberty bodices, jim-jams, flashing hockey sticks, and furtive events in the dorm. The most daring scene in the narrative describes the thrills of knickerless horse riding (Larkin was a devout Lawrentian at this period). Other highpoints identify the author's niche 'preference' for bondage and sadism, as in the following 'six of the best' episode:

> As Pam finally pulled Marie's tunic down over her black-stockinged legs, Miss Holden, pausing only to snatch a cane from the cupboard on the wall, gripped Marie by the hair and, with a strength lent by anger, forced her head down until she was bent nearly double. Then she began thrashing her unmercifully, her face a mask of ferocity, caring little where the blows fell as long as they found a mark somewhere on Marie's squirming body.

This is as hot as the story gets.

The plot centres on Hilary, 'a semi-intellectual sixth-former', a strapping (in every sense) girl, 'with a strongly-moulded body, damp lips, and smouldering, discontented eyes'. Hilary smokes and has graduated into suspenders and bra – flagrantly displayed in the dorm. She develops a crush on fourth-former Mary, downy-skinned, mordant-toothed, possessing 'a figure that a Spartan girl might have envied', and something of a swot. The wooing climaxes with vaguely described groping beneath the poplin pyjamas. Hilary is eventually expelled for sexual misconduct, after a complicated business which involves a stolen £5 note, blackmail, and acts of naughtiness which stop well short of the 'real thing'.

An unthrilled Kingsley Amis, one of the Oxford pals to whom Larkin read out the story, called it a 'soft-porn fairy story'. Let's leave it at that. Interesting, though, to know what first-class minds were fantasising about in 1943.

Troubles, J. G. Farrell, 1970

Reviewers were not enthusiastic about *Troubles* when it was first published. It took time for its brilliance to shine through. It was recognised for the great novel it is when in 2010 it won the 'Lost Booker' (i.e. for the year 1970, when a change of eligibility rules meant no prize was awarded to books published that year). By then long-dead, Farrell was not around to collect the award.

The birth of the novel was a freezing St Patrick's Day in New York. Farrell was, as he liked to put it, 'half Irish'. The day itself was, as it always is, all blarney, plastic shamrocks, and Guinness belches. But while watching the parade Farrell was struck by the idea of writing a novel about modern Ireland's birth pangs. He had recently been reading Giuseppe Tomasi di Lampedusa's chronicle of the decay and survival of Sicilian aristocratic society, THE LEOPARD. There was another epiphanic moment on Block Island (near New York) when, while vacationing, Farrell saw the ruins of the Ocean View Hotel. Once majestic – with two hundred and fifty suites, the world's longest bar, and a magnificent outlook over the Atlantic – the Ocean View had welcomed presidents. Now it was a crumbling shell. *Sic transit*. . . His authorial canvas had acquired its central theme: ruined grandeur.

Novelists, like generals, need luck. Farrell's chronicle of the aftermath of the 1916 Irish uprising came out in 1970, a few months after Ulster had exploded once more into flames. Few novels have been more timely. *Troubles* is set in 1919–21. The hero, so to call him, is an English ex-Major (still addressed by that now honorary title) who did his duty in the trenches. And survived. What the Great War was all about he was never quite sure. Shell-shock has, in the medical description of the time, rendered him 'neurasthenic' – chronically passive. Farrell had been impressed, a couple of years before, by reading *The Man without Qualities*. Robert Musil's use of his passive hero, Ulrich, as an inert reflecting surface rather than an agent of change had struck Farrell as a device to copy.

As the novel opens Major Brendan Archer

has come to Kilnalough, on the south-eastern coast of Ireland, to claim his bride. He has not rushed to do so, having received months of medical treatment for his post-war nervous breakdown. Nor is he even entirely sure that he is engaged to Miss Angela Spencer. There was a brief wartime encounter, while he was on leave in 1916, in Brighton. Did he propose? Did she accept? He has no distinct memory – although her letters to him during his time in the trenches make it clear that she regards him as her fiancé. Angela, once a belle but now an invalid (dying, although Archer does not yet know it), lives in a hotel called the Majestic, owned and managed by her father Edward – 'ex-India' and a fanatical Unionist. The Majestic is majestic no longer. The statue of Queen Victoria on horseback at its entrance is stained green (ominous colour) by time and mould. During the climactic siege by the Sinn Feiners it will be violated by gelignite – incompetently, alas, leaving the monarch still mounted but obscenely skirt-less. The hotel's fabric is in a condition of advanced decomposition. Its only residents are a crew of genteel old ladies no longer capable of paying their bills but with nowhere else to go.

After Angela's surprising death Archer falls in love with a local Catholic woman. She is much smarter than he and is disinclined to do more than toy, cat-and-mouse-style, with her bumbling English admirer. Spencer meanwhile goes certifiably mad. The civil unrest heats up to the point of rebellion. There is the *de rigueur* siege, but so parlous is the condition of the Majestic that it collapses and burns down leaving, among the ashes, a wilderness of two hundred and fifty indestructible toilet pans and wash basins. *Sic transit* empires and hotels.

True Names, Vernor Vinge, 1981

Vinge established himself as a genre leader with this novella. It was, he geekily recalls, 'the first story I ever wrote with a word processor – a Heathkit LSI 11/03'. Grand claims have been made for *True Names*. 'It inspired a generation of computer scientists', says Mark Pearce (himself a 'virtual

reality pioneer'), 'to think about life online in new ways.' It can also be claimed to have created a new map of cyberspace and was one of the stepping stones to 'social networking', 'hacktivism', and MMORPG gaming (i.e. 'Massively Multiplayer Online Role Playing Game'). Vinge's novel was instrumental in laying down the 'idea' substratum of the shape of things techno-logical to come. He had a vision. And a Heathkit (self-assembled) computer to write that vision up.

Vernor Vinge, a man as unusual as his name (which looks as if it came from the science-fiction props cupboard), was, by day, a distinguished mathematician. Science fiction was, for him, a mental lab in which mind games could be played. *True Names* is set in 2014 and takes as its premise Arthur C. Clarke's paradox that, at its extremes (its cutting edge), technology is indistinguish-able from magic. The computer screen and the crystal ball meet in superhuman unison. It opens:

> In the once-upon-a-time days of the First Age of Magic, the prudent sorcerer regarded his own true name as his most valued possession but also the greatest threat to his continued good health, for – the stories go – once an enemy, even a weak unskilled enemy, learned the sorcerer's true name, then routine and widely known spells could destroy or enslave even the most powerful. As times passed, and we graduated to the Age of Reason and thence to the first and second industrial revolutions, such notions were discredited. Now it seems that the Wheel has turned full circle (even if there never really was a First Age) and we are back to worrying about true names again.

As the narrative continues a 'coven' of 'warlocks' – effectively anarchist hackers – go to war against the 'Great Adversary', the American Government. Their protection (their magic cloak, in Hogwartian terms) lies in their pseudonyms. Revelation of their 'true names' would be suicidal. They hide behind such *noms de guerre cyber* as 'Mr Slippery'. Warlocks are forever finding ways of slipping the nooses of the all-seeing state.

Enter a third player in the cybergame, 'The Mailman', a doughtier foe. He, it emerges, is an AI construct. The warlocks now have two adversaries. One is the government; the other the out-of-control machine they themselves operate against the government. Once the Mailman has, vampire-like, sucked in every computer avatar on the web, he – the machine – will rule. Exit humanity – destroyed by humanity's greatest invention.

True Names, as Vinge recalls, was inspired by a real-life experience in which he and an unknown person were logged into the same computer anonymously and struck up a conversation via its TALK program:

> The TALKer claimed some implausible name, and I responded in kind. We chatted for a bit, each trying to figure out the other's true name. Finally I gave up, and told the other person I had to go – that I was actually a personality simulator, and if I kept talking my artificial nature would become obvious. Afterward, I realised that I had just lived a science-fiction story.

The basic idea in *True Names* is simplified, and popularised, in the *Terminator* series of movies. It's a good place to start and work back to the remarkably prophetic novel. The world we now live in may not be that different from what Vernor foresaw three decades earlier.

The Turner Diaries, William L. Pierce, 1978

A prime candidate for the nastiest novel ever written (worse by far than the hardest of hard-core porn), *The Turner Diaries* was the bedtime reading of Timothy McVeigh, the Oklahoma bomber, perpetrator of the worst domestic act of terrorism in American history. McVeigh actually took some pages of the novel on his bombing raid of 19 April 1995, in which he killed one hundred and eighty fellow Americans. The FBI labelled

William L. Pierce's novel 'The Bible of the Racist Right'. The author impudently adopted the condemnation as the front-cover strapline. The book was self-published by Pierce's neo-Nazi sect, the National Vanguard. It has sold, by now, around a million copies, by direct mail and at gun shows. (McVeigh had a stall selling the book at these events, where firearms are routinely and illegally purchased.) It has never been stocked in respectable bookstores.

The Turner Diaries takes the form of a posthumous memoir by a foot soldier in the 'Great Revolution' of 1991–9 (i.e. well into the future at the time of writing). Earl Turner, an ordinary 'Joe Q. Public' American, is politicised by the Washington DC 'gun raids' of September 1991. These have been sanctioned by the 'Cohen Act'. Posses of deputised black men (egged on by the Jewish-owned *Washington Post*) raid the homes of white people, seizing their weapons and violating the women (recent legislation has decriminalised rape and hard-drug use by African-Americans). Turner is rounded up after his trusty .357 revolver is discovered. On his release from prison, he drifts into the Organization, a radical-right grouping dedicated to the overthrow of the System, as they call the federal government, and is recruited to blow up the FBI national headquarters. The explosion kills seven hundred people. Having proved his mettle, Turner is now inducted into the inner corps of the Organization – the Order – a secret élite open only to those who have passed 'the test of the deed'. Meanwhile, the Organization continues its campaign of terrorist disruption. On 20 April 1993 (Hitler's birthday, as the initiated reader will immediately apprehend), the Israeli Embassy in Washington is hit by heavy mortars, and three hundred people are killed. 'Jews, your day is coming!' Turner exults on hearing the news.

Their day comes a few months later. The Organization seizes Vandenberg Air Force Base on the West Coast, and re-targets its missiles on New York and Tel Aviv. Under this nuclear shield, a white Aryan enclave is created. Seven million black people and Chicanos ('mestizos') are transported to the Californian border, and decanted into the eastern territory still held by the System.

Hundreds of thousands of black Americans (who have turned to cannibalism) are marched into the desert, and executed. All Jews are summarily shot, clubbed or lynched. There follows the 'Day of the Rope' (1 August 1993). At every intersection in Los Angeles, there hangs a corpse bearing one of two placards: 'I betrayed my race' (for traitors) or 'I defiled my race' (for women 'who were married to or living with blacks, with Jews or other non-white males').

In a cunning triple strike, the Order nukes Israel, New York and the Soviet Union, simultaneously wiping out the Red and Jewish evil empires. In the Middle East, Arab hordes swarm across the borders of 'occupied Palestine . . . within a week the throat of the last Jewish survivor in the last kibbutz and in the last smoking ruin of Tel Aviv had been cut.' On 9 November 1993 (marked ever after as the Day of Martyrs), Turner takes off on a suicide mission. He flies a nuke-bearing converted crop-duster on a kamikaze raid on the Pentagon, the System's last surviving nerve centre. An epilogue records the success of his mission and briefly outlines the measures then taken by the triumphant New Order. China is carpeted by a nuclear bombardment, which leaves it the Great Eastern Waste. All black Africans are exterminated, and the continent is given over to the Afrikaners. Only fifty million Americans have survived, but the nation is at last racially pure. All this is achieved 'in the year 1999, according to the chronology of the Old Era – just 110 years after the birth of the Great One' (Adolf Hitler, 1889–1945).

Pierce died in 2002. *The Turner Diaries* sells on, year after year, in the tens of thousands. I find that very sad.

Two Crimes, Jorge Ibargüengoitia, 1979

Jorge Ibargüengoitia is, in every sense, a strange name to Anglophone ears. It belonged to a Mexican journalist, dramatist and occasional writer of upmarket thrillers. He published only three of them; but more would have been demanded (so good are they) had he not been killed, aged fifty-five, in the Madrid air disaster of 1983. It was in that year that his first crime novel, *The Dead Girls* (*Las Muertas*), was published in the Anglophone market. It was warmly received ('startlingly good', declared Salman Rushdie). The story was one of mass murder in a Mexican brothel and the narrative artfully uncovered behind the newspaper version: a farcically accidental chain of violence. Fiction is fictional, but journalism is lies. What seemed sensational, when screamed out in headlines, turned out to be banal. Ironic and documentary in tone, *The Dead Girls* carries the teasing epigraph: 'Some of the events described herein are real'. But which ones?

The novel sets up a sharply comic juxta-position of the business superstructure of prostitution with Mexico's formal charades of law enforcement, public morality, and government bureaucracy. Rushdie was right. It's startlingly good. Following up the interest in Ibargüengoitia provoked by *The Dead Girls*, an earlier work, *Two Crimes* (*Dos Crímenes*), was translated and published in English. It is a better novel. It is less starkly objective than *The Dead Girls* and gives the impression of being more wearily tolerant of Mexican corruption. The narrative takes the form of an autobiographical retrospect by the hero, Marcos González, also known as 'El Negro'. Marcos is a political radical in the evening and a minor civil servant by day. He is forced into hiding after giving refuge to a terrorist. This, his first 'crime', is not exactly an act of commitment: Marcos is too embarrassed to tell the man to go away.

He is forced to flee Mexico City, a step or two ahead of the police, and makes for Muerdago, where a rich uncle lives. At first he merely intends to cheat his relative out of enough money to stake a few months' comfortable asylum in some luxury hotel with his girlfriend, 'the Chamuca'. But Marcos is gradually sucked into his family's furious competition for the old man's fortune when he does them all the favour of dying. Comic and melodramatic compli-cations ensue. Inheritance hunting, adul-tery, and finally murder for gain (the second crime) take over as the main preoccupations of Marcos' existence. Insidiously he is trans-formed into a *petit bourgeois*. He is no longer a revolutionary on the run but a nephew on the make. The moral regression, of which the hero is unaware, is handled with the remote, understated finesse which was Ibargüengoitia's stock in trade. And again the novel makes sly points about Mexico's extraordinary confusion of revolutionary idealism and low capitalist greed. The play of contradictions is evident in the novel's opening sentences:

The story I am going to tell begins on a night the Police violated the Constitution. It was the same night the Chamuca and I threw a party to celebrate the fifth anniversary, not of our wedding, because we aren't married, but of 13 April, the 'day she gave herself to me' on one of the drafting tables in the government planning office.

There is a finely measured disproportion here between violated Constitution, government plans, anti-bourgeois gestures, and cheerful desk-top copulation. *The Dead Girls* unfolded the real story behind the newspaper story. *Two Crimes* employs the more traditional techniques of suspense, surprise and denouement.

Ulysses, James Joyce, 1922

Joyce began to work seriously on this Dublin novel at the period in which he left the city for ever. In a tenuous sense, it follows on from the work that preceded it, *A Portrait of the Artist as a Young Man*. The not-quite-so-young man, Stephen Dedalus (now a writer and teacher), is central to the opening sections of *Ulysses* – the 'Telemachiad'. The Ulysses figure (Telemachus' father) is temporarily elsewhere. He emerges as Leopold Bloom, a middle-aged, part-Jewish advertising canvasser. A childless cuckold, Bloom assumes the role of father figure to Stephen in later sections of the narrative. Why Joyce chose this most un-Homeric figure as his hero is much disputed by professors of literature, whom Joyce promised to keep busy for centuries.

The action of the novel covers one day and night – that of 16 June 1904 (now celebrated annually as Bloomsday). The easiest point of entry into *Ulysses* is the last section, 'Penelope', a long, unpunctuated stream-of-consciousness slide into unconsciousness episode in which Molly Bloom's mind wanders, increasingly freely, over her past and present.

From its first publication, in Paris, *Ulysses* offended. The most prominent articles of offence were the descriptions of defecation, urination, nose-picking and – worst of all – sex, as it is imagined, privately, in the free range of the male and female minds. At a deeper level, however, what offended most grievously was the literary novelty of the thing – 'the shock of the new'. For early readers, *Ulysses* must have been like sticking their fingers into an electric light socket. One of the earliest, most eloquently disgusted, objectors was Alfred Noyes, author of that all-time favourite poem, 'The Highwayman'. Noyes' diatribe was reported on for the *Sunday Chronicle* in October 1922 (a date on which having a copy of *Ulysses* in England was a crime):

> [*Ulysses*] is simply the foulest book that has ever found its way into print . . . there is no foulness conceivable to the mind of madman or ape that has not been poured into its imbecile pages . . . it is the extreme case of complete reduction to absurdity of what I have I called the 'literary Bolshevism of the Hour'.

As it happened, the Bolsheviks did not at all regard *Ulysses* as congenial fiction. In the USSR Congress of Soviet Writers of 1934, Karl Radek, to spontaneous applause, anathematised it as a plague sore of dying capitalism.

> A heap of dung, crawling with worms, photographed by a cinema apparatus through a microscope – such is Joyce's work.

Radek may have slavishly toed the party line but it did not help him; Stalin had him liquidated in a purge, five years later.

'Dying capitalism' was having just as much difficulty with *Ulysses*. In New York in 1933, Judge John M. Woolsey gave his verdict that the novel was not 'aphrodisiac' but 'emetic'. It could therefore be published, but should be kept not on the shelf but in the sick-bag. In Britain *Ulysses* remained banned, locked up in literature's 'poison cabinet' (there was such a physical receptacle in the British Museum Library, called the Private Case, and a special P.C. pressmark, as shameful as Hester Prynne's scarlet letter). The magisterial critic F. R. Leavis was warned that he faced prosecution if he mentioned *Ulysses* in his lectures (though he was probably not so inclined anyway; he thought the book a 'dead end' for fiction).

Ulysses eventually made it into publication in Britain (not Ireland) in the late 1930s, but a dark shadow of suspicion remained over it. In the 1950s, when I was picking up my higher education from Colchester Public Library, Ulysses was shelved not on the fiction shelves, but in the remote recesses of the upstairs Reference Library. A page, I discovered, had been razored out. Some laborious hunting in more liberal bookshops revealed that it was that containing the description of analingus, in Molly's Penelope reverie:

> if he wants to kiss my bottom I'll drag open my drawers and bulge it right out in his face as large as life he can stick his tongue seven miles up my hole

Who, one wondered, looking around at the demurely aproned library assistants, had wielded the censorious Gillette Blue blade?

Times change. It's nice to note that both 'The Highwayman' and James Joyce nestle together nowadays on the National Curriculum – state-approved bedfellows.

The Unbearable Lightness of Being, Milan Kundera, 1984

Kundera's novel opens, ominously, with one of Nietzsche's weightier theses:

> The idea of eternal return is a mysterious one, and Nietzsche has often perplexed other philosophers with it: to think that everything recurs as we once experienced it, and that the recurrence itself recurs ad infinitum! What does this mad myth mean?

Count me among the 'perplexed', Milan. The German edict 'Einmal ist keinmal' is repeated at strategic points in the book. The irreverent reader will recall Jacqueline Susann's saucy 'Once is not enough'. We are, the reader will apprehend with a sigh, in that most demanding of literary territories: the philosophical novel. Flex your neurons.

Since human lives are, by their nature, shapeless (although Kundera plays with the idea, at one point, that they may resemble musical composition), they are doomed by the Nietzschean calculus to be 'light' – in the avoirdupois, not the luminous, sense. The point is made explicit in reference to the novel's flightiest character, the artist Sabina, who likes to welcome her lovers into her studio while wearing her grandfather's bowler hat and nothing else:

> When we want to give expression to a dramatic situation in our lives, we tend to use metaphors of heaviness. We say that something has become a great burden to us. We either bear the burden or fail and go down with it, we struggle with it, win or lose. And Sabina – what had come over her? Nothing. She had left a man because she felt like leaving him. Had he

persecuted her? Had he tried to take revenge on her? No. Her drama was a drama not of heaviness but of lightness. What fell to her lot was not the burden, but the unbearable lightness of being.

The novel takes place against a historical background: the repeated invasions of Czechoslovakia. From 1938, when it was the opening move in the Second World War, through the incorporation into the Soviet Bloc in 1948, to the failure of the 1968 Prague Spring (exhaustively analysed by Kundera), it has happened over and again until, after 1989, the 'former' Czechoslovakia broke into pieces. Kundera tracks the lives of four 'light' personages, to say nothing (as Jerome K. Jerome would add) of the dog Karenin. Tomáš, a gifted surgeon, is an incorrigible womaniser. He marries Tereza, a waitress and (at her peak) photographer. After the Russian invasion they decamp to Switzerland. Homesick and tired of his infidelities, she returns to Prague. He follows and offends the now iron-strict regime with a published allegory on Oedipus (self-inflicted blindness to facts too awful to live with is the theme) and takes a job washing windows in an effort to embrace obscurity. After he moves to the country with Tereza, they both die, obscurely, in a car accident (or is it?).

The other strand, commingled, centres on a Genovese philosopher, Franz. He shares his mistress (the artist Sabina) with the satyromaniac Tomáš – whose hair, Tereza distastefully notes, smells of sex as other men's smell of hair cream. Sabina dumps Franz because he is too nice.

Discussing Trollope, Henry James described as 'suicidal' the other novelist's habit of reaching out to the reader – telling them, for example, that Eleanor Bold will not end up, as the current scene threatens, the wife of the abominable Mr Slope. By that Jamesian rule Kundera is very suicidal indeed. Hence such statements as the following:

> It would be senseless for the author to try and convince the reader that characters once actually lived. They were not born of a mother's womb; they were born of a stimulating

phrase or two or from a basic situation. Tomáš was born of the saying 'Einmal ist keinmal'. Tereza was born of the rumbling of a stomach.

Did ever a novelist point a gun to his own head so self-destructively?

One of the more poignant scenes in Kundera's novel plays with the Camus-like proposition that the only rational response to totalitarian tyranny is suicide – and it is noted, as a statistical fact, that after the 1968 invasion, Czech death rates soared; not from Soviet guns, but from heaviness of spirit: despair. The most amiable character in the narrative, the canine Karenin, is named after the most famous suicide in history. This is a novel that is cleverer, and glummer, than most of its readers (me, certainly), but none the less hugely enjoyable.

Uncle Tom's Cabin: or, Life among the Lowly, Harriet Beecher Stowe, 1852

Legend has it that in 1862, Abraham Lincoln greeted Harriet Beecher Stowe in the White House with a request to shake the hand of 'the little woman who made this great war'. If so, it would have been a very bloody hand and POTUS' politeness would not have pleased the pacifically minded little woman one bit: the last thing Uncle Tom's Cabin was meant to do was start wars. Stowe is supposed to have been inspired to write her novel after being told the story of the slave Eliza Harris. On discovering that her master (whose concubine she had been) intended to sell her, Harris jumped from the slave wagon, scooped up her youngest child and ran. When she reached the vast expanse of the Ohio River, it was only partially frozen over. She jumped across it from floe to floe. As a fugitive slave she was still liable to capture by bounty hunters, but abolitionists transported her and her child to safety via the underground railway to Canada.

Stowe, in Chapters 7 and 8 of Uncle Tom's Cabin, makes Harris' daring flight the melodramatic highpoint of her novel:

nerved with strength such as God gives only to the desperate, with one wild cry and flying leap, [Eliza] vaulted sheer over the turbid current by the shore, on to the raft of ice beyond . . . The huge green fragment of ice on which she alighted pitched and creaked as her weight came on it, but she stayed there not a moment. With wild cries and desperate energy she leaped to another and still another cake; – stumbling – leaping, – slipping – springing upwards again! Her shoes are – gone – her stockings cut from her feet – while blood marked every step; but she saw nothing, felt nothing, till dimly, as in a dream, she saw the Ohio side, and a man helping her up the bank.

This one scene, it is claimed, 'inspired countless previously neutral Americans to embrace the cause of abolitionism'. It also (see CRY, THE BELOVED COUNTRY) inspired a much finer novel.

Stowe's story, written as it was by a school-teacher with a mission, is baby-talk simple. A Kentucky farmer, Arthur Shelby, and his wife are obliged to sell off two of their slaves in order to remain, financially, in the slave-owning class. 'Uncle Tom' and the young son of the house servant Eliza are selected. Eliza flees, jumping the ice floes, to the dubious safety of the North. Tom accepts his fate with Christ-like fortitude. On the river journey, he dives in to save the life of a little white girl and is bought by her grateful father, in whose service he is a model Christian slave: pull that rope, tote that bale, etc. A series of accidents (introducing, on the way, Stowe's most beloved character, little black Topsy who just 'growed') ends with Tom becoming the property of the sadistic – and sexually predatory – plantation owner Simon Legree, in deepest, dankest Louisiana. When Tom refuses to whip a fellow slave, as ordered, Legree resolves to destroy his Christian spirit.

'You've always stood it out agin' me: now, I'll conquer ye, or kill ye! – one or t' other. I'll count every drop of blood there is in you, and take 'em one by one, till ye give up!'

Tom looked up to his master, and answered, 'Mas'r, if you was sick, or in trouble, or dying, and I could save ye, I'd *give* ye my heart's blood; and, if taking every drop of blood in this poor old body would save your precious soul, I'd give 'em freely, as the Lord gave his for me. O, Mas'r! don't bring this great sin on your soul! It will hurt you more than 'twill me! Do the worst you can, my troubles'll be over soon; but, if ye don't repent, yours won't *never* end!'

Tom is beaten to death, forgiving his 'Mas'r' with his last breath. Vague happy endings are prophesied for the luckier slaves in Canada or Liberia.

Stowe's novel has increasingly disgusted modern readers, and 'Uncle Tom' is now a term of abuse among the African-American community. The imagination rather balks at the thought of the 44th President of the United States shaking the little lady's hand.

The Uncommon Reader, Alan Bennett, 2012

This was published as a jubilee tribute to the monarch from her realm's most beloved tale-teller, but like most of Bennett's fiction it has a slyly dissident undertone. It's curious to recall that fifty years ago (when Bennett was delighting the British public in *Beyond the Fringe*), *The Uncommon Reader* would have been even less publishable than LADY CHAT-TERLEY'S LOVER – not on grounds of obscenity, but the still-observed conventions of *lèse-majesté*. From the eighteenth century until 1968, new British drama was reviewed by the censorial eye of the Lord Chamberlain (a member of the Royal Household). Among the things proscribed from being shown on stage was any representation of living monarchs and/or their immediate families. (And the Lord Chamberlain himself, of course.) This was, from the authorities' point of view, sensible. Audiences (like football fans) become mobs very readily. Representations of living monarchs also offended the 'King's Two Bodies' principle (outlined authoritatively by the historian E. H.

Kantorowicz) – namely that the monarch has two bodies, one 'politic' the other 'natural'. One is mortal, the other immortal – hence the patriotic proclamation: 'The King is Dead! Long live the King!' The embargo on the stage representation of living monarchs, in their 'natural' guise, was observed, voluntarily, by other genres of fiction too. One doubts whether any publisher would have looked at *The Uncommon Reader* before 1968.

At this same time, the House of Windsor became PR-conscious and 'modernised' itself. They adopted the common touch – going one hundred per cent natural, other than on state occasions. Bennett's title is cunningly allusive: to Dr Johnson (who declared that he loved to concur with 'the common reader') via Virginia Woolf (who used the title *The Common Reader* for her collected non-fiction prose). The Queen is, of course, by definition, not a 'commoner'.

The narrative opens with a state banquet at Windsor. The Queen (identifiably Elizabeth II, although the name is never spelled out) is entertaining the president of France:

'Now that I have you to myself,' said the Queen, smiling to left and right as they glided through the glittering throng, 'I've been longing to ask you about the writer Jean Genet'.

The president thinks it's going to be a long evening. The story then flashes back to recall how it was that the Queen belatedly became a lover of literature. A mishap with escaping corgis (they scamper more than once across Bennett's oeuvre) leads to an encounter with a library van and a helpful lower servant, Norman Seakins, who is a 'great reader' – and gay (a 'nancy', as the jealous equerries call him). Norman, now a bookman not a footman, feeds Her Majesty a curriculum of selected literary works. Gay classics feature strongly: E. M. Forster, J. R. Ackerley, Marcel Proust, Denton Welch and, of course, Genet. The Palace *apparat* hate their sovereign's dangerous new passion for the printed word. The corgis themselves tear the books to bits when they can:

Ian McEwan had ended up like this and even A. S. Byatt. Patron of the

London Library though she was, Her Majesty regularly found herself on the phone apologising to the renewals clerk for the loss of yet another volume.

If I may digress, I have been fined (quite heavily) by the London Library for dog-damage: the books in that venerable institution are old, much handled, and as irresistible as smelly eclairs to Fido.

Despite the Royal Household's exiling Norman to the Creative Writing Course at the University of East Anglia, the Queen's appetite for good literature proves unquenchable. It changes her world view, as exposure to literature always does. 'The appeal of reading', she realises, 'lay in its indifference . . . Books did not care who was reading them . . . All readers were equal, herself included. Literature, she thought, is a commonwealth; letters a republic.' The Queen becomes first literate, then cultivated, then her own woman, then a genuine 'commoner'. It ends with her summoning the Privy Council to declare – what? That she will abdicate. Read all about it.

Under the Net, Iris Murdoch, 1954

When it first came out this novel was lumped together with LUCKY JIM, SATURDAY NIGHT AND SUNDAY MORNING, and ROOM AT THE TOP. Iris Murdoch was viewed as an Angry Young Man in skirts. She wasn't anything of the sort, of course, but the low-life, vagrant, rebellious, 'outsider' hero-narrator of this, her first novel, made the affiliation plausible.

The narrative opens with Jake Donaghue (a rogue's name) back from a bit of flaneuring and *dernier cri* book-collecting (some stolen, doubtless, like his prized copies of Beckett and Queneau) in Paris. A writer, he keeps body and soul together by translating French literature. Jake discovers that he and his pal, Finn, have been kicked out of their Earls Court pad to make way for the landlady Madge's rich bookie fancy man. Jake has nowhere to lay his head unless he pays rent, which he is disinclined to do. His first port of call is Mrs Trinckham, who runs a corner shop, a home for unwanted cats, and looks after Jake's manuscripts. The novel moves forward from this point in a kind of artful incoherence. Girlfriends whom Jake wants to sponge off give him the brush off. He never does find a room but has escapades, increasingly unpredictable, involving film stars, film sets and a film-star Alsatian dog called Mr Mars.

In her private notebooks Murdoch called *Under the Net* a 'philosophical adventure story'; in the novel itself the Oxford Professor of Philosophy regularly takes over from the debut novelist. Jake despises relationships – 'I hate solitude, but I am afraid of intimacy. The substance of my life is a private conversation with myself which to turn into a dialogue would be equivalent to self-destruction' – but he has an indissoluble connection with Hugo Belfounder, a fireworks manufacturer and film producer (both 'evanescent' arts, cultural acts without permanence) who is fascinated by metaphysics. Murdoch leaves numerous signposts as to what the novel's inner concern is. It can be summed up as 'contingency versus theory'. As in chess, your moves take you merely to the point you cannot predict where any following moves (two ahead for most players) will take you. Despite this fact of life (and the chessboard), we plan and theorise our moves continuously. Hugo eventually becomes a watchmaker – watches having wholly predictable 'movements'.

Language – what Hugo is escaping from and Jake, the writer, wrestles with – is unable to throw its nets round real life. The novel's title is a quotation from Wittgenstein in which, as Murdoch's biographer Peter J. Conradi explains, the philosopher describes:

> the net of discourse behind which the world's particulars hide, a net which is necessary in order to elicit and describe them . . .

We are, it is clear, a long way from the worlds of Joe Lampton and Arthur Seaton. I read the novel, uncomprehendingly, fifty-five years ago, and before re-reading it recently (I still have the Penguin edition) tried to recall what residue remained in my mind. One thing only with any vividness – one of the set-pieces which were always Murdoch's specialisms as a novelist. I never met her but I knew well someone who knew her well, who said that if she and her husband, John Bayley, saw a puddle in the street they would want to strip off, put on their bathing togs, and swim in it. And *Under the Net* has a magnificent swimming scene. Jake and two friends have been on a pub crawl around Fleet Street (that site of the *cloaca maxima*, London's river of sewage). The Thames tide is full and on the turn – that daily cleansing of the city – and the three young men strip and dip:

> The sky opened out above me like an unfurled banner, cascading with stars and blanched by the moon. The black hulls of barges darkened the water behind me and murky towers and pinnacles rose indistinctly on the other bank. I swam well out into the river. It seemed enormously wide; and as I looked up and down stream I could see on one side the dark pools under Blackfriars Bridge, and on the other the pillars of Southwark Bridge glistening under the moon. The whole expanse of water was running with light. It was like swimming in quicksilver.

It remains one of the loveliest watery passages in fiction that I know – rivalled only by passages in another of Murdoch's novels, *The Sea, the Sea*.

Under the Volcano, Malcolm Lowry, 1947

Lowry's life was one of continuous and spectacular crack-up (to borrow Scott Fitzgerald's term). Out of that self-inflicted, drink-sodden chaos came a masterpiece. The raw material of *Under the Volcano* was two shiftless years Lowry spent with his wife (from whom he was painfully separating) in Cuernavaca (Quauhnahuac in the novel), nestled under the lowering volcanoes Popocatepetl and Iztaccihuatl. It is now self-advertised as 'The Beverly Hills of Mexico', but for Lowry it was hell (Dante is

specifically evoked), a 'dormitory for vultures and city Moloch!'

The Lowrys arrived in Mexico, it pleased Malcolm to observe, on the country's Day of the Dead festival, in 1936. The germ of the novel was their seeing an 'Indian', bleeding to death on the side of the road, with no one helping him. There are no Samaritans in Mexico, but there is much death. The episode features, passingly, in the novel, which opens with a snapshot:

> Towards sunset on the Day of the Dead in November 1939, two men in white flannels sat on the main terrace of the Casino drinking *anís*.

Given that date they might, of course, have been preoccupied with the outbreak of world war or fascist dictatorship in Mexico. Instead they are discussing an Englishman who died exactly one year ago, Geoffrey Firmin. The events of his last day, from blood-red sunrise to darkest night, are covered in what follows.

Firmin's background is disclosed in occasional glimpses. He is drinking himself to death, and has long been doing it – although this is not a novel about alcoholism. He is well educated. His father, when Firmin was still a child, wandered into the Himalayan mountains, never to return. The Mexican volcanoes remind him of his father, constantly. In the First World War, Firmin commanded a Q-boat (called, ironically, the *Samaritan*). Q-boats were faux-merchant vessels which lured German U-boats to the surface in order to destroy them. He won a DSO (a medal second only in prestige to the Victoria Cross) but was court-martialled for throwing Germans prisoners, alive, into his ship's furnaces.

One of the leitmotifs in the novel (which is stuffed to bursting with symbolism) is the film *The Hands of Orlac*, in which a concert pianist loses his hands in an accident and is then traumatised by accepting the transplant of a murderer's hands. Firmin's warcrime has been hushed up, and he has been shunted into minor diplomatic jobs – most recently becoming British Consul in Quauhnahuac. He intends to write a great work – but mescal (his drink of choice) gets in the way. With Mexico's expropriation of its oil production in March 1938, diplomatic relations with Britain are broken off and Firmin is no longer a consul. More ominously, Germany is preparing, visibly, for war. Drunkenness is a rational response: 'if our civilisation were to sober up for a couple of days', says Firmin, between glasses of mescal, 'it'd die of remorse on the third'.

On his personal Day of the Dead, Firmin's divorced ex-wife Yvonne has returned to him. Once a child actress (who may have been the victim of predatory paedophiles in the film business), she wants to understand him. Why does he drink? There is a striking episode in the second chapter in which he and Yvonne are sitting in a *cantina*, drinking. It is morning. '. . . oh Geoffrey, why can't you turn back? Must you', Yvonne asks, 'go on and on forever into this stupid darkness?' But it's not darkness, Geoffrey replies. 'Look at that sunlight there, ah, then perhaps you'll get the answer, see, look at the way it falls through the window: what beauty can compare to that of a *cantina* in the early morning?' And suddenly, uncannily, Yvonne sees that it is beautiful: light, not darkness. That luminescence is worth even the 'horripilating' hangovers he suffers. Geoffrey's artistically gifted half-brother, Hugh (who has cuckolded him), is also in Cuernavaca. Everyone around Geoffrey Firmin is magnetically fascinated by this unhappy man.

It all ends in a squalid bar, after sunset. Fascistic police accuse him of being a 'Jew chingao' [fucking Jew] and shoot him dead, throwing his corpse down a nearby ravine, for the vultures. Somebody throws a dead dog down to keep him company. 'He had', the novel enigmatically comments, 'reached the summit.'

Under Two Flags, Ouida, 1867

'*Je n'écris pas pour les femmes, j'écris pour les militaires*', was the author's proud boast. Despite the grand pen-name she was born, humbly enough, Maria Louise Ramé at Bury St Edmunds. Her Guernsey-born father, Louis Ramé, was a teacher of French; her mother (née Sutton) was as English as Suffolk mutton. M. Ramé gave his quick-witted, artistic and precocious daughter an unusually good education for a country girl of her background, but paternal care he did not give. In the 1860s he went off to Paris and – as she liked to think – disappeared during the upheaval of the 1871 Commune. Or he may just have walked out on what had proved to be an uninteresting entanglement in the English provinces.

Ouida made her name, young and glamorously, as a writer of sporting novels. *Under Two Flags* became a perennial bestseller, and the archetype of innumerable French Foreign Legion novels (see BEAU GESTE) – although this rag-tag scum were not the *militaires* Ouida claimed to cater for.

The Hon. Bertie Cecil of the Life Guards is a dashing man about town, a champion of the race course, a lover of beautiful women and a gambler 'known generally in the Brigades as "Beauty." The appellative, gained at Eton, was in no way undeserved'. He is 'one of the cracks of the Household'.

But the good life ends when he fakes his own death and leaves London in order to protect the reputation of a lady and the honour of his unworthy younger brother Berkeley. Using the name 'Louis Victor', Bertie enlists as a *chasseur d'Afrique* and performs prodigies of horsey valour against the Arab rebels in Algeria. He also incurs the implacable enmity of the sadistic Colonel Chateauroy. Bertie is loved by the beautiful camp follower, Cigarette. Although he treats her courteously, he gives his heart to the mysterious Princess Corona (who eventually turns out to be Bertie's best friend's sister).

The hero's elder brother dies and the Royallieu title (rightfully Bertie's) goes to Berkeley, who also turns up in North Africa, which by this time is becoming rather crowded with aristocratic English folk. In a tremendous climax Bertie strikes Chateauroy for daring to insult the Princess Corona and is sentenced to death. Cigarette takes to her horse to inform a marshal of France of the condemned man's true identity and wins his reprieve. She gallops back, neck and crop, but a smidgen too late. Bertie has already given the firing squad the signal for his own 'deathshot'. Fingers are tightening on triggers. Cigarette hurls herself into the fusillade, taking into her heart the bullets intended for Bertie. Ouida describes it rather more richly:

The flash of fire was not so fleet as the
swiftness of her love; and on his
breast she threw herself, and flung her
arms about him, and turned her head
backward with her old, dauntless,
sunlit smile as the balls pierced her
bosom, and broke her limbs, and were
turned away by the shield of warm
young life from him.

She dies a martyr for love and Bertie marries
the princess. The 'little one' will lie, for ever
honoured, in a North African grave, under
a white stone:

troops, as they passed it by, saluted
and lowered their arms in tender
reverence, in faithful, unasked
homage, because beneath the Flag
they honoured there was carved in
the white stone one name that spoke
to every heart within the army she
had loved, one name on which the
Arab sun streamed as with a martyr's
glory:
    'CIGARETTE, "ENFANT DE L'ARMEE,
SOLDAT DE LA FRANCE.'

Vive la France! Vive l'amour!

Up the Junction, Nell Dunn, 1963

Very much a document of the year in which
it was written – 1963 – *Up the Junction* is a
series of episodic sketches, which introduced a new note of authenticity into
English fiction – the female working-class
voice. It was gender- and class-specific,
belonging to that interval between puberty
and (too) early marriage. In this interval,
working-class young women ('birds' as they
were then called – or sometimes, more
patronisingly, 'dolly-birds') were most free
to be themselves, before the dreary life-
script already written for them took over.
They faced the prospect of being slags or
old scrubbers in ten years' time. Or, worse
than both, wives and mothers. But for a
glorious few years they were free to smoke
fags, back-comb their hair into bee-hives
(damn the split ends), wear stilettos, winkle

pickers or baby-doll pyjamas, and enjoy
wild nights at the pub – all of it funded (for
the girl gang chronicled here) by work at
the local factory at two-and-fivepence an
hour.

It is the early sixties – the pill is still only
available to married women and the Abortion Act (1967) seems a long way off. One
brown ale too many, a moment's recklessness, and a girl can easily find herself in the
club. One episode describes a horrific, but
common enough, home abortion. Petty
crime is winked at and brushes with the Bill,
or the beak, are routine. What gives the novel
its particular kick is the record of what
women talk about among themselves –
something that always gives men the shudders. For example, Sylvia on the subject of
'it':

If I have it once I want it three or four
times. Let's face it, you get a bit irri-
tated seeing the same man all the
time, it's boring. Remember I got
married when I was sixteen. Now I've
got rid of him I like to be out and
about. I mean I've sat in watching telly
for the last five years – he even used
to time me when I run round the
corner for a quarter of tea. Trouble is
I can see that Ray turning out the
same if I go and live with him.

The episodes gathered together as *Up the
Junction* were first published in the socialist
magazine the *New Statesman* (at the invitation of its then literary editor, Karl Miller).
The book appeared a few months before
Harold Wilson's 1964 election, from which
great things were expected. Too optimistically, as it turned out.

Dunn wrote a nostalgic introduction for
the republication of *Up the Junction*, under
the feminist Virago imprint in 2013:

I went to live in Battersea in 1959. The
house was a two-storey cottage near
a stream running into the Wandle,
and in the garden were an apple tree
and a pear tree – the remains of the
market garden it once was. The next-
door family kept hens. The old mother
lived downstairs and her children and
grandchildren upstairs, and whenever

they had a row the old lady locked her door and they couldn't get to the toilet which was out the back, so they had to come in to use mine. I had the only bath in the street so there was always a queue for it because my friends opposite had to fill a plastic bowl with water from the kitchen tap and then take it up to the tiny back bedroom they shared to wash. You washed your feet last because that was the dirtiest part of your body.

It's another world. The house Dunn describes would come in now at around a million pounds and there's talk of turning Battersea Power Station, that ruined cathedral of the area, into luxury flats.

V for Vendetta, Alan Moore and David Lloyd, 1982–9

This is a graphic novel (Alan Moore being responsible for the text and David Lloyd for the illustrations), conceived and published as a comic for adults. It remains a cult best-seller thanks, in large part, to a face mask. Read on. Or should that be 'look on'?

V for Vendetta, upon its original eighties publication (first in the aptly named Warrior magazine), foresaw a grim future for the world. It is set in 1997. Nuclear war has laid waste the globe, and destroyed the natural environment. Britain – thanks to its leftist government under Michael Foot, whose first act (as part of the 'clean up Thatcherism' programme) was to get rid of the US bases on its soil – has survived more or less intact. But a far-right, fascist regime, Norsefire, now governs. A puppet queen, Zara, makes an occasional appearance for show, dressed in demeaning sexy lingerie. All civil liberties have been abolished. Britons of colour, homosexuals, all 'undesirables', are liquidated. Old people, viewed as burdens on the state, are beaten to death with iron bars by homicidal Sonder-Kommandos. Whole areas of London are 'quarantined' – turned into concentration camps for those with Aids.

The narrative opens with a sixteen-year-old streetwalker, Evey Hammond, mistakenly propositioning a likely-looking client who turns out to be a member of the dreaded 'Fingermen' anti-vice unit. The Fingermen set about raping her, intending to kill her by summary execution afterwards, their lusts satisfied and their duty still to do. Enter a masked man. Is it Zorro, the Lone Ranger, Batman? No, it is a man wearing a mask resembling Guy Fawkes. He does for the Fingermen and takes Evey to his underground hideaway, the Shadow Gallery – a cavern rich with the cultural artefacts the regime has otherwise destroyed: rock and roll records (on a jukebox), books, works of art. The mystery man's nom de guerre is V. His goddess is Anarchy:

> She has taught me that justice is meaningless without freedom. She is honest. She makes no promises and breaks none.

More efficient than his mask-sake, V bombs the Houses of Parliament to the ground, following up with a wonderful firework display for the oppressed people of London.

The plot thereafter grows more complicated with a series of assassinations (that of a paedophiliac bishop in Westminster Abbey is particularly gruesome). The background of V is gradually disclosed. Although we never see his face or learn his birth-name, we learn that he was a prisoner in a special experimental unit in a concentration camp, cell number 5 (or Roman V). He has methodically destroyed the camp with his trusty gunpowder and, one by one, ingeniously, all its staff.

V's final act of revolution is an address to the nation from the Post Office Tower before blowing it up and returning to the Shadow Gallery to die. But, miraculously, he comes back from the dead. Before an assault on Number Ten Downing Street, he offers the people of Britain a choice:

> We've seen where their way leads, through camps and wars towards the slaughterhouse. In Anarchy there is another way. With Anarchy, from rubble comes new life, hope reinstated . . . Tomorrow Downing Street will be destroyed, the Head reduced to ruins, an end to what has gone before. Tonight, you must choose what comes next. Lives of our own, or a return to chains. Choose carefully. And so, adieu.

The reanimated V is, of course, Evey, his apostle, who has donned his mask and mantle.

In an essay written during the publication of the novel, Moore disclosed that he and Lloyd tried all sorts of personas for V. Finally he and Lloyd hit on the ideal character to lend coherence to the narrative – Guy Fawkes. Instead of being burned in effigy, as a demonised enemy of the state, he should be celebrated as its potential saviour. Vive l'anarchie.

V for Vendetta was adapted into a big-budget film in 2006, and was further popularised by the Occupy movement who adopted V's mask as their uniform (it also helped prevent photographic identification by the police). As one blogger put it: 'By appropriating the masks as a symbol, the Occupy protesters are putting a face on their movement – a face of revolution'. Moore disowned any association with the film, viewing it as a product of the kind of big business he despised, but he approved of Occupy's adoption of his facial symbol, telling the *New Musical Express*:

'It's obviously a romantic symbol that's seized people's imaginations, and perhaps that story that I wrote does touch on today's protest movements in some interesting ways. I'm not claiming I was prescient, it's just the way we've been unfortunate enough for the world to work out.'

The Valley of Amazement, Amy Tan, 2013

Tan's breakthrough work, *The Joy Luck Club*, mapped out what would become familiar territory for her: the stories of Chinese-American women – Americanised variously by immigration (as were Tan's parents), acculturation (as is Tan), or intermarriage (Tan has been married for forty years to Louis DeMattei, a man of Italian extraction: they have, by choice, no children but a Yorkshire terrier instead). *The Valley of Amazement* explores, sensitively, the edges of some currently thorny topics. China is, geopolitically, the newly awakened giant (Napoleon's prophetic image) of the twenty-first century. Chinese-Americans are among the most dynamic, and socially cohesive, ethnic groups in the US. They are on the rise. And Tan is one of their leading voices.

The novel opens with a sentence practically flung into the reader's face:

When I was seven, I knew exactly who I was: a thoroughly American girl in race, manners, and speech, whose mother, Lulu Minturn, was the only white woman who owned a first-class courtesan house in Shanghai.

The date is 1905 and the 'exactitude' is misplaced. Violet has a Chinese father – prevented by his family (imposing a weight heavy as a 'thousand tombstones'), and by the laws of both countries, from marrying her mother.

Lulu's 'courtesan house' (the b-word is studiously avoided) is called 'Hidden Jade Path' (no 'knock twice and ask for Fifi' in Shanghai). Violet is brought up in the 'flower' world of courtesans. They are virtuosi of the oldest profession, trained in the creation of the 'illusions' that separate male customers ('suitors', as they are euphemistically called) from their money and leave them eager to return. American silver dollars are the preferred currency. The courtesans have a repertoire of 'song poems' for every male mood. Wives drop by to politely enquire as to 'the unusual positions their husbands enjoy'. There is a 'Ten Beauties in Shanghai' competition for courtesans run by the city's tabloid newspaper.

With the downfall of the Qing dynasty in 1912, Shanghai becomes dangerous. Lulu returns to San Francisco, where (Violet learns) she has another child, a boy. Daughters matter less (they still do in China). Male chicanery and her mother's neglect lead to Violet being sold as a virgin-courtesan to another 'house': baggage not wanted on the voyage.

She is tutored in the arts of love for a year in the House of Tranquility, until, aged fifteen, she blooms and is sold for defloration to a customer for an unprecedented pile of silver dollars. After the uncomfortable event she is signed over, by contract, for the exclusive use of a young man, who treats her as well as a courtesan can expect. She is no longer a 'thoroughly American girl' but a 'half breed' and 'Eurasian'.

The first half of the novel is a guided tour of the traditional Shanghai commercial sex industry. Thereafter, plot kicks in. Violet has a child by an American and is tricked into parting with her babe. Her charms fade. She finds herself the third wife (i.e. concubine) of a brute in the country – beaten and violated at will. Abruptly, the narrative goes back in time to chronicle how Violet's mother became Shanghai's leading whoremonger. The theme throughout is that women's only true friends are women. Men the world over want only one thing – preferably in a hundred and twenty-five different positions accompanied by a pleasant soundtrack. The anger felt about this is muted, but palpable, throughout.

Tan's fiction is illuminating about one of the more discreet divisions of the world's oldest profession, and hugely readable – preferably alongside its clear predecessor, Pearl S. Buck's THE GOOD EARTH. There is also a teasing sidelight. Scanning her family photograph album, Tan realised – to her shock – that her grandmother (whom she had been told was eminently respectable) was dressed exactly in the uniform of Shanghai's 'ten beauties' and must have been . . . Enough said.

Valley of the Dolls, Jacqueline Susann, 1966

Susann's views on the art of fiction were refreshingly primitive: 'I don't think any novelist should be concerned with literature . . . Literature should be left to essayists.' Essayist Gore Vidal famously exclaimed on reading Valley of the Dolls, 'She doesn't write, she types!' But, truth to tell, Jackie was not even that great a typist. The first draft of the novel, as one of the publisher's rewrite team recalled, was 'hardly written in English', and it took a lot of work to bring it up to the standard of 'readable mediocrity'. But then, Jackie liked to ask, when did Shakespeare ever top the New York Times bestseller list for two years straight?

Jacqueline Susann's father, Bob Susan (Jacqueline's mother decided to add the final 'n' to clarify the pronunciation), was a painter of society portraits, and a philanderer. 'I could have had all the women whose portraits I painted,' he boasted, 'plus all their mothers and their daughters.' It was no idle boast. Jackie learned the 'facts of life' when, aged four, she blundered into her father's studio and found him 'humping' (her word) one of his sitters. She remained incurably curious about 'humping' all her life.

As a bright schoolgirl with a mind of her own, Jackie decided against college (although in later life, when necessary, she would claim an Ivy League background). Like Anne Welles in Valley of the Dolls, Jackie found freedom in Manhattan: there she could 'breathe'. She arrived at eighteen years old and gravitated straight to café society. The Stork Club,

Copacabana, El Morocco and 21 called irresistibly to her. But stardom as an actress and fame as a cover girl eluded the young Jackie. Nor could she sing. Of course, she tried the casting couch – any couch. To use one of her own phrases, she was a love machine. One of her friends suggested she should install a revolving door and a cloakroom checkout service outside her bedroom.

In late 1962 she was diagnosed as having cancer and underwent a radical mastectomy. Jackie, who firmly believed that 'women only own the world when they are very young' and that '40 is Hiroshima', felt herself on the terrible brink of menopause – were she to live that long. A year before her mastectomy, aged forty-three, she had undergone her first face-lift because: 'I'm a realist.' Her 'good years' were behind her: what could she do in the bad years to come? She wrote a novel meditating on how fast the good years pass by – and how tragically they end for some.

This is how it goes. It's September 1945. Anne Welles leaves small-town nowhere in Massachusetts for Manhattan, sharing a building with a bunch of other girls determined to make it. She takes up office work and, later on, modelling. A future screen star, the sassy Neely O'Hara (based, supposedly, on Judy Garland), is one of her bosom friends, as is the dumb starlet Jennifer North (reportedly based on Marilyn Monroe). Complications multiply for the young women, and looming over all is the awful spectre of that time when they will no longer be young. That inescapable fate is vividly depicted in the characterisation of the singer Helen Lawson, a generation older than they are (based, it is surmised, on the great song-belter, Ethel Merman). Jennifer North is the most unlucky of the girls. She aborts a child, lest it inherits the Huntington's chorea which, she discovers too late, her lover carries genetically. Diagnosed with breast cancer, she finally kills herself with an overdose of pills rather than face a mutilated middle age – or middle age on any terms.

'Dolls' carries a double meaning. It indicates 'young women' – or dolly birds, as they were called in 1960s Britain. But in Susann's own argot, 'dolls' are pills. The author herself was a long-time unrepentant prescription junkie. She took 'tranks' (Librium by choice) to get through the day; amphetamines (Preludin) to help her clear the daily hurdles and suppress her appetite; and to get to sleep at night, lots of barbiturates, or 'barbies' (hence 'dolls').

Jackie's first thought was to call her novel *The Pink Dolls*. The eventual title was a private joke. Although you would never guess it from the book, the author's favoured form of 'doll' was the suppository; it is not difficult to imagine what the 'doll valley' is. We (Gore Vidal et al.) may sneer at Susann, but she's laughing at us ('Assholes!') – all the way to the bank.

The Vampyre, John Polidori, 1819

It's one of the curiosities of fiction that two of its most popular genres owe their birth to rain. The wet summer of 1816 and the inconvenience it caused a party of distinguished literary tourists (Lord Byron, Percy Shelley, Mary Godwin, Claire Clairmont and John Polidori) is the stuff of literary legend. Novels have been written and films made about it. The bad weather began, far away in Indonesia, with the eruption of Mount Tambora. The result, worldwide, was the 'year without a summer' – and a less deadly eruption of Gothicism in Villa Diodati, alongside Lake Geneva, where the English tourists were staying. Pent up by the foul weather, they beguiled the rainy days and nights with light reading and a competition to write the most spine-chilling story. Mary Godwin (soon to be Mary Shelley) was evidently struck by the fact that Milton was supposed to have visited Villa Diodati. She elected to rewrite *Paradise Lost* as *Frankenstein*. Shelley and Byron's efforts rather fizzled out. But by then, science fiction and horror were born.

The author of 'The Vampyre' was a graduate of Edinburgh medical school (the youngest ever to qualify, supposedly). Polidori had learned his sawbones trade on cadavers supplied by Edinburgh's famous 'resurrectionists' – i.e. grave robbers. He had written his thesis on somnambulism and was fascinated by the paranormal. A second generation Italo-Englishman, he had found himself at the Villa Diodati by a once-in-a-lifetime stroke of luck. Byron needed a travelling companion – preferably a physician. He was taken with Polidori, whom he had met socially. The young man was recruited for the duration of the tour abroad.

Polidori was flattered to the point of intoxication. But the gauche young doctor soon began to annoy Byron and matters were not improved by the subject matter of Polidori's short story 'The Vampyre'. It opens (imagine a chilly evening, rain pelting on the windowpanes, guttering candles, roaring fire casting fleeting shadows on the walls):

> It happened that in the midst of the dissipations attendant upon a London winter, there appeared at the various parties of the leaders of the *ton* a nobleman more remarkable for his singularities, than his rank.

Clearly (not least to the first auditors) the hero of this tale, Lord Ruthven, as we learn his name to be, *is* Byron. 'Ruthven' was one of the titles of the villain-hero in the revenge novel *Glenarvon*, by Byron's discarded mistress Lady Caroline Lamb, which came out in May 1816. Lamb's book too may well have been light reading for the inhabitants of the Villa. Byron, with studied insouciance, dismissed her novel as so much 'fuck and publish'.

Intended as flattery, Polidori's story was in fact grossly tactless. The plot of 'The Vampyre' is simple. The sinister Lord Ruthven takes the handsome young Aubrey, 'an orphan left with an only sister in the possession of great wealth', on a continental tour with him during which Ruthven destroys, teeth flashing, every young person who comes his way. Finally, while the young man is dying of a burst blood vessel, Ruthven turns his dead, grey, irresistible eye on Aubrey's sister:

> Aubrey's weakness increased; the effusion of blood produced symptoms of the near approach of death. He desired his sister's guardians might be called, and when the midnight hour had struck, he related composedly what the reader has

perused – he died immediately after. The guardians hastened to protect Miss Aubrey; but when they arrived, it was too late. Lord Ruthven had disappeared, and Aubrey's sister had glutted the thirst of a VAMPYRE!

Finding the young doctor insufferable, Byron sent him on his way to cross the Alps – alone, friendless and penniless. At least he still had his blood. On his return to England, Polidori drifted, gambled wildly, and suffered a disastrous head injury in a coach accident in 1817, which exacerbated a temperamental disposition towards melancholy.

'The Vampyre' – that failed compliment – was long forgotten until it rose from the grave in suspicious circumstances. Henry Colburn, the most unscrupulous publisher in London (responsible for the publication of *Glenarvon*), issued it in 1819 as being 'by Lord Byron'. With his name attached to it, the trashy tale proved sensationally popular. But Polidori hardly profited at all from the runaway success of his story. He died aged twenty-five, suicidally depressed, probably by a self-administered dose of prussic acid. His name is forgotten: 'The VAMPYRE!' lives on.

Vanity Fair, William Makepeace Thackeray, 1847–8

Vanity Fair confirms the wisdom of waiting until you have a novel to write. Thackeray published it, his first full-length work of fiction, at the age of thirty-five. While one is dropping big literary names, he had also (as in one of his favourite quotes from Schiller) '*gelebt und geliebt*', lived and loved, when he finally got round to putting his masterwork down on paper.

Born with money and social position, young William Thackeray lost his patrimony in card games at university. He dissipated a second fortune speculating in newspapers, and proved to himself, after studying in bohemian Paris, that he was, at best, a second-rate artist (if, as would eventually become clear, a brilliant illustrator of his own fiction). He married improvidently: a

poor woman who, poor woman, lost her mind to post-natal depression after the birth of their third child. She would be confined to an asylum for the rest of her life, and he, because divorce from a lunatic was impossible, would remain a lifelong, sexually restless bachelor. In the period running up to the publication of *Vanity Fair* he was a 'penny a liner', writing for his life, with the wolves and printers' devils at his door.

Thackeray had been born in India, the son of a high-ranking official in the East India Company. He was, as was usual with children of his class, sent back to England to attend public school (Charterhouse) in order to be made into a 'gentleman' (redefining what that word meant would be one of Thackeray's great enterprises in authorship). On the way his ship stopped at St Helena, where he caught a glimpse of the Corsican Monster, 'Boney'. These were the seeds from which his great novel of empire, his 'Waterloo Novel', as he called it, sprang.

He began writing it in early 1845 with a view to publishing in that same anniversary year of the 1815 battle. The 1840s was a decade in which victory in the Napoleonic Wars was still being triumphantly crowed over by the British nation. Nelson's towering column was erected in 1843 in Trafalgar Square – his good eye pointing for ever over Admiralty Arch towards the scene of the naval victory which had scuppered the French as a naval power. Subscriptions were being gathered for the triumphal arch to Wellington to be raised at the entrance to Hyde Park. Everyone was aware those pivotal few days in Belgium, in June 1815, had made possible 'Britain's Century' and the global expansion of the British Empire. But for that 'damned close-run thing', as the Iron Duke called it, there would have been a French Century and a French Empire covering the globe. Horrible thought. Thank God for Eton's playing fields.

Thackeray's first working titles were 'Pen and Pencil Sketches of English Society' (the kind of thing he routinely did for *Punch*) and 'The Novel without a Hero' (a marker for his quarrel with Thomas Carlyle, and the latter's doctrine of Hero Worship). It was only a few weeks before the first serial part was published that he came up with the superb Bunyan-esque title.

In a sense, *Vanity Fair* is indeed a novel without a hero. Instead it follows, from their leaving school on a sunny morning in 1813, the fortunes of two heroines: Amelia Sedley, daughter of a nouveau-riche merchant, and Becky Sharp, daughter of a Bohemian ne'er-do-well. They marry and both marriages reach crisis point in Belgium, on the eve of the Great Battle. The heroines' respective fortunes see-saw over the twenty years that the narrative covers. As one goes up, the other goes down. They finally meet, survivors, across a charity stall in Vanity Fair.

Virginia Woolf applauded *Middlemarch* as the first novel for 'grown-up people' in English literature. *Vanity Fair* is, I think, the first 'middle-aged' novel in English literature – infused, via Thackeray's exquisitely relaxed prose style, with that wise weariness that comes in the middle of life. Relish, for example, those last words of the narrative:

> Ah! *Vanitas Vanitatum!* Which of us is happy in this world? Which of us has his desire? or, having it, is satisfied? – Come, children, let us shut up the box and the puppets, for our play is played out.

All life, as they say, is there. For what it's worth.

Vertigo, W. G. Sebald, 1990

German by origin (and language), British by choice, Sebald everywhere indulges – in some form or another – the national German pastime of 'wandering'. The solitary wanderer's thoughts ramble in aimless rhythm (there is a dearth of dialogue in Sebald's fiction – it is virtually soundless). He labelled his narrative technique 'tangential', 'hypotactic', 'periscopic'. Thoughts, he said, 'disintegrated before I can fully grasp them'. Among the many oddities of British public life that fascinated him was the London Tube injunction, 'Mind the gap!' Sebald minds little else.

On a stylistic level, the effect is one of unechoing emptiness. There is little or no antecedent information offered to his narratives. Why, when he walks, is he always

walking alone? In *Vertigo* there is a vaguely indicated 'personal crisis' in the background – but no detail is given. The first leg of the wander is to Vienna – the home of the talking cure. Is the novel (if that is what it is), which constantly teeters on the brink of confessional memoir, an attempt at curative self-analysis? Sebald's prose, while formal at the level of the sentence (one of which goes on for nine pages), notoriously lacks paragraph breaks. One whole novel, *Austerlitz*, lacks any white space whatsoever. Sebald's prose drones, monotonously. But if he is talking to himself (mining 'the salt mines of the soul', as he puts it) why shouldn't his discourse be toneless and formless? The stream is broken only by captionless photographs – typically grainy and badly reproduced. Does one think in words, or pictures? If the latter, then the pictures need no labels.

In *Vertigo* (in German, more disjointedly, *Schwindel. Gefühle.*) he wanders to and through Austria, Italy, and finally his native Bavaria. Along the way, he chronicles the post-war life of a Napoleonic soldier, 'Marie-Henri Beyle' – his fraught love affairs, syphilis and wretched end. Nowhere does Sebald trouble to tell the reader that Beyle is the novelist Stendhal (author of THE CHARTERHOUSE OF PARMA). Another section centres on 'Dr K.' – Kafka. Casanova is glimpsed. Sebald walks alone, but ghosts accompany him:

> Often, probably because I was so very tired, I believed I saw someone I knew walking ahead of me. Those who appeared in these hallucinations, for that is what they were, were always people I had not thought of for years . . . On one occasion, in Gonzagagasse, I even thought I recognised the poet Dante, banished from his home town on pain of being burned at the stake. For some considerable time he walked a short distance ahead of me, with the familiar cowl on his head, distinctly taller than the people in the street, yet he passed by them unnoticed. When I walked faster in order to catch him up he went down Heinrichsgasse, but when I reached the corner he was nowhere to be seen. After one or two turns of this kind I began to sense in

me a vague apprehension, which manifested itself as a feeling of vertigo.

In the last of the novel's sections, 'Il ritorno in patria' (an allusion to Ulysses, returning to Ithaca after his wanderings), a nameless W. G. Sebald goes back to a similarly nameless hometown, 'W' (Wertach im Allgäu). He traces its history via a record of its dead: in 1511 the Black Death claims five hundred and eleven lives; in 1569, a fire destroys a hundred houses; seven hundred people die of the plague in 1635. The casualty list goes on through war after war until one hundred and twenty-five deaths are recorded in the Second World War. It is a catalogue of death, but not quite (even in a village of 1,000 souls) a never-ending holocaust. Such death rates can be lived with. The total destruction of the European Jewish population is, by contrast, the uneasy truth pervading Sebald's fiction. He despised both the shroud of silence in Germany after the war and the exploitative 'Holocaust Industry'. In Sebald's view of things the Holocaust could not be forgotten, but neither could it be directly confronted. It is something always there but beyond thinking about, even in the privacy of one's own mind. Finally one apprehends – W. G. Sebald is not wandering *to* somewhere ('returning home'), he is wandering *away* from something. For ever. If there is such a thing as the Wandering Jew, he is the Wandering German.

The Vicar of Wakefield, Oliver Goldsmith, 1766

This endlessly reprinted novel's initial route into print is legendary. In 1762, Goldsmith found himself in more-than-usual financial distress with his landlady. His friend Samuel Johnson dispatched the necessary guinea. A little later, he called by only to find the guinea had been expended on a bottle of Madeira. Johnson stuck the cork back in the bottle and 'began to talk to him of the means by which he might be extricated'. Goldsmith ('Polly' to his friends):

then told me [Johnson] he had a novel ready for the press, which he produced

to me. I looked into it and saw its merit; told the landlady I should soon return; and, having gone to a bookseller, sold it for sixty pounds. I brought Goldsmith the money, and he discharged his rent, not without rating his landlady in a high tone for having used him so ill.

On what evidence we have, Goldsmith had little time for fiction. How, one wonders, could the author of a life of Voltaire produce a work as sentimental as *The Vicar of Wakefield*? How could a man who never troubled to marry (his sexual life is entirely obscure and probably shameful) put his name to this extended eulogy on 'monogamy'? The Revd Primrose outlines his uplifting theories of life in the novel's opening sentences:

I was ever of opinion that the honest man, who married and brought up a large family, did more service than he who continued single, and only talked of population. From this motive, I had scarce taken orders a year, before I began to think seriously of matrimony, and chose my wife as she did her wedding-gown, not for a fine glossy surface, but such qualities as would wear well.

Mrs Primrose not only wears, but bears well. The couple have six children: 'the offspring of temperance', Primrose is in haste to assure us). The family lives comfortably off the father's invested wealth; his £35 a year clerical stipend he gives to the poor.

Disaster strikes when Primrose's fortune is lost through the malfeasance of a city speculator, who leaves not 'a shilling in the pound' for his investors. Job-like tribulation ensues. The most famous episode in the novel is that in which the young Moses Primrose is sent off to the fair in order to sell one of the few assets left to the family, the horse. He:

came slowly on foot, and sweating under the deal box, which he had strapt round his shoulders like a pedlar. – 'Welcome, welcome, Moses! Well, my boy, what have you brought us from the fair?' – 'I have brought you myself,' cried Moses, with a sly look, and resting the box on the dresser. - 'Ay, Moses,' cried my wife, 'that we know; but where is the horse?' 'I have sold him,' cried Moses, 'for three pounds five shillings and twopence.' - 'Well done, my good boy,' returned she, 'I knew you would touch them off. Between ourselves, three pounds five shillings and twopence is no bad day's work. Come, let us have it then.' - 'I have brought back no money,' cried Moses again. 'I have laid it all out in a bargain, and here it is,' pulling out a bundle from his breast: 'here they are; a groce of green spectacles, with silver rims and shagreen cases.' - 'A groce of green spectacles!' repeated my wife in a faint voice. 'And you have parted with the colt, and brought us back nothing but a groce of green paltry spectacles!'

Moses is forgiven. The Primroses are a forgiving family. Adversity does not destroy but strengthens their inherent goodness. God takes note and all ends providentially. The last image we have is of good Parson Primrose with his whole family 'assembled once more by a cheerful fireside':

> My two little ones sat upon each knee, the rest of the company by their partners. I had nothing now on this side of the grave to wish for, all my cares were over, my pleasure was unspeakable. It now only remained that my gratitude in good fortune should exceed my former submission in adversity.

The Vicar of Wakefield was, along with THE PILGRIM'S PROGRESS, one of the books which children were encouraged to read on Sundays. A sermon in story form, it indoctrinated the youth of the country with wholesome ideas about the virtues of innocence, a relaxed approach to religion, social optimism and the kindness of God. Amen.

A Visit from the Goon Squad, Jennifer Egan, 2010

First - the title. In a promotional interview Egan disclosed:

> I knew as far back as 2001 that I would write a book called *A Visit from the Goon Squad*, though I had no idea what kind of book it would be. As I worked on it, I kept wondering, 'Who is the goon?' I liked the sense that there were many answers. And then I found myself writing 'Time is a goon', and realized that of course that's true - time is the stealth goon, the one you ignore because you are so busy worrying about the goons right in front of you.

Tony Soprano, *capo di tutti* goons, was another inspiration, she elsewhere confided.

The main player in Egan's novel is rock and roll. Its tempo, the novel suggests, has speeded up American life and splintered it. The narrative is fractured and slips across time and place. Everything is lateral and tangential. It's called a 'visit' because the squad doesn't hang around. It's here, it's gone. And so are you. One's reminded of the joke:

> 'Whoosh!'
> 'What's that noise?'
> 'That was your life'
> 'Can I have it back?'
> 'No.'

The first chapter (short-story length) centres on Sasha, a young (but no longer as young as she was) woman in New York, and a chronic kleptomaniac. It's her way of creating a kind of permanence, holding on to things before the great whoosh takes them away. She has a one-night stand with Alex, a guy whom she meets through online dating, whose wallet she rifles through (post-coitally), eventually stealing a worthless slip of paper. Alex, many hundreds of pages later, will resurface. He vaguely remembers (or can he) that chick who went through his pants, after he took them off.

When we first meet her, Sasha is the

ex-assistant to a music impresario, Bennie Salazar, the big wheel at Sow's Ear records. He, as the story develops, will become its lead player. As we first encounter him, he is middle-aged, burned out, divorced, and trying, vainly, to reignite his libido with gold flakes sprinkled on his coffee and roach exterminator under his arms. Eventually – again, many hundreds of pages hence – he will resign from his job by serving up the money men in his company a lunch of cow pats with the memorable instruction that if they want to sell shit they should know what it tastes like.

Well before this point we slip back to Bennie's adolescent glory years as a member of the Flaming Dildos The group has 'had a lot of names: the Crabs, the Croks, the Crimps, the Crunch, the Scrunch, the Gawks, the Gobs, the Flaming Spiders, the Black Widows'. They are punk by style and piss poor. They play in bars where patrons pelt them with whatever garbage comes to hand. The teenage Bennie is a bass player, talentless, overawed by the dashingly handsome Lou, later encountered as a coke-destroyed seducer of young girls and, like Bennie, something big in the music industry. The only Flaming Dildo with any musical talent is frontman Scott Hausmann. He drops out and lives a bum's life, fishing in the East River for toxic fish (which he eats – what the hell? Everything's toxic). Late in the novel, Sasha's children (one of whom is mildly autistic) produce a seventy-page PowerPoint presentation of Great Rock and Roll Pauses (it's the most skippable section of the book). But in life there is no pause button. Language itself is accelerated into textese.

At the furthermost point of its chronology the narrative leaps into the near future, 2020, which has been ravaged by fifteen years of war. Scotty's hyper-grunge guitar is now the music *du jour*. He is promoted by that Alex whom we encountered pantless in Sasha's apartment all those pages, and all that time, ago. Scotty's songs are an anthem to wreckage – all the Goon Squad leaves behind it.

Among many other things, Egan's novel is a satire on celebrity. A once-great pop idol, Bosco, discovers the only way he can bring his career back to life is with a suicide tour,

at the end of which he will publicly kill himself. 'Genius', thinks his agent.

A Visit from the Goon Squad won every prize going. It will last, be sure of that.

Voss, Patrick White, 1957

Chronically at odds with his country, stigmatised as 'Australia's most unreadable novelist' (he returned the insult with the remark that Australia proved that 'it is possible to recycle shit'), Patrick White was nonetheless the first Australian to win the Nobel Prize for Literature. Cross-grained as ever, he declined to turn up in Sweden to accept it. 'I don't want to pretend to be me,' was his baffling explanation.

Voss is a novel of exploration: of Australia and of what White obscurely called 'the deep end of the unconscious'. Set in the mid-1840s, the novel's hero is a version of the life of an actual explorer, the German Ludwig Leichhardt, who died, it is assumed, in the desert on his third expedition across the continent. His aim was to discover an overland route from Brisbane to Perth. All he discovered was death and sand. In an interview, White said that his other inspiration was the 'arch megalomaniac' Adolf Hitler, whose Afrika Korps had done their best to kill White in the great deserts of North Africa during World War Two.

Johann Ulrich Voss's motives are uncertain even to himself. He is given to such utterances as: 'If I were not obsessed . . . I would be purposeless' and 'I am compelled into this country' – like the transported convict, one thinks. But Australia, he believes, is where the most valuable things about the human condition are to be discovered:

> . . . in this disturbing country, so far as I have become acquainted with it already, it is possible more easily to discard the inessential and to attempt the infinite. You will be burned up, most likely, you will have the flesh torn from your bones, you will be tortured probably in many horrible and primitive ways, but you will realise that genius of which you sometimes suspect you are possessed.

Australia, as Voss believes, cannot be explored, mapped or understood. It can only be imagined. On his final journey into the interior, Voss is sustained by a Platonic relationship with a young woman in Sydney, Laura Trevelyan, whose uncle – a rich, vulgar draper – has financed Voss' venture. The relationship with Laura is mysterious. There is, apparently, some spiritual communication across the vast barren wastes. She is, he confides to his journal, 'locked inside him'.

Voss' journey takes him through the outskirts of civilisation (always a marginal, coastal thing in Australia) to the outback, guided by aborigines. The explorers' party breaks down under the strain of isolation and what becomes increasingly clear – the utter pointlessness of what they are doing. One member, Judd, an ex-convict, makes it back to civilisation – but can't accurately recall what happened or why. It is Laura alone who understands Voss' fascination with 'desert places' while the rest of Australia 'huddles' in its ports. His 'legend', she asserts, 'will be written down, eventually, by those who are troubled by it'.

At the end of the novel, years later, Laura and her cousin Belle have dedicated themselves to good works. Australia must be built, not explored: that is the more achievable task. Sydney raises a monument to Voss – though the city is still not at all clear what, if anything, he has achieved. Cross-grained to the end, White said, 'I wish I had never written Voss, which is going to be everybody's albatross.' Most readers, and not only those in Sweden, are likely to think very differently.

The Voyeur, Alain Robbe-Grillet, 1955

Robbe-Grillet's work can be seen as a response to the violent interruption imposed on French literature by the 'Occupation'. Henceforth continuity was impossible; a fresh start was required. He called it 'New Fiction' (le nouveau roman).

The Voyeur was very much a French thing. In an interview with the Paris Review, in 1986, the author recalled, with wry amusement:

In England, critics have been very hostile. When The Voyeur was published, Philip Toynbee wrote in the Observer that it was one of the two most boring novels he had ever read. I wrote to him asking what the second one was. He never replied.

Or, one suspects, finished reading the book. The phrase bandied about at the time was 'higher froggy nonsense'.

'Voyeur' has two meanings: 'observer' and 'illicit watcher'. Bafflement begins on the title-page – as do problems with translation (what best to call it? 'Onlooker', or 'Nosy Parker', or 'Dirty Old Man'? If in doubt, stick with the French). What Robbe-Grillet aimed to do, in the broadest sense, was to free the novel from its chains – those directional shapes imposed by narrative, sequence, rhetoric, prioritisation of certain details over others. Above all, to 'erase' (a favourite ARG term) the dictatorship of 'story'. Call it liberation.

The situation of The Voyeur, in so far as one can assemble it (one feels like a blind person with a jigsaw puzzle), is as follows. A watch salesman (implying clockwork, machinery, predictable 'movement' – and, of course, watching/voyeurism) called Mathias returns to the island off the coast of France where he was brought up. He cycles (on a rented machine) round the island in a figure-of-eight configuration, calling at houses, door-stepping prospective customers. He's not a very successful salesman: never has been. But he's very 'watchful'.

He arrives at ten o'clock on a Tuesday. If he sells enough watches, quickly enough, Mathias can get off the island by the evening boat – otherwise he'll have to wait four days. For some reason he's very keen to get away from a place which one would think held fond memories for him. He is also obsessed by the layout of the pier, which is his point of entry and exit.

Dates and place-names – history and geography – are withheld. Past and present flow into each other. Names are 'Jean' at one moment, 'Pierre' the next. Facts are fluid. Characters are said to be dead but then turn up alive. Rather late on there is a mention of the hideous rape, mutilation and murder of a thirteen-year-old girl, Jacqueline Leduc. Her body has been found on the rocks.

Is Mathias responsible for the crime? Has his mind suppressed what he did? Is he engaged on constructing an elaborate alibi or is he genuinely just an onlooker? Did it even happen? Mathias starts fantasising evil things when he sees a salacious film poster. Is Jacqueline's brutal death a private fantasy? He overhears some sailors in a bar (called L'Espérance – hope/expectation) discussing what may be an act of violence. Are they the guilty parties?

Robbe-Grillet called his novel a *policier* – a detective novel. But the reader acts as investigator. There is no storyline to carry us to a conventional denouement (or unknotting). Just the knots. The Voyeur is one of the most discussed novels of modern times. The novelist André Brink is amusing on the way in which it 'has been flogged to near death by generations of critics', before indulging in some ingenious flogging of his own (he tends towards the idea that Mathias has committed a perfect murder). My own introduction to the novel was indirect, via the script and screenplay Robbe-Grillet wrote for Alain Resnais' 1961 film *Last Year at Marienbad*. I sat there, mystified, in Colchester's Hippodrome, trying to make a story out of a film dedicated to destroying story. It was Higher Froggy Nonsense to me then. But I dutifully went on and bought the John Calder translation of *Le Voyeur*, when, a few years later, it became available. I think I can now see what Robbe-Grillet was trying to do. But it's hard work: more fun to write than to read, I suspect. Sadly I'm with Philip Toynbee on this one.

War and Peace, Leo Tolstoy, 1869

To summarise Tolstoy's novel in seven hundred words is, to borrow an image from Emily Brontë, to plant an oak tree in a flower pot. But needs must. The novel opens in 1805 – for Britain, the comforting year of Trafalgar; for Russia the year in which Napoleonic invasion became uncomfortably imminent. Central to the narrative are Pierre Bezukhov, the favourite illegitimate son of a rich count, and his friend, Prince Andrei Bolkonski. Pierre is, in his rather ineffectual way, a drunkard, a whoremonger, and – when first encountered – what Anthony Trollope (a favourite author of Tolstoy's) would have called a 'hobbledehoy'. Andrei has more purpose in life. With war coming, breeding and money behind him, he will pursue a military career. His prospects, as aide de camp to the supreme commander of the Russian army, are brilliant: insofar, that is, as the Russian army's prospects are hopeful in the face of the greatest general since Alexander.

The early parts of the narrative paint, on Tolstoy's panoramic canvas, the social life of aristocratic Moscow and St Petersburg (Tolstoy was inspired by another of his favourite English authors, Thackeray, the author of Vanity Fair). Another central family are the Rostovs: principally the beautiful Natasha and her brother, another young man with a bright military future, Nicholas. Pierre becomes heir to his father's estate. He has married, disastrously. Infidelities, discord and duel ensue. His prospects are not bright.

Russia joins Austria in the ill-fated battle of Austerlitz. The battle which will reshape Europe is begun. Andrei is reported dead and (rescued by Napoleon himself) returns a broken man. Pierre meanwhile thrashes around, looking for some meaning in life. Freemasonry proves of dubious assistance to him, as does a project to liberate the serfs. History is not ready for that momentous event. Much space is devoted to Nicholas Rostov's gambling and his ill-assorted marriage. Pierre is attracted to the now nubile Natasha, who prefers Andrei. Andrei's father stands in the way of any marriage.

Fathers are all-powerful in this world, most of all the 'little father' of the nation, Tsar Alexander, whose global struggle with the French emperor is reaching a climax. Natasha looks around for substitute lovers – but overlooks Pierre.

War is conclusively opened in 1812 when Napoleon invades, over-running the estates of several of the novel's principals. Pierre, clownish as always, determines to save the fatherland by assassinating the foreign tyrant and goes, as a civilian, to the front. At the battle of Borodino the Russian forces, against expectation, are victorious. God, it would seem, loves them. There are vivid scenes of Napoleon's discovery that merely occupying Moscow does not yield him Russia, which prefers to burn than surrender. The grand army's retreat, through the snows, is a slow massacre of the invaders by harrying partisans, hunger, and Russia's greatest general, 'Mother Winter' (Hitler would have been wise to ponder the novel). Pierre finds himself a prisoner and is rescued by partisans. His hobbledehoyhood is now behind him. He has seen war – or, at least, the fog that swirls around it. With peace, he and Natasha finally marry (his wife has destroyed herself, attempting an ill-administered abortion).

Natasha is foreseen, in the novel's epilogue, as having lost her beauty. In her middle age she is merely another Russian mother whose happiest moments are discovering her children's nappies are stained brown rather than dangerous green. Passages such as the following invariably irritate women readers I've discussed the novel with:

> Natasha did not follow the golden rule advocated by clever folk, especially by the French, which says that a girl should not let herself go when she marries, should not neglect her accomplishments, should be even more careful of her appearance than when she was unmarried, and should fascinate her husband as much as she did before he became her husband. Natasha on the contrary had at once abandoned all her witchery, of which her singing had been an unusually powerful part . . . There were then as

now conversations and discussions about women's rights, the relations of husband and wife and their freedom and rights, though these themes were not yet termed questions as they are now; but these topics were not merely uninteresting to Natasha, she positively did not understand them.

Perhaps true happiness lies in the direction of 'not understanding'. The novel's vast, eloquent, perplexity is summed up in an epigram: 'We can know only that we know nothing. And that is the highest degree of human wisdom.' Forget flower pots. One could put it in a Christmas cracker.

The War in the Air, H. G. Wells, 1908

The War in the Air has been overshadowed for posterity by the more filmable, and less futuristically plausible, The War of the Worlds and The Shape of Things to Come. This 'scientific romance' (as Wells called it) is more genuinely prescient – eerily so, in fact.

The narrative sets its scene obliquely, in the manner of Kipps and The History of Mr Polly. The hero, we apprehend, is another one of Wells' trademark 'little men':

Bert Smallways was a vulgar little creature, the sort of pert, limited soul that the old civilisation of the early twentieth century produced by the million in every country of the world. He had lived all his life in narrow streets, and between mean houses he could not look over, and in a narrow circle of ideas from which there was no escape.

One relaxes, looking forward to another dose of the familiar Wellsian comedy. Bert, a handy young fellow in his small way, helps run a cycle-repair business in Bun Hill (transparently Wells' hometown, Bromley). Wells, like other political commentators, saw the 'bike' as an instrument of proletarian liberation. Cycling clubs were, in historical fact, one of the foundation elements in the emergence of the Independent Labour Party. Wells' time machine, closely observed, is a bicycle with science-fiction knobs on.

There is no grand future for Bert's business, alas, which goes bust. By a complicated sequence of comic disasters he finds himself soaring into the upper atmosphere in a balloon. It belongs to a Mr Butteridge, who has invented the flying machine of the future – a monoplane capable of manoeuvre, something that the airship (effectively a balloon with a propeller) can't do. Wells, as he admitted, was inspired by the Wright Brothers' first powered flight in 1903 and Bleriot's monoplane with which he would cross the Channel a few months after The War in the Air was published. Bert's balloon drifts him deep into Germany, where, under the bellicose Kaiser, a huge aerial navy is preparing a sneak attack on the United States, prefatory to colonising the whole of South America. Bert finds himself a passenger on the Prussian aerial armada – an unwilling, and uncomprehending, witness to what will be the greatest war in human history.

After a ruthless bombardment of New York, America hoists the white flag. But Germany's triumph is short-lived. Enter the massed aerial forces of the Orient, the Sino-Japanese axis, who have been building in secrecy an even greater, and more sophisticated, aerial navy. Thus, the 'Yellow Peril' is now airborne and invincible. The various imperial powers combat each other to mutual extermination. The world is returned to pre-industrial, pre-imperial medievalism. Bert Smallways survives and is reunited with his 'girl', Edna – a little man in a little world:

From that time forth life became a succession of peasant encounters, an affair of pigs and hens and small needs and little economies and children, until Clapham and Bun Hill and all the life of the Scientific Age became to Bert no more than the fading memory of a dream. He never knew how the War in the Air went on, nor whether it still went on . . . They lived and did well, as well was understood in those days. They went the way of all flesh, year by year.

On the eve of the Second World War's Blitz on London, Wells authorised an ominous republication of the novel, with the bitter preface:

> Here in 1941 *The War in the Air* is being reprinted once again. It was written in 1907 and first published in 1908. It was reprinted in 1921, and then I wrote a preface which also I am reprinting. Again I ask the reader to note the warnings I gave in that year, twenty years ago. Is there anything to add to that preface now? Nothing except my epitaph. That, when the time comes, will manifestly have to be: 'I told you so. You *damned* fools.' (The italics are mine.)

Wells lived through the Blitz and survived to witness the dropping of the first atomic bombs. Then he died.

The Wasp Factory, Iain Banks, 1984

In the obituaries for Iain Banks – who died in 2013, gallantly and prematurely, aged fifty-nine – it was agreed that his major novel was his first, *The Wasp Factory*. It was a memorable debut – not merely for the control of narrative surprise and its display of dark gothic imagination. *The Wasp Factory* provoked a moral panic in a readership not yet ready for it. The alarmed comments of first readers ring comically thirty years on, calloused as sensibilities now are. The shuddering *TLS* critic, for example, called Banks' novel the 'literary equivalent of the nastiest brand of juvenile delinquency' (the author was a stripling twenty-nine years old when he wrote it – the average *TLS* reviewer in those days rather older).

Young male novelists routinely seek to give offence. Martin Amis did so in 1975 by calling a novel *Dead Babies*. In *The Wasp Factory*, Banks recounts acts of child-on-child sadism in a sixteen-year-old's deadpan, Holden Caulfield-style monologue which suggests that serial killing is a minor rite of passage, as insignificant in adult retrospect as squeezing pimples or playing conkers:

Two years after I killed Blyth I murdered my young brother Paul, for quite different and more fundamental reasons than I'd disposed of Blyth, and then a year after that I did for my young cousin Esmerelda, more or less on a whim. That's my score to date. Three. I haven't killed anybody for years, and don't intend to ever again. It was just a stage I was going through.

He has carried out his homicides with a scrupulous attention to gender fairness. He is a thoughtful monster:

> I killed little Esmerelda because I felt I owed it to myself and to the world in general. I had, after all, accounted for two male children and thus done womankind something of a statistical favour. If I really had the courage of my convictions, I reasoned, I ought to redress the balance at least slightly. My cousin was simply the easiest and most obvious target.

Frank Cauldhame has been raised on a remote Scottish 'near-island', by his father, in an isolation which allows his psychopathy to bloom. He invents, for his own pleasure, what he calls a 'wasp factory'. The ubiquitously unloved insects are put in a machine – half grandfather clock, half Poe's pit and the pendulum – to be killed in unpredictable, but ingeniously horrible, ways. He has a necropolis of other dead animals – rather like Stephen King's *Pet Sematary* (1983), a likely influence.

'All our lives', thinks Frank, 'are symbols. Everything we do is part of a pattern we have at least some say in. The strong make their own patterns and influence other people's, the weak have their courses mapped out for them.' At sacramental moments he holds his crotch, and repeats his private catechism. For Frank, who can read the auguries, the wasp factory is as prophetic as the entrails of live chickens were for the ancients. The novel opens:

> I had been making the rounds of the Sacrifice Poles [sticks with skulls on them] the day we heard my brother

had escaped. I already knew something was going to happen; the Factory told me.

His brother has escaped from an asylum for the criminally insane and is on his way 'home' for a family reunion.

What sticks in the mind from reading *The Wasp Factory* is the surprise ending in which Frank discovers himself/herself not, as he tormentedly imagined, a castrated boy, but a hormonally interfered-with girl. His cruelties arose from his mistaken belief that he had been genitally mauled by a dog. In fact, he was the subject of an experiment by his scientist father; an evil man, too big, alas, to fit in the wasp factory for the punishment he deserves.

Watership Down, Richard Adams, 1972

The 1970s, a decade more conscious and worried than its predecessors about the 'environment' (what the Romantics called 'Nature'), was notable for a number of best-selling animal narratives directed as much at adults as the traditional young-persons market. Three qualified as super sellers: *Jonathan Livingston Seagull*, JAWS, and *Watership Down*. Adams' was the most subtle of the three. He invented it as a tale told to his daughters (to whom it is dedicated) on long car journeys. It would have resonated as powerfully with any grown-up passengers.

The novel introduces a rabbit cosmogony establishing the animal as central to the universe. In this creation myth Frith, maker of the world, punishes the Adamic rabbit, El-ahrairah, for his insolent progenitiveness (he goes at it, as the crude idiom puts it, 'like a rabbit') by making all other animals his born enemy, and he their prey. In compensation, and in a spirit of divine fair play, Frith bestows on the chastened El-ahrairah speed and cunning wherewith to survive:

All the world will be your enemy, Prince with a Thousand Enemies, and whenever they catch you, they will kill you. But first they must catch you, digger, listener, runner, prince with the swift warning. Be cunning and full of tricks and your people shall never be destroyed.

This mixed curse and blessing creates the terms of the natural world in which the rabbits in the story exist. But the environmental covenant, drawn up by Frith, is soon to be breached by man. A new threat emerges from which the rabbits cannot run or dig and against which their cunning is futile. The inexplicable notice board is sensed by the precognitive Fiver as betokening blood: the 'developers' with their poison gas and bulldozers are imminent. 'Men', observes one of the rabbits, 'will never rest till they've spoiled the earth and destroyed the animals.'

Migration, the all-or-nothing animal gamble for survival, is counselled. They leave their warren at Sandleford, and in the course of their adventure discover and escape new animal and human foes. They also discover other warrens which have devised their own ways of surviving. One such is the 'Warren of the Shining Wires', whose rabbits have reached an accommodation with man – a kind of *modus vivendi*. Men put out food for them, but a terrible price is paid: the snare. They are being fattened for the pot. This is not the destiny Frith created them for. The Cowslip warren:

knew well enough what was happening. But even to themselves they pretended that all was well, for the food was good, they were protected, they had nothing to fear but the one fear; and that struck here and there, never enough at a time to drive them away. They forgot the ways of wild rabbits. They forgot El-ahrairah, for what use had they for tricks and cunning, living in the enemy's warren and paying his price?

More significantly the Sandleford rabbits discover 'political' opposition in the totalitarian regime of the Efrafan warren. The Efrafans have replaced the benign tribal hierarchy of Sandleford and its wise 'chief rabbit' with a military apparatus under the fearsome General Woundwort. Woundwort substitutes, for the Frithian survival strategies of speed and cunning, a 'revolutionary' reliance on ferocity and the rule of tooth and claw. He and his order are destroyed by the farm dog whom Frith, in his wisdom, has more liberally endowed with teeth and claws.

At the end of the tale, with Woundwort dead and the resettlement of the warren achieved, the natural, Frith-approved life of the Sandlefordians is re-established in Watership Down. The eco-system is restored, old ways rule again, and the narrative subsides into the timeless legend with which it began. The journey is over – for the rabbits and Mr Adams' entranced little girls.

The Way of All Flesh, Samuel Butler, 1903

The least Victorian of Victorian writers (as Anthony Trollope, see THE WAY WE LIVE NOW, is the most Victorian), Butler published two works which have achieved literary immortality. One is the dystopian satire *Erewhon* (1872). Set in New Zealand, its hero Higgs journeys over a mountain range to a country where everything, like the name ('nowhere') is back to front. Crime is regarded as an ailment and is humanely treated, while illness is regarded as a crime, and punished. Other nonsenses (as Butler saw them) of Victorian life and times are satirised. Many of those nonsenses are still with us.

The other work of Butler's which has lasted is this *Bildungsroman*, a thinly fictionalised version of the author's own early life. One of his typically cross-grained observations on the human condition was the fervent wish that society would set up orphanages – refuges – for those luckless children who had families, rather than their luckier fellows who didn't. Butler began *The Way of All Flesh* in 1873 and completed it ten years later. It would not be published until the year after his death and two years after Queen Victoria's. It cut, as that precautionary delay indicates, very close to the bone: too much so, unfortunately, to be published when it would have had maximum impact. The narrative covers three generations of the Pontifexes,

satirically named for their patriarchs' habits of laying down the law – pontificating. George Pontifex, a successful publisher, of stern evangelical views, has a son, Theobald, whom he forces (against his inclinations) to go into the Church. Ordained, the dull-spirited Theobald is snapped up by Christina Allaby, who plays at cards with her sisters for first go at the eligible young clergyman.

The couple set up a conventional middle-class household. Their son Ernest is born in the same year, 1835, as was Butler. Ernest is mercilessly tyrannised by his father and regarded as a 'mollycoddle' at Roughborough School. But he is saved from being utterly crushed by his warm-hearted spinster aunt, Alethea, and her rationalist friend, Overton. Alethea brings out Ernest's interest in music. Overton nurtures a saving sense of contrarian scepticism.

Browbeaten into it by his father, Ernest enrols to study at Cambridge with a view to taking orders in an Anglican Church in whose religion he does not believe (Butler wrote a pamphlet denouncing the Crucifixion as a gigantic confidence trick). In London, a city wholly immune to his Christian message, Ernest is cheated out of his inheritance. By a series of misadventures, and total innocence about sex, he is convicted of indecent assault while serving as a curate. Disastrously, his lusts have been inflamed by the easy conquests related to him by a friend. He mistakes a girl who won't for a girl who will. Twenty-three years of sexual repression explode into crime:

> Then it flashed upon him that if he could not see Miss Snow he could at any rate see Miss Maitland. He knew well enough what he wanted now, and as for the Bible, he pushed it from him to the other end of his table.
>
> About ten minutes after we last saw Ernest, a scared, insulted girl, flushed and trembling, was seen hurrying from Mrs Jupp's house as fast as her agitated state would let her, and in another ten minutes two policemen were seen also coming out of Mrs Jupp's, between whom there shambled rather than walked our

unhappy friend Ernest, with staring eyes, ghastly pale, and with despair branded upon every line of his face.

Six months later, after release from prison – and no longer a member of decent society – Ernest is free, at last, to grow up and become a rational, and joyously un-Victorian, human being. He has, at last, realised the importance of being un-earnest. He marries 'beneath him': one of his family's former servants. She turns out to be a doltish drunkard and it is with relief that he discovers that his marriage was bigamous, and marriage itself just another Victorian sham. Henceforth he will find more rational ways of satisfying his sexual needs. Profiting by Overton's advice and Aunt Alethea's wealth, Ernest becomes a successful, icono-clastic, man of letters. Just like his creator.

The Way We Live Now, Anthony Trollope, 1875

In December 1872, Anthony Trollope, by then an angry old man with twenty-seven published novels to his name, returned to England. After a year and a half spent in the colonies putting his errant son's affairs in order, he found the moral stench of London intolerable. Like some enraged father of the old school, he resolved to horsewhip a gener-ation grown delinquent in his absence. He justified *The Way We Live Now*'s corrective fury in a passage written the following year and published posthumously in his *Auto-biography*:

a certain class of dishonesty, dishon-esty magnificent in its proportions, and climbing into high places, has become at the same time so rampant and so splendid that there seems to be reason for fearing that men and women will be taught to feel that dishonesty, if it can become splendid, will cease to be abominable. If dishonesty can live in a gorgeous palace with pictures on all its walls, and gems in all its cupboards, with marble and ivory in all its corners, and can give Apician dinners, and get into Parliament, and

deal in millions, then dishonesty is not disgraceful, and the man dishonest after such a fashion is not a low scoun-drel. Instigated, I say, by some such reflections as these, I sat down in my new house to write *The Way We Live Now*. And as I had ventured to take the whip of the satirist into my hand, I went beyond the iniquities of the great speculator who robs everybody, and made an onslaught also on other vices; – on the intrigues of girls who want to get married, on the luxury of young men who prefer to remain single, and on the puffing propensities of authors who desire to cheat the public into buying their volumes.

In its satirical design *The Way We Live Now* attacks this all-pervasive 'dishonesty'. Trol-lope (as any good annotated edition of the novel will make clear – try mine) had precise contemporary targets in mind.

The dishonesty of the literary world is shown in Lady Carbury's career in author-ship. Good reviews of bad books are paid for in flirtation, and not worth the paper they are printed on. Dishonesty among the younger set is pictured at the Bear Garden Club, where Sir Felix Carbury and his upper-class, layabout cronies pay their gambling debts with IOUs that will not be honoured. Dishonesty on a grand financial scale is magnificently displayed in the career of Augustus Melmotte, the great financier. A rootless cosmopolitan (Trollope toyed with the idea of making him Jewish, then French, and finally decided on Irish-American), he creates a vast empire by the issue of worth-less paper shares. His *grand projet* is an American railway construction scheme. Millions are made, but not a yard of line is laid. The daring 'wealth creator' Melmotte becomes the hero of the City of London and is elected MP for Westminster (Tory: Trol-lope was a Liberal). He is escorted into the House by Disraeli – a politician novelist Trol-lope cordially loathed and thought (inevit-ably) 'dishonest'.

But the bubble bursts. Melmotte is ruined (along with the usual widows and children) and commits suicide. Trollope toyed with the idea of putting him on trial but decided, on reflection, that the 'Roman

Death' was more appropriate. He was, by the standards of the way they lived in 1875, a great man. By those standards, the jaundiced reader of the present day might think, Bernie Madoff was a great man (how much was it he filched? $18 billion?).

There is perennial debate about which of Trollope's forty-seven novels is his masterpiece. I would argue that *The Way We Live Now* is indisputably his most powerful work. It also, not least in its title, identifies the unique quality of Trollope's fiction. He is, quite reasonably, regarded as not quite in the same class as Dickens, George Eliot, or (his idol) Thackeray. But they all habitually 'antedated' their fiction historically. MIDDLEMARCH, published in 1871–2, is antedated forty years, to the period of the First Reform Bill. The action of *Vanity Fair*, published in 1847–8, revolves around the Battle of Waterloo, thirty years in the past. So too does GREAT EXPECTATIONS, published in 1860–1, present itself as a 'period piece'. *Wuthering Heights*, published in 1847, is set in the first decades of the nineteenth century. Of the top tiers of Victorian novelists, Trollope alone truly writes about 'the way we live now'. Or, as his favourite Latin writer, Cicero, put it: *'sic vivitur'*.

We, Yevgeny Zamyatin, 1924

On 4 January 1946 an excited George Orwell informed readers of his 'As I Please' column in the socialist weekly *Tribune*:

> Several years after hearing of its existence, I have at last got my hands on a copy of Zamyatin's *We*, which is one of the literary curiosities of this bookburning age.

He went on to describe the literary curiosity:

> In the twenty-sixth century, in Zamyatin's vision of it, the inhabitants of Utopia have so completely lost their individuality as to be known only by numbers. They live in glass houses (this was written before television was invented), which enables the political police, known as the 'Guardians', to supervise them more easily. They all

wear identical uniforms, and a human being is commonly referred to either as 'a number' or 'a unif' (uniform). They live on synthetic food, and their usual recreation is to march in fours while the anthem of the Single State is played through loudspeakers. At stated intervals they are allowed for one hour (known as 'the sex hour') to lower the curtains round their glass apartments ... The Single State is ruled over by a personage known as The Benefactor, who is annually re-elected by the entire population, the vote being always unanimous.

Orwell started, almost immediately, on his own great work: 'The Last Man in Europe', as he provisionally called it. And, as commentators have noted, he did not stray far from his source. The Guardians? Thought police. The Benefactor? Big Brother. One can draw up a long list of Zamyatin's inspirations for NINETEEN EIGHTY-FOUR.

The hero of *We* is a mathematician, D-503. He falls in love, against regulations, with a dissident woman, I-330 (men have 'consonant + uneven number' names, women's names are made up of a vowel + even number). Winston and Julia's love tryst in the countryside is paralleled by Zamyatin's couple's visit to 'The Ancient House' – a museum piece (with walls, curtains, and privacy) – where they catch a whiff of old freedoms, now for ever lost. *Nineteen Eighty-Four*'s climactic and horrific 'Do it to Julia' plot is similarly reproduced. D-503, in the last paragraphs, watches, with perfect equanimity, his former lover being tortured. He has, at this point, been tied to a table and subjected to the 'Great Operation', which has removed his 'imagination' and all capacity for sympathy. He loves only the Benefactor.

It would be easy and wrong to indict Orwell for plagiarism. The image that comes to mind is of a virtuoso musician (Nigel Kennedy, say) picking up someone of lesser ability's instrument and performing, to a much higher standard, on it. *Nineteen Eighty-Four* is miles superior to *We*. But it is also heavily indebted.

Zamyatin's novel is set in a post-apocalyptic world. A two-hundred-year war between the city-dwellers and land-dwellers has abolished agriculture. However, 'it is likely that savage Christians stubbornly clung to their "bread" out of religious prejudice'. That word, D-503 adds in a footnote, is 'now unknown to us'. Human diet is now supplied by petroleum derivatives. A gigantic wall divides the city state from the wasteland outside. The planet is cities and deserts. The novel is narrated by D-503 as a testament for generations to come. Mankind is on the brink of its greatest leap – into space (here a metaphor for world-wide communism). The 'Integral' project will carry the revolution throughout the universe, leaving behind a planet it has destroyed. D-503 is part of the team working on the pioneer spaceship. He intends his notes to serve as a history manual for the extra-terrestrial generations of his species (no species, other than man, is mentioned in We).

For all its technological marvels the foundations of the twenty-sixth-century state are shaky – even with its population's minds reduced to 'human tractor' status by the 'Great Operation', and a state-of-the-art guillotine that reduces those the operation cannot re-educate to ash and puddle. An underground movement, MEPHI, is threatening counter-revolution. Where it will lead is left open.

An early Bolshevik, Zamyatin was, by 1921, having serious doubts about collectivisation, the state annihilation of 'I' and the institutionalisation of 'We'. Extraordinarily, in 1931 he petitioned Stalin, by personal letter, to let him leave the USSR for France. This was just before the great purges, when authors would be liquidated en masse for being authors. Having consulted Maxim Gorky on the subject, Stalin assented. For which the monster should receive one less day in hell.

We Need to Talk About Kevin, Lionel Shriver, 2003

The novel opens with a letter, dated 8 November 2000, to 'Franklin' from 'Eva':

Dear Franklin,

I'm unsure why one trifling incident this afternoon has moved me to write to you. But since we've been separated, I may most miss coming home to deliver the narrative curiosities of my day, the way a cat might lay mice at your feet.

Franklin is, we deduce, her husband. Why did they separate? She has remained in the marital home, Gladstone, New York State, to be near Kevin. What was the 'trifling incident'? A trip to the supermarket, we learn. In the aisles she met someone she was once close to – now looking prematurely and shockingly aged. For some reason, she could not greet or face her former friend and rushed to the checkout where another little drama awaited:

'Khatchadourian,' the girl pronounced when I handed her my debit card. She spoke loudly, as if to those waiting in line. It was late afternoon, the right shift for an after-school job; plausibly about seventeen, this girl could have been one of Kevin's classmates. Sure, there are half a dozen high schools in this area, and her family might have just moved here from California. But from the look in her eye I didn't think so. She fixed me with a hard stare. 'That's an unusual name.'

She bags the packet of eggs she's handling so hard they break. 'I'm exhausted with shame,' Eva writes. She kept her birth name after marriage (her husband's surname is Plaskett) as witness to the fact that, as a people, the Armenians are closest of all to massacre, genocide, and diaspora. Their surnames do not usually inspire prejudice.

Kevin, we will discover, was the perpetrator of a Columbine massacre-style 'incident' in Gladstone's middle school. Eva can only think of it as that 'Thursday'. Her letters are a long introspection on where, if anywhere, she can indict herself. It is not something easily 'talked about'. Eva is, by profession, a writer. That comes easier. Her self-analysis, via a stream of apparently unanswered letters to Franklin, returns to primal problems with conception (she hated all that 'trying for a baby' stuff) and breast-feeding issues: baby Kevin was uninterested in the teat; she contracted double mastitis.

He was surly, sulky, mewling and hair-pulling from birth. Destructive rampages began as soon as he was strong enough to rampage. He put domestic pets down the garbage disposal and (although it was never proved) blinded his baby sister, Celia, in one eye with drain cleaner. Franklin, ever the soft cop, did not help. Kevin's problems brought the couple to divorce. Was Eva partly responsible? She is haunted by her breaking the infant Kevin's arm when, enraged by his deliberate underwear soiling, she hurled him across the room. He covered for her – it was 'an accident', he fell, he tells people. It gives him a hold over his mother, which he exploits cruelly.

Climactically, at the end of a very long narrative, the 'Thursday' event is described in agonised detail. Kevin carried out the school massacre (seven pupils, a cafeteria worker and a teacher) with a crossbow – Robin Hood was always his idol and archery his only hobby. A final horror awaits. Released from the initial police investigation, Eva goes home to find Franklin and little Celia slaughtered ('Her body was affixed to the target by five arrows, which held her torso like stick-pins'). Franklin took an arrow through the throat. Locked away for life, Kevin protests he would do it again. There are two kinds of people in life – watchers and watchees. He is a watchee. Need proof? Look at what headed the TV news that Thursday night.

The novel ends with a final surprise. Aged eighteen, Kevin is about to be transferred to Sing Sing and lifelong 'hard time'. He and Eva have, oddly, bonded over the course of her prison visits. Now, at last, she discovers herself a loving mother and him a loving son:

When I hugged him goodbye, he clung to me childishly, as he never had in childhood proper. I'm not quite sure, since he muttered it into the upturned collar of my coat, but I like to think that he choked '*I'm sorry*'. Taking the risk that I'd heard correctly, I said distinctly myself, '*I'm sorry too*, Kevin. I'm sorry too.'

Reviewers were divided as to whether they liked that ending. I don't. The rest of the novel, very much yes.

The Well of Loneliness, Radclyffe Hall, 1928

The epigraph is to 'our three selves'. One of the things which has dated this novel is its sexology and its idea of the 'third self'. Radclyffe Hall (she went by the name 'John') followed the Havelock Ellis theory current at the time, including the view that lesbianism was a condition of 'inversion' – men trapped in female bodies (and homosexuality the reverse, women trapped in male bodies).

The story opens with a sweeping pen picture of Morton Hall, the ancestral seat of the Gordons of Bramley – 'well-timbered, well-cottaged, well-fenced and well-watered'. All is well, it seems. To Morton Hall comes Lady Anna Gordon, a twenty-year-old bride, 'lovely as only an Irish woman can be'. She has married Sir Stephen, a fine English gentleman nine years her senior. He had, in his younger days, 'sown no few wild oats', but now he has settled down, resolved to be as virtuous as the Vicar of Wakefield himself.

Alas, the Mortons will sow something more problematic than the wildest of oats. It's hard to say where things went awry. Sir Stephen requires a male heir. 'It never seemed to cross his mind for a moment that Anna might very well give him a daughter.' They are obliged to wait ten years for a child to come. The child is named in the womb 'Stephen'. What emerges is 'a narrow-hipped, wide-shouldered little tadpole of a baby'. But 'Stephen' she must be. The girl develops into a tomboy: a lover of rough and tumble, horses and, a bit later, housemaids. After puberty (a trial) she eerily resembles her father, broad and flat in the chest, slim in the flank, lean and aquiline in the face. She is a daring hunter of the fox (the day she is 'blooded' is the happiest of her young life).

Sir Stephen, observing his daughter's ungirly strangeness and possessing 'one of the finest libraries in England', bones up on theories of advanced psychology and discovers that Stephen occupies 'the loneliest place in this world ... the no-man's-land of sex'. His mission to help her find her way is frustrated when a large cedar tree falls on him. He dies desperately trying to enlighten his wife as to what they have brought into the world:

he goaded his ebbing strength to the making of one great and terrible effort: 'Anna – it's Stephen – listen.' They were holding hands. 'It's – Stephen – our child – she's, she's – it's Stephen – not like–'

He dies before finishing his sentence.

After a scandalous episode with a woman who half succumbs to Stephen, the uncomprehending and unsympathetic Anna disowns her daughter with a curse:

And this thing that you are is a sin against creation . . . I would rather see you dead at my feet than standing before me with this thing upon you – this unspeakable outrage that you call love.

Stephen goes off to Paris, freedom, and an independent life, supported by a handsome allowance. She makes her way as a novelist. Serving, gallantly, as an ambulance driver in the Great War, she at last has a full experience of love with a young comrade at the wheel, Mary Llewellyn. The climactic act of union is described, loftily but vaguely: 'and that night, they were not divided'. As for the vagueness, Hall would probably have retorted that the Bible does not tell us what the undivided David and Jonathan did, carnally.

Post-war Paris is indulgent but even French society does not tolerate open lesbian union. To protect Mary, and as a mark of love, Stephen forces her lover back to heterosexuality. The novel ends with Stephen's plea to the God who made her:

We have not denied You, then rise up and defend us. Acknowledge us, oh God, before the whole world. Give us also the right to our existence!

The publisher, Jonathan Cape, took a risk with *The Well of Loneliness*, issuing a small, vastly expensive edition. Unluckily they drew the wrath of the *Sunday Express*, whose James Douglas declared: 'I would rather give a healthy boy or a healthy girl a phial of prussic acid than this novel.' Even more unluckily 'God's Policeman', William Joynson-Hicks, was occupying the Home Office. The verdict went against the novel.

Critical verdicts still do. It's an execrably written novel making an irrefutable case for enlightenment. No answer has yet been received from God, although the Sexual Offences Act of 1967 was a step in the right direction.

The Well-Beloved, Thomas Hardy, 1897

This is the last published of Hardy's novels (he would continue, as a poet, for three decades), the oddest of his fictional works, and the least revisited by posterity, which prefers for one reason or another to see his career as a novelist finishing, on a note of terminal pessimism, with *Jude the Obscure*.

The story is most memorable for its evocation of Portland, the tongue of land off Dorset, connected to the shore by a stony causeway. It's called by Hardy the Isle of Slingers (stones being what slingers throw). Say 'Portland' today and various images will come to mind – the magnificent lighthouse, for example, constructed in 1906; or the 'Portland' report on the BBC long-wave shipping forecast (one of the great *poèmes trouvés* of the radio era), or the high-security prison (Britain's Château d'If). Most recently Hardy's Isle of Slingers evokes the catastrophic storms of early 2014. As one of Britain's most threatened beauty spots it will soon, alas, suffer the fate of Atlantis.

This is how Hardy describes this 'Gibraltar of Wessex' in his opening sentence:

A person who differed from the local wayfarers was climbing the steep road which leads through the sea-skirted townlet definable as the Street of Wells, and forms a pass into that Gibraltar of Wessex, the singular peninsula once an island, and still called such, that stretches out like the head of a bird into the English Channel. It is connected with the mainland by a long thin neck of pebbles 'cast up by rages of the sea', and unparalleled in its kind in Europe.

The island, and its causeway, is the setting of Ian McEwan's novel *On Chesil Beach* (2007). His description is more richly flavoured. Newly-weds are at a hotel, celebrating a union about to be disastrously unconsummated:

> A shift or a strengthening of the wind brought them the sound of waves breaking, like a distant shattering of glass. The mist was lifting to reveal in part the contours of the low hills, curving away above the shoreline to the east. They could see a luminous grey smoothness that may have been the silky surface of the sea itself, or the lagoon, or the sky – it was difficult to tell.

Hardy's novel, like McEwan's, is about love gone wrong.

Jocelyn Pierston, a sculptor (and the 'wayfarer' of the first sentence) is brought up on the island, the son of a stone merchant. He devotes his life to the pursuit of ideal female beauty – the 'well-beloved'. A Platonic quest. Jocelyn first discovers what he is looking for in the person of a local woman on the island, Avice Caro, to whom he becomes engaged. He later jilts her for Marcia Bencombe, the daughter of a rival stone merchant. A misunderstanding drives Marcia and Jocelyn apart.

As Jocelyn ages, he glimpses the ideal of the well-beloved once more in Avice's daughter. But she, he discovers, is already secretly married. Finally, aged sixty (Hardy was fifty-seven in 1897) he proposes, hopelessly, to Avice's eerily lookalike granddaughter, also called Avice Caro. He fails to capture any incarnation of his ideal and accepts time's victory over beauty by returning to the now aged and widowed Marcia.

The plot of *The Well-Beloved* (subtitled 'A Sketch of a Temperament') has the implausibility and perfect symmetry – and inner truth – of a fable. The novel serves, coming where it does in Hardy's career, as a fitting touchstone: small and perfect enough to remind us of his extraordinary and persistently idiosyncratic genius.

What I Loved, Siri Hustvedt, 2003

The *roman à clef* – fiction which draws on real events and persons, flimsily veiled – has a venerable history and gives a special pleasure to readers 'in the know'. Hustvedt's emergence as something other than the novel-writing wife of novelist Paul Auster was established, sensationally, with her third effort, *What I Loved*, described by some as a *roman à clef* which engrossed and fascinated knowing readers – particularly those resident in New York.

In 1998 Hustvedt's twenty-year-old stepson, Daniel Auster, had been arrested for involvement in a murder, horrific even by New York standards. The victim was a drug dealer, Andre Melendez, who supplied the Manhattan club world with its necessaries. After a quarrel about money Melendez was murdered by a New York 'party promoter', Michael Alig, who forced Drano down the luckless pusher's throat, strangled him with a rope and finished him off with a hammer. He and an accomplice then chopped the body into pieces, stuffed the dismembered flesh and bone into a cardboard box, and threw it into the Hudson River. Melendez' remains were identified, months later, by dental records. Alig, meanwhile, had partied on.

The trial was sensational – and was further sensationalised by the movie *Party Monster*, with Macaulay Culkin in the Alig role. Hustvedt's novel was released a few months before the film. The connection between them was transparent – at least to anyone who read New York newspapers. Daniel Auster (reportedly) admitted being actually present at the murder, but passed out on heroin at the time. He pleaded guilty to stealing $3,000 from Melendez and was sentenced to five years' probation. Alig and his accomplice got twenty years in prison after pleading down to manslaughter.

Paul Auster has never spoken publicly about his son's crime or written about it. Hustvedt, in this novel, appears to have used the dramatic events as creative inspiration. *What I Loved* is narrated by an aged Jewish art history professor at Columbia, Leo Hertzberg, who is slowly going blind as his past

life becomes clearer to him. The most important person in that life is not his wife, Erica,
from whom Leo eventually separates, but
his friend, the conceptual artist Bill Wechsler.
Wechsler's art is marked by 'his almost
brutal desire for purity and his resistance to
compromise'. After the death of his own son,
Matt, in a freak accident at summer camp,
Leo assumes the role of favourite uncle to
Bill's son, Mark. He (an exact contemporary
of Leo's lost son) is, it gradually emerges, an
incorrigible psychopath.

It gets complicated. Bill, having broken up
with his wife, Lucille, made a second marriage
with a young woman of Scandinavian descent
and Minnesota background, Violet Blom. She
is engaged upon writing a dissertation at NYU
when they meet. The subject of the dissertation is women's hysteria and their spectacular nervous ailments, as something
culturally conditioned and narrativised (why,
for example, did Victorian women faint so
epidemically?). Hustvedt eventually
published a book along these lines, The
Shaking Woman: or, A History of My Nerves,
in 2009. She is of American-Norwegian
descent, and she and Auster first met at a
Columbia University event.

Mark falls in with the demonic Teddy
Giles, a transvestite 'she monster', whose
preferred art-form is homicidal sadism. The
action climaxes with the torture, murder
and dismemberment of a Spanish kid, Rafael
Hernandez, whose remains are stuffed into
a suitcase and deposited in the river. Mark
is present and implicated in the murder but
finally exonerated, although his stepmother,
Violet, continues to have 'doubts' and, as her
final comment on the matter, says, 'I hate
Mark'. The title, What I Loved, echoes ironically.

The novel's correspondence with the
crime and the movie triggered consternation. As the commentator Joe Hagan put it,
what Daniel Auster had gone through was:

> not the sort of event any father would
> want his son to be involved in, and
> not the sort of story a father would
> want the world to spend too much
> time pondering. But now the world
> – or at least the New York literary
> community – can do just that, thanks
> to Ms Hustvedt's new novel.

On the face of it What I Loved is less a roman
à clef than a bunch of keys hurled in the face
of the reader. Hustvedt, without conceding
transcription, has confessed to the work
being 'emotionally autobiographical'.

What's Wrong with America, Scott Bradfield, 1994

Scott Bradfield's fiction is most at home in
California, the quintessential place: 'California is America squared,' one of his characters says. 'It's the place where you go to
find more America than you ever thought
possible.' Bradfield's thoroughly American
theme is broken families – broken, that is,
by violence. Convenience killing comes up
everywhere in his fiction. It's Bradfield's
human comedy.

In What's Wrong with America, a grandmother – Emma O'Hallahan – blasts the
head off her spouse with a twelve-gauge
shotgun so that she can bond again with her
estranged family, most of whom have been
recruited by cults. The novel takes the form
of a long journal-letter to her 'Dear Kids,
Grand-kids, In-Laws, Cousins, Assorted
Genetic Riff-raff and so on'. Among other
good things, familial homicide offers Pentecostal liberations.

Emma is quaintly garrulous rather than
eloquent. She never breaks out of the prefab-
ricated language of TV commercials and
self-help manuals that has surrounded her
all her life. Her dead husband Marvin is, in
her words, 'permanently defunct in the
living department'. The effect of removing
Marvin from the living department and
disposing of his remains in the gardening
department is that of uncorking a gaseous
talkativeness stoppered for fifty years. For
the duration of their marriage her husband
bullied Emma into silence, submission and
nervous foolishness. On the basis of his
appearances in the narrative (which are all
posthumous and visionary) Marvin got
what was coming to him. For Emma, what's
wrong with America is (hilariously): 'Not
enough gun control.' For Marvin – a John
Bircher and addict of Rush Limbaugh slob
conservatism – what's wrong with America
is 'coloureds and hispanics' (the Jews he can

live with, since 'they only sell drugs and prostitutes in the *coloured* districts').

Marvin built the best fall-out shelter in the block in the sixties, assembled a home arsenal (including some impressive high explosives which Emma does creative things with) in the seventies, and in the eighties favoured nuking 'the communistical trouble makers jigaboos and diaperheads'. He was a paid-up member of the Church of Immaculate Reason (a thinly veiled version of the Church of Scientology). All in all, Marvin was what is wrong with America squared. Freed from Marvin, Emma reads junk fiction and binges on junk food. She buys a leotard and does TV jazzercise. She has an affair with a manager at the local (and financially shaky) Savings and Loans, and fools around with her Colt .357. She writes lists of self-improving things to do and 'amends' letters to her children. Alas, she has made her move too late in life. She declares at the outset that she blasted her spouse 'being of very sound mind and generally sound body'. But it emerges over the next few months that emancipation has coincided with the onset of senile dementia – a mental deterioration not helped by a diet of brandy, Valium and too many Kit-Kats. As her neurones backfire and splutter, Emma becomes unstuck in reality. Marvin (smelling of mulch and, in his later appearances, festooned with worms) returns to berate her as he did in life – an addle-pated, big-butted moron. Like her namesake, Emma discovers in widowhood the platitudes of marriage. Unlike Madame Bovary, she goes down fighting. She uses the pick of his own impressive gun collection to blast at Marvin's corpse in its shallow grave and takes pot shots when it returns to make itself turkey and cheese sandwiches from the refrigerator and leaves the door open ('his most annoying habit'). She buys a stout garden stake from the local hardware store, and drives it through the place where his heart should be.

Even in California these noisy do-it-yourself exorcisms are unusual. When Mrs Stansfield, a particularly nosy neighbour, asks too many questions she joins Marvin in the garden. Her death does not simplify things domestically. She, too, comes back from the bourn to nag about how cold and wet it is underground. It all works up to a 'comedy of death' climax to rival that of Don DeLillo's WHITE NOISE, a novel which has clearly exercised its idiosyncratic influence on Bradfield.

Whisky Galore, Compton Mackenzie, 1947

On 6 May 2013 two very unappetising-looking bottles of whisky were sold by public auction. They fetched a good price, £12,050. *Slàinte mhath!* (Gaelic for 'Cheers!' if you don't know). Behind the sale was a story – and more than that, a bestselling novel and a classic film. The bottles were the last bootlegged from a cargo ship, the SS *Politician*, which ran aground in 1941 just off the island of Eriskay, in the Outer Hebrides. It had been loaded (but not for long) with thousands of cases of whisky bound for export to America. For the Eriskay islanders, denied their *usquebaugh* ('water of life') by wartime rationing and shortages, this was manna. The islanders trusted in the complex laws of salvage of abandoned ships (effectively 'finders keepers') to exonerate them from criminal charges.

In 1947 – an era of even greater shortage of the sweeteners of life (sweets themselves did not come 'off ration' until 1953) – Compton Mackenzie published his fantasia closely based (despite the ritual 'no resemblance' shibboleth) on the historical event. The title of his novel has become proverbial, putting the word 'galore' into general circulation (it derives from the Gaelic gu leóir, 'sufficiently, enough').

The story is simple. The setting is two Hebridean islands, Little Todday and Great Todday (toddy being another name for whisky and water), many miles from the western coast of Scotland. Inbreeding has made the islands very different. Little Todday is Catholic, Great Todday Protestant. One island calls the day of rest 'the Sabbath' (and is relaxed about it), the other 'Sunday' (and is fanatical about making the day of rest a day of paralysis). Little Todday is green, Great Todday rocky. Both of the islands, the official history records, were formerly under the protection of St Tod who is said to have sailed there from Donegal on a log, his monkish habit providing the sail, his arm uplifted in benediction the mast.

The inhabitants of the two islands co-exist in a state of simmering feud. What they have in common are appalling weather (sometimes so bad even the sheep commit suicide), a love of whisky (more particularly 'a dram and a pint of heavy', drunk in that order), a total indifference to what is going on in the outside world and a visceral dislike of England. They listen to German radio by preference. The young men of the islands, unwilling to wear English uniform, enlist in the Mercantile Marine (they are, by tradition, skilled sailors). One of the islanders hopes that in his next rousing address to the nation, Winston Churchill will mention the lamentable shortage of whisky his people are afflicted by. Anything else the prime minister has to say is of no interest to the two Toddays.

It being 1943 and therefore wartime, the islands are under the bumbling supervision of an English *gauleiter*, Captain Waggett, a man driven to distraction by the islanders' 'defeatism', their total lack of wartime spirit, and his Home Guard troops' disinclination to obey his orders. The constant rumbling of sedition is fuelled by the fact that the islands have almost run dry. Worse still, it is the run-up to Lent when, traditionally (as in Mardi Gras), deep drinking is a quasi-religious observance.

Following the historical precedent a cargo ship, the SS *Cabinet Minister*, runs aground on a tricky rock. Being a Sunday, the observant islanders hold back before their looting of the salvageable vessel, empty of crew but loaded with thousands of cases of malt whisky – the nectar of the Gods, life blood of the Hebrides. Saint Tod has seen them right. The narrative of the novel is loosely framed around two weddings. By tradition marriage cannot be celebrated without the proper libation – whisky, that is.

Whisky Galore did well as a novel but was immensely popularised by the 1949 Ealing Comedy film, directed by Alexander Mackendrick. The film played up the knockabout farce of the islanders' ingenuities in hiding the whisky from a Whitehall-dispatched team of inspectors from the Ministry of Shipping (there was, for instance, nary a hot water bottle on the island not a hundred per cent proof).

Mackenzie was a lifelong nationalist (Mackendrick less so, he came close to disowning his film in later life). The novel records the fact that Scotland, that country which England likes to forget, has its own ways and will, one day, go its own way. Beware, English cabinet ministers.

White Noise, Don DeLillo, 1985

DeLillo's hugely successful novel opens with the onset of the new academic year at an unprestigious college in a small town called Blacksmith. The town is populated by obese people who overeat because they are unhappy. The college is staffed by professors whose preferred reading is 'nothing but cereal boxes'. It's hardly Harvard.

It's fall: the leaves come tumbling down and the students come tumbling back. It's 'the day of the station wagons' – a locution recalling the pioneer days of America:

> The station wagons arrived at noon, a long shining line that coursed through the west campus. In single file they eased around the orange I-beam sculpture and moved toward the dormitories. The roofs of the station wagons were loaded down with carefully secured suitcases full of light and heavy clothing; with boxes of blankets, boots and shoes, stationery and books, sheets, pillows, quilts; with rolled-up rugs and sleeping bags; with bicycles, skies, rucksacks, English and Western saddles, inflated rafts.

What follows is an academic year in the life of the hero-narrator Jack Gladney, 'chairman of the department of Hitler Studies'. His career progress to the top of his little pile has been unimpeded by the fact that he does not yet 'have' German. 'I invented Hitler Studies in North America in March 1968,' he modestly records. He confided the idea to his chancellor, who was 'quick to see the possibilities'. The chancellor, a bright fellow, 'went on to serve as adviser to Nixon, Ford and Carter before his death in a ski lift in Austria'.

Jack's closest friend is Murray Jay Siskind. 'I'm the Jew,' he says. Murray dresses entirely in corduroy. His views on Hitler are withheld but he torments himself with questions such as 'Did his mother know that Elvis would die young?' Jack has family like other people (to borrow one of James Thurber's jokes) have mice. He has been married five times, leaving children behind after every rupture. Typically he gives them German names (e.g. Heinrich Gerhardt), which may not help them in later life. Nonetheless he worries about those later lives and obsesses constantly about mortality. Currently he is married to Babette – a mate with 'girth and heft'.

White Noise, never orthodox in its narrative moves, changes gear into the outright bizarre in its second part, labelled 'The Airborne Toxic Event'. A rail crash releases a poisonous black cloud over Blacksmith. 'Only a catastrophe gets our attention,' muses one of Jack's students. Everything else is white noise. Evacuation follows to a scout camp in the woods. This, thinks Jack, is the kind of thing which normally happens to people who live in trailer parks or 'low-lying areas', not heads of Hitler Studies departments. Worse still, he has been exposed to a dose of Nyodene D., which may – or may not – be lethal. The good news is that the toxic event has left sunsets which are very beautiful. 'To die for', as the idiom has it.

The third part of *White Noise*, 'Dylarama', continues the *Totentanz* theme. Jack discovers that Babette has been conspiring to get hold of a medication, Dylar, which relieves thanatophobia – fear of death. She pays for the illicit deal with sex. What she then finds is that fear of death is essential to living in any practical sense. Jack has his own issues with death, or black noiselessness. It's driving him to drink and reckless acts. Murray suggests, helpfully, that murder might be therapeutic. Jack selects the cuckolding Dylar dealer, Willie Mink, as his victim.

The novel ends with two images. One is of six-year-old Wilder, Jack's youngest child,

running his plastic tricycle, death-defyingly, across the path of a rush-hour expressway. Drivers veer, brake, and sound their horns. Wilder lives. The other terminal image is of Jack in the supermarket, scanning the papers (specifically, we guess, the *National Enquirer*) in the checkout lane:

> Everything we need that is not food or love is here in the tabloid racks. The tales of the supernatural and the extraterrestrial. The miracle vitamins, the cures for cancer, the remedies for obesity. The cults of the famous and the dead.

The last word resonates. DeLillo delivers a comic masterpiece with black, surreal, fringes. You may die laughing.

White Teeth, Zadie Smith, 2000

Smith wrote the bulk of *White Teeth* while still a student (a brilliant one) at Cambridge. Aged twenty-four, she circulated a sample among leading London publishers. Hamish Hamilton, on the strength reportedly of nothing more than the opening pages, came up with a bid of a quarter of a million pounds. *White Teeth* went on to pick up golden reviews and a cabinet full of prizes.

The opening paragraph will give some idea of what whetted the publisher's appetite and unclamped their wallet:

> Early in the morning, late in the century, Cricklewood Broadway. At 06.27 hours on 1 January 1975, Alfred Archibald Jones was dressed in corduroy and sat in a fume-filled Cavalier Musketeer Estate face down on the steering wheel, hoping the judgement would not be too heavy upon him. He lay forward in a prostrate cross, jaw slack, arms splayed either side like some fallen angel; scrunched up in each fist he held his army service medals (left) and his marriage licence (right), for he had decided to take his mistakes with him. A little green light flashed in his eye, signalling a right turn he had resolved

never to make. He was resigned to it. He was prepared for it. He had flipped a coin and stood staunchly by its conclusions. This was a decided-upon suicide. In fact it was a New Year's resolution.

1975 was Smith's birth year. She was brought up in North-West London, the daughter of a Jamaican mother and an English father. She probably knows, to this day, every crack on every paving stone on Cricklewood Broadway.

The luckless Archie has just had his Italian wife, Ophelia, walk out on him. She couldn't stand his dullness. She left him the Hoover – that housewife's manacle. He has resolved to put it to more manly use by attaching its tube to the exhaust pipe of his unlovely car and poisoning himself. But 'luck was with him that morning'. A local halal butcher, Mo Hussein-Ishmael, outside whose premises the Cavalier is parked, discovers what Archie is doing ('I am gassing myself, leave me alone') and orders him to move on. 'No one gasses himself on my property. We are not licensed.' Archie (who makes the important decisions in his life by the flip of a coin) takes it as a sign. He does not merely move on, but lives on – and loves on. He drops in on a New Year's party and in no time at all he has found a new mate, Clara. She is from Jamaica via Lambeth (South London), two faraway places. She does not find Archie dull. A 'peculiar marriage' ensues. New Year, new life.

The sheer zest of Smith's writing is like breathing oxygen off the page. The plot, however, skitters maddeningly, returning in time to 1945 when Archie was best mates with a Bangladeshi Muslim, Samad Iqbal. They served together in the last months of the war, in the 'Buggers Battalion', which did not the slightest harm to the Germans. Samad's marriage to his wife Alsana was arranged before her birth: not for a devout Muslim the flip of any coin. He is proud of an ancestor who fired the first shot in what used to be called the Indian Mutiny and is now, more properly, called the Indian Rebellion. That ancestor, Mangal Pandey, missed his target. Samad cannot quite work out whether he has forsaken Allah or Allah has forsaken him.

Leapfrogging back to 1975, Archie and Samad find themselves becoming parents. Archie and Clara's daughter Irie (whose mixed parentage matches the author's) is shy and bright. Samad and Alsana have twin boys, Magid and Millat (Alsana likes the sound of 'M'). Magid becomes a scientist, Millat a fundamentalist. Both intend to change the world. Another ethnic, North London-based, clan, the Jewish professional Chalfens, are woven into Smith's by now many-coloured tapestry. Rather awkwardly, a genetically engineered mouse precipitates a final farcical scene which is the one thing in the novel some reviewers disliked.

There are all the colours of global human pigmentation in Willesden, but all teeth are white (at least, to start with). The image witnesses to a generosity of spirit in Smith's novel which matches the effervescence of her prose. All in all, it's worth a quarter of a million of any publisher's money.

Wide Sargasso Sea, Jean Rhys, 1966

Wide Sargasso Sea, 'the anti-JANE EYRE', is routinely read as an outrider to a revisionary work of feminist literary criticism, Sandra Gilbert and Susan Gubar's The Madwoman in the Attic (1979). Rhys proclaimed that she intended to write Bertha Mason 'a life'– in retaliation against the crudely dismissive characterisation spat out by Rochester, in self-exculpation, after his bigamous ruse has been tumbled:

> Bertha Mason is mad; and she came of a mad family; idiots and maniacs through three generations! Her mother, the Creole, was both a madwoman and a drunkard! – as I found out after I had wed the daughter: for they were silent on family secrets before. Bertha, like a dutiful child, copied her parent in both points.

Put thus, Wide Sargasso Sea sounds like a roman à thèse – a novel with a purpose, that purpose being to do the right thing by Bertha Mason, to 'de-monster' the madwoman in the attic.

Biographical accounts record that Jean Rhys was in no shape while writing this novel to do anything so purposive. She spent twenty years writing *Wide Sargasso Sea*, in a continuously teetering state of breakdown. As one commentator bluntly puts it: 'She ended up [in her seventies] drinking cheap wine in a draughty cottage in Devon, scribbling on her writing pad, generally presumed dead.' The novel, in a condition of manuscript incoherence, was extracted and pulled into shape by her friend and editor, Diana Athill.

Rhys had been brought up in the last years of the nineteenth century and was, like Brontë's Bertha, a 'Creole' (i.e. a generations-long established white resident) in the West Indies. As we first meet her, the novel's heroine is called Antoinette Cosway. Her Christian name witnesses to a French mother. The West Indian economy, and the life of the colonial elite, is in crisis. Slave-trading was abolished in 1807 but emancipation (freedom for slaves) was not enacted by Parliament until 1833. Without the whip ('No more slavery – why should anybody work?') the sugar plantations have withered.

In the wake of this disaster (for the whites) Antoinette's family, who had prospered mightily as slave-owners, find themselves in a spiral of destitution on their decayed Coulibri estate. The father drank himself to death five years since. Antoinette's brother Pierre shows ominous signs of the family tendency to madness. Her mother, Annette, has become a moody recluse. Antoinette finds consolation in the company of her black nurse Christophine (an adept in 'obeah' – voodoo) and a servant's daughter, Tia, who tells her, bluntly, 'Old time white people nothing but white nigger now, and black nigger better than white nigger.' Annette, still young and beautiful, marries a rich Englishman called Mason who restores Coulibri to its former glory. It comes to grief. His intention to bring in Chinese coolies provokes a black uprising: the house is burned; the family flees. Antoinette is nearly killed by Tia, who hurls a 'jagged rock' in her face. Pierre dies and Annette falls into a condition of 'zombie' madness.

The second section shows Antoinette at seventeen. Having 'come out', she is courted by a young Englishman (the never-named Rochester, hereafter 'NNR') who takes over the narrative. They marry speedily. It emerges that NNR has been bribed to take Antoinette off the Mason family's hands. He renames her, on a whim, 'Bertha'. He does not love her under either her French or her English name, but the money he is very glad to have. An illegitimate half-black, half-brother of Antoinette's causes mischief by warning NNR about the strains of madness, drunkenness and sexual delinquency in the family. There is bad blood on both sides. NNR sleeps with a 'half-caste' servant. Discovering his infidelity, a rum-maddened Bertha bites him, venomously, on the arm. The bad blood has come out.

The third section is narrated, incoherently, by Antoinette. The couple have returned to England where, having been certified a lunatic, she is incarcerated in an English mansion. She is last seen escaping at night, her wardress Grace Poole having drunk herself into a stupor:

> I got up, took the keys, and unlocked the door. I was outside holding my candle. Now at last I know why I was brought here and what I have to do. There must have been a draught for the flame flickered and I thought it was out. But I shielded it with my hand and it burned up again to light me along the dark passage.

Jean Rhys wrote Bertha a life, but – with the most delicate artistic tact – left it to Charlotte Brontë to write her fiery death.

Wise Blood, Flannery O'Connor, 1952

In 1951, aged twenty-six, O'Connor was diagnosed with systemic lupus erythematosus. It meant a life in the care (devoted but overbearing) of her mother. This was the situation in which she wrote her first published novel.

After seven years perfecting her 'opus nauseous', O'Connor published *Wise Blood* in 1952. In a later preface (1962), she asserted it was 'a comic novel about a Christian *malgré lui*' – an interpretation with which most readers find it difficult to agree. As the book opens, it is 1947. Hazel Motes (the biblical allusion to eyes is meaningful) has come back from the war but we know nothing of his four years' service other than that the army 'sent him half way round the world and forgot him'. He was wounded, and the shrapnel that remains in his body is poisoning him, rusting round his heart. Motes is first encountered on the train back to Taulkinham, Tennessee, wearing a suit of 'glaring blue', with the price tag attached ($11.98), and a 'fierce black hat'. He is resolved to be a preacher. Religion is buzzing around in his head 'like a wasp'.

The problem with this vocation is that he 'doesn't believe in anything'. Hazel solves the problem by establishing the 'Church of Truth without Jesus Christ Crucified'. He preaches his Christless Christianity from the hood of his beat-up car, 'a rat-colored machine'.

> I preach there are all kinds of truth, your truth and somebody else's, but behind all of them, there's only one truth and that is that there is no truth ... No truth behind all truths is what I and this church preach! Where you come from is gone, where you thought you were going to never was there, and where you are is no good unless you can get away from it. Where is there a place for you to be? No place ... In yourself right now is all the place you've got.

Hazel recruits two disciples: one is an idiot boy, Enoch Emery, who has 'wise blood' but an unwise head. A guard at the local zoo, Enoch is obsessed with a movie-star gorilla, 'Gonga', and beats up the man promoting the movie in order to steal his gorilla suit. As an act of devotion, he also steals a holy relic for Hazel from the city museum – a shrunken mummy ('a dead part-nigger shriveled up dwarf' is the recipient's blunt description). Hazel's other disciple is a pubescent, underage nymphomaniac, Sabbath Lily Hawks, who affords him cheaper relief than the local whorehouse (a setting which, as unkind male critics pointed out, did not show O'Connor at her most knowledgeable).

In the climax of the story, Hazel blinds himself with quick lime, mortifies his body with barbed wire, and puts sharp stones in his shoes. Why? he is asked. 'To pay', is his reply. He finally ends up in a ditch, dying of exposure. His body is picked up by some cruising police:

> He died in the squad car but they didn't notice and took him on to the landlady's. She had them put him on her bed and when she had pushed them out the door, she locked it behind them and drew up a straight chair and sat down close to his face where she could talk to him. 'Well Mr Motes,' she said, 'I see you've come home!'

Wise Blood was published to largely perplexed reviews ('Southern Gothic' was not yet an established genre) and a surge of scandalised protest in O'Connor's hometown of Milledgeville, where bookstores sold it in brown paper bags. The American publishers sent a proof copy to Evelyn Waugh in the hope that, as a Catholic, he would recognise its genius. He replied, frigidly: 'If this is really the unaided work of a young lady, it is a remarkable product.' T. S. Eliot (Anglo-Catholic, and a Southerner by birth) was also shown the text, with a view to Faber publishing it, and returned it with the wry observation: 'my nerves are just not strong enough.'

Wolf Hall, Hilary Mantel, 2009

Wolf Hall is the most applauded British novel of the twenty-first century. If literature had rafters they would ring to Hilary Mantel's praise. On the face of it the applause and impressive sales are odd. The novel is about a historical figure whose surname is better known attached to 'Oliver'. The action is set half a millennium ago, when language, both literary and vernacular, was different. How would Mantel avoid 'gadzookery'?

The novel is narrated in an unfamiliar 'camcorder in the head' style which some readers found off-putting. The book is very long, over six hundred and fifty pages, prefaced by a deterrent five-page 'cast of characters'. Long as it is, the story covers only eight years (1527–35) of Henry VIII's reign and Thomas Cromwell's period in office. Wolf Hall itself is barely mentioned in *Wolf Hall*. It will come later. This book, as not all first readers realised, is the first part of a trilogy. It will be a long haul, some two thousand pages and many years (as I write, impatiently) before the story is brought to Cromwell's execution (no spoiler alert required) on 28 July 1540.

Why did *Wolf Hall* work so well with readers? Two reasons, I suggest. One is a spirit of the age thing (Mantel's age, not Cromwell's). The other reason is peculiar to Mantel herself. As anyone who has read her harrowing memoirs will know, she has experienced a huge amount of pain – arising both from a family broken in childhood and from chronic disease. *Wolf Hall* opens with a horribly painful scene. It is 1500. Fifteen-year-old Thomas is being beaten to a pulp by his drunken blacksmith father:

'So now get up.'
Felled, dazed, silent, he has fallen; knocked full length on the cobbles of the yard. His head turns sideways; his eyes are turned towards the gate, as if someone might arrive to help him out. One blow, properly placed, could kill him now.

Blood from the gash in his head – which was his father's first effort – is trickling across his face. Add to this, his left eye is blinded; but if he squints sideways, with his right eye he can see that the stitching of his father's boot is unravelling. The twine has sprung clear of the leather, and a hard knot in it has caught his eyebrow and opened another cut . . .

I'll miss my dog, he thinks.

Pain, as Mantel sees it, is as formative as the potter's hand. Few, I suspect, reading the opening passage will find it easy to put the book down until the last page is turned.

The other reason that *Wolf Hall* hit the mark so successfully is that Thomas Cromwell was an 'adviser'. Mafiosi call them *consiglieri*. The first decade of the twenty-first century, like the reign of Henry VIII, was one in which 'special advisers' wielded world-shaping power. Karl Rove was called 'Bush's Brain'. It was not paranoid, at times, to think that Alastair Campbell wasn't the power behind

the Blair throne. He *was* the power.

A bruised Thomas leaves home (so to call it) and the dog behind, for a life of adventure. Having got that out of his system, he turns to money-making and the law. In his thirties (he never knows his precise age) he is recruited as 'secretary' by Cardinal Wolsey, the King's adviser. This is the point at which Mantel picks up the story again, after the initial paternal battery. The intervening years are 'lost'. Cromwell has by now educated himself to the level of a university-trained humanist scholar. He can quote the whole New Testament in Latin and the new poets in Italian. He studies Machiavelli, whose political science is more useful than Petrarch's verse. It is a crucial moment in English history. The King has tired of one childless wife and wishes to move on to the next, Anne Boleyn. To do so he must change the world. Wolsey fails his master and is succeeded by Thomas More. Mantel depicts him, against received opinion, as a bloodthirsty papist and a sadist.

Finally, it is Cromwell who manages the Boleyn affair. Family distractions are removed when his own wife and children succumb to the plague. But Cromwell is more than a marriage broker and problem fixer. It is he, behind the scenes, who brings about the so-called Henrician Reformation, dismantling the revenue-sucking monasteries and installing a sound system of taxation. Henry called Cromwell: 'A good household manager, but not fit to meddle in the affairs of kings'. As Mantel convinces us, he was royally wrong.

Wuthering Heights, Emily Brontë, 1847

Even, a century and a half later, the title throbs radio-actively. Fewer roentgens, one feels, would radiate from a work announcing itself as 'Windy Peak' by 'Emily Prunty' (the Brontë family name: their clergyman father changed it, to rid it of any taint of his native Irishness). A bracing gust of moorland wind, mingled with faint Celtic keening, blows off the title page.

The *OED*, while helpfully defining 'wuther' ('A violent or impetuous movement, a rush; an attack, onset; a smart blow or stroke; a blast or gust of wind; a quivering movement, a tremble; a rushing or whizzing sound') cannot come up with a convincing example of any one else using it. It's Emily's word. In a later, more mercenary, age she could have trademarked it.

The title-page didn't help the novel. It was published (aborted is the fairer description) by the greatest rogue in London, Thomas Cautley Newby, and fell doomed from the press. Sadly Emily died never knowing that her book would be judged one of the glories of English literature.

The three Brontë sisters were, by the time their first novels were published, accomplished story tellers, having woven in their 'web of childhood', the alternative universes of Gondal and Angria. Those years of fictional practice, together with some hints from the Haworth parsonage's favourite novelist, Scott, enabled Emily to write a first novel with precocious masterly sophistication. Everything was precocious about the Brontë sisters. None of them had long to live.

The first narrator, Mr Lockwood, a 'fashionable gentleman', rents a mansion on the Yorkshire moors. He has retired to the wilderness to mend a broken heart. He makes an ill-advised visit through the bleak, snowy, hills to his landlord, Heathcliff, who lives in a rugged farmhouse, Wuthering Heights. Overnighting there Lockwood is frightened out of his wits by a ghost calling herself 'Cathy' and – chilled to near death – is nursed back to health by his house-keeeper Nellie Dean who entertains him through convalescence with a mysterious back story.

It begins with Heathcliff (no Christian name – the holy water would fizzle on his forehead) being brought back from Liverpool, where the then owner of the Heights, Mr Earnshaw, allegedly found him in the gutter. The swarthy foundling hisses in a strange tongue. Is he the offspring of some slave mother (it's the 1770s, the trade is roaring)? Irish, perhaps (Emily was writing when the great famine was raging)? Is he 'an imp of satan'? Is he (a wholly plausible supposition) an illegitimate brat of Earnshaw's, engendered on some raggle-taggle gypsy?

Heathcliff is installed as a son of the house and becomes closer than even a brother to Catherine Earnshaw. So close, indeed, that she can exclaim in a moment of passion (she has several), 'I *am* Heathcliff'. There ensues a

double blow – old Earnshaw dies. His vindictive son demotes Heathcliff to the status of a menial servant. Cathy – wanting more out of life than farmhouse drudgery – elects to marry a 'gentleman' tenant of nearby Thrushcross Grange (where bedridden Lockwood is now listening to Nellie's strange tale).

A furiously despairing Heathcliff leaves only to return, three years later, a vengeful, wealthy 'gentleman' himself (how that transformation happened we are not told). He embarks on a long, vengeful, campaign to repossess the now married Cathy (unsuccessfully: she dies of frustrated passion) and take possession of both great houses (he succeeds). Finally, his victory dust in his mouth, he is haunted to death by his dead lover: it is not clear whether she wishes to destroy him, or be united with him in happy union beyond the grave.

I first read *Wuthering Heights* in my school library edition, aged sixteen. I've read it many times since but certain problems have always tormented me. I have wrestled with them in print, in classrooms, and in conversation. They are:

1. Is the relationship between Cathy and Heathcliff adulterous or, more horrible thought, incestuous?
2. Is Heathcliff a murderer – does he kill Hindley to take possession of Wuthering Heights?
3. What is Cathy's 'game' in haunting him to death – revenge or a desire for eternal union? Is she really a 'revenant', or merely Heathcliff's conscience punishing him?
4. Most perplexing, why are we drawn, sympathetically, to this brute of a man (if that is what he is) who beats up women and, cardinal sin, kills puppy-dogs out of sheer malice and abuses children. And, quite likely, kills people.

I have never myself come up with satisfactory answers, nor have I encountered any in the hugely voluminous commentary on the novel. That's probably why it's so voluminous and why I, and others, read the novel so often.

The Yellow Birds, Kevin Powers, 2012

A first novel by a young veteran, who served, honourably, in the shabby conflict it chronicles, *The Yellow Birds* won a basketful of prizes and glowing reviews on both sides of the Atlantic. Powers' title alludes to a sentimental song, 'The Yellow Bird', which was originally a Haitian ditty and then popularised by Harry Belafonte in the 1960s. It is burlesqued in US Army training camps as:

> A yellow bird
> With a yellow bill
> Was perched upon
> My windowsill.
> I lured him in
> With a piece of bread
> And then I smashed
> His fucking head.

The novel opens grimly: 'The war tried to kill us in the spring.' The lushly described killing ground is the northern Iraq city of Al Tafar, where Powers himself served as a machine gunner in the romantically entitled 'Desert Storm' (itself a name worthy of Edith M. Hull's original Arabian bodice-ripper, *The Sheik*). *The Yellow Birds* is a grunt's novel. Only the enlisted men have names; the officers merely have ranks: Lieutenant, Major, Colonel.

The higher up the ranks you go, the more full of shit you find them. A colonel in a crisply ironed uniform delivers a (typewritten) 'once more into the breach' speech to the men about to go into action:

> 'If you die, know this: we'll put you on the first bird to Dover. Your families will have a distinction beyond all others. If these bastards want a fight, we're going to give them one.' He paused. A look of great sentimentality came over him. 'I can't go with you boys,' he explained with regret, 'but I'll be in contact from the operation center the whole time. Give 'em hell.'

No actual entering the breach for this colonel. It might crease his uniform.

Comradeship, the novel contends, extends no farther than each soldier's platoon: the men who may be killed alongside him. War is wholly inglorious and ruinously sleepless. The men keep themselves alert with amphetamines, dabs of Tabasco sauce to the eyes, and callous jests. There's the routine R&R, booze and bargirls, but for most who have girls at home there's also the inevitable 'Dear John'. Absence makes the female heart treacherous. There is no attempt to work out what the war is about – risking your life on behalf of people who are doing their best to take your life? Shooting up the country to save the country? That seems to be it.

At the heart of the novel is a triangular relationship between three characters: Private Bartle, Private Daniel Murphy and Sergeant Sterling. Bart and Murph become best buddies – what the British army would call 'muckers'. Sterling, an NCO, is basically a good man, but stern and aloof. When he hears Bart, in the air-embarcation departure scene, promise Murph's mother that he will take care of her son, he promptly beats Bart senseless. You're not in the army to protect buddies but to kill 'fucking hajis', he claims.

Murph eventually buckles. His girl dumps him. He stops talking and wants out – as Sterling puts it, 'he's gone home' in all but body. Unfortunately, there's only one way back for him. After a particularly bloody mortar bombardment, Murph commits suicide by wandering alone and unarmed into hostile territory. Sterling and Bart recover his body and, reverently, consign it to the Tigris river. They know that this way Murph will be honourably described as MIA /KIA (missing in action, killed in action), not branded a coward. Sterling, aware that he has betrayed his military oath, shoots himself, while Bart succumbs to PTSD and is invalided out to his 'little shit-hole town in Virginia'. There, he lives with his mother and drinks himself stupid, unaware that the military courts are catching up with him. The whole truth never comes out, but enough of it emerges to get Bart a sentence in a military prison. He has, as he sees it, done his duty: to his comrade, not the US army or his country. *Semper fidelis*.

The Yellow Wallpaper, Charlotte Perkins Gilman, 1892

The Yellow Wallpaper has, with the madwoman in the attic and the Stepford wife, become a militant emblem of the oppression of woman. Gilman's story takes the form of a monologue by an unnamed doctor's wife, who has been confined to convalescent inactivity by her ostensibly well-meaning husband, John. He has taken a short locum position for three months in an unnamed resort town. It is suggested that she has suffered a post-natal breakdown – in her husband's parlance, 'a temporary nervous depression – a slight hysterical tendency'.

John has brought his sister, a severe woman, to act as housekeeper in their rented mansion during his wife's indisposition. A servant looks after the baby. John is a firm believer in the 'rest cure' therapy, and his wife is kept in a state of virtual sensory deprivation. She is denied reading materials, forbidden visitors, and may not even see her baby, because it makes her 'so nervous'. She is confined to what seems like a nursery at the top of the house, but which may have served a more sinister purpose. It is described as:

> a big, airy room, the whole floor nearly, with windows that look all ways, and air and sunshine galore. It was a nursery first and then playroom and gymnasium, I should judge; for the windows are barred for little children, and there are rings and things in the walls.

Over the subsequent weeks, the woman's *idée fixe* about the room's yellow wallpaper develops into full-blown psychosis. The narrative, delivered entirely in her own words, chronicles her descent into homicidal madness. Underlying it all is the implication that her condition may be 'iatrogenic' – caused, not relieved, by the medical treatment to which she is subjected. The treatment itself may be merely a mask for patriarchal oppression, the cruelties of which are hinted at by the apparatus of Bedlam which surrounds her ('rings and things in the walls').

The Yellow Wallpaper is a fragmentary narrative, which disintegrates into one-sentence, barely grammatical paragraphs, with no apparent internal architecture other than that of the fugùe from neurosis to psychosis. There is, however, a significant middle point in the story when the woman declares: 'Well, the Fourth of July is over!' The day's celebration of Independence is marked in the story by a tacit change in the mode of address. Before Independence Day, it is clear that the woman, who is 'literary' by nature, is writing her own narrative. We see her attempting to hide her work:

> There comes John's sister. Such a dear girl as she is, and so careful of me! I must not let her find me writing . . . I verily believe she thinks it is the writing which made me sick!

After the Fourth of July, there are no more references to this independent, if hidden, written record. We now understand that what we are listening to is a stream of consciousness, and finally mad babble. The nursery has become Bertha Mason's attic.

There is an enigma at the heart of *The Yellow Wallpaper*: is the woman mentally ill, in any clinical sense, or has she been driven mad by solitary confinement? Is she unusual, or in some sense representative of a whole class of married women and mothers, locked in what Ibsen called the bourgeois 'doll's house'? This uncertainty parallels Gilman's own experience and the severe post-natal depression from which she suffered after the birth of her first child. In a 1913 essay, 'Why I Wrote *The Yellow Wallpaper*', she describes how her husband (an artist, not a doctor) referred her to the great Dr Silas Weir Mitchell. The doctor prescribed his famous rest cure – based on his Quaker religious beliefs – with the solemn advice to 'live as domestic a life as possible . . . And never touch pen, brush, or pencil again as long as you live.' Gilman followed the advice for three months, 'and came so near the borderline of utter mental ruin that I could see over'.

After this glimpse into the heart of marital darkness Gilman divorced her husband, on the grounds that marriage was driving her insane, in 1894, two years after her story was published. The 'divorce cure' wasn't entirely successful, although as history records, it worked better than Mitchell's rest cure.

Young Törless, Robert Musil, 1906

Musil's novel has two attractions. The first is that it is a much less daunting read than *The Man without Qualities*. The second is that, for readers with historical interests, it probes one of the great questions of the twentieth century. How did Germany create such an (almost) world-beating army – more particularly, how was it that their officer corps was so extraordinarily, ruthlessly efficient? And so horrifically cruel? The answer, Musil suggests, is more likely to be found in Nietzsche than Clausewitz.

Musil's German title was *Die Verwirrungen des Zöglings Törless*. It translates as 'The Confusions of the Boarding School Pupil Törless'. Confusion, according to the novel, is the essential human condition. The epigraph is from Maeterlinck: 'As soon as we put something into words, we devalue it in a strange way.' But what, other than words, do we have to put it in?

The action is set in a prestigious Austrian military academy called 'W', based on the one that Musil attended in his adolescent years, before deciding that philosophy and literature were his vocation. In the Austro-Hungarian Empire, and post-Bismarck Germany, these were nurseries for the officer corps, as they still are in the US. In the Britain of the time, the task was left to the more diffusely purposed public schools.

No first names are given in Musil's novel. This is, we apprehend, the story of a necessary dehumanising process. Nor are we given details of the curriculum and the military training regime. Instead, it is the pupils' private world which is the author's focus. 'W' is the kind of school which tolerates smoking, drinking and – in modest measure – whoring. But some things the system does not tolerate. There was, shortly before the novel's action opens, an outbreak of 'beastliness' in the school, which 'went too far',

and a purgative round of expulsions followed.

The central characters are four young men: Reiting, Beineberg, Törless, and Basini. They are radically different both by nature and by beliefs. Beineberg is a mystic, infatuated with Indian philosophy. Reiting is a nihilist who reveres Napoleon. Törless, in turn, is a 'confused' observer for most of the novel, but finally a participant in the central events.

At the outset of the book Basini is discovered stealing money from the lockers and should, by regulations, be denounced and expelled. But Reiting and Beineberg resolve that they will make him the subject of an experiment in the exercise of power. 'We're holding Basini in the palm of our hand,' they tell Törless, 'we can do whatever we like with him.' What they like intensifies into ritualised sadism: specifically flagellation with wire whips. Basini's back is soon a mass of scars.

Törless is fascinated and horrified but, above all, interested. A visit to the local whore, Bozena, confirms what he suspects. Basini is 'effeminate'. He is rich, and has returned the stolen money without difficulty. Was his theft a kind of masochistic experiment of his own? Does he want what is happening to him?

A confused Törless begins to 'cultivate his moods'. He becomes fascinated by the idea of infinity – no boundaries, no 'stopping points'. He resolves to become shameless: 'Shame is yet another loneliness, a new dark wall.' He recalls the time when, before he went to school, he wore dresses (as infants of both sexes did at the time) and 'there were times when he felt a quite inexpressible longing to be a girl'. While watching the flagellation of Basini he discovers himself 'in a state of sexual arousal' which he necessarily hides from his comrades. Finally, alone with his victim, he rapes Basini. It generates a 'secret, unspecific, melancholy sensuality'. The degradation supplies:

> that tiny quantity of poison that is needed to rid the soul of its overly calm, complacent health and instead give it a kind of health that is more refined, acute and understanding.

After the act he feels purged of confusion, and healthy. Basini (who now loves him) is just so much waste material. Törless has discovered that there is no rational connection in life, any more than there is between pre-coital lust and post-coital gloom.

> It is always the case that what we experience in one moment, whole and unquestioning, becomes incomprehensible and confused when we seek to bind it to our enduring ownership with the chains of thought.

The school's lesson has been learned, and it all ends anticlimactically. Basini is expelled and Törless goes off to philosophise. Reiting and Beineberg, and their kind, go off to win wars.

The Young Visiters, Daisy Ashford, 1919

Young Daisy Ashford wrote novels after tea and before bedtime (a strict six o'clock) for the delectation of her father, a civil servant in the War Office. It was the high point of the day for both of them. He duly copied the stories out, retaining her quaintly juvenile grammar and orthography, as well as the stunningly precocious vocabulary picked up from romance novels left around by her older sisters.

The novel on which Miss Ashford's eternal fame rests, *The Young Visiters*, was published in 1919 as a curiosity. It contained an introduction by J. M. Barrie, who – manuscript in hand – vouched for the bona fides of the 'authoress of nine years'. It went on to be a huge bestseller and still is.

The narrative opens (imagine the ubiquitous '[sic]'):

> Mr Salteena was an elderly man of 42 and was fond of asking peaple to stay with him. He had quite a young girl staying with him of 17 named Ethel Monticue. Mr Salteena had dark short hair and mustache and wiskers which were very black and twisty. He was middle sized and he had very pale blue eyes. He had a pale brown suit but on Sundays he had a black one and he had a topper every day as he thorght it more becoming.
>
> Ethel Monticue had fair hair done on the top and blue eyes. She had a blue velvet frock which had grown rarther short in the sleeves. She had a black straw hat and kid gloves.

Ethel is given to 'sneery' looks and a 'snappy tone' when crossed.

Mr Salteena is invited by his young 'very grand' friend, Bernard Clark, to visit Clark's 'sumpshous' mansion. 'Please bring one of your young ladies whichever is the prettiest in the face', he is instructed. When the morning of the visit comes: 'Mr Salteena did not have an egg for his brekfast in case he should be sick on the jorney.' 'I shall put some red ruge on my face', decides Ethel, 'because I am very pale owing to the drains in this house.'

Exposed to Bernard's style of life, Alfred Salteena is forced to realise 'I am not quite a gentleman.' The young people fall in love on the spot. Bernard kindly takes his not-quite-gentlemanly friend in hand, introducing him to the Prince of Wales, no less, at Buckingham Palace. Alfred is clad for the occasion in 'black satin knickerbockers and a hat with white feathers also garters and a star or two'. The event is quite worthy of his black satin unmentionables:

> They all went out by a private door and found themselves in a smaller but gorgous room. The Prince tapped on the table and instantly two menials in red tunics appeared.
>
> Bring three glasses of champaigne commanded the prince and some ices he added majestikally. The goods appeared as if by majic and the prince drew out a cigar case and passed it round.
>
> One grows weary of Court Life he remarked.

The expected 'proposale' ensues:

> Bernard placed one arm tightly round her. When will you marry me Ethel he uttered you must be my wife it has come to that I love you so intensly

that if you say no I shall perforce dash my body to the brink of yon muddy river he panted wildly.

Oh dont do that implored Ethel breathing rarther hard.

Then say you love me he cried.

Oh Bernard she sighed fervently I certinly love you madly you are to me like a Heathen god she cried looking at his manly form and handsome flashing face I will indeed marry you.

Mr Salteena has also fallen in love with Ethel. But she is not for him. 'This is agony', he cries, 'my life will be sour grapes and ashes without you.' So be it. Bernard and Ethel marry in Westminster Abbey. By way of consolation, the rejected Mr Salteena 'marrid one of the maids in waiting at Buckingham palace by name Bessie Topp a plesant girl of 18 with a round red face and rarther stary eyes'.

Young Miss Ashford may not have known about sex, but she knew all about the English class system. Even in black silk knickerbockers poor Mr Salteena ('Fred') will never be a gent.

The Zayat Kiss, Sax Rohmer, 1912

This is the first of Rohmer's 'yellow peril' Fu Manchu stories, centred on the arch-evil Mandarin. 'The Zayat Kiss' was delivered to the world in the *Story-Teller* magazine in 1912 and, as republished together with other follow-up tales in *The Mystery of Dr Fu Manchu*, became a runaway bestseller. It ran through sixteen editions in as many years (1913–29), and by the 1920s it was selling by the hundred thousand in Methuen two-shilling editions. What it did for race relations in Britain is not recorded.

The success of Rohmer's exotic fiend inspired innumerable sequels and imitations on page and screen. His influence can be distantly felt in Ian Fleming's Dr No, as well as in Ming the Merciless – that inscrutably sadistic demon of the Flash Gordon comic strips – and Michael Myers' Dr Evil. Rohmer was also clearly influenced by M. P. Shiel's *The Yellow Danger* (which was followed some years later by his novel *The Yellow Peril*).

As one of the 'Seven of the Si-Fan' (hinting at the anti-Semitic myth of the Elders of Zion), Fu Manchu is bent on nothing less than world domination. How he will achieve it is not always clear. As the critic Colin Watson wearily notes:

> The plots, such as they are, of the Fu Manchu novels would be quite meaningless in paraphrase. They are a jumble of incredible encounters, pursuits, traps, and escapes. Who is trying to accomplish what, and why? – this is never explained. All that seems certain is that a titanic struggle is being waged by a man called [Sir Denis] Nayland Smith to thwart the designs of Fu Manchu.

The narrative of 'The Zayat Kiss' opens with Smith – a salt-of-the-earth British government official in Burma – making a surprise call on his old London friend Dr Petrie (Smith's Dr Watson, as he is to be). Smith has taken a spot of furlough in order to save 'the White Race' from the fiendish plots of a Chinese mastermind, Dr Fu Manchu. 'He is no ordinary criminal', Smith announces:

> He is the greatest genius which the powers of evil have put on earth for centuries. He has the backing of a political group whose wealth is enormous and his mission in Europe is *to pave the way*! Do you follow me? He is the advance-agent of a movement so epoch-making that not one Britisher, and not one American, in fifty thousand has ever dreamed of it.

An opium addict, Fu Manchu is physically deformed. He is possessed of viridescent eyes, with which he is capable of hypnotising his victims. In addition to being a 'profound chemist', he is also a white slaver, and 'the genius of the Yellow Peril'. Like other arch-criminals, he has a sinister pet – a trained marmoset.

It emerges that the fiend's immediate aim is to kill all high-ranking Britons, particularly 'old hands' who know anything whatsoever about the East, and he plans to start with Nayland Smith. Fu Manchu uses extravagantly ingenious methods to accomplish this prophylactic goal: poisonous centipedes in 'The Zayat Kiss', Thuggee assassins in 'The Call of Siva', toxic gas in 'Green Mist' and – at his most infernal – fungi cellars in 'The Spores of Death', in which poisonous mushrooms pump out lethal particles to dispatch his victims in agony. He despises guns, bludgeons, and knives – the weapons of lesser criminals.

In the first series of stories, headed by 'The Zayat Kiss', Smith finally foils his adversary, but the yellow fiend leaves a letter promising an even more fiendish return. Meanwhile, Petrie falls in love with one of Fu Manchu's former henchwomen, the luscious Kâramanèh, whom he sends back to her home in Egypt (there is a hint that they may marry one day, as indeed they do, and their daughter figures in later instalments). Fu Manchu's own daughter, Fah lo Suee, has a weakness for Nayland Smith, and helpfully saves him from a variety of fates worse than death.

Fu Manchu tales poured from Rohmer's pen (mainly to support his gambling addiction) until 'Emperor Fu Manchu' in 1959, by which time the former villain was somewhat rehabilitated as an opponent of Communism. Red perils turned out to be worse than yellow.

Zazie dans le métro, Raymond Queneau, 1959

Pity the translator. This is the first paragraph, as rendered into English, gallantly, by Barbara Wright:

Howcanaystinksotho, wondered Gabriel, exasperated. Ts incredible, they never clean themselves. It says in the paper that not eleven percent of the flats in Paris have bathrooms.

(Queneau's French for that first neologism is 'Doukipudonktan?' – 'D'où qu'ils puent donc tant?')

The setting is the railway station and Gabriel is waiting for his niece, Zazie. Gabriel is, it will emerge, a female impersonator. There are lively exchanges between him and his niece, in slang, as to whether he is a 'hormosessual' or not (we never find out). Zazie has been dispatched from the country for a seventy-two-hour holiday in Paris so that her mother can be alone with her lover. Zazie is, it will emerge, a vexatiously perceptive Keyhole Kate.

Zazie gives her uncle the slip and falls in with a gallery of Parisian types, acquiring for herself a longed-for pair of 'blewgenes'. She sees the sights of the city for the first time and easily avoids molestation, the thought of which gives her uncle the heeby-jeebies.

But the great monuments of Paris leave Zazie cold. Her dearest wish is to see the Underground. However, in one of the wildcat strikes for which 1950s Paris was notorious, it's closed. Via a trip into the sewers she contrives to get underground and, finally, sees the 'métro'. It's a life-changing experience – and a sinister one.

There is an even more disturbing moment in the narrative when the young heroine recalls the death of her father:

I got home, then, and there he was boozed as a coot, my papa, so he starts

to kiss me which was quite natural seeing he was my papa, but then he starts pawing me (wolf whistle), so I say oh you don't because I could see what he was getting at, the bastard, but when I'd said ah no, not that, never, he flings himself on to the door and he locks it.

Her mother then broke in and buried an axe in the filthy molester's skull, making Zazie a half-orphan.

The novel – written by the most mandarin (to use de Beauvoir's term) of French intellectuals – was a runaway success. The name 'Zazie' was bestowed on the new-born generation (notably the pop singer Zazie, born in 1964). At the high point of French nouvelle vague creativity, in 1960, it was adapted into a film by the brilliant director Louis Malle.

In adapting the novel, Malle faced a crux. Should the heroine be sexy? Malle makes Zazie a boyish twelve-year-old LOLITA (a clear influence), although the book places Zazie at fourteen, already pubescent. Queneau gave the subject some thought (he spent six years writing the novel). His answer in interview to the issue of age and sex is careful, and depicts it as something inherently ambiguous. When a man, Queneau suggests, looks at what Nabokov called a 'nymphet' (and Queneau, 'une fillette') there is a radical uncertainty as to which side of the age of consent the male mind should categorise her.

This equivocation resonates uncomfortably, particularly after the so-called 'Jimmy Savile effect' which agonised the British nation in 2013. Our nearest neighbours are, it would seem, less shockable. In France, in 1977, a group of leading intellectuals under the leadership of Michel Foucault, author of The History of Sexuality and darling of the 'theorists', submitted a petition to abolish the 'contractual' age of consent in France. There should be no artificial constraint where Zazies were concerned, it argued. The petition was signed by among others, Louis Althusser, Jean-Paul Sartre, Simone de Beauvoir and Roland Barthes. Had he not died in 1976 one suspects Queneau would have added his name.

Zuleika Dobson, Max Beerbohm, 1911

I first read *Zuleika Dobson* as a schoolboy with grand hopes (dashed, alas) of going to study in the dreaming spires myself. I was tickled to death (as the phrase is) by Beerbohm's stylistic dandyism. While reading parts of the novel I burst out laughing. I relished the cunningly overcooked Beerbohmian prose. Reading the novel again, fifty years on, *Zuleika Dobson* strikes me very differently. It's always been a mystery to me that novels change as you change, but they do. Sometimes, as in this case, totally.

Nowadays, *Zuleika*'s comedy strikes me as blacker than black, and much of it no laughing matter at all. The plot is easily summarised. A orphaned young maiden, having gained wealth and praise as a conjurer and socialite, eventually comes 'to rest' in the house of her grandfather, the Warden of Judas College.

Zuleika duly explodes on the sex-starved, all-male undergraduates, and the central narrative is devoted to her love affair with the Duke of Dorset. The most golden of *jeunesse*, the Duke is a paragon, a non-pareil. He achieves effortless 'firsts' without reading; a prodigy without needing to extend himself or strain his blue-blooded elegance:

He was fluent in all modern languages, had a very real talent in water-colour, and was accounted, by those who had had the privilege of hearing him, the best amateur pianist on this side of the Tweed.

He also owns 340,000 acres of England and most of Scotland (for shooting, since it's good for nothing else). The less grand members of the university are all referred to by him as 'Smith' – it saves time to give them the same name. Oicks – that is, ungowned townees – remain nameless.

A *femme fatale* of the first water, Zuleika plays a cat-and-mouse game with her paramour – whom, for all his lustre, she regards as a 'snob'. He is astonished by such an allegation. He has, he indignantly retorts,

adapted his lifestyle to the monastic tradition of Oxford, bringing no larger entourage with him than a butler.

Having failed to win over Zuleika, he resolves to throw himself into the Isis, dressed in full ducal regalia, and to die for love: *Liebestod*. He selects the day of the great inter-collegiate boat race, with all the undergraduate population either competing on the water or watching from the bank. Zuleika serenely accepts his amorous sacrifice, imposing the sole condition that, as he plunges to his death, he should shout her name for all the world to hear. It will immortalise her. Proof of his mortality is a small price to pay for that.

Her spell has been exercised not merely on the noblest of Oxford's gilded youth but on every single undergraduate. Like lemmings they too die a noble Oxonian death. All shout the word 'Zuleika!' as they plunge into the water:

Victory and defeat alike forgotten, the crews staggered erect and flung themselves into the river, the slender boats capsizing and spinning futile around in a melley of oars.

From the towing-path – no more din there now, but great single cries of 'Zuleika!' – leaped figures innumerable through rain to river. The arrested boats of the other crews drifted zigzag hither and thither. The dropped oars rocked and clashed, sank and rebounded, as the men plunged across them into the swirling stream.

That evening, at high table, the dons fail to notice that the whole undergraduate population has mysteriously disappeared. There are more important things on their minds. Zuleika, surveying what she has done, commands her maid to book the fastest train to Cambridge.

The novel, for all its comedy, is about slaughter. At one rather more serious moment in the narrative, Beerbohm observes in passing that 'youth' and 'death' do not belong together. *Zuleika Dobson* came out three years before the Great War, in which the death toll among alumnae was horrific, as plaques in every college now attest. The overwhelming mass of 'those whose name liveth for evermore' (it doesn't) were youthful; many abandoned their studies to answer their country's call. They died for a cause which, many might think, was no worthier of the 'highest price' than 'Zuleika!'

Ever one to love trivia, Beerbohm devotes his preface to the instruction that his ear has been offended by mis-pronunciation of 'Zulike-a'. It should be 'Zuleeka'.

Appendix

The 500 novels covered in the first edition of this book all appeared in or before 2014; its publication date. Since then there have been marked changes of emphasis in contemporary writing, reflecting what's going on in the world beyond fiction's tides and currents.

One major drift is towards what Jean-Paul Sartre termed *littérature engagée*. 'Fiction with a Purpose', Victorians called it. Novels of the last decade have engaged with feminism's #MeToo and the Black Lives Matter insurgencies in the US. In the UK, major reassessments of what the British Empire was have found expression and spurred debate, sometimes heated, in fiction.

A substantial number of the authors in this supplement earned qualifications in 'creative writing'. Once scorned, these educational programs have – I believe – sophisticated the fabric of modern fiction. It is craftier.

As interesting is what has happened to the reading of novels. I detect two major forces. One is the growth of the reading group and 'collective response' (typically, fruitful disagreement) after discussion. This has gone well beyond front-room, tea and biscuits gatherings into 'Zoominars' and internet quarrels. Goodreads.com is to novels what rottentomatoes.com is to movies. Old critic-reader circuits have been elaborated and discussion widened. Vast free internet libraries such as Project Gutenberg have given historical depth to reader response. The reading public has acquired new agency.

Related to this is a new refinement of sensibility. I find nothing to mock in institutionally imposed 'trigger warnings' or publishers making preparatory use of 'sensitivity readers'. It indicates, I believe, a welcome fullness of literary response. We are relearning the Victorian ability to read with the emotions as well as the mind.

To talk about novels is to talk about oneself. What follows is a small bag of nails – they are, however, my nails. Others would have selected a different supplementary twenty titles. Diversity and disagreement are what being 'well read' is all about.

Elizabeth is Missing, Emma Healey, 2014

The form of this novel is traditional in fiction: it's an 'I' narrative. But JANE EYRE or *David Copperfield* it isn't. This 'I' is a Miss Marple (named Martha Horsham) whose mind is in terminal decline. She's following up a murder – perhaps two. But she can't for the life of her (what's left of it) hold the clues in her mind.

Martha lives alone in her own house – which suggests she is 'dotty' rather than afflicted with one of the recognised forms of dementia (vascular, Alzheimer's, frontotemporal) that – with the dubious benefit of longer life – have become first-world countries' second most common cause of death.

Martha has a daughter, Helen, who is dutiful but preoccupied with her own life. 'Households' and 'nuclear families' are history. The council and its carers are kind but too busy for empathy. Martha has little thought for her dead husband. Hour-to-hour, she organises her life and mind with post-it notes written to herself and with recurrent compulsive obsessions: the need to buy cans of peach slices, her childhood comfort food, or deciding the best place to plant summer squash. She wants to go back in time and dig something up from there. A seventy-year-old 'vanity compact' comes to her hand while she is scrabbling in her friend Elizabeth's back garden in a kind of confused effort to do something useful. It means something. But what? Why is it there?

Elizabeth has now gone missing. She was the last of Martha's friends who isn't in a coffin or in a (miscalled) 'care' home. There was someone else who went missing. Martha's elder sister Sukey disappeared in the postwar period.

Sukey had a spiv husband. She was also involved with Douglas (nice on the surface but really not), a lodger with Martha's family after he was bombed out of his own home. Men are largely absent from the book and those recollected by Martha are all bad lots. A madwoman in the street knows something, but what? And how is she related to Douglas?

There is an explanation of where Elizabeth is but Maud constantly forgets or suppresses the knowledge. What's missing is her obsession. Something is not there. Exhumation, digging up the past, will be her last enterprise before her own inhumation. Solution then dissolution.

Elizabeth is Missing is a debut novel: Healey was a graduate of creative writing courses, which manifestly worked well for her. Her novel takes on something impossible – telling a story through the mind of someone incapable of telling a story. I would bet that in the earlier drafts of this novel there is one in which Elizabeth returns for a *dea ex machina* denouement. If so there is no such untying in the work as published. Strands of mystery still dangle for reading groups to form their own hypotheses. What should we make of Douglas? How in life do Elizabeth and Sukey conjoin?

TV adaptation is nowadays as important a subsidiary as paperback publication. The novel was adapted into a TV drama in 2019 by the BBC. Glenda Jackson (eighty-two years old, Martha's age) played the central character. Jackson had recently portrayed male cognitive impairment in a cross-gender *King Lear*. Together film and novel unite to make a statement: age beyond the biblical threescore and ten can help you uncover the truth – but do you want to know it?

The Buried Giant, Kazuo Ishiguro, 2015

Between the publication of this book and his next, *Klara and the Sun* (2021), Kazuo

Ishiguro won the Nobel Prize for Literature. You can never foresee from which direction his next novel will come – nor how long you'll have to wait for what's coming. In this case, a strange mix of Kafka and *Gawain and the Green Knight*. One waited ten years for it, a mere six for its successor.

The Buried Giant is set in the Dark Ages, two centuries after the Roman departure from Britain, forty or so years after Arthur's failed attempts to set up a modern nation state. 'An odd setting', Ishiguro conceded, musingly, in an interview.

Things have slipped back into primeval darkness. Britons, in the West, and Saxons inconclusively contest ownership of the island. It's the murkiest, least 'remembered' era of British history. Here be ogres, giants, dragons – legend and superstition maintain.

Axl and Beatrice know their names, that they are Britons, and that they're married. Otherwise they exist in a state of utter forgetfulness about themselves, their past, and the world around them. A 'mist' has fallen on the country. Universal amnesia covers all. Axl and Beatrice mistily recall they once had a son. They think he lives, or has died, in the eastern, Saxon, regions of the island. They resolve to leave their primitive village in search of him. His name, and what he looked like, they cannot recollect. They journey east as unconsciously as homing pigeons.

Quests – journeys – figure centrally in Ishiguro's fiction. In his previous novel, *Never Let Me Go*, the genetically manufactured characters set out, forlornly, to find who made them, and why. IN THE REMAINS OF THE DAY, the butler, Stevens, journeys west to bring back Miss Kenton to Darlington Hall. I would guess Don Quixote – that archetypal quester – has an honoured place on the Ishiguro bookshelf.

On the journey they 'must take', Axl and Beatrice encounter boatmen ferrying passengers to an island of the living dead. In a Saxon village they are joined by a 'warrior', Wistan, and a strange boy, Edwin, who nurses a wound that never heals, inflicted on him by a she-dragon, Querig.

There are a series of close-run things with bandits, villains and treacherous monks. Sir Gawain, now a geriatric relic of

Arthur's Round Table, on a worn-out nag called Horace, makes up another of the motley band. Axl dimly recollects he too was once one of Arthur's men. Details elude him. But there was an atrocity. He is glad to have forgotten his part in it.

Eventually the couple's mission changes. They resolve to destroy the she-dragon whose deadly breath has brought down this 'mist' on the country. The narrative moves towards a terminal surprise when they finally confront the monster in her lair.

Dragons are central to the mythic foundations of modern Britain. Saint George whose cross is now the English emblem killed a dragon. A dragon killed the first hero in British literature, Beowulf. And, of course, looming over the whole, is the scholar-fabulist Tolkien and his gold-hoarding dragon Smaug.

It was Tolkien who decreed, in his classic essay on *Beowulf*, that we should simply enjoy dragons as dragons in our fables, as children enjoy them, not lumber the beasts with deep symbolisms. One can certainly enjoy the sheer quest-and-adventure surface of Ishiguro's fable. Nonetheless, it is impossible to escape the sense that it is 'about' something weighty.

Seven years ago Ishiguro put on record that he'd wanted, for some time, 'to write a novel about how societies remember and forget . . . When is it better to just *forget*?' The moral? If a society doesn't forget the past, it will never move forward into the future but will be forever locked in its own Dark Age. It is the mist, 'forgetfulness', that allows Britain, at its formative stage, to solder itself together – 'move on', and put the past behind it.

Ishiguro is the most British of novelists since P. G. Wodehouse (doubtless theses have been written on Stevens's debt to Jeeves). But Ishiguro was born in one of the only two cities which, seventy years ago, were destroyed by the atom bomb. To move forward, Japan has had to forget. So too America, which perpetrated the inhuman slaughter of Japanese civilians. Instead of festivals of 'remembrance' for World War One, Dresden, Auschwitz or Hiroshima, it would, according to Ishiguro, be healthier to have festivals of forgetfulness.

He wrote THE REMAINS OF THE DAY in four hectic weeks. *The Buried Giant* took him ten slow years to bring to completion. Its progress was not helped by his wife telling him the first draft was rubbish and to start again from scratch. Which he did.

An American Marriage, Tayari Jones, 2015

This novel received endorsement from the then most powerful man in the world, Barack Obama. The first lady shared the presidential opinion. Jones had written four earlier novels; none was published in the UK. The potent mix of Pulitzer, Obama and Oprah installed the author of *An American Marriage* in the pantheon of early-twenty-first-century fiction and its preoccupation with matters of social urgency. It sits alongside Colin Kaepernick's 'taking the knee', the murder of George Floyd, and Black Lives Matter protests.

Obama's description – 'A moving portrayal of the effects of a wrongful conviction on a young African-American couple' – is only partly true. Racial injustice is the plot's kick-off point but the novel is in essence a meditation on not just African-American marriage but what its title promises: modern marriage in America.

The storyline is drawn out over the best part of a decade, in which the main characters become different people. A young couple have been married for eighteen months. They met at Morehouse College, founded for black students. He was there on scholarship; she had private means. Celestial has a history at college she does not share with Roy; he has secrets about his birth he does not share with her. Secrecy – not intimately knowing each other – is corroding their marriage. Class differences cause additional friction: his background is blue-collar, hers is moneyed middle-class. He believes home is where you launch from in life: leaving it behind. It's a poker card you swap to get a better hand. She believes background is heritage. You live with what gave you life. Your roots are there. Without roots, life has no direction. Each of the facts of their situation poses a question, and these disparate questions combine to form one giant overriding question about the key word in the title. There are many marriages but only one America. Has it 'married' all the elements that make it what it is in the twentieth century?

As the novel's action starts they are living in Atlanta and succeeding as the city – historically a centre of race conflict – booms. Roy is in business and a man of action. He lost a tooth apprehending a robber on their first date. Celestial treasures the tooth as a relic. She has artistic ambitions. She makes black baby dolls – all with Roy's face. But she fiercely does not want actual babies. Her work is critically admired. At this point one wonders: is this a uniquely particular marriage? Or is it, in its way, typical?

On a visit to Roy's parents in small-town Louisiana, marital stresses provoke an argument. They stay overnight at a local seedy motel – Piney Woods. After some bickering, Roy takes a bucket to the landing's ice machine. While there he helps a middle-aged guest with her arm in a sling carry her bucket back to her room. Is she white? Or is she black? The novel does not say, leaving it open. As the questionnaire appended to the back of the narrative suggests, it is something left, by design, for reading groups to mull over. Roy and Celestial make up and make love – but with a strange, ominous urgency.

Police break in and arrest them both. They are forced to lie, handcuffed, on the tarmac outside the motel 'like two corpses' – flesh of each other's flesh at last, Celestial thinks. Roy is railroaded on a rape charge and given twelve years. An unusual act of (mis)justice or typical? There is no evidence offered other than the statement given by the woman on the landing, who may be deluded or malicious in her claim to have been assaulted – something else for the reading group to mull over.

The marital relationship is thereafter largely conducted by letter and the occasional visit: unsatisfying for Roy, degrading for Celestial. He is unmanned. In prison, however, he discovers a crucial fact about himself – he was born outside marriage. Her career as an artist takes off: she enters into a relationship with Andre, the friend who got them together at college. She is becoming more herself and moving away. But still married. You cannot, she thinks, unlove.

Roy is released early. There is no reunion. The last third of the novel is a tangle of marital breakup, making up, and painful 'moving on'. All three principal characters are looking, as Roy puts it, for a new kind of 'happy marriage'. A new kind of 'knot' as Celestial pictures it, to hold two people together in a relationship that is more fulfilling than a hitching post. Jones says that what was on her mind, when she was writing, was Homer's Penelope, waiting twenty years for her husband to return, sewing every day and unsewing every night, not a doll but a shroud.

The novel is told through the three principals' interwoven streams of thought. It is subtly and skilfully voiced. One 'hears' it more than with most novels. Placing the drama in a suprapersonal dimension is Jones's extraordinary skill with proverbial wisdom – the communal truths that make sense of life's mess and are passed on from generation to generation. There are twelve pages of them on Goodreads.com. For example:

> 'One is the left shoe and the other is the right. They are the same but not interchangeable';
> 'Marriage is between two people. There is no studio audience';
> 'When a spectral voice says, get out, you should do it. But in real life, you don't know that you're in a scary movie'.

One may wonder if the last of these saws was perhaps picked up in the title of the Oscar-winning, (very) scary movie, about insidious forms of modern black exploitation by white Americans, *Get Out* (2017).

Sweet Caress, William Boyd, 2015

One of the joys of William Boyd's fiction is that you never know where the next one is coming from (see THE NEW CONFESSIONS, earlier). This is no exception.

The appended Acknowledgments is a list of names, some of which look familiar – and then you realise that's because they're all great women photographers. This is a novel it's useful to back, rather than nose, into.

From the beginning *Sweet Caress* is a rattling good story and a meditation, in fiction, on women and the lens – more particularly what Susan Sontag, partner of the photographer Annie Leibovitz, called 'the woman photographer of conscience'.

Cameras are different tools in the hands of men and women. For men – vividly depicted in Antonioni's film *Blow Up* – photographers are latent sexual violators. Peeping Toms. Pornography is male lens-craft. And conscienceless. Great women photographers, the novel suggests, are different. They 'capture' image receptively, feelingly. The avatar is Vivian Maier, that recluse who wandered the streets of Chicago with her Rollei, taking thousands of 'real life' pictures, which she never cared if anyone looked at.

Sweet Caress opens with a lonely old woman, recalling her life as a world-class photographer while living out her last years on the west coast of Scotland. She has not long to go: she has multiple sclerosis.

Amory Clay, born 1908, is so called because her father wanted a boy. A war hero who gave his sanity for his country, he tries to kill Amory. Thereafter the family falls apart. A gay, society photographer uncle gives her a Box Brownie camera. From behind it, Amory can face life. Having, at her uncle's suggestion, surrendered her virginity, simply to get the damn thing out of the way, she spurns Oxford to become a *Tatler*-style fashion photographer. She loses the job by making her subjects look like real women.

She takes off to Weimar Germany to photograph its lesbian underworld club life, puts the pictures she brings back on display in London and is duly prosecuted for obscenity. England isn't ready for her honesty. While covering a Black Shirt march in the East End, she is savagely kicked in the womb and rendered sterile. Once recovered, it's off to America, to work in the glossy magazine industry. She takes lovers – rich, sophisticated men of the world. They are her conquests.

In the Second World War, by now a frontline photo-journalist, she meets the man she will marry. A war hero, he turns out to be lord of a castle as well. Like her father, he has been destroyed, mentally, by war. It turns out Amory is not sterile. She has twins. Her husband commits suicide by alcohol. She reaches the peak of her career in Vietnam, not photographing the front-line but capturing on film the trauma of those who have been through battle and survived to suffer. The long strands of her life as daughter, wife, mother and photographer have been woven into a single design.

Go Set a Watchman, Harper Lee, 2015

The background to TO KILL A MOCKINGBIRD, one of the pre-eminently famous novels of our times, is given in earlier pages. Harper Lee was born in 1926 in Monroeville, Alabama (Maycomb in her fiction).

Were it not for her novel her birthplace would be just another municipal drive-thru – or 'flag stop' for trains in the 1930s. It was where she would spend most of her life before and after writing MOCKINGBIRD and where she would choose to die. She drew attention to Maycomb's topography as a place where ancient trails met. Her own began and finished there.

Her father, the dedicatee of TO KILL A MOCKINGBIRD, was a lawyer. He had defended two black men accused of murdering a white man. They were hanged. Lee herself studied law but gave up college to go to New York and write. She left her forename 'Nelle' (Ellen backwards) behind her; henceforth she would be, to the world, 'Harper Lee' – a male-sounding name. In New York she kept herself alive by working as an airline travel agent – something that left not the slightest residue in her fiction or her life. No great writer of the era was less 'travelled'. She wrote by night and in her spare time. There was interest but no revenue from publishers. Friends clubbed together to give her money enough for a sabbatical year. (Who says New York has no heart?). Those few who knew her, loved her.

The rest is literary history. She submitted a manuscript of what became MOCKINGBIRD in 1957. It was published three years later and won a Pulitzer. The film, which did as much for Gregory Peck's reputation as for hers, followed. (Lee gave Peck her father's watch – he was someone she let into her life, along with his family.) Both novel and film created a powerful side-wind to the Civil Rights Act of 1964. For generations after, Lee's novel was prescribed reading for the young of America. Atticus's injunction to Scout became proverbial: 'You never really understand a person . . . until you climb inside of his skin and walk around in it.'

Having written MOCKINGBIRD, in her mid-thirties Lee retired to Monroeville; a place she had never, in her heart, left. She certainly wrote thereafter but she did not publish. The world eventually reconciled itself to the fact she never would. Then, in 2015, a bombshell. She was going to publish a second novel. It emerged that it was the 'proto-MOCKINGBIRD', the raw material out of which her masterwork had been fashioned. The news it was coming set the reading world agog.

Go Set a Watchman takes place in the 1950s, twenty years on from MOCKINGBIRD. Scout discovers, returning to Maycomb, that Atticus may once have been a lawyer with a good heart, but he, like his white fellow citizens, is furious at the 1954 federal instruction that the South must desegregate its schools. There are some skins, it appears, Atticus does not want to walk around in. As he explains to his thunderstruck daughter:

> Let's put this on a practical basis right now. Do you want Negroes by the carload in our schools and churches and theaters? Do you want them in our world? . . . Honey, you do not seem to understand that the Negroes down here are still in their childhood as a people.

Racist reading matter in his study reveals active connection with the Ku Klux Klan. No sequel has been more disturbing. It has been suggested it was her brilliant first editor, Tay Hohoff, who advised her to rework the primal *Watchman*, setting it in the Depression era and giving it a liberal spin.

It used to be joked that Mount Rushmore's fifth face should be that of Atticus Finch. No more.

Mothering Sunday: A Romance, Graham Swift, 2016

Up to World War One some 90 per cent of working women and 70 per cent of working men were in 'domestic service'. Britain was more of a slave state than Periclean Athens. War, supertax to pay for 'Victory', female emancipation ('The Vote'), and mass urbanisation changed all that over the interwar years.

My mother (born in 1916) began life as a domestic servant, emptying chamber pots and changing sheets for luckier women than her at Bedford College. She could be quite bitter on the subject. But, enterprising person that she was, she went on to a better life. Her parents couldn't. A door was left slightly ajar for her – 'narrow is the way'.

Mothering Sunday is set, principally, on one day: 30 March 1924. Sanctioned by the Church, this was the only day in the year when female domestic servants were guaranteed time off. When their superiors holidayed on other occasions – Christmas, New Year, or some Tory Party victory – the servants would be expected to work for their betters twice as hard.

Jane Fairchild is motherless – a foundling. She is twenty-two and a maid at a large house that has seen better days prewar. A comely lass, as the phrase was, she has attracted the seigneurial attentions of a young gent from a neighbouring country house. One recalls Tess Durbeyfield. Sensible young fellow that he is, Paul Sheringham is engaged to an heiress. He has a horror of work.

He snatches some time with Jane before motoring off to lunch with his fiancée. His family home is empty. For once his and Jane's love-making takes place, lubriciously described, in a luxurious bedroom, not – as it has done, furtively, for some years – behind bushes or in empty corridors.

Jane can have a hot bath afterwards: not the cat-lick servants usually make do with. The lovers leave tell-tale stains on the sheets. Let the servants, she thinks, momentarily 'upper', take care of that. This is the first time she has seen her lover naked. He has placed his ashtray on her bare belly, as if she were a piece of furniture. In a fortnight's time, when he marries, she, like his cigarette, will be stubbed out. Paul has, however, misjudged 'Jay'. She is observing his 'kind' critically. She has raided the house's library and is currently deep into Joseph Conrad. Her mind is expanding. A servant who thinks? Dangerous.

Out of the blue, something awful happens that jolts Jane out of her life in service. She leaves to work in a bookshop in Oxford. Books become her university. She marries a philosopher who, after helping win the war at Bletchley, dies of a brain tumour. 'Too brainy by half' is his funereal jest. Jane goes on to become a renowned novelist.

What actual novelist(s) is Swift thinking of? I can't think of any who fit Jane's profile. Alison Light (like me, the child of a domestic servant, I believe) in her applauded *Mrs Woolf and the Servants* (2008) is eloquent about the unbridgeable gap between great authors and those who emptied their chamber pots and filled their coal scuttles and didn't have full names. But, however unlikely it is historically, *Mothering Sunday* recommends itself as an antidote to the cloying sentimentality of Downton Abbey. Empty your own damn chamber pots.

Lullaby, Leïla Slimani, 2016

This is a novel with many titles: in France, where it won the Prix Goncourt, it is called *Chanson Douce*; in America *The Perfect Nanny*; and in England *Lullaby*. The variety of names witnesses to a slipperiness in the text – its refusal to answer the question it painfully poses.

True to its origins the novel probes at a French literary theme – purposeless, or *absurde*, murder. 'Motiveless malignity', Coleridge called it. André Gide, in his discussion of Dostoevsky's CRIME AND PUNISHMENT, referred to it as *le crime gratuit*. In Camus's THE OUTSIDER (the English-translated title) Meursault murders an Arab he does not know on the beach. The title of the novel in French, *L'Étranger*, means both stranger (its American title is *The Stranger*) and foreigner. Meursault is a Frenchman from Algiers, *pied-noir*. He lives in North Africa without belonging there: an insider-outsider.

That fact, in terms of his defining act, explains nothing.

Slimani is French-Moroccan. Her novel took as its subject a peculiarly horrible, apparently gratuitous crime. In October 2012 two children, aged six and two, were brutally murdered, with kitchen knives and battery, by their 'perfect' nanny, Yoselyn Ortega (Dominican-American), in an Upper West Side Manhattan apartment. On the parents' return, Ortega tried to stab herself but failed and lived to be tried. Neither she, the police nor the court furnished any explanation. It was absurd. The crime was written up in *Paris Match* under the headline '*la nounou de l'horreur*' – the nanny of horror – where, presumably, it came to Slimani's notice.

Myriam and Paul Massé are successful professional Parisians. She is a rising lawyer, he in the music promotion business. They live well, if modestly, in Paris's 10th arrondissement. They have what would appear to be fulfilling lives. A good marriage, good careers and two adorable children, six and two years old. There are, however, wormholes. He works long hours: home is a dormitory: his *élan vital* is elsewhere. She finds 'motherhood' downright tedious. She feels it is 'eating her alive'. She takes to minor shoplifting, as one might scratch an itch. She dearly wants to get back to her profession.

The problem is solved. They find an ideal day-time nanny who not only takes on the tasks of a pseudo-mother but does them 'miraculously'. Meals, clothes, laundry, cooking, house cleaning, play – even the bedtime stories and lullabies – are put in an apple-pie order they never had under Myriam's resentful regime. But why do the mythic stories Louise invents for the children have such a dark, Voldemort tinge to them? 'In what black lake, in what deep forest has she found these cruel tales'?

Louise, the perfect nanny, is now forty with no partner and has a daughter who has left her. She was not a perfect mother. She lives in a single room as comfortless as a prison cell. Mothering the Massé children, as they should be mothered, becomes a mania with her – she resents Myriam's periods because it means no more children to mother. It is monthly murder. She herself, one presumes, is perimenopausal.

The novel opens with Louise's own act of murder – in its ending is its beginning:

> The baby is dead. It took only a few seconds. The doctor said he didn't suffer . . . The little girl was still alive when the ambulance arrived . . . On the way to the hospital she was agitated, her body shaken by convulsions . . . Her lungs had been punctured . . . her head smashed violently against the blue chest of drawers.

Suicidal Louise is saved by the paramedics who hate her. 'She didn't know how to die. She only knew how to give death'. The police photograph the crime scene forensically – the camera may never lie but it cannot explain. The investigating police captain, a woman, dips her hands into Louise's 'rotting soul' only to find there is nothing there.

The novel can be seen as dramatising what the French sociologist Emile Durkehim called *anomie* – the rootlessness of urban life, and its spiritual vacuums. But that would be trite applied to Slimani's complex narrative. There is more to it – but what?

The novel, as critics observed almost in unison, 'disturbs'. There can be happy marriages, but can there be a happy mistress-servant relationship between a working mother and a 'perfect nanny'? How much enslavement of others does it take to be free? And what revenge should we fear from those others? Is this novel – at least one angry reviewer asked – a 'guilt trip' for working mothers with time left to read a novel?

Home Fire, Kamila Shamsie, 2017

Shamsie's title evokes Ivor Novello's schmaltzy World War One song – 'Keep the Home Fires Burning'. In 2017 for the Briton of Pakistani origin and Muslim faith, 'home' meant something more complex than dear old Blighty did in 1917. *Home Fire* is set then with a small number of characters. The novel opens, tautly, with Isma, an LSE-taught sociologist, suffering the indignity of an 'immigrant' interview at Heathrow. She is in fact emigrating to a career in a top university in the US. She misses her plane. Britain neither wants her nor is willing to let her go.

Two Muslim families resident in Britain, the Pashas and the Lones, make up the intercoiled strands of *Home Fire*. Underlying it is a retelling of the ancient Greek tragedy *Antigone* and a consideration of Sophocles' question: what does the honourable person owe their family? The ultimate sacrifice?

The Pashas, Isma's family, had a Jihadi-warrior father, Adil, who fought everywhere Islam was in conflict with the West. He appears in the narrative only by heroic repute. We are to assume he killed, in battle, Russian soldiers in Chechnya, and British and American soldiers while with the Taliban. He is presumed killed (suspiciously) in transit to Guantanamo. In a life devoted to war Adil visited his British family occasionally, and undercover, to impregnate his wife – who has since died prematurely of the stress of her marriage. Some would call it shame. Adil Pasha is not talked about among his family. But his memory still interests MI5 intensely.

Isma has escaped after playing the part of mother to her younger twin siblings, who are now adult. Parvaiz yearns to find out for himself what fire (call it faith) burned within his father. After grooming he allows himself to be recruited into ISIS. The Caliphate, he learns, is the only 'home' on earth for a devout Muslim. Parvaiz does not fight. He is a weakling. But, as an audio engineer, he puts soundtracks to crucifixions, beheadings and the tortures ISIS perpetrates and publicises world-wide. His end, like his father's, could be seen as martyrdom.

Each of the main characters has a long section devoted to them. Parvaiz's is the most challenging. In a high-achieving family, he is the under-achiever. He drifts. He travels to the Caliphate voluntarily – enthusiastically, even – beguiled by his extremist recruiters. We are to assume that he genuinely believes the 'State' is paradisal. He is a misled youth.

Parvaiz's twin sister, Aneeka, is a law student. For her, being Muslim is a matter of personal identity. It defines what she is. She proudly defies thugs who spit on her in the tube for wearing the hijab.

The other family, the Lones, have assimilated in Britain to the point of invisibility.

The patriarch, Karamat (nickname 'the lone wolf'), has married out to an Irish American. After a ruthless career in business he is now Britain's Home Secretary. It's not tokenism: he does the job better than the other guy.

Karamat's pampered son Eamonn wastes his life just this side of being a playboy. But an encounter, in America, with Isma leads to his falling desperately in love with Aneeka. He discovers, through her, what it is to be Muslim in the modern world. His father does not regard union with the daughter of a Jihadi warrior as something that will help his own advance to Number 10. The plot thickens to explosive, Sophoclean, tragedy.

The question Shamsie asks, in this fearless but hugely troubling novel, is: why did Britain, so ineffably proud of its post-colonial 'liberal tolerance', think multi-culturalism would be easy?

Milkman, Anna Burns, 2018

Milkman won the last Man Booker Prize. It was 'controversial' and provoked headlines – always a good thing for an award claiming to be the Anglophone world's most prestigious fiction prize.

I was a judge on the Booker in 1999 (when DISGRACE won) and in 2005 (when THE SEA won). These awards were made before the prize was opened to US contenders in 2014.

Having ploughed through some 140 submissions, the chair of the 2018 judging panel, Kwame Anthony Appiah, likened reading *Milkman* to climbing Snowdon. Wonderful view when you've yomped to the top and can forget your blisters. *Milkman* defies conventional narrative structure and pours onto the page like lumpy porridge. Characters are described by role, not name. It is a novel about 'the Troubles'. But where is it set? Belfast? No mention of that city in the text. And when is it set? The 1970s, most reviewers assumed. But the *Irish Times*, which knows a thing or two about its country's history and its times, went for the 'uneasy nineties'. Don't ask, said Ms Burns in a post-award interview. Any time from Bloody Sunday to Good Friday.

Giving the award to Burns's novel laid bare the cross-purposes (troubles?) that the Booker Prize has lived with annually. At its inception the award had two godfathers: the late publisher Tom Maschler and the late Martyn Goff, a bookseller-turned-literary entrepreneur. Mr Maschler wanted a British version of France's Prix Goncourt, with all its severe Gallic purity: a token few francs as a prize, permanent judges and a mission to certify, chauvinistically, French literary *gloire*. Goff, on the other hand, saw the Booker as something to fire up the British book trade. His mission was to make more people buy more novels. Preferably, granted, the best of novels. The Booker apparatus has served Goff's ulterior purpose while honouring Mr Maschler's higher purpose. It recruits judges with high-profile names and, largely, non-literary-world day jobs, plus the occasional 'celebrity'. The prize has been funded (most expensively, the slap-up Guildhall banquet) by big business. Goff would leak shamelessly to get a mention in the press of what the judges were arguing about. Publicity, he believed, is not the enemy of literature. It is wind in the sails.

Maschlerism and Goffism created a strange arrhythmia between literary high-mindedness and what Stella Rimington, the 2011 chair of judges, called 'readability'– novels that make you want to turn the page and that sell (Julian Barnes's more than readable *The Sense of an Ending* won that year). The split was manifest in the composition of the panel that went for *Milkman*. It comprised two stellar professors, a literary journalist, a distinguished graphic storyteller and a queen of detective fiction. The last two had the consolation of a pictorial novel and a crime thriller on the longlist. It created the kind of headline furore Goff would have loved.

Milkman goes a long way to joining up the Maschler-Goff bipolarity. On its narrative surface it's funny – as funny as that other Irish novel of the year, Sally Rooney's *Normal People*. But *Milkman* is also what we awkwardly term 'literary fiction'. Historical blur? It's artful. The pre-Good Friday conflict was a civil war, masked by the euphemism 'Troubles'. Women, *Milkman* insists, may survive war, but not unscathed.

Above all, the novel's entwined themes were and still are burningly topical: the Northern Irish 'problem' and, as Prof Appiah stressed in his award speech, the #MeToo uprising. Ms Burns's protagonist, 'middle sister', is a victim of sexual predation by the codenamed 'Milkman'.

Without its topicalities, *Milkman* would probably never have won through. But even the best novels need a little luck. Ms Burns, charmingly as she received the award, still couldn't believe the great finger in the sky had pointed at her.

The Patrick Melrose Novels, Edward St Aubyn, 2018

St Aubyn's pentateuch was published over the years 1992 to 2011. The omnibus edition of the collected works was republished to coincide with a five-part TV series in 2018. Among much else the novels, in toto, and their adaptation bear witness to a new symbiosis in which two equivalent narrative forms enhance and serve each other. Page or screen first? Doesn't matter.

Edward St Aubyn qualifies as one of the many best British novelists never to have won the Booker Prize. Only once, in 2006 when *Mother's Milk* was shortlisted, has he come within spitting distance. It rankles. He responded, scathingly, with a novel, *Lost for Words* (2014), satirising the nonsensical prize. Disdain is St Aubyn's trump card.

The life and times of Patrick Melrose over five novels and between the ages of five to forty-five, from the sixties to the first decade of the twenty-first century, could feasibly have qualified for the Ballie Gifford Prize for Non-fiction. It's vouched for as autofiction, memoir in novel's clothing.

St Aubyn, like his hero, was raped as a small child by his father. The opening Melrose novel, *Never Mind*, recounts the event in carnal detail. The TV version shirked any close-up of the 'cold pool of slime' running down the violated Patrick's thighs. It was, his father thinks as he goes downstairs to lunch, 'short and brutish but not altogether nasty'. For him, that is. He proceeds to tuck into his *brochette* of lamb.

Unsurprisingly a poem that catches Patrick's fancy in later life is Philip Larkin's 'This Be The Verse', with its first line 'They f*** you up, your mum and dad'. Most of us are lucky enough not to be physically effed by our dads (I euphemise the word – in the novels St Aubyn never does).

When he confided to his mother he was being paternally sodomised, her reported reply was 'Me too' (oddly, St Aubyn seems to have come up with the later angry feminist slogan). In the novel Patrick is conceived when his father jams his fleeing wife's head through the staircase uprights and rapes her ('too'?). Why did his father do it? The novels ponder the question to their last pages.

His father declares that what he does will make a man of Patrick. He will now be able to say: 'If I survived that, I can survive anything'. There are deeper reasons. David Melrose could have been a concert pianist. Rheumatic fever crippled his fingers. He qualified instead in medicine. But he despises the human race too much to heal them. Someone must pay.

The Melrose line began, on the bar sinister, with Charles II's liaison with a prostitute. David, Patrick's father, has inherited aristocratic charm and uses it to win an American heiress wife. Her dollars bestow on him a French chateau alongside the town of Lacoste, made famous by the Marquis de Sade. David has taken lessons from the master. At a lunch party he obliges his wife to eat rotting figs off the terrace paving. On all fours. Such is the world they live in no one stops him, although they do think it a trifle irregular.

Bad News, the second in the series, centres on the adult Patrick collecting his father's ashes. David has died penniless, divorced and crippled, in New York while Patrick has inherited a huge slab of his mother's family wealth. He crosses the Atlantic by Concorde. He is the most stylish of dustmen.

More to the point he is now a junkie – spending five grand a week on cocaine and heroin. There are loving descriptions of mainline injection, replaying the penetration of childhood rape. *Bad News* is the funniest of the novels: but then, you could say Hieronymus Bosch is a wonderfully funny cartoonist.

Mother's Milk, fourth in the series, ponders his mother's role in effing up Patrick. Unable to protect her offspring, she squanders her vast wealth on 'save the children' good causes. The unsaved Patrick cannot love her.

The only defence he can erect against the awfulness of things are irony, wit, style and cold indifference. St Aubyn's fiction has two elements. One is the conversation novel – St Aubyn is as brilliant as those masters of the genre, Thomas Love Peacock and Aldous Huxley. Below that is 'the slowly simmering scum of [Patrick's] thoughts'. Scum-dipping: welcome to the *Melrosiad*.

Why do we admire Edward St Aubyn as a writer so hugely but not warm to his fiction as we surely should? By any measure he should be up there with Amis, McEwan and Hollinghurst. It comes down to class and money. Take one of Patrick's clever-clever wisecracks: 'Most people wait for their parents to die with a mixture of tremendous sadness and plans for a new swimming pool.' What jars the most is 'new'. How many of St Aubyn's readers have a replaceable swimming pool? Or could shell out five thousand a week for their little helpers? Does he, we wonder, look down on us, his readers?

St Aubyn, to do him credit, has as little time for Royal Highnesses as for his underlings. The big scene in the third novel, *Some Hope* (1994), is a dinner party graced by the presence of Princess Margaret. She was still alive to read such silly-woman words put into her mouth as: 'The Queen was saying only the other day that London property prices are so high she doesn't know how she'd cope without Buckingham Palace'. That doubtless has done for Mr St Aubyn's attendance at any future Royal Garden party.

The fifth novel, *At Last*, finds a male menopausal Patrick – an unsuccessful barrister, no longer wholly addicted but teetering on divorce, stony broke, living in a bedsit so awful he can't even bring waitresses back for one-night stands. It is the final horror. He is middle class. Lower middle class.

Benedict Cumberbatch's superb fleshing out of Melrose did wonders for the second-wind bestsellerdom of St Aubyn's towering literary achievement.

Convenience Store Woman, Sayaka Murata (translated by Ginny Tapley Takemori), 2018 (published in Japan, 2016)

This novel is what it says it is. You can add the article 'A' to make the heroine narrator like so many others; or 'The' to make Keiko Furukura a unique woman. The Japanese language does not have much use for articles, one gathers, except those the country exports so brilliantly.

The term 'Convenience Store' was originally an urban American term for a place to snatch a sandwich and a coffee or beer, before running off to deal with the inconvenient things in life. In Britain they used to be called 'corner shops'. Japan burnishes the notion of convenience into something delicatessen-like: scrupulously clean, formally courteous, with delicious foodstuffs; not BLT and potato crisps, but rice balls and bonito shavings.

Keiko Furukura is born into a good family but realises early on in life that 'I am rather a strange child' and at university that 'I wouldn't survive in the real world'. There is a murderous violence in her, which must be controlled.

Beyond control Keiko wants to conform – to inhabit and fit in a world: an artificial world if necessary. On graduating she turns her part-time job at the local Smile Mart into her life's work. ('Life?' the narrative subversively enquires.) At the training sessions she feels 'reborn'. In this 'light-filled box' in which the 'manual' explains everything, she feels 'normal'. Western readers may recall Isaac Asimov's robots.

Keiko accepts she is componential. Her circadian clock ticks with the chronologies and routine tasks of the Smile Mart. She adopts the speech patterns of those in her store to ease her relationship with them. She is a gifted mimic.

Keiko has escaped from personality into role. So far, after eighteen years, it has brought her peace. Does the cog ask questions of the machine that wears it out? What is life itself, the novel asks, other than a series of roles? The roles Japan expects of women, as fellow workers and her family remind her, are wife and mother. Japan's population is ageing and declining simultaneously. She opts for Smile Mart. Let Japan decay.

The first half of the novel centres on the routines of Convenience Store work. The second half centres on a crisis. A layabout dismissed from Smile Mart attaches himself to Keiko. More correctly, he leeches on her. There is no sex – Shiraha would not dream of 'penetrating' a dried-up husk like Keiko. She is grateful. Cogs have no sex life.

Her family and fellow workers mistakenly congratulate Keiko – she has accepted her roles: wife and mother. It's a sham of course. She has merely adopted Shiraha, as one might a pet not yet house-trained.

He is possessed of as simplistic a world view as she. Japanese society, he believes, is just a plasti-wrapped version of the Stone Age village. You either belong – which means gainful work for him, marriage and children for her – or you are expelled. His rational choice has been to drop out. Self-expulsion. The two of them cohabit without love or mutual understanding or even much interest in each other.

She loses her job. It is a little death. She falls apart: a cog without a machine to call her own. Finally, she happens to call in at another Convenience Store: epiphany. She applies for a vacant post and is taken on. Call it resurrection. Or call it the third submersion of a drowning woman. But call it a gem of a novel as well.

This Mournable Body, Tsitsi Dangarembga, 2018

Zimbabwean fiction has transformed since Wilbur Smith's Rhodesian war sagas and Doris Lessing's *The Grass is Singing*. It wars and sings less but, as Dangarembga's fiction testifies, inspires profoundly disturbing novels.

This Mournable Body concludes the trilogy begun with *Nervous Conditions* (1988) and continued with *The Book of Not* (2006). The three novels recount the life story of Tambudzai ('Tambu') Sigauke from birth in a village in colonised 'Southern Rhodesia' to higher education, won entirely by her own

efforts. Tambu comes into this third phase of her life with a degree in sociology. It has taken her nowhere but gives her a sharper sense of her, and her country's, mournful condition.

Her childhood was passed against the background of the people's fight for independence. She separated herself from the struggle by choosing to learn instead. Her sister lost a leg in the struggle. More was lost. Their natal village is now destitute, its intricate clan system fractured. Everyone is alone, scattered like dust. Such is victory.

In this novel, set in the second decade of the twenty-first century (it took its author four years to get it published), Tambu is in her late thirties, 'past it' by the misogynistic standards of the Harare sexual scene.

Meanwhile the world itself is withering: wind and water have left the Zimbabwean land. This is the white colonisers' last bequest to Africa: global warming. As if Africa needed more heat. There is, by way of compensation, Nollywood TV – the great urban fashion influencer.

Is Tambu thinking and speaking throughout in English or Shona? Is the novel's text a gigantic subtitle to its real language and thought? Dangarembga's previous novels were told, Jane Eyre-style, in the first person. This final novel is given in vocative second-person address. Tambu is now no longer 'I' but 'you'. She has transformed from subject to object.

Her life has gone from bad to worse. She chucked 'a good job', copywriting in an advertising agency with the archaic colonial name Steers, D'Arcy and MacPedius. Colonial remnants litter her world – there is still a Churchill Avenue in Harare apparently. Credit for her work at the agency was filched by colleagues. Her creativity stifled, she still has her degree – a 'solid second' in sociology. Northlea High School employs her to teach biology; sociology . . . Just another 'ology', what's the difference?

The biological 'facts of life' are visible at the school gate every afternoon. Men lie in wait outside, like lions hunting prey, in their Mercs and BMWs. The young 'bornfrees' require little tempting. This is the only dolce vita available.

Men have no interest in Tambu beyond the occasional insult – good only for gang rape, it is suggested in one awful scene. She has had no sexual relationships. Love is a void in her life. Her day-to-day existence in the capital city has returned to the base village realities of food, a roof over her head, menial work. The novel opens with a lengthy description of her finding somewhere to live. She has outgrown the Twiss Youth Hostel 'for single girls' where she found temporary refuge. She has outgrown not merely youth but marriage, career, children – so what lies beyond for Tambu? She breaks the hostel mirror that returns her image. Sometimes, she thinks, 'forgetting is better than remembering when there is nothing to be done.' But some things must be done. She is now looking for a job in 'service' – maid's work. She will 'do' for a mistress. So much for independence.

Spasmodic outbursts of violence lead to her finding herself in a psychiatric hospital. Demons in the form of hyenas and ants haunt her. 'The snakes that hold your womb inside you' wriggle restlessly. Her reason fails her.

The novel's title and a central theme were inspired by a *New Yorker* essay by Teju Cole responding to the Charlie Hebdo massacre in Paris. Observing France's spasm of national grief, Cole concluded that first-world victims are 'mournable' while third-world victims are 'unmournable'. They merely happen.

The novel's final section is sourly ironic. A former friend/boss at the advertising agency with as faux a British name as can be, Tracey Stevenson, has devised a scheme. 'We're going backward, Tambu,' she says. 'Peasants, serfs, running sewage. It's so Middle Ages.' They will set up, Tracey suggests, an 'eco-tourist' business for Europeans and Americans and advertise it on the internet. It will be a kind of safari holiday experience for Europeans and Americans, not to wonder at wild animals but at primitive human life: the 'real Zimbabwe'. Tambu, a copywriter again, suggests the perfect name: Green Jacaranda Getaways. The project takes off wonderfully. Tambu has finally found her job as a 'village rural hostess'.

One recalls Julian Barnes's ENGLAND, ENGLAND in which the country converts itself into a theme park. Zimbabwe, as Dangarembga fantasises it, will recolonise itself. Rhodes may fall in Oxford, but not Harare (formerly Salisbury).

Putney, Sofka Zinovieff, 2018

There are some topics so hot that, one feels, only psychoanalysis or the novel can touch them. LOLITA got by under the net with the liberating Obscene Publications Act of 1959, Penguin Books' acquittal of obscenity charges after publishing LADY CHATTERLEY'S LOVER, and the 'swinging', anything goes, sixties and seventies. Attitudes had changed by the second decade of the twenty-first century. Some things could no longer 'go'.

LOLITA reached the page as one paedophile's word-crazed, but perversely beautiful, thought stream. *Putney* emerges triple-streamed: as thought streams of the paedophile, the victim, and the observing moralist. It's a complex, jolting weave.

The novel's epigraph is from Stendhal's treatise on love: 'Man is not free to avoid doing what gives him greater pleasure than any other action'. Such has always been the conviction of Ralph Boyd.

We encounter him in his last days. He has terminal prostate cancer. That his genitals are killing him may be seen as just desserts. He has a durable, loving marriage and gratifyingly high-performing children. A distinguished composer, Ralph is coming up to his seventieth birthday. There will be a celebratory concert in the Barbican, a big do in the Garrick Club, newspaper tributes. It is, as only he and his doctors know, a race with the undertaker.

With unease (that worrying MeToo thing) he recalls his 'affair' (as he thinks of it) with Daphne Greenslay back in the free and easy seventies. The relationship began when Daphne was nine and he twenty-seven. Ralph had been commissioned to compose the music for an adaptation of her excessively Bohemian father's novel *Oedipus Blues*.

He first saw Daphne on a visit to the Greenslay house in Putney. What he fancied he saw (his 'intestines juddering') was a half-Greek 'sprite' in striped tee shirt, ripped shorts and sandaled grubby feet. She 'inspired' him and he was 'oddly freed' by his lust for her. Over the next four years he devoted himself to charming her (the 2018 word is 'grooming'). There were exquisitely chosen gifts; the two of them created their own 'little language' and teased each other. It was their secret. For them, particularly him, 'the risky element was part of the pleasure'.

Ralph reassures himself he is not a 'career' paedophile – though there were, he recalls, those boys in the Youth Orchestras he worked with. His relationship with Daphne was something sublime. He composes it, as carefully as a symphony. He uses her in the choir for a musical performance of his adaptation of William Blake's *Songs of Innocence* – unwilling to face his robbery of just that innocence from her. 'Consent', he reassures himself, does not come into it: she is a willing participant. It is love. By now he is married.

The relationship reaches consummation when Daphne is thirteen. She and Ralph are on a Greek island – a place infused with myth. For Daphne it is mess, stain, pain and shame. For him, ecstasy. Soon afterwards the relationship with Daphne ends – no one else, except for one of her school friends, Jane, has ever known about it.

The next mind the narrative enters is Daphne's. Her life after Ralph dumped her was a fugue of self-harm, anorexia and mental disorder. In her teens she took to drugs and the faux-freedoms of the hippy life. A marriage of sorts produced a daughter, Libby ('liberty'). Now fifty, Daphne has cleaned up and lives, a shell of herself, in Putney, where her great love and only happiness happened: that being the affair with Ralph.

She is an artist working with *appliqué* design on textile and cushions. Like Penelope in the *Odyssey*, she sews to keep the world at bay. Her subject? She and Ralph. She has mythologised her rape as something beautiful, Leda and Zeus.

The third mind is that of Jane. No sprite but large and lumpy, she was Daphne's best friend, Plain Jane, the clever girl. She knew all about Ralph and what was going on, but kept mum. Did she, confusedly, envy Daphne? No matter. Embarked on the world, Jane went straight as Daphne went hippy. Jane is now a researcher into cancer, a happily married woman with two well-adjusted children.

She gets an email from Daphne suggesting after all these years they should meet up again. They do and Jane, learning the whole story, explains that Daphne's 'mythic love' was grooming and rape. Daphne finally realises the truth and sets the wheels of justice in motion.

Ralph is advised by his bluff-spoken, friendly solicitor that if he admits the truth he will die in jail, and suffer the same posthumous obloquy as Jimmy Savile. His only defence is denial it ever happened. He tries to win Daphne over but repents nothing. She lures him into a walk beside the Thames and, having followed her into the river, he emerges covered in slime. The metaphorical truth escapes him.

[Spoiler Alert] As Ralph comes up to trial – judgement or acquittal (unlikely, those former choir boys will also testify) – Daphne drops the charge when he at last admits to himself and her that what he did was not merely wrong, not merely criminal, but sinful. He could have followed the example of Oedipus at his moment of anagnorisis. Having endured the wretchedness of public adulation for his seventieth, he now follows the instruction of Jesus: 'But whoso shall offend one of these little ones which believe in me, it were better for him that a millstone were hanged about his neck, and that he were drowned in the depth of the sea'. His obituaries, unjustifiably, praise him to the skies.

Speaking for myself, this is one of the most disturbing novels I can recall reading.

After the Party, Cressida Connolly, 2018

One of Cyril Connolly's much-quoted remarks about the writer's perennial foes in *Enemies of Promise* (1938) is that heading the list is 'the pram in the hall'. One pram occupant for him was his daughter Cressida (born 1960). Perhaps that damned pram explains why Cyril only has one novel to his / their name. Cressida has five, including this applauded work.

After the Party did not make the Booker listings that year – the woes of middle-class, Home Counties ladies in the 1930s were not favoured in 2018 (*Milkman* won: see below) – though Connolly's novel would surely have won any prize for witty titles. *After the Party* makes play with semantic blur and allusion – Party in the sense of political and party in the sense of making whoopee. The story has two confluent streams. One is centred on events between 1938 and 1945 told as straightforward narrative. The other is autobiographical recollection, in italics, spoken by the heroine Phyllis to an anonymous, unresponsive researcher writing a book on pre-World War Two British fascism and the English would-be Führer, Oswald Mosley.

'The Old Man', as followers called him, was glamorous and lecherous: a quarter of his followers, like Phyllis, were women. They, as a class, had lived on to grieve after the First World War and wish to avoid further conflict. Phyllis has a son. She does not want him to die fighting Germans. Mosley – more sexily than weak old Neville Chamberlain – promises 'peace for our time' and wins over the female vote.

The lengthy 1938 eve-of-war narrative concentrates on the British Union of Fascists' summer camp by the sea in West Sussex, a 'Strength Through Joy' indoctrination event – working classes welcome. The climax is to be a great ball (for toffs only): a party for the Party, the 'Leader' as hoped for guest of honour.

Phyllis is the youngest of three sisters – the Mitfords are recalled (one of whom, Diana, married Mosley; another, Unity, adored Hitler who, in his way, adored her). Phyllis's sister Nina is the most devoted to the 'Cause'. What does 'Perish Judah' mean? Phyllis innocently asks. Nina explains the necessities of anti-Semitism. The brightest and most self-seeking of the sisters, Patricia, keeps her own counsel. The relationship between the sisters would furnish another, very different novel. Their childhood is spent in a country house, The Grange, but thereafter they go their separate ways and seem never much to have liked each other. Again, the Mitford sisters are evoked.

Phyllis had, in her late teens, loved a man but marriage was out of the question – he was 'the son of a tenant'. A suitable match of the right class was found. She is nowadays 'just a wife and mother' who goes along with whatever her husband, Hugh Forrester, says or does. Love doesn't come into it. In Phyllis's class good marriages are not necessarily the same as happy marriages.

A senior naval officer in the First World War, Hugh went on to be something big in British colonial rubber. Two generations older than Phyllis, now in her thirties, he has decided to retire to Sussex, not far from The Grange – sponsor of the summer camps. Until their new home is built, the Forresters and their children accept an invitation from Phyllis's sisters to move in to The Grange.

The Forresters have been living abroad for years. She knows nothing of Britain's current political ferment. But 'People tended to tell me things,' she says; because she doesn't matter. Hugh is 'no great age' and still a handsome, masterful man. As Phyllis meekly comments: 'he has such a lot of opinions about everything'. Including the man to put everything right in an England going to the dogs. Hugh, it turns out, is more deeply involved with Mosley than she realises.

When she actually hears a speech by him, Phyllis is converted. 'From the ashes of the past shall rise a Merrie England of gay and serene manhood,' its future Leader promises. And, of course, peace everlasting. Phyllis eagerly joins the 'Women's Campaign' – her 'bit' for Fascism and serene manhood.

The novel opens with the first interview session in 1979. It is the 'Winter of Discontent'. What with the strikes (communists!), uncollected rubbish (strikers!) and rats (ugh!) foraging in the streets, Phyllis tells her interviewer, '[H]istory has proved us right'.

She cannot, in this opening interview, go into her wartime experiences. She can only talk about how her hair turned white during internment:

> Of course I had never been the beauty of the family, but my hair was the one thing people admired; it was long and abundant, not quite the colour of a conker.

Now, chestnut no longer, it is 'like the mane of an old wooden rocking-horse.'

The novel has an epigraph from Iris Murdoch, whose key line is: 'Those who make one mistake wreck all the rest' (i.e. the lives of other people). What was Phyllis's 'one mistake' and whom did she 'wreck'? At the great party in 1938, having had too much drink forced on her, she danced with her dearest friend Sarita's husband. It goes beyond smooching on his part; he grinds against her, lustfully. Phyllis is revolted. But Sarita assumes they are having an affair and kills herself that night.

The party ends and so does the Party. War breaks out. Hugh is arrested – the 'Leader' had advised those closest to him to get firearms. Hugh has kept his old service revolver in the children's bedroom. The last third of the novel centres – as narrative and testimony – on Phyllis's imprisonment and internment. She is bundled off to Holloway and encounters, for the first time in her upper-class life, maggots in food, unbearable stench, filth that gets under the skin and abuse from 'decently' criminal inmates.

Conditions are more bearable in an internment camp on the Isle of Man where a self-comforting community of erstwhile women fascists forms. Feminism in extremis. Phyllis never recants but endures the punishment in private reparation for the death of Sarita. She deserves to suffer because of her 'one mistake'. 'It all gets muddled up together, the political and the personal,' she tells her interviewer.

On release she and Hugh are ostracised – even by their own family. Her children do not recognise, and have no intention of loving, 'this haggish-looking old person' who used to be their mother. The Forresters are impoverished – another new experience. Nina, ostraciser-in-chief, gets off scot-free and has a good war. Why? Because she informed on Hugh and Phyllis to gain immunity for her husband and herself. Phyllis, alone in the world after Hugh's death and her family's filching what inheritance should have come her way, takes up work as a 'lady's companion' to an ancient relic of the aristocracy, Lady Prendergast.

After the Party was well received though there were objections that Phyllis was too frail a vessel to contain political ideas of world historical significance. That quibble misses Connolly's point. 'Extremism' (as it's now called) is not the work solely of demagogues and fanatics, but also of 'nice' ordinary people, swept irresistibly along with it. It can be their ruinous 'one mistake'.

This Storm, James Ellroy, 2019

This Storm requires, by my count, twenty close-reading hours (abandon TV, all ye who enter here). And the novel is a mere foothill around the mountain of the two intermeshing 'Los Angeles Quartets' of which this is part six. James Ellroy writes big. *This Storm* follows on from *Perfidia*, published five years earlier, with many of the same characters. The title is a quotation from W. H. Auden ('noted British poet of the homosexual ilk' – Ellroy calls him), 'this storm, this savaging disaster'.

Perfidia covered, in real time, the public hysteria that lasted for twenty-three days after Pearl Harbor. *This Storm* covers the first forty-eight days of 1942. The indiscriminate rounding up of American-Japanese citizens for exile in distant concentration camps is underway. 'Outside of Tokyo', says a character in *Perfidia*, 'Los Angeles is the Jap capital of the world', but a bad place to be Japanese in 1942.

Ellroy disdains the apparatus of realistic fiction – plotwork, character development, scene build-up, fine writing. He is disinclined to read other novelists lest they put un-Ellrovian ideas into his head. Dostoevsky may be an exception. Reading his fiction is a buffeting experience.

Ellroy sees LA as a 'corrupt copocracy'. Corruption understates it. One copocrat in *This Storm* keeps a scorpion in a bottle ('El Buggo') to let loose on uncommunicative informants' genitals. They talk.

The character occupying most space is LAPD Sergeant Dudley Liam Smith (aka 'The Dudster'), a psycho former IRA killer. His rival is Sergeant Elmer Jackson (a historical character) who runs a call-girl ring on the side while 'working Vice' (i.e. the Vice Unit). There is a squad of sexually hyperactive female characters already familiar to devoted Ellroy readers. Dipping in and out of the action is (historical) Captain William H. Parker. Ten years later, by various acts of skulduggery, 'Whiskey Bill' will be the LAPD Chief. He consoles himself during the wait to meet his destiny with comely redheads and Jameson's Irish.

There are forlorn structural plot elements holding the narrative sprawl together. A US Mint train was robbed in 1931 and its hoard of gold never recovered: who has it, and for what crazed ends, gradually emerges. The Dudster is assigned to work undercover in Mexico. He supplements his pay by illegally shipping busloads of press-ganged Mexicans across the border to pick California's seasonal crops. Heroin is packed in the hubcaps for LA's black ghetto. 'Serve and Protect' is not Dudley's motto.

In 1933 there was a catastrophic wildfire in Griffith Park, central LA. Seven years later, when *This Storm* opens, a Pacific storm and mudslides have uncovered a body. Clues from the scene start a treasure hunt for the missing gold. The city goes collectively mad when, on the night of 24 February 1942, it deludes itself that a Pearl Harbor-style air-raid is happening. Searchlights and artillery rake and blast the empty sky. Riots erupt ghettoside. Fires rage.

Well-publicised demons torment James Ellroy. His mother was raped and murdered when he was ten. It's a cold case for the LAPD nowadays but still white hot for Ellroy. His father was an erstwhile business manager for Rita Hayworth, who married Orson Welles in 1943. 'El Porko' has a scummy role in *This Storm*. He snitches on fellow commies to the Feds and makes 'smut films' featuring big-name movie stars. Historically, he didn't.

A full cast of other Hollywood stars make their entrance. Clark Gable does star-turn sex acts for select audiences. No Oscar special category award for that, alas. Nor for the orgy Ellroy describes at a f*** flophouse where Cary Grant, Barbara 'Butch' Stanwyck, Mickey Rooney and other Hollywood headliners take their interpenetrating pleasures with (fictional) 'Ten-Inch' Tony Mangano, who 'tricks switcheroosky'. An audience clandestinely watches through peepholes for fifty bucks a peep. Katharine Hepburn's abortionist sells her purloined pubic hair for a hundred dollars a clump. Hepburn has an unaborted 'mulatto love child' by Duke Ellington. Ellroy, in short, uses Hollywood history like a latrine. Unflushed.

It's a mad, mad novel. But, Ellroy would say, in madness lies truth.

Girl, Woman, Other, Bernardine Evaristo, 2019

The Man Booker Prize, as it was then known, tacitly enforces the Highlander rule – 'There can be only one'. The one, in the last century, was largely white, male and British. The Prize has widened its dimensions in the present century. In 2019 the judges awarded it to two women: one North American, one British: one white, one mixed-race but defiantly black. It was, the judges insisted, in no sense a 'shared' prize – half a loaf. It was 'an equal first'. Photographs showed Margaret Atwood alongside Bernardine Evaristo: shoulder to shoulder. What came to mind was the passing of the torch from one generation to the next. The fight goes on. Atwood's winning novel was *The Testaments* – a follow-up to THE HANDMAID'S TALE. Over the years and with its TV adaptation, that novel (originally an SF classic) had changed the Western world. Handmaidenly uniform had become feminism's battle dress.

Evaristo's novel (her eighth) challenges conventional modalities of women's fiction. As a writer she is not rebellious – but resistant. 'Oppositional' in her own words. Evaristo's stated aim was to create what she calls 'fusion fiction'. This is writing that – while keeping semantic unities – melts into itself. There are no full stops in her text, no capitals fronting sentences, indifference to paragraphing. Punctuation is patriarchal.

Before she won, and criticism was drowned out by acclaim, some commentators had been nervous of Evaristo's stylistic heterodoxy. But (a feeble jest) it made its point. It accompanied a structural defiance of narrative linearity – the Aristotelian beginning, middle and end. Also discarded were old character typologies. Who is the hero(ine) of *Girl, Woman, Other*? All and none.

Traditional fiction is teleological – moving to conclusion through invented narrative time – whereas Evaristo's quilted narrative lies as flat on the page as geometry. As Wikipedia neatly puts it:

> Girl, Woman, Other follows the lives of each of 12 principal characters as they navigate the world. The book is divided into four chapters, each containing episodes about three women who are connected directly to one another in some way.

The reader is left to draw in the connecting lines for themself. The novel ends where it begins – with the performance of a play, The Last Amazon of Dahomey, whose storyline, if there is one, is never revealed. Evaristo's way of writing fiction, evolved over a quarter of a century, may have been worked out for herself alone or as broader innovation for the genre to incorporate. For a certainty her novelties will be influential.

The majority of Evaristo's dramatis personae are women of colour – but no more one colour or genetic heritage than individual daubs of paint on an artist's palette. Each has togetherness with others; each, one way or another, 'others' others. What does a middle-aged schoolteacher like Shirley have in common with the dissident university student Yazz?

Shirley 'wants to be a great teacher for every black person in the world'. Student Yazz defies the 'greyhead' (average age a hundred) canon of 'English' Literature. She and her band of 'unf*ckwithables' see feminism as 'herdlike' – a lot of cows mooing in unison. They want their own voices. Bohemian Dominique sees Shirley as a 'dry heterosexual schoolteacher'. What does Waris, a devoted daughter whose Islamic family fled Mogadishu for their lives, have in common with Courtney, a white daughter of the shires? Or Courtney herself have in common with the cleaner Bummi who insists, brandishing her mop, she is not British but Nigerian and always will be? Or Bummi with Nenet, the sophisticated daughter of an Egyptian diplomat? But they do, the novel asserts, have commonality. It simply takes subtle forms – so subtle that only the novel can anatomise them. Evaristo, incidentally, has much the same hostility to question marks as full stops. This is a novel founded on conviction.

The character who dominates is Amma whose mission, as a lesbian Amazonian dramatist, is to throw hand grenades into white Britain's theatrical world. Yet even she – the most aggressive of the twelve central girls, women and others – stops short of violence. Actual grenades. There is resistance but no flag-waving protest in the novel. Britain and, by implication, the US are regarded in a spirit of opportunism, not rejection. Things can be done there. Evaristo herself has done what she proclaims was her intention in writing the novel:

> I wanted to put presence into absence. I was very frustrated that black British women weren't visible in literature.

She was, nonetheless, amazed by winning the Booker. She was, overnight, world famous, superselling and potentially, like Atwood, a contributor to global change for her sex and gender. She remains, nonetheless, cautious: 'Social inclusion is more important than success'. Success ('sickcess'), Amma thinks, can be repressive tolerance. Fame can hobble. Winning the Nobel, said Saul Bellow, was like swimming for the rest of your career with your tombstone on your back. Whether she sinks or swims under 'sickcess', Evaristo will over the next decade be a major force in Brit(ish) fiction – to borrow Afua Hirsch's witty neologism – for the edginess of the mixed-race woman in modern Britain.

A Theatre for Dreamers, Polly Samson, 2020

A group of cosmopolitan creatives, identifiably 'real-life' people, find themselves together on the Greek island of Hydra in the early 1960s. This chronicle of what the island does for them and they, children of the sun, do to and for each other, is not quite historical fiction nor a travelogue. People on the island still remember Samson's principal characters. In this book they are scrutinised through the innocent eyes of a youthful narrator who lacks their gifts. Their complex, destructive and creative interplay is recalled by her in age, the survivor. An artistic gift, she concludes, is like the shirt of Nessus that tormented Hercules. Only demigods can bear to wear it.

For me, *A Theatre for Dreamers* occupies the same literary territory as *Tender is the Night* – F. Scott Fitzgerald's novel about Americans of the Lost Generation, finding their personal and literary destinies in interwar France. What is lost, what is won, by expatriation: the severing of roots?

Centre-stage in Samson's theatre are poet, performer and songsmith Leonard Cohen; the classic Australian writers George Johnston and Charmian Clift; the wildly bohemian Norwegian novelist Axel Jensen; and Axel's wife, Cohen's lover, Marianne Ihlen, who inspired his exquisitely elegiac love song 'So Long, Marianne'. They are 'Beautiful Losers' all of them, a phrase coined by Cohen in his 1960s novel. Beautiful dreamers too.

The island is the novel's principal character but the characters do not 'live' there. They 'are' there and live in each other. Hydra is, despite its name, waterless. It is a rock the sea no longer claims. George, impotent by virtue of his TB, sees it as the place to which Prometheus is chained while harpies come every night to feast on his liver: his wife leading them.

The grecophile traveller Patrick Leigh Fermor wastes few words on Hydra, dismissing it with the joke that when a person dies on the island, they have to send to Athens for the dirt to bury them. It is uniquely unspoiled by tourism because it has so little to offer. Mules remain the principal mode of transport. The island's unique character was forged over centuries by its symbiotic relationship with the surrounding sea – night fishing, piracy, sponge farming. Hydra hosts, it does not home, the book's characters.

Like Fitzgerald, again, Samson's descriptive prose can have a velvety texture. Her audio version rewards the listener. It's a voiced novel that moves at its own speed and thinks its own thoughts. Hydra abides.

The Space Between Worlds, Micaiah Johnson, 2020

This is a work walking high wires between SF, fantasy, and subtle feminist, LGBTQ+ and BLM tract. Unusually for its genre mix and theses it was a transgeneric bestseller. It won prizes, including The Kitschies Golden Tentacle Award.

The young author gives a sprightly self-portrait:

> Micaiah Johnson was raised in California's Mojave Desert surrounded by trees named Joshua and women who told stories.

She has learned to tell her woman's stories in creative writing degree courses and is now (in 2022) a postgraduate at Vanderbilt University where 'she focuses on critical race theory . . . and automatons'.

This is Johnson's 'debut' novel: a term that for elderly British readers (e.g. me) evokes young ladies in ball gowns. *The Space Between Worlds* does not set out to chronicle the lives of begowned debutantes, nor does it, as *Star Trek* used to, declare an aim:

> To explore strange new worlds, to seek out new life and new civilisations, to boldly go where no man has gone before.

Instead Johnson's unmanly hero boldly skips *between* worlds – all earthly – in a 'multiverse'.

One of the novel's many glowing reviews – in *New Scientist* – offers a helpful guide to multiversality. 'More of the same' sums it up sufficiently for the average reader.

I was once deep into SF of the hard Fred Pohl, Richard Heinlein and Ballardian kind, before the genre began surfing the 1970s 'new wave' and multivolume sword-and-sorcery sagas, moving at the fringes in and out of 'gaming'. After that it was, for me, an occasional guilty pleasure (see ENDERS GAME, BABEL-17, in the previous pages).

This novel is a pleasurable experience – but it may stick a few darts in the male reader's hide. The hero, Cara, is a 'multiverser'. She can trip between 400-odd earths (some odder than others, all different). A paranoid concept.

She is not a tourist, nor an explorer, but an information-gatherer for her employer. She inhabits the walled Wiley City on 'Zero

Earth'. This is a corporate dictatorship under the rule of CEO Adam Bosch and his Eldridge Institute. The Institute worked out multiversality and the means of inter-earth multitraversing. It has mineral exploitation, not exploration (forget *Star Trek*) in mind.

There's a catch. Cara can only visit worlds where she is already dead, lest she upset the cosmic applecart by meeting herself – doppelgängers negate each other and their worlds. She is dead on so many planets because she was brought up outside Wiley City, in the Wasteland's Ashtown, and – given the deprived nature of that environment – has died on some 372 of the alternate worlds. The Institute only uses multiverses of colour because they have – elsewhere – died earlier than whites. Allusions to T. S. Eliot may be recognised. *The Matrix* is recalled everywhere.

In some worlds Cara discovers alternate histories of her dead selves. All bleak. The difference between worlds is typically fractional, though – and in Bosch's eyes, those differences are ripe for plundering. To understand this, look what we've done to Africa on this earth. If Cara completes four years' service for the Institute, under the supervision of her female handler, Dell (with whom romance develops), she may earn Wiley citizenship. Good luck with that. The institute is already working on automation.

Given its gimmick, the novel sounds like a return to classic hard SF. In fact, it is more concerned with Cara and her prismatic identities. She holds a great secret about herself (divulged early on) and she has a mission (details withheld till late on).

The novel aroused incidental interest because of its LGBTQ+ dramatis personae and the theme of investigating alternate-self identities, and the spaces they create within worlds and within selves. Johnson's narrative plays with intersectionality and its frictional spark points; between human entities, individuals and groups, in society and in one's self. The great liberal endeavour to iron out all social difference in the name of liberty, equality, fraternity (sorority?), is satirised as a grand illusion or a cynical hoax. Take your pick. Johnson, still working out her ideas here, is a writer to bookmark.

Real Life, Brandon Taylor, 2020

Taylor's title is a tease. As critics pointed out, the novel is, as regards narrative externals, very close to autofiction. This is a first novel. Taylor wrote it in five weeks, fuelled by an excoriating anger whose source was a mystery to him. The novel, as it emerged, helped explain things. To him, and to us.

The hero is Wallace. His surname is never given – another tease: is it Taylor? He is a postgraduate student at a university recognisable as the University of Wisconsin-Madison. His subject is biochemistry – he works with cans of worms: literally, not symbolically. Specifically, he studies their ambiguous sexuality.

Wallace is the one black student in his year's intake. He is clever, but not the cleverest of his cohort. He is on fellowship: his fees are paid for him. He attends a social meeting with his donor-benefactors: 'wealthy white people'. They speak in lowered voices when he comes in earshot. Are they saying 'look at the good thing we've done for that black kid, (what's his name?) from Alabama'.

Wallace's talent as a scientist 'is not for looking, exactly, but waiting' – watching how it turns out. In experimental science it is useful. But this is not a 'waiting' narrative. It covers a frantic weekend of research, love and violating sex.

Wallace never encounters outright racism from his fellow students, with whom he hangs out and can sometimes, guardedly, like; nor from his departmental supervisors whom he cannot bring himself to like. But racist vibration is always there – like a social tinnitus. The phrase 'white people' recurs over and over again in the narrative. It is not a phrase white people ever use. There are no black 'people' around – only a black person: him. He does not fit – the white world 'makes room' for him. Should he, misfit that he is, give back what 'white people' have given him? 'It was not so much that he wanted to leave graduate school as that he wanted to leave his life'. But what is 'real life'?

The novel opens with the fact that his father has died a few weeks before. Wallace did not go to the funeral. His father 'did nothing for him' – hated him, in fact, like a 'glowing hot wire' in their family life. His mother has disowned him with a volley of objurgation among which the word 'son' never comes up. Why? Because he is black and gay. No son of hers. He permitted a stranger to rape him. He is unclean. (Taylor, we are told, was born in Alabama in a strict Baptist home.)

The young white people, his 'semblance' buddies, gays among them, have no such problems as his. When they ask him, politely, about his life, he replies: 'I am from Alabama.' How could these white, middle-class, people understand what that means?

Over the weekend he has an abrupt affair with a white fellow student, Miller, who claims he is not gay and is given to outbursts of psycho-sexual violence. Their brief encounter climaxes in teeth, fists and genitals. Homicidal mutual rape. Real love?

In another line of the novel's twined narrative, Wallace's experiment – which requires months of attention – is sabotaged by a 'gifted' white female student who has taken against him. Why? Her hatred is made plain. Because he's gay and black.

'Women', she sneeringly tells him, 'are the new n*gg*rs, the new f*gg*ts.' His enemy goes on to accuse him before the female head of their department of abusive misogyny. He does not defend himself. Wallace is, his chief says, a 'dysfunctional' element in their team. Has he thought of moving on?

It's unfair, Wallace thinks. When you tell white people that something is racist, they hold it up to the light and try to discern if you are telling the truth. It's not 'telling' for him. He feels racism as he'd feel a white-hot poker: no need to hold it up to the light and check. He keeps all this to himself 'because people don't know what to do with the reality of other people's feelings'. Those 'others'? Black people. So it was and so it is. How can his companions know what it is to be brought up in a trailer park up a dirt road with the prospect of dying in the same? That's Wallace's reality. How do they put it? 'You come from a challenging background.' What they mean is that he has a 'deficiency of whiteness'. Or fairness.

His only stroke of luck was to have had a good middle-school chemistry teacher. Where has that luck brought him? He will leave – as did Taylor in the same circumstances, we are told – to be a chemist-turned-novelist. Or so we may assume. Why else would these words be here?

The novel ends by looping back four years to Wallace arriving at Wisconsin-Madison, getting off a Greyhound bus, thrilled: 'He had never been out of the south before'. Everyone is welcoming. He has arrived: but in a world, he will find, that does not make it possible for him to stay.

This novel gives the sense of being something thrown in the face of the 'white people' who will read it – guided by encomiastic reviews in the usual places or its being on the shortlist of the Man Booker Prize in the year, and to the month, in which George Floyd was murdered. Taylor remains defiant: 'I could have written this book to be more sympathetic to the white gaze, but it would've been a worse book.' The word 'gaze' hurts.

Tokyo Redux, David Peace, 2021

David Peace made his authorial name as a dyed-in-the-wool man of Yorkshire. His headline success was with the 2009 beyond-noir TV adaptation of his *Red Riding* quartet. After that Peace reportedly found that Yorkshire was stifling his imagination. The raw material was too close. He cut his roots and went off to Japan to teach at Tokyo University. There he eventually embarked on what is, with *Tokyo Redux*, his 'Tokyo Trilogy'.

The novels are set in the seven years of the post-war US Occupation. The conquered superpower was, effectively, America's to reshape as it willed. Its will, ruthlessly enforced, was to stop Japan going the same way as Mao's China. Japan was the domino that would not fall. The occupiers mainlined American capitalism into the country: only to find, like Dr Frankenstein, they had created a monster: but a geopolitically useful monster.

Three historical events – symptomatic of the dark depths underneath the emergence of 'New Japan' – feature in Peace's trilogy. In *Tokyo Year Zero* (2007) it is the hunt for the 'Japanese Bluebeard', who strangles prostitutes with their scarves. The connection with the Yorkshire Ripper is clear enough. So too is Peace's theme in his police novels that investigation brings the detective into a relationship as intimate as sex with the criminal. Finally, the hunter recognises himself in what he hunts. The second in the series, *Occupied City* (2009), takes as its subject the true crime of a robber who impersonated an occupying-force medic to trick bank employees, en masse, into drinking cyanide.

This concluding work, which took Peace ten years to write, has as its central event the death, on 5 July 1949, of the newly appointed president of the national railway system, Sadanori Shimoyama. He was appointed to strip out 100,000 workers in the cause of free enterprise, American-style. Peace's novel about the miners' strike, *GB84* (2004), whose loss tore the heart out of industrial Yorkshire, will come to mind.

The communist-infiltrated unions hate and threaten Shimoyama – a good man, obeying American orders. His body is found smashed to pieces on a railway line alongside a favoured suicide site. Who killed Shimoyama? Or was it suicide – an act of conscience? His marriage was troubled, his finances in ruins, he was physically at the end of his tether.

The Occupation detective assigned to the case, Harry Sweeney, is himself suicidal, his wrists bandaged. His marriage, too, is on the rocks, something that torments his Catholic conscience. He sees himself in Shimoyama. But a verdict of suicide is not what the Americans want.

The unions are to be found guilty, to justify a crackdown on the commies. Just like Joe McCarthy in the US. Behind it all may be invisible hands – Unit Zed, a clandestine American outfit, or the Kremlin, which simply wants to destabilise Japan in the cause of the same kind of revolution that worked for them in China. Suicide, murder, set up. Cold War games?

To this day, no one knows. Nonetheless, David Peace would have us believe that fiction, with its creative paranoia, can suggest plausible solutions. The second half of the novel shifts to 1964. A seedy private investigator is hired by a mystery employer. He is charged with finding a missing person, a hack novelist who has written a manuscript about the Shimoyama case that no one must be allowed to read. The novelist has also written potboilers about the Japanese Bluebeard and the criminal who attempted bank robbery by cyanide. Is David Peace mocking David Peace? Tokyo novelist Kuroda Roman has been on the edge of the narrative throughout. Does he really know the truth about the 'Shimoyama Incident'? If so, how? Read on. It's a long book, by the way, some 450 dense pages.

David Peace mixes true crime with crime fiction. It is only in this mixture, he asserts with his Tokyo novels, that you will find any worthwhile truth about crime. Or it may be, as in Kurosawa's *Rashomon* – a film Peace much admires – that there are many truths. That's life.

Index

L